Fundamentals of
Corporate Finance

THE McGRAW-HILL/IRWIN SERIES IN FINANCE, INSURANCE, AND REAL ESTATE

Stephen A. Ross, Franco Modigliani Professor of Financial Economics
Sloan School of Management, Massachusetts Institute of Technology
Consulting Editor

Financial Management

Block, Hirt, and Danielsen
Foundations of Financial Management
Sixteenth Edition

Brealey, Myers, and Allen
Principles of Corporate Finance
Twelfth Edition

Brealey, Myers, and Allen
Principles of Corporate Finance, Concise
Second Edition

Brealey, Myers, and Marcus
Fundamentals of Corporate Finance
Ninth Edition

Brooks
FinGame Online 5.0

Bruner
Case Studies in Finance: Managing for Corporate Value Creation
Eighth Edition

Cornett, Adair, and Nofsinger
Finance: Applications and Theory
Fourth Edition

Cornett, Adair, and Nofsinger
M: Finance
Third Edition

DeMello
Cases in Finance
Third Edition

Grinblatt (editor)
Stephen A. Ross, Mentor: Influence through Generations

Grinblatt and Titman
Financial Markets and Corporate Strategy
Second Edition

Higgins
Analysis for Financial Management
Eleventh Edition

Ross, Westerfield, Jaffe, and Jordan
Corporate Finance
Eleventh Edition

Ross, Westerfield, Jaffe, and Jordan
Corporate Finance: Core Principles and Applications
Fifth Edition

Ross, Westerfield, and Jordan
Essentials of Corporate Finance
Ninth Edition

Ross, Westerfield, and Jordan
Fundamentals of Corporate Finance
Eleventh Edition

Shefrin
Behavioral Corporate Finance: Decisions That Create Value
Second Edition

Investments

Bodie, Kane, and Marcus
Essentials of Investments
Tenth Edition

Bodie, Kane, and Marcus
Investments
Tenth Edition

Hirt and Block
Fundamentals of Investment Management
Tenth Edition

Hirschey and Nofsinger
Investments: Analysis and Behavior
Second Edition

Jordan, Miller, and Dolvin
Fundamentals of Investments: Valuation and Management
Eighth Edition

Stewart, Piros, and Heisler
Running Money: Professional Portfolio Management
First Edition

Sundaram and Das
Derivatives: Principles and Practice
Second Edition

Financial Institutions and Markets

Rose and Hudgins
Bank Management and Financial Services
Ninth Edition

Rose and Marquis
Financial Institutions and Markets
Eleventh Edition

Saunders and Cornett
Financial Institutions Management: A Risk Management Approach
Ninth Edition

Saunders and Cornett
Financial Markets and Institutions
Sixth Edition

International Finance

Eun and Resnick
International Financial Management
Eighth Edition

Real Estate

Brueggeman and Fisher
Real Estate Finance and Investments
Fifteenth Edition

Ling and Archer
Real Estate Principles: A Value Approach
Fifth Edition

Financial Planning and Insurance

Allen, Melone, Rosenbloom, and Mahoney
Retirement Plans: 401(k)s, IRAs, and Other Deferred Compensation Approaches
Eleventh Edition

Altfest
Personal Financial Planning
Second Edition

Harrington and Niehaus
Risk Management and Insurance
Second Edition

Kapoor, Dlabay, and Hughes
Focus on Personal Finance: An Active Approach to Help You Develop Successful Financial Skills
Fifth Edition

Kapoor, Dlabay, and Hughes
Personal Finance
Twelve Edition

Walker and Walker
Personal Finance: Building Your Future
Second Edition

Fundamentals of
Corporate Finance

Ninth EDITION

Richard A. Brealey
London Business School

Stewart C. Myers
Sloan School of Management,
Massachusetts Institute of Technology

Alan J. Marcus
Carroll School of Management,
Boston College

McGraw
Hill
Education

FUNDAMENTALS OF CORPORATE FINANCE, NINTH EDITION

Published by McGraw-Hill Education, 2 Penn Plaza, New York, NY 10121. Copyright © 2018 by McGraw-Hill Education. All rights reserved. Printed in the United States of America. Previous editions © 2015, 2012, 2009, 2007, 2004, 2001, 1999, and 1995. No part of this publication may be reproduced or distributed in any form or by any means, or stored in a database or retrieval system, without the prior written consent of McGraw-Hill Education, including, but not limited to, in any network or other electronic storage or transmission, or broadcast for distance learning.

Some ancillaries, including electronic and print components, may not be available to customers outside the United States.

This book is printed on acid-free paper.

4 5 6 7 8 9 LWI 21 20 19 18

ISBN 978-1-259-72261-5
MHID 1-259-72261-9

Chief Product Officer, SVP Products & Markets: *G. Scott Virkler*
Vice President, General Manager, Products & Markets: *Marty Lange*
Vice President, Content Design & Delivery: *Betsy Whalen*
Managing Director: *James Heine*
Director, Finance: *Chuck Synovec*
Director, Product Development: *Rose Koos*
Product Developer: *Noelle Bathurst*
Marketing Director: *Melissa Caughlin*
Marketing Manager: *Trina Mauer*
Director of Digital Content Development: *Douglas Ruby*
Digital Product Developer: *Tobi Philips*
Director, Content Design & Delivery: *Linda Avenarius*
Program Manager: *Mark Christianson*
Content Project Managers: *Kathryn D. Wright, Kristin Bradley, and Karen Jozefowicz*
Buyer: *Jennifer Pickel*
Design: *Matt Diamond*
Content Licensing Specialists: *Beth Thole and Melissa Homer*
Cover Image: *© Ximo Michavila/Getty Images*
Compositor: *SPi Global*
Printer: *LSC Communications*

All credits appearing on page or at the end of the book are considered to be an extension of the copyright page.

Library of Congress Cataloging-in-Publication Data

Names: Brealey, Richard A., author. | Myers, Stewart C., author. | Marcus, Alan J., author.
Title: Fundamentals of corporate finance / Richard A. Brealey, London
Business School, Stewart C. Myers, Sloan School of Management, Massachusetts Institute of Technology,
Alan J. Marcus, Carroll School of Management, Boston College.
Description: Ninth edition. | New York, NY : McGraw-Hill, [2017]
Identifiers: LCCN 2016031933 | ISBN 9781259722615 (alk. paper)
Subjects: LCSH: Corporations--Finance.
Classification: LCC HG4026 .B6668 2017 | DDC 658.15--dc23 LC record available at https://lccn.loc.gov/2016031933

The Internet addresses listed in the text were accurate at the time of publication. The inclusion of a website does not indicate an endorsement by the authors or McGraw-Hill Education, and McGraw-Hill Education does not guarantee the accuracy of the information presented at these sites.

mheducation.com/highered

Dedication To Our Families

Courtesy of Richard A. Brealey

Richard A. Brealey

Professor of Finance at the London Business School
Professor Brealey is the former president of the European Finance Association and a former director of the American Finance Association. He is a fellow of the British Academy and has served as Special Adviser to the Governor of the Bank of England and as director of a number of financial institutions. Professor Brealey is also the author (with Professor Myers and Franklin Allen) of this book's sister text, *Principles of Corporate Finance* (McGraw-Hill Education).

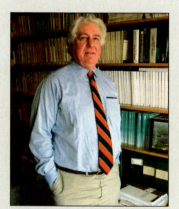

Courtesy of Stewart C. Myers

Stewart C. Myers

Gordon Y Billard Professor of Finance at MIT's Sloan School of Management
Dr. Myers is past president of the American Finance Association and a research associate of the National Bureau of Economic Research. His research has focused on financing decisions, valuation methods, the cost of capital, and financial aspects of government regulation of business. Dr. Myers is a director of The Brattle Group, Inc. and is active as a financial consultant. He is also the author (with Professor Brealey and Franklin Allen) of this book's sister text, *Principles of Corporate Finance* (McGraw-Hill Education).

Courtesy of Alan J. Marcus

Alan J. Marcus

Mario Gabelli Professor of Finance in the Carroll School of Management at Boston College
Professor Marcus's main research interests are in derivatives and securities markets. He is co-author (with Zvi Bodie and Alex Kane) of the texts *Investments* and *Essentials of Investments* (McGraw-Hill Education). Professor Marcus has served as a research fellow at the National Bureau of Economic Research. Professor Marcus also spent two years at Freddie Mac, where he helped to develop mortgage pricing and credit risk models. He currently serves on the Research Foundation Advisory Board of the CFA Institute.

Preface

This book is an introduction to corporate finance. It focuses on how companies invest in real assets, how they raise the money to pay for the investments, and how those assets ultimately affect the value of the firm. It also provides a broad overview of the financial landscape, discussing, for example, the major players in financial markets, the role of financial institutions in the economy, and how securities are traded and valued by investors. The book offers a framework for systematically thinking about most of the important financial problems that both firms and individuals are likely to confront.

Financial management is important, interesting, and challenging. It is *important* because today's capital investment decisions may determine the businesses that the firm is in 10, 20, or more years ahead. Needless to say, a firm's success or failure depends, in large part, on its ability to find the capital that it requires.

Finance is *interesting* for several reasons. Financial decisions often involve huge sums of money. Large investment projects or acquisitions may involve billions of dollars. Also, the financial community is international and fast-moving, with colorful heroes and a sprinkling of unpleasant villains.

Finance is *challenging*. Financial decisions are rarely cut and dried, and the financial markets in which companies operate are changing rapidly. Good managers can cope with routine problems, but only the best managers can respond to change. To handle new problems, you need more than rules of thumb; you need to understand why companies and financial markets behave as they do and when common practice may not be best practice. Once you have a consistent framework for making financial decisions, complex problems become more manageable.

This book provides that framework. It is not an encyclopedia of finance. It focuses instead on setting out the basic *principles* of financial management and applying them to the main decisions faced by the financial manager. It explains why the firm's owners would like the manager to increase firm value and shows how managers make choices between investments that may pay off at different points of time or have different degrees of risk. It also describes the main features of financial markets and discusses why companies may prefer a particular source of finance.

We organize the book around the key concepts of modern finance. These concepts, properly explained, simplify the subject. They are also practical. The tools of financial management are easier to grasp and use effectively when presented in a consistent conceptual framework. This text provides that framework.

Modern financial management is not "rocket science." It is a set of ideas that can be made clear by words, graphs, and numerical examples. The ideas provide the "why" behind the tools that good financial managers use to make investment and financing decisions.

We wrote this book to make financial management clear, useful, and fun for the beginning student. We set out to show that modern finance and good financial practice go together, even for the financial novice.

Fundamentals and Principles of Corporate Finance

This book is derived in part from its sister text *Principles of Corporate Finance*. The spirit of the two books is similar. Both apply modern finance to give students a working ability to make financial decisions. However, there are also substantial differences between the two books.

First, we provide in *Fundamentals* much more detailed discussion of the principles and mechanics of the time value of money. This material underlies almost all of this text, and we spend a lengthy chapter providing extensive practice with this key concept.

Second, we use numerical examples in this text to a greater degree than in *Principles*. Each chapter presents several detailed numerical examples to help the reader become familiar and comfortable with the material.

Third, we have streamlined the treatment of most topics. Whereas *Principles* has 34 chapters, *Fundamentals* has only 25. The relative brevity of *Fundamentals* necessitates a broader-brush coverage of some topics, but we feel that this is an advantage for a beginning audience.

Fourth, we assume little in the way of background knowledge. While most users will have had an introductory accounting course, we review the concepts of accounting that are important to the financial manager in Chapter 3.

Principles is known for its relaxed and informal writing style, and we continue this tradition in *Fundamentals*. In addition, we use as little mathematical notation as possible. Even when we present an equation, we usually write it in words rather than symbols. This approach has two advantages. It is less intimidating, and it focuses attention on the underlying concept rather than the formula.

Organizational Design

Fundamentals is organized in eight parts.

Part 1 (Introduction) provides essential background material. In the first chapter, we discuss how businesses are organized, the role of the financial manager, and the financial markets in which the manager operates. We explain how shareholders want managers to take actions that increase the value of their investment, and we introduce the concept of the opportunity cost of capital and the trade-off that the firm needs to make when assessing investment proposals. We also describe some of the mechanisms that help to align the interests of managers and shareholders. Of course, the task of increasing shareholder value does not justify corrupt and unscrupulous behavior. We, therefore, discuss some of the ethical issues that confront managers.

Chapter 2 surveys and sets out the functions of financial markets and institutions. This chapter also reviews the crisis of 2007–2009. The events of those years illustrate clearly why and how financial markets and institutions matter.

A large corporation is a team effort, so the firm produces financial statements to help the players monitor its progress. Chapter 3 provides a brief overview of these financial statements and introduces two key distinctions—between market and book values and between cash flows and profits. This chapter also discusses some of the shortcomings in accounting practice. The chapter concludes with a summary of federal taxes.

Chapter 4 provides an overview of financial statement analysis. In contrast to most introductions to this topic, our discussion is motivated by considerations of valuation and the insight that financial ratios can provide about how management has added to the firm's value.

Part 2 (Value) is concerned with valuation. In Chapter 5, we introduce the concept of the time value of money, and because most readers will be more familiar with their own financial affairs than with the big leagues of finance, we motivate our discussion by looking first at some personal financial decisions. We show how to value long-lived streams of cash flows and work through the valuation of perpetuities and annuities. Chapter 5 also contains a short concluding section on inflation and the distinction between real and nominal returns.

Chapters 6 and 7 introduce the basic features of bonds and stocks and give students a chance to apply the ideas of Chapter 5 to the valuation of these securities. We show how to find the value of a bond given its yield, and we show how prices of bonds fluctuate as interest rates change. We look at what determines stock prices and how stock valuation formulas can be used to infer the return that investors expect. Finally, we see how investment opportunities are reflected in the stock price and why analysts focus on the price-earnings multiple. Chapter 7 also introduces the concept of market efficiency. This concept is crucial to interpreting a stock's valuation; it also provides a framework for the later treatment of the issues that arise when firms issue securities or make decisions concerning dividends or capital structure.

The remaining chapters of Part 2 are concerned with the company's investment decision. In Chapter 8, we introduce the concept of net present value and show how to calculate the NPV of a simple investment project. We then consider more complex investment proposals, including choices between alternative projects, machine replacement decisions, and decisions of when to invest. We also look at other measures of an investment's attractiveness—its internal rate of return, profitability index, and payback period. We show how the profitability index can be used to choose between investment projects when capital is scarce. The appendix to Chapter 8 shows how to sidestep some of the pitfalls of the IRR rule.

The first step in any NPV calculation is to decide what to discount. Therefore, in Chapter 9, we work through a realistic example of a capital budgeting analysis, showing how the manager needs to recognize the investment in working capital and how taxes and depreciation affect cash flows.

We start Chapter 10 by looking at how companies organize the investment process and ensure everyone works toward a common goal. We then go on to look at various techniques to help managers identify the key assumptions in their estimates, such as sensitivity analysis, scenario analysis, and break-even analysis. We explain the distinction between accounting break-even and NPV break-even. We conclude the chapter by describing how managers try to build future flexibility into projects so that they can capitalize on good luck and mitigate the consequences of bad luck.

Part 3 (Risk) is concerned with the cost of capital. Chapter 11 starts with a historical survey of returns on bonds and stocks and goes on to distinguish between the specific risk and market risk of individual stocks. Chapter 12 shows how to measure market risk and discusses the relationship between risk and expected return. Chapter 13 introduces the weighted-average cost of capital and provides a practical illustration of how to estimate it.

Part 4 (Financing) begins our discussion of the financing decision. Chapter 14 provides an overview of the securities that firms issue and their relative importance as sources of finance. In Chapter 15, we look at how firms issue securities, and we follow a firm from its first need for venture capital, through its initial public offering, to its continuing need to raise debt or equity.

Part 5 (Debt and Payout Policy) focuses on the two classic long-term financing decisions. In Chapter 16, we ask how much the firm should borrow, and we summarize bankruptcy procedures that occur when firms can't pay their debts. In Chapter 17, we study how firms should set dividend and payout policy. In each case, we start with Modigliani and Miller's (MM's) observation that in well-functioning markets, the decision should not matter, but we use this initial observation to help the reader understand why financial managers in practice *do* pay attention to these decisions.

Part 6 (Financial Analysis and Planning) starts with long-term financial planning in Chapter 18, where we look at how the financial manager considers the combined effects of investment and financing decisions on the firm as a whole. We also show how measures of internal and sustainable growth help managers check that the firm's planned growth is consistent with its financing plans. Chapter 19 is an introduction to short-term financial planning. It shows how managers ensure that the firm will have enough cash to pay its bills over the coming year. Chapter 20 addresses working capital management. It describes the basic steps of credit management, the principles of inventory management, and how firms handle payments efficiently and put cash to work as quickly as possible. It also describes how firms invest temporary surpluses of cash and how they can borrow to offset any temporary deficiency. Chapter 20 is conceptually straightforward, but it contains a large dollop of institutional material.

Part 7 (Special Topics) covers several important but somewhat more advanced topics—mergers (Chapter 21), international financial management (Chapter 22), options (Chapter 23), and risk management (Chapter 24). Some of these topics are touched on in earlier chapters. For example, we introduce the idea of options in Chapter 10, when we show how companies build flexibility into capital projects. However, Chapter 23 generalizes this material, explains at an elementary level how options are valued, and provides some examples of why the financial manager needs to be concerned about options. International finance is also not confined to Chapter 22. As one might expect from a book that is written by an international group of authors, examples from different countries and financial systems are scattered throughout the book. However, Chapter 22 tackles the specific problems that arise when a corporation is confronted by different currencies.

Part 8 (Conclusion) contains a concluding chapter (Chapter 25), in which we review the most important ideas covered in the text. We also introduce some interesting questions that either were unanswered in the text or are still puzzles to the finance profession. Thus, the last chapter is an introduction to future finance courses as well as a conclusion to this one.

Routes through the Book

There are about as many effective ways to organize a course in corporate finance as there are teachers. For this reason, we have ensured that the text is modular so that topics can be introduced in different sequences.

We like to discuss the principles of valuation before plunging into financial planning. Nevertheless, we recognize that many instructors will prefer to move directly from Chapter 4 (Measuring Corporate Performance) to Chapter 18 (Long-Term Financial Planning) in order to provide a gentler transition from the typical prerequisite accounting course. We have made sure that Part 6 (Financial Analysis and Planning) can easily follow Part 1.

Similarly, we like to discuss working capital after the student is familiar with the basic principles of valuation and financing, but we recognize that here also many instructors prefer to reverse our order. There should be no difficulty in taking Chapter 20 out of order.

When we discuss project valuation in Part 2, we stress that the opportunity cost of capital depends on project risk. But we do not discuss how to measure risk or how return and risk are linked until Part 3. This ordering can easily be modified. For example, the chapters on risk and return can be introduced before, after, or midway through the material on project valuation.

Changes in the Ninth Edition

Users of previous editions of this book will not find dramatic changes in either the material or the ordering of topics. But, throughout, we have made the book more up to date and easier to read. Here are some of the ways that we have done this.

Beyond the Page The biggest change in the last edition was the introduction of Beyond the Page digital extensions and applications. These digital extensions are not, as they may sound, artificial fingernails; they are additional examples, anecdotes, spreadsheet programs, and more thoroughgoing explanations of some topics. This material is very easily accessed on the web. In this edition, we have added a number of additional applications and made them easier to access. For example, the applications are seamlessly available with a click on the e-version of the book, but they are also readily accessible in the traditional hard copy of the text using the shortcut URLs provided in the margins of relevant pages.

Improving the Flow A major part of our effort in revising this text was spent on improving the flow. Often this has meant a word change here or a redrawn diagram there, but sometimes we have made more substantial changes. One example is the discussion of WACC in Chapter 13. Rather than chop and change between our two illustrative companies, Geothermal and Big Oil, we now follow through the Geothermal example to the end. By then, the reader should understand when one can and can't use WACC and can move on to tackling the practical problems of estimating Big Oil's capital structure and expected returns. The material is substantially unchanged, but we think that the flow is much improved.

Updating Of course, in each new edition we try to ensure that any statistics are as up to date as possible. For example, since the previous edition, we have available an extra 3 years of data on security returns. These show up in the figures in Chapter 11 of the long-run returns on stocks, bonds, and bills. Measures of EVA, data on security ownership, dividend payments, and stock repurchases are just a few of the other cases where data have been brought up to date.

Recent Events We discussed the financial crisis of 2007–2009 in the previous edition, but we have now been able to revise our discussion to include the spillover to the crisis in the eurozone and to draw some general lessons. The eurozone crisis was also a reminder that government debt is not risk free. We come back to that issue in Chapter 6 when we discuss default risk.

Concepts There are several places where we have introduced new conceptual material. For example, students who have learned about the dividend discount model are often confused about how to value the many companies that also repurchase their stock. We introduce the issue in Chapters 7 and 13, and in Chapter 17, we explain how to value stocks of companies that both pay dividends and repurchase stock.

New Illustrative Boxes The text contains a number of boxes with illustrative real-world examples. Many of these are new. Look, for example, at the box in Chapter 2 that describes prediction markets and what they had to say about the 2016 primaries. Or look at the box in Chapter 15 that shows how HUDWAY used crowdfunding to finance its Head-Up Display project.

More Worked Examples We have added more worked examples in the text, many of them taken from real companies.

Specific Chapter Changes in the Ninth Edition

Here are a few of the additions to chapter material:

Chapter 1 contains a discussion of the ethical implications of Volkswagen's suppression of emissions data for its diesel cars.

Chapter 2 includes a new box on mortgage-backed securities and their role in the financial crisis.

Chapter 3 includes updated discussions of accounting malfeasance and of the ebb and flow of attempts to harmonize GAAP and IFRS accounting standards.

Chapter 5 has a reorganized and integrated discussion of calculators and spreadsheets.

Chapter 6 includes a new Finance in Practice box to show how to find bond information on the web.

Chapter 7 contains a new section on using discounted cash flow to value entire businesses. The section on the efficient market theory has also been substantially revised and given a more up-to-date feel.

Chapter 9 now includes a short section that looks ahead to the techniques of project analysis in Chapter 10.

Chapter 10 has been substantially rewritten and better integrated with Chapter 9. It continues with the Blooper example from the earlier chapter to show how capital budgeting practices and project analysis techniques combine to ensure that investment decisions truly add value.

Chapter 14 now includes a discussion of shareholder votes on management compensation.

Chapter 16 now includes a section warning of the effects of hidden debt and a summary section that discusses how a thoughtful financial manager should set the company's debt strategy.

Chapter 17 contains a quick overview of trends in taxation and payout policy.

Chapter 18 has been considerably revised with a new example. It takes the example of Dynamic Mattress and sets out the three steps needed to derive a financial plan for the company.

Chapter 19 now offers a more focused look at short-term planning models. Discussions of working capital and the sources of short-term finance have been deferred until the next chapter.

Chapter 20 introduces the components of working capital and the determinants of the cash cycle. It then looks briefly at each of the components including short-term debt. Chapter 20 is longer than in the previous edition, but we think that it stands much better on its own.

Chapter 21 features numerous updates to reflect merger news of recent years, including the Allergan/Valeant battle.

Assurance of Learning

Assurance of learning is an important element of many accreditation standards. *Fundamentals of Corporate Finance,* Ninth Edition, is designed specifically to support your assurance-of-learning initiatives. Each chapter in the book begins with a list of numbered learning objectives, which are referred to in the end-of-chapter problems and exercises. Every test bank question is also linked to one of these objectives, in addition to level of difficulty, topic area, Bloom's Taxonomy level, and AACSB skill area. Connect, McGraw-Hill's online homework solution, and *EZ Test,* McGraw-Hill's easy-to-use test bank software, can search the test bank by these and other categories, providing an engine for targeted assurance-of-learning analysis and assessment.

AACSB Statement

McGraw-Hill Education is a proud corporate member of AACSB International. Understanding the importance and value of AACSB accreditation, *Fundamentals of*

Corporate Finance, Ninth Edition, has sought to recognize the curricula guidelines detailed in the AACSB standards for business accreditation by connecting selected questions in the test bank to the general knowledge and skill guidelines found in the AACSB standards.

The statements contained in *Fundamentals of Corporate Finance,* Ninth Edition, are provided only as a guide for the users of this text. The AACSB leaves content coverage and assessment within the purview of individual schools, the mission of the school, and the faculty. While *Fundamentals of Corporate Finance,* Ninth Edition, and the teaching package make no claim of any specific AACSB qualification or evaluation, we have, within the test bank, labeled selected questions according to the six general knowledge and skills areas.

Unique Features

What makes *Fundamentals of Corporate Finance* such a powerful learning tool?

Integrated Examples

Numbered and titled examples are integrated in each chapter. Students can learn how to solve specific problems step-by-step as well as gain insight into general principles by seeing how they are applied to answer concrete questions and scenarios.

> **Example 5.8 ▶** Winning Big at the Lottery
>
> In September 2015, a 50-year-old Michigan woman bought a Powerball lottery ticket and won $310.5 million. We suspect that she received unsolicited congratulations, good wishes, and requests for money from dozens of more or less worthy charities, relations, and newly devoted friends. In response, she could fairly point out that the prize wasn't really worth $310.5 million. That sum was to be paid in 30 equal annual installments of $10.35 million each. Assuming that the first payment occurred at the end of 1 year, what was the present value of the prize? The interest rate at the time was about 3.2%.
>
> The present value of these payments is simply the sum of the present values of each annual payment. But rather than valuing the payments separately, it is much easier to treat them as a 30-year annuity. To value this annuity, we multiply $10.35 million by the 30-year annuity factor:
>
> $$PV = 10.35 \times \text{30-year annuity factor}$$
>
> $$= 10.35 \times \left[\frac{1}{r} - \frac{1}{r(1+r)^{30}} \right]$$
>
> At an interest rate of 3.2%, the annuity factor is
>
> $$\left[\frac{1}{.032} - \frac{1}{.032(1.032)^{30}} \right] = 19.1033$$

Spreadsheet Solutions Boxes

These boxes provide the student with detailed examples of how to use Excel spreadsheets when applying financial concepts. The boxes include questions that apply to the spreadsheet, and their solutions are given at the end of the applicable chapter. These spreadsheets are available for download in Connect.

> **Spreadsheet Solutions** Bond Valuation
>
> Excel and most other spreadsheet programs provide built-in functions to compute bond values and yields. They typically ask you to input both the date you buy the bond (called the *settlement date*) and the maturity date of the bond.
>
> The Excel function for bond value is:
>
> =PRICE(settlement date, maturity date, annual coupon rate, yield to maturity, redemption value as percent of face value, number of coupon payments per year)
>
> (If you can't remember the formula, just remember that you can go to the Formulas tab in Excel, and from the Financial tab pull down the PRICE function, which will prompt you for the necessary inputs.) For our 1.25% coupon bond, we would enter the values shown in the spreadsheet below. Alternatively, we could simply enter the following function in Excel.
>
> The value of the bond assuming annual coupon payments is 100.164% of face value, or $1,001.64. If we wanted to assume semiannual coupon payments, as in Example 6.1, we would simply change the entry in cell B10 to 2 (see column D), and the bond value would change to 100.165% of face value, as we found in that example.
>
> We have also assumed that the first coupon payment comes in exactly one period (either a year or a half-year). In other words, the settlement date is precisely at the beginning of the period. However, the PRICE function will make the necessary adjustments for intraperiod purchase dates.
>
> Suppose now that you wish to find the price of a 30-year maturity bond with a coupon rate of 6% (paid annually) selling at a yield to maturity of 7%. You are not given a specific settlement or maturity date. You can still use the PRICE function to value the bond. Simply choose an arbitrary settlement date

Excel Exhibits

Selected exhibits are set as Excel spreadsheets. The accompanying files are available for instructors and students in Connect.

SPREADSHEET 5.3 Using a spreadsheet to find the present value of multiple cash flows

	A	B	C	D	E
1	Finding the present value of multiple cash flows using a spreadsheet				
2					
3	Time until CF	Cash flow	Present value	Formula in Col C	Alternative formula for Col C
4	0	8000	$8,000.00	=PV(B10, A4,0, −B4)	=B4/(1 + B10)^A4
5	1	4000	$3,703.70	=PV(B10, A5,0, −B5)	=B5/(1 + B10)^A5
6	2	4000	$3,429.36	=PV(B10, A6,0, −B6)	=B6/(1 + B10)^A6
7					
8	SUM		$15,133.06	=SUM(C4:C6)	=SUM(C4:C6)
9					
10	Discount rate:	0.08			
11					
12	Notice that the time until each payment is found in column A.				
13	Once we enter the formula for present value in cell C4, we can copy it to cells C5 and C6.				
14	The present value for other interest rates can be found by changing the entry in cell B10.				

values (column C) therefore appear as positive numbers. Column E shows an alternative to the use of the PV function, where we calculate present values directly.

Finance in Practice Boxes

These are excerpts that appear in most chapters, often from the financial press, providing real-life illustrations of the chapter's topics, such as ethical choices in finance, disputes about stock valuation, financial planning, and credit analysis.

Finance in Practice Ethical Disputes in Finance

Short-Selling

Investors who take short positions are betting that securities will fall in price. Usually they do this by borrowing the security, selling it for cash, and then waiting in the hope that they will be able to buy it back cheaply.* In 2007, hedge fund manager John Paulson took a huge short position in mortgage-backed securities. The bet paid off, and that year Paulson's trade made a profit of $1 billion for his fund.[1]

Was Paulson's trade unethical? Some believe not only that he was profiting from the misery that resulted from the crash in mortgage-backed securities, but that his short trades accentuated the collapse. It is certainly true that short-sellers have never been popular. For example, following the crash of 1929, one commentator compared short-selling to the ghoulishness of "creatures who, at all great earthquakes and fires, spring up to rob broken homes and injured and dead

But sometimes raids can enhance shareholder value. For example, in 2012 and 2013, Relational Investors teamed up with the California State Teachers' Retirement System (CSTRS, a pension fund) to try to force Timken Co. to split into two separate companies, one for its steel business and one for its industrial bearings business. Relational and CSTRS believed that Timken's combination of unrelated businesses was unfocused and inefficient. Timken management responded that breakup would "deprive our shareholders of long-run value—all in an attempt to create illusory short-term gains through financial engineering." But Timken's stock price rose at the prospect of a breakup, and a nonbinding shareholder vote on Relational's proposal attracted a 53% majority. Finally in 2014 Timken spun off its steel business in a new corporation, Timken Steel.

How do you see the ethical line in such examples? Was

Financial Calculator Boxes and Exercises

In a continued effort to help students grasp the critical concept of the time value of money, many pedagogical tools have been added throughout the first section of the text. Financial Calculator boxes provide examples for solving a variety of problems, with directions for the most popular financial calculators.

Financial Calculator Using a Financial Calculator to Compute Bond Yield

You can use a financial calculator to calculate the yield to maturity on our 1.25% Treasury bond. The inputs are:

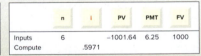

	n	i	PV	PMT	FV
Inputs	3		−1001.64	12.5	1000
Compute		1.194			

Now compute *i* and you should get an answer of 1.194%.

Let's now redo this calculation but recognize that the coupons are paid semiannually. Instead of three annual coupon payments of $12.50, the bond makes six semiannual

payments of $6.25. Therefore, we can find the semiannual yield as follows:

	n	i	PV	PMT	FV
Inputs	6		−1001.64	6.25	1000
Compute		.5971			

This yield to maturity, of course, is a 6-month yield, not an annual one. Bond dealers would typically annualize the semiannual rate by doubling it, so the yield to maturity would be quoted as .5971 × 2 = 1.1942%.

Self-Test Questions

Provided in each chapter, these helpful questions enable students to check their understanding as they read. Answers are worked out at the end of each chapter.

6.4 Self-Test

Suppose that the market interest rate is 4% and then drops overnight to 2%. Calculate the present values of the 1.25%, 3-year bond and of the 1.25%, 30-year bond both before and after this change in interest rates. Assume annual coupon payments. Confirm that your answers correspond with Figure 6.5. Use your financial calculator or a spreadsheet. You can find a box on bond pricing using Excel later in this chapter.

"Beyond the Page" Interactive Content and Applications

Additional resources and hands-on applications are just a click away. Students can tap or click the icons in the e-version or use the direct web links to learn more about key concepts and try out calculations, tables, and figures when they go "Beyond the Page."

BEYOND THE PAGE

How changes in interest rates affect long- and short-term bonds

mhhe.com/brealey9e

BEYOND THE PAGE

Which is the longer-term bond?

mhhe.com/brealey9e

the market interest rate rises, the value of their investment falls.

A change in interest rates has only a modest impact on the present value of near-term cash flows but a much greater impact on the value of distant cash flows. Therefore, any change has a greater impact on the price of long-term bonds than the price of short-term bonds. For example, compare the two curves in Figure 6.5. The blue line shows how the value of the 3-year, 1.25% coupon bond varies with the interest rate. The green line shows how the price of a 30-year, 1.25% bond varies. You can see that the 30-year bond is more sensitive to interest rate fluctuations than the 3-year bond. This should not surprise you. If you buy a 3-year bond and rates then rise, you will be stuck with a bad deal—you could have got a better interest rate if you had waited. However, think how much worse it would be if the loan had been for 30 years rather than 3 years. The longer the loan, the more income you have lost by accepting what turns out to be a low interest rate. This shows up in a bigger decline in the price of the longer-term bond. Of course, there is a flip side to this effect, which you can also see from Figure 6.5. When interest rates fall, the longer-term bond responds with a greater increase in price.

Web Exercises

Select chapters include Web Exercises that allow students to utilize the Internet to apply their knowledge and skills with real-world companies.

WEB EXERCISES

1. Log on to www.investopedia.com to find a simple calculator for working out bond prices. (Start by clicking the *Investing* link.) Check whether a change in yield has a greater effect on the price of a long-term or a short-term bond.

2. When we plotted the yield curve in Figure 6.7, we used the prices of Treasury strips. You can find current prices of strips by logging on to *The Wall Street Journal* website (www.wsj.com) and clicking on *Market*, *Market Data*, and then *Rates*. Try plotting the yields on stripped coupons against maturity. Do they currently increase or decline with maturity? Can you explain why? You can also use *The Wall Street Journal* site to compare the yields on nominal Treasury bonds with those on TIPS. Suppose that you are confident that inflation will be 3% per year. Which bonds are the better buy?

3. You can find the most recent bond rating for many companies by logging on to finance.yahoo.com and going to the Bond Center. Find the bond rating for some major companies. Were they investment-grade or below?

4. In Figure 6.9, we showed how bonds with greater credit risk have promised higher yields to maturity. This yield spread goes up when the economic outlook is particularly uncertain. You can check how much extra yield low-grade bonds offer today by logging on to www.

Minicases

Integrated minicases allow students to apply their knowledge to relatively complex, practical problems and typical real-world scenarios.

MINICASE

Old Alfred Road, who is well-known to drivers on the Maine Turnpike, has reached his 70th birthday and is ready to retire. Mr. Road has no formal training in finance but has saved his money and invested carefully.

Mr. Road owns his home—the mortgage is paid off—and does not want to move. He is a widower, and he wants to bequeath the house and any remaining assets to his daughter.

He has accumulated savings of $180,000, conservatively invested. The investments are yielding 9% interest. Mr. Road also has $12,000 in a savings account at 5% interest. He wants to keep the savings account intact for unexpected expenses or emergencies.

Mr. Road's basic living expenses now average about $1,500 per

inflation. That is, they will be automatically increased in proportion to changes in the consumer price index.

Mr. Road's main concern is with inflation. The inflation rate has been below 3% recently, but a 3% rate is unusually low by historical standards. His Social Security payments will increase with inflation, but the interest on his investment portfolio will not.

What advice do you have for Mr. Road? Can he safely spend all the interest from his investment portfolio? How much could he withdraw at year-end from that portfolio if he wants to keep its real value intact?

Suppose Mr. Road will live for 20 more years and is willing to use up all of his investment portfolio over that period. He also

Supplements

In addition to the overall refinement and improvement of the text material, considerable effort was put into developing an exceptional supplement package to provide students and instructors with an abundance of teaching and learning resources.

Instructor Library

The Connect Instructor Library is your repository for additional resources to improve student engagement in and out of class. You can select and use any asset that enhances your lecture. The Connect Instructor Library includes all of the instructor supplements for this text.

Solutions Manual

Mishal Rawaf worked with the authors to prepare this resource containing detailed and thoughtful solutions to all the end-of-chapter problems.

Instructor's Manual

This manual, updated and enhanced by Matthew Will at the University of Indianapolis, includes a descriptive preface containing alternative course formats and case teaching methods, a chapter overview and outline, key terms and concepts, a description of the PowerPoint slides, video teaching notes, related web links, and pedagogical ideas.

Test Bank

Author Richard Brealey has thoroughly reviewed and revised the test bank, adding new questions and ensuring that all of the content is closely correlated to the text. More than 2,000 true/false, multiple-choice, and discussion questions/problems are available to the instructor at varying levels of difficulty and comprehension. All questions are tagged by learning objective, topic, AACSB category, and Bloom's Taxonomy level. Complete answers are provided for all test questions and problems. The test bank is available as downloadable Word files, and tests can also be created online within McGraw-Hill's Connect or through TestGen.

TestGen is a complete, state-of-the-art test generator and editing application software that allows instructors to quickly and easily select test items from McGraw-Hill's test bank content. The instructors can then organize, edit, and customize questions and answers to rapidly generate tests for paper or online administration. Questions can include stylized text, symbols, graphics, and equations that are inserted directly into questions using built-in mathematical templates. TestGen's random generator provides the option to display different text or calculated number values each time questions are used. With both quick-and-simple test creation and flexible and robust editing tools, TestGen is a complete test generator system for today's educators.

PowerPoint Presentations

These visually stimulating slides have been fully updated by Matthew Will, with colorful graphs, charts, and lists. The slides can be edited or manipulated to fit the needs of a particular course.

Beyond the Page Content

The authors have created a wealth of additional examples, explanations, and applications, available for quick access by instructors and students. Each "Beyond the Page" feature is called out in the text with an icon that links directly to the content.

Excel Solutions and Templates

Excel templates are available in Connect for select exhibits and various end-of-chapter problems that have been set as Excel spreadsheets. They correlate with specific concepts in the text and allow students to work through financial problems and gain experience using spreadsheets. Also refer to the valuable Spreadsheet Solutions Boxes that are sprinkled throughout the text for some helpful prompts on working in Excel.

Student Study Center

The Connect Student Study Center is the place for students to access additional resources. The Student Study Center:

- Offers students quick access to the Beyond the Page features, Excel files and templates, lectures, eBooks, and more.
- Provides instant practice material and study questions, easily accessible on the go.

Student Progress Tracking

Connect keeps instructors informed about how each student, section, and class is performing, allowing for more productive use of lecture and office hours. The progress-tracking function enables you to:

- View scored work immediately and track individual or group performance with assignment and grade reports.
- Access an instant view of student or class performance relative to learning objectives.
- Collect data and generate reports required by many accreditation organizations, such as AACSB and AICPA.

McGraw-Hill Customer Care Contact Information

At McGraw-Hill, we understand that getting the most from new technology can be challenging. That's why our services don't stop after you purchase our products. You can e-mail our product specialists 24 hours a day to get product training online. Or you can search our knowledge bank of frequently asked questions on our support website.

For customer support, call **800-331-5094** or visit **www.mhhe.com/support**. One of our technical support analysts will be able to assist you in a timely fashion.

©Getty Images/iStockphoto

McGraw-Hill Connect®
Learn Without Limits

Connect is a teaching and learning platform that is proven to deliver better results for students and instructors.

Connect empowers students by continually adapting to deliver precisely what they need, when they need it, and how they need it, so your class time is more engaging and effective.

73% of instructors who use Connect require it; instructor satisfaction increases by 28% when Connect is required.

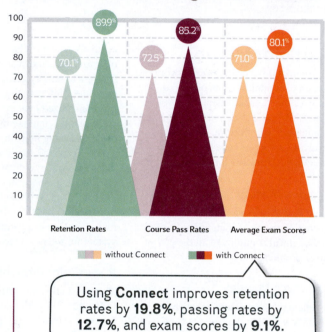

Connect's Impact on Retention Rates, Pass Rates, and Average Exam Scores

- Retention Rates: 70.1% without Connect, 89.9% with Connect
- Course Pass Rates: 72.5% without Connect, 85.2% with Connect
- Average Exam Scores: 71.0% without Connect, 80.1% with Connect

without Connect / with Connect

Using **Connect** improves retention rates by **19.8%**, passing rates by **12.7%**, and exam scores by **9.1%**.

Analytics

Connect Insight®

Connect Insight is Connect's new one-of-a-kind visual analytics dashboard that provides at-a-glance information regarding student performance, which is immediately actionable. By presenting assignment, assessment, and topical performance results together with a time metric that is easily visible for aggregate or individual results, Connect Insight gives the user the ability to take a just-in-time approach to teaching and learning, which was never before available. Connect Insight presents data that helps instructors improve class performance in a way that is efficient and effective.

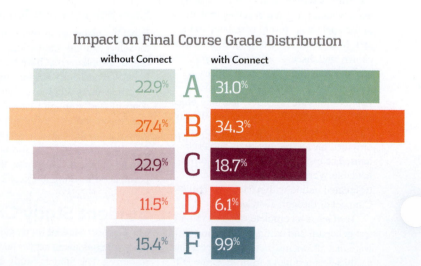

Impact on Final Course Grade Distribution

	without Connect	with Connect
A	22.9%	31.0%
B	27.4%	34.3%
C	22.9%	18.7%
D	11.5%	6.1%
F	15.4%	9.9%

Adaptive

THE ADAPTIVE READING EXPERIENCE DESIGNED TO TRANSFORM THE WAY STUDENTS READ

More students earn **A's** and **B's** when they use McGraw-Hill Education **Adaptive** products.

SmartBook®

Proven to help students improve grades and study more efficiently, SmartBook contains the same content within the print book, but actively tailors that content to the needs of the individual. SmartBook's adaptive technology provides precise, personalized instruction on what the student should do next, guiding the student to master and remember key concepts, targeting gaps in knowledge and offering customized feedback, and driving the student toward comprehension and retention of the subject matter. Available on tablets, SmartBook puts learning at the student's fingertips—anywhere, anytime.

Over **8 billion questions** have been answered, making McGraw-Hill Education products more intelligent, reliable, and precise.

www.mheducation.com

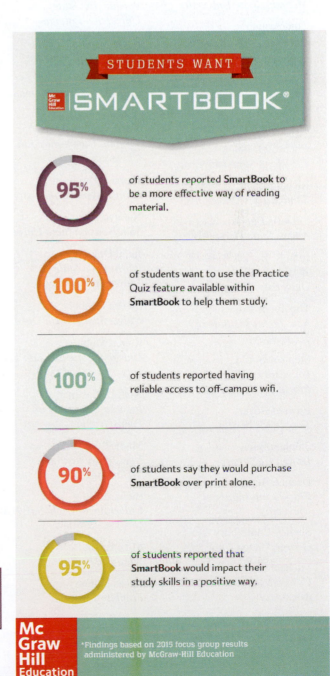

STUDENTS WANT

SMARTBOOK®

95% of students reported SmartBook to be a more effective way of reading material.

100% of students want to use the Practice Quiz feature available within SmartBook to help them study.

100% of students reported having reliable access to off-campus wifi.

90% of students say they would purchase SmartBook over print alone.

95% of students reported that SmartBook would impact their study skills in a positive way.

*Findings based on 2015 focus group results administered by McGraw-Hill Education

Acknowledgments

We take this opportunity to thank all of the individuals who helped us prepare this and previous editions. We want to express our appreciation to those instructors whose insightful comments and suggestions were invaluable to us during this revision.

Marlena Akhbari
Wright State University

Timothy Alzheimer
Montana State University

Tom Arnold
University of Richmond

Robert Balik
Western Michigan University

Anindam Bandopadhyaya
University of Massachusetts–Boston

Chenchu Bathala
Cleveland State University

Richard Bauer
Saint Mary's University

LaDoris Baugh
Athens State University

John R. Becker Blease
Washington State University–Vancouver

Theologos Bonitsis
New Jersey Institute of Technology

Stephen Borde
University of Central Florida

Edward Boyer
Temple University

Stephen Buell
Lehigh University

Deanne Butchey
Florida International University

Shelley Canterbury
George Mason University

Michael Casey
University of Central Arkansas

Fan Chen
University of Mississippi

Nicole Choi
Washington State University–Pullman

Bruce Costa
University of Montana

Ernie Dancer
Columbus State Community College

Kenneth Daniels
Virginia Commonwealth University

Morris Danielson
Saint Joseph's University

Natalya Delcoure
Sam Houston State University

Jared DeLisle
Washington State University–Vancouver

Steven Dennis
University of North Dakota

Robert Dubil
University of Utah–Salt Lake City

Alan D. Eastman
Indiana University of Pennsylvania

Michael Ehrlich
New Jersey Institute of Technology

Richard Elliot
University of Utah–Salt Lake City

Mike Evans
Winthrop University

James Falter
Franklin University

John Fay
Santa Clara University

Richard Fedler
Georgia State University

Michael Ferguson
University of Cincinnati

Dov Fobar
Brooklyn College

Eric Fricke
California State University–East Bay

Steve Gallaher
Southern New Hampshire University

Sharon Garrison
University of Arizona

Ashley Geisewite
Southwest Tennessee Community College

Homaifar Ghassem
Middle Tennessee State University

Phillip Giles
Columbia University

Gary Gray
Penn State University–University Park

John Halstead
Liberty University

Mahfuzul Haque
Indiana State University

Andrew Hession-Kunz
Boston College

Larry Holland
University of Arkansas–Little Rock

James J. Hopper
Mississippi State University

Jian "Emily" Huang
California State University–Chico

Stoyu Ivanov
San Jose State University

Raymond Jackson
University of Massachusetts–Dartmouth

Keith Jacob
University of Montana

Bharat Jain
Towson University

Benjamas Jirasakuldech
Slippery Rock University of Pennsylvania

Mark Johnson
Loyola University Maryland

Steve Johnson
Sam Houston State University

Daniel Jubinski
Saint Joseph's University

Alan Jung
San Francisco State University

Ayala Kayhan
Louisiana State University

Marvin Keene
Coastal Carolina University

Eric Kelley
University of Arizona

Dong Man Kim
California State University–San Bernardino

Jullavut Kittiakarasakun
University of Texas at San Antonio

Ladd Kochman
Kennesaw State University

David Kuipers
University of Missouri–Kansas City

Mark Lane
Hawaii Pacific University–Honolulu

Linda Lange
Regis University

Doug Letsch
Walden University

Paul Lewandowski
Saginaw Valley State University

Scott W. Lowe
James Madison University

Yuming Li
California State University–Fullerton

Qianqiu Liu
University of Hawaii–Manoa

Sheen Liu
Washington State University–Vancouver

Wilson Liu
James Madison University

Qingzhong Ma
Cornell University–Ithaca

Yulong Ma
California State University–Long Beach

Brian Maris
Northern Arizona University

Jinghan Meng
University of North Carolina–Chapel Hill

Jose Mercardo
University of Central Missouri

Paulo Miranda
Purdue University–Calumet Hammond

Derek Mohr
State University of New York at Buffalo

Helen Moser
University of Minnesota–Minneapolis

Tammie Mosley
California State University–East Bay

Vivian Nazar
Ferris State University

Steve Nenninger
Sam Houston State University

Bonnie Van Ness
University of Mississippi

Srinivas Nippani
Texas A&M University–Commerce

Prasad Padmanabhan
Saint Mary's University

Ohaness Paskelian
University of Houston–Downtown

Jeffrey Phillips
Colby-Sawyer College

Richard Ponarul
California State University–Chico

Gary Porter
John Carroll University

Eric Powers
University of South Carolina

Ronald Prange
Western Michigan University

Robert Puelz
Southern Methodist University

Sunder Raghavan
Embry-Riddle University

Vedpauri Raghavan
Embry-Riddle University–Daytona Beach

Ganas K. Rakes
Ohio University

Adam Reed
University of North Carolina–Chapel Hill

Thomas Rhee
California State University–Long Beach

Jong Rhim
University of Southern Indiana

Joe Riotto
New Jersey City University

Mukunthan Santhanakrishnan
Idaho State University

Maria Schutte
Michigan Technological University

Adam Schwartz
Washington & Lee University

John Settle
Portland State University

Michael G. Sher
Metropolitan State University

Henry Silverman
Roosevelt University

Ron Spicer
Colorado Tech University

Roberto Stein
Tulane University

Tom Strickland
Middle Tennessee State University

Jan Strockis
Santa Clara University

Joseph Tanimura
San Diego State University

Steve Tokar
University of Indianapolis

Damir Tokic
University of Houston–Downtown

Michael Toyne
Northeastern State University

James Turner
Weber State Universtiy

Joe Walker
University of Alabama–Birmingham

Kenneth Washer
Texas A&M University–Commerce

K. Matthew Wong
St. John's University

Qiang Wu
Rensselaer Polytechnic University

David Yamoah
Kean University

Fred Yeager
St. Louis University

Kevin Yost
Auburn University

Emilio R. Zarruk
Florida Atlantic University

Athena Zhang
California State University–Chico

Shaorong Zhang
Marshall University

Yilei Zhang
University of North Dakota

Yiling Zhang
University of Texas–Arlington

Zhong-Guo Zhou
California State University–Northridge

In addition, we would like to thank the dedicated experts who have helped with updates to our instructor materials and online content in Connect and LearnSmart, including Kay Johnson, Annie Treinen, Mishal Rawaf, Matt Will, Blaise Roncagli, Peter Crabb, Deb Bauer, Marc-Anthony Isaacs, and Nicholas Racculia. Their efforts are much appreciated as they will help both students and instructors. We also appreciate help from Aleijda de Cazenove Balsan and Malcolm Taylor.

We are grateful to the talented staff at McGraw-Hill Education, especially Noelle Bathurst, Senior Product Developer; Chuck Synovec, Director, Finance; Kevin Shanahan, Digital Product Analyst; Tobi Philips, Digital Product Developer; Kathryn Wright and Kristin Bradley, Content Project Managers; Matthew Diamond, Senior Designer; Melissa Caughlin, Marketing Director; Trina Mauer, Senior Marketing Manager; Dave O'Donnell, Marketing Specialist; and Melissa Homer and Valerie Moring Schubert, Photo Researchers.

Finally, as was the case with the last eight editions, we cannot overstate the thanks due to our families.

Richard A. Brealey
Stewart C. Myers
Alan J. Marcus

Contents in Brief

Part One
Introduction

1 Goals and Governance of the Corporation   2
2 Financial Markets and Institutions   32
3 Accounting and Finance   56
4 Measuring Corporate Performance   86

Part Two
Value

5 The Time Value of Money   118
6 Valuing Bonds   166
7 Valuing Stocks   196
8 Net Present Value and Other Investment Criteria   238
9 Using Discounted Cash-Flow Analysis to Make Investment Decisions   274
10 Project Analysis   302

Part Three
Risk

11 Introduction to Risk, Return, and the Opportunity Cost of Capital   330
12 Risk, Return, and Capital Budgeting   360
13 The Weighted-Average Cost of Capital and Company Valuation   390

Part Four
Financing

14 Introduction to Corporate Financing   418
15 How Corporations Raise Venture Capital and Issue Securities   440

Part Five
Debt and Payout Policy

16 Debt Policy   466
17 Payout Policy   504

Part Six
Financial Analysis and Planning

18 Long-Term Financial Planning   528
19 Short-Term Financial Planning   550
20 Working Capital Management   570

Part Seven
Special Topics

21 Mergers, Acquisitions, and Corporate Control   610
22 International Financial Management   638
23 Options   664
24 Risk Management   692

Part Eight
Conclusion

25 What We Do and Do Not Know about Finance   712

Appendix: Present Value and Future Value Tables   A-1
Glossary   G-1
Global Index   IND-1
Subject Index   IND-5

Contents

Part One — Introduction

Chapter 1
Goals and Governance of the Corporation   2

1.1   **Investment and Financing Decisions**   4
The Investment (Capital Budgeting) Decision   6
The Financing Decision   6

1.2   **What Is a Corporation?**   8
Other Forms of Business Organization   9

1.3   **Who Is the Financial Manager?**   10

1.4   **Goals of the Corporation**   12
Shareholders Want Managers to Maximize Market Value   12

1.5   **Agency Problems, Executive Compensation, and Corporate Governance**   15
Executive Compensation   16
Corporate Governance   17

1.6   **The Ethics of Maximizing Value**   18

1.7   **Careers in Finance**   21

1.8   **Preview of Coming Attractions**   22

1.9   **Snippets of Financial History**   23
Summary   25
Questions and Problems   26

Chapter 2
Financial Markets and Institutions   32

2.1   **The Importance of Financial Markets and Institutions**   34

2.2   **The Flow of Savings to Corporations**   35
The Stock Market   37
Other Financial Markets   38
Financial Intermediaries   40
Financial Institutions   42
Total Financing of U.S. Corporations   43

2.3   **Functions of Financial Markets and Intermediaries**   44
Transporting Cash across Time   45
Risk Transfer and Diversification   45
Liquidity   46
The Payment Mechanism   46
Information Provided by Financial Markets   47

2.4   **The Crisis of 2007–2009**   49
Summary   51
Questions and Problems   52

Chapter 3
Accounting and Finance   56

3.1   **The Balance Sheet**   58
Book Values and Market Values   61

3.2   **The Income Statement**   63
Income versus Cash Flow   64

3.3   **The Statement of Cash Flows**   67
Free Cash Flow   69

3.4   **Accounting Practice and Malpractice**   70

3.5   **Taxes**   73
Corporate Tax   73
Personal Tax   74

Summary   76
Questions and Problems   76

Chapter 4
Measuring Corporate Performance   86

4.1   **How Financial Ratios Relate to Shareholder Value**   88

4.2   **Measuring Market Value and Market Value Added**   89

4.3   **Economic Value Added and Accounting Rates of Return**   91
Accounting Rates of Return   93
Problems with EVA and Accounting Rates of Return   95

4.4   **Measuring Efficiency**   96

4.5   **Analyzing the Return on Assets: The Du Pont System**   97
The Du Pont System   98

4.6   **Measuring Financial Leverage**   100
Leverage and the Return on Equity   102

4.7   **Measuring Liquidity**   103

4.8   **Interpreting Financial Ratios**   104

4.9   **The Role of Financial Ratios**   108
Summary   109
Questions and Problems   110
Minicase   116

Part Two | Value

Chapter 5
The Time Value of Money   118

5.1   **Future Values and Compound Interest**   120

5.2   **Present Values**   123

Finding the Interest Rate   127

5.3   **Multiple Cash Flows**   128

Future Value of Multiple Cash Flows   128

Present Value of Multiple Cash Flows   130

5.4   **Reducing the Chore of the Calculations: Part 1**   131

Using Financial Calculators to Solve Simple Time-Value-of-Money Problems   131

Using Spreadsheets to Solve Simple Time-Value-of-Money Problems   132

5.5   **Level Cash Flows: Perpetuities and Annuities**   135

How to Value Perpetuities   135

How to Value Annuities   136

Future Value of an Annuity   140

Annuities Due   143

5.6   **Reducing the Chore of the Calculations: Part 2**   144

Using Financial Calculators to Solve Annuity Problems   145

Using Spreadsheets to Solve Annuity Problems   145

5.7   **Effective Annual Interest Rates**   146

5.8   **Inflation and the Time Value of Money**   148

Real versus Nominal Cash Flows   148

Inflation and Interest Rates   150

Valuing Real Cash Payments   151

Real or Nominal?   153

Summary   *153*

Questions and Problems   *154*

Minicase   *165*

Chapter 6
Valuing Bonds   166

6.1   **The Bond Market**   168

Bond Characteristics   168

6.2   **Interest Rates and Bond Prices**   169

How Bond Prices Vary with Interest Rates   172

Interest Rate Risk   174

6.3   **Yield to Maturity**   174

Calculating the Yield to Maturity   176

6.4   **Bond Rates of Return**   176

6.5   **The Yield Curve**   178

Nominal and Real Rates of Interest   181

6.6   **Corporate Bonds and the Risk of Default**   182

Protecting against Default Risk   185

Not All Corporate Bonds Are Plain Vanilla   187

Summary   *187*

Questions and Problems   *188*

Chapter 7
Valuing Stocks   196

7.1   **Stocks and the Stock Market**   198

Reading Stock Market Listings   199

7.2   **Market Values, Book Values, and Liquidation Values**   201

7.3   **Valuing Common Stocks**   203

Valuation by Comparables   203

Price and Intrinsic Value   204

The Dividend Discount Model   206

7.4   **Simplifying the Dividend Discount Model**   209

Case 1: The Dividend Discount Model with No Growth   209

Case 2: The Dividend Discount Model with Constant Growth   209

Case 3: The Dividend Discount Model with Nonconstant Growth   214

7.5   **Valuing a Business by Discounted Cash Flow**   218

Valuing the Concatenator Business   218

Repurchases and the Dividend Discount Model   219

7.6   **There Are No Free Lunches on Wall Street**   220

Random Walks and Efficient Markets   221

7.7   **Market Anomalies and Behavioral Finance**   225

Market Anomalies   225

Bubbles and Market Efficiency   226

Behavioral Finance   227

Summary   *228*

Questions and Problems   *229*

Minicase   *236*

Chapter 8
Net Present Value and Other Investment Criteria   238

8.1   **Net Present Value**   240

A Comment on Risk and Present Value   241

Valuing Long-Lived Projects   242

Choosing between Alternative Projects   244

8.2   **The Internal Rate of Return Rule**   245

A Closer Look at the Rate of Return Rule   246

Calculating the Rate of Return for Long-Lived Projects   246

A Word of Caution   248

Some Pitfalls with the Internal Rate of Return Rule   248

8.3   **The Profitability Index**   253

Capital Rationing 254

Pitfalls of the Profitability Index 254

8.4 The Payback Rule 255

Discounted Payback 256

8.5 More Mutually Exclusive Projects 256

Problem 1: The Investment Timing Decision 257

Problem 2: The Choice between Long- and Short-Lived Equipment 258

Problem 3: When to Replace an Old Machine 260

8.6 A Last Look 261

Summary 262

Questions and Problems 263

Minicase 270

Appendix: *More on the IRR Rule 271*

Using the IRR to Choose between Mutually Exclusive Projects 271

Using the Modified Internal Rate of Return When There Are Multiple IRRs 271

Chapter 9

Using Discounted Cash-Flow Analysis to Make Investment Decisions 274

9.1 Identifying Cash Flows 276

Discount Cash Flows, Not Profits 276

Discount *Incremental* Cash Flows 278

Discount Nominal Cash Flows by the Nominal Cost of Capital 281

Separate Investment and Financing Decisions 282

9.2 Calculating Cash Flow 283

Element 1: Capital Investment 283

Element 2: Operating Cash Flow 283

Element 3: Changes in Working Capital 285

9.3 An Example: Blooper Industries 286

Cash-Flow Analysis 286

Calculating the NPV of Blooper's Project 288

Further Notes and Wrinkles Arising from Blooper's Project 289

Summary 293

Questions and Problems 294

Minicase 301

Chapter 10

Project Analysis 302

10.1 How Firms Organize the Investment Process to Draw on Their Competitive Strengths 304

The Capital Budget 304

Problems and Some Solutions 305

10.2 Reducing Forecast Bias 305

10.3 Some "What-If" Questions 306

Sensitivity Analysis 307

Scenario Analysis 310

10.4 Break-Even Analysis 310

Accounting Break-Even Analysis 311

NPV Break-Even Analysis 312

Operating Leverage 315

10.5 Real Options and the Value of Flexibility 317

The Option to Expand 317

A Second Real Option: The Option to Abandon 319

A Third Real Option: The Timing Option 319

A Fourth Real Option: Flexible Production Facilities 320

Summary 321

Questions and Problems 322

Minicase 328

Part Three Risk

Chapter 11

Introduction to Risk, Return, and the Opportunity Cost of Capital 330

11.1 Rates of Return: A Review 332

11.2 A Century of Capital Market History 333

Market Indexes 333

The Historical Record 333

Using Historical Evidence to Estimate Today's Cost of Capital 336

11.3 Measuring Risk 338

Variance and Standard Deviation 338

A Note on Calculating Variance 341

Measuring the Variation in Stock Returns 341

11.4 Risk and Diversification 343

Diversification 343

Asset versus Portfolio Risk 344

Market Risk versus Specific Risk 350

11.5 Thinking about Risk 351

Message 1: Some Risks Look Big and Dangerous but Really Are Diversifiable 351

Message 2: Market Risks Are Macro Risks 352

Message 3: Risk Can Be Measured 353

Summary 354

Questions and Problems 355

Chapter 12
Risk, Return, and Capital Budgeting   360

12.1 Measuring Market Risk   362
    Measuring Beta   362
    Betas for U.S. Steel and PG&E   365
    Total Risk and Market Risk   365

12.2 What Can You Learn from Beta?   367
    Portfolio Betas   367
    The Portfolio Beta Determines the Risk of a Diversified Portfolio   370

12.3 Risk and Return   371
    Why the CAPM Makes Sense   373
    The Security Market Line   374
    Using the CAPM to Estimate Expected Returns   375
    How Well Does the CAPM Work?   375

12.4 The CAPM and the Opportunity Cost of Capital   378
    The Company Cost of Capital   380
    What Determines Project Risk?   380
    Don't Add Fudge Factors to Discount Rates   381

    Summary   *381*
    Questions and Problems   *382*

Chapter 13
The Weighted-Average Cost of Capital and Company Valuation   390

13.1 Geothermal's Cost of Capital   392
13.2 The Weighted-Average Cost of Capital   393

Calculating Company Cost of Capital as a Weighted Average   394
Use Market Weights, Not Book Weights   396
Taxes and the Weighted-Average Cost of Capital   396
What If There Are Three (or More) Sources of Financing?   398
The NPV of Geothermal's Expansion   398
Checking Our Logic   399

13.3 Interpreting the Weighted-Average Cost of Capital   400
    When You Can and Can't Use WACC   400
    Some Common Mistakes   400
    How Changing Capital Structure Affects Expected Returns   401
    What Happens When the Corporate Tax Rate Is Not Zero   401

13.4 Practical Problems: Measuring Capital Structure   401

13.5 More Practical Problems: Estimating Expected Returns   403
    The Expected Return on Bonds   403
    The Expected Return on Common Stock   404
    The Expected Return on Preferred Stock   405
    Adding It All Up   406
    Real-Company WACCs   406

13.6 Valuing Entire Businesses   406
    Calculating the Value of the Deconstruction Business   408

    Summary   *409*
    Questions and Problems   *410*
    Minicase   *415*

Part Four   Financing

Chapter 14
Introduction to Corporate Financing   418

14.1 Creating Value with Financing Decisions   420
14.2 Patterns of Corporate Financing   420
    Are Firms Issuing Too Much Debt?   423
14.3 Common Stock   424
    Ownership of the Corporation   426
    Voting Procedures   427
    Classes of Stock   428
14.4 Preferred Stock   428
14.5 Corporate Debt   429
    Debt Comes in Many Forms   429
    Innovation in the Debt Market   432
14.6 Convertible Securities   434

    Summary   *435*
    Questions and Problems   *436*

Chapter 15
How Corporations Raise Venture Capital and Issue Securities   440

15.1 Venture Capital   442
    Venture Capital Companies   443
15.2 The Initial Public Offering   444
    Arranging a Public Issue   445
    Other New-Issue Procedures   449
    The Underwriters   449
15.3 General Cash Offers by Public Companies   450
    General Cash Offers and Shelf Registration   451
    Costs of the General Cash Offer   452
    Market Reaction to Stock Issues   452
15.4 The Private Placement   453

    Summary   *454*
    Questions and Problems   *454*
    Minicase   *459*
    Appendix: *Hotch Pot's New-Issue Prospectus*   *461*

Part Five — Debt and Payout Policy

Chapter 16
Debt Policy 466

16.1 How Borrowing Affects Value in a Tax-Free Economy 468
MM's Argument—A Simple Example 469
How Borrowing Affects Earnings per Share 470
How Borrowing Affects Risk and Return 472

16.2 Debt and the Cost of Equity 473
No Magic in Financial Leverage 476

16.3 Debt, Taxes, and the Weighted-Average Cost of Capital 477
Debt and Taxes at River Cruises 478
How Interest Tax Shields Contribute to the Value of Stockholders' Equity 479
Corporate Taxes and the Weighted-Average Cost of Capital 480
The Implications of Corporate Taxes for Capital Structure 481

16.4 Costs of Financial Distress 482
Bankruptcy Costs 482
Costs of Bankruptcy Vary with Type of Asset 484
Financial Distress without Bankruptcy 485

16.5 Explaining Financing Choices 487
The Trade-Off Theory 487
A Pecking Order Theory 488
The Two Faces of Financial Slack 489
Is There a Theory of Optimal Capital Structure? 490

Summary 491

Questions and Problems 492
Minicase 499
Appendix: *Bankruptcy Procedures* 501

Chapter 17
Payout Policy 504

17.1 How Corporations Pay Out Cash to Shareholders 506
How Firms Pay Dividends 507
Limitations on Dividends 507
Stock Dividends and Stock Splits 508
Stock Repurchases 509

17.2 The Information Content of Dividends and Repurchases 509

17.3 Dividends or Repurchases? The Payout Controversy 511
Dividends or Repurchases? An Example 512
Repurchases and the Dividend Discount Model 513
Dividends and Share Issues 514

17.4 Why Dividends May Increase Value 515

17.5 Why Dividends May Reduce Value 517
Taxation of Dividends and Capital Gains under Current Tax Law 518
Taxes and Payout—A Summary 518

17.6 Payout Policy and the Life Cycle of the Firm 518

Summary 519
Questions and Problems 520
Minicase 526

Part Six — Financial Analysis and Planning

Chapter 18
Long-Term Financial Planning 528

18.1 What Is Financial Planning? 530
Why Build Financial Plans? 530

18.2 Financial Planning Models 531
Components of a Financial Planning Model 531

18.3 A Long-Term Financial Planning Model for Dynamic Mattress 532
Pitfalls in Model Design 537
Choosing a Plan 538

18.4 External Financing and Growth 539

Summary 542
Questions and Problems 543
Minicase 549

Chapter 19
Short-Term Financial Planning 550

19.1 Links between Long-Term and Short-Term Financing 552

19.2 Tracing Changes in Cash 554

19.3 Cash Budgeting 556
Preparing the Cash Budget 556

19.4 Dynamic's Short-Term Financial Plan 559
Dynamic Mattress's Financing Plan 559
Evaluating the Plan 560
A Note on Short-Term Financial Planning Models 561

Summary 563
Questions and Problems 563
Minicase 568

Chapter 20
Working Capital Management 570

20.1 Working Capital 572
Components of Working Capital 572
Working Capital and the Cash Cycle 572

20.2 Accounts Receivable and Credit Policy 575
Terms of Sale 576
Credit Agreements 577
Credit Analysis 578
The Credit Decision 579
Collection Policy 584

20.3 Inventory Management 586

20.4 Cash Management 588
Check Handling and Float 589

Other Payment Systems 590
Electronic Funds Transfer 591
International Cash Management 592

20.5 Investing Idle Cash: The Money Market 593
Money Market Investments 593
Calculating the Yield on Money Market Investments 594
Yields on Money Market Investments 595
The International Money Market 595

20.6 Managing Current Liabilities: Short-Term Debt 596
Bank Loans 596
Commercial Paper 597

Summary 598
Questions and Problems 600
Minicase 608

Part Seven   Special Topics

Chapter 21
Mergers, Acquisitions, and Corporate Control 610

21.1 Sensible Motives for Mergers 612
Economies of Scale 614
Economies of Vertical Integration 614
Combining Complementary Resources 615
Mergers as a Use for Surplus Funds 616
Eliminating Inefficiencies 616
Industry Consolidation 616

21.2 Dubious Reasons for Mergers 617
Diversification 617
The Bootstrap Game 617

21.3 The Mechanics of a Merger 619
The Form of Acquisition 619
Mergers, Antitrust Law, and Popular Opposition 619
Cross-Border Mergers and Tax Inversion 620

21.4 Evaluating Mergers 620
Mergers Financed by Cash 620
Mergers Financed by Stock 622
A Warning 623
Another Warning 623

21.5 The Market for Corporate Control 624

21.6 Method 1: Proxy Contests 625

21.7 Method 2: Takeovers 625

21.8 Method 3: Leveraged Buyouts 627
Barbarians at the Gate? 628

21.9 Method 4: Divestitures, Spin-Offs, and Carve-Outs 630

21.10 The Benefits and Costs of Mergers 630
Merger Waves 630

Summary 632
Questions and Problems 633
Minicase 636

Chapter 22
International Financial Management 638

22.1 Foreign Exchange Markets 640
Spot Exchange Rates 640
Forward Exchange Rates 642

22.2 Some Basic Relationships 643
Exchange Rates and Inflation 643
Real and Nominal Exchange Rates 646
Inflation and Interest Rates 646
The Forward Exchange Rate and the Expected Spot Rate 649
Interest Rates and Exchange Rates 650

22.3 Hedging Currency Risk 651
Transaction Risk 651
Economic Risk 652

22.4 International Capital Budgeting 653
Net Present Values for Foreign Investments 653
Political Risk 655
The Cost of Capital for Foreign Investment 656
Avoiding Fudge Factors 656

Summary 657
Questions and Problems 658
Minicase 663

Chapter 23

Options   664

23.1 **Calls and Puts   666**

Selling Calls and Puts   668

Payoff Diagrams Are Not Profit Diagrams   669

Financial Alchemy with Options   670

Some More Option Magic   671

23.2 **What Determines Option Values?   672**

Upper and Lower Limits on Option Values   672

The Determinants of Option Value   673

Option-Valuation Models   675

23.3 **Spotting the Option   678**

Options on Real Assets   678

Options on Financial Assets   679

Summary   682

Questions and Problems   683

Chapter 24

Risk Management   692

24.1 **Why Hedge?   694**

The Evidence on Risk Management   695

24.2 **Reducing Risk with Options   696**

24.3 **Futures Contracts   696**

The Mechanics of Futures Trading   699

Commodity and Financial Futures   700

24.4 **Forward Contracts   701**

24.5 **Swaps   702**

Interest Rate Swaps   702

Currency Swaps   704

And Some Other Swaps   704

24.6 **Innovation in the Derivatives Market   705**

24.7 **Is "Derivative" a Four-Letter Word?   705**

Summary   706

Questions and Problems   707

Part Eight Conclusion

Chapter 25

What We Do and Do Not Know about Finance   712

25.1 **What We Do Know: The Six Most Important Ideas in Finance   714**

Net Present Value (Chapter 5)   714

Risk and Return (Chapters 11 and 12)   714

Efficient Capital Markets (Chapter 7)   715

MM's Irrelevance Propositions (Chapters 16 and 17)   715

Option Theory (Chapter 23)   715

Agency Theory   716

25.2 **What We Do Not Know: Nine Unsolved Problems in Finance   716**

What Determines Project Risk and Present Value?   716

Risk and Return—Have We Missed Something?   717

Are There Important Exceptions to the Efficient-Market Theory?   718

Is Management an Off-Balance-Sheet Liability?   718

How Can We Explain Capital Structure?   719

How Can We Resolve the Payout Controversy?   719

How Can We Explain Merger Waves?   719

What Is the Value of Liquidity?   720

Why Are Financial Systems Prone to Crisis?   720

25.3 **A Final Word   721**

Questions and Problems   721

Appendix A   A-1

Glossary   G-1

Global Index   IND-1

Subject Index   IND-5

Fundamentals of
Corporate Finance

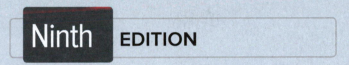
Ninth EDITION

1

Goals and Governance of the Corporation

LEARNING OBJECTIVES

After studying this chapter, you should be able to:

1-1 Give examples of the investment and financing decisions that financial managers make.

1-2 Distinguish between real and financial assets.

1-3 Cite some of the advantages and disadvantages of organizing a business as a corporation.

1-4 Describe the responsibilities of the CFO, treasurer, and controller.

1-5 Explain why maximizing market value is the natural financial goal of the corporation.

1-6 Understand what is meant by "agency problems," and cite some of the ways that corporate governance helps mitigate agency problems.

1-7 Explain why unethical behavior does not maximize market value.

RELATED WEBSITES FOR THIS CHAPTER CAN BE FOUND IN CONNECT.

To grow from small beginnings to a major corporation, FedEx needed to make good investment and financing decisions.
Frank Kovalchek via Alaskan Dude/Flickr/CC BY 2.0

To carry on business, a corporation needs an almost endless variety of assets. Some are tangible assets such as plant and machinery, office buildings, and vehicles; others are intangible assets such as brand names and patents. Corporations finance these assets by borrowing, by reinvesting profits back into the firm, and by selling additional shares to the firm's shareholders.

Financial managers, therefore, face two broad questions. First, what investments should the corporation make? Second, how should it pay for these investments? *Investment decisions* spend money. *Financing decisions* raise money for investment.

We start this chapter with examples of recent investment and financing decisions by major U.S. and foreign corporations. We review what a corporation is and describe the roles of its top financial managers. We then turn to the financial goal of the corporation, which is usually expressed as *maximizing value*, or at least adding value. Financial managers add value whenever the corporation can invest to earn a higher return than its shareholders can earn for themselves.

But managers are human beings; they cannot be perfect servants who always and everywhere maximize value. We will consider the conflicts of interest that arise in large corporations and how corporate governance helps to align the interests of managers and shareholders.

If we ask managers to maximize value, can the corporation also be a good citizen? Won't the managers be tempted to try unethical or illegal financial tricks? They may sometimes be tempted, but wise managers realize that such tricks are not just dishonest; they almost always destroy value, not increase it. More challenging are the gray areas where the line between ethical and unethical financial actions is hard to draw.

Finally, we look ahead to the rest of this book and look back to some entertaining snippets of financial history.

1.1 Investment and Financing Decisions

Fred Smith is best known today as the founder of FedEx. But in 1965 he was still a sophomore at Yale, where he wrote an economics term paper arguing that delivery systems were not keeping up with increasing needs for speed and dependability.[1] He later joined his stepfather at a struggling equipment and maintenance firm for air carriers. He observed firsthand the difficulties of shipping spare parts on short notice. He saw the need for an integrated air and ground delivery system with a central hub that could connect a large number of points more efficiently than a point-to-point delivery system. In 1971, at the age of 27, Smith founded Federal Express.

Like many start-up firms, Federal Express flirted again and again with failure. Smith and his family had an inheritance of a few million dollars, but this was far from enough. The young company needed to purchase and retrofit a small fleet of aging Dassault Falcon jets; build a central-hub facility; and hire and train pilots, delivery, and office staff. The initial source of capital was short-term bank loans. Because of the company's shaky financial position, the bank demanded that the planes be used as collateral and that Smith personally guarantee the loan with his own money.

In April 1973, the company went live with a fleet of 14 jets, servicing 25 U.S. cities out of its Memphis hub. By then, the company had spent $25 million and was effectively flat broke, without enough funds to pay for its weekly delivery of jet fuel. In desperation, it managed to acquire a bank loan for $23.7 million. This loan had to be backed by a guarantee from General Dynamics, which in return acquired an option to buy the company. (Today, General Dynamics must regret that it never exercised this option.)

In November of that year, the company finally achieved some financial stability when it raised $24.5 million from venture capitalists, investment firms that provide funds and advice to young companies in return for a partial ownership share. Eventually, venture capitalists invested about $90 million in Federal Express.

In 1977, private firms were allowed for the first time to compete with the Postal Service in package delivery. Federal Express responded by expanding its operations. It acquired seven Boeing 727s, each with about seven times the capacity of the Falcon jets. To pay for these new investments, Federal Express raised about $19 million by selling shares of stock to the general public in an *initial public offering (IPO)*. The new stockholders became part-owners of the company in proportion to the number of shares they purchased.

From this point on, success followed success, and the company invested heavily to expand its air fleet as well as its supporting infrastructure. It introduced an automated shipping system and a bar-coded tracking system. In 1994, it launched its **fedex.com** website for online package tracking. It opened several new hubs across the United States as well as in Canada, France, the Philippines, and China. In 2007, FedEx (as the company was now called) became the world's largest airline measured by number of planes. FedEx also invested in other companies, capped by the acquisition of Kinko's for $2.4 billion in 2004. By 2016, FedEx had 325,000 employees, annual revenue of $49 billion, and a stock market value of almost $40 billion. Its name had become a verb—to "FedEx a package" was to ship it overnight.

Even in retrospect, FedEx's success was hardly a sure thing. Fred Smith's idea was inspired, but its implementation was complex and difficult. FedEx had to make *good investment decisions*. In the beginning, these decisions were constrained by lack of financing. For example, used Falcon jets were the only option, given the young company's precarious financial position. At first it could service only a short list of the major cities. As the company grew, its investment decisions became more complex. Which type of planes should it buy? When should it expand coverage to Europe and

---

[1] Legend has it that Smith received a grade of C on this paper. In fact, he doesn't remember the grade.

Asia? How many operations hubs should it build? What computer and tracking systems were necessary to keep up with the increasing package volume and geographic coverage? Which companies should it acquire as it expanded its range of services?

FedEx also needed to make *good financing decisions.* For example, how should it raise the money it needed for investment? In the beginning, these choices were limited to family money and bank loans. As the company grew, its range of choices expanded. Eventually it was able to attract funding from venture capitalists, but this posed new questions. How much cash did the firm need to raise from the venture capitalists? How big a share in the firm would the venture capitalists demand in return? The initial public offering of stock prompted similar questions. How many shares should the company try to sell? At what price? As the company grew, it raised more funds by borrowing money from its banks and by selling publicly traded bonds to investors. At each point, it needed to decide on the proper form and terms of financing as well as the amounts to be raised.

In short, FedEx needed to be *good at finance.* It had a head start over potential competitors, but a series of bad financial decisions would have sunk the company. No two companies' histories are the same, but, like FedEx, all successful companies must make good investment and financing decisions. And, as with FedEx, those decisions range from prosaic and obvious to difficult and strategically crucial.

Let's widen our discussion. Table 1.1 gives an example of a recent investment and financing decision for 11 corporations. Seven are U.S. corporations. Four are foreign: Virgin Atlantic's headquarters are in London, TransCanada's in Calgary, LVMH's in Paris,[2] and Vale's in Rio de Janeiro. We have chosen very large public corporations that you are likely to be familiar with. You may have flown with Virgin Atlantic, shopped at Walmart, or posted a picture on Facebook.

TABLE 1.1 Examples of recent investment and financing decisions by major public corporations

Company	Recent Investment Decisions	Recent Financing Decisions
Entergy	Purchased the Union Power generating station near El Dorado, Arkansas, for $948 million.	Entergy's Arkansas subsidiary issued $325 million of bonds maturing in 2026.
ExxonMobil	Cut total capital investment for 2016 to $34 billion, down 12% because of plummeting oil prices.	Eliminated share repurchases for 2016, thus reducing payout to stockholders.
Facebook	Spent $60 million to acquire Pebbles, an Israeli company developing virtual reality software.	Financed capital investment and acquisitions with operating cash flow.
Ford	Announced plan to invest $1 billion to build an assembly plant in Mexico.	Ford's credit subsidiary issued $3.5 billion in long-term debt.
John Deere	Total capital investment fell to $655 million, after completing investments for producing clean-burning diesel engines.	Maintained credit lines with banks that allowed it to borrow up to $7.2 billion.
LVMH	Acquired Luxola, a Singapore cosmetics e-commerce start-up.	Repaid €750 million in debt issued in 2009 and 2011.
Procter & Gamble	Spent $2.0 billion on research and development in 2015.	Spent $4.6 billion to repurchase its common stock.
TransCanada	Announced purchase of Columbia Pipeline Group for $10.2 billion.	Will pay Columbia shareholders in cash and also assume $2.8 billion of existing Columbia debt.
Vale	Started up the Caue Itabiritos iron-ore project after capital investment of $927 million.	Announced plan to issue at least $750 million of 30-year debt.
Virgin Atlantic Airlines	Ordered 12 new Airbus A350-1000 planes.	Used value of its landing slots at London's Heathrow Airport as collateral for a £220 million bond issue.
Walmart	Announced plans to open more than 200 new stores in 2016.	Raised its annual dividend to $2.00 a share.

----

[2] LVMH (Moët Hennessy Louis Vuitton) markets perfumes and cosmetics, wines and spirits, leather goods, watches, and other luxury products. And, yes, we know what you are thinking, but "LVMH" really is short for "Moët Hennessy Louis Vuitton."

Take a look at the decisions now. We think you will agree that they appear sensible—at least there is nothing obviously wrong with them. But if you are new to finance, it may be difficult to think about why these companies made these decisions and not others.

The Investment (Capital Budgeting) Decision

Investment decisions, such as those shown in Table 1.1, are also called **capital budgeting or capital expenditure (CAPEX) decisions.** Some of the investments in the table, such as Walmart's new stores or Virgin Atlantic's new planes, involve tangible assets—assets that you can touch and kick. Others involve intangible assets, such as research and development (R&D), advertising, and the design of computer software. For example, major pharmaceutical manufacturers invest billions every year on R&D for new drugs.

Most of the investments in Table 1.1 have long-term consequences. For example, the planes acquired by Virgin Atlantic may still be flying 20 or 30 years from now. Other investments may pay off in only a few months. For example, with the approach of the Christmas holidays, Walmart spends nearly $50 billion to stock up its ware-houses and retail stores. As the goods are sold over the following months, the company recovers its investment in these inventories.

The world of business can be intensely competitive, and corporations prosper only if they can keep launching new products or services. In some cases, the costs and risks of doing so are amazingly large. For example, the cost of developing the Gorgon natural gas field in Australia has been estimated at $54 billion. It's not surprising that this cost is being shared among several major energy companies. But do not think of companies as making billion-dollar investments on a daily basis. Most investment decisions are smaller, such as the purchase of a truck, machine tool, or computer system. Corporations make thousands of such investments each year. The cumulative amount of these small expenditures can be just as large as the occasional jumbo invest-ments, such as those shown in Table 1.1.

Not all investments succeed. In October 2011 Hewlett-Packard (HP) paid $11.1 billion to acquire the British software company Autonomy. Just 13 months later, HP wrote down the value of this investment by $8.8 billion. HP claimed that it was misled by improper accounting at Autonomy. Nevertheless, the Autonomy acquisition was a disastrous investment for HP. HP's CEO was fired in short order.

There are no free guarantees in finance. But you can tilt the odds in your favor if you learn the tools of investment analysis and apply them intelligently. We cover these tools in detail later in this book.

The Financing Decision

The financial manager's second main responsibility is to raise the money that the firm requires for its investments and operations. This is the **financing decision.** When a company needs to raise money, it can invite investors to put up cash in exchange for a share of future profits, or it can promise to pay back the investors' cash plus a fixed rate of interest. In the first case, the investors receive shares of stock and become shareholders, part-owners of the corporation. The investors in this case are referred to as *equity investors,* who contribute *equity financing.* In the second case, the investors are lenders, that is, *debt investors,* who one day must be repaid. The choice between debt and equity financing is often called the *capital structure decision.* Here "capital" refers to the firm's sources of long-term financing. A firm that is seeking to raise long-term financing is said to be "raising capital."

Notice the essential difference between the investment and financing decisions. When the firm invests, it acquires **real assets,** which are then used to produce the firm's goods and services. The firm finances its investment in real assets by issuing **financial assets** to investors. A share of stock is a financial asset, which has value as a

---

capital budgeting or capital expenditure (CAPEX) decision
Decision to invest in tangible or intangible assets.

financing decision
Decision on the sources and amounts of financing.

real assets
Assets used to produce goods and services.

financial assets
Financial claims to the income generated by the firm's real assets.

claim on the firm's real assets and on the income that those assets will produce. A bank loan is a financial asset also. It gives the bank the right to get its money back plus interest. If the firm's operations can't generate enough income to repay the bank, the bank can force the firm into bankruptcy and stake a claim on its real assets. Financial assets that can be purchased and traded by investors in public markets are called *securities*. The shares of stock issued by the public corporations in Table 1.1 are all securities. Entergy's 10-year bond in Table 1.1 is a security. But a bank loan from JPMorgan to Entergy is not called a security unless the bank resells the loan to public investors.

The firm can issue an almost endless variety of financial assets. Suppose it decides to borrow. It can issue debt to investors, or it can borrow from a bank. It can borrow for 1 year or 20 years. If it borrows for 20 years, it can reserve the right to pay off the debt early if interest rates fall. It can borrow in Paris, receiving and promising to repay euros, or it can borrow dollars in New York. (As Table 1.1 shows, Ford chose to borrow U.S. dollars, but it could have borrowed euros or Japanese yen instead.)

In some ways, financing decisions are less important than investment decisions. Financial managers say that "value comes mainly from the investment side of the balance sheet." Also, the most successful corporations sometimes have the simplest financing strategies. Take Microsoft as an example. It is one of the world's most valuable corporations. In early 2016, Microsoft shares traded for $53 each. There were 7.91 billion shares outstanding. Therefore Microsoft's market value—its *market capitalization* or *market cap*—was 53 × 7.91 = $419 billion. Where did this market value come from? It came from Microsoft's products, from its brand name and worldwide customer base, from its R&D, and from its ability to make profitable future investments. It did not come from sophisticated financing. Microsoft's financing strategy is very simple: It finances almost all investment by retaining and reinvesting operating cash flow.

Financing decisions may not add much value compared to good investment decisions, but they can destroy value if they are stupid or ambushed by bad news. For example, when a consortium of investment companies bought the energy giant TXU in 2007, the company took on an additional $40 billion in debt. This may not have been a stupid decision, but it did prove fatal. The consortium did not foresee the expansion of shale gas production and the resulting sharp fall in natural gas and electricity prices, and in April 2014 the company (renamed Energy Future Holdings) was bankrupt.

1.1   Self-Test

Are the following capital budgeting or financing decisions? (*Hint:* In one case the answer is "both.")

a. Intel decides to spend $7 billion to develop a new microprocessor factory.
b. BMW borrows 350 million euros (€350 million) from Deutsche Bank.
c. Royal Dutch Shell constructs a pipeline to bring natural gas onshore from a production platform in Australia.
d. Avon spends €200 million to launch a new range of cosmetics in European markets.
e. Pfizer issues new shares to buy a small biotech company.

We have emphasized the financial manager's responsibility for two decisions:

The investment decision = purchase of real assets
The financing decision = sale of financial assets

But this is an oversimplification because the financial manager is also involved in many other day-to-day activities that are essential to the smooth operation of a business.

For example, if the firm sells goods or services on credit, it needs to make sure that its customers pay on time. Corporations that operate internationally must constantly transfer cash from one currency to another. And the manager must keep an eye on the risks that the firm runs and ensure that they don't land the firm in a pickle.

1.2   Self-Test

Which of the following are financial assets, and which are real assets?

a. A patent.
b. A share of stock issued by Wells Fargo Bank.
c. A blast furnace in a steelmaking factory.
d. A mortgage loan taken out to help pay for a new home.
e. After a successful advertising campaign, potential customers trust FedEx to deliver packages promptly and reliably.
f. An IOU ("I owe you") from your brother-in-law.

1.2   What Is a Corporation?

We have been referring to "corporations." But before going too far or too fast, we need to offer some basic definitions.

corporation
A business organized as a separate legal entity owned by stockholders.

A **corporation** is a distinct, permanent legal entity. Suppose you decide to create a new corporation.[3] You would work with a lawyer to prepare *articles of incorporation,* which set out the purpose of the business and how it is to be financed, managed, and governed. These articles must conform to the laws of the state in which the business is incorporated. For many purposes, the corporation is considered a resident of its state. For example, it can enter into contracts, borrow or lend money, and sue or be sued. It pays its own taxes (but it cannot vote!).

A corporation's owners are called *shareholders* or *stockholders.*[4] The shareholders do not directly own the business's real assets (factories, oil wells, stores, etc.). Instead they have indirect ownership via financial assets (the shares of the corporation).

limited liability
The owners of a corporation are not personally liable for its obligations.

A corporation is legally distinct from the shareholders. Therefore, the shareholders have **limited liability** and cannot be held personally responsible for the corporation's debts. When the U.S. financial corporation Lehman Brothers failed in 2008, no one demanded that its stockholders put up more money to cover Lehman's massive debts. Shareholders can lose their entire investment in a corporation, but no more.

Example 1.1 ▶   Business Organization

Suppose you buy a building and open a restaurant. You have invested in the building itself, kitchen equipment, dining-room furnishings, plus various other assets. If you do not incorporate, you own these assets personally, as the *sole proprietor* of the business. If you have borrowed money from a bank to start the business, then you are personally responsible for this debt. If the business loses money and cannot pay the bank, then the bank can demand

---

[3] In the United States, corporations are identified by the label "Corporation," "Incorporated," or "Inc.," as in *Caterpillar Inc.* The United Kingdom identifies public corporations by "plc" (short for "Public Limited Corporation"). French corporations have the suffix "SA" ("Société Anonyme"). The corresponding labels in Germany are "GmbH" ("Gesellschaft mit beschränkter Haftung") and "AG" ("Aktiengesellschaft").

[4] "Shareholder" and "stockholder" mean exactly the same thing and are used interchangeably.

that you raise cash by selling other assets—your car or house, for example—in order to repay the loan. But if you incorporate the restaurant business, and then the corporation borrows from the bank, your other assets are shielded from the restaurant's debts. Of course, incorporation also means that the bank will be more cautious in lending, because the bank will have no recourse to your other assets.[5]

Notice that if you incorporate your business, you exchange direct ownership of its real assets (the building, kitchen equipment, etc.) for indirect ownership via financial assets (the shares of the new corporation). ■

When a corporation is first established, its shares may be privately owned by a small group of investors, perhaps the company's managers and a few backers. In this case, the shares are not publicly traded and the company is *closely held*. Eventually, when the firm grows and new shares are issued to raise additional capital, its shares are traded in public markets such as the New York Stock Exchange. Such corporations are known as *public companies*. Most well-known corporations in the United States are public companies with widely dispersed shareholdings. In other countries, it is more common for large corporations to remain in private hands, and many public companies may be controlled by just a handful of investors.

A large public corporation may have hundreds of thousands of shareholders, who together own the business. An individual may have 100 shares, receive 100 votes, and be entitled to a tiny fraction of the firm's income and value. On the other hand, a pension fund or insurance company may own millions of shares, receive millions of votes, and have a correspondingly large stake in the firm's performance.

Public shareholders cannot possibly manage or control the corporation directly. Instead, they elect a *board of directors,* who in turn appoint the top managers and monitor their performance. This *separation of ownership and control* gives corporations permanence. Even if managers quit or are dismissed, the corporation survives. Today's stockholders can sell all their shares to new investors without disrupting the operations of the business. Corporations can, in principle, live forever, and in practice they may survive many human lifetimes. One of the oldest corporations is the Hudson's Bay Company, which was formed in 1670 to profit from the fur trade between northern Canada and England. The company still operates as one of Canada's leading retail chains.

The separation of corporate ownership and control can also have a downside, for it can open the door for managers and directors to act in their own interests rather than in the stockholders' interest. We return to this problem later in the chapter.

There are other disadvantages to being a corporation. One is the cost, in both time and money, of managing the corporation's legal machinery. These costs are particularly burdensome for small businesses.

There is also an important tax drawback to corporations in the United States. Because the corporation is a separate legal entity, it is taxed separately. So corporations pay tax on their profits, and shareholders are taxed again when they receive dividends from the company or sell their shares at a profit. By contrast, income generated by businesses that are not incorporated is taxed just once as personal income.[6]

BEYOND THE PAGE

🌐 | S-corporations

mhhe.com/brealey9e

Other Forms of Business Organization

Corporations do not have to be prominent, multinational businesses such as those listed in Table 1.1. You can organize a local plumbing contractor or barber shop as a corporation if you want to take the trouble. But most corporations are larger

---

[5] The bank may ask you to put up personal assets as collateral for the loan to your restaurant corporation. But it has to ask and get your agreement. It doesn't have to ask if your business is a sole proprietorship.

[6] The U.S. tax system is somewhat unusual in this respect. To avoid taxing the same income twice, many other countries give shareholders at least some credit for the taxes that the corporation has already paid.

businesses or businesses that aspire to grow. Small "mom-and-pop" businesses are usually organized as sole proprietorships.

What about the middle ground? What about businesses that grow too large for sole proprietorships but don't want to reorganize as corporations? For example, suppose you wish to pool money and expertise with some friends or business associates. You can form a *partnership* and enter into a partnership agreement that sets out how decisions are to be made and how profits are to be split up. Partners, like sole proprietors, face unlimited liability. If the business runs into difficulties, each partner can be held responsible for *all* the business's debts.

Partnerships have a tax advantage. Partnerships, unlike corporations, do not have to pay income taxes. The partners pay personal income taxes on their shares of the profits.

Some businesses are hybrids that combine the tax advantage of a partnership with the limited liability advantage of a corporation. In a *limited partnership,* partners are classified as general or limited. General partners manage the business and have unlimited personal liability for its debts. Limited partners are liable only for the money they invest and do not participate in management.

Many states allow *limited liability partnerships (LLPs)* or *limited liability companies (LLCs).* These are partnerships in which all partners have limited liability. Another variation on the theme is the *professional corporation (PC),* which is commonly used by doctors, lawyers, and accountants. In this case, the business has limited liability, but the professionals can still be sued personally, for example, for malpractice.

Most large investment banks such as Morgan Stanley and Goldman Sachs started life as partnerships. But eventually these companies and their financing requirements grew too large for them to continue as partnerships, and they reorganized as corporations. The partnership form of organization does not work well when ownership is widespread and separation of ownership and management is essential.

1.3   Who Is the Financial Manager?

chief financial officer (CFO)
Supervises all financial functions and sets overall financial strategy.

What do financial managers do for a living? That simple question can be answered in several ways. We can start with financial managers' job titles. Most large corporations have a **chief financial officer (CFO),** who oversees the work of all financial staff. As you can see from Figure 1.1, the CFO is deeply involved in financial policy and financial planning and is in constant contact with the chief executive officer (CEO) and other top management. The CFO is the most important financial voice of the corporation and explains earnings results and forecasts to investors and the media.

FIGURE 1.1 Financial managers in large corporations

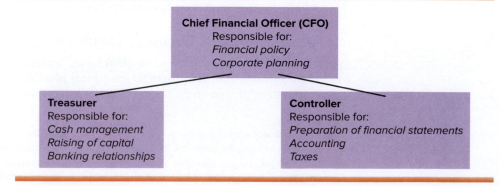

treasurer
Responsible for financing, cash management, and relationships with banks and other financial institutions.

controller
Responsible for budgeting, accounting, and taxes.

BEYOND THE PAGE

The role of the corporate treasurer

mhhe.com/brealey9e

Below the CFO are usually a **treasurer** and a **controller.** The treasurer looks after the firm's cash, raises new capital, and maintains relationships with banks and other investors that hold the firm's securities. The controller prepares the financial statements, manages the firm's internal budgets and accounting, and looks after its tax affairs. Thus the treasurer's main function is to obtain and manage the firm's capital, whereas the controller ensures that the money is used efficiently.

1.3	Self-Test

Fritz and Frieda went to business school together 10 years ago. They have just been hired by a midsize corporation that wants to bring in new financial managers. Fritz studied finance, with an emphasis on financial markets and institutions. Frieda majored in accounting and became a CPA 5 years ago. Who is more suited to be treasurer and who controller? Briefly explain.

In large corporations, financial managers are responsible for organizing and supervising the capital budgeting process. However, major capital investment projects are so closely tied to plans for product development, production, and marketing that managers from these other areas are inevitably drawn into planning and analyzing the projects. If the firm has staff members specializing in corporate planning, they are naturally involved in capital budgeting too. For this reason, we will use the term *financial manager* to refer to anyone responsible for an investment or financing decision. Often we will use the term collectively for all the managers drawn into such decisions.

Now let's go beyond job titles. What is the essential role of the financial manager? Figure 1.2 gives one answer. The figure traces how money flows from investors to the corporation and back again to investors. The flow starts when cash is raised from investors (arrow 1 in the figure). The cash could come from banks or from securities sold to investors in financial markets. The cash is then used to pay for the real assets (investment projects) needed for the corporation's business (arrow 2). Later, as the business operates, the assets generate cash inflows (arrow 3). That cash is either reinvested (arrow 4a) or returned to the investors who furnished the money in the first place (arrow 4b). Of course, the choice between arrows 4a and 4b is constrained by the promises made when cash was raised at arrow 1. For example, if the firm borrows money from a bank at arrow 1, it must repay this money plus interest at arrow 4b.

You can see examples of arrows 4a and 4b in Table 1.1. Facebook financed its investments by reinvesting earnings (arrow 4a). Procter & Gamble decided to return cash to shareholders by buying back its stock (arrow 4b). It could have chosen instead to pay the money out as additional cash dividends, also on arrow 4b.

Notice how the financial manager stands between the firm and outside investors. On the one hand, the financial manager is involved in the firm's operations,

FIGURE 1.2 Flow of cash between investors and the firm's operations. Key: (1) Cash raised by selling financial assets to investors; (2) cash invested in the firm's operations; (3) cash generated by the firm's operations; (4a) cash reinvested; (4b) cash returned to investors.

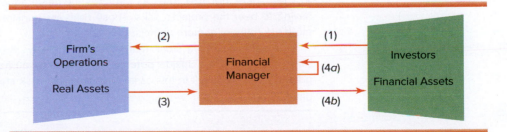

particularly by helping to make good investment decisions. On the other hand, he or she deals with financial institutions and other investors and with financial markets such as the New York Stock Exchange. We say more about these financial institutions and markets in the next chapter.

1.4 Goals of the Corporation

Shareholders Want Managers to Maximize Market Value

For small corporations, shareholders and management may be one and the same. But for large corporations, separation of ownership and management is a practical necessity. For example, Walmart has nearly 300,000 shareholders. There is no way that these shareholders can be actively involved in management; it would be like trying to run New York City by town meetings. Authority has to be delegated.

How can shareholders effectively delegate decision making when they all have different tastes, wealth, time horizons, personal opportunities, and tolerance for risk? Delegation can work only if the shareholders have a common goal. Fortunately there is a natural financial objective on which almost all shareholders can agree: Maximize the current market value of shareholders' investment in the firm.

This simple, unqualified goal makes sense when the shareholders have access to well-functioning financial markets and institutions. Access gives them the flexibility to manage their own savings and consumption plans, leaving the corporation's financial managers with only one task, to increase market value. For example, a corporation's roster of shareholders will usually include both risk-averse and risk-tolerant investors. You might expect the risk-averse to say, "Sure, maximize value, but don't touch too many high-risk projects." Instead, they say, "Risky projects are okay, provided that expected profits are more than enough to offset the risks. If this firm ends up too risky for my taste, I'll adjust my investment portfolio to make it safer." For example, the risk-averse shareholder can shift more of his or her portfolio to safe assets, such as U.S. government bonds. Shareholders can also just say good-bye, selling off shares of the risky firm and buying shares in a safer one. If the risky investments increase market value, the departing shareholders are better off than they would be if the risky investments were turned down.

BEYOND THE PAGE

Foundations of the NPV rule

mhhe.com/brealey9e

Example 1.2 ▶ Value Maximization

Fast-Track Wireless shares trade for $20. It has just announced a "bet the company" investment in a high-risk, but potentially revolutionary, WhyFi technology. Investors note the risk of failure but are even more impressed with the technology's upside. They conclude that the possibility of very high future profits justifies a higher share price. The price goes up to $23.

Caspar Milquetoast, a thoughtful but timid shareholder, notes the downside risks and decides that it's time for a change. He sells out to more risk-tolerant investors. But he sells at $23 per share, not $20. Thus he captures the value added by the WhyFi project without having to bear the project's risks. Those risks are transferred to other investors, who are more risk-tolerant or more optimistic.

In a well-functioning stock market, there is always a pool of investors ready to bear downside risks if the upside potential is sufficiently attractive. We know that the upside potential was sufficient in this case, because Fast-Track stock attracted investors willing to pay $23 per share. ■

The same principles apply to the timing of a corporation's cash flows, as the following Self-Test illustrates.

1.4   Self-Test

Rhonda and Reggie Hotspur are working hard to save for their children's college education. They don't need more cash for current consumption but will face big tuition bills in 2025. Should they therefore avoid investing in stocks that pay generous current cash dividends? (*Hint:* Are they required to spend the dividends on current consumption?) Explain briefly.

Sometimes you hear managers speak as if the corporation has other goals. For example, they may say that their job is to "maximize profits." That sounds reasonable. After all, don't shareholders want their company to be profitable? But taken literally, profit maximization is not a well-defined corporate objective. Here are two reasons:

1. Maximize profits? Which year's profits? A corporation may be able to increase current profits by cutting back on outlays for maintenance or staff training, but that will not add value unless the outlays were wasteful in the first place. Shareholders will not welcome higher short-term profits if long-term profits are damaged.
2. A company may be able to increase future profits by cutting this year's dividend and investing the freed-up cash in the firm. That is not in the shareholders' best interest if the company earns only a very low rate of return on the extra investment.

Maximizing—or at least maintaining—value is necessary for the long-run survival of the corporation. Suppose, for example, that its managers forget about value and decide that the only goal is to increase the market share of its products. So the managers cut prices aggressively to attract new customers, even when this leads to continuing losses. As losses mount, the corporation finds it more and more difficult to borrow money and sooner or later cannot pay existing debts. Nor can it raise new equity financing if shareholders see that new equity investment will follow previous investments down the drain.

This firm's managers would probably pay the price for this business malpractice. For example, outside investors would see an opportunity for easy money. They could buy the firm from its current shareholders, toss out the managers, and reemphasize value rather than market share. The investors would profit from the increase in value under new management.

Managers who pursue goals that destroy value often end in early retirement— another reason that the natural financial goal of the corporation is to maximize market value.

The Investment Trade-Off   Okay, let's take the objective as maximizing market value, or at least adding market value. But why do some investments increase market value, while others reduce it? The answer is given by Figure 1.3, which sets out the fundamental trade-off for corporate investment decisions. The corporation has a proposed investment project (the purchase of a real asset). Suppose it has sufficient cash on hand to finance the project. The financial manager is trying to decide whether to go ahead. If he or she decides not to invest, the corporation can pay out the cash to shareholders, say as an extra dividend. (The investment and dividend arrows in Figure 1.3 are arrows 2 and 4*b* in Figure 1.2.)

Assume that the financial manager is acting in the interests of the corporation's owners, its stockholders. What do these stockholders want the financial manager to do?

BEYOND THE PAGE

B-corporations

mhhe.com/brealey9e

FIGURE 1.3 The firm can either keep and reinvest cash or return it to investors. (Arrows represent possible cash flows or transfers.) If cash is reinvested, the opportunity cost is the expected rate of return that shareholders could have obtained by investing in financial assets.

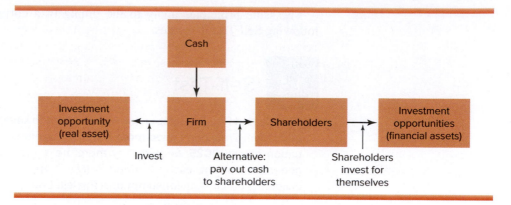

The answer depends on the rate of return on the investment project and on the rate of return that stockholders can earn by investing in financial markets. If the return offered by the investment project is higher than the rate of return that shareholders can get by investing on their own, then the shareholders would vote for the investment project. If the investment project offers a lower return than shareholders can achieve on their own, the shareholders would vote to cancel the project and take the cash instead.

Figure 1.3 could apply to Virgin Atlantic's decisions to invest in new aircraft. Suppose the company has cash set aside to buy five more Airbus A350-1000s. It could go ahead with the purchase, or it could choose to cancel the investment and instead pay out the cash to its stockholders. If it pays out the cash, the stockholders could then invest for themselves.

Suppose that Virgin's investment in new planes is just about as risky as the stock market and that investment in the stock market offers a 10% expected rate of return. If the new planes offer a superior rate of return, say 20%, then Virgin's stockholders would be happy to let the company keep the cash and invest it in the new planes. If the planes offer only a 5% return, then the stockholders are better off with the cash and without the new project; in that case, the financial manager should turn down the project.

As long as a corporation's proposed investments offer higher rates of return than its shareholders can earn for themselves in the stock market (or in other financial markets), its shareholders will applaud the investments and the market value of the firm will increase. But if the company earns an inferior return, shareholders boo, market value falls, and stockholders clamor to get their money back so that they can invest on their own.

opportunity cost of capital
Expected rate of return given up by investing in a project rather than in the capital market.

In our example, the minimum acceptable rate of return on Virgin's new aircraft is 10%. This minimum rate of return is called the *hurdle rate* or **opportunity cost of capital.** It is called an *opportunity cost* of capital because it depends on the alternative investment *opportunities* available to shareholders in financial markets. Whenever a corporation invests cash in a new project, its shareholders lose the opportunity to invest the cash on their own. Corporations increase value by accepting investment projects that earn more than the opportunity cost of capital.

Figure 1.3, which compares rates of return on investment projects with the opportunity cost of capital, illustrates a general principle: A corporation should direct cash to investments that *add market value,* compared with the investments that shareholders could make on their own.[7]

---

[7] We have mentioned 5% or 20% as possible future rates of return on Virgin Atlantic's new planes. We will see in Chapter 8 that future rates of return are sometimes difficult to calculate and interpret. The general principle always holds, however. In Chapters 8 and 9 we show you how to apply the principle by calculating the net present value (NPV) of investment projects.

Notice that the opportunity cost of capital depends on the risk of the proposed investment project. Why? It's not just because shareholders are risk-averse. It's also because shareholders have to trade off risk against return when they invest on their own. The safest investments, such as U.S. government debt, offer low rates of return. Investments with higher expected rates of return—the stock market, for example—are riskier and sometimes deliver painful losses. (The U.S. stock market fell 38% in 2008, for example.) Other investments are riskier still. For example, high-tech growth stocks offer the prospect of higher rates of return than typical stocks but are also more volatile than typical stocks.

Managers look to the financial markets to measure the opportunity cost of capital for the firm's investment projects. They can observe the opportunity cost of capital for safe investments by looking up current interest rates on safe debt securities. For risky investments, the opportunity cost of capital has to be estimated. We start to tackle this task in Chapter 11.

1.5   Self-Test

Investing $100,000 in additional raw materials, mostly palladium, should allow Cryogenic Concepts to increase production and earn an additional $112,000 next year. This payoff could cover the investment, plus a 12% return. Palladium is traded in commodity markets. The CFO has studied the history of returns from investments in palladium and believes that investors in the precious metal can reasonably expect a 15% return. What is the opportunity cost of capital? Is Cryogenic's proposed investment in palladium a good idea? Why or why not?

1.5   Agency Problems, Executive Compensation, and Corporate Governance

Sole proprietors face no conflicts in financial management. They are both owners and managers, reaping the rewards of good decisions and hard work and suffering when they make bad decisions or slack off. Their personal wealth is tied to the value of their businesses.

In most large corporations, the owners are mostly outside investors, and so the managers may be tempted to act in their own interests rather than maximize shareholder value. For example, they may shy away from valuable but risky investment projects because they worry more about job security than maximizing value. They may build empires by overaggressive investment or overconfident acquisitions of other companies.

The temptation for such value-destroying actions arises because the managers are not the shareholders, but *agents* of the shareholders. Therefore, the actions are called **agency problems.** Losses in value from agency problems—or from costs incurred to mitigate the problems—are called **agency costs.**

Agency problems sometimes lead to outrageous behavior. When Dennis Kozlowski, the former CEO of Tyco, threw a $2 million birthday bash for his wife, he charged half the cost to the company. Conrad Black, the former boss of Hollinger International, used the company jet for a trip with his wife to Bora Bora. These, of course, are extreme examples. The agency problems encountered in the ordinary course of business are often subtle and mundane. But agency problems do arise whenever managers think just a little less hard about spending money that is not their own.

---

agency problem
Managers are agents for stockholders and are tempted to act in their own interests rather than maximizing value.

agency cost
Value lost from agency problems or from the cost of mitigating agency problems.

stakeholder

Anyone with a financial
interest in the corporation.

Think of the corporation's value as a pie that is divided among several classes of claimants. These include managers and workers as well as shareholders and lenders. The government is a claimant, too, because it taxes sales and profits. The claimants are called **stakeholders** because each has a stake in the firm. Agency problems arise whenever the stakeholders' interests do not coincide.

1.6   Self-Test

What are agency problems and agency costs? Give two or three examples of decisions by managers that can lead to agency costs.

Agency problems are controlled in practice in three ways. First, corporations set up internal controls and decision-making procedures to prevent wasteful spending and discourage careless investment. We discuss the controls and procedures in several later chapters. For example, Chapters 8, 9, and 10 cover procedures for disciplined, value-maximizing capital investment decisions. Second, corporations try to design compensation schemes that align managers' and shareholders' interests. Third, the corporations are constrained by corporate governance. We comment on compensation and governance here.

Executive Compensation

The compensation packages of top executives are almost always tied to the financial performance of their companies. The package typically includes a fixed base salary plus an annual award tied to earnings or other measures of financial performance. The more senior the manager, the smaller the base salary as a fraction of total compensation. Also, compensation is not all in cash, but partly in shares. The shares are usually *restricted stock,* which the manager is required to hold onto while employed by the corporation.[8] Many corporations also include stock options in compensation packages. Stock options, which we cover in Chapter 23, give especially powerful incentives to maximize stock price per share.

The upside compensation potential for a few top managers is enormous. For example, Larry Ellison, CEO of the business software giant Oracle, received total compensation of $64 million for 2015. Only $1 of that amount was base salary. The rest came from grants of stock and options. The options will be worthless if Oracle's stock price falls from its 2015 level but will pay off handsomely if the price rises. In addition, as a founder of Oracle, Ellison owns shares worth $49 billion. No one can say for certain how hard Ellison would have worked with a different compensation package, but one thing is clear: He has a huge personal stake in Oracle's market value.

Well-designed compensation schemes alleviate agency problems by encouraging managers to maximize shareholder wealth. But some schemes are not well designed; they reward managers even when value is destroyed. For example, during Robert Nardelli's 6-year tenure as CEO, Home Depot's stock price fell by 20% while shares of its rival Lowe's nearly doubled. When Nardelli was ousted in January 2007, he received a farewell package worth $210 million. Needless to say, many shareholders were livid.

In 2010, the Dodd-Frank financial reform law gave U.S. shareholders the right to express their opinion on executive compensation through nonbinding "say on pay" votes at 1- or 3-year intervals. (Shareholders of U.K. companies have a similar right.)

---

[8] Most restricted stock does not "vest" immediately. Suppose the vesting period is 3 years. If the manager quits or is fired in year 2, the restricted stock stays behind. Vesting gives the managers an incentive to stay at the corporation, in this example, for at least 3 years.

Most votes have endorsed compensation policy, but occasionally shareholders refuse. For example, in 2011 Hewlett-Packard's shareholders voted against a $40 million compensation package for its new CEO. When there is a "no" vote, the company generally changes the pay package to make it less generous; other companies look anxiously over their shoulders to check that their compensation package is not next in the spotlight.

Corporate Governance

Financial markets and institutions are supposed to direct financing to firms that can invest to add value. But financing moves from investors to firms only if investors are protected and if agency problems within firms are absent or at least tolerable. Thus there is a need for a system of **corporate governance** so that money can flow to the right firms at the right times. "Corporate governance" refers to the laws, regulations, institutions, and corporate practices that protect shareholders and other investors. When scandals happen, we say that corporate governance has broken down. When corporations compete to deliver value to shareholders, we are comforted that corporate governance is working properly.

Good corporate governance relies in part on well-designed management compensation packages. Other elements of good corporate governance include the following.

Legal Requirements   Good governance requires laws and regulations that protect investors from self-dealing by insiders. CEOs and financial managers have a fiduciary duty to stockholders. That is, they are required to act fairly and responsibly in the stockholders' interests. If they don't, they may end up in jail like Tyco's Dennis Kozlowski and Hollinger's Conrad Black.

Boards of Directors   The board of directors appoints top managers, including the CEO and CFO, and must approve important financial decisions. For example, only the board has legal authority to approve a dividend or a public issue of securities. The board approves compensation schemes and awards to top management. Boards usually delegate decision making for small and medium-size investments, but the authority to approve large investments is almost never delegated.

The board of directors is elected by shareholders and is supposed to represent their interests. Boards have been portrayed as passive supporters of top management, but the balance has tipped toward independence. The Sarbanes-Oxley Act of 2002 (SOX) requires that more directors be independent—that is, not affiliated with management. The majority of directors are now independent. Boards must also meet in executive sessions with the CEO not present. SOX also requires CEOs and CFOs to sign off personally on the corporation's accounting procedures and results.

Activist Shareholders   Institutional shareholders, including pension funds, have become more active in monitoring management and pushing for changes. CEOs have been forced out as a result, including the CEOs of JCPenney, Procter & Gamble, Barnes & Noble, Citigroup, Yahoo!, and Carnival. Boards outside the United States, which have traditionally been more management-friendly, have also become more willing to replace underperformers. The list of foreign companies with CEO departures includes Barclays, Carrefour, Siemens, Barrick, and Rio Tinto.

Although U.S. corporations typically have thousands of individual shareholders, they often also have *blockholders,* that is, investors who own 5%, 10%, or more of outstanding shares. The blockholders may include wealthy individuals or families— for example, descendants of a founder. They may also include other corporations, pension funds, or foundations.[9] When a 5% blockholder calls, the CFO answers.

corporate governance
The laws, regulations, institutions, and corporate practices that protect shareholders and other investors.

---

[9] A large block of shares may give effective control even when there is no majority owner. For example, Larry Ellison's billion-plus shares give him a 25% stake in Oracle. Barring some extreme catastrophe, this holding means that he can run the company as long as he wants to.

Disgruntled shareholders can also take the "Wall Street Walk" by selling out and moving on to other investments. The Wall Street Walk can send a powerful message. If enough shareholders bail out, the stock price tumbles, which damages top managers' compensation and reputation.

Takeovers   The Wall Street Walk also opens the door for takeovers. The further the stock price falls, the easier it is for another company to buy up the majority of shares and take over. The old management team is then likely to find itself out on the street. We discuss takeovers in Chapter 21.

Information for Investors   Corporate governance can't work unless outside investors get detailed, up-to-date information. If a firm is transparent—if investors can see its true profitability and prospects—then problems will show up right away in a falling stock price. That in turn generates extra scrutiny from security analysts, bond rating agencies, and banks and other lenders, who keep an eagle eye on the progress of their borrowers.

The U.S. Securities and Exchange Commission (SEC) sets accounting and reporting standards for public companies. We cover accounting and finance in Chapter 3.

Chapter 1 is not the right place for a worldwide tour of corporate governance. But be aware that governance laws, regulations, and practice vary. The differences are more dramatic in continental Europe and Japan than in Canada, the United Kingdom, Australia, and other English-speaking countries. In Germany, for example, banks often control large blocks of stock and can push hard for changes in the management or strategy of poorly performing companies. (Banks in the United States are prohibited from large or permanent holdings of the stock of nonfinancial corporations.) Large German firms also have two boards of directors: the supervisory board *(Aufsichtsrat)* and the management board *(Vorstand)*. Half of the supervisory board's members are elected by employees. Some French firms also have two boards, one including employee representatives.

1.6   The Ethics of Maximizing Value

Shareholders want managers to maximize the market value of their shares. But perhaps this begs the question: Is it desirable for managers to act in the narrow, selfish interest of their shareholders? Does a focus on shareholder value mean that the managers must act as greedy mercenaries riding roughshod over widows and orphans?

Most of this book is devoted to financial policies that increase value. None of these policies requires galloping over widows and orphans. In most instances, there is little conflict between doing well (maximizing value) and doing good. The first step in doing well is doing good by your customers. Here is how Adam Smith put the case in 1776:

> It is not from the benevolence of the butcher, the brewer, or the baker, that we expect our dinner, but from their regard to their own interest. We address ourselves, not to their humanity but to their self-love, and never talk to them of our own necessities but of their advantages.[10]

Profitable firms are those with satisfied customers and loyal employees; firms with dissatisfied customers and a disgruntled workforce will probably end up with declining profits and a low stock price.[11]

Of course, ethical issues do arise in business as in other walks of life. When the stakes are high, it is often tempting for managers to cut corners. Laws and regulations seek to prevent managers from undertaking dishonest actions. But written rules and laws can help only so much. In business, as in other day-to-day affairs, there are also

BEYOND THE PAGE

Things are not always fair in love or business

mhhe.com/brealey9e

---

[10] Adam Smith, *An Inquiry into the Nature and Causes of the Wealth of Nations* (New York: Random House, 1937; first published 1776), p. 14.

[11] Shareholders value integrity. Firms that are regarded as trustworthy by their employees and that are voted as good places to work tend to be more highly valued by investors and to perform better. See A. Edmans, "Does the Stock Market Fully Value Intangibles? Employee Satisfaction and Equity Prices," *Journal of Financial Economics* 101, no. 3 (September 2011), pp. 621–640; and L. Guiso, P. Sapienza, and L. Zingales, "The Value of Corporate Culture," *Journal of Financial Economics* 117, no. 1 (July 2015), pp. 60–76.

unwritten rules of behavior. They are reinforced because good managers know that their firm's reputation is one of its most important assets, and therefore playing fair and keeping one's word are simply good business practices. Thus financial deals are regularly sealed by a handshake, and each side knows that the other will not renege later if things turn sour.

Reputation is particularly important in finance. If you buy a well-known brand in a supermarket, you can be fairly sure of what you are getting. But in financial transactions, the other party often has more information than you, and it is less easy to be sure of the quality of what you are buying. Therefore, honest financial firms seek to build long-term relationships with their customers and to establish a name for fair dealing and financial integrity. Major banks and securities firms protect their reputations.

When something happens to undermine reputations, the costs can be enormous. Volkswagen (VW) is a recent case in point. VW had installed secret software that cut back pollution from its diesel cars, but only when the cars were tested. Actual pollution in regular driving was much higher—and far in excess of legal maximums. Discovery of the software scandal in 2015 caused a tidal wave of opprobrium. VW's stock price dropped by 35%. Its CEO was fired. VW diesel vehicles piled up unsold on car dealers' lots. Potential fines imposed by the U.S. and European governments could be enormous. VW set aside $7.3 billion to cover costs and losses, but some analysts viewed this amount as much too low.

Charlatans and swindlers sometimes prey on individual investors, especially in booming markets. (It's only "when the tide goes out that you learn who's been swimming naked."[12]) The tide went out in 2008 and a number of frauds were exposed. One notorious example was the Ponzi scheme run by the disgraced financier Bernard Madoff (pronounced "Made-off").[13] Individuals and institutions invested around $20 billion with Madoff and were told that their investments had grown to $65 billion. That figure turned out to be completely fictitious. (It's not clear what Madoff did with all this money, but much of it was apparently paid out to early investors in the scheme to create an impression of superior investment performance.) With hindsight, the investors should not have trusted Madoff or the financial advisers who steered money to him.

Madoff's Ponzi scheme was (we hope) a once-in-a-lifetime event. (Ponzi schemes pop up frequently, but few have approached the scope and duration of Madoff's.) It was astonishingly unethical and illegal and was bound to end in tears. Needless to say, it was not designed to add value for investors.

BEYOND THE PAGE

Business culture and unethical behavior

mhhe.com/brealey9e

BEYOND THE PAGE

The Great Albanian Ponzi Scheme

mhhe.com/brealey9e

1.7   Self-Test

Without knowing anything about the personal ethics of the owners, which company would you trust more to keep its word in a business deal?

a. Harry's Hardware has been in business for 50 years. Harry's grandchildren, now almost adults, plan to take over and operate the business. Successful hardware stores depend on long-term loyal customers.

b. Victor's Videos just opened for business. It rents a storefront in a strip mall and has financed its inventory with a bank loan. Victor has little of his own money invested in the business. Video shops usually command little customer loyalty.

---

[12] The quotation is from Warren Buffett's annual letter to the shareholders of Berkshire Hathaway, March 2008.

[13] Ponzi schemes are named after Charles Ponzi, who founded an investment company in 1920 that promised investors unbelievably high returns. He was soon deluged with funds from investors in New England, taking in $1 million during one 3-hour period. Ponzi invested only about $30 of the money that he raised. But he used part of the cash provided by later investors to pay generous dividends to the original investors, thus promoting the illusion of high profits and quick payoffs. Within months the scheme collapsed and Ponzi started a 5-year prison sentence.

Short-Selling

Investors who take short positions are betting that securities will fall in price. Usually they do this by borrowing the security, selling it for cash, and then waiting in the hope that they will be able to buy it back cheaply.* In 2007, hedge fund manager John Paulson took a huge short position in mortgage-backed securities. The bet paid off, and that year Paulson's trade made a profit of $1 billion for his fund.†

Was Paulson's trade unethical? Some believe not only that he was profiting from the misery that resulted from the crash in mortgage-backed securities, but that his short trades accentuated the collapse. It is certainly true that short-sellers have never been popular. For example, following the crash of 1929, one commentator compared short-selling to the ghoulishness of "creatures who, at all great earthquakes and fires, spring up to rob broken homes and injured and dead humans."

Short-selling in the stock market is the Wall Street Walk on steroids. Not only do short-sellers sell all the shares they may have previously owned, but they borrow more shares and sell them too, hoping to buy them back for less when the stock price falls. Poorly performing companies are natural targets for short-sellers, and the companies' incumbent managers naturally complain, often bitterly. Governments sometimes listen to such complaints. For example, in 2008 the U.S. government temporarily banned short sales of financial stocks in an attempt to halt their decline.

But defendants of short-selling argue that selling securities that one believes are overpriced is no less legitimate than buying those that appear underpriced. The object of a well-functioning market is to set the correct stock prices, not always higher prices. Why impede short-selling if it conveys truly bad news, puts pressure on poor performers, and helps corporate governance work?

Corporate Raiders

In the movie *Pretty Woman,* Richard Gere plays the role of an asset stripper, Edward Lewis. He buys companies, takes them apart, and sells the bits for more than he paid for the total package. In the movie *Wall Street,* Gordon Gekko buys a failing airline, Blue Star, in order to break it up and sell the bits. Real corporate raiders may not be as ruthless as Edward Lewis or Gordon Gekko, but they do target companies whose assets can be profitably split up and redeployed.

This has led some to complain that raiders seek to carve up established companies, often leaving them with heavy debt burdens, basically in order to get rich quick. One German politician has likened them to "swarms of locusts that fall on companies, devour all they can, and then move on."

But sometimes raids can enhance shareholder value. For example, in 2012 and 2013, Relational Investors teamed up with the California State Teachers' Retirement System (CSTRS, a pension fund) to try to force Timken Co. to split into two separate companies, one for its steel business and one for its industrial bearings business. Relational and CSTRS believed that Timken's combination of unrelated businesses was unfocused and inefficient. Timken management responded that breakup would "deprive our shareholders of long-run value—all in an attempt to create illusory short-term gains through financial engineering." But Timken's stock price rose at the prospect of a breakup, and a nonbinding shareholder vote on Relational's proposal attracted a 53% majority. Finally in 2014 Timken spun off its steel business in a new corporation, Timken Steel.

How do you draw the ethical line in such examples? Was Relational Investors a "raider" (sounds bad) or an "activist investor" (sounds good)? Breaking up a portfolio of businesses can create difficult adjustments and job losses. Some stakeholders lose. But shareholders and the overall economy can gain if businesses are managed more efficiently.

Tax Avoidance

In 2012 it was revealed that during the 14 years that Starbucks had operated in the United Kingdom, it paid hardly any taxes. Public outrage led to a boycott of Starbucks shops, and the company responded by promising that it would voluntarily pay to the taxman about $16 million more than it was required to pay by law. Several months later, a U.S. Senate committee investigating tax avoidance by U.S. technology firms reported that Apple had used a "highly questionable" web of offshore entities to avoid billions of dollars of U.S. taxes.

Multinational companies, such as Starbucks and Apple, could reduce their tax bills using legal techniques with exotic names such as the "Dutch Sandwich," "Double Irish," and "Check-the-Box." But the public outcry over the revelations suggested that many believed that use of these techniques, though legal, was unethical. If they were unethical, that leaves an awkward question: How do companies decide which tax schemes are ethical and which are not? Can a company act in shareholders' interest if it voluntarily pays more taxes than it is legally obligated to pay?

---

*We need not go into the mechanics of short sales here, but note that the seller is obligated to buy back the security, even if its price skyrockets far above what he or she sold it for. As the saying goes, "He who sells what isn't his'n, buys it back or goes to prison."

†The story of Paulson's trade is told in G. Zuckerman, *The Greatest Trade Ever* (Broadway Business, 2009). The trade was controversial for reasons beyond short-selling. Scan the nearby Beyond the Page icon "Goldman Sachs causes a ruckus" to learn more.

BEYOND THE PAGE

Goldman Sachs causes a ruckus

mhhe.com/brealey9e

It is not always easy to know what is ethical behavior, and there can be many gray areas. The nearby box presents three ethical controversies in finance. Think about where you stand on these issues and where you would draw the ethical line.

1.7 Careers in Finance

Well over 1 million people work in the financial services industry in the United States, and many others work as financial managers in corporations. We can't tell you what each one does all day, but we can give you some idea of the variety of careers in finance. The nearby box summarizes the experience of a small sample of recent graduates.[14]

We explained earlier that corporations face two principal financial decisions: the investment decision and the financing decision. Therefore, as a newly recruited financial analyst, you may help to analyze a major new investment project. Or you may instead help to raise the money to pay for it, perhaps by negotiating a bank loan or by arranging to lease the plant and equipment. Other financial analysts work on short-term finance, managing collection and investment of the company's cash or checking whether customers are likely to pay their bills. Financial analysts are also involved in monitoring and controlling risk. For example, they may help to arrange insurance for the firm's plant and equipment, or they may assist with the purchase and sale of options, futures, and other exotic tools for managing risk.

Instead of working in the finance department of a corporation, you may join a financial institution. The largest employers are banks. Banks collect deposits and relend the cash to corporations and individuals. If you join a bank, you may start in a branch office, where individuals and small businesses come to deposit cash or to seek a loan. You could also work in the head office, helping to analyze a $500 million loan to a large corporation.

Banks do many things in addition to lending money, and they probably provide a greater variety of jobs than other financial institutions. For example, if you work in the cash management department of a large bank, you may help companies to transfer huge sums of money electronically as wages, taxes, and payments to suppliers. Banks also buy and sell foreign exchange, so you could find yourself working in front of one of those computer screens in a foreign exchange trading room. Another glamorous bank job is in the derivatives group, which helps companies to manage their risk by buying and selling options, futures, and so on. This is where the mathematicians and the computer buffs thrive.

Investment banks, such as Goldman Sachs or Morgan Stanley, help companies sell their securities to investors. They also have large corporate finance departments that assist firms in mergers and acquisitions. When firms issue securities or try to take over another firm, a lot of money is at stake and the firms may need to move fast. Thus, working for an investment bank can be a high-pressure activity with long hours. It can also pay very well.

The insurance industry is another large employer. Much of the insurance industry is involved in designing and selling insurance policies on people's lives and property, but businesses are also major customers. So, if you work for an insurance company or a large insurance broker, you could find yourself arranging insurance on a Boeing 787 in the United States or an oil rig in Indonesia.

Life insurance companies are major lenders to corporations and to investors in commercial real estate. (Life insurance companies deploy the insurance premiums received from policyholders into medium- or long-term loans; banks specialize in shorter-term financing.) So you could end up negotiating a $50 million loan for construction of a new shopping center or investigating the creditworthiness of a family-owned manufacturing company that has applied for a loan to expand production.

Then there is the business of "managing money," that is, deciding which companies' shares to invest in or how to balance investment in shares with safer securities, such as the bonds (debt securities) issued by the U.S. Treasury. Take mutual funds, for example. A mutual fund collects money from individuals and invests in a portfolio of

---

[14] The careers are fictitious but based on the actual experiences of several of the authors' students.

Susan Webb, Research Analyst, Mutual Fund Group

After majoring in biochemistry, I joined the research department of a large mutual fund group. Because of my background, I was assigned to work with the senior pharmaceuticals analyst. I start the day by reading *The Wall Street Journal* and reviewing the analyses that come in each day from stock-broking firms. Sometimes we need to revise our earnings forecasts and meet with the portfolio managers to discuss possible trades. The remainder of my day is spent mainly in analyzing companies and developing forecasts of revenues and earnings. I meet frequently with pharmaceutical analysts in stockbroking firms, and we regularly visit company management. In the evenings I study for the Chartered Financial Analyst (CFA) exam. I did not study finance at college, so this is quite challenging. I hope eventually to move from a research role to become a portfolio manager.

Richard Gradley, Project Finance, Large Energy Company

After leaving college, I joined the finance department of a large energy company. I spent my first year helping to analyze capital investment proposals. I then moved to the project finance group, which is responsible for analyzing independent power projects around the world. Recently, I have been involved in a proposal to set up a company that would build and operate a large new electricity plant in southeast Asia. We built a spreadsheet model of the project to make sure that it was viable. We had to check that the contracts with the builders, operators, suppliers, and so on, were all in place before we could arrange bank financing for the project.

Albert Rodriguez, European Markets Group, Major New York Bank

I joined the bank after majoring in finance. I spent the first 6 months in the bank's training program, rotating among departments. I was assigned to the European markets team just before the 2010 Greek crisis, when worries about a possible default caused interest rates on Greek government debt to jump to more than 4% above the rate on comparable German government debt. Those rates soon went much higher! There was a lot of activity, with everyone trying to figure out whether Greece might be forced to abandon the euro and how this would affect our business. My job is largely concerned with analyzing economies and assessing the prospects for bank business. There are plenty of opportunities to work abroad, and I hope to spend some time in Madrid or one of our other European offices.

Sherry Solera, Branch Manager, Regional Bank

I took basic finance courses in college, but nothing specific for banking. I started here as a teller. I was able to learn about banking through the bank's training program and also by evening courses at a local college. Last year I was promoted to branch manager. I oversee the branch's operations and help customers with a wide variety of problems. I'm also spending more time on credit analysis of business loan applications. I want to expand the branch's business customers, but not by making loans to shaky companies.

---

stocks or bonds. A financial analyst in a mutual fund analyzes the prospects for the securities and works with the investment manager to decide which should be bought and sold. Many other financial institutions also contain investment management departments. For example, you might work as a financial analyst in the investment department of an insurance company. (Insurance companies also invest in traded securities.) Or you could be a financial analyst in the trust department of a bank that manages money for retirement funds, universities, and charities.

Stockbroking firms help investment management companies and private individuals to invest in securities. They employ sales staff and dealers who make the trades. They also employ financial analysts to analyze the securities and help customers to decide which to buy or sell.

Investment banks and stockbroking firms are largely headquartered in New York, as are many of the large commercial banks. Insurance companies and investment management companies tend to be more scattered. For example, some of the largest insurance companies are headquartered in Hartford, Connecticut, and many investment management companies are located in Boston. Of course, some U.S. financial institutions have large businesses outside the United States. Finance is a global business. So you may spend some time working in a branch overseas or making the occasional trip to one of the other major financial centers, such as London, Tokyo, Hong Kong, or Singapore.

1.8 Preview of Coming Attractions

This book covers investment decisions, then financing decisions, and finally a variety of planning issues that require an understanding of both investment and financing. But first there are three further introductory chapters that should be helpful to readers who are making a first acquaintance with financial management. Chapter 2 is an overview of financial markets and institutions. Chapter 3 reviews the basic concepts of accounting, and Chapter 4 demonstrates the techniques of financial statement analysis.

We have said that the financial manager's task is to make investment and financing decisions that add value for the firm's shareholders. But that statement opens up a treasure chest of follow-up questions that will occupy us from Chapter 4 onward:

- *How do I calculate the value of a stream of future cash flows?* A dollar that you receive today is worth more than the promise of a dollar in 10 or 20 years' time. So, when measuring the effect of a new project on firm value, the financial manager needs to recognize the *timing* of the cash flows. In Chapters 5 through 10, we show how to calculate the present value of an investment that produces a stream of future cash flows. We begin by calculating the present value of bonds and stocks and then look at how to value the cash flows resulting from capital investment projects. Present value is a workhorse concept of corporate finance that shows up in almost every chapter.
- *How do I measure risk?* In Chapters 5 through 10, we largely ignore the issue of risk. But risky cash flows are less valuable than safe ones. In Chapters 11, 12, and 13, we look at how to measure risk and how it affects present values.
- *Where does financing come from?* Broadly speaking, it comes from borrowing or from cash invested or reinvested by stockholders. But financing can get complicated when you get down to specifics. Chapter 14 gives an overview of the sources of finance. Chapters 15, 16, and 17 then look at how companies sell their securities to investors, the choice between debt and equity, and the decision to pay out cash to stockholders.
- *How do I ensure that the firm's financial decisions add up to a sensible whole?* There are two parts to this question. The first is concerned with making sure that the firm can finance its future growth strategy. This is the role of long-term planning. The second is concerned with ensuring that the firm has a sensible plan for managing and financing its short-term assets such as cash, inventories, and money due from customers. We cover long- and short-term planning in Chapters 18, 19, and 20.
- *What about some of those other responsibilities of the financial manager that you mentioned earlier?* Not all of the financial manager's responsibilities can be classified simply as an investment decision or a financing decision. In Chapters 21 through 24, we review four such topics. First we look at mergers and acquisitions. Then we consider international financial management. All the financial problems of doing business at home are present overseas, but the international financial manager faces the additional complications created by multiple currencies, different tax systems, and special regulations imposed by foreign institutions and governments. Finally, we look at risk management and the specialized securities, including futures and options, which managers can use to hedge or lay off risks.

That's enough material to start, but as you reflect on this chapter, you can see certain themes emerging that you will encounter again and again throughout this book:

1. Corporate finance is about adding value.
2. The opportunity cost of capital sets the standard for investments.
3. A safe dollar is worth more than a risky one.
4. Smart investment decisions create more value than smart financing decisions.
5. Good governance matters.

1.9   Snippets of Financial History

Now let's lighten up a little. In this book we are going to describe how financial decisions are made today. But financial markets also have an interesting history. Look at the nearby box, which lays out bits of this history, starting in prehistoric times, when the growth of bacteria anticipated the mathematics of compound interest, and continuing nearly to the present. We have keyed each of these episodes to the chapter of the book that discusses its topic.

Date unknown *Compound Growth* Bacteria start to propagate by subdividing. They thereby demonstrate the power of compound growth. (*Chapter 5*)

c. 1800 B.C. *Interest Rates* In Babylonia, Hammurabi's Code established maximum interest rates on loans. Borrowers often mortgaged their property and sometimes their spouses, but lenders were obliged to return spouses in good condition within 3 years. (*Chapter 6*)

c. 1000 B.C. *Options* One of the earliest recorded options is described by Aristotle. The philosopher Thales knew by the stars that there would be a great olive harvest, so, having a little money, he bought options for the use of olive presses. When the harvest came, Thales was able to rent the presses at great profit. Today financial managers need to be able to evaluate options to buy or sell a wide variety of assets. (*Chapter 23*)

15th century *International Banking* Modern international banking had its origins in the great Florentine banking houses. But the entire European network of the Medici empire employed only 57 people in eight offices. Today the London-based bank HSBC has around 260,000 employees in 71 different countries. (*Chapter 14*)

1650 *Futures* Futures markets allow companies to protect themselves against fluctuations in commodity prices. During the Tokugawa era in Japan, feudal lords collected rents in the form of rice, but often they wished to trade their future rice deliveries. Rice futures therefore came to be traded on what was later known as the Dojima Rice Market. Rice futures are still traded, but now companies can also trade in futures on a range of items from pork bellies to stock market indexes. (*Chapter 24*)

17th century *Joint Stock Corporations* Although investors have for a long time combined together as joint owners of an enterprise, the modern corporation with a large number of stockholders originated with the formation in England of trading firms like the East India Company (est. 1599). (*Chapter 15*)

17th century *Money* America has been in the forefront in the development of new types of money. Early settlers often used a shell known as wampum. For example, Peter Stuyvesant raised a loan in wampum, and in Massachusetts it was legal tender. Unfortunately, the enterprising settlers found that with a little dye the relatively common white wampum shells could be converted profitably into the more valuable black ones, which confirmed Gresham's law that bad money drives out good. The first issue of paper money in America was by the Massachusetts Bay Colony in 1690, and other colonies soon set their printing presses to producing money. In 1862 Congress agreed to an issue of paper money that would be legal tender. These notes, printed in green ink, immediately became known as "greenbacks." (*Chapters 19, 20*)

1720 *New-Issue Speculation* From time to time investors have been tempted by speculative new issues. During the South Sea Bubble in England, one company was launched to develop perpetual motion. Another enterprising individual announced a company "for carrying on an undertaking of great advantage but nobody to know what it is." Within 5 hours he had raised £2,000; within 6 hours he was on his way out of the country. Readers nearly two centuries later could only wonder at the naïve or foolhardy investors in these ventures—that is, until they had a chance to participate in the follies unearthed by the financial crisis of 2008–2009. (*Chapter 2*)

1792 *Formation of the New York Stock Exchange* The New York Stock Exchange (NYSE) was founded in 1792 when a group of brokers met under a buttonwood tree* and arranged to trade shares with one another at agreed rates of commission. Today the NYSE is the largest stock exchange in the world, trading on average about 1.5 billion shares a day. (*Chapter 7*)

1929 *Stock Market Crashes* Common stocks are risky investments. In September 1929 stock prices in the United States reached an all-time high, and the economist Irving Fisher forecast that they were at "a permanently high plateau." Some 3 years later, stock prices were almost 90% lower, and it was to be a quarter of a century before the prices of September 1929 were seen again. Eighty years later, history came close to repeating itself. After stock prices peaked in July 2007, they slumped over the next 20 months by 54%. (*Chapter 11*)

1960s *Eurodollar Market* In the 1950s the Soviet Union transferred its dollar holdings from the United States to a Russian-owned bank in Paris. This bank was best known by its telex address, eurobank, and consequently dollars held outside the United States came to be known as eurodollars. In the 1960s, U.S. taxes and regulation made it much cheaper to borrow and lend dollars in Europe than in the United States, and a huge market in eurodollars arose. (*Chapter 14*)

1971 *Corporate Bankruptcies* Every generation of investors is shocked and surprised by a major corporate bankruptcy. In 1971 the Penn Central Railroad, a pillar of American industry, suddenly collapsed. At that time, it was the largest corporate bankruptcy in history. In 2008, the investment bank Lehman Brothers smashed Penn Central's record. (*Chapter 16*)

1972 *Financial Futures* Financial futures allow companies to protect themselves against fluctuations in interest rates, exchange rates, and so on. It is said that they originated from a remark by the economist Milton Friedman that he was unable to profit from his view that sterling (the U.K. currency) was overpriced. The Chicago Mercantile Exchange founded the first financial futures market. Today futures exchanges trade 6 billion contracts a year of financial futures. (*Chapter 24*)

1986 *Capital Investment Decisions* The largest investment project undertaken by a single private company was the construction of the tunnel under the English Channel. This started in 1986 and was completed in 1994 at a total cost of $15 billion. The cost of the Gorgon natural gas project in Australia is estimated at $54 billion. (*Chapters 8, 9*)

1988 *Mergers* The 1980s saw a wave of takeovers culminating in the $25 billion takeover of RJR Nabisco. Over a period of 6 weeks, three groups battled for control of the company. As one of the contestants put it, "We were charging through the rice paddies, not stopping for anything and taking no prisoners." The takeover was the largest in history and generated almost $1 billion in fees for the banks and advisers. (*Chapter 21*)

1993 *Inflation* Financial managers need to recognize the effect of inflation on interest rates and on the profitability of the firm's investments. In the United States inflation has been relatively modest, but some countries have suffered from hyperinflation. In Hungary after World War II, the government issued banknotes worth 1,000 trillion pengoes. In Yugoslavia in October 1993, prices rose by nearly 2,000% and a dollar bought 105 million dinars. The inflation rate in Venezuela in late 2015 was about 180%. (*Chapter 5*)

1780 and 1997 *Inflation-Indexed Debt* In 1780, Massachusetts paid Revolutionary War soldiers with interest-bearing notes rather than its rapidly eroding currency. Interest and principal payments on the notes were tied to the subsequent rate of inflation. After a 217-year hiatus, the U.S. Treasury issued inflation-indexed notes called TIPS (Treasury Inflation Protected Securities). Many other countries, including Britain and Israel, had done so previously. (*Chapter 6*)

1993 *Controlling Risk* When a company fails to keep close tabs on the risks being taken by its employees, it can get into serious trouble. This was the fate of Barings, a 220-year-old British bank that numbered the queen among its clients. In 1993 it discovered that Nick Leeson, a trader in its Singapore office, had hidden losses of $1.3 billion (£869 million) from unauthorized bets on the Japanese equity market. The losses wiped out Barings and landed Leeson in jail, with a 6-year sentence. In 2008 a rogue trader at Morgan Stanley established a new record by losing $9 billion on unauthorized deals. (*Chapter 24*)

1999 *The Euro* Large corporations do business in many currencies. In 1999 a new currency came into existence when 11 European countries adopted the euro in place of their separate currencies. They have since been joined by eight other countries. This is not the first time that different countries have agreed on a common currency. In 1865 France, Belgium, Switzerland, and Italy came together in the Latin Monetary Union, and they were joined by Greece and Romania the following year. Members of the European Monetary Union (EMU) hope that the euro will be a longer-lasting success than this earlier experiment. As we write this in early 2016, the euro appears to have weathered the worst of the crisis caused by the Greek government's debt default. (*Chapter 23*)

2002 *Financial Scandals* A seemingly endless series of financial and accounting scandals climaxed in this year. Resulting bankruptcies included the icons Enron (and its accounting firm, Arthur Andersen), WorldCom, and the Italian food company Parmalat. Congress passed the Sarbanes-Oxley Act to increase the accountability of corporations and executives. (*Chapters 1, 14*)

2007–2009 *Subprime Mortgages* Subprime mortgages are housing loans made to homeowners with shaky credit standing. After a decade in which housing prices had consistently gone up, lenders became complacent about the risks of these home loans and progressively loosened lending standards. When housing prices stalled and interest rates increased in 2007, many of these loans went bad. Some large banks such as Lehman Brothers went to the wall, while others such as Wachovia and Merrill Lynch were rescued with the aid of government money. (*Chapters 2, 14*)

2011 *Defaults on Sovereign Debt* By 2010 the Greek government had amassed a huge $460 billion of debt. Other eurozone governments and the International Monetary Fund (IMF) rushed to Greece's aid, but their assistance was insufficient, and in 2011 the Greek government defaulted on $100 billion of debt. It was the largest-ever sovereign default. Investors nervously eyed other highly indebted eurozone countries. (*Chapter 2*)

_____

* The American sycamore, *Planatus occidentalis*.

SUMMARY

What are the two major decisions made by financial managers? (*LO1-1*)

Financial management can be broken down into (1) the investment or **capital budgeting decision** and (2) the **financing decision.** The firm has to decide (1) which real assets to invest in and (2) how to raise the funds necessary to pay for those investments.

What does "real asset" mean? (*LO1-2*)

Real assets include all assets used in the production or sale of the firms' products or services. They can be tangible (plant and equipment, for example) or intangible (patents or trademarks, for example). In contrast, **financial assets** (such as stocks or bonds) are claims on the income generated by real assets.

What are the advantages and disadvantages of forming a corporation? (*LO1-3*)

Corporations are distinct, permanent legal entities. They allow for separation of ownership and control, and they can continue operating without disruption even as management or ownership changes. They provide **limited liability** to their owners. On the other hand, managing the corporation's legal machinery is costly. Also, corporations are subject to double taxation, because they pay taxes on their profits and the shareholders are taxed again when they receive dividends or sell their shares at a profit.

Who are the principal financial managers in a corporation? (*LO1-4*)

Almost all managers are involved to some degree in investment decisions, but some managers specialize in finance, for example, the treasurer, controller, and CFO. The **treasurer** is most directly responsible for raising capital and maintaining relationships with banks and investors that hold the firm's securities. The **controller** is responsible for preparing financial statements and managing budgets. In large firms, a **chief financial officer** oversees both the treasurer and the controller and is involved in financial policymaking and corporate planning.

Why does it make sense for corporations to maximize shareholder wealth? (*LO1-5*)

Value maximization is the natural financial goal of the firm. Shareholders can invest or consume the increased wealth as they wish, provided that they have access to well-functioning financial markets.

What is the fundamental trade-off in investment decisions? (*LO1-5*)

Companies either can invest in real assets or can return the cash to shareholders, who can invest it for themselves. The return that shareholders can earn for themselves is called the **opportunity cost of capital.** Companies create value for shareholders whenever they can earn a higher return on their investments than the opportunity cost of capital.

How do corporations ensure that managers act in the interest of stockholders? (*LO1-6*)

Conflicts of interest between managers and stockholders can lead to **agency problems** and **agency costs.** Agency problems are kept in check by financial controls, by well-designed compensation packages for managers, and by effective corporate governance.

Is value maximization ethical? (*LO1-7*)

Shareholders do not want the maximum possible stock price; they want the maximum honest price. But there need be no conflict between value maximization and ethical behavior. The surest route to maximum value starts with products and services that satisfy customers. A good reputation with customers, employees, and other stakeholders is important for the firm's long-run profitability and value.

QUESTIONS AND PROBLEMS

1. **Vocabulary Check.** Choose the term within the parentheses that best matches each of the following descriptions. (*LO1-1–LO1-7*)
   a. Expenditure on research and development (*financing decision / investment decision*)
   b. A bank loan (*real asset / financial asset*)
   c. Listed on a stock exchange (*closely held corporation / public corporation*)
   d. Has limited liability (*partnership / corporation*)
   e. Responsible for bank relationships (*the treasurer / the controller*)
   f. Agency cost (*the cost resulting from conflicts of interest between managers and shareholders / the amount charged by a company's agents such as the auditors and lawyers*)

2. **Financial Decisions.** Which of the following are investment decisions, and which are financing decisions? (*LO1-1*)
   a. Should we stock up with inventory ahead of the holiday season?
   b. Do we need a bank loan to help buy the inventory?
   c. Should we develop a new software package to manage our inventory?
   d. With a new automated inventory management system, it may be possible to sell off our Birdlip warehouse.
   e. With the savings we make from our new inventory system, it may be possible to increase our dividend.
   f. Alternatively, we can use the savings to repay some of our long-term debt.

3. **Financial Decisions.** What is the difference between capital budgeting decisions and capital structure decisions? (*LO1-1*)

4. **Real versus Financial Assets.** Which of the following are real assets, and which are financial? (*LO1-2*)

   a. A share of stock
   b. A personal IOU
   c. A trademark
   d. A truck
   e. Undeveloped land
   f. The balance in the firm's checking account
   g. An experienced and hardworking sales force
   h. A bank loan agreement

5. **Real and Financial Assets.** Read the following passage and fit each of the following terms into the most appropriate space*: financing, real, bonds, investment, executive airplanes, financial, capital budgeting, brand names.* (*LO1-2*)

   Companies usually buy _____ assets. These include both tangible assets such as _____ and intangible assets such as _____. To pay for these assets, they sell _____ assets such as _____. The decision about which assets to buy is usually termed the _____ or _____ decision. The decision about how to raise the money is usually termed the _____ decision.

6. **Corporations.** Choose in each case the type of company that best fits the description. (*LO1-3*)

   a. The business is owned by a small group of investors. (*private corporation / public corporation*)
   b. The business does not pay income tax. (*private corporation / partnership*)
   c. The business has limited liability. (*sole proprietorship / public corporation*)
   d. The business is owned by its shareholders. (*partnership / public corporation*)

7. **Corporations.** What do we mean when we say that corporate income is subject to *double taxation?* (*LO1-3*)

8. **Corporations.** Which of the following statements always apply to corporations? (*LO1-3*)

   a. Unlimited liability
   b. Limited life
   c. Ownership can be transferred without affecting operations
   d. Managers can be fired with no effect on ownership

9. **Corporations.** What is limited liability, and who benefits from it? (*LO1-3*)

10. **Corporations.** Which of the following are correct descriptions of large corporations? (*LO1-3*)

    a. Managers no longer have the incentive to act in their own interests.
    b. The corporation survives even if managers are dismissed.
    c. Shareholders can sell their holdings without disrupting the business.
    d. Corporations, unlike sole proprietorships, do not pay tax; instead, shareholders are taxed on any dividends they receive.

11. **Corporations.** Is limited liability always an advantage for a corporation and its shareholders? (*Hint:* Could limited liability reduce a corporation's access to financing?) (*LO1-3*)

12. **Financial Managers.** Which of the following statements more accurately describes the treasurer than the controller? (*LO1-4*)

    a. Monitors capital expenditures to make sure that they are not misappropriated
    b. Responsible for investing the firm's spare cash
    c. Responsible for arranging any issue of common stock
    d. Responsible for the company's tax affairs

13. **Financial Managers.** Explain the differences between the CFO's responsibilities and the treasurer's and controller's responsibilities. (*LO1-4*)

14. **Goals of the Firm.** Give an example of an action that might increase short-run profits but at the same time reduce stock price and the market value of the firm. (*LO1-5*)

15. **Cost of Capital.** Why do financial managers refer to the *opportunity* cost of capital? How would you find the opportunity cost of capital for a safe investment? (*LO1-5*)

16. **Goals of the Firm.** You may have heard big business criticized for focusing on short-term performance at the expense of long-term results. Explain why a firm that strives to maximize

stock price should be *less* subject to an overemphasis on short-term results than one that simply maximizes profits. (*LO1-5*)

17. **Goals of the Firm.** Fritz is risk-averse and is content with a relatively low but safe return on his investments. Frieda is risk-tolerant and seeks a very high rate of return on her invested savings. Yet both shareholders will applaud a high-risk capital investment if it offers a superior rate of return. Why? What is meant by "superior"? (*LO1-5*)

18. **Goals of the Firm.** We claim that the goal of the firm is to maximize current market value. Could the following actions be consistent with that goal? (*LO1-5*)

    a. The firm adds a cost-of-living adjustment to the pensions of its retired employees.
    b. The firm reduces its dividend payment, choosing to reinvest more earnings in the business.
    c. The firm buys a corporate jet for its executives.
    d. The firm drills for oil in a remote jungle. The chance of finding oil is only 1 in 5.

19. **Goals of the Firm.** Fill in the blanks in the following passage by choosing the most appropriate term from the following list (some of the terms may be used more than once or not used at all): *expected return, financial assets, lower, market value, higher, opportunity cost of capital, real assets, dividend, shareholders.* (*LO1-5*)

    Shareholders want managers to maximize the _____ of their investments. The firm faces a trade-off. Either it can invest its cash in _____ or it can give the cash back to _____ in the form of a(n) _____ and they can invest it in _____. Shareholders want the company to invest in _____ only if the _____ is _____ than they could earn for themselves in equivalent risk investments. The return that shareholders could earn for themselves is therefore the _____ for the firm.

20. **Goals of the Firm.** Explain why each of the following may not be appropriate corporate goals. (*LO1-5*)

    a. Increase market share
    b. Minimize costs
    c. Underprice any competitors
    d. Expand profits

21. **Goals of the Firm.** We can imagine the financial manager doing several things on behalf of the firm's stockholders. For example, the manager might do the following:

    a. Make shareholders as wealthy as possible by investing in real assets.
    b. Modify the firm's investment plan to help shareholders achieve a particular time pattern of consumption.
    c. Choose high- or low-risk assets to match shareholders' risk preferences.
    d. Help balance shareholders' checkbooks.

    However, in well-functioning capital markets, shareholders will vote for only one of these goals. Which one will they choose? (*LO1-5*)

22. **Cost of Capital.** British Quince comes across an average-risk investment project that offers a rate of return of 9.5%. This is less than the company's normal rate of return, but one of Quince's directors notes that the company can easily borrow the required investment at 7%. "It's simple," he says. "If the bank lends us money at 7%, then our cost of capital must be 7%. The project's return is higher than the cost of capital, so let's move ahead." How would you respond? (*LO1-5*)

23. **Cost of Capital.** In a stroke of good luck, your company has uncovered an opportunity to invest for 10 years at a guaranteed 6% rate of return. How would you determine the opportunity cost of capital for this investment? (*LO1-5*)

24. **Cost of Capital.** Pollution Busters Inc. is considering a purchase of 10 additional carbon sequesters for $100,000 apiece. The sequesters last for only 1 year before becoming saturated. Then the carbon is sold to the government. (*LO1-5*)

    a. Suppose the government guarantees the price of carbon. At this price, the payoff after 1 year is $115,000 for sure. How would you determine the opportunity cost of capital for this investment?
    b. Suppose instead that the sequestered carbon has to be sold on the London Carbon Exchange. Carbon prices have been extremely volatile, but Pollution Busters' CFO learns that average rates of return from investments on that exchange have been about 20%. She thinks this is a

reasonable forecast for the future. What is the opportunity cost of capital in this case? Is the purchase of additional sequesters a worthwhile capital investment?

25. **Goals of the Firm.** It is sometimes suggested that instead of seeking to maximize shareholder value and, in the process, pursuing profit, the firm should seek to maximize the welfare of all its stakeholders, such as its employees, its customers, and the community in which it operates. How far would this objective conflict with one of maximizing shareholder value? Do you think such an objective is feasible or desirable? (*LO1-5*)

26. **Agency Issues.** Many firms have devised defenses that make it much more costly or difficult for other firms to take them over. How might such takeover defenses affect the firm's agency problems? Are managers of firms with formidable takeover defenses more or less likely to act in the firm's interest rather than their own? (*LO1-6*)

27. **Agency Issues.** Sometimes lawyers work on a contingency basis. They collect a percentage of their clients' settlements instead of receiving fixed fees. Why might clients prefer this arrangement? Would the arrangement mitigate an agency problem? Explain. (*LO1-6*)

28. **Agency Issues.** One of the "Finance through the Ages" episodes that we cited is the 1993 collapse of Barings Bank, when one of its traders lost $1.3 billion. Traders are compensated in large part according to their trading profits. How might this practice have contributed to an agency problem? (*LO1-6*)

29. **Agency Issues.** When a company's stock is widely held, it may not pay an individual shareholder to spend time monitoring managers' performance and trying to replace poor performers. Explain why. Do you think that a bank that has made a large loan to the company is in a different position? (*LO1-6*)

30. **Agency Issues.** Company A pays its managers a fixed salary. Company B ties compensation to the performance of the stock. Which company's compensation package would most effectively mitigate conflicts of interest between managers and shareholders? (*LO1-6*)

31. **Corporate Governance.** How do clear and comprehensive financial reports promote effective corporate governance? (*LO1-6*)

32. **Corporate Governance.** Some commentators have claimed that the U.S. system of corporate governance is "broken" and needs thorough reform. What do you think? Do you see systematic failures in corporate governance or just a few "bad apples"? (*LO1-6*)

33. **Agency Issues.** Which of the following forms of compensation is most likely to align the interests of managers and shareholders? (*LO1-6*)
    a. A fixed salary
    b. A salary linked to company profits
    c. A salary that is paid partly in the form of the company's shares

34. **Agency Costs.** What are agency costs? List some ways by which agency costs are mitigated. (*LO1-6*)

35. **Reputation.** As you drive down a deserted highway, you are overcome with a sudden desire for a hamburger. Fortunately, just ahead are two hamburger outlets; one is owned by a national brand, and the other appears to be owned by "Joe." Which outlet has the greater incentive to serve you cat meat? Why? (*LO1-7*)

36. **Ethics.** In some countries, such as Japan and Germany, corporations develop close long-term relationships with one bank and rely on that bank for a large part of their financing needs. In the United States, companies are more likely to shop around for the best deal. Do you think that this practice is more or less likely to encourage ethical behavior on the part of the corporation? (*LO1-7*)

37. **Ethics.** Is there a conflict between "doing well" and "doing good"? In other words, are policies that increase the value of the firm (doing well) necessarily at odds with socially responsible policies (doing good)? When there are conflicts, how might government regulations or laws tilt the firm toward doing good? For example, how do taxes or fees charged on pollutants affect the firm's decision to pollute? Can you cite other examples of "incentives" used by governments to align private interests with public ones? (*LO1-7*)

38. **Ethics.** Look at some of the practices described in the Finance in Practice box on ethic disputes in finance. What, if any, do you believe are the ethical issues involved? (*LO1-7*)

SOLUTIONS TO SELF-TEST QUESTIONS

1.1 a. The development of a microprocessor is a capital budgeting decision. The investment of $1 billion will purchase a real asset, the microprocessor design and production facilities.

b. The bank loan is a financing decision. This is how BMW will raise money for its investment.

c. Capital budgeting.

d. Capital budgeting. The marketing campaign should generate a real, though intangible, asset.

e. Both. The acquisition is an investment decision. The decision to issue shares is a financing decision.

1.2 a. A real asset. Real assets can be intangible assets.

b. Financial.

c. Real.

d. Financial.

e. Real.

f. Financial.

1.3 Fritz would more likely be the treasurer and Frieda the controller. The treasurer raises money from the financial markets and requires a background in financial institutions. The controller requires a background in accounting.

1.4 There is no reason for the Hotspurs to avoid high-dividend stocks, even if they wish to invest for tuition bills in the distant future. Their concern should be only with the risk and expected return of the shares. If a particular stock pays a generous cash dividend, they always have the option of reinvesting the dividend in that stock or, for that matter, in other securities. The dividend payout does not affect their ability to redirect current investment income to their future needs as they plan for their anticipated tuition bills.

1.5 Because investors can reasonably expect a 15% return in other investments in palladium, the firm should take this as the opportunity cost of capital for its proposed investment. Although the project is expected to show an accounting profit, its expected return is only 12%. Therefore, the firm should reject the project: Its expected return is less than the 15% expected return offered by equivalent-risk investments.

1.6 Agency problems arise when managers and shareholders have different objectives. Managers may empire-build with excessive investment and growth. Managers may be unduly risk-averse, or they may try to take excessive salaries or perquisites.

1.7 Harry's has a far bigger stake in the reputation of its business than Victor's. The store has been in business for a long time. The owners have spent years establishing customer loyalty. In contrast, Victor's has just been established. The owner has little of his own money tied up in the firm, and so has little to lose if the business fails. In addition, the nature of the business results in little customer loyalty. Harry's is probably more reliable.

2

Financial Markets and Institutions

LEARNING OBJECTIVES

After studying this chapter, you should be able to:

2-1   Understand how financial markets and institutions channel savings to corporate investment.

2-2   Understand the basic structure of banks, insurance companies, mutual funds, and pension funds.

2-3   Explain the functions of financial markets and institutions.

2-4   Understand the main events behind the financial crisis of 2007–2009 and the subsequent eurozone crisis.

RELATED WEBSITES FOR THIS CHAPTER CAN BE FOUND IN CONNECT.

Read this chapter before you visit the New York Stock Exchange. *Alexander Baxevanis/Flickr/CC BY 2.0*

If a corporation needs to issue more shares of stock, then its financial manager had better understand how the stock market works. If it wants to take out a bank loan, the financial manager had better understand how banks and other financial institutions work. If the firm contemplates a capital investment, such as a factory expansion or a new product launch, the financial manager needs to think clearly about the cost of the capital that the firm raises from outside investors. As we pointed out in Chapter 1, the opportunity cost of capital for the firm is the rate of return that its stockholders expect to get by investing on their own in financial markets. This means that the financial manager must understand how prices are determined in the financial markets in order to make wise investment decisions.

Financial markets and institutions are the firm's financial environment. You don't have to know everything about that environment to begin the study of financial management, but a general understanding provides useful context for the work ahead. For example, it will help you to understand why you are calculating the yield to maturity of a bond in Chapter 6, the net present value of a capital investment in Chapter 9, or the weighted-average cost of capital for a company in Chapter 13.

This chapter does three things. First, it surveys financial markets and institutions. We will cover the stock and bond markets, banks and insurance companies, and mutual and pension funds. Second, we will set out the functions of financial markets and institutions and look at how they help corporations and the economy. Third, we will discuss the financial crisis of 2007–2009 and the eurozone crisis that followed. An understanding of what happens when financial markets do *not* function well is important for understanding why and how financial markets and institutions matter.

2.1 The Importance of Financial Markets and Institutions

In the previous chapter, we explained why corporations need to be good at finance in order to survive and prosper. All corporations face important investment and financing decisions. But, of course, those decisions are not made in a vacuum. They are made in a financial environment. That environment has two main segments: financial markets and financial institutions.

Businesses have to go to financial markets and institutions for the financing they need to grow. When they have a surplus of cash, and no need for immediate financing, they have to invest the cash, for example, in bank accounts or in securities. Let's take Apple Computer Inc. as an example.

Table 2.1 presents a time line for Apple and examples of the sources of financing tapped by Apple from its start-up in a California garage in 1976 to its cash-rich status in 2016. The initial investment in Apple stock was $250,000. Apple was also able to get short-term financing from parts suppliers who did not demand immediate payment. Apple got the parts, assembled and sold the computers, and afterward paid off its accounts payable to the suppliers. (We discuss accounts payable in Chapter 19.) Then,

TABLE 2.1 Examples of financing decisions by Apple Computer

April 1976: Apple Computer Inc. founded	Mike Makkula, Apple's first chairman, invests $250,000 in Apple shares.
1976: First 200 computers sold	Parts suppliers give Apple 30 days to pay. (Financing from accounts payable.)
1978–79	Apple raises $3.5 million from venture capital investors.
December 1980: Initial public offering	Apple raises $91 million, after fees and expenses, by selling shares to public investors.
May 1981	Apple sells 2.6 million additional shares at $31.25 per share.
April 1987	Apple pays its first dividend at an annual rate of $.12 per share.
Early 1990s	Apple carries out several share repurchase programs.
1994	Apple issues $300 million of debt at an interest rate of 6.5%.
1996–97: Apple reports a $740 million loss in the second quarter of 1996. Lays off 2,700 employees in 1997.	Dividend is suspended in February 1996. Apple sells $661 million of debt to private investors in June 1996. The borrowing provides "sufficient liquidity" to execute Apple's strategic plans and to "return the company to profitability."
September 1997: Acquires assets of Power Computing Corp.	Acquisition is financed with $100 million of Apple stock.
2004: Apple is healthy and profitable, thanks to iMac, iPod, and other products.	Apple pays off the $300 million in long-term debt issued in 1994, leaving the company with no long-term debt outstanding.
2005–13	Apple's profits grow rapidly. It invests in marketable securities, which accumulate to $147 billion by June 2013.
2012–13	Apple announces plans to pay out $100 billion to shareholders over the next 3 years. It also borrows a record $17 billion.
2013–15	Apple's Capital Return Program distributes cash to shareholders by paying dividends and repurchasing shares. The planned total distribution is $200 billion by 2017.
2015	Apple issues $14.5 billion in dollar-denominated debt, €4.8 billion in euro debt, as well as debt issued in U.K. pounds, Swiss francs, and Japanese yen.
February 2016	Apple's market capitalization, the total market value of all its outstanding shares, is $521 billion, far in excess of the $119 billion cumulative investment by Apple's shareholders. The cumulative investment includes $92 billion of retained earnings.

as Apple grew, it was able to obtain several rounds of financing by selling Apple shares to private venture capital investors. (We discuss venture capital in Chapter 15.) In December 1980, it raised $91 million in an initial public offering (IPO) of its shares to public investors. There was also a follow-up share issue in May 1981.[1]

After Apple became a public company, it could raise financing from many sources, and it was able to pay for acquisitions by issuing more shares. We show a few examples in Table 2.1.

Apple started paying cash dividends to shareholders in 1987, and it also distributed cash to investors by stock repurchases in the early 1990s. But Apple hit a rough patch in 1996 and 1997, and regular dividends were eliminated. The company had to borrow $661 million from a group of private investors in order to cover its losses and finance its recovery plan. However, the rough patch ended with the release of the iMac in 1998 and the iPod in 2001. Apple's profitability increased rapidly, and it was able to finance its growth by plowing back earnings into operations. These retained earnings had grown to $92 billion by September 2015.

As the twenty-first century progressed, Apple's profits grew so fast that it piled up a cash mountain, which grew to more than $200 billion by 2016. It resumed cash dividends and started a massive program of share repurchases. Its Capital Return Program, which began in 2012, will distribute $200 billion in cash to its shareholders by 2017.

Apple is well known for its product innovations, including the Macintosh computer, the iPhone, and the iPad. Apple is not special because of financing. In fact, the story of its financing is not too different from that of many other successful companies. But access to financing was vital to Apple's growth and profitability. Would we have iMac computers, iPhones, or iPads if Apple had been forced to operate in a country with a primitive financial system? Definitely not. A prosperous economy requires a well-functioning financial system.

A modern financial system offers financing in many different forms, depending on the company's age, its growth rate, and the nature of its business. For example, Apple relied on venture capital financing in its early years and only later floated its shares in public stock markets. Still later, as the company matured, it turned to other forms of financing, including the examples given in Table 2.1. But the table does not begin to cover the range of financing channels open to modern corporations. We will encounter many other channels later in the book, and new channels are opening up regularly. The nearby box describes one recent financial innovation, micro-lending funds that make small loans to businesspeople in the poorer parts of the world.

2.2 The Flow of Savings to Corporations

The money that corporations invest in real assets comes ultimately from savings by investors. But there can be many stops on the road between savings and corporate investment. The road can pass through financial markets, financial intermediaries, or both.

Let's start with the simplest case of a small, closely held corporation, like Apple in its earliest years. The orange arrows in Figure 2.1 show the flow of savings from shareholders in this simple setting. There are two possible paths: The firm can sell new shares, or it can reinvest cash back into the firm's operations. Reinvestment means additional savings by existing shareholders. The reinvested cash could have been paid out to those shareholders and spent by them on personal consumption. By *not* taking and spending the cash, shareholders have reinvested their savings in the corporation.

---

[1] Many of the shares sold in the 1981 issue were previously held by Apple employees. Sale of these shares allowed the employees to cash out and diversify some of their Apple holdings but did not raise additional financing for Apple.

Vahid Hujdur had dreams of opening his own business. With about $200 of his own money and a $1,500 loan, he was able to rent space in the old section of Sarajevo, and he began repairing and selling discarded industrial sewing machines. After just 8 years, Hujdur has 10 employees building, installing, and fixing this industrial machinery. Hujdur didn't get his initial loan from a local bank. "They were asking for guarantees that were impossible to get," he recalls. Instead, the capital came from LOKmicro, a local financial institution specializing in microfinance—the lending of small amounts to the poor in developing nations to help them launch small enterprises.

Microfinance institutions get capital from individual and institutional investors via microfinance funds, which collect the investors' money, vet the local lenders, offer them management assistance, and administer investors' accounts.

The interest rates on these micro loans are relatively high; this is because the cost of writing and administering such small loans is high and the loans are made in nations with weak currencies. However, default rates on the loans are only about 4%. "There is a deep pride in keeping up with payments," says Deidre Wagner, an executive vice president of Starbucks, who invested $100,000 in a microfinance fund in 2003. "In some instances, when an individual is behind on payments, others in the village may make up the difference." Investors and borrowers know that when the micro loans are repaid, the money gets recycled into new loans, giving still more borrowers a chance to move up the economic ladder.

Source: Adapted from Eric Uhlfelder, "Micro Loans, Solid Returns," *Business-Week,* May 9, 2005, pp. 100–102.

FIGURE 2.1 Flow of savings to investment in a closely held corporation. Investors use savings to buy additional shares. Investors also save when the corporation reinvests on their behalf.

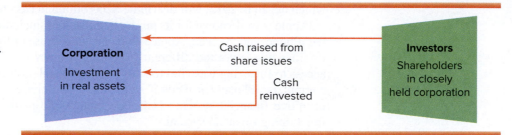

Cash retained and reinvested in the firm's operations is cash saved and invested on behalf of the firm's shareholders.

Of course, a small corporation has other financing choices. It could take out a bank loan, for example. The bank in turn may have raised money by attracting savings accounts. In this case, investors' savings flow through the bank to the firm.

Now consider a large, public corporation, for example, Apple Computer in September 2015. What's different? Scale, for one thing: Apple's annual revenues for the previous 12 months were $234 billion, and its balance sheet showed total assets of $290 billion. The scope of Apple's activities has also expanded: It now has dozens of product lines and operates worldwide. Because of this scale and scope, Apple attracts investors' savings by a variety of different routes. It can do so because it is a large, profitable, public firm.

The flow of savings to large public corporations is shown in Figure 2.2. Notice two key differences from Figure 2.1. First, public corporations can draw savings from investors worldwide. Second, the savings flow through financial markets, financial intermediaries, or both. Suppose, for example, that Bank of America raises $900 million by a new issue of shares. An Italian investor buys 4,000 of the new shares for $15 per share. Now Bank of America takes that $60,000, along with money raised by the rest of the issue, and makes a $300 million loan to Apple. The Italian investor's savings end up flowing through financial markets (the stock market), to a financial intermediary (Bank of America), and finally to Apple.

Of course, our Italian friend's $60,000 doesn't literally arrive at Apple in an envelope marked "From L. DaVinci." Investments by the purchasers of the Bank of America's stock issue are pooled, not segregated. Signor DaVinci would own a share of all of Bank of America's assets, not just one loan to Apple. Nevertheless, investors' savings are flowing through the financial markets and the bank to finance Apple's capital investments.

FIGURE 2.2 Flow of savings to investment for a large, public corporation. Savings come from investors worldwide. The savings may flow through financial markets or financial intermediaries. The corporation also reinvests on shareholders' behalf.

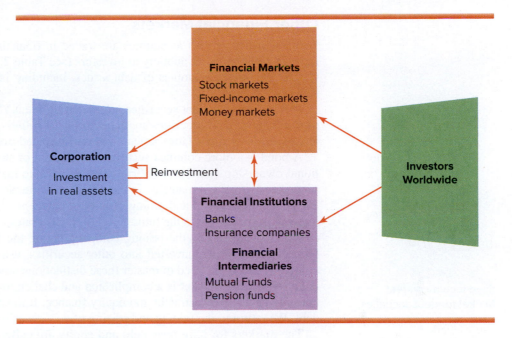

The Stock Market

financial market
Market where securities are issued and traded.

A **financial market** is a market where securities are issued and traded. A security is just a traded financial asset, such as a share of stock. For a corporation, the stock market is probably the most important financial market.

As corporations grow, their requirements for outside capital can expand dramatically. At some point the firm will decide to "go public" by issuing shares on an organized exchange such as the New York Stock Exchange (NYSE) or NASDAQ; that first issue is called an *initial public offering* or *IPO.* The buyers of the IPO are helping to finance the firm's investment in real assets. In return, the buyers become part-owners of the firm and participate in its future success or failure. (Most investors in the Internet IPOs of 1999 and 2000 are by now sorely disappointed, but many IPOs pay off handsomely. If only we had bought Apple shares on their IPO day in 1980 . . .) Of course a corporation's IPO is not its last chance to issue shares. For example, Bank of America went public in the 1930s, but it could make a new issue of shares tomorrow.

BEYOND THE PAGE

 Stock exchanges: From clubs to commercial businesses

mhhe.com/brealey9e

A new issue of shares increases both the amount of cash held by the company and the number of shares held by the public. Such an issue is known as a *primary issue,* and it is sold in the **primary market.** But in addition to helping companies raise new cash, financial markets also allow investors to trade securities among themselves. For example, Smith might decide to raise some cash by selling her Apple stock at the same time that Jones invests his spare cash in Apple. The result is simply a transfer of ownership from Smith to Jones, which has no effect on the company itself. Such purchases and sales of existing securities are known as *secondary transactions,* and they take place in the **secondary market.** Notice that Smith and Jones might be less happy for Apple to raise new capital and invest in long-term projects if they could not sell their stock in the secondary market when they needed the cash for personal use.

primary market
Market for the sale of new securities by corporations.

secondary market
Market in which previously issued securities are traded among investors.

Stock markets are also called *equity markets* because stockholders are said to own the common equity of the firm. You will hear financial managers refer to the capital structure decision as "the choice between debt and equity financing."

Now may be a good time to stress that the financial manager plays on a global stage and needs to be familiar with markets around the world. For example, Apple's stock is traded on the NASDAQ market and also in Germany on the Deutsche Börse. China Telecom, Deutsche Bank, Ferrari, Novartis, Petrobras (Brazil), Sony, Unilever, Manchester United football club, and more than 500 other overseas firms have listed their shares on the NYSE. We return to the trading and pricing of shares in Chapter 7.

Other Financial Markets

Debt securities as well as equities are traded in financial markets. The Apple bond issue in 1994 was sold publicly to investors (see Table 2.1). Table 1.1 in the previous chapter also gives examples of debt issues, including issues by Virgin Atlantic and Entergy Arkansas.

A few corporate debt securities are traded on the NYSE and other exchanges, but most corporate debt securities are traded *over the counter,* through a network of banks and securities dealers. Government debt is also traded over the counter.

A bond is a more complex security than a share of stock. A share is just a proportional ownership claim on the firm, with no definite maturity. Bonds and other debt securities can vary in maturity, in the degree of protection or collateral offered by the issuer, and in the level and timing of interest payments. Some bonds make "floating" interest payments tied to the future level of interest rates. Many can be "called" (repurchased and retired) by the issuing company before the bonds' stated maturity date. Some bonds can be converted into other securities, usually the stock of the issuing company. You don't need to master these distinctions now; just be aware that the debt or **fixed-income market** is a complicated and challenging place. A corporation must not only decide between debt and equity finance. It must also consider the design of debt. We return to the trading and pricing of debt securities in Chapter 6.

The markets for *long-term* debt and equity are called **capital markets.** A firm's *capital* is its long-run financing. Short-term securities are traded in the **money markets.** "Short term" means less than 1 year. For example, large, creditworthy corporations raise short-term financing by issues of *commercial paper,* which are debt issues with maturities of no more than 270 days. Commercial paper is issued in the money market.

fixed-income market
Market for debt securities.

capital market
Market for long-term financing.

money market
Market for short-term financial assets.

2.1 Self-Test

Do you understand the following distinctions? Briefly explain in each case.

a. Primary market vs. secondary market.
b. Capital market vs. money market.
c. Stock market vs. fixed-income market.

The financial manager regularly encounters other financial markets. Here are three examples, with references to the chapters where they are discussed:

- *Foreign exchange markets* (Chapter 22). Any corporation engaged in international trade must be able to transfer money back and forth between dollars and other currencies. Foreign exchange is traded over the counter through a network of the largest international banks.
- *Commodities markets* (Chapter 24). Dozens of commodities are traded on organized exchanges, such as the Chicago Mercantile Exchange (CME) or the Intercontinental Exchange. You can buy or sell corn, wheat, cotton, fuel oil, natural gas, copper, silver, platinum, and so on.
- *Markets for options and other derivatives* (Chapters 23 and 24). Derivatives are securities whose payoffs depend on the prices of other securities or commodities. For example, you can buy an option to purchase IBM shares at a fixed price on a fixed future date. The option's payoff depends on the price of IBM shares on that date. Commodities can be traded by a different kind of derivative security called a futures contract.

Stock markets allow investors to bet on their favorite stocks. Prediction markets allow them to bet on almost anything else. These markets reveal the collective guess of traders on issues as diverse as New York City snowfall, an avian flu outbreak, and the occurrence of a major earthquake.

Prediction markets are conducted on a number of online exchanges such as PredictIt (www.predictit.org) and Iowa Electronic Markets (tippie.uiowa.edu/iem). Take the 2016 presidential primaries as an example. On the Iowa Electronic Markets you could have bet that Donald Trump would win the Republican nomination by buying one of his contracts. Each Trump contract promised to pay $1 if he won the nomination and nothing if he lost. If you thought that the probability of a Trump victory was 55% (say), you would have been prepared to pay up to $.55 for his contract. Someone who was relatively pessimistic about Trump's chances would have been happy to *sell* you such a contract because that sale would turn a profit if he were to lose. With many participants buying and selling, the market price of a contract revealed the collective wisdom of the crowd.

Take a look at the accompanying figure from the Iowa Electronic Markets. It shows the contract prices for the various contenders for the Republican nomination between January and May 2016. You can see that as Ted Cruz beat Trump in a series of primaries and caucuses during March, the price of

Trump contracts declined. But as it became clear that Trump was headed toward a big victory in the New York primary in April, the price of Trump contracts dramatically recovered.

The red line in the figure is for "Rest of field" (i.e., a contract that will pay off $1 if anyone other than the named candidates in the figure wins the nomination). The 20 cent price for this contract in early April is evidence that even at this late date, there was meaningful uncertainty about the prospects for a contested convention in which someone other than the current leaders would be selected as the Republican candidate. By May, however, Trump futures were selling for $.92, and the "Rest of field" price had fallen to $.06.

Participants in prediction markets are putting their money where their mouth is. So the forecasting accuracy of these markets compares favorably with that of major polls. Some businesses have formed internal prediction markets to survey the views of their staff. For example, Google operates an internal market to forecast product launch dates, the number of Gmail users, and other strategic questions.*

* Google's experience is analyzed in B. Cowgill, J. Wolfers, and E. Zitzewitz, "Using Prediction Markets to Track Information Flows: Evidence from Google," working paper, Dartmouth College, January 2009.

2016 U.S. Republican Convention Nomination Market

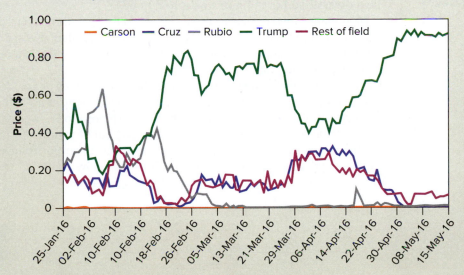

Source: Iowa Electronic Markets, **www.tippie.uiowa.edu/iem/**, May 16, 2016.

Commodity and derivative markets are not sources of financing but markets where the financial manager can adjust the firm's exposure to business risks. For example, an electric generating company may wish to lock in the future price of natural gas by trading in commodity markets, thus eliminating the risk of a sudden jump in the price of its raw materials.

Wherever there is uncertainty, investors may be interested in trading, either to speculate or to lay off their risks, and a market may arise to meet that trading demand. In recent years, several smaller markets have been created that allow punters to bet on a single event. The nearby box discusses how prices in these markets can reveal people's predictions about the future.

financial intermediary
An organization that raises money from investors and provides financing for individuals, corporations, or other organizations.

Financial Intermediaries

A **financial intermediary** is an organization that raises money from investors and provides financing for individuals, companies, and other organizations. For corporations, intermediaries are important sources of financing. Intermediaries are a stop on the road between savings and real investment.

Why is a financial intermediary different from a manufacturing corporation? First, it may raise money in different ways, for example, by taking deposits or selling insurance policies. Second, it invests that money in *financial* assets, for example, in stocks, bonds, or loans to businesses or individuals. In contrast, a manufacturing company's main investments are in plant, equipment, or other *real* assets.

We will start with two important classes of intermediaries, mutual funds and pension funds.

mutual funds
An investment company that pools the savings of many investors and invests in a portfolio of securities.

Mutual funds raise money by selling shares to investors. The investors' money is pooled and invested in a portfolio of securities. Investors can buy or sell shares in mutual funds as they please, and initial investments are often $3,000 or less. Vanguard's Explorer Fund, for example, held a portfolio of more than 700 stocks with a market value of about $10 billion in early 2016. An investor in Explorer can increase her stake in the fund's portfolio by buying additional shares, and so gain a higher share of the portfolio's subsequent dividends and price appreciation.[2] She can also sell her shares back to the fund if she decides to cash out of her investment.[3]

The advantages of a mutual fund should be clear: Unless you are very wealthy, you cannot buy and manage a 700-stock portfolio on your own, at least not efficiently. **Mutual funds offer investors low-cost diversification and professional management. For most investors, it's more efficient to buy a mutual fund than to assemble a diversified portfolio of stocks and bonds.**

Most mutual fund managers also try their best to "beat the market," that is, to generate superior performance by finding the stocks with better-than-average returns. Whether they can pick winners consistently is another question, which we address in Chapter 7.

In exchange for their services, the fund's managers take out a management fee. There are also the expenses of running the fund. For Explorer, fees and expenses absorb about .5% of portfolio value each year. This seems reasonable, but watch out: The typical mutual fund charges more than Explorer does. In some cases, fees and expenses add up to 2% per year. That's a big bite out of your investment return.

Mutual funds are a stop on the road from savings to corporate investment. Suppose Explorer purchases part of the new issue of shares by Bank of America. Again we show the flow of savings to investment by orange arrows:

BEYOND THE PAGE

   U.S. mutual funds

mhhe.com/brealey9e

There are about 8,000 mutual funds in the United States. In fact, there are more mutual funds than public companies! The funds pursue a wide variety of investment strategies. Some funds specialize in safe stocks with generous dividend payouts. Some specialize in high-tech growth stocks. Some "balanced" funds offer mixtures of stocks and bonds. Some specialize in particular countries or regions. For example, the Fidelity Investments mutual fund group sponsors funds for Canada, Japan, China, Europe, and Latin America.

---

[2] Mutual funds are not corporations but investment companies. They pay no tax, providing that all income from dividends and price appreciation is passed on to the funds' shareholders. The shareholders pay personal tax on this income.

[3] Explorer, like most mutual funds, is an *open-end* fund. It stands ready to issue shares to new investors in the fund and to buy back existing shares when its shareholders decide to cash out. The purchase and sale prices depend on the fund's net asset value (NAV) on the day of purchase or redemption. *Closed-end* funds have a fixed number of shares traded on an exchange. If you want to invest in a closed-end fund, you must buy shares from another stockholder in the fund.

hedge funds
Private investment fund that pursues complex, high-risk investment strategies.

Like mutual funds, **hedge funds** also pool the savings of different investors and invest on their behalf. But they differ from mutual funds in at least two ways. First, because hedge funds usually follow complex, high-risk investment strategies, access is usually restricted to knowledgeable investors such as pension funds, endowment funds, and wealthy individuals. Don't try to send a check for $3,000 or $5,000 to a hedge fund; most hedge funds are not in the "retail" investment business. Second, hedge funds try to attract the most talented managers by compensating them with potentially lucrative, performance-related fees.[4] In contrast, mutual funds usually charge a fixed percentage of assets under management.

Hedge funds follow many different investment strategies. Some try to make a profit by identifying *over*valued stocks or markets and selling short. (We will not go into procedures for short-selling here. Just remember that short-sellers profit when prices *fall*.[5]) "Vulture funds" specialize in the securities of distressed corporations. Some hedge funds take bets on firms involved in merger negotiations, others look for mispriced convertible bonds, and some take positions in currencies and interest rates. Hedge funds manage less money than mutual funds, but they sometimes take very big positions and have a large impact on the market.

There are other ways of pooling and investing savings. Consider a pension plan set up by a corporation or other organization on behalf of its employees. There are several types of pension plan. The most common type of plan is the *defined-contribution* plan. In this case, a percentage of the employee's monthly paycheck is contributed to a **pension fund.** (The employer and employee may each contribute 5%, for example.) Contributions from all participating employees are pooled and invested in securities or mutual funds. (Usually the employees can choose from a menu of funds with different investment strategies.) Each employee's balance in the plan grows over the years as contributions continue and investment income accumulates. The balance in the plan can be used to finance living expenses after retirement. The amount available for retirement depends on the accumulated contributions and on the rate of return earned on the investments.[6]

pension fund
Fund set up by an employer to provide for employees' retirement.

Pension funds are designed for long-run investment. They provide professional management and diversification. They also have an important tax advantage: Contributions are tax-deductible, and investment returns inside the plan are not taxed until cash is finally withdrawn.[7]

Pension plans are among the most important vehicles for savings. Total assets held by U.S. pension plans were about $15 trillion in 2015.

2.2   Self-Test

Individual investors can buy bonds and stocks directly, or they can put their money in a mutual fund or a defined-contribution pension fund. What are the advantages of the second strategy?

---

[4] Sometimes these fees can be very large indeed. For example, *Forbes* estimated that the top hedge fund manager in 2012 earned $2.2 billion in fees.

[5] A short-seller borrows a security from another investor and sells it. Of course, the seller must sooner or later buy the security back and return it to its original owner. The short-seller earns a profit if the security can be bought back at a lower price than it was sold for.

[6] In a *defined-benefit* plan, the employer promises a certain level of retirement benefits (set by a formula) and the *employer* invests in the pension plan. The plan's accumulated investment value has to be large enough to cover the promised benefits. If not, the employer must put in more money. Defined-benefit plans are gradually giving way to defined-contribution plans.

[7] Defined-benefit pension plans share these same advantages, except that the employer invests rather than the employees. In a defined-benefit plan, the advantage of tax deferral on investment income accrues to the employer. This deferral reduces the cost of funding the plan.

Financial Institutions

Banks and insurance companies are **financial institutions.**[8] A financial institution is an intermediary that does more than just pool and invest savings. Institutions raise financing in special ways, for example, by accepting deposits or selling insurance policies, and they provide additional financial services. Unlike a mutual fund, they not only invest in securities but also lend money directly to individuals, businesses, or other organizations.

BEYOND THE PAGE

The world's largest banks

mhhe.com/brealey9e

Commercial Banks   There are about 5,400 commercial banks in the United States.[9] They vary from giants such as JPMorgan Chase with $2.6 trillion of assets to relative dwarfs like Cambridge Bancorp with assets of $1.7 billion.

Commercial banks are major sources of loans for corporations. (In the United States, they are generally not allowed to make equity investments in corporations, although banks in most other countries can do so.) Suppose that a local forest products company negotiates a 9-month bank loan for $2.5 million. The flow of savings is:

The bank provides debt financing for the company and, at the same time, provides a place for depositors to park their money safely and withdraw it as needed.

Investment Banks   We have discussed commercial banks, which raise money from depositors and other investors and then make loans to businesses and individuals. *Investment banks* are different. Investment banks do not generally take deposits or make loans to companies.[10] Instead, they advise and assist companies in obtaining finance. For example, investment banks *underwrite* stock offerings by purchasing the new shares from the issuing company at a negotiated price and reselling the shares to investors. Thus the issuing company gets a fixed price for the new shares, and the investment bank takes responsibility for distributing the shares to investors. We discuss share issues in more detail in Chapter 15.

Investment banks also advise on takeovers, mergers, and acquisitions. They offer investment advice and manage investment portfolios for individual and institutional investors. They run trading desks for foreign exchange, commodities, bonds, options, and other derivatives.

Investment banks can invest their own money in start-ups and other ventures. For example, the Australian Macquarie Bank has invested in airports, toll highways, electric transmission and generation, and other infrastructure projects around the world.

---

[8] We may be drawing too fine a distinction between financial intermediaries and institutions. A mutual fund could be considered a financial institution. But "financial institution" usually suggests a more complicated intermediary, such as a bank.

[9] Banks that accept deposits and provide financing mostly to businesses are called commercial banks. Savings banks and savings & loans (S&Ls) accept deposits and lend mostly to individuals, for example, as mortgage loans to home buyers.

[10] Investment banks do not take deposits and do not lend money to businesses or individuals, except as *bridge loans* made as temporary financing for takeovers or other transactions. Investment banks are sometimes called *merchant banks.*

The largest investment banks are financial powerhouses. They include Goldman Sachs, Morgan Stanley, Lazard, Nomura (Japan), and Macquarie Bank.[11] In addition, the major commercial banks, including Bank of America and Citigroup, all have investment banking operations.[12]

Insurance Companies   Insurance companies are more important than banks for the *long-term* financing of business. They are massive investors in corporate stocks and bonds, and they often make long-term loans directly to corporations.

Suppose a company needs a loan of $2.5 million for 9 years, not 9 months. It could issue a bond directly to investors, or it could negotiate a 9-year loan with an insurance company:

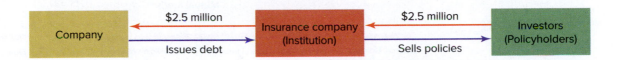

The money to make the loan comes mainly from the sale of insurance policies. Say you buy a fire insurance policy on your home. You pay cash to the insurance company and get a financial asset (the policy) in exchange. You receive no interest payments on this financial asset, but if a fire does strike, the company is obliged to cover the damages up to the policy limit. This is the return on your investment. (Of course, a fire is a sad and dangerous event that you hope to avoid. But if a fire does occur, you are better off getting a payoff on your insurance policy than not having insurance at all.)

The company will issue not just one policy but thousands. Normally the incidence of fires "averages out," leaving the company with a predictable obligation to its policyholders as a group. Of course, the insurance company must charge enough for its policies to cover selling and administrative costs, pay policyholders' claims, and generate a profit for its stockholders.

2.3   Self-Test

What are the key differences between a mutual fund and a bank or an insurance company?

Total Financing of U.S. Corporations

The pie chart in Figure 2.3 shows the investors in bonds and other debt securities. Notice the importance of institutional investors—mutual funds, pension funds, insurance companies, and banks. Households (individual investors) hold less than 5% of the debt pie. The other slices represent the rest of the world (investors from outside the United States) and other, smaller categories of investors.

The pie chart in Figure 2.4 shows holdings of the shares issued by U.S. corporations. Here, households make a stronger showing, with 37.2% of the total. Pension

---

[11] The distinction between investment and commercial banks is not a legal one. Since 2008 both Goldman Sachs and Morgan Stanley have held banking licenses and are supervised by the Federal Reserve. However, they are not in the business of taking retail deposits or providing loans.

[12] Bank of America owns Merrill Lynch, one of the largest investment banks. Merrill was rescued by Bank of America in 2009 after making huge losses from mortgage-related investments.

FIGURE 2.3 Holdings of corporate and foreign bonds, September 30, 2015. The total amount is $11.9 trillion.

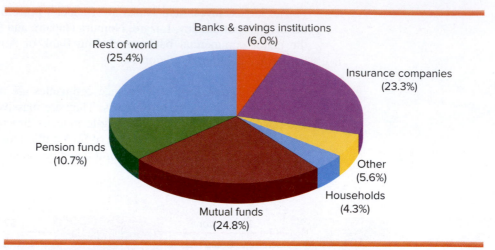

Source: Board of Governors of the Federal Reserve System, Division of Research and Statistics, *Flow of Funds Accounts,* Table L.213 (**www.federalreserve.gov**).

FIGURE 2.4 Holdings of corporate equities, September 30, 2015. The total amount is $34.1 trillion.

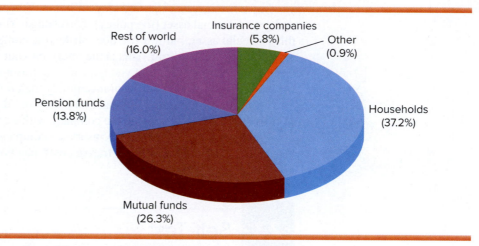

Source: Board of Governors of the Federal Reserve System, Division of Research and Statistics, *Flow of Funds Accounts,* Table L.223 (**www.federalreserve.gov**).

funds, insurance companies, and mutual funds add up to 45.9% of the total. Remember, banks in the United States do not usually hold stock in other companies. The rest-of-the-world slice is 16.0%.

The aggregate amounts represented in these figures are enormous. There is $11.9 trillion of debt behind Figure 2.3 and $34.1 trillion of equity behind Figure 2.4 ($34,100,000,000,000).

Chapter 14 reviews corporate financing patterns in more detail.

2.3 Functions of Financial Markets and Intermediaries

Financial markets and intermediaries provide financing for business. They channel savings to real investment. That much should be loud and clear from Sections 2.1 and 2.2 of this chapter. But there are other functions that may not be quite so obvious.

Transporting Cash across Time

Individuals need to transport expenditures in time. If you have money now that you wish to save for a rainy day, you can (for example) put the money in a savings account at a bank and withdraw it with interest later. If you don't have money today, say to buy a car, you can borrow money from the bank and pay off the loan later. Modern finance provides a kind of time machine. Lenders transport money forward in time; borrowers transport it back. Both are happier than if they were forced to spend income as it arrives. Of course, individuals are not alone in needing to raise cash from time to time. Firms with good investment opportunities, but a shortage of internally generated cash, raise cash by borrowing or selling new shares. Many governments run deficits and finance current outlays by issuing debt.

Young people saving for retirement may transport their current earnings 30 or 40 years into the future by means of a pension fund. They can even transport income to their heirs by purchase of a life insurance policy.

In principle, individuals or firms with cash surpluses could take out newspaper advertisements or surf the web looking for counterparties with cash shortages. But it is usually cheaper and more convenient to use financial markets and intermediaries. It is not just a matter of avoiding the cost of searching for the right counterparty. Follow-up is needed. For example, banks don't just lend money and walk away. They monitor the borrower to make sure that the loan is used for its intended purpose and that the borrower's credit stays solid.

Risk Transfer and Diversification

Financial markets and intermediaries allow investors and businesses to reduce and reallocate risk. Insurance companies are an obvious example. When you buy homeowner's insurance, you greatly reduce the risk of loss from fire, theft, or accidents. But your policy is not a very risky bet for the insurance company. It diversifies by issuing thousands of policies, and it expects losses to average out over the policies.[13] The insurance company allows you to pool risk with thousands of other homeowners.

Investors should diversify too. For example, you can buy shares in a mutual fund that holds hundreds of stocks. In fact, you can buy *index funds* that invest in all the stocks in the popular market indexes. For example, the Vanguard 500 Index Fund holds the stocks in the Standard & Poor's Composite stock market index. (The "S&P 500" tracks the performance of the largest U.S. stocks. It is the index most used by professional investors.) If you buy this fund, you are insulated from the company-specific risks of the 500 companies in the index. These risks are averaged out by diversification. Of course you are still left with the risk that the level of the stock market as a whole will fall. In fact, we will see in Chapter 11 that investors are mostly concerned with *market risk,* not the specific risks of individual companies.

Index mutual funds are one way to invest in widely diversified portfolios at low cost. Another route is provided by exchange-traded funds (ETFs), which are portfolios of stocks that can be bought or sold in a single trade. For example, Standard & Poor's Depositary Receipts (SPDRs, or "spiders") invest in portfolios that match Standard & Poor's stock market indexes. The total amount invested in the spider that tracks the benchmark S&P 500 index was $134 billion in early 2016.

ETFs are in some ways more efficient than mutual funds. To buy or sell an ETF, you simply make a trade, just as if you bought or sold shares of stock.[14] This is

---

[13] Unfortunately for insurance companies, the losses don't always average out. Hurricanes and earthquakes can damage thousands of homes at once. The potential losses are so great that property insurance companies buy *reinsurance* against such catastrophes.

[14] ETFs are in this respect like closed-end mutual funds (see footnote 3). But ETFs do not have managers with the discretion to try to "pick winners." ETF portfolios are tied down to indexes or fixed baskets of securities. ETF issuers make sure that the ETF price tracks the price of the underlying index or basket.

different from investing in an open-end mutual fund. In that case you have to send money to the fund in exchange for newly issued shares. And, if you want to withdraw the investment, you have to notify the fund, which redeems your shares and sends you a check. Also, many of the larger ETFs charge lower fees than mutual funds. State Street Global Advisors charges just .11% a year for managing the Standard & Poor's 500 Index Spider. For a $100,000 investment, the fee is only .0011 × 100,000 = $110.

Financial markets provide other mechanisms for sharing risks. For example, a wheat farmer and a baking company are each exposed to fluctuations in the price of wheat after the harvest. The farmer worries about low prices, the baker about high prices. They can both rest easier if the baker can agree with the farmer to buy wheat in the future at a fixed price. Of course, it would be difficult, to say the least, if the baker and the farmer had to contact an Internet dating service to get together to make a deal. Fortunately, no dating service is needed: Each can trade in commodity markets, the farmer as a seller and the baker as a buyer.

Liquidity

liquidity
The ability to sell an asset on short notice at close to the market value.

Markets and intermediaries also provide **liquidity,** that is, the ability to turn an investment back into cash when needed. Suppose you deposit $5,000 in a savings bank on February 1. During that month, the bank uses your deposit and other new deposits to make a 6-month construction loan to a real estate developer. On March 1, you realize that you need your $5,000 back. The bank can give it to you. Because the bank has thousands of depositors, and other sources of financing if necessary, it can make an illiquid loan to the developer financed by liquid deposits made by you and other customers. If you lend your money for 6 months directly to the real estate developer, you will have a hard time retrieving it 1 month later.[15]

The shares of public companies are liquid because they are traded more or less continuously in the stock market. An Italian investor who puts $60,000 into Bank of America shares can recover that money on short notice. (A $60,000 sell order is a drop in the bucket compared with the normal trading volume of Bank of America shares.) Mutual funds can redeem their shares for cash on short notice because the funds invest in traded securities, which can be sold as necessary.

Of course, liquidity is a matter of degree. Foreign exchange markets for major currencies are exceptionally liquid. Bank of America or Deutsche Bank could buy $200 million worth of yen or euros in the blink of an eye, with hardly any effect on foreign exchange rates. U.S. Treasury securities are also very liquid, and the shares of the largest companies on the major international stock exchanges are only slightly less so.

Liquidity is most important when you're in a hurry. If you try to sell $500,000 worth of the shares of a small, thinly traded company all at once, you will probably knock down the price to some extent. If you're patient and don't surprise other investors with a large, sudden sell order, you may be able to unload your shares on better terms. It's the same problem that you may face in selling real estate. A house or condominium is not a liquid asset in a panic sale. If you're determined to sell in an afternoon, you're not going to get full value.

The Payment Mechanism

Think how inconvenient life would be if you had to pay for every purchase in cash or if Boeing had to ship truckloads of hundred-dollar bills around the country to pay its suppliers. Checking accounts, credit cards, and electronic transfers allow individuals

---

[15] Of course, the bank can't repay all depositors simultaneously. To do so, it would have to sell off its loans to the real estate developer and other borrowers. These loans are *not* liquid. This raises the specter of bank runs, where doubts about a bank's ability to pay off its depositors cause a rush of withdrawals, with each depositor trying to get his or her money out first. Bank runs are rare because bank deposits are backed up by the U.S. Federal Deposit Insurance Corporation, which insures bank accounts up to $250,000 per account.

and firms to send and receive payments quickly and safely over long distances. Banks are the obvious providers of payment services, but they are not alone. For example, if you buy shares in a money market mutual fund, your money is pooled with that of other investors and used to buy safe, short-term securities. You can then write checks on this mutual fund investment, just as if you had a bank deposit.

Information Provided by Financial Markets

In well-functioning financial markets, you can *see* what securities and commodities are worth, and you can see—or at least estimate—the rates of return that investors can expect on their savings. The information provided by financial markets is often essential to a financial manager's job. Here are three examples of how this information can be used.

Commodity Prices   Catalytic converters are used in the exhaust systems of cars and light trucks to reduce pollution. The catalysts include platinum, which is traded on the New York Mercantile Exchange (NYMEX).

In March a manufacturer of catalytic converters is planning production for October. How much per ounce should the company budget for purchases of platinum in that month? Easy: The company's CFO looks up the futures price of platinum on the New York Mercantile Exchange—$972 per ounce for delivery in October (this was the closing price for platinum in March 2016, for delivery in October). The CFO can lock in that price if she wishes. The details of such a trade are covered in Chapter 24.

Interest Rates   The CFO of Catalytic Concepts has to raise $400 million in new financing. She considers an issue of long-term bonds. What will the interest rate on the bonds be? To find out, the CFO looks up interest rates on existing bonds traded in financial markets.

The results are shown in Table 2.2. Notice how the interest rate climbs as credit quality deteriorates: The largest, safest companies, which are rated AAA ("triple-A"), can raise long-term debt at a 2.59% interest rate. The interest rates for AA, A, and BBB rise to 2.62%, 3.03%, and 4.32%, respectively. BBB companies are still regarded as *investment grade,* that is, good quality, but the next step down takes the investor into *junk bond* territory. The interest rate for BB debt climbs to 5.62%. Single-B companies are riskier still, so investors demand 8.32%.

There will be more on bond ratings and interest rates in Chapter 6. But you can see how a financial manager can use information from fixed-income markets to forecast the interest rate on new debt financing. For example, if Catalytic Concepts can qualify as a BBB-rated company, and interest rates are as shown in Table 2.2, it should be able to raise new debt financing for approximately 4.32%.

Company Values   How much was Callaway Golf worth in March 2016? How about Alaska Air Group, Entergy, Yum! Brands, or GE? Table 2.3 shows the *market capitalization* of each company. We simply multiply the number of shares outstanding by the price per share in the stock market. Investors valued Callaway Golf at $821 million and GE at $283 *billion.*

TABLE 2.2 Interest rates on long-term corporate bonds, March 2016. The interest rate is lowest for top-quality (AAA) issuers. The rate rises as credit quality declines.

Credit Rating	Interest Rate
AAA	2.59%
AA	2.62
A	3.03
BBB	4.32
BB	5.62
B	8.32

Source: Thomson Reuters.

TABLE 2.3 Calculating the market capitalization of Callaway Golf and other companies in March 2016. (Shares and market values in millions. Ticker symbols in parentheses.)

	Number of Shares	×	Stock Price	=	Market Capitalization ($ millions)
Callaway Golf (ELY)	93.8	×	$8.76	=	$821
Alaska Air Group (ALK)	124.7	×	$80.77	=	$10,074
Entergy (ETR)	178.5	×	$75.92	=	$13,551
Yum! Brands (YUM)	408.7	×	$77.77	=	$31,875
General Electric (GE)	9,331.0	×	$30.34	=	$283,091

Source: Yahoo! Finance, finance.yahoo.com.

Stock prices and company values summarize investors' collective assessment of how well a company is doing, both its current performance and its future prospects. Thus an increase in stock price sends a positive signal from investors to managers.[16] That is why top management's compensation is linked to stock prices. A manager who owns shares in his or her company will be motivated to increase the company's market value. This reduces agency costs by aligning the interests of managers and stockholders.

This is one important advantage of going public. A private company can't use its stock price as a measure of performance. It can still compensate managers with shares, but the shares will not be valued in a financial market.

cost of capital
Minimum acceptable rate of return on capital investment.

Cost of Capital   Financial managers look to financial markets to measure, or at least estimate, the **cost of capital** for the firm's investment projects. The cost of capital is the minimum acceptable rate of return on the project. Investment projects offering rates of return higher than their cost of capital are worthwhile because they add value; they make both the firm and its shareholders better off financially. Projects offering rates of return less than the cost of capital subtract value and should not be undertaken.[17]

Thus the hurdle rate for investments inside the corporation is actually set outside the corporation. The expected rate of return on investments in financial markets determines the opportunity cost of capital.

The opportunity cost of capital is generally *not* the interest rate that the firm pays on a loan from a bank or insurance company. If the company is making a risky investment, the opportunity cost of capital is the expected rate of return that investors can achieve in financial markets at the same level of risk. The expected rate of return on risky securities is normally well above the interest rate on corporate borrowing.

We introduced the cost of capital in Chapter 1, but this brief reminder may help to fix the idea. We cover the cost of capital in detail in Chapters 11 and 12.

2.4   Self-Test

Which of the functions described in this section require financial markets? Explain briefly.

---

[16] We can't claim that investors' assessments of value are always correct. Finance can be a risky and dangerous business—dangerous for your wealth, that is. With hindsight we see horrible mistakes by investors, for example, the gross overvaluation of Internet and telecom companies in 2000. On average, however, it appears that financial markets collect and assess information quickly and accurately. We'll discuss this issue again in Chapter 7.

[17] Of course, the firm may invest for other reasons. For example, it may invest in pollution control equipment for a factory. The equipment may not generate a cash return but may still be worth investing in to meet legal and ethical obligations.

2.4 The Crisis of 2007–2009

The financial crisis of 2007–2009 raised many questions, but it settled one question conclusively: Yes, *financial markets and institutions are important*. When financial markets and institutions ceased to operate properly, the world was pushed into a global recession.

The financial crisis had its roots in the easy-money policies that were pursued by the U.S. Federal Reserve and other central banks following the collapse of the Internet and telecom stock bubble in 2000. At the same time, large balance-of-payments surpluses in Asian economies were invested back into U.S. debt securities. This also helped to push down interest rates and contribute to lax credit.

Banks took advantage of this cheap money to expand the supply of *subprime mortgages* to low-income borrowers. Many banks tempted would-be homeowners with low initial payments, offset by significantly higher payments later.[18] (Some home buyers were betting on escalating housing prices so that they could resell or refinance before the higher payments kicked in.) One lender is even said to have advertised what it dubbed its "NINJA" loan—*NINJA* standing for "No Income, No Job, and No Assets." Most subprime mortgages were then packaged together into *mortgage-backed securities (MBSs)* that could be resold. But, instead of selling these securities to investors who could best bear the risk, many banks kept large quantities of the loans on their own books or sold them to other banks.

BEYOND THE PAGE

Housing prices in the financial crisis

mhhe.com/brealey9e

The widespread availability of mortgage finance fueled a dramatic increase in house prices, which doubled in the 5 years ending June 2006. At that point, prices started to slide and homeowners began to default on their mortgages. A year later, Bear Stearns, a large investment bank, announced huge losses on the mortgage investments that were held in two of its hedge funds. By the spring of 2008, Bear Stearns was on the verge of bankruptcy, and the U.S. Federal Reserve arranged for it to be acquired by JPMorgan Chase.

BEYOND THE PAGE

Time line of the financial crisis

mhhe.com/brealey9e

The crisis peaked in September 2008, when the U.S. government was obliged to take over the giant federal mortgage agencies Fannie Mae and Freddie Mac, both of which had invested several hundred billion dollars in subprime mortgage-backed securities. Over the next few days, the financial system started to melt down. Both Merrill Lynch and Lehman Brothers were in danger of failing. On September 14, the government arranged for Bank of America to take over Merrill in return for financial guarantees. However, it did nothing to rescue Lehman Brothers, which filed for bankruptcy protection the next day. Two days later, the government reluctantly lent $85 billion to the giant insurance company AIG, which had insured huge volumes of mortgage-backed securities and other bonds against default. The following day, the Treasury unveiled its first proposal to spend $700 billion to purchase "toxic" mortgage-backed securities.

BEYOND THE PAGE

The rise and fall of Lehman Brothers

mhhe.com/brealey9e

After the failure of Lehman and the forced rescues of Bear Stearns, Fannie Mae, Freddie Mac, Merrill Lynch, and AIG, investors and financial institutions had to ask, "Who will be next? Do I dare trade with or lend money to Bank X?" In many situations, the cautious answer was "No." Customary day-to-day financial transactions were canceled or completed on onerous terms.[19] At the same time, trading in MBSs and other hard-to-value securities dried up; it therefore became even harder to know what these securities were worth. As banks and other financial institutions became reluctant to trade securities or lend to one another, the supply of credit to the economy contracted and business investment was cut back. The U.S. economy suffered one of its worst setbacks since the Great Depression. Unemployment rose rapidly and business bankruptcies tripled.

---

[18] With a so-called *option ARM loan,* the minimum mortgage payment was often not even sufficient to cover that month's interest on the loan. The unpaid interest was then added to the amount of the mortgage, so the homeowner was burdened by an ever-increasing mortgage that one day would need to be paid off.

[19] The interest rate on interbank loans rose in 2008 to 4.6% above the rate on U.S. Treasury debt. The normal spread over Treasuries is less than .5%.

Mortgage-backed securities (MBSs) provide another example of how financial markets convey savings to finance investment in real assets. In this case, the real assets are homes, which homeowners finance in part with mortgage loans.

In the old days—the 1960s, for example—most mortgage loans were made by local banks, savings banks, and savings and loan institutions (S&Ls), which accepted deposits and savings accounts and made mortgage and other local loans. We will use an S&L as the example. The flow of savings would be as described by the figure in Panel *a*, at the bottom of this box.

The typical mortgage was long term, up to 30 years maturity, with a fixed interest rate. The S&Ls' liabilities—chiefly savings accounts—had much shorter maturities, perhaps a year or two on average. The S&Ls were therefore "borrowing short, lending long," a dangerous investment strategy. When interest rates rose in the 1970s and 1980s, the S&Ls' interest costs on savings accounts rose, too, but their interest income was locked up in long-term, fixed-rate mortgages. Losses mounted. The S&L crisis of the 1980s followed.*

The invention of the MBS allowed S&Ls to eliminate the risks of borrowing short and lending long. You can still get a mortgage from your local S&L, but now the S&L does not have to keep it. The S&L originates the mortgage, but will probably resell it to an MBS issuer—for example, Fannie Mae (Federal National Mortgage Association or FNMA†) or Bank of America. The issuer combines your mortgage with hundreds or thousands of others and issues an MBS backed by the combined portfolio. The MBS is sold to investors such as life insurance companies that want to hold long-term, fixed-rate obligations. Cash flows from the mortgage portfolio are passed through to investors.‡

Suppose a life insurance company purchases an MBS. The flow of savings would now match the figure in Panel *b*.

The invention of MBSs also made mortgages liquid. They are actively traded among banks, insurance companies, mutual funds, pension funds, and endowments.

The MBS market has grown explosively. With the growth came more and more complexity. Issuers were not content with the simple pass-through MBS described earlier. They issued complicated packages of securities called *tranches*. The most senior tranches were given first call on all cash flows from the mortgage portfolio and were viewed as almost risk-free. Bond-rating agencies gave their highest, triple-A ratings to the senior tranches, even for MBSs based on *subprime* mortgages for homeowners with weak credit. Many investors in triple-A tranches lost a lot of money in the crisis of 2007–2009. We discuss bond ratings in Chapter 6.

The MBS market survived. It is still by far the largest source of mortgage financing. By 2015, the aggregate MBSs outstanding exceeded $2 trillion. MBSs are part of a broader market for asset-backed securities, which include securities that work like MBSs but are based on portfolios of other types of assets, including car loans, bank loans to businesses, and financing for commercial real estate.

---

* For a history of the crisis, see Edward *J. Kane, The S&L Insurance Mess: How Did It Happen?* (Washington, D.C.: Urban Institute Press, 1989).

† Fannie Mae and Freddie Mac (Federal Home Loan Mortgage Corp.) are government-sponsored entities (GSEs) charged with increasing the availability of mortgage credit. The GSEs purchase "conforming loans" and package and resell them as MBSs. Nonconforming loans—for example, large, "jumbo" mortgages—are packaged by banks such as Citigroup or Bank of America.

‡ You still send monthly payments to your local S&L. The S&L extracts a small servicing fee and sends your payments along to the MBS issuer, which also extracts a small servicing fee. Net cash flows from the portfolio of mortgages then go to the MBS investors.

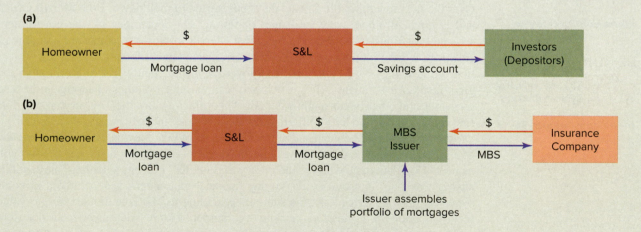

Few developed economies escaped the crisis. As well as suffering from a collapse in their own housing markets, a number of foreign banks had made large investments in U.S. subprime mortgages and had to be rescued by their governments. Many European governments were already heavily in debt and, as the cost of the bank bailouts mounted, investors began to worry about the ability of the governments to repay their debts. Thus in Europe, the banking crisis became entwined with a sovereign debt crisis.

Greece was in the worst shape. It had accumulated €350 billion (about $460 billion) of government debt. Greece is a member of the single-currency euro club, so it had no control over its currency and could not just print more euros to service its debts. In 2011 it defaulted on debts totaling €100 billion.

Greece was still on shaky ground in early 2016, despite a series of rescue packages from the European Union, the European Central Bank, and the International Monetary Fund. Spain, Portugal, Ireland, and other European countries that had also worried investors avoided default and seemed to be recovering. But unemployment in many European countries remained stubbornly high and economic growth anemic.

What lessons can you, as a student of finance, draw from these financial crises? Here are three. First, note the sorry consequences for the economy when financial markets and institutions do not carry out the functions described in this chapter. For example, the crisis was amplified by the sudden disappearance of liquidity in many markets, including the market for MBSs. That meant that potential buyers of the illiquid assets could not know for sure what they were worth. Thus, the informational function of financial markets was also compromised.

Second, why were Bear Stearns, Lehman, Merrill Lynch, and the other distressed firms so fragile? One reason is that they were mostly financed with borrowed money, much of it short-term debt that had to be refinanced frequently. Investment banks like Lehman typically were financed with more than 95% debt and less than 5% equity capital. Thus a 5% fall in their asset values could wipe out their equity "cushions" and leave the banks insolvent. Regulators since the crisis have therefore required banks to finance with much more equity. This requirement has also affected payout to shareholders. A U.S. bank's dividend payments can be stopped by regulators if the bank's equity capital ratio is not up to snuff. We cover decisions about debt versus equity financing and payout in Chapters 16 and 17.

Third, some causes of the crisis can be traced back to agency problems noted in Chapter 1. Managers in the mortgage business were probably at least dimly aware that promoting and selling massive amounts of subprime MBSs was likely to end badly. They didn't wake up in the morning thinking, "Hey, maybe I can cause a financial crisis," but their incentives did call for trying to squeeze out one more fat bonus before the game ended. Their incentives were not aligned with shareholders'. The value of their firms suffered accordingly.

BEYOND THE PAGE

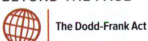 The Dodd-Frank Act

mhhe.com/brealey9e

SUMMARY

Where does the financing for corporations come from? (*LO2-1*)	The ultimate source of financing is individuals' savings. The savings may flow through **financial markets** and **intermediaries.** The intermediaries include mutual funds, pension funds, and financial institutions, such as banks and insurance companies.
Why do nonfinancial corporations need modern financial markets and institutions? (*LO2-1*)	It's simple: Corporations need access to financing in order to innovate and grow. A modern financial system offers different types of financing, depending on a corporation's age and the nature of its business. A high-tech start-up will seek venture capital financing, for example. A mature firm will rely more on bond markets.
What if a corporation finances investment by retaining and reinvesting cash generated from its operations? (*LO2-1*)	In that case, the corporation is saving on behalf of its shareholders.
What are the key advantages of mutual funds and pension funds? (*LO2-2*)	**Mutual** and **pension funds** allow investors to diversify in professionally managed portfolios. Pension funds offer an additional tax advantage, because the returns on pension investments are not taxed until withdrawn from the plan.

What are the functions of financial markets? (*LO2-3*)	**Financial markets** help channel savings to corporate investment, and they help match up borrowers and lenders. They provide **liquidity** and diversification opportunities for investors. Trading in financial markets provides a wealth of useful information for the financial manager.
Do financial institutions have different functions? (*LO2-3*)	**Financial institutions** carry out a number of similar functions to financial markets but in different ways. They channel savings to corporate investment, and they serve as **financial intermediaries** between borrowers and lenders. Banks also provide liquidity for depositors and, of course, play a special role in the economy's payment systems. Insurance companies allow policyholders to pool risks.
What happens when financial markets and institutions no longer function well? (*LO2-4*)	The financial crisis of 2007–2009 provided a dramatic illustration. The huge expansion in subprime mortgage lending in the United States led to a collapse of the banking system. The government was forced into costly bailouts of banks and other financial institutions. As the credit markets seized up, the country suffered a deep recession. In much of Europe, the financial crisis did not end in 2009. As governments struggled to reduce their debt mountains and to strengthen their banking systems, many countries suffered sharp falls in economic activity and severe unemployment.

QUESTIONS AND PROBLEMS

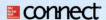

1. **Corporate Financing.** How can a small, private firm finance its capital investments? Give two or three examples of financing sources. (*LO2-1*)

2. **Financial Markets.** The stock and bond markets are not the only financial markets. Give two or three additional examples. (*LO2-1*)

3. **Financial Markets and Institutions.** True or false? (*LO2-1*)
   a. Financing for public corporations must flow through financial markets.
   b. Financing for private corporations must flow through financial intermediaries.
   c. Almost all foreign exchange trading occurs on the floors of the FOREX exchanges in New York and London.
   d. Derivative markets are a major source of finance for many corporations.
   e. The opportunity cost of capital is the capital outlay required to undertake a real investment opportunity.
   f. The cost of capital is the interest rate paid on borrowing from a bank or other financial institution.

4. **Corporate Financing.** Financial markets and intermediaries channel savings from investors to corporate investment. The savings make this journey by many different routes. Give a specific example for each of the following routes: (*LO2-1*)
   a. Investor to financial intermediary, to financial markets, and to the corporation
   b. Investor to financial markets, to a financial intermediary, and to the corporation
   c. Investor to financial markets, to a financial intermediary, back to financial markets, and to the corporation

5. **Financial Intermediaries.** You are a beginning investor with only $5,000 in savings. How can you achieve a widely diversified portfolio at reasonable cost? (*LO2-2*)

6. **Financial Intermediaries.** Is an insurance company also a financial intermediary? How does the insurance company channel savings to corporate investment? (*LO2-2*)

7. **Corporate Financing.** Choose the most appropriate term to complete each sentence. (*LO2-2*)
   a. Households hold a greater percentage of (*corporate equities / corporate bonds*).
   b. (*Pension funds / Banks*) are major investors in corporate equities.
   c. (*Investment banks / Commercial banks*) raise money from depositors and make loans to individuals and businesses.

8. **Financial Markets.** Which of the following are financial markets? (*LO2-2*)
   a. NASDAQ
   b. Vanguard Explorer Fund
   c. JPMorgan Chase
   d. Chicago Mercantile Exchange

9. **Financial Intermediaries.** True or false? (*LO2-2*)
   a. Exchange traded funds are hedge funds that can be bought and sold on the stock exchange.
   b. Hedge funds provide small investors with low-cost diversification.
   c. The sale of insurance policies is a source of financing for insurance companies.
   d. In defined-contribution pension plans, the pension pot depends on the rate of return earned on the contributions by the employer and employee.

10. **Liquidity.** Securities traded in active financial markets are liquid assets. Explain why liquidity is important to individual investors and to mutual funds. (*LO2-2*)

11. **Liquidity.** Bank deposits are liquid; you can withdraw money on demand. How can the bank provide this liquidity and at the same time make illiquid loans to businesses? (*LO2-2*)

12. **Financial Institutions.** Summarize the differences between a commercial bank and an investment bank. (*LO2-2*)

13. **Mutual Funds.** Why are mutual funds called financial intermediaries? Why does it make sense for an individual to invest her savings in a mutual fund rather than directly in financial markets? (*LO2-2*)

14. **Functions of Financial Markets.** Fill in the blanks in the following passage by choosing the most appropriate term from the following list: *CFO, save, financial intermediaries, stock market, savings, real investment, bonds, commodity markets, mutual funds, shares, liquid, ETFs, banks*. Each term should be used once only. (*LO2-3*)

    Financial markets and _____ channel _____ to _____. They also channel money from individuals who want to _____ for the future to those who need cash to spend today. A third function of financial markets is to allow individuals and businesses to adjust their risk. For example, _____, such as the Vanguard Index fund, and _____, such as SPDRs or "spiders," allow individuals to spread their risk across a large number of stocks. Financial markets provide other mechanisms for sharing risks. For example, a wheat farmer and a baker may use the _____ to reduce their exposure to wheat prices. Financial markets and intermediaries allow investors to turn an investment into cash when needed. For example, the _____ of public companies are _____ because they are traded in huge volumes on the _____. _____ are the main providers of payment services by offering checking accounts and electronic transfers. Finally, financial markets provide information. For example, the _____ of a company that is contemplating an issue of debt can look at the yields on existing _____ to gauge how much interest the company will need to pay.

15. **Financial Markets and Intermediaries.** List the major functions of financial markets and intermediaries in a modern financial system. (*LO2-3*)

16. **Functions of Financial Markets.** On a mountain trek, you discover a 6-ounce gold nugget. A friend offers to pay you $2,500 for it. How do you check whether this is a fair price? (*LO2-3*)

17. **Functions of Financial Markets.** What kinds of useful information can a financial manager obtain from financial markets? Give examples. (*LO2-3*)

18. **Functions of Financial Markets.** Look back at Section 2.3 and then answer the following questions: (*LO2-3*)
    a. The price of Entergy stock has risen to $90. What is the market value of the firm's equity if the number of outstanding shares does not change?
    b. The rating agency has revised Catalytic Concepts' bond rating to A. What interest rate, approximately, would the company now need to pay on its bonds?
    c. A farmer and a meatpacker use the commodity markets to reduce their risk. One agrees to buy live cattle in the future at a fixed price, and the other agrees to sell. Which one sells?

19. **The Financial Crisis.** True or false? (*LO2-4*)
    a. The financial crisis was largely caused by banks taking large positions in the options and futures markets.
    b. The prime cause of the financial crisis was an expansion in bank lending for the overheated commercial real estate market.

c. Many subprime mortgages were packaged together by banks for resale as mortgage-backed securities (MBSs).

d. The crisis could have been much more serious if the government had not stepped in to rescue Merrill Lynch and Lehman Brothers.

e. The crisis in the eurozone finally ended when other eurozone countries and the IMF provided a massive bailout package to stop Greece from defaulting on its debts.

WEB EXERCISES

1. Log on to **finance.yahoo.com** and use the website to update Table 2.3. How have market values of these companies changed?

2. Find the websites for the Vanguard Group, Fidelity Investments, and Putnam Investments. Pick three or four funds from these sites and compare their investment objectives, risks, past returns, fund fees, and so on. Read the prospectuses for each fund. Who do you think should, or should not, invest in each fund?

3. Morningstar provides data on mutual fund performance. Log on to its website. Which category of funds has performed unusually well or badly?

SOLUTIONS TO SELF-TEST QUESTIONS

2.1   a. Corporations sell securities in the primary market. The securities are later traded in the secondary market.

b. The capital market is for long-term financing; the money market, for short-term financing.

c. The market for stocks versus the market for bonds and other debt securities.

2.2   Efficient diversification and professional management. Pension funds offer an additional advantage, because investment returns are not taxed until withdrawn from the fund.

2.3   Mutual funds pool investor savings and invest in portfolios of traded securities. Financial institutions such as banks or insurance companies raise money in special ways, for example, by accepting deposits or selling insurance policies. They not only invest in securities but also lend directly to businesses. They provide various other financial services.

2.4   Liquidity, risk reduction by investment in diversified portfolios of securities (through a mutual fund, for example), information provided by trading.

3

Accounting and Finance

LEARNING OBJECTIVES

After studying this chapter, you should be able to:

3-1 Interpret the information contained in the balance sheet, income statement, and statement of cash flows.

3-2 Distinguish between market and book values.

3-3 Explain why income differs from cash flow.

3-4 Understand the essential features of the taxation of corporate and personal income.

RELATED WEBSITES FOR THIS CHAPTER CAN BE FOUND IN CONNECT.

In Chapter 1 we pointed out that a large corporation is a team effort. All the players—the shareholders, lenders, directors, management, and employees—have a stake in the company's success, and all therefore need to monitor its progress. For this reason, the company prepares regular financial accounts and arranges for an independent firm of auditors to certify that these accounts present a "true and fair view."

Until the mid-nineteenth century, most businesses were owner-managed and seldom required outside capital beyond personal loans to the proprietor. There was little need, therefore, for firms to produce comprehensive accounting information. But with the industrial revolution and the creation of large railroad and canal companies, the shareholders and bankers demanded information that would help them gauge a firm's financial strength. That was when the accounting profession began to come of age.

We don't want to get lost in the details of accounting practice. But because we will refer to financial statements throughout this book, it may be useful to review briefly their main features. In this chapter, we introduce the major financial statements: the balance sheet, the income statement, and the statement of cash flows. We discuss the important differences between income and cash flow and between book values and market values. We also discuss the federal tax system.

This chapter is our first look at financial statements and is meant primarily to serve as a brief review of your accounting class. It will be far from our last look. For example, we will see in the next chapter how managers use financial statements to analyze a firm's performance and assess its financial strength.

Accounting is not the same as finance, but the two are related.
© g-stockstudio/iStock/Getty Images RF

3.1   The Balance Sheet

Public companies are obliged to file their financial statements with the SEC each quarter. These quarterly reports (or 10Qs) provide the investor with information about the company's earnings during the quarter and its assets and liabilities at the end of the quarter. In addition, companies need to file annual financial statements (or 10Ks) that provide rather more detailed information about the outcome for the entire year.

The financial statements show the firm's balance sheet, the income statement, and a statement of cash flows. We will review each in turn.[1]

Firms need to raise cash to pay for the many assets used in their businesses. In the process of raising that cash, they also acquire obligations or "liabilities" to those who provide the funding. The **balance sheet** presents a snapshot of the firm's assets and liabilities at one particular moment. The assets—representing the uses of the funds raised—are listed on the left-hand side of the balance sheet. The liabilities—representing the sources of that funding—are listed on the right.

Some assets can be turned more easily into cash than others; these are known as *liquid* assets. The accountant puts the most liquid assets at the top of the list and works down to the least liquid. Look, for example, at Table 3.1, which shows the consolidated balance sheet for Home Depot (HD), at the end of its 2014 fiscal year.[2] ("Consolidated" simply means that the balance sheet shows the position of Home Depot and any companies it owns.) You can see that Home Depot had $1,723 million of cash and marketable securities. In addition, it had sold goods worth $1,484 million but had not yet received payment. These payments are due soon, and therefore the balance sheet shows the unpaid bills or *accounts receivable* (or simply *receivables*) as a current asset. The next asset consists of inventories. These may be (1) raw materials and ingredients that the firm bought from suppliers, (2) work in progress, and (3) finished products waiting to be shipped from the warehouse. For Home Depot, inventories consist largely of goods in the warehouse or on the store shelves; for manufacturing companies, inventories would be more skewed toward raw materials and work in progress. Of course, there are always some items that don't fit into neat categories. So there is a fourth entry, *other current assets*.

Up to this point, all the assets in Home Depot's balance sheet are likely to be used or turned into cash in the near future. They are therefore described as *current assets*. The next assets listed in the balance sheet are longer-lived or *fixed assets* and include items such as buildings, equipment, and vehicles.

The balance sheet shows that the gross value of Home Depot's property, plant, and equipment is $40,353 million. This is what the assets originally cost. But they are unlikely to be worth that now. For example, suppose the company bought a delivery van 2 years ago; that van may be worth far less now than Home Depot paid for it. It might, in principle, be possible for the accountant to estimate separately the value today of the van, but this would be costly and somewhat subjective. Accountants rely instead on rules of thumb to estimate the *depreciation* in the value of assets, and with rare exceptions they stick to these rules. For example, in the case of that delivery van, the accountant may deduct a third of the original cost each year to reflect its declining value. So if Home Depot bought the van 2 years ago for $15,000, the balance sheet would show that accumulated depreciation is $2 \times \$5,000 = \$10,000$. Net of depreciation the value is only $5,000. Table 3.1 shows that Home Depot's total accumulated

---

balance sheet
Financial statement that shows the firm's assets and liabilities at a particular time.

---

[1] In addition, the company provides a statement of the shareholders' equity, which shows how much of the firm's earnings has been retained in the business rather than paid out as dividends and how much money has been raised by issuing new shares or spent by repurchasing stock. We will not review in detail the statement of shareholders' equity.

[2] Home Depot's fiscal 2014 ended February 1, 2015. The balance sheet in Table 3.1, therefore, shows the firm's assets and liabilities on this date. We have simplified and eliminated some of the detail in the company's published financial statements.

TABLE 3.1 Home Depot's balance sheet (figures in $ millions)

Assets	End of Fiscal 2014	End of Fiscal 2013	Liabilities and Shareholders' Equity	End of Fiscal 2014	End of Fiscal 2013
Current assets			Current liabilities		
Cash and marketable securities	$ 1,723	$ 1,929	Debt due for repayment	$ 328	$ 33
Receivables	1,484	1,398	Accounts payable	9,473	9,379
Inventories	11,079	11,057	Other current liabilities	1,468	1,337
Other current assets	1,016	895	Total current liabilities	$11,269	$10,749
Total current assets	$15,302	$15,279			
Fixed assets			Long-term debt	$16,869	$14,691
Tangible fixed assets			Deferred income taxes	642	514
Property, plant, and equipment	$40,353	$39,064	Other long-term liabilities	1,844	2,042
Less accumulated depreciation	17,633	15,716			
Net tangible fixed assets	$22,720	$23,348	Total liabilities	$30,624	$27,996
Intangible assets (goodwill)	1,353	1,289	Shareholders' equity		
Other assets	571	602	Common stock and other paid-in capital	$ 8,521	$ 8,536
			Retained earnings	26,995	23,180
Total assets	$39,946	$40,518	Treasury stock	(26,194)	(19,194)
			Total shareholders' equity	$ 9,322	$12,522
			Total liabilities and shareholders' equity	$39,946	$40,518

Note: Column sums subject to rounding error.
Source: Derived from Home Depot annual reports.

depreciation on fixed assets is $17,633 million. So while the assets cost $40,353 million, their net value in the accounts is only $40,353 − $17,633 = $22,720 million.

In addition to its tangible assets, Home Depot also has valuable intangible assets, such as its brand name, skilled management, and a well-trained labor force. Accountants are generally reluctant to record these intangible assets in the balance sheet unless they can be readily identified and valued.

There is, however, one important exception. When Home Depot has acquired other businesses in the past, it has paid more for their assets than the value shown in the firms' accounts. This difference is shown in Home Depot's balance sheet as "goodwill." Most of the intangible assets on Home Depot's balance sheet consist of goodwill.

Now look at the right-hand portion of Home Depot's balance sheet, which shows where the money to buy its assets came from. The accountant starts by looking at the company's liabilities—that is, the money owed by the company. First come those liabilities that are likely to be paid off most rapidly. For example, Home Depot has borrowed $328 million, due to be repaid shortly. It also owes its suppliers $9,473 million for goods that have been delivered but not yet paid for. These unpaid bills are shown as *accounts payable* (or *payables*). Both the borrowings and the payables are debts that Home Depot must repay within the year. They are therefore classified as *current liabilities.*

Home Depot's current assets total $15,302 million; its current liabilities amount to $11,269 million. Therefore, the difference between the value of Home Depot's current assets and its current liabilities is $15,302 − $11,269 = $4,033 million. This figure is known as Home Depot's *net current assets* or *net working capital.* It roughly measures the company's potential reservoir of cash.

Below the current liabilities Home Depot's accountants have listed the firm's long-term liabilities, such as debts that come due after the end of a year. You can see that banks and other investors have made long-term loans to Home Depot of $16,869 million.

Home Depot's liabilities are financial obligations to various parties. For example, when Home Depot buys goods from its suppliers, it has a liability to pay for them; when it borrows from the bank, it has a liability to repay the loan. Thus the suppliers and the bank have first claim on the firm's assets. What is left over after the liabilities

FIGURE 3.1 Assets and liabilities on the balance sheet

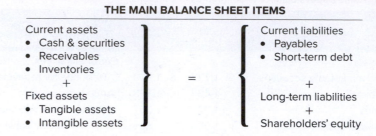

have been paid off belongs to the shareholders. This figure is known as the shareholders' *equity*. For Home Depot the total value of shareholders' equity amounts to $9,322 million. Table 3.1 shows that Home Depot's equity is made up of three parts. One portion, $8,521 million, has resulted from the occasional sale of new shares to investors. A much larger amount, $26,995 million, has come from earnings that Home Depot has retained and reinvested in the business on the shareholders' behalf.[3] Finally, treasury stock is a large negative number, −$26,194 million. This represents the amount that Home Depot has spent on buying back its shares. The money to repurchase them has gone out of the firm and reduced shareholders' equity.

Figure 3.1 shows how the separate items in the balance sheet link together. There are two classes of assets—current assets, which will soon be used or turned into cash, and long-term or "fixed" assets, which may be either tangible or intangible. There are also two classes of liability—current liabilities, which are due for payment shortly, and long-term liabilities.

The difference between the assets and the liabilities represents the amount of the shareholders' equity. This is the basic balance sheet identity. Shareholders are sometimes called "residual claimants" on the firm. We mean by this that shareholders' equity is what is left over when the liabilities of the firm are subtracted from its assets:

$$\text{Shareholders' equity} = \text{net assets} = \text{total assets} - \text{total liabilities} \qquad (3.1)$$

3.1 | Self-Test

Suppose that Home Depot borrows $500 million by issuing new long-term bonds. It places $100 million of the proceeds in the bank and uses $400 million to buy new machinery. What items of the balance sheet would change? Would shareholders' equity change?

common-size balance sheet
All items in the balance sheet are expressed as a percentage of total assets.

When comparing financial statements, analysts often calculate a **common-size balance sheet**, which re-expresses all items as a percentage of total assets. Table 3.2 is Home Depot's common-size balance sheet. The financial manager might look at this common-size balance sheet and notice right away that in 2014 receivables accounted for a higher proportion of the firm's assets than they did in the previous year. There may be good reasons for this, but the manager might wish to check that the company has not become lazy in collecting its customers' unpaid bills.

---

[3] Here is an occasional source of confusion. You may be tempted to think of retained earnings as a pile of cash that the company has built up from its past operations. But there is absolutely no link between retained earnings and cash balances. The earnings that Home Depot has plowed back into the business may have been used to buy new equipment, trucks, warehouses, and so on. Typically only a small proportion will be kept in the bank. Notice that Home Depot's balance sheet lists $26,995 in retained earnings but only $1,723 in cash and marketable securities.

TABLE 3.2 Common-size balance sheet of Home Depot (all items expressed as a percentage of total assets)

Assets	End of Fiscal 2014	End of Fiscal 2013	Liabilities and Shareholders' Equity	End of Fiscal 2014	End of Fiscal 2013
Current assets			Current liabilities		
Cash and marketable securities	4.3%	4.8%	Debt due for repayment	0.8%	0.1%
Receivables	3.7	3.5	Accounts payable	23.7	23.1
Inventories	27.7	27.3	Other current liabilities	3.7	3.3
Other current assets	2.5	2.2	Total current liabilities	28.2%	26.5%
Total current assets	38.3%	37.7%			
Fixed assets			Long-term debt	42.2%	36.3%
Tangible fixed assets			Deferred income taxes	1.6	1.3
Property, plant, and equipment	101.0%	96.4%	Other long-term liabilities	4.6	5.0
Less accumulated depreciation	44.1	38.8			
Net tangible fixed assets	56.9%	57.6%	Total liabilities	76.7%	69.1%
Intangible assets (goodwill)	3.4%	3.2%	Shareholders' equity:		
Other assets	1.4%	1.5%	Common stock and other paid-in capital	21.3%	21.1%
			Retained earnings	67.6	57.2
Total assets	100.0%	100.0%	Treasury stock	(65.6)	(47.4)
			Total shareholders' equity	23.3%	30.9%
			Total liabilities and shareholders' equity	100.0%	100.0%

Note: Column sums subject to rounding error.

By the way, it is easy to obtain the financial statements of almost any publicly traded firm. Most firms make their annual reports available on the web. You also can find key financial statements of most firms at Yahoo! Finance (**finance.yahoo.com**) or Google Finance (**finance.google.com**).

Book Values and Market Values

Throughout this book, we will frequently make a distinction between the book values of the assets shown in the balance sheet and their market values.

generally accepted accounting principles (GAAP)
U.S. procedures for preparing financial statements.

Items in the balance sheet are valued according to **generally accepted accounting principles,** commonly called **GAAP.** These state that assets must be shown in the balance sheet at their *historical cost* adjusted for depreciation. **Book values** are therefore "backward-looking" measures of value. They are based on the past cost of the asset, not its current market price or value to the firm. For example, suppose that 2 years ago Home Depot built an office building for $30 million and that in today's market the building would sell for $40 million. The book value of the building would be less than its market value, and the balance sheet would understate the value of Home Depot's asset.

book value
Net worth of the firm according to the balance sheet.

Or consider a specialized plant that Intel develops for producing special-purpose computer chips at a cost of $800 million. The book value of the plant is $800 million less accumulated depreciation. But suppose that shortly after the plant is constructed, a new chip makes the existing one obsolete. The market value of Intel's new plant could fall by 50% or more. In this case, market value would be less than book value.

The difference between book value and market value is greater for some assets than for others. It is zero in the case of cash but potentially very large for fixed assets where the accountant starts with initial cost and then depreciates that figure according to a prespecified schedule. The purpose of depreciation is to allocate the original cost of the asset over its life, and the rules governing the depreciation of asset values do not reflect actual loss of market value. Usually the market value of fixed assets is much higher than the book value, but sometimes it is less.

The same goes for the right-hand side of the balance sheet. In the case of liabilities, the accountant simply records the amount of money that you have promised to pay. For short-term liabilities, this figure is generally close to the market value of that promise. For example, if you owe the bank $1 million tomorrow, the accounts show a book liability of $1 million. As long as you are not bankrupt, that $1 million is also roughly the value to the bank of your promise. But now suppose that $1 million is not due to be repaid for several years. The accounts still show a liability of $1 million, but how much your debt is worth depends on what happens to interest rates. If interest rates rise after you have issued the debt, lenders may not be prepared to pay as much as $1 million for your debt; if interest rates fall, they may be prepared to pay more than $1 million.[4] Thus the market value of a long-term liability may be higher or lower than the book value. **Market values of assets and liabilities do not generally equal their book values. Book values are based on historical or *original* values. Market values measure *current* values of assets and liabilities.**

The difference between book value and market value is likely to be greatest for shareholders' equity. The book value of equity measures the cash that shareholders have contributed in the past plus the cash that the company has retained and reinvested in the business on their behalf. But this often bears little resemblance to the total market value that investors place on the shares.

If the market price of the firm's shares falls through the floor, don't try telling the shareholders that the book value is satisfactory—they won't want to hear. Shareholders are concerned with the market value of their shares; market value, not book value, is the price at which they can sell their shares. Managers who wish to keep their shareholders happy will focus on market values.

We will often find it useful to think about the firm in terms of a **market-value balance sheet.** Like a conventional balance sheet, a market-value balance sheet lists the firm's assets, but it records each asset at its current market value rather than at historical cost less depreciation. Similarly, each liability is shown at its market value. **The difference between the market values of assets and liabilities is the market value of the shareholders' equity claim. The stock price is simply the market value of shareholders' equity divided by the number of outstanding shares.**

market-value balance sheet
Balance sheet showing market rather than book values of assets, liabilities, and stockholders' equity.

Example **3.1 ▶**   Market- versus Book-Value Balance Sheets

Jupiter has developed a revolutionary auto production process that enables it to produce cars 20% more efficiently than any rival. It has invested $10 billion in building its new plant. To finance the investment, Jupiter borrowed $4 billion and raised the remaining funds by selling new shares of stock in the firm. There are currently 100 million shares of stock outstanding. Investors are very excited about Jupiter's prospects. They believe that the flow of profits from the new plant justifies a stock price of $75.

If these are Jupiter's only assets, the book-value balance sheet immediately after it has made the investment is as follows:

BOOK-VALUE BALANCE SHEET FOR JUPITER MOTORS (Figures in $ billions)			
Assets		**Liabilities and Shareholders' Equity**	
Auto plant	10	Debt	4
		Shareholders' equity	6

---
[4] We will show you how changing interest rates affect the market value of debt in Chapter 6.

Investors are placing a *market value* on Jupiter's equity of $7.5 billion ($75 per share times 100 million shares). We assume that the debt outstanding is worth $4 billion.[5] Therefore, if you owned all Jupiter's shares and all its debt, the value of your holdings would be $7.5 + $4 = $11.5 billion. In this case, you would own the company lock, stock, and barrel and would be entitled to all its cash flows. Because you can buy the entire company for $11.5 billion, the total value of Jupiter's assets must also be $11.5 billion. In other words, the market value of the assets must be equal to the market value of the liabilities plus the market value of the shareholders' equity.

We can now draw up the market-value balance sheet as follows:

MARKET-VALUE BALANCE SHEET FOR JUPITER MOTORS (Figures in $ billions)			
Assets		**Liabilities and Shareholders' Equity**	
Auto plant	11.5	Debt	4
		Shareholders' equity	7.5

Notice that the market value of Jupiter's plant is $1.5 billion more than the plant cost to build. The difference is due to the superior profits that investors expect the plant to earn. **Thus, in contrast to the balance sheet shown in the company's books, the market-value balance sheet is forward-looking. It depends on the profits that investors expect the assets to provide.** ■

Is it surprising that market value generally exceeds book value? It shouldn't be. Firms find it attractive to raise money to invest in various projects because they believe the projects will be worth more than they cost. Otherwise, why bother? You will usually find that shares of stock sell for more than the value shown in the company's books.

3.2   Self-Test

a. What would be Jupiter's price per share if the auto plant had a market value of $14 billion?
b. How would you reassess the value of the auto plant if the value of outstanding stock was $8 billion?

3.2   The Income Statement

income statement
Financial statement that shows the revenues, expenses, and net income of a firm over a period of time.

If Home Depot's balance sheet resembles a snapshot of the firm at a particular time, its **income statement** is like a video. It shows how profitable the firm has been during the past year.

Look at the summary income statement in Table 3.3. You can see that during fiscal 2014, Home Depot sold goods worth $83,176 million and that the total cost of acquiring and selling those goods was $54,222 + $16,699 = $70,921 million. The largest expense item, amounting to $54,222 million, consisted of the cost of goods sold. This included the acquisition cost of Home Depot's goods, the wages of its employees, and the other expenses incurred to obtain and sell its wares. Almost all the remaining

---

[5] Jupiter has borrowed $4 billion to finance its investment, but if the interest rate has changed in the meantime, the debt could be worth more or less than $4 billion.

TABLE 3.3 Home Depot's income statement, fiscal 2014

	$ Million	% of Sales
Net sales	$83,176	100.0%
Other income	337	0.4
Cost of goods sold	54,222	65.2
Selling, general, and administrative expenses	16,699	20.1
Depreciation	1,786	2.1
Earnings before interest and income taxes (EBIT)	$10,806	13.0%
Interest expense	830	1.0
Taxable income	$ 9,976	12.0%
Taxes	3,631	4.4
Net income	$ 6,345	7.6%
Allocation of net income		
Dividends	$ 2,530	3.0%
Addition to retained earnings	$ 3,815	4.6%

Source: Derived from Home Depot annual reports.

expenses were administrative expenses such as head office costs, advertising, and distribution.

In addition to these out-of-pocket expenses, Home Depot also made a deduction for the value of the plant and equipment used up in producing the goods. In 2014, this charge for depreciation was $1,786 million. Thus Home Depot's *earnings before interest and taxes (EBIT)* were

$$\text{EBIT} = \text{total revenues} + \text{other income} - \text{costs} - \text{depreciation}$$
$$= 83,176 + 337 - (54,222 + 16,699) - 1,786$$
$$= \$10,806 \text{ million}$$

The remainder of the income statement shows where these earnings went. As we saw earlier, Home Depot has partly financed its investment in plant and equipment by borrowing. In 2014, it paid $830 million of interest on this borrowing. A further slice of the profit went to the government in the form of taxes. This amounted to $3,631 million. The $6,345 million that was left over after paying interest and taxes belonged to the shareholders. Of this sum, Home Depot paid out $2,530 million in dividends and reinvested the remaining $3,815 million in the business. Presumably, these reinvested funds made the company more valuable.

The $3,815 of earnings that Home Depot retained and reinvested in the firm show up on its balance sheet as an increase in retained earnings. Notice that retained earnings in Table 3.1 increased by $3,815 million in 2014, from $23,180 million to $26,995 million. However, shareholders' equity fell during the year because Home Depot also repurchased some of its stock.

Just as it is sometimes useful to prepare a common-size balance sheet, we can also prepare a **common-size income statement.** In this case, all items are expressed as a percentage of revenues. The last column of Table 3.3 is Home Depot's common-size income statement. You can see, for example, that the cost of goods sold consumed 65.2% of revenues and that selling, general, and administrative expenses absorbed a further 20.1%.

common-size income statement
All items on the income statement are expressed as a percentage of revenues.

Income versus Cash Flow

It is important to distinguish between Home Depot's income and the cash that the company generated. Here are two reasons that income and cash are not the same:

1. *Depreciation.* When Home Depot's accountants prepare the income statement, they do not simply count the cash coming in and the cash going out. Instead, the accountant starts with the cash payments but then divides these payments into two

groups—current expenditures (such as wages) and capital expenditures (such as the purchase of new machinery). Current expenditures are deducted from current profits. However, rather than deducting the cost of long-lived machinery in the year it is purchased, the accountant spreads its acquisition cost over its forecasted life by making an annual charge for depreciation.

Thus, when calculating profits, the accountant does *not* deduct the expenditure on new equipment that year, even though cash is paid out. However, the accountant *does* deduct depreciation on assets previously purchased, even though no cash is currently paid out. For example, suppose a $100,000 investment is depreciated by $10,000 a year for 10 years.[6] This depreciation is treated as an annual expense, although the cash actually went out of the door when the asset was first purchased. For this reason, the deduction for depreciation is classified as a *noncash* expense.

To calculate the cash produced by the business, it is necessary to *add* the depreciation charge (which is not a cash payment) back to accounting profits and to *subtract* the expenditure on new capital equipment (which is a cash payment).

2. *Cash versus accrual accounting.* Consider a manufacturer that spends $60 to produce goods in period 1. In period 2 it sells these goods for $100, but its customers pay their bills with a delay, so payment is not received until period 3. The following diagram shows the firm's cash flows. In period 1 there is a cash *outflow* of $60. Then, when customers pay their bills in period 3, there is an *inflow* of $100.

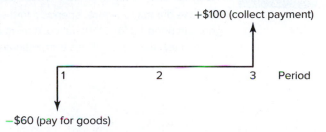

It would be misleading to say that the firm was running at a loss in period 1 (when cash flow was negative) or that it was extremely profitable in period 3 (when cash flow was positive). Therefore, to construct the income statement, the accountant looks at when the sale was made (period 2 in our example) and gathers together all the revenues and expenses associated with that sale. For our company, the income statement would show:

Revenue	$100
Less cost of goods sold	60
Profit	$ 40

This practice of matching revenues and expenses is known as *accrual accounting*. Of course, the accountant does not ignore the actual timing of the cash expenditures and payments. So the cash outlay in the first period will be treated not as an expense but as an *investment* in inventories. Subsequently, in period 2, when the goods are taken out of inventory and sold, the accountant shows a *reduction* in inventories.

To go from the cost of goods sold in the income statement to the cash outflows, we need to subtract the investment in inventories that is shown in the balance sheet:

Period:	1	2
Cost of goods sold (income statement)	0	60
+ Investment in inventories (balance sheet)	60	−60
= Cash paid out	60	0

---

[6] We discuss depreciation rules in Chapter 9.

The accountant also does not ignore the fact that the firm has to wait until period 3 to collect its bills. When the sale is made in period 2, the figure for accounts receivable in the balance sheet is increased to show that the company's customers owe an extra $100 in unpaid bills. Later, when the customers pay those bills in period 3, accounts receivable are reduced by $100. Therefore, to go from the sales shown in the income statement to the cash inflows, we need to subtract the investment in receivables:

Period:	2	3
Sales (income statement)	100	0
− Investment in receivables (balance sheet)	100	−100
= Cash received	0	+100

We will return to these issues in more detail in Chapter 9, but for now we summarize the key points as follows: Cash *outflow* is equal to the cost of goods sold, which is shown in the income statement, *plus* the change in inventories. Cash *inflow* is equal to the sales shown in the income statement *less* the change in uncollected bills.

Example 3.2 ▶ Profits versus Cash Flows

Suppose our manufacturer spends a further $80 to produce goods in period 2. It sells these goods in period 3 for $120, but customers do not pay their bills until period 4.
  The cash flows from these transactions are now as follows:

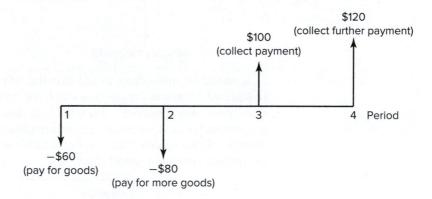

How do the new transactions affect the income statement and the balance sheet? The income statement will match costs with revenues and record the cost of goods sold when the sales are made in periods 1 and 2. The difference between the costs shown in the income statement and the cash flows is recorded as an investment (and later, disinvestment) in inventories. Thus, in period 1 the accountant shows an investment in inventories of $60 just as before. In period 2, these goods are taken out of inventory and sold, but the firm also produces a further $80 of goods. Thus, there is a net increase in inventories of $20. As these goods in turn are sold in period 3, inventories are reduced by $80. The following table confirms that the cash outflow in each period is equal to the cost of goods sold that is shown in the income statement plus the change in inventories.

Period:	1	2	3
Cost of goods sold (income statement)	0	60	80
+ Investment in inventories (balance sheet)	60	−60 + 80 = 20	−80
= Cash paid out	60	80	0

The following table provides a similar reconciliation of the difference between the revenues shown in the income statement and the cash inflow:

Period:	2	3	4
Sales (income statement)	100	120	0
− Investment in receivables (balance sheet)	100	−100 + 120 = 20	−120
= Cash received	0	+100	+120

In the income statement the accountant records sales of $100 in period 1 and $120 in period 2. The fact that the firm has to wait for payment is recognized in the balance sheet as an investment in receivables. The cash that the company *receives* is equal to the sales shown in the income statement *less* the investment in receivables. ■

3.3 Self-Test

Consider a firm that spends $200 to produce goods in period 1. In period 2, it sells half of those goods for $150, but it doesn't collect payment until one period later. In period 3, it sells the other half of the goods for $150, and it collects payment on these sales in period 4. Calculate the profits and the cash flows for this firm in periods 1 to 4.

3.3 The Statement of Cash Flows

The firm requires *cash* when it buys new plant and machinery or when it pays interest to the bank and dividends to the shareholders. Therefore, the financial manager needs to keep track of the cash that is coming in and going out.

We have seen that the firm's cash flow can be quite different from its net income. These differences can arise for at least two reasons:

1. The income statement does not recognize capital expenditures as expenses in the year that the capital goods are paid for. Instead, it spreads those expenses over time in the form of an annual deduction for depreciation.
2. The income statement uses the accrual method of accounting, which means that revenues and expenses are recognized when sales are made, rather than when the cash is received or paid out.

statement of cash flows
Financial statement that shows the firm's cash receipts and cash payments over a period of time.

The **statement of cash flows** shows the firm's cash inflows and outflows from operations as well as from its investments and financing activities. Table 3.4 is the cash-flow statement for Home Depot. It contains three sections. The first shows the cash flow from operations. This is the cash generated from Home Depot's normal business activities. Next comes the cash that Home Depot has invested in plant and equipment or in the acquisition of new businesses. The final section reports cash flows from financing activities such as the sale of new debt or stock. We will look at each of these sections in turn.

The first section, cash flow from operations, starts with net income but adjusts that figure for those parts of the income statement that do not involve cash coming in or going out. Therefore, it adds back the allowance for depreciation because depreciation is not a cash outflow, even though it is treated as an expense in the income statement.

Any additions to current assets (other than cash itself) need to be *subtracted* from net income because these absorb cash but do not show up in the income statement. Conversely, any additions to current liabilities need to be *added* to net income because these release cash. For example, you can see that the increase of $86 million in accounts

TABLE 3.4 Home Depot's statement of cash flows (figures in $ millions)

Cash Provided by Operations	
Net income	$6,345
Depreciation	1,786
Changes in working capital items	
Decrease (increase) in accounts receivable	−86
Decrease (increase) in inventories	−22
Decrease (increase) in other current assets	−121
Increase (decrease) in accounts payable	94
Increase (decrease) in other current liabilities	131
Total decrease (increase) in working capital	−$ 4
Cash provided by operations	$8,127
Cash Flows from Investments	
Cash provided by (used for) disposal of (additions to) property, plant, and equipment	−$1,289
Sales (acquisitions) of other long-term assets	31
Cash provided by (used for) investments	−$1,258
Cash Provided by (Used for) Financing Activities	
Increase (decrease) in short-term debt	$ 295
Increase (decrease) in long-term debt	2,178
Dividends	−2,530
Repurchases of stock	−7,000
Other	−18
Cash provided by (used for) financing activities	−$7,075
Net increase (decrease) in cash and cash equivalents	−$ 206

Source: Calculated from data in Tables 3.1 and 3.3.

receivable is deducted from income. In addition, Home Depot increased inventories by $22 million. This increase in inventory levels also absorbed cash and must be deducted from net income when calculating cash flows. On the other hand, Home Depot does not pay all its bills immediately. These delayed payments show up as payables. In 2014, Home Depot had larger bills outstanding than a year earlier: Accounts payable *increased* by $94 million. Delaying these payments freed up extra cash.

We have pointed out that depreciation is not a cash payment; it is simply the accountant's allocation to the current year of the original cost of the capital equipment. However, cash does flow out the door when the firm actually buys and pays for new capital equipment. Therefore, these capital expenditures are set out in the second section of the cash-flow statement. You can see that Home Depot spent $1,289 million on new capital equipment. Notice that (gross) property, plant, and equipment on Home Depot's balance sheet increased by precisely this amount. On the other hand, Home Depot freed up $31 million by selling off other investments. Total cash used by investments was $1,258 million.

Finally, the third section of the cash-flow statement shows the cash from financing activities. For example, Home Depot raised $2,178 million by issuing long-term debt. But it paid out $2,530 million to stockholders in the form of dividends and used another $7,000 million to repurchase stock.[7]

To summarize, the cash-flow statement tells us that Home Depot generated $8,127 million from operations, spent $1,258 million on new investments, and used $7,075 million in financing activities. Home Depot earned and raised less cash than it spent.

---

[7] You might think that interest payments also ought to be listed in this section. However, it is usual to include interest in the first section with cash flow from operations. This is because, unlike dividends, interest payments are not discretionary. The firm must pay interest when a payment comes due, so these payments are treated as a business expense rather than as a financing decision.

Therefore, its cash balance decreased by $206 million. To calculate this change in cash balance, we subtract the uses of cash from the sources:

	In Millions
Cash flow from operations	$8,127
− Cash flow for new investment	−1,258
+ Cash provided by new financing	−7,075
= Change in cash balance	−$ 206

Look back at Table 3.1 and you will see that cash accounts on the balance sheet did indeed decrease by $206 million in 2014.[8]

3.4 Self-Test

Would the following activities increase or decrease the firm's cash balance?

a. Inventories are increased.
b. The firm reduces its accounts payable.
c. The firm issues additional common stock.
d. The firm buys new equipment.

free cash flow
Cash available for distribution to investors after firm pays for new investments or additions to working capital.

Free Cash Flow

The value of a company depends on how much cash it can generate for investors after it has paid for any new capital investments. This cash is called the company's **free cash flow.** Free cash flow is available to be paid out to investors as interest or dividends or to repay debt or buy back stock.

Example 3.3 ▶ Free Cash Flow for Home Depot

Let's use Home Depot's income and cash-flow statements to calculate its free cash flow in 2014. We start with the earnings produced by the firm's ongoing operations. This is equal to

$$\text{Net income} + \text{debt interest} = \$6,345 + \$830 = \$7,175 \text{ million}$$

We need to make two adjustments to this figure for those parts of the income statement that do not involve cash coming in or going out. First, we must add back depreciation because depreciation is not a cash outflow, even though it is treated as an expense in the income statement. Second, accounting income is not cash in the bank. For example, the firm may need to lay out money to buy materials ahead of time, or its customers may not pay for their purchases immediately. Therefore, to measure the cash from ongoing operations, we need to subtract those additions to net working capital shown in the top panel of the statement of cash flows. This gives us cash flow from operations:

$$\text{Cash flow from operations} = (\text{net income} + \text{interest}) + \text{depreciation} - \text{additions to}$$
$$\text{net working capital}$$
$$= \$7,175 + \$1,786 - \$4 = \$8,957 \text{ million}$$

---

[8] Home Depot's published statement of cash flows differs from the cash-flow statement that we derived from the balance sheet and income statement. This is a common occurrence, particularly if the company has engaged in mergers or divestitures during the year.

This cash is not all available to be paid out to investors, for the company needs some of the cash for new capital expenditures. So the capital that is free for distribution is

$$\text{Free cash flow} = \text{cash flow from operations} - \text{capital expenditures}$$
$$= \$8{,}957 - \$1{,}258 = \$7{,}699 \text{ million}$$

Notice that free cash flow differs from the addition-to-cash balances found in the statement of cash flows (Table 3.4). First, when we calculate free cash flow, we ignore altogether items in the last panel of Table 3.4, "Cash provided by financing activities."[9] This is because free cash flow measures how much cash the company's operations generate for possible distribution to investors. The *available* amount should not be confused with the amount that the company actually raised by financing activities. Second, we add back interest payments when computing free cash flow, as those payments are part of the distributions made to investors.[10]

It is often useful to ask what Home Depot's free cash flow would have been if the company had been financed entirely by equity. In that case, all the free cash flow would belong to the shareholders. However, if Home Depot no longer paid out $830 million as interest, pretax income would be increased by that amount, and the company would pay an additional .35 × 830 = $290.50 million in tax. Thus, if the company was financed solely by equity, free cash flow would have been $7,699 − $290.50 = $7,408.50 million. ∎

3.4 Accounting Practice and Malpractice

Managers of public companies face constant scrutiny. Much of that scrutiny focuses on earnings. Security analysts forecast earnings per share, and investors then wait to see whether the company can meet or beat the forecasts. A shortfall, even if it is only a cent or two, can be a big disappointment. Investors might judge that if you could not find that extra cent or two of earnings, the firm must be in a really bad way.

Managers complain about this pressure, but do they do anything about it? Unfortunately, the answer appears to be yes, according to Graham, Harvey, and Rajgopal, who surveyed about 400 senior managers.[11] Most of the managers said that accounting earnings were the single most important number reported to investors. Most admitted to adjusting their firms' operations and investments to produce the earnings that investors were looking for. For example, 80% were prepared to decrease discretionary spending on R&D, advertising, or plant maintenance to meet earnings targets.

Of course, managers may not need to adjust the firm's operations if they can instead adjust their accounting methods. U.S. accounting rules are spelled out by the Financial Accounting Standards Board (FASB) and its generally accepted accounting principles (GAAP). Yet, inevitably, rules and principles leave room for discretion, and managers under pressure to perform are tempted to take advantage of this leeway to satisfy

---

[9] For this reason, when we calculated cash flow from operations, we ignored the change in holdings of short-term debt, even though this short-term debt is listed under current liabilities. We were interested only in the items of working capital that arose from the firm's operations.

[10] We can check the logic linking free cash flow to the statement of cash flows as follows:

Increase in cash balance from Table 3.4	−$ 206
+ Cash used for financing activities from Table 3.4	7,075
+ Interest payments	830
Free cash flow	$7,699

[11] J. R. Graham, C. R. Harvey, and S. Rajgopal, "The Economic Implications of Corporate Financial Reporting," *Journal of Accounting and Economics* 40 (2005), pp. 3–73.

investors. Investors worry about the fact that some companies seem particularly prone to inflate their earnings by playing fast and loose with accounting practice. They refer to such companies as having "low-quality" earnings, and they place a correspondingly lower value on the firms' stock.

Here are some examples of ambiguities in accounting rules that have been used by companies to conceal unflattering information:

- *Revenue recognition.* As we saw earlier, firms record a sale when it is made, not when the customer actually pays. But the date of sale is not always obvious. Suppose it is November and you are concerned that if your firm does not meet its sales target, you can forget about your annual bonus. You contact your main customers, and they agree to increase their December orders as long as they have the right to return any unsold goods. Your firm then books these shipments as "sales," even though there is a high likelihood that many of the goods will be returned. That is almost certainly illegal and will get you into serious trouble. But suppose instead that you tell your customers that the price of your product may rise in the new year and suggest that they place an extra order in December. This practice, known as "channel stuffing," increases this year's sales at the expense of next year's sales.

  Many companies have been thought to use channel stuffing to overstate their earnings, but very blatant instances are liable to attract the SEC's attention. For example, in 2002 the pharmaceutical giant, Bristol Myers Squibb, disclosed that wholesalers were holding hundreds of millions of dollars in excessive inventories of its products and the company's earnings for 2002 might be just half of its 2001 earnings as wholesalers worked down these inventories. Following an investigation by the SEC, the company agreed to pay $150 million to settle accusations that this channel stuffing had improperly inflated its sales and earnings. In Chapter 1, we mentioned Hewlett-Packard's disastrous acquisition of the British company Autonomy. Hewlett-Packard paid $11.1 billion for Autonomy. Just over a year later, it wrote down the value of the company by $8.8 billion, alleging that Autonomy had used channel stuffing to greatly inflate its revenues.

- *Cookie-jar reserves.* The giant mortgage-pass-through firm Freddie Mac earned the Wall Street nickname "Steady Freddie" for its unusually smooth and predictable pattern of earnings growth, at least until 2008 when it suddenly collapsed in the wake of the meltdown in subprime mortgages. Unfortunately, it emerged in 2003 that Freddie achieved this predictability in part by misusing its reserve accounts. Normally, such accounts are intended to allow for the likely impact of events that might reduce earnings, such as the failure of customers to pay their bills. But Freddie seemed to "overreserve" against such contingencies so that it could "release" those reserves and bolster income in a bad year. Its steady growth was largely a matter of earnings management.

- *Off–balance sheet assets and liabilities.* Before its bankruptcy in 2001 (at that time, the second largest in U.S. history), Enron had accumulated large debts and had also guaranteed the debts of other companies in which it had an ownership stake. To present a fair view of the firm, Enron should have recognized these potential liabilities on its balance sheet. But the firm created and placed paper firms— so-called special-purpose entities (SPEs)—in the middle of its transactions and excluded these liabilities from its financial statements.

The collapse of Enron illustrates how dishonest managers with creamy compensation packages may be tempted to conceal the truth from investors. If the company had been more transparent to outsiders—that is, if they could have assessed its true profitability and prospects—its problems would have shown up right away in a falling stock price. This in turn would have generated extra scrutiny from security analysts, bond rating agencies, lenders, and investors.

The International Financial Reporting Standards (IFRS), which are set by the London-based International Accounting Standards Board (IASB), aim to harmonize financial reporting around the world. They are the basis for reporting throughout the European Union. In addition, some 100 other countries, such as Australia, Canada, Brazil, India, and China, have adopted them or plan to do so.

For some years, the SEC has worked to bring U.S. accounting standards more in line with international rules. For example, until 2007 foreign companies that traded on U.S. stock exchanges were required to show how their accounts differed from U.S. GAAP. This was a very expensive exercise that cost some companies millions of dollars annually and caused many to delist their stocks. These companies can now simply report results using international accounting standards. Subsequently, in August 2008, the SEC released its plans to allow some large U.S. multinationals, representing approximately $2.5 trillion in market capitalization, to eventually use IFRS for financial statements.

This shift from GAAP to IFRS would involve a major change in the way that accountants in the United States approach their task. IFRS tend to be "principles-based," which means that there are no hard-and-fast codes to follow. Instead, companies must be ready to defend their accounting practices in light of the general principles laid out in the IFRS. By contrast, in the United States, GAAP are accompanied by thousands of pages of prescriptive regulatory guidance and interpretations from auditors and accounting groups. For example, more than 160 pieces of authoritative literature relate to how and when companies record revenue. This leaves less room for judgment, but detailed rules rapidly become out of date, and unscrupulous companies have been able to structure transactions so that they keep to the letter but not the spirit of the rules.

By 2014, it had become clear that the SEC's plan to move to IFRS was effectively dead and that, while the SEC and IASB would continue to collaborate on accounting rules, there was little prospect of any agreement over a single global standard that included the United States.

BEYOND THE PAGE

Accounting acronyms

mhhe.com/brealey9e

With transparency, corporate troubles generally lead to corrective action. But the top management of a troubled and opaque company may be able to maintain its stock price and postpone the discipline of the market. Market discipline caught up with Enron only a month or two before bankruptcy.

Enron was not the only company to be mired in accounting scandals in the early years of the century. Firms such as Global Crossing, Qwest Communications, and WorldCom misstated profits by billions of dollars. Overseas, the Italian dairy company Parmalat falsified the existence of a bank account to the tune of $5.5 billion, and the French media and entertainment company Vivendi came close to bankruptcy after it was accused of accounting fraud. In response to these scandals, Congress passed the Sarbanes-Oxley Act, widely known as SOX. A major goal of SOX is to increase transparency and ensure that companies and their accountants provide directors, lenders, and shareholders with the information they need to monitor progress.

SOX created the Public Accounting Oversight Board to oversee the auditing of public companies; it banned accounting firms from offering other services to companies whose accounts they audit; it prohibited any individual from heading a firm's audit for more than 5 years; and it required that the board's audit committee consist of directors who are independent of the company's management. Sarbanes-Oxley also required that management certify that the financial statements present a fair view of the firm's financial position and demonstrate that the firm has adequate controls and procedures for financial reporting. All this has come at a price. Managers and investors worry that the costs of SOX and the burden of meeting detailed, inflexible regulations are pushing some corporations to return from public to private ownership. Some blame SOX and onerous regulation in the United States for the fact that an increasing number of foreign companies have chosen to list their shares in London rather than New York.

There is also a vigorous debate over "rules-based" versus "principles-based" approaches to accounting standards. The United States follows a rules-based approach, with detailed rules governing virtually every circumstance that possibly can be anticipated. In contrast, the European Union takes a principles-based approach to accounting. Its International Financial Reporting Standards set out general approaches that financial statements should take to valuing assets. Europe and the United States have been engaged for years in attempts to coordinate their systems, and many in the United States have lobbied for the greater simplicity that principles-based accounting standards might offer. The nearby box reports on these efforts.

3.5 Taxes

Taxes often have a major effect on financial decisions. Therefore, we should explain how corporations and investors are taxed.

Corporate Tax

Companies pay tax on their income. Table 3.5 shows that there are special low rates of corporate tax for small companies, but for large companies (those with income over $18.33 million) the corporate tax rate is 35%.[12] Thus for every $100 that the firm earns it pays $35 in corporate tax.

When firms calculate taxable income, they are allowed to deduct expenses. These expenses include an allowance for depreciation. However, the Internal Revenue Service (IRS) specifies the rates of depreciation that the company can use for different types of equipment. The rates of depreciation used to calculate taxes are not the same as the rates used when the firm reports its profits to shareholders.[13]

The company is also allowed to deduct interest paid to debtholders when calculating its taxable income, but dividends paid to shareholders are not deductible. These dividends are therefore paid out of after-tax income. Table 3.6 provides an example of how interest payments reduce corporate taxes. Although EBIT for both firms A and B

TABLE 3.5 Corporate tax rates, 2016

Taxable Income ($)	Tax Rate (%)
0–50,000	15
50,001–75,000	25
75,001–100,000	34
100,001–18,333,333	Varies between 39 and 34
Over 18,333,333	35

TABLE 3.6 Firms A and B both have earnings before interest and taxes (EBIT) of $100 million, but A pays out part of its profits as debt interest. This reduces the corporate tax paid by A.

	Firm A	Firm B
EBIT	$100	$100
Interest	40	0
Pretax income	$ 60	$100
Tax (35% of pretax income)	21	35
Net income	$ 39	$ 65

Note: Figures in millions of dollars.

---

[12] In addition, corporations pay state income taxes, which we ignore here for simplicity.

[13] If the company assumes a slower rate of depreciation in its income statement than the Internal Revenue Service assumes, the tax charge shown in the income statement will be higher in the early years of a project's life than the actual tax payment. This difference is recorded in the balance sheet as a liability for deferred tax. We will tell you more about depreciation allowances in Chapter 9.

is $100 million, firm A, which has $40 million of interest expense, has lower pretax income and therefore pays less taxes.

The bad news about taxes is that each extra dollar of revenue increases taxable income by $1 and results in 35 cents of extra taxes. The good news is that each extra dollar of expense *reduces* taxable income by $1 and therefore reduces taxes by 35 cents. For example, if the firm borrows money, every dollar of interest it pays on the loan reduces taxes by 35 cents. Therefore, a dollar of interest reduces after-tax income by only 65 cents.

3.5 | Self-Test

Recalculate the figures in Table 3.6, assuming that firm A now has to make interest payments of $60 million. What happens to taxes paid? Does net income fall by the additional $20 million interest payment compared with the case considered in Table 3.6, where interest expense was only $40 million?

When firms make profits, they pay 35% of the profits to the Internal Revenue Service. But the process doesn't work in reverse; if the firm suffers a loss, the IRS does not send it a check for 35% of the loss. However, the firm can carry the losses back, deduct them from taxable income in earlier years, and claim a refund of past taxes. Losses can also be carried forward and deducted from taxable income in the future.[14]

Personal Tax

Table 3.7 shows the U.S. rates of personal tax. Notice that as income increases, the tax rate also increases. Notice also that the top personal tax rate is higher than the top corporate rate.

marginal tax rate
Additional taxes owed per dollar of additional income.

The tax rates presented in Table 3.7 are **marginal tax rates.** The marginal tax rate is the tax that the individual pays on each *extra* dollar of income. For example, as a single taxpayer, you would pay 10 cents of tax on each extra dollar you earn when your income is below $9,275, but once income exceeds $9,275, you would pay 15 cents of tax on each extra dollar of income up to an income of $37,650. If your total income is $50,000, your tax bill is 10% of the first $9,275 of income, 15% of the next $28,375 (i.e., 37,650 − 9,275), and 25% of the remaining $12,350:

$$\text{Tax} = (.10 \times \$9{,}275) + (.15 \times \$28{,}375) + (.25 \times \$12{,}350) = \$8{,}271.25$$

TABLE 3.7 Personal tax rates, 2016

Taxable Income ($)		Tax Rate (%)
Single Taxpayers	**Married Taxpayers Filing Joint Returns**	
0–9,275	0–18,550	10.0
9,276–37,650	18,551–75,300	15.0
37,651–91,150	75,301–151,900	25.0
91,151–190,150	151,901–231,450	28.0
190,151–413,350	231,451–413,350	33.0
413,351–415,050	413,351–466,950	35.0
415,051 and above	466,951 and above	39.6

---

[14] Losses can be carried back for a maximum of 3 years and forward for up to 15 years.

average tax rate
Total taxes owed divided by total income.

The **average tax rate** is simply the total tax bill divided by total income. In this example it is $8,271.25/$50,000 = .165, or 16.5%. Notice that the average rate is lower than the marginal rate. This is because of the lower rates on the first $37,650.

BEYOND THE PAGE

Average and marginal tax rates

mhhe.com/brealey9e

3.6	Self-Test

What are the average and marginal tax rates for a single taxpayer with a taxable income of $80,000? What are the average and marginal tax rates for married taxpayers filing joint returns if their joint taxable income is also $80,000?

The tax rates in Table 3.7 apply to "ordinary income," primarily income earned as salary or wages. Interest earnings also are treated as ordinary income.

The U.S. government also taxes investment earnings, for example dividends or capital gains. The treatment of dividend income in the United States leads to what is commonly dubbed the "double taxation" of corporate earnings. Each dollar the company earns is taxed at the corporate rate. Then, if the company pays a dividend out of this after-tax income, the shareholder pays personal income taxes on the distribution. The original earnings are taxed first as corporate income and again as dividend income. Suppose instead that the company earns a dollar which is paid out as interest. The dollar escapes corporate tax because the interest payment is considered a business expense that reduces the firm's taxable income.

Capital gains are also taxed, but only when the gains are realized. Suppose that you bought Bio-technics stock when it was selling for 10 cents a share. Its market price today is $1 a share. As long as you hold on to your stock, there is no tax to pay on your gain. But if you sell, the 90 cents of capital gain is taxed.

Table 3.8 shows tax rates on investment income. For most investors, the effective tax rate is either 15% or 18.8% (15% plus a potential 3.8% surcharge), but the highest income investors pay an effective rate of 23.8%.

Financial managers need to worry about the tax treatment of investment income because tax policy will affect the prices individuals are willing to pay for the company's stock or bonds. We will return to these issues in Part 5 of the text.

The tax rates in Table 3.7 and Table 3.8 apply to individuals. But financial institutions are major investors in corporate securities. These institutions often have special tax provisions. For example, pension funds are not taxed on interest or dividend income or on capital gains.

TABLE 3.8 Tax rates on investment income* corresponding to 2016 tax brackets**

Taxable Income ($)		Tax Rate (%)
Single Taxpayers	**Married Taxpayers Filing Joint Returns**	
0–9,275	0–18,550	0
9,276–37,650	18,551–75,300	0
37,651–91,150	75,301–151,900	15
91,151–190,150	151,901–231,450	15
190,151–413,350	231,451–413,350	15
413,351–415,050	413,351–466,950	15
415,051 and above	466,951 and above	20

*These rates apply to capital gains and dividends on assets held for at least one year.

**In addition to these nominal rates, an additional 3.8% surtax is assessed on net investment income for taxpayers with total income over $200,000 (single filers) or $250,000 (married filing jointly).

SUMMARY

What information is contained in the balance sheet, income statement, and statement of cash flows? (*LO3-1*)

Investors and other stakeholders in the firm need regular financial information to help them monitor the firm's progress. Accountants summarize this information in a balance sheet, income statement, and statement of cash flows.

The **balance sheet** provides a snapshot of the firm's assets and liabilities. The assets consist of current assets that can be rapidly turned into cash and fixed assets such as plant and machinery. The liabilities consist of current liabilities that are due for payment within a year and long-term debts. The difference between the assets and the liabilities represents the amount of the shareholders' equity.

The **income statement** measures the profitability of the company during the year. It shows the difference between revenues and expenses.

The **statement of cash flows** measures the sources and uses of cash during the year. The change in the company's cash balance is the difference between sources and uses.

What is the difference between market and book values? (*LO3-2*)

It is important to distinguish between the book values that are shown in the company accounts and the market values of the assets and liabilities. **Book values** are historical measures based on the original cost of an asset. For example, the assets in the balance sheet are shown at their historical cost less an allowance for depreciation. Similarly, the figure for shareholders' equity measures the cash that shareholders have contributed in the past or that the company has reinvested on their behalf. In contrast, **market value** is the current price of an asset or liability.

Why does accounting income differ from cash flow? (*LO3-3*)

Income is not the same as cash flow. There are two reasons for this: (1) Investment in fixed assets is not deducted immediately from income but is instead spread (as charges for depreciation) over the expected life of the equipment, and (2) the accountant records revenues when the sale is made, rather than when the customer actually pays the bill, and at the same time deducts the production costs even though those costs may have been incurred earlier.

What are the essential features of the taxation of corporate and personal income? (*LO3-4*)

For large companies the **marginal rate of tax** on income is 35%. In calculating taxable income the company deducts an allowance for depreciation and interest payments. It cannot deduct dividend payments to the shareholders.

Individuals are also taxed on their income, which includes dividends and interest on their investments. Capital gains are taxed, but only when the investment is sold and the gain realized.

LISTING OF EQUATION

3.1   Shareholders' equity = net assets = total assets − total liabilities

QUESTIONS AND PROBLEMS

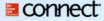

1. **Financial Statements.** Earlier in the chapter, we characterized the balance sheet as providing a snapshot of the firm at one point in time and the income statement as providing a video. What did we mean by this? Is the statement of cash flow more like a snapshot or a video? (*LO3-1*)

2. **Balance Sheet.** Balance sheet items are usually entered in order of declining liquidity. Place each of the terms below in the appropriate place in the following balance sheet. (*LO3-1*)

    Accounts payable   Total current assets
    Net fixed assets   Accounts receivable
    Debt due for repayment   Total current liabilities
    Cash and marketable securities Inventories
    Equity   Long-term debt

Assets	Liabilities and Equity
a.	f.
b.	g.
c.	h.
d.	i.
e.	j.
Total assets	Total liabilities and equity

3. **Balance Sheet.** Construct a balance sheet for Sophie's Sofas given the following data. What is shareholders' equity? (*LO3-1*)

Cash balances = $10,000

Inventory of sofas = $200,000

Store and property = $100,000

Accounts receivable = $22,000

Accounts payable = $17,000

Long-term debt = $170,000

4. **Income Statement.** A firm's income statement included the following data. The firm's average tax rate was 20%. (*LO3-1*)

Cost of goods sold	$8,000
Income taxes paid	$2,000
Administrative expenses	$3,000
Interest expense	$1,000
Depreciation	$1,000

a. What was the firm's net income?

b. What must have been the firm's revenues?

c. What was EBIT?

5. **Balance Sheet/Income Statement.** The year-end 2015 balance sheet of Brandex Inc. listed common stock and other paid-in capital at $1,100,000 and retained earnings at $3,400,000. The next year, retained earnings were listed at $3,700,000. The firm's net income in 2016 was $900,000. There were no stock repurchases during the year. What were the dividends paid by the firm in 2016? (*LO3-1*)

6. **Financial Statements.** South Sea Baubles has the following (incomplete) balance sheet and income statement. (*LO3-1, LO3-4*)

BALANCE SHEET AT END OF YEAR (Figures in $ millions)					
Assets	2015	2016	Liabilities and Shareholders' Equity	2015	2016
Current assets	$ 90	$140	Current liabilities	$ 50	$ 60
Net fixed assets	800	900	Long-term debt	600	750

INCOME STATEMENT, 2016 (Figures in $ millions)	
Revenue	$1,950
Cost of goods sold	1,030
Depreciation	350
Interest expense	240

a. What is shareholders' equity in 2015?

b. What is shareholders' equity in 2016?

c. What is net working capital in 2015?

d. What is net working capital in 2016?

e. What are taxes paid in 2016? Assume the firm pays taxes equal to 35% of taxable income.

f. What is cash provided by operations during 2016? Pay attention to changes in net working capital, using Table 3.4 as a guide.

g. Net fixed assets increased from $800 million to $900 million during 2016. What must have been South Sea's *gross* investment in fixed assets during 2016?

h. If South Sea reduced its outstanding accounts payable by $35 million during the year, what must have happened to its other current liabilities?

7. **Financial Statements.** Here are the 2015 and 2016 (incomplete) balance sheets for Newble Oil Corp. (*LO3-1*)

<table>
<tr><th colspan="7">BALANCE SHEET AT END OF YEAR
(Figures in $ millions)</th></tr>
<tr><th>Assets</th><th>2015</th><th>2016</th><th>Liabilities and Shareholders' Equity</th><th>2015</th><th>2016</th></tr>
<tr><td>Current assets</td><td>$ 310</td><td>$ 420</td><td>Current liabilities</td><td>$210</td><td>$240</td></tr>
<tr><td>Net fixed assets</td><td>1,200</td><td>1,420</td><td>Long-term debt</td><td>830</td><td>920</td></tr>
</table>

a. What was shareholders' equity at the end of 2015?

b. What was shareholders' equity at the end of 2016?

c. If Newble paid dividends of $100 in 2016 and made no stock issues, what must have been net income during the year?

d. If Newble purchased $300 in fixed assets during 2016, what must have been the depreciation charge on the income statement?

e. What was the change in net working capital between 2015 and 2016?

f. If Newble issued $200 of new long-term debt, how much debt must have been paid off during the year?

8. **Financial Statements.** Henry Josstick has just started his first accounting course and has prepared the following balance sheet and income statement for Omega Corp. Unfortunately, although the data for the individual items are correct, he is very confused as to whether an item should go in the balance sheet or income statement and whether it is an asset or liability. Help him by rearranging the items and filling in the blanks.

<table>
<tr><th colspan="4">BALANCE SHEET</th></tr>
<tr><td>Payables</td><td>$ 35</td><td>Inventories</td><td>$50</td></tr>
<tr><td>Less accumulated depreciation</td><td>120</td><td>Receivables</td><td>35</td></tr>
<tr><td>Total current assets</td><td>_____</td><td>Total current liabilities</td><td></td></tr>
<tr><td>Long-term debt</td><td>$350</td><td>Interest expense</td><td>$25</td></tr>
<tr><td>Property, plant, and equipment</td><td>520</td><td>Total liabilities</td><td></td></tr>
<tr><td>Net fixed assets</td><td>_____</td><td>Shareholders' equity</td><td>$90</td></tr>
<tr><td>Total assets</td><td>_____</td><td>Total liabilities and shareholders' equity</td><td>_____</td></tr>
</table>

<table>
<tr><th colspan="2">INCOME STATEMENT</th></tr>
<tr><td>Net sales</td><td>$700</td></tr>
<tr><td>Cost of goods sold</td><td>580</td></tr>
<tr><td>Selling, general, and administrative expenses</td><td>38</td></tr>
<tr><td>EBIT</td><td></td></tr>
<tr><td>Debt due for repayment</td><td>$ 25</td></tr>
<tr><td>Cash</td><td>15</td></tr>
<tr><td>Taxable income</td><td></td></tr>
<tr><td>Taxes</td><td>$ 15</td></tr>
<tr><td>Depreciation</td><td>12</td></tr>
<tr><td>Net income</td><td></td></tr>
</table>

What is the correct total for the following? (*LO3-1*)

a. Current assets

b. Net fixed assets

c. Total assets

    d. Current liabilities

    e. Total liabilities

    f. Total liabilities and shareholders' equity

    g. EBIT

    h. Taxable income

    i. Net income

9. **Market versus Book Values.** The founder of Alchemy Products Inc. discovered a way to turn gold into lead and patented this new technology. He then formed a corporation and invested $200,000 in setting up a production plant. He believes that he could sell his patent for $50 million. (*LO3-2*)

    a. What is the book value of the firm?

    b. What is the market value of the firm?

    c. If there are 2 million shares of stock in the new corporation, what is the book value per share?

    d. What is the price per share?

10. **Market versus Book Values.** State whether each of the following events would increase or decrease the ratio of market value to book value. (*LO3-2*)

    a. Big Oil announces the discovery of a major new oil field in Costaguana.

    b. Big Autos increases its depreciation provision.

    c. Since Big Stores purchased its assets, inflation has risen sharply.

11. **Market versus Book Values.** (*LO3-2*)

    a. In early 2015, the market values of the shares of many banks (e.g., Bank of America or Citigroup) were less than book value per share. How would you interpret this pattern?

    b. At the same time, Google's market value per share was more than four times its book value. Is this consistent with your analysis in part (a)?

12. **Income versus Cash Flow.** Explain why accounting income generally differs from a firm's cash inflows. (*LO3-3*)

13. **Cash Flows.** Will the following actions increase or decrease the firm's cash balance? (*LO3-3*)

    a. The firm sells some goods from inventory.

    b. The firm sells some machinery to a bank and leases it back for a period of 20 years.

    c. The firm buys back 1 million shares of stock from existing shareholders.

14. **Income versus Cash Flow.** Butterfly Tractors had $14 million in sales last year. Cost of goods sold was $8 million, depreciation expense was $2 million, interest payment on outstanding debt was $1 million, and the firm's tax rate was 35%. (*LO3-3*)

    a. What was the firm's net income?

    b. What was the firm's cash flow?

    c. What would happen to net income and cash flow if depreciation were increased by $1 million?

    d. Would you expect the change in depreciation to have a positive or negative impact on the firm's stock price?

    e. What would be the impact on net income if depreciation was $1 million and interest expense was $2 million?

    f. What would be the impact on cash flow if depreciation was $1 million and interest expense was $2 million?

15. **Working Capital.** QuickGrow is in an expanding market, and its sales are increasing by 25% per year. Would you expect its net working capital to be increasing or decreasing? (*LO3-3*)

16. **Income Statement.** Sheryl's Shipping had sales last year of $10,000. The cost of goods sold was $6,500, general and administrative expenses were $1,000, interest expenses were $500, and depreciation was $1,000. The firm's tax rate is 35%. (*LO3-3*)

    a. What are earnings before interest and taxes?

    b. What is net income?

    c. What is cash flow from operations?

17. **Income versus Cash Flow.** Start-up firms typically have negative net cash flows for several years. (*LO3-3*)

    a. Does this mean that they are failing?

    b. Accounting profits for these firms are also commonly negative. How would you interpret this pattern? Is there a shortcoming in our accounting rules?

18. **Income versus Cash Flow.** Can cash flow from operations be positive if net income is negative? Can it be negative if net income is positive? Give examples. (*LO3-3*)

19. **Income versus Cash Flow.** During the last year of operations, Theta's accounts receivable increased by $10,000, accounts payable increased by $5,000, and inventories decreased by $2,000. What is the total impact of these changes on the difference between profits and cash flow? (*LO3-3*)

20. **Income versus Cash Flow.** Candy Canes Inc. spends $100,000 to buy sugar and peppermint in April. It produces its candy and sells it to distributors in May for $150,000, but it does not receive payment until June. For each month, find the firm's sales, net income, and net cash flow, and fill in the following table. (*LO3-3*)

	Sales	Net Income	Cash Flow
April	a.	b.	c.
May	d.	e.	f.
June	g.	h.	i.

21. **Income versus Cash Flow.** Ponzi Products produced 100 chain-letter kits this quarter, resulting in a total cash outlay of $10 per unit. It will sell 50 of the kits next quarter at a price of $11, and the other 50 kits in the third quarter at a price of $12. It takes a full quarter for Ponzi to collect its bills from its customers. (Ignore possible sales in earlier or later quarters.) (*LO3-3*)

   a. What is the net income for Ponzi next quarter?
   b. What are the cash flows for the company this quarter?
   c. What are the cash flows for the company in the third quarter?
   d. What is Ponzi's net working capital in the next quarter?

22. **Income versus Cash Flow.** Value Added Inc. buys $1 million of sow's ears at the beginning of January but doesn't pay immediately. Instead, it agrees to pay the bill in March. It processes the ears into silk purses, which it sells for $2 million in February. However, it will not collect payment on the sales until April. (*LO3-3*)

   a. What is the firm's net income in February?
   b. What is its net income in March?
   c. What is the firm's net new investment in working capital in January?
   d. What is its net new investment in working capital in April?
   e. What is the firm's cash flow in January?
   f. What is the firm's cash flow in February?
   g. What is the cash flow in March?
   h. What is the cash flow in April?

23. **Free Cash Flow.** Free cash flow measures the cash available for distribution to debtholders and shareholders. Look at Section 3.3, where we calculate free cash flow for Home Depot. Show how this cash was distributed to investors. How much was used to build up cash reserves? (*LO3-3*)

24. **Free Cash Flow.** The following table shows an abbreviated income statement and balance sheet for Quick Burger Corporation for 2016.

INCOME STATEMENT OF QUICK BURGER CORP., 2016 (Figures in $ millions)	
Net sales	$27,567
Costs	17,569
Depreciation	1,402
Earnings before interest and taxes (EBIT)	$ 8,596
Interest expense	517
Pretax income	8,079
Taxes	2,614
Net income	$ 5,465

BALANCE SHEET OF QUICK BURGER CORP., 2016 (Figures in $ millions)					
Assets	**2016**	**2015**	**Liabilities and Shareholders' Equity**	**2016**	**2015**
Current assets			**Current liabilities**		
Cash and marketable securities	$ 2,336	$ 2,336	Debt due for repayment	—	$ 367
Receivables	1,375	1,335	Accounts payable	$ 3,403	3,143
Inventories	122	117	Total current liabilities	$ 3,403	$ 3,509
Other current assets	1,089	616			
Total current assets	$ 4,922	$ 4,403			
Fixed assets			Long-term debt	$13,633	$12,134
Property, plant, and equipment	$24,677	$22,835	Other long-term liabilities	3,057	2,957
Intangible assets (goodwill)	2,804	2,653	Total liabilities	$20,093	$18,600
Other long-term assets	2,983	3,099	Total shareholders' equity	15,294	14,390
Total assets	$35,387	$32,990	Total liabilities and shareholders' equity	$35,387	$32,990

In 2016 Quick Burger had capital expenditures of $3,049. (*LO3-3*)

a. Calculate Quick Burger's free cash flow in 2016.

b. If Quick Burger was financed entirely by equity, how much more tax would the company have paid? (Assume a tax rate of 35%.)

c. What would the company's free cash flow have been if it was all-equity financed?

25. **Tax Rates.** (*LO3-4*)

a. What would be the marginal tax rate for a married couple with income of $90,000?

b. What would be the average tax rate for a married couple with income of $90,000?

c. What would be the marginal tax rate for an unmarried taxpayer with income of $90,000?

d. What would be the average tax rate for an unmarried taxpayer with income of $90,000?

26. **Tax Rates.** Using Table 3.7, calculate the marginal and average tax rates for a single taxpayer with the following incomes: (*LO3-4*)

a. $20,000

b. $50,000

c. $300,000

d. $3,000,000

27. **Taxes.** A married couple earned $95,000 in 2016. How much did they pay in taxes? (*LO3-4*)

a. What was their marginal tax bracket?

b. What was their average tax bracket?

28. **Tax Rates.** What would be the marginal and average tax rates for a corporation with an income level of $100,000? (*LO3-4*)

29. **Tax Rates.** You have set up your tax preparation firm as an incorporated business. You took $70,000 from the firm as your salary. The firm's taxable income for the year (net of your salary) was $30,000. Assume you pay personal taxes as an unmarried taxpayer. (*LO3-4*)

a. How much tax must be paid to the federal government, including both your personal taxes and the firm's taxes? Use the tax rates presented in Tables 3.5 and 3.7.

b. By how much will you reduce the total tax bill if you cut your salary to $50,000, thereby leaving the firm with taxable income of $50,000?

c. What allocation will minimize the total tax bill? *Hint:* Think about marginal tax rates and the ability to shift income from a higher marginal bracket to a lower one.

30. **Tax Rates.** Turn back to Table 3.7, which shows marginal personal tax rates. Make a table in Excel that calculates taxes due for income levels ranging from $10,000 to $10 million. (*LO3-4*)

a. For each income, calculate the average tax rate of a single taxpayer. Plot the average tax rate as a function of income.

b. What happens to the difference between the average and top marginal tax rates as income becomes very large?

The table below contains data on Fincorp Inc. that you should use for Problems 31–38. The balance sheet items correspond to values at year-end 2015 and 2016, while the income statement items correspond to revenues or expenses during the year ending in either 2015 or 2016. All values are in thousands of dollars.

	2015	2016
Revenue	$4,000	$4,100
Cost of goods sold	1,600	1,700
Depreciation	500	520
Inventories	300	350
Administrative expenses	500	550
Interest expense	150	150
Federal and state taxes*	400	420
Accounts payable	300	350
Accounts receivable	400	450
Net fixed assets†	5,000	5,800
Long-term debt	2,000	2,400
Notes payable	1,000	600
Dividends paid	410	410
Cash and marketable securities	800	300

*Taxes are paid in their entirety in the year that the tax obligation is incurred.

†Net fixed assets are fixed assets net of accumulated depreciation since the asset was installed.

31. **Balance Sheet.** Construct a balance sheet for Fincorp for 2015 and 2016. What is shareholders' equity? (*LO3-1*)

32. **Working Capital.** What was the change in net working capital during the year? (*LO3-1*)

33. **Income Statement.** Construct an income statement for Fincorp for 2015 and 2016. What were reinvested earnings for 2016? (*LO3-1*)

34. **Earnings per Share.** Suppose that Fincorp has 500,000 shares outstanding. What were earnings per share? (*LO3-1*)

35. **Balance Sheet.** Examine the values for depreciation in 2016 and net fixed assets in 2015 and 2016. What was Fincorp's gross investment in plant and equipment during 2016? (*LO3-1*)

36. **Book versus Market Value.** Suppose that the market value (in thousands of dollars) of Fincorp's fixed assets in 2016 is $6,000 and that the value of its long-term debt is only $2,200. In addition, the consensus among investors is that Fincorp's past investments in developing the skills of its employees are worth $2,900. This investment of course does not show up on the balance sheet. What will be the price per share of Fincorp stock? (*LO3-2*)

37. **Income versus Cash Flows.** Construct a statement of cash flows for Fincorp for 2016. (*LO3-3*)

38. **Tax Rates.** (*LO3-4*)

    a. What was the firm's average tax bracket for each year?
    b. Do you have enough information to determine the marginal tax bracket?

WEB EXERCISES

1. Find Microsoft (MSFT) and Ford (F) on **finance.yahoo.com**, and examine the financial statements of each. Which firm uses more debt finance? Which firm has higher cash as a percentage of total assets? Which has higher EBIT per dollar of total assets? Which has higher profits per dollar of shareholders' equity?

2. Now choose two highly profitable technology firms, such as Intel (INTC) and Microsoft (MSFT), and two electric utilities, such as American Electric Power (AEP) and Duke Energy (DUK). Which firms have the higher ratio of market value to book value of equity? Does this

make sense to you? Which firms pay out a higher fraction of their profits as dividends to share-holders? Does this make sense?

3. Log on to the website of a large nonfinancial company and find its latest financial statements. Draw up a simplified balance sheet, income statement, and statement of cash flows as in Tables 3.1, 3.3, and 3.4. Some companies' financial statements can be extremely complex; try to find a relatively straightforward business. Also, as far as possible, use the same headings as in these tables, and don't hesitate to group some items as "other current assets," "other expenses," and so on. Look first at your simplified balance sheet. How much was the company owed by its cus-tomers in the form of unpaid bills? What liabilities does the company need to meet within a year? What was the original cost of the company's fixed assets? Now look at the income state-ment. What were the company's earnings before interest and taxes (EBIT)? Finally, turn to the cash-flow statement. Did changes in working capital add to cash or use it up?

4. The schedule of tax rates for individuals changes frequently. Check the latest schedules on either www.irs.gov or www.bankrate.com. What is your marginal tax rate if you are single with a taxable income of $70,000? What is your average tax rate?

SOLUTIONS TO SELF-TEST QUESTIONS

3.1 Cash and equivalents would increase by $100 million. Property, plant, and equipment would increase by $400 million. Long-term debt would increase by $500 million. Shareholders' equity would not increase: Assets and liabilities have increased equally, leaving shareholders' equity unchanged.

3.2 a. If the auto plant were worth $14 billion, the equity in the firm would be worth $14 − $4 = $10 billion. With 100 million shares outstanding, each share would be worth $100.
b. If the outstanding stock were worth $8 billion, we would infer that the market values the auto plant at $8 + $4 = $12 billion.

3.3 The profits for the firm are recognized in periods 2 and 3 when the sales take place. In both of those periods, profits are $150 − $100 = $50. Cash flows are derived as follows.

Period:	1	2	3	4
Sales	$ 0	$150	$150	$ 0
− Change in accounts receivable	0	150	0	− 150
− Cost of goods sold	0	100	100	0
− Change in inventories	− 200	−100	− 100	0
= Net cash flow	−$200	$ 0	+$150	+$150

In period 2, half the units are sold for $150 but no cash is collected, so the entire $150 is treated as an increase in accounts receivable. Half the $200 cost of production is recognized, and a like amount is taken out of inventory. In period 3, the firm sells another $150 of product but collects $150 from its previous sales, so there is no change in outstanding accounts receivable. Net cash flow is the $150 collected in this period on the sale that occurred in period 2. In period 4, cash flow is again $150, as the accounts receivable from the sale in period 3 are collected.

3.4 a. An increase in inventories uses cash, reducing the firm's net cash balance.
b. A reduction in accounts payable uses cash, reducing the firm's net cash balance.
c. An issue of common stock is a source of cash.
d. The purchase of new equipment is a use of cash, and it reduces the firm's net cash balance.

3.5

	Firm A	Firm B
EBIT	100	100
Interest	60	0
Pretax income	40	100
Tax (35% of pretax income)	14	35
Net income	26	65

Note: Figures in millions of dollars.

Taxes owed by firm A fall from $21 million to $14 million. The reduction in taxes is 35% of the extra $20 million of interest income. Net income does not fall by the full $20 million of extra interest expense. It instead falls by interest expense less the reduction in taxes, or $20 million − $7 million = $13 million.

3.6   For a single taxpayer with taxable income of $80,000, total taxes paid are

$$(.10 \times 9{,}275) + [.15 \times (37{,}650 - 9{,}275)] + [.25 \times (80{,}000 - 37{,}650)] \ = \ \$15{,}771.25$$

The marginal tax rate is 25%, but the average tax rate is only 15,771.25/80,000 = .197, or 19.7%. For the married taxpayers filing jointly with taxable income of $80,000, total taxes paid are

$$(.10 \times 18{,}550) + [.15 \times (75{,}300 - 18{,}550)] + [.25 \times (80{,}000 - 75{,}300)] \ = \ \$11{,}542.50$$

The marginal tax rate is 25%, and the average tax rate is 11,542.50/80,000 = .144, or 14.4%.

4

Measuring Corporate Performance

LEARNING OBJECTIVES

After studying this chapter, you should be able to:

4-1   Calculate and interpret the market value and market value added of a public corporation.

4-2   Calculate and interpret key measures of financial performance, including economic value added (EVA) and rates of return on capital, assets, and equity.

4-3   Calculate and interpret key measures of operating efficiency, leverage, and liquidity.

4-4   Show how profitability depends on the efficient use of assets and on profits as a fraction of sales.

4-5   Compare a company's financial standing with that of its competitors and its own position in previous years.

RELATED WEBSITES FOR THIS CHAPTER CAN BE FOUND IN CONNECT.

When managers need to judge a firm's performance, they start with some key financial ratios. © *Wavebreakmedia Ltd UC4/ Alamy RF*

In Chapter 1 we introduced the basic objective of corporate finance: Maximize the current *value* of shareholders' investment in the firm. For public corporations, this value is set in the stock market. It equals market price per share multiplied by the number of shares outstanding. Of course, the fluctuations in market value partly reflect events that are outside the manager's control. Nevertheless, good managers always strive to *add value* by superior investment and financing decisions.

How can we judge whether managers are doing a good job at adding value or where there may be scope for improvement? We need measures of value added. We also need measures that help explain where the value added comes from. For example, value added depends on profitability, so we need measures of profitability. Profitability depends in turn on profit margins and on how efficiently the firm uses its assets. We will describe the standard measures of profitability and efficiency in this chapter.

Value also depends on sound financing. Value is destroyed if the firm is financed recklessly and can't pay its debts. Value is also destroyed if the firm does not maintain adequate liquidity and therefore has difficulty finding the cash to pay its bills. Therefore, we will describe the measures that financial managers and investors use to assess debt policy and liquidity.

These financial measures are mostly *financial ratios* calculated from the firm's income statement and balance sheet. Therefore, we will have to take care to remember the limitations of these accounting data.

You have probably heard stories of whizzes who can take a company's accounts apart in minutes, calculate a list of financial ratios, and divine the company's future. Such people are like abominable snowmen: often spoken of but never truly seen. Financial ratios are no substitute for a crystal ball. They are just a convenient way to summarize financial data and to assess and compare financial performance. The ratios help you to ask the right questions, but they seldom answer them.

4.1   How Financial Ratios Relate to Shareholder Value

The good news about financial ratios is that they are usually easy to calculate. The bad news is that there are so many of them. To make it worse, the ratios are often presented in long lists that seem to require memorization first and understanding maybe later.

We can mitigate the bad news by taking a moment to preview what the ratios are measuring and how the ratios connect to the ultimate objective of value added for shareholders.

Shareholder value depends on good investment decisions. The financial manager evaluates investment decisions by asking several questions, including: How profitable are the investments relative to the cost of capital? How should profitability be measured? What does profitability depend on? (We will see that it depends on efficient use of assets and on the bottom-line profits on each dollar of sales.)

Shareholder value also depends on good financing decisions. Again, there are obvious questions: Is the available financing sufficient? The firm cannot grow unless financing is available. Is the financing strategy prudent? The financial manager should not put the firm's assets and operations at risk by operating at a dangerously high debt ratio, for example. Does the firm have sufficient liquidity (a cushion of cash or assets that can be readily sold for cash)? The firm has to be able to pay its bills and respond to unexpected setbacks.

Figure 4.1 summarizes these questions in somewhat more detail. The boxes on the left are for investment, the boxes on the right for financing. In each box, we have posed a question and, where appropriate, given examples of financial ratios or other measures that the financial manager can use to answer the question. For example, the bottom box on the far left of Figure 4.1 asks about efficient use of assets. Three financial ratios that measure asset efficiency are turnover ratios for assets, inventory, and accounts receivable.

The two bottom boxes on the right ask whether financial leverage (the amount of debt financing) is prudent and whether the firm has enough liquidity for the coming year. The ratios for tracking financial leverage include debt ratios, such as the ratio of debt to equity, and interest coverage ratios. The ratios for liquidity are the current, quick, and cash ratios.

FIGURE 4.1 An organization chart for financial ratios. The figure shows how common financial ratios and other measures relate to shareholder value.

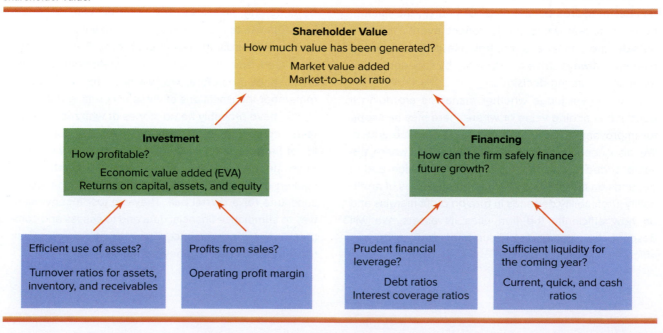

We will explain how to calculate and interpret these and the other ratios in Figure 4.1. For now you can read the figure as an organization chart that locates some important financial ratios and shows how they relate to the objective of shareholder value.

Now we start at the top of the figure. Our first task is to measure value. We will explain market capitalization, market value added, and the market-to-book ratio.

4.2 Measuring Market Value and Market Value Added

Twenty years have passed since your introductory finance class. You are well into your career, and Home Depot is on your mind. Perhaps you are a mutual fund manager trying to decide whether to allocate $25 million of new money to Home Depot stock. Perhaps you are a major shareholder pondering a sellout. You could be an investment banker seeking business from Home Depot or a bondholder concerned with Home Depot's credit standing. You could be the treasurer or CFO of Home Depot or of one of its competitors. You want to understand Home Depot's value and financial performance. How would you start?

market capitalization
Total market value of equity, equal to share price times number of shares outstanding.

Home Depot's common stock closed fiscal 2014 at a price of $114.75 per share. There were 1,307 million shares outstanding, so Home Depot's **market capitalization** or "market cap" was $114.75 × 1,307 = $149,978 million, or nearly $150 billion. This is a big number, of course, but Home Depot is a big company. Home Depot's shareholders have, over the years, invested billions in the company. Therefore, you decide to compare Home Depot's market capitalization with the book value of Home Depot's equity. The book value measures shareholders' cumulative investment in the firm.

market value added
Market capitalization minus book value of equity.

You turn to Home Depot's income statement and balance sheet, which are reproduced in Tables 4.1 and 4.2.[1] At the end of 2014, the book value of Home Depot's equity was $9,322 million. Therefore, Home Depot's **market value added,** the difference between the market value of the firm's shares and the amount of money that shareholders have invested in the firm, was $149,978 − $9,322 = $140,656 million. In other words, Home Depot shareholders have contributed about $9.3 billion and ended up with shares worth almost $150 billion. They have accumulated $140.7 billion in market value added.

TABLE 4.1 Income statement for Home Depot, fiscal 2014

	$ Millions
Net sales	$83,176
Other income	337
Cost of goods sold	54,222
Selling, general, and administrative expenses	16,699
Depreciation	1,786
Earnings before interest and income taxes (EBIT)	$10,806
Interest expense	830
Taxable income	$ 9,976
Taxes	3,631
Net income	$ 6,345
Allocation of net income	
Dividends	$ 2,530
Addition to retained earnings	$ 3,815

---
[1] For convenience the statements are repeated from Chapter 3. We are pretending that you actually had these statements on February 3, 2015, the close of Home Depot's fiscal year. They were not published until March.

TABLE 4.2 Home Depot's balance sheet (figures in $ millions)

Assets	End of Fiscal 2014	End of Fiscal 2013	Liabilities and Shareholders' Equity	End of Fiscal 2014	End of Fiscal 2013
Current assets					
Cash and marketable securities	$ 1,723	$ 1,929	Current liabilities		
Receivables	1,484	1,398	Debt due for repayment	$ 328	$ 33
Inventories	11,079	11,057	Accounts payable	9,473	9,379
Other current assets	1,016	895	Other current liabilities	1,468	1,337
Total current assets	$15,302	$15,279	Total current liabilities	$11,269	$10,749
Fixed assets			Long-term debt	$16,869	$14,691
Tangible fixed assets			Deferred income taxes	642	514
Property, plant, and equipment	$40,353	$39,064	Other long-term liabilities	1,844	2,042
Less accumulated depreciation	17,633	15,716			
Net tangible fixed assets	$22,720	$23,348	Total liabilities	$30,624	$27,996
Intangible assets (goodwill)	1,353	1,289	Shareholders' equity		
Other assets	571	602	Common stock and other paid-in capital	$ 8,521	$ 8,536
			Retained earnings	26,995	23,180
Total assets	$39,946	$40,518	Treasury stock	(26,194)	(19,194)
			Total shareholders' equity	$ 9,322	$12,522
			Total liabilities and shareholders' equity	$39,946	$40,518

Note: Column sums subject to rounding error.

The consultancy firm EVA Dimensions calculates market value added for a large sample of U.S. companies. Table 4.3 shows a few of the firms from EVA's list. They include some of the most and least successful companies. Apple heads the group. It has created $627.6 billion of wealth for its shareholders. Bank of America languishes near the bottom: The market value of its shares is $118 billion *less* than the amount of shareholders' money invested in the firm.

The top-listed companies in Table 4.3 are large firms. Their managers have lots of assets to work with. A small firm could not hope to create so much extra value. Therefore, financial managers and analysts also like to calculate how much value has been added *for each dollar that shareholders have invested*. To do this, they compute the *ratio* of market value to book value. For example, Home Depot's **market-to-book ratio** in early 2015 (at the end of its 2014 fiscal year) was[2]

market-to-book ratio
Ratio of market value of equity to book value of equity.

$$\text{Market-to-book ratio} = \frac{\text{market value of equity}}{\text{book value of equity}} = \frac{\$149,978}{\$9,322} = 16.1$$

TABLE 4.3 Stock market measures of company performance, February 2015. Companies are ranked by market value added (dollar values in millions).

	Market Value Added	Market-to-Book Ratio
Apple	$627,589	6.41
Microsoft	242,343	2.55
Walmart	185,339	3.99
ExxonMobil	171,465	2.30
Coca-Cola	150,102	5.95
Delta Airlines	2,850	1.41
Time Warner	75	1.02
Alcoa	−7,772	0.93
Sprint	−42,682	0.87
Bank of America	−118,151	0.60

Source: We are grateful to EVA Dimensions for providing these statistics.

[2] The market-to-book ratio can also be calculated by dividing stock price by book value per share.

In other words, Home Depot has multiplied the value of its shareholders' investment 16.1 times.

Table 4.3 shows a sample of market-to-book ratios for 2014. Notice that Coca-Cola has a much higher market-to-book ratio than ExxonMobil. But Exxon's market value added is higher because of its larger scale.

4.1   Self-Test

Shares of Notung Cutlery Corp. closed 2015 at $75 per share. Notung had 14.5 million shares outstanding. The book value of equity was $610 million. Compute Notung's market capitalization, market value added, and market-to-book ratio.

The market-value performance measures in Table 4.3 have three drawbacks. First, the market value of the company's shares reflects investors' expectations about *future* performance. Investors pay attention to current profits and investment, of course, but they also avidly forecast investment and growth. Second, market values fluctuate because of many risks and events that are outside the financial manager's control. Thus, market values are noisy measures of how well the corporation's management is performing. Third, you can't look up the market value of privately owned companies whose shares are not traded. Nor can you observe the market value of divisions or plants that are parts of larger companies. You may use market values to satisfy yourself that Home Depot as a whole has performed well, but you can't use them to drill down to compare the performance of the lumber and home improvement divisions. To do this, you need accounting measures of profitability. We start with economic value added (EVA).

4.3   Economic Value Added and Accounting Rates of Return

When accountants draw up an income statement, they start with revenues and then deduct operating and other costs. But one important cost is *not* included: the cost of the capital the firm employs. Therefore, to see whether the firm has truly created value, we need to measure whether it has earned a profit after deducting *all* costs, including the cost of its capital.

Recall from Chapters 1 and 2 that the cost of capital is the minimum acceptable rate of return on capital investment. It is an *opportunity* cost of capital because it equals the expected rate of return on opportunities open to investors in financial markets. The firm creates value only if it can earn more than its cost of capital, that is, more than its investors can earn by investing on their own.

economic value added (EVA)
Net income minus a charge for the cost of capital employed. Also called *residual income.*

The profit after deducting all costs, *including the cost of capital,* is called the company's **economic value added** or **EVA.** The term "EVA" was coined by Stern Stewart & Co., which did much to develop and promote the concept. EVA is also called *residual income.*

In calculating EVA, it's customary to take account of all the long-term capital contributed by investors in the corporation. That means including bonds and other long-term debt as well as equity capital. Total long-term capital, usually called *total capitalization,* is the sum of long-term debt and shareholders' equity.

Home Depot entered fiscal 2014 with a total capitalization of $27,213 million, which was made up of $14,691 million of long-term debt and $12,522 million of shareholders' equity. This was the cumulative amount that had been invested by Home Depot's debt and equity investors. Home Depot's cost of capital was about 9%.[3] So we can convert the cost of capital into dollars by multiplying total capitalization by 9%: .09 × $27,213 million = $2,449.2 million. To satisfy its debt and equity investors, Home Depot needed to earn total income of $2,449.2 million.

Now we can compare this figure with the income that Home Depot actually generated for its debt and equity investors. In 2014, debt investors received interest income of $830 million. The after-tax equivalent, using Home Depot's 35% tax rate, is (1 − .35) × 830 = $539.5 million.[4] Net income to shareholders was $6,345 million. Therefore, Home Depot's after-tax interest and net income totaled 539.5 + 6,345 = $6,884.5 million. If you deduct the dollar cost of capital from this figure, you can see that the company earned 6,884.5 − 2,449.2 = $4,435.3 million *more* than investors required. This was Home Depot's EVA or residual income:

$$\text{EVA} = \text{after-tax interest} + \text{net income} - (\text{cost of capital} \times \text{total capitalization})$$
$$= 539.5 + 6,345 - 2,449.2 = \$4,435.3 \text{ million}$$

The sum of Home Depot's net income and after-tax interest is its after-tax *operating income.* This is what Home Depot would earn if it had no debt and could not take interest as a tax-deductible expense. After-tax operating income is what the company would earn if it were all-equity-financed. In that case it would have no (after-tax) interest expense and all operating income would go to shareholders.

Thus EVA also equals:

$$\text{EVA} = \text{after-tax operating income} - (\text{cost of capital} \times \text{total capitalization})$$
$$= 6,884.5 - 2,449.2 = \$4,435.3 \text{ million}$$

Of course Home Depot and its competitors do use debt financing. Nevertheless, EVA comparisons are more useful if focused on operating income, which is not affected by interest tax deductions.

Table 4.4 shows estimates of EVA for our sample of large companies. Apple again heads the list. It earned $30.3 billion more than was needed to cover its cost of capital. By contrast, Bank of America was a laggard. Although it earned an accounting profit of $13.7 billion, this figure was calculated *before* deducting the cost of capital. *After* deducting the cost of capital, the company made an EVA loss of $7.5 billion.

Notice how the cost of capital differs across the 10 firms in Table 4.4. The variation is due to differences in business risk. Relatively safe companies like Walmart and Coca-Cola tend to have low costs of capital. Riskier companies like Apple and Microsoft have high costs of capital.

EVA, or residual income, is a better measure of a company's performance than is accounting income. Accounting income is calculated after deducting all costs *except* the cost of capital. By contrast, EVA recognizes that companies need to cover their opportunity costs before they add value.

---

[3] This is an after-tax weighted-average cost of capital, or WACC. A company's WACC depends on the risk of its business. The WACC is almost the same as the opportunity cost of capital, but with the cost of debt calculated after tax. We will explain WACC and how to calculate it in Chapter 13.

[4] Why do we take interest after tax? Remember from Chapter 3 that when a firm pays interest, it reduces its taxable income and therefore its tax bill. This tax saving, or *tax shield,* will vary across firms depending on the amounts of debt financing. But we want to focus here on operating results. To put all firms on a common basis, we subtract the interest tax shield from reported income, or, equivalently, we look at after-tax interest payments. By ignoring the tax shield, we calculate each firm's income as if it had no debt outstanding and shareholders got the (after-tax) interest. To be consistent, the cost of capital is defined as an after-tax weighted-average cost of capital (WACC). We have more to say about these issues in Chapters 13 and 16.

TABLE 4.4 EVA and ROC, 2015. Companies are ranked by EVA (dollar values in millions).

	1. After-Tax Interest + Net Income	2. Cost of Capital (WACC) (%)	3. Total Long-Term Capital	4. EVA = 1 − (2 × 3)	5. Return on Capital (ROC) (%) = 1 ÷ 3
Apple	$43,337	9.14%	$142,657	$30,298	30.4%
Microsoft	22,738	8.66	48,992	18,495	46.4
Walmart	17,194	5.26	154,846	9,049	11.1
ExxonMobil	39,467	6.77	301,902	19,028	13.1
Coca-Cola	8,671	5.28	59,742	5,517	14.5
Alcoa	1,340	8.36	30,463	−1,207	4.4
Delta Airlines	1,509	7.39	49,253	−2,131	3.1
Time Warner	4,313	6.76	112,137	−3,267	3.8
Sprint	1,269	6.54	122,304	−6,730	1.0
Bank of America	13,692	7.50	283,138	−7,543	4.8

Source: We are grateful to EVA Dimensions for providing these statistics.

EVA makes the cost of capital *visible* to operating managers. There is a clear target: Earn *at least* the cost of capital on assets employed. A plant or divisional manager can improve EVA by reducing assets that aren't making an adequate contribution to profits. Evaluating performance by EVA pushes managers to flush out and dispose of such underutilized assets. Therefore, a growing number of firms now calculate EVA and tie managers' compensation to it.

4.2 Self-Test

> Roman Holidays Inc. had operating income of $30 million on a start-of-year total capitalization of $188 million. Its cost of capital was 11.5%. What was its EVA?

Accounting Rates of Return

EVA measures how many dollars a business is earning after deducting the cost of capital. Other things equal, the more assets the manager has to work with, the greater the opportunity to generate a large EVA. The manager of a small division may be highly competent, but if that division has few assets, she is unlikely to rank high in the EVA stakes. Therefore, when comparing managers, it can be helpful to measure the firm's profits *per dollar of assets*. Three common measures are the return on capital (ROC), the return on equity (ROE), and the return on assets (ROA). These are called *book rates of return,* because they are based on accounting information.

return on capital (ROC)
Net income plus after-tax interest as a percentage of long-term capital.

Return on Capital (ROC)   The return on capital is equal to after-tax operating income divided by total capitalization. In 2014, Home Depot's operating income was $6,885 million. It started the year with total capitalization (long-term debt plus shareholders' equity) of $27,213 million. Therefore, its **return on capital (ROC)** was[5]

$$\text{ROC} = \frac{\text{after tax operating income}}{\text{total capitalization}} = \frac{6,885}{27,213} = .253, \text{ or } 25.3\%$$

---

[5] The numerator of Home Depot's ROC is again its after-tax operating income, calculated by adding back after-tax interest to net income. More often than not, financial analysts forget that interest is tax-deductible and use pretax interest to calculate operating income. This complicates comparisons of ROC for companies that use different fractions of debt financing. It also muddies comparisons of ROC with the after-tax weighted-average cost of capital (WACC). We cover WACC in Chapter 13.

BEYOND THE PAGE

 Average or start-of-year assets

mhhe.com/brealey9e

As we noted earlier, Home Depot's cost of capital was about 9%. This was the return that investors could have expected to earn at the start of 2014 if they invested their money in other companies or securities with the same risk as Home Depot's business. So in 2014 the company earned $25.3 − 9.0 = 16.3\%$ more than investors required.

When we calculated ROC, we compared a flow measure (income earned over the year) with a snapshot measure (capital at the start of the year). We therefore ignored the company's additional financing and investment during that year. If the additional investment contributed a significant part of the year's operating income, it may be better to divide by the average of the total capitalization at the beginning and end of the year. In the case of Home Depot, the company increased long-term debt in 2014 and repurchased some of its stock. So it actually ended the year with less capital than it had at the start. Therefore, if we divide operating income by average capitalization, Home Depot's ROC for 2014 increases slightly to

$$\text{ROC} = \frac{\text{after-tax operating income}}{\text{average total capitalization}} = \frac{6,885}{(26,191 + 27,213)/2} = .258, \text{ or } 25.8\%$$

Is one measure better than another? It is difficult to generalize, but if you would like to know more about *when* one might prefer to use average rather than start-of-year figures to calculate a financial ratio, the icon in the margin provides a link to a short discussion of the issue.[6]

The last column in Table 4.4 shows ROC for our sample of well-known companies. Notice that Microsoft's return on capital was 46.4%, over 37 percentage points above its cost of capital. Although Microsoft had a higher return on capital than ExxonMobil, it had a lower EVA. This was partly because it was riskier than Exxon and so had a higher cost of capital, but also because it had far fewer dollars invested than Exxon.

The five companies in Table 4.4 with negative EVAs all have ROCs less than their cost of capital. The spread between ROC and the cost of capital is really the same thing as EVA but expressed as a percentage return rather than in dollars.

return on assets (ROA)
Net income plus after-tax interest as a percentage of total assets.

Return on Assets (ROA)   **Return on assets (ROA)** measures after-tax operating income as a fraction of the firm's *total* assets. Total assets (which equal total liabilities plus shareholders' equity) are greater than total capitalization because total capitalization does not include current liabilities. For Home Depot, ROA was

$$\text{Return on assets} = \frac{\text{after-tax operating income}}{\text{total assets}} = \frac{6,885}{40,518} = .170 \text{ or } 17.0\%$$

Using average total assets, ROA was slightly higher:

$$\text{ROA} = \frac{\text{after-tax operating income}}{\text{average total assets}} = \frac{6,885}{(39,946 + 40,518)/2} = .171, \text{ or } 17.1\%$$

For both ROA and ROC, we use after-tax operating income, which is calculated by adding after-tax interest to net income. We are again asking how profitable the company would have been if it were all-equity-financed. This what-if calculation is helpful when comparing the profitability of firms with different capital structures. The tax deduction for interest is often ignored, however, and operating income is calculated using pretax interest. Some financial analysts take *no* account of interest payments and measure ROA as net income for shareholders divided by total assets. This calculation is *really*—we were about to say "stupid," but don't want to offend anyone. The calculation ignores entirely the income that the firm's assets have generated for debt investors.

---

[6] Sometimes it's convenient to use a snapshot figure at the end of the year, although this procedure is not strictly correct.

4.3 Self-Test

What is the difference between after-tax operating income and net income to shareholders? How is after-tax operating income calculated? Why is it useful in calculating EVA, ROC, and ROA?

return on equity (ROE)
Net income as a percentage of shareholders' equity.

Return on Equity (ROE)   We measure the **return on equity (ROE)** as the income to shareholders per dollar that they have invested. Home Depot had net income of $6,345 million in fiscal 2014 and shareholders' equity of $12,522 million at the start of the year. So Home Depot's ROE was

$$\text{Return on equity} = \text{ROE} = \frac{\text{net income}}{\text{equity}} = \frac{6,345}{12,522} = .507, \text{ or } 50.7\%$$

Using average equity, ROE was

$$\text{ROE} = \frac{\text{net income}}{\text{average equity}} = \frac{6,345}{(9,322 + 12,522)/2} = .581, \text{ or } 58.1\%$$

4.4 Self-Test

Explain the *differences* among ROE, ROC, and ROA.

Problems with EVA and Accounting Rates of Return

Rates of return and economic value added have some obvious attractions as measures of performance. Unlike market-value-based measures, they show current performance and are not affected by all the other things that move stock market prices. Also, they can be calculated for an entire company or for a particular plant or division. However, remember that both EVA and accounting rates of return are based on book (balance sheet) values for assets. Debt and equity are also book values. As we noted in the previous chapter, accountants do not show every asset on the balance sheet, yet our calculations take accounting data at face value. For example, we ignored the fact that Home Depot has invested large sums in marketing in order to establish its brand name. This brand name is an important asset, but its value is not shown on the balance sheet. If it were shown, the book values of assets, capital, and equity would increase, and Home Depot would not appear to earn such high returns.

EVA Dimensions, which produced the figures in Tables 4.3 and 4.4, does make a number of adjustments to the accounting data. However, it is impossible to include the value of all assets or to judge how rapidly they depreciate. For example, did Microsoft really earn a return on capital of 46.4%? It's difficult to say because its investment over the years in operating systems and other software is not shown in the balance sheet and cannot be measured exactly.

Remember also that the balance sheet does not show the current market values of the firm's assets. The assets in a company's books are valued at their original cost less any depreciation. Older assets may be grossly undervalued in today's market conditions and prices. So a high return on assets indicates that the business has performed well by making profitable investments in the past, but it does not necessarily mean that you could buy the same assets today at their reported book values. Conversely, a low return suggests some poor decisions in the past, but it does not always mean that today the assets could be employed better elsewhere.

4.4 Measuring Efficiency

We began our analysis of Home Depot by calculating how much value that company has added for its shareholders and how much profit the company is earning after deducting the cost of the capital that it employs. We examined its rates of return on equity, capital, and total assets, which were all impressively high. Our next task is to probe a little deeper to understand the reasons for Home Depot's success. What factors contribute to this firm's overall profitability? One is the efficiency with which it uses its various assets.

Asset Turnover Ratio   The asset turnover, or sales-to-assets, ratio shows how much sales are generated by each dollar of total assets, and therefore it measures how hard the firm's assets are working. For Home Depot, each dollar of assets produced $2.05 of sales:

$$\text{Asset turnover} = \frac{\text{sales}}{\text{total assets at start of year}} = \frac{83{,}176}{40{,}518} = 2.05$$

Like some of our profitability ratios, the sales-to-assets ratio compares a flow measure (sales over the entire year) to a snapshot measure (assets on one day). Therefore, financial managers and analysts often calculate the ratio of sales over the entire year to the *average* level of assets over the same period. In this case, the value is about the same:

$$\text{Asset turnover} = \frac{\text{sales}}{\text{average total assets}} = \frac{83{,}176}{(39{,}946 + 40{,}518)/2} = 2.07$$

The asset turnover ratio measures how efficiently the business is using its entire asset base. But you also might be interested in how hard *particular types* of assets are being put to use. A couple of examples are provided next.

Inventory Turnover   Efficient firms don't tie up more capital than they need in raw materials and finished goods. They hold only a relatively small level of inventories of raw materials and finished goods, and they turn over those inventories rapidly.

The balance sheet shows the cost of inventories rather than the amount that the finished goods will eventually sell for. So it is usual to compare the level of inventories with the cost of goods sold rather than with sales. In Home Depot's case,

$$\text{Inventory turnover} = \frac{\text{cost of good sold}}{\text{inventory at start of year}} = \frac{54{,}222}{11{,}057} = 4.9$$

Another way to express this measure is to look at how many days of output are represented by inventories. This is equal to the level of inventories divided by the daily cost of goods sold:

$$\text{Average days in inventory} = \frac{\text{inventory at start of year}}{\text{daily cost of good sold}} = \frac{11{,}057}{54{,}222/365} = 74 \text{ days}$$

You could say that on average Home Depot has sufficient inventories to maintain operations for 74 days.

In Chapter 20 we will see that many firms have managed to increase their inventory turnover in recent years. Toyota has been the pioneer in this endeavor. Its *just-in-time* inventory system ensures that auto parts are delivered exactly when they are needed. Toyota now keeps only about one month's supply of parts and finished cars in inventory and turns over its inventory about 11 times a year.

Receivables Turnover   Receivables are sales for which you have not yet been paid. The receivables turnover ratio measures the firm's sales as a multiple of its receivables. For Home Depot,

$$\text{Receivables turnover} = \frac{\text{sales}}{\text{receivables at start of year}} = \frac{83{,}176}{1{,}398} = 59.5$$

If customers are quick to pay, unpaid bills will be a relatively small proportion of sales and the receivables turnover will be high. Therefore, a high ratio often indicates an efficient credit department that is quick to follow up on late payers. Sometimes, however, a high ratio may indicate that the firm has an unduly restrictive credit policy and offers credit only to customers who can be relied on to pay promptly.[7]

Another way to measure the efficiency of the credit operation is by calculating the average length of time for customers to pay their bills. The faster the firm turns over its receivables, the shorter the collection period. On average, Home Depot's customers pay their bills in about 6.1 days:

$$\text{Average collection period} = \frac{\text{receivables at start of year}}{\text{average daily sales}} = \frac{1,398}{83,176/365} = 6.1 \text{ days}$$

4.5   Self-Test

The average collection period measures the number of days it takes Home Depot to collect its bills. But Home Depot also delays paying its own bills. Use the information in Tables 4.1 and 4.2 to calculate the average number of days that it takes Home Depot to pay its bills. [Like days in inventory, payment delay should be calculated using only direct cost of goods sold—these do not include indirect costs (i.e., selling, general, and administrative).]

The receivables turnover ratio and the inventory turnover ratio may help to highlight particular areas of inefficiency, but they are not the only possible indicators. For example, a retail chain might compare its sales per square foot with those of its competitors, an airline might look at revenues per passenger-mile, and a law firm might look at revenues per partner. A little thought and common sense should suggest which measures are likely to produce the most helpful insights into your company's efficiency.

4.5   Analyzing the Return on Assets: The Du Pont System

We have seen that every dollar of Home Depot's assets generates $2.05 of sales. But Home Depot's success depends not only on the efficiency with which it uses its assets to generate sales but also on how profitable those sales are. This is measured by Home Depot's profit margin.

Profit Margin   The profit margin measures the proportion of sales that finds its way into profits. It is sometimes defined as

$$\text{Profit margin} = \frac{\text{net income}}{\text{sales}} = \frac{6,345}{83,176} = .076, \text{ or } 7.6\%$$

This definition can be misleading. When companies are partly financed by debt, a portion of the revenue produced by sales must be paid as interest to the firm's lenders. So profits from the firm's operations are divided between the debtholders and the shareholders. We would not want to say that a firm is less profitable than its rivals simply because it employs debt finance and pays out part of its income as interest. Therefore, when we are calculating the profit margin, it makes sense to add back the

---

[7] Where possible, it makes sense to look only at *credit* sales. Otherwise, a high receivables turnover ratio (or, equivalently, a low average collection period) might simply indicate that a small proportion of sales are made on credit. For example, if a retail customer pays cash for a purchase at Home Depot, that transaction will have a collection period of zero, regardless of any policies of the firm's credit department.

operating profit margin
After-tax operating income
as a percentage of sales.

after-tax debt interest to net income. This leads us again to after-tax operating income and to the **operating profit margin:**

$$\text{Operating profit margin} = \frac{\text{after-tax operating income}}{\text{sales}}$$

$$= \frac{6{,}345 + (1 - .35) \times 830}{83{,}176} = .083, \text{ or } 8.3\%$$

The Du Pont System

We calculated earlier that Home Depot has earned a return of 17.0% on its assets. The following equation shows that this return depends on two factors—the sales that Home Depot generates from its assets (asset turnover) and the profit that it earns on each dollar of sales (operating profit margin):

$$\text{Return on assets} = \frac{\text{after-tax operating income}}{\text{assets}} \tag{4.1}$$

$$= \frac{\text{sales}}{\text{assets}} \times \frac{\text{after-tax operating income}}{\text{sales}}$$

$$\underset{\text{asset turnover}}{\uparrow} \qquad \underset{\substack{\text{operating} \\ \text{profit margin}}}{\uparrow}$$

Du Pont formula
ROA equals the product of
asset turnover and
operating profit margin.

This breakdown of ROA into the product of turnover and margin is often called the **Du Pont formula,** after the chemical company that popularized the procedure. In Home Depot's case, the formula gives the following breakdown of ROA:

$$\text{ROA} = \text{asset turnover} \times \text{operating profit margin}$$
$$= 2.05 \times .0803 = .170$$

The Du Pont formula is a useful way to think about a company's strategy. For example, a retailer may strive for high turnover at the expense of a low profit margin (a "Walmart strategy"), or it may seek a high profit margin even if that results in low turnover (a "Bloomingdales strategy"). You would naturally prefer both high profit margin and high turnover, but life isn't that easy. A high-price and high-margin strategy will typically result in lower sales per dollar of assets, so firms must make trade-offs between these goals. The Du Pont formula can help sort out which strategy the firm is pursuing.

All firms would like to earn a higher return on their assets, but their ability to do so is limited by competition. The Du Pont formula helps to identify the constraints that firms face. Fast-food chains, which have high asset turnover, tend to operate on low margins. Classy hotels have relatively low turnover ratios but tend to compensate with higher margins.

Example 4.1 ▶ Turnover versus Margin

Firms often seek to improve their profit margins by acquiring a supplier. The idea is to capture the supplier's profit as well as their own. Unfortunately, unless they have some special skill in running the new business, they are likely to find that any gain in profit margin is offset by a decline in asset turnover.

A few numbers may help to illustrate this point. Table 4.5 shows the sales, profits, and assets of Admiral Motors and its components supplier, Diana Corporation. Both earn a 10% return on assets, though Admiral has a lower operating profit margin (20% versus Diana's 25%). Because all of Diana's output goes to Admiral, Admiral's management reasons that it would be better to merge the two companies. That way, the merged company would capture the profit margin on both the auto components and the assembled car.

TABLE 4.5 Merging with suppliers or customers will generally increase the profit margin, but this will be offset by a reduction in asset turnover

	Sales	Profits	Assets	Asset Turnover	Profit Margin	ROA
Admiral Motors	$20	$4	$40	0.50	20%	10%
Diana Corp.	8	2	20	0.40	25	10
Diana Motors (the merged firm)	20	6	60	0.33	30	10

The bottom row of Table 4.5 shows the effect of the merger. The merged firm does indeed earn the combined profits. Total sales remain at $20 million, however, because all the components produced by Diana are used within the company. With higher profits and unchanged sales, the profit margin increases. Unfortunately, the asset turnover is *reduced* by the merger since the merged firm has more assets. This exactly offsets the benefit of the higher profit margin. The return on assets is unchanged. ∎

Figure 4.2 shows evidence of the trade-off between turnover and profit margin. You can see that industries with high average turnover ratios tend to have lower average profit margins. Conversely, high margins are typically associated with low turnover. The classic examples here are electric or water utilities, which have enormous capital requirements and therefore low asset turnover ratios. However, they have extremely low marginal costs for each unit of additional output and therefore earn high markups. The two curved lines in the figure trace out the combinations of profit margin and turnover that result in an ROA of either 3% or 10%. Despite the enormous dispersion across industries in both margin and turnover, that variation tends to be offsetting, so for most industries the return on assets lies between 3% and 10%. The notable exception is mining, which was suffering badly in 2015 from the slump in commodity prices.

FIGURE 4.2 Operating profit margin and asset turnover for 45 industries

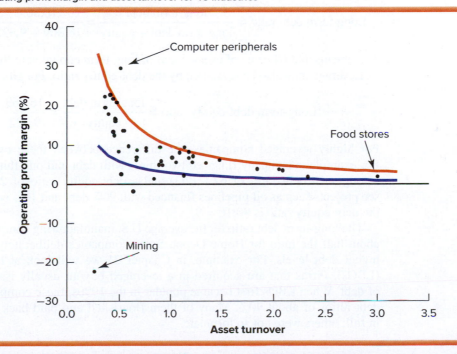

Source: U.S. Census Bureau, *Quarterly Report for Manufacturing and Trade Corporations, Second Quarter 2015* (www.census.gov/econ/qfr). This is an updated version of a figure that first appeared in Thomas I. Selling and Clyde P. Stickney, "The Effects of Business Environments and Strategy on a Firm's Rate of Return on Assets," *Financial Analysts Journal*, January–February 1989, pp. 43–52.

4.6 Self-Test

The Du Pont formula (Equation 4.1) seems to suggest that companies with above-average asset turnover ratios generally will have above-average ROAs. Why may this not be so?

4.6 Measuring Financial Leverage

As Figure 4.1 indicates, shareholder value depends not only on good investment decisions and profitable operations, but also on sound financing decisions. We look first at measures of financial leverage and then at measures of liquidity.

When a firm borrows money, it promises to make a series of interest payments and then to repay the amount that it has borrowed. If profits rise, the debtholders continue to receive only the fixed interest payment, so all the gains go to the shareholders. Of course, the reverse happens if profits fall. In this case, shareholders bear most of the pain. If times are sufficiently hard, a firm that has borrowed heavily may not be able to pay its debts. The firm is then bankrupt, and shareholders lose most or all of their entire investment.

Because debt increases returns to shareholders in good times and reduces them in bad times, it is said to create *financial leverage.* Leverage ratios measure how much financial leverage the firm has taken on. CFOs keep an eye on leverage ratios to ensure that lenders are happy to continue to take on the firm's debt.

Debt Ratio   Financial leverage is usually measured by the ratio of long-term debt to total long-term capital (that is, to total capitalization). Here long-term debt should include not just bonds or other borrowing, but also financing from long-term leases.[8] For Home Depot,

$$\text{Long-term debt ratio} = \frac{\text{long-term debt}}{\text{long-term debt} + \text{equity}} = \frac{16,869}{16,869 + 9,322} = .64, \text{ or } 64\%$$

This means that 64 cents of every dollar of long-term capital is in the form of debt.

Leverage may also be measured by the debt-equity ratio. For Home Depot,

$$\text{Long-term debt-equity ratio} = \frac{\text{long-term debt}}{\text{equity}} = \frac{16,869}{9,322} = 1.81$$

For highly leveraged companies, the difference between these two ratios is large. For example, a company financed two-thirds with debt and one-third with equity has a long-term debt ratio of 67% (2/3) and a debt-equity ratio of 2. Sometimes you see projects such as oil pipelines financed with 90% debt and 10% equity. In that case, the debt-equity ratio is 90/10 = 9.

The long-term debt ratio for the average U.S. manufacturing company is about 33%, about half the ratio for Home Depot. Some companies deliberately operate at much higher debt levels. For example, in Chapter 21 we will look at leveraged buyouts (LBOs). Firms that are acquired in a leveraged buyout usually issue large amounts of debt. When LBOs first became popular in the 1990s, these companies had average debt ratios of about 90%. Many of them flourished and paid back their debtholders in full; others were not so fortunate.

---

[8] A finance lease is a long-term rental agreement that commits the firm to make regular payments. This commitment is just like the obligation to make payments on an outstanding loan.

Notice that debt ratios make use of book (accounting) values rather than market values.[9] In principle, lenders should be more interested in the *market value* of the company, which reflects the actual value of the company's assets and the actual cash flows those assets will produce. If the market value of the company covers its debts, then lenders should get their money back. Thus, you would expect to see the debt ratio computed using the market values of debt and equity. Yet book debt ratios are used almost universally.

Does use of book rather than market leverage ratios matter much? Perhaps not; after all, the market value of the firm includes the value of intangible assets generated by research and development, advertising, staff training, and so on. These assets are not easy to sell, and if the company falls on hard times, their value may disappear altogether. Thus, when banks demand that a borrower keep within a maximum debt ratio, they usually define that ratio in terms of book values, and they ignore the intangible assets that contribute to the market value of the firm but are not shown on the balance sheet.

Notice also that these measures of leverage ignore short-term debt. That probably makes sense if the short-term debt is temporary or is matched by similar holdings of cash, but if the company is a regular short-term borrower, it may be preferable to widen the definition of debt to include all liabilities. In this case,

$$\text{Total debt ratio} = \frac{\text{total liabilities}}{\text{total assets}} = \frac{30,624}{39,946} = .77, \text{ or } 77\%$$

Therefore, Home Depot is financed 77% with long- and short-term debt and 23% with equity.[10] We could also say that its ratio of total debt to equity is $30,624/9,322 = 3.28$.

Managers sometimes refer loosely to a company's debt ratio, but we have just seen that the debt ratio may be measured in several different ways. For example, Home Depot has a debt ratio of .64 (the long-term debt ratio) and also .77 (the total debt ratio). This is not the first time we have come across several ways to define a financial ratio. There is no law stating how a ratio should be defined. So be warned: Do not use a ratio without understanding how it has been calculated.

Times Interest Earned Ratio   Another measure of financial leverage is the extent to which interest obligations are covered by earnings. Banks prefer to lend to firms with earnings that cover interest payments with room to spare. *Interest coverage* is measured by the ratio of earnings before interest and taxes (EBIT) to interest payments. For Home Depot,

$$\text{Times interest earned} = \frac{\text{EBIT}}{\text{interest payments}} = \frac{10,806}{830} = 13.0$$

By this measure, Home Depot is conservatively financed. Sometimes lenders are content with coverage ratios as low as 2 or 3.

The regular interest payment is a hurdle that companies must keep jumping if they are to avoid default. The interest coverage ratio measures how much clear air there is between hurdle and hurdler. The ratio is only part of the story, however. For example, it doesn't tell us whether Home Depot is generating enough cash to repay its debt as it becomes due.

Cash Coverage Ratio   As we explained in Chapter 3, depreciation is not a cash expense. Depreciation is deducted when calculating the firm's earnings, even though

---

[9] In the case of leased assets, accountants estimate the value of the lease commitments. In the case of long-term debt, they simply show the face value, which can be very different from market value.

[10] In this case, the 77% of debt includes other liabilities, including accounts payable and other current liabilities.

no cash goes out the door. Suppose we add back depreciation to EBIT in order to calculate operating cash flow. We then calculate a *cash* coverage ratio.[11] For Home Depot,

$$\text{Cash coverage ratio} = \frac{\text{EBIT} + \text{depreciation}}{\text{interest payments}} = \frac{10{,}806 + 1{,}786}{830} = 15.2$$

4.7   Self-Test

A firm repays $10 million face value of outstanding debt and issues $10 million of new debt with a lower rate of interest. What happens to its long-term debt ratio? What happens to its times interest earned and cash coverage ratios?

Leverage and the Return on Equity

When the firm raises cash by borrowing, it must make interest payments to its lenders. This reduces net profits. On the other hand, if a firm borrows instead of issuing equity, it has fewer equityholders to share the remaining profits. Which effect dominates? An extended version of the Du Pont formula helps us answer this question. It breaks down the return on equity (ROE) into four parts:

$$\text{ROE} = \frac{\text{net income}}{\text{equity}} = \underset{\substack{\uparrow \\ \text{leverage} \\ \text{ratio}}}{\frac{\text{assets}}{\text{equity}}} \times \underset{\substack{\uparrow \\ \text{asset} \\ \text{turnover}}}{\frac{\text{sales}}{\text{assets}}} \times \underset{\substack{\uparrow \\ \text{operating} \\ \text{profit margin}}}{\frac{\text{after-tax} \\ \text{operating income}}{\text{sales}}} \times \underset{\substack{\uparrow \\ \text{"debt burden"}}}{\frac{\text{net income}}{\text{after-tax} \\ \text{operating income}}} \qquad (4.2)$$

Notice that the product of the two middle terms in Equation 4.2 is the return on assets. It depends on the firm's production and marketing skills and is unaffected by the firm's financing mix.[12] However, the first and fourth terms do depend on the debt-equity mix. The first term, assets/equity, which we call the *leverage ratio,* can be expressed as (equity + liabilities)/equity, which equals 1 + total-debt-to-equity ratio. The last term, which we call the "debt burden," measures the proportion by which interest expense reduces profits.

Suppose that the firm is financed entirely by equity. In this case, both the leverage ratio and the debt burden are equal to 1, and the return on equity is identical to the return on assets. If the firm borrows, however, the leverage ratio is greater than 1 (assets are greater than equity) and the debt burden is less than 1 (part of the profits is absorbed by interest). Thus leverage can either increase or reduce return on equity. In fact, we will see in Chapter 16 that leverage increases ROE when the firm's return on assets is higher than the interest rate it pays on its debt. Because Home Depot's return on capital exceeds the interest rate on its debt, return on equity is higher than return on capital.

---

[11] Depreciation of intangible assets is called *amortization* and is therefore also added back to EBIT. This gives EBIT + depreciation + amortization = EBITDA. EBITDA coverage ratios are common. You may also encounter still other ratios, in addition to the standard ratios covered here.

[12] Again, we use after-tax operating income, which is the sum of net income and after-tax interest.

4.8 Self-Test

a. Sappy Syrup has a profit margin below the industry average, but its ROA equals the industry average. How is this possible?

b. Sappy Syrup's ROA equals the industry average, but its ROE exceeds the industry average. How is this possible?

4.7 Measuring Liquidity

liquidity
The ability to sell an asset on short notice at close to the market value.

If you are extending credit to a customer or making a short-term bank loan, you are interested in more than the borrower's financial leverage. You want to know whether the company can lay its hands on the cash to repay you. That is why credit analysts and bankers look at several measures of **liquidity.** Liquid assets can be converted into cash quickly and cheaply.

Think, for example, what you would do to meet a large unexpected bill. You might have some money in the bank or some investments that are easily sold, but you would not find it so easy to turn your old sweaters into cash. Companies, likewise, own assets with different degrees of liquidity. For example, accounts receivable and inventories of finished goods are generally quite liquid. As inventories are sold off and customers pay their bills, money flows into the firm. At the other extreme, real estate may be quite *illiquid.* It can be hard to find a buyer, negotiate a fair price, and close a deal at short notice.

There is another reason to focus on liquid assets: Their book (balance sheet) values are usually reliable. The book value of a catalytic cracker may be a poor guide to its true value, but at least you know what cash in the bank is worth.

Liquidity ratios also have some *less* desirable characteristics. Because short-term assets and liabilities are easily changed, measures of liquidity can rapidly become outdated. You might not know what the catalytic cracker is worth, but you can be fairly sure that it won't disappear overnight. Cash in the bank can disappear in seconds.

Also, assets that seem liquid sometimes have a nasty habit of becoming illiquid. This happened during the subprime mortgage crisis in 2008. Some financial institutions had set up funds known as *structured investment vehicles (SIVs)* that issued short-term debt backed by residential mortgages. As mortgage default rates began to climb, the market in this debt dried up and dealers became very reluctant to quote a price.

Bankers and other short-term lenders applaud firms that have plenty of liquid assets. They know that when they are due to be repaid, the firm will be able to get its hands on the cash. But more liquidity is not always a good thing. For example, efficient firms do not leave excess cash in their bank accounts. They don't allow customers to postpone paying their bills, and they don't leave stocks of raw materials and finished goods littering the warehouse floor. In other words, high levels of liquidity may indicate sloppy use of capital. Here, EVA can highlight the problem because it penalizes managers who keep more liquid assets than they really need.

Net Working Capital to Total Assets Ratio   Current assets include cash, marketable securities, inventories, and accounts receivable. Current assets are mostly liquid. The difference between current assets and current liabilities is known as *net working capital.* It roughly measures the company's potential net reservoir of cash. Because current assets usually exceed current liabilities, net working capital is usually positive. For Home Depot,

$$\text{Net working capital} = 15,302 - 11,269 = \$4,033 \text{ million}$$

Home Depot's net working capital was 10% of total assets:

$$\frac{\text{Net working capital}}{\text{Total assets}} = \frac{4,033}{39,946} = .10, \text{ or } 10\%$$

Current Ratio   The current ratio is just the ratio of current assets to current liabilities:

$$\text{Current ratio} = \frac{\text{current assets}}{\text{current liabilities}} = \frac{15,302}{11,269} = 1.36$$

Home Depot has $1.36 in current assets for every dollar in current liabilities.

Changes in the current ratio can be misleading. For example, suppose that a company borrows a large sum from the bank and invests it in marketable securities. Current liabilities rise and so do current assets. If nothing else changes, net working capital is unaffected but the current ratio changes. For this reason, it is sometimes preferable to net short-term investments against short-term debt when calculating the current ratio.

Quick (Acid-Test) Ratio   Some current assets are closer to cash than others. If trouble comes, inventory may not sell at anything above fire-sale prices. (Trouble typically comes *because* the firm can't sell its inventory of finished products for more than production cost.) Thus managers often exclude inventories and other less liquid components of current assets when comparing current assets to current liabilities. They focus instead on cash, marketable securities, and bills that customers have not yet paid. This results in the quick ratio:

$$\text{Quick ratio} = \frac{\text{cash + marketable securities + receivables}}{\text{current liabilities}} = \frac{1,723 + 1,484}{11,269} = .28$$

Cash Ratio   A company's most liquid assets are its holdings of cash and marketable securities. That is why analysts also look at the cash ratio:

$$\text{Cash ratio} = \frac{\text{cash + marketable securities}}{\text{current liabilities}} = \frac{1,723}{11,269} = .15$$

A low cash ratio may not matter if the firm can borrow on short notice. Who cares whether the firm has actually borrowed from the bank or whether it has a guaranteed line of credit that lets it borrow whenever it chooses? None of the standard measures of liquidity takes the firm's "reserve borrowing power" into account.

4.9   Self-Test

a. A firm has $1.2 million in current assets and $1 million in current liabilities. If it uses $.5 million of cash to pay off some of its accounts payable, what will happen to the current ratio? What happens to net working capital?
b. A firm uses cash on hand to pay for additional inventories. What will happen to the current ratio? To the quick ratio?

4.8   Interpreting Financial Ratios

We have shown how to calculate some common summary measures of Home Depot's performance and financial condition. These are summarized in Table 4.6.

Now that you have calculated these measures, you need some way to judge whether they are a matter for concern or congratulation. In some cases, there may be a natural

TABLE 4.6 Summary of Home Depot's performance measures

Performance Measures		
Market value added ($ millions)	market value of equity − book value of equity	$140,656
Market-to-book ratio	market value of equity ÷ book value of equity	16.1
Profitability Measures		
Return on assets (ROA)	after-tax operating income/total assets	17.0%
Return on capital (ROC)	after-tax operating income/(long-term debt + equity)	25.3%
Return on equity (ROE)	net income/equity	50.7%
EVA ($ millions)	after-tax operating income − cost of capital × capital	$4,435
Efficiency Measures		
Asset turnover	sales/total assets at start of year	2.05
Receivables turnover	sales/receivables at start of year	59.5
Average collection period (days)	receivables at start of year/daily sales	6.1
Inventory turnover	cost of goods sold/inventory at start of year	4.9
Days in inventory	inventories at start of year/daily cost of goods sold	74
Profit margin	net income/sales	7.6%
Operating profit margin	after-tax operating income/sales	8.3%
Leverage Measures		
Long-term debt ratio	long-term debt/(long-term debt + equity)	64%
Long-term debt-equity ratio	long-term debt/equity	181%
Total debt ratio	total liabilities/total assets	77%
Times interest earned	EBIT/interest payments	13.0
Cash coverage ratio	(EBIT + depreciation)/interest payments	15.2
Liquidity Measures		
Net working capital to assets	net working capital/total assets	0.10
Current ratio	current assets/current liabilities	1.36
Quick ratio	(cash + marketable securities + receivables)/current liabilities	0.28
Cash ratio	(cash + marketable securities)/current liabilities	0.15

benchmark. For example, if a firm has negative value added or a return on capital that is less than the cost of that capital, it is not creating wealth for its shareholders.

But what about some of our other measures? There is no right level for, say, the asset turnover or profit margin, and if there were, it would almost certainly vary from year to year and industry to industry. When assessing company performance, managers usually look first at how the financial ratios have changed over time, and then they look at how their measures stack up in comparison with companies in the same line of business.

We will first compare Home Depot's position in 2014 with its performance in earlier years. For example, Figure 4.3 plots Home Depot's return on assets since 1996. We know that ROA = asset turnover × operating profit margin. Figure 4.3 shows that beginning in 1999 there was a steady decline in the company's ability to generate sales from its assets, though for a while this effect was largely offset by a rise in the profit margin. When the downturn in the housing market in 2008 also led to a sharp decline in the profit margin, Home Depot's ROA fell dramatically. The turnaround came under new management in 2009, and in each of the following years, the company was able to increase both the rate of asset turnover and the profit margin.

Managers also need to ask themselves how the company's performance compares with that of its principal competitors. Table 4.7 sets out some key performance measures for Home Depot and Lowe's. Home Depot's ROA is higher, due to its higher asset turnover ratio and its better operating profit margin. Home Depot has higher debt ratios, but, thanks to its greater profitability, it has the higher interest cover. Home Depot turns over its inventory more rapidly. However, its longer collection period

FIGURE 4.3 Home Depot's financial ratios over time

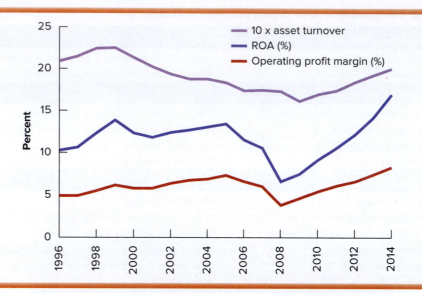

TABLE 4.7 Selected financial measures for Home Depot and Lowe's, 2014

	Home Depot	Lowe's
Performance Measures		
Market value added ($ millions)	$140,656	$58,582
Market-to-book ratio	16.1	6.9
Profitability Measures		
Return on assets (ROA)	17.0%	9.3%
Return on capital (ROC)	25.3%	13.8%
Return on equity (ROE)	50.7%	22.8%
EVA* ($ millions)	$ 4,435	$ 1,163
Efficiency Measures		
Asset turnover	2.05	1.72
Receivables turnover	59	223
Average collection period (days)	6.1	1.6
Inventory turnover	4.9	4.0
Days in inventory	74	91
Profit margin	7.6%	4.8%
Operating profit margin	8.3%	5.4%
Leverage Measures		
Long-term debt ratio	64%	52%
Long-term debt-equity ratio	181%	108%
Total debt ratio	77%	69%
Times interest earned	13.0	9.3
Cash coverage ratio	15.2	12.2
Liquidity Measures		
Net working capital to assets	0.10	0.02
Current ratio	1.36	1.08
Quick ratio	0.28	0.09
Cash ratio	0.15	0.06

*Authors' calculation.

seems to suggest that it is much less efficient in collecting its bills. This is actually an illusion. Lowe's tends to sell its accounts receivable to other parties, and thus maintains lower receivables on its balance sheet. The lesson? Ratios can tip you off to differences in strategy as well as to emerging business strengths or problems, but you will generally have to probe further to fully understand the implications of the numbers.

TABLE 4.8 Financial ratios for major industry groups

	LT Debt/ Assets	Interest Coverage	Current Ratio	Quick Ratio	Asset Turnover	Receivables Turnover	Inventory Turnover	Profit Margin (%)	Return on Assets (%)	Return on Equity (%)
All manufacturing	0.22	4.31	1.36	0.93	0.76	2.45	2.02	7.17	5.43	14.35
Food products	0.27	6.19	1.62	1.01	1.13	3.29	2.43	7.39	8.35	10.14
Retail trade	0.24	8.96	1.29	0.57	2.14	10.54	2.44	5.53	11.84	18.99
Publishing	0.23	5.19	1.15	1.10	0.41	1.68	9.78	15.96	6.57	17.28
Chemicals	0.28	3.10	1.21	0.90	0.46	1.81	1.76	10.31	4.73	14.73
Pharmaceuticals	0.28	3.16	1.27	1.00	0.36	1.69	1.74	13.31	4.77	17.88
Machinery	0.19	5.70	1.50	0.97	0.81	2.00	1.50	7.63	6.16	15.13
Electrical	0.12	6.21	1.20	0.80	0.55	2.17	1.58	8.78	4.87	13.69
Motor vehicles	0.15	5.32	1.20	0.90	1.24	3.67	3.47	4.82	5.97	15.34
Computer and electronic	0.18	6.80	1.38	1.14	0.51	2.15	2.66	12.64	6.41	22.34

Source: U.S. Department of *Commerce, Quarterly Financial Report for Manufacturing, Mining and Trade Corporations,* fourth quarter 2014 (March 2015). Available at **www2.census.gov/econ/qfr/current/qfr_pub.pdf**.

BEYOND THE PAGE

Financial ratios for U.S. companies

mhhe.com/brealey9e

Home Depot and Lowe's are fairly close competitors, and it makes sense to compare their financial ratios. However, all financial ratios must be interpreted in the context of industry norms. For example, you would not expect a soft-drink manufacturer to have the same profit margin as a jeweler or the same leverage as a finance company. You can see this from Table 4.8, which presents some financial ratios for a sample of industry groups.

Notice the large variation across industries. Some of these differences, particularly in profitability measures, may arise from chance; in 2014 the sun shone more kindly on some industries than others. But other differences may reflect more fundamental factors. For example, notice the comparatively high debt ratios of pharmaceutical and chemical product companies. In comparison, computer and electronic companies tend to borrow far less, and these differences persist in both good times and bad. We pointed out earlier that some businesses are able to generate a high level of sales from relatively few assets. Differences in turnover ratios also tend to be relatively stable. For example, you can see that the asset turnover ratio for electrical companies is higher than that for pharmaceutical companies. But competition ensures that electrical businesses earn a correspondingly lower margin on their sales. The net effect is that the return on assets in the two industries is broadly similar.

Now that you know how to interpret financial ratios, you can use the nearby Beyond the Page feature to compare the ratios of other U.S. companies.

4.10 Self-Test

Even within an industry, there can be a considerable difference in the type of business that companies do, and this shows up in their financial ratios. Here are some data on assets, sales, and income for two companies. Calculate for each company the asset turnover, the operating profit margin, and the return on assets. In each case, the values are expressed as a percentage of sales. One of these two companies is Walmart. The other is Tiffany. Which one is which? Explain.

	Company A	Company B
Sales	100	100
Assets	41.2	109.6
Net income + after-tax interest	4.1	12.0

4.9 The Role of Financial Ratios

Whenever two managers get together to talk business and finance, it's a good bet that they will refer to financial ratios. Let's drop in on two conversations.

Conversation 1   The CEO was musing out loud: "How are we going to finance this expansion? Would the banks be happy to lend us the $30 million that we need?"

"I've been looking into that," the financial manager replies. "Our current debt ratio is 30%. If we borrow the full cost of the project, the ratio would be about 45%. When we took out our last loan from the bank, we agreed that we would not allow our debt ratio to get above 50%. So if we borrow to finance this project, we wouldn't have much leeway to respond to possible emergencies. Also, the rating agencies currently give our bonds an investment-grade rating. They too look at a company's leverage when they rate its bonds. I have a table here (Table 4.9), which shows that when firms are highly leveraged, their bonds receive a lower rating. I don't know whether the rating agencies would downgrade our bonds if our debt ratio increased to 45%, but they might. That wouldn't please our existing bondholders, and it could raise the cost of any new borrowing.

"We also need to think about our interest cover, which is beginning to look a bit thin. Debt interest is currently covered three times, and if we borrowed the entire $30 million, interest cover would fall to about two times. Sure, we expect to earn additional profits on the new investment, but it could be several years before they come through. If we run into a recession in the meantime, we could find ourselves short of cash."

"Sounds to me as if we should be thinking about a possible equity issue," concluded the CEO.

Conversation 2   The CEO was not in the best of moods after his humiliating defeat at the company golf tournament by the manager of the packaging division: "I see our stock was down again yesterday," he growled. "It's now selling below book value, and the stock price is only six times earnings. I work my socks off for this company; you would think that our stockholders would show a little more gratitude."

"I think I can understand a little of our shareholders' worries," the financial manager replies. "Just look at our book rate of return on assets. It's only 6%, well below the cost of capital. Sure we are making a profit, but that profit does not cover the cost of the funds that investors provide. Our economic value added is actually negative. Of course, this doesn't necessarily mean that the assets could be used better elsewhere, but we should certainly be looking carefully at whether any of our divisions should be sold off or the assets redeployed.

TABLE 4.9 Median financial ratios by rating class for nonfinancial North American corporations

Rating Category	Operating Margin (%)[a]	Long-Term Debt Ratio (%)[b]	Cash Coverage Ratio[c]
Aaa	22.0	19.3	28.9
Aa	17.1	50.2	15.1
A	17.6	38.6	9.7
Baa	14.1	46.2	5.9
Ba	11.2	51.7	3.5
B	8.9	72.0	1.7
C	4.1	98.0	0.6

[a] Operating profit/net revenues
[b] Long-term debt/(book value of total capital).
[c] EBITDA/interest expense, where EBITDA is earnings before interest, tax, depreciation, and amortization.
Source: Moody's Financial Metrics, "Key Ratios by Rating and Industry for North American Non-Financial Corporations," December 2013.

"In some ways we're in good shape. We have very little short-term debt, and our current assets are three times our current liabilities. But that's not altogether good news because it also suggests that we may have more working capital than we need. I've been looking at our main competitors. They turn over their inventory 12 times a year compared with our figure of just 8 times. Also, their customers take an average of 45 days to pay their bills. Ours take 67. If we could just match their performance on these two measures, we would release $300 million that could be paid out to shareholders."

"Perhaps we could talk more about this tomorrow," said the CEO. "In the meantime I intend to have a word with the production manager about our inventory levels and with the credit manager about our collections policy. You've also got me thinking about whether we should sell off our packaging division. I've always worried about the divisional manager there. Spends too much time practicing his backswing and not enough worrying about his return on assets."

SUMMARY

How do you measure whether a public corporation has delivered value for its shareholders? *(LO4-1)*

For a public corporation, this is relatively easy. Start with **market capitalization,** which equals price per share times the number of shares outstanding. The difference between market capitalization and the book value of equity measures the **market value added** by the firm's investments and operations. The book value of equity is the cumulative investment (including reinvested earnings) by shareholders in the company. The ratio of market value to book value is another way of expressing value added.

For private corporations, financial managers and analysts have to turn to other performance measures, because stock prices are not available.

What measures are used to assess financial performance? *(LO4-2)*

Financial managers and analysts track **return on equity (ROE),** which is the ratio of net income to shareholders' equity. But net income is calculated after interest expense, so ROE depends on the debt ratio. The **return on capital (ROC)** and the **return on assets (ROA)** are better measures of operating performance. These are the ratios of after-tax operating income to total capitalization (long-term debt plus shareholders' equity) and to total assets. ROC should be compared with the company's cost of capital. **EVA (economic value added** or residual income) deducts the cost of capital from operating income. If EVA is positive, then the firm's operations are adding value for shareholders.

What are the standard measures of profitability, efficiency, leverage, and liquidity? *(LO4-3)*

Financial managers and analysts have to condense the enormous volume of information in a company's financial statements. They rely on a handful of ratios to summarize financial performance, operating efficiency, and financial strength. Look back at Table 4.6, which summarizes the most important ratios. Remember that the ratios sometimes appear under different names and may be calculated differently.

Profitability ratios measure return on investment. Efficiency ratios measure how intensively the firm uses its assets. Leverage ratios measure how much the firm has borrowed and its obligations to pay interest. Liquidity ratios measure how easily the firm can obtain cash.

Financial ratios crop up repeatedly in financial discussions and contracts. For example, banks and bondholders usually demand limits on debt ratios or interest coverage.

What determines the return on assets and equity? *(LO4-4)*

The **Du Pont system** links financial ratios together to explain the return on assets and equity. Return on assets is the product of asset turnover and operating profit margin. Return on equity is the product of the leverage ratio, asset turnover, operating profit margin, and debt burden.

What are some potential pitfalls in financial statement analysis? (*LO4-5*)

Financial statement analysis will rarely be useful if done mechanically. Financial ratios do not provide final answers, although they should prompt the right questions. In addition, accounting entries do not always reflect current market values, and in rare cases accounting is not transparent, because unscrupulous managers make up good news and hide bad news in financial statements.

You will need a benchmark to assess a company's financial condition. Therefore, analysts usually compare financial ratios with the company's ratios in earlier years and with ratios of other firms in the same business.

LISTING OF EQUATIONS

4.1 $\text{Return on assets} = \dfrac{\text{after-tax operating income}}{\text{assets}}$

$$= \underset{\underset{\text{asset turnover}}{\uparrow}}{\dfrac{\text{sales}}{\text{assets}}} \times \underset{\underset{\substack{\text{operating} \\ \text{profit margin}}}{\uparrow}}{\dfrac{\text{after-tax operating income}}{\text{sales}}}$$

4.2 $\text{ROE} = \dfrac{\text{net income}}{\text{equity}} = \underset{\underset{\substack{\text{leverage} \\ \text{ratio}}}{\uparrow}}{\dfrac{\text{assets}}{\text{equity}}} \times \underset{\underset{\substack{\text{asset} \\ \text{turnover}}}{\uparrow}}{\dfrac{\text{sales}}{\text{assets}}} \times \underset{\underset{\substack{\text{operating} \\ \text{profit margin}}}{\uparrow}}{\dfrac{\text{after-tax} \\ \text{operating income}}{\text{sales}}} \times \underset{\underset{\text{"debt burden"}}{\uparrow}}{\dfrac{\text{net income}}{\text{after-tax} \\ \text{operating income}}}$

QUESTIONS AND PROBLEMS

1. **Market Value Added.** Here is a simplified balance sheet for Locust Farming:

Current assets	$42,524	Current liabilities	$29,755
Long-term assets	46,832	Long-term debt	27,752
		Other liabilities	14,317
		Equity	17,532
Total	$89,356	Total	$89,356

Locust has 657 million shares outstanding with a market price of $83 a share. (*LO4-1*)

a. Calculate the company's market value added.

b. Calculate the market-to-book ratio.

c. How much value has the company created for its shareholders?

2. **Market Value Added.** Suppose the broad stock market falls 20% in a year and Home Depot's stock price falls by 10%. (*LO4-1*)

a. Will the company's market value added rise or fall?

b. Should this change affect our assessment of the performance of Home Depot's managers?

c. Would you feel differently about Home Depot's managers if the stock market were unchanged and Home Depot's stock fell by 10%?

3. **Measuring Performance.** Here are simplified financial statements for Watervan Corporation:

INCOME STATEMENT (Figures in $ millions)	
Net sales	$881
Cost of goods sold	741
Depreciation	31
Earnings before interest and taxes (EBIT)	109
Interest expense	12
Income before tax	97
Taxes	34
Net income	63

BALANCE SHEET (Figures in $ millions)	End of Year	Start of Year
Assets		
Current assets	$369	$312
Long-term assets	258	222
Total assets	$627	$534
Liabilities and shareholders' equity		
Current liabilities	$194	$157
Long-term debt	108	121
Shareholders' equity	325	256
Total liabilities and shareholders' equity	$627	$534

The company's cost of capital is 8.5%. (*LO4-2*)

a. Calculate Watervan's economic value added (EVA).
b. What is the company's return on capital? (Use start-of-year rather than average capital.)
c. What is its return on equity? (Use start-of-year rather than average equity.)
d. Is the company creating value for its shareholders?

4. **Measuring Performance.** Recalculate Home Depot's economic value added as we did in Section 4.3, but assuming its cost of capital is 10%. (*LO4-2*)

5. **Economic Value Added.** EVA will be positive whenever ROC is positive and greater than the cost of capital. Explain why this is so. (*LO4-2*)

6. **Return on Capital.** Microlimp does not raise any new finance during the year, but it generates a lot of earnings, which are immediately reinvested. If you were calculating the company's return on capital, would it make more sense to use capital at the start of the year or an average of the starting and ending capital? Would your answer change if Microlimp made a large issue of debt early in the year? Illustrate your answer with simple examples. (*LO4-2*)

7. **Financial Ratios.** Here are simplified financial statements for Phone Corporation in a recent year:

INCOME STATEMENT (Figures in $ millions)	
Net sales	$13,193
Cost of goods sold	4,060
Other expenses	4,049
Depreciation	2,518
Earnings before interest and taxes (EBIT)	$ 2,566
Interest expense	685
Income before tax	$ 1,881
Taxes (at 35%)	658
Net income	$ 1,223
Dividends	856

BALANCE SHEET (Figures in $ millions)		
	End of Year	**Start of Year**
Assets		
Cash and marketable securities	$ 89	$ 158
Receivables	2,382	2,490
Inventories	187	238
Other current assets	867	932
Total current assets	$ 3,525	$ 3,818
Net property, plant, and equipment	19,973	19,915
Other long-term assets	4,216	3,770
Total assets	$27,714	$27,503
Liabilities and shareholders' equity		
Payables	$ 2,564	$ 3,040
Short-term debt	1,419	1,573
Other current liabilities	811	787
Total current liabilities	$ 4,794	$ 5,400
Long-term debt and leases	7,018	6,833
Other long-term liabilities	6,178	6,149
Shareholders' equity	9,724	9,121
Total liabilities and shareholders' equity	$27,714	$27,503

Calculate the following financial ratios for Phone Corporation using the methodologies listed for each part: (*LO4-3*)

a. Return on equity (use average balance sheet figures)
b. Return on assets (use average balance sheet figures)
c. Return on capital (use average balance sheet figures)
d. Days in inventory (use start-of-year balance sheet figures)
e. Inventory turnover (use start-of-year balance sheet figures)
f. Average collection period (use start-of-year balance sheet figures)
g. Operating profit margin
h. Long-term debt ratio (use end-of-year balance sheet figures)
i. Total debt ratio (use end-of-year balance sheet figures)
j. Times interest earned
k. Cash coverage ratio
l. Current ratio (use end-of-year balance sheet figures)
m. Quick ratio (use end-of-year balance sheet figures)

8. **Financial Ratios.** Consider this simplified balance sheet for Geomorph Trading: (*LO4-3*)

Current assets	$100	Current liabilities	$ 60
Long-term assets	500	Long-term debt	280
		Other liabilities	70
		Equity	190
	$600		$600

a. What is the company's debt-equity ratio?
b. What is the ratio of total long-term debt to total long-term capital?
c. What is its net working capital?
d. What is its current ratio?

9. **Receivables.** Chik's Chickens has accounts receivable of $6,333. Sales for the year were $9,800. What is its average collection period? (*LO4-3*)

10. **Inventory.** Salad Daze maintains an inventory of produce worth $400. Its total bill for produce over the course of the year was $73,000. How old on average is the lettuce it serves its customers? (*LO4-3*)

11. **Times Interest Earned.** In the past year, TVG had revenues of $3 million, cost of goods sold of $2.5 million, and depreciation expense of $200,000. The firm has a single issue of debt

outstanding with book value of $1 million on which it pays an interest rate of 8%. What is the firm's times interest earned ratio? (*LO4-3*)

12. **Leverage Ratios.** Lever Age pays an 8% rate of interest on $10 million of outstanding debt with face value $10 million. The firm's EBIT was $1 million. (*LO4-3*)

   a. What is its times interest earned?
   b. If depreciation is $200,000, what is its cash coverage ratio?

13. **Financial Ratios.** There are no universally accepted definitions of financial ratios, but some of the following ratios make no sense at all. Substitute correct definitions. (*LO4-3*)

   a. Debt-equity ratio = long-term debt/(long-term debt + equity)
   b. Return on equity = net income/average equity
   c. Operating profit margin = after-tax operating income/sales
   d. Inventory turnover = total sales/average inventory
   e. Current ratio = current liabilities/current assets
   f. Average collection period = sales/(average receivables/365)
   g. Quick ratio = (cash + marketable securities + receivables)/current liabilities

14. **Asset Turnover.** In each case, choose the firm that you expect to have the higher asset turnover ratio. (*LO4-3*)

   a. Economics Consulting Group or Home Depot
   b. Catalog Shopping Network or Gucci
   c. Electric Utility Co. or Standard Supermarkets

15. **Inventory Turnover.** (*LO4-3*)

   a. If a firm's inventory level of $10,000 represents 30 days' sales, what is the annual cost of goods sold?
   b. What is the inventory turnover ratio?

16. **Leverage.** A firm has a long-term debt-equity ratio of .4. Shareholders' equity is $1 million. Current assets are $200,000, and the current ratio is 2. The only current liabilities are notes payable. What is the total debt ratio? (*LO4-3*)

17. **Leverage Ratios.** A firm has a debt-to-equity ratio of .5 and a market-to-book ratio of 2. What is the ratio of the book value of debt to the market value of equity? (*LO4-3*)

18. **Liquidity Ratios.** A firm uses $1 million in cash to purchase inventories. (*LO4-3*)
   a. Will its current ratio rise or fall?
   b. Will its quick ratio rise or fall?

19. **Current Ratio.** Would the following events increase or decrease a firm's current ratio? (*LO4-3*)

   a. Inventory is sold.
   b. The firm takes out a bank loan to pay its suppliers.
   c. The firm arranges a line of credit with a bank that allows it to borrow at any time to pay its suppliers.
   d. A customer pays its overdue bills.
   e. The firm uses cash to buy additional inventory.

20. **Financial Ratios.** True or false? (*LO4-3*)

   a. A company's debt-equity ratio is always less than 1.
   b. The quick ratio is always less than the current ratio.
   c. For a profitable company, the return on equity is always less than the return on assets.

21. **Interpreting Financial Ratios.** In each of the following cases, state which of the two companies is likely to be characterized by the higher ratio. (*LO4-3*)

   a. Debt-equity ratio: a shipping company or a computer software company
   b. Payout ratio: United Foods Inc. or Computer Graphics Inc.
   c. Ratio of sales to assets: an integrated pulp and paper manufacturer or a paper mill
   d. Average collection period: Regional Electric Power Company or Z-Mart Discount Outlets

22. **Financial Ratios.** As you can see, someone has spilled ink over some of the entries in the balance sheet and income statement of Transylvania Railroad. Use the information from the tables to work out the following missing entries, and then calculate the company's return on equity. Note: Inventory turnover, average collection period, and return on equity are calculated using start-of-year, not average, values. (*LO4-3*)

Long-term debt ratio	0.4
Times interest earned	8.0
Current ratio	1.4
Quick ratio	1.0
Cash ratio	0.2
Inventory turnover	5.0
Average collection period	73 days

INCOME STATEMENT
(Figures in $ millions)

Net sales	▨▨▨
Cost of goods sold	▨▨▨
Selling, general, and administrative expenses	10
Depreciation	20
Earnings before interest and taxes (EBIT)	▨▨▨
Interest expense	▨▨▨
Income before tax	▨▨▨
Tax (35% of income before tax)	▨▨▨
Net income	▨▨▨

BALANCE SHEET
(Figures in $ millions)

	This Year	Last Year
Assets		
Cash and marketable securities	▨▨▨	20
Accounts receivable	▨▨▨	34
Inventories	▨▨▨	26
Total current assets	▨▨▨	80
Net property, plant, and equipment	▨▨▨	25
Total assets	▨▨▨	105
Liabilities and shareholders' equity		
Accounts payable	25	20
Notes payable	30	35
Total current liabilities	▨▨▨	55
Long-term debt	▨▨▨	20
Shareholders' equity	▨▨▨	30
Total liabilities and shareholders' equity	115	105

a. Total assets
b. Total current liabilities
c. Total current assets
d. Cash and marketable securities
e. Accounts receivable
f. Inventory
g. Fixed assets
h. Long-term debt
i. Shareholders' equity
j. Net sales
k. Cost of goods sold
l. EBIT
m. Interest expense
n. Income before tax
o. Tax
p. Net income

23. **Interpreting Financial Ratios.** (*LO4-3*)

   a. Turn back to Table 4.8. For the sample of industries in that table, plot operating profit margin against asset turnover in a scatter diagram. What is the apparent relationship between these two variables? Does this make sense to you?

   b. Now plot a scatter diagram of the cash ratio versus quick ratio. Do these two measures of liquidity tend to move together? Would you conclude that once you know one of these ratios, there is little to be gained by calculating the other?

24. **Du Pont Analysis.** Last year Electric Autos had sales of $100 million and assets at the start of the year of $150 million. If its return on start-of-year assets was 15%, what was its operating profit margin? (*LO4-4*)

25. **Du Pont Analysis.** Torrid Romance Publishers has total receivables of $3,000, which represents 20 days' sales. Total assets are $75,000. The firm's operating profit margin is 5%. Find: (*a*) the firm's ROA and (*b*) its asset turnover ratio. (*LO4-4*)

26. **Du Pont Analysis.** Keller Cosmetics maintains an operating profit margin of 5% and asset turnover ratio of 3. (*LO4-4*)

   a. What is its ROA?

   b. If its debt-equity ratio is 1, its interest payments and taxes are each $8,000, and EBIT is $20,000, what is its ROE?

27. **Du Pont Analysis.** CFA Corp. has a debt-equity ratio that is lower than the industry average, but its cash coverage ratio is also lower than the industry average. What might explain this seeming contradiction? (*LO4-4*)

28. **Using Financial Ratios.** For each category of financial ratios discussed in this chapter, give some examples of who would be likely to examine these ratios and why. (*LO4-5*)

WEB EXERCISE

1. Log on to finance.yahoo.com to find the latest simplified financial statements for Home Depot. Recalculate HD's financial ratios. What have been the main changes from the financial statements shown in this chapter? If you owned some of HD's debt, would these changes make you feel more or less happy?

SOLUTIONS TO SELF-TEST QUESTIONS

4.1   Market capitalization is $75 × 14.5 million = $1,087.5 million. Market value added is $1,087.5 − $610 = $477.5 million. Market to book is 1,087.5/610 = 1.78. You can also calculate book value per share at $610/14.5 = $42.07, and use price per share to calculate market to book: $75/$42.07 = 1.78.

4.2   The cost of capital in dollars is .115 × $188 million = $21.62 million. EVA is $30 − $21.62 = $8.38 million.

4.3   After-tax operating income is calculated before interest expense. Net income is calculated after interest expense. Financial managers usually start with net income, so they add back after-tax interest to get after-tax operating income. After-tax operating income measures the profitability of the firm's investment and operations. If properly calculated, it is not affected by financing.

4.4   ROE measures return to equity as net income divided by the book value of equity. ROC and ROA measure the return to all investors, including interest paid as well as net income to shareholders. ROC measures return versus long-term debt and equity. ROA measures return versus total assets.

4.5   Average daily expenses are 54,222/365 = $148.6 million. Accounts payable at the start of the year are $9,379 million. The average payment delay is therefore 9,379/148.6 = 63.1 days.

4.6   In industries with rapid asset turnover, competition forces prices down, reducing profit margins.

4.7   Nothing will happen to the long-term debt ratio computed using book values, since the face values of the old and new debt are equal. However, times interest earned and cash coverage will increase since the firm will reduce its interest expense.

4.8   a. The firm must compensate for its below-average profit margin with an above-average turn-over ratio. Remember that ROA is the *product* of operating margin × turnover.

b. If ROA equals the industry average but ROE exceeds the industry average, the firm must have above-average leverage. As long as ROA exceeds the borrowing rate, leverage will increase ROE.

4.9   a. The current ratio starts at 1.2/1.0 = 1.2. The transaction will reduce current assets to $.7 million and current liabilities to $.5 million. The current ratio increases to .7/.5 = 1.4. Net working capital is unaffected: Current assets and current liabilities fall by equal amounts.

b. The current ratio is unaffected because the firm merely exchanges one current asset (cash) for another (inventories). However, the quick ratio will fall because inventories are not included among the most liquid assets.

4.10

	Company A	Company B
1. Asset turnover	2.4	0.91
2. Operating profit margin (%)	4.1	12.0
3. Return on assets (%) (= 1 × 2)	10.0	10.9

Company A is Walmart; it generates a high volume of sales from its assets, but earns a relatively low profit margin on these sales. The reverse is true of Tiffany (company B). The two companies differ enormously in their asset turnover and profit margin, but much less in their return on assets.

MINICASE

Burchetts Green had enjoyed the bank training course, but it was good to be starting his first real job in the corporate lending group. Earlier that morning the boss had handed him a set of financial statements for The Hobby Horse Company Inc. (HH). "Hobby Horse," she said, "has a $45 million loan from us due at the end of September, and it is likely to ask us to roll it over. The company seems to have run into some rough weather recently, and I have asked Furze Platt to go down there this afternoon and see what is happening. It might do you good to go along with her. Before you go, take a look at these financial statements and see what you think the problems are. Here's a chance for you to use some of that stuff they taught you in the training course."

Mr. Green was familiar with the HH story. Founded in 1990, it had rapidly built up a chain of discount stores selling materials for crafts and hobbies. However, last year a number of new store openings coinciding with a poor Christmas season had pushed the company into loss. Management had halted all new construction and put 15 of its existing stores up for sale.

Mr. Green decided to start with the 6-year summary of HH's balance sheet and income statement (Table 4.10). Then he turned to examine in more detail the latest position (Tables 4.11 and 4.12).

What appear to be the problem areas in HH? Do the financial ratios suggest questions that Ms. Platt and Mr. Green need to address?

TABLE 4.10 Financial highlights for The Hobby Horse Company Inc., year ending March 31

	2016	2015	2014	2013	2012	2011
Net sales	3,351	3,314	2,845	2,796	2,493	2,160
EBIT	−9	312	256	243	212	156
Interest	37	63	65	58	48	46
Taxes	3	60	46	43	39	34
Net profit	−49	189	145	142	125	76
Earnings per share	−0.15	0.55	0.44	0.42	0.37	0.25
Current assets	669	469	491	435	392	423
Net fixed assets	923	780	753	680	610	536
Total assets	1,592	1,249	1,244	1,115	1,002	959
Current liabilities	680	365	348	302	276	320
Long-term debt	236	159	297	311	319	315
Stockholders' equity	676	725	599	502	407	324
Number of stores	240	221	211	184	170	157
Employees	13,057	11,835	9,810	9,790	9,075	7,825

TABLE 4.11 Income statement for The Hobby Horse Company Inc., year ending March 31, 2016 (figures in $ millions)

Net sales	$3,351
Cost of goods sold	1,990
Selling, general, and administrative expenses	1,211
Depreciation expense	159
Earnings before interest and taxes (EBIT)	−$ 49
Net interest expense	37
Taxable income	−$ 46
Income taxes	3
Net income	−$ 49
Allocation of net income	
Addition to retained earnings	−$ 49
Dividends	0

TABLE 4.12 Consolidated balance sheet for The Hobby Horse Company Inc. (figures in $ millions)

Assets	Mar. 31, 2016	Mar. 31, 2015
Current assets		
Cash and marketable securities	$ 14	$ 72
Receivables	176	194
Inventories	479	203
Total current assets	$ 669	$ 469
Fixed assets		
Property, plant, and equipment	$1,077	$ 910
Less accumulated depreciation	154	130
Net fixed assets	$ 923	$ 780
Total assets	$1,592	$1,249

Liabilities and Shareholders' Equity	Mar. 31, 2016	Mar. 31, 2015
Current liabilities		
Debt due for repayment	$ 484	$ 222
Accounts payable	94	58
Other current liabilities	102	85
Total current liabilities	$ 680	$ 365
Long-term debt	$ 236	$ 159
Stockholders' equity		
Common stock and other paid-in capital	$ 155	$ 155
Retained earnings	521	570
Total stockholders' equity	$ 676	$ 725
Total liabilities and stockholders' equity	$1,592	$1,249

Note: Column sums subject to rounding error.

5

The Time Value of Money

LEARNING OBJECTIVES

After studying this chapter, you should be able to:

5-1 Calculate the future value of money that is invested at a particular interest rate.

5-2 Calculate the present value of a future payment.

5-3 Calculate present and future values of a level stream of cash payments.

5-4 Compare interest rates quoted over different time intervals—for example, monthly versus annual rates.

5-5 Understand the difference between real and nominal cash flows and between real and nominal interest rates.

RELATED WEBSITES FOR THIS CHAPTER CAN BE FOUND IN CONNECT.

Time affects the value of a dollar.   © David Zalubowski/AP Images

Companies invest in lots of things. Some are *tangible assets*—that is, assets you can kick, like factories, machinery, and offices. Others are *intangible assets,* such as patents or trademarks. In each case the company lays out some money now in the hope of receiving even more money later.

Individuals also make investments. For example, your college education may cost you $30,000 per year. That is an investment you hope will pay off in the form of a higher salary later in life. You are sowing now and expecting to reap later.

Companies pay for their investments by raising money and, in the process, assuming liabilities. For example, they may borrow money from a bank and promise to repay it with interest later. You also may have financed your investment in a college education by borrowing money that you plan to pay back out of that fat salary.

All these financial decisions require comparisons of cash payments at different dates. Will your future salary be sufficient to justify the current expenditure on college tuition? How much will you have to repay the bank if you borrow to finance your education?

In this chapter, we take the first steps toward understanding the time value of money, that is, the relationship between the values of dollars today and dollars in the future. We start by looking at how funds invested at a specific interest rate will grow over time. We next ask how much you would need to invest today to produce a specified future sum of money, and we describe some shortcuts for working out the value of a series of cash payments. Then we consider how inflation affects these financial calculations.

There is nothing complicated about the calculations, but if they are to become second nature, you should read the chapter thoroughly, work carefully through the examples (we have provided plenty), and make sure you tackle the self-test questions. We are asking you to make an investment now in return for a payoff later. One of the payoffs is that you will understand what is going on behind the screen when you value cash flows using a spreadsheet program or a financial calculator. We show how to use spreadsheets and financial calculators later in the chapter.

For simplicity, almost every example in this chapter is set out in dollars, but the concepts and calculations are identical in euros, yen, tugrik, or drams.[1]

---

[1] The tugrik is the currency of Mongolia, and the dram is the currency of Armenia.

5.1 Future Values and Compound Interest

You have $100 invested in a bank account. Suppose banks are currently paying an interest rate of 6% per year on deposits. So after a year, your account will earn interest of $6:

$$\text{Interest} = \text{interest rate} \times \text{initial investment}$$
$$= .06 \times \$100 = \$6$$

You start the year with $100 and you earn interest of $6, so the value of your investment will grow to $106 by the end of the year:

$$\text{Value of investment after 1 year} = \$100 + \$6 = \$106$$

Notice that the $100 invested grows by the factor $(1 + .06) = 1.06$. In general, for any interest rate r, the value of the investment at the end of 1 year is $(1 + r)$ times the initial investment:

$$\text{Value after 1 year} = \text{initial investment} \times (1 + r)$$
$$= \$100 \times (1.06) = \$106$$

What if you leave this money in the bank for a second year? Your balance, now $106, will continue to earn interest of 6%. So

$$\text{Interest in year 2} = .06 \times \$106 = \$6.36$$

You start the second year with $106, on which you earn interest of $6.36. So by the end of the year the value of your account will grow to $106 + $6.36 = $112.36.

In the first year, your investment of $100 increases by a factor of 1.06 to $106; in the second year the $106 again increases by a factor of 1.06 to $112.36. Thus the initial $100 investment grows twice by a factor 1.06:

$$\text{Value of investment after 2 years} = \$100 \times 1.06 \times 1.06$$
$$= \$100 \times (1.06)^2 = \$112.36$$

If you keep your money invested for a third year, your investment multiplies by 1.06 each year for 3 years. By the end of the third year it will total $100 \times (1.06)^3 = $119.10, scarcely enough to put you in the millionaire class, but even millionaires have to start somewhere.

Clearly, if you invest your $100 for t years, it will grow to $100 \times (1.06)^t$. For an interest rate of r and a horizon of t years, the **future value (FV)** of your investment will be

$$\text{Future value (FV) of } \$100 = \$100 \times (1 + r)^t \qquad \text{(5.1)}$$

future value (FV)
Amount to which an investment will grow after earning interest.

Notice in our example that your interest income in the first year is $6 (6% of $100) and in the second year is $6.36 (6% of $106). Your income in the second year is higher because you now earn interest on *both* the original $100 investment *and* the $6 of interest earned in the previous year. Earning interest on interest is called *compounding* or **compound interest.** In contrast, if the bank calculated the interest only on your original investment, you would be paid **simple interest.** With simple interest, the value of your investment would grow each year by .06 × $100 = $6.

compound interest
Interest earned on interest.

simple interest
Interest earned only on the original investment; no interest is earned on interest.

Table 5.1 and Figure 5.1 illustrate the mechanics of compound interest. Table 5.1 shows that in each year, you start with a greater balance in your account—your savings have been increased by the previous year's interest. As a result, your interest income also is higher.

Obviously, the higher the rate of interest, the faster your savings will grow. Figure 5.2 shows the balance in your savings account after a given number of years for several interest rates. Even a few percentage points added to the (compound) interest rate can dramatically affect the future balance. For example, after 10 years $100

TABLE 5.1 How your savings grow; the future value of $100 invested to earn 6% with compound interest

Year	Balance at Start of Year	Interest Earned during Year	Balance at End of Year
1	$100.00	0.06 × $100.00 = $6.00	$106.00
2	$106.00	0.06 × $106.00 = $6.36	$112.36
3	$112.36	0.06 × $112.36 = $6.74	$119.10
4	$119.10	0.06 × $119.10 = $7.15	$126.25
5	$126.25	0.06 × $126.25 = $7.57	$133.82

FIGURE 5.1 A plot of the data in Table 5.1, showing the future values of an investment of $100 earning 6% with compound interest

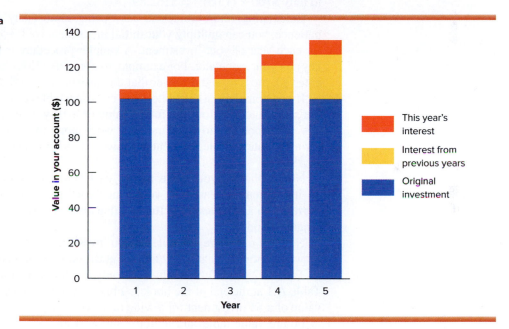

FIGURE 5.2 How an investment of $100 grows with compound interest at different interest rates

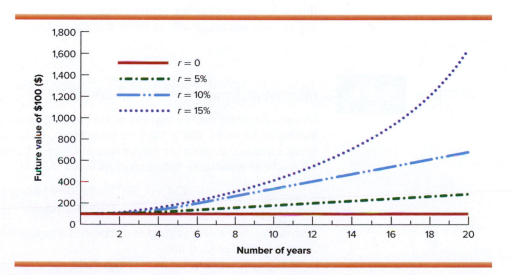

TABLE 5.2 An example of a future value table, showing how an investment of $1 grows with compound interest

Number of Years	Interest Rate per Year					
	5%	6%	7%	8%	9%	10%
1	1.0500	1.0600	1.0700	1.0800	1.0900	1.1000
2	1.1025	1.1236	1.1449	1.1664	1.1881	1.2100
3	1.1576	1.1910	1.2250	1.2597	1.2950	1.3310
4	1.2155	1.2625	1.3108	1.3605	1.4116	1.4641
5	1.2763	1.3382	1.4026	1.4693	1.5386	1.6105
10	1.6289	1.7908	1.9672	2.1589	2.3674	2.5937
20	2.6533	3.2071	3.8697	4.6610	5.6044	6.7275
30	4.3219	5.7435	7.6123	10.0627	13.2677	17.4494

invested at 10% will grow to $100 \times (1.10)^{10} = \$259.37$. If invested at 5%, it will grow to only $100 \times (1.05)^{10} = \$162.89$.

Calculating future values is easy using almost any calculator. If you have the patience, you can multiply your initial investment by $1 + r$ (1.06 in our example) once for each year of your investment. A simpler procedure is to use the power key (the y^x key) on your calculator. For example, to compute $(1.06)^{10}$, enter 1.06, press the y^x key, enter 10, press =, and discover that the answer is 1.7908. (Try this!)

If you don't have a calculator, you can use a table of future values such as Table 5.2. Let's use it to work out the future value of a 10-year investment at 6%. First find the row corresponding to 10 years. Now work along that row until you reach the column for a 6% interest rate. The entry shows that $1 invested for 10 years at 6% grows to $1.7908.

Notice that as you move across each *row* in Table 5.2, the future value of a $1 investment increases, as your funds compound at a higher interest rate. As you move down any *column*, the future value also increases, as your funds compound for a longer period.

Now try one more example. If you invest $1 for 20 years at 10% and do not withdraw any money, what will you have at the end? Your answer should be $6.7275.

Table 5.2 gives future values for only a small selection of years and interest rates. Table A.1 at the end of the book is a bigger version of Table 5.2. It presents the future value of a $1 investment for a wide range of time periods and interest rates.

Future value tables are tedious, and as Table 5.2 demonstrates, they show future values only for a limited set of interest rates and time periods. For example, suppose that you want to calculate future values using an interest rate of 7.835%. The power key on your calculator will be faster and easier than future value tables.

Example 5.1 ▶   Manhattan Island

Almost everyone's favorite example of the power of compound interest is the purchase of Manhattan Island for $24 in 1626 by Peter Minuit. Based on New York real estate prices today, it seems that Minuit got a great deal. But did he? Consider the future value of that $24 if it had been invested for 390 years (2016 minus 1626) at an interest rate of 8% per year:

$$\$24 \times (1.08)^{390} = \$260{,}301{,}027{,}018{,}004$$
$$= \$260 \text{ trillion}$$

Perhaps the deal wasn't as good as it appeared. The total value of land on Manhattan today is only a fraction of $260 trillion.

Though entertaining, this analysis is actually somewhat misleading. The 8% interest rate we've used to compute future values is high by historical standards. At a 3.5% interest rate, more consistent with historical experience, the future value of the $24 would be *dramatically* lower, only $24 \times (1.035)^{390} = \$16,104,515$! On the other hand, we have understated the returns to Mr. Minuit and his successors: We have ignored all the rental income that the island's land has generated over the last four centuries.

All things considered, if we had been around in 1626, we would have gladly paid $24 for the island. ■

The power of compounding is not restricted to money. Foresters try to forecast the compound growth rate of trees, demographers the compound growth rate of populations. A social commentator once observed that the number of lawyers in the United States is increasing at a higher compound rate than the population as a whole (3.6% versus .9% in the 1980s) and calculated that in about two centuries there will be more lawyers than people. In all these cases, the principle is the same: **Compound growth means that value increases each period by the factor (1 + growth rate). The value after *t* periods will equal the initial value times (1 + growth rate)^*t*. When money is invested at compound interest, the growth rate is the interest rate.**

5.1   Self-Test

Suppose that Peter Minuit did not become the first New York real estate tycoon but instead had invested his $24 at a 5% interest rate in New Amsterdam Savings Bank. What would have been the balance in his account after 5 years? 50 years?

5.2   Self-Test

In 1973 Gordon Moore, one of Intel's founders, predicted that the number of transistors that could be placed on a single silicon chip would double every 18 months, equivalent to an annual growth of 59% (i.e., $1.59^{1.5} = 2.0$). The first microprocessor was built in 1971 and had 2,250 transistors. By 2015, high-end Intel chips contained 5.5 billion transistors, nearly 2.5 million times the number of transistors 44 years earlier. What has been the annual compound rate of growth in processing power? How does it compare with the prediction of Moore's law?

5.2   Present Values

Money can be invested to earn interest. If you are offered the choice between $100,000 now and $100,000 at the end of the year, you naturally take the money now to get a year's interest. Financial managers make the same point when they say that money in hand today has a *time value* or when they quote perhaps the most basic financial principle: **A dollar today is worth more than a dollar tomorrow.**

We have seen that $100 invested for 1 year at 6% will grow to a future value of $100 \times 1.06 = \$106$. Let's turn this around: How much do we need to invest *now* in

present value (PV)
Value today of a future cash flow.

order to produce $106 at the end of the year? In other words, what is the **present value (PV)** of the $106 payoff?

To calculate future value, we multiply today's investment by 1 plus the interest rate, .06, or 1.06. To calculate present value, we simply reverse the process and divide the future value by 1.06:

$$\text{Present value} = PV = \frac{\text{future value}}{1.06} = \frac{\$106}{1.06} = \$100$$

What is the present value of, say, $112.36 to be received 2 years from now? Again we ask, How much would we need to invest now to produce $112.36 after 2 years? The answer is obviously $100; we've already calculated that at 6% interest, $100 grows to $112.36:

$$\$100 \times (1.06)^2 = \$112.36$$

However, if we don't know, or forgot the answer, we just divide future value by $(1.06)^2$:

$$\text{Present value} = PV = \frac{\$112.36}{(1.06)^2} = \$100$$

In general, for a future value or payment t periods away, present value is

$$\text{Present value} = \frac{\text{future value after } t \text{ periods}}{(1 + r)^t} \qquad (5.2)$$

discounted cash flow (DCF)
Method of calculating present value by discounting future cash flows.

To calculate present value, we *discounted* the future value at the interest rate r. The calculation is therefore termed a **discounted cash-flow (DCF)** calculation, and the interest rate r is known as the **discount rate.**

In this chapter, we will be working through a number of more or less complicated DCF calculations. All of them involve a present value, a discount rate, and one or more future cash flows. If ever a DCF problem leaves you confused and flustered, just pause and write down which of these measures you know and which one you need to calculate.

discount rate
Interest rate used to compute present values of future cash flows.

Example 5.2 ▶   Saving for a Future Purchase

Suppose you need $3,000 next year to buy a new computer. The interest rate is 8% per year. How much money must you set aside now in order to pay for the purchase? Just calculate the present value at an 8% interest rate of a $3,000 payment at the end of 1 year. To the nearest dollar, this value is

$$PV = \frac{\$3,000}{1.08} = \$2,778$$

Notice that $2,778 invested for 1 year at 8% will prove just enough to buy your computer:

$$\text{Future value} = \$2,778 \times 1.08 = \$3,000$$

The longer the time before you must make a payment, the less you need to invest today. For example, suppose that you can postpone buying that computer until the end of 2 years. In this case, we calculate the present value of the future payment by dividing $3,000 by $(1.08)^2$:

$$PV = \frac{\$3,000}{(1.08)^2} = \$2,572$$

Thus you need to invest $2,778 today to provide $3,000 in 1 year but only $2,572 to provide the same $3,000 in 2 years. ∎

You now know how to calculate future and present values: **To work out how much you will have in the future if you invest for *t* years at an interest rate *r*, *multiply* the initial investment by $(1 + r)^t$. To find the present value of a future payment, run the process in reverse and *divide* by $(1 + r)^t$.**

Present values are always calculated using compound interest. The ascending lines in Figure 5.2 showed the future value of $1 invested with compound interest. In contrast, present values decline, other things equal, when future cash payments are delayed. The longer you have to wait for money, the less it's worth today.

The descending line in Figure 5.3 shows the present value today of $100 to be received at some future date. Notice how even small variations in the interest rate can have a powerful effect on the value of distant cash flows. At an interest rate of 5%, a payment of $100 in year 20 is worth $37.69 today. If the interest rate increases to 10%, the value of the future payment falls by about 60% to $14.86.

The present value formula is sometimes written differently. Instead of dividing the future payment by $(1 + r)^t$, we could equally well multiply it by $1/(1 + r)^t$:

$$PV = \frac{\text{future payment}}{(1 + r)^t} = \text{future payment} \times \frac{1}{(1 + r)^t}$$

discount factor

Present value of a $1 future payment.

The expression $1/(1 + r)^t$ is called the **discount factor.** It measures the present value of $1 received in year *t*.

The simplest way to find the discount factor is to use a calculator, but financial managers sometimes find it convenient to use tables of discount factors. For example, Table 5.3 shows discount factors for a small range of years and interest rates. Table A.2 at the end of the book provides a set of discount factors for a wide range of years and interest rates.

Try using Table 5.3 to check our calculations of how much to put aside for that $3,000 computer purchase. If the interest rate is 8%, the present value of $1 paid at the end of 1 year is $.9259. So the present value of $3,000 is (to the nearest dollar)

$$PV = \$3,000 \times \frac{1}{1.08} = \$3,000 \times .9259 = \$2,778$$

which matches the value we obtained in Example 5.2.

FIGURE 5.3 **Present value of a future cash flow of $100. Notice that the longer you have to wait for your money, the less it is worth today**

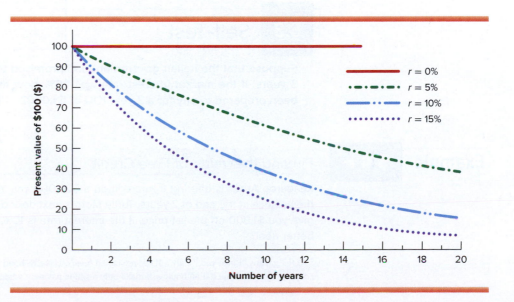

TABLE 5.3 An example of a present value table, showing the value today of $1 received in the future

Number of Years	Interest Rate per Year					
	5%	6%	7%	8%	9%	10%
1	0.9524	0.9434	0.9346	0.9259	0.9174	0.9091
2	0.9070	0.8900	0.8734	0.8573	0.8417	0.8264
3	0.8638	0.8396	0.8163	0.7938	0.7722	0.7513
4	0.8227	0.7921	0.7629	0.7350	0.7084	0.6830
5	0.7835	0.7473	0.7130	0.6806	0.6499	0.6209
10	0.6139	0.5584	0.5083	0.4632	0.4224	0.3855
20	0.3769	0.3118	0.2584	0.2145	0.1784	0.1486
30	0.2314	0.1741	0.1314	0.0994	0.0754	0.0573

What if the computer purchase is postponed until the end of 2 years? Table 5.3 shows that the present value of $1 paid at the end of 2 years is .8573. So the present value of $3,000 is

$$PV = \$3,000 \times \frac{1}{(1.08)^2} = \$3,000 \times .8573 = \$2,572$$

as we found in Example 5.2.

Notice that as you move along the rows in Table 5.3, moving to higher interest rates, present values decline. As you move down the columns, moving to longer discounting periods, present values again decline. (Why does this make sense?)

Example 5.3 ▶ Italy Borrows Some Cash

In September 2014, the Italian government needed to borrow several billion euros. It did so by selling IOUs.[2] Each IOU was a promise to pay the holder €1,000 at the end of 2 years. Investors demanded an interest rate of .385% to lend to the Italian government. How much, therefore, were they prepared to pay for that IOU? Easy! Because the IOU matured in 2 years, we calculate its present value by multiplying the €1,000 future payment by the 2-year discount factor:

$$PV = €1,000 \times \frac{1}{(1.00385)^2}$$
$$= €1,000 \times .99234 = €992.34 \ \blacksquare$$

5.3   Self-Test

Suppose that the Italian government had promised to pay €1,000 at the end of 3 years. If the market interest rate was 1.0%, how much would investors have been prepared to pay for a 3-year IOU of €1,000?

Example 5.4 ▶ Finding the Value of Free Credit

Kangaroo Autos is offering free credit on a $20,000 car. You pay $8,000 down and then the balance at the end of 2 years. Turtle Motors next door does not offer free credit but will give you $1,000 off the list price. If the interest rate is 10%, which company is offering the better deal?

---

[2] "IOU" means "I owe you." Italy's IOUs are called *bonds*. Usually, bond investors receive a regular *interest* or *coupon* payment. This Italian bond will make only a single payment when it matures. It is therefore known as a *zero-coupon bond*. More on this in the next chapter.

FIGURE 5.4 Drawing a time line can help us to calculate the present value of the payments to Kangaroo Autos

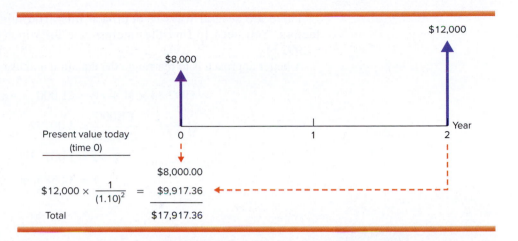

Notice that you pay more in total by buying through Kangaroo, but because part of the payment is postponed, you can keep this money in the bank where it will continue to earn interest. To compare the two offers, you need to calculate the present value of your payments to Kangaroo. The *time line* in Figure 5.4 shows the cash payments. The first payment, $8,000, takes place today. The second payment, $12,000, takes place at the end of 2 years. To find its present value, we need to multiply by the 2-year discount factor. The total present value of the payments to Kangaroo is therefore

$$PV = \$8,000 + \$12,000 \times \frac{1}{(1.10)^2}$$

$$= \$8,000 + \$9,917.36 = \$17,917.36$$

Suppose you start with $17,917.36. You make a down payment of $8,000 to Kangaroo Autos and invest the balance of $9,917.36. At an interest rate of 10%, this will grow over 2 years to $9,917.36 \times 1.10^2 = \$12,000$, just enough to make the final payment on your automobile. The total cost of $17,917.36 is a better deal than the $19,000 charged by Turtle Motors. ∎

These calculations illustrate how important it is to use present values when comparing alternative patterns of cash payment. **You should *never* compare cash flows occurring at different times without first discounting them to a common date. By calculating present values, we see how much cash must be set aside today to pay future bills.**
Calculating present and future values can entail a considerable amount of tedious arithmetic. Fortunately, financial calculators and spreadsheets are designed with present value and future value formulas already programmed. They can make your work much easier. In Section 5.4, we will show how they do so.

Finding the Interest Rate

When we looked at the Italian government's IOUs in Example 5.3, we used the interest rate to compute a fair market price for each IOU. Sometimes, however, you are given the price and have to calculate the interest rate that is being offered.
For example, when Italy borrowed money, it did not announce an interest rate. It simply offered to sell each IOU for €992.34 (see Example 5.3). Thus we know that

$$PV = €1,000 \times \frac{1}{(1 + r)^2} = €992.34$$

What is the interest rate?

There are several ways to approach this. You might use a table of discount factors. You need to find the interest rate for which the 2-year discount factor = .99234.

A better approach is to rearrange the equation and use your calculator:

$$€992.34 \times (1 + r)^2 = €1,000$$

$$(1 + r)^2 = \frac{€1,000}{€992.34} = 1.00772$$

$$1 + r = 1.00772^{1/2} = 1.00385$$

$$r = .00385, \text{ or } .385\%$$

Example 5.5 ▶   Double Your Money

How many times have you heard of an investment adviser who promises to double your money? Is this really an amazing feat? That depends on how long it will take for your money to double. With enough patience, your funds eventually will double even if they earn only a very modest interest rate. Suppose your investment adviser promises to double your money in 8 years. What interest rate is implicitly being promised?

The adviser is promising a future value of $2 for every $1 invested today. Therefore, we find the interest rate by solving for r as follows:

$$\text{Future value (FV)} = PV \times (1 + r)^t$$

$$\$2 = \$1 \times (1 + r)^8$$

$$1 + r = 2^{1/8} = 1.0905$$

$$r = .0905, \text{ or } 9.05\% \blacksquare$$

5.3 Multiple Cash Flows

So far, we have considered problems involving only a single cash flow. This is obviously limiting. Most real-world investments, after all, will involve many cash flows over time. When there are many payments, you'll hear managers refer to a *stream of cash flows.*

Future Value of Multiple Cash Flows

Recall the computer you hope to purchase in 2 years (see Example 5.2). Now suppose that instead of putting aside one sum in the bank to finance the purchase, you plan to save some amount of money each year. You might be able to put $1,200 in the bank now, and another $1,400 in 1 year. If you earn an 8% rate of interest, how much will you be able to spend on a computer in 2 years?

The time line in Figure 5.5 shows how your savings grow. There are two cash inflows into the savings plan. The first cash flow will have 2 years to earn interest and therefore will grow to $1,200 \times (1.08)^2 = $1,399.68$, while the second deposit, which comes a year later, will be invested for only 1 year and will grow to $1,400 \times (1.08) = $1,512$. After 2 years, then, your total savings will be the sum of these two amounts, or $2,911.68.

FIGURE 5.5 Drawing a time line can help to calculate the future value of your **savings**.

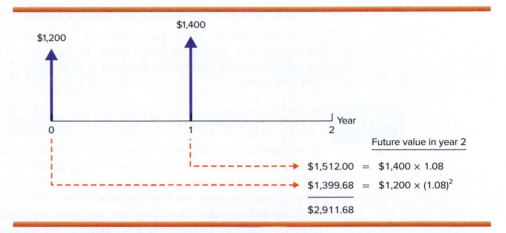

Example 5.6 ▶ Even More Savings

Suppose that the computer purchase can be put off for an additional year and that you can make a third deposit of $1,000 at the end of the second year. How much will be available to spend 3 years from now?

Again we organize our inputs using a time line as in Figure 5.6. The total cash available will be the sum of the future values of all three deposits. Notice that when we save for 3 years, the first two deposits each have an extra year for interest to compound:

$$\$1,200 \times (1.08)^3 = \$1,511.65$$
$$\$1,400 \times (1.08)^2 = 1,632.96$$
$$\$1,000 \times (1.08) = \underline{1,080.00}$$
$$\text{Total future value} = \$4,224.61 \blacksquare$$

Our examples show that problems involving multiple cash flows are simple extensions of single cash-flow analysis. **To find the value at some future date of a stream of cash flows, calculate the future value of each cash flow and then add up these future values.**

As we will now see, a similar adding-up principle works for present value calculations.

FIGURE 5.6 **To find the future value of a stream of cash flows, you just calculate the future value of each flow and then add them.**

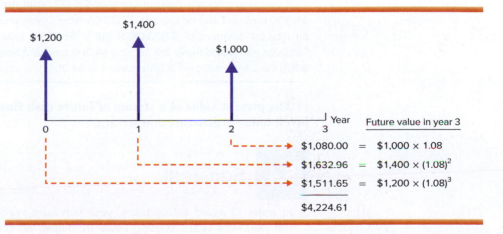

Present Value of Multiple Cash Flows

When we calculate the present value of a future cash flow, we are asking how much that cash flow would be worth today. If there is more than one future cash flow, we simply need to work out what each flow would be worth today and then add these present values.

Example **5.7 ▶** Cash Up Front versus an Installment Plan

Suppose that your auto dealer gives you a choice between paying $15,500 for a used car or entering into an installment plan where you pay $8,000 down today and make payments of $4,000 in each of the next 2 years. Which is the better deal? Before reading this chapter, you might have compared the total payments under the two plans: $15,500 versus $16,000 in the installment plan. Now, however, you know that this comparison is wrong because it ignores the time value of money. For example, the last installment of $4,000 is less costly to you than paying out $4,000 now. The true cost of that last payment is the present value of $4,000.

Assume that the interest rate you can earn on safe investments is 8%. Suppose you choose the installment plan. As the time line in Figure 5.7 illustrates, the present value of the plan's three cash flows is:

	Present Value		
Immediate payment	$8,000	=	$ 8,000.00
Second payment	$4,000/1.08	=	3,703.70
Third payment	$4,000/(1.08)^2	=	3,429.36
Total present value		=	$15,133.06

Because the present value of the three payments is less than $15,500, the installment plan is in fact the cheaper alternative.

The installment plan's present value is the amount that you would need to invest now to cover the three payments. Let's check.

Here is how your bank balance would change as you make each payment:

Year	Initial Balance	−	Payment	=	Remaining Balance	+	Interest Earned	=	Balance at Year-End
0	$15,133.06		$8,000		$7,133.06		$570.64		$7,703.70
1	7,703.70		4,000		3,703.70		296.30		4,000.00
2	4,000.00		4,000		0		0		0

If you start with the present value of $15,133.06 in the bank, you could make the first $8,000 payment and be left with $7,133.06. After 1 year, your savings account would receive an interest payment of $7,133.06 × .08 = $570.64, bringing your account to $7,703.70. Similarly, you would make the second $4,000 payment and be left with $3,703.70. This sum left in the bank would grow with interest to $4,000, just enough to make the last payment. ■

The present value of a stream of future cash flows is the amount you need to invest today to generate that stream.

5.4   Self-Test

In order to avoid estate taxes, your rich aunt Frederica will pay you $10,000 per year for 4 years, starting 1 year from now. What is the present value of your benefactor's planned gifts? The interest rate is 7%. How much will you have 4 years from now if you invest each gift at 7%?

FIGURE 5.7 To find the present value of a stream of cash flows, you just calculate the present value of each flow and then add them.

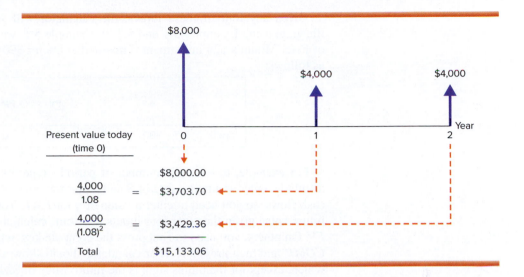

Present value today (time 0)	0	1	2
	$8,000.00		
$\dfrac{4{,}000}{1.08}$ =	$3,703.70		
$\dfrac{4{,}000}{(1.08)^2}$ =	$3,429.36		
Total	$15,133.06		

5.4 Reducing the Chore of the Calculations: Part 1

We have worked through a number of present value problems by hand because it is important that you understand *how* present values are calculated. But calculating values in this way can be laborious. Therefore, financial managers generally turn to financial calculators or computer spreadsheets to remove much of the tedium. In this section, we show how these calculators and spreadsheets are used to solve the future and present value problems that we have encountered so far. Later in the chapter, we will look at how they can also help to solve problems where there are recurring payments.

We start with an introduction to financial calculators and then look at spreadsheets.

Using Financial Calculators to Solve Simple Time-Value-of-Money Problems

The basic financial calculator uses five keys that correspond to the inputs for common problems involving the time value of money:

Each key represents the following input:

- *n* is the number of periods. (We have been using *t* to denote the length of time or the number of periods.)
- *i* is the interest rate, expressed as a percentage (not a decimal). For example, if the interest rate is 8%, you would enter 8, not .08. On some calculators, this key appears as *I/YR, I/Y,* or just *i.* (We have been using *r* to denote the interest rate.)
- *PV* is the present value.
- *FV* is the future value.
- *PMT* is the amount of any recurring payment, that is, any intermediate payments that come before the date when future value, FV, is calculated. We will start with examples where there are no recurring payments, so for now we just set this key to zero.

Given any four of these inputs, the calculator will solve for the fifth. We can illustrate using Examples 5.1 and 5.2. In Example 5.1, we calculated the future value of Peter Minuit's $24 investment if invested at 8% for 390 years. Our inputs would be as follows:

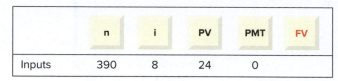

	n	i	PV	PMT	FV
Inputs	390	8	24	0	

For example, to enter the number of periods, type 390 and then press the *n* key. Similarly, enter an interest rate of 8 and a present value of 24. There are no recurring cash flows, so you need to enter a value of 0 for *PMT*. You now wish to solve for the future value given the other four inputs. On some calculators, you do this by pressing *FV*. On others, you need to first press the compute key, which may be labeled *CPT* or *COMP,* and then press *FV.* Your calculator should show a value of −$260.30 trillion, which, except for the minus sign, is the future value of $24. Try it.

Why does the minus sign appear? Most calculators treat cash flows as either inflows (shown as positive numbers) or outflows (negative numbers). For example, if you borrow $100 today at an interest rate of 12%, you receive money now (a positive cash flow), but you will have to pay back $112 in a year, a negative cash flow at that time. Therefore, the calculator displays FV as a negative number. The following time line of cash flows shows the reasoning employed. The final negative cash flow of $112 is the payment that you will need to make to clear your debt.

PV = $100

Year: 0 ————————————————— 1

FV = $112

If, instead of borrowing, you were to invest $100 today to reap a future benefit, you would enter PV as a negative number (first press 100, then press the + / − key to change the value to negative, and finally press *PV* to enter the value into the PV register). In this case, FV would appear as a positive number, showing that you will reap a cash inflow when your investment comes to fruition.

In Example 5.2, we consider a simple savings problem. We need to solve for the amount that you must put aside today to produce $3,000 in 2 years. So our inputs look like this:

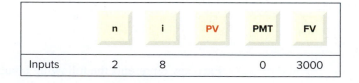

	n	i	PV	PMT	FV
Inputs	2	8		0	3000

Now compute PV; you should get an answer of −2572.02. Again the answer is displayed as a negative number because you need to make a cash outflow today (an investment) of $2,572.02 in order to reap a cash flow of $3,000 in 2 years.

BEYOND THE PAGE

Using financial calculators

mhhe.com/brealey9e

Using Spreadsheets to Solve Simple Time-Value-of-Money Problems

Just as financial calculators largely replaced interest rate tables in the 1980s, these calculators are today giving way to spreadsheets. Spreadsheets have a particular advantage when a problem involves a number of uneven cash flows. Such problems can rapidly become tedious and prone to errors from "typos," even if you use a financial calculator.

Like financial calculators, spreadsheets provide built-in functions that solve the equations linking the five variables in a time-value-of-money problem: the number of periods, the interest rate per period, the present value, the future value, and any recurring payment. For now we ignore recurring payments; later we will show you how to solve problems involving recurring payments.

Single Cash Flows   We show first how spreadsheets, such as Microsoft Excel, can be used to solve the single cash-flow problems in Examples 5.1 and 5.2.

The two Excel functions for these single cash-flow problems are:

$$\text{Future value} = \text{FV(rate, nper, pmt, PV)}$$

$$\text{Present value} = \text{PV(rate, nper, pmt, FV)}$$

As you can see, each spreadsheet formula requires four inputs—just as financial calculators require four inputs. The spreadsheet then provides the solution for the fifth variable. Also, as with most calculators, the spreadsheet functions interpret cash inflows as positive values and cash outflows as negative values. Unlike financial calculators, however, most spreadsheets require that interest rates be input as decimals rather than whole numbers (e.g., .06 rather than 6%). Note also the use of = in front of the formulas to alert Excel to the fact that these are predefined formulas.

Spreadsheet 5.1 solves for the future value of the $24 spent to acquire Manhattan Island (Example 5.1). The interest rate is entered as a decimal in cell B3. The number of periods is 390 (cell B4). We enter the recurring payment as zero in cell B5. The present value is entered as −24 (cell B6), representing the purchase price, and therefore the future value is a positive cash flow.

Of course, memorizing Excel functions such as the one in cell B8 may not come easily to everyone. (We admit that we're still working on it.) But there is an easy cure for those of us with bad memories. You can pull down the appropriate function from Excel's built-in functions (from the Formulas tab), and you will be prompted for the necessary inputs. Spreadsheet 5.2 illustrates. Go to the Formula tab, click Financial formulas, and then select FV. The "Function Arguments" screen shown in Spreadsheet 5.2 should now appear. At the bottom left of the function box there is a Help facility with an example of how the function is used.

Now let's solve Example 5.2 in a spreadsheet. We can type the Excel function = PV(rate, nper, pmt, FV) = PV(.08, 2, 0, 3000), or we can select the PV function from the pull-down menu of financial functions and fill in our inputs as shown in the dialog box below. Either way, you should get an answer of −$2,572. (Notice that you

SPREADSHEET 5.1 Using a spreadsheet to find the future value of $24

	A	B	C
1	**Finding the future value of $24 using a spreadsheet**		
2	**INPUTS**		
3	Interest rate	0.08	
4	Periods	390	
5	Payment	0	
6	Present value (PV)	−24	
7			Formula in cell B8
8	Future value	$260,301,027,018,004	=FV(B3,B4,B5,B6)
9			
10	Notice that we enter the present value in cell B6 as a negative number,		
11	since the "purchase price" is a cash outflow. The interest rate in cell B3		
12	is entered as a decimal, not a percentage.		
13			
14			

SPREADSHEET 5.2 Using the financial function pull-down menu

	A	B	C
1	**Finding the future value of $24 using a spreadsheet**		
2	**INPUTS**		
3	Interest rate	0.08	
4	Periods	390	
5	Payment	0	
6	Present value (PV)	−24	
7			Formula in cell B8
8	Future value	$260,301,027,018,004	= FV(B3,B4,B5,B6)
9			
10			

Function Arguments

FV

Rate	.08	= 0.08
Nper	390	= 390
Pmt	0	= 0
Pv	-24	= -24
Type		= number

= 2.60301E+14

Returns the future value of an investment based on periodic, constant payments and a constant interest rate.

Pv is the present value, or the lump-sum amount that a series of future payments is worth now. If omitted, Pv = 0.

Formula result = 2.60301E+14

Help on this function   OK   Cancel

don't type the comma in 3,000 when entering the number in the spreadsheet. If you did, Excel would interpret the entry as two different numbers, 3 followed by zero.)

Finding the present value of a future amount using the pull-down menu in Excel. This is the solution for the savings problem in Example 5.2.

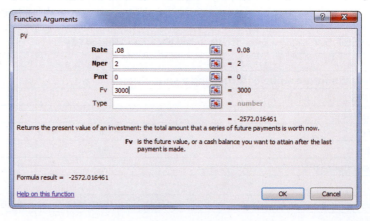

Function Arguments

PV

Rate	.08	= 0.08
Nper	2	= 2
Pmt	0	= 0
Fv	3000	= 3000
Type		= number

= -2572.016461

Returns the present value of an investment: the total amount that a series of future payments is worth now.

Fv is the future value, or a cash balance you want to attain after the last payment is made.

Formula result = -2572.016461

Help on this function   OK   Cancel

BEYOND THE PAGE

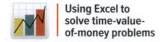 **Using Excel to solve time-value-of-money problems**

mhhe.com/brealey9e

Multiple Cash Flows   Valuing multiple cash flows with a spreadsheet is no different from valuing single cash flows. You simply find the present value of each flow and then add them up. Spreadsheet 5.3 shows how to find the solution to Example 5.7.

The time until each payment is listed in column A. This value is then used to set the number of periods (nper) in the formula in column C. The values for the cash flow in each future period are entered as negative numbers in the PV formula. The present

SPREADSHEET 5.3 Using a spreadsheet to find the present value of multiple cash flows

	A	B	C	D	E
1	Finding the present value of multiple cash flows using a spreadsheet				
2					
3	Time until CF	Cash flow	Present value	Formula in Col C	Alternative formula for Col C
4	0	8000	$8,000.00	=PV(B10, A4,0, −B4)	=B4/(1 + B10)^A4
5	1	4000	$3,703.70	=PV(B10, A5,0, −B5)	=B5/(1 + B10)^A5
6	2	4000	$3,429.36	=PV(B10, A6,0, −B6)	=B6/(1 + B10)^A6
7					
8	SUM		$15,133.06	=SUM(C4:C6)	=SUM(C4:C6)
9					
10	Discount rate:	0.08			
11					
12	Notice that the time until each payment is found in column A.				
13	Once we enter the formula for present value in cell C4, we can copy it to cells C5 and C6.				
14	The present value for other interest rates can be found by changing the entry in cell B10.				

values (column C) therefore appear as positive numbers. Column E shows an alternative to the use of the PV function, where we calculate present values directly. This allows us to see exactly what we are doing.

The Beyond the Page icon will take you to an application that shows how each of the examples in this chapter can be solved using a spreadsheet.

5.5 Level Cash Flows: Perpetuities and Annuities

annuity
Level stream of cash flows at regular intervals with a finite maturity.

perpetuity
Stream of level cash payments that never ends.

Frequently, you may need to value a stream of equal cash flows. For example, a home mortgage might require the homeowner to make equal monthly payments for the life of the loan. For a 30-year loan, this would result in 360 equal payments. A 4-year car loan might require 48 equal monthly payments. Any such sequence of equally spaced, level cash flows is called an **annuity.** If the payment stream lasts forever, it is called a **perpetuity.**

How to Value Perpetuities

Some time ago, the British government borrowed by issuing loans known as consols. Consols are perpetuities. In other words, instead of repaying these loans, the British government pays the investors a fixed annual payment in perpetuity (forever).

How might we value such a security? Suppose that you could invest $100 at an interest rate of 10%. You would earn annual interest of $.10 \times \$100 = \$10$ per year and could withdraw this amount from your investment account each year without ever running down your balance. In other words, a $100 investment could provide a perpetuity of $10 per year. In general,

$$\text{Cash payment from perpetuity} = \text{interest rate} \times \text{present value}$$
$$C = r \times \text{PV}$$

We can rearrange this relationship to derive the present value of a perpetuity, given the interest rate r and the cash payment C:

$$\text{PV of perpetuity} = \frac{C}{r} = \frac{\text{cash payment}}{\text{interest rate}} \qquad (5.3)$$

Suppose some worthy person wishes to endow a chair in finance at your university. If the rate of interest is 10% and the aim is to provide $100,000 a year forever, the amount that must be set aside today is

$$\text{Present value of perpetuity} = \frac{C}{r} = \frac{\$100,000}{.10} = \$1,000,000$$

Two warnings about the perpetuity formula. First, at a quick glance you can easily confuse the formula with the present value of a single cash payment. A payment of $1 at the end of 1 year has a present value $1/(1 + r)$. The perpetuity has a value of $1/r$. At a 10% interest rate, a perpetuity is 11 times more valuable than a single cash flow.

Second, the perpetuity formula tells us the value of a regular stream of payments starting one period from now. Thus our endowment of $1 million would provide the university with its first payment of $100,000 one year hence. If the worthy donor wants to provide the university with an additional payment of $100,000 up front, he or she would need to put aside $1,100,000.

Sometimes you may need to calculate the value of a perpetuity that does not start to make payments for several years. For example, suppose that our philanthropist decides to provide $100,000 a year with the first payment 4 years from now. We know that in year 3, this endowment will be an ordinary perpetuity with payments starting at the end of 1 year. So our perpetuity formula tells us that in year 3 the endowment will be worth $100,000/r$. But it is not worth that much now. To find today's value we need to multiply by the 3-year discount factor. Thus, at an interest rate of 10%, the "delayed" perpetuity is worth

$$\$100,000 \times \frac{1}{r} \times \frac{1}{(1 + r)^3} = \$1,000,000 \times \frac{1}{(1.10)^3} = \$751,315$$

5.5   Self-Test

A British government perpetuity pays £4 a year forever and is selling for £48. What is the interest rate?

How to Value Annuities

Let us return to Kangaroo Autos for (almost) the last time. Most installment plans call for level streams of payments. So let us suppose that Kangaroo now offers an "easy payment" scheme of $8,000 a year at the end of each of the next 3 years.

The payments on the Kangaroo plan constitute a 3-year annuity. Figure 5.8 shows a time line of these cash flows and calculates the present value of each year's flow assuming an interest rate of 10%. You can see that the total present value of the payments is $19,894.82.

You can always value an annuity by calculating the present value of each cash flow and finding the total. However, it is usually quicker to use a simple formula that states

FIGURE 5.8 To find the value of an annuity, you can calculate the value of each cash flow. It is usually quicker to use the annuity formula.

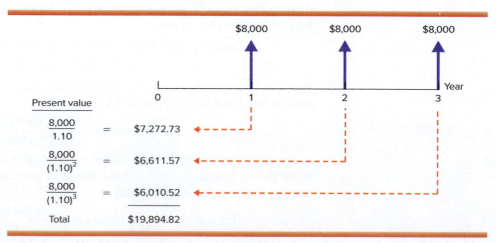

that if the interest rate is r, then the present value of an annuity that pays C dollars a year for each of t periods is

$$\text{Present value of } t\text{-year annuity} = C\left[\frac{1}{r} - \frac{1}{r(1+r)^t}\right] \qquad (5.4)$$

annuity factor
Present value of an annuity of $1 per period.

The expression in brackets shows the present value of a t-year annuity of $1 starting in period 1. It is generally known as the t-year **annuity factor.** Therefore, another way to write the value of an annuity is

$$\text{Present value of } t\text{-year annuity} = \text{payment} \times \text{annuity factor}$$

You can use this formula to calculate the present value of the payments to Kangaroo. The annual payment (C) is $8,000, the interest rate (r) is 10%, and the number of years (t) is 3. Therefore,

$$\text{Present value} = C\left[\frac{1}{r} - \frac{1}{r(1+r)^t}\right]$$

$$= 8,000\left[\frac{1}{.10} - \frac{1}{.10(1.10)^3}\right]$$

$$= \$19,894.82$$

This is exactly the same answer that we got by separately valuing each cash flow. If the number of periods is small, there is little to choose between the two methods, but when you are valuing long-term annuities, it is far easier to use the formula.

If you are wondering where the annuity formula comes from, look at Figure 5.9. It shows the payments and values of three investments.

Row 1   The investment in the first row provides a perpetual stream of $1 starting at the end of the first year. We have already seen that this perpetuity has a present value of $1/r$.

Row 2   Now look at the investment shown in the second row of Figure 5.9. It also provides a perpetual stream of $1 payments, but these payments don't start until year 4. This stream of payments is identical to the payments in row 1, except that they are delayed for an additional 3 years. In year 3, the investment will be an ordinary perpetuity with payments starting in 1 year and will therefore be worth $1/r$ in year 3. To find the value *today,* we simply multiply this figure by the 3-year discount factor. Thus

$$PV = \frac{1}{r} \times \frac{1}{(1+r)^3} = \frac{1}{r(1+r)^3}$$

Row 3   Finally, look at the investment shown in the third row of Figure 5.9. This provides a level payment of $1 a year for each of 3 years. In other words, it is a 3-year annuity. You can also see that, taken together, the investments in rows 2 and 3 provide exactly the same cash payments as the investment in row 1. Thus the value of our annuity (row 3) must be equal to the value of the row 1 perpetuity less the value of the delayed row 2 perpetuity:

$$\text{Present value of a 3-year \$1 annuity} = \frac{1}{r} - \frac{1}{r(1+r)^3}$$

FIGURE 5.9 The value of an annuity is equal to the difference between the value of two perpetuities.

	Cash Flow						Present Value
Year:	1	2	3	4	5	6 . . .	
1. Perpetuity A	$1	$1	$1	$1	$1	$1 . . .	$\frac{1}{r}$
2. Perpetuity B				$1	$1	$1 . . .	$\frac{1}{r(1+r)^3}$
3. Three-year annuity	$1	$1	$1				$\frac{1}{r} - \frac{1}{r(1+r)^3}$

TABLE 5.4 An example of an
annuity table, showing the
present value today of $1 a year
received for each of *t* years

Number of Years	Interest Rate per Year					
	5%	6%	7%	8%	9%	10%
1	0.9524	0.9434	0.9346	0.9259	0.9174	0.9091
2	1.8594	1.8334	1.8080	1.7833	1.7591	1.7355
3	2.7232	2.6730	2.6243	2.5771	2.5313	2.4869
4	3.5460	3.4651	3.3872	3.3121	3.2397	3.1699
5	4.3295	4.2124	4.1002	3.9927	3.8897	3.7908
10	7.7217	7.3601	7.0236	6.7101	6.4177	6.1446
20	12.4622	11.4699	10.5940	9.8181	9.1285	8.5136
30	15.3725	13.7648	12.4090	11.2578	10.2737	9.4269

Remembering formulas is about as difficult as remembering other people's birthdays. But as long as you bear in mind that an annuity is equivalent to the difference between an immediate and a delayed perpetuity, you shouldn't have any difficulty.

You can use a calculator or spreadsheet to work out annuity factors (we show you how momentarily), or you can use a set of annuity tables. Table 5.4 is an abridged annuity table (an extended version is shown in Table A.3 at the end of the book). Check that you can find the 3-year annuity factor for an interest rate of 10%.

Compare Table 5.4 with Table 5.3, which presented the present value of a *single* cash flow. In both tables, present values fall as we move across the rows to higher discount rates. But in contrast to those in Table 5.3, present values in Table 5.4 increase as we move down the columns, reflecting the greater number of payments made by longer annuities.

5.6   Self-Test

If the interest rate is 8%, what is the 4-year discount factor? What is the 4-year annuity factor? What is the relationship between these two numbers? Explain.

Example 5.8 ▶   Winning Big at the Lottery

In September 2015, a 50-year-old Michigan woman bought a Powerball lottery ticket and won $310.5 million. We suspect that she received unsolicited congratulations, good wishes, and requests for money from dozens of more or less worthy charities, relations, and newly devoted friends. In response, she could fairly point out that the prize wasn't really worth $310.5 million. That sum was to be paid in 30 equal annual installments of $10.35 million each. Assuming that the first payment occurred at the end of 1 year, what was the present value of the prize? The interest rate at the time was about 3.2%.

The present value of these payments is simply the sum of the present values of each annual payment. But rather than valuing the payments separately, it is much easier to treat them as a 30-year annuity. To value this annuity, we multiply $10.35 million by the 30-year annuity factor:

$$PV = 10.35 \times 30\text{-year annuity factor}$$

$$= 10.35 \times \left[\frac{1}{r} - \frac{1}{r(1+r)^{30}} \right]$$

At an interest rate of 3.2%, the annuity factor is

$$\left[\frac{1}{.032} - \frac{1}{.032(1.032)^{30}} \right] = 19.1033$$

The present value of the cash payments is $10.35 × 19.1033 = $197.7 million, much less than the much-advertised prize, but still not a bad day's haul.

Lottery operators generally make arrangements for winners with big spending plans to take an equivalent lump sum. In our example, the winner could either take the $310.5 million spread over 30 years or receive $197.7 million up front. Both arrangements have the same present value. ∎

Example 5.9 ▶ How Much Luxury and Excitement Can $79 Billion Buy?

Bill Gates is one of the world's richest persons, with wealth in 2015 reputed to be about $79 billion. Mr. Gates has devoted a large part of his fortune to the Bill and Melinda Gates Foundation; but suppose that he decided instead to allocate his entire wealth to a life of luxury and entertainment (L&E). What annual expenditures on L&E could $79 billion support over a 30-year period? Assume that Mr. Gates can invest his funds at 6%.

The 30-year, 6% annuity factor is 13.7648. We set the present value of Mr. Gates's spending stream equal to his total wealth:

$$\text{Present value} = \text{annual spending} \times \text{annuity factor}$$

$$79,000,000,000 = \text{annual spending} \times 13.7648$$

$$\text{Annual spending} = 5,739,300,000, \text{ or about } \$5.7 \text{ billion}$$

Warning to Mr. Gates: We haven't considered inflation. The cost of buying L&E will increase, so $5.7 billion won't buy as much L&E in 30 years as it will today. More on that later. ∎

5.7 Self-Test

Suppose you retire at age 70. You expect to live 20 more years and to spend $55,000 a year during your retirement. How much money do you need to save by age 70 to support this consumption plan? Assume an interest rate of 7%.

Example 5.10 ▶ Home Mortgages

Sometimes you may need to find the series of cash payments that would provide a given value today. For example, home purchasers typically borrow the bulk of the house price from a lender. The most common loan arrangement is a 30-year loan that is repaid in equal monthly installments. Suppose that a house costs $125,000 and that the buyer puts down 20% of the purchase price, or $25,000, in cash, borrowing the remaining $100,000 from a mortgage lender such as the local savings bank. What is the appropriate monthly mortgage payment?

The borrower repays the loan by making monthly payments over the next 30 years (360 months). The savings bank needs to set these monthly payments so that they have a present value of $100,000. Thus

$$\text{Present value} = \text{mortgage payment} \times \text{360-month annuity factor}$$
$$= \$100,000$$
$$\text{Mortgage payment} = \frac{\$100,000}{\text{360-month annuity factor}}$$

Suppose that the interest rate is 1% a month. Then

$$\text{Mortgage payment} = \frac{\$100{,}000}{\left[\dfrac{1}{.01} - \dfrac{1}{.01(1.01)^{360}}\right]} = \frac{\$100{,}000}{97.218} = \$1{,}028.61 \blacksquare$$

The mortgage loan in Example 5.10 is an example of an *amortizing loan*. "Amortizing" means that part of the monthly payment is used to pay interest on the loan and part is used to reduce the amount of the loan. Table 5.5 illustrates a 4-year amortizing loan of $1,000 with an interest rate of 10% and annual payments starting in 1 year. The annual payment (annuity) that would repay the loan is $315.47. (Confirm this for yourself.) At the end of the first year, the interest payment is 10% of $1,000, or $100. So $100 of your first payment is used to pay interest, and the remaining $215.47 is used to reduce (or "amortize") the loan balance to $784.53.

Next year, the outstanding balance is lower, so the interest charge is only $78.45. Therefore, $315.47 − $78.45 = $237.02 can be applied to amortization. Amortization in the second year is higher than in the first because the amount of the loan has declined, and therefore, less of the payment is taken up in interest. This procedure continues until the last year, when the amortization is just enough to reduce the outstanding balance on the loan to zero.

Because the loan is progressively paid off, the fraction of each payment devoted to interest steadily falls over time, while the fraction used to reduce the loan (the amortization) steadily increases. Figure 5.10 illustrates the amortization of the mortgage loan in Example 5.10. In the early years, almost all of the mortgage payment is for interest. Even after 15 years, the bulk of the monthly payment is interest.

5.8   Self-Test

What will be the monthly payment if you take out a $100,000 15-year mortgage at an interest rate of 1% per month? How much of the first payment is interest, and how much is amortization?

Future Value of an Annuity

You are back in savings mode again. This time you are setting aside $3,000 at the end of every year. If your savings earn interest of 8% a year, how much will they be worth at the end of 4 years? We can answer this question with the help of the time line in Figure 5.11. Your first year's savings will earn interest for 3 years, the second will earn interest for 2 years, the third will earn interest for 1 year, and the final savings in year 4 will earn no interest. The sum of the future values of the four payments is

$$(\$3{,}000 \times 1.08^3) + (\$3{,}000 \times 1.08^2) + (\$3{,}000 \times 1.08) + \$3{,}000 = \$13{,}518$$

TABLE 5.5 An example of an amortizing loan. If you borrow $1,000 at an interest rate of 10%, you would need to make an annual payment of $315.47 over 4 years to repay the loan with interest.

Year	Beginning-of-Year Balance	Year-End Interest Due on Balance	Year-End Payment	Amortization of Loan	End-of-Year Balance
1	$1,000.00	$100.00	$315.47	$215.47	$784.53
2	784.53	78.45	315.47	237.02	547.51
3	547.51	54.75	315.47	260.72	286.79
4	286.79	28.68	315.47	286.79	0

FIGURE 5.10 Mortgage amortization. This figure shows the breakdown of mortgage payments between interest and amortization. Monthly payments within each year are summed, so the figure shows the annual payment on the mortgage.

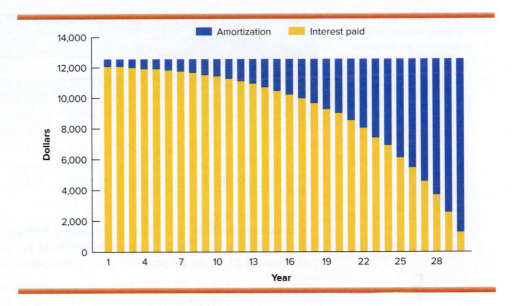

FIGURE 5.11 Calculating the future value of an ordinary annuity of $3,000 a year for 4 years (interest rate = 8%)

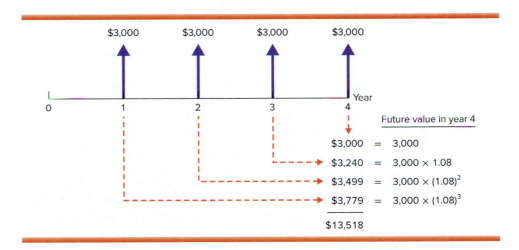

But wait a minute! We are looking here at a level stream of cash flows—an annuity. We have seen that there is a shortcut formula to calculate the *present* value of an annuity. So there ought to be a similar formula for calculating the *future* value of a level stream of cash flows.

Think first how much your stream of savings is worth today. You are setting aside $3,000 in each of the next 4 years. The *present* value of this 4-year annuity is therefore equal to

$$PV = \$3,000 \times 4\text{-year annuity factor}$$

$$= \$3,000 \times \left[\frac{1}{.08} - \frac{1}{.08(1.08)^4}\right] = \$9,936$$

Now think how much you would have after 4 years if you invested $9,936 today. Simple! Just multiply by $(1.08)^4$:

$$\text{Value at end of year 4} = \$9,936 \times 1.08^4 = \$13,518$$

TABLE 5.6 An example of a
table showing the future value of
an investment of $1 a year for
each of *t* years

Number of Years	Interest Rate per Year					
	5%	6%	7%	8%	9%	10%
1	1.0000	1.0000	1.0000	1.0000	1.0000	1.0000
2	2.0500	2.0600	2.0700	2.0800	2.0900	2.1000
3	3.1525	3.1836	3.2149	3.2464	3.2781	3.3100
4	4.3101	4.3746	4.4399	4.5061	4.5731	4.6410
5	5.5256	5.6371	5.7507	5.8666	5.9847	6.1051
10	12.5779	13.1808	13.8164	14.4866	15.1929	15.9374
20	33.0660	36.7856	40.9955	45.7620	51.1601	57.2750
30	66.4388	79.0582	94.4608	113.2832	136.3075	164.4940

We calculated the future value of the annuity by first calculating the present value and then multiplying by $(1 + r)^t$. The general formula for the future value of a stream of cash flows of $1 a year for each of t years is therefore

$$\begin{matrix} \text{Future value (FV) of} \\ \text{annuity of \$1 a year} \end{matrix} = \begin{matrix} \text{present value of annuity} \\ \text{of \$1 a year} \times (1 + r)^t \end{matrix} \qquad (5.5)$$

$$= \left[\frac{1}{r} - \frac{1}{r(1 + r)^t} \right] \times (1 + r)^t$$

$$= \frac{(1 + r)^t - 1}{r}$$

If you need to find the future value of just four cash flows as in our example, it is a toss-up whether it is quicker to calculate the future value of each cash flow separately (as we did in Figure 5.11) or to use the annuity formula. If you are faced with a stream of 10 or 20 cash flows, there is no contest.

You can find the future value of an annuity in Table 5.6 or the more extensive Table A.4 at the end of the book. You can see that in the row corresponding to $t = 4$ and the column corresponding to $r = 8\%$, the future value of an annuity of $1 a year is $4.5061. Therefore, the future value of the $3,000 annuity is $3,000 \times 4.5061 = \$13,518$. In practice, you will tend to use a calculator or spreadsheet to find these values.

Example 5.11 ▶   Saving for Retirement

In only 50 more years, you will retire. (That's right—by the time you retire, the retirement age will be around 70 years. Longevity is not an unmixed blessing.) Have you started saving yet? Suppose you believe you will need to accumulate $500,000 by your retirement date in order to support your desired standard of living. How much savings each year would be necessary to produce $500,000 at the end of 50 years? Let's say that the interest rate is 10% per year. You need to find how large the annuity in the following figure must be to provide a future value of $500,000:

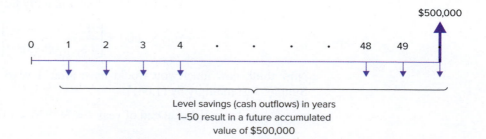

We know that if you were to save $1 each year your funds would accumulate to

$$\text{Future value (FV) of annuity of \$1 a year} = \frac{(1 + r)^t - 1}{r} = \frac{(1.10)^{50} - 1}{.10}$$

$$= \$1,163.91$$

We need to choose C to ensure that $C \times 1,163.91 = \$500,000$. Thus $C = \$500,000/1,163.91 = \$429.59$. This appears to be surprisingly good news. Saving $429.59 a year does not seem to be an extremely demanding savings program. Don't celebrate yet, however. Your goal will appear far more daunting once we consider the impact of inflation. ■

Annuities Due

BEYOND THE PAGE

Valuing annuities

mhhe.com/brealey9e

annuity due
Level stream of cash flows
starting immediately.

Remember that our annuity formulas assume that the first cash flow does not occur until the end of the first period. The present value of an annuity is the value today of a stream of payments that starts in one period. Similarly, the future value of an annuity assumes that the first cash flow comes at the end of one period.

But in many cases, cash payments start immediately. For example, when Kangaroo Autos (see Figure 5.8) sells you a car on credit, it may insist that the first payment be made at the time of the sale. A level stream of payments starting immediately is known as an **annuity due.**

Figure 5.12 depicts the cash-flow streams of an ordinary annuity and an annuity due. Comparing panels *a* and *b*, you can see that each of the three cash flows in the annuity due comes one period earlier than the corresponding cash flow of the ordinary annuity. Therefore, each is discounted for one less period, and its present value increases by a factor of $(1 + r)$. Therefore,

$$\text{Present value of annuity due} = \text{present value of ordinary annuity} \times (1 + r) \quad \textbf{(5.6)}$$

Figure 5.12 shows that bringing the Kangaroo loan payments forward by 1 year increases their present value from $19,894.82 (as an ordinary annuity) to $21,884.30 (as an annuity due). Notice that $21,884.30 = \$19,894.82 \times 1.10$.

5.9   Self-Test

In Example 5.11, we showed that an annual savings stream of **$429.59 invested for 50 years at 10% a year would satisfy a savings goal of $500,000. Suppose instead that you made 50 annual investments, but you made these investments at the beginning of each year rather than at the end. How much would these savings amount to by the end of year 50?**

You may also want to calculate the *future* value of an annuity due. If the first cash flow comes immediately, the future value of the cash-flow stream is greater because each flow has an extra year to earn interest. For example, at an interest rate of 10%, the future value of an annuity due would be exactly 10% greater than the future value of an ordinary annuity. More generally,

$$\text{Future value of annuity due} = \text{future value of ordinary annuity} \times (1 + r) \quad \textbf{(5.7)}$$

FIGURE 5.12 The cash payments on the ordinary annuity in panel *a* start in year 1. The first payment on the annuity due in panel *b* occurs immediately. The annuity due is therefore more valuable.

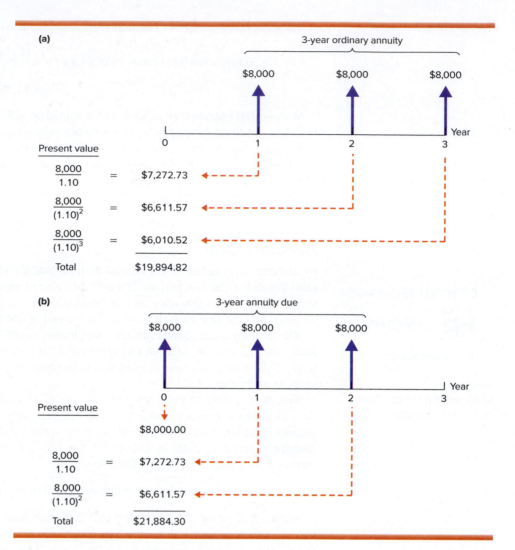

Example 5.12 ▶ Good News for the Powerball Lottery Winner

When calculating the value of the Powerball lottery prize in Example 5.8, we assumed that the first of the payments occurred at the end of 1 year. However, if the winner of the lottery had chosen to receive the prize in installments, she would not, in fact, have needed to wait before receiving any cash. She would have gotten her first installment of $10.35 million up front, and the remaining payments would have been spread over the following 29 years. How would this affect the value of the prize?

We saw in Example 5.8 that the 30-year annuity factor for an ordinary annuity is 19.1033. Therefore, the 30-year *annuity-due* factor would be 19.1033 × 1.032 = 19.7146. The present value of the winnings would be $10.35 × 19.7146 = $204 million, an increase of about $6.3 million. ∎

5.6 Reducing the Chore of the Calculations: Part 2

In Section 5.4, we showed how managers use financial calculators or spreadsheets to solve present value problems. At that point we had not encountered annuities, and we assumed that there were no recurring cash flows. We were simply concerned with the present value (PV) and the future value (FV). However, when we need to value an annuity, we are concerned with the present value, the future value, and the regular annuity payment (PMT). Here are some examples of how you can use a financial calculator and a spreadsheet to value annuities.

Using Financial Calculators to Solve Annuity Problems

We looked earlier at the "easy payment" scheme offered by Kangaroo Autos. It called for a payment of $8,000 at the end of each of the next 3 years. What is the present value of these payments if the interest rate is 10%?

To find the answer on your financial calculator, you must enter the following numbers:

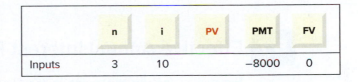

	n	i	PV	PMT	FV
Inputs	3	10		−8000	0

Notice that PMT is no longer set at zero; instead, you need to enter the regular annuity payment (−8000). Note also that PMT is entered as a negative number; you are paying out $8,000 a year to Kangaroo Autos. There are no other payments involved, so FV is set at zero. (If, say, you were also required to pay an *additional* $5,000 in year 3, you would need to enter a future value, FV, of −5000.) Now compute PV; you should get an answer of 19,894.82.

Now let us use a financial calculator to solve Example 5.10. A savings bank needed to set the monthly payments on a mortgage so that they would have a present value, PV, of $100,000. There were 360 monthly payments, and the interest rate was 1% per month. To find the regular monthly payment (PMT), you need to enter the following data:

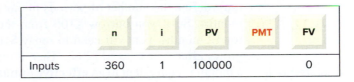

	n	i	PV	PMT	FV
Inputs	360	1	100000		0

BEYOND THE PAGE

 Annuities and financial calculators

mhhe.com/brealey9e

Notice that we enter PV as a positive number: You get a cash inflow when the bank lends you the money. When you press the *PMT* key, you should get the answer −1,028.61 because the payment is a cash outflow.

Suppose that the mortgage is an annuity due with the first monthly payment made immediately. You can solve for annuities due by pressing the *begin* key on your calculator. The calculator will automatically interpret the cash-flow series as an annuity due with the cash flows coming at the beginning of each period. To return to the ordinary annuity mode, just press the *begin* key again.

Using Spreadsheets to Solve Annuity Problems

Solving annuity problems with a spreadsheet involves exactly the same functions that we used to solve single cash-flow problems. However, with an annuity, the recurring payment (*PMT*) is no longer zero.

Think again of the "easy payment" scheme offered by Kangaroo Autos. This called for a payment of $8,000 at the end of each of the next 3 years. We need to calculate the present value of these payments at an interest rate of 10%. The following spreadsheet shows the solution to this problem.

	A	B	C
1	**Finding the present value of an annuity using a spreadsheet**		
2			
3	Interest rate (i)	0.1	
4	Number of periods (nper)	3	
5	Payment per period (pmt)	8000	
6			
7			Formula in cell B8
8	Present value (PV)	$19,894.82	=PV(B3,B4,−B5,0)
9			
10	Notice that the interest rate is entered as a decimal, not a percentage.		

5.7 Effective Annual Interest Rates

We realize that by this point in the chapter you probably feel overwhelmed by formulas. We have, however, two more tasks; so, if your head is spinning, now might be a good time to take a break and drink a strong cup of coffee.

So far in this chapter we have mainly used *annual* interest rates to value a series of *annual* cash flows. But interest rates may be quoted for days, months, years, or any convenient interval. How should we compare rates when they are quoted for different periods, such as monthly versus annually?

Consider your credit card. Suppose you have to pay interest on any unpaid balances at the rate of 1% *per month*. What is it going to cost you if you neglect to pay off your unpaid balance for a year?

Don't be put off because the interest rate is quoted per month rather than per year. The important thing is to maintain consistency between the interest rate and the number of periods. If the interest rate is quoted as a percent per month, then we must define the number of periods in our future value calculation as the number of months. So if you borrow $100 from the credit card company at 1% per month for 12 months, you will need to repay $100 \times (1.01)^{12} = \$112.68$. Thus your debt grows after 1 year to $112.68. Therefore, we can say that the interest rate of 1% a month is equivalent to an **effective annual interest rate,** or *annually compounded rate,* of 12.68%.

effective annual interest rate
Interest rate that is annualized using compound interest.

In general, the effective annual interest rate is defined as the rate at which your money grows, allowing for the effect of compounding. Therefore, for the credit card,

$$1 + \text{effective annual rate} = (1 + \text{monthly rate})^{12}$$

When comparing interest rates, it is best to use effective annual rates. This compares interest paid or received over a common period (1 year) and allows for possible compounding during the period. Unfortunately, short-term rates are sometimes annualized by multiplying the rate per period by the number of periods in a year. In fact, truth-in-lending laws in the United States *require* that rates be annualized in this manner. Such rates are called **annual percentage rates (APRs).**[3] The interest rate on your credit card loan was 1% per month. Because there are 12 months in a year, the APR on the loan is $12 \times 1\% = 12\%$.[4]

annual percentage rate (APR)
Interest rate that is annualized using simple interest.

---

[3] The truth-in-lending laws apply to credit card loans, auto loans, home improvement loans, and some loans to small businesses. The term "APR" is not commonly used or quoted in the big leagues of finance.

[4] The rules for calculating the APR differ from one country to another. For example, in the EU, companies are obliged to quote the effective annual interest rate on most loans.

If the credit card company quotes an APR of 12%, how can you find the effective annual interest rate? The solution is simple:

Step 1. Take the quoted APR and divide by the number of compounding periods in a year to recover the rate per period actually charged. In our example, the interest was calculated monthly. So we divide the APR by 12 to obtain the interest rate per month:

$$\text{Monthly interest rate} = \frac{\text{APR}}{12} = \frac{12\%}{12} = 1\%$$

Step 2. Now convert to an annually compounded interest rate:

$$1 + \text{effective annual rate} = (1 + \text{monthly rate})^{12} = (1 + .01)^{12} = 1.1268$$

The effective annual interest rate is .1268, or 12.68%.

In general, if an investment is quoted with a given APR and there are m compounding periods in a year, then \$1 will grow to $\$1 \times (1 + \text{APR}/m)^m$ after 1 year. The effective annual interest rate is $(1 + \text{APR}/m)^m - 1$. For example, a credit card loan that charges a monthly interest rate of 1% has an APR of 12% but an effective annual interest rate of $(1.01)^{12} - 1 = .1268$, or 12.68%. To summarize: **The effective annual rate is the rate at which invested funds will grow over the course of a year. It equals the rate of interest per period compounded for the number of periods in a year.**

Example 5.13 ▶   The Effective Interest Rates on Bank Accounts

Back in the 1960s and 1970s, federal regulation limited the APR interest rates banks could pay on savings accounts. Banks were hungry for depositors, and they searched for ways to increase the *effective* rate of interest that could be paid within the rules. Their solution was to keep the same APR but to calculate the interest on deposits more frequently. As interest is compounded at shorter and shorter intervals, less time passes before interest can be earned on interest. Therefore, the effective annually compounded rate of interest increases. Table 5.7 shows the calculations assuming that the maximum APR that banks could pay was 6%. (Actually, it was a bit less than this, but 6% is a nice round number to use for illustration.)

You can see from Table 5.7 how banks were able to increase the effective interest rate simply by calculating interest at more frequent intervals.

The ultimate step was to assume that interest was paid in a continuous stream rather than at fixed intervals. With 1 year's *continuous compounding*, \$1 grows to e^{APR}, where $e = 2.718$ (a figure that may be familiar to you as the base for natural logarithms). Thus if you deposited \$1 with a bank that offered a continuously compounded rate of 6%, your investment would grow by the end of the year to $(2.718)^{.06} = \$1.061837$, just a hair's breadth more than if interest were compounded daily. ∎

TABLE 5.7 These investments all have an APR of 6%, but the more frequently interest is compounded, the higher is the effective annual rate of interest.

Compounding Period	Periods per Year (m)	Per-Period Interest Rate	Growth Factor of Invested Funds	Effective Annual Rate
1 year	1	6%	1.06	6.0000%
Semiannually	2	3	$1.03^2 = 1.0609$	6.0900
Quarterly	4	1.5	$1.015^4 = 1.061364$	6.1364
Monthly	12	0.5	$1.005^{12} = 1.061678$	6.1678
Weekly	52	0.11538	$1.0011538^{52} = 1.061800$	6.1800
Daily	365	0.01644	$1.0001644^{365} = 1.061831$	6.1831
Continuous			$e^{.06} = 1.061837$	6.1837

5.10 **Self-Test**

A car loan requiring quarterly payments carries an APR of 8%. What is the effective annual rate of interest?

5.8 ## Inflation and the Time Value of Money

When a bank offers to pay 6% on a savings account, it promises to pay interest of $60 for every $1,000 you deposit. The bank fixes the number of dollars that it pays, but it doesn't provide any assurance of how much those dollars will buy. If the value of your investment increases by 6% while the prices of goods and services increase by 10%, you actually lose ground in terms of the goods you can buy.

Real versus Nominal Cash Flows

Prices of goods and services continually change. Textbooks may become more expensive (sorry) while computers become cheaper. An overall general rise in prices is known as **inflation.** If the inflation rate is 5% per year, then goods that cost $1.00 a year ago typically cost $1.05 this year. The increase in the general level of prices means that the purchasing power of money has eroded. If a dollar bill bought one loaf of bread last year, the same dollar this year buys only part of a loaf.

Economists track the general level of prices using several different price indexes. The best known of these is the *consumer price index,* or *CPI.* This measures the number of dollars needed to buy a specified basket of goods and services that is supposed to represent the typical family's purchases.[5] Thus the percentage increase in the CPI from one year to the next measures the rate of inflation.

Table 5.8 shows the CPI for selected years. The base period for the index is 1982–1984, so the index shows the price level in each year as a percentage of the average price level during these 3 years. For example, the index in 1950 was 25.0. This means that on average $25 in 1950 would have bought the same quantity of goods and services as $100 in 1982–1984. By the end of 2015, the index had risen to 236.5. In other words, prices in 2015 were 9.46 times their level in 1950 (236.5/25.0 = 9.46).[6]

It is interesting to look at annual inflation rates over a somewhat longer period. These are shown in Figure 5.13. The peak year for inflation was 1918, when prices rose by 20%, but you can see that there have also been a few years when prices have fallen quite sharply.

inflation
Rate at which prices as a whole are increasing.

BEYOND THE PAGE

 World inflation rates

mhhe.com/brealey9e

TABLE 5.8 The consumer price index (CPI) shows how inflation has increased the cost of a typical family's purchases.

	CPI	Percent Change since 1950
1950	25.0	
1960	29.8	+ 19.2%
1970	39.8	+ 59.2
1980	86.3	+245.2
1990	133.8	+435.2
2000	174.0	+596.0
2010	219.2	+776.8
2015	236.5	+846.0

[5] Don't ask how you buy a "basket" of services.

[6] The choice by the Bureau of Labor Statistics of 1982–1984 as a base period is arbitrary. For example, it could have set December 1950 as the base period. In this case the index would have been 100 in 1950 and 946.0 in 2015.

FIGURE 5.13 Annual rates of inflation in the United States from 1900 to 2015

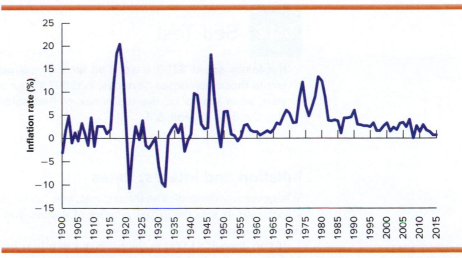

Source: Bureau of Labor Statistics.

As we write this in early 2016, all appears quiet on the inflation front. In the United States the inflation rate is close to zero and a few countries are even experiencing falling prices, or *deflation*. This has led some economists to argue that inflation is dead; others are less sure.

Example 5.14 ▶ The Price of Gasoline

Motorists in late 2015, who were paying about $2.00 for a gallon of gasoline, may have looked back longingly to 1980, when they were paying just $1.08 a gallon. But how much had the real price of gasoline changed over this period? Let's check.

In 2015, the consumer price index was about 2.74 times its level in 1980. If the price of gasoline had risen in line with inflation, it would have cost 2.74 × $1.08 = $2.96 a gallon in 2015. That was the cost of gasoline in 1980 but measured in terms of 2015 dollars rather than 1980 dollars. Thus the real price of gasoline had actually *declined* over the 35-year period. ∎

5.11 Self-Test

Consider a telephone call to London that currently would cost $5. If the real price of telephone calls does not change in the future, how much will it cost you to make a call to London in 50 years if the inflation rate is 5% (roughly its average over the past 30 years)? What if inflation is 10%?

Economists sometimes talk about *current* or *nominal dollars* versus *constant* or *real dollars*. Current or nominal dollars refer to the actual number of dollars of the day; constant or real dollars refer to the amount of purchasing power.

Some expenditures are fixed in nominal terms and therefore *decline* in real terms when the CPI increases. Suppose you took out a 30-year house mortgage in 1990. The monthly payment was $800. It was still $800 in 2015, even though the CPI increased by a factor of 236.5/133.8 = 1.77 over those years.

What's the monthly payment for 2015 expressed in real 1990 dollars? The answer is $800/1.77, or $452 per month. The real burden of paying the mortgage was much less in 2015 than in 1990.

5.12   Self-Test

If a family spent $250 a week on their typical purchases in 1950, how much would those purchases have cost in 1980? If your salary in 1980 was $30,000 a year, what would be the real value of that salary in terms of 1950 dollars? Use the data in Table 5.8.

Inflation and Interest Rates

Whenever anyone quotes an interest rate, you can be fairly sure that it is a *nominal,* not a *real,* rate. It sets the actual number of dollars you will be paid with no offset for future inflation.

nominal interest rate
Rate at which money invested grows.

If you deposit $1,000 in the bank at a **nominal interest rate** of 6%, you will have $1,060 at the end of the year. But this does not mean you are 6% better off. Suppose that the inflation rate during the year is also 6%. Then the goods that cost $1,000 last year will now cost $1,000 × 1.06 = $1,060, so you've gained nothing:

$$\text{Real future value of investment} = \frac{\$1,000 \times (1 + \text{nominal interest rate})}{(1 + \text{inflation rate})}$$

$$= \frac{\$1,000 \times 1.06}{1.06} = \$1,000$$

real interest rate
Rate at which the purchasing power of an investment increases.

In this example, the nominal rate of interest is 6%, but the **real interest rate** is zero.

The real rate of interest is calculated by

$$1 + \text{real interest rate} = \frac{1 + \text{nominal interest rate}}{1 + \text{inflation rate}} \qquad \textbf{(5.8)}$$

In our example, both the nominal interest rate and the inflation rate were 6%. So

$$1 + \text{real interest rate} = \frac{1.06}{1.06} = 1$$

$$\text{Real interest rate} = 0$$

What if the nominal interest rate is 6% but the inflation rate is only 2%? In that case the real interest rate is 1.06/1.02 − 1 = .039, or 3.9%. Imagine that the price of a loaf of bread is $1, so that $1,000 would buy 1,000 loaves today. If you invest that $1,000 at a nominal interest rate of 6%, you will have $1,060 at the end of the year. However, if the price of loaves has risen in the meantime to $1.02, then your money will buy you 1,060/1.02 = 1,039 loaves. The real rate of interest is 3.9%.

5.13   Self-Test

a. Suppose that you invest your funds at an interest rate of 8%. What will be your real rate of interest if the inflation rate is zero? What if it is 5%?
b. Suppose that you demand a real rate of interest of 3% on your investments. What nominal interest rate do you need to earn if the inflation rate is zero? If it is 5%?

Here is a useful approximation. The real rate approximately equals the difference between the nominal rate and the inflation rate:[7]

$$\text{Real interest rate} \approx \text{nominal interest rate} - \text{inflation rate} \qquad \textbf{(5.9)}$$

Our example used a nominal interest rate of 6%, an inflation rate of 2%, and a real rate of 3.9%. If we round to 4%, the approximation gives the same answer:

$$\text{Real interest rate} \approx \text{nominal interest rate} - \text{inflation rate}$$
$$\approx 6 - 2 = 4\%$$

The approximation works best when both the inflation rate and the real rate are small. When they are not small, throw the approximation away and do it right.

Example **5.15 ▶**   **Real and Nominal Rates**

In the United States in late 2015, long-term high-grade Aa-rated corporate bonds offered a yield of 2.66%. If inflation in the coming year is expected to be about 1%, the real yield is

$$1 + \text{real interest rate} = \frac{1 + \text{nominal interest rate}}{1 + \text{inflation rate}} = \frac{1.0266}{1.01} = 1.0164$$

$$\text{Real interest rate} = .0164, \text{ or } 1.64\%$$

BEYOND THE PAGE

German
hyperinflation

mhhe.com/brealey9e

The approximation rule gives a similar value of 2.66 − 1.0 = 1.66%. But the approximation would not have worked in the German hyperinflation of 1922–1923, when the inflation rate was well over 100% per *month* (at one point you needed 1 million marks to mail a letter). ∎

Valuing Real Cash Payments

Think again about how to value future cash payments. Earlier in the chapter, you learned how to value payments in current dollars by discounting at the nominal interest rate. For example, suppose that the nominal interest rate is 10%. How much do you need to invest now to produce $100 in a year's time? Easy! Calculate the present value of $100 by discounting by 10%:

$$\text{PV} = \frac{\$100}{1.10} = \$90.91$$

You get exactly the same result if you discount the *real* payment by the *real interest rate*. For example, assume that you expect inflation of 7% over the next year. The real value of that $100 is therefore only $100/1.07 = $93.46. In one year's time your $100 will buy only as much as $93.46 today. Also, with a 7% inflation rate the real rate of interest is only about 3%. We can calculate it exactly from the formula

$$1 + \text{real interest rate} = \frac{1 + \text{nominal interest rate}}{1 + \text{inflation rate}} = \frac{1.10}{1.07} = 1.028$$

$$\text{Real interest rate} = .028, \text{ or } 2.8\%$$

If we now discount the $93.46 real payment by the 2.8% real interest rate, we have a present value of $90.91, just as before:

$$\text{PV} = \frac{\$93.46}{1.028} = \$90.91$$

The two methods should always give the same answer.

---

[7] The squiggle (≈) means "approximately equal to."

Remember: **Current dollar cash flows must be discounted by the nominal interest rate; real cash flows must be discounted by the real interest rate.**

Mixing up nominal cash flows and real discount rates (or real rates and nominal flows) is an unforgivable sin. It is surprising how many sinners one finds.

5.14 Self-Test

You are owed $5,000 by a relative who will pay it back in 1 year. The nominal interest rate is 8%, and the inflation rate is 5%. What is the present value of your relative's IOU? Show that you get the same answer (a) discounting the nominal payment at the nominal rate and (b) discounting the real payment at the real rate.

Example 5.16 ▶ How Inflation Might Affect Bill Gates

We showed earlier (Example 5.9) that at an interest rate of 6% Bill Gates could, if he wished, turn his $79 billion wealth into a 30-year annuity of $5.7 billion per year of luxury and excitement (L&E). Unfortunately, L&E expenses inflate just like gasoline and groceries. Thus Mr. Gates would find the purchasing power of that $5.7 billion steadily declining. If he wants the same luxuries in 2045 as in 2015, he'll have to spend less in 2015 and then increase expenditures in line with inflation. How much should he spend in 2015? Assume the long-run inflation rate is 3%.

Mr. Gates needs to calculate a 30-year *real* annuity. The real interest rate is a little less than 3%:

$$1 + \text{real interest rate} = \frac{1 + \text{nominal interest rate}}{1 + \text{inflation rate}}$$

$$= \frac{1.06}{1.03} = 1.029$$

so the real rate is 2.9%. The 30-year annuity factor at 2.9% is 19.8562. Therefore, annual spending (in 2015 dollars) should be chosen so that

$$\$79,000,000,000 = \text{annual spending} \times 19.8562$$
$$\text{Annual spending} = \$3,979,000,000$$

Mr. Gates could spend that amount on L&E in 1 year's time and 3% more (in line with inflation) in each subsequent year. This is only about 70% of the value we calculated when we ignored inflation. Life has many disappointments, even for tycoons. ∎

5.15 Self-Test

You have reached age 60 with a modest fortune of $3 million and are considering early retirement. How much can you spend each year for the next 30 years? Assume that spending is stable in real terms. The nominal interest rate is 10%, and the inflation rate is 5%.

Real or Nominal?

Any present value calculation done in nominal terms can also be done in real terms, and vice versa. Most financial analysts forecast in nominal terms and discount at nominal rates. However, in some cases real cash flows are easier to deal with. In our example of Bill Gates, the *real* expenditures were fixed. In this case, it was easiest to use real quantities. On the other hand, if the cash-flow stream is fixed in nominal terms (for example, the payments on a loan), it is easiest to use all nominal quantities.

SUMMARY

If you invest money at a given interest rate, what will be the future value of your investment? (*LO5-1*)

An investment of $1 earning an interest rate of r will increase in value each period by the factor $(1 + r)$. After t periods its value will grow to $\$(1 + r)^t$. This is the **future value** of the $1 investment with compound interest.

What is the present value of a cash flow to be received in the future? (*LO5-2*)

The **present value** of a future cash payment is the amount that you would need to invest today to produce that future payment. To calculate present value, we divide the cash payment by $(1 + r)^t$ or, equivalently, multiply by the **discount factor** $1/(1 + r)^t$. The discount factor measures the value today of $1 received in period t.

How can we calculate present and future values of streams of cash payments? (*LO5-3*)

A level stream of cash payments that continues indefinitely is known as a **perpetuity;** one that continues for a limited number of years is called an **annuity.** The present value of a stream of cash flows is simply the sum of the present value of each individual cash flow. Similarly, the future value of an annuity is the sum of the future value of each individual cash flow. Shortcut formulas make the calculations for perpetuities and annuities easy.

How should we compare interest rates quoted over different time intervals, for example, monthly versus annual rates? (*LO5-4*)

Interest rates for short time periods are often quoted as annual rates by multiplying the per-period rate by the number of periods in a year. These **annual percentage rates (APRs)** do not recognize the effect of compound interest; that is, they annualize assuming simple interest. The **effective annual rate** annualizes using compound interest. It equals the rate of interest per period compounded for the number of periods in a year.

What is the difference between real and nominal cash flows and between real and nominal interest rates? (*LO5-5*)

A dollar is a dollar, but the amount of goods that a dollar can buy is eroded by **inflation.** If prices double, the real value of a dollar halves. Financial managers and economists often find it helpful to reexpress future cash flows in terms of real dollars—that is, dollars of constant purchasing power.

Be careful to distinguish the **nominal interest rate** and the **real interest rate**—that is, the rate at which the real value of the investment grows. Discount nominal cash flows (that is, cash flows measured in current dollars) at nominal interest rates. Discount real cash flows (cash flows measured in constant dollars) at real interest rates. *Never* mix and match nominal and real.

LISTING OF EQUATIONS

5.1 $\text{Future value} = \text{present value} \times (1 + r)^t$

5.2 $\text{Present value} = \dfrac{\text{future value after } t \text{ periods}}{(1 + r)^t}$

5.3 $\text{PV of perpetuity} = \dfrac{C}{r} = \dfrac{\text{cash payment}}{\text{interest rate}}$

5.4   Present value of t-year annuity $= C \left[\dfrac{1}{r} - \dfrac{1}{r(1 + r)^t} \right]$

5.5   Future value (FV) of annuity of $1 a year = present value of annuity of
$1 a year $\times (1 + r)^t$

$$= \left[\frac{1}{r} - \frac{1}{r(1 + r)^t} \right] \times (1 + r)^t$$

$$= \frac{(1 + r)^t - 1}{r}$$

5.6   Present value of annuity due = present value of ordinary annuity $\times (1 + r)$

5.7   Future value of annuity due = future value of ordinary annuity $\times (1 + r)$

5.8 $1 + \text{real interest rate} = \dfrac{1 + \text{nominal interest rate}}{1 + \text{inflation rate}}$

5.9   Real interest rate $\approx$ nominal interest rate $-$ inflation rate

QUESTIONS AND PROBLEMS

connect

1.   **Compound Interest.** Old Time Savings Bank pays 4% interest on its savings accounts. If you deposit $1,000 in the bank and leave it there: (*LO5-1*)

   a. How much interest will you earn in the first year?
   b. How much interest will you earn in the second year?
   c. How much interest will you earn in the 10th year?

2.   **Compound Interest.** New Savings Bank pays 4% interest on its deposits. If you deposit $1,000 in the bank and leave it there, will it take more or less than 25 years for your money to double? You should be able to answer this without a calculator or interest rate tables. (*LO5-1*)

3.   **Compound Interest.** Suppose that the value of an investment in the stock market has increased at an average compound rate of about 5% since 1900. It is now 2016. (*LO5-1*)

   a. If your great grandfather invested $1,000 in 1900, how much would that investment be worth today?
   b. If an investment in 1900 has grown to $1 million, how much was invested in 1900?

4.   **Future Values.** Compute the future value of a $100 cash flow for the following combinations of rates and times. (*LO5-1*)

   a. $r = 8\%$, $t = 10$ years
   b. $r = 8\%$, $t = 20$ years
   c. $r = 4\%$, $t = 10$ years
   d. $r = 4\%$, $t = 20$ years

5.   **Future Values.** You deposit $1,000 in your bank account. (*LO5-1*)

   a. If the bank pays 4% simple interest, how much will you accumulate in your account after 10 years?
   b. How much will you accumulate if the bank pays compound interest?

6.   **Future Values.** If you earn 6% per year on your bank account, how long will it take an account with $100 to double to $200? (*LO5-1*)

7.   **Future Values.** In 1880 five aboriginal trackers were each promised the equivalent of 100 Australian dollars for helping to capture the notorious outlaw Ned Kelley. In 1993 the grand-daughters of two of the trackers claimed that this reward had not been paid. The Victorian prime minister stated that if this was true, the government would be happy to pay the $100. However, the granddaughters also claimed that they were entitled to compound interest. (*LO5-1*)

   a. How much was each granddaughter entitled to if the interest rate was 4%?
   b. How much was each entitled to if the interest rate was 8%?

8. **Future Values.** How long will it take for $400 to grow to $1,000 at the following interest rates? (*LO5-1*)

   a. 4%
   b. 8%
   c. 16%

9. **Future Values.** You invest $1,000 today and expect to sell your investment for $2,000 in 10 years. (*LO5-1*)

   a. Is this a good deal if the interest rate is 6%?
   b. What if the interest rate is 10%?

10. **Future Values.** Your wealthy uncle established a $1,000 bank account for you when you were born. For the first 8 years of your life, the interest rate earned on the account was 6%. Since then, rates have been only 4%. Now you are 21 years old and ready to cash in. How much is in your account? (*LO5-1*)

11. **Present Values.** You can buy property today for $3 million and sell it in 5 years for $4 million. (You earn no rental income on the property.) (*LO5-2*)

   a. If the interest rate is 8%, what is the present value of the sales price?
   b. Is the property investment attractive to you?
   c. Would your answer to part (b) change if you also could earn $200,000 per-year rent on the property? The rent is paid at the end of each year.

12. **Present Values.** Compute the present value of a $100 cash flow for the following combinations of discount rates and times. (*LO5-2*)

   a. $r = 8\%, t = 10$ years
   b. $r = 8\%, t = 20$ years
   c. $r = 4\%, t = 10$ years
   d. $r = 4\%, t = 20$ years

13. **Present Values.** You will require $700 in 5 years. If you earn 5% interest on your funds, how much will you need to invest today in order to reach your savings goal? (*LO5-2*)

14. **Present Values.** What is the present value of the following cash-flow stream if the interest rate is 6%? (*LO5-2*)

Year	Cash Flow
1	$200
2	400
3	300

15. **Calculating the Interest Rate.** Find the interest rate implied by the following combinations of present and future values. (*LO5-2*)

Present Value	Years	Future Value
$400	11	$684
183	4	249
300	7	300

16. **Calculating the Interest Rate.** Find the annual interest rate. (*LO5-2*)

Present Value	Future Value	Time Period
$100	$115.76	3 years
200	262.16	4
100	110.41	5

17. **Calculating the Interest Rate.** A zero-coupon bond that will pay $1,000 in 10 years is selling today for $422.41. What interest rate does the bond offer? (*LO5-2*)

18. **Present Values.** A factory costs $400,000. You forecast that it will produce cash inflows of $120,000 in year 1, $180,000 in year 2, and $300,000 in year 3. The discount rate is 12%. (*LO5-2*)

    a. What is the value of the factory?
    b. Is the factory a good investment?

19. **Present Values.** The 2-year discount factor is .92. What is the present value of $1 to be received in year 2? What is the present value of $2,000? (*LO5-2*)

20. **Annuities.** A famous quarterback just signed a $15 million contract providing $3 million a year for 5 years. A less famous receiver signed a $14 million 5-year contract providing $4 million now and $2 million a year for 5 years. The interest rate is 10%. Who is better paid? (*LO5-3*)

21. **Annuities.** Would you rather receive $1,000 a year for 10 years or $800 a year for 15 years if the interest rate is 5%? What if the interest rate is 20%? (*LO5-3*)

22. **Perpetuities.** A local bank advertises the following deal: "Pay us $100 a year for 10 years and then we will pay you (or your beneficiaries) $100 a year forever." Is this a good deal if the interest rate is 6%? (*LO5-3*)

23. **Perpetuities.** A local bank will pay you $100 a year for your lifetime if you deposit $2,500 in the bank today. If you plan to live forever, what interest rate is the bank paying? (*LO5-3*)

24. **Perpetuities.** A property will provide $10,000 a year forever. If its value is $125,000, what must be the discount rate? (*LO5-3*)

25. **Perpetuities.** British government 4% perpetuities pay £4 interest each year forever. Another bond, 2.5% perpetuities, pays £2.50 a year forever. (*LO5-3*)

    a. What is the value of 4% perpetuities if the long-term interest rate is 6%?
    b. What is the value of 2.5% perpetuities?

26. **Annuities.** (*LO5-3*)

    a. What is the present value of a 3-year annuity of $100 if the discount rate is 6%?
    b. What is the present value of the annuity in part (a) if you have to wait 2 years instead of 1 year for the first payment?

27. **Annuities.** Professor's Annuity Corp. offers a lifetime annuity to retiring professors. For a payment of $80,000 at age 65, the firm will pay the retiring professor $600 a month until death. (*LO5-3*)

    a. If the professor's remaining life expectancy is 20 years, what is the monthly interest rate on this annuity?
    b. What is the effective annual interest rate?
    c. If the monthly interest rate is .5%, what monthly annuity payment can the firm offer to the retiring professor?

28. **Annuities.** You want to buy a new car, but you can make an initial payment of only $2,000 and can afford monthly payments of at most $400. (*LO5-3*)

    a. If the APR on auto loans is 12% and you finance the purchase over 48 months, what is the maximum price you can pay for the car?
    b. How much can you afford if you finance the purchase over 60 months?

29. **Annuities.** You can buy a car that is advertised for $24,000 on the following terms: (a) pay $24,000 and receive a $2,000 rebate from the manufacturer; (b) pay $500 a month for 4 years for total payments of $24,000, implying zero percent financing. Which is the better deal if the interest rate is 1% per month? (*LO5-3*)

30. **Annuities.** You have just borrowed $100,000 to buy a condo. You will repay the loan in equal monthly payments of $804.62 over the next 30 years. (*LO5-4*)

    a. What monthly interest rate are you paying on the loan?
    b. What is the APR?
    c. What is the effective annual rate on that loan?
    d. What rate is the lender more likely to quote on the loan?

31. **Future Value of Annuities.** I now have $20,000 in the bank earning interest of .5% per month. I need $30,000 to make a down payment on a house. I can save an additional $100 per month. How long will it take me to accumulate the $30,000? (*LO5-3*)

32. **Real Annuities.** A retiree wants level consumption in real terms over a 30-year retirement. If the inflation rate equals the interest rate she earns on her $450,000 of savings, how much can she spend in real terms each year over the rest of her life? (*LO5-3*)

33. **Delayed Annuities.** Suppose that you will receive annual payments of $10,000 for a period of 10 years. The first payment will be made 4 years from now. If the interest rate is 5%, what is the present value of this stream of payments? (*LO5-3*)

34. **Annuity Due.** Your landscaping company can lease a truck for $8,000 a year (paid at year-end) for 6 years. It can instead buy the truck for $40,000. The truck will be valueless after 6 years. The interest rate your company can earn on its funds is 7%. (*LO5-3*)
    a. What is the present value of the cost of leasing?
    b. Is it cheaper to buy or lease?
    c. What is the present value of the cost of leasing if the lease payments are an annuity due, so the first payment comes immediately?
    d. Is it now cheaper to buy or lease?

35. **Annuity Due.** Recall that an annuity due is like an ordinary annuity except that the first payment is made immediately instead of at the end of the first period. (*LO5-3*)
    a. Why is the present value of an annuity due equal to $(1 + r)$ times the present value of an ordinary annuity?
    b. Why is the future value of an annuity due equal to $(1 + r)$ times the future value of an ordinary annuity?

36. **Annuity Due.** A store offers two payment plans. Under the installment plan, you pay 25% down and 25% of the purchase price in each of the next 3 years. If you pay the entire bill immediately, you can take a 10% discount from the purchase price. (*LO5-3*)
    a. Which is a better deal if you can borrow or lend funds at a 5% interest rate?
    b. How will your answer change if the payments on the 4-year installment plan do not start for a full year?

37. **Annuity Due.** (*LO5-3*)
    a. If you borrow $1,000 and agree to repay the loan in five equal annual payments at an interest rate of 12%, what will your payment be?
    b. What will your payment be if you make the first payment on the loan immediately instead of at the end of the first year?

38. **Annuity Due.** The $40 million lottery payment that you have just won actually pays $2 million per year for 20 years. The interest rate is 8%. (*LO5-3*)
    a. If the first payment comes in 1 year, what is the present value of the winnings?
    b. What is the present value if the first payment comes immediately?

39. **Amortizing Loan.** You take out a 30-year $100,000 mortgage loan with an APR of 6% and monthly payments. In 12 years you decide to sell your house and pay off the mortgage. What is the principal balance on the loan? (*LO5-3*)

40. **Amortizing Loan.** Consider a 4-year amortizing loan. You borrow $1,000 initially and repay it in four equal annual year-end payments. (*LO5-3*)
    a. If the interest rate is 8%, what is the annual payment?
    b. Fill in the following table, which shows how much of each payment is interest versus principal repayment (that is, amortization) and the outstanding balance on the loan at each date.

Time	Loan Balance ($)	Year-End Interest Due on Loan Balance ($)	Total Year-End Payment ($)	Amortization of Loan ($)
0	1,000	_____	_____	_____
1	_____	_____	_____	_____
2	_____	_____	_____	_____
3	_____	_____	_____	_____
4	0	0		

41. **Retirement Savings.** A couple will retire in 50 years; they plan to spend about $30,000 a year in retirement, which should last about 25 years. They believe that they can earn 8% interest on retirement savings. (*LO5-3*)

    a. If they make annual payments into a savings plan, how much will they need to save each year? Assume the first payment comes in 1 year.
    b. How would the answer to part (a) change if the couple also realize that in 20 years they will need to spend $60,000 on their child's college education?

42. **Retirement Savings.** You believe you will need to have saved $500,000 by the time you retire in 40 years in order to live comfortably. If the interest rate is 6% per year, how much must you save each year to meet your retirement goal? (*LO5-3*)

43. **Retirement Savings.** You believe you will need to have saved $500,000 by the time you retire in 40 years in order to live comfortably. You also believe that you will inherit $100,000 in 10 years. If the interest rate is 6% per year, how much must you save each year to meet your retirement goal? (*LO5-3*)

44. **Retirement Savings.** You believe you will spend $40,000 a year for 20 years once you retire in 40 years. If the interest rate is 6% per year, how much must you save each year until retirement to meet your retirement goal? (*LO5-3*)

45. **Retirement Savings.** A couple thinking about retirement decide to put aside $3,000 each year in a savings plan that earns 8% interest. In 5 years they will receive a gift of $10,000 that also can be invested. (*LO5-3*)

    a. How much money will they have accumulated 30 years from now?
    b. If their goal is to retire with $800,000 of savings, how much extra do they need to save every year?

46. **Perpetuities and Effective Interest Rate.** What is the value of a perpetuity that pays $100 every 3 months forever? The interest rate quoted on an APR basis is 6%. (*LO5-3*)

47. **Amortizing Loans and Inflation.** Suppose you take out a $100,000, 20-year mortgage loan to buy a condo. The interest rate on the loan is 6%. To keep things simple, we will assume you make payments on the loan annually at the end of each year. (*LO5-3*)

    a. What is your annual payment on the loan?
    b. Construct a mortgage amortization table in Excel similar to Table 5.5 in which you compute the interest payment each year, the amortization of the loan, and the loan balance each year. (Allow the interest rate to be an input that the user of the spreadsheet can enter and change.)
    c. What fraction of your initial loan payment is interest?
    d. What fraction of your initial loan payment is amortization?
    e. What fraction of the loan has been paid off after 10 years (halfway through the life of the loan)?
    f. If the inflation rate is 2%, what is the real value of the first (year-end) payment?
    g. If the inflation rate is 2%, what is the real value of the last (year-end) payment?
    h. Now assume the inflation rate is 8% and the real interest rate on the loan is unchanged. What must be the new nominal interest rate?
    i. Recompute the amortization table. What is the real value of the first (year-end) payment in this high-inflation scenario?
    j. What is the real value of the last payment in this high-inflation scenario?

48. **Mortgage with Points.** Home loans typically involve "points," which are fees charged by the lender. Each point charged means that the borrower must pay 1% of the loan amount as a fee. For example, if the loan is for $100,000 and 2 points are charged, the loan repayment schedule is calculated on a $100,000 loan but the net amount the borrower receives is only $98,000. Assume the interest rate is 1% per month. What is the effective annual interest rate charged on such a loan, assuming loan repayment occurs over 360 months? (*LO5-4*)

49. **Effective Interest Rate.** A store will give you a 3% discount on the cost of your purchase if you pay cash today. Otherwise, you will be billed the full price with payment due in 1 month. What is the implicit borrowing rate being paid by customers who choose to defer payment for the month? (*LO5-4*)

50. **Effective Interest Rate.** You've borrowed $4,248.68 and agreed to pay back the loan with monthly payments of $200. If the interest rate is 12% stated as an APR, how long will it take you to pay back the loan? What is the effective annual rate on the loan? (*LO5-4*)

51. **Effective Interest Rate.** You invest $1,000 at a 6% annual interest rate, stated as an APR. Interest is compounded monthly. How much will you have in 1 year? In 1.5 years? (*LO5-4*)

52. **Effective Interest Rate.** If a bank pays 6% interest with continuous compounding, what is the effective annual rate? (*LO5-4*)

53. **Effective Interest Rate.** In a discount interest loan, you pay the interest payment up front. For example, if a 1-year loan is stated as $10,000 and the interest rate is 10%, the borrower "pays" .10 × $10,000 = $1,000 immediately, thereby receiving net funds of $9,000 and repaying $10,000 in a year. (*LO5-4*)

    a. What is the effective interest rate on this loan?
    b. What is the effective annual rate on a 1-year loan with an interest rate quoted on a discount basis of 20%?

54. **Effective Interest Rate.** Banks sometimes quote interest rates in the form of "add-on interest." In this case, if a 1-year loan is quoted with a 20% interest rate and you borrow $1,000, then you pay back $1,200. But you make these payments in monthly installments of $100 each. (*LO5-4*)

    a. What is the true APR on this loan?
    b. What is the effective annual rate on the loan?

55. **Effective Interest Rate.** You borrow $1,000 from the bank and agree to repay the loan over the next year in 12 equal monthly payments of $90. However, the bank also charges you a loan initiation fee of $20, which is taken out of the initial proceeds of the loan. What is the effective annual interest rate on the loan, taking account of the impact of the initiation fee? (*LO5-4*)

56. **Effective Interest Rate.** First National Bank pays 6.2% interest compounded semiannually. Second National Bank pays 6% interest compounded monthly. Which bank offers the higher effective annual interest rate? (*LO5-4*)

57. **Loan Payments.** You take out an $8,000 car loan that calls for 48 monthly payments starting after 1 month at an APR of 10%. (*LO5-4*)

    a. What is your monthly payment?
    b. What is the effective annual interest rate on the loan?
    c. Now assume the payments are made in four annual year-end installments. What annual payment would have the same present value as the monthly payment you calculated?

58. **Continuous Compounding.** How much will $100 grow to if invested at a continuously compounded interest rate of 10% for 8 years? What if it is invested for 10 years at 8%? (*LO5-4*)

59. **Effective Interest Rate.** Find the effective annual interest rate for each case. (*LO5-4*)

APR	Compounding Period
12%	1 month
8	3
10	6

60. **Effective Interest Rate.** Find the APR (the stated interest rate) for each case. (*LO5-4*)

Effective Annual Interest Rate	Compounding Period
10.00%	1 month
6.09	6
8.24	3

61. **Effective Interest Rate.** Lenny Loanshark charges "1 point" per week (i.e., 1% per week) on his loans. What APR must he report to consumers? Assume exactly 52 weeks in a year. What is the effective annual rate? (*LO5-4*)

62. **Effective Interest Rate.** Suppose you can borrow money at 8.6% per year (APR) compounded semiannually or 8.4% per year (APR) compounded monthly. Which is the better deal? (*LO5-4*)

63. **Effective Interest Rate.** If you take out an $8,000 car loan that calls for 48 monthly payments of $240 each, what is the APR of the loan? What is the effective annual interest rate on the loan? (*LO5-4*)

64. **Real versus Nominal Perpetuities.** If the interest rate is 6% per year, how long will it take for your money to quadruple in value? If the inflation rate is 4% per year, what will be the change in the purchasing power of your money over this period? (*LO5-5*)

65. **Inflation.** In April 2016 a pound of apples cost $1.41, while oranges cost $1.05. Four years earlier the price of apples was only $1.20 a pound and that of oranges was $.91 a pound. (*LO5-5*)

    a. What was the annual compound rate of growth in the price of apples?
    b. What was the annual compound rate of growth in the price of oranges?
    c. If the same rates of growth persist in the future, what will be the price of apples in 2030?
    d. What about the price of oranges?

66. **Real versus Nominal Dollars.** An engineer in 1950 was earning $6,000 a year. In 2015 she earned $80,000 a year. However, on average, prices in 2015 were higher than in 1950. What was her real income in 2015 in terms of constant 1950 dollars? Use the data in Table 5.8. (*LO5-5*)

67. **Real versus Nominal Dollars.** Your consulting firm will produce cash flows of $100,000 this year, and you expect cash flow thereafter to keep pace with any increase in the general level of prices. The interest rate currently is 6%, and you anticipate inflation of about 2%. (*LO5-5*)

    a. What is the present value of your firm's cash flows for years 1 through 5?
    b. How would your answer to part (a) change if you anticipated no growth in cash flow?

68. **Real versus Nominal Rates.** If investors are to earn a 3% real interest rate, what nominal interest rate must they earn if the inflation rate is: (a) zero? (b) 4%? (c) 6%? (*LO5-5*)

69. **Real versus Nominal Rates.** If investors receive a 6% interest rate on their bank deposits, what real interest rate will they earn if the inflation rate over the year is: (a) zero? (b) 3%? (c) 6%? (*LO5-5*)

70. **Real versus Nominal Annuities.** Good news: You will almost certainly be a millionaire by the time you retire in 50 years. Bad news: The inflation rate over your lifetime will average about 3%. (*LO5-5*)

    a. What will be the real value of $1 million by the time you retire in terms of today's dollars?
    b. What real annuity (in today's dollars) will $1 million support if the real interest rate at retirement is 2% and the annuity must last for 20 years?

71. **Inflation.** In the summer of 2007, Zimbabwe's official inflation rate was about 110% per month. What was the annual inflation rate? (*LO5-5*)

72. **Real versus Nominal Annuities.** You plan to retire in 30 years and want to accumulate enough by then to provide yourself with $30,000 a year for 15 years. (*LO5-5*)

    a. If the interest rate is 10%, how much must you accumulate by the time you retire?
    b. How much must you save each year until retirement in order to finance your retirement consumption?
    c. Now you remember that the annual inflation rate is 4%. If a loaf of bread costs $1 today, what will it cost by the time you retire?
    d. You really want to consume $30,000 a year in real dollars during retirement and wish to save an equal real amount each year until then. What is the real amount of savings that you need to accumulate by the time you retire?
    e. Calculate the required preretirement real annual savings necessary to meet your consumption goals.
    f. What is the nominal value of the amount you need to save during the first year? (Assume the savings are put aside at the end of each year.)
    g. What is the nominal value of the amount you need to save during the 30th year?

73. **Retirement and Inflation.** A couple will retire in 50 years; they plan to spend about $30,000 a year (in current dollars) in retirement, which should last about 25 years. They believe that they can earn 8% interest on retirement savings. The inflation rate over the next 75 years is expected to average 5%. (*LO5-5*)

    a. What is the real annual savings the couple must set aside?
    b. How much do they need to save in nominal terms in the first year?
    c. How much do they need to save in nominal terms in the last year?
    d. What will be their nominal expenditures in the first year of retirement?
    e. What will be their nominal expenditures in the last year of retirement?

74. **Real versus Nominal Cash Flows.** *(LO5-5)*

    a. It is 2016, you've just graduated college, and you are contemplating your lifetime budget. You think your general living expenses will average around $50,000 a year. For the next 8 years, you will rent an apartment for $16,000 a year. After that, you will want to buy a house that should cost around $250,000. In addition, you will need to buy a new car roughly once every 10 years, costing around $30,000 each. In 25 years, you will have to put aside around $150,000 to put a child through college, and in 30 years you'll need to do the same for another child. In 50 years, you will retire and will need to have accumulated enough savings to support roughly 20 years of retirement spending of around $35,000 a year on top of your Social Security benefits. The interest rate is 5% per year. What average salary will you need to earn to support this lifetime consumption plan?

    b. Whoops! You just realized that the inflation rate over your lifetime is likely to average about 3% per year, and you need to redo your calculations. As a rough cut, it seems reasonable to assume that all relevant prices and wages will increase at around the rate of inflation. What is your new estimate of the required salary (in today's dollars)?

75. **Real versus Nominal Rates.** You will receive $100 from a savings bond in 3 years. The nominal interest rate is 8%. *(LO5-5)*

    a. What is the present value of the proceeds from the bond?

    b. If the inflation rate over the next few years is expected to be 3%, what will the real value of the $100 payoff be in terms of today's dollars?

    c. What is the real interest rate?

    d. Show that the real payoff from the bond [from part (b)] discounted at the real interest rate [from part (c)] gives the same present value for the bond as you found in part (a).

76. **Time Value of Money.** Solve the following crossword. (Round your final answers to the nearest dollar, but do not round intermediate calculations.)

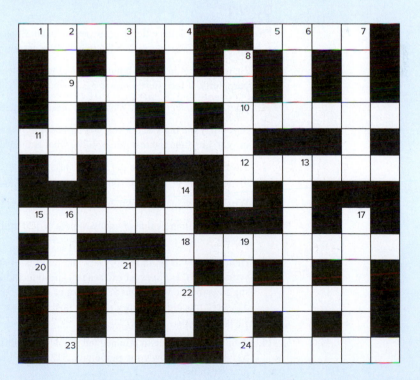

ACROSS

1. A rich uncle has promised to pay you $3,160 at the end of each of the next 25 years. If you invest this money at 4.9%, how much will you have at the end of the 25 years?

5. Hepsibah Sloop put $10,000 under his mattress 20 years ago. Since then, inflation has averaged 1%. What is the real value of his savings?

9. A 20-year annuity has a present value of $42,419,233. If the interest rate is 15%, what is the annual cash flow?

10. A Treasury bond pays $1 million at the end of 20 years. What is its present value if the interest rate is 4%?

11. A project is forecast to produce a safe cash flow of $800,000 a year for 20 years. If the cost of capital is 4%, what is the present value of the project?

12. If you invest $100,000 today, how much will your savings be worth at the end of 9 years if the interest rate is 10%?

15. An annuity due with 10 annual payments has a present value of 1,244,353. If the interest rate is 15%, what is the annual payment?

18. Investment in a Dustinbourne grinder is expected to produce cash flows over the following 7 years of $7 million, $8 million, $9 million, $10 million, $9 million, $8 million, and $7 million. What is the present value of the project if the cost of capital is 5%?

20. You invest $95,525 for 20 years at 11.7%. Inflation over the same period is 4% a year. What is the real value of your savings at the end of that period?

22. You invest $1 million for 7 years at 5% and then for a further 7 years at 8%. How much will you have at the end of this time?

23. The discount factor is .8, and the present value of a cash flow is $2,703. What is the cash flow?

24. A deferred annuity makes four equal payments of $129,987 a year starting at the end of year 8. If the interest rate is 12%, what is its present value?

DOWN

2. The winning lottery ticket promises to make 30 payments of $30,000 a year starting immediately. If the interest rate is 5.8%, what is the present value of these payments?

3. An investment in consol bonds promises to provide an interest payment of $2.5 million a year in perpetuity. If the interest rate is 3.3%, what is the value of this investment?

4. The discount factor is .9. What is the present value of $63,269?

6. If you pay the bank $50 a year for 10 years, it promises to pay you $100 a year forever starting in year 11. If the interest rate is 4.2%, what is the value of this proposal to you?

7. The nominal interest rate is 13% and inflation is 4%. If you invest $100,000 today, what will be the real value of your investment at the end of 20 years?

8. What is the value of a payment of $2,125,000 in year 30 if the interest rate is 3.8%?

13. What is the future value of an investment of $20 million at the end of 11 years if the interest rate is 9%?

14. Henry Hub will retire in 25 years and expects to spend a further 20 years in retirement (i.e., years 26–45). He lives an extravagant lifestyle and has drawn up a detailed spreadsheet which suggests that he will spend $256,880 a year in real terms in retirement. If the real interest rate is 3%, how much does Henry need to save each year in real terms until retirement to attain his spending goal?

16. A factory is forecast to produce the following cash flows: year 1, $6,516; year 2, $7,000; year 3, $11,400; year 4 onward in perpetuity, $12,000. If the cost of capital is 6%, what is the factory's present value?

17. What is the future value of $189,956 at the end of 7 years if the interest rate is 11%?

19. Natasha Petrov has savings of $78,780. If she invests the full amount in a bank at an interest rate of 4%, how much will she have after 4 years?

21. You plan to save $1,000 a year in each of years 1 through 5. If the interest rate is 8%, how much will you have saved by the end of year 5?

WEB EXERCISES

1. In Example 5.10, we showed you how to work out mortgage payments. Log on to the personal finance page of www.bankrate.com and find the mortgage payment calculator. Assume a 20-year mortgage loan of $100,000 and an interest rate (APR) of 12%. What is the amount of the monthly payment? Check that you get the same answer when using the annuity formula. Now look at how much of the first month's payment goes to reduce the size of the mortgage. How much of the payment by the 10th year? Can you explain why the figure changes? If the interest rate doubles, would you expect the mortgage payment to double? Check whether you are right.

2. You can find data on the consumer price index (CPI) on the Bureau of Labor Statistics website, www.bls.gov/cpi/home.htm. Tables of historical data can be formatted to provide either levels of the index or changes in the index (i.e., the rate of inflation). Construct a table of annual inflation rates since 1913. When did the USA last experience a year of deflation (i.e., falling prices)? Find the inflation rate in the latest year. Now log on to www.bloomberg.com, and on the first page find a measure of the short-term interest rate (e.g., the 2-year rate). Use the recent level of inflation to calculate the *real* interest rate. Consider the case of Herbert Protheroe, who in 1920 was an eligible bachelor with an income of $2,000 a year. What is that equivalent to today?

SOLUTIONS TO SELF-TEST QUESTIONS

5.1   Value after 5 years would have been $24 \times (1.05)^5 = \$30.63$; after 50 years, $24 \times (1.05)^{50} = \$275.22$.

5.2   Call g the annual growth rate of transistors over the 44-year period between 1971 and 2015. Then

$$2{,}250 \times (1 + g)^{44} = 5{,}500{,}000{,}000$$

$$(1 + g)^{44} = 2{,}444{,}444$$

$$1 + g = 2{,}444{,}444^{1/44} = 1.40$$

So the actual growth rate was $g = .40$, or 40%, not quite as high as Moore's prediction, but not so shabby either.

5.3   Multiply the €1,000 payment by the 3-year discount factor:

$$PV = €1{,}000 \times \frac{1}{(1.01)^3} = €970.59$$

5.4

Gift at Year	Present Value
1	$10{,}000/(1.07) = \$9{,}345.79$
2	$10{,}000/(1.07)^2 = 8{,}734.39$
3	$10{,}000/(1.07)^3 = 8{,}162.98$
4	$10{,}000/(1.07)^4 = 7{,}628.95$
	33,872.11

Gift at Year	Future Value
1	$10{,}000 \times (1.07)^3 = \$12{,}250.43$
2	$10{,}000 \times (1.07)^2 = 11{,}449$
3	$10{,}000 \times (1.07) = 10{,}700$
4	$10{,}000 = 10{,}000$
	$44,399.43

5.5   The rate is 4/48 = .0833, about 8.3%.

5.6   The 4-year discount factor is $1/(1.08)^4 = .7350$. The 4-year annuity factor is $[1/.08 - 1/(.08 \times 1.08^4)] = 3.3121$. This is the difference between the present value of a $1 perpetuity starting next year and the present value of a $1 perpetuity starting in year 5:

$$\text{PV (perpetuity starting next year)} = \frac{1}{.08} = 12.50$$

$$- \text{PV (perpetuity starting in year 5)} = \frac{1}{.08} \times \frac{1}{(1.08)^4} = 9.1879$$

$$= \text{PV (4-year annuity)}   = 12.50 - 9.1879 = 3.3121$$

which matches the annuity factor.

5.7   You will need the present value at 7% of a 20-year annuity of $55,000:

$$\text{Present value} = \text{annual spending} \times \text{annuity factor}$$

The annuity factor is $[1/.07 - 1/(.07 \times 1.07^{20})] = 10.5940$. Thus, you need $55,000 \times 10.594 = \$582,670$.

5.8   Fifteen years means 180 months.

$$\text{Mortgage payment} = \frac{100,000}{180\text{-month annuity factor}}$$

$$= \frac{100,000}{83.32}$$

$$= \$1,200.17 \text{ per month}$$

$1,000 of the first payment is interest. The remainder, $200.17, is amortization.

5.9   We know that the future value of an annuity due is equal to the future value of an ordinary annuity $\times (1 + r)$. Therefore, if you make the first of your 50 annual investments immediately, then by the end of the 50 years your retirement savings will be 10% higher, $550,000.

5.10   The quarterly rate is 8/4 = 2%. The effective annual rate is $(1.02)^4 - 1 = .0824$, or 8.24%.

5.11   The cost in dollars will increase by 5% each year, to a value of $5 \times (1.05)^{50} = \$57.34$. If the inflation rate is 10%, the cost will be $5 \times (1.10)^{50} = \$586.95$.

5.12   The CPI in 1980 was 3.452 times its value in 1950 (see Table 5.8). Therefore, purchases that cost $250 in 1950 would have cost $250 \times 3.452 = \$863$ in 1980. The value of a 1980 salary of $30,000, expressed in real 1950 dollars, is $30,000 \times (1/3.452) = \$8,691$.

5.13   a. If there's no inflation, real and nominal rates are equal at 8%. With 5% inflation, the real rate is $(1.08/1.05) - 1 = .02857$, a bit less than 3%.
       b. If you want a 3% *real* interest rate, you need a 3% nominal rate if inflation is zero and an 8.15% rate if inflation is 5%. Note that $1.03 \times 1.05 = 1.0815$.

5.14   The present value is

$$PV = \frac{\$5,000}{1.08} = \$4,629.63$$

The real interest rate is 2.857% (see Self-Test 5.13a). The real cash payment is $5,000/1.05 = $4,761.90. Thus,

$$PV = \frac{\$4,761.90}{1.02857} = \$4,629.63$$

5.15   Calculate the real annuity. The real interest rate is $1.10/1.05 - 1 = .0476$. We'll round to 4.8%. The real annuity is

$$\text{Annual payment} = \frac{\$3,000,000}{30\text{-year annuity factor}} = \frac{\$3,000,000}{\dfrac{1}{.048} - \dfrac{1}{.048(1.048)^{30}}} = \frac{\$3,000,000}{15.7292} = \$190,728$$

You can spend this much each year in dollars of constant purchasing power. The purchasing power of each dollar will decline at 5% per year, so you'll need to spend more in nominal dollars: $190,728 \times 1.05 = $200,264 in the second year, $190,728 \times 1.05^2 = $210,278 in the third year, and so on.

MINICASE

Old Alfred Road, who is well-known to drivers on the Maine Turnpike, has reached his 70th birthday and is ready to retire. Mr. Road has no formal training in finance but has saved his money and invested carefully.

Mr. Road owns his home—the mortgage is paid off—and does not want to move. He is a widower, and he wants to bequeath the house and any remaining assets to his daughter.

He has accumulated savings of $180,000, conservatively invested. The investments are yielding 9% interest. Mr. Road also has $12,000 in a savings account at 5% interest. He wants to keep the savings account intact for unexpected expenses or emergencies.

Mr. Road's basic living expenses now average about $1,500 per month, and he plans to spend $500 per month on travel and hobbies. To maintain this planned standard of living, he will have to rely on his investment portfolio. The interest from the portfolio is $16,200 per year (9% of $180,000), or $1,350 per month.

Mr. Road will also receive $750 per month in Social Security payments for the rest of his life. These payments are indexed for inflation. That is, they will be automatically increased in proportion to changes in the consumer price index.

Mr. Road's main concern is with inflation. The inflation rate has been below 3% recently, but a 3% rate is unusually low by historical standards. His Social Security payments will increase with inflation, but the interest on his investment portfolio will not.

What advice do you have for Mr. Road? Can he safely spend all the interest from his investment portfolio? How much could he withdraw at year-end from that portfolio if he wants to keep its real value intact?

Suppose Mr. Road will live for 20 more years and is willing to use up all of his investment portfolio over that period. He also wants his monthly spending to increase along with inflation over that period. In other words, he wants his monthly spending to stay the same in real terms. How much can he afford to spend per month?

Assume that the investment portfolio continues to yield a 9% rate of return and that the inflation rate will be 4%.

CHAPTER

6

Valuing Bonds

LEARNING OBJECTIVES

After studying this chapter, you should be able to:

6-1 Distinguish among a bond's coupon rate, current yield, and yield to maturity.

6-2 Find the market price of a bond given its yield to maturity, find a bond's yield given its price, and demonstrate why prices and yields move in opposite directions.

6-3 Show why bonds exhibit interest rate risk.

6-4 Understand why investors draw a plot of bond yields against maturity.

6-5 Understand why investors pay attention to bond ratings and demand a higher interest rate for bonds with low ratings.

RELATED WEBSITES FOR THIS CHAPTER CAN BE FOUND IN CONNECT.

Bondholders once received a beautifully engraved certificate like this one issued by a railroad. Nowadays their ownership is simply recorded on an electronic database. © CPC Collection/Alamy

When a corporation needs external financing, it can borrow money. If it needs the money for a month, quarter, or year, it will probably borrow from a bank. If it needs to make a long-term investment, it may instead issue a bond, which is a debt security held by individual and institutional investors.

Companies are not the only bond issuers. State and local governments also raise money by selling bonds. So does the U.S. Treasury. Most investors would regard the risk of default on Treasury bonds as negligible, and therefore, these issues offer a lower rate of interest than corporate bonds. Nevertheless, the interest rates on government bonds provide a benchmark for all interest rates. When government interest rates go up or down, corporate rates follow more or less proportionally. Thus, in the first part of this chapter, we focus on Treasury bonds and sidestep the issue of default.

We begin by showing you how to understand the bond pages in the financial press, and we explain what bond dealers mean when they quote yields to maturity. We look at why short-term rates are usually lower (but sometimes higher) than long-term rates and why the longest-term bond prices are most sensitive to fluctuations in interest rates. We distinguish real (inflation-adjusted) interest rates and nominal (money) rates and explain how future inflation can affect interest rates.

Toward the end of the chapter, we return to corporate bonds, which carry a possibility of default. We look at how bond ratings provide a guide to that default risk and how low-rated bonds offer higher promised yields. There is enormous variation in the design of corporate bonds. We introduce here some of the main ways in which they differ, but we will revisit the topic in Chapter 14.

<table>
<tr><td>**6.1**</td><td></td></tr>
</table>

6.1 The Bond Market

bond
Security that obligates the issuer to make specified payments to the bondholders.

Governments and corporations borrow money by selling **bonds** to investors. The market for these bonds is huge. At the start of 2016, public holdings of U.S. government bonds was almost $14 trillion ($14,000,000,000,000). Companies also raise very large sums of money by selling bonds. For example, in 2015 Apple borrowed $6.5 billion by an issue of bonds. The market for bonds is sophisticated and active. Bond traders frequently make massive trades motivated by tiny price discrepancies.

Bonds sometimes go under different names. For example, Treasury bonds with maturities of 2 to 10 years at the time of issue are called "notes." Some corporate bonds are called notes or "debentures." In this chapter, we will simplify and just say "bonds."

When governments or companies issue bonds, they promise to make a series of interest payments and then to repay the debt. But don't get the idea that all bonds are alike. For example, most bonds make a fixed interest payment, but in other cases, the payment may go up or down as short-term interest rates change. Bonds may also have different maturities. Sometimes a company may borrow for only a few years, but there have been a few occasions when bonds have been issued with maturities of 100 years or more.

Bond Characteristics

face value
Payment at the maturity of the bond. Also called *principal* or *par value*.

coupon
The interest payments paid to the bondholder.

In November 2013, the U.S. government made a typical issue of a Treasury bond. It auctioned off 1.25% coupon bonds maturing in 2018. The bonds have a **face value** (also called the *principal* or *par value*) of $1,000. Each year until the bond matures, the bondholder receives an interest payment of 1.25% of the face value, or $12.50. This 1.25% interest payment is called the bond's **coupon.** (In the old days, most bonds used to have coupons that the investor clipped off and mailed to the bond issuer to claim the interest payment.) When the 1.25% coupon bond matures in 2018, the government must pay the $1,000 face value of the bond in addition to the final coupon payment.

At any moment, there are more than 200 different Treasury bonds outstanding. The prices at which you can buy and sell each of these bonds are shown each day in the financial press and on the web. Table 6.1, which is compiled from *The Wall Street Journal*'s web page, shows the prices for just a small sample of issues. The entry for the 1.25% bond maturing in November 2018 is highlighted.

Anyone buying the 1.25% bond would need to pay the *asked price,* which is $100.164. This means that the price is 100.164% of face value. Therefore, each bond costs $1,001.64. An investor who *already* owns the bond and wishes to *sell* it would receive the *bid price,* which is shown as 100.148. Just as the used-car dealer earns a living by reselling cars at higher prices than he paid for them, so the bond dealer needs to charge a *spread* between the bid and the asked price. Notice that the spread for these 1.25% bonds is about .016% of the bond's value. Don't you wish that used-car dealers charged similar spreads?

The final column in the table shows the *asked yield to maturity.* This measures the return to investors if they buy the bond at the asked price and hold it to maturity in 2018. You can see that the 1.25% coupon Treasury bond offers a yield to maturity of 1.194%. We will explain shortly how this figure was calculated.

6.1 Self-Test

How much would an investor pay to buy one 1.625% Treasury bond of 2022 (see Table 6.1)? If a Treasury bond costs $1,106.25, how would this price be quoted? How much would the investor receive if he sold the 3% Treasury bond of 2044?

TABLE 6.1 Sample Treasury bond quotes in November 2015

Maturity	Coupon	Bid Price	Asked Price	Chg	Asked Yield to Maturity (%)
2017, Nov 15	4.25	106.6250	106.6406	0.0078	0.888
2018, Nov 15	**1.25**	**100.1484**	**100.1641**	**0.1094**	**1.194**
2022, Nov 15	1.625	97.3047	97.3203	0.3281	2.038
2025, Nov 15	2.25	99.7500	99.7656	0.3516	2.276
2028, Nov 15	5.25	130.3906	130.4531	0.3828	2.493
2039, Nov 15	4.375	124.6406	124.6719	0.4766	2.935
2044, Nov 15	3	98.5859	98.6172	0.3750	3.072

Source: The Wall Street Journal Online, November 15, 2015, www.wsj.com.

FIGURE 6.1 Cash flows to an investor in the 1.25% coupon bond maturing in 2018

You can't buy Treasury bonds on the stock exchange. Instead, they are traded by a network of bond dealers, who quote bid and ask prices at which they are prepared to buy and sell. For example, suppose that in 2015 you decide to buy the "1.25s of 2018," that is, the 1.25% coupon bonds maturing in 2018. You approach a broker who checks the current price on her screen. If you are happy to go ahead with the purchase, your broker will contact a bond dealer and the trade is done.

If you plan to hold your bond until maturity, you can look forward to the cash flows shown in Figure 6.1. For the first 2 years, the cash flows equal the 1.25% coupon payment. Then, when the bond matures in 2018, you receive the $1,000 face value of the bond plus the final coupon payment.

6.2 Self-Test

Find the 5.25% coupon 2028 Treasury bond in Table 6.1.

a. How much does it cost to buy the bond?
b. If you already owned the bond, how much would a bond dealer pay you for it?
c. What annual interest payment does the bond make?
d. What is the bond's yield to maturity?

6.2 Interest Rates and Bond Prices

In Figure 6.1, we set out the cash flows from your 1.25% Treasury bond. The value of the bond is the present value of these cash flows. To find this value, you need to discount each future payment by the current interest rate.

The 1.25s were not the only Treasury bonds that matured in 2018. Almost identical bonds maturing at the same time offered an interest rate of just under 1.2%. If the 1.25s had offered a lower return than this, no one would have been willing to hold them. Equally, if they had offered a *higher* return, everyone would have rushed to sell their other bonds and buy the 1.25s. In other words, if investors were on their toes, the 1.25s had to offer the same rate of interest as similar Treasury bonds. You might recognize this as the opportunity cost of the funds invested in the bond, as we discussed in Chapter 1. This is the rate that investors could earn by placing their funds in similar securities rather than in this bond.

We can now calculate the present value of the 1.25s of 2018 by discounting the cash flows at 1.194%, or a shade under 1.2%:

$$PV = \frac{\$12.50}{(1+r)} + \frac{\$12.50}{(1+r)^2} + \frac{\$1,012.50}{(1+r)^3}$$

$$= \frac{\$12.50}{(1.01194)} + \frac{\$12.50}{(1.01194)^2} + \frac{\$1,012.50}{(1.01194)^3} = \$1,001.64$$

Bond prices are usually expressed as a percentage of their face value. Thus we can say that your 1.25% Treasury bond is worth 100.164% of face value.[1]

Did you notice that your bond is like a package of two investments? The first provides a level stream of coupon payments of $12.50 a year for each of 3 years. The second consists of the final repayment of the $1,000 face value. Therefore, you can use the annuity formula to value the coupon payments and then add on the present value of the final payment of face value:

$$PV = PV(\text{coupons}) + PV(\text{face value}) \tag{6.1}$$

$$= (\text{coupon} \times \text{annuity factor}) + (\text{face value} \times \text{discount factor})$$

$$= \$12.50 \times \left[\frac{1}{.01194} - \frac{1}{.01194(1.01194)^3} \right] + \$1,000 \times \frac{1}{1.01194^3}$$

$$= \$36.62 + \$965.02 = \$1,001.64$$

If you need to value a bond with many years to run before maturity, it is usually easiest to value the coupon payments as an annuity and then add on the present value of the final payment.

6.3   Self-Test

Calculate the present value of a 6-year bond with a 9% coupon. The interest rate is 12%.

You can calculate bond prices easily using a financial calculator or spreadsheet. The trick is to recognize that the bond provides its owner *both* a recurring payment (the coupons) *and* an additional one-time cash flow (the face value). For the 1.25% bond, the time to maturity is 3 years, annual coupon payment is $12.50, and face value is $1,000. The interest rate is 1.194%. Therefore, the inputs for a financial calculator would be:

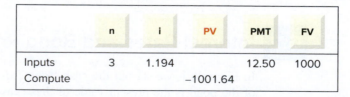

	n	i	PV	PMT	FV
Inputs	3	1.194		12.50	1000
Compute			−1001.64		

---

[1] You will often find that your calculated value is slightly different from the asked price quoted in the financial press. One reason is minor rounding error in the interest rate. Another is that the bond's actual coupon is not $12.50 per year, but $6.25 every 6 months. In the next example, we'll show how to handle semiannual coupons.

Now compute PV, and you should get an answer of −1,001.64, which is the initial cash outflow required to purchase the bond.

For an introduction to bond pricing using Excel, turn to the box later in the chapter.

| Example | 6.1 ▶ | Bond Prices and Semiannual Coupon Payments |

When we valued our Treasury bond, we assumed that interest payments occur annually. This is the case for bonds in many European countries, but in the United States, most bonds make coupon payments *semiannually*. So when you hear that a bond in the United States has a coupon rate of 1.25%, you can generally assume that the bond makes a payment of $12.50/2 = $6.25 every 6 months. Similarly, when investors in the United States refer to the bond's interest rate, they usually mean the semiannually compounded interest rate. Thus, an interest rate quoted at 1.194% really means that the 6-month rate is 1.194/2 = .597%.[2] The actual cash flows on the Treasury bond are illustrated in Figure 6.2. To value the bond a bit more precisely, we should have discounted the series of semiannual payments by the semiannual rate of interest as follows:

$$PV = \frac{\$6.25}{(1.00597)} + \frac{\$6.25}{(1.00597)^2} + \frac{\$6.25}{(1.00597)^3} + \frac{\$6.25}{(1.00597)^4}$$

$$+ \frac{\$6.25}{(1.00597)^5} + \frac{\$1,006.25}{(1.00597)^6}$$

$$= \$1,001.65$$

FIGURE 6.2 Cash flows to an investor in the 1.25% coupon bond maturing in 2018. The bond pays semiannual coupons, so there are two payments of $6.25 each year.

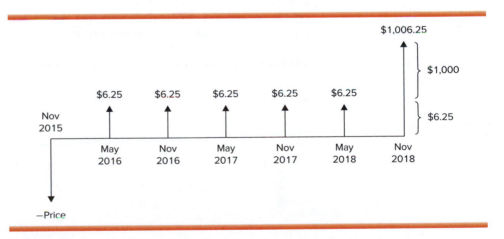

---

[2] You may have noticed that the semiannually compounded interest rate on the bond is also the bond's APR, although this term is not generally used by bond investors. To find the effective rate, we can use a formula that we presented in Section 5.7:

$$\text{Effective annual rate} = \left(1 + \frac{\text{APR}}{m}\right)^m - 1$$

where m is the number of payments each year. In the case of our Treasury bond,

$$\text{Effective annual rate} = \left(1 + \frac{.01194}{2}\right)^2 - 1 = 1.00597^2 - 1 = .01198, \text{ or } 1.198\%$$

When interest rates are low, there is negligible difference between the annually compounded interest rate and the semiannually compounded rate. The difference is greater when rates are high.

Thus, once we allow for the fact that coupon payments are semiannual, the value of the 1.25s is 100.165% of face value, which is slightly higher than the value that we obtained when we assumed annual coupon payments.[3] Because semiannual coupon payments just add to the arithmetic, we will stick for the most part to our simplification and assume annual interest payments. ∎

How Bond Prices Vary with Interest Rates

Figure 6.3 plots the interest rate on 10-year maturity Treasury bonds from 1900 to 2015. Notice how much the interest rate fluctuates. For example, interest rates climbed steeply after 1979 when the Federal Reserve instituted a policy of tight money to rein in inflation. Within 2 years, the rate on 10-year government bonds rose from 10% to 14%. Contrast this with 2015, when long-term Treasuries offered a measly 1.9% rate of interest.

As interest rates change, so do bond prices. For example, suppose that investors demanded an interest rate of 1.25% on 3-year Treasury bonds. What would be the price of the Treasury 1.25s of 2018? Just repeat our PV calculation with a discount rate of $r = .0125$:

$$\text{PV at } 1.25\% = \frac{\$12.50}{(1.0125)} + \frac{\$12.50}{(1.0125)^2} + \frac{\$1,012.50}{(1.0125)^3} = \$1,000.00$$

Thus when the interest rate is the same as the coupon rate (1.25% in our example), the bond sells for its face value.

We first valued the Treasury bond using an interest rate of 1.194%, which is lower than the coupon rate. In that case, the price of the bond was *higher* than its face value. We then valued it using an interest rate that is equal to the coupon and found that bond price equaled face value. You have probably already guessed that when the cash flows are discounted at a rate that is *higher* than the bond's coupon rate, the bond is worth *less* than its face value. The following example confirms that this is the case.

FIGURE 6.3 The interest rate on 10-year U.S. Treasury bonds, 1900–2015

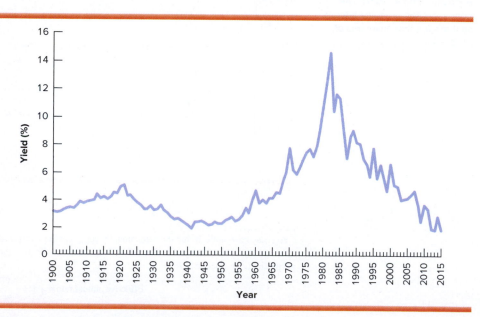

Source: www.econ.yale.edu/~shiller/data.htm.

---

[3] Why is the present value a bit higher in this case? Because now we recognize that half the annual coupon payment is received only 6 months into the year, rather than at year-end. Because part of the coupon income is received earlier, its present value is higher.

Example 6.2 ▶ Interest Rates and Bond Prices

Investors will pay $1,000 for a 1.25%, 3-year Treasury bond when the interest rate is 1.25%. Suppose that the interest rate is higher than the coupon rate at (say) 10%. Now what is the value of the bond? Simple! We just repeat our calculation but with $r = .10$:

$$\text{PV at } 10\% = \frac{\$12.50}{(1.10)} + \frac{\$12.50}{(1.10)^2} + \frac{\$1,012.50}{(1.10)^3} = \$782.40$$

The bond sells for 78.24% of face value. ■

This is a general result. When the market interest rate exceeds the coupon rate, bonds sell for less than face value. When the market interest rate is below the coupon rate, bonds sell for more than face value.

Suppose that interest rates rise. On hearing the news, bond investors appear disconsolate. Why? Don't they like higher interest rates? If you are not sure of the answer, look at Figure 6.4, which shows the present value of the 1.25% Treasury bond for different interest rates. For example, imagine yields soar from 1.194% to 10%. Our bond would then be worth only $782.40, creating a loss to bondholders of some 22%. Conversely, bondholders have reason to celebrate when market interest rates fall. You can see this also from Figure 6.4. For instance, if interest rates fall to zero, the value of our 1.25% bond would increase to $1,037.50. That was just about the biggest profit that investors in the 1.25s could hope for.

Figure 6.4 illustrates a fundamental relationship between interest rates and bond prices: **When the interest rate rises, the present value of the payments to be received by the bondholder falls and bond prices fall. Conversely, a decline in the interest rate increases the present value of those payments and the price of bonds.**

A warning! People sometimes confuse the interest, or coupon, *payment* on the bond with the *interest rate*—that is, the return that investors require. The $12.50 coupon payments on our Treasury bond are *fixed* when the bond is issued. The **coupon rate,** 1.25%, measures the coupon payment ($12.50) as a percentage of the bond's face value ($1,000) and is therefore also fixed. **However, the interest rate changes from day to day. These changes affect the *present value* of the coupon payments but not the payments themselves.**

coupon rate
Annual interest payment as a percentage of face value.

FIGURE 6.4 The value of the 1.25% bond falls as interest rates rise

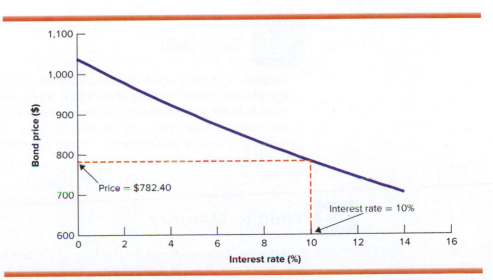

Price = $782.40

Interest rate = 10%

FIGURE 6.5 Plot of bond prices as a function of the interest rate. The price of long-term bonds is more sensitive to changes in the interest rate than is the price of short-term bonds.

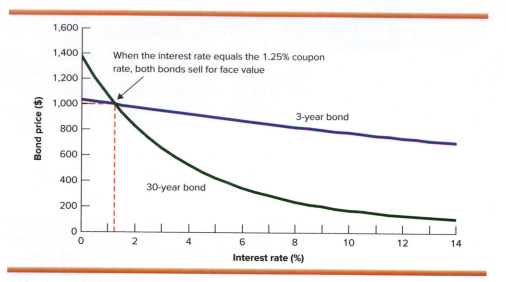

Interest Rate Risk

We have just seen that bond prices fluctuate as interest rates change. In other words, bonds are subject to **interest rate risk.** Bond investors cross their fingers that market interest rates will fall, so that the price of their bond will rise. If they are unlucky and the market interest rate rises, the value of their investment falls.

A change in interest rates has only a modest impact on the present value of near-term cash flows but a much greater impact on the value of distant cash flows. Therefore, any change has a greater impact on the price of long-term bonds than the price of short-term bonds. For example, compare the two curves in Figure 6.5. The blue line shows how the value of the 3-year, 1.25% coupon bond varies with the interest rate. The green line shows how the price of a 30-year, 1.25% bond varies. You can see that the 30-year bond is more sensitive to interest rate fluctuations than the 3-year bond. This should not surprise you. If you buy a 3-year bond and rates then rise, you will be stuck with a bad deal—you could have got a better interest rate if you had waited. However, think how much worse it would be if the loan had been for 30 years rather than 3 years. The longer the loan, the more income you have lost by accepting what turns out to be a low interest rate. This shows up in a bigger decline in the price of the longer-term bond. Of course, there is a flip side to this effect, which you can also see from Figure 6.5. When interest rates fall, the longer-term bond responds with a greater increase in price.

6.4   Self-Test

Suppose that the market interest rate is 4% and then drops overnight to 2%. Calculate the present values of the 1.25%, 3-year bond and of the 1.25%, 30-year bond both before and after this change in interest rates. Assume annual coupon payments. Confirm that your answers correspond with Figure 6.5. Use your financial calculator or a spreadsheet. You can find a box on bond pricing using Excel later in this chapter.

6.3   Yield to Maturity

Suppose you are considering the purchase of a 3-year bond with a coupon rate of 10%. Your investment adviser quotes a price for the bond. How do you calculate the rate of return the bond offers?

For bonds priced at face value the answer is easy. The rate of return is the coupon rate. We can check this by setting out the cash flows on your investment:

	Cash Paid to You in Year:			
You Pay	1	2	3	Rate of Return
$1,000	$100	$100	$1,100	10%

Notice that in each year you earn 10% on your money ($100/$1,000). In the final year, you also get back your original investment of $1,000. Therefore, your total return is 10%, the same as the coupon rate.

Now suppose that the market price of the 3-year bond rises to $1,200. Your cash flows are as follows:

	Cash Paid to You in Year:			
You Pay	1	2	3	Rate of Return
$1,200	$100	$100	$1,100	?

Notice that you are paying out $1,200 and receiving an annual income of $100. So your income as a proportion of the initial outlay is $100/$1,200 = .083, or 8.3%. This is sometimes called the bond's **current yield.**

current yield
Annual coupon payment divided by bond price.

However, your *total* return depends on both interest income and any capital gains or losses. A current yield of 8.3% may sound attractive until you realize that the bond's price must fall. The price today is $1,200, but when the bond matures 3 years from now, the bond will sell for its face value, or $1,000. A price decline (i.e., a *capital loss*) of $200 is guaranteed, so the overall return over the next 3 years must be less than the 8.3% current yield.

Let us generalize. A bond that is priced above its face value is said to sell at a *premium*. Investors who buy a bond at a premium must absorb a capital loss over the life of the bond, so the return on these bonds is always less than the bond's current yield. A bond priced below face value sells at a *discount*. Investors in discount bonds receive a capital *gain* over the life of the bond; the return on these bonds is *greater* than the current yield: **Because it focuses only on current income and ignores prospective price increases or decreases, the *current* yield does not measure the bond's total rate of return. It overstates the return of premium bonds and understates that of discount bonds.**

yield to maturity
Discount rate at which the present value of the bond's payments equals the price.

We need a measure of return that takes account of both coupon payments and the change in a bond's value over its life. The standard measure is called **yield to maturity.** The yield to maturity is the answer to the following question: At what interest rate would the bond be correctly priced? **The yield to maturity is defined as the discount rate that makes the present value of the bond's payments equal to its price.**

If you can buy the 3-year bond at face value, the yield to maturity is the coupon rate, 10%. We can check this by noting that when we discount the cash flows at 10%, the present value of the bond is equal to its $1,000 face value:

$$PV \text{ at } 10\% = \frac{\$100}{(1.10)} + \frac{\$100}{(1.10)^2} + \frac{\$1,100}{(1.10)^3} = \$1,000.00$$

But what if our 3-year bond is priced at $1,200? In this case, the yield to maturity is only 2.94%. At that discount rate, the bond's present value equals its actual market price, $1,200:

$$PV \text{ at } 2.94\% = \frac{\$100}{(1.0294)} + \frac{\$100}{(1.0294)^2} + \frac{\$1,100}{(1.0294)^3} = \$1,200$$

The yield to maturity is a measure of a bond's total return, including both coupon income and capital gain. If you buy the bond today and hold it to maturity, your return will be the yield to maturity. Bond investors often refer loosely to a bond's "yield." It's a safe bet that they are talking about its yield to maturity rather than its current yield.

Calculating the Yield to Maturity

To find the price of the 1.25% Treasury bond, we discounted the cash payments at the interest rate r. If $r = 1.194\%$, then bond price $= \$1,001.64$:

$$\text{Price} = \frac{\$12.50}{(1 + r)} + \frac{\$12.50}{(1 + r)^2} + \frac{\$1,012.50}{(1 + r)^3}$$

$$= \frac{\$12.50}{(1.01194)} + \frac{\$12.50}{(1.01194)^2} + \frac{\$1,012.50}{(1.01194)^3} = \$1,001.64$$

We could have phrased the question the other way round and asked, "If the price of the bond is $1,001.64, what is the bond's yield to maturity?"

To calculate yield, we need to find the discount rate, r, that gives the correct bond price. The only general procedure for doing this is trial and error. You guess at an interest rate and calculate the present value of the bond's payments. If the present value is greater than the actual price, your discount rate must have been too low, so you try a higher interest rate (because a higher rate results in a lower PV). Conversely, if PV is less than price, you must reduce the interest rate. Of course, this would be a mind-numbing procedure to do by hand. Fortunately, financial calculators or spreadsheet programs can rapidly find a bond's yield to maturity, using a similar trial-and-error process. We give examples in the nearby boxes.

> ### 6.5 Self-Test
>
> A 4-year maturity bond with a 14% coupon rate can be bought for $1,200. What is the yield to maturity if the coupon is paid annually? What if it is paid semiannually? You will need a spreadsheet or a financial calculator to answer this question.

6.4 Bond Rates of Return

The yield to maturity is defined as the discount rate that equates the bond's price to the present value of all its promised future cash flows. It measures the rate of return that you will earn if you buy the bond today and hold it to maturity. However, as interest rates fluctuate, the return that you earn in the interim may be very different from the yield to maturity. If interest rates rise in a particular week, month, or year, the price of your bond will fall and your return for that period will be lower than the yield to maturity. Conversely, if rates fall, the price of your bond will rise and your return will be higher. This is emphasized in the following example.

Example 6.3 ▶ Rate of Return versus Yield to Maturity

On May 15, 2008, the U.S. Treasury sold $9 billion of 4.375% bonds maturing in February 2038. The bonds were issued at a price of 96.38% and offered a yield to maturity of 4.60%. This was the return to anyone buying at the issue price and holding the bonds to maturity. In the months following the issue, the financial crisis reached its peak. Lehman Brothers filed for bankruptcy with assets of $691 billion, and the government poured money into rescuing Fannie Mae, Freddie Mac, AIG, and a host of banks. As investors rushed to the safety of

You can use a financial calculator to calculate the yield to maturity on our 1.25% Treasury bond. The inputs are:

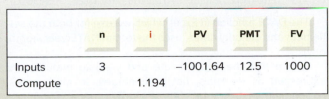

	n	i	PV	PMT	FV
Inputs	3		−1001.64	12.5	1000
Compute		1.194			

Now compute *i* and you should get an answer of 1.194%.

Let's now redo this calculation but recognize that the coupons are paid semiannually. Instead of three annual coupon payments of $12.50, the bond makes six semiannual payments of $6.25. Therefore, we can find the semiannual yield as follows:

	n	i	PV	PMT	FV
Inputs	6		−1001.64	6.25	1000
Compute		.5971			

This yield to maturity, of course, is a 6-month yield, not an annual one. Bond dealers would typically annualize the semiannual rate by doubling it, so the yield to maturity would be quoted as .5971 × 2 = 1.1942%.

---

rate of return

Total income per period per dollar invested.

Treasury bonds, their prices soared. By mid-December, the price of the 4.375s of 2038 had reached 138.05% of face value and the yield had fallen to 2.5%. Anyone fortunate enough to have bought the bond at the issue price would have made a capital gain of $1,380.50 − $963.80 = $416.70. In addition, on August 15 the bond made its first coupon payment of $21.875 (this is the semiannual payment on the 4.375% coupon bond with a face value of $1,000). Our lucky investor would therefore have earned a 7-month **rate of return** of 45.5%:

$$\text{Rate of return} = \frac{\text{coupon income} + \text{price change}}{\text{investment}} \quad (6.2)$$

$$= \frac{\$21.875 + \$416.70}{\$963.80} = .455 = 45.5\%$$

Suddenly, government bonds did not seem quite so boring as before. ■

6.6 Self-Test

Suppose that you purchased 8% coupon, 10-year bonds for $1,324.4 when they were yielding 4% (we assume annual coupon payments). One year later, you receive the annual coupon payment of $80, but the yield to maturity has risen to 6%. Confirm that the rate of return on your bond over the year is less than the original 4% yield to maturity.

Is there *any* connection between the yield to maturity and the rate of return during a particular period? Yes: If the bond's yield to maturity remains unchanged during the period, the bond price changes with time so that the total return on the bond is equal to the yield to maturity. The rate of return will be less than the yield to maturity if interest rates rise, and it will be greater than the yield to maturity if interest rates fall.

6.7 Self-Test

Suppose that you buy 8%, 2-year bonds for $1,036.67 when they yield 6%. At the end of the year, they still yield 6%. Show that if you continue to hold the bond until maturity, your return in *each* of the two years will also be 6%.

Excel and most other spreadsheet programs provide built-in functions to compute bond values and yields. They typically ask you to input both the date you buy the bond (called the *settlement date*) and the maturity date of the bond.

The Excel function for bond value is:

=PRICE(settlement date, maturity date, annual coupon rate, yield to maturity, redemption value as percent of face value, number of coupon payments per year)

(If you can't remember the formula, just remember that you can go to the Formulas tab in Excel, and from the Financial tab pull down the PRICE function, which will prompt you for the necessary inputs.) For our 1.25% coupon bond, we would enter the values shown in the spreadsheet below.

Alternatively, we could simply enter the following function in Excel:

=PRICE(DATE(2015,11,15), DATE(2018,11,15),.0125,.01194,100,1)

The DATE function in Excel, which we use for both the settlement and maturity dates, uses the format DATE(year,month, day).

Notice that the coupon rate and yield to maturity are expressed as decimals, not percentages. In most cases, redemption value will be 100 (i.e., 100% of face value), and the resulting price will be expressed as a percent of face value. Occasionally, however, you may encounter bonds that pay off at a premium or discount to face value. One example would be callable bonds, which give the company the right to buy back the bonds at a premium before maturity.

	A	B	C	D	E	F
1		**1.25% annual**		**1.25% semiannual**		**6% annual**
2		**coupon bond,**		**coupon bond,**		**coupon bond,**
3		**maturing Nov 2018**	**Formula in column B**	**maturing Nov 2018**		**30-year maturity**
4						
5	Settlement date	11/15/2015	=DATE(2015,11,15)	11/15/2015		1/1/2000
6	Maturity date	11/15/2018	=DATE(2018,11,15)	11/15/2018		1/1/2030
7	Annual coupon rate	0.0125		0.0125		0.06
8	Yield to maturity	0.01194		0.01194		0.07
9	Redemption value (% of face value)	100		100		100
10	Coupon payments per year	1		2		1
11						
12						
13	Bond price (% of par)	100.164	=PRICE(B5,B6,B7,B8,B9,B10)	100.165		87.591

The solid curve in Figure 6.6 plots the price of a 30-year maturity, 6% coupon bond over time assuming that its yield to maturity is currently 4% and does not change. The price declines gradually until the maturity date, when it finally reaches face value. In each period, the price decline offsets the coupon income by just enough to reduce total return to 4%. The dashed curve in Figure 6.6 shows the corresponding price path for a bond with a 2% coupon that sells at a discount to face value. In this case, the coupon income would provide less than a competitive rate of return, so the bond sells below face value. Its price gradually approaches face value, however, and the price gain each year brings its total return up to the market interest rate.

6.5 The Yield Curve

When you buy a bond, you buy a package of coupon payments plus the final repayment of face value. But sometimes it is inconvenient to buy things in packages. For example, perhaps you do not need a regular income and would prefer to buy just the final repayment. That's not a problem. The Treasury is prepared to split its bonds

The value of the bond assuming annual coupon payments is 100.164% of face value, or $1,001.64. If we wanted to assume semiannual coupon payments, as in Example 6.1, we would simply change the entry in cell B10 to 2 (see column D), and the bond value would change to 100.165% of face value, as we found in that example.

We have also assumed that the first coupon payment comes in exactly one period (either a year or a half-year). In other words, the settlement date is precisely at the beginning of the period. However, the PRICE function will make the necessary adjustments for intraperiod purchase dates.

Suppose now that you wish to find the price of a 30-year maturity bond with a coupon rate of 6% (paid annually) selling at a yield to maturity of 7%. You are not given a specific settlement or maturity date. You can still use the PRICE function to value the bond. Simply choose an arbitrary settlement date

(January 1, 2000, is convenient) and let the maturity date be 30 years hence. The appropriate inputs appear in column F of the preceding spreadsheet, with the resulting price, 87.591% of face value, appearing in cell F13.

Excel also provides a function for yield to maturity. It is:

=YIELD(settlement date, maturity date, annual coupon rate, bond price, redemption value as percent of face value, number of coupon payments per year)

For example, to find the yield to maturity of our 1.25% bond, we would use column B of the following spreadsheet if the coupons were paid annually. If the coupons were paid semiannually, we would change the entry for payments per year to 2 (see cell D8), and the yield would increase slightly.

	A	B	C	D	E
1		**Annual coupons**		**Semiannual coupons**	
2					
3	Settlement date	11/15/2015		11/15/2015	
4	Maturity date	11/15/2018		11/15/2018	
5	Annual coupon rate	0.0125		0.0125	
6	Bond price	100.164		100.164	
7	Redemption value (% of face value)	100		100	
8	Coupon payments per year	1		2	
9					
10	**Yield to maturity (decimal)**	**0.011940**		**0.011942**	
11					
12					
13		The formula entered here is =YIELD(B3,B4,B5,B6,B7,B8)			
14					

FIGURE 6.6 How bond prices change as they approach maturity, assuming an unchanged yield to maturity of 4%. Prices of both premium and discount bonds approach face value as their maturity date approaches.

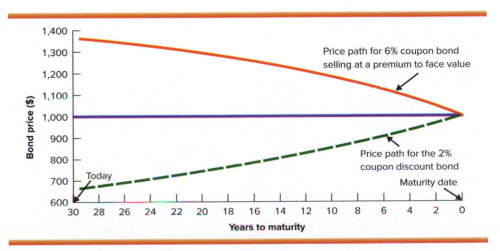

into a series of mini-bonds, each of which makes a single payment. These single-payment bonds are called *strips*.

The prices of strips are shown regularly in the financial press or on the web. For example, in November 2015 it would have cost you $962.85 to buy a strip that

yield curve
Plot of relationship between bond yields to maturity and time to maturity.

would pay out $1,000 in November 2018. The yield on this 3-year mini-bond was 1.27%. In other words, $962.85 × 1.0127^3 = $1,000.

Bond investors often draw a plot of the relationship between bond yields and maturity. This is known as the **yield curve.** Treasury strips provide a convenient way to measure this yield curve. For example, if you look at Figure 6.7, you will see that in November 2015 one-year strips offered a yield to maturity of just .60%; those with 20 or more years to run provided a yield above 3%. In this case, the yield curve sloped upward.[4] This is usually the case, though long-term bonds sometimes offer *lower* yields, and so the yield curve slopes downward.

But that raises a question. If long-term bonds offered much higher yields, why didn't everyone buy them? Who were the (foolish?) investors who put their money into short-term Treasuries at such low yields?

Even when the yield curve is upward-sloping, investors might rationally stay away from long-term bonds for two reasons. First, the prices of long-term bonds fluctuate much more than prices of short-term bonds. We saw in Figure 6.5 that long-term bond prices are more sensitive to shifting interest rates. A sharp increase in interest rates could easily knock 20% or 30% off long-term bond prices. If investors don't like price fluctuations, they will invest their funds in short-term bonds unless they receive a higher yield to maturity on long-term bonds.

Second, short-term investors can profit if interest rates rise. Suppose you hold a 1-year bond. A year from now, when the bond matures, you can reinvest the proceeds and enjoy whatever rates the bond market offers then. These rates may be high enough to offset the first year's relatively low yield on the 1-year bond. Thus, you often see an upward-sloping yield curve when future interest rates are expected to rise.

6.8   Self-Test

One-year Treasury bonds yield 5%, while 2-year bonds yield 6%. You are quite confident that in 1 year's time 1-year bonds will yield 8%. Would you buy the 2-year bond today? Show that there is a better strategy.

FIGURE 6.7 Treasury strips are bonds that make a single payment. The yields on Treasury strips in November 2015 show that investors received a higher yield to maturity on longer-term bonds.

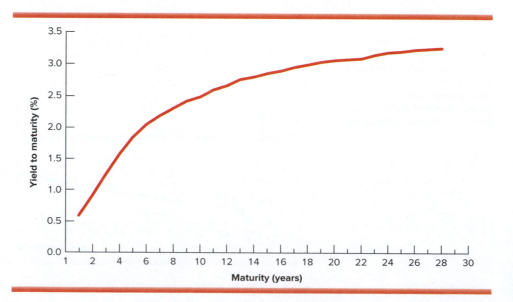

---

[4] Coupon bonds are like packages of strips. Investors often plot the yield curve using the yields on these packages. For example, you could plot the yields on the small sample of bonds in Table 6.1 against their maturity.

Nominal and Real Rates of Interest

In Chapter 5, we drew a distinction between nominal and real rates of interest. The cash flows on the Treasury bonds that we have been discussing are fixed in nominal terms. Investors are sure to receive a fixed interest payment each year, but they do not know what that money will buy. The *real* interest rate on the Treasury bonds depends on the rate of inflation. For example, if the nominal rate of interest is 8% and the inflation rate is 4%, then the real interest rate is calculated as follows:

$$1 + \text{real interest rate} = \frac{1 + \text{nominal interest rate}}{1 + \text{inflation rate}} = \frac{1.08}{1.04} = 1.0385$$

$$\text{Real interest rate} = .0385 = 3.85\%$$

Because the inflation rate is uncertain, so is the real rate of interest on the Treasury bonds.

You *can* nail down a real rate of interest by buying an indexed bond, whose payments are linked to inflation. Indexed bonds have been available in some countries for many years, but they were almost unknown in the United States until 1997 when the U.S. Treasury began to issue inflation-indexed bonds known as *Treasury Inflation-Protected Securities,* or *TIPS.*[5] The real cash flows on TIPS are fixed, but the nominal cash flows (interest and principal) are increased as the consumer price index increases. For example, suppose the U.S. Treasury issues 3% coupon, 2-year TIPS. The *real* cash flows on the 2-year TIPS are therefore:

	Year 1	Year 2
Real cash flows	$30	$1,030

The *nominal* cash flows on TIPS depend on the inflation rate. For example, assume that inflation turns out to be 5% in year 1 and a further 4% in year 2. Then the *nominal* cash flows would be:

	Year 1	Year 2
Nominal cash flows	$30 × 1.05 = $31.50	$1,030 × 1.05 × 1.04 = $1,124.76

These cash payments are just sufficient to provide the holder with a 3% real rate of interest.

As we write this in late 2016, 10-year TIPS offer a yield of about .2%. This yield is a *real* interest rate. It measures the amount of extra goods your investment will allow you to buy. The .2% real yield on TIPS was 1.6% less than the 1.8% nominal yield on nominal 10-year Treasury bonds. If the annual inflation rate proves to be higher than 1.6%, you will earn a higher real return by holding TIPS; if the inflation rate is lower than 1.6%, the reverse will be true.

Figure 6.8 shows the history of both real and nominal rates of interest in the United States since 2003. During this period, the two rates have moved pretty much together and inflation has been quite moderate, so it is primarily variations in the real rate that have caused the nominal rate to move. Notice that in 2012 and 2013, real rates were negative. This means that your savings in these bonds would buy less and less each year.

Since 2003, the outlook for inflation has been benign, but when inflation is expected to be high, investors demand a higher nominal interest rate to compensate for the declining purchasing power of each dollar. For example, suppose that investors revise

BEYOND THE PAGE

Inflation and nominal interest rates

mhhe.com/brealey9e

BEYOND THE PAGE

How to make a certain loss

mhhe.com/brealey9e

---

[5] Indexed bonds were not completely unknown in the United States before 1997. For example, in 1780 American Revolution soldiers were compensated with indexed bonds that paid the value of "five bushels of corn, 68 pounds and four-sevenths part of a pound of beef, ten pounds of sheep's wool, and sixteen pounds of sole leather."

FIGURE 6.8 The bottom line shows the real yield on 7-year indexed bonds issued by the U.S. government. The top line shows the yield on 7-year U.S. government nominal bonds.

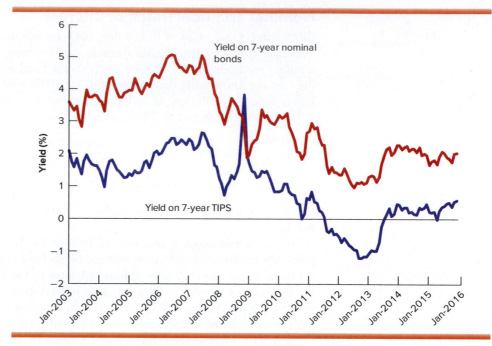

upward their forecast of inflation by 1%. If investors demand the same *real* rate of interest on their savings, the *nominal* interest rate must rise by 1% to compensate for the higher inflation prospects. Therefore, in periods of high and variable inflation, we would expect to see much more variation in the nominal rate than the real rate. For example, in 1980 U.S. inflation rose to greater than 14%. The interest rate on Treasury bills rose correspondingly to top 15%; the real rate remained at a relatively modest value of about 1%.

6.9   Self-Test

Notice from Figure 6.8 that the yield on nominal bonds was *less* than that on TIPS bonds in late 2008. What does that signify about expected inflation at the time? What was the state of the economy in late 2008?

6.6   Corporate Bonds and the Risk of Default

Our focus so far has been on U.S. Treasury bonds. But the federal government is not the only issuer of bonds. State and local governments borrow by selling bonds.[6] So do corporations. Many foreign governments and corporations also borrow in the United States. At the same time, U.S. corporations may borrow dollars or other currencies by issuing their bonds in other countries. For example, they may issue dollar bonds in London that are then sold to investors throughout the world.

---

[6] These *municipal bonds* enjoy a special tax advantage; investors are exempt from federal income tax on the coupon payments on state and local government bonds. As a result, investors are prepared to accept lower yields on this debt.

BEYOND THE PAGE

Sovereign defaults

mhhe.com/brealey9e

default risk
The risk that a bond issuer may default on its bonds. Also called *credit risk.*

credit risk
See *default risk.*

default premium
The additional yield on a bond that investors require for bearing credit risk.

investment grade
Bonds rated Baa or above by Moody's or BBB or above by Standard & Poor's or Fitch.

junk bond
Bond with a rating below Baa or BBB.

Investors usually regard bonds issued by the U.S. Treasury as completely safe. They know that the government can always print the money needed to pay off the debt. But when a foreign government borrows dollars, investors do worry that in some future crisis the government may not be able to come up with enough dollars to repay the debt. This worry shows up in bond prices and yields to maturity. For example, in 2001 the Argentinian government defaulted on $95 billion of dollar-denominated loans. As the prospect of default loomed, the price of Argentinian bonds slumped and the promised yield climbed to more than 40 percentage points above the yield on U.S. Treasuries.

Unlike governments, corporations cannot print their own money, and the specter of default is always lurking in the shadows. The payments promised to the bondholders, therefore, represent a best-case scenario: The firm will never pay more than the promised cash flows, but in hard times it may pay less.[7]

The risk that a bond issuer may default on its obligations is called **default risk** (or **credit risk**). Companies need to compensate for this default risk by promising a higher rate of interest on their bonds. The difference between the promised yield on a corporate bond and the yield on a U.S. Treasury bond with the same coupon and maturity is called the **default premium.** The greater the chance that the company will get into trouble, the higher the default premium demanded by investors.

The safety of most corporate bonds can be judged from bond ratings provided by Moody's, Standard & Poor's, or other bond rating firms. Table 6.2 lists the possible bond ratings in declining order of quality. For example, the bonds that receive the highest Moody's rating are known as *Aaa* (or "triple A") bonds. Then come *Aa* ("double A"), *A, Baa* bonds, and so on. Bonds rated Baa and above are called **investment grade,** while those with a rating of Ba or below are referred to as *speculative grade, high yield,* or **junk bonds.**[8]

Table 6.2 shows how the chances of default vary by Moody's bond rating. You can see that it is rare for highly rated bonds to default. Since 1981, only 8 in 1,000 triple-A

TABLE 6.2 Key to Moody's and Standard & Poor's bond ratings. The highest-quality bonds are rated triple A, then come double-A bonds, and so on.

Moody's	Standard & Poor's	Percent of Bonds Defaulting within 10 Years of Issue	Safety
Investment-Grade Bonds			
Aaa	AAA	0.8%	The strongest rating; ability to repay interest and principal is very strong.
Aa	AA	2.4	Very strong likelihood that interest and principal will be repaid.
A	A	3.6	Strong ability to repay, but some vulnerability to changes in circumstances.
Baa	BBB	6.5	Adequate capacity to repay; more vulnerability to changes in economic circumstances.
High-Yield Bonds			
Ba	BB	18.1	Considerable uncertainty about ability to repay.
B	B	33.5	Likelihood of interest and principal payments over sustained periods is questionable.
Caa Ca	CCC CC	52.4	Bonds that may already be in default or in danger of imminent default.
C	C	—	Little prospect for interest or principal on the debt ever to be repaid.

---

[7] Municipalities also cannot print their own money, and they too are liable to default. This was brought home to investors in 2013 when the city of Detroit, with $18.5 billion of debt outstanding, stopped making payments on some of its bonds.

[8] Rating agencies also distinguish between bonds in the same class. For example, the most secure A-rated bonds would be rated A1 by Moody's and A+ by Standard & Poor's. The least secure bonds in this risk class would be rated A3 by Moody's and A- by Standard & Poor's.

BEYOND THE PAGE

Bond rating definitions

mhhe.com/brealey9e

U.S. corporate bonds have defaulted within 10 years of issue. However, when an investment-grade bond is downgraded or defaults, the shock waves can be considerable. For example, in May 2001 WorldCom sold $11.8 billion of bonds with an investment-grade rating. Within little more than a year, WorldCom filed for bankruptcy, and its bondholders lost more than 80% of their investment. For low-grade issues, defaults are more common. For example, more than 50% of the bonds that were rated CCC or below by Moody's at issue have defaulted within 10 years.[9]

Table 6.3 shows prices and yields to maturity in September 2015 for a sample of corporate bonds. As you would expect, corporate bonds offer higher yields than U.S. Treasuries. You can see that the yield differential generally rises as safety falls off.

Investors also prefer liquid bonds that they can easily buy and sell. So, additionally we find that the heavily traded bonds are more highly prized and offer lower yields than their less liquid brethren. This became important during the banking crisis of 2007–2009 when the market for many corporate bonds effectively dried up and investors found it almost impossible to sell their holdings.

Figure 6.9 shows the yield spread between corporate bonds and Treasuries since 1953. During periods of uncertainty, the spread shoots up. For example, as worries about the economy intensified at the end of 2008, the promised yield on Baa bonds climbed to 6% above the yield on Treasuries. You might have been tempted by the higher promised yields on the lower-grade bonds. But remember, these bonds do not always keep their promises.

TABLE 6.3 Prices and yields of a sample of senior corporate bonds, September 2015

Issuer Name	Coupon (%)	Maturity	S&P Rating	Price (%)	Yield (%)
Johnson & Johnson	3.55	2021	AAA	109.08	1.84
Walmart	3.3	2024	AA	104.21	2.73
Bristol Myers	2.0	2022	A	96.76	2.52
Corning	3.7	2023	BBB	103.75	3.16
Sprint	6.0	2022	BB	75.37	11.10
AMD	7.0	2024	B	62.34	14.81

Source: TRACE.

FIGURE 6.9 Yield spreads between corporate and 10-year Treasury bonds

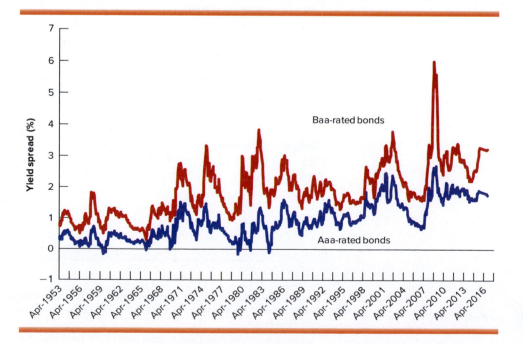

---

[9] Moody's Investor Service, "Annual Default Study: Corporate Default and Recovery Rates, 1920–2014."

You can find considerable information about most corporate bonds, including their rating, at the website of the Financial Industry Regulatory Authority (FINRA). See the nearby box for more information.

Example 6.4 ▶   Promised versus Expected Yield to Maturity

Bad Bet Inc. issued bonds several years ago with a coupon rate (paid annually) of 10% and face value of $1,000. The bonds are due to mature in 6 years. However, the firm is currently in bankruptcy proceedings, the firm has ceased to pay interest, and the bonds sell for only $200. Based on *promised* cash flow, the yield to maturity on the bond is 63.9%. (On your calculator, set PV = −200, FV = 1000, PMT = 100, n = 6, and compute i.) But this calculation is based on the very unlikely possibility that the firm will resume paying interest and come out of bankruptcy. Suppose that the most likely outcome is that after 3 years of litigation, during which no interest will be paid, debtholders will receive 27 cents on the dollar—that is, they will receive $270 for each bond with $1,000 face value. In this case, the expected yield on the bond is 10.5%. (On your calculator, set PV = −200, FV = 270, PMT = 0, n = 3, and compute i.) When default is a real possibility, the promised yield can depart considerably from the expected return. ■

Protecting against Default Risk

Corporate debt can be dependable or as risky as a dizzy tightrope walker—it depends on the value and the risk of the firm's assets. Bondholders can never eliminate default risk, but they can take steps to minimize it. Here are some of the ways that they do so.

Seniority   Some debts are subordinated. In the event of default, the subordinated lender gets in line behind the firm's general creditors. The subordinated lender holds a junior claim and is paid only after all senior creditors are satisfied. Therefore, investors who want to limit their risk will hold senior claims.

When you lend money to a firm, you can assume that you hold a senior claim unless the debt agreement says otherwise. However, this does not always put you at the front of the line because the firm may have set aside some of its assets specifically for the protection of other lenders. That brings us to our next classification.

Security   When you borrow to buy your home, the lender will take out a mortgage on the house. The mortgage acts as security for the loan. If you default on the loan payments, the lender can seize your home.

secured debt
Debt that, in the event of a default, has first claim on specified assets.

When companies borrow, they also may set aside some assets as security for the loan. These assets are termed *collateral,* and the debt is said to be **secured.** In the event of default, the secured lender has first claim on the collateral but has the same claim as other lenders on the rest of the firm's assets.

Protective Covenants   When investors lend to a company, they know that they might not get their money back. But they expect that the company will use the money well and not take unreasonable risks. To help ensure this, lenders usually impose a number of conditions, or **protective covenants,** on companies that borrow from them. An honest firm is willing to accept these conditions because it knows that they allow the firm to borrow at a reasonable rate of interest.

protective covenants
Conditions imposed on borrowers to protect lenders from unreasonable risks.

Companies that borrow in moderation are less likely to get into difficulties than those that are up to the gunwales in debt. So lenders usually restrict the amount of extra debt that the firm can issue. Lenders are also eager to prevent others from pushing ahead of them in the queue if trouble occurs. So they may not allow the company to create new debt that is senior to theirs or to set aside assets for other lenders.

A firm may sell many, even dozens, of issues of bonds to the public. For example, there are currently 25 FedEx bond issues outstanding with various maturity dates and coupon rates. Because of the plethora of bonds, many issues do not trade on any particular day, so pricing information can be, at best, irregular. Moreover, most bonds do not trade on public exchanges. Instead, they trade through an electronic network linking together bond dealers. It can be quite difficult for individual investors to find current information on any particular bond.

The Financial Industry Regulatory Authority (FINRA) is a so-called *self-regulatory organization* that oversees brokerage and securities firms making markets in bonds and other securities. One of its goals has been to foster transparency. To this end, its website makes it far easier for individuals to obtain up-to-date information on bonds.

Go to **finra-markets.morningstar.com/BondCenter**, click on the *Bonds* tab on the left side of the page, click on the *Search* tab, and enter a company ticker symbol, e.g., FDX for FedEx. When you submit your request, you will be given a list of all bonds issued by FedEx. Click on any bond, and you will find a page like the one in this box. The page contains information about the bond's coupon, yield, issue size, and the price and date of its most recent trade.

Bond detail for FedEx

Last Updated: 11/11/2015

Bond Detail

Lookup Symbol: FDX.GD [GO]

FEDERAL EXPRESS CORP

[+ ADD TO WATCHLIST]

Coupon Rate	Maturity Date	Symbol	CUSIP	Next Call Date	Callable
7.600%	**07/01/2097**	FDX.GD	313309AP1	—	—

		Last Trade Price	Last Trade Yield	Last Trade Date	US Treasury Yield
		$129.42	5.860%	10/27/2015	—

Trade History

Price Chart | Yield Chart

04/16/2003 - 10/27/2015   Zoom: 5D 1M 3M YTD 1Y 3Y 10Y Max

Price

Classification Elements

Bond Type	US Corporate Debentures
Debt Type	—
Industry Group	Industrial
Industry Sub Group	Transportation
Sub-Product Asset	CORP
Sub-Product Asset Type	Corporate Bond
State	—
Use of Proceeds	—
Security Code	—

Special Characteristics

Medium Term Note	N

Issue Elements

Offering Data	07/07/1997
Dated Data	07/01/1997
First Coupon Date	01/01/1998
Original Offering*	$250,000.00
Amount Outstanding*	$250,000.00
Series	—
Issue Description	—

Credit and Rating Elements

Moody's Rating	Baa1 (04/07/2015)
Standard & Poor's Rating	BBB (07/09/1997)

Source: http://finra-markets.morningstar.com/BondCenter, November 11, 2015.

6.10 Self-Test

In 1987 RJR Nabisco, the food and tobacco giant, had $5 billion of A-rated debt outstanding. In that year, the company was taken over, and $19 billion of debt was issued and used to buy back equity. The debt ratio skyrocketed, and the debt was downgraded to a BB rating. The holders of the previously issued debt were furious, and one filed a lawsuit claiming that RJR had violated an implicit obligation not to undertake major financing changes at the expense of existing bondholders. Why did these bondholders believe they had been harmed by the massive issue of new debt? What type of explicit restriction would you have wanted if you had been one of the original bondholders?

Not All Corporate Bonds Are Plain Vanilla

In finance, "plain vanilla" means simple, standard, and common. In this chapter, we have stuck with plain-vanilla bonds. In Chapter 14, we will introduce bonds and other ways of borrowing money that are *not* plain vanilla, but here are just a few examples:

- *Zero-coupon bonds* repay principal at maturity but do not have coupon payments along the way. (Zero-coupon Treasuries are called "strips" because coupons are stripped away from the bonds and sold separately.)
- *Floating-rate bonds* have coupon payments that are not fixed but fluctuate with short-term interest rates.
- *Convertible bonds* can be exchanged for a specified number of shares of the issuing corporation's common stock.

SUMMARY

What are the differences between the bond's coupon rate, current yield, and yield to maturity? (LO6-1)

A bond is a long-term debt of a government or corporation. When you own a bond, you receive a fixed interest payment each year until the bond matures. This payment is known as the coupon. The **coupon rate** is the annual coupon payment expressed as a fraction of the bond's **face value.** At maturity the bond's face value is repaid. In the United States most bonds have a face value of $1,000. The **current yield** is the annual coupon payment expressed as a percentage of the bond price. The **yield to maturity** measures the rate of return to an investor who purchases the bond and holds it until maturity, accounting for coupon income as well as the difference between purchase price and face value.

How can one find the market price of a bond given its yield to maturity or find a bond's yield given its price? Why do prices and yields vary inversely? (LO6-2)

Bonds are valued by discounting the coupon payments and the final repayment by the yield to maturity on comparable bonds. The bond payments discounted at the bond's yield to maturity equal the bond price. You may also start with the bond price and ask what interest rate the bond offers. The interest rate that equates the present value of bond payments to the bond price is the yield to maturity. Because present values are lower when discount rates are higher, price and yield to maturity vary inversely.

Why do bonds exhibit interest rate risk? (LO6-3)

Bond prices are subject to **interest rate risk,** rising when market interest rates fall and falling when market rates rise. Long-term bonds exhibit greater interest rate risk than short-term bonds.

What is the yield curve and why do investors pay attention to it? (LO6-4)

The yield curve plots the relationship between bond yields and maturity. Yields on long-term bonds are usually higher than those on short-term bonds. These higher yields compensate holders for the fact that prices of long-term bonds are more sensitive to changes in interest rates. Investors may also be prepared to accept a lower interest rate on short-term bonds when they expect interest rates to rise.

Why do investors pay attention to bond ratings and demand a higher interest rate for bonds with low ratings? (*LO6-5*)

Investors demand higher promised yields if there is a high probability that the borrower will run into trouble and default. **Credit risk** implies that the promised yield to maturity on the bond is higher than the expected yield. The additional yield investors require for bearing credit risk is called the **default premium.** Bond ratings measure the bond's credit risk.

LISTING OF EQUATIONS

6.1   Bond price = PV(coupons) + PV(face value)

= (coupon × annuity factor) + (face value × discount factor)

6.2   Bond rate of return = $\dfrac{\text{coupon income + price change}}{\text{investment}}$

QUESTIONS AND PROBLEMS

1. **Financial Pages.** Turn back to Table 6.1. (*LO6-1*)
   a. What is the current yield of the 5.25% 2028 maturity bond?
   b. "The current yield is less than the yield to maturity whenever the bond price is greater than the face value." True or false?

2. **Bond Yields.** A 30-year Treasury bond is issued with face value of $1,000, paying interest of $60 per year. If market yields increase shortly after the T-bond is issued, what happens to the bond's: (*LO6-1*)
   a. coupon rate?
   b. price?
   c. yield to maturity?
   d. current yield?

3. **Bond Yields.** If a bond with face value of $1,000 and a coupon rate of 8% is selling at a price of $970, is the bond's yield to maturity more or less than 8%? (*LO6-1*)

4. **Bond Yields.** A bond with face value $1,000 has a current yield of 6% and a coupon rate of 8%. (*LO6-1*)
   a. If interest is paid annually, what is the bond's price?
   b. Is the bond's yield to maturity more or less than 8%?

5. **Bond Pricing.** A General Power bond carries a coupon rate of 8%, has 9 years until maturity, and sells at a yield to maturity of 7%. (Assume annual interest payments.) (*LO6-1* and *LO6-2*)
   a. What interest payments do bondholders receive each year?
   b. At what price does the bond sell?
   c. What will happen to the bond price if the yield to maturity falls to 6%?
   d. If the yield to maturity falls to 6%, will the current yield be less, or more, than the yield to maturity?

6. **Bond Yields.** A bond has 8 years until maturity, carries a coupon rate of 8%, and sells for $1,100. (*LO6-1* and *LO6-2*)
   a. What is the current yield on the bond?
   b. What is the yield to maturity if interest is paid once a year?
   c. What is the yield to maturity if interest is paid semiannually?

7. **Bond Prices and Returns.** One bond has a coupon rate of 8%, another a coupon rate of 12%. Both bonds pay interest annually, have 10-year maturities, and sell at a yield to maturity of 10%. (*LO6-2*)

   a. If their yields to maturity next year are still 10%, what is the rate of return on each bond?
   b. Does the higher-coupon bond give a higher rate of return over this period?

8. **Bond Pricing.** A 6-year Circular File bond pays interest once a year of $80 and sells for $950. (*LO6-2*)

   a. What is its coupon rate?
   b. What is its yield to maturity?
   c. If Circular wants to issue a new 6-year bond at face value, what coupon rate must the bond offer?

9. **Coupon Rate.** General Matter's outstanding bond issue has a coupon rate of 10%, and it sells at a yield to maturity of 9.25%. The firm wishes to issue additional bonds to the public at face value. What coupon rate must the new bonds offer in order to sell at face value? (*LO6-2*)

10. **Bond Pricing.** A 30-year maturity bond with face value of $1,000 makes annual coupon payments and has a coupon rate of 8%. What is the bond's yield to maturity if the bond is selling for: (*LO6-2*)

    a. $900?
    b. $1,000?
    c. $1,100?

11. **Bond Pricing.** A 30-year maturity bond with face value of $1,000 makes *semiannual* coupon payments and has a coupon rate of 8%. What is the bond's yield to maturity if the bond is selling for: (*LO6-2*)

    a. $900?
    b. $1,000?
    c. $1,100?

12. **Bond Pricing.** The following table shows some data for three zero-coupon bonds. The face value of each bond is $1,000. (*LO6-2*)

Bond	Price	Maturity (years)	Yield to Maturity
A	$300	30	—
B	300	—	8%
C	—	10	10

    a. What is the yield to maturity of bond A? (Express your answer as a percentage rather than a decimal.)
    b. What is the maturity of B?
    c. What is the price of C?

13. **Pricing Consol Bonds.** Perpetual Life Corp. has issued consol bonds with coupon payments of $60. (Consols pay interest forever and never mature. They are perpetuities.) (*LO6-2*)

    a. If the required rate of return on these bonds at the time they were issued was 6%, at what price were they sold to the public?
    b. If the required return today is 10%, at what price do the consols sell?

14. **Bond Pricing.** Sure Tea Co. has issued 9% annual coupon bonds that are now selling at a yield to maturity of 10% and current yield of 9.8375%. What is the remaining maturity of these bonds? (*LO6-2*)

15. **Bond Pricing.** Maxcorp's bonds sell for $1,065.15. The bond life is 9 years, and the yield to maturity is 7%. What is the coupon rate on the bonds? (Assume annual coupon payments.) (*LO6-2*)

16. **Bond Returns.** You buy an 8% coupon, 10-year maturity bond for $980. A year later, the bond price is $1,200. (Assume annual coupon payments.) (*LO6-2*)

    a. What is the new yield to maturity on the bond?
    b. What is your rate of return over the year?

17. **Bond Returns.** A bond has 10 years until maturity, carries a coupon rate of 9%, and sells for $1,100. Interest is paid annually. (*LO6-2* and *LO6-3*)

    a. If the bond has a yield to maturity of 9% 1 year from now, what will its price be at that time?
    b. What will be the rate of return on the bond?
    c. Now assume that interest is paid semiannually. What will be the rate of return on the bond?
    d. If the inflation rate during the year is 3%, what is the real rate of return on the bond? (Assume annual interest payments.)

18. **Bond Returns.** You buy an 8% coupon, 20-year maturity bond when its yield to maturity is 9%. (Assume semiannual coupon payments.) Six months later, the yield to maturity is 10%. What is your return over the 6 months? (*LO6-3*)

19. **Interest Rate Risk.** Consider three bonds with 8% coupon rates, all making annual coupon payments and all selling at face value. The short-term bond has a maturity of 4 years, the intermediate-term bond has a maturity of 8 years, and the long-term bond has a maturity of 30 years. (*LO6-3*)

    a. What will be the price of the 4-year bond if its yield increases to 9%?
    b. What will be the price of the 8-year bond if its yield increases to 9%?
    c. What will be the price of the 30-year bond if its yield increases to 9%?
    d. What will be the price of the 4-year bond if its yield decreases to 7%?
    e. What will be the price of the 8-year bond if its yield decreases to 7%?
    f. What will be the price of the 30-year bond if its yield decreases to 7%?
    g. Comparing your answers to parts (a), (b), and (c), are long-term bonds more or less affected than short-term bonds by a rise in interest rates?
    h. Comparing your answers to parts (d), (e), and (f), are long-term bonds more or less affected than short-term bonds by a decline in interest rates?

20. **Rate of Return.** A 2-year maturity bond with face value of $1,000 makes annual coupon payments of $80 and is selling at face value. What will be the rate of return on the bond if its yield to maturity at the end of the year is: (a) 6%? (b) 8%? (c) 10%? (*LO6-3*)

21. **Rate of Return.** A bond is issued with a coupon of 4% paid annually, a maturity of 30 years, and a yield to maturity of 7%. What rate of return will be earned by an investor who purchases the bond for $627.73 and holds it for 1 year if the bond's yield to maturity at the end of the year is 8%? (*LO6-3*)

22. **Real Returns.** Suppose that you buy a 1-year maturity bond with a coupon of 7% paid annually. If you buy the bond at its face value, what real rate of return will you earn if the inflation rate is: (a) 4%? (b) 6%? (c) 8%? (*LO6-3*)

23. **Real Returns.** Suppose that you buy a TIPS (inflation-indexed) bond with a 1-year maturity and a coupon of 4% paid annually. If you buy the bond at its face value, and the inflation rate is 8%: (*LO6-3*)

    a. What will be your cash flow at the end of the year?
    b. What will be your real return?
    c. What will be your nominal return?

24. **Real Returns.** Suppose that you buy a TIPS (inflation-indexed) bond with a 2-year maturity and a coupon of 4% paid annually. If you buy the bond at its face value, and the inflation rate is 8% in each year: (*LO6-3*)

    a. What will be your cash flow in year 1?
    b. What will be your cash flow in year 2?
    c. What will be your real rate of return over the two-year period?

25. **Interest Rate Risk.** Consider two bonds, a 3-year bond paying an annual coupon of 5% and a 10-year bond also with an annual coupon of 5%. Both currently sell at face value. Now suppose that interest rates rise to 10%. (*LO6-3*)

    a. What is the new price of the 3-year bonds?
    b. What is the new price of the 10-year bonds?
    c. Do you conclude that long-term or short-term bonds are more sensitive to a change in interest rates?

26. **Interest Rate Risk.** Suppose interest rates increase from 8% to 9%. Which bond will suffer the greater percentage decline in price: a 30-year bond paying annual coupons of 8% or a 30-year zero-coupon bond? (*LO6-3*)

27. **Interest Rate Risk.** Look again at the previous question. Can you explain intuitively why the zero exhibits greater interest rate risk even though it has the same maturity as the coupon bond? (*LO6-3*)

28. **Interest Rate Risk.** Consider two 30-year maturity bonds. Bond A has a coupon rate of 4%, while bond B has a coupon rate of 12%. Both bonds pay their coupons semiannually. (*LO6-3*)

    a. Construct an Excel spreadsheet showing the prices of each of these bonds for yields to maturity ranging from 2% to 15% at intervals of 1%. Column A should show the yield to maturity (ranging from 2% to 15%), and columns B and C should compute the prices of the two bonds (using Excel's bond price function) at each interest rate.

    b. Suppose Bond A is currently priced to offer a yield to maturity of 8%. Calculate the (percentage) capital gain or loss on the bond if its yield immediately changes to each value in column A. Report the capital gain or loss corresponding to the new yield in column D.

    c. Now repeat part (b) for Bond B. Show the capital gain or loss corresponding to each yield to maturity in column E.

    d. Plot the values in columns D and E as a function of the yield to maturity. Which bond's price exhibits greater proportional sensitivity to changes in its yield? In other words, which bond has greater interest rate risk?

    e. Can you explain the result you found in part (*d*)? (*Hint:* Is there any sense in which a bond that pays a high coupon rate has lower "average" or "effective" maturity than a bond that pays a low coupon rate?)

29. **The Yield Curve.** Suppose that investors expect interest rates to fall sharply. Would you expect short-term bonds to offer higher or lower yields than long-term bonds? (*LO6-4*)

30. **Yield Curve.** The following table shows the prices of a sample of Treasury strips. Each strip makes a single payment at maturity. (*LO6-4*)

Years to Maturity	Price (% of face value)
1	96.852%
2	93.351
3	89.544
4	85.480

    a. What is the 1-year interest rate?
    b. What is the 2-year interest rate?
    c. What is the 3-year interest rate?
    d. What is the 4-year interest rate?
    e. Is the yield curve upward-sloping, downward-sloping, or flat?
    f. Is this the usual shape of the yield curve?

31. **Yield Curve.** In Figure 6.7, we saw a plot of the yield curve on stripped Treasury bonds and pointed out that bonds of different maturities may sell at different yields to maturity. In principle, when we are valuing a stream of cash flows, each cash flow should be discounted by the yield appropriate to its particular maturity. Suppose the yield curve on (zero-coupon) Treasury strips is as follows: (*LO6-4*)

Years to Maturity	Yield to Maturity
1	4.0%
2	5.0
3–5	5.5
6–10	6.0

You wish to value a 10-year bond with a coupon rate of 10%, paid annually.

    a. Set up an Excel spreadsheet to value each of the bond's annual cash flows using this table of yields. Add up the present values of the bond's 10 cash flows to obtain the bond price.

    b. What is the bond's yield to maturity?

    c. Compare the yield to maturity of the 10-year, 10% coupon bond with that of a 10-year zero-coupon bond or Treasury strip. Which is higher? Why does this result make sense given this yield curve?

32. **Credit Risk.** (*LO6-5*)

    a. Several years ago, Castles in the Sand Inc. issued bonds at face value at a yield to maturity of 7%. Now, with 8 years left until the maturity of the bonds, the company has run into hard times and the yield to maturity on the bonds has increased to 15%. What is now the price of the bond? (Assume semiannual coupon payments.)

    b. Suppose that investors believe that Castles can make good on the promised coupon payments but that the company will go bankrupt when the bond matures and the principal comes due. The expectation is that investors will receive only 80% of face value at maturity. If they buy the bond today, what yield to maturity do they *expect* to receive?

33. **Credit Risk.** Suppose that Casino Royale has issued bonds that mature in 1 year. They currently offer a yield of 20%. However, there is a 50% chance that Casino will default and bondholders will receive nothing. What is the *expected* yield on the bonds? (*LO6-5*)

34. **Credit Risk.** Bond A is a 10-year U.S. Treasury bond. Bond B is a 10-year corporate bond. True or false? (*LO6-3* and *LO6-5*)

    a. If you hold bond A to maturity, your return will be equal to the yield to maturity.

    b. If you hold bond B to maturity, your return will be equal to or less than the yield to maturity.

    c. If you hold bond A for 5 years and then sell it, your return could be greater than the yield to maturity.

35. **Credit Risk.** A bond's credit rating provides a guide to its risk. Suppose that long-term bonds rated Aa currently offer yields to maturity of 7.5%. A-rated bonds sell at yields of 7.8%. Suppose that a 10-year bond with a coupon rate of 7.6% is downgraded by Moody's from an Aa to A rating. (*LO6-5*)

    a. Is the bond likely to sell above or below par value before the downgrade?

    b. Is the bond likely to sell above or below par value after the downgrade?

36. **Credit Risk.** Sludge Corporation has two bonds outstanding, each with a face value of $2 million. Bond A is a senior bond; bond B is subordinated. Sludge has suffered a severe downturn in demand, and its assets are now worth only $3 million. If the company defaults, what payoff can the holders of bond B expect? (*LO6-5*)

37. **Credit Risk.** Slush Corporation has two bonds outstanding, each with a face value of $2 million. Bond A is secured on the company's head office building; bond B is unsecured. Slush has suffered a severe downturn in demand. Its head office building is worth $1 million, but its remaining assets are now worth only $2 million. If the company defaults, what payoff can the holders of bond B expect? (*LO6-5*)

WEB EXERCISES

1. Log on to **www.investopedia.com** to find a simple calculator for working out bond prices. (Start by clicking the *Investing* link.) Check whether a change in yield has a greater effect on the price of a long-term or a short-term bond.

2. When we plotted the yield curve in Figure 6.7, we used the prices of Treasury strips. You can find current prices of strips by logging on to *The Wall Street Journal* website (**www.wsj.com**) and clicking on *Market, Market Data,* and then *Rates.* Try plotting the yields on stripped coupons against maturity. Do they currently increase or decline with maturity? Can you explain why? You can also use *The Wall Street Journal* site to compare the yields on nominal Treasury bonds with those on TIPS. Suppose that you are confident that inflation will be 3% per year. Which bonds are the better buy?

3. You can find the most recent bond rating for many companies by logging on to **finance.yahoo.com** and going to the Bond Center. Find the bond rating for some major companies. Were they investment-grade or below?

4. In Figure 6.9, we showed how bonds with greater credit risk have promised higher yields to maturity. This yield spread goes up when the economic outlook is particularly uncertain. You can check how much extra yield lower-grade bonds offer today by logging on to **www.federalreserve.gov** and comparing the yields on Aaa and Baa bonds. Look for the *Economic Research & Data* tab. How does the spread in yields compare with the spread in November 2008 at the height of the financial crisis?

SOLUTIONS TO SELF-TEST QUESTIONS

6.1 The asked price of the 1.625s is 97.3203. So one bond would cost $973.203. A bond selling for $1,106.25 would be quoted at 110.625. The bid price of the 3s of 2044 is 98.5859. So you would receive $985.859.

6.2 a. The asked price is 130.4531% of face value, or $1,304.531.
b. The bid price is 130.3906% of face value, or $1,303.906.
c. The annual coupon is 5.25% of face value, or $52.50, a year.
d. The yield to maturity, based on the asked price, is given as 2.493%.

6.3 The coupon is 9% of $1,000, or $90 a year. First value the 6-year annuity of coupons:

$$PV = \$90 \times (\text{6-year annuity factor})$$

$$= \$90 \times \left[\frac{1}{.12} - \frac{1}{.12(1.12)^6} \right]$$

$$= \$90 \times 4.1114 = \$370.03$$

Then value the final payment and add:

$$PV = \frac{\$1,000}{(1.12)^6} = \$506.63$$

$$PV \text{ of bond} = \$370.03 + \$506.63 = \$876.66$$

Using a financial calculator, your inputs would be: $n = 6$; $i = 12$; PMT $= 90$; FV $= 1000$. Now compute PV.

6.4 At an interest rate of 4%, the 3-year bond sells for $923.68. If the interest rate drops to 2%, the bond price rises to $978.37, an increase of 5.9%. The 30-year bond sells for $524.47 when the interest rate is 4%, but its price rises to $832.03 at an interest rate of 2%, a much larger percentage increase of 58.6%.

6.5 The yield to maturity assuming annual coupons is about 8%, because the present value of the bond's cash returns is $1,199, almost exactly $1,200, when discounted at 8%:

$$PV = PV(\text{coupons}) + PV(\text{final payment})$$

$$= (\text{coupon} \times \text{annuity factor}) + (\text{face value} \times \text{discount factor})$$

$$= \$140 \times \left[\frac{1}{.08} - \frac{1}{.08(1.08)^4} \right] + \$1,000 \times \frac{1}{1.08^4}$$

$$= \$463.70 + \$735.03 = \$1,199$$

To obtain a more precise solution on your calculator, these would be your inputs:

	Annual Payments	Semiannual Payments
n	4	8
PV	−1200	−1200
FV	1000	1000
PMT	140	70

Compute i to find yield to maturity (annual payments) = 7.97%. Yield to maturity (semiannual payments) = 4.026% per 6 months, which would be reported in the financial press as 8.05% annual yield.

6.6 With a yield of 4%, the 8% coupon, 10-year bond sells for $1,324.44. At the end of the year, the bond has only 9 years to maturity and investors demand an interest rate of 6%. Therefore, the value of the bond becomes $1,136.03. (On your calculator, input $n = 9$; $i = 6$; PMT $= 8$; FV $= 1000$; compute PV.) Thus, you have received a coupon payment of $80 but have a capital *loss* of 1,324.44 − 1,136.03 = $188.41. Your total return is therefore (80 − 188.41)/1,324.44 = −.082, or −8.2%. Because interest rates rose over the year, your return was *less* than the yield to maturity.

6.7   By the end of the year, the bond will have only 1 year left until maturity. So its price will be $1,080/1.06 = \$1,018.87$. You will therefore receive a coupon payment of \$80 and make a capital loss of $\$1,036.67 - \$1,018.87 = \$17.80$. Your total return over the year is $(80 - 17.80)/1,036.67 = .060$, or 6.0%. When the bond matures, you receive the face value of \$1,000. So, in the final year, you receive a coupon payment of \$80 and make a capital loss of \$18.87. Your total return over this year is $(80 - 18.87)/1,018.87 = .060$, or 6.0%. When the yield to maturity does not change, your return is equal to the yield to maturity.

6.8   If you invest in a 2-year bond, you will have $\$1,000 \times 1.06^2 = \$1,123.60$. If you are right in your forecast about 1-year rates, then an investment in 1-year bonds will produce $\$1,000 \times 1.05 \times 1.08 = \$1,134.00$ by the end of 2 years. You would do better to invest in the 1-year bond.

6.9   The difference between the nominal yield and the real yield is a rough guide to inflation expectations. That difference turned negative in late 2008, signifying that prices were generally expected to decrease, or equivalently, that inflation would be negative. This was the beginning of the so-called Great Recession resulting from the financial crisis. In deep recessions like that one, inflationary pressures can disappear, and prices are more prone to actually decline.

6.10   The extra debt makes it more likely that the firm will not be able to make good on its promised payments to its creditors. If the new debt is not junior to the already-issued debt, then the original bondholders suffer a loss when their bonds become more susceptible to default risk. A protective covenant limiting the amount of new debt that the firm can issue would have prevented this problem. Investors, having witnessed the problems of the RJR bondholders, generally demanded the covenant on later debt issues.

7

Valuing Stocks

LEARNING OBJECTIVES

After studying this chapter, you should be able to:

7-1 Understand the stock trading reports on the Internet or in the financial pages of the newspaper.

7-2 Calculate the present value of a stock given forecasts of future dividends and show how growth opportunities are reflected in stock prices and price-earnings ratios.

7-3 Apply valuation models to an entire business.

7-4 Understand what professionals mean when they say that there are no free lunches on Wall Street.

RELATED WEBSITES FOR THIS CHAPTER CAN BE FOUND IN CONNECT.

Charts of stock prices. Looking at past fluctuations in stock prices can be mesmerizing, but what determines those prices?
© *woraput chawalitphon/Getty Images RF*

A corporation can either raise cash for investment by borrowing or by selling new shares of common stock to investors. If it borrows, it has a fixed obligation to repay the lender. If it issues shares, there is no fixed obligation, but the new stockholders become partial owners of the firm. All old and new stockholders share in its fortunes, in proportion to the number of shares that they hold. In this chapter, we take a first look at common stocks, the stock market, and the principles of stock valuation.

We start by looking at how stocks are bought and sold. Then we look at what determines stock prices and how stock valuation formulas can be used to value individual stocks as well as entire businesses. We will see how the firm's investment opportunities are reflected in its stock price and why stock market analysts focus so much attention on the price-earnings, or P/E, ratio of the company.

Why should you care how stocks are valued? After all, if you want to know the value of a firm's stock, you can look up the stock price on the Internet or in *The Wall Street Journal*. But you need to know what determines prices for at least two reasons. First, you may need to value the common stock of a business that is *not* traded on a stock exchange. For example, you may be the founder of a successful business that plans to sell stock to the public for the first time. You and your advisers need to estimate the price at which those shares can be sold.

Second, in order to make good capital budgeting decisions, corporations need to have some understanding of how the market values firms. A project is attractive if it increases shareholders' wealth. But you can't judge that unless you know how their shares are valued.

There may be a third reason that you would like to know how stocks are valued. You may be hoping that the knowledge will allow you to make a killing on Wall Street. It's a pleasant thought, but we will see that even professional investors find it difficult to outsmart the competition and to earn consistently superior returns.

7.1 Stocks and the Stock Market

In Chapter 1, we saw how FedEx was founded and how it then grew and prospered. To fund this growth, FedEx needed capital. Initially, that capital came largely from borrowing, but in 1978 FedEx sold shares of **common stock** to the public for the first time. Those investors who bought shares in the **initial public offering,** or **IPO,** became part-owners of the business, and as shareholders they shared in the company's future successes and setbacks.[1]

A company's initial public offering is rarely its last, and since 1978 FedEx has raised more capital by selling additional shares. These sales of shares by the company are called **primary offerings** and are said to be made in the **primary market.**

Owning shares is a risky occupation. For example, if at the start of 2015 you had the misfortune to buy shares in Chesapeake Energy, you would have lost 78% of your money by the year-end. You can understand, therefore, why investors would be reluctant to buy shares if they were forced to tie the knot with a particular company forever. So large companies usually arrange for their common stock to be listed on a stock exchange so that investors can trade shares among themselves. Exchanges are really markets for secondhand stocks, but they prefer to describe themselves as **secondary markets,** which sounds more important.

The two principal stock markets in the United States are the New York Stock Exchange (NYSE) and NASDAQ.[2] In addition, there are many computer networks called *electronic communication networks (ECNs)* that connect traders with each other. All of these markets compete vigorously for the business of traders and just as vigorously tout the advantages of their own trading venue. The volume of trades in these markets is immense. For example, every day the NYSE alone trades more than a billion shares with market value exceeding $40 billion.

Of course, there are stock exchanges in many other countries. Some are tiny, such as the stock exchange in the Maldives, which trades shares in just six companies. Others, such as the London, Tokyo, Frankfurt, and pan-European Euronext exchanges, trade the shares of thousands of firms.

Suppose that Ms. Jones, a longtime FedEx shareholder, no longer wishes to hold her shares in the company. She can sell them via a stock exchange to Mr. Brown, who wishes to increase his stake in the firm. The transaction merely transfers (partial) ownership of the firm from one investor to another. No new shares are created, and FedEx usually will neither care nor even be aware that such a trade has taken place.[3]

Ms. Jones and Mr. Brown do not buy or sell FedEx shares themselves. Instead, each must hire a brokerage firm with trading privileges on an exchange to arrange the transaction for them. Not so long ago, such trades would have involved hands-on negotiation. The broker would have had to agree on an acceptable price with a dealer in the stock or would have brought the trade to the floor of an exchange where a *specialist* in FedEx would have coordinated the transaction. But today, the vast majority of trades are executed automatically and electronically, even on the more traditional exchanges.

When Ms. Jones and Mr. Brown decide to buy or sell FedEx stock, they need to give their brokers instructions about the price at which they are prepared to transact. Ms. Jones, who is anxious to sell quickly, might give her broker a *market order* to sell

---

common stock
Ownership shares in a publicly held corporation.

initial public offering (IPO)
First offering of stock to the general public.

primary offering
The corporation sells shares in the firm.

primary market
Market for the sale of new securities by corporations.

secondary market
Market in which previously issued securities are traded among investors.

BEYOND THE PAGE

The world's stock exchanges

mhhe.com/brealey9e

---

[1] We use the terms "shares," "stock," and "common stock" interchangeably, as we do "shareholders" and "stockholders."

[2] This originally was an acronym for National Association of Security Dealers Automated Quotation system, but now is simply known as the NASDAQ market.

[3] Eventually, FedEx must know to whom it should send dividend checks, but this information is needed only when such payments are being prepared. In some cases, FedEx might care about a stock transaction, for example, if a large investor is building a big stake in the firm. But this is the exception.

FIGURE 7.1 A portion of the limit order book for FedEx on the BATS Exchange, November 11, 2015

FedEx Corporation (FDX) - NYSE ★ Watchlist
160.09 ↓1.41 (0.87%) 10:53AM EST - NYSE Real Time Price

Order Book

Top of Book

Bid		Ask	
Price	Size	Price	Size
159.78	100	159.99	100
159.77	100	160.00	100
159.74	100	160.10	10
159.30	100	160.60	100
159.20	100	160.66	100

Source: BATS, accessed from Yahoo! Finance, November 11, 2015.

stock at the best available price. On the other hand, Mr. Brown might give his broker a price limit at which he is willing to buy FedEx stock. If his order cannot be executed immediately, it is recorded in the exchange's *limit order book* until it can be executed.

Figure 7.1 shows a portion of the limit order book for FedEx from the BATS Exchange, one of the largest electronic markets. The last trade in FedEx took place earlier in the day at a share price of $160.09. The bid prices on the left are the prices (and numbers of shares) at which investors are currently willing to buy. The Ask column presents offers to sell. The prices are arranged from best to worst, so the highest bids and lowest asks are at the top of the list. The broker might electronically enter Ms. Jones's market order to sell 100 shares on the BATS Exchange, where it would be automatically matched or *crossed* with the best offer to buy, which at that moment was $159.78 a share. Similarly, a market order to *buy* would be crossed with the best ask price, $159.99. The *bid-ask spread* at that moment was therefore 21 cents per share.

Reading Stock Market Listings

If you are thinking about buying shares in FedEx, you will wish to see its current price. Until recently, you probably would have looked for that information in *The Wall Street Journal* or the financial pages of your local newspaper. But those pages contain less and less information about individual stocks, and most investors today turn to the Internet for their information. For example, if you go to **finance.yahoo.com**, enter FedEx's ticker symbol, FDX, and ask to "Get Quotes," you will find recent trading data such as those presented in Figure 7.2.[4]

The most recent price at which the stock traded on November 11 was $160.39 per share, which was $1.11 lower than the previous day's closing price of $161.50. The range of prices at which the stock traded that day, as well as over the previous 52 weeks, is provided in the set of columns on the right. Yahoo! also tells us that the average daily trading volume over the last 3 months was 1,987,080 shares. So far, by 10:57 a.m. on November 11, 596,716 shares had traded. FedEx's *market cap* (shorthand for market capitalization) is the total value of its outstanding shares of stock, $45.29 billion. You will frequently hear traders referring to large-cap or small-cap firms, which is a convenient way to summarize the size of the company.

---

[4] Other good sources of trading data are **moneycentral.msn.com/investor/home.asp** or the online edition of *The Wall Street Journal* at **www.wsj.com** (look for the Market and then Market Data tabs).

FIGURE 7.2 Trading
information for FedEx

FedEx Corporation (FDX) - NYSE

160.39 ↓1.11 (0.69%) 10:57 AM EST - Nasdaq Real Time Price

Prev Close:	161.50	Day's Range:	159.00 — 160.64
Open:	160.01	52wk Range:	130.13 — 185.19
Bid:	159.45 × 200	Volume:	596,716
Ask:	159.52 × 200	Avg Vol (3m)	1,987,080
1y Target Est:	185.09	Market Cap:	45.29B
Beta:	1.19525	P/E (ttm):	42.25
Next Earnings Date:	16-Dec-15 📅	EPS (ttm):	3.80
		Div & Yield:	1.00 (0.65%)

Source: Yahoo! Finance, November 11, 2015.

P/E ratio
Ratio of stock price to
earnings per share.

FedEx earned $3.80 per share in the past year. (The abbreviation "ttm" in the parentheses stands for *trailing 12 months.*) Therefore, the ratio of price per share to earnings per share, known as the *price-earnings multiple* or, equivalently, **P/E ratio,** is (aside from a little rounding error) 160.39/3.80 = 42.25. The P/E ratio is a key tool of stock market analysts, and we will have much to say about it later in the chapter.

The *dividend yield* tells you how much dividend income you would receive for every $100 invested in the stock. FedEx paid annual dividends of $1.00 per share, so its yield was 1.00/160.39 = about .65%. For every $100 invested in the stock, you would have received $.65 in dividends. Of course, this would not be the total rate of return on your investment, as you would also hope for some increase in the stock price. The dividend yield is thus much like the current yield of a bond. Both measures ignore prospective capital gains or losses.

The price at which you can buy shares in FedEx changes day to day and minute to minute as investors change their estimates of the company's prospects. Figure 7.3 shows the share price of FedEx over several months in 2015. The price rose by 5% in just over 1 week at the end of May. Why would the price that investors were willing to pay for each share change so suddenly? And, for that matter, why were they willing that month to pay $180 a share for FedEx but only $47 a share for Microsoft? To answer these questions, we need to look at what determines value.

FIGURE 7.3 Share price history for FedEx

Source: Yahoo! Finance, November 10, 2015.

7.2   Market Values, Book Values, and Liquidation Values

Finding the value of FedEx stock may sound like a simple problem. Each quarter, the company publishes a balance sheet, which lists the value of the firm's assets and liabilities. The simplified balance sheet in Table 7.1 shows that in May 2015, the book value of all FedEx's assets—plant and machinery, inventories of materials, cash in the bank, and so on—was $37,069 million. FedEx's debt and other liabilities—money that it owes the banks, taxes that are due to be paid, and the like—amounted to $22,076 million. The difference between the value of the assets and the liabilities was $14,993 million. This was the **book value** of the firm's equity.[5] Book value records all the money that FedEx has raised from its shareholders plus all the earnings that have been plowed back on their behalf.

Book value is a reassuringly definite number. But does the stock price equal book value? FedEx shares in November 2015 were selling at around $161, but as Table 7.2 shows, its book value per share was only $54.12. So the shares were worth about 3 times book value. This and the other cases shown in Table 7.2 tell us that investors in the stock market do *not* just buy and sell at book value per share.

Accountants don't even try to estimate market values. The value of the assets reported on the firm's balance sheet is equal to their original (or "historical") cost less an allowance for depreciation. But that may not be a good guide to what the firm could sell its assets for today.

Well, maybe stock price equals **liquidation value** per share, that is, the amount of cash per share a company could raise if it sold off all its assets in secondhand markets and paid off all its debts. Wrong again. A successful company ought to be worth more

book value
Net worth of the firm according to the balance sheet.

liquidation value
Net proceeds that could be realized by selling the firm's assets and paying off its creditors.

TABLE 7.1 Simplified balance sheet for FedEx, May 30, 2015 (figures in $ millions)

Assets		Liabilities and Shareholders' Equity	
Current assets	$10,941	Current liabilities	$ 5,957
Plant, equipment and other long-term assets	26,128	Debt and other long-term liabilities	16,119
		Shareholders' equity	14,993
Total assets	$37,069	Total liabilities and equity	$37,069

Note: Shares of stock outstanding: 277.0 million. Book value of equity (per share): 14,993/277.0 = $54.12.

TABLE 7.2 Market values versus book values, November 2015

	Ticker	Stock Price	Book Value per Share	Market-to-Book-Value Ratio
FedEx	FDX	$161.50	$54.12	3.0
Johnson & Johnson	JNJ	101.45	25.96	3.9
Campbell Soup	CPB	48.30	4.45	10.9
PepsiCo	PEP	98.83	9.31	10.6
Walmart	WMT	58.68	24.53	2.4
Dow Chemical	DOW	51.71	17.55	2.9
Amazon	AMZN	659.68	26.50	24.9
McDonald's	MCD	112.93	9.05	12.5
American Electric Power	AEP	55.10	36.06	1.5
General Electric	GE	30.12	11.00	2.7

Source: Yahoo! Finance, finance.yahoo.com.

---

[5] "Equity" is still another word for stock. Thus, stockholders are often referred to as *equity investors*.

than liquidation value. After all, that's the goal of bringing all those assets together in the first place.

The difference between a company's actual value and its book or liquidation value is often attributed to *going-concern value,* which refers to three factors:

1. *Extra earning power.* A company may have the ability to earn more than an adequate rate of return on assets. In this case the value of those assets will be higher than their book value or secondhand value.

2. *Intangible assets.* There are many assets that accountants don't put on the balance sheet. Some of these assets are extremely valuable. Take Johnson & Johnson, a health care product and pharmaceutical company. As you can see from Table 7.2, it sells at 3.9 times book value per share. Where did all that extra value come from? Largely from the cash flow generated by the drugs it has developed, patented, and marketed. These drugs are the fruits of a research and development (R&D) program that has grown to more than $8 billion per year. But U.S. accountants don't recognize R&D as an investment and don't put it on the company's balance sheet. Nevertheless, expertise, experience, and knowledge are crucial assets, and their values do show up in stock prices.

3. *Value of future investments.* If investors believe a company will have the opportunity to make very profitable investments in the future, they will pay more for the company's stock today. When eBay, the Internet auction house, first sold its stock to investors in 1998, the book value of shareholders' equity was about $100 million. Yet 1 day after the issue investors valued the equity at more than $6 *billion.* In part, this difference reflected an intangible asset, eBay's unique platform for trading a wide range of goods over the Internet. But investors also judged that eBay was a *growth company.* In other words, they were betting that the company's know-how and brand name would allow it to expand internationally and make it easier for customers to trade and pay online. By 2015, eBay had operating income of $3.5 billion and a market capitalization of $35 billion.

Market price is not the same as book value or liquidation value. Market value, unlike book value and liquidation value, treats the firm as a going concern.

It is not surprising that stocks virtually never sell at book or liquidation values. Investors buy shares on the basis of present and *future* earning power. Two key features determine the profits the firm will be able to produce: first, the earnings that can be generated by the firm's tangible and intangible assets, and second, the opportunities the firm has to invest in lucrative projects that will increase future earnings.

Example   7.1 ▶   Amazon and Consolidated Edison

Amazon is a growth company. As recently as 2014, its profit was actually negative, −$241 million. Yet investors in December 2014 were prepared to pay about $110 billion for Amazon's common stock. The value of the stock came from the company's market position, its highly regarded distribution system, and the promise of new related products that will generate increased future earnings. Amazon was a growth firm because its market value depended so heavily on intangible assets and the anticipated profitability of new investments.

Contrast this with Consolidated Edison (Con Ed), the electric utility servicing the New York City area. Con Ed is not a growth company. Its market is limited, and it is expanding capacity at a very deliberate pace. More important, it is a regulated utility, so its returns on present and future investments are constrained. Con Ed's value derives mostly from the stream of income generated by its existing assets. Therefore, while Amazon shares sold for 24.9 times book value, Con Ed shares sold at only about 1.4 times book value. ∎

Investors refer to Amazon as a *growth stock* and Con Ed as an *income stock*. A few stocks, like Alphabet (the parent company of Google), offer both income and growth. Alphabet earns plenty from its current products, such as the Google search engine. These earnings are part of what makes the stock attractive to investors. In addition, investors are willing to pay for the company's ability to invest profitably in new ventures that will increase future earnings.

Let's summarize. Just remember:

- *Book value* records what a company has paid for its assets, less a deduction for depreciation. It does not capture the true value of a business.
- *Liquidation value* is what the company could net by selling its assets and repaying its debts. It does not capture the value of a successful going concern.
- *Market value* is the amount that investors are willing to pay for the shares of the firm. This depends on the earning power of *today's* assets and the expected profitability of *future* investments.

The next question is, What determines market value?

7.1 Self-Test

In the 1970s, the computer industry was growing rapidly. In the 1980s, many new competitors entered the market, and computer prices fell. Since then, computer makers have struggled with thinning profit margins and intense competition. How has the industry's market-value balance sheet changed over time? Have assets in place become proportionately more or less important? Do you think this progression is unique to the computer industry?

7.3 Valuing Common Stocks

Valuation by Comparables

When financial analysts need to value a business, they often start by identifying a sample of similar firms. They then examine how much investors in these companies are prepared to pay for each dollar of assets or earnings. This is often called *valuation by comparables*. Look, for example, at Table 7.3. The first column of numbers shows, for some well-known companies, the ratio of the market value of the equity to the book value. Notice that in each case market value is higher than book value.

The second column of numbers shows the market-to-book ratio for competing firms. For example, you can see from the second row of the table that the stock of the typical large pharmaceutical firm sells for 4.7 times its book value. If you did not have a market price for the stock of Johnson & Johnson (J&J), you might estimate that it would also sell at 4.7 times book value. In this case, your estimate of J&J's market price would have been a bit high.

An alternative would be to look at how much investors in other pharmaceutical stocks are prepared to pay for each dollar of earnings. The second row of Table 7.3 shows that the typical price-earnings (P/E) ratio for pharmaceutical stocks in 2015 was 18.1. If you assumed that Johnson & Johnson should sell at a similar multiple of earnings, you would have gotten a value for the stock of $117, somewhat higher than its actual price of $101.45 in November 2015.

	Market-to-Book-Value Ratio		Price-Earnings Ratio	
	Company	Industry*	Company	Industry*
FedEx	3.0	2.2	13.2	20.7
Johnson & Johnson	3.9	4.7	15.8	18.1
Campbell Soup	10.9	4.2	17.6	20.0
PepsiCo	10.6	5.5	20.4	23.9
Walmart	2.4	3.2	14.0	21.5
Dow Chemical	2.9	3.7	14.7	12.5
Amazon	24.9	5.4	116.8	26.5
McDonald's	12.5	8.1	21.4	22.2
American Electric Power	1.5	1.7	14.8	16.5
General Electric	2.7	3.1	19.8	14.7

*Figures are median values for companies in the same industry.

Market-to-book and price-earnings ratios are the most popular rules of thumb for valuing common stocks, but financial analysts sometimes look at other multiples. For example, infant firms often do not have any earnings. So, rather than calculate a price-earnings ratio, analysts may look at the price-to-sales ratio for these firms. In the late 1990s, when dot-com companies were growing rapidly and losing lots of money, multiples were often based on the number of subscribers or website visits.

There is nothing wrong with such rules of thumb if intelligently applied. For example, you can see that valuation by comparables would have worked fairly well for American Electric Power and Johnson & Johnson in 2015. However, that is not the case for all the companies shown in Table 7.3. For example, if you had naively assumed that Amazon stock would sell at similar ratios to comparable Internet retail stocks, you would have been out by a wide margin. Both the market-to-book ratio and the price-earnings ratio can vary considerably from stock to stock even for firms that are in the same line of business. To understand why this is so, we need to dig deeper and look at what determines a stock's market value.

Price and Intrinsic Value

In the previous chapter, we saw that the value of a bond is the present value of its coupon payments plus the present value of its final payment of face value. You can think of stocks in a similar way. Instead of receiving coupon payments, investors may receive dividends, and instead of receiving the bond's face value, they will receive the stock price at the time they sell their shares.

Consider, for example, an investor who buys a share of Blue Skies Inc. today and plans to sell it in 1 year. Call the predicted stock price in 1 year P_1, the expected dividend per share DIV_1, and the discount rate for the stock's expected cash flows r.[6] Remember, the discount rate reflects the risk of the stock. Riskier firms will have higher discount rates. Then the present value of the cash flows the investor will receive from Blue Skies is

$$V_0 = \frac{DIV_1 + P_1}{1 + r} \tag{7.1}$$

We call V_0 the **intrinsic value** of the share. Intrinsic value is just the present value of the cash payoffs anticipated by the investor in the stock.

To illustrate, suppose investors expect a cash dividend next year of $3 ($DIV_1 = \$3$) and expect the stock to sell for $81 a year hence ($P_1 = \$81$). If the discount rate is 12%, then intrinsic value is $75:

$$V_0 = \frac{3 + 81}{1.12} = \$75$$

intrinsic value
Present value of future cash payoffs from a stock or other security.

---

[6] For simplicity we assume that the dividend is paid at the end of the year.

You can think of intrinsic value as the "fair" price for the stock. If investors buy the stock for \$75, their expected rate of return will precisely equal the discount rate—in other words, their investment return will just compensate them for the opportunity cost of their money.

To confirm this, note that the expected rate of return over the next year is the expected dividend plus the expected increase in price, $P_1 - P_0$, all divided by price at the start of the year, P_0. If the investor buys the shares for intrinsic value, then $P_0 = \$75$ and

$$\text{Expected return} = \frac{\text{DIV}_1 + P_1 - P_0}{P_0} = \frac{3 + 81 - 75}{75} = .12, \text{ or } 12\%$$

Notice that this expected return comes in two parts, the dividend yield and the capital gain:

$$\text{Expected rate of return} = \text{expected dividend yield} + \text{expected capital gain}$$

$$= \frac{\text{DIV}_1}{P_0} + \frac{P_1 - P_0}{P_0}$$

$$= \frac{3}{75} + \frac{81 - 75}{75}$$

$$= .04 + .08 = .12, \text{ or } 12\%$$

Of course, the actual return for Blue Skies may turn out to be more or less than investors expect. For example, in 2015, retail stocks were one of the best performing sectors with an average return of almost 20%. This was almost certainly better than investors expected at the start of the year. At the other extreme, the share prices of energy service firms declined by more than 20%. No investor at the start of the year would have purchased these shares anticipating such a loss. Never confuse the actual outcome with the expected outcome.

The dream of every investor is to buy shares at a bargain price—that is, a price less than intrinsic value. But in competitive markets, no price other than intrinsic value could survive for long. To see why, imagine that Blue Skies' current price was above \$75. Then the expected rate of return on Blue Skies stock would be *lower* than that on other securities of equivalent risk. *(Check this!)* Investors would bail out of Blue Skies stock and move into other securities. In the process, they would force down the price of Blue Skies stock. If P_0 were less than \$75, Blue Skies stock would offer a *higher* expected rate of return than equivalent-risk securities. *(Check this, too.)* Everyone would rush to buy, forcing the price up to \$75. When the stock is priced correctly (that is, price equals present value), the *expected* rate of return on Blue Skies stock is also the rate of return that investors *require* to hold the stock. **In a well-functioning market, all equally risky securities are priced to offer the same expected rate of return. This is a fundamental characteristic of prices in competitive markets. It is also common sense.**

Equation 7.1 is just a *definition* of intrinsic value, which works for any discount rate r. Now we can go beyond that definition and identify r as the expected rate of return on all securities with a particular level of risk. If a stock is priced correctly, it will offer an expected rate of return equal to that of other equally risky stocks and price will equal intrinsic value:

$$P_0 = \frac{\text{DIV}_1 + P_1}{1 + r}$$

Thus, today's price will equal the present value of dividend payments plus the present value of future price. But now we need to take a further step: How do we estimate the future price P_1?

7.2   Self-Test

Androscoggin Copper is increasing next year's dividend to $5 per share. The forecast stock price next year is $105. Equally risky stocks of other companies offer expected rates of return of 10%. What should Androscoggin common stock sell for?

Of course, many corporations do not currently pay cash dividends. Investors in a young, growing company may have to wait a decade or more before the firm matures and starts paying out cash to shareholders. Our formula for P_0 still applies to such firms if we set the immediate dividend DIV_1 equal to zero. In this case value depends on the subsequent dividends. But let's begin with a mature firm that is paying dividends now. We will say more about growth firms later.

The Dividend Discount Model

Our equation for stock price depends on $DIV_1 + P_1$, that is, next period's dividend and next period's price. Suppose you have forecast the dividend. How do you forecast the price P_1? We can answer this question by moving our stock price equation forward one period and applying it in period 1. The equation then says that P_1 depends on the second period's dividend DIV_2 and the second-period price P_2. The second-period price P_2 in turn depends on the third period's dividend DIV_3 and the third-period price P_3, which depends on DIV_4 . . . you can see where this logic is going.

As it turns out, we can express a stock's intrinsic value (and, therefore, price) as the present value of *all* the forecasted future dividends paid by the company to its shareholders without referring to the future stock price. This is the **dividend discount model:**

dividend discount model
Discounted cash-flow model that states that today's stock price equals the present value of all expected future dividends.

$$P_0 = \text{present value of } (DIV_1, DIV_2, DIV_3, \cdots, DIV_t, \cdots)$$

$$= \frac{DIV_1}{1 + r} + \frac{DIV_2}{(1 + r)^2} + \frac{DIV_3}{(1 + r)^3} + \cdots + \frac{DIV_t}{(1 + r)^t} + \cdots$$

How far out in the future could we look? In principle, 40, 60, or 100 years or more—corporations are potentially immortal. However, far-distant dividends will not have significant present values. For example, the present value of $1 received in 30 years using a 10% discount rate is only $.057. Most of the value of established companies comes from dividends to be paid within a person's working lifetime.

How do we get from the one-period formula $P_0 = (DIV_1 + P_1)/(1 + r)$ to the dividend discount model? We look at increasingly long investment horizons.

Let's consider investors with different investment horizons. Each investor will value the share of stock as the present value of the dividends that she or he expects to receive plus the present value of the price at which the stock is eventually sold. Unlike bonds, however, the final horizon date for stocks is not specified—stocks do not "mature." Moreover, both dividends and final sales price can only be estimated. But the general valuation approach is the same. For a one-period investor, the valuation formula looks like this:

$$P_0 = \frac{DIV_1 + P_1}{1 + r}$$

A 2-year investor would value the stock as

$$P_0 = \frac{DIV_1}{1 + r} + \frac{DIV_2 + P_2}{(1 + r)^2}$$

and a 3-year investor would use the formula

$$P_0 = \frac{DIV_1}{1 + r} + \frac{DIV_2}{(1 + r)^2} + \frac{DIV_3 + P_3}{(1 + r)^3}$$

In fact, we can look as far out into the future as we like. Suppose we call our horizon date H. Then the stock valuation formula would be

$$P_0 = \frac{DIV_1}{1+r} + \frac{DIV_2}{(1+r)^2} + \cdots + \frac{DIV_H + P_H}{(1+r)^H} \qquad (7.2)$$

In words, the value of a stock is the present value of the dividends it will pay over the investor's horizon plus the present value of the expected stock price at the end of that horizon.

Does this mean that investors with different horizons will come to different conclusions about the value of the stock? No! Regardless of the investment horizon, the stock value will be the same. This is because the stock price at the horizon date is determined by expectations of dividends from that date forward. Therefore, as long as investors agree about a firm's prospects, they will also agree on its present value. Let's confirm this with an example.

Example **7.2 ▶** **Valuing Blue Skies Stock**

Take Blue Skies. The firm is growing steadily, and investors expect both the stock price and the dividend to increase at 8% per year. Now consider three investors, Erste, Zweiter, and Dritter. Erste plans to hold Blue Skies for 1 year, Zweiter for 2, and Dritter for 3. Compare their payoffs:

	Year 1	Year 2	Year 3
Erste	$DIV_1 = 3$ $P_1 = 81$		
Zweiter	$DIV_1 = 3$	$DIV_2 = 3.24$ $P_2 = 87.48$	
Dritter	$DIV_1 = 3$	$DIV_2 = 3.24$	$DIV_3 = 3.50$ $P_3 = 94.48$

Remember, we assumed that dividends and stock prices for Blue Skies are expected to grow at a steady 8%. Thus, $DIV_2 = \$3 \times 1.08 = \$3.24$, $DIV_3 = \$3.24 \times 1.08 = \$3.50$, and so on.

Each investor requires the same 12% expected return. So we can calculate present value over Erste's 1-year horizon:

$$PV = \frac{DIV_1 + P_1}{1+r} = \frac{\$3 + \$81}{1.12} = \$75$$

or Zweiter's 2-year horizon:

$$PV = \frac{DIV_1}{1+r} + \frac{DIV_2 + P_2}{(1+r)^2}$$

$$= \frac{\$3}{1.12} + \frac{\$3.24 + \$87.48}{(1.12)^2}$$

$$= \$2.68 + \$72.32 = \$75$$

or Dritter's 3-year horizon:

$$PV = \frac{DIV_1}{1+r} + \frac{DIV_2}{(1+r)^2} + \frac{DIV_3 + P_3}{(1+r)^3}$$

$$= \frac{\$3}{1.12} + \frac{\$3.24}{(1.12)^2} + \frac{\$3.50 + \$94.48}{(1.12)^3}$$

$$= \$2.68 + \$2.58 + \$69.74 = \$75$$

All agree the stock is worth $75 per share. This illustrates our basic principle: The value of a common stock equals the present value of dividends received out to the investment horizon plus the present value of the forecast stock price at the horizon. Moreover, when you move the horizon date, the stock's present value should not change. The principle holds for horizons of 1, 3, 10, 20, and 50 years or more. ∎

> ### 7.3 Self-Test
>
> Refer to Self-Test 7.2. Assume that Androscoggin Copper's dividend and share price are expected to grow at a constant 5% per year. Calculate the current value of Androscoggin stock with the dividend discount model using a 3-year horizon. You should get the same answer as in Self-Test 7.2.

BEYOND THE PAGE

The dividend discount model

mhhe.com/brealey9e

Look at Table 7.4, which continues the Blue Skies example for various time horizons, still assuming that the dividends are expected to increase at a steady 8% compound rate. The expected price increases at the same 8% rate. Each row in the table represents a present value calculation for a different horizon year. Note that total present value does not depend on the investment horizon. Figure 7.4 presents the same data in a graph. Each column shows the present value of the dividends up to the horizon and the present value of the price at the horizon. As the horizon recedes, the dividend stream accounts for an increasing proportion of present value but the *total* present value of dividends plus terminal price always equals $75.

TABLE 7.4 Value of Blue Skies

Horizon (years)	PV (dividends)	+	PV (terminal price)	=	Value per Share
1	$2.68		$72.32		$75
2	5.26		69.74		75
3	7.75		67.25		75
10	22.87		52.13		75
20	38.76		36.24		75
30	49.81		25.19		75
50	62.83		12.17		75
100	73.02		1.98		75

FIGURE 7.4 Value of Blue Skies for different horizons

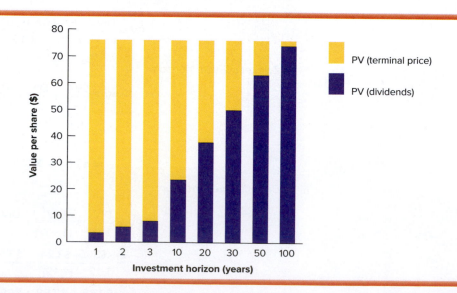

BEYOND THE PAGE

Value and the
investor's horizon

mhhe.com/brealey9e

If the horizon is infinitely far away, then we can forget about the final horizon price—it has almost no present value—and simply say,

$$\text{Stock price} = \text{PV(all future dividends per share)}$$

This is the dividend discount model.

7.4   Simplifying the Dividend Discount Model

The dividend discount model requires a forecast of dividends for every year into the future, which poses a bit of a problem for stocks with potentially infinite lives. If the model is to be of practical use, we need some simplifying assumptions. We will look at three cases, beginning with the most basic and ending with the most general.

Case 1: The Dividend Discount Model with No Growth

Consider a company that pays out all its earnings to its common shareholders. Such a company does not grow because it does not reinvest.[7] Stockholders might enjoy a generous immediate dividend, but they could not look forward to higher future dividends. The company's stock would offer a perpetual stream of equal cash payments, $\text{DIV}_1 = \text{DIV}_2 = \cdots = \text{DIV}_t = \cdots$.

The dividend discount model says that these no-growth shares should sell for the present value of a constant, perpetual stream of dividends. We learned how to do that calculation when we valued perpetuities in Chapter 5. Just divide the annual cash payment by the discount rate. The discount rate is the rate of return demanded by investors in other stocks with the same risk:

$$\text{Value of a no-growth stock} = P_0 = \frac{\text{DIV}_1}{r}$$

Because our company pays out all its earnings as dividends, dividends and earnings are the same, and we could just as well calculate stock value by

$$\text{Value of a no-growth stock} = P_0 = \frac{\text{EPS}_1}{r}$$

where EPS_1 represents next year's earnings per share of stock. Thus some people loosely say, "Stock price is the present value of future earnings," and calculate value by this formula. Be careful—this is a special case.

7.4   Self-Test

Moonshine Industries has produced a barrel per week for the past 20 years but cannot grow because of certain legal hazards. It earns $25 per share per year and pays it all out to stockholders. The stockholders have alternative, equivalent-risk ventures yielding 20% per year on average. How much is one share of Moonshine worth? Assume the company can keep going indefinitely.

Case 2: The Dividend Discount Model with Constant Growth

Here's another simplification that finds a good deal of practical use. Suppose forecast dividends grow at a constant rate into the indefinite future. Then instead of forecasting an infinite number of dividends, we need to forecast only the next dividend and the dividend growth rate.

---

[7] We assume it does not raise money by issuing new shares.

Suppose that a stock is expected to pay a dividend of DIV_1 next year, and thereafter, the dividend is expected to grow each year by the rate g. Thus the expected dividend in year 2 is $DIV_1 \times (1 + g)$, the dividend in year 3 is $DIV_1 \times (1 + g)^2$, and so on. The present value of this stock is, therefore:

$$P_0 = \frac{DIV_1}{1 + r} + \frac{DIV_1(1 + g)}{(1 + r)^2} + \frac{DIV_1(1 + g)^2}{(1 + r)^3} + \frac{DIV_1(1 + g)^3}{(1 + r)^4} + \cdots$$

Although there is an infinite number of terms, each of them is proportionately smaller than the preceding one as long as the dividend growth rate g is less than the discount rate r. Because the present value of distant dividends will be ever closer to zero, the sum of all of these terms is finite despite the fact that an infinite number of dividends will be paid. The sum can be shown to equal

$$P_0 = \frac{DIV_1}{r - g} \tag{7.3}$$

constant-growth dividend discount model
Version of the dividend discount model in which expected dividends grow at a constant rate.

This equation is called the **constant-growth dividend discount model,** or the *Gordon growth model* after Myron Gordon, who did much to popularize it.[8]

The formula for the present value of a no-growth perpetuity (our first case) is simply a special case of this constant-growth formula. Suppose you forecast no growth in dividends ($g = 0$). Then the dividend stream is a simple perpetuity, and the valuation formula reduces to $P_0 = DIV_1/r$. This is precisely the formula you used in Self-Test 7.4 to value Moonshine, a no-growth common stock.

Our task in this section is to show how the constant growth model can be used to estimate P_0, the value of a common stock. But sometimes managers find it useful to rearrange the constant-growth formula as:

$$r = \frac{DIV_1}{P_0} + g \tag{7.4}$$

$$= \text{dividend yield} + \text{growth rate}$$

Thus, if you know a stock's dividend yield and the expected growth rate, you can deduce its expected return. We will come back to this version of the formula in Chapter 13, when we look at how managers estimate the cost of equity capital.

Example **7.3** ▶ **Using the Constant-Growth Model to Value the Stock of Aqua America**

Aqua America (ticker symbol WTR) is a water utility serving parts of 14 states from Maine to Texas. In October 2015, its stock was selling for $26.83 a share. Because there were 176 million shares outstanding, investors were placing a total value on the stock of 176 million × $26.83 = $4.7 billion. Can we explain this valuation?

In 2015 Aqua America could point to a remarkably consistent growth record. For each of the past two decades, it had steadily increased its dividend payment (see Figure 7.5), and, with one minor hiccup, earnings had also grown steadily. The constant-growth model, therefore, seems tailor-made for valuing Aqua America's stock.

In 2015 investors were forecasting that, in the following year, Aqua America would pay a dividend of $.74 ($DIV_1 = \$.74$). The forecast growth in dividend (g) was about 5% a year over the foreseeable future (we explain in a moment where this figure comes from). If investors required a return of 7.8% from Aqua America's stock, then the constant-growth model predicts a current share value (P_0) of $26.43, almost identical to the market price:

$$P_0 = \frac{DIV_1}{r - g} = \frac{\$.74}{.078 - .05} = \$26.43 \quad ■$$

---

[8] Notice that the first dividend is assumed to come at the *end* of the first period and is discounted for a full period. If the stock has just paid a dividend DIV_0, then next year's dividend will be $(1 + g)$ times the dividend just paid. So another way to write the valuation formula is

$$P_0 = \frac{DIV_1}{r - g} = \frac{DIV_0 \times (1 + g)}{r - g}$$

FIGURE 7.5 Aqua America's dividends have grown steadily

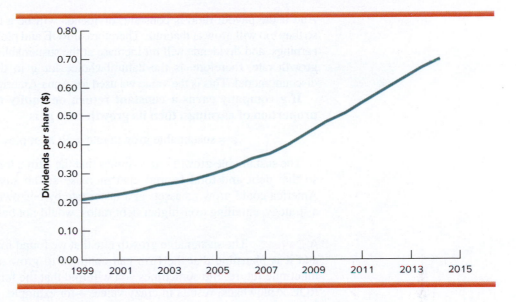

Estimating the Growth Rate for Aqua America

The constant-growth model generalizes the perpetuity formula to allow for constant growth in dividends. But how do we estimate that growth rate? Mature companies grow mainly by reinvesting earnings. How rapidly they grow depends on both the proportion of earnings reinvested into the business and the profits generated by those new investments. The firm's **sustainable growth rate** is the rate at which the firm can grow by reinvesting earnings, keeping its long-term debt ratio constant.

sustainable growth rate
The firm's growth rate if it plows back a constant fraction of earnings, maintains a constant return on equity, and keeps its debt ratio constant.

Aqua America has a book value per share of $9.86 in 2015. Suppose that it will generate a return on this book value of 12.5%.[9] Then in 2016 earnings per share will be

$$\text{EPS} = \text{book value per share} \times \text{ROE}$$
$$= \$9.86 \times .125 = \$1.233$$

payout ratio
Fraction of earnings paid out as dividends.

Over the next several years, the firm is expected to maintain a **payout ratio** (the proportion of earnings to be paid out as dividends) of 60%, so next year's dividend will be .60 × $1.233 = $.74. The **plowback ratio** (the fraction of earnings reinvested in the firm) is 1 − .60 = .40. Therefore, in the first year, Aqua America will plow back .40 × $1.233 = $.493 a share into new plant and equipment. Book value per share will increase by $.493 to $9.86 + $.493 = $10.353. The growth rate of equity generated by reinvesting earnings is

plowback ratio
Fraction of earnings retained by the firm.

$$\text{Growth rate in book equity} = \frac{\text{plowed-back earnings}}{\text{initial equity}} = \frac{\$.493}{\$9.86} = .05, \text{ or } 5.0\%$$

To see how growth depends on plowback and ROE, we can rewrite this equation as follows:

$$\text{Growth rate} = \frac{\text{plowed-back earnings}}{\text{initial equity}} = \frac{\text{plowed-back earnings}}{\text{total earnings}} \times \frac{\text{total earnings}}{\text{initial equity}}$$

$$= \text{plowback ratio} \times \text{ROE}$$

$$= .40 \times .125 = .050, \text{ or } 5.0\%$$

This is the growth rate of the book value of equity. What about dividends and earnings? If ROE is constant, then earnings per share will grow in direct proportion to equity (remember that EPS = ROE × book equity), so earnings also will grow at 5%.

---

[9] We construct estimates of trend earnings and dividends using data from the *Value Line Investment Survey,* October 16, 2015.

And if the payout ratio is constant, dividends will be a fixed proportion of earnings, so they too will grow at that rate. Therefore, if ROE and plowback are stable, book equity, earnings, and dividends will *all* increase at the sustainable growth rate. The sustainable growth rate, therefore, is the natural choice for g in the constant-growth dividend discount model. This is the value we used for Aqua America in Example 7.3.

If a company earns a constant return on equity and plows back a constant proportion of earnings, then its growth rate, *g*, is

$$g = \text{sustainable growth rate} = \text{ROE} \times \text{plowback ratio} \tag{7.5}$$

The sustainable growth rate assumes that the firm's long-term debt ratio is constant so that debt and total capital also increase at the sustainable growth rate. Aqua America could grow its assets at a faster rate by borrowing more and more, but such a strategy, entailing ever-higher debt ratios, would not be sustainable.

A Caveat   The sustainable growth rate that we found for Aqua America is moderate, and it is plausible that the firm can continue to grow at a trend rate of 5% for the indefinite future. But sometimes you will find that the formula for sustainable growth, ROE × plowback, results in crazy values—for example, growth rates of 20% or even more. No company could expect to maintain growth rates like these forever. After all, the (real) growth rate of the economy as a whole is only around 2.5%. If a firm or industry grew indefinitely at 20%, it eventually would outgrow the entire economy and then move on to take over the galaxy!

Other things equal, the constant-growth formula implies that the stock price will be higher when the dividend growth rate, *g*, is higher. But the formula is valid only if the growth rate is sustainable *and* is less than the discount rate. If you forecast perpetual dividend growth at a rate higher than investors' required return, *r*, then two things happen:

1. The formula explodes and gives nutty values. (For example, what would be the "value" of Aqua America in Example 7.3 if you assumed a growth rate of 10%?)
2. You know your forecasts must be wrong because the present value of far-distant dividends would be incredibly high. If projected dividends grow at a higher rate than the discount rate, the present value of each successive dividend will grow without limit. (Again, try a numerical example using Aqua America. Calculate the present value of a dividend paid after 100 years, assuming $\text{DIV}_1 = \$.74$, $r = .078$, and $g = .128$.)

Clearly, the constant-growth model cannot handle cases where there is temporary rapid growth. We will show you how to deal with this situation shortly.

Example **7.4 ▶**   Aqua America Gets a Windfall

Suppose that a shift in water usage allows Aqua America to generate 6% per year expected future growth without sacrificing immediate dividends. Will that increase *r*, the expected rate of return?

This is good news for the firm's stockholders. The stock price will jump to

$$P_0 = \frac{\text{DIV}_1}{r - g} = \frac{\$.74}{.078 - .06} = \$41.11$$

Aqua America's good news is reflected in a higher stock price *today*. But the good news does not imply a higher expected rate of return in the future. At this price, Aqua's expected rate of return is unchanged at 7.8%, consistent with its unchanged risk. ∎

7.5 Self-Test

Androscoggin Copper can grow at 5% per year for the indefinite future. It's selling at $100, and next year's dividend is $5. What is the expected rate of return from investing in Carrabasset Mining common stock? Carrabasset and Androscoggin shares are equally risky.

BEYOND THE PAGE

 Estimating stock value with non-constant growth

mhhe.com/brealey9e

The Sources of Aqua America's Value   We often hear investors speak of *growth stocks* and *income stocks*. They buy growth stocks primarily in the expectation of capital gains, and they are interested in the future growth of earnings rather than in next year's dividends. On the other hand, they buy income stocks principally for the cash dividends. Let us see whether these distinctions make sense, and what we can learn about the sources of Aqua America's value.

Aqua America is expected to pay a dividend in 2016 of $.74 ($DIV_1 = .74$), and this dividend is expected to grow at a steady rate of 5% a year ($g = .05$). If investors require a return of 7.8% ($r = .078$), then the price of Aqua America should be

$$P_0 = \frac{DIV_1}{r - g} = \frac{\$.74}{.078 - .05} = \$26.43$$

What if Aqua America did not plow back *any* of its earnings into new plant and equipment? In that case, it would pay out all of its earnings, $1.233 a share, but would forgo any further growth in earnings and dividends:

g = sustainable growth rate = return on equity × plowback ratio = .125 × 0 = 0

We could recalculate the value of Aqua America assuming it paid out all its forecast earnings and forwent any growth:

$$P_0 = \frac{DIV_1}{r - g} = \frac{EPS_1}{r} = \frac{\$1.233}{.078} = \$15.81$$

Thus, if Aqua America did not reinvest any of its earnings, its stock price would not be $26.43, but instead it would be only $15.81. The $15.81 represents the value of earnings from assets that are already in place. The rest of the stock price ($26.43 − $15.81 = $10.62) is the net present value of the *future* investments that Aqua America is expected to make.

What if the company kept to its policy of reinvesting 40% of its profits but the forecast return on new investments was only 7.8%? In that case, the sustainable growth rate would also be lower:

g = sustainable growth rate = return on equity × plowback ratio
= .078 × .40 = .0312, or 3.12%

If we plug this new figure into our valuation formula, we come up again with a value of $15.81 for Aqua America stock, no different from the value if it had chosen not to grow at all:

$$P_0 = \frac{DIV_1}{r - g} = \frac{.74}{.078 - .0312} = \$15.81$$

Plowing earnings back into new investments may result in growth in earnings and dividends, but it does not add to the current stock price if that money is expected to earn only the return that investors require. Plowing earnings back

***does* add value if investors believe that the reinvested earnings will earn a higher rate of return.**

To repeat, if Aqua America did not reinvest any of its earnings, the value of its stock would simply derive from the stream of earnings from the existing assets. The price of its stock would be $15.81. If the company *did* reinvest each year but earned only the return that investors require, then those new investments would not add any value, and therefore, the price of the stock would still be $15.81. In this case, both dividends and earnings are expected to grow, but this growth makes no contribution to firm value. Be careful not to equate firm performance with the growth in earnings per share.

Fortunately, investors believe that Aqua America has the opportunity to earn 12.5% on its new investments, somewhat above the 7.8% return that investors require. This is reflected in the $26.43 that investors are prepared to pay for the stock. The total value of Aqua America stock is equal to the value of its assets in place *plus* the **present value of its growth opportunities,** or **PVGO:**

present value of growth opportunities (PVGO)
Net present value of a firm's expected future investments.

Value of assets in place	$15.81
+ Present value of growth opportunities (PVGO)	10.62
= Total value of Aqua America's stock	$26.43

A true "growth stock" is one where the net present value of its future investments accounts for a significant fraction of the stock's price.

The investment prospects of Aqua America are reflected in its price-earnings ratio. With a stock price of $26.43 and forecast earnings of $1.233, the P/E ratio is $26.43/$1.233 = 21.4. If the company had no growth opportunities, its stock price would be only $15.81 and its P/E would be $15.81/$1.233 = 12.8. The P/E ratio is, therefore, an indicator of Aqua's prospects and the profitability of its growth opportunities.

Does this mean that the financial manager should celebrate if the firm's stock sells at a high P/E? The answer is usually yes. The high P/E suggests that investors think that the firm has good growth opportunities. However, firms can have high P/E ratios not because the price is high but because earnings are temporarily depressed. A firm that earns *nothing* in a particular period will have an *infinite* P/E.

7.6 │ Self-Test

Suppose that instead of plowing money back into lucrative ventures, Aqua America's management is investing at an expected return on equity of 5%, which is *below* the return of 7.8% that investors could expect to get from comparable securities.

a. Find the sustainable growth rate of dividends and earnings in these circumstances. Continue to assume a 40% plowback ratio.

b. Find the new value of its investment opportunities. Explain why this value is negative despite the positive growth rate of earnings and dividends.

c. If you were a corporate raider, would Aqua America be a good candidate for an attempted takeover?

Case 3: The Dividend Discount Model with Nonconstant Growth

Water companies and other utilities tend to have steady rates of growth and are, therefore, natural candidates for application of the constant-growth model. But many companies grow at rapid or irregular rates for several years before settling down.

Obviously, in such cases, we can't use the constant-growth model to estimate value. However, there is an alternative approach. It involves three steps:

Step 1: Set the *investment horizon* (year *H*) as the future year after which you expect the company's growth to settle down to a stable rate. Then calculate the present value of dividends from now to this horizon year.

Step 2: Forecast the stock price at the horizon, and discount it also to give its present value today. That price can be estimated using the constant-growth formula to value the dividends that will be paid after the horizon date because by then they will be growing at a sustainable rate.

Step 3: Finally, sum the total present value of dividends plus the present value of the ending stock price.

The formula is

$$P_0 = \underbrace{\frac{DIV_1}{1+r} + \frac{DIV_2}{(1+r)^2} + \cdots + \frac{DIV_H}{(1+r)^H}}_{\text{PV of dividends from year 1 to horizon}} + \underbrace{\frac{P_H}{(1+r)^H}}_{\text{PV of stock price at horizon}}$$

Example 7.5 ▶ Estimating the Value of McDonald's Stock

In mid-2015, the price of McDonald's stock was just about $100. The company earned about $4.75 a share and was projected to pay out about 60% of earnings as dividends. Let's see how we might use the dividend discount model to estimate McDonald's intrinsic value.

Investors in 2015 were optimistic about the prospects for McDonald's and were forecasting that earnings would grow over the next 5 years by about 10% a year.[10] This growth rate is almost certainly higher than the return, *r*, that investors required from McDonald's stock, and it is implausible to suppose that such rapid growth could continue indefinitely. Therefore, we cannot use the simple constant-growth formula to value the shares. Instead, we will break the problem down into our three steps:

Step 1: Our first task is to value McDonald's dividends over the next 5 years. If dividends keep pace with the growth in earnings, then forecast earnings and dividends are as follows:

Year	1	2	3	4	5
Earnings	4.75	5.23	5.75	6.32	6.95
Dividends (60% of earnings)	2.85	3.14	3.45	3.79	4.17

In 2015, investors required a return of about 8.5% from McDonald's stock.[11] Therefore, the present value of the forecast dividends for years 1 to 5 was:

$$\text{PV of dividends years } 1-5 = \frac{\$2.85}{1.085} + \frac{\$3.14}{(1.085)^2} + \frac{\$3.45}{(1.085)^3} + \frac{\$3.79}{(1.085)^4} + \frac{\$4.17}{(1.085)^5}$$

$$= \$13.50$$

Step 2: The trickier task is to estimate the price of McDonald's stock in the horizon year 5. The most likely scenario is that after year 5 growth will gradually settle down to a

---

[10] Consensus analysts' forecasts are collected by Zack's, First Call, and IBES. They are available on the web at **moneycentral.com** and **finance.yahoo.com.**

[11] For now, you can take this value purely as an assumption. In Chapter 12, we will show you how to estimate required returns. This value is about 4 percentage points higher than the 2015 yield to maturity on McDonald's long-term bonds. The stock requires a higher discount rate because it is riskier than the bonds.

sustainable rate, but to keep life simple, we will assume that in year 6 the growth rate falls *immediately* to 5% a year.[12] Thus, the forecast dividend in year 6 is

$$DIV_6 = 1.05 \times DIV_5 = 1.05 \times \$4.17 = \$4.38$$

and the expected price at the end of year 5 is

$$P_5 = \frac{DIV_6}{r - g} = \frac{\$4.38}{.085 - .05} = \$125.14$$

Step 3: Remember, the value of McDonald's today is equal to the present value of forecast dividends up to the horizon date plus the present value of the price at the horizon. Thus,

$$P_0 = PV(\text{dividends years } 1 - 5) + PV(\text{price in year 5})$$

$$= \$13.50 + \frac{\$125.14}{1.085^5} = \$96.72 \ \blacksquare$$

A Reality Check   Our estimate of McDonald's value looks reasonable and almost matches McDonald's actual market price in mid-2015. But does it make you nervous to note that your estimate of the terminal price accounts for such a large proportion of the stock's value? It should. Only very minor changes in your assumptions about growth beyond year 5 could change your estimate of this terminal price by 10%, 20%, or 30%. In other words, it's easy for a discounted-cash-flow business valuation to be mechanically perfect and practically wrong.

In the case of McDonald's, we *know* what the market price really was in the middle of 2015, but suppose that you are using the dividend discount model to value a company going public for the first time or that you are wondering whether to buy Blue Skies' concatenator division. In such cases you do not have the luxury of looking up the market price in *The Wall Street Journal*. A valuation error of 30% could amount to serious money. Wise managers, therefore, check that their estimate of value is in the right ballpark by looking at what the market is prepared to pay for similar businesses. For example, suppose you can find mature, public companies whose scale, risk, and growth prospects today roughly match those projected for McDonald's at the investment horizon. You look back at Table 7.3 and discover that the stocks in McDonald's industry group typically sell at 22.2 times recent earnings. Then you can reasonably guess that McDonald's value in year 5 will be about 22.2 times the earnings forecast for that year, that is, $22.2 \times \$6.95 = \$154.29$, somewhat higher than the $125.14 horizon value that we obtained from the dividend discount model.

Table 7.3 shows that the market–book ratios of companies in McDonald's industry group average around 8.1. If McDonald's plows back 40% of its earnings, then book value per share will increase to $20.7 by the end of year 5. If McDonald's market–book ratio is 8.1 in year 5, then

$$PV(\text{horizon value}) = (8.1 \times \$20.7) = \$167.67$$

It's easy to poke holes in our last two calculations. Book value, for example, is often a poor measure of the true value of a company's assets. It can fall far behind actual asset values when there is rapid inflation, and it often entirely misses important intangible assets. Earnings may also be biased by inflation and a long list of arbitrary accounting choices. Finally, you never know when you have found a sample of truly

---

[12] We showed earlier that if a company plows back a constant proportion of earnings and earns a constant return on these new investments, then earnings and dividends will grow by $g =$ plowback ratio $\times$ return on new investment. Thus, if from year 5 onward McDonald's continues to reinvest 40% of its earnings and earns an ROE of 12.5% on this investment, earnings and dividends will grow by $.40 \times .125 = .05$, or 5%.

What is Facebook worth? This was the question that confronted investors as the company's highly anticipated initial public offering approached in May 2012. Estimates of value in the months before the IPO ranged from as little as $50 billion to as much as $125 billion. The difference in these estimates turned on questions of growth.

Facebook's revenue grew by 88% in 2011, and net income grew by 65%. Such growth was impressive but was sharply lower than in the previous few years. From 2009 to 2010, for example, revenue had increased by around 150%. What was a reasonable projection of growth in the years following the IPO?

It is notoriously difficult to guess what future opportunities may be available to a high-tech company. Rather than attempting to make detailed growth forecasts, many investors used valuation by comparables, comparing Facebook to rival companies with similar business models.

Facebook's reported profits in 2011 were around $1 billion. Even at the low range for the IPO of $50 billion, this would imply a P/E ratio of 50, well above even successful Internet firms such as Google. At the higher end of the valuation estimates—say, $100 billion—investors would

be valuing Facebook at around half of Google's value at the time, even though Google's profits that year were 10 times Facebook's. But optimists argued that Facebook could generate much higher growth than Google in its advertising revenue, which would justify higher earnings multiples. Clearly, valuation by comparables was tricky given the difficulties in projecting and comparing growth opportunities.

In the end, investors were overly optimistic. Facebook's closing stock price on the day of its IPO was $38 per share, implying total market capitalization of just over $100 billion. But the stock price almost immediately fell, bottoming out at $18 by September 2012; the price did not again reach $38 for about another year.

Does this mean that Facebook's IPO was a failure? While some firms seem to covet an "IPO pop"—that is, a stock price run-up on the day of the IPO—it is hard to see why a pop is in their interest. A pop signifies that investors would have been willing to pay more for the shares or, in other words, that the IPO was underpriced and the issuing firm "left money on the table." In contrast, Facebook seems to have received all it could from its IPO.

---

similar companies to use as comparables. But remember, the purpose of discounted cash flow is to estimate market value—to estimate what investors would pay for a stock or business. When you can observe what they actually pay for similar companies, that's valuable evidence. Try to figure out a way to use it. One way to use it is through valuation by comparables, based on price-earnings or market–book ratios. Valuation rules of thumb, artfully employed, sometimes beat a complex discounted-cash-flow calculation hands down.

Valuing stocks is always harder in practice than in principle. Forecasting cash flows and settling on an appropriate discount rate require skill and judgment. The difficulties are often greatest in the case of young companies such as Facebook or Twitter, whose value comes largely from growth opportunities rather than assets that are already in place. These companies usually pay no cash dividends, and their current growth rates cannot be sustained for the longer run. Here, the dividend discount model still works logically—we could project dividends as zero out to some distant date when the firm matures and payout commences. But forecasting far-off dividends is easier said than done. In these cases, it's more helpful to think about the value of a stock as the sum of the value of assets in place plus PVGO, the present value of growth opportunities. As the nearby box shows, in these cases there is plenty of room for disagreement about value.

BEYOND THE PAGE

 **Valuing Google**

mhhe.com/brealey9e

7.7 Self-Test

Suppose that on further analysis you decide that after year 5 McDonald's earnings and dividends will grow by a constant 4% a year. How does this affect your estimate of the value of McDonald's stock at year 0?

7.5   Valuing a Business by Discounted Cash Flow

Investors buy or sell shares of common stock. Companies often buy or sell entire businesses. For example, in 2015 Johnson & Johnson announced that it had sold a medical device subsidiary for $2 billion. The business was not a public company, and therefore, there was no stock price to look at. It's a safe bet that before the sale, J&J and its advisers were doing their best to value that business by discounted cash flow. You can be equally sure that they were endeavoring to identify the most appropriate comparables for the business and checking what it would be worth if it traded at similar P/E and P/B ratios to these other firms.

One more example should help you to understand that DCF models work just as well for entire businesses as for shares of common stock. It doesn't matter whether you forecast dividends per share or the total free cash flow of a business. Value today always equals future cash flow discounted at the opportunity cost of capital.

Valuing the Concatenator Business

Blue Skies is interested in selling its concatenator manufacturing operation. Its problem is to figure out what the business is worth.

Table 7.5 gives a forecast of **free cash flow (FCF)** for the concatenator business. Free cash flow is the amount of cash that a firm can pay out to investors after paying for all investments necessary for growth. As we will see, free cash flow can be zero or negative for rapidly growing businesses. Growth for the concatenator business starts out at a rapid 12% per year, then falls in two steps to a moderate 6% rate for the long run. The growth rate determines the net additional investment required, and the return on equity determines the earnings thrown off by the business.

Free cash flow, the fourth line in Table 7.5, is equal to the firm's earnings less the new investment expenditures. Free cash flow is zero in years 1 to 3, even though the parent company is earning more than $3 million during this period.

Are the early zeros for free cash flow a bad sign? No: Free cash flow is zero because the business is growing rapidly, not because it is unprofitable. Rapid growth is good news, not bad, because the business is earning a return of 12%, 2 percentage points over the 10% cost of capital.

free cash flow (FCF)
Cash flow available for distribution to investors after firm pays for new investments or additions to working capital.

TABLE 7.5 Forecasts of free cash flow in $ millions for the concatenator division, with input assumptions in boldface type. Free cash flow is zero for periods 1 to 3 because investment absorbs all of net income. Free cash flow turns positive when growth slows down after period 3.

	Year									
	1	2	3	4	5	6	7	8	9	10
Asset value	10.00	11.20	12.54	14.05	15.31	16.69	18.19	19.29	20.44	21.67
Earnings	1.20	1.34	1.51	1.69	1.84	2.00	2.18	2.31	2.45	2.60
Net investment	1.20	1.34	1.51	1.26	1.38	1.50	1.09	1.16	1.23	1.30
Free cash flow (FCF)	0.00	0.00	0.00	0.42	0.46	0.50	1.09	1.16	1.23	1.30
Return on equity (ROE)	0.12	0.12	0.12	0.12	0.12	0.12	0.12	0.12	0.12	0.12
Asset growth rate	0.12	0.12	0.12	0.09	0.09	0.09	0.06	0.06	0.06	0.06
Earnings growth rate		0.12	0.12	0.12	0.09	0.09	0.09	0.06	0.06	0.06

Notes:
1. Starting asset value is $10 million. Assets grow at 12% to start, then at 9%, and finally at 6% in perpetuity. Profitability (ROE) is assumed constant at 12%.
2. Free cash flow equals earnings minus net investment. Net investment equals total capital outlays minus depreciation. We assume that investment for replacement of existing assets is covered by depreciation and that net investment is devoted to growth. Earnings are also net of depreciation.

The value of a business is usually computed as the discounted value of free cash flows out to a *valuation horizon (H)*, plus the forecasted value of the business at the horizon, also discounted back to present value. That is,

$$PV = \underbrace{\frac{FCF_1}{1+r} + \frac{FCF_2}{(1+r)^2} + \cdots + \frac{FCF_H}{(1+r)^H}}_{PV(\text{free cash flow})} + \underbrace{\frac{PV_H}{(1+r)^H}}_{PV(\text{horizon value})}$$

Of course, the concatenator business will continue after the horizon, but it's not practical to forecast free cash flow year-by-year to infinity. PV_H stands in for the total present value of the project's free cash flows in periods $H + 1$, $H + 2$, and so on.

Valuation horizons are often chosen arbitrarily. Sometimes the boss tells everybody to use 10 years because that's a round number. We will try year 6, because growth of the concatenator business seems to settle down to a long-run trend after year 7.

There are several common formulas or rules of thumb for estimating horizon value. We will just use the constant-growth DCF formula. This requires free cash flow for year 7, which we have from Table 7.5; a long-run growth rate, which is projected at 6%; and a discount rate, which some high-priced consultant has told us is 10%.

$$\text{Horizon value (PV looking forward from period 6)} = PV_H = \frac{1.09}{.10 - .06} = \$27.3 \text{ million}$$

$$\text{Horizon value (discounted back to PV in period 0)} = \frac{27.3}{(1.1)^6} = \$15.4 \text{ million}$$

Given the forecasts in Table 7.5, the PV of the near-term free cash flows is $.9 million. Thus the present value of the concatenator division is

$$PV(\text{business}) = PV(\text{free cash flow}) + PV(\text{horizon value})$$
$$= .9 + 15.4 = \$16.3 \text{ million}$$

Repurchases and the Dividend Discount Model

We assumed that the concatenator business was a division of Blue Skies, not a free-standing corporation. But suppose it was a separate corporation with 1 million shares outstanding. How would we calculate price per share? Simple: Calculate the PV of the business and divide by 1 million. If we decide that the business is worth $16.3 million, the price per share is $16.30.

If the concatenator business were a public Concatenator Corp. with no other assets and operations, it could pay out its free cash flow as dividends. Dividends per share would be the free cash flow shown in Table 7.5 divided by 1 million shares: $0 in periods 1 to 3, then $.42 per share in period 4, $.46 per share in period 5, and so forth.

Dividends are not the only way that firms can return cash to their equity investors. They also can, and commonly do, engage in stock repurchases. In a repurchase, the firm buys back a small fraction of the outstanding shares of its shareholders. In some years, repurchases may exceed dividend payouts. Repurchases are attractive to firms that wish to distribute cash to equityholders but do not want to signal to them, even informally, that they should expect to receive such distributions on a regular basis in the future. In contrast, investors (rightly) interpret dividends as a repeated cash distribution that the firm will, in most circumstances, try to maintain or even increase. We discuss repurchases in some detail in Chapter 17.

When we use the dividend discount model, we should recognize that repurchases act much like dividends. For example, if the firm buys back 1% of all the shares of each of its shareholders, that action is very similar to paying a dividend equal to 1% of the share price.

Repurchases do not invalidate the dividend discount model. The value of any share is still the present value of the dividends that the holder will receive. But repurchases do complicate the implementation of the model because, as the number of shares changes, it can be hard to forecast dividends on a "per share" basis. This can lead to difficult bookkeeping and complications working out the correct value for sustainable growth. Here is our suggestion: When repurchases are important, it is usually simpler to value the firm's total free cash flow, as we did for the concatenator division, rather than just per share dividends. By free cash flow, we mean the cash the firm has available to distribute after paying for all investments necessary for its growth.

In a sense, imagine that you own all the shares in the firm. Free cash flow is what you could receive as the single shareholder in the firm; importantly, it will not depend on the breakdown between dividends and repurchases. After all, as the sole shareholder, you won't care whether you get free cash flow by receiving dividends or by selling some of your shares back to the firm. If you value the whole firm by applying the dividend discount model to free cash flow, then you can find the share price by dividing the value of the firm by the current number of shares outstanding.

7.6 There Are No Free Lunches on Wall Street

Corporations rely on both comparables and the dividend discount model to value entire businesses. Investors in the stock market regularly use comparables in their quest for undervalued stocks. For example, an investor might judge that Kappa Pharmaceuticals is undervalued because it is selling at a lower P/E than Omicron and Upsilon despite the potential profits from its new carboglutin drug. Major investment management companies also use dividend discount models to estimate the value of common stocks and to compare those estimates with stock market prices. In each case, the investor is betting that once others have realized that a stock is undervalued, its price will shoot up and earn her juicy profits.

We will look shortly at how challenging it is for investors to find undervalued stocks. But before we do so, we should explain why a corporate financial manager, who is more concerned with issuing or purchasing securities, should care whether investors can "beat the market." The reason is that, if even professional investors cannot consistently find undervalued stocks, then financial managers should generally assume that market prices provide a good estimate of intrinsic value. A similar message applies to the financial manager when setting the firm's exchange rate policy or deciding on an issue of debt. If it is impossible to identify when a currency or a bond is wrongly valued, then the financial manager should trust market prices rather than engage in risky attempts to "beat the market."

Let's start with a quick look at the performance of amateur investors. Brad Barber and Terrance Odean examined the common stock investments of more than 66,000 households during the period 1991 to 1996.[13] After controlling for differences in risk, they found that the average household underperformed the market by about 1.8% a year before trading costs and by 3.7% after costs.

It may not be surprising that the amateurs don't beat the market, but what about the pros? Presumably, if the amateurs lose before trading costs, the professional investors must gain. Figure 7.6 provides some evidence on the matter. It shows the average performance of equity mutual funds over 3 decades. You can see that in some years, these mutual funds did beat the market, but more often than not (in fact, in 27 of the 44 years since 1970), it was the other way around. On average, these funds underperformed the market by about 1% a year. It looks as if any gains that the professionals made at the expense of the amateurs were more than eaten up by expenses. Of course,

---

[13] B. Barber and T. Odean, "Trading Is Hazardous to Your Wealth: The Stock Market Investment Performance of Individual Investors," *Journal of Finance* 55 (2000), pp. 773–806.

FIGURE 7.6 Annual returns on the Wilshire 5000 Market Index and equity mutual funds, 1971–2014. The market index provided a higher return than the average mutual fund in 27 of the 44 years.

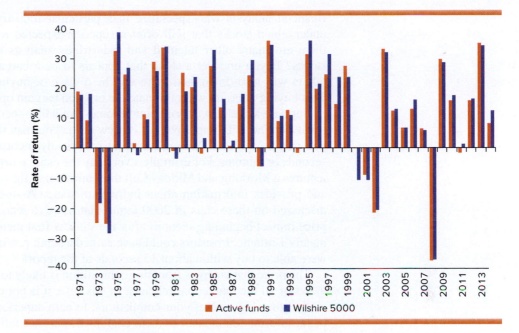

it would be surprising if some managers were not smarter than others and able to earn superior returns. But, as Example 7.6 shows, it seems hard to spot the smart ones, and the top-performing managers one year have about an average chance of falling on their face the next year.

Example 7.6 ▶   Performance of Money Managers

Standard & Poor's regularly examines the investment performance of professional money managers. One study looked at 2,862 stock mutual funds. It took the top quartile of performers in 2010 and asked how many of those funds were top-quartile performers in 2011. The study then repeated the exercise for each year through 2014. If performance is persistent, then the top performers in one year might be expected to continue as top performers in the following years. But only two of the original 2,862 firms were top-quartile performers in each of the five years, almost exactly the same number as would be produced from chance. It appears that even professional managers cannot consistently outperform the market.[14] ∎

As this kind of discouraging evidence has accumulated, many investors have given up the search for superior investment returns. Instead, they simply buy and hold index funds or exchange-traded portfolios (ETFs) that track the entire stock market. We discussed index funds and ETFs in Chapter 2. Recall that they provide maximum diversification, with very low management fees. Why pay higher fees to managers who attempt to "beat the market" but can't do so consistently? Corporate pension funds now invest over one-quarter of their U.S. equity holdings in index funds.

Random Walks and Efficient Markets

Why is it so difficult to earn superior returns? Suppose that you manage a portfolio of common stocks. You try to gauge the business prospects of each firm by studying the financial and trade press, the company's financial accounts, the president's annual statements, and other items of news. You attend company presentations and speak to

---

[14] The study is summarized in Jeff Sommer, "How Many Mutual Funds Routinely Rout the Market? Zero." *The New York Times,* March 14, 2015.

financial analysts who specialize in a particular industry. Your aim is to uncover undervalued stocks that will offer a superior expected return. But what happens if there are many other talented and industrious analysts trying to find undervalued stocks? If you uncover a stock that appears to be a bargain, it stands to reason that others will also do so, and there will be a wave of buying that pushes up its price. This buying pressure will eliminate the original bargain opportunity.

Suppose some new information becomes available—perhaps Kappa announces that it has obtained FDA approval for its new drug. You rush to buy. The chances are that you will be too late. New information is typically incorporated into stock prices in seconds or minutes. For example, every day the cable television news provider CNBC features a Morning and Midday Call that summarizes the opinions of security analysts and provides information about individual stocks. A study of 322 stocks that were discussed on these calls in 2000 found that positive reports resulted in a significant price impact beginning seconds after the stock is first mentioned and lasting approximately 1 minute. Investors could have earned a small profit after expenses only if they were able to buy within about 15 seconds of the report.[15]

The price that emerges from this competition is likely to reflect the information and views of all the market participants. In this case, it is not enough to have better information than any one of your competitors; to earn superior returns, you need to have better information than all of them combined. This is a tall order.

If a stock is fairly priced, it will reflect all existing information and respond only to new information. But new information is necessarily unanticipated. Therefore, the resulting change in the stock price must be a surprise and cannot be predicted from earlier changes in the stock price. So in a market where stocks are fairly valued, their prices will wander randomly. Stocks will be equally likely to offer a high or low return on any particular day, regardless of what occurred on previous days. In other words, prices will follow a random walk.

If you are not sure what we mean by "random walk," consider the following example: You are given $100 to play a game. At the end of each week, a coin is tossed. If it comes up heads, you win 3% of your investment; if it is tails, you lose 2.5%. Therefore, your payoff at the end of the first week is either $103 or $97.50. At the end of the second week, the coin is tossed again. Now the possible outcomes are as follows:

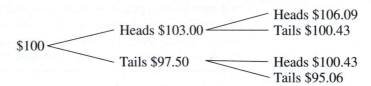

This process is a random walk because successive changes in the value of your stake are independent and determined by the flip of a fair coin. That is, the odds of making money each week are the same, regardless of the value at the start of the week or the pattern of heads or tails in the previous weeks. If a stock's price follows a random walk, the odds of an increase or decrease during any day, month, or year do not depend at all on the stock's previous price moves. In this case, the patterns that investors sometimes see in stock prices are a mirage, and the historical path of prices gives no useful information about the future—just as a long series of recorded heads and tails gives no information about the next toss.

The notion that successive stock prices follow something close to a random walk has been confirmed in countless ways. Look, for example, at Figure 7.7a. The horizontal axis shows the return on the New York Composite Index in 1 week (5 business days), while the vertical axis shows the return in the following week. Each point in the chart represents a different week over a 40-year period. If a market rise one week

---

[15] The price response to negative reports was more gradual, lasting 15 minutes, perhaps due to the higher costs of short selling. See J. A. Busse and T. C. Green, "Market Efficiency in Real Time," *Journal of Financial Economics* 65 (2002), pp. 415–437.

tended to be followed by a rise the next week, the points in the chart would plot along an upward-sloping line. But you can see that there was no such tendency; the points are scattered randomly across the chart. Statisticians sometimes measure the relationship between these changes by the correlation coefficient. In our example, the correlation between the market movements in successive weeks is −.022, in other words, effectively zero. Figure 7.7*b* shows a similar plot for monthly (20-business-day) moves. Again, you can see that this month's change in the index gives you almost no

FIGURE 7.7a Each dot shows the returns on the New York Composite Index on two successive weeks over a 40-year period. The circled dot shows a weekly return of +3.1%, followed by +5.2% in the next week. The scatter diagram shows no significant relationship between returns on successive weeks.

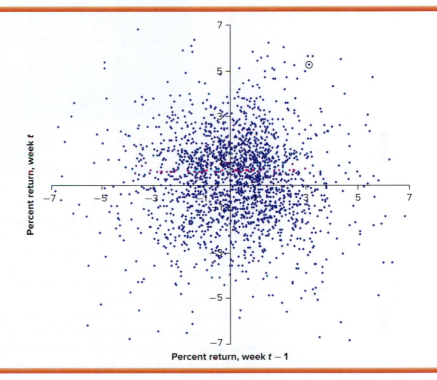

FIGURE 7.7b This scatter diagram shows that there is also no relationship between market returns in successive months.

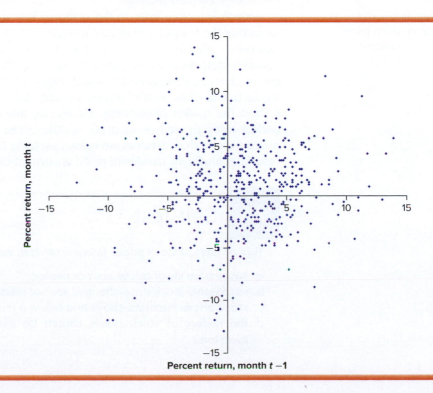

FIGURE 7.8 Cycles self-destruct as soon as they are recognized by investors. The stock price instantaneously jumps to the present value of the expected future price.

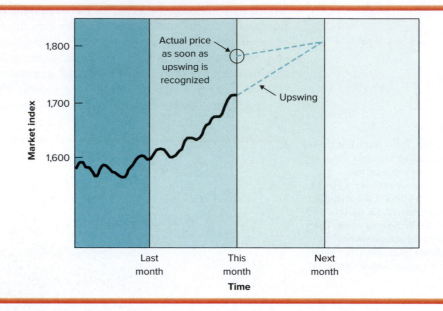

clue as to the likely change next month. The correlation between successive monthly changes is −.004. This is almost exactly what we would expect in a market where new information was rapidly impounded in stock prices.

Does it surprise you that stocks seem to follow a random walk? If so, imagine that it was not the case and that changes in stock prices were expected to persist for several months. Figure 7.8 provides a hypothetical example of such a predictable cycle. You can see that an upswing in the market started when the index was 1,600 and is expected to carry the price to 1,800 next month. What will happen when investors perceive this bonanza? Because stocks are a bargain at their current level, investors will rush to buy and, in so doing, will push up prices. They will stop buying only when stocks are fairly priced. Thus, as soon as a cycle becomes apparent to investors, they immediately eliminate it by their trading.

efficient market
Market in which prices reflect all available information.

Economists often refer to the stock market as an **efficient market.** By this they mean that the competition to find misvalued stocks is intense. So when new information comes out, investors rush to take advantage of it and thereby eliminate any profit opportunities. As a result, each new change in the price of a stock is independent of earlier changes. Professional investors express the same idea when they say that there are no free lunches on Wall Street. It is very difficult to detect undervalued stocks and to beat the market consistently. Of course, this does not mean that investors have perfect foresight and never make mistakes. The large fluctuations in stock market prices suggest that investors are being caught by surprise every day, and that with the benefit of hindsight wonderful profit opportunities were dangling from every tree.

7.8 Self-Test

True or false: If stock prices follow a random walk,

a. successive stock prices are not related.
b. successive stock price changes are not related.
c. stock prices fluctuate above and below a normal long-run price.
d. the history of stock prices cannot be used to predict future returns to investors.

7.7   Market Anomalies and Behavioral Finance

Market Anomalies

Almost without exception, early researchers concluded that the efficient-market hypothesis was a remarkably good description of reality. They tested three versions of the hypothesis. The *weak form* of the hypothesis maintains that stock prices follow a random walk, so that it is impossible to make superior returns just from a study of past price changes. Figure 7.7, which shows that price changes are essentially independent from one period to the next, provides just one example of a test of the weak-form hypothesis. The *semi-strong form* of the hypothesis maintains that public information is impounded in the stock price, so that it is impossible to earn superior returns by a study of information that is also available to other investors. Researchers have tested this hypothesis by looking at how rapidly prices incorporate different types of news such as our example of the CNBC Morning and Midday Calls. The *strong form* of the hypothesis holds that no group of investors with whatever information and skill-sets that they possess can earn consistently superior returns. Figure 7.6, which shows that even professional managers do not generally outperform the market, offers some evidence that the market is strong-form efficient.

But eventually, cracks in the evidence began to appear, and soon the finance journals were packed with examples of anomalies, or seeming profit opportunities, that investors have apparently failed to exploit. Some of these concern very short-term stock returns. To have any chance of making money from anomalies that may last for only a few seconds, you need to be a high-frequency trader with one eye on the computer screen and the other on your annual bonus. If you are a corporate financial manager, these patterns may be intriguing conundrums, but they are unlikely to change major financial decisions about which projects to invest in and how they should be financed. Corporate managers should be more concerned about possible mispricing that lasts months or years.

Economists have unearthed a number of these longer-term anomalies. Here are a couple examples.

The Momentum Factor   We said earlier that stock prices follow something close to a random walk. That is true, but there do appear to be some exceptions. For example, researchers who have looked at stock market returns over long periods have found a tendency for price rises to persist for some 6 to 9 months and then to revert.[16] Investors refer to this persistence of returns as *momentum.*

The New-Issue Puzzle   When firms issue stock to the public, investors typically rush to buy. On average, those lucky enough to receive stock receive an immediate capital gain. However, researchers have found that these early gains often turn into losses. For example, suppose that you bought stock immediately following each initial public offering (IPO) and then held that stock for three years. Over the period 1980–2014, your average return would have been 6.3% less than the return on a portfolio of stocks with a similar size and book-to-market value.[17]

The jury is still out on such studies of longer-term anomalies. We can't be sure whether they are important exceptions to the efficient-market theory or a coincidence that stems from the efforts of many researchers to find interesting patterns in the data. It does appear to be the case that anomalies become less pronounced once their existence becomes known.

---

[16] See, for example, N. Jegadeesh, "Evidence of Predictable Behavior of Stock Returns," *Journal of Finance* 45, (1990), pp. 881–898; and T. J. Moskowitz, Y. H. Ooi, and L. H. Pedersen, "Time Series Momentum," *Journal of Financial Economics* (2011), pp. 104, 228–250.

[17] An excellent resource for data and analysis of initial public offerings is Professor Jay Ritter's web page, site.warrington.ufl.edu/ritter/ipo-data/.

Market anomalies such as the *new-issue puzzle* suggest that there may be occasions when prices of individual stocks can get out of line. But are there also cases in which prices as a whole can no longer be justified by fundamentals? We will look at the evidence in a moment, but first we should note how difficult it is to value common stocks and to determine whether their prices are irrational.

For example, imagine that in December 2015 you wanted to check whether the stocks forming Standard & Poor's Composite Index were fairly valued. As a first stab, you might use the constant-growth formula that we introduced earlier. In 2015, the annual dividends paid by the companies in the index totaled just over $400 billion. Suppose that these dividends were expected to grow at a steady rate of 4.0% and that investors required a return of 6.0%. Then the constant-growth formula gives a value for the common stocks of

$$PV = \frac{DIV_1}{r - g} = \frac{\$400 \text{ billion}}{.06 - .04} = \$20,000 \text{ billion}$$

which was slightly more than their value in December 2015. But how confident could you be about these figures? Perhaps the likely dividend growth was only 3.5% per year. In that case, your estimate of the value of the common stocks would decline to

$$PV = \frac{DIV_1}{r - g} = \frac{\$400 \text{ billion}}{.06 - .035} = \$16,000 \text{ billion}$$

In other words, a reduction of just half a percentage point in the expected rate of dividend growth would reduce the value of common stocks by 20%. The extreme sensitivity of price to even minor changes in assumptions tells us that valuing common stocks from scratch is always going to be very imprecise. This conclusion has two important consequences.

First, investors find it easier to price a common stock relative to yesterday's price or relative to today's price of comparable securities. In other words, they generally take yesterday's price as correct, adjusting upward or downward on the basis of today's information. If information arrives smoothly, then, as time passes, investors become increasingly confident that today's price level is correct. But when investors lose confidence in the benchmark of yesterday's price, there may be a period of confused trading and volatile prices before a new benchmark is established.

Second, most of the tests of market efficiency are concerned with relative prices and focus on whether there are easy profits to be made. It is almost impossible to test whether stocks are correctly valued, because no one can measure true value with any precision.

Bubbles and Market Efficiency

It may be impossible to prove that market levels are, or are not, consistent with fundamentals. However, every now and again investors seem to be caught up in a speculative frenzy, and asset prices then reach levels that (at least with hindsight) cannot easily be justified by the outlook for profits and dividends. Investors refer to such occasions as bubbles.

The Japanese bubble is a good example. Between 1985 and 1989, the Japanese Nikkei index roughly quadrupled. But in 1990, interest rates rose and stock prices started to fall. By October the Nikkei had sunk to about half its peak, and by March 2009 it was down 80% from its peak value 19 years earlier.

The boom in Japanese stock prices was matched by an even greater explosion in land prices. For example, Ziemba and Schwartz document that the few hundred acres of land under the Emperor's Palace in Tokyo, evaluated at neighborhood land prices, was worth as much as all the land in Canada or California.[18] But then the real estate

---

[18] See W. T. Ziemba and S. L. Schwartz, *Invest Japan* (Chicago: Probus Publishing, 1992), p. 109.

BEYOND THE PAGE

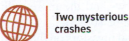

Two mysterious crashes

mhhe.com/brealey9e

bubble also burst. By 2005 land prices in the six major Japanese cities had slumped to just 13% of their peak.

The dot-com bubble in the United States was almost as dramatic. The technology-heavy NASDAQ stock index rose 580% from the start of 1995 to its eventual high in March 2000. But then, as rapidly as it began, the boom ended, and by October 2002 the index had fallen 78% from its peak.

Looking back at these episodes, it seems difficult to believe that expected future cash flows could ever have been sufficient to justify the initial price run-ups. If that is the case, we have two important exceptions to the theory of efficient markets.

But beware of jumping to the conclusion that prices are always arbitrary and capricious. First, most bubbles become obvious only after they have burst. At the time, there often seems to be a plausible explanation for the price run-up. In the dot-com boom, for example, many contemporary observers rationalized stock price gains as justified by the prospect of a new and more profitable economy, driven by technological advances.

Behavioral Finance

Why *might* prices depart from fundamental values? Some scholars believe that the answer to this question lies in behavioral psychology. People are not 100% rational 100% of the time. This shows up in three broad areas—their attitudes to risk, the way that they assess probabilities, and their sentiment about the economy:

1. *Attitudes toward risk.* Psychologists have observed that, when making risky decisions, people are particularly loath to incur losses, even if those losses are small. Losers are liable to regret their actions and kick themselves for having been so foolish. To avoid this unpleasant possibility, individuals will tend to shun those actions that may result in loss.

   The pain of a loss seems to depend on whether it comes on the heels of earlier losses. Once investors have suffered a loss, they may be even more cautious not to risk a further loss. Conversely, just as gamblers are known to be more willing to take large bets when they are ahead, so investors may be more prepared to run the risk of a stock market dip after they have experienced a period of substantial gains. If they do then suffer a small loss, they at least have the consolation of being up on the year.

   You can see how this sort of behavior could lead to a stock price bubble. For example, early investors in the technology firms that boomed during the dot-com bubble were big winners. They may have stopped worrying about the risk of loss. They may have thrown caution to the winds and piled even more investment into these companies, driving stock prices far above fundamental values. The day of reckoning came when investors woke up and realized how far above fundamental value prices had soared.

2. *Beliefs about probabilities.* Most investors do not have a Ph.D. in probability theory and may make common errors in assessing the probability of uncertain outcomes. Psychologists have found that, when judging the possible future outcomes, individuals commonly look back to what has happened in recent periods and then assume that this is representative of what may occur in the future. The temptation is to project recent experience into the future and to forget the lessons learned from the more distant past. For example, an investor who places too much weight on recent events may judge that glamorous growth companies are very likely to continue to grow rapidly, even though very high rates of growth cannot persist indefinitely.

   A second common bias is overconfidence. Most of us believe that we are better-than-average drivers, and most investors think that they are better-than-average stock pickers. We know that two speculators who trade with one another cannot both make money from the deal; for every winner there must be a loser. But presumably investors are prepared to continue trading because each is confident that it is the other one who is the patsy.

BEYOND THE PAGE

Overconfident CFOs

mhhe.com/brealey9e

You can see how such characteristics may have reinforced the dot-com boom. As the bull market developed, it generated increased optimism about the future and stimulated demand for shares. The more that investors racked up profits on their stocks, the more confident they became in their views and the more willing they became to bear the risk that the next month might not be so good.

3. *Sentiment.* Efficient markets bring to mind absolutely rational investors on the lookout for every possible profit opportunity. But real investors are people, and people are subject to emotion. Sentiment may be interpreted as their general level of optimism or pessimism about the economy. If the sentiment of large groups of investors varies in tandem, it potentially could have a noticeable impact on security pricing.

Sentiment is offered as another reason that stock market bubbles might develop. An improvement in sentiment can lead to an increase in stock prices. That increase can feed on itself, with investors extrapolating recent performance into the future and deciding that it is a good time to buy, thus pushing prices up even further.

Now it is not difficult to believe that your uncle Harry or aunt Hetty may become caught up in a scatty whirl of irrational exuberance,[19] but why don't hardheaded professional investors bail out of the overpriced stocks and force their prices down to fair value? Perhaps they feel that it is too difficult to predict when the boom will end and that their jobs will be at risk if they move aggressively into cash when others are raking up profits. In this case, sales of stock by the pros are simply not large enough to stem the tide of optimism sweeping the market.

It is too early to say how far behavioral finance scholars can help to sort out some of the puzzles and explain events like the dot-com boom. One thing, however, seems clear: It is relatively easy for statisticians to spot anomalies with the benefit of hindsight and for psychologists to provide an explanation for them. It is much more difficult for investment managers who are at the sharp end to spot and invest in mispriced securities. And that is the basic message of the efficient-market theory. For corporate financial managers there is a clear lesson: Trust market prices unless you have a clear advantage that ensures the odds are in your favor.

SUMMARY

What information is included in stock trading reports, and how can stock-price information about other firms be used to help you value a particular firm? (*LO7-1*)

Large companies usually arrange for their stocks to be traded on a stock exchange. The stock listings report the stock's price, price change, volume, dividend yield, and **price-earnings (P/E)** ratio.

To value a stock financial analysts often start by identifying similar firms and looking at how much investors in these companies are prepared to pay for each dollar of earnings or book assets.

How can one calculate the present value of a stock given forecasts of future dividends and future stock price, and how do a company's growth opportunities show up in its stock price and price-earnings ratio? (*LO7-2*)

Stockholders generally expect to receive (1) cash dividends and (2) capital gains or losses. The rate of return that they expect over the next year is defined as the expected dividend per share DIV_1 plus the expected increase in price $P_1 - P_0$, all divided by the price at the start of the year P_0.

Unlike the fixed interest payments that the firm promises to bondholders, the dividends that are paid to stockholders depend on the fortunes of the firm. That's why a company's common stock is riskier than its debt. The return that investors expect on any one stock is also the return that they demand on all stocks subject to the same degree of risk.

The present value of a share is equal to the stream of expected dividends per share up to some horizon date plus the expected price at this date, all discounted at the return that

---

[19] The term "irrational exuberance" was coined by Alan Greenspan, former chairman of the Federal Reserve Board, to describe the dot-com boom. It was also the title of a book by Robert Shiller that examined the boom. See R. Shiller, *Irrational Exuberance* (New York City: Broadway Books, 2001).

investors require. If the horizon date is far away, we simply say that stock price equals the present value of all future dividends per share. This is the **dividend discount model.**

If forecast dividends grow at a constant rate, g, then the value of a stock is $P_0 = DIV_1/(r - g)$. This is the **constant-growth dividend discount model.** Sometimes, it is feasible to discount forecasted dividends for the next few years and then to discount the expected price at the end of this period. The expected price is often estimated using the constant-growth model.

You can think of a share's value as the sum of two parts—the value of the assets in place and the **present value of growth opportunities,** that is, of future opportunities for the firm to invest in high-return projects. The price-earnings (P/E) ratio reflects the market's assessment of the firm's growth opportunities.

How can these stock valuation formulas be used to infer the value of an entire business? (*LO7-3*)

Similar valuation methods can be used to estimate the value of an entire business. In this case, you need to forecast and discount the free cash flows provided by the business. These are the cash flows that are not plowed back into the business but can be used to pay dividends or repurchase stock.

How does competition among investors lead to efficient markets? (*LO7-4*)

Competition between investors will tend to produce an **efficient market**—that is, a market in which prices rapidly reflect new information and investors have difficulty making consistently superior returns. Of course, we all *hope* to beat the market, but if the market is efficient, all we can rationally *expect* is a return that is sufficient on average to compensate for the time value of money and for the risks we bear.

The evidence for market efficiency is voluminous, and there is little doubt that skilled professional investors find it difficult to win consistently. Nevertheless, there remain some puzzling instances where markets do not seem to be efficient. Some financial economists attribute these apparent anomalies to behavioral foibles.

LISTING OF EQUATIONS

7.1 $\quad V_0 = \dfrac{DIV_1 + P_1}{1 + r}$

7.2 $\quad P_0 = \dfrac{DIV_1}{1 + r} + \dfrac{DIV_2}{(1 + r)^2} + \cdots + \dfrac{DIV_H + P_H}{(1 + r)^H}$

7.3 $\quad P_0 = \dfrac{DIV_1}{r - g}$ (Constant-growth dividend discount model)

7.4 $\quad r = \dfrac{DIV_1}{P_0} + g = $ dividend yield + growth rate

7.5 $\quad g = $ sustainable growth rate = return on equity × plowback ratio

QUESTIONS AND PROBLEMS

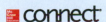

1. **Stock Markets.** True or false? (*LO7-1*)

   a. The bid price is always greater than the ask price.

   b. An investor who wants to sell his stock immediately should enter a limit order.

   c. The sale of shares by a large investor is usually termed a "primary offering."

   d. Electronic Communications Network refers to the automated ticker tape on the New York Stock Exchange.

2. **Stock Quotes.** Go to finance.yahoo.com and get trading quotes for IBM. (*LO7-1*)

   a. What is the latest stock price and market cap?
   b. What is the bid-ask spread?
   c. What is IBM's dividend payment and dividend yield?
   d. What is IBM's P/E ratio?

3. **Stock Quotes.** Here is a small part of the order book for Mesquite Foods: (*LO7-1*)

Bid		Ask	
Price	Size	Price	Size
103	100	103.5	200
102.5	200	103.8	200
101	400	104	300
99.8	300	104.5	400

   a. Georgina Sloberg submits a market order to sell 100 shares. What price will she receive?
   b. Norman Pilbarra submits a market order to buy 400 shares. What is the maximum price that he will pay?
   c. Carlos Ramirez submits a limit bid order at 105. Will it execute immediately?

4. **P/E Ratios.** Favorita Candy's stock is expected to earn $2.40 per share this year. Its P/E ratio is 18. What is the stock price? (*LO7-1*)

5. **Dividend Yield.** BMM Industries pays a dividend of $2 per quarter. The dividend yield on its stock is reported at 4.8%. What is the stock price? (*LO7-1*)

6. **Valuation by Comparables.** Look up the P/E and P/B ratios for American Electric Power (ticker symbol AEP), using Yahoo! Finance or another online source. Calculate the same ratios for the following potential comparables: Duke Energy (DUK), FirstEnergy Corporation (FE), PG&E Corporation (PCG), CenterPoint Energy (CNP), and Southern Company (SO). Are the ratios for these electric companies tightly grouped or scattered? If you didn't know AEP's stock price, would the comparables give a good estimate? (*LO7-2*)

7. **Valuation by Comparables.** Valuation by comparables worked much better for some of the companies in Table 7.3 than for others. Update the table using data from Yahoo! Finance. Do you still find that valuation by comparables works well or badly for the same companies? (*LO7-2*)

8. **Dividend Discount Model.** Rework Table 7.4 for horizon years 1, 2, 3, and 10, assuming that investors expect the dividend and the stock price to increase at only 6% a year and that each investor requires the same 12% expected return. (*LO7-2*)

   a. What value would Dritter place on the stock?
   b. Add a new row to Table 7.4 for a new investor, Zehnte, who has a 10-year horizon.

9. **Dividend Discount Model.** Amazon has never paid a dividend, but in December 2015, the market value of its stock was greater than $300 billion. Does this invalidate the dividend discount model? (*LO7-2*)

10. **Dividend Discount Model.** How can we say that price equals the present value of all future dividends when many actual investors may be seeking capital gains and planning to hold their shares for only a year or two? Explain. (*LO7-2*)

11. **Dividend Discount Model.** True or False? (*LO7-2*)

    a. Investors will invest in a stock only if it gives a higher return than they could get elsewhere. Therefore, if a stock is fairly priced, its expected return will be greater than the cost of equity capital.
    b. A stock that is expected to pay a level dividend in perpetuity has a value of $P_0 = DIV_1/r$. Any company that can reinvest to grow its earnings will have a greater value.
    c. The dividend discount model is still logically correct even for stocks that do not currently pay a dividend.

12. **Dividend Discount Model.** Integrated Potato Chips just paid a $1 per share dividend. You expect the dividend to grow steadily at a rate of 4% per year. (*LO7-2*)

   a. What is the expected dividend in each of the next 3 years?
   b. If the discount rate for the stock is 12%, at what price will the stock sell?
   c. What is the expected stock price 3 years from now?
   d. If you buy the stock and plan to sell it 3 years from now, what are your expected cash flows in (i) year 1; (ii) year 2; (iii) year 3?
   e. What is the present value of the stream of payments you found in part (d)? Compare your answer to part (b).

13. **Preferred Stock.** Preferred Products has issued preferred stock with an $8 annual dividend that will be paid in perpetuity. (*LO7-2*)

   a. If the discount rate is 12%, at what price should the preferred sell?
   b. At what price should the stock sell 1 year from now?
   c. What are (i) the dividend yield; (ii) the capital gains yield; (iii) the expected rate of return of the stock?

14. **Constant-Growth Model.** Arts and Crafts Inc. will pay a dividend of $5 per share in 1 year. It sells at $50 a share, and firms in the same industry provide an expected rate of return of 14%. What must be the expected growth rate of the company's dividends? (*LO7-2*)

15. **Constant-Growth Model.** A stock sells for $40. The next dividend will be $4 per share. If the rate of return earned on reinvested funds is a constant 15% and the company reinvests a constant 40% of earnings in the firm, what must be the discount rate? (*LO7-2*)

16. **Constant-Growth Model.** Gentleman Gym just paid its annual dividend of $3 per share, and it is widely expected that the dividend will increase by 5% per year indefinitely. (*LO7-2*)

   a. What price should the stock sell at? The discount rate is 15%.
   b. How would your answer change if the discount rate was only 12%? Why does the answer change?

17. **Constant-Growth Model.** Eastern Electric currently pays a dividend of $1.64 per share and sells for $27 a share. (*LO7-2*)

   a. If investors believe the growth rate of dividends is 3% per year, what rate of return do they expect to earn on the stock?
   b. If investors' required rate of return is 10%, what must be the growth rate they expect of the firm?
   c. If the sustainable growth rate is 5% and the plowback ratio is .4, what must be the rate of return earned by the firm on its new investments?

18. **Constant-Growth Model.** You believe that the Non-Stick Gum Factory will pay a dividend of $2 on its common stock next year. Thereafter, you expect dividends to grow at a rate of 6% a year in perpetuity. If you require a return of 12% on your investment, how much should you be prepared to pay for the stock? (*LO7-2*)

19. **Constant-Growth Model.** Horse and Buggy Inc. is in a declining industry. Sales, earnings, and dividends are all shrinking at a rate of 10% per year. (*LO7-2*)

   a. If $r = 15\%$ and $DIV_1 = \$3$, what is the value of a share?
   b. What price do you forecast for the stock next year?
   c. What is the expected rate of return on the stock?
   d. Can you distinguish between "bad stocks" and "bad companies"? Does the fact that the industry is declining mean that the stock is a bad buy?

20. **Constant-Growth Model.** Metatrend's stock will generate earnings of $6 per share this year. The discount rate for the stock is 15%, and the rate of return on reinvested earnings also is 15%. (*LO7-2*)

   a. Find both the growth rate of dividends and the price of the stock if the company reinvests the following fraction of its earnings in the firm: (i) 0%; (ii) 40%; (iii) 60%.
   b. Redo part (a) now assuming that the rate of return on reinvested earnings is 20%. What is the present value of growth opportunities for each reinvestment rate?
   c. Considering your answers to parts (a) and (b), can you briefly state the difference between companies experiencing growth and companies with growth opportunities?

21. **Constant-Growth Model.** Here are data on two stocks, both of which have discount rates of 15%: (*LO7-2*)

	Stock A	Stock B
Return on equity	15%	10%
Earnings per share	$2.00	$1.50
Dividends per share	$1.00	$1.00

    a. What are the dividend payout ratios for each firm?
    b. What are the expected dividend growth rates for each stock?
    c. What is the value of each stock?

22. **Constant-Growth Model.** Fincorp will pay a year-end dividend of $2.40 per share, which is expected to grow at a 4% rate for the indefinite future. The discount rate is 12%. (*LO7-2*)

    a. What is the stock selling for?
    b. If earnings are $3.10 a share, what is the implied value of the firm's growth opportunities?

23. **Dividend Discount Model.** Consider the following three stocks:

    a. Stock A is expected to provide a dividend of $10 a share forever.
    b. Stock B is expected to pay a dividend of $5 next year. Thereafter, dividend growth is expected to be 4% a year forever.
    c. Stock C is expected to pay a dividend of $5 next year. Thereafter, dividend growth is expected to be 20% a year for 5 years (i.e., years 2 through 6) and zero thereafter.

    If the market capitalization rate for each stock is 10%, which stock is the most valuable? What if the capitalization rate is 7%? (*LO7-2*)

24. **Rate of Return.** Steady As She Goes Inc. will pay a year-end dividend of $3 per share. Investors expect the dividend to grow at a rate of 4% indefinitely. (*LO7-2*)

    a. If the stock currently sells for $30 per share, what is the expected rate of return on the stock?
    b. If the expected rate of return on the stock is 16.5%, what is the stock price?

25. **Dividend Growth.** Grandiose Growth has a dividend growth rate of 20%. The discount rate is 10%. The end-of-year dividend will be $2 per share. (*LO7-2*)

    a. What is the present value of the dividend to be paid in: (i) year 1? (ii) Year 2? (iii) Year 3?
    b. Could anyone rationally expect this growth rate to continue indefinitely?

26. **Valuing Businesses.** Start-Up Industries is a new firm that has raised $200 million by selling shares of stock. Management plans to earn a 24% rate of return on equity, which is more than the 15% rate of return available on comparable-risk investments. Half of all earnings will be reinvested in the firm. (*LO7-3*)

    a. What will be Start-Up's ratio of market value to book value?
    b. How would that ratio change if the firm can earn only a 10% rate of return on its investments?

27. **Nonconstant Growth.** You expect a share of stock to pay dividends of $1.00, $1.25, and $1.50 in each of the next 3 years. You believe the stock will sell for $20 at the end of the third year. (*LO7-2*)

    a. What is the stock price if the discount rate for the stock is 10%?
    b. What is the dividend yield for year 1?
    c. What will be the dividend yield at the start of year 2?

28. **Nonconstant Growth.** Planned Obsolescence has a product that will be in vogue for 3 years, at which point the firm will close up shop and liquidate the assets. As a result, forecast dividends are $DIV_1 = $2, $DIV_2 = $2.50, and $DIV_3 = $18. What is the stock price if the discount rate is 12%? (*LO7-2*)

29. **Nonconstant Growth.** Tattletale News Corp. has been growing at a rate of 20% per year, and you expect this growth rate in earnings and dividends to continue for another 3 years. (*LO7-2*)

    a. If the last dividend paid was $2, what will the next dividend be?
    b. If the discount rate is 15% and the steady growth rate after 3 years is 4%, what should the stock price be today?

30. **Nonconstant Growth.** Reconsider Tattletale News from the previous problem. *(LO7-2)*
    a. What is your prediction for the stock price in 1 year?
    b. Show that the expected rate of return equals the discount rate.

31. **Nonconstant Growth.** Phoenix Industries has pulled off a miraculous recovery. Four years ago it was near bankruptcy. Today, it announced a $1 per share dividend to be paid a year from now, the first dividend since the crisis. Analysts expect dividends to increase by $1 a year for another 2 years. After the third year (in which dividends are $3 per share), dividend growth is expected to settle down to a more moderate long-term growth rate of 6%. If the firm's investors expect to earn a return of 14% on this stock, what must be its price? *(LO7-2)*

32. **Nonconstant Growth.** A company will pay a $2 per share dividend in 1 year. The dividend in 2 years will be $4 per share, and it is expected that dividends will grow at 5% per year thereafter. The expected rate of return on the stock is 12%. *(LO7-2)*
    a. What is the current price of the stock?
    b. What is the expected price of the stock in a year?
    c. Show that the expected return, 12%, equals dividend yield plus capital appreciation.

33. **Nonconstant Growth.** Better Mousetraps has come out with an improved product, and the world is beating a path to its door. As a result, the firm projects growth of 20% per year for 4 years. By then, other firms will have copycat technology, competition will drive down profit margins, and the sustainable growth rate will fall to 5%. The most recent annual dividend was $DIV_0 = \$1$ per share. *(LO7-2)*
    a. What are the expected values of: (i) DIV_1, (ii) DIV_2, (iii) DIV_3, and (iv) DIV_4?
    b. What is the expected stock price 4 years from now? The discount rate is 10%.
    c. What is the stock price today?
    d. Find the dividend yield, DIV_1/P_0.
    e. What will next year's stock price, P_1, be?
    f. What is the expected rate of return to an investor who buys the stock now and sells it in 1 year?

34. **Nonconstant Growth.** *(LO7-2)*
    a. Return to the previous problem, and compute the value of Better Mousetraps for assumed sustainable growth rates of 6% through 9%, in increments of .5%.
    b. Compute the percentage change in the value of the firm for each 1 percentage point increase in the assumed final growth rate, g.
    c. What happens to the sensitivity of intrinsic value to changes in g? What do you conclude about the reliability of estimates based on the dividend growth model when the assumed sustainable growth rate begins to approach the discount rate?

35. **Valuing Businesses.** Construct a new version of Table 7.5, assuming that competition drives down profitability (on existing assets as well as new investment) to 11.5% in year 6, 11% in year 7, 10.5% in year 8, and 8% in year 9 and all later years. What is the value of the concatenator business? *(LO7-3)*

36. **P/E Ratios.** No-Growth Industries pays out all of its earnings as dividends. It will pay its next $4 per share dividend in a year. The discount rate is 12%. *(LO7-2)*
    a. What is the price-earnings ratio of the company?
    b. What would the P/E ratio be if the discount rate were 10%?

37. **P/E Ratios.** Castles in the Sand generates a rate of return of 20% on its investments and maintains a plowback ratio of .30. Its earnings this year will be $4 per share. Investors expect a 12% rate of return on the stock. *(LO7-2)*
    a. Find the price and P/E ratio of the firm.
    b. What happens to the P/E ratio if the plowback ratio is reduced to .20? Why?
    c. Show that if plowback equals zero, the earnings-price ratio, E/P, falls to the expected rate of return on the stock.

38. **P/E Ratios.** Web Cites Research projects a rate of return of 20% on new projects. Management plans to plow back 30% of all earnings into the firm. Earnings this year will be $3 per share, and investors expect a 12% rate of return on stocks facing the same risks as Web Cites. *(LO7-2)*
    a. What is the sustainable growth rate?
    b. What is the stock price?

  c. What is the present value of growth opportunities?

  d. What is the P/E ratio?

  e. What would the price and P/E ratio be if the firm paid out all earnings as dividends?

  f. What do you conclude about the relationship between growth opportunities and P/E ratios?

39. **P/E Ratios.** Investors in Rance Electric's stock require a return of 8%. If the company simply earns the cost of capital on its new investments, what is the stock's P/E? (*LO7-2*)

40. **Growth Opportunities.** Stormy Weather has no attractive investment opportunities. Its return on equity equals the discount rate, which is 10%. Its expected earnings this year are $4 per share. Fill in the following table. (*LO7-2*)

Plowback Ratio	Growth Rate	Stock Price	P/E Ratio
0	a.	b.	c.
0.4	d.	e.	f.
0.8	g.	h.	i.

41. **Growth Opportunities.** Trend-Line Inc. has been growing at a rate of 6% per year and is expected to continue to do so indefinitely. The next dividend is expected to be $5 per share. (*LO7-2*)

  a. If the market expects a 10% rate of return on Trend-Line, at what price must it be selling?

  b. If Trend-Line's earnings per share will be $8 next year, what part of its value is due to assets in place?

  c. What part of its value is due to growth opportunities?

42. **Efficient Markets.** Which if any of these statements are true? Stock prices appear to behave as though successive values (*LO7-4*)

  a. are random numbers.

  b. follow regular cycles.

  c. differ by a random number.

43. **Forms of Efficient Markets.** Fill in the missing words from the following list: *semi-strong, strong, weak.* (*LO7-4*)

There are three forms of the efficient-market theory. Tests that have found there are no patterns in share price changes provide evidence for the (a) form of the theory. Evidence for the (b) form of the theory is provided by tests that look at how rapidly markets respond to new public information, and evidence for the (c) form of the theory is provided by tests that look at the performance of professionally managed portfolios.

44. **Information and Efficient Markets.** "It's competition for information that makes securities markets efficient." Is this statement correct? Explain. (*LO7-4*)

45. **Behavioral Finance.** Some finance scholars cite well-documented behavioral biases to explain apparent cases of market inefficiency. Describe two of these biases. (*LO7-4*)

46. **Interpreting the Efficient-Market Theory.** How would you respond to the following comments? (*LO7-4*)

  a. "Efficient market, my eye! I know lots of investors who do crazy things."

  b. "Efficient market? Balderdash! I know at least a dozen people who have made a bundle in the stock market."

  c. "The trouble with the efficient-market theory is that it ignores investors' psychology."

47. **Real versus Financial Investments.** Why do investments in financial markets almost always have zero NPVs, whereas firms can find many investments in their product markets with positive NPVs? (*LO7-4*)

48. **Investment Performance.** It seems that every month we read an article in *The Wall Street Journal* about a stock picker with a marvelous track record. Do these examples mean that financial markets are not efficient? (*LO7-4*)

49. **Implications of Efficient Markets.** The president of Good Fortunes Inc. states at a press conference that the company has a 30-year history of ever-increasing dividend payments. Good Fortunes is widely regarded as one of the best-run firms in its industry. Does this make the firm's stock a good buy? Explain. (*LO7-4*)

50. **Implications of Efficient Markets.** "Long-term interest rates are at record highs. Most companies, therefore, find it cheaper to finance with common stock or relatively inexpensive short-term bank loans." Discuss. (*LO7-4*)

51. **Expectations and Efficient Markets.** Geothermal Corp. just announced good news: Its earnings have increased by 20%. Most investors had anticipated an increase of 25%. Will Geothermal's stock price increase or decrease when the announcement is made? (*LO7-4*)

52. **Behavioral Finance.** True or false? (*LO7-4*)
    a. Most managers tend to be overconfident.
    b. Psychologists have found that, once people have suffered a loss, they are more relaxed about the possibility of incurring further losses.
    c. Psychologists have observed that people tend to put too much weight on recent events when forecasting.
    d. Behavioral biases open up the opportunity for easy arbitrage profits.

WEB EXERCISES

1. Review Table 7.2, which lists the market values of several stocks. Update the table. Which stock's value has changed by the greatest percentage since 2015, when the table was created? Now recalculate book value per share. Have the book values for any firm changed? Which seems to be more stable, book or market value? Why?

2. From finance.yahoo.com, obtain the price-earnings ratios of Adobe Systems (ADBE) and American Electric Power (AEP). Which of these two firms seems to be more of a "growth stock"? Now obtain a forecast of each firm's expected earnings per share in the coming year. You can find earnings forecasts on yahoo.com under "Analysts Estimates." What is the present value of growth opportunities for each firm as a fraction of the stock price? (Assume, for simplicity, that the required rate of return on the stocks is $r = 8\%$.) Are the relative values you obtain for PVGO consistent with the P/E ratios?

SOLUTIONS TO SELF-TEST QUESTIONS

7.1 Expected industry profitability has fallen. Thus, the value of future investment opportunities has fallen relative to the value of assets in place. This happens in all growth industries sooner or later, as competition increases and profitable new investment opportunities shrink.

7.2 $$P_0 = \frac{DIV_1 + P_1}{1 + r} = \frac{\$5 + \$105}{1.10} = \$100$$

7.3 Because dividends and share price grow at 5%,

$$DIV_2 = \$5 \times 1.05 = \$5.25, DIV_3 = \$5 \times 1.05^2 = \$5.51$$

$$P_3 = \$100 \times 1.05^3 = \$115.76$$

$$P_0 = \frac{DIV_1}{1 + r} + \frac{DIV_2}{(1 + r)^2} + \frac{DIV_3 + P_3}{(1 + r)^3}$$

$$= \frac{\$5.00}{1.10} + \frac{\$5.25}{(1.10)^2} + \frac{\$5.51 + \$115.76}{(1.10)^3} = \$100$$

7.4 $$P_0 = \frac{DIV}{r} = \frac{\$25}{.20} = \$125$$

7.5 The two firms have equal risk, so we can use the data for Androscoggin to find the expected return on either stock:

$$r = \frac{DIV_1}{P_0} + g = \frac{\$5}{\$100} + .05 = .10, \text{ or } 10\%$$

7.6   a. The sustainable growth rate is

$$g = \text{return on equity} \times \text{plowback ratio}$$
$$= .05 \times .40 = .02, \text{ or } 2\%$$

b. First value the company. At a 60% payout ratio, $\text{DIV}_1 = \$.74$ as before. Using the constant-growth model,

$$P_0 = \frac{\$.74}{.078 - .02} = \$12.76$$

which is $3.05 per share less than the company's no-growth value of $15.81. In this example, Aqua America would be throwing away $3.05 of potential value by investing in projects with unattractive rates of return.

c. Sure. A raider could take over the company and generate a profit of $3.05 per share just by halting all investments offering less than the 7.8% rate of return demanded by investors. This assumes the raider could buy the shares for $12.76.

7.7   The present value of dividends in years 1 to 5 is still $13.50. However, with a lower terminal growth rate after year 5, the stock price in year 5 will be lower. If we assume a 4% growth rate, then the forecast dividend in year 6 is

$$\text{DIV}_6 = 1.04 \times \text{DIV}_5 = 1.04 \times 4.17 = \$4.34$$

and the expected price at the end of year 5 is

$$P_5 = \frac{\text{DIV}_6}{r - g} = \frac{\$4.34}{.085 - .04} = \$96.44$$

Therefore, present value is

$$P_0 = \text{PV (dividends years 1–5)} + \text{PV (price in year 5)}$$

$$= \$13.50 + \frac{\$96.44}{1.085^5} = \$77.64$$

7.8   a. False. The *levels* of successive stock prices are related. If a stock is selling for $100 per share today, the best guess of its price tomorrow is about $100.

b. True. *Changes* in stock prices are unrelated. Whether a stock price increases or decreases today has no bearing on whether it will do so tomorrow.

c. False. There is no such thing as a "normal" price. If there were, you could make easy profits by buying shares selling below their normal prices (which would tend to be rising back toward those normal levels) and selling shares currently selling above their normal prices. Under a random walk, prices are equally likely to rise or fall.

d. True. Under a random walk, prices are equally likely to over- or underperform regardless of their past history.

MINICASE

Terence Breezeway, the CEO of Prairie Home Stores, wondered what retirement would be like. It was almost 20 years to the day since his uncle Jacob Breezeway, Prairie Home's founder, had asked him to take responsibility for managing the company. Now it was time to spend more time riding and fishing on the old Lazy Beta Ranch.

Under Mr. Breezeway's leadership, Prairie Home had grown slowly but steadily and was solidly profitable. (Table 7.6 shows earnings, dividends, and book asset values for the last 5 years.) Most of the company's supermarkets had been modernized, and its brand name was well known.

Mr. Breezeway was proud of this record, although he wished that Prairie Home could have grown more rapidly. He had passed up several opportunities to build new stores in adjacent counties. Prairie Home was still just a family company. Its common stock was distributed among 15 grandchildren and nephews of Jacob Breezeway, most of whom had come to depend on generous regular dividends. The commitment to high dividend payout[20] had reduced the earnings available for reinvestment and thereby constrained growth.

Mr. Breezeway believed the time had come to take Prairie Home public. Once its shares were traded in the public market, the

_____
[20] The company traditionally paid out cash dividends equal to 10% of start-of-period book value. See Table 7.6.

TABLE 7.6 Financial data for Prairie Home Stores, 2016–2020 (figures in millions)

	2016	2017	2018	2019	2020
Book value, start of year	$62.7	$66.1	$69.0	$73.9	$76.5
Earnings	9.7	9.5	11.8	11.0	11.2
Dividends	6.3	6.6	6.9	7.4	7.7
Retained earnings	3.4	2.9	4.9	2.6	3.5
Book value, end of year	66.1	69.0	73.9	76.5	80.0

Notes:
1. Prairie Home Stores has 400,000 common shares.
2. The company's policy is to pay cash dividends equal to 10% of start-of-year book value.

Breezeway descendants who needed (or just wanted) more cash to spend could sell off part of their holdings. Others with more interest in the business could hold on to their shares and be rewarded by higher future earnings and stock prices.

But if Prairie Home did go public, what should its shares sell for? Mr. Breezeway worried that shares would be sold, either by Breezeway family members or by the company itself, at too low a price. One relative was about to accept a private offer for $200, the current book value per share, but Mr. Breezeway had intervened and convinced the would-be seller to wait.

Prairie Home's value depended not just on its current book value or earnings but on its future prospects, which were good. One financial projection (shown in the top panel of Table 7.7) called for growth in earnings of more than 100% by 2027. Unfortunately, this plan would require reinvestment of all of Prairie Home's earnings from 2021 to 2024. After that, the company could resume its normal dividend payout and growth rate. Mr. Breezeway believed this plan was feasible.

He was determined to step aside for the next generation of top management. But before retiring, he had to decide whether to recommend that Prairie Home Stores "go public"—and before that decision he had to know what the company was worth.

The next morning, he rode thoughtfully to work. He left his horse at the south corral and ambled down the dusty street to Mike Gordon's Saloon, where Francine Firewater, the company's CFO, was having her usual steak-and-beans breakfast. He asked Ms. Firewater to prepare a formal report to Prairie Home stockholders, valuing the company on the assumption that its shares were publicly traded.

Ms. Firewater asked two questions immediately. First, what should she assume about investment and growth? Mr. Breezeway suggested two valuations, one assuming more rapid expansion (as in the top panel of Table 7.7) and another just projecting past growth (as in the bottom panel of Table 7.7).

Second, what rate of return should she use? Mr. Breezeway said that 15%, Prairie Home's usual return on book equity, sounded right to him, but he referred her to an article in the *Journal of Finance* indicating that investors in rural supermarket chains, with risks similar to Prairie Home Stores, expected to earn about 11% on average.

TABLE 7.7 Financial projections for Prairie Home Stores, 2021–2026 (figures in millions)

	2021	2022	2023	2024	2025	2026
			Rapid-Growth Scenario			
Book value, start of year	$80	$ 92.0	$105.8	$121.7	$139.9	$146.9
Earnings	12	13.8	15.9	18.3	21.0	22.0
Dividends	0	0	0	0	14	14.7
Retained earnings	12	13.8	15.9	18.3	7.0	7.4
Book value, end of year	92	105.8	121.7	139.9	146.9	154.3
			Constant-Growth Scenario			
Book value, start of year	$80	$84.0	$88.2	$92.6	$ 97.2	$102.1
Earnings	12	12.6	13.2	13.9	14.6	15.3
Dividends	8	8.4	8.8	9.3	9.7	10.2
Retained earnings	4	4.2	4.4	4.6	4.9	5.1
Book value, end of year	84	88.2	92.6	97.2	102.1	107.2

Notes:
1. Both panels assume earnings equal to 15% of start-of-year book value. This profitability rate is constant.
2. The top panel assumes all earnings are reinvested from 2021 to 2024. In 2025 and later years, two-thirds of earnings are paid out as dividends and one-third reinvested.
3. The bottom panel assumes two-thirds of earnings are paid out as dividends in all years.
4. Columns may not add up because of rounding.

8

Net Present Value and Other Investment Criteria

LEARNING OBJECTIVES

After studying this chapter, you should be able to:

8-1 Calculate the net present value of a project.

8-2 Calculate the internal rate of return of a project and know what to look out for when using the internal rate of return rule.

8-3 Calculate the profitability index and use it to choose between projects when funds are limited.

8-4 Understand the payback rule and explain why it *doesn't* always make shareholders better off.

8-5 Use the net present value rule to analyze three common problems that involve competing projects: (a) when to postpone an investment expenditure, (b) how to choose between projects with unequal lives, and (c) when to replace equipment.

RELATED WEBSITES FOR THIS CHAPTER CAN BE FOUND IN CONNECT.

High-tech businesses often require huge investments. How do companies decide which investments are worth pursuing?
© Erik Isakson/Blend Images LLC RF

The investment decision, also known as the *capital budgeting decision,* is central to the success of the company. We have already seen that capital investments can sometimes absorb substantial amounts of cash; they also have very long-term consequences. The assets you buy today may determine the business you are in many years hence.

For some investment projects, "substantial" is an understatement. Consider the following examples:

- Verizon spent $23 billion rolling out its fiber-optic network.

- The cost of bringing one new prescription drug to market has been estimated to be as high as $2.6 billion.

- The eventual cost of the Gorgon natural gas project in Western Australia is forecast at $54 billion.

- General Motors' research and development costs for the Chevrolet Volt have been about $1.2 billion.

- Estimated production costs for *The Hobbit* movie trilogy were over $600 million.

- The development costs of the Boeing 787 Dreamliner jet were over $30 billion.

Notice that many of these big capital projects require heavy investment in intangible assets. For example, almost all the cost of drug development is for research and testing. So is much of the cost of developing the electric auto. Any expenditure made in the hope of generating more cash later can be called a *capital investment project,* regardless of whether the cash outlay goes to tangible or intangible assets.

A company's shareholders prefer to be rich rather than poor. Therefore, they want the firm to invest in every project that is worth more than it costs. The difference between a project's value and its cost is termed the *net present value.* Companies can best help their shareholders by investing in projects with a *positive* net present value.

We start this chapter by showing how to calculate the net present value of some simple investment projects. We then examine three other criteria that companies sometimes use to evaluate investments. Often, they compare the expected rate of return offered by a project to the return that their shareholders could earn on equivalent-risk investments in the capital market. They accept only projects that provide a higher return than shareholders could earn for themselves. Generally, this rule will give the same guidance as the net present value rule, but, as we shall see, it presents some pitfalls, especially when choosing between alternative projects. We explore the key pitfalls of the rate of return rule, and in the appendix we show you some tricks for avoiding them.

Another measure of project worth is the *profitability index*, which is net present value per dollar invested. This can be a handy tool when the company does not have enough money to take on every project with a positive net present value.

The third measure, the *payback rule*, is a simple rule of thumb that companies may use to separate the no-brainers from more marginal cases. But we shall see that this rule is an unreliable guide to project viability and is even more unreliable when used to choose between competing projects. We will spend relatively little time on it.

We start the chapter by looking at some simple take-it-or-leave-it decisions. However, in practice, projects can rarely be considered in isolation. Usually, there are several alternatives, only one of which can be chosen. For example, suppose you are considering whether to build a new factory. Should you build a 100,000-square-foot factory or 150,000? Should you design it to last 20 years or 30? Should it be built today, or should you wait a year? Later in the chapter we explain how to make such choices.

8.1 Net Present Value

In Chapters 6 and 7, you learned how to value bonds and stocks by adding up the present values of the cash flows that they are expected to provide to their investors. Now we will do the same for investment projects.

Suppose that you are in the real estate business. You are considering construction of an office block. The land would cost $50,000, and construction would cost a further $300,000. You foresee a shortage of office space and predict that a year from now you will be able to sell the building for $400,000. Thus, you would be investing $350,000 now in the expectation of realizing $400,000 at the end of the year. The projected cash flows may be summarized in a simple time line as follows:

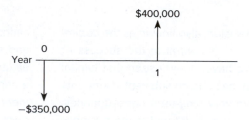

You should go ahead if the present value of the $400,000 payoff is greater than the investment of $350,000.

Assume for the moment that the $400,000 payoff is certain. The office building is not the only way to obtain a sure-fire $400,000 a year from now. You could instead invest in 1-year U.S. Treasury bills. Suppose Treasury securities offer interest of 7%. How much would you have to invest in them in order to receive $400,000 at the end of the year? That's easy: You would have to invest

$$\$400,000 \times \frac{1}{1.07} = \$400,000 \times .9346 = \$373,832$$

Let's assume that as soon as you have purchased the land and laid out the money for construction, you decide to cash in on your project. How much could you sell it for? Because the property will be worth $400,000 in a year, investors would be willing to pay, at most, $373,832 for it now. That's the amount it would cost them to get precisely the same $400,000 payoff by investing in government securities. Of course, you could always sell your property for less, but why sell for less than the market will bear?

Therefore, at an interest rate of 7%, the present value of the $400,000 payoff from the office building is $373,832. The $373,832 present value is the only price that satisfies both buyer and seller. In general, the present value is the only feasible price, and the present value of the property is also its *market price* or *market value*.

To calculate present value, we discounted the expected future payoff by the rate of return offered by comparable investment alternatives. The discount rate—7% in our example—is often known as the **opportunity cost of capital.** It is called the *opportunity cost* because if you decide to invest in this project, you will forgo other similar investment opportunities such as the purchase of Treasury securities.

opportunity cost of capital
Expected rate of return given up by investing in a project rather than in the capital market.

The building is worth $373,832, but this does not mean that you are $373,832 better off. You committed $350,000, and therefore your **net present value (NPV)** is $23,832. Net present value is found by subtracting the required initial investment from the present value of the project cash flows:[1]

net present value (NPV)
Present value of cash flows minus investment.

$$NPV = PV - \text{required investment} \qquad (8.1)$$
$$= \$373{,}832 - \$350{,}000 = \$23{,}832$$

In other words, your office development is worth more than it costs—it makes a *net* contribution to value. **The net present value *rule* states that managers increase shareholders' wealth by accepting projects that are worth more than they cost. Therefore, they should accept all projects with a positive net present value.**

A Comment on Risk and Present Value

In our discussion of the office development, we assumed that we knew the value of the completed project. In practice, you will never be *certain* about the future values of office buildings. The $400,000 represents the best *forecast,* but it is not a sure thing.

In this case, our initial conclusion about how much investors would pay for the building is premature. Because they could achieve $400,000 *risklessly* by investing in $373,832 worth of U.S. Treasury bills, they would not buy your risky project for that amount. You would have to cut your asking price to attract investors' interest.

Here we can invoke a basic financial principle: **A risky dollar is worth less than a safe one.**

Most investors avoid risk when they can do so without sacrificing return. However, the concepts of present value and the opportunity cost of capital still apply to risky investments. It is still proper to discount the payoff by the rate of return offered by a comparable investment. But we have to think of *expected* payoffs and the *expected* rates of return on other investments. And we need to make sure that those other investments have comparable risk.

Not all investments are equally risky. The office development is riskier than a Treasury bill but is probably less risky than investing in a start-up biotech company. Suppose you believe the office development is as risky as an investment in the stock market and that you forecast a 12% rate of return for stock market investments. Then 12% would be the appropriate opportunity cost of capital. That is what you are giving up by not investing in securities with similar risk. You can now recompute NPV:

$$PV = \$400{,}000 \times \frac{1}{1.12} = \$400{,}000 \times .8929 = \$357{,}143$$

$$NPV = PV - \$350{,}000 = \$7{,}143$$

If other investors agree with your forecast of a $400,000 payoff and with your assessment of a 12% opportunity cost of capital, then the property ought to be worth $357,143 once construction is under way. If you tried to sell for more than that, there would be no takers because the property would then offer a lower expected rate of return than the 12% available in the stock market. Even at a discount rate of 12%, the office building still makes a net contribution to value, but it is much smaller than our earlier calculations indicated.

---

[1] You often hear financial innocents talk about net present value when they really mean present value. Remember, the present value measures what a project is worth. Net present value deducts the cost of the investment.

Valuing Long-Lived Projects

The net present value rule works for projects of any length. For example, suppose that you are approached by a possible tenant who is prepared to rent your office block for 3 years at a fixed annual rent of $25,000. You would need to expand the reception area and add some other tailor-made features. This would increase the initial investment to $375,000, but you forecast that after you have collected the third year's rent, the building could be sold for $450,000. The projected cash flow (denoted C) in each year is shown here (the final cash flow is the sum of rental income plus the proceeds from selling the building).

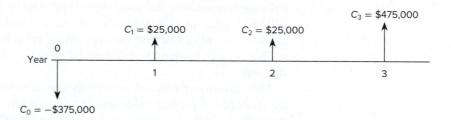

Notice that the initial investment shows up as a negative cash flow. That first cash flow, C_0, is −$375,000. For simplicity, we will again assume that these cash flows are certain and that the opportunity cost of capital is $r = 7\%$.

Figure 8.1 shows a time line of the cash inflows and their present values. To find the present value of the project, we discount these cash inflows at the 7% opportunity cost of capital:

$$PV = \frac{C_1}{1+r} + \frac{C_2}{(1+r)^2} + \frac{C_3}{(1+r)^3}$$

$$= \frac{\$25,000}{1.07} + \frac{\$25,000}{1.07^2} + \frac{\$475,000}{1.07^3} = \$432,942$$

BEYOND THE PAGE

The revised office project

mhhe.com/brealey9e

The *net* present value of the revised project is NPV = $432,942 − $375,000 = $57,942. Constructing the office block and renting it for 3 years makes a greater addition to your wealth than selling it at the end of the first year.

Of course, rather than subtracting the initial investment from the project's present value, you could calculate NPV directly, as in the following equation, where C_0 denotes the initial cash outflow required to build the office block.

$$NPV = C_0 + \frac{C_1}{1+r} + \frac{C_2}{(1+r)^2} + \frac{C_3}{(1+r)^3}$$

$$= -\$375,000 + \frac{\$25,000}{1.07} + \frac{\$25,000}{1.07^2} + \frac{\$475,000}{1.07^3} = \$57,942$$

FIGURE 8.1 Cash flows and their present values for the office-block project. Final cash flow of $475,000 is the sum of the rental income in year 3 plus the forecast sales price for the building.

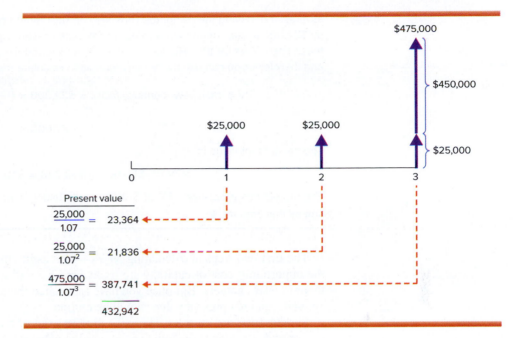

Let's check that the owners of this project really are better off. Suppose you put up $375,000 of your own money, commit to build the office building, and sign a lease that will bring in $25,000 a year for 3 years. Now you can cash in by selling the project to other investors.

Suppose you sell 1,000 shares in the project. Each share represents a claim to 1/1,000 of the future cash flows. Because the cash flows are certain, and the interest rate offered by other certain investments is 7%, investors will value each share at

$$\text{Price per share} = \frac{\$25}{1.07} + \frac{\$25}{1.07^2} + \frac{\$475}{1.07^3} = \$432.94$$

Thus, you can sell the project to outside investors for $1,000 \times \$432.94 = \$432,940$, which, save for rounding, is exactly the present value we calculated earlier. Your net gain is

$$\text{Net gain} = \$432,942 - \$375,000 = \$57,942$$

which is the project's NPV. This equivalence should be no surprise because the present value calculation is *designed* to calculate the value of future cash flows to investors in the capital markets.

Notice that, in principle, there could be a different opportunity cost of capital for each period's cash flow. In that case, we would discount C_1 by r_1, the discount rate for 1-year cash flows; C_2 would be discounted by r_2; and so on. However, here we assume that the cost of capital is the same regardless of the date of the cash flow. We do this for one reason only—simplicity. But we are in good company: With only rare exceptions, firms decide on an appropriate discount rate and then use it to discount all cash flows from the project.

Example 8.1 ▶ Valuing a New Computer System

Obsolete Technologies is considering the purchase of a new computer system to help handle its warehouse inventories. The system costs $50,000 and is expected to last 4 years and to reduce the cost of managing inventories by $22,000 a year. The opportunity cost of capital is 10%. Should Obsolete go ahead?

Don't be put off by the fact that the computer system does not generate any sales. If the expected cost savings are realized, the company's cash flows will be $22,000 a year higher as a result of buying the computer. Thus, we can say that the computer increases cash flows by $22,000 a year for each of 4 years. To calculate present value, you can discount each of these cash flows by 10%. However, it is smarter to recognize that the cash flows are level, and therefore, you can use the annuity formula to calculate the present value:

$$PV = \text{cash flow} \times \text{annuity factor} = \$22,000 \times \left(\frac{1}{.10} - \frac{1}{.10(1.10)^4} \right)$$

$$= \$22,000 \times 3.1699 = \$69,738$$

The net present value is

$$NPV = -\$50,000 + \$69,738 = \$19,738$$

The project has a positive NPV of $19,738. Undertaking it would increase the value of the firm by that amount. ∎

The first two steps in calculating NPVs—forecasting the cash flows and estimating the opportunity cost of capital—are tricky, and we will have a lot more to say about them in later chapters. But once you have assembled the data, the calculation of present value and net present value should be routine.

Spreadsheets are ideal for taking the drudgery out of these calculations. The nearby box provides guidance on how they are used to calculate NPVs.

Choosing between Alternative Projects

So far, the simple projects that we have considered all involved take-it-or-leave-it decisions. But real-world decisions are rarely straightforward go-or-no-go choices; rather, you will almost always be forced to choose between several alternatives. In these cases, you need to rank your alternatives and select the most attractive one. In principle, the decision rule is easy:

When choosing between mutually exclusive projects, choose the one that offers the highest net present value.

In reality, however, it can be surprisingly tricky to compare projects properly. We treat some of the challenging cases later in the chapter, in Section 8.5. For now, we illustrate the general rule with a simple example.

| Example | 8.2 ▶ | Choosing between Two Projects |

It has been several years since your office last upgraded its office networking software. Two competing systems have been proposed. Both have an expected useful life of 3 years, at which point it will be time for another upgrade. One proposal is for an expensive, cutting-edge system, which will cost $800,000 and increase firm cash flows by $350,000 a year through increased productivity. The other proposal is for a cheaper, somewhat slower system. This system would cost only $700,000 but would increase cash flows by only $300,000 a year. If the cost of capital is 7%, which is the better option?

The following table summarizes the cash flows and the NPVs of the two proposals:

System	Cash Flows (thousands of dollars)				NPV at 7%
	C_0	C_1	C_2	C_3	
Faster	−800	+350	+350	+350	118.5
Slower	−700	+300	+300	+300	87.3

In both cases, the software systems are worth more than they cost, but the faster system would make the greater contribution to value and, therefore, should be your preferred choice. ∎

Computer spreadsheets are tailor-made to calculate the present value of a series of cash flows. Spreadsheet 8.1 is an Excel spreadsheet for the revised office project (see Figure 8.1). Cells C3 through C6 calculate the PV of each year's cash flow by discounting at 7% for the length of time given in column A. Cell C7 calculates NPV as the sum of the PVs of all years' cash flows. Column D shows the Excel formulas used to calculate the results in column C.

Excel also provides a built-in function to calculate NPVs. The formula is = NPV(discount rate, list of cash flows). So, instead of calculating the PV of each cash flow and summing up, we can use the NPV function in cell C9. (The formula used in that cell is shown in D9.) The first entry in the function is the discount rate expressed as a decimal, in this case .07. That is followed by B4:B6, which tells Excel to discount all cash flows in column B from cells B4 to B6.

Why is the first cash flow in the NPV formula from cell B4, which contains the cash flow for year 1, rather than B3, which contains the immediate investment in year 0? It turns out that Excel always assumes that the first cash flow comes after one period, the next after two periods, and so on. If the first cash flow actually comes at year 0, we do not want it discounted, nor do we want later cash flows discounted for an extra period. Therefore, we don't include the immediate cash flow in the NPV function. Instead, we add it undiscounted to the NPV of other cash flows. See cell D9 for the formula.

Be careful with the timing of cash flows when you use the NPV function. If in doubt, discount each cash flow and add them up, as in cell C7.

The formulas used in column C (specifically, in cells C3 through C7) and spelled out in column D all contain 1.07. What if you want to see how the PVs change at a different discount rate, say, 9%? You would have to change each of the formulas manually. However, there is an easier way. Instead of repeatedly replacing 1.07 with 1.09 in each of those cells, first enter the appropriate discount rate in cell B1, and then replace every incidence of 1.07 with (1 + B1) in column C. This tells Excel that the discount factor is 1 plus the number in cell B1, where the discount rate resides. (The dollar signs in B1 ensure that the Excel formula always refers to exactly that cell, regardless of where the formula is located in the spreadsheet.) Now you can easily experiment with different discount rates by changing just one number, the rate entered in cell B1; Excel will recalculate the PVs and NPV automatically using that rate.

For example, the formula used in cell C4 and displayed in D4 become =C4/(1 + B1)^A4. The NPV formula becomes =NPV(B1, B4:B6) + B3. The "live" version of Spreadsheet 8.1, which is available in Connect, is set up in this way.

Spreadsheet Questions

1. Go to the spreadsheet version of Spreadsheet 8.1. How does NPV change if the discount rate increases? What discount rate would drive NPV down to zero?

2. Try calculating the office project's NPV using the formula =NPV(B1, B3:B6), using a discount rate of 7%. You should find that NPV decreases by a factor of exactly 1/1.07. Why?

Brief solutions appear at the end of the chapter.

SPREADSHEET 8.1 Forecast cash flows and present values for the revised office project

	A	B	C	D
1	Cost of Capital:	0.07		
2	Year	Cash Flow ($ millions)	PV	Formula for Column C (Note the = sign before formula)
3	0	−375	−375.0	=B3
4	1	25	23.4	=B4/1.07^A4
5	2	25	21.8	=B5/1.07^A5
6	3	475	387.7	=B6/1.07^A6
7		Sum (NPV):	57.9	=SUM(C3:C6)
8				
9		Using Excel's NPV function:	57.9	=NPV(.07,B4:B6) + B3

8.2 The Internal Rate of Return Rule

Instead of calculating a project's net present value, companies often prefer to ask whether the project's return is higher or lower than the opportunity cost of capital. For example, think back to the original proposal to build an office block. You planned to invest $350,000 to get back a cash flow of $C_1 = \$400,000$ in 1 year. Therefore, you forecast a profit on the venture of $400,000 − $350,000 = $50,000. In a one-period project like this one, it is easy to calculate the rate of return. Simply compute end-of-year profit per dollar invested in the project:

$$\text{Rate of return} = \frac{\text{profit}}{\text{investment}} = \frac{C_1 - \text{investment}}{\text{investment}} = \frac{\$400{,}000 - \$350{,}000}{\$350{,}000}$$

$$= .1429, \text{ or about } 14.3\%$$

The alternative of investing in a U.S. Treasury bill would provide a return of only 7%. Thus the return on your office building is higher than the opportunity cost of capital.[2]

This suggests two rules for deciding whether to go ahead with an investment project:

1. **The NPV rule.** Invest in any project that has a positive NPV when its cash flows are discounted at the opportunity cost of capital.
2. **The rate of return rule.** Invest in any project offering a rate of return that is higher than the opportunity cost of capital.

Both rules set the same cutoff point. An investment that is on the knife edge with an NPV of zero will also have a rate of return that is just equal to the cost of capital.

Suppose that the rate of interest on Treasury securities is not 7% but 14.3%. Because your office project also offers a return of 14.3%, the rate of return rule suggests that there is now nothing to choose between taking the project and leaving your money in Treasury securities.

The NPV rule likewise tells you that if the interest rate is 14.3%, the project is evenly balanced with an NPV of zero:

$$\text{NPV} = C_0 + \frac{C_1}{1 + r} = -\$350{,}000 + \frac{\$400{,}000}{1.143} = 0$$

The project would make you neither richer nor poorer; it is worth just what it costs. Thus, the NPV rule and the rate of return rule both give the same decision on accepting the project.

A Closer Look at the Rate of Return Rule

We know that if the office project's cash flows are discounted at a rate of 7%, the project has a net present value of $23,832. If they are discounted at a rate of 14.3%, it has an NPV of zero. Figure 8.2 plots the project's NPV for a variety of discount rates. This is often called the *NPV profile* of the project. Notice two important things about Figure 8.2:

BEYOND THE PAGE

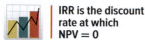

IRR is the discount rate at which NPV = 0

mhhe.com/brealey9e

1. The project rate of return (in our example, 14.3%) is also the discount rate that would give the project a zero NPV. This gives us a useful definition: **The rate of return is the discount rate at which NPV equals zero.**
2. If the opportunity cost of capital is less than the project rate of return, then the NPV of your project is positive. If the cost of capital is greater than the project rate of return, then NPV is negative. Thus, for this accept-or-reject decision, the rate of return rule and the NPV rule are equivalent.

Calculating the Rate of Return for Long-Lived Projects

There is no ambiguity in calculating the rate of return for an investment that generates a single payoff after one period. But how do we calculate return when the project produces cash flows in several periods? Just think back to the definition that we introduced above—*the project rate of return is also the discount rate that gives the project*

---

[2] Recall that we are assuming the profit on the office building is risk-free. Therefore, the opportunity cost of capital is the rate of return on other risk-free investments.

FIGURE 8.2 The value of the office project is lower when the discount rate is higher. The project has a positive NPV if the discount rate is less than 14.3%.

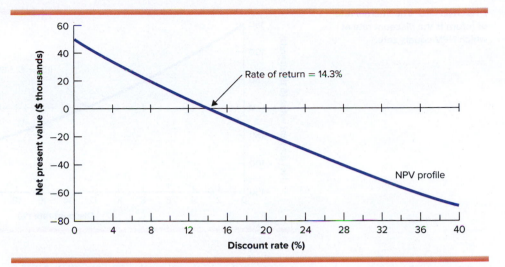

a zero NPV. We can use this idea to find the return on a project that has many cash flows. **The discount rate that gives the project a zero NPV is known as the project's internal rate of return, or IRR. It is also called the discounted cash-flow (DCF) rate of return.**

Let's calculate the IRR for the revised office project. If you rent out the office block for 3 years, the cash flows are as follows:

Year:	0	1	2	3
Cash flows	−$375,000	+$25,000	+$25,000	+$475,000

The IRR is the discount rate at which these cash flows would have zero NPV. Thus,

$$\text{NPV} = -\$375,000 + \frac{\$25,000}{1 + \text{IRR}} + \frac{\$25,000}{(1 + \text{IRR})^2} + \frac{\$475,000}{(1 + \text{IRR})^3} = 0$$

There is no simple general method for solving this equation to find the IRR. You have to rely on a little trial and error. Let us arbitrarily try a zero discount rate. This gives an NPV of $150,000:

$$\text{NPV} = -\$375,000 + \frac{\$25,000}{1.0} + \frac{\$25,000}{(1.0)^2} + \frac{\$475,000}{(1.0)^3} = \$150,000$$

With a zero discount rate the NPV is positive. So it looks as if the IRR is greater than zero.

The next step might be to try a discount rate of 50%. In this case, NPV is –$206,481:

$$\text{NPV} = -\$375,000 + \frac{\$25,000}{1.50} + \frac{\$25,000}{(1.50)^2} + \frac{\$475,000}{(1.50)^3} = -\$206,481$$

At this higher discount rate, NPV turns negative. So the IRR should lie somewhere between zero and 50%. In Figure 8.3, we have plotted the net present values for a range of discount rates. You can see that a discount rate of 12.56% gives an NPV of zero. Therefore, the IRR is 12.56%. You can always find the IRR by plotting an NPV profile, as in Figure 8.3, but it is quicker and more accurate to let a spreadsheet or specially programmed financial calculator do the trial and error for you. The nearby Spreadsheet Solution and Financial Calculator boxes illustrate how to do so.

The rate of return rule tells you to accept a project if the rate of return exceeds the opportunity cost of capital. You can see from Figure 8.3 why this makes sense. Because the NPV profile is downward-sloping, the project has a positive NPV as long as the opportunity cost of capital is less than the project's 12.56% IRR. If the opportunity

FIGURE 8.3 The internal rate of return is the discount rate at which NPV equals zero.

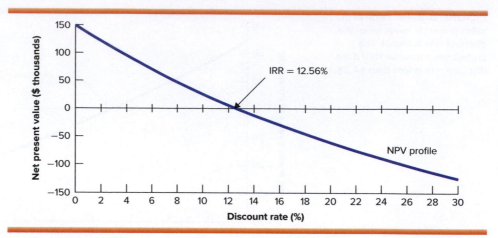

FIGURE 8.3 The internal rate of return is the discount rate at which NPV equals zero.

cost of capital is higher than the 12.56% IRR, NPV is negative. Therefore, when we compare the project IRR with the opportunity cost of capital, we are effectively asking whether the project has a positive NPV. This was true for our one-period office project. It is also true for our three-period office project. Thus, **the rate of return rule will give the same answer as the NPV rule** *as long as the NPV of a project declines smoothly as the discount rate increases.*[3]

The usual agreement between the net present value and internal rate of return rules should not be a surprise. Both are *discounted cash-flow* methods of choosing between projects. Both are concerned with identifying those projects that make shareholders better off, and both recognize that companies always have a choice: They can invest in a project, or if the project is not sufficiently attractive, they can give the money back to shareholders and let them invest it for themselves in the capital market.

BEYOND THE PAGE

Interpreting the IRR

mhhe.com/brealey9e

8.2 Self-Test

Suppose the cash flow in year 3 is only $420,000. Redraw Figure 8.3. How would the IRR change?

A Word of Caution

Some people confuse the internal rate of return on a project with the opportunity cost of capital. Remember that the project IRR measures the profitability of the project. It is an *internal* rate of return in the sense that it depends only on the project's own cash flows. The opportunity cost of capital is the standard for deciding whether to accept the project. It is equal to the return offered by equivalent-risk investments in the capital market.

Some Pitfalls with the Internal Rate of Return Rule

Many firms use the internal rate of return rule instead of net present value. We think that this is a pity. When used properly, the two rules lead to the same decision, but the rate of return rule has several pitfalls that can trap the unwary. In particular, it is poorly suited to choosing between two (or more) competing proposals. Here are three examples.

---

[3] In Chapter 6, we showed how to calculate the yield to maturity on a bond. A bond's yield to maturity is simply its IRR by another name.

Calculating internal rate of return in Excel is as easy as listing the project cash flows. For example, to calculate the IRR of the office-block project, you could simply type in its cash flows as in the spreadsheet shown here, and then calculate IRR as we do in cell E4. As always, the interest rate is returned as a decimal.

	A	B	C	D	E	F
1	**Calculating IRR by using a spreadsheet**					
2						
3	Year	Cash Flow				Formula
4	0	−375,000		IRR=	0.1256	=IRR(B4:B7)
5	1	25,000				
6	2	25,000				
7	3	475,000				

Pitfall 1: Mutually Exclusive Projects   We have seen that firms are seldom faced with take-it-or-leave-it projects. Usually, they need to choose from a number of mutually exclusive alternatives. Given a choice between several competing projects, you should accept the one that adds most to shareholder wealth. This is the one with the highest NPV.

But what about the rate of return rule? Would it make sense just to choose the project with the highest internal rate of return? Unfortunately, no. Mutually exclusive projects involve a dangerous pitfall for users of the IRR rule.

Consider once more the two office-block proposals from Section 8.1. You initially intended to invest $350,000 in the building and then sell it at the end of the year for $400,000. Under the revised proposal, you planned to invest $375,000, rent out the offices for 3 years at a fixed annual rent of $25,000, and then sell the building for $450,000. The following table shows the cash flows, IRRs, and NPVs for the two projects:

Year:	0	1	2	3	IRR	NPV at 7%
Initial proposal	−350,000	+400,000			14.29%	+$23,832
Revised proposal	−375,000	+25,000	+25,000	+475,000	12.56%	+$57,942

Both projects are good investments; both offer a positive NPV. But the revised proposal has the higher net present value and, therefore, is the better choice. Unfortunately, the superiority of the revised proposal doesn't show up as a higher rate of return. The IRR rule seems to say you should go for the initial proposal because it has the higher IRR. If you follow the IRR rule, you have the satisfaction of earning a 14.29% rate of return; if you use NPV, you are nearly $58,000 richer.

Figure 8.4 shows why the IRR rule gives the wrong signal. The figure plots the NPV of each project for different discount rates. These two NPV profiles cross at an interest rate of 11.72%. So if the opportunity cost of capital is higher than 11.72%, the initial proposal, with its rapid cash inflow, is the superior investment. If the cost of capital is lower than 11.72%, then the revised proposal dominates. Depending on the discount rate, either proposal may be superior. For the 7% cost of capital that we have assumed, the revised proposal is the better choice.

Now consider the IRR of each proposal. The IRR is simply the discount rate at which NPV equals zero, that is, the discount rate at which the NPV profile crosses the horizontal axis in Figure 8.4. As noted, these rates are 14.29% for the initial proposal and 12.56% for the revised proposal. However, as you can see from Figure 8.4, the higher IRR for the initial proposal does not mean that it has a higher NPV.

We saw in Chapter 5 that the formulas for the present and future values of level annuities and one-time cash flows are built into financial calculators. However, as the example of the office block illustrates, most investment projects entail multiple cash flows that cannot be expected to remain level over time. Fortunately, many calculators are equipped to handle problems involving a sequence of uneven cash flows. In general, the procedure is quite simple. You enter the cash flows one by one into the calculator, and then you press the *IRR* key to find the project's internal rate of return. The first cash flow you enter is interpreted as coming immediately, the next cash flow is interpreted as coming at the end of one period, and so on. We can illustrate using the office block as an example. To find the project IRR, you would use the following sequence of keystrokes:*

−375,000	CFj
25,000	CFj
25,000	CFj
475,000	CFj
	⬜ (IRR/YR)

The calculator should display the value 12.56%, the project's internal rate of return.

To calculate project NPV, the procedure is similar. You need to enter the discount rate in addition to the project cash flows, and then simply press the *NPV* key. Here is the specific sequence of keystrokes, assuming that the opportunity cost of capital is 7%:

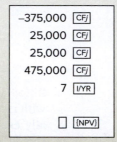

−375,000	CFj
25,000	CFj
25,000	CFj
475,000	CFj
7	I/YR
	⬜ (NPV)

The calculator should display the value 57,942, the project's NPV when the discount rate is 7%.

By the way, you can check that NPV = 0 when the discount rate equals the IRR. Enter 12.56 (the project's IRR) as the interest rate, and you will find that NPV is just about zero (it is not exactly zero, because we are rounding off the IRR to only two decimal places).

---

* Various calculators entail minor variations on these key strokes. For example, on the HP12C, the first cash flow is entered using the CF_0 key, to signify that the cash flow comes immediately and not after 1 year. The other cash flows are entered using the CF_j key. On the Texas Instruments BAII Plus calculator, you would begin by hitting the *CF* key to signify that the following entries should be interpreted as cash flows. Each cash flow entry is then followed by the down arrow, rather than the CF_j key. After hitting the *IRR* key, you would then hit *CPT* (the compute key). If you don't have your own financial calculator, you can download an emulator onto your computer or phone and practice using that. See the nearby Beyond the Page icon.

BEYOND THE PAGE

Finding NPV and IRR on financial calculators

mhhe.com/brealey9e

In our example, both projects involved the same outlay, but the revised proposal had the longer life. The IRR rule mistakenly favored the quick payback project with the high percentage return but the lower NPV. **Remember, a high IRR is not an end in itself. You want projects that increase the value of the firm. Projects that earn a good rate of return for a long time often have higher NPVs than those that offer high percentage rates of return but die young.**

FIGURE 8.4 The initial proposal offers a higher IRR than the revised proposal, but its NPV is lower if the discount rate is less than 11.72%

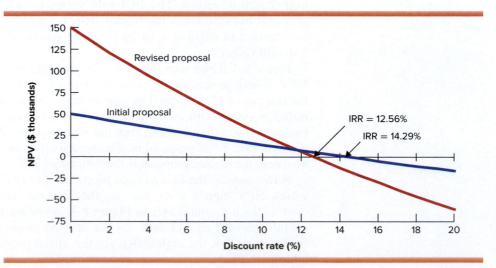

8.3 | Self-Test

A rich, friendly, and probably slightly unbalanced benefactor offers you the opportunity to invest $1 million in two mutually exclusive ways. The payoffs are:

a. $2 million after 1 year, a 100% return.
b. $300,000 a year forever.

Neither investment is risky, and safe securities are yielding 7%. Which investment will you take? You can't take both, so the choices are mutually exclusive. Do you want to earn a high percentage return, or do you want to be rich?

Pitfall 1a: Mutually Exclusive Projects Involving Different Outlays   A similar misranking also may occur when comparing projects with the same lives but different outlays. In this case, the IRR may mistakenly favor small projects with high rates of return but low NPVs. When you are faced with a straightforward either-or choice, the simple solution is to compare their NPVs. However, if you are determined to use the IRR rule, there is a way to do so. We explain how in the appendix.

8.4 | Self-Test

Your wacky benefactor (see Self-Test 8.3) now offers you the choice of two opportunities:

a. Invest $1,000 today and quadruple your money—a 300% return—in 1 year with no risk.
b. Invest $1 million for 1 year at a guaranteed 50% return.

Which will you take? Do you want to earn a wonderful rate of return (300%), or do you want to be rich? Safe securities still yield 7%.

Pitfall 2: Lending or Borrowing?   Remember our condition for the IRR rule to work: The project's NPV must fall as the discount rate increases. Now consider the following projects:

Project	Cash Flows (dollars)		IRR (%)	NPV at 10%
	C_0	C_1		
A	−100	+150	+50	+$36.4
B	+100	−150	+50	−36.4

Each project has an IRR of 50%. In other words, if you discount the cash flows at 50%, both projects would have zero NPV.

Does this mean that the two projects are equally attractive? Clearly not. In the case of project A we are paying out $100 now and getting $150 back at the end of the year. That is better than any bank account. But what about project B? Here we are getting paid $100 now, but we have to pay out $150 at the end of the year. That is equivalent to borrowing money at 50%.

If someone asked you whether 50% was a good rate of interest, you could not answer unless you also knew whether that person was proposing to lend or borrow at that rate. Lending money at 50% is great (as long as the borrower does not flee the country), but borrowing at 50% is not usually a good deal (unless, of course, you plan to flee the country). When you lend money, you want a *high* rate of return; when you borrow, you want a *low* rate of return.

If you plot a graph like Figure 8.2 for project B, you will find the NPV *increases* as the discount rate increases. (*Try it!*) Obviously, the rate of return rule will not work in this case.

Project B is a fairly obvious trap, but if you want to make sure you don't fall into it, calculate the project's NPV. For example, suppose that the cost of capital is 10%. Then the NPV of project A is +$36.4 and the NPV of project B is −$36.4. The NPV rule correctly warns us away from a project that is equivalent to borrowing money at 50%.

When NPV rises as the interest rate rises, the rate of return rule is reversed: A project is acceptable only if its internal rate of return is *less* than the opportunity cost of capital.

Pitfall 3: Multiple Rates of Return   Here is a tricky problem: King Coal Corporation is considering a project to strip-mine coal. The project requires an investment of $210 million and is expected to produce a cash inflow of $125 million in the first 2 years, building up to $175 million in years 3 and 4. However, the company is obliged in year 5 to reclaim the land at a cost of $400 million. At a 20% opportunity cost of capital the project has an NPV of $5.9 million.

To find the IRR of King Coal's project, we have calculated the NPV for various discount rates and plotted the results in Figure 8.5. You can see that there are *two* discount rates at which NPV = 0. That is, *each* of the following statements holds:

$$\text{NPV} = -210 + \frac{\$125}{1.03} + \frac{125}{1.03^2} + \frac{175}{1.03^3} + \frac{175}{1.03^4} - \frac{400}{1.03^5} = 0$$

and

$$\text{NPV} = -210 + \frac{\$125}{1.25} + \frac{125}{1.25^2} + \frac{175}{1.25^3} + \frac{175}{1.25^4} - \frac{400}{1.25^5} = 0$$

In other words, the investment has an IRR of both 3% *and* 25%. The reason for this is the double change in the sign of the cash flows. There can be as many different internal rates of return as there are changes in the sign of the cash-flow stream.[4]

FIGURE 8.5 King Coal's project has two internal rates of return. NPV = 0 when the discount rate is either 3% or 25%.

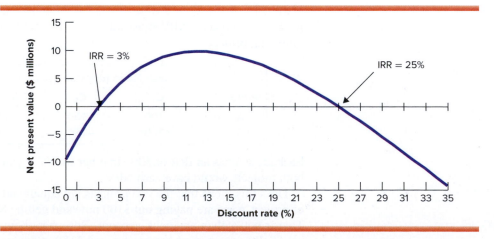

_____

[4] There may be *fewer* IRRs than the number of sign changes. You may even encounter projects for which there is *no* IRR. For example, there is no IRR for a project that has cash flows of +$1,000 in year 0, −$3,000 in year 1, and +$2,500 in year 2. If you don't believe us, try plotting NPV for different discount rates. Can such a project ever have a negative NPV?

Is the coal mine worth developing? The simple IRR rule—accept if the IRR is greater than the cost of capital—won't help. For example, you can see from Figure 8.5 that with a low cost of capital (less than 3%) the project has a negative NPV. It has a positive NPV only if the cost of capital is between 3% and 25%.

Decommissioning and clean-up costs, which make King Coal's final cash flow negative, can sometimes be huge. For example, the ultimate cost of removing North Sea oil platforms in the United Kingdom is estimated to be more than $60 billion. It can cost more than $300 million to decommission a nuclear power plant. These are obvious examples where cash flows go from positive to negative, but you can probably think of a number of other cases where the company needs to plan for later expenditures. Ships periodically need to go into dry dock for a refit, hotels may receive a major facelift, machine parts may need replacement, and so on.

Whenever the cash-flow stream is expected to change sign more than once, the project typically has more than one IRR and there is no simple IRR rule. It is possible to get around the problem of multiple rates of return by calculating a *modified internal rate of return (MIRR)*. We explain how to do so in the appendix to this chapter. However, it is much easier in such cases to abandon the IRR rule and just calculate project NPV.

8.3 The Profitability Index

profitability index
Ratio of net present value to initial investment.

The **profitability index** measures the net present value of a project *per dollar of investment:*

$$\text{Profitability index} = \frac{\text{net present value}}{\text{initial investment}} \qquad (8.2)$$

For example, our initial proposal to construct an office building involved an investment of $350,000 and had an NPV of $23,832. Its profitability index[5] was

$$\frac{23,832}{350,000} = .068$$

The profitability index is also known as the *benefit-cost ratio*. The "benefit" of the project is its net present value. The "cost" is the required investment. The index measures the benefit realized per dollar of cost.

Any project with a positive profitability index must also have a positive NPV, so it would seem that either criterion must result in identical decisions. Why go to the trouble of calculating the profitability index? The answer is that whenever there is a limit on the amount the company can spend, it makes sense to concentrate on getting the biggest bang for each investment buck. In other words, when there is a shortage of funds, the firm needs to pick those projects that have the highest profitability index.

Let us illustrate. Assume that you are faced with the following investment opportunities:

	Cash Flows ($ millions)				
Project	C_0	C_1	C_2	NPV at 10%	Profitability Index
C	−10	+30	+5	21	21/10 = 2.1
D	−5	+5	+20	16	16/5 = 3.2
E	−5	+5	+15	12	12/5 = 2.4

---

[5] Sometimes the profitability index is defined as the ratio of total present value (rather than *net* present value) to required investment. By this definition, all the profitability indexes calculated below are increased by 1. For example, the office building's profitability index would be PV/investment = 373,832/350,000 = 1.068. Note that project rankings under either definition are identical.

All three projects are attractive, but suppose that the firm is limited to spending $10 million. In that case, you can invest either in project C *or* in projects D and E, but you can't invest in all three. The solution is to start with the project that has the highest profitability index and continue until you run out of money. In our example, D provides the highest NPV per dollar invested, followed by E. These two projects exactly use up the $10 million budget. Between them they add $28 million to shareholder wealth. The alternative of investing in C would have added only $21 million.

Capital Rationing

capital rationing
Limit set on the amount of funds available for investment.

Economists use the term **capital rationing** to refer to a shortage of funds available for investment. In simple cases of capital rationing, the profitability index can measure which projects to accept.[6] But that raises a question. Most large corporations can obtain very large sums of money on fair terms and at short notice. So why does top management sometimes tell subordinates that capital is limited and that they may not exceed a specified amount of capital spending? There are two reasons.

Soft Rationing   For many firms, the limits on capital funds are "soft." By this we mean that the capital rationing is not imposed by investors. Instead, the limits are imposed by top management. For example, suppose that you are an ambitious, upwardly mobile junior manager. You are keen to expand your part of the business, and as a result you tend to overstate the investment opportunities. Rather than trying to determine which of your many bright ideas are truly worthwhile, senior management may find it simpler to impose a limit on the amount that you and other junior managers can spend. This limit forces you to set your own priorities.

Even if capital is not rationed, other resources may be. For example, very rapid growth can place considerable strains on management and the organization. A somewhat rough-and-ready response to this problem is to ration the amount of capital that the firm spends.

Hard Rationing   Soft rationing should never cost the firm anything. If the limits on investment become so tight that truly good projects are being passed up, then management should raise more money and relax the limits it has imposed on capital spending. But what if there is "hard rationing," meaning that the firm actually *cannot* raise the money it needs? This may not be a common problem for large, publicly owned corporations, but in many countries some of the largest businesses are owned by the government. Suppose that you are the manager of a state-owned enterprise (SEI), where you do not have the freedom to raise new capital. In that case, you may be forced to pass up positive-NPV projects. You may still be interested in net present value, but you now need to select the package of projects that is within the company's resources and yet gives the highest net present value. This is when the profitability index can be useful.

Pitfalls of the Profitability Index

The profitability index is sometimes used to rank projects even when there is neither soft nor hard capital rationing. In this case the unwary user may be led to favor small projects over larger projects that have higher NPVs. The profitability index was designed to select projects with the most bang per buck—the greatest NPV per dollar spent. That's the right objective when bucks are limited. When they are not, a bigger bang is always better than a smaller one, even when more bucks are spent. This is another case where project comparisons can go awry once we abandon the NPV rule. Self-Test 8.5 is a numerical example.

---

[6] Unfortunately, when capital is rationed in more than one period, or when personnel, production capacity, or other resources are rationed in addition to capital, it isn't always possible to get the NPV-maximizing package just by ranking projects on their profitability index. Tedious trial and error may be called for, or linear programming methods may be used.

8.5   Self-Test

Calculate the profitability indexes of the two pairs of mutually exclusive investments in Self-Tests 8.3 and 8.4. Use a 7% discount rate. Does the profitability index give the right ranking in each case?

8.4   The Payback Rule

A project with a positive net present value is worth more than it costs. So whenever a firm invests in such a project, it is making its shareholders better off.

These days almost every large corporation calculates the NPV of proposed investments, but management may also consider other criteria when making investment decisions. When properly used, the internal rate of return and profitability index lead to the same decisions as net present value. However, payback is no better than a very rough guide to an investment's worth.

We suspect that you have often heard conversations that go something like this: "A washing machine costs about $800. But we are currently spending $6 a week, or around $300 a year, at the Laundromat. So the washing machine should pay for itself in less than 3 years." You have just encountered the payback rule.

payback period
Time until cash flows recover the initial investment in the project.

A project's **payback period** is the length of time before you recover your initial investment. For the washing machine the payback period was just under 3 years. **The payback rule states that a project should be accepted if its payback period is less than a specified cutoff period.** For example, if the cutoff period is 4 years, the washing machine makes the grade; if the cutoff is 2 years, it doesn't.

As a rough rule of thumb, the payback rule may be adequate, but it is easy to see that it can lead to nonsensical decisions, especially when used to compare projects. For example, compare projects F and G. Project F has a 2-year payback and a large positive NPV. Project G also has a 2-year payback but a negative NPV. Project F is clearly superior, but the payback rule ranks both equally. This is because payback does not consider any cash flows that arrive after the payback period. A firm that uses the payback criterion with a cutoff of 2 or more years would accept both F and G despite the fact that only F would increase shareholder wealth.

Project	Cash Flows (dollars)				Payback Period (years)	NPV at 10%
	C_0	C_1	C_2	C_3		
F	−2,000	+1,000	+1,000	+10,000	2	$7,249
G	−2,000	+1,000	+1,000	0	2	−264
H	−2,000	0	+2,000	0	2	−347

A second problem with payback is that it gives equal weight to all cash flows arriving *before* the cutoff period, despite the fact that the more distant flows are less valuable. For example, look at project H. It also has a payback period of 2 years, but it has an even lower NPV than project G. Why? Because its cash flows arrive later within the payback period.

To use the payback rule, a firm has to decide on an appropriate cutoff period. If it uses the same cutoff regardless of project life, it will tend to accept too many short-lived projects and reject too many long-lived ones. The payback rule will bias the firm against accepting long-term projects because cash flows that arrive after the payback period are ignored.

The primary attraction of the payback criterion is its simplicity. But remember that the hard part of project evaluation is forecasting the cash flows, not doing the arithmetic. Today's spreadsheets make discounting a trivial exercise. Therefore, the payback rule saves you only the easy part of the analysis.

We have had little good to say about payback. So why do many companies continue to use it? Senior managers don't truly believe that all cash flows after the payback period are irrelevant. It seems more likely (and more charitable to those managers) that payback survives because there are some offsetting benefits. Thus, managers may point out that payback is the simplest way to *communicate* an idea of project desirability. Investment decisions require discussion and negotiation between people from all parts of the firm, and it is important to have a measure that everyone can understand. Perhaps, also, managers favor quick payback projects even when the projects have lower NPVs because they believe that quicker profits mean quicker promotion. That takes us back to Chapter 1, where we discussed the need to align the objectives of managers with those of the shareholders.

In practice, payback is most commonly used when the capital investment is small or when the merits of the project are so obvious that more formal analysis is unnecessary. For example, if a project is expected to produce constant cash flows for 10 years and the payback period is only 2 years, the project in all likelihood has a positive NPV.

Discounted Payback

Sometimes managers calculate the *discounted-payback period.* This is the number of periods before the present value of prospective cash flows equals or exceeds the initial investment. The discounted-payback measure asks, How long must the project last in order to offer a positive net present value? If the discounted payback meets the company's cutoff period, the project is accepted; if not, it is rejected. The discounted-payback rule has the advantage that it will never accept a negative-NPV project. On the other hand, it still takes no account of cash flows after the cutoff date, so a company that uses the discounted-payback rule risks rejecting good long-term projects and can easily misrank competing projects.

Rather than automatically rejecting any project with a long discounted-payback period, many managers simply use the measure as a warning signal. These managers don't unthinkingly reject a project with a long discounted-payback period. Instead, they check that the proposer is not unduly optimistic about the project's ability to generate cash flows into the distant future. They satisfy themselves that the equipment truly has a long life or that competitors will not enter the market and eat into the project's cash flows.

8.6   Self-Test

A project costs $5,000 and will generate annual cash flows of $660 for 20 years. What is the payback period? If the interest rate is 6%, what is the discounted payback period? What is the project NPV? Should the project be accepted?

8.5   More Mutually Exclusive Projects

We've seen that almost all real-world decisions entail either-or choices between competing alternatives. A real estate developer can build an apartment block or an office block on an available lot. Either can be heated with oil or with natural gas. Building can start today or a year from now. All of these choices are said to be *mutually exclusive*. When choosing between mutually exclusive projects, we must calculate the NPV of each alternative and choose the one with the highest positive NPV.

Sometimes, it is enough simply to compare the NPV of two or more projects. But in other cases, the choices you make today will affect your *future* investment opportunities. In that case, choosing between competing projects can be trickier. Here are three important, but often challenging, problems:

- *The investment timing problem.* Should you buy a computer now or wait and think about it again next year? (Here, today's investment is competing with possible future investments.)
- *The choice between long- and short-lived equipment.* Should the company save money today by installing cheaper machinery that will not last as long? (Here, today's decision would accelerate a later investment in machine replacement.)
- *The replacement problem.* When should existing machinery be replaced? (Using it another year could delay investment in more modern equipment.)

We will look at each of these problems in turn.

Problem 1: The Investment Timing Decision

In Example 8.1, Obsolete Technologies is contemplating the purchase of a new computer system. The proposed investment has a net present value of almost $20,000, so it appears that the cost savings would easily justify the expense of the system. However, the financial manager is not persuaded. She reasons that the price of computers is continually falling and, therefore, suggests postponing the purchase, arguing that the NPV of the system will be even higher if the firm waits until the following year. Unfortunately, she has been making the same argument for 10 years, and the company is steadily losing business to competitors with more efficient systems. Is there a flaw in her reasoning?

This is a problem in investment timing. When is it best to commit to a positive-NPV investment? Investment timing problems all involve choices between mutually exclusive investments. You can either proceed with the project now or do so later. You can't do both.

Table 8.1 lays out the basic data for Obsolete. You can see that the cost of the computer is expected to decline from $50,000 today to $45,000 next year, and so on. The new computer system is expected to last for 4 years from the time it is installed. The present value of the savings *at the time of installation* is expected to be $70,000. Thus, if Obsolete invests today, it achieves an NPV of $70,000 − $50,000 = $20,000; if it invests next year, it will have an NPV of $70,000 − $45,000 = $25,000.

Isn't a gain of $25,000 better than one of $20,000? Well, not necessarily—you may prefer to be $20,000 richer *today* than $25,000 richer *next year*. Your decision should depend on the cost of capital. The final column of Table 8.1 shows the value today (year 0) of those net present values at a 10% cost of capital. For example, you can see

TABLE 8.1 Obsolete Technologies: The gain from purchase of a computer is rising, but the NPV today is highest if the computer is purchased in year 3 (dollar values in thousands)

Year of Purchase	Cost of Computer	PV Savings	NPV at Year of Purchase ($r = 10\%$)	NPV Today	
0	$50	$70	$20	$20.0	
1	45	70	25	22.7	
2	40	70	30	24.8	
3	36	70	34	25.5	← optimal purchase date
4	33	70	37	25.3	
5	31	70	39	24.2	

that the discounted value of that $25,000 gain is $25,000/1.10 = $22,700. The financial manager has a point. It is worth postponing investment in the computer: Today's NPV is higher if she waits a year. But the investment should not be postponed indefinitely. You maximize net present value today by buying the computer in year 3.

Notice that you are involved in a trade-off. The sooner you can capture the $70,000 savings the better, but if it costs you less to realize those savings by postponing the investment, it may pay for you to wait. If you postpone purchase by 1 year, the gain from buying a computer rises from $20,000 to $25,000, an increase of 25%. Because the cost of capital is only 10%, it pays to postpone at least until year 1. If you postpone from year 3 to year 4, the gain rises from $34,000 to $37,000, a rise of just under 9%. Because this is less than the cost of capital, this postponement would not make sense. **The decision rule for investment timing is to choose the investment date that produces the highest net present value** *today.*

BEYOND THE PAGE

 Investment timing decisions

mhhe.com/brealey9e

8.7   Self-Test

Unfortunately, Obsolete Technologies' business is shrinking as the company dithers and dawdles. Its chief financial officer realizes that the savings from installing the new computer will likewise shrink by $4,000 per year, from a present value of $70,000 now, to $66,000 next year, then to $62,000, and so on. Redo Table 8.1 with this new information. When should Obsolete buy the new computer?

Problem 2: The Choice between Long- and Short-Lived Equipment

Suppose the firm is forced to choose between two machines, I and J. The machines are designed differently but have identical capacity and do exactly the same job. Machine I costs $15,000 and will last 3 years. It costs $4,000 per year to run. Machine J is an "economy" model, costing only $10,000, but it will last only 2 years and costs $6,000 per year to run.

Because the two machines produce exactly the same product, the only way to choose between them is on the basis of cost. Suppose we compute the present value of the costs:

	Costs (thousands of dollars)				
Year:	0	1	2	3	PV at 6%
Machine I	15	4	4	4	$25.69
Machine J	10	6	6	—	21.00

Should we take machine J, the one with the lower present value of costs? Not necessarily. All we have shown is that machine J offers 2 years of service for a lower total cost than 3 years of service from machine I. But is the *annual* cost of using J lower than that of I?

Suppose the financial manager in corporate headquarters agrees to buy machine I and pay for its operating costs out of her budget. She then charges the plant manager an annual amount for use of the machine. There will be three equal payments starting in year 1. Obviously, the financial manager has to make sure that the present value of these payments equals the present value of the costs of machine I, $25,690. When the

equivalent annual annuity
The cash flow per period with the same present value as the cost of buying and operating a machine.

discount rate is 6%, the payment stream with such a present value turns out to be $9,610 a year. In other words, the cost of buying and operating machine I over its 3-year life is equivalent to an annual charge of $9,610 a year for 3 years. This figure is therefore termed the **equivalent annual annuity** of operating machine I.

	Costs (thousands of dollars)				
Year:	0	1	2	3	PV at 6%
Machine I	15	4	4	4	$25.69
Equivalent annual annuity		9.61	9.61	9.61	25.69

How did we know that an annual charge of $9,610 has a present value of $25,690? The annual charge is a 3-year annuity. So we calculate the value of this annuity and set it equal to $25,690:

Equivalent annual annuity × 3-year annuity factor = PV of costs = $25,690

If the cost of capital is 6%, the 3-year annuity factor is 2.6730. So

$$\text{Equivalent annual annuity} = \frac{\text{PV of costs}}{\text{3-year annuity factor}} \qquad (8.3)$$

$$= \frac{\$25,690}{\text{3-year annuity factor}} = \frac{\$25,690}{2.6730} = \$9,610$$

If we make a similar calculation of costs for machine J, we get:

	Costs (thousands of dollars)			
Year:	0	1	2	PV at 6%
Machine J	10	6	6	$21.00
Equivalent annual annuity		11.45	11.45	21.00

We see now that machine I is better because its equivalent annual cost is less ($9,610 for I versus $11,450 for J). In other words, the financial manager could afford to set a lower *annual* charge for the use of I. **We thus have a rule for comparing assets with different lives:** *Select the machine that has the lowest equivalent annual annuity.*

BEYOND THE PAGE

Equivalent annual annuities

mhhe.com/brealey9e

Think of the equivalent annual annuity as the level annual charge that is necessary to recover the present value of investment outlays and operating costs.[7] The annual charge continues for the life of the equipment. Calculate the equivalent annual annuity by dividing the present value by the annuity factor.

Example **8.3 ▶**   Equivalent Annual Annuity

You need a new car. You can either purchase one outright for $15,000 or lease one for 7 years for $3,000 a year. If you buy the car today, you can sell it in 7 years for $500. The discount rate is 10%. Should you buy or lease? What is the maximum lease payment you would be willing to pay?

The present value of the cost of purchasing is

$$PV = \$15,000 - \frac{\$500}{(1.10)^7} = \$14,743$$

---

[7] We have implicitly assumed that inflation is zero. If that is not the case, it would be better to calculate the equivalent annual annuities for machines I and J in real terms, using the real rate of interest to calculate the annuity factor.

Thus, the equivalent annual cost of purchasing the car is the annuity with this present value:

$$\text{Equivalent annual annuity} \times \text{7-year annuity factor at 10\%} = \text{PV costs of buying}$$
$$= \$14{,}743$$

$$\text{Equivalent annual annuity} = \frac{\$14{,}743}{\text{7-year annuity factor}} = \frac{\$14{,}743}{4.8684} = \$3{,}028$$

Therefore, the annual lease payment of $3,000 is less than the equivalent annual annuity of buying the car. You should be willing to pay up to $3,028 annually to lease. ∎

Example 8.4 ▶ Another Equivalent Annual Annuity

Low-energy light bulbs typically cost $3.50, have a life of 9 years, and use about $1.60 of electricity a year. Conventional light bulbs are cheaper to buy because they cost only $.50. On the other hand, they last only about a year and use about $6.60 of energy. If the discount rate is 5%, which product is cheaper to use?

To answer this question, you need first to convert the initial cost of each bulb to an annual figure and then to add in the annual energy cost.[8] The following table sets out the calculations:

	Low-Energy Bulb	Conventional Bulb
1. Initial cost ($)	3.50	0.50
2. Estimated life (years)	9	1
3. Annuity factor at 5%	7.1078	0.9524
4. Equivalent annual annuity ($) = (1)/(3)	0.49	0.52
5. Annual energy cost ($)	1.60	6.60
6. Total annual cost ($) = (4) + (5)	2.09	7.12
Assumption: Energy costs are incurred at the end of each year.		

It seems that a low-energy bulb provides an annual saving of about $7.12 – $2.09 = $5.03. ∎

Problem 3: When to Replace an Old Machine

Our earlier comparison of machines I and J took the life of each machine as fixed. In practice, the point at which equipment is replaced reflects economics, not physical collapse. We, rather than nature, usually decide when to replace. For example, we usually replace a car not when it finally breaks down but when it becomes more expensive and troublesome to maintain than a replacement.

Here is an example of a replacement problem: You are operating an old machine that will last 2 more years before it gives up the ghost. It costs $12,000 per year to operate. You can replace it now with a new machine that costs $25,000 but is much more efficient (only $8,000 per year in operating costs) and will last for 5 years. Should you replace the machine now or stick with it for a while longer? The opportunity cost of capital is 6%.

We calculate the NPV of the new machine and its equivalent annual annuity in the following table:

	Costs (thousands of dollars)						
Year:	0	1	2	3	4	5	PV at 6%
New machine	25	8	8	8	8	8	$58.70
Equivalent annual annuity		13.93	13.93	13.93	13.93	13.93	58.70

---

[8] Our calculations ignore any environmental costs.

The cash flows of the new machine are equivalent to an annuity of $13,930 per year. So we can equally well ask whether you would want to replace your old machine, which costs $12,000 a year to run, with a new one costing $13,930 a year. When the question is posed this way, the answer is obvious. As long as your old machine costs only $12,000 a year, why replace it with a new machine that costs $1,930 a year more?

8.8   Self-Test

Machines K and L are mutually exclusive and have the following investment and operating costs. Note that machine K lasts for only 2 years.

Year:	0	1	2	3
K	$10,000	$1,100	$1,200	—
L	12,000	1,100	1,200	$1,300

a. Calculate the equivalent annual annuity of each investment by using a discount rate of 10%. Which machine is the better buy?
b. Now suppose you have an existing machine. You can keep it going for 1 more year only, but it will cost $2,500 in repairs and $1,800 in operating costs. Is it worth replacing now with either K or L?

8.6   A Last Look

We've covered several investment criteria, each with its own nuances. If your head is spinning, you might want to take a look at Table 8.2, which gives an overview and summary of these decision rules.

TABLE 8.2 A comparison of investment decision rules

Criterion	Definition	Investment Rule	Comments
Net present value (NPV)	Present value of cash flows minus initial investment	Accept project if NPV is positive. For mutually exclusive projects, choose the one with the highest (positive) NPV.	The "gold standard" of investment criteria. Only criterion necessarily consistent with maximizing the value of the firm. Provides appropriate rule for choosing between mutually exclusive investments. Only pitfall involves capital rationing, when one cannot accept all positive-NPV projects.
Internal rate of return (IRR)	The discount rate at which project NPV equals zero	Accept project if IRR is greater than opportunity cost of capital.	If used properly, results in same accept-reject decision as NPV in the absence of project interactions. However, beware of the following pitfalls: IRR cannot rank mutually exclusive projects—the project with higher IRR may have lower NPV. The simple IRR rule cannot be used in cases of multiple IRRs or an upward-sloping NPV profile.
Profitability index	Ratio of net present value to initial investment	Accept project if profitability index is greater than 0. In case of capital rationing, accept projects with highest profitability index.	Results in same accept-reject decision as NPV in the absence of project interactions. Useful for ranking projects in case of capital rationing, but misleading in the presence of interactions. Cannot rank mutually exclusive projects.
Payback period	Time until the sum of project cash flows equals the initial investment	Accept project if payback period is less than some specified number of years.	A quick and dirty rule of thumb, with several critical pitfalls. Ignores cash flows beyond the acceptable payback period. Ignores discounting. Tends to improperly reject long-lived projects.

TABLE 8.3 Capital budgeting techniques used in practice

Investment Criterion	Percentage of Firms That Always or Almost Always Use Criterion	Average Score on 0–4 Scale (0 = never use; 4 = always use)		
		All Firms	Small Firms	Large Firms
Internal rate of return	76	3.1	2.9	3.4
Net present value	75	3.1	2.8	3.4
Payback period	57	2.5	2.7	2.3
Profitability index	12	0.8	0.9	0.8

Source: J. R. Graham and C. R. Harvey, "The Theory and Practice of Corporate Finance: Evidence from the Field," from *Journal of Financial Economics,* Vol. 60, Issue 2–3, May 2001, pp. 187–243. Copyright © 2001 Elsevier Science.

Clearly, NPV is the gold standard. It is designed to tell you whether an investment will increase the value of the firm and by how much it will do so. It is the only rule that can always be used to rank and choose between mutually exclusive investments. The time that you need to be careful when applying the NPV rule occurs when the firm faces capital rationing. In this case, there may not be enough cash to take every project with a positive NPV, and the firm must then rank projects by the profitability index, that is, net present value per dollar invested.

For managers in the field, discounted cash-flow analysis is in fact the dominant tool for project evaluation. Table 8.3 provides a sample of the results of a large survey of chief financial officers (CFOs). Notice that 75% of firms either always or almost always use NPV or IRR to evaluate projects. The dominance of these criteria is even stronger in larger, presumably more sophisticated, firms. Despite the clear advantages of discounted cash-flow methods, however, firms do use other investment criteria to evaluate projects. For example, just over half of corporations always or almost always compute a project's payback period. The profitability index is routinely computed by about 12% of firms.

What explains such wide use of presumably inferior decision rules? To some extent, these rules present rough reality checks on the project. As we noted in Section 8.4, managers might want to consider some simple ways to describe project profitability, even if they present obvious pitfalls. For example, managers talk casually about quick-payback projects in the same way that investors talk about high-P/E stocks. The fact that they talk about payback does not mean that the payback rule governs their decisions. Shortcuts like payback may work for very simple go-or-no-go decisions, but they are dangerous when used to compare projects.

SUMMARY

What is the net present value of an investment, and how do you calculate it? (*LO8-1*)

The **net present value** of a project measures the difference between its value and cost. NPV is, therefore, the amount that the project will add to shareholder wealth. A company maximizes shareholder wealth by accepting all projects that have a positive NPV.

How is the internal rate of return of a project calculated, and what must one look out for when using the internal rate of return rule? (*LO8-2*)

Instead of asking whether a project has a positive NPV, many businesses prefer to ask whether it offers a higher return than shareholders could expect to get by investing in the capital market. Return is usually defined as the discount rate that would result in a zero NPV. This is known as the **internal rate of return,** or **IRR.** The project is attractive if the IRR exceeds the **opportunity cost of capital.**

There are some pitfalls in using the internal rate of return rule. Be careful about using the IRR when (1) you need to choose between two **mutually exclusive projects,** (2) there is more than one change in the sign of the cash flows, or (3) the early cash flows are positive.

How is the profitability index calculated, and how can it be used to choose between projects when funds are limited? (*LO8-3*)

Why doesn't the payback rule always make shareholders better off? (*LO8-4*)

How can the net present value rule be used to analyze three common problems that involve competing projects: when to postpone an investment expenditure, how to choose between projects with unequal lives, and when to replace equipment? (*LO8-5*)

If there is a shortage of capital, companies need to choose projects that offer the highest net present value per dollar of investment. This measure is known as the **profitability index.**

The net present value rule and the rate of return rule both properly reflect the time value of money. But companies sometimes use rules of thumb to judge projects. One is the payback rule, which states that a project is acceptable if you get your money back within a specified period. The payback rule takes no account of any cash flows that arrive after the payback period and fails to discount cash flows within the payback period.

Sometimes, a project may have a positive NPV if undertaken today but an even higher NPV if the investment is delayed. Choose between these alternatives by comparing their NPVs *today*.

When you have to choose between projects with different lives, you should put them on an equal footing by comparing the **equivalent annual annuity** of the two projects. When you are considering whether to replace an aging machine with a new one, you should compare the annual cost of operating the old one with the equivalent annual annuity of the new one.

LISTING OF EQUATIONS

8.1 $NPV = PV - \text{required investment}$

8.2 $\text{Profitability index} = \dfrac{\text{net present value}}{\text{initial investment}}$

8.3 $\text{Equivalent annual annuity} = \dfrac{\text{present value of costs}}{\text{annuity factor}}$

QUESTIONS AND PROBLEMS

Problems 1–9 refer to two projects with the following cash flows:

Year	Project A	Project B
0	−$200	−$200
1	80	100
2	80	100
3	80	100
4	80	

1. **IRR/NPV.** If the opportunity cost of capital is 11%, which of these projects is worth pursuing? (*LO8-1*)

2. **Mutually Exclusive Investments.** Suppose that you can choose only one of these projects. Which would you choose? The discount rate is still 11%. (*LO8-1*)

3. **IRR/NPV.** Which project would you choose if the opportunity cost of capital is 16%? (*LO8-1*)

4. **IRR.** What are the internal rates of return on projects A and B? (*LO8-2*)

5. **Investment Criteria.** In light of your answers to Problems 2, 3, and 4, is the project with the higher IRR the better project? (*LO8-2*)

6. **Profitability Index.** If the opportunity cost of capital is 11%, what is the profitability index for each project? (*LO8-3*)

7. **Profitability Index.** Is the project with the highest profitability index also the one with the highest NPV? (*LO8-3*)

8. **Payback.** What is the payback period of each project? (*LO8-4*)

9. **Investment Criteria.** Is the project with the shortest payback period also the one with the highest NPV? (*LO8-4*)

10. **NPV and IRR.** A project that costs $3,000 to install will provide annual cash flows of $800 for each of the next 6 years. (*LO8-1 and LO8-2*)
    a. What is NPV if the discount rate is 10%?
    b. How high can the discount rate be before you would reject the project?

11. **NPV.** A proposed nuclear power plant will cost $2.2 billion to build and then will produce cash flows of $300 million a year for 15 years. After that period (in year 15), it must be decommissioned at a cost of $900 million. (*LO8-1 and LO8-2*)
    a. What is project NPV if the discount rate is 5%?
    b. What if the discount rate is 18%?

12. **NPV/IRR.** A new computer system will require an initial outlay of $20,000, but it will increase the firm's cash flows by $4,000 a year for each of the next 8 years. (*LO8-1*)
    a. Is the system worth installing if the required rate of return is 9%?
    b. What if the required return is 14%?
    c. How high can the discount rate be before you would reject the project?

13. **NPV/IRR.** Here are the cash flows for a project under consideration: (*LO8-1 and LO8-2*)
    a. Calculate the project's net present value for discount rates of 0, 50%, and 100%.
    b. What is the IRR of the project?

C_0	C_1	C_2
−$6,750	+$4,500	+$18,000

14. **NPV versus IRR.** Here are the cash flows for two mutually exclusive projects: (*LO8-1 and LO8-2*)

Project	C_0	C_1	C_2	C_3
A	−$20,000	+$8,000	+$8,000	+$ 8,000
B	−20,000	0	0	+25,000

   a. At what interest rates would you prefer project A to B? (*Hint:* Try drawing the NPV profile of each project.)
   b. What is the IRR of each project?

15. **NPV/IRR.** Growth Enterprises believes its latest project, which will cost $80,000 to install, will generate a perpetual growing stream of cash flows. Cash flow at the end of the first year will be $5,000, and cash flows in future years are expected to grow indefinitely at an annual rate of 5%. (*LO8-1 and LO8-2*)
    a. If the discount rate for this project is 10%, what is the project NPV?
    b. What is the project IRR?

16. **IRR/NPV.** Consider the following project with an internal rate of return of 13.1%. (*LO8-2*)
    a. Should you accept or reject the project if the discount rate is 12%?
    b. What is project NPV?

Year	Cash Flow
0	+$100
1	−60
2	−60

17. **Multiple IRRs.** Strip Mining Inc. can develop a new mine at an initial cost of $5 million. The mine will provide a cash flow of $30 million in 1 year. The land then must be reclaimed at a cost of $28 million in the second year. (*LO8-2*)

a. What are the IRRs of this project?
b. Should the firm develop the mine if the discount rate is 10%?
c. What if it is 20%?
d. What if it is 350%?
e. What if it is 400%?

18. **IRR.** Marielle Machinery Works forecasts the following cash flows on a project under consideration. It uses the internal rate of return rule to accept or reject projects. (*LO8-2*)

a. What is the project's IRR?
b. Should this project be accepted if the required return is 12%?

C_0	C_1	C_2	C_3
−$10,000	0	+$7,500	+$8,500

19. **NPV/IRR.** Consider projects A and B: (*LO8-2*)

	Cash Flows (dollars)			
Project	C_0	C_1	C_2	NPV at 10%
A	−30,000	21,000	21,000	+$6,446
B	−50,000	33,000	33,000	+7,273

a. Calculate IRRs for A and B.
b. Which project does the IRR rule suggest is best?
c. Which project is really best?

20. **IRR.** You are offered the chance to participate in a project that produces the following cash flows:

C_0	C_1	C_2
+$5,000	+$4,000	−$11,000

The internal rate of return is 13.6%. If the opportunity cost of capital is 12%, would you accept the offer? (What is the net present value of the project?) (*LO8-2*)

21. **Multiple IRRs.** Consider the following cash flows: (*LO8-2*)

C_0	C_1	C_2	C_3	C_4
−$22	+$20	+$20	+$20	−$40

a. Which two of the following rates are the IRRs of this project: 2.5%, 7.2%. 14.3%, 33.7%, 40.0%?
b. What is project NPV if the discount rate is 5%?
c. What if it is 20%?
d. What if it is 40%?

22. **Profitability Index.** What is the profitability index of a project that costs $10,000 and provides cash flows of $3,000 in years 1 and 2 and $5,000 in years 3 and 4? The discount rate is 9%. (*LO8-3*)

23. **Profitability Index.** Consider the following projects: (*LO8-3*)

Project	C_0	C_1	C_2
A	−$2,100	+$2,000	+$1,200
B	−2,100	+1,440	+1,728

a. Calculate the profitability index for A and B assuming a 22% opportunity cost of capital.
b. According to the profitability index rule, which project(s) should you accept?

24. **Capital Rationing.** You are a manager with an investment budget of $8 million. You may invest in the following projects. Investment and cash-flow figures are in millions of dollars. (*LO8-3*)

Project	Discount Rate (%)	Investment	Annual Cash Flow	Project Life (years)
A	10	3	1	5
B	12	4	1	8
C	8	5	2	4
D	8	3	1.5	3
E	12	3	1	6

a. Which projects should the manager choose?
b. Which projects will be chosen if there is no capital rationing?

25. **Profitability Index versus NPV.** Consider projects A and B with the following cash flows: (*LO8-3*)

	C_0	C_1	C_2	C_3
A	−$36	+$20	+$20	+$20
B	−50	+25	+25	+25

a. Which project has the higher NPV if the discount rate is 10%?
b. Which has the higher profitability index?
c. Which project is most attractive to a firm that can raise an unlimited amount of funds to pay for its investment projects?
d. Which project is most attractive to a firm that is limited in the funds it can raise?

26. **Investment Criteria.** If you insulate your office for $10,000, you will save $1,000 a year in heating expenses. These savings will last forever. (*LO8-1, LO8-2, and LO8-4*)

a. What is the NPV of the investment when the cost of capital is 8%?
b. What if it is 10%?
c. What is the IRR of the investment?
d. What is the payback period on this investment?

27. **Payback.** A project that costs $2,500 to install will provide annual cash flows of $600 for the next 6 years. (*LO8-4*)

a. The firm accepts projects with payback periods of less than 5 years. What is this project's payback period?
b. Will it be accepted?
c. Should this project be pursued if the discount rate is 2%? (What is its NPV?)
d. What if the discount rate is 12%?
e. Will the firm's decision change as the discount rate changes?

28. **Payback and NPV.** A project has a life of 10 years and a payback period of 10 years. Is the project NPV positive or negative? (*LO8-4*)

29. **Payback and NPV.** Here are the expected cash flows for three projects: (*LO8-4*)

Project	Year:	0	1	2	3	4
				Cash Flows (dollars)		
A		−5,000	+1,000	+1,000	+3,000	0
B		−1,000	0	+1,000	+2,000	+3,000
C		−5,000	+1,000	+1,000	+3,000	+5,000

a. What is the payback period on each of the projects?
b. Given that you wish to use the payback rule with a cutoff period of 2 years, which projects would you accept?

    c. If you use a cutoff period of 3 years, which projects would you accept?

    d. If the opportunity cost of capital is 10%, which projects have positive NPVs?

    e. "Payback gives too much weight to cash flows that occur after the cutoff date." True or false?

30. **Investment Criteria.** A new furnace for your small factory will cost $27,000 a year to install and will require ongoing maintenance expenditures of $1,500 a year. But it is far more fuel-efficient than your old furnace and will reduce your consumption of heating oil by 2,400 gallons per year. Heating oil this year will cost $3 a gallon; the price per gallon is expected to increase by $.50 a year for the next 3 years and then to stabilize for the foreseeable future. The furnace will last for 20 years, at which point it will need to be replaced and will have no salvage value. The discount rate is 8%. (*LO8-1, LO8-2, LO8-4, and LO8-5*)

    a. What is the net present value of the investment in the furnace?

    b. What is the IRR?

    c. What is the payback period?

    d. What is the equivalent annual cost of the furnace?

    e. What is the equivalent annual savings derived from the furnace?

    f. Compare the PV of the difference between the equivalent annual cost and savings to your answer to part (a). Are the two measures the same or is one larger?

31. **Mutually Exclusive Investments.** Here are the cash-flow forecasts for two mutually exclusive projects: (*LO8-5*)

	Cash Flows (dollars)	
Year	Project A	Project B
0	−100	−100
1	30	49
2	50	49
3	70	49

    a. Which project would you choose if the opportunity cost of capital is 2%?

    b. Which would you choose if the opportunity cost of capital is 12%?

32. **Equivalent Annual Annuity.** A precision lathe costs $10,000 and will cost $20,000 a year to operate and maintain. If the discount rate is 10% and the lathe will last for 5 years, what is the equivalent annual cost of the tool? (*LO8-5*)

33. **Equivalent Annual Annuity.** A firm can lease a truck for 4 years at a cost of $30,000 annually. It can instead buy a truck at a cost of $80,000, with annual maintenance expenses of $10,000. The truck will be sold at the end of 4 years for $20,000. (*LO8-5*)

    a. What is the equivalent annual cost of buying and maintaining the truck if the discount rate is 10%?

    b. Which is the better option: leasing or buying?

34. **Equivalent Annual Annuity.** Econo-Cool air conditioners cost $300 to purchase, result in electricity bills of $150 per year, and last for 5 years. Luxury Air models cost $500, result in electricity bills of $100 per year, and last for 8 years. The discount rate is 21%. (*LO8-5*)

    a. What is the equivalent annual cost of the Econo-Cool model?

    b. What is the equivalent annual cost of the Luxury Air model?

    c. Which model is more cost-effective?

    d. Now you remember that the inflation rate is expected to be 10% per year for the foreseeable future. Redo parts (a) and (b).

35. **Investment Timing.** You can purchase an optical scanner today for $400. The scanner provides benefits worth $60 a year. The expected life of the scanner is 10 years. Scanners are expected to decrease in price by 20% per year. Suppose the discount rate is 10%. (*LO8-5*)

    1. Should you purchase the scanner today or wait to purchase?

    2. When is the best purchase time?

36. **Replacement Decision.** You are operating an old machine that is expected to produce a cash inflow of $5,000 in each of the next 3 years before it fails. You can replace it now with a new machine that costs $20,000 but is much more efficient and will provide a cash flow of $10,000 a year for 4 years. Should you replace your equipment now? The discount rate is 15%. (*LO8-5*)

37. **Investment Timing.** A classic problem in management of forests is determining when it is most economically advantageous to cut a tree for lumber. When the tree is young, it grows very rapidly. As it ages, its growth slows down. Why is NPV maximized if you cut the tree when its growth rate equals the discount rate? (*LO8-5*)

38. **Replacement Decision.** A forklift will last for only 2 more years. It costs $5,000 a year to maintain. For $20,000 you can buy a new lift that can last for 10 years and should require maintenance costs of only $2,000 a year. (*LO8-5*)

   a. If the discount rate is 4% per year, should you replace the forklift?
   b. What if the discount rate is 12% per year?

SOLUTIONS TO SELF-TEST QUESTIONS

8.1   Even if construction costs are $355,000, NPV is still positive:

$$NPV = PV - \$355,000 = \$357,143 - \$355,000 = \$2,143$$

Therefore, the project is still worth pursuing. The project is viable as long as construction costs are less than the PV of the future cash flow, that is, as long as construction costs are less than $357,143. However, if the opportunity cost of capital is 20%, the PV of the $400,000 sales price is lower and NPV is negative:

$$PV = \$400,000 \times \frac{1}{1.20} = \$333,333$$

$$NPV = PV - \$355,000 = -\$21,667$$

The present value of the future cash flow is not as high when the opportunity cost of capital is higher. The project would need to provide a higher payoff in order to be viable in the face of the higher opportunity cost of capital.

8.2   The IRR is now about 8.3% because

$$NPV = -\$375,000 + \frac{\$25,000}{1.083} + \frac{\$25,000}{(1.083)^2} + \frac{\$420,000}{(1.083)^3} = 0$$

Note in Figure 8.6 that NPV falls to zero as the discount rate reaches 8.3%.

8.3   You want to be rich. The NPV of the long-lived investment is much larger.

$$Short: NPV = -\$1 + \frac{\$2}{1.07} = +\$.869 \text{ million}$$

$$Long: NPV = -\$1 + \frac{\$.3}{.07} = +\$3.286 \text{ million}$$

FIGURE 8.6 NPV falls to zero at an interest rate of 8.3%.

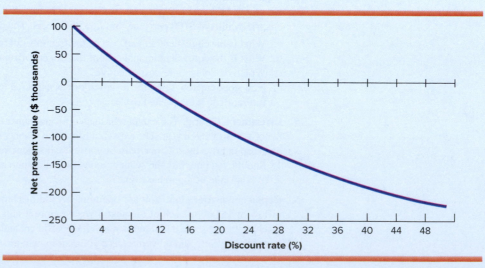

8.4   You want to be richer. The second alternative generates greater value at any reasonable discount rate. Other risk-free investments offer 7%. Therefore,

$$NPV = -\$1,000 + \frac{\$4,000}{1.07} = +\$2,738$$

$$NPV = -\$1,000,000 + \frac{\$1,500,000}{1.07} = +\$401,869$$

8.5   The profitability index gives the correct ranking for the first pair, but the incorrect ranking for the second:

Project	PV	Investment	NPV	Profitability Index (NPV/Investment)
Short	$1,869,159	$1,000,000	$ 869,159	0.869
Long	4,285,714	1,000,000	3,285,714	3.286
Small	3,738	1,000	2,738	2.738
Large	1,401,869	1,000,000	401,869	0.402

8.6   The payback period is $5,000/$660 = 7.6 years. Discounted payback is just over 11 years. Calculate NPV as follows. The present value of a $660 annuity for 20 years at 6% is

$$PV\ annuity = \$7,570$$
$$NPV = -\$5,000 + \$7,570 = +\$2,570$$

The project should be accepted.

8.7

Year of Purchase	Cost of Computer	PV Savings	NPV at Year of Purchase	NPV Today
0	$50	$70	$20	$20
1	45	66	21	19.1
2	40	62	22	18.2
3	36	58	22	16.5
4	33	54	21	14.3
5	31	50	19	11.8

Purchase the new computer now.

8.8

	Year:	0	1	2	3	PV of Costs
K Cash flows		$10,000	$1,100	$1,200		$11,992
Equivalent annual annuity			6,910	6,910		11,992
L Cash flows		12,000	1,100	1,200	$1,300	14,968
Equivalent annual annuity			6,019	6,019	6,019	14,968

Machine L is the better buy. However, it's even better to keep the old machine going for 1 more year. That costs $4,300, which is less than L's equivalent annual cost, $6,019.

SOLUTIONS TO SPREADSHEET QUESTIONS

1.   NPV is zero at .1256, or 12.56%. This is the office project's IRR.

2.   The answer is 54.2. The correct NPV of 57.9 is 7% higher. The Excel function treats the initial cash flow as if it occurs at the end of 1 year, and discounts each successive cash flow by an extra year.

MINICASE

Flowton Products enjoys a steady demand for stainless steel infiltrators used in a number of chemical processes. Revenues from the infiltrator division are $50 million a year, and production costs are $47.5 million. However, the 10 high-precision Munster stamping machines that are used in the production process are coming to the end of their useful life. One possibility is simply to replace each existing machine with a new Munster. These machines would cost $800,000 each and would not involve any additional operating costs. The alternative is to buy 10 centrally controlled Skilboro stampers. Skilboros cost $1.25 million each, but compared with the Munster, they would produce a total saving in operator and material costs of $500,000 a year. Moreover, the Skilboro is sturdily built and would last 10 years, compared with an estimated 7-year life for the Munster.

Analysts in the infiltrator division have produced the accompanying summary table, which shows the forecast total cash flows from the infiltrator business over the life of each machine. Flowton's standard procedures for appraising capital investments involve calculating net present value, internal rate of return, and payback, and these measures are also shown in the table.

As usual, Emily Balsam arrived early at Flowton's head office. She had never regretted joining Flowton. Everything about the place, from the mirror windows to the bell fountain in the atrium, suggested a classy outfit. Ms. Balsam sighed happily and reached for the envelope at the top of her in-tray. It was an analysis from the infiltrator division of the replacement options for the stamper machines. Pinned to the paper was the summary table of cash flows and a note from the CFO, which read, "Emily, I have read through 20 pages of excruciating detail and I still don't know which of these machines we should buy. The NPV calculation seems to indicate that the Skilboro is best, while IRR and payback suggest the opposite. Would you take a look and tell me what we should do and why. You also might check that the calculations are OK."

Can you help Ms. Balsam by writing a memo to the CFO? You need to justify your solution and also to explain why some or all of the measures in the summary table are inappropriate.

		Cash Flows (millions of dollars)				
Year:	0	1–7	8	9	10
Munster					
Investment	−8.0		0	0	0
Revenues		50.0	0	0	0
Costs		47.5	0	0	0
Net cash flow	−8.0	2.5			
NPV at 15%	$2.40 million				
IRR	24.5%				
Payback period	3.2 years				
Skilboro					
Investment	−12.5				
Revenues		50.0	50.0	50.0	50.0
Costs		47.0	47.0	47.0	47.0
Net cash flow	−12.5	3.0	3.0	3.0	3.0
NPV at 15%	$2.56 million				
IRR	20.2%				
Payback period	4.2 years				

APPENDIX

More on the IRR Rule

In Section 8.2, we described several pitfalls that lie in wait for users of the IRR rule. However, there are some tricks that users of the rule may use to circumvent these hazards. In this appendix, we show how you can adapt the IRR rule when you need to choose between competing projects or when there are multiple IRRs.

Using the IRR to Choose between Mutually Exclusive Projects

When you need to choose between mutually exclusive projects, a simple comparison of internal rates of return is liable to lead to poor decisions. We illustrated this by looking at our two office building projects. Your initial proposal involved constructing the office building and then selling it. Under the revised proposal you would construct a more expensive building and rent it out before selling it at the end of 3 years. The cash flows from the two projects were as follows:

	Cash Flows					
	C_0	C_1	C_2	C_3	IRR	NPV at 7%
Initial proposal	−350,000	+400,000			14.29%	+$23,832
Revised proposal	−375,000	+25,000	+25,000	+475,000	12.56%	+$57,942

Although the initial proposal has the higher IRR, it has the lower net present value. If you were misled into choosing the initial rather than the revised proposal, you would have been more than $30,000 poorer.

You can salvage the IRR rule in these cases; you do so by calculating the IRR on the *incremental* cash flows, that is, the difference in cash flows between the two projects. Start with the smaller project, where you plan to invest $350,000 and sell the office building after 1 year. It has an IRR of 14.29%, which is well in excess of the 7% cost of capital. So you know that it is worthwhile. You now ask yourself whether it is worth investing the additional $25,000 and renting out the building for 3 years. Here are the incremental cash flows from doing so, together with their IRR and NPV:

Cash Flows:	C_0	C_1	C_2	C_3	IRR	NPV at 7%
Incremental cash flows	−25,000	−375,000	+25,000	+475,000	11.72%	+$34,110

The IRR on the incremental cash flows is 11.72%. Since this is greater than the opportunity cost of capital, you should prefer the revised proposal.

BEYOND THE PAGE

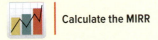

Calculate the MIRR

mhhe.com/brealey9e

Using the Modified Internal Rate of Return When There Are Multiple IRRs

Whenever there is more than one change in the sign of the cash flows, there is generally more than one internal rate of return and, therefore, no simple IRR rule. Companies sometimes get around this problem by calculating a *modified IRR (MIRR)*, which can then be compared with the cost of capital.

Think back to King Coal's strip-mining project. Its cash flows are as follows:

Cash Flows:	C_0	C_1	C_2	C_3	C_4	C_5
Cash flows ($ millions)	−210	+125	+125	+175	+175	−400

The problem with the IRR rule arises because the cash flow in year 5 is negative. So let us try replacing the last two cash flows with a *single* year 4 cash flow that has the same present value. If the cost of capital is 20%, then we can replace the cash flows in years 4 and 5 with a single cash flow in year 4 of

$$+175 - \frac{400}{1.20} = -158$$

This figure is also negative. So we still have a problem. Therefore, we need to step back a further year and combine the last *three* cash flows into a single year 3 cash flow with the same present value:

$$+175 + \frac{175}{1.20} - \frac{400}{1.20^2} = +43$$

This value is positive, so if we use it in place of the last three cash flows, we will have only one change of sign. Now we can compute IRR using the *modified* cash-flow sequence:

Year:	0	1	2	3	4	5
Cash flows ($ millions)	−210	+125	+125	+43	—	—

The modified IRR (MIRR) is the discount rate at which the net present value of these cash flows is zero:

$$-210 + \frac{125}{1 + \text{MIRR}} + \frac{125}{(1 + \text{MIRR})^2} + \frac{43}{(1 + \text{MIRR})^3} = 0$$

We solve to find that MIRR = .22, or 22%, which is greater than the cost of capital of 20%. If the modified IRR is greater than the cost of capital, then the project must have a positive NPV.

9

Using Discounted Cash-Flow Analysis to Make Investment Decisions

LEARNING OBJECTIVES

After studying this chapter, you should be able to:

9-1   Identify the cash flows from a proposed new project.

9-2   Calculate the cash flows of a project from standard financial statements.

9-3   Understand how the company's tax bill is affected by depreciation and how this affects project value.

9-4   Understand how changes in working capital affect project cash flows.

RELATED WEBSITES FOR THIS CHAPTER CAN BE FOUND IN CONNECT.

A working magnoosium mine. But how do you find its net present value? © *Andrey Rudakov/Bloomberg/Getty Images*

Think of the problems that Toyota's managers face when considering whether to introduce a new model. What investment must be made in new plant and equipment? What will it cost to market and promote the new car? How soon can the car be put into production? What is the likely production cost? How much must be invested in inventories of raw materials and finished cars? How many cars can be sold each year and at what price? What credit arrangements should be given to dealers? How long will the model stay in production? When production comes to an end, can the plant and equipment be used elsewhere in the company? All of these issues affect the level and timing of project cash flows. In this chapter we continue our analysis of the capital budgeting decision by turning our focus to how the financial manager should prepare cash-flow estimates for use in net present value analysis.

In Chapter 8, you used the net present value rule to make a simple capital budgeting decision. You tackled the problem in four steps:

Step 1. Forecast the project cash flows.

Step 2. Estimate the opportunity cost of capital—that is, the rate of return that your shareholders could expect to earn if they invested their money in the capital market.

Step 3. Use the opportunity cost of capital to discount the future cash flows. The project's present value (PV) is equal to the sum of the discounted future cash flows.

Step 4. Net present value (NPV) measures whether the project is worth more than it costs. To calculate NPV, you need to subtract the required investment from the present value of the future payoffs: NPV = PV − required investment

If NPV is positive, you should go ahead with the project.

We now need to consider how to apply the net present value rule to practical investment problems. The first step is to decide what to discount. We know the answer in principle: Discount cash flows. This is why capital budgeting is often referred to as *discounted cash-flow,* or *DCF,* analysis. But useful forecasts of cash flows do not arrive on a silver platter. Often, the financial manager has to make do with raw data supplied by specialists in design, production, marketing, and so on. In addition, most financial forecasts are prepared in accordance with accounting principles that do not necessarily recognize cash flows when they occur. These forecasts must also be adjusted.

275

We look first at what cash flows should be discounted. We then present an example that shows how cash flows can be derived from standard accounting information and why cash flows and accounting income

usually differ. The example will lead us to various further points, including the links between depreciation and taxes and the importance of tracking investments in working capital.

9.1 Identifying Cash Flows

Discount Cash Flows, Not Profits

Up to this point we have been concerned mainly with the mechanics of discounting and with the various methods of project appraisal. We have had almost nothing to say about the problem of *what* you should discount. The first and most important point is this: To calculate net present value, you need to discount cash flows, *not* accounting profits.

We stressed the difference between cash flows and profits in Chapter 3. Here we stress it again. Income statements are intended to show how well the firm has performed. They do not track cash flows.

If the firm lays out a large amount of money on a big capital project, you do not conclude that the firm performed poorly that year, even though a lot of cash is going out the door. Therefore, the accountant does not deduct capital expenditure when calculating the year's income but, instead, depreciates it over several years.

That is fine for computing year-by-year profits, but it could get you into trouble when working out net present value. For example, suppose that you are analyzing an investment proposal. It costs $2,000 and is expected to bring in a cash flow of $1,500 in the first year and $500 in the second. You think that the opportunity cost of capital is 10% and so calculate the present value of the cash flows as follows:

$$PV = \frac{\$1,500}{1.10} + \frac{\$500}{(1.10)^2} = \$1,776.86$$

The project is worth less than it costs; it has a negative NPV:

$$NPV = \$1,776.86 - \$2,000 = -\$223.14$$

The project costs $2,000 today, but accountants would not treat that outlay as an immediate expense. They would depreciate that $2,000 over 2 years and deduct the depreciation from the cash flow to obtain accounting income:

	Year 1	Year 2
Cash inflow	+$1,500	+$ 500
Less depreciation	− 1,000	− 1,000
Accounting income	+ 500	− 500

Thus, an accountant would forecast income of $500 in year 1 and an accounting loss of $500 in year 2.

Suppose you were given this forecast income and loss and naively discounted them. Now NPV *looks* positive:

$$\text{Apparent NPV} = \frac{\$500}{1.10} + \frac{-\$500}{(1.10)^2} = \$41.32$$

Of course we know that this is nonsense. The project is obviously a loser; we are spending money today ($2,000 cash outflow), and we are simply getting our money back later ($1,500 in year 1 and $500 in year 2). We are earning a zero return when we could get a 10% return by investing our money in the capital market.

The message of the example is this: **When calculating NPV, recognize investment expenditures when they occur, not later when they show up as depreciation. Projects are financially attractive because of the cash they generate, either for**

distribution to shareholders or for reinvestment in the firm. Therefore, the focus of capital budgeting must be on cash flow, not profits.

We saw another example of the distinction between cash flow and accounting profits in Chapter 3. Accountants try to show profit as it is earned, rather than when the company and the customer get around to paying their bills. For example, an income statement will recognize revenue when the sale is made, even if the bill is not paid for months. This practice also results in a difference between accounting profits and cash flow. The sale generates immediate profits, but the cash flow comes later.

Example 9.1 ▶   **When Cash Flow Comes Later than Sales**

Your firm's ace computer salesman closed a $500,000 sale on December 15, just in time to count it toward his annual bonus. How did he do it? Well, for one thing he gave the customer 180 days to pay. The income statement will recognize the sale in December, even though cash will not arrive until June.

To take care of this timing difference, the accountant adds $500,000 to accounts receivable in December and then reduces accounts receivable when the money arrives in June. (The total of accounts receivable is just the sum of all cash due from customers.)

You can think of the increase in accounts receivable as an investment—it's effectively a 180-day loan to the customer—and, therefore, a cash outflow. That investment is recovered when the customer pays. Thus financial analysts often find it convenient to calculate cash flow as follows:

December		June	
Sales	$500,000	Sales	0
Less investment in accounts receivable	−500,000	Plus recovery of accounts receivable	+$500,000
Cash flow	0	Cash flow	$500,000

Note that this procedure gives the correct cash flow of $500,000 in June. ■

It is not always easy to translate accounting data back into actual dollars. If you are in doubt about what is a cash flow, simply count the dollars coming in and take away the dollars going out.

9.1   Self-Test

A regional supermarket chain is deciding whether to install a tewgit machine in each of its stores. Each machine costs $250,000. Projected income per machine is as follows:

Year:	1	2	3	4	5
Sales	$250,000	$300,000	$300,000	$250,000	$250,000
Operating expenses	200,000	200,000	200,000	200,000	200,000
Depreciation	50,000	50,000	50,000	50,000	50,000
Accounting income	0	50,000	50,000	0	0

Why would a store continue to operate a machine in years 4 and 5 if it produces no profits? What are the cash flows from investing in a machine? Assume each tewgit machine has no salvage value at the end of its 5-year life.

Discount *Incremental* Cash Flows

A project's present value depends on the *extra* cash flows that it produces. So you need to forecast first the firm's cash flows if you go ahead with the project. Then forecast the cash flows if you *don't* accept the project. Take the difference and you have the extra (or *incremental*) cash flows produced by the project:

$$\frac{\text{Incremental}}{\text{cash flow}} = \frac{\text{cash flow}}{\text{with project}} - \frac{\text{cash flow}}{\text{without project}}$$

Example 9.2 ▶   Launching a New Product

Consider the decision by Apple to develop the iPhone 7. If successful, the 7 could lead to several billion dollars in profits.

But are these profits all incremental cash flows? Certainly not. Our with-versus-without principle reminds us that we need also to think about what the cash flows would be *without* the new phone. By launching the iPhone 7, Apple will reduce demand for the iPhone 6S. The incremental cash flows therefore are

Cash flow with 7   cash flow without 7
(including lower cash flow − (with higher cash flow
from iPhone 6S)   from iPhone 6S) ■

The trick in capital budgeting is to trace all the incremental flows from a proposed project. Here are some things to look out for.

Include All Indirect Effects   The decision to launch a new smartphone illustrates a common indirect effect. New products often damage sales of an existing product. Of course, companies frequently introduce new products anyway, usually because they believe that their existing product line is under threat from competition. Even if Apple doesn't go ahead with a new product, Samsung and other competitors will surely continue to improve their Android phones, so there is no guarantee that sales of the existing product line will continue at their present level. Sooner or later they will decline.

Sometimes, a new project will *help* the firm's existing business. Suppose that you are the financial manager of an airline that is considering opening a new short-haul route from Peoria, Illinois, to Chicago's O'Hare Airport. When considered in isolation, the new route may have a negative NPV. But once you allow for the additional business that the new route brings to your other traffic out of O'Hare, it may be a very worthwhile investment. **To forecast incremental cash flow, you must trace out all indirect effects of accepting the project.**

Some capital investments have very long lives once all indirect effects are recognized. Consider the introduction of a new jet engine. Engine manufacturers often offer attractive pricing to achieve early sales because, once an engine is installed, 15 years' sales of replacement parts are almost ensured. Also, because airlines prefer to limit the number of different engines in their fleet, selling jet engines today improves sales tomorrow as well. Later sales will generate further demands for replacement parts. Thus, the string of incremental effects from the first sales of a new-model engine can run for 20 years or more.

Forget Sunk Costs   Sunk costs are like spilled milk: They are past and irreversible outflows. **Sunk costs remain the same whether or not you accept the project. Therefore, they do not affect project NPV.**

Unfortunately, managers often are influenced by sunk costs. A classic case occurred in 1971, when Lockheed sought a federal guarantee for a bank loan to continue development of the Tristar airplane. Lockheed and its supporters argued that it would be foolish to abandon a project on which nearly $1 billion had already been spent.

This was a poor argument, however, because the $1 billion was sunk. The relevant questions were how much more needed to be invested and whether the finished product warranted the *incremental* investment.

Lockheed's supporters were not the only ones to appeal to sunk costs. Some of its critics claimed that it would be foolish to continue with a project that offered no prospect of a satisfactory return on that $1 billion. This argument too was faulty. The $1 billion was gone, and the decision to continue with the project should have depended only on the return on the incremental investment.

Include Opportunity Costs   Resources are almost never free, even when no cash changes hands. For example, suppose a new manufacturing operation uses land that could otherwise be sold for $100,000. This resource is costly; by using the land, you pass up the opportunity to sell it. There is no out-of-pocket cost, but there is an **opportunity cost,** that is, the value of the forgone alternative use of the land.

This example prompts us to warn you against judging projects "before versus after" rather than "with versus without." A manager comparing before versus after might not assign any value to the land because the firm owns it both before and after:

Before	Take Project	After	Cash Flow, Before versus After
Firm owns land	⟶	Firm still owns land	0

The proper comparison, with versus without, is as follows:

Before	Take Project	After	Cash Flow, with Project
Firm owns land	⟶	Firm still owns land	0

Before	Do Not Take Project	After	Cash Flow, without Project
Firm owns land	⟶	Firm sells land for $100,000	$100,000

If you compare the cash flows with and without the project, you see that $100,000 is given up by undertaking the project. The original cost of purchasing the land is irrelevant—that cost is sunk. **The opportunity cost equals the cash that could be realized from selling the land now; you lose that cash if you take the project.**

When the resource can be freely traded, its opportunity cost is simply the market price.[1] However, sometimes opportunity costs are difficult to estimate. Suppose that you go ahead with a project to develop Computer Nouveau, pulling your software team off their work on a new operating system that some existing customers are not-so-patiently awaiting. The exact cost of infuriating those customers may be impossible to calculate, but you'll think twice about the opportunity cost of moving the software team to Computer Nouveau.

Recognize the Investment in Working Capital   **Net working capital** (often referred to simply as *working capital*) is the difference between a company's short-term assets and its liabilities. The principal short-term assets that you need to consider are accounts receivable (customers' unpaid bills) and inventories of raw materials and finished goods, and the principal short-term liabilities are accounts payable (bills that *you* have not paid) and accruals (liabilities for items such as wages or taxes that have recently been incurred but have not yet been paid).

opportunity cost
Benefit or cash flow forgone as a result of an action.

net working capital
Current assets minus current liabilities. Often called *working capital*.

---

[1] If the value of the land to the firm were less than the market price, the firm would sell it. On the other hand, the opportunity cost of using land in a particular project cannot exceed the cost of buying an equivalent parcel to replace it.

Most projects entail an additional investment in working capital. For example, before you can start production, you need to invest in inventories of raw materials. Then, when you deliver the finished product, customers may be slow to pay and accounts receivable will increase. (Remember the computer sale described in Example 9.1. It required a $500,000, 6-month investment in accounts receivable.) Next year, as business builds up, you may need a larger stock of raw materials and you may have even more unpaid bills. **Investments in working capital, just like investments in plant and equipment, result in cash outflows.**

Working capital is one of the most common sources of confusion in forecasting project cash flows.[2] Here are the most common mistakes:

1. *Forgetting about working capital entirely.* We hope that you never fall into that trap.
2. *Forgetting that working capital may change during the life of the project.* Imagine that you sell $100,000 of goods per year and customers pay on average 6 months late. You will, therefore, have $50,000 of unpaid bills. Now you increase prices by 10%, so revenues increase to $110,000. If customers continue to pay 6 months late, unpaid bills increase to $55,000, and therefore, you need to make an *additional* investment in working capital of $5,000.
3. *Forgetting that working capital is recovered at the end of the project.* When the project comes to an end, inventories are run down, any unpaid bills are (you hope) paid off, and you can recover your investment in working capital. This generates a cash *inflow*.

Remember Terminal Cash Flows   The end of a project almost always brings additional cash flows. For example, you might be able to sell some of the plant, equipment, or real estate that was dedicated to it. Also, as we just mentioned, you may recover some of your investment in working capital as you sell off inventories of finished goods and collect on outstanding accounts receivable.

Sometimes, there may be *costs* to shutting down a project. For example, the decommissioning costs of nuclear power plants can soak up several hundred million dollars. Similarly, when a mine is exhausted, the surrounding environment may need rehabilitation. The mining company Freeport-McMoRan has earmarked $450 million to cover the future closure and reclamation costs of its New Mexico mines. Don't forget to include these terminal cash flows.

Beware of Allocated Overhead Costs   We have already mentioned that the accountant's objective in gathering data is not always the same as the project analyst's. A case in point is the allocation of overhead costs such as rent, heat, or electricity. These overhead costs may not be related to a particular project, but they must be paid for nevertheless. Therefore, when the accountant assigns costs to the firm's projects, a charge for overhead is usually made. But our principle of incremental cash flows says that in investment appraisal we should include only the *extra* expenses of the project.

A project may generate extra overhead costs, but then again it may not. We should be cautious about assuming that the accountant's allocation of overhead costs represents the *incremental* cash flow that would be incurred by accepting the project.

> ## 9.2   Self-Test
>
> **A firm is considering an investment in a new manufacturing plant. The site already is owned by the company, but existing buildings would need to be demolished. Which of the following should be treated as incremental cash flows?**

---

[2] If you are not clear *why* working capital affects cash flow, look back to Chapter 3, where we gave a primer on working capital and a couple of simple examples.

a. The market value of the site.
b. The market value of the existing buildings.
c. Demolition costs and site clearance.
d. The cost of a new access road put in last year.
e. Lost cash flows on other projects due to executive time spent on the new facility.
f. Future depreciation of the new plant.
g. The reduction in the firm's tax bill resulting from depreciation of the new plant.
h. The initial investment in inventories of raw materials.
i. Money already spent on engineering design of the new plant.

Discount Nominal Cash Flows by the Nominal Cost of Capital

Interest rates are usually quoted in *nominal* terms. If you invest $100 in a bank deposit offering 6% interest, then the bank promises to pay you $106 at the end of the year. It makes no promises about what that $106 will buy. The real rate of interest on the bank deposit depends on inflation. If inflation is 2%, that $106 will buy you only 4% more goods at the end of the year than your $100 could buy today. The nominal rate of interest is 6%, but the *real* rate is about 4%.[3]

If the discount rate is nominal, consistency requires that cash flows be estimated in nominal terms as well, taking account of trends in selling price, labor and materials costs, and so on. This calls for more than simply applying a single assumed inflation rate to all components of cash flow. Some costs or prices increase faster than inflation, some slower. For example, perhaps you have entered into a 5-year fixed-price contract with a supplier. No matter what happens to inflation over this period, this part of your costs is fixed in nominal terms.

Of course, there is nothing wrong with discounting real cash flows at the real interest rate, although this is not commonly done. We saw in Chapter 5 that real cash flows discounted at the real discount rate give exactly the same present values as nominal cash flows discounted at the nominal rate.

While the need to maintain consistency may seem like an obvious point, analysts sometimes forget to account for the effects of inflation when forecasting future cash flows. As a result, they end up discounting real cash flows at a nominal discount rate. This can grossly understate project values.

It should go without saying that you cannot mix and match real and nominal quantities. Real cash flows must be discounted at a real discount rate, nominal cash flows at a nominal rate. Discounting real cash flows at a nominal rate is a *big* mistake.

Example 9.3 ▶   Cash Flows and Inflation

City Consulting Services is considering moving into a new office building. The cost of a 1-year lease is $8,000, paid immediately. This cost will increase in future years at the annual inflation rate of 3%. The firm believes that it will remain in the building for 4 years. What is the present value of its rental costs if the discount rate is 10%?

---

[3] Remember from Chapter 5,

$$\text{Real rate of interest} \approx \text{nominal rate of interest} - \text{inflation rate}$$

The exact formula is

$$1 + \text{real rate of interest} = \frac{1 + \text{nominal rate of interest}}{1 + \text{inflation rate}} = \frac{1.06}{1.02} = 1.0392$$

Therefore, the real interest rate is .0392, or 3.92%.

The present value can be obtained by discounting the nominal cash flows at the 10% discount rate as follows:

Year	Cash Flow	Present Value at 10% Discount Rate
0	8,000	8,000
1	$8,000 \times 1.03 = 8,240$	$8,240/1.10 = 7,491$
2	$8,000 \times 1.03^2 = 8,487$	$8,487/(1.10)^2 = 7,014$
3	$8,000 \times 1.03^3 = 8,742$	$8,742/(1.10)^3 = 6,568$
		$29,073$

Alternatively, the real discount rate can be calculated as $1.10/1.03 - 1 = .06796 = 6.796\%$.[4] The present value can then be computed by discounting the real cash flows at the real discount rate as follows:

Year	Real Cash Flow	Present Value at 6.796% Discount Rate
0	8,000	8,000
1	8,000	$8,000/1.06796 = 7,491$
2	8,000	$8,000/(1.06796)^2 = 7,014$
3	8,000	$8,000/(1.06796)^3 = 6,568$
		$29,073$

Notice the real cash flow is a constant, since the lease payment increases at the rate of inflation. The present value of *each* cash flow is the same regardless of the method used to discount it. The sum of the present values is, of course, also identical. ■

9.3   Self-Test

Nasty Industries is closing down an outmoded factory and throwing all of its workers out on the street. Nasty's CEO is enraged to learn that the firm must continue to pay for workers' health insurance for 4 years. The cost per worker next year will be $2,400 per year, but the inflation rate is 4%, and health costs have been increasing at 3 percentage points faster than inflation. What is the present value of this obligation? The (nominal) discount rate is 10%.

Separate Investment and Financing Decisions

Suppose you finance a project partly with debt. How should you treat the proceeds from the debt issue and the interest and principal payments on the debt? The answer: You should *neither* subtract the debt proceeds from the required investment *nor* recognize the interest and principal payments on the debt as cash outflows. Regardless of the actual financing, you should view the project as if it were all-equity-financed, treating all cash outflows required for the project as coming from stockholders and all cash inflows as going to them.[5]

This procedure focuses exclusively on the *project* cash flows, not the cash flows associated with alternative financing schemes. It, therefore, allows you to separate the

---

[4] We calculate the real discount rate to three decimal places to avoid confusion from rounding. Such precision is rarely necessary in practice.

[5] Notice that this means that when you calculate the working capital associated with the project, you should assume zero short-term debt or holdings of cash.

analysis of the investment decision from that of the financing decision. First, you ask whether the project has a positive net present value, assuming all-equity financing. Then you can undertake a separate analysis of any potential impact of your financing strategy. Financing decisions are considered later in the text.

9.2 Calculating Cash Flow

It is helpful to think of a project's cash flow as composed of three elements:

$$\text{Total cash flow} = \text{cash flows from capital investments} \quad \text{(9.1)}$$
$$+ \text{ operating cash flows}$$
$$+ \text{ cash flows from changes in working capital}$$

We will look at each of these components in turn.

Element 1: Capital Investment

To get a project off the ground, a company typically needs to make considerable up-front investments in plant, equipment, research, marketing, and so on. For example, development of a new car model typically involves expenditure of $500 million or more. This expenditure is a negative cash flow—negative because cash goes out the door.

When the model finally goes out of production, the company can either sell the plant and equipment or redeploy the assets elsewhere in the business. This salvage value (net of any taxes if the equipment is sold) represents a positive cash flow to the firm. However, remember our earlier comment that final cash flows can be negative if there are significant shutdown costs.

Example 9.4 ▶   Cash Flow from Capital Investment

Slick Corporation plans to invest $800 million to develop the Mock4 razor blade. The specialized blade factory will run for 7 years until it is replaced by more advanced technology. At that point, the machinery will be sold for $50 million. Taxes of $10 million will be assessed on the sale.

The initial cash flow from Slick's investment is −$800 million. In year 7, when the firm sells the land and equipment, there will be a net inflow of $50 million − $10 million = $40 million. Thus, the initial investment involves a negative cash flow, and the salvage value results in a positive flow. ∎

Element 2: Operating Cash Flow

Suppose that you are establishing a firm to launch a new product. In this case, the operating cash flow consists of revenues from the sale of the new product less the costs of production and any taxes:

$$\text{Operating cash flow} = \text{revenues} - \text{costs} - \text{taxes}$$

Undoubtedly, the revenues are expected to outweigh the costs, and therefore, operating cash flows are positive.

Many investments do not result in additional revenues; they are simply designed to reduce the costs of the company's existing operations. For example, a new computer system may provide labor savings, or a new heating system may be more energy-efficient than the one it replaces. Such projects also contribute to the operating cash flow of the firm—not by increasing revenues but by reducing costs. These cost savings, therefore, represent a positive contribution to net cash flow.

Example 9.5 ▶   Operating Cash Flow of Cost-Cutting Projects

Suppose a new heating system would reduce heating costs by $30,000 a year. The firm's tax rate is 35%. The new system does not change revenues, but, thanks to the cost savings, income increases by $30,000. Therefore, incremental operating cash flow is:

Increase in (revenues less expenses)	$30,000
− Incremental tax at 35%	− 10,500
= Increase in operating cash flow	+$19,500

Notice that because the cost savings increase profits, the company must pay more tax. The *net* increase in cash flow equals the after-tax cost savings:

$$(1 - .35) \times \$30,000 = \$19,500 \ \blacksquare$$

Here is another matter that you need to look out for when calculating cash flow. When the firm calculates its taxable income, it makes a deduction for depreciation. This depreciation charge is an accounting entry. It affects the tax that the company pays, but it is not a cash expense and should not be deducted when calculating operating cash flow. (Remember from our earlier discussion that you want to discount cash flows, not profits.)

When you work out a project's cash flows, there are three possible ways to deal with depreciation.

Method 1: Dollars In Minus Dollars Out   Take only the items from the income statement that represent actual cash flows. This means that you start with cash revenues and subtract cash expenses and taxes paid. You do not, however, subtract a charge for depreciation because this does not involve cash going out the door. Thus,

$$\text{Operating cash flow} = \text{revenues} - \text{cash expenses} - \text{taxes} \qquad \textbf{(9.2)}$$

Method 2: Adjusted Accounting Profits   Alternatively, you can start with after-tax accounting profits and add back any noncash "accounting expenses," specifically, the depreciation deduction. This gives

$$\text{Operating cash flow} = \text{after-tax profit} + \text{depreciation} \qquad \textbf{(9.3)}$$

Method 3: Add Back Depreciation Tax Shield   Although the depreciation deduction is *not* a cash expense, it does affect the firm's tax payment, which certainly is a cash item. Each additional dollar of depreciation reduces taxable income by $1. So, if the firm's tax bracket is 35%, tax payments fall by $.35, and cash flow increases by the same amount. Financial managers often refer to this tax saving as the **depreciation tax shield.** It equals the product of the tax rate and the depreciation charge:

depreciation tax shield
Reduction in taxes attributable to depreciation.

$$\text{Depreciation tax shield} = \text{tax rate} \times \text{depreciation}$$

This suggests a third way to calculate operating cash flow. First, calculate net profit, initially assuming zero depreciation. This is equal to (revenues − cash expenses) × (1 − tax rate). Now add back the tax shield based on the amount of depreciation actually claimed to find operating cash flow:

$$\text{Operating cash flow} = (\text{revenues} - \text{cash expenses}) \times (1 - \text{tax rate}) \qquad \textbf{(9.4)}$$
$$+ (\text{tax rate} \times \text{depreciation})$$

The following example confirms that the three methods all give the same figure for operating cash flow.

Example 9.6 ▶ Operating Cash Flow

A project generates revenues of $1,000, cash expenses of $600, and depreciation charges of $200 in a particular year. The firm's tax bracket is 35%. Net income is calculated as follows:

Revenues	1,000
− Cash expenses	600
− Depreciation charge	200
= Profit before tax	200
− Tax at 35%	70
= Net profit	130

Methods 1, 2, and 3 all show that operating cash flow is $330:

Method 1: Operating cash flow = revenues − cash expenses − taxes

$$= 1{,}000 - 600 - 70 = 330$$

Method 2: Operating cash flow = net profit + depreciation = 130 + 200 = 330

Method 3: Operating cash flow = (revenues − cash expenses)

$$\times (1 - \text{tax rate}) + (\text{depreciation} \times \text{tax rate})$$

$$= (1{,}000 - 600) \times (1 - .35) + (200 \times .35) = 330 \ \blacksquare$$

9.4 Self-Test

A project generates revenues of **$600**, expenses of **$300**, and depreciation charges of **$200** in a particular year. The firm's tax bracket is **35%**. Find the operating cash flow of the project by using all three approaches.

Element 3: Changes in Working Capital

We pointed out earlier in the chapter that when a company builds up inventories of raw materials or finished product, the company's cash is reduced; the reduction in cash reflects the firm's investment in inventories. Similarly, cash is reduced when customers are slow to pay their bills—in this case, the firm makes an investment in accounts receivable. Investment in working capital, just like investment in plant and equipment, represents a negative cash flow. On the other hand, later in the life of a project, when inventories are sold off and accounts receivable are collected, the firm's investment in working capital is reduced as it converts these assets into cash.

Example 9.7 ▶ Cash Flow from Changes in Working Capital

Slick makes an initial (year 0) investment of $10 million in inventories of plastic and steel for its blade plant. Then in year 1 it accumulates an additional $20 million of raw materials. The total level of inventories is now $10 million + $20 million = $30 million, but the cash outlay in year 1 is simply the $20 million addition to inventory. The $20 million investment in additional inventory results in a cash flow of −$20 million. Notice that the increase in working capital is an *investment* in the project. Like other investments, a buildup of working capital requires cash. Increases in the *level* of working capital, therefore, show up as *negative* cash flows.

Later on, say, in year 5, the company begins planning for the next-generation blade. At this point, it decides to reduce its inventory of raw material from $30 million to $25 million. This reduction in inventory investment frees up $5 million of cash, which is a positive cash flow. Therefore, the cash flows from inventory investment are −$10 million in year 0, −$20 million in year 1, and +$5 million in year 5.

These calculations can be summarized in a simple table, as follows:

Year:	0	1	2	3	4	5
1. Total working capital, year-end ($ million)	10	30	30	30	30	25
2. Change in working capital ($ million)	10	20	0	0	0	−5
3. Cash flow from changes in working capital	−10	−20	0	0	0	+5

In years 0 and 1, there is a net investment in working capital (line 2), corresponding to a negative cash flow (line 3), and an increase in the *level* of total working capital (line 1). In years 2 to 4, the level of working capital is unchanged at $30 million, so the *net investment* in working capital in those years is zero. But in year 5, the firm begins to disinvest in working capital, which frees up cash and thereby provides a positive cash flow. ∎

In general: **An *increase* in working capital is an investment and therefore implies a *negative* cash flow; a decrease in working capital implies a positive cash flow. The cash flow is measured by the *change* in working capital, not the *level* of working capital.**

9.3   An Example: Blooper Industries

Now that we have examined the basic elements of a cash-flow analysis, let's try to put them together into a coherent whole. As the newly appointed financial manager of Blooper Industries, you are about to analyze a proposal for mining and selling a small deposit of high-grade magnoosium ore.[6] You are given the forecasts shown in Spreadsheet 9.1. We will walk through the lines in the table.

Cash-Flow Analysis

Capital Investment   Panel A of the spreadsheet summarizes our assumptions. Panel B details capital investments and disinvestments. The project requires an initial investment of $10 million, as shown in cell B14. After 5 years, the ore deposit is exhausted, so the mining equipment may be sold for $2 million (cell B3), a forecast that already reflects the likely impact of inflation.

When you sell the equipment, the IRS will check to see whether any taxes are due on the sale. Any difference between the sale price ($2 million) and the book value of the equipment will be treated as a taxable gain.

We assume that Blooper depreciates the equipment to a final value of zero. Therefore, the book value of the equipment when it is sold in year 6 will be zero, and you will be subject to taxes on the full $2 million proceeds. Your sale of the equipment will land you with an additional tax bill in year 6 of .35 × $2 million = $.70 million. The net cash flow from the sale in year 6 is, therefore,

Salvage value − tax on gain = $2 million − $.70 million = $1.30 million

BEYOND THE PAGE

Blooper Industries

mhhe.com/brealey9e

---

[6] Readers have inquired whether magnoosium is a real substance. Here, now, are the facts: Magnoosium was created in the early days of television, when a splendid-sounding announcer closed a variety show by saying, "This program has been brought to you by Blooper Industries, proud producer of aleemiums, magnoosium, and stool." We forget the company, but the blooper really happened.

SPREADSHEET 9.1 Financial projections for Blooper's magnoosium mine (dollar values in thousands)

	A	B	C	D	E	F	G	H
1	**A. Inputs**		Spreadsheet Name					
2	Initial investment	10,000	Investment					
3	Salvage value	2,000	Salvage					
4	Initial revenue	15,000	Initial_rev					
5	Initial expenses	10,000	Initial_exp					
6	Inflation rate	0.05	Inflation					
7	Discount rate	0.12	Disc_rate					
8	Acct receiv. as fraction of sales	= 2/12	A_R					
9	Inven. as fraction of expenses	0.15	Inv_pct					
10	Tax rate	0.35	Tax_rate					
11								
12	Year:	**0**	**1**	**2**	**3**	**4**	**5**	**6**
13	**B. Capital investment**							
14	Investment in fixed assets	10,000						
15	Sales of fixed assets							1,300
16	CF, invest. in fixed assets	− 10,000	0	0	0	0	0	1,300
17								
18	**C. Operating cash flow**							
19	Revenues		15,000	15,750	16,538	17,364	18,233	
20	Expenses		10,000	10,500	11,025	11,576	12,155	
21	Depreciation		2,000	2,000	2,000	2,000	2,000	
22	Pretax profit		3,000	3,250	3,513	3,788	4,078	
23	Tax		1,050	1,138	1,229	1,326	1,427	
24	Profit after tax		1,950	2,113	2,283	2,462	2,650	
25	Operating cash flow		3,950	4,113	4,283	4,462	4,650	
26								
27	**D. Changes in working capital**							
28	Working capital	1,500	4,075	4,279	4,493	4,717	3,039	0
29	*Change* in working cap	1,500	2,575	204	214	225	−1,679	−3,039
30	CF, invest. in wk capital	−1,500	−2,575	−204	−214	−225	1,679	3,039
31								
32	**E. Project valuation**							
33	Total project cash flow	−11,500	1,375	3,909	4,069	4,238	6,329	4,339
34	Discount factor	1.0	0.8929	0.7972	0.7118	0.6355	0.5674	0.5066
35	PV of cash flow	−11,500	1,228	3,116	2,896	2,693	3,591	2,198
36	Net present value	4,223						

This amount is recorded in cell H15. Blooper does not expect to incur any reclamation costs when the project comes to an end. If it did, these costs would need to be subtracted from the salvage value.

Row 16 summarizes the cash flows from investments in and sales of fixed assets. The entry in each cell equals the after-tax proceeds from asset sales (row 15) minus the investments in fixed assets (row 14).

Operating Cash Flow   The company expects to be able to sell 750,000 pounds of magnoosium a year at a price of $20 a pound in year 1. That points to initial revenues of 750,000 × $20 = $15,000,000. But be careful; inflation is running at about 5% a year. If magnoosium prices keep pace with inflation, you should increase your forecast of the second-year revenues by 5%. Third-year revenues should increase by a further 5%, and so on. Row 19 in Spreadsheet 9.1 shows revenues rising in line with inflation.

The sales forecasts in Spreadsheet 9.1 are cut off after 5 years. That makes sense if the ore deposit will run out at that time. But if Blooper could make sales for year 6, you should include them in your forecasts. We have sometimes encountered financial managers who assume a project life of (say) 5 years, even when they confidently expect revenues for 10 years or more. When asked the reason, they explain that forecasting beyond 5 years is too hazardous. We sympathize, but you just have to do your best. Do not arbitrarily truncate a project's life.

Expenses in year 1 are $10,000 (cell C20). We assume that the expenses of mining and refining (row 20) also increase in line with inflation at 5% a year.

straight-line depreciation
Constant depreciation for
each year of the asset's
accounting life.

We also assume for now that the company applies **straight-line depreciation** to the mining equipment over 5 years. This means that it deducts one-fifth of the initial $10 million investment from profits. Thus, row 21 shows that the annual depreciation deduction is $2 million.

Pretax profit, shown in row 22, equals (revenues − expenses − depreciation). Taxes (row 23) are 35% of pretax profit. For example, in year 1,

$$\text{Tax} = .35 \times 3,000 = 1,050, \text{ or } \$1,050,000$$

Profit after tax (row 24) equals pretax profit less taxes.

The last row of panel C presents operating cash flow. We calculate cash flow as the sum of after-tax profits plus depreciation (method 2, above). Therefore, row 25 is the sum of rows 24 and 21.

Changes in Working Capital   Row 28 shows the *level* of working capital. As the project gears up in the early years, working capital increases, but later in the project's life, the investment in working capital is recovered and the level declines.

Row 29 shows the *change* in working capital from year to year. Notice that in years 1 to 4, the change is positive; in these years, the project requires additional investments in working capital. Starting in year 5, the change is negative; there is a disinvestment as working capital is recovered. Cash flow associated with investments in working capital (row 30) is the negative of the change in working capital. Just like investment in plant and equipment, investment in working capital produces a negative cash flow, and disinvestment produces a positive cash flow.

Total Project Cash Flow   Total cash flow is the sum of cash flows from each of the three elements: cash flow from investments in fixed assets and working capital and operating cash flow. Therefore, total cash flow in row 33 is just the sum of rows 16, 25, and 30.

Calculating the NPV of Blooper's Project

You have now derived (in row 33) the forecast cash flows from Blooper's magnoosium mine. Suppose that investors expect a return of 12% from investments in the capital market with the same risk as the magnoosium project. This is the opportunity cost of the shareholders' money that Blooper is proposing to invest in the project. Therefore, to calculate NPV, you need to discount the cash flows at 12%.

Rows 34 and 35 set out the calculations. Remember that to calculate the present value of a cash flow in year t you can divide the cash flow by $(1 + r)^t$ or you can multiply by a discount factor that is equal to $1/(1 + r)^t$. Row 34 presents the discount factors for each year, and row 35 calculates the present value of each cash flow by multiplying the cash flow (row 33) by the discount factor. When all cash flows are discounted and added up, the magnoosium project is seen to offer a positive net present value of $4,223 thousand (cell B36), or about $4.2 million.

Now here is a small point that often causes confusion: To calculate the present value of the first year's cash flow, we divide by $(1 + r) = 1.12$. Strictly speaking, this makes sense only if all the sales and all the costs occur exactly 365 days, zero hours, and zero minutes from now. Of course, the year's sales don't all take place on the stroke of midnight on December 31. However, when making capital budgeting decisions, companies are usually happy to pretend that all cash flows occur at 1-year intervals. They pretend this for one reason only—simplicity. When sales forecasts are sometimes little more than intelligent guesses, it may be pointless to inquire how the sales are likely to be spread out during the year.[7]

Further Notes and Wrinkles Arising from Blooper's Project

Before we leave Blooper and its magnoosium project, we should cover a few extra wrinkles.

Forecasting Working Capital   Spreadsheet 9.1 shows that Blooper expects its magnoosium mine to produce revenues of $15,000 in year 1 and $15,750 in year 2. But Blooper will not actually receive these amounts in years 1 and 2, because some of its customers will not pay up immediately. We have assumed that, on average, customers pay with a 2-month lag, so that 2/12 of each year's sales are not paid for until the following year. These unpaid bills show up as accounts receivable. For example, in year 1 Blooper will have accounts receivable of $(2/12) \times 15,000 = \$2,500$.[8]

Consider now the mine's expenses. These are forecast at $10,000 in year 1 and $10,500 in year 2. But some of this cash will go out the door earlier, for Blooper must produce the magnoosium before selling it. Each year, Blooper mines magnoosium ore, but some of this ore is not sold until the following year. The ore is put into inventory, but the accountant does not deduct the cost of its production until it is taken out of inventory and sold. We assume that 15% of each year's expenses represent an investment in inventory that took place in the previous year. Thus, the investment in inventory is forecast at $.15 \times 10,000 = \$1,500$ in year 0 and at $.15 \times \$10,500 = \$1,575$ in year 1.[9]

We can now see how Blooper arrives at its forecast of working capital (row 28 of the spreadsheet):

	0	**1**	**2**	**3**	**4**	**5**	**6**
1. Receivables (2/12 × revenues)	$ 0	$2,500	$2,625	$2,756	$2,894	$3,039	0
2. Inventories (.15 × following year's expenses)	1,500	1,575	1,654	1,736	1,823	0	0
3. Working capital (1 + 2)	1,500	4,075	4,279	4,493	4,717	3,039	0

Note: Columns may not sum due to rounding.

Notice that working capital builds up in years 1 to 4, as sales of magnoosium increase. Year 5 is the last year of sales, so Blooper can reduce its inventories to zero in that year. In year 6, the company expects to collect any unpaid bills from year 5, and so in that year receivables also fall to zero. This decline in working capital increases cash flow. For example, in year 6, cash flow is increased as the $3,039 of outstanding bills are paid (see row 30 of the spreadsheet).

The construction of the Blooper spreadsheet is discussed further in the Spreadsheet Solutions box. Once the spreadsheet is set up, it is easy to try out different assumptions for working capital. For example, you can adjust the level of receivables and inventories by changing the values in cells B8 and B9.

---

[7] Financial managers sometimes assume cash flows arrive in the middle of the calendar year, that is, at the end of June. This midyear convention is roughly equivalent to assuming cash flows are distributed evenly throughout the year. This is a bad assumption for some industries. In retailing, for example, most of the cash flow comes late in the year, as the holiday season approaches.

[8] For convenience, we assume that, although Blooper's customers pay with a lag, Blooper pays all its bills on the nail. If it didn't, these unpaid bills would be recorded as accounts payable. Working capital would be reduced by the amount of the accounts payable.

[9] It might make more sense to assume that inventories are 15% of just the direct costs of production (i.e., cost of goods sold), not 15% of total expenses, which also include fixed costs. However, to avoid complicating the spreadsheet, we will ignore this distinction.

A Further Note on Depreciation   We warned you earlier not to assume that all cash flows are likely to increase with inflation. The depreciation tax shield is a case in point because the Internal Revenue Service lets companies depreciate only the amount of the original investment. For example, if you go back to the IRS to explain that inflation mushroomed since you made the investment and you should be allowed to depreciate more, the IRS won't listen. The *nominal* amount of depreciation is fixed, and therefore the higher the rate of inflation, the lower the *real* value of the depreciation that you can claim.

We assumed in our calculations that Blooper could depreciate its investment in mining equipment by $2 million a year. That produced an annual tax shield of $2 million × .35 = $.70 million per year for 5 years. These tax shields increase cash flows from operations and therefore increase present value. So if Blooper could get those tax shields sooner, they would be worth more, right? Fortunately for corporations, tax law allows them to do just that. It allows *accelerated depreciation.*

The rate at which U.S. firms are permitted to depreciate equipment is known as the **modified accelerated cost recovery system,** or **MACRS.** MACRS places assets into one of six classes, each of which has an assumed life. Table 9.1 shows the rate of depreciation that the company can use for each of these classes. Most industrial equipment falls into the 5- and 7-year classes. To keep life simple, we will assume that all of Blooper's mining equipment goes into 5-year assets. Thus, Blooper can depreciate 20% of its $10 million investment in year 1. In the second year it can deduct depreciation of .32 × 10 = $3.2 million, and so on.[10]

How does MACRS depreciation affect the value of the depreciation tax shield for the magnoosium project? Table 9.2 gives the answer. Notice that MACRS does not

modified accelerated cost recovery system (MACRS) Depreciation method that allows higher tax deductions in early years and lower deductions later.

BEYOND THE PAGE

 | MACRS classes

mhhe.com/brealey9e

TABLE 9.1 Tax depreciation allowed under the modified accelerated cost recovery system (MACRS), figures in percent of depreciable investment

Year(s)	Recovery Period Class					
	3 Year	5 Year	7 Year	10 Year	15 Year	20 Year
1	33.33	20.00	14.29	10.00	5.00	3.75
2	44.45	32.00	24.49	18.00	9.50	7.22
3	14.81	19.20	17.49	14.40	8.55	6.68
4	7.41	11.52	12.49	11.52	7.70	6.18
5		11.52	8.93	9.22	6.93	5.71
6		5.76	8.92	7.37	6.23	5.28
7			8.93	6.55	5.90	4.89
8			4.46	6.55	5.90	4.52
9				6.56	5.91	4.46
10				6.55	5.90	4.46
11				3.28	5.91	4.46
12					5.90	4.46
13					5.91	4.46
14					5.90	4.46
15					5.91	4.46
16					2.95	4.46
17–20						4.46
21						2.23

Notes:
1. Tax depreciation is lower in the first year because assets are assumed to be in service for 6 months.
2. Real property is depreciated straight-line over 27.5 years for residential property and 39 years for nonresidential property.

―――――――――
[10] You might wonder why the 5-year asset class provides a depreciation deduction in years 1 through 6. This is because the tax authorities assume that the assets are in service for only 6 months of the first year and 6 months of the last year. The total project life is 5 years, but that 5-year life spans parts of 6 calendar years. This assumption also explains why the depreciation allowance is lower in the first year than it is in the second.

TABLE 9.2 The switch from straight-line to 5-year MACRS depreciation increases the value of Blooper's depreciation tax shield from $2,523,000 to $2,583,000 (figures in $ thousands)

	Straight-Line Depreciation			MACRS Depreciation		
Year	Depreciation	Tax Shield	PV Tax Shield at 12%	Depreciation	Tax Shield	PV Tax Shield at 12%
1	$ 2,000	$ 700	$ 625	$ 2,000	$ 700	$ 625
2	2,000	700	558	3,200	1,120	893
3	2,000	700	498	1,920	672	478
4	2,000	700	445	1,152	403	256
5	2,000	700	397	1,152	403	229
6	0	0	0	576	202	102
Totals	$10,000	$3,500	$2,523	$10,000	$3,500	$2,583

Note: Column sums subject to rounding error.

affect the total amount of depreciation that is claimed. This remains at $10 million just as before. But MACRS allows companies to get the depreciation deduction earlier, which increases the present value of the depreciation tax shield from $2,523,000 to $2,583,000, an increase of $60,000. Before we recognized MACRS depreciation, we calculated project NPV as $4,223,000. When we recognize MACRS, we should increase that figure by $60,000.

All large corporations in the United States keep two sets of books—one for stockholders and one for the Internal Revenue Service. It is common to use straight-line depreciation on the stockholder books and MACRS depreciation on the tax books. Only the tax books are relevant in capital budgeting.

BEYOND THE PAGE

The value of MACRS tax savings

mhhe.com/brealey9e

9.5   Self-Test

Suppose that Blooper's mining equipment could be put in the 3-year recovery period class. What is the present value of the depreciation tax shield? Confirm that the change in the value of the depreciation tax shield equals the increase in project NPV from Question 1 of the Spreadsheet Solutions box.

More on Salvage Value   When you sell equipment, you must pay taxes on the difference between the sales price and the book value of the asset. The book value in turn equals the initial cost minus cumulative charges for depreciation. It is common when figuring tax depreciation to assume a salvage value of zero at the end of the asset's depreciable life.

However, reports to shareholders often assume positive salvage values. For example, Blooper's financial statements might assume that its $10 million investment in mining equipment would be worth $2 million in year 6. In this case, the depreciation reported to shareholders would be based on the difference between the investment and the salvage value, that is, $8 million. Straight-line depreciation then would be $1.6 million annually.

Project Analysis   Let us review. Earlier in the chapter, you embarked on an analysis of Blooper's proposed mining project. You started with a simplified statement of assets and income for the project. You used these to develop a series of cash-flow forecasts, and you then calculated the project's NPV.

Discounted cash-flow analysis of proposed capital investments is tailor-made for spreadsheet analysis. The formula view of the Excel spreadsheet used in the Blooper example appears below. (Columns E and F of the spreadsheet are not shown.)

Notice that most of the entries in the spreadsheet are formulas rather than specific numbers. Once the relatively few input values in panel A are entered, the spreadsheet does most of the work.

Revenues and expenses in each year equal the value in the previous year times (1 + inflation rate). To make the spreadsheet easier to read, we have defined names for a few cells, such as B6 (*Inflation*) and B7 (*Disc_rate*). These names can be assigned using the Define Name command (right-click on the cell you wish to name) and thereafter can be used to refer to specific cells.

Row 28 sets out the level of working capital, which is the sum of accounts receivable and inventories. Because inventories tend to rise with production, we set them equal to .15 times expenses recognized in the following year when the product is sold. Similarly, accounts receivable rise with sales, so we assume that they will be 2/12 times current year's revenues (in other words, that Blooper's customers pay, on average, 2 months after purchasing the product). Each entry in row 28 is the sum of these two quantities.

We calculate the discount factor in row 34, compute present values of each cash flow in row 35, and find NPV in cell B36.

Once the spreadsheet is up and running, "what-if" analyses are easy. Here are a few questions to try your hand.

	A	B	C	D	G	H
1	**A. Inputs**		Spreadsheet Name			
2	Initial investment	10,000	Investment			
3	Salvage value	2,000	Salvage			
4	Initial revenue	15,000	Initial_rev			
5	Initial expenses	10,000	Initial_exp			
6	Inflation rate	0.05	Inflation			
7	Discount rate	0.12	Disc_rate			
8	Acct receiv. as fraction of sales	= 2/12	A_R			
9	Inven. as fraction of expenses	0.15	Inv_pct			
10	Tax rate	0.35	Tax_rate			
11						
12	Year:	0	1	2	5	6
13	**B. Capital investment**					
14	Investment in fixed assets	=Investment				
15	Sales of fixed assets					=Salvage*(1−Tax_rate)
16	CF, invest. in fixed assets	=−B14+B15	=−C14+C15	=−D14+D15	=−G14+G15	=−H14+H15
17						
18	**C. Operating cash flow**					
19	Revenues		=Initial_rev	=C19*(1+Inflation)	=F19*(1+Inflation)	
20	Expenses		=Initial_exp	=C20*(1+Inflation)	=F20*(1+Inflation)	
21	Depreciation		=Investment/5	=Investment/5	=Investment/5	
22	Pretax profit		=C19−C20−C21	=D19−D20−D21	=G19−G20−G21	
23	Tax		=C22*Tax rate	=D22*Tax rate	=G22*Tax rate	
24	Profit after tax		=C22−C23	=D22−D23	=G22−G23	
25	Operating cash flow		=C21 + C24	=D21 + D24	=G21 + G24	
26						
27	**D. Changes in working capital**					
28	Working capital	=Inv_pct*C20+A_R*B19	=Inv_pct*D20+A_R*C19	=Inv_pct*E20+A_R*D19	=Inv_pct*H20+A_R*G19	=Inv_pct*I20+A_R*H19
29	*Change* in working cap	=B28	=C28−B28	=D28−C28	=G28−F28	=H28−G28
30	CF, invest. in wk capital	=−B29	=−C29	=−D29	=−G29	=−H29
31						
32	**E. Project valuation**					
33	Total project cash flow	=B16+B30+B25	=C16+C30+C25	=D16+D30+D25	=G16+G30+G25	=H16+H30+H25
34	Discount factor	=1/(1+Disc_rate)^B12	=1/(1+Disc_rate)^C12	=1/(1+Disc_rate)^D12	=1/(1+Disc_rate)^G12	=1/(1+Disc_rate)^H12
35	PV of cash flow	=B33*B34	=C33*C34	=D33*D34	=G33*G34	=H33*H34
36	Net present value	=SUM(B35:H35)				

The Blooper Spreadsheet Model (continued)

Spreadsheet Questions

1. What happens to cash flow in each year and the NPV of the project if the firm uses MACRS depreciation assuming a 3-year recovery period? Assume year 1 is the first year that depreciation is taken.

2. Suppose the firm can economize on working capital by managing inventories more efficiently. If it reduces inventories from 15% to 10% of next year's cost of goods sold, what will be the effect on project NPV? (Assume straight-line depreciation.)

3. What happens to NPV if the inflation rate falls from 5% to zero and the discount rate falls from 12% to 7%? Given that the real discount rate is almost unchanged, why does project NPV increase? [To be consistent, you should assume that nominal salvage value will be lower in a zero-inflation environment. If you set (before-tax) salvage value to $1.492 million, you will maintain its real value unchanged. Assume straight-line depreciation and inventories equal to 15% of cost of goods sold.]

Brief solutions appear at the end of the chapter.

Does that mean you are now done? The positive NPV suggests that you should go ahead, but you would almost certainly wish to analyze some alternatives. For example, you might want to explore different access methods for the mine or different ways to support the rock as the ore is removed. You might wish to look at alternative ways to transport and refine the ore.

You will also want to ask some "what-if" questions. What if technical problems delay start-up? What if you have underestimated labor costs? Managers employ a variety of techniques to develop a better understanding of the effect of such unpleasant surprises on NPV. If they know what could go wrong with the project, they may be able to collect more information today that will reduce these uncertainties. We will practice using several "what-if " techniques in Chapter 10.

When surprises do occur, you need to have the flexibility to respond. For example, if the price of magnoosium falls through the floor, you might wish to halt operations or to close the mine permanently. It can be worth spending money up-front to position the company to better adapt to changing conditions in the future.

As we shall see in the next chapter, your calculation of Blooper's project NPV was just the first step in making the investment decision.

SUMMARY

How should the cash flows of a proposed new project be calculated? *(LO9-1)*

Here is a checklist to bear in mind when forecasting a project's cash flows:

- Discount cash flows, not profits.
- Estimate the project's *incremental* cash flows—that is, the difference between the cash flows with the project and those without the project.
- Include all indirect effects of the project, such as its impact on the sales of the firm's other products.
- Forget sunk costs.
- Include **opportunity costs,** such as the value of land that you could otherwise sell.
- Beware of allocated overhead charges for heat, light, and so on. These may not reflect the incremental effects of the project on these costs.
- Remember the investment in working capital. As sales increase, the firm may need to make additional investments in working capital, and as the project finally comes to an end, it will recover these investments.
- Treat inflation consistently. If cash flows are forecast in nominal terms (including the effects of future inflation), use a nominal discount rate. Discount real cash flows at a real rate.
- Do not include debt interest or the cost of repaying a loan. When calculating NPV, assume that the project is financed entirely by the shareholders and that they receive all the cash flows. This separates the investment decision from the financing decision.

How can the cash flows of a project be computed from standard financial statements? *(LO9-2)*	Project cash flow does not equal profit. You must allow for noncash expenses such as depreciation as well as changes in working capital.
How is the company's tax bill affected by depreciation, and how does this affect project value? *(LO9-3)*	Depreciation is not a cash flow. However, because depreciation reduces taxable income, it reduces taxes. This tax reduction is called the **depreciation tax shield. Modified accelerated cost recovery system (MACRS)** depreciation schedules allow more of the depreciation allowance to be taken in early years than is possible under **straight-line depreciation.** This increases the present value of the tax shield.
How do changes in working capital affect project cash flows? *(LO9-4)*	Increases in **net working capital** such as accounts receivable or inventory are investments and therefore use cash—that is, they reduce the net cash flow provided by the project in that period. When working capital is run down, cash is freed up, so cash flow increases.

LISTING OF EQUATIONS

9.1   Total cash flow = cash flows from capital investments
$$+ \text{ operating cash flows}$$
$$+ \text{ cash flows from changes in working capital}$$

9.2   Operating cash flow = revenues − cash expenses − taxes

9.3   Operating cash flow = after-tax profit + depreciation

9.4   Operating cash flow = (revenues − cash expenses) × (1 − tax rate)
$$+ \text{ (tax rate} \times \text{depreciation)}$$

QUESTIONS AND PROBLEMS

1. **Cash Flows.** Quick Computing currently sells 10 million computer chips each year at a price of $20 per chip. It is about to introduce a new chip, and it forecasts annual sales of 12 million of these improved chips at a price of $25 each. However, demand for the old chip will decrease, and sales of the old chip are expected to fall to 3 million per year. The old chips cost $6 each to manufacture, and the new ones will cost $8 each. What is the proper cash flow to use to evaluate the present value of the introduction of the new chip? *(LO9-1)*

2. **Incremental Cash Flows.** A corporation donates a valuable painting from its private collection to an art museum. Which of the following are incremental cash flows associated with the donation? *(LO9-1)*

   a. The price the firm paid for the painting
   b. The current market value of the painting
   c. The deduction from income that it declares for its charitable gift
   d. The reduction in taxes due to its declared tax deduction

3. **Cash Flows.** Conference Services Inc. has leased a large office building for $4 million per year. The building is larger than the company needs; two of the building's eight stories are almost empty. A manager wants to expand one of her projects, but this will require using one of the empty floors. In calculating the net present value of the proposed expansion, senior management allocates one-eighth of $4 million of building rental costs (i.e., $.5 million) to the project expansion, reasoning that the project will use one-eighth of the building's capacity. *(LO9-1)*

   a. Is this a reasonable procedure for purposes of calculating NPV?
   b. Can you suggest a better way to assess a cost of the office space used by the project?

4. **Cash Flows.** A new project will generate sales of $74 million, costs of $42 million, and depreciation expense of $10 million in the coming year. The firm's tax rate is 35%. In Section 9.2, we described three methods for dealing with depreciation. Calculate cash flow for the year using: (*LO9-2*)

    a. Method 1: Dollars in minus dollars out.
    b. Method 2: Adjusted accounting profits.
    c. Method 3: Add back depreciation tax shield.

5. **Cash Flows.** Tubby Toys estimates that its new line of rubber ducks will generate sales of $7 million, operating costs of $4 million, and a depreciation expense of $1 million. If the tax rate is 35%, what is the firm's operating cash flow? (*LO9-2*)

6. **Cash Flows.** True or false? (*LO9-2*)

    a. A project's depreciation tax shields depend on the actual future rate of inflation.
    b. Project cash flows should take account of interest paid on borrowings undertaken to finance the project.
    c. Accelerated depreciation reduces near-term cash flows and, therefore, reduces project NPV.

7. **Calculating Net Income.** The owner of a bicycle repair shop forecasts revenues of $160,000 a year. Variable costs will be $50,000, and rental costs for the shop are $30,000 a year. Depreciation on the repair tools will be $10,000. Prepare an income statement for the shop based on these estimates. The tax rate is 35%. (*LO9-2*)

8. **Cash Flows.** Calculate the operating cash flow for the repair shop in the previous problem using all three methods suggested in the chapter. All three approaches should result in the same value for cash flow. (*LO9-2*)

    a. Dollars in minus dollars out.
    b. Adjusted accounting profits.
    c. Add back depreciation tax shield.

9. **Cash Flows.** Reliable Electric is considering a proposal to manufacture a new type of industrial electric motor that would replace most of its existing product line. A research breakthrough has given Reliable a 2-year lead on its competitors. The project proposal is summarized in Table 9.3. Read the notes to the table, and in each case, explain whether the note makes sense or not. (*LO9-2*)

    Notes:

    a. *Capital investment:* $8 million for new machinery and $2.4 million for a warehouse extension. The full cost of the extension has been charged to this project, although only about half the space is currently needed. Because the new machinery will be housed in an existing factory building, no charge has been made for land and building.
    b. *Research and development:* $1.82 million spent in 2016. This figure was adjusted for 10% inflation from the time of expenditure to date. Thus, 1.82 × 1.1 = $2 million.
    c. *Working capital:* Initial investment in inventories.
    d. *Revenue:* These figures assume sales of 2,000 motors in 2018, 4,000 in 2019, and 10,000 per year from 2020 through 2027. The initial unit price of $4,000 is forecasted to remain constant in real terms.

TABLE 9.3 Estimated cash flows and present value of Reliable Electric's proposed investment ($ thousands) (See Problem 9)

	2017	2018	2019	2020–2027
1. Capital investment	−10,400			
2. Research and development	−2,000			
3. Working capital	−4,000			
4. Revenue		8,000	16,000	40,000
5. Operating costs		−4,000	−8,000	−20,000
6. Overhead		−800	−1,600	−4,000
7. Depreciation		−1,040	−1,040	−1,040
8. Interest		−2,160	−2,160	−2,160
9. Income	−2,000	0	3,200	12,800
10. Tax	0	0	420	4,480
11. Net cash flow	−16,400	0	2,780	8,320
12. Net present value = +13,932				

e. *Operating costs:* These include all direct and indirect costs. Indirect costs (heat, light, power, fringe benefits, etc.) are assumed to be 200% of direct labor costs. Operating costs per unit are forecasted to remain constant in real terms at $2,000.

f. *Overhead:* Marketing and administrative costs, assumed equal to 10% of revenue.

g. *Depreciation:* Straight-line for 10 years.

h. *Interest:* Charged on capital expenditure and working capital at Reliable's current borrowing rate of 15%.

i. *Income:* Revenue less the sum of research and development, operating costs, overhead, depreciation, and interest.

j. *Tax:* 35% of income. However, income is negative in 2017. This loss is carried forward and deducted from taxable income in 2019.

k. *Net cash flow:* Assumed equal to income less tax.

l. *Net present value:* NPV of net cash flow at a 15% discount rate.

10. **Operating Cash Flows.** Laurel's Lawn Care Ltd. has a new mower line that can generate revenues of $120,000 per year. Direct production costs are $40,000, and the fixed costs of maintaining the lawn mower factory are $15,000 a year. The factory originally cost $1 million and is being depreciated for tax purposes over 25 years using straight-line depreciation. Calculate the operating cash flows of the project if the firm's tax bracket is 35%. (*LO9-2*)

11. **Equivalent Annual Cost.** Gluon Inc. is considering the purchase of a new high pressure glueball. It can purchase the glueball for $120,000 and sell its old low-pressure glueball, which is fully depreciated, for $20,000. The new equipment has a 10-year useful life and will save $28,000 a year in expenses. The opportunity cost of capital is 12%, and the firm's tax rate is 40%. What is the equivalent annual saving from the purchase if Gluon uses straight-line depreciation? (*LO9-2*)

12. **Cash Flows and NPV.** Johnny's Lunches is considering purchasing a new, energy-efficient grill. The grill will cost $40,000 and will be depreciated according to the 3-year MACRS schedule. It will be sold for scrap metal after 3 years for $10,000. The grill will have no effect on revenues but will save Johnny's $20,000 in energy expenses. The tax rate is 35%. (*LO9-2*)

   a. What are the operating cash flows in each year?
   b. What are the total cash flows in each year?
   c. If the discount rate is 12%, should the grill be purchased?

13. **Project Evaluation.** PC Shopping Network may upgrade its modem pool. It last upgraded 2 years ago, when it spent $115 million on equipment with an assumed life of 5 years and an assumed salvage value of $15 million for tax purposes. The firm uses straight-line depreciation. The old equipment can be sold today for $80 million. A new modem pool can be installed today for $150 million. This will have a 3-year life and will be depreciated to zero using straight-line depreciation. The new equipment will enable the firm to increase sales by $25 million per year and decrease operating costs by $10 million per year. At the end of 3 years, the new equipment will be worthless. Assume the firm's tax rate is 35% and the discount rate for projects of this sort is 10%. (*LO9-2*)

   a. What is the net cash flow at time 0 if the old equipment is replaced?
   b. What are the incremental cash flows in years: (i) 1; (ii) 2; (iii) 3?
   c. What is the NPV of the replacement project?
   d. What is the IRR of the replacement project?

14. **Project Evaluation.** Revenues generated by a new fad product are forecast as follows:

Year	Revenues
1	$40,000
2	30,000
3	20,000
4	10,000
Thereafter	0

Expenses are expected to be 40% of revenues, and working capital required in each year is expected to be 20% of revenues in the following year. The product requires an immediate investment of $45,000 in plant and equipment. (*LO9-2*)

    a. What is the initial investment in the product? Remember working capital.

    b. If the plant and equipment are depreciated over 4 years to a salvage value of zero using straight-line depreciation, and the firm's tax rate is 40%, what are the project cash flows in each year?

    c. If the opportunity cost of capital is 12%, what is project NPV?

    d. What is project IRR?

15. **Project Evaluation.** Kinky Copies may buy a high-volume copier. The machine costs $100,000 and will be depreciated straight-line over 5 years to a salvage value of $20,000. Kinky antici-pates that the machine actually can be sold in 5 years for $30,000. The machine will save $20,000 a year in labor costs but will require an increase in working capital, mainly paper supplies, of $10,000. The firm's marginal tax rate is 35%, and the discount rate is 8%. What is the NPV of this project? (*LO9-2*)

16. **Project Evaluation.** Blooper Industries must replace its magnoosium purification system. Quick & Dirty Systems sells a relatively cheap purification system for $10 million. The system will last 5 years. Do-It-Right sells a sturdier but more expensive system for $12 million; it will last for 8 years. Both systems entail $1 million in operating costs; both will be depreciated straight-line to a final value of zero over their useful lives; neither will have any salvage value at the end of its life. The firm's tax rate is 35%, and the discount rate is 12%. (*Hint:* Check the discussion of equivalent annual annuities in the previous chapter.) (*LO9-2*)

    a. What is the equivalent annual cost of investing in the cheap system?

    b. What is the equivalent annual cost of investing in the more expensive system?

    c. Which system should Blooper install?

17. **Project Evaluation.** Ilana Industries Inc. needs a new lathe. It can buy a new high-speed lathe for $1 million. The lathe will cost $35,000 per year to run, but it will save the firm $125,000 in labor costs and will be useful for 10 years. Suppose that, for tax purposes, the lathe will be depreciated on a straight-line basis over its 10-year life to a salvage value of $100,000. The actual market value of the lathe at that time also will be $100,000. The discount rate is 8%, and the corporate tax rate is 35%. What is the NPV of buying the new lathe? (*LO9-2*)

18. **Project Evaluation.** Better Mousetraps has developed a new trap. It can go into production for an initial investment in equipment of $6 million. The equipment will be depreciated straight-line over 6 years to a value of zero, but, in fact, it can be sold after 6 years for $500,000. The firm believes that working capital at each date must be maintained at a level of 10% of next year's forecast sales. The firm estimates production costs equal to $1.50 per trap and believes that the traps can be sold for $4 each. Sales forecasts are given in the following table. The project will come to an end in 5 years when the trap becomes technologically obsolete. The firm's tax bracket is 35%, and the required rate of return on the project is 12%. (*LO9-2 and LO9-3*)

Year:	0	1	2	3	4	5	6	Thereafter
Sales (millions of traps)	0	0.5	0.6	1.0	1.0	0.6	0.2	0

    a. What is project NPV?

    b. By how much would NPV increase if the firm depreciated its investment using the 5-year MACRS schedule?

19. **Project Evaluation.** United Pigpen is considering a proposal to manufacture high-protein hog feed. The project would require use of an existing warehouse, which is currently rented out to a neighboring firm. The next year's rental charge on the warehouse is $100,000, and thereafter, the rent is expected to grow in line with inflation at 4% a year. In addition to using the warehouse, the proposal envisages an investment in plant and equipment of $1.2 million. This could be depreciated for tax purposes straight-line over 10 years. However, Pigpen expects to terminate the project at the end of 8 years and to resell the plant and equipment in year 8 for $400,000. Finally, the project requires an immediate investment in working capital of $350,000. Thereafter, working capital is forecasted to be 10% of sales in each of years 1 through 7. Work-ing capital will be run down to zero in year 8 when the project shuts down. Year 1 sales of hog feed are expected to be $4.2 million, and thereafter, sales are forecasted to grow by 5% a year, slightly faster than the inflation rate. Manufacturing costs are expected to be 90% of sales, and profits are subject to tax at 35%. The cost of capital is 12%. What is the NPV of Pigpen's project? (*LO9-2 and LO9-3*)

20. **Cash Flows.** We've emphasized that the firm should pay attention only to cash flows when assessing the net present value of proposed projects. Depreciation is a noncash expense. Why then does it matter whether we assume straight-line or MACRS depreciation when we assess project NPV? (*LO9-3*)

21. **Salvage Value.** Quick Computing (from Problem 1) installed its previous generation of computer chip manufacturing equipment 3 years ago. Some of that older equipment will become unnecessary when the company goes into production of its new product. The obsolete equipment, which originally cost $40 million, has been depreciated straight-line over an assumed tax life of 5 years, but it can be sold now for $18 million. The firm's tax rate is 35%. What is the after-tax cash flow from the sale of the equipment? (*LO9-3*)

22. **Salvage Value.** Your firm purchased machinery with a 7-year MACRS life for $10 million. The project, however, will end after 5 years. If the equipment can be sold for $4.5 million at the completion of the project, and your firm's tax rate is 35%, what is the after-tax cash flow from the sale of the machinery? (*LO9-3*)

23. **Depreciation and Project Value.** Bottoms Up Diaper Service is considering the purchase of a new industrial washer. It can purchase the washer for $6,000 and sell its old washer for $2,000. The new washer will last for 6 years and save $1,500 a year in expenses. The opportunity cost of capital is 16%, and the firm's tax rate is 40%. (*LO9-3*)

    a. If the firm uses straight-line depreciation to an assumed salvage value of zero over a 6-year life, what are the cash flows of the project in years 0 to 6? The new washer will in fact have zero salvage value after 6 years, and the old washer is fully depreciated.
    b. What is project NPV?
    c. What is NPV if the firm uses MACRS depreciation with a 5-year tax life?

24. **Depreciation and Project Value.** Ms. T. Potts, the treasurer of Ideal China, has a problem. The company has just ordered a new kiln for $400,000. Of this sum, $50,000 is described by the supplier as an installation cost. Ms. Potts does not know whether the Internal Revenue Service (IRS) will permit the company to treat this cost as a tax-deductible current expense or as a capital investment. In the latter case, the company could depreciate the $50,000 using the five-year MACRS tax depreciation schedule. The tax rate is 35% and the opportunity cost of capital is 5%.

    a. What is the present value of the cost of the kiln if the installation cost is treated as a separate current expense?
    b. What is the present value of the cost of the kiln if the installation cost is treated as a part of the capital investment?

25. **Operating Cash Flows.** Talia's Tutus bought a new sewing machine for $40,000 that will be depreciated using the MACRS depreciation schedule for a 5-year recovery period. (*LO9-3*)

    a. Find the depreciation charge each year.
    b. If the sewing machine is sold after 3 years for $22,000, what will be the after-tax proceeds on the sale if the firm's tax bracket is 35%?

26. **Cash Flows.** Canyon Tours showed the following components of working capital last year: (*LO9-4*)

	Beginning of Year	End of Year
Accounts receivable	$24,000	$23,000
Inventory	12,000	12,500
Accounts payable	14,500	16,500

    a. What was the change in net working capital during the year?
    b. If sales were $36,000 and costs were $24,000, what was cash flow for the year? Ignore taxes.

27. **Cash Flows and Working Capital.** A house painting business had revenues of $16,000 and expenses of $9,000 last summer. There were no depreciation expenses. However, the business reported the following changes in working capital:

	Beginning of Year	End of Year
Accounts receivable	$1,200	$4,500
Accounts payable	700	300

Calculate net cash flow for the business for this period. (*LO9-4*)

28. **Cash Flows and Working Capital.** A firm had after-tax income last year of $1.2 million. Its depreciation expenses were $.4 million, and its total cash flow was $1.2 million. What happened to net working capital during the year? (*LO9-4*)

29. **Cash Flows and Working Capital.** The only capital investment required for a small project is investment in inventory. Profits this year were $10,000, and inventory increased from $4,000 to $5,000. What was the cash flow from the project? (*LO9-4*)

30. **Cash Flows and Working Capital.** A firm's balance sheets for year-end 2016 and 2017 contain the following data. What happened to investment in net working capital during 2017? All items are in millions of dollars. (*LO9-4*)

	Dec. 31, 2016	Dec. 31, 2017
Accounts receivable	32	36
Inventories	25	30
Accounts payable	12	26

BEYOND THE PAGE

 Blooper Industries

mhhe.com/brealey9e

31. **Project Evaluation.** Suppose that Blooper's customers paid their bills with an average 3-month delay (instead of 2 months) and that Blooper's inventories were 20% rather than 15% of next year's expenses. (*LO9-4*)

    a. Would project NPV be higher or lower than that in the worked example in the chapter?
    b. Calculate Blooper's working capital in each year of its project.
    c. What is the change in project NPV (use the Blooper spreadsheet)?

32. **Project Evaluation.** The efficiency gains resulting from a just-in-time inventory management system will allow a firm to reduce its level of inventories permanently by $250,000. What is the most the firm should be willing to pay for installing the system? (*LO9-4*)

33. **Working Capital.** Return to Better Mousetraps in Problem 18. Suppose the firm can cut its requirements for working capital in half by using better inventory control systems. By how much will this increase project NPV? (*LO9-4*)

34. **Project Evaluation.** The following table presents sales forecasts for Golden Gelt Giftware. The unit price is $40. The unit cost of the giftware is $25.

Year	Unit Sales
1	22,000
2	30,000
3	14,000
4	5,000
Thereafter	0

It is expected that net working capital will amount to 20% of sales in the following year. For example, the store will need an initial (year 0) investment in working capital of .20 × 22,000 × $40 = $176,000. Plant and equipment necessary to establish the giftware business will require an additional investment of $200,000. This investment will be depreciated using MACRS and a 3-year life. After 4 years, the equipment will have an economic and book value of zero. The firm's tax rate is 35%. What is the net present value of the project? The discount rate is 20%. (*LO9-4*)

WEB EXERCISE

1. Go to finance.yahoo.com and obtain the financial statements for Ford (F) and Microsoft (MSFT). What were capital expenditures and sales for each firm? What were the ratios of capital expenditure to sales for the last 3 years for both companies? What were the sales and net capital expenditures relative to total assets? What might explain the variation in these ratios for these two large corporations? Did the company make an investment or disinvestment in working capital in each of the 3 years?

SOLUTIONS TO SELF-TEST QUESTIONS

9.1 Remember, discount cash flows, not profits. Each tewgit machine costs $250,000 right away. Recognize that outlay, but forget accounting depreciation. Cash flows per machine are:

Year:	0	1	2	3	4	5
Investment (outflow)	−250,000					
Sales		250,000	300,000	300,000	250,000	250,000
Operating expenses		−200,000	−200,000	−200,000	−200,000	−200,000
Cash flow	−250,000	+ 50,000	+100,000	+100,000	+ 50,000	+ 50,000

Each machine is forecast to generate $50,000 of cash flow in years 4 and 5. Thus it makes sense to keep operating for 5 years.

9.2 a,b. The site and buildings could have been sold or put to another use. Their values are opportunity costs, which should be treated as incremental cash outflows.
c. Demolition costs are incremental cash outflows.
d. The cost of the access road is sunk and not incremental.
e. Lost cash flows from other projects are incremental cash outflows.
f. Depreciation is not a cash expense and should not be included, except as it affects taxes. (Taxes are discussed later in this chapter.)
g. The reduction in tax due to depreciation is an addition to cash flow.
h. The initial investment in inventories is a cash outflow.
i. The expenditure on design is a sunk cost and not an incremental cash flow.

9.3 Actual health costs will be increasing at about 7% a year.

Year:	1	2	3	4
Cost per worker	$2,400	$2,568	$2,748	$2,940

The present value at 10% of these four cash flows is $8,377.

9.4 The tax rate is $T = 35\%$. Taxes paid will be

$$T \times (\text{revenue} - \text{expenses} - \text{depreciation}) = .35 \times (600 - 300 - 200) = \$35$$

Operating cash flow can be calculated as follows.
a. Revenue − expenses − taxes = 600 − 300 − 35 = $265
b. Net profit + depreciation = (600 − 300 − 200 − 35) + 200 = 65 + 200 = 265
c. (Revenues − cash expenses) × (1 − tax rate) + (depreciation × tax rate) = (600 − 300) × (1 − .35) + (200 × .35) = 265

9.5

Year	MACRS 3-Year Depreciation	Tax Shield	PV Tax Shield at 12%
1	3,333	1,167	1,042
2	4,445	1,556	1,240
3	1,481	518	369
4	741	259	165
Totals	10,000	3,500	2,816

The present value increases to 2,816, or $2,816,000.

SOLUTIONS TO SPREADSHEET QUESTIONS

9.1   NPV = $4,515

9.2   NPV = $4,459

9.3   NPV = $5,741. NPV rises because the real value of depreciation allowances and the depreciation tax shield is higher when the inflation rate is lower.

MINICASE

Jack Tar, CFO of Sheetbend & Halyard Inc., opened the internal company confidential envelope. It contained a draft of a competitive bid for a contract to supply duffel canvas to the U.S. Navy. The cover memo from Sheetbend's CEO asked Mr. Tar to review the bid before it was submitted.

The bid and its supporting documents had been prepared by Sheetbend's sales staff. It called for Sheetbend to supply 100,000 yards of duffel canvas per year for 5 years. The proposed selling price was fixed at $30 per yard.

Mr. Tar was not usually involved in sales, but this bid was unusual in at least two respects. First, if accepted by the navy, it would commit Sheetbend to a fixed-price, long-term contract. Second, producing the duffel canvas would require an investment of $1.5 million to purchase machinery and to refurbish Sheetbend's plant in Pleasantboro, Maine.

Mr. Tar set to work and, by the end of the week, had collected the following facts and assumptions:

- The plant in Pleasantboro had been built in the early 1900s and is now idle. The plant was fully depreciated on Sheetbend's books, except for the purchase cost of the land of $10,000.
- Now that the land was valuable shorefront property, Mr. Tar thought the land and the idle plant could be sold, immediately or in the near future, for $600,000.
- Refurbishing the plant would cost $500,000. This investment would be depreciated for tax purposes on the 10-year MACRS schedule.

- The new machinery would cost $1 million. This investment could be depreciated on the 5-year MACRS schedule.
- The refurbished plant and new machinery would last for many years. However, the remaining market for duffel canvas was small, and it was not clear that additional orders could be obtained once the navy contract was finished. The machinery was custom-built and could be used only for duffel canvas. Its secondhand value at the end of 5 years was probably zero.
- Table 9.4 shows the sales staff's forecasts of income from the navy contract. Mr. Tar reviewed this forecast and decided that its assumptions were reasonable, except that the forecast used book, not tax, depreciation.
- But the forecast income statement contained no mention of working capital. Mr. Tar thought that working capital would average about 10% of sales.

Armed with this information, Mr. Tar constructed a spreadsheet to calculate the NPV of the duffel canvas project, assuming that Sheetbend's bid would be accepted by the navy.

He had just finished debugging the spreadsheet when another confidential envelope arrived from Sheetbend's CEO. It contained a firm offer from a Maine real estate developer to purchase Sheetbend's Pleasantboro land and plant for $1.5 million in cash.

Should Mr. Tar recommend submitting the bid to the navy at the proposed price of $30 per yard? The discount rate for this project is 12%.

TABLE 9.4 Forecast income statement for the U.S. Navy duffel canvas project (dollar values in thousands, except price per yard)

Year:	1	2	3	4	5
1. Yards sold	100.00	100.00	100.00	100.00	100.00
2. Price per yard	30.00	30.00	30.00	30.00	30.00
3. Revenue (1 × 2)	3,000.00	3,000.00	3,000.00	3,000.00	3,000.00
4. Cost of goods sold	2,100.00	2,184.00	2,271.36	2,362.21	2,456.70
5. Operating cash flow (3 − 4)	900.00	816.00	728.64	637.79	543.30
6. Depreciation	250.00	250.00	250.00	250.00	250.00
7. Income (5 − 6)	650.00	566.00	478.64	387.79	293.30
8. Tax at 35%	227.50	198.10	167.52	135.72	102.65
9. Net income (7 − 8)	$422.50	$367.90	$311.12	$252.07	$190.65

Notes:

1. Yards sold and price per yard would be fixed by contract.
2. Cost of goods includes fixed cost of $300,000 per year plus variable costs of $18 per yard. Costs are expected to increase at the inflation rate of 4% per year.
3. Depreciation: A $1 million investment in machinery is depreciated straight-line over 5 years ($200,000 per year). The $500,000 cost of refurbishing the Pleasantboro plant is depreciated straight-line over 10 years ($50,000 per year).

10

Project Analysis

LEARNING OBJECTIVES

After studying this chapter, you should be able to:

10-1 Understand how companies organize the investment process so that it capitalizes on their strengths.

10-2 Appreciate the problems of obtaining unbiased inputs for valuing projects.

10-3 Use sensitivity, scenario, and break-even analyses to see how project profitability would be affected by an error in your forecasts.

10-4 Understand why an overestimate of sales is more serious for projects with high operating leverage.

10-5 Recognize the importance of managerial flexibility in capital budgeting.

RELATED WEBSITES FOR THIS CHAPTER CAN BE
FOUND IN CONNECT.

When undertaking capital investments, good managers maintain maximum flexibility. © fizkes/Shutterstock RF

I n the last chapter, we looked at a simple but fairly realistic example in which the financial manager calculated the NPV of Blooper's new mine. But we should not leave you with the idea that project evaluation is simply a mechanical exercise in which the manager takes a set of cash-flow forecasts and cranks out a net present value. When presented with an (apparently) attractive proposal, wise financial managers ask a series of questions:

1. **Does the project draw on the company's competitive strengths?** Positive NPVs are only believable if the company has some special advantage. It may be that your firm is well-placed to expand production capacity more quickly and cheaply than your competitors. Or perhaps it has some proprietary technology or brand name that competitors can't match. You need to make sure that your investments capitalize on such advantages.

2. **Do the cash-flow forecasts give due weight to possible favorable and unfavorable outcomes?** The forecasts used to calculate NPVs should be unbiased. This means that they will be correct on average. But project proposers may have many reasons to present an overly rosy picture. The company needs to establish a set of procedures to ensure that the forecasts it gets are honest and consistent.

3. **What are the things that could go wrong with the project?** Managers need to look behind the cash-flow forecasts to try to understand what makes the project tick and what could go wrong. They try to identify the key assumptions in their analysis. This involves asking a number of "what-if" questions. What if your market share turns out to be higher or lower than forecast? What if energy costs increase rapidly? What if . . . ? A number of techniques have been developed to help answer such questions. They include sensitivity analysis, scenario analysis, and break-even analysis. If managers can identify the future danger points, they may be able to avoid a costly mistake by undertaking more analysis up-front or by modifying the project.

4. **Does the project have built-in flexibility that would allow the company to respond to unexpected events?** Books about capital budgeting sometimes create the impression that once the manager has made an investment decision, there is nothing to do but sit back and watch the cash flows develop. But because cash flows rarely proceed as anticipated, companies constantly need to modify their operations. If cash flows are better than anticipated, the project may be expanded. If they are worse, it may be scaled back or abandoned altogether. Projects need to be designed to provide this flexibility.

5. **Does a proposal consider possible variations on the project?** For example, would it be better to go for a larger or smaller project? Would a project's NPV be higher if the factory is built in northern South Dakota rather than the planned investment in southern North Dakota? Is there a case for investing in more durable but also more expensive equipment?

Should the existing equipment be kept in operation for a further year?

We looked briefly at the last set of questions in Chapter 8, when we showed how companies compare mutually exclusive versions of a project. It is now time to look at how companies tackle the remaining questions.

How Firms Organize the Investment Process to Draw on Their Competitive Strengths

The Capital Budget

Potential projects and accurate cash-flow forecasts don't fall from the sky. Promising investment opportunities have to be identified, and they must fit in with the firm's strategic goals. Therefore, once a year, the head office generally asks each of its divisions to provide a list of the investments that it would like to make. These are gathered together into a proposed **capital budget.** Smaller investments won't be itemized separately in the budget. For example, they may be grouped into the broad category of "machine replacement." Larger investments that will significantly affect the company's future will receive greater attention. The budget is then reviewed and pruned by senior management and staff specializing in planning and financial analysis. Usually, there are negotiations between senior management and divisional management, and there may also be special analyses of major outlays or ventures into new areas.

Once the budget has been approved, it generally remains the basis for planning over the ensuing year. However, inclusion of a project in the budget does not confer permission to go ahead with it. Before each investment gets the final go-ahead, it will need to be supported by a more detailed analysis setting out particulars of the project, cash-flow forecasts, and present value calculations.

Many of the investment proposals that are included in the budget bubble up from the bottom of the organization. But ideas are also likely to come from higher up. For example, the managers of plants A and B cannot be expected to see the potential benefits of closing their plants and consolidating production at a new plant C. We expect divisional managers to propose plant C. Similarly, divisions 1 and 2 may not be eager to give up their own data processing operations to a large central computer. That proposal would come from senior management.

The construction of a capital budget provides a good opportunity for senior management to ensure that the firm's investments match its corporate strategy. Corporate strategy aims to find and exploit sources of competitive advantage. It focuses on the firm's existing strengths—not just ones that it would be nice to have—and then identifies the markets where these capabilities can add the most value.

A competitive advantage may arise in several ways. It may come from relationships that the firm has built up over time with its customers, from the skills and experience of employees, from brand names and reputation, from the ability to innovate, or simply from the fact that you are lucky enough to own a particularly valuable building or piece of land. Managers with a clear idea of the firm's competitive strengths are better placed to separate significant investments that truly have a positive NPV from those that do not.

Analyzing competitive advantage can also help to ferret out projects that incorrectly appear to have a negative NPV. If you are the lowest-cost producer of a profitable product in a growing market, then you should probably invest to expand along with the market. If your calculations show a negative NPV for such an expansion, then it is likely that you have made a mistake.

capital budget
List of planned investment projects.

Investment strategy also involves understanding the likely response of the firm's competitors. If your firm is earning juicy profits, other companies will try to muscle in on your success. You should, therefore, be suspicious of any investment that predicts a stream of excess profits stretching into the indefinite future.

Problems and Some Solutions

Evaluating capital investment opportunities is hard enough when you can do the entire job yourself. In most firms, however, capital budgeting is a group effort, and this brings with it some challenges.

Ensuring that Forecasts Are Consistent   Inconsistent assumptions often creep into investment proposals. For example, suppose that the manager of the furniture division is bullish (optimistic) on housing starts, but the manager of the appliance division is bearish (pessimistic). This inconsistency makes the projects proposed by the furniture division look more attractive than those of the appliance division.

To ensure consistency, many firms begin the capital budgeting process by establishing forecasts of economic indicators, such as inflation and the growth in national income, as well as forecasts of particular items that are important to the firm's business, such as housing starts or the price of raw materials. These forecasts can then be used as the basis for all project analyses.

Eliminating Conflicts of Interest   In Chapter 1, we pointed out that while managers want to do a good job, they are also concerned about their own futures. If the interests of managers conflict with those of stockholders, the result is likely to be poor investment decisions.

We also discussed in Chapter 1 that, in the case of senior managers, these conflicts are alleviated partly by compensation schemes that reward management for investing in projects that offer high returns and partly by good systems of corporate governance that oversee management's actions. But senior managers also need to ensure that more junior staff are also not simply looking after their own interests. For example, new plant managers naturally want to demonstrate good performance right away. So they might propose quick-payback projects even if NPV is sacrificed. Unfortunately, many firms measure performance and reward managers in ways that encourage such behavior. If the firm always demands quick results, it is unlikely that plant managers will concentrate only on NPV.

10.2 Reducing Forecast Bias

Project cash flows are supposed to be *unbiased* forecasts that give due weight to all possible outcomes. Sometimes, the cash flow will turn out to be higher than the expected level and, at other times, it will be lower, but the errors should average out over many projects. Suppose that you expect project Z to produce just one cash flow, forecasted at $1 million. But now you discover that the company's engineers are behind schedule in developing the technology required for the project. They are confident that it will work, but they admit to a small chance that it will not. You still see the *most likely* outcome as $1 million, but you also see some chance that project Z will generate *zero* cash flow next year. If you forecast a cash flow of $1 million for projects such as Z, you will overestimate the average cash flow because, every now and again, you will hit a zero. Those zeros should be averaged in to your estimates of the expected cash flow. For example, if the technological uncertainty introduces a 10% chance of a zero cash flow, the unbiased forecast would drop to $900,000:

Expected cash flow = unbiased forecast = .10 × $0 + .90 × $1 million = $900,000

BEYOND THE PAGE

Overoptimism and
cost overruns

mhhe.com/brealey9e

The problem of obtaining unbiased forecasts is complicated by the fact that some-one who is keen to get a project proposal accepted is likely to look on the bright side when forecasting the project's cash flows. Such overoptimism is a common feature in financial forecasts. For example, think of large public expenditure proposals. How often have you heard of a new missile, dam, or highway that actually cost less than was originally forecast?

Overoptimism is not altogether bad. Psychologists stress that optimism and confidence are likely to increase effort, commitment, and persistence. The problem is that it is difficult for senior managers to judge the true prospects for each project.

Sometimes, senior management seems to actually encourage project sponsors to overstate their case. For example, if middle managers believe that success depends on having the largest division rather than the most profitable one, they will propose large expansion projects that they do not believe have the highest net present value. Or if divisions must compete for limited resources, they will try to outbid each other for those resources. The fault in such cases is top management's—if lower-level managers are not rewarded on the basis of net present value and contribution to firm value, it should not be surprising that they focus their efforts elsewhere.

Other problems stem from sponsors' eagerness to obtain approval for their favorite projects. As the proposal travels up the organization, alliances are formed. Thus, once a division has screened its own plants' proposals, the plants in that division unite in competing against outsiders. The result is that the head office may receive several thousand investment proposals each year, all essentially sales documents presented by united fronts and designed to persuade. The forecasts have been doctored to ensure that NPV appears positive. One response of senior managers to this problem of biased information is to impose rigid expenditure limits on individual plants or divisions. These limits force the subunits to choose among projects. The firm ends up using capital rationing not because capital is unobtainable but as a way of decentralizing decisions.[1]

Sometimes, senior managers try to offset bias by increasing the hurdle rate for capital expenditures. Suppose the true cost of capital is 10%, but the CEO is frustrated by the large fraction of projects that don't subsequently earn 10%. Therefore, she directs project sponsors to use a 15% discount rate. In other words, she adds a 5% fudge factor in an attempt to offset forecast bias. But it doesn't work; it *never* works. Brealey, Myers, and Marcus's Second Law explains why. The law states: *The proportion of projects that promise positive NPVs at the corporate hurdle rate is independent of the hurdle rate.*[2]

10.3 Some "What-If" Questions

"What-if" questions ask what will happen to a project in various circumstances. For example, what will happen if the economy enters a recession? What if a competitor enters the market? What if costs turn out to be higher than anticipated?

You might wonder why one would bother with these sorts of questions. For instance, suppose your project seems to have a positive NPV based on the best available forecasts, in which you have already factored in the chances of both positive and negative surprises. Won't you commit to this project regardless of possible future surprises? If things later don't work out as you had hoped, that is too bad, but you don't have a crystal ball.

In fact, what-if analysis is crucial to capital budgeting. First recall that cash-flow forecasts are just estimates. You often have the opportunity to improve on those estimates if you are willing to commit additional resources to the task. For example,

---

[1] We discussed capital rationing in Chapter 8.

[2] There is no First Law. We think "Second Law" sounds better.

if you wish to improve the precision of an estimate of the demand for a product, you might conduct additional market research. Or if cost uncertainty is a concern, you might commission additional engineering studies to evaluate the feasibility of a novel production process. But how do you know when to keep sharpening your forecasts or where it is best to devote your efforts? What-if analysis can help identify the inputs that are most worth refining before you commit to a project. These will be the ones that have the greatest potential to alter project NPV.

Moreover, managers don't simply turn a key to start a project and then walk away and let the cash flows roll in. There are always surprises, adjustments, and refinements. What-if analysis indicates where the most likely need for adjustments will arise and where to undertake contingency planning. In this section, therefore, we examine some of the standard tools managers use when considering important types of what-if questions.

Sensitivity Analysis

Uncertainty means that more things *can* happen than *will* happen. Therefore, whenever managers are given a cash-flow forecast, they try to determine what else might happen and the implications of those possible events. This is called **sensitivity analysis.**

Put yourself again in the well-heeled shoes of the financial manager of Blooper Industries. In the last chapter we assessed a proposal by Blooper to develop a magnoosium mine. The proposal contained detailed forecasts of the cash flows from this mine and a calculation of its NPV. Spreadsheet 10.1 reproduces the analysis in Spreadsheet 9.1 except that we have broken down expenses into **variable costs** and **fixed costs.** Fixed costs are those that do not change if output is above or below expectations.[3] For example, Blooper's machine rental costs, environmental expenses, and management costs may be fixed. By contrast, its expenditure on labor, explosives, drill bits, and fuel are likely to increase with the quantity of ore mined. We assume that variable costs will equal 40% of revenues (see cell B5).

The mine appears to have a positive NPV, but there is inevitable uncertainty in the forecasts. Cash flows could turn out to be better or worse than expected. So, before you agree to go ahead, you want to delve behind the forecasts and identify the key variables that will determine whether the project succeeds or fails.

Spreadsheet 10.1 seems to comprise the important factors that will determine success or failure, but look out for things you may have forgotten. Perhaps there will be delays in obtaining planning permission, or perhaps you will need to undertake costly re-landscaping. The greatest dangers often lie in these *unknown unknowns,* or "unk-unks," as scientists call them.

Having found no unk-unks (no doubt you will find them later), you look at how NPV may be affected if you have made a wrong forecast of revenues, costs and so on. To do this, you first obtain optimistic and pessimistic estimates for the underlying variables. These are set out in the left-hand columns of Table 10.1. For example, you can see that in the worst case, revenues each year could fall 20% short of expectations. The good news is that they could also exceed expectations by 15%.

Now you see what happens to NPV under the optimistic and pessimistic forecasts for each variable. The right-hand side of Table 10.1 shows the project's net present value if the variables are set *one at a time* to their optimistic and pessimistic values. For example, if revenues in each year turn out to be 20% below forecast and all other forecasts are unchanged from Spreadsheet 10.1, then the project would be a loser with an NPV of −$91,000.[4] Your project, it seems, is by no means a sure thing. The principal uncertainties appear to be revenues and variable costs. By contrast, even a major uplift in

sensitivity analysis
Analysis of the effects on project profitability of changes in sales, costs, and so on.

variable costs
Costs that change as the level of output changes.

fixed costs
Costs that do not depend on the level of output.

BEYOND THE PAGE

 Project analysis

mhhe.com/brealey9e

---

[3] This doesn't mean that the level of fixed costs is the same in each year. Indeed, we assume that they are expected to rise annually with inflation.

[4] Notice that when we changed revenues, we did not change variable costs. An alternative would be to calculate how NPV changes if revenues change but variable costs remain at 40% of revenues.

SPREADSHEET 10.1 Financial projections for Blooper's magnoosium mine (dollar values in thousands). This table repeats the analysis in Spreadsheet 9.1 except that expenses are now broken down into variable and fixed expenses.

	A	B	C	D	E	F	G	H
1	**A. Inputs**							
2	Initial investment ($ thousands)	10,000						
3	Salvage value ($ thousands)	2,000						
4	Initial revenues ($ thousands)	15,000						
5	Variable costs (% of revenues)	40.0%						
6	Initial fixed costs ($ thousands)	4,000						
7	Inflation rate (%)	5.0%						
8	Discount rate (%)	12.0%						
9	Receivables (% of sales)	16.7%						
10	Inventory (% of next year's costs)	15.0%						
11	Tax rate (%)	35.0%						
12								
13	**Year:**	**0**	**1**	**2**	**3**	**4**	**5**	**6**
14	**B. Fixed assets**							
15	Investments in fixed assets	10,000						
16	Sales of fixed assets							1,300
17	Cash flow from investment in fixed assets	−10,000						1,300
18								
19	**C. Operating cash flow**							
20	Revenues		15,000	15,750	16,538	17,364	18,233	
21	Variable expenses		6,000	6,300	6,615	6,946	7,293	
22	Fixed expenses		4,000	4,200	4,410	4,631	4,862	
23	Depreciation		2,000	2,000	2,000	2,000	2,000	
24	Pretax profit		3,000	3,250	3,513	3,788	4,078	
25	Tax		1,050	1,138	1,229	1,326	1,427	
26	Profit after tax		1,950	2,113	2,283	2,462	2,650	
27	Operating cash flow		3,950	4,113	4,283	4,462	4,650	
28								
29	**D. Working capital**							
30	Working capital	1,500	4,075	4,279	4,493	4,717	3,039	0
31	Change in working capital	1,500	2,575	204	214	225	−1,679	−3,039
32	Cash flow from investment in working capital	−1,500	−2,575	−204	−214	−225	1,679	3,039
33								
34	**E. Project valuation**							
35	Total project cash flow	−11,500	1,375	3,909	4,069	4,238	6,329	4,339
36	Discount factor	1.000	0.893	0.797	0.712	0.636	0.567	0.507
37	PV of cash flow	−11,500	1,228	3,116	2,896	2,693	3,591	2,198
38	Net present value	4,223						

TABLE 10.1 Sensitivity analysis for Blooper magnoosium mine

	Possible Annual Deviation from Expected Values		NPV (thousands of dollars)		
Variable	Pessimistic	Optimistic	Pessimistic	Expected	Optimistic
Investment	+35%	−25%	+$1,606	+$4,223	+$6,092
Revenues	−20	+15	−91	+4,223	+7,458
Variable costs	+30	−25	−515	+4,223	+8,170
Fixed costs	+40	−25	+11	+4,223	+6,855
Working capital	+100	−50	+2,458	+4,223	+5,105

working capital requirements would not have a serious impact on project NPV. Trendy consultants sometimes present the results of a sensitivity analysis by a *tornado diagram,* such as the one in Figure 10.1. The blue bars show how far NPV falls short of its expected value when each variable is set at its pessimistic value. The red bars show how far NPV *exceeds* its expected value when each variable is set at its *optimistic* value.

Value of Information   Now that you know the project could be thrown badly off course by a poor estimate of revenues, you might like to see whether it is possible to resolve some of this uncertainty. You would surely wish to understand the reason for the uncertainty about revenues. For example, if it stems from doubts about the size of the deposit, a further test hole may be worthwhile. If it reflects uncertainty about magnoosium prices, some more economic analysis may be warranted, or you may investigate whether a buyer would be prepared to enter into a fixed price contract to buy the magnoosium.

On the other hand, there is less value to gathering additional information about the amount of the initial investment or the working capital requirements. Because the project is marginally profitable even under pessimistic assumptions about these variables, a misestimate is unlikely to get you in trouble.

Limits to Sensitivity Analysis   Sensitivity analysis expresses cash flows in terms of unknown variables and then calculates the consequences of misestimating those variables. It forces the manager to identify the underlying factors, indicates where

FIGURE 10.1 Tornado diagram for Blooper project showing the effect on NPV of changes in forecasts

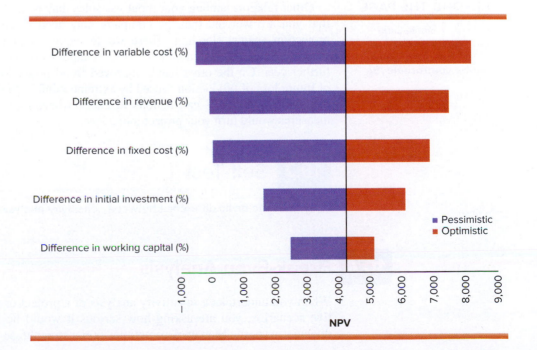

additional information would be most useful, and helps to expose confused or inappropriate forecasts.

Of course, there is no law stating which variables you should consider in your sensitivity analysis. For example, it would probably have made sense for Blooper to look separately at the quantity of ore extracted and the selling price. Or if you are concerned about a possible change in the corporate tax rate, you may wish to look at the effect of such a change on the project's NPV.

One drawback to sensitivity analysis is that it gives somewhat ambiguous results. For example, what exactly does "optimistic" or "pessimistic" mean? One person may be interpreting the terms in a different way from another. Ten years from now, after hundreds of projects, hindsight may show that somebody's pessimistic limit was exceeded twice as often as the other's; but hindsight won't help you now while you're making the investment decision.

Another problem with sensitivity analysis is that the underlying variables are likely to be interrelated. For example, if geological problems cause a delay in opening the mine, the initial costs are likely to be higher than expected, and initial revenues will be lower than forecast.

Because of these connections, you cannot push one-at-a-time sensitivity analysis too far. It is impossible to obtain optimistic and pessimistic values for total project cash flows from the information in Table 10.1. Still, it does give a sense of which variables should be most closely monitored.

Scenario Analysis

When variables are interrelated, managers often find it helpful to look at how their project would fare under different scenarios. **Scenario analysis** allows them to look at different but consistent combinations of variables. Forecasters generally prefer to give an estimate of revenues or costs under a particular scenario rather than to give some absolute optimistic or pessimistic value. For example, a general economic expansion might increase the market price of magnoosium but, at the same time, result in higher wages for your employees and, therefore, higher variable costs of production. When revenue and variable costs are linked, it does not make sense to do sensitivity analysis on each of them separately. Instead, you probably want to see the effect of changes in the two variables that are mutually consistent with particular economic forecasts.

Other relations among your input variables may be particular to the firm. Suppose that you are worried that the company may need to construct costly levees as a protection against flooding. These would require regulatory approval and involve construction delays and additional costs. Output from the mine would not start for a further year. On the other hand, improved flood protection would limit the chances of future loss of production caused by extreme rainfall. In this case, it might be worth re-running your NPV calculations to check whether the up-front flood protection measures would turn your project into a loser.

10.2 Self-Test

What is the basic difference between sensitivity analysis and scenario analysis?

10.4 Break-Even Analysis

When you undertake a sensitivity analysis of a project or when you look at alternative scenarios, you are asking how serious it would be if you have misestimated revenues or costs. Managers sometimes prefer to rephrase this question and ask how far off the estimates could be before the project begins to lose money. This exercise is known as **break-even analysis.**

For many projects, the make-or-break variable is sales volume. Therefore, managers most often focus on the break-even level of revenues. However, you might also look at other project variables, such as how high costs could be before the project goes into the red. Then, having calculated the break-even level of costs, management might say, "We really can't be sure of costs, but we can be confident that they will be less than the break-even level. It looks as if we can give the project the go-ahead."

As it turns out, "losing money" can be defined in more than one way. Most often, the break-even condition is defined in terms of accounting profits. More properly, however, it should be defined in terms of net present value. We will start with accounting break-even, show that it can lead you astray, and then show how NPV break-even can be used as an alternative.

Accounting Break-Even Analysis

The *accounting break-even* point is the level of sales at which profits are zero or, equivalently, at which total revenues equal total costs. As we have seen, some costs are fixed regardless of the level of output. Other costs vary as output changes.

When you first analyzed Blooper's mining project, you came up with the following estimates for initial revenues and costs:

Revenues	$15 million
Variable costs	6 million
Fixed costs	4 million
Depreciation	2 million

How large must revenues be to avoid losses? If the revenues are zero, the income statement will show fixed costs and depreciation totaling $6 million. Thus, there will be an accounting loss before tax of $6 million. Now notice that variable costs are 40% of revenues. So each additional dollar of revenues increases costs by only $.40 and thus reduces losses by $.60. Therefore, to cover fixed costs plus depreciation, you need annual revenues of 6 million/.60 = $10 million. Table 10.2 confirms that at this level of revenues, the firm will just break even. More generally,

$$\text{Break-even level of revenues} = \frac{\text{fixed costs including depreciation}}{\text{additional profit from each additional dollar of sales}} \qquad (10.1)$$

Table 10.2 shows the income statement with only $10 million of sales.

Figure 10.2 shows how the break-even point is determined. The blue 45-degree line shows project revenues. The dashed cost line shows how costs vary with revenues. When revenues are $10 million, the two lines cross, indicating that costs equal

break-even analysis
Analysis of the level of sales at which the project breaks even.

BEYOND THE PAGE

Project analysis

mhhe.com/brealey9e

TABLE 10.2 Income statement, break-even sales volume

Item	$ Thousands	
Revenues	$10,000	
Variable costs	4,000	(40% of revenues)
Fixed costs	4,000	
Depreciation	2,000	
Pretax profit	0	
Taxes	0	
Profit after tax	$ 0	

FIGURE 10.2 Accounting break-even analysis

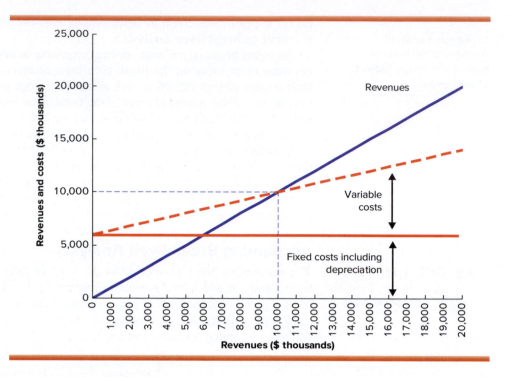

revenues. For lower revenues, revenues are less than costs and the project is in the red; for higher revenues, revenues exceed costs and the project moves into the black.

But consider this question: Is a project that breaks even in accounting terms an acceptable investment? If you are not sure about the answer, here's a possibly easier question: Would you be happy about an investment in a stock that, after 5 years, gave you a total rate of return of zero? We hope not. You might break even on such a stock, but a zero return does not compensate you for the time value of money or the risk that you have taken.

A project that simply breaks even on an accounting basis gives you your money back but does not cover the opportunity cost of the capital tied up in the project. A project that breaks even in accounting terms will surely have a negative NPV.

NPV Break-Even Analysis

A manager who calculates an accounting-based measure of break-even may be tempted to think that any project that earns more than this figure will help shareholders. But projects that break even on an accounting basis are really making a loss—they are failing to cover the costs of capital employed.[5] Managers who accept such projects are not helping their shareholders. Therefore, instead of asking what sales must be to produce an accounting profit, it is more useful to focus on the point at which NPV switches from negative to positive. This is called the **NPV break-even point.**

NPV break-even point
Minimum level of sales needed to cover all costs including the cost of capital.

Because revenues are not constant, but are expected to increase over time, it makes most sense to ask what *percentage* shortfall in each year's revenues would push the project into a negative NPV. To find the NPV break-even point, start by looking back at Spreadsheet 10.1, which showed that when revenues are $15 million, NPV is $4.223 million. Now calculate the impact on present value of a 1% decrease

[5] Think back to our discussion of economic value added (EVA) in Chapter 4. A project that breaks even on a present value basis will have a positive accounting profit but zero economic value added. In other words, it will just cover all its costs, including the cost of capital.

in initial year revenue. Go back to the Blooper spreadsheet, reduce initial revenues by 1% to $14.85 million, and compute the change in project NPV. (Changing initial revenues changes future revenues as well because revenue over time is assumed to increase from its initial level by the inflation rate.) You should find that NPV declines by $.2156 million. Each 1% decline in the revenue stream decreases NPV by $.2156 million. Therefore, a decline of 4.223/.2156 = .196, or about 20%, will reduce NPV from its base-case value all the way to zero.

Figure 10.3 shows how the present values of the revenues and costs from Blooper's mine vary with initial revenues. The present value of revenues rises in direct proportion to initial revenue, but the present value of costs rises at a slower pace because part of the costs is fixed. On the other hand, even when sales are zero, costs are positive because the project still incurs these fixed costs. At revenues of $15 million (where the deviation from the base case is zero), the present value of revenues exceeds that of costs by $4.223 million. The two lines cross when revenues in each year are about 20% below forecast. In other words, the project would have zero NPV if revenues started at .8 × $15 million = $12 million and then increased by 5% each year with inflation. This is the project's NPV break-even point. Notice that it is significantly higher than the point at which the project has zero profit.

10.3 Self-Test

What would be the accounting break-even level of sales if the capital investment was only $8 million? (Continue to assume that variable costs are 40% of revenues.)

FIGURE 10.3 NPV breakeven analysis

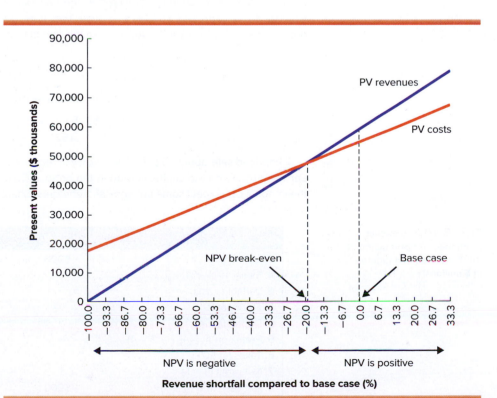

Example 10.1 ▶ Break-Even Analysis

We have said that projects that break even on an accounting basis are really making a loss—they are losing the opportunity cost of their investment. Here is a dramatic example. Lophead Aviation is contemplating investment in a new passenger aircraft, code-named the Trinova. Lophead's financial staff has gathered the following estimates:

1. The cost of developing the Trinova is forecast at $900 million, and this investment can be depreciated in six equal annual amounts.
2. Production of the plane is expected to take place at a steady annual rate over the following 6 years.
3. The average price of the Trinova is expected to be $15.5 million.
4. Fixed costs are forecast at $175 million a year.
5. Variable costs are forecast at $8.5 million a plane.
6. The tax rate is 50%.
7. The cost of capital is 10%.

Lophead's financial manager has used this information to construct a forecast of the profitability of the Trinova program. This is shown in rows 1 through 7 of Table 10.3 (ignore row 8 for a moment).

How many aircraft does Lophead need to sell to break even? The answer depends on what is meant by "break even." In accounting terms, the venture will break even when net profit (row 7 in the table) is zero. In this case,

$$(3.5 \times \text{planes sold}) - 162.5 = 0$$
$$\text{Planes sold} = 162.5/3.5 = 46.4$$

Thus, Lophead needs to sell about 46 planes a year, or a total of 280 planes, over the 6 years to show a profit. With a price of $15.5 million a plane, Lophead will break even in accounting terms with annual revenues of 46.4 × $15.5 million = $719 million.

We would have arrived at the same answer if we had used our formula to calculate the break-even level of revenues. Notice that the variable cost of each plane is $8.5 million, which is 54.8% of the $15.5 million sale price. Therefore, each dollar of sales increases pretax profits by $1 − $.548 = $.452. Now we use the formula for the accounting break-even point:

$$\text{Break-even revenues} = \frac{\text{fixed costs including depreciation}}{\text{additional profit from each additional dollar of sales}}$$

$$= \frac{\$325 \text{ million}}{.452} = \$719 \text{ million}$$

If Lophead sells about 46 planes a year, it will recover its original investment, but it will not earn any return on the capital tied up in the project. Companies that earn a zero return on their capital can expect some unhappy shareholders. Shareholders will be content only if the

TABLE 10.3 Forecast profitability for production of the Trinova airliner (figures in $ millions)

	Year 0	Years 1–6
Investment	$900	
1. Sales		$15.5 × planes sold
2. Variable costs		8.5 × planes sold
3. Fixed costs		175
4. Depreciation		900/6 = 150
5. Pretax profit (1 − 2 − 3 − 4)		(7 × planes sold) − 325
6. Taxes (at 50%)		(3.5 × planes sold) − 162.5
7. Net profit (5 − 6)		(3.5 × planes sold) − 162.5
8. Net cash flow (4 + 7)	−$900	(3.5 × planes sold) − 12.5

company's investments earn at least the cost of the capital invested. True break-even occurs when the projects have zero NPV.

How many planes must Lophead sell to break even in terms of net present value? Development of the Trinova costs $900 million. If the cost of capital is 10%, the 6-year annuity factor is 4.3553. The last row of Table 10.3 shows that net cash flow (in millions of dollars) in years 1–6 equals (3.5 × planes sold − 12.5). We can now find the annual plane sales necessary to break even in terms of NPV:

$$4.3553 \times (3.5 \times \text{planes sold} - 12.5) = 900$$
$$15.2436 \times \text{planes sold} - 54.44 = 900$$
$$\text{Planes sold} = 954.44/15.2436 = 62.6$$

Thus, while Lophead will break even in terms of accounting profits with sales of 46.4 planes a year (about 280 in total), it needs to sell 62.6 a year (or about 375 in total) to recover the opportunity cost of the capital invested in the project and break even in terms of NPV. ■

Our example may seem fanciful, but it is based loosely on reality. In 1971, Lockheed was in the middle of a major program to bring out the L-1011 TriStar airliner. This program was to bring Lockheed to the brink of failure, and it tipped Rolls-Royce (supplier of the TriStar engine) over the brink. In giving evidence to Congress, Lockheed argued that the TriStar program was commercially attractive and that sales would eventually exceed the break-even point of about 200 aircraft. But in calculating this break-even point, Lockheed appears to have ignored the opportunity cost of the huge capital investment in the project. Lockheed probably needed to sell about 500 aircraft to reach a zero net present value.[6]

10.4   Self-Test

What is the basic difference between sensitivity analysis and break-even analysis?

Operating Leverage

A project's break-even point depends on both its fixed costs, which do not vary with sales, and the profit on each extra sale. Managers often face a trade-off between these variables. For example, Blooper may be able to increase the number of part-time workers that it employs. In this case, Blooper replaces a fixed cost with a variable cost that is linked to output. Because a greater proportion of the company's expenses will fall when its output falls, its break-even point is reduced.

Of course, a high proportion of fixed costs is not all bad. The firm whose costs are largely fixed fares poorly when demand is low, but it may make a killing during a boom. Let us illustrate.

Suppose that increased use of part-time workers would reduce Blooper's fixed costs from $4 million to $2 million, but variable costs would rise from 40% to 53% of revenues. Table 10.4 shows that at the forecast level of revenues, the two policies fare equally, but if output falls short of forecast, the mine that relies on casual labor does better because its costs fall along with revenue. At high levels of output, the reverse is true, and the mine with the higher proportion of fixed costs has the advantage.

operating leverage
Degree to which costs are fixed.

A business with high fixed costs is said to have high **operating leverage** because small changes in sales will result in large changes in profits. We can measure operating

---

[6] The true break-even point for the TriStar program is estimated in U. E. Reinhardt, "Break-Even Analysis for Lockheed's TriStar: An Application of Financial Theory," *Journal of Finance* 28 (September 1973), pp. 821–838.

TABLE 10.4 A mine with high operating leverage performs relatively badly in a slump but flourishes in a boom (figures in $ thousands)

	High Fixed Costs			High Variable Costs		
	Slump	Normal	Boom	Slump	Normal	Boom
Revenues	11,250	15,000	20,000	11,250	15,000	20,000
− Variable costs	4,500	6,000	8,000	6,000	8,000	10,667
− Fixed costs	4,000	4,000	4,000	2,000	2,000	2,000
− Depreciation	2,000	2,000	2,000	2,000	2,000	2,000
= Pretax profit	750	3,000	6,000	1,250	3,000	5,333

degree of operating leverage (DOL)
Percentage change in profits given a 1% change in sales.

leverage by asking how much profits change for each 1% change in revenues. This measure is called the **degree of operating leverage,** often abbreviated as **DOL:**

$$DOL = \frac{\text{percentage change in profits}}{\text{percentage change in sales}} \qquad (10.2)$$

For example, Table 10.4 shows that as the mine moves to a high level of output, revenues increase from $15 million to $20 million, a rise of 33%. For the policy with high fixed costs, profits increase from $3 million to $6 million, a rise of 100%. Therefore,

$$DOL = \frac{100}{33} = 3$$

BEYOND THE PAGE

Project analysis

mhhe.com/brealey9e

The percentage change in sales is magnified threefold in terms of the percentage impact on profits.

Now look at the operating leverage of the mine if it uses the policy with low fixed costs but high variable costs. As the mine moves from normal times to high output levels, profits increase from $3 million to $5.333 million, a rise of 77%. Therefore,

$$DOL = \frac{77}{33} = 2.33$$

Because some costs remain fixed, a change in sales still generates a larger percentage change in profits, but the degree of operating leverage is lower.

In fact, one can show that degree of operating leverage depends on fixed charges (including depreciation) in the following manner:[7]

$$DOL = 1 + \frac{\text{fixed costs}}{\text{profits}} \qquad (10.3)$$

Example 10.2 ▶   Operating Leverage

Suppose Blooper adopts the high-fixed-cost policy. Then fixed costs, including depreciation, will be 4 + 2 = $6 million. Because the mine produces profits of $3 million at a normal level of sales, DOL should be

$$DOL = 1 + \frac{\text{fixed costs}}{\text{profits}} = 1 + \frac{6}{3} = 3$$

---

[7] This formula for DOL can be derived as follows: If sales increase by 1%, then variable costs also should increase by 1%, and profits will increase by .01 × (sales − variable costs) = .01 × (profits + fixed costs). Now recall the definition of DOL:

$$DOL = \frac{\text{percentage change in profits}}{\text{percentage change in sales}} = \frac{\text{change in profits/level of profits}}{.01}$$

$$= 100 \times \frac{\text{change in profits}}{\text{level of profits}} = 100 \times \frac{.01 \times (\text{profits + fixed costs})}{\text{level of profits}}$$

$$= 1 + \frac{\text{fixed costs}}{\text{profits}}$$

This value matches the one we obtained by comparing the actual percentage changes in sales and profits. Use this formula to confirm for yourself that DOL under the low-fixed-cost strategy is only 2.33, as we found just above. ■

Mining companies generally have high levels of fixed costs. So do steel producers and paper companies. By contrast, many service businesses such as restaurants have low fixed costs. When business is poor, they can reduce their expenditure on materials and labor.

Notice that operating leverage will affect the risk of a project. The greater the degree of operating leverage, the greater the sensitivity of profits to variation in sales. **Risk varies with operating leverage. If a large proportion of costs is fixed, a shortfall in sales has a magnified effect on profits.**

We will have more to say about risk in the next three chapters.

> ### 10.5   Self-Test
>
> Suppose that sales of magnoosium and variable costs increase by 10% from the values in the normal scenario. Compute the percentage change in pretax profits from the normal level for both policies in Table 10.4. Compare your answers to the values predicted by the DOL formula.

10.5   Real Options and the Value of Flexibility

When you use discounted cash flow (DCF) to value a project, you implicitly assume that the firm will hold the assets passively. But managers are not paid to be dummies. After they have invested in a project, they do not simply sit back and watch the future unfold. If things go well, the project may be expanded; if they go badly, the project may be cut back or abandoned altogether. Most tools for project analysis ignore these opportunities. Projects that can easily be modified in these ways are more valuable than those that do not provide such flexibility. The more uncertain the outlook, the more valuable this flexibility becomes.

That sounds obvious, but notice that sensitivity analysis does not recognize the opportunity to modify projects. For example, if the price of magnoosium collapses, Blooper might be able to abandon its mine or close it temporarily. If so, the worst outcomes would not be as devastating as our sensitivity analysis suggested.

real options
Options to invest in, modify, postpone, or dispose of a capital investment project.

Options to modify projects are known as **real options.** Managers may not always use this term to describe these opportunities; for example, they may refer to "intangible advantages" of projects that are easy to modify. But when they review major investment proposals these option intangibles are often the key to their decisions.

The Option to Expand

The scientists at MacCaugh have developed a diet whiskey, and the firm is ready to go ahead with pilot production and test marketing. The preliminary phase will take a year and cost $200,000. Management feels that there is only a 50–50 chance that the pilot production and market tests will be successful. If they are, then MacCaugh will build a $2 million production plant that will generate an expected annual cash flow in perpetuity of $480,000 after taxes. Given an opportunity cost of capital of 12%, project NPV in this case will be −$2 million + $480,000/.12 = $2 million. If the tests are not successful, MacCaugh will discontinue the project and the cost of the pilot production will be wasted.

Notice that MacCaugh's expenditure on the pilot program buys a valuable managerial option. The firm is not obliged to enter full production, but it has the option to do so depending on the outcome of the tests. If there is some doubt as to whether the project will take off, expenditure on the pilot operation could help the firm to avoid a costly mistake. Therefore, when it proposed the expenditure, MacCaugh's management was simply following the fundamental rule of swimmers: If you know the water temperature (and depth), dive in; if you don't, try putting a toe in first.

When faced with projects like this that involve future decisions, it is often helpful to draw a **decision tree** as in Figure 10.4. You can think of the problem as a game between MacCaugh and fate. Each square represents an action or decision by the company. Each circle represents an outcome revealed by fate. MacCaugh starts the play at the left-hand square. If it decides to test, then fate will cast the enchanted dice and decide the results of the tests. Once the results are known, MacCaugh faces a second decision: Should it wind up the project, or should it invest $2 million and start full-scale production?

The second-stage decision is obvious: *Invest if the tests indicate that NPV is positive, and stop if they indicate that NPV is negative.* So now MacCaugh can move back to consider whether it should invest in the test program. This first-stage decision boils down to a simple problem: Should MacCaugh invest $200,000 now to obtain a 50% chance of a project with an NPV of $2 million a year later? At any reasonable discount rate the test program has a positive NPV.

You can probably now think of many other investments that take on added value because of the options they provide to expand in the future. For example:

- When designing a factory, it can make sense to provide extra land or floor space to reduce the future cost of a second production line.
- When building a four-lane highway, it may pay to build six-lane bridges so that the road can be converted later to six lanes if traffic proves higher than expected.
- An airline may acquire an option to buy a new aircraft (the nearby box explains how Korean Air bought options on the Boeing 737 airliner).

In each of these cases you are paying out money today to give you the option to invest in real assets at some time in the future. These options do not show up in the assets that the company lists in its balance sheet, but investors are very aware of their existence, and value more highly companies with important real options. We consider the valuation of options in Chapter 23.

decision tree
Diagram of sequential decisions and possible outcomes.

BEYOND THE PAGE

| Decision tree examples

mhhe.com/brealey9e

FIGURE 10.4 Decision tree for the diet-whiskey project

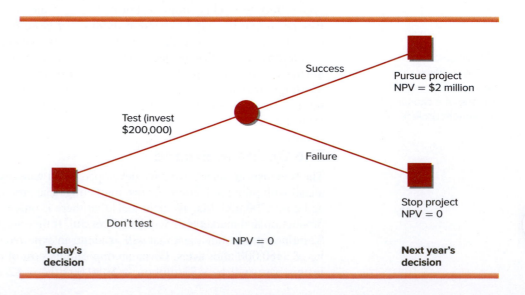

A Second Real Option: The Option to Abandon

If the option to expand has value, what about the decision to bail out? Projects don't just go on until the assets expire of old age. The decision to terminate a project is usually taken by management, not by nature. Once the project is no longer profitable, the company will cut its losses and exercise its option to abandon the project.

Some assets are simpler to bail out of than others. Tangible assets are usually easier to sell than intangible ones. It helps to have active secondhand markets, which really exist only for standardized items. Real estate, airplanes, trucks, and certain machine tools are likely to be relatively easy to sell. On the other hand, the knowledge accumulated by a software company's research and development program is a specialized intangible asset and probably would not have significant abandonment value. (Some assets, such as old mattresses, even have *negative* abandonment value; you have to pay to get rid of them. It is costly to decommission nuclear power plants or to reclaim land that has been strip-mined.)

Example 10.3 ▶ Abandonment Option

Suppose that the Widgeon Company must choose between two technologies for the manufacture of a new product, a Wankel-engined outboard motor:

1. Technology A uses custom-designed machinery to produce the complex shapes required for Wankel engines at low cost. But if the Wankel engine doesn't sell, this equipment will be worthless.
2. Technology B uses standard machine tools. Labor costs are much higher, but the tools can easily be sold if the motor doesn't sell.

Technology A looks better in an NPV analysis of the new product because it is designed to have the lowest possible cost at the planned production volume. Yet you can sense the advantage of technology B's flexibility if you are unsure whether the new outboard will sink or swim in the marketplace. ∎

10.6 Self-Test

Draw a decision tree showing how the choices open to the Widgeon Company depend on demand for the new product. Pick some plausible numbers to illustrate why it might make sense to adopt the more expensive technology B.

A Third Real Option: The Timing Option

Suppose that you have a project that could be a big winner or a big loser. The project's upside potential outweighs its downside potential, and it has a positive NPV if undertaken today. However, the project is not "now or never." So should you invest right away or wait? It's hard to say. If the project turns out to be a winner, waiting means the loss or deferral of its early cash flows. But if it turns out to be a loser, it would have been better to wait and get a better fix on the likely demand.

You can think of any project proposal as giving you the *option* to invest today. You don't have to exercise that option immediately. Instead, you need to weigh the value of the cash flows lost by delaying against the possibility that you will pick up some valuable information. Suppose, for example, you are considering development of a new oil field. At current oil prices, the investment has a small positive NPV. But oil prices are highly volatile, occasionally halving or doubling in the space of a few years. If a small decline in crude prices could push your project into the red, it might be better to wait a little before investing.

Our example illustrates why companies sometimes turn down apparently profitable projects. For example, imagine that you approach your boss with a proposed project. It involves spending $1 million and has an NPV of $1,000. You explain to him how carefully you have analyzed the project, but nothing seems to convince him that the company should invest. Is he being irrational to turn down a positive-NPV project?

Faced by such marginal projects, it often makes sense to wait. One year later, you may have much better information about the prospects for the project, and it may become clear whether it is really a winner or a loser. In the former case you can go ahead with confidence, but if it looks like a loser, the delay will have helped you to avoid a bad mistake.[8]

A Fourth Real Option: Flexible Production Facilities

A sheep is not a flexible production facility. It produces mutton and wool in roughly fixed proportions. If the price of mutton suddenly rises and that of wool falls, there is little that the farmer with a flock of sheep can do about it. Many manufacturing operations are different because they have built-in flexibility to vary their output mix as demand changes. Because we have mentioned sheep, we might point to the knitwear industry as a case in which manufacturing flexibility has become particularly important in recent years. Fashion changes have made the pattern of demand in the knitwear industry notoriously difficult to predict, and firms have increasingly invested in computer-controlled knitting machines, which provide an option to vary the product mix as demand changes.

Companies also try to avoid becoming dependent on a single source of raw materials. For example, when high-tech firms realized that they were almost wholly dependent on China for supplies of rare-earth metals (a key ingredient in applications such as lasers, solar panels, and smartphones), they began to develop new recycling methods and search for new suppliers. These strategies gave them options to shift toward cheaper sources of supply in response to changing market conditions.

10.7   Self-Test

Investments in new products or production capacity often include an option to expand. What are other major types of options encountered in capital investment decisions?

---

[8] Does this conclusion contradict our earlier dictum (see Chapter 8) that the firm should accept all positive-NPV projects? No. Notice that the investment timing problem involves a choice among mutually exclusive alternatives. You can build the project today or next year, but not both. In such cases, we have seen that the right choice is the one with the *highest* NPV. The NPV of the project today, even if positive, may well be less than the NPV of deferring investment and keeping alive the option to invest later.

SUMMARY

How do companies ensure that projects capitalize on the company's competitive advantages? (*LO10-1*)

Project evaluation should never be a mechanical exercise in which the financial manager takes a set of cash flow forecasts and cranks out a net present value. Managers need to ensure that projects fit in with the company's strategic goals. By this, we mean that a company's strategic investments should take advantage of its competitive strengths. Therefore, most companies will draw up an annual **capital budget** that contains an inventory of planned investments. The process of constructing the capital budget helps to ensure that the investments fit the corporate strategy and form a coherent package.

How do companies obtain the unbiased forecasts that are needed for good investment decisions (*LO10-2*)

NPVs are only believable if the forecasts on which they are based are unbiased. In other words, the forecasts need to factor in the chances that the cash flows may exceed or fall short of the most likely outcome. That is hard enough when you can be dispassionate about a particular investment proposal. But management needs to recognize that forecasts are more likely to be biased when project sponsors have their own axes to grind or are overly enthusiastic about their proposals.

How are sensitivity, scenario, and break-even analyses used to see the effect of an error in forecasts on project profitability? (*LO10-3*)

Good managers realize that the forecasts behind NPV calculations are imperfect. Therefore, they explore the consequences of a poor forecast and check whether it is worth doing some more homework. They use the following principal tools to answer these what-if questions:

- **Sensitivity analysis,** where one variable at a time is changed.
- **Scenario analysis,** where the manager looks at the project under alternative scenarios.
- **Break-even analysis,** where the focus is on how far sales could fall before the project begins to lose money. Often, the phrase "lose money" is defined in terms of accounting losses, but it makes more sense to define it as "failing to cover the opportunity cost of capital"—in other words, as a negative NPV.

Why is an overestimate of sales more serious for projects with high operating leverage? (*LO10-4*)

Operating leverage is the degree to which costs are fixed. A project's break-even point will be affected by the extent to which costs can be reduced as sales decline. If the project has mostly **fixed costs,** it is said to have *high operating leverage.* High operating leverage implies that profits are more sensitive to changes in sales.

Why is managerial flexibility important in capital budgeting? (*LO10-5*)

Some projects may take on added value because they give the firm the option to bail out if things go wrong or to capitalize on success by expanding. These options are known as **real options.** Other real options include the possibility to delay a project or to choose flexible production facilities. We showed how **decision trees** may be used to set out the possible choices.

LISTING OF EQUATIONS

10.1 Break-even level of revenues $= \dfrac{\text{fixed costs including depreciation}}{\text{additional profit from each additional dollar of sales}}$

10.2 $\text{DOL} = \dfrac{\text{percentage change in profits}}{\text{percentage change in sales}}$

10.3 $\text{DOL} = 1 + \dfrac{\text{fixed costs}}{\text{profits}}$

QUESTIONS AND PROBLEMS

connect

1. **Terminology.** Match each of the following terms to one of the definitions or descriptions listed below: *sensitivity analysis, scenario analysis, break-even analysis, operating leverage, decision tree, real option.* (*LO10-1 through LO10-5*)

    a. Recalculation of project NPV by changing several inputs to new but consistent values.
    b. Opportunity to modify a project at a future date.
    c. Analysis of how project NPV changes if different assumptions are made about sales, costs, and other key variables.
    d. The degree to which fixed costs magnify the effect on profits of a shortfall in sales.
    e. A graphical technique for displaying possible future events and decisions taken in response to those events
    f. Determination of the level of future sales at which project profitability or NPV equals zero

2. **The Capital Budget.** True or false? (*LO10-1 and LO10-2*)

    a. Approval of the capital budget allows manager to go ahead with any project included in the budget.
    b. Project authorizations are mostly developed "bottom-up." Strategic planning is a "top-down" process.
    c. Project sponsors are likely to be overoptimistic.
    d. The problem of overoptimism in cash-flow forecasts can always be solved by setting a higher discount rate.

3. **Project Analysis.** True or false? (*LO10-3*)

    a. Sensitivity analysis can be used to identify the variables most crucial to a project's success.
    b. Sensitivity analysis is used to obtain expected, optimistic, and pessimistic values for total project cash flows.
    c. Rather than basing one's estimate of NPV just on expected cash flows, it makes more sense to average the NPVs calculated from the pessimistic and optimistic estimates of cash flow.
    d. Risk is reduced when a high proportion of costs are fixed.
    e. The break-even level of sales for a project is higher when break-even is defined in terms of NPV rather than accounting income.

4. **Fixed and Variable Costs.** In a slow year, Deutsche Burgers will produce 2 million hamburgers at a total cost of $3.5 million. In a good year, it can produce 4 million hamburgers at a total cost of $4.5 million. (*LO10-3*)

    a. What are the fixed costs of hamburger production?
    b. What are the variable costs?
    c. What is the average cost per burger when the firm produces 1 million hamburgers?
    d. What is the average cost when the firm produces 2 million hamburgers?
    e. Why is the average cost lower when more burgers are produced?

5. **Sensitivity Analysis.** A project currently generates sales of $10 million, variable costs equal 50% of sales, and fixed costs are $2 million. The firm's tax rate is 35%. What are the effects of the following changes on cash flow? (*LO10-3*)

    a. Sales increase from $10 million to $11 million.
    b. Variable costs increase to 65% of sales.

6. **Sensitivity Analysis.** Blooper's analysts have come up with the following revised estimates for its magnoosium mine (see Section 10.3):

	Range	
	Pessimistic	**Optimistic**
Initial investment	+50%	−25%
Revenues	−15%	+20%
Variable costs	+10%	−10%
Fixed costs	+50%	−30%
Working capital	+50%	−50%

Conduct a sensitivity analysis using the revised data. Label your answers as follows: (*LO10-3*)

	Project NPV		
	Pessimistic	**Expected**	**Optimistic**
Initial investment	a.	b.	c.
Revenues	d.	e.	f.
Variable costs	g.	h.	i.
Fixed costs	j.	k.	l.
Working capital	m.	n.	o.

7. **Sensitivity Analysis.** The Rustic Welt Company is proposing to replace its old welt-making machinery with more modern equipment. The new equipment costs $9 million (the existing equipment has zero salvage value). The attraction of the new machinery is that it is expected to cut manufacturing costs from their current level of $8 a welt to $4. However, as the following table shows, there is some uncertainty about both the future sales and the performance of the new machinery:

	Pessimistic	**Expected**	**Optimistic**
Sales (million welts)	0.4	0.5	0.7
Manufacturing cost ($ per welt)	6	4	3
Life of new machinery (years)	7	10	13

Conduct a sensitivity analysis of the replacement decision assuming a discount rate of 12%. Rustic does not pay taxes. Label your answers as follows: (*LO10-3*)

	NPV of Replacement Decision		
	Pessimistic	**Expected**	**Optimistic**
Sales (million welts)	a.	b.	c.
Manufacturing cost ($ per welt)	d.	e.	f.
Life of new machinery (years)	g.	h.	i.

8. **Sensitivity Analysis.** Emperor's Clothes Fashions can invest $5 million in a new plant for producing invisible makeup. The plant has an expected life of 5 years, and expected sales are 6 million jars of makeup a year. Fixed costs are $2 million a year, and variable costs are $1 per jar. The product will be priced at $2 per jar. The plant will be depreciated straight-line over 5 years to a salvage value of zero. The opportunity cost of capital is 10%, and the tax rate is 40%. (*LO10-3*)

   a. What is project NPV under these base-case assumptions?
   b. What is NPV if variable costs turn out to be $1.20 per jar?
   c. What is NPV if fixed costs turn out to be $1.5 million per year?
   d. At what price per jar would project NPV equal zero?

9. **Scenario Analysis.** The most likely outcomes for a particular project are estimated as follows:

   Unit price: $50
   Variable cost: $30
   Fixed cost: $300,000
   Expected sales: 30,000 units per year

   However, you recognize that some of these estimates are subject to error. Suppose that each variable may turn out to be either 10% higher or 10% lower than the initial estimate. The project will last for 10 years and requires an initial investment of $1 million, which will be depreciated straight-line over the project life to a final value of zero. The firm's tax rate is 35%, and the required rate of return is 12%. (*LO10-3*)

   a. What is project NPV in the best-case scenario, that is, assuming all variables take on the best possible value?
   b. What about the worst-case scenario?

10. **Break-Even Analysis.** The following estimates have been prepared for a project:

    Fixed costs: $20,000
    Depreciation: $10,000
    Sales price: $2
    Accounting break-even: 60,000 units

    What must be the variable cost per unit? (*LO10-3*)

11. **Break-Even Analysis.** Dime a Dozen Diamonds makes synthetic diamonds by treating carbon. Each diamond can be sold for $100. The materials cost for a standard diamond is $40. The fixed costs incurred each year for factory upkeep and administrative expenses are $200,000. The machinery costs $1 million and is depreciated straight-line over 10 years to a salvage value of zero. (*LO10-3*)

    a. What is the accounting break-even level of sales in terms of number of diamonds sold?

    b. What is the NPV break-even level of sales assuming a tax rate of 35%, a 10-year project life, and a discount rate of 12%?

12. **Break-Even Analysis.** You are evaluating a project that will require an investment of $10 million that will be depreciated over a period of 7 years. You are concerned that the corporate tax rate will increase during the life of the project. (*LO10-3*)

    a. Would this increase the accounting break-even point?

    b. Would it increase the NPV break-even point?

13. **Break-Even Analysis.** Define the *cash-flow break-even* point as the sales volume (in dollars) at which cash flow equals zero. (*LO10-3*)

    a. Is the cash-flow break-even level of sales higher or lower than the zero-profit (accounting) break-even point?

    b. If a project operates at cash-flow break-even [see part (a)] for all future years, is its NPV positive or negative?

14. **NPV Break-Even Analysis.** Modern Artifacts can produce keepsakes that will be sold for $80 each. Nondepreciation fixed costs are $1,000 per year, and variable costs are $60 per unit. The initial investment of $3,000 will be depreciated straight-line over its useful life of 5 years to a final value of zero, and the discount rate is 10%. (*LO10-3*)

    a. What is the accounting break-even level of sales if the firm pays no taxes?

    b. What is the NPV break-even level of sales if the firm pays no taxes?

    c. What is the accounting break-even level of sales if the firm's tax rate is 35%?

    d. What is the NPV break-even level of sales if the firm's tax rate is 35%?

15. **NPV Break-Even Analysis.** A financial analyst has computed both accounting and NPV break-even sales levels for a project using straight-line depreciation over a 6-year period. The project manager wants to know what will happen to these estimates if the firm uses MACRS depreciation instead. The capital investment will be in a 5-year recovery-period class under MACRS rules (see Table 9.2). The firm is in a 35% tax bracket. (*LO10-3*)

    a. Would the accounting break-even level of sales in the first years of the project increase or decrease?

    b. Would the NPV break-even level of sales in the first years of the project increase or decrease?

    c. If you were advising the analyst, would the answer to part (a) or (b) be important to you? Specifically, would you say that the switch to MACRS makes the project more or less attractive?

16. **NPV Break-Even Analysis.** Reconsider Blooper's mining project. Suppose that by investing an additional $1,000,000 initially, Blooper could reduce variable costs to 35% of sales. (*LO10-3*)

    a. Using the base-case assumptions (Spreadsheet 10.1), find the NPV of this alternative scheme.

    b. At what level of sales will accounting profits be unchanged if the firm makes the new investment? Assume the equipment receives the same straight-line depreciation treatment as in the original example. (*Hint:* Focus on the project's incremental effects on fixed and variable costs.)

    c. What is the NPV break-even point?

17. **Break-Even Analysis and NPV.** If the Blooper project from Problem 16 operates at accounting break-even, will net present value be positive or negative? (*LO10-3*)

18. **Operating Leverage.** You estimate that your cattle farm will generate $1 million of profits on sales of $4 million under normal economic conditions and that the degree of operating leverage is 8. (*LO10-4*)

    a. What will profits be if sales turn out to be $3.5 million?
    b. What if they are $4.5 million?

19. **Operating Leverage.** (*LO10-4*)

    a. What is the degree of operating leverage of Modern Artifacts (in Problem 14) when sales are $7,000?
    b. What is the degree of operating leverage when sales are $12,000?
    c. Why is operating leverage different at these two levels of sales?

20. **Operating Leverage.** What is the lowest possible value for the degree of operating leverage for a profitable firm? Show with a numerical example that if Modern Artifacts (see Problem 14) has zero fixed costs and zero depreciation, then DOL = 1 and, in fact, sales and profits are directly proportional, so a 1% change in sales results in a 1% change in profits. (*LO10-4*)

21. **Operating Leverage.** A project has fixed costs of $1,000 per year, depreciation charges of $500 a year, annual revenue of $6,000, and variable costs equal to two-thirds of revenues. (*LO10-4*)

    a. If sales increase by 10%, what will be the increase in pretax profits?
    b. What is the degree of operating leverage of this project?

22. **Project Options.** Section 10.5 describes four types of real options. For each of the following cases, state which type of option is involved: (*LO10-5*)

    a. Deutsche Metall postpones a major plant expansion. The expansion has a positive NPV on a discounted cash-flow basis, but before proceeding, management wants to see how product demand grows.
    b. Western Telecom commits to production of digital switching equipment specially designed for the European market. The project has a negative NPV, but it is justified on strategic grounds by the need for a strong market position in a rapidly growing and potentially very profitable market.
    c. Western Telecom vetoes a fully integrated, automated production line for the new switches. It relies on standard, less expensive equipment. The automated production line is more efficient overall, according to a discounted cash-flow calculation.
    d. Mount Fuji Airways buys a jumbo jet with special equipment that allows the plane to be switched quickly from freight to passenger use and vice versa.

23. **Project Options.** Your midrange guess as to the amount of oil in a prospective field is 10 million barrels, but, in fact, there is a 50% chance that the amount of oil is 15 million barrels and a 50% chance of 5 million barrels. If the actual amount of oil is 15 million barrels, the present value of the cash flows from drilling will be $8 million. If the amount is only 5 million barrels, the present value will be only $2 million. It costs $3 million to drill the well. Suppose that a seismic test costing $100,000 can verify the amount of oil under the ground. Is it worth paying for the test? Use a decision tree to justify your answer. (*LO10-5*)

24. **Project Options.** A silver mine can yield 10,000 ounces of silver at a variable cost of $32 per ounce. The fixed costs of operating the mine are $40,000 per year. In half the years, silver can be sold for $48 per ounce; in the other years, silver can be sold for only $24 per ounce. Ignore taxes. (*LO10-5*)

    a. What is the average cash flow you will receive from the mine if it is always kept in operation and the silver always is sold in the year it is mined?
    b. Now suppose you can costlessly shut down the mine in years of low silver prices. What happens to the average cash flow from the mine?

25. **Project Options.** An auto plant that costs $100 million to build can produce a line of flex-fuel cars. The investment will produce cash flows with a present value of $140 million if the line is successful but only $50 million if it is unsuccessful. You believe that the probability of success

is only about 50%. You will learn whether the line is successful immediately after building the plant. (*LO10-5*)

a. Would you build the plant?

b. Suppose that the plant can be sold for $95 million to another automaker if the auto line is not successful. Now would you build the plant?

c. Illustrate the option to abandon in part (b) using a decision tree.

26. **Project Options.** Explain why options to expand or contract production are most valuable when forecasts about future business conditions are most uncertain. (*LO10-5*)

27. **Decision Trees.** The Finance in Practice box in Section 10.5 describes Korean Air's option to buy additional 737 airliners. Draw a decision tree showing the future choices faced by the airline. (*LO10-5*)

28. **Project Analysis.** New Energy is evaluating a new biofuel facility. The plant would cost $4,000 million to build and has the potential to produce up to 40 million barrels of synthetic oil a year. The product is a close substitute for conventional oil and would sell for the same price. The market price of oil currently is fluctuating around $100 per barrel, but there is considerable uncertainty about future prices. Variable costs for the organic inputs to the production process are estimated at $82 per barrel and are expected to be stable. In addition, annual upkeep and maintenance expenses on the facility will be $100 million regardless of the production level. The plant has an expected life of 15 years, and it will be depreciated using MACRS and a 10-year recovery period. Salvage value net of cleanup costs is expected to be negligible.

Demand for the product is difficult to forecast. Depending on consumer acceptance, sales might range from 25 million to 35 million barrels annually. The discount rate is 12%, and New Energy's tax bracket is 35%. (*LO10-3, LO10-4, and LO10-5*)

a. Find the project NPV for the following combinations of oil price and sales volume. Which source of uncertainty seems most important to the success of the project?

	Oil Price		
Annual Sales	**$80/Barrel**	**$100/Barrel**	**$120/Barrel**
25 million barrels	(i)	(ii)	(iii)
30 million barrels	(iv)	(v)	(vi)
35 million barrels	(vii)	(viii)	(ix)

b. At an oil price of $100, what level of annual sales, maintained over the life of the plant, is necessary for NPV break-even? (This will require trial and error unless you are familiar with more advanced features of Excel, such as the Goal Seek command.)

c. At an oil price of $100, what is the accounting break-even level of sales in each year? Why does it change each year? Does this notion of break-even seem reasonable to you?

d. If each of the scenarios in the grid in part (a) is equally likely, what is the NPV of the facility?

e. Why might the facility be worth building despite your answer to part (d)? (*Hint:* What real option may the firm have to avoid losses in low-oil-price scenarios?)

WEB EXERCISE

1. Can you guess Hewlett-Packard's incremental cost for producing one computer? You probably have that amount in your wallet or purse! This gives the company considerable operating leverage. Let's estimate the degree of operating leverage for HP (ticker symbol HPQ). Go to the annual income statement, which you can find at finance.yahoo.com. Assume that selling, general, administrative, R&D, and depreciation expenses are fixed and cost of goods sold (which Yahoo! calls *cost of revenue*) are variable. Estimate the degree of operating leverage for HP for the last year (annual).

SOLUTIONS TO SELF-TEST QUESTIONS

10.1   The revised valuation of the Blooper mine is as follows:

Year:	0	1	2	3	4	5	6
B. Fixed assets							
Investments in fixed assets	10,000						
Sales of fixed assets							1,300
CF, invest. in fixed assets	−10,000						1,300
C. Operating cash flow							
Revenues		12,000	12,600	13,230	13,892	14,586	
Variable expenses		4,800	5,040	5,292	5,557	5,834	
Fixed expenses		4,000	4,200	4,410	4,631	4,862	
Depreciation		2,000	2,000	2,000	2,000	2,000	
Pretax profit		1,200	1,360	1,528	1,704	1,890	
Tax		420	476	535	597	661	
Profit after tax		780	884	993	1,108	1,228	
Operating cash flow		2,780	2,884	2,993	3,108	3,228	
D. Working capital							
Working capital	1,320	3,386	3,555	3,733	3,920	2,431	0
Change in working capital	1,320	2,066	169	178	187	−1,489	−2,431
CF, invest. in wk. capital	−1,320	−2,066	−169	−178	−187	1,489	2,431
E. Project valuation							
Total project cash flow	−11,320	714	2,715	2,815	2,921	4,717	3,731
Discount factor	1.000	0.893	0.797	0.712	0.636	0.567	0.507
PV of cash flow	−11,320	637	2,164	2,004	1,856	2,677	1,890
Net present value	−91						

10.2   Both calculate how NPV depends on input assumptions. Sensitivity analysis changes inputs one at a time, whereas scenario analysis changes several variables at once. The changes should add up to a consistent scenario for the project as a whole.

10.3   In the normal scenario, break-even occurs at revenues of $10 million. If initial investment is now only $8 million, annual depreciation expense falls by $2,000,000/5 = $400,000. Because each dollar of sales contributes $.60 to profits, sales can fall by $400,000/.6 = $666,666 before accounting profit turns negative. Therefore, accounting break-even would occur with revenues of $9.333 million. Let's check:

Revenues	$9,333,333
Variable expenses	3,733,333
Fixed expenses	4,000,000
Depreciation	1,600,000
Pretax profit	0

10.4   Break-even analysis finds the level of sales or revenue at which NPV = 0. Sensitivity analysis changes these and other input variables to optimistic and pessimistic values and recalculates NPV.

FIGURE 10.5 Example of a decision tree for Widgeon Company

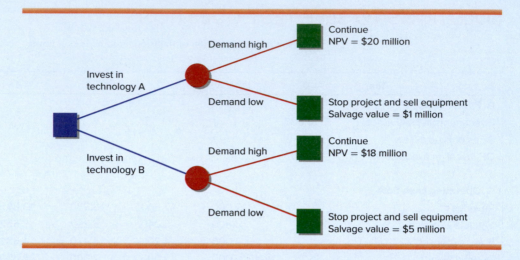

10.5   Reworking Table 10.4 for the normal level of sales and 10% higher sales gives the following (figures in thousands of dollars):

	High Fixed Costs		High Variable Costs	
	Normal	**10% Higher Sales**	**Normal**	**10% Higher Sales**
Sales	15,000	16,500	15,000	16,500
− Variable costs	6,000	6,600	8,000	8,800
− Fixed costs	4,000	4,000	2,000	2,000
− Depreciation	2,000	2,000	2,000	2,000
= Pretax profit	3,000	3,900	3,000	3,700

For the high-fixed-cost policy, profits increase by 30%, from $3,000,000 to $3,900,000. For the high variable-cost policy, profits increase by 23.3%. In both cases the percentage increase in profits equals DOL times the percentage increase in sales. This illustrates that DOL measures the sensitivity of profits to changes in sales.

10.6   See Figure 10.5. Note that while technology A delivers the higher NPV if demand is high, technology B has the advantage of a higher salvage value if demand is unexpectedly low.

10.7   Abandonment options, options due to flexible production facilities, investment timing options.

MINICASE

Maxine Peru, the CEO of Peru Resources, hardly noticed the plate of savory quenelles de brochet and the glass of Corton Charlemagne '94 on the table before her. She was absorbed by the engineering report handed to her just as she entered the executive dining room.

The report described a proposed new mine on the North Ridge of Mt. Zircon. A vein of transcendental zirconium ore had been discovered there on land owned by Ms. Peru's company. Test borings indicated sufficient reserves to produce 340 tons per year of transcendental zirconium over a 7-year period.

The vein probably also contained hydrated zircon gemstones. The amount and quality of these zircons were hard to predict because they tended to occur in "pockets." The new mine might come across one, two, or dozens of pockets. The mining engineer guessed that 150 pounds per year might be found. The current price for high-quality hydrated zircon gemstones was $3,300 per pound.

Peru Resources was a family-owned business with total assets of $45 million, including cash reserves of $4 million. The outlay required for the new mine would be a major commitment. Fortunately, Peru Resources was conservatively financed, and Ms. Peru believed that the company could borrow up to $9 million at an interest rate of about 8%.

The mine's operating costs were projected at $900,000 per year, including $400,000 of fixed costs and $500,000 of variable costs. Ms. Peru thought these forecasts were accurate. The big question marks seemed to be the initial cost of the mine and the selling price of transcendental zirconium.

Opening the mine, and providing the necessary machinery and ore-crunching facilities, was supposed to cost $10 million, but cost overruns of 10% or 15% were common in the mining business. In addition, new environmental regulations, if enacted, could increase the cost of the mine by $1.5 million.

There was a cheaper design for the mine, which would reduce its cost by $1.7 million and eliminate much of the uncertainty about cost overruns. Unfortunately, this design would require much higher fixed operating costs. Fixed costs would increase to $850,000 per year at planned production levels.

The current price of transcendental zirconium was $10,000 per ton, but there was no consensus about future prices.[9] Some experts were projecting rapid price increases to as much as $14,000 per ton. On the other hand, there were pessimists saying that prices could be as low as $7,500 per ton. Ms. Peru did not have strong views either way: Her best guess was that price would just increase

with inflation at about 3.5% per year. (Mine operating costs would also increase with inflation.)

Ms. Peru had wide experience in the mining business, and she knew that investors in similar projects usually wanted a forecast nominal rate of return of at least 14%.

You have been asked to assist Ms. Peru in evaluating this project. Lay out the base-case NPV analysis, and undertake sensitivity, scenario, or break-even analyses as appropriate. Assume that Peru Resources pays tax at a 35% rate. For simplicity, also assume that the investment in the mine could be depreciated for tax purposes straight-line over 7 years.

What forecasts or scenarios should worry Ms. Peru the most? Where would additional information be most helpful? Is there a case for delaying construction of the new mine?

---

[9] There were no traded forward or futures contracts on transcendental zirconium. See Chapter 24.

11

Introduction to Risk, Return, and the Opportunity Cost of Capital

LEARNING OBJECTIVES

After studying this chapter, you should be able to:

11-1 Estimate the opportunity cost of capital for an "average-risk" project.

11-2 Calculate returns and standard deviation of returns for individual common stocks or for a stock portfolio.

11-3 Understand why diversification reduces risk.

11-4 Distinguish between specific risk, which can be diversified away, and market risk, which cannot.

RELATED WEBSITES FOR THIS CHAPTER CAN BE FOUND IN CONNECT.

Investing in risky assets is not the same as gambling. After reading this chapter, you should be able to explain the difference and understand the rewards for bearing risk in the stock market. © *All kind of people/Shutterstock RF*

In earlier chapters, we skirted the issue of project risk; now it is time to confront it head-on. We can no longer be satisfied with vague statements like, "The opportunity cost of capital depends on the risk of the project." We need to know how to measure risk, and we need to understand how risk affects the cost of capital. These are the topics of the next two chapters.

Think for a moment what the cost of capital for a project means. It is the rate of return that shareholders could expect to earn if they invested in equally risky securities. So one way to estimate the cost of capital is to find securities that have the same risk as the project and then estimate the expected rate of return on these securities.

We start our analysis by looking at the rates of return earned in the past from different investments, concentrating on the *extra* return that investors have received for investing in risky rather than safe securities. We then show how to measure the risk of a portfolio, and we look again at past history to find out how risky it is to invest in the stock market.

Finally, we explore the concept of diversification. Most investors do not put all their eggs into one basket—they diversify. Thus investors are not concerned with the risk of each security in isolation; instead, they are concerned with how much it contributes to the risk of a diversified portfolio. Therefore, we need to distinguish between the risk that can be eliminated by diversification and the risk that cannot be eliminated.

11.1   Rates of Return: A Review

When investors buy a stock or a bond, their return comes in two forms: (1) a dividend or interest payment and (2) a capital gain or a capital loss. For example, Starbucks was one of the star performers of 2015. Suppose you bought its stock at the beginning of the year when its price was $40.20 a share. By the end of the year the value of that investment had appreciated to $60.03, giving a capital gain of $60.03 − $40.20 = $19.83. In addition, in 2015 Starbucks paid a dividend of $.80 a share.

The *percentage* return on your investment was, therefore,

$$\text{Percentage return} = \frac{\text{capital gain} + \text{dividend}}{\text{initial share price}} \qquad \textbf{(11.1)}$$

$$= \frac{\$19.83 + \$.80}{\$40.20} = .513, \text{ or } 51.3\%$$

The percentage return can also be expressed as the sum of the *dividend yield* and *percentage capital gain*. The dividend yield is the dividend expressed as a percentage of the stock price at the beginning of the year:

$$\text{Dividend yield} = \frac{\text{dividend}}{\text{initial share price}}$$

$$= \frac{\$.80}{\$40.20} = .020, \text{ or } 2.0\%$$

Similarly, the percentage capital gain is

$$\text{Percentage capital gain} = \frac{\text{capital gain}}{\text{initial share price}}$$

$$= \frac{\$19.83}{\$40.20} = .493, \text{ or } 49.3\%$$

Thus the total return is the sum of 2.0% + 49.3% = 51.3%, which is the same as we calculated above.

Remember that in Chapter 5, we made a distinction between the *nominal* rate of return and the *real* rate of return. The nominal return measures how much more money you will have at the end of the year if you invest today. The return that we just calculated for Starbucks stock is, therefore, a nominal return. The real rate of return tells you how much more you will be able to *buy* with your money at the end of the year. To convert from a nominal to a real rate of return, we use the following relationship:

$$1 + \text{real rate of return} = \frac{1 + \text{nominal rate of return}}{1 + \text{inflation rate}}$$

In 2015, inflation was .5%. So we calculate the real rate of return on Starbucks stock as follows:

$$1 + \text{real rate of return} = \frac{1.513}{1.005} = 1.505$$

Therefore, the real rate of return equals .505, or 50.5%. Inflation in 2015 was very modest, so the real return was only slightly less than the nominal return.

11.1   Self-Test

Suppose you buy a bond for $1,020 with a 15-year maturity paying an annual coupon of $80. A year later, interest rates have dropped and the bond's price has increased to $1,050. What are your nominal and real rates of return? Assume the inflation rate is 4%.

11.2 **A Century of Capital Market History**

When you invest in a stock, you don't know what return you will earn. But by looking at the history of security returns, you can get some idea of the return that investors might reasonably expect from different types of securities and of the risks that they face. Let us look, therefore, at the risks and returns that investors have experienced in the past.

Market Indexes

Investors can choose from an enormous number of different securities. For example, about 2,800 U.S. and foreign companies currently list their stocks on the New York Stock Exchange, and a further 3,100 stocks are traded on the NASDAQ stock market.

> **market index**
> Measure of the investment performance of the overall market.

Financial analysts can't track every stock, so they rely on **market indexes** to summarize the return on different classes of securities. The best-known stock market index in the United States is the **Dow Jones Industrial Average,** generally known as the *Dow.* The Dow tracks the performance of a portfolio that holds one share in each of 30 large firms. For example, suppose that the Dow starts the day at a value of 15,000 and then rises by 150 points to a new value of 15,150. An investor with a $15,000 investment in the Dow portfolio would make a capital gain of 150/15,000 = .01, or 1%.[1]

> **Dow Jones Industrial Average**
> Index of the investment performance of a portfolio of 30 "blue-chip" stocks.

The Dow Jones Industrial Average was first computed in 1896. Most people are used to it and expect to hear it on the 6 o'clock news. However, it is far from the best measure of the performance of the stock market. First, with only 30 large stocks, it is not representative of the performance of stocks generally. Second, investors don't usually hold an equal number of shares in each company. For example, in 2015 there were 6.2 billion shares in Pfizer and .62 billion in 3M. So, on average, investors did *not* hold the same number of shares in the two firms. Instead, they held 10 times as many shares in Pfizer as in 3M. It doesn't make sense, therefore, to look at an index that measures the performance of a portfolio with an equal number of shares in the two firms.

> **Standard & Poor's Composite Index**
> Index of the investment performance of a portfolio of 500 large stocks. Also called the *S&P 500.*

The **Standard & Poor's Composite Index,** better known as the *S&P 500,* includes the stocks of 500 major companies and is, therefore, a more comprehensive index than the Dow. Also, it measures the performance of a portfolio that holds shares in each firm in proportion to the number of shares that have been issued to investors. For example, the S&P portfolio would hold 10 times as many shares in Pfizer as in 3M. Thus, the S&P 500 shows the *average* performance of investors in the 500 firms.

Only a small proportion of the publicly traded companies are represented in the S&P 500. However, these firms are among the largest in the country, and they account for about 75% of the market value of traded stocks. Therefore, success for professional investors usually means "beating the S&P."

Some stock market indexes, such as the Dow Jones Wilshire 5000, include an even larger number of stocks, while others focus on special groups of stocks such as the stocks of small companies. There are also stock market indexes for other countries, such as the Nikkei Index for Tokyo and the Financial Times Stock Exchange (FTSE) Index for London. Morgan Stanley Capital International (MSCI) even computes a world stock market index. The Financial Times Company and Standard & Poor's have combined to produce their own world index.

The Historical Record

The historical returns of stock or bond market indexes can give us an idea of the typical performance of different investments. For example, Elroy Dimson, Paul Marsh,

---

[1] Most stock market indexes record the market value of the portfolio. To calculate the total return on the portfolio, we need to add in any dividends that are paid.

and Mike Staunton have compiled measures of the investment performance of three portfolios of securities since 1900:

1. A portfolio of 3-month loans issued each week by the U.S. government. These loans are known as *Treasury bills*.
2. A portfolio of long-term *Treasury bonds* issued by the U.S. government and maturing in about 10 years.
3. A diversified portfolio of common stocks.

These portfolios are not equally risky. Treasury bills are about as safe an investment as you can make. Because they are issued by the U.S. government, you can be confident that you will get your money back. Their short-term maturity means that their prices are relatively stable. In fact, investors who wish to lend money for 3 months can achieve a certain payoff by buying 3-month bills. Of course, they can't be sure what that money will buy; there is still some uncertainty about inflation.

Long-term Treasury bonds are also certain to be repaid when they mature, but the prices of these bonds fluctuate more as interest rates vary. When interest rates fall, the values of long-term bonds rise; when rates rise, the values of the bonds fall.

Common stocks are the riskiest of the three groups of securities. When you invest in common stocks, there is no promise that you will get your money back. As a part-owner of the corporation, you receive what is left over after the bonds and any other debts have been repaid.

Figure 11.1 shows the performance of the three groups of securities assuming that all dividends or interest income had been reinvested in the portfolios. You can see that the performance of the portfolios fits our intuitive risk ranking. Common stocks were the riskiest investment, but they also offered the greatest gains. One dollar invested at the start of 1900 in a portfolio of common stocks would have grown to $35,100 by the start of 2016. At the other end of the spectrum, an investment in Treasury bills would have accumulated to only $74.

Table 11.1 shows the average of the annual returns from each of these portfolios. These returns are comparable to the return that we calculated for Starbucks. In other words, they include (1) dividends or interest and (2) any capital gains or losses.

The safest investment, Treasury bills, had the lowest rates of return—they averaged 3.8% a year. Long-term government bonds gave slightly higher returns than Treasury bills. This difference is called the **maturity premium.** Common stocks

BEYOND THE PAGE

Arithmetic averages and compound annual returns

mhhe.com/brealey9e

maturity premium
Extra annual return from investing in long- versus short-term Treasury securities.

FIGURE 11.1 How an investment of $1 at the start of 1900 would have grown by the start of 2016 (index values plotted on log scale)

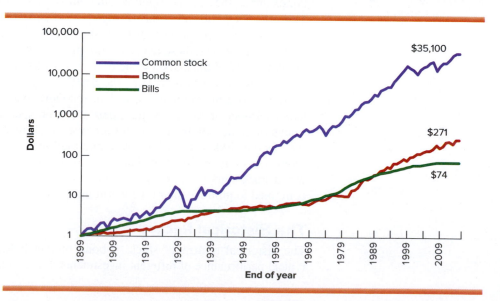

Source: E. Dimson, P. R. Marsh, and M. Staunton, *Triumph of the Optimists: 101 Years of Global Investment Returns* (Princeton, NJ: Princeton University Press, 2002), with updates kindly provided by *Triumph's* authors.

TABLE 11.1 Average rates of return on Treasury bills, government bonds, and common stocks, 1900–2015 (figures in percent per year)

Portfolio	Average Annual Rate of Return	Average Premium (Extra return versus Treasury bills)
Treasury bills	3.8%	
Treasury bonds	5.3	1.5%
Common stocks	11.4	7.6

Source: E. Dimson, P. R. Marsh, and M. Staunton, *Triumph of the Optimists: 101 Years of Global Investment Returns* (Princeton, NJ: Princeton University Press, 2002), with updates kindly provided by *Triumph's* authors.

risk premium
Expected return in excess of risk-free return as compensation for risk.

were in a class by themselves. Investors who accepted the risk of common stocks received on average an extra return of 7.6% a year over the return on Treasury bills. This compensation for taking on the risk of common stock ownership is known as the market **risk premium:**

$$\frac{\text{Rate of return}}{\text{on common stocks}} = \frac{\text{interest rate on}}{\text{Treasury bills}} + \frac{\text{market risk}}{\text{premium}}$$

The historical record shows that investors have received a risk premium for holding risky assets. Average returns on high-risk assets have been higher than those on low-risk assets.

You may ask why we look back over such a long period to measure average rates of return. The reason is that annual rates of return for common stocks fluctuate so much that averages taken over short periods are extremely unreliable. In some years, investors in common stocks had a disagreeable shock and received a substantially lower return than they expected. In other years, they had a pleasant surprise and received a higher-than-expected return. By averaging the returns across both the rough years and the smooth, we should get a fair idea of the typical return that investors might justifiably expect.

While common stocks have offered the highest average returns, they have also been riskier investments. Figure 11.2 shows the 116 annual rates of return on common stocks since 1900. The fluctuations in year-to-year returns on common stocks are remarkably wide. There were 2 years (1933 and 1954) when investors earned a return of more than 50%. However, Figure 11.2 shows that you can also lose money, and lots

FIGURE 11.2 Rates of return on common stocks, 1900–2015

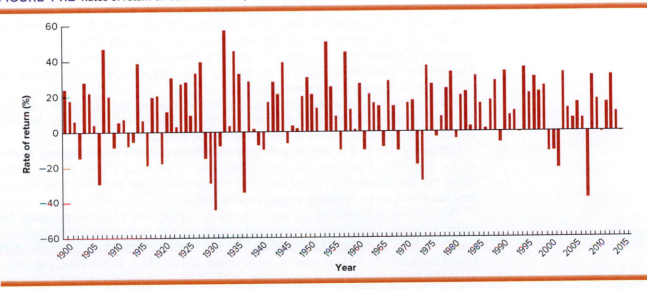

Source: E. Dimson, P. R. Marsh, and M. Staunton, *Triumph of the Optimists: 101 Years of Global Investment Returns* (Princeton, NJ: Princeton University Press, 2002), with updates kindly provided by *Triumph's* authors.

of it, by investing in the stock market. The most dramatic case was the stock market crash of 1929–1932. Shortly after President Coolidge joyfully observed that stocks were "cheap at current prices," stocks rapidly became even cheaper. By July 1932, the Dow Jones Industrial Average had fallen in a series of agonizing slides by 89%.

You don't have to look that far back to see that the stock market is a risky place. Investors who bought at the stock market peak in March 2000 saw little but falling stock prices over the next 2½ years. By October 2002, the S&P 500 had declined by 49%, while the tech-heavy NASDAQ market fell by 78%. But this was not the end of the roller-coaster ride. After recovering sharply, share prices plunged 57% between October 2007 and March 2009 as the financial crisis unfolded.

Bond prices also fluctuate, but far less than stock prices. The worst year for investors in our portfolio of Treasury bonds was 2009; their return that year was −14.9%.

11.2   Self-Test

Here are the average rates of return for common stocks and Treasury bills for four different periods:

	1900–1928	1929–1957	1958–1986	1987–2015
Stocks	12.0%	9.8%	12.2%	12.0%
Treasury bills	4.9	1.0	6.1	3.8

What was the risk premium on stocks for each of these periods?

Using Historical Evidence to Estimate Today's Cost of Capital

Think back now to Chapter 8, where we showed how firms calculate the present value of a new project by discounting the expected cash flows by the opportunity cost of capital. The opportunity cost of capital is the return that the firm's shareholders are giving up by investing in the project rather than in comparable-risk alternatives.

Measuring the cost of capital is easy if the project is a sure thing. Because shareholders can obtain a surefire payoff by investing in a U.S. Treasury bill, the firm should invest in a risk-free project only if it can at least match the rate of interest on such a loan. If the project is risky—and most projects are—then the firm needs to at least match the return that shareholders could expect to earn if they invested in securities of similar risk. It is not easy to put a precise figure on this, but our skim through history provides an idea of the average return an investor might expect from an investment in risky common stocks.

Suppose there is an investment project that you *know*—don't ask how—has the same risk as an investment in a diversified portfolio of U.S. common stocks. We will say that it has the same degree of risk as the *market portfolio*.

Instead of investing in the project, your shareholders could invest directly in this market portfolio. Therefore, the opportunity cost of capital for your project is the return that the shareholders could expect to earn on the market portfolio. This is what they are giving up by investing money in your project.

The problem of estimating the project's cost of capital boils down to estimating the currently expected rate of return on the market portfolio. One way to estimate the expected market return is to assume that the future will be like the past and that today's investors expect to receive the average rates of return shown in Table 11.1. In this case, you might judge that the expected market return today is 11.4%, the average of past market returns.

Unfortunately, this is *not* the way to do it. Investors are not likely to demand the same return each year on an investment in common stocks. For example, we know that the interest rate on safe Treasury bills varies over time. At their peak in 1981, Treasury bills offered a return of 14%, more than 10 percentage points above the 3.8% average return on bills shown in Table 11.1.

What if you were called upon to estimate the expected return on common stocks in 1981? Would you have said 11.4%? That doesn't make sense. Who would invest in the risky stock market for an expected return of 11.4% when you could get a safe 14% from Treasury bills?

A better procedure is to take the *current* interest rate on Treasury bills plus 7.6%, the average *risk premium* shown in Table 11.1. In 1981, when the rate on Treasury bills was 14%, that would have given

$$\text{Expected market return (1981)} = \text{interest rate on Treasury bills (1981)} + \text{normal risk premium}$$
$$= 14 + 7.6 = 21.6\%$$

The first term on the right-hand side tells us the time value of money in 1981; the second term measures the compensation for risk. **The expected return on an investment provides compensation to investors both for waiting (the time value of money) and for worrying (the risk of the particular asset).**

What about today? As we write this in early 2016, Treasury bills offer a return of about .3%. This suggests that investors in common stocks are looking for a return of around 7.9%:[2]

$$\text{Expected market return (2016)} = \text{interest rate on Treasury bills (2016)} + \text{normal risk premium}$$
$$= .3 + 7.6 = 7.9\%$$

These calculations assume that there is a normal, stable risk premium on the market portfolio, so the expected *future* risk premium can be measured by the average past risk premium. But even with more than 100 years of data, we can't estimate the market risk premium exactly; nor can we be sure that investors today are demanding the same reward for risk that they were in the early 1900s. All this leaves plenty of room for argument about what the risk premium *really* is.

Many financial managers and economists believe that long-run historical returns are the best measure available. Others have a gut instinct that investors don't need such a large risk premium to persuade them to hold common stocks. For example, surveys of financial economists and chief financial officers commonly suggest a risk premium that is 1% to 2% lower than the historical average.[3]

We may be able to gain some further insights into the question by looking at the experience of other countries. Figure 11.3 shows that the United States is roughly average in terms of the risk premium. Swiss common stocks come bottom of the league; the average risk premium in Switzerland was only 5.4%. Top of the form is Portugal, with a premium of 10.1%. Some of these variations between countries may reflect differences in risk. But remember how difficult it is to make precise estimates of what investors expected. You probably would not be too far out if you concluded that the *expected* risk premium was the same in each country.

BEYOND THE PAGE

The market risk premium

mhhe.com/brealey9e

---

[2] In practice, things might be a bit more complicated. In 2016, short-term interest rates were unusually low and probably not appropriate for judging the required return on a long-term project. We will return to this problem in the next chapter.

[3] For example, a 2015 survey of U.S. CFOs reported an average expected risk premium of 4.5% over the 10-year Treasury rate, which was equivalent to 6.6% over the rate on short-term Treasury bills. See J. R. Graham and C. R. Harvey, "The Equity Risk Premium in 2015," October 1, 2015, available at http://dx.doi.org/10.2139/ssrn.2611793. However, a 2015 survey of nearly 2,000 U.S. economists, financial analysts, and managers reported an average risk premium of 5.5% over a long-term interest rate of 2.4%. Because the Treasury bill rate in 2015 was about 0.2%, this figure is equivalent to a premium of 7.7% over the Treasury bill rate. See P. Fernandez, A. Ortiz, and I. F. Acin. "Discount Rate (Risk-Free Rate and Market Risk Premium) Used for 41 Countries in 2015: A Survey," November 19, 2015, available at http://dx.doi.org/10.2139/ssrn.2598104.

FIGURE 11.3 The risk premium in 20 countries, 1900–2015. For these 20 countries, the average return on common stocks has been 7.4% more than the interest rate on bills.

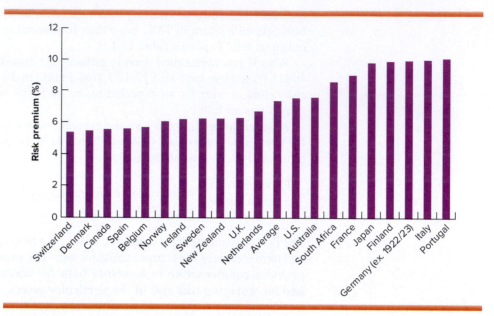

Note: The data for Germany omit the hyperinflation years 1922 and 1923.
Source: Author's calculations using data from E. Dimson, P. R. Marsh, and M. Staunton, *Triumph of the Optimists: 101 Years of Global Investment Returns* (Princeton, NJ: Princeton University Press, 2002), with updates kindly provided by *Triumph*'s authors.

11.3   Measuring Risk

You now have some benchmarks. You know that the opportunity cost of capital for safe projects must be the rate of return offered by safe Treasury bills, and you know that the opportunity cost of capital for "average-risk" projects must be the expected return on the market portfolio. But you *don't* know how to estimate the cost of capital for projects that do not fit these two simple cases. Before you can do this, you need to understand more about investment risk.

The average fuse time for army hand grenades is 5 seconds, but that average hides a lot of potentially relevant information. If you are in the business of throwing grenades, you need some measure of the variation around the average fuse time.[4] Similarly, if you are in the business of investing in securities, you need some measure of how far the returns may differ from the average.

One way to present the spread of possible investment returns is by using histograms, such as the ones in Figure 11.4. The bars in each histogram show the number of years between 1900 and 2015 that the investment's return fell within a specific range. Look first at the performance of common stocks. Their risk shows up in the wide spread of outcomes. For example, you can see that in one year, the return was between +55% and +60%, but there was also one year that investors lost between 40% and 45%.

The corresponding histograms for Treasury bonds and bills show that extreme returns, either high or low, are much less common. Investors in these securities could have been much more confident of the outcome than common stockholders.

Variance and Standard Deviation

Investment risk depends on the dispersion or spread of possible outcomes. For example, Figure 11.4 showed that on past evidence, there is greater uncertainty about the possible returns from common stocks than about the returns from bills or bonds.

---

[4] We can reassure you; the variation around the standard fuse time is very small.

FIGURE 11.4 Historical returns on major asset classes, 1900–2015

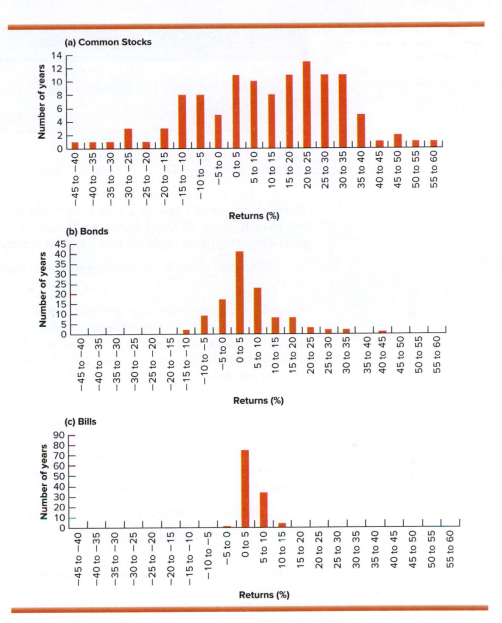

Source: Authors' calculations using data from E. Dimson, P. R. Marsh, and M. Staunton, *Triumph of the Optimists: 101 Years of Global Investment Returns* (Princeton, NJ: Princeton University Press, 2002), with updates kindly provided by *Triumph's* authors.

Sometimes, a picture like Figure 11.4 tells you all you need to know about (past) dispersion. But, in general, pictures do not suffice. The financial manager needs a numerical measure of dispersion to quantify risk. The standard measures are **variance** and **standard deviation.**

Here is a very simple example showing how variance and standard deviation are calculated. Suppose that you are offered the opportunity to play the following game: You start by investing $100. Then two coins are flipped. For each head that comes up your starting balance will be *increased* by 20%, and for each tail that comes up your starting balance will be *reduced* by 10%. Clearly, there are four equally likely outcomes:

- Head + Head: You make 20 + 20 = 40%
- Head + Tail: You make 20 − 10 = 10%
- Tail + Head: You make − 10 + 20 = 10%
- Tail + Tail: You make − 10 − 10 = −20%

variance
Average value of squared deviations from mean. A measure of volatility.

standard deviation
Square root of variance. A measure of volatility.

TABLE 11.2 The coin-toss game; calculating variance and standard deviation

(1) Rate of Return (%)	(2) Deviation from Expected Return (%)	(3) Squared Deviation
+40	+30	900
+10	0	0
+10	0	0
−20	−30	900

Notes:
1. Variance = average of squared deviations = 1,800/4 = 450.
2. Standard deviation = square root of variance = $\sqrt{450}$ = 21.2, about 21%.

There is a chance of 1 in 4, or .25, that you will make 40%; a chance of 2 in 4, or .5, that you will make 10%; and a chance of 1 in 4, or .25, that you will lose 20%. The game's expected return is, therefore, a weighted average of the possible outcomes:

Expected return = probability-weighted average of possible outcomes

$$= (.25 \times 40) + (.5 \times 10) + (.25 \times -20) = +10\%$$

If you play the game a very large number of times, your average return should be 10%.

Table 11.2 shows how to calculate the variance and standard deviation of the returns on your game. Column 1 shows the four equally likely outcomes. In column 2, we calculate the difference between each possible outcome and the expected outcome. You can see that at best the return could be 30% higher than expected; at worst, it could be 30% lower.

These deviations in column 2 illustrate the spread of possible returns. But if we want a measure of this spread, it is no use just averaging the deviations in column 2—the average is always going to be zero because the positive and negative deviations cancel out. To get around this problem, we *square* the deviations in column 2 before averaging them. These squared deviations are shown in column 3. The variance is the average of these squared deviations and, therefore, is a natural measure of dispersion:

Variance = average of squared deviations around the average   **(11.2)**

$$= \frac{1,800}{4} = 450$$

When we squared the deviations from the expected return, we changed the units of measurement from *percentages* to *percentages squared*. Our last step is to get back to percentages by taking the square root of the variance. This is the standard deviation:

Standard deviation = square root of variance   **(11.3)**

$$= \sqrt{450} = 21\%$$

BEYOND THE PAGE

How to calculate variance and standard deviation

mhhe.com/brealey9e

Because standard deviation is simply the square root of variance, it too is a natural measure of risk. If the outcome of the game had been certain, the standard deviation would have been zero because there would then be no deviations from the expected outcome. The actual standard deviation is positive because we *don't* know what will happen.

Now think of a second game: It is the same as the first except that each head means a 35% gain and each tail means a 25% loss. Again, there are four equally likely outcomes:

- Head + Head: You gain 70%
- Head + Tail: You gain 10%
- Tail + Head: You gain 10%
- Tail + Tail: You lose 50%

The expected return of this game is 10%, the same as that of the first game, but it is riskier. For example, in the first game, the worst possible outcome is a loss of 20%, which is 30% worse than the expected outcome. In the second game, the downside is a loss of 50%, or 60% below the expected return. This increased spread of outcomes shows up in the standard deviation, which is double that of the first game, 42% versus 21%. By this measure, the second game is twice as risky as the first.

A Note on Calculating Variance

When we calculated variance in Table 11.2, we recorded separately each of the four possible outcomes. An alternative would have been to recognize that in two of the four possible cases the outcomes are the same. In other words, if you were to play the game a large number of times, you would find that on 50% of the occasions the deviation from the expected return is 0%, 25% of the time it is +30%, and the remaining 25% of the time it is −30%. This suggests a simple way to calculate variance: Just weight each squared deviation by its probability:

$$\text{Variance} = \text{sum of squared deviations weighted by probabilities}$$
$$= .25 \times 30^2 + .5 \times 0 + .25 \times (-30)^2 = 450$$

11.3	Self-Test

> Calculate the variance and standard deviation of the second (higher-risk) coin-tossing game.

Measuring the Variation in Stock Returns

When estimating the spread of possible outcomes from investing in the stock market, most financial analysts start by assuming that the spread of returns in the past is a reasonable indication of what could happen in the future. Therefore, they calculate the standard deviation of past returns. To illustrate, suppose that you were presented with the data for stock market returns shown in Table 11.3. The average return over the 6 years from 2010 to 2015 was 12.47%. This is just the sum of the returns over the 6 years divided by 6 (74.84/6 = 12.47%).

Column 2 in Table 11.3 shows the difference between each year's return and the average return. For example, in 2013 the return of 31.71% on common stocks was

TABLE 11.3 The average return and standard deviation of stock market returns, 2010–2015

Year	Rate of Return (%)	Deviation from Average Return (%)	Squared Deviation
2010	17.86	5.39	29.02
2011	−0.90	−13.37	178.85
2012	15.97	3.50	12.23
2013	31.71	19.24	370.05
2014	10.86	−1.61	2.60
2015	−0.66	−13.13	172.48
Total	74.84		765.23
Average return = 74.84/6 = 12.47%			
Variance = average of squared deviations = 765.23/6 = 127.54			
Standard deviation = square root of variance = 11.29%			

Note: Returns shown in the table are rounded to 2 decimal places. The squared deviation in the last column uses the actual returns, without rounding.

Source: Authors' calculations using data from E. Dimson, P. R. Marsh, and M. Staunton, *Triumph of the Optimists: 101 Years of Global Investment Returns* (Princeton, NJ: Princeton University Press, 2002), with updates kindly provided by *Triumph*'s authors.

TABLE 11.4 Standard deviation of returns, 1900–2015

Portfolio	Standard Deviation (%)
Treasury bills	2.9
Long-term government bonds	9.0
Common stocks	19.9

Source: Authors' calculations using data from E. Dimson, P. R. Marsh, and M. Staunton, *Triumph of the Optimists: 101 Years of.Global Investment Returns* (Princeton, NJ: Princeton University Press, 2002), with updates kindly provided by *Triumph*'s authors.

above the 6-year average by 19.24%. In column 3, we square these deviations from the average. The variance is then the average of these squared deviations:[5]

$$\text{Variance} = \text{average of squared deviations}$$

$$= \frac{765.23}{6} = 127.54$$

Because standard deviation is the square root of the variance,

$$\text{Standard deviation} = \text{square root of variance}$$

$$= \sqrt{127.54} = 11.29\%$$

It is difficult to measure the risk of securities on the basis of just six past outcomes. Therefore, Table 11.4 lists the annual standard deviations for our three portfolios of securities over the period 1900–2015. As expected, Treasury bills were the least variable security, and common stocks were the most variable. Treasury bonds hold the middle ground.

Of course, there is no reason to believe that the market's variability should stay the same over many years. Indeed many people believe that, in recent years, the stock market has become more volatile due to irresponsible speculation by . . . (fill in here the name of your preferred guilty party). Figure 11.5 provides a chart of the volatility of the U.S. stock market for each year from 1900 to 2015.[6] Notice how volatility spiked

FIGURE 11.5 Annualized standard deviation of weekly percent changes in the Dow Jones Industrial Average, 1900–2015

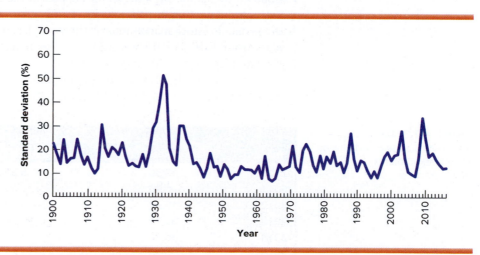

Source: www.djaverages.com.

[5] *Technical note:* When variance is estimated from a sample of observed returns, it is common to add the squared deviations and divide by $N - 1$, rather than N, where N is the number of observations. This procedure adjusts the estimate for what is called *the loss of a degree of freedom*. We will ignore this fine point, emphasizing the interpretation of variance as an average squared deviation. In any event, the correction for the lost degree of freedom is negligible when there are plentiful observations. For example, with 100 years of data, the difference between dividing by 99 or 100 will affect the estimated variance by only 1% (i.e., a factor of 1.01).

[6] We converted the weekly variance to an annual variance by multiplying by 52. In other words, the variance of annual returns is 52 times that of weekly returns. The longer you hold a security, the more risk you have to bear.

upward during the Great Crash of 1929. The past decade has also experienced unusually high volatility as the dot-com boom unwound in 2002 and as the financial crisis reached its climax in 2009. But recent years have also seen some of the most tranquil stock prices. Market volatility, it seems, may rise and fall, but there is little sign of an upward trend.

11.4 Risk and Diversification

Diversification

We can calculate our measures of variability equally well for individual securities and portfolios of securities. Of course, the level of variability over 100 years is less interesting for specific companies than for the market portfolio because it is a rare company that faces the same business risks today as it did a century ago.

Table 11.5 presents estimated standard deviations for some well-known common stocks for a recent 5-year period.[7] The standard deviation of the market portfolio in these years was 11.6%, well below the long-term average. However, the standard deviation of the returns on each of our stocks was much higher than 11.6%.

This raises an important question: The market portfolio is made up of individual stocks, so why isn't its variability equal to the average variability of its components? The answer is that **diversification** *reduces variability.*

Selling umbrellas is a risky business; you may make a killing when it rains, but you are likely to lose your shirt in a heat wave. Selling ice cream is no safer; you do well in the heat wave, but business is poor in the rain. Suppose, however, that you invest in both an umbrella shop and an ice cream shop. By diversifying your investment across the two businesses, you make an average level of profit come rain or shine.

Portfolio diversification works because prices of different stocks do not move exactly together. Statisticians make the same point when they say that stock price changes are less than perfectly correlated. Diversification works best when the returns are negatively correlated, as is the case of our umbrella and ice cream businesses. When one business does well, the other does badly. Unfortunately, in practice, stocks that are negatively correlated are as rare as a summer snowstorm.

diversification
Strategy designed to reduce risk by spreading the portfolio across many investments.

TABLE 11.5 Standard deviations for selected common stocks, January 2011–December 2015

Stock	Standard Deviation (%)	Stock	Standard Deviation (%)
U.S. Steel	43.7	Union Pacific	18.3
Newmont Mining	36.6	PG&E	16.6
Amazon	27.5	Campbell Soup	16.5
Ford	25.3	Walmart	16.5
Monsanto	21.3	IBM	15.6
Alphabet	21.2	ExxonMobil	15.5
Intel	21.2	Pfizer	15.3
Disney	20.6	Coca-Cola	13.5
Starbucks	19.7	McDonald's	12.6
General Electric	19.2	S&P 500	11.6
Boeing	19.1		

---

[7] We pointed out earlier that five annual observations are insufficient to give a reliable estimate of variability. Therefore, these estimates are derived from 60 monthly rates of return, and then the monthly variance is multiplied by 12.

Asset versus Portfolio Risk

The history of returns on different asset classes provides compelling evidence of a risk–return trade-off and suggests that the variability of the rate of return on a broad asset class is a useful measure of risk. However, volatility of returns can be a misleading measure of risk for an *individual* asset held as part of a portfolio. To see why, consider the following example.

Suppose there are three equally likely outcomes, or *scenarios,* for the economy: a recession, normal growth, and a boom. An investment in an auto stock will have a rate of return of −8% in a recession, 5% in a normal period, and 18% in a boom. Auto firms are *cyclical:* They do well when the economy does well. In contrast, gold firms are often said to be *countercyclical,* meaning that they do well when other firms do poorly. Suppose that stock in a gold mining firm will provide a rate of return of 20% in a recession, 3% in a normal period, and −20% in a boom. These assumptions are summarized in Table 11.6.

It appears that gold is the more volatile investment. The difference in return across the boom and bust scenarios is 40% (−20% in a boom versus +20% in a recession), compared with a spread of only 26% for the auto stock. In fact, we can confirm the higher volatility by measuring the variance or standard deviation of returns of the two assets. The calculations are set out in Table 11.7.

Because all three scenarios are equally likely, the expected return on each stock is simply the average of the three possible outcomes.[8] For the auto stock, the expected return is 5%; for the gold stock, it is 1%. The variance is the average of the squared deviations from the expected return, and the standard deviation is the square root of the variance.

TABLE 11.6 Rate of return assumptions for two stocks

		Rate of Return (%)	
Scenario	Probability	Auto Stock	Gold Stock
Recession	1/3	−8	+20
Normal	1/3	+5	+3
Boom	1/3	+18	−20

TABLE 11.7 Expected return and volatility for two stocks

	Auto Stock			Gold Stock		
Scenario	Rate of Return (%)	Deviation from Expected Return (%)	Squared Deviation	Rate of Return (%)	Deviation from Expected Return (%)	Squared Deviation
Recession	−8	−13	169	+20	+19	361
Normal	+5	0	0	+3	+2	4
Boom	+18	+13	169	−20	−21	441
Expected return	$\frac{1}{3}(-8+5+18)=5\%$			$\frac{1}{3}(+20+3-20)=1\%$		
Variance*	$\frac{1}{3}(169+0+169)=112.7$			$\frac{1}{3}(361+4+441)=268.7$		
Standard deviation (= √variance)	$\sqrt{112.7}=10.6\%$			$\sqrt{268.7}=16.4\%$		

* Variance = average of squared deviations from the expected value.

---

[8] If the probabilities were not equal, we would need to weight each outcome by its probability in calculating the expected outcome and the variance.

> ## 11.4 Self-Test
>
> Suppose the probability of the recession or boom is .30, while the probability of a normal period is .40. Would you expect the variance of returns on these two investments to be higher or lower? Why? Confirm by calculating the standard deviation of the auto stock. (Refer to Section 11.3 if you are unsure of how to do this.)

The gold mining stock offers a lower expected rate of return than the auto stock and *more* volatility—a loser on both counts, right? Would anyone be willing to hold gold mining stocks in an investment portfolio? The answer is a resounding yes.

To see why, suppose you do believe that gold is a lousy asset, and therefore, you hold your entire portfolio in the auto stock. Your expected return is 5% and your standard deviation is 10.6%. We'll compare that portfolio to a partially diversified one, invested 75% in autos and 25% in gold. For example, if you have a $10,000 portfolio, you could put $7,500 in autos and $2,500 in gold.

First, we need to calculate the return on this portfolio in each scenario. The portfolio return is the weighted average of returns on the individual assets with weights equal to the proportion of the portfolio invested in each asset. For a portfolio formed from only two assets,

$$
\begin{array}{l}
\text{Portfolio rate} \\
\text{of return}
\end{array} = \left(\begin{array}{l} \text{fraction of portfolio} \\ \text{in first asset} \end{array} \times \begin{array}{l} \text{rate of return} \\ \text{on first asset} \end{array} \right) \qquad \textbf{(11.4)}
$$

$$
+ \left(\begin{array}{l} \text{fraction of portfolio} \\ \text{in second asset} \end{array} \times \begin{array}{l} \text{rate of return} \\ \text{on second asset} \end{array} \right)
$$

For example, autos have a weight of .75 and a rate of return of −8% in the recession, and gold has a weight of .25 and a return of 20% in a recession. Therefore, the portfolio return in the recession is the following weighted average:[9]

$$
\text{Portfolio return in recession} = [.75 \times (-8\%)] + (.25 \times 20\%)
$$
$$
= -1\%
$$

Table 11.8 expands Table 11.6 to include the portfolio of the auto stock and the gold mining stock. The expected returns and volatility measures are summarized at the bottom of the table. The surprising finding is this: When you shift part of your funds from the auto stock to the more volatile gold mining stock, your portfolio variability actually *decreases*. In fact, the volatility of the auto-plus-gold stock portfolio is considerably less than the volatility of *either* stock separately. This is the payoff to diversification.

We can understand this more clearly by focusing on asset returns in the two extreme scenarios, boom and recession. In the boom, when auto stocks do best, the poor return on gold reduces the performance of the overall portfolio. However, when auto stocks are stalling in a recession, gold shines, providing a substantial positive return that boosts portfolio performance. The gold stock offsets the swings in the performance of the auto stock, reducing the best-case return but improving the worst-case return. The inverse relationship between the returns on the two stocks means that returns are more stable when the gold mining stock is added to an all-auto portfolio.

---

[9] Let's confirm this. Suppose you invest $7,500 in autos and $2,500 in gold. If the recession hits, the rate of return on autos will be −8%, and the value of the auto investment will fall by 8% to $6,900. The rate of return on gold will be 20%, and the value of the gold investment will rise 20% to $3,000. The value of the total portfolio falls from its original value of $10,000 to $6,900 + $3,000 = $9,900, which is a rate of return of −1%. This matches the rate of return given by the formula for the weighted average.

Scenario	Probability	Rate of Return (%)		Portfolio Return (%)*
		Auto Stock	Gold Stock	
Recession	1/3	−8	+20	−1.0
Normal	1/3	+5	+3	+4.5
Boom	1/3	+18	−20	+8.5
Expected return		5	1	4
Variance		112.7	268.7	15.2
Standard deviation		10.6	16.4	3.9

* Portfolio return = (.75 × auto stock return) + (.25 × gold stock return).

A gold stock is really a *negative-risk* asset to an investor starting with an all-auto portfolio. Adding it to the portfolio reduces the volatility of returns. The *incremental* risk of the gold stock (i.e., the *change* in overall risk when gold is added to the portfolio) is *negative* despite the fact that gold returns are highly volatile.

In Table 11.9, we consider several other potential portfolios, all formed by mixing our gold and auto stocks in varying proportions. Portfolio A is invested fully in the auto stock, portfolio B shifts 20% of the portfolio from the auto stock to gold, and so on, until we reach portfolio F, which is fully invested in gold. The table shows the rate of return of each portfolio in each scenario; the expected value and standard deviation of returns across the three scenarios appear in the last two columns. Notice that the standard deviation of portfolio A is 10.6%, which of course is just the standard deviation of the auto stock. When we shift 20% of the portfolio to more volatile gold, as in portfolio B, standard deviation actually falls. As we've seen, this is the benefit of diversification.

How much more can we reduce risk? The standard deviation of portfolio C, which has a 40% weight in gold, is even lower. But this is about the best we can do. Beyond this point, adding more gold *increases* standard deviation, to 5.6% for portfolio D and 11% for portfolio E. These portfolios are already heavily invested in gold, so adding more of it increases risk. Thus, the incremental risk of gold depends on where you are starting from. Portfolios A and B are dominated by the auto stock, so adding gold *reduces* volatility. But portfolios D and E are already dominated by gold, so adding more now *increases* volatility.

Figure 11.6 plots the expected return–standard deviation pairs of our six portfolios. The "extreme" portfolios, A and F, which are fully invested in either autos or gold, are at the two ends of the plot. When we "connect the dots" corresponding to each portfolio, we trace out the possible combinations of expected return and portfolio risk. This plot is called the **investment opportunity frontier.** The frontier dramatically illustrates the benefit of diversification. In our example, as portfolio C shows, risk can be driven almost to zero. The great power of diversification in this case derives from the strong inverse relation between the gold and the auto stock. If the relationship were less strong, the investment opportunity frontier would have the same general shape, but it would not come so close to the vertical axis.

In general, the incremental risk of a stock depends on whether its returns tend to vary with or against the returns of the other assets in the portfolio. Incremental risk does not

investment opportunity frontier
Plot of the combinations of expected return versus standard deviation for various portfolio weights.

	Portfolio Weights		Portfolio Rate of Return (%)			Expected Return	Standard Deviation
	Gold	Autos	Recession	Normal	Boom		
A	0.0	1.0	−8.0	5.0	18.0	5.0	10.6
B	0.2	0.8	−2.4	4.6	10.4	4.2	5.2
C	0.4	0.6	3.2	4.2	2.8	3.4	0.6
D	0.6	0.4	8.8	3.8	−4.8	2.6	5.6
E	0.8	0.2	14.4	3.4	−12.4	1.8	11.0
F	1.0	0.0	20.0	3.0	−20.0	1.0	16.4

FIGURE 11.6 The investment opportunity frontier for the gold and auto stocks. Each point on the curve represents a feasible combination of expected return and volatility. The six labeled points correspond to the portfolios in Table 11.9.

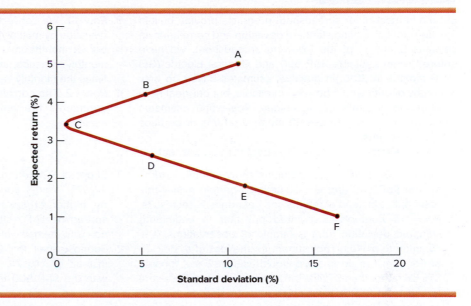

just depend on a stock's volatility. If returns do not move closely with those of the rest of the portfolio, the stock generally will reduce the volatility of portfolio returns.

The degree to which two stocks move together can be measured by the *correlation* between their returns. If the gold and auto stocks in Table 11.7 moved in perfect lockstep, the correlation would be 1.0. If their returns were completely unrelated, the correlation would be zero. Because their returns actually move inversely, that is, one stock goes up when the other goes down, the correlation is negative. The lowest possible correlation is −1.0, which indicates that returns move in perfect lockstep but in opposite directions. In our example, the correlation between the gold and auto stocks was nearly this extreme at −.996. Unfortunately, in practice, negative correlations are rare because most stocks have a common dependence on the overall economy.

Table 11.10 shows correlations across a few major industries calculated from 5 years of monthly stock returns ending in 2015. You can find the correlation between any industry pair by picking off the number in the relevant row and column. Of course, each industry is perfectly correlated with itself, so every entry on the diagonal is exactly 1.

As we would expect, most correlations in the table are positive, but the correlations are highest between pairs of industries that are very sensitive to the business cycle. The maximum correlation in the table, .86, is between the machinery and auto industries. Correlations between these industries and less "cyclical" industries such

TABLE 11.10 Correlations across some major industries

	Food	Drugs	Construction	Machinery	Autos	Gold	Oil	Utilities	Telecom	Retail	Banks
Food	1.00										
Drugs	0.64	1.00									
Construction	0.46	0.52	1.00								
Machinery	0.40	0.43	0.85	1.00							
Autos	0.37	0.42	0.74	0.86	1.00						
Gold	−0.01	0.01	0.09	0.21	0.11	1.00					
Oil	0.38	0.35	0.68	0.84	0.64	0.31	1.00				
Utilities	0.48	0.53	0.28	0.28	0.19	0.01	0.36	1.00			
Telecom	0.63	0.65	0.63	0.63	0.57	−0.03	0.65	0.41	1.00		
Retail	0.58	0.68	0.63	0.62	0.63	−0.02	0.45	0.35	0.64	1.00	
Banks	0.45	0.52	0.80	0.75	0.77	−0.09	0.62	0.20	0.69	0.63	1.00

Source: Authors' calculations using monthly value-weighted industry index returns for the 5-year period ending December 2015, downloaded from the Fama-French data library: http://mba.tuck.dartmouth.edu/pages/faculty/ken.french/Data_Library/det_10_ind_port.html.

Excel and most other spreadsheet programs provide built-in functions for calculating standard deviation and correlation. In columns B and C of the following spreadsheet, we have entered returns for the S&P 500 and General Electric (GE) for 6 months in 2015. In practice, estimates based on only 6 months of data would be *very* unreliable, but our goal here is simply to illustrate the technique. Real-world estimates would be more likely to use 60 monthly returns or perhaps 52 weekly returns.

Here are some points to notice about the spreadsheet:

1. *Columns B and C.* These columns show monthly *returns* for the S&P 500 and GE. Sometimes people mistakenly enter prices instead of returns and get nonsensical results.
2. *Row 10.* Footnote 5 pointed out that in estimating standard deviation from a sample of observations, it is common to make an adjustment for the loss of a "degree of freedom." To do this, we would use the Excel formula STDEV rather than STDEVP. In some versions of Excel, the formulas are STDEV.S (which corrects for degrees of freedom) and STDEV.P (which does not).

3. *Row 11.* We converted from monthly to annual standard deviation by multiplying by the square root of 12 (the number of months in a year). Annual variance is 12 times monthly variance, so annual *standard deviation* is $\sqrt{12}$ times the monthly value.
4. *Row 12.* The correlation function, CORREL, takes as its arguments the entire series of returns on the two assets.

Spreadsheet Questions

1. Suppose GE's return in October had been 3.0% instead of 14.67%. Would you expect GE's standard deviation to be higher or lower than the value obtained in the spreadsheet? Reestimate the annualized standard deviation with the new value to confirm your intuition.
2. Suppose again that GE's return in October had been 3.0% instead of 14.67%. Would you expect GE's correlation with the S&P 500 to be higher or lower than the value obtained in the spreadsheet? Reestimate the correlation with the new value to confirm your intuition.

	A	B	C	D
		Returns (%)		Formula Used in
1		**S&P 500**	**GE**	**Column C**
2	**Month**			
3	Jul-15	1.97	−1.77	
4	Aug-15	−6.26	−4.90	
5	Sep-15	−2.64	2.52	
6	Oct-15	8.30	14.67	
7	Nov-15	0.05	2.77	
8	Dec-15	−1.75	4.81	
9				
10	Mean return	−0.05	3.02	=AVERAGE(C3:C8)
11	Standard deviation (monthly)	4.51	6.12	=STDEVP(C3:C8)
12	Standard deviation (annualized)	15.62	21.21	=C11*SQRT(12)
13	Correlation		0.82	=CORREL(C3:C8,B3:B8)

as gold are considerably lower. The real-life correlation between gold and autos is .11, quite low, but still not negative as the value used in our example.

Excel provides built-in formulas that make calculating correlations as well as standard deviations pretty easy. We show you how in the nearby box.

We can summarize as follows:

1. Investors care about the expected return and risk of their *portfolio* of assets. The risk of the overall portfolio can be measured by the volatility of returns, that is, the variance or standard deviation.
2. The standard deviation of the returns of an individual security measures how risky that security would be if held in isolation. But an investor who holds a portfolio of securities is interested only in how each security affects the risk of the entire portfolio. The contribution of a security to the risk of the portfolio depends on how the security's returns vary with the investor's other holdings. Thus, a security that is risky if held in isolation may, nevertheless, serve to reduce the variability of the portfolio if its returns do not move in lockstep with the rest of the portfolio.
3. You can calculate how risky a portfolio has been by collecting its historical returns and calculating the standard deviation or variance. The reduction in portfolio risk

BEYOND THE PAGE

How to calculate correlation coefficients

mhhe.com/brealey9e

FIGURE 11.7 The rate of return of a portfolio evenly divided between U.S. Steel and Newmont was less volatile than either stock on its own.

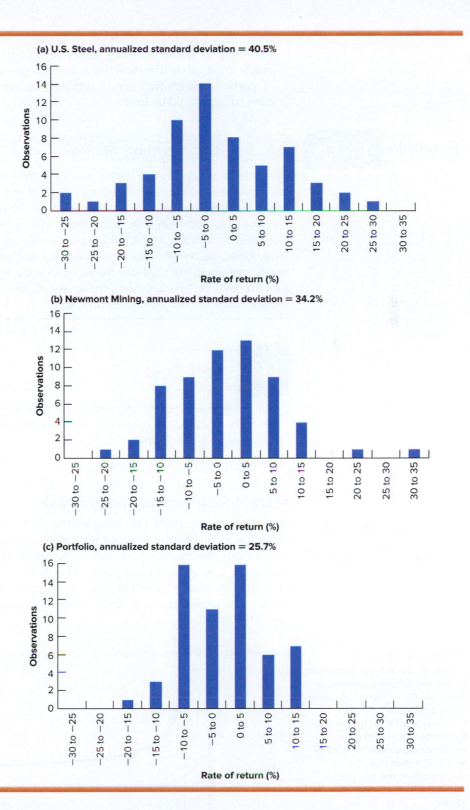

(a) U.S. Steel, annualized standard deviation = 40.5%

(b) Newmont Mining, annualized standard deviation = 34.2%

(c) Portfolio, annualized standard deviation = 25.7%

from diversification depends on the correlations between stocks in the portfolio. Portfolios of stocks all taken from one industry, for example, would not benefit much from diversification because the returns would be highly correlated. A portfolio diversified across different industries would benefit more because correlations would be lower.

Example 11.1 ▶   U.S. Steel and Newmont Mining

Our example of the auto and gold mining stocks was entirely fanciful, but we can make the same point by looking at two real firms, U.S. Steel and Newmont Mining. Panels *a* and *b* of Figure 11.7 show the spread of monthly returns on the two stocks for the 5-year period ending June 2015. Although both stocks had a wide spread of monthly returns, they did not move in exact lockstep. Often, a decline in the value of one stock was offset by a rise in the price of the other. Panel *c* shows that if you had split your portfolio equally between the two stocks, you would have reduced the variation in the returns on your investment. The standard deviation of the combined portfolio would have been more than 30% less than the average risk of the two individual stocks. ■

11.5   Self-Test

An investor is currently fully invested in gold mining stocks. Which action would do more to reduce portfolio risk: diversification into silver mining stocks or into automotive stocks? Why?

Market Risk versus Specific Risk

BEYOND THE PAGE

How diversification reduces risk

mhhe.com/brealey9e

Our examples illustrate that even a little diversification can provide a substantial reduction in variability. Suppose you calculate and compare the standard deviations of randomly chosen one-stock portfolios, two-stock portfolios, five-stock portfolios, and so on. You can see from Figure 11.8 that diversification can cut the variability of returns by nearly half. But you can get most of this benefit with relatively few stocks: The improvement is slight when the number of stocks is increased beyond, say, 20 or 30.

FIGURE 11.8 The risk (standard deviation) of portfolios containing different numbers of New York Stock Exchange stocks. The stocks were selected randomly from New York Stock Exchange stocks that were continuously quoted from 2010 to 2014. Notice that diversification reduces risk rapidly at first and then more slowly.

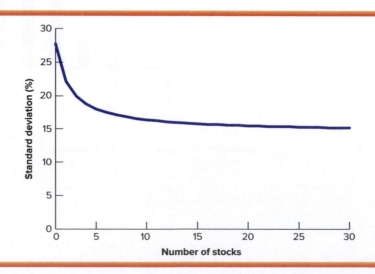

FIGURE 11.9 Diversification eliminates specific risk. But there is some risk that diversification cannot eliminate. This is called market risk.

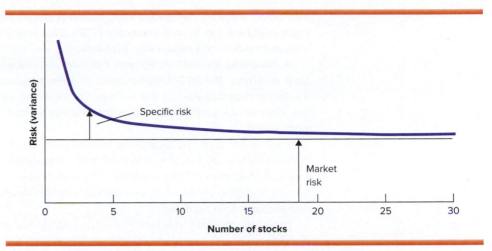

Technical note: Risk here is measured by the variance. The total variance of a portfolio is the sum of the variance due to the market and the specific variance.

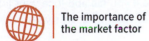
specific risk
Risk factors affecting only that firm. Also called *diversifiable risk.*

market risk
Economywide (macroeconomic) sources of risk that affect the overall stock market. Also called *systematic risk.*

Figure 11.8 also illustrates that no matter how many securities you hold, you cannot eliminate all risk. If the economy as a whole tanks, then most stocks, and even diversified portfolios, are likely to plummet.

The risk that can be eliminated by diversification is called **specific risk.** The risk that you can't avoid regardless of how much you diversify is generally known as **market risk** or *systematic risk. Specific risk* **arises because many of the perils that surround an individual company are peculiar to that company and perhaps its direct competitors.** *Market risk* **stems from economywide perils that threaten all businesses. Market risk explains why stocks have a tendency to move together, so even well-diversified portfolios are exposed to market movements.**

Figure 11.9 divides risk into its two parts—specific risk and market risk. If you have only a single stock, specific risk is very important; but once you have a portfolio of 30 or more stocks, diversification has done most of what it can to eliminate risk. **For a reasonably well-diversified portfolio, only market risk matters.**

11.5   Thinking about Risk

How can you tell which risks are specific and diversifiable? Where do market risks come from? Here are three messages to help you think clearly about risk.

Message 1: Some Risks Look Big and Dangerous but Really Are Diversifiable

Managers confront risks "up close and personal." They must make decisions about particular investments. The failure of such an investment could cost a promotion, bonus, or otherwise steady job. Yet that same investment may not seem risky to an investor who can stand back and combine it in a diversified portfolio with many other assets or securities.

Example   11.2 ▶   Wildcat Oil Wells

You have just been promoted to director of exploration, Western Hemisphere, of MPS Oil. The manager of your exploration team in far-off Costaguana has appealed for $20 million extra to drill in an even steamier part of the Costaguanan jungle. The manager thinks there may be an "elephant" field worth $500 million or more hidden there. But the chance of finding it is at best 1 in 10, and yesterday MPS's CEO sourly commented on the $100 million already "wasted" on Costaguanan exploration.

Is this a risky investment? For you it probably is; you may be a hero if oil is found and a goat otherwise. But MPS drills hundreds of wells worldwide; for the company as a whole, it's the *average* success rate that matters. Geologic risks (is there oil or not?) should average out. The risk of a worldwide drilling program is much less than the apparent risk of any single wildcat well.

Back up one step, and think of the investors who buy MPS stock. The investors may hold other oil companies, too, as well as companies producing steel, computers, clothing, cement, and breakfast cereal. They naturally—and realistically—assume that your successes and failures in drilling oil wells will average out with the thousands of other bets made by the companies in their portfolio.

Therefore, the risks you face in Costaguana do not affect the rate of return investors demand for holding the stock of MPS Oil. Diversified investors in MPS stock will be happy if you find that elephant field, but they probably will not notice if you fail and lose your job. In any case, they will not demand a higher *average* rate of return for worrying about geologic risks in Costaguana. ■

Example 11.3 ▶   Fire Insurance

Would you be willing to write a $100,000 fire insurance policy on your neighbor's house? The neighbor is willing to pay you $100 for a year's protection, and experience shows that the chance of fire damage in a given year is substantially less than 1 in 1,000. But if your neighbor's house is damaged by fire, you would have to pay up.

Few of us have deep enough pockets to insure our neighbors, even if the odds of fire damage are very low. Insurance seems a risky business if you think policy by policy. But a large insurance company, which may issue a million policies, is concerned only with average losses, which can be predicted with excellent accuracy. ■

11.6   Self-Test

Imagine a laboratory at Intel, late at night. One scientist speaks to another.

"You're right, Watson, I admit this experiment will consume all the rest of this year's budget. I don't know what we'll do if it fails. But if this yttrium–magnoosium alloy superconducts, the patents will be worth millions."

Would this be a good or bad investment for Intel? Can't say. But from the ultimate investors' viewpoint this is *not* a risky investment. Explain why.

Message 2: Market Risks Are Macro Risks

We have seen that diversified portfolios are not exposed to the specific risks of individual stocks but are exposed to the uncertain events that affect the entire securities market and the entire economy. These are macroeconomic, or "macro," factors such as changes in interest rates, industrial production, inflation, foreign exchange rates, and energy costs. These factors affect most firms' earnings and stock prices. When the relevant macro risks turn generally favorable, stock prices rise and investors do well; when the same variables go the other way, investors suffer.

You can often assess relative market risks just by thinking through exposures to the business cycle and other macro variables. The following businesses have substantial macro and market risks:

- *Airlines.* Because business travel falls during a recession, and individuals postpone vacations and other discretionary travel, the airline industry is subject to the swings of the business cycle. On the positive side, airline profits really take off when business is booming and personal incomes are rising.
- *Machine tool manufacturers.* These businesses are especially exposed to the business cycle. Manufacturing companies that have excess capacity rarely buy new machine tools to expand. During recessions, excess capacity can be quite high.

Here, on the other hand, are two industries with less-than-average macro exposures:

- *Food companies.* Companies selling staples, such as breakfast cereal, flour, and dog food, find that demand for their products is relatively stable in good times and bad.
- *Electric utilities.* Business demand for electric power varies somewhat across the business cycle, but by much less than demand for air travel or machine tools. Also, many electric utilities' profits are regulated. Regulation cuts off upside profit potential but also gives the utilities the opportunity to increase prices when demand is slack.

Remember, investors holding diversified portfolios are mostly concerned with macroeconomic risks. They do not worry about microeconomic risks peculiar to a particular company or investment project. Micro risks wash out in diversified portfolios. Company managers may worry about both macro and micro risks, but only the former affect diversified investors and the cost of capital.

11.7 Self-Test

Which company of each of the following pairs would you expect to be more exposed to macro risks?

a. A luxury Manhattan restaurant or an established Burger Queen franchise?
b. A paint company that sells through small paint and hardware stores to do-it-yourselfers or a paint company that sells in large volumes to Ford, GM, and Chrysler?

Message 3: Risk Can Be Measured

Delta Airlines clearly has more exposure to macro risks than food companies such as Kellogg or General Mills. These are easy cases. But is IBM stock a riskier investment than ExxonMobil? That's not an easy question to reason through. We can, however, *measure* the risk of IBM and ExxonMobil by looking at how their stock prices fluctuate.

We've already hinted at how to do this. Remember that diversified investors are concerned with market risks. The movements of the stock market sum up the net effects of all relevant macroeconomic uncertainties. If the market portfolio of all traded stocks is up in a particular month, we conclude that the net effect of macroeconomic news is positive. Remember, the performance of the market is barely affected by a firm-specific event. These cancel out across thousands of stocks in the market.

How do we measure the risk of a single stock like IBM or ExxonMobil? We do not look at the stocks in isolation because the risks that loom when you're up close to a single company are often diversifiable. Instead, we measure the individual stock's sensitivity to the fluctuations of the overall stock market. We will show you how this works in the next chapter.

SUMMARY

How can one estimate the opportunity cost of capital for an "average-risk" project? (*LO11-1*)

Over the past century the return on the **Standard & Poor's Composite Index** of common stocks has averaged 7.6% a year higher than the return on safe Treasury bills. This is the **risk premium** that investors have received for taking on the risk of investing in stocks. Long-term bonds have offered a higher return than Treasury bills but less than stocks.

If the risk premium in the past is a guide to the future, we can estimate the expected return on the market today by adding that 7.6% expected risk premium to today's interest rate on Treasury bills. This would be the opportunity cost of capital for an average-risk project, that is, one with the same risk as the broad market index.

How is the standard deviation of returns for individual common stocks or for a stock portfolio calculated? (*LO11-2*)

The spread of outcomes on different investments is commonly measured by the **variance** or **standard deviation** of the possible outcomes. The variance is the average of the squared deviations around the average outcome, and the standard deviation is the square root of the variance. The standard deviation of the returns on a market portfolio of common stocks has averaged around 20% a year.

Why does diversification reduce risk? (*LO11-3*)

The standard deviation of returns is generally higher on individual stocks than it is on the market. Because individual stocks do not move in exact lockstep, much of their risk can be diversified away. By spreading your portfolio across many investments, you smooth out the risk of your overall position. The risk that can be eliminated through diversification is known as **specific risk.**

What is the difference between specific risk, which can be diversified away, and market risk, which cannot? (*LO11-4*)

Even if you hold a well-diversified portfolio, you will not eliminate all risk. You will still be exposed to macroeconomic changes that affect most stocks and the overall stock market. These macro risks combine to create **market risk**—that is, the risk that the market as a whole will slump.

Stocks are not all equally risky. But what do we mean by a "high-risk stock"? We don't mean a stock that is risky if held in isolation; we mean a stock that makes an above-average contribution to the risk of a diversified portfolio. In other words, investors don't need to worry much about the risk that they can diversify away; they *do* need to worry about risk that can't be diversified. This depends on the stock's sensitivity to macroeconomic conditions.

LISTING OF EQUATIONS

11.1 Percentage return $= \dfrac{\text{capital gain} + \text{dividend}}{\text{initial share price}}$

11.2 Variance = average of squared deviations around the average

11.3 Standard deviation = square root of variance

11.4 $\begin{aligned}\text{Portfolio rate} \atop \text{of return}\end{aligned} = \left(\begin{aligned}&\text{fraction of portfolio} \\ &\text{in first asset}\end{aligned} \times \begin{aligned}&\text{rate of return} \\ &\text{on first asset}\end{aligned}\right)$

$\qquad\qquad + \left(\begin{aligned}&\text{fraction of portfolio} \\ &\text{in second asset}\end{aligned} \times \begin{aligned}&\text{rate of return} \\ &\text{on second asset}\end{aligned}\right)$

QUESTIONS AND PROBLEMS

connect

1. **Stock Market History.** Use the data in Tables 11.1 and 11.4 to answer these questions: (*LO11-1*)
   a. What was the average rate of return on large U.S. common stocks from 1900 to 2015?
   b. What was the average risk premium on large stocks?
   c. What was the standard deviation of returns on the market portfolio?

2. **Maturity Premiums.** Investments in long-term government bonds produced a negative average return during the period 1977–1981. How should we interpret this? Did bond investors in 1977 expect to earn a negative maturity premium? What do these 5 years of bond returns tell us about the normal future maturity premium? (*LO11-1*)

3. **Risk Premiums.** What will happen to the opportunity cost of capital if investors suddenly become especially conservative and less willing to bear investment risk? (*LO11-1*)

4. **Risk Premium.** If the stock market return next year turns out to be −20%, will our estimate of the "normal" risk premium increase or decrease? Does this make sense? (*LO11-1*)

5. **Risk Premiums and Discount Rates.** Top hedge fund manager Sally Buffit believes that a stock with the same market risk as the S&P 500 will sell at year-end at a price of $50. The stock will pay a dividend at year-end of $2. What price should she be willing to pay for the stock today? Assume that risk-free Treasury securities currently offer an interest rate of 2%. Use Table 11.1 to find a reasonable discount rate. (*LO11-1*)

6. **Risk Premiums.** Here are rates of return on a broad stock market index and on Treasury bills between 2011 and 2015: (*LO11-1*)

Year	Stock Market Return (%)	T-Bill Return (%)
2011	0.98	0.03
2012	16.06	0.05
2013	33.06	0.07
2014	12.71	0.05
2015	0.67	0.21

   a. What was the risk premium on common stock in each year?
   b. What was the average risk premium?
   c. What was the standard deviation of the risk premium?

7. **Rate of Return.** A stock is selling today for $40 per share. At the end of the year, it pays a dividend of $2 per share and sells for $44. (*LO11-2*)
   a. What is the total rate of return on the stock?
   b. What are the dividend yield and percentage capital gain?
   c. Now suppose the year-end stock price after the dividend is paid is $36. What are the dividend yield and percentage capital gain in this case?

8. **Real versus Nominal Returns.** You purchase 100 shares of stock for $40 a share. The stock pays a $2 per share dividend at year-end. (*LO11-2*)
   a. What is the rate of return on your investment if the end-of-year stock price is (i) $38; (ii) $40; (iii) $42?
   b. What is your real (inflation-adjusted) rate of return if the inflation rate is 4%?

9. **Real versus Nominal Returns.** The Costaguanan stock market provided a rate of return of 95%. The inflation rate in Costaguana during the year was 80%. In Ruritania, in contrast, the stock market return was only 12%, but the inflation rate was only 2%. Which country's stock market provided the higher real rate of return? (*LO11-2*)

10. **Real versus Nominal Returns.** The inflation rate in the United States has averaged 3% a year since 1900. What was the average real rate of return on Treasury bills, Treasury bonds, and common stocks in that period? Use the data in Table 11.1. (*LO11-2*)

11. **Market Indexes.** The accompanying table shows annual stock prices on the Sulaco Stock Exchange in the republic of Costaguana for 2010–2015. Construct two stock market indexes, one using weights as in the Dow Jones Industrial Average and the other using weights as in the Standard & Poor's Composite Index. (*LO11-2*)

Annual prices in Costaguanan pegos for trading on the Sulaco Stock Exchange (only five stocks were traded at the start of 2010)					
	San Tomé Mining (184 million*)	Sulaco Markets (42 million*)	National Central Railway (64 million*)	Minerva Shipping (38 million*)	Azuera Inc. (16 million*)
2010	55.10	80.00	21.45	82.50	135.00
2011	58.15	144.62	24.04	115.52	151.22
2012	58.45	135.93	26.53	138.90	166.99
2013	52.43	74.61	23.53	121.02	149.42
2014	52.50	75.01	32.46	174.62	177.27
2015	54.82	67.22	34.48	164.48	165.52

* Number of shares outstanding.

12. **Market Indexes.** In February 2009, the Dow Jones Industrial Average was at a level of about 8,000. In January 2016, it was about 17,150. Would you expect the Dow in 2016 to be more or less likely to move up or down by more than 40 points in a day than in 2009? Does this mean the market was riskier in 2016 than it was in 2009? (*LO11-2*)

13. **Scenario Analysis.** Consider the following scenario analysis: (*LO11-2*)

		Rate of Return	
Scenario	Probability	Stocks	Bonds
Recession	0.20	−5%	+14%
Normal economy	0.60	+15	+8
Boom	0.20	+25	+4

a. Is it reasonable to assume that Treasury bonds will provide higher returns in recessions than in booms?
b. Calculate the expected rate of return and standard deviation for each investment.
c. Which investment would you prefer?

14. **Risk and Expected Return.** A stock will provide a rate of return of either −18% or +26%. If both possibilities are equally likely, calculate the stock's expected return and standard deviation. (*LO11-2*)

15. **Scenario Analysis and Portfolio Risk.** The common stock of Leaning Tower of Pita Inc., a restaurant chain, will generate payoffs to investors next year, which depend on the state of the economy, as follows: (*LO11-2 and LO11-3*)

	Dividend	Stock Price
Boom	$8	$240
Normal economy	4	90
Recession	0	0

a. The company goes out of business if a recession hits. Calculate the expected rate of return and standard deviation of return to Leaning Tower of Pita shareholders. Assume for simplicity that the three possible states of the economy are equally likely. The stock is selling today for $80.
b. Who would view the stock of Leaning Tower of Pita as a risk-reducing investment—the owner of a gambling casino or a successful bankruptcy lawyer? Explain.

16. **Scenario Analysis.** The common stock of Escapist Films sells for $25 a share and offers the following payoffs next year: (*LO11-3*)

	Dividend	Stock Price
Boom	$0	$18
Normal economy	1	26
Recession	3	34

a. Calculate the expected return and standard deviation of Escapist. All three scenarios are equally likely.

b. Now calculate the expected return and standard deviation of a portfolio half invested in Escapist and half in Leaning Tower of Pita (from Problem 15). Show that the portfolio standard deviation is lower than that of either stock. Explain why this happens.

17. **Average Return and Standard Deviation.** In 2011–2015, mutual fund manager Diana Sauros produced the following percentage rates of return for the Mesozoic Fund. Rates of return on the market index are given for comparison. Calculate (a) the average return on both the fund and the index, and (b) the standard deviation of the returns on each. Did Ms. Sauros do better or worse than the market index on these measures? *(LO11-3)*

	2011	2012	2013	2014	2015
Fund	−1.2	+24.8	+40.7	+11.1	+0.3
Market index	−0.9	+16.0	+31.7	+10.9	−0.7

18. **Portfolio Analysis.** Use the data in the scenario analysis from Problem 13 and consider a portfolio with weights of .60 in stocks and .40 in bonds. *(LO11-3)*

a. What is the rate of return on the portfolio in each scenario?

b. What are the expected rate of return and standard deviation of the portfolio?

c. Would you prefer to invest in the portfolio, in stocks only, or in bonds only? Explain the benefit of diversification.

19. **Diversification.** Here are the returns on two stocks. *(LO11-3)*

a. Calculate the variance and standard deviation of each stock. Which stock is riskier if held on its own?

b. Now calculate the returns in each month of a portfolio that invests an equal amount each month in the two stocks.

c. Is the variance more or less than halfway between the variance of the two individual stocks?

	Digital Cheese	Executive Fruit
January	+15	+7
February	−3	+1
March	+5	+4
April	+7	+13
May	−4	+2
June	+3	+5
July	−2	−3
August	−8	−2

20. **Diversification.** In which of the following situations would you get the largest reduction in risk by spreading your portfolio across two stocks? Why? *(LO11-3)*

a. The stock returns vary with each other.

b. The stock returns are independent.

c. The stock returns vary against each other.

21. **Diversification.** Log in to Connect or ask your instructor for access to the materials for Chapter 11. You will find a spreadsheet containing 5 years of monthly rates of return on ExxonMobil (XOM), Chevron (CVX), and Walmart (WMT). *(LO11-3)*

a. What was the average return and standard deviation of returns for each firm?

b. What was the correlation of returns between each pair of firms? Try using Excel's CORREL function, which calculates the correlation between two series of numbers. Which pair of firms exhibits the highest correlation of returns? Is this surprising?

c. Now imagine that you held an equally weighted portfolio of ExxonMobil and Walmart (i.e., a portfolio with equal dollar investments in each stock). Compute the portfolio's rate of return for each month, and calculate the standard deviation of the portfolio's monthly rate of return. Is the portfolio standard deviation more or less than the average of the standard deviations of the two component stocks?

d. Repeat part (c), but this time calculate the results for a portfolio of Chevron and ExxonMobil.

e. Compare your answers to parts (c) and (d). Which pair of firms provides greater benefits from diversification? Relate your answer to the correlation coefficients you found in part (a).

22. **Market Risk.** Which firms of each pair below would you expect to have greater market risk? (*LO11-4*)

   a. General Steel or General Food Supplies
   b. Club Med or General Cinemas

23. **Specific versus Market Risk.** Sassafras Oil is staking all its remaining capital on wildcat exploration off the Côte d'Huile. There is a 10% chance of discovering a field with reserves of 50 million barrels. If it finds oil, it will immediately sell the reserves to Big Oil at a price depending on the state of the economy. Thus, the possible payoffs are as follows:

	Value of Reserves per Barrel	Value of Reserves (50 Million Barrels)	Value of Dryholes
Boom	$4	$200,000,000	0
Normal economy	5	250,000,000	0
Recession	6	300,000,000	0

Is Sassafras Oil a risky investment for a diversified investor in the stock market—compared, say, with the stock of Leaning Tower of Pita, described in Problem 15? Explain. (*LO11-4*)

24. **Portfolio Risk.** True or false? (*LO11-4*)

   a. Investors prefer diversified portfolios because they are less risky.
   b. If stocks were perfectly correlated, diversification would not reduce risk.
   c. Diversification with an indefinitely large number of securities completely eliminates risk.
   d. Diversification works only when returns are uncorrelated.
   e. The risk of a diversified portfolio depends on the specific risk of the individual stocks.
   f. The risk that you can't avoid no matter how much you diversify is known as market risk.
   g. For a well-diversified portfolio, only market risk matters.

WEB EXERCISES

1. Go to finance.yahoo.com, and find the monthly rates of return over a 2-year period for five companies of your choice. Now assume you form each month an equally weighted portfolio of the five firms (i.e., a portfolio with equal investments in each firm). What is the rate of return each month on your portfolio? Compare the standard deviation of the monthly portfolio return with that of each firm and with the average standard deviation across the five firms. What do you conclude about portfolio diversification?

2. Return to the monthly returns of the five companies you chose in the previous question.

   a. Use the Excel functions for average (AVERAGE) and sample standard deviation (STDEV) to calculate the average and the standard deviation of the returns for each of the firms.
   b. Use Excel's correlation function (CORREL) to find the correlations between each pair of five stocks. What are the highest and lowest correlations?
   c. Try finding correlations between pairs of stocks in the same industry. Are the correlations higher than those you found in part (b)? Is this surprising?

3. A large mutual fund group such as Fidelity offers a variety of funds. Some, called *sector funds*, specialize in particular industries; others, known as *index funds*, simply invest in the market index. Log on to www.fidelity.com and look up the standard deviation of returns on the Fidelity 500 Index Fund (FUSEX), which replicates the S&P 500. Now find the standard deviation of fund returns for different industry (sector) funds. Are they larger or smaller than the index fund? How do you interpret your findings?

SOLUTIONS TO SELF-TEST QUESTIONS

11.1 The bond price at the end of the year is $1,050. Therefore, the capital gain on each bond is $1,050 − $1,020 = $30. Your dollar return is the sum of the income from the bond, $80, plus the capital gain, $30, or $110. The rate of return is

$$\frac{\text{Income plus capital gain}}{\text{Original price}} = \frac{80 + 30}{1,020} = .108, \text{ or } 10.8\%$$

Real rate of return is

$$\frac{1 + \text{nominal return}}{1 + \text{inflation rate}} - 1 = \frac{1.108}{1.04} - 1 = .065, \text{ or } 6.5\%$$

11.2 The risk premium on stocks is the average return in excess of Treasury bills. It was 7.1% in period 1, 8.8% in period 2, 6.1% in period 3, and 8.2% in period 4.

11.3

Rate of Return (%)	Deviation (%)	Squared Deviation
+70	+60	3,600
+10	0	0
+10	0	0
−50	−60	3,600

Variance = average of squared deviations = 7,200/4 = 1,800

Standard deviation = square root of variance = $\sqrt{1,800}$ = 42.4, about 42%

11.4 The standard deviation should decrease because there is now a lower probability of the more extreme outcomes. The expected rate of return on the auto stock is now

$$[.3 \times (-8\%)] + (.4 \times 5\%) + (.3 \times 18\%) = 5\%$$

The variance is

$$[.3 \times (-8 - 5)^2] + [.4 \times (5 - 5)^2] + [.3 \times (18 - 5)^2] = 101.4$$

The standard deviation is $\sqrt{101.4}$ = 10.07%, which is lower than the value assuming equal probabilities of each scenario.

11.5 The gold mining stock's returns are more highly correlated with the silver mining company than with a car company. As a result, the automotive firm will offer a greater diversification benefit. The power of diversification is lowest when rates of return are highly correlated, performing well or poorly in tandem. Shifting part of the portfolio from one such firm to another has little impact on overall risk.

11.6 The success of this project depends on the experiment. Success does *not* depend on the performance of the overall economy. The experiment creates a diversifiable risk. A portfolio of many stocks will embody "bets" on many such specific risks. Some bets will work out and some will fail. Because the outcomes of these risks do not depend on common factors, such as the overall state of the economy, the risks will tend to cancel out in a well-diversified portfolio.

11.7 a. The luxury restaurant will be more sensitive to the state of the economy because expense account meals will be curtailed in a recession. Burger Queen meals should be relatively recession-proof.

b. The paint company that sells to the auto producers will be more sensitive to the state of the economy. In a downturn, auto sales fall dramatically as consumers stretch the lives of their cars. In contrast, in a recession, more people "do it themselves," which makes paint sales through small stores more stable and less sensitive to the economy.

SOLUTIONS TO SPREADSHEET QUESTIONS

11.1 If the return on GE had been 3.0% in October, you should observe a lower standard deviation because the performance in this month is now less extreme. In fact, using this rate of return, the annualized standard deviation falls from 21.21% to 11.52%.

11.2 You should expect to observe a lower correlation. GE now has an average return in this month, which is when the market has its best performance. The correlation falls from .82 to .42.

12

Risk, Return, and Capital Budgeting

LEARNING OBJECTIVES

After studying this chapter, you should be able to:

12-1 Measure and interpret the market risk, or beta, of a security.

12-2 Relate the market risk of a security to the rate of return that investors demand.

12-3 Understand why and how project risk determines the opportunity cost of capital.

RELATED WEBSITES FOR THIS CHAPTER CAN BE FOUND IN CONNECT.

If you want big rewards, you generally need to take big risks.   *© ZUMA Press, Inc./Alamy*

I n Chapter 11, we began to come to grips with risk. We stressed the distinction between *specific* risk and *market* risk. Specific risk arises from events that affect only the individual firm or its immediate competitors; it can be eliminated by diversification. But regardless of how much you diversify, you cannot avoid the macroeconomic events that create market risk. This is why investors do not require a higher rate of return to compensate for specific risk but do need a higher return to persuade them to take on market risk.

How can you measure the market risk of a security or a project? We will see that market risk is usually measured by *beta*—that is, by the sensitivity of the investment's returns to fluctuations in the market. We will also see that the risk premium investors demand should be proportional to beta. This relationship between risk and return is a useful way to estimate the return that investors expect from investing in common stocks.

Finally, we will distinguish the risk of the company's securities and the risk of an individual project. We will also consider what managers should do when the risk of the project is different from that of the company's existing business.

12.1   Measuring Market Risk

market portfolio
Portfolio of all assets in the economy. In practice a broad stock market index is used to represent the market.

Changes in interest rates, government spending, oil prices, foreign exchange rates, and other macroeconomic events affect almost all companies and the returns on almost all stocks. We can, therefore, assess the impact of "macro" news by tracking the rate of return on a **market portfolio** of all securities. If the market is up on a particular day, then the net impact of macroeconomic changes must be positive. We know the performance of the market reflects only macro events, because firm-specific events—that is, specific risks—average out when we look at the combined performance of thousands of securities.

In principle, the market portfolio should contain all assets in the world economy—not just stocks but bonds, foreign securities, real estate, and so on. In practice, however, financial analysts make do with indexes of the stock market, such as the Standard & Poor's Composite Index (the S&P 500).[1]

Our task here is to define and measure the risk of *individual* common stocks. Because risk depends on exposure to macroeconomic events, we measure it as the sensitivity of a stock's returns to fluctuations in returns on the market portfolio. This sensitivity is called the stock's **beta.** Beta is often written as the Greek letter β.

beta
Sensitivity of a stock's return to the return on the market portfolio.

Measuring Beta

In the last chapter, we looked at the variability of several individual securities. U.S. Steel had one of the highest standard deviations, and McDonald's had the lowest. If you had held U.S. Steel on its own, your returns would have varied more than three times as much as they would have if you had held McDonald's. But wise investors don't put all their eggs in just one basket: They reduce their risk by diversification. An investor with a diversified portfolio will be interested in the effect each stock has on the risk of the entire portfolio.

Diversification can eliminate the risk that is unique to individual stocks but not the risk that the market as a whole may decline, carrying your stocks with it.

Some stocks are less affected than others by market fluctuations. Investment managers talk about "defensive" and "aggressive" stocks. Defensive stocks are not very sensitive to market fluctuations and, therefore, have low betas. In contrast, aggressive stocks amplify any market movements and have higher betas. If the market goes up, it is good to be in aggressive stocks; if it goes down, it is better to be in defensive stocks (and better still to leave your money in the bank).

Aggressive stocks have high betas, betas greater than 1.0. Their returns tend to respond more than one-for-one to returns on the overall market. The betas of defensive stocks are less than 1.0. The returns of these stocks vary less than one-for-one with market returns. The average beta of all stocks is—no surprises here—1.0 exactly.

Now we'll show you how betas are measured.

Example 12.1 ▶   Measuring Beta for Turbot-Charged Seafoods

Suppose we look back at the trading history of Turbot-Charged Seafoods and pick out 6 months when the return on the market portfolio was plus or minus 1%.

Month	Market Return (%)	Turbot-Charged Seafoods Return (%)	
1	+1	+0.8	
2	+1	+1.8	Average = 0.8%
3	+1	−0.2	
4	−1	−1.8	
5	−1	+0.2	Average = − 0.8
6	−1	−0.8	

---

[1] We discussed the most popular stock market indexes in Section 11.2.

FIGURE 12.1 This figure is a plot of the data presented in the table in Example 12.1. Each point shows the performance of Turbot-Charged Seafoods stock when the overall market is either up or down by 1%. On average, Turbot-Charged moves in the same direction as the market, but not as far. Therefore, Turbot-Charged's beta is less than 1.0. We can measure beta by the slope of a line fitted to the points in the figure. In this case, it is .8.

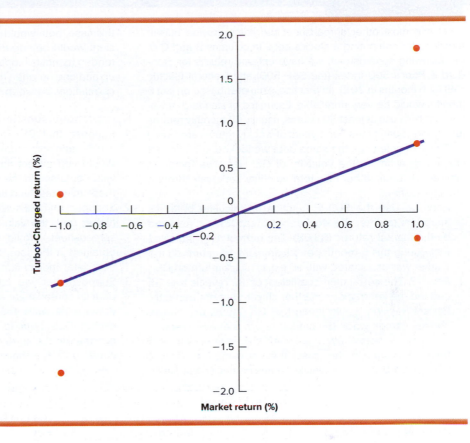

Look at Figure 12.1, where these observations are plotted. We've drawn a line through the average performance of Turbot when the market is up or down by 1%. *The slope of this line is Turbot's beta.* You can see right away that the beta is .8, because on average, Turbot stock gains or loses .8% when the market is up or down by 1%. Notice that a 2-percentage-point difference in the market return (−1 to +1) generates, on average, a 1.6-percentage-point difference for Turbot shareholders (−.8 to +.8). The ratio, 1.6/2 = .8, is beta.

In 4 months, Turbot's returns lie above or below the line in Figure 12.1. The distance from the line shows the response of Turbot's stock returns to news or events that affected Turbot but did *not* affect the overall market. For example, in month 2, investors in Turbot stock benefited from good macroeconomic news (the market was up 1%) and also from some favorable news specific to Turbot. The market rise gave a boost of .8% to Turbot stock (beta of .8 times the 1% market return). Then, firm-specific news gave Turbot stockholders an extra 1% return, for a total return that month of 1.8%. ∎

As this example illustrates, we can break down common stock returns into two parts: the part explained by market returns and the firm's beta and the part due to news that is specific to the firm. Fluctuations in the first part reflect market risk; fluctuations in the second part reflect specific risk.

Of course, diversification can get rid of the specific risks. That's why wise investors, who don't put all their eggs in one basket, will look to Turbot's less-than-average beta and call its stock "defensive."

Excel and most other spreadsheet programs provide built-in functions for computing a stock's beta. In columns B and C of the following spreadsheet, we have entered returns for Standard & Poor's 500 Index (the S&P 500) and General Electric (GE) for 6 months in 2015. (In practice, estimates based on just 6 months would be *very* unreliable. Estimates of standard deviation and beta use at least 50 returns, usually 60 monthly returns for 5 years. Sometimes 1 or 2 years of weekly returns are used.)

This example uses the same data we looked at in the last chapter to estimate the volatility of GE. Here, we focus on market risk (beta) rather than total volatility. Let's walk through the spreadsheet.

1. *Row 12.* Use the SLOPE function to calculate beta. It's important to enter the stock returns (C3:C8) first, followed by the market returns (B3:B8). The beta of 1.11 indicates that during this 6-month period, an extra 1% return on the market was associated with an extra 1.11% return on GE.

2. *Row 13.* The correlation coefficient of .82 reveals that GE and the market track each other closely, but not perfectly. Perfect tracking would mean that GE returns are always above average when the market return is above average, and always below average when the market return is below average. In this case, the correlation coefficient would be 1.0. Zero correlation means no tracking at all—in this case, beta would also be zero. The correlation coefficient would be *negative* if returns on GE and the market tended to move in opposition, one down when the other is up and one up when the other is down. However, negative correlations between stocks are rare.

Spreadsheet Questions

1. Suppose that GE's return in October 2015 had been +10%, and its return in August 2015 had been −2%. Would you expect its beta to be more or less than the value obtained in the spreadsheet? Reestimate beta with these new data, and confirm your intuition.

2. Suppose that GE's return in each month had been 1% higher than the values presented in the accompanying spreadsheet. Would GE's beta differ from the value obtained in the spreadsheet? Reestimate beta with these new data, and confirm your intuition.

3. Suppose that you add 1 more month of data to your original spreadsheet and find that, in that month, GE was down 8.6% while the market was up 4.0%. Would you expect GE's beta to be more or less than the value obtained in the spreadsheet? What about the correlation coefficient? Reestimate beta and the correlation coefficient with this new data point, and confirm your intuition.

BEYOND THE PAGE

 Calculating beta

mhhe.com/brealey9e

	A	B	C	D
1		**Returns (%)**		**Formula Used in**
2	**Month**	**S&P 500**	**GE**	**Column C**
3	Jul-15	1.97	−1.77	
4	Aug-15	−6.26	−4.90	
5	Sep-15	−2.64	2.52	
6	Oct-15	8.30	14.67	
7	Nov-15	0.05	2.77	
8	Dec-15	−1.75	4.81	
9				
10	Mean return	−0.05	3.02	=AVERAGE(C3:C8)
11	Standard deviation (monthly)	4.51	6.12	=STDEVP(C3:C8)
12	Standard deviation (annualized)	15.62	21.21	=C11*SQRT(12)
13	Beta		1.11	=SLOPE(C3:C8:B3:B8)
14	Correlation		0.82	=CORREL(C3:C8,B3:B8)

12.1 Self-Test

Here are 6 months' returns to stockholders in the Anchovy Queen restaurant chain:

Month	Market Return (%)	Anchovy Queen Return (%)
1	+1	+2.0
2	+1	+0
3	+1	+1.0
4	−1	−1.0
5	−1	+0
6	−1	−2.0

Draw a figure like Figure 12.1 and check the slope of the fitted line. What is Anchovy Queen's beta?

Real life doesn't serve up numbers quite as convenient as those in our examples so far. However, the procedure for measuring real companies' betas is exactly the same:

1. Observe rates of return, usually monthly or weekly, for the stock and the market.
2. Plot the observations as in Figure 12.1.
3. Fit a line showing the average return to the stock at different market returns.

Beta is the slope of the fitted line.

This may sound like a lot of work, but in practice, computers do it for you. The nearby box shows how to use the SLOPE function in Excel to calculate a beta. Here are two real examples.

Betas for U.S. Steel and PG&E

Each point in Figure 12.2*a* shows the return on U.S. Steel stock and the return on the market index in a different month. For example, the upper circled point shows that in October 2013, U.S. Steel's stock price rose by 20.9%, whereas the market index rose by 4.5%. Notice that more often than not, U.S. Steel outperformed the market when the index rose and underperformed the market when the index fell. Thus, U.S. Steel was a relatively aggressive, high-beta stock.

We have drawn a line of best fit through the points in the figure.[2] The slope of this line is 1.85. For each extra 1% rise in the market, U.S. Steel's stock price moved on average an extra 1.85%. For each extra 1% fall in the market, U.S. Steel's stock price fell an extra 1.85%. Thus U.S. Steel's beta was 1.85.

BEYOND THE PAGE

 Beta estimates for U.S. stocks

mhhe.com/brealey9e

Of course, U.S. Steel's stock returns are not perfectly related to market returns. For example, in October 2013, the point highlighted in Figure 12.2*a*, U.S. Steel performed better than one would have predicted given the return on the market index. We know this because U.S. Steel's return in that month lies above the upward-sloping line in the figure—the line that describes the typical relation between the market return and U.S. Steel's return. The vertical distance from this "beta line" to U.S. Steel's return in October 2013 shows the impact of the firm-specific events that lifted U.S. Steel's fortunes in that month. At other times, such as November 2014, U.S. Steel flew south when the market went north. In that month, firm-specific events conspired to reduce U.S. Steel's return.

Thus, while the slope of the line in Figure 12.2*a* measures beta and exposure to market risk, firm-specific risk shows up in the scatter of points *around* the line: Wider scatter means more firm-specific risk.

BEYOND THE PAGE

 Comparing beta estimates

mhhe.com/brealey9e

Figure 12.2*b* shows a similar plot of the monthly returns for the regulated electric utility, PG&E. In contrast to U.S. Steel, PG&E was a defensive, low-beta stock. It was not highly sensitive to market movements, usually lagging when the market rose, but doing better (or less badly) when the market fell. The slope of the line of best fit shows that on average an extra 1% change in the index resulted in an extra .23% change in the price of PG&E stock. Thus, PG&E's beta was .23.

Estimates of beta can be accessed easily, for example, at **finance.yahoo.com**, but you may find it interesting to look at Table 12.1, which shows betas of several well-known stocks. PG&E had the lowest beta: Its stock return was only .23 times as sensitive as the average stock to market movements. U.S. Steel was at the other extreme: Its return was 1.85 times as sensitive as the average stock to market movements.

Total Risk and Market Risk

U.S. Steel tops our list of betas in Table 12.1. It was also at the top of Table 11.5, which showed the total variability of the same group of stocks. But total risk is not the

---

[2] The line of best fit is a *regression* line. The slope of the line can be calculated using *ordinary least squares* regression. The dependent variable is the return on the stock (U.S. Steel). The independent variable is the return on the market index–in this case, the S&P 500.

FIGURE 12.2 (*a*) Each point in this figure shows the returns on U.S. Steel common stock and the overall market in a particular month between January 2011 and December 2015. U.S. Steel's beta is the slope of the line fitted to these points. U.S. Steel has a very high beta of 1.85. (*b*) In this plot of 60 months' returns for PG&E and the overall market, the slope of the fitted line is much less than U.S. Steel's beta in panel *a*. PG&E has a relatively low beta of .23.

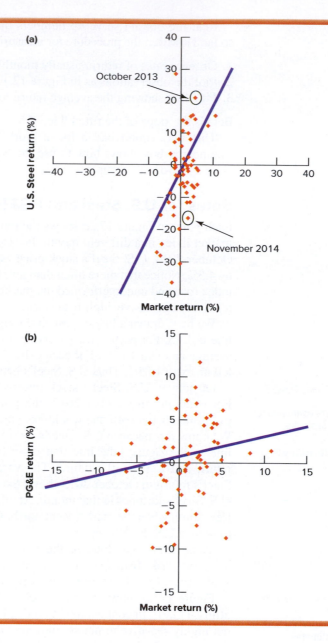

same as market risk. Some of the most variable stocks have below-average betas, and vice versa.

Consider, for example, Newmont Mining. Newmont is the world's largest gold producer. The company cites the many risks that the company faces as "gold and other metals' price volatility, increased costs and variances in ore grade or recovery rates from those assumed in mining plans, as well as political and operational risks in the countries in which we operate and governmental regulation and judicial outcomes."

These risks are considerable and are reflected in the high standard deviation of the returns on Newmont's stock (see Table 11.5). But they are mostly firm-specific, not macro, risks. When the U.S. economy is booming, gold prices are just as likely to slump, and a mine in some distant part of the world may well be hit by political unrest. So, while Newmont stock has above-average total volatility, it has a relatively low beta.

TABLE 12.1 Betas for selected common stocks, January 2011–December 2015

	Beta
U.S. Steel	1.85
Disney	1.42
Ford	1.31
General Electric	1.20
Monsanto	1.19
Boeing	1.01
Union Pacific	1.00
Alphabet	0.96
ExxonMobil	0.94
Amazon	0.93
Intel	0.91
Pfizer	0.90
Starbucks	0.79
IBM	0.59
McDonald's	0.51
Coca-Cola	0.49
Campbell Soup	0.47
Walmart	0.26
Newmont Mining	0.24
PG&E	0.23

Note: Betas are calculated from 5 years of monthly data.

Firm-specific risk is, of course, diversifiable and of no concern to an investor tracking the performance of his or her fully diversified portfolio. Newmont's CEO and financial managers are acutely interested in firm-specific risk, however, always hoping that the next return will plot above the beta line. Investors analyzing Newmont's financial performance will likewise watch total return, even if much of the risk in that return will, in the end, be diversified away.

12.2 What Can You Learn from Beta?

You can learn a lot from beta. First, if you don't know whether a stock is defensive or aggressive, you can check whether its beta has been less than or greater than 1.0. Second, you can predict the beta of a portfolio.

Portfolio Betas

The beta of a portfolio is just an average of the betas of the individual securities in the portfolio, weighted by the investment in each security. For example, the beta of a two-stock portfolio is calculated as:

$$\text{Portfolio beta} = (\text{fraction of portfolio in stock 1} \times \text{beta of stock 1}) \tag{12.1}$$
$$+ (\text{fraction of portfolio in stock 2} \times \text{beta of stock 2})$$

Thus, a portfolio invested 50–50 in U.S. Steel and PG&E would have a beta of $(.5 \times 1.85) + (.5 \times .23) = 1.04$.

Suppose you formed a portfolio of the 20 stocks in Table 12.1 with an equal amount invested in each stock. You could predict the portfolio beta as a simple average of the betas listed in the table. If you decided to invest more money in some stocks than others, you would have to calculate a weighted average.

12.2 Self-Test

Rosa Rugonis receives a bequest of $1 million and decides to invest it as follows: $200,000 each in Ford, Starbucks, Union Pacific, and IBM, and $100,000 each in Newmont Mining and Walmart. Rosa is, of course, undiversified. But what is her portfolio beta? Use the stock betas in Table 12.1.

Example 12.2 ▶   How Risky Are Mutual Funds?

You don't have to be wealthy to own a diversified portfolio. You can buy shares in one of the more than 8,000 mutual funds in the United States.

Investors buy shares of the funds, and the funds use the money to buy portfolios of securities. The returns on the portfolios are passed through to the funds' owners in proportion to their shareholdings. Therefore, the funds act like investment cooperatives, providing even the smallest investors with diversification and professional management at low cost.

Panel *a* of Figure 12.3 shows the calculation of beta for both an individual stock, Union Pacific, and a stock mutual fund, Vanguard's Growth & Income (G&I) Fund. As in Figure 12.1, each dot in the diagram shows the return in a particular month for the S&P 500 and a particular investment, either Union Pacific or the mutual fund. The orange dots are for Union Pacific, and the black dots are for the mutual fund. During this period, both Union Pacific and the Vanguard fund displayed average sensitivity to market fluctuations, with betas of almost exactly 1. Therefore, if Union Pacific and the G&I fund had no specific risk, their returns would have been precisely as variable as the market's. But they both do have specific risk, so their returns actually were more variable than the market's.

FIGURE 12.3 (*a*) Betas of Union Pacific and Vanguard's Growth & Income Fund.

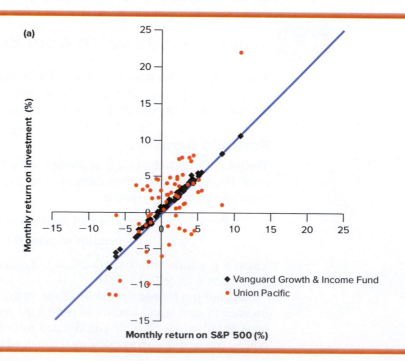

FIGURE 12.3 (*b*) The beta of Vanguard's 500 Index Fund. This is a fully diversified index fund designed to track the performance of the market. Note the index fund's beta (1.0) and the absence of specific risk. The fund's returns lie almost precisely on the fitted line relating its returns to those of the S&P 500 portfolio.

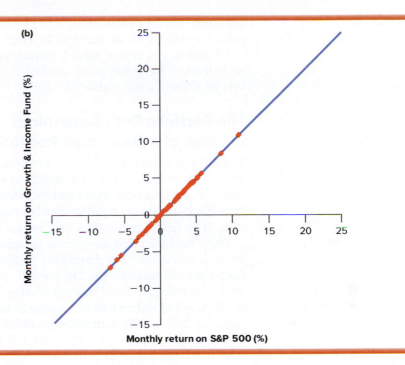

Union Pacific's returns exhibit a wide scatter, reflecting its considerable firm-specific risk. As a result, its total volatility is substantially greater than that of the market. Turn back to Table 11.5 and you will see that Union Pacific's standard deviation was 18.3% annually, versus only 11.6% for the S&P 500. Vanguard's G&I fund is highly diversified—it holds more than 800 different stocks—and its dots cluster tightly around the fitted line. Its total volatility is almost identical to that of the market and is considerably less than Union Pacific's; this is the benefit of diversification.

How did the G&I fund achieve a beta of almost exactly 1.0? By acquiring stocks with an average beta of 1.0. Remember, a portfolio beta equals the weighted-average beta of its component securities. The weights are the proportions invested in each security. If G&I were not a mutual fund (whose returns we can directly observe and plot as in Figure 12.3) but a privately held portfolio—say, a private pension fund—we could calculate its beta as the weighted-average beta of its holdings.

Figure 12.3, panel *b,* shows a similar plot for Vanguard's 500 Index mutual fund. Notice that this fund has a beta of 1.0 and only the tiniest level of specific risk—each month's return on the fund matches almost exactly that of the index. The managers of an index fund do not attempt to pick stocks but just work to achieve full diversification at very low cost. Investors in this fund buy the market as a whole and don't need to worry at all about specific risk. ∎

By the way, knowing a mutual or pension fund's beta will help you ask the right questions when a portfolio manager brags about "beating the market." Suppose, for example, that in January 2014, you met the manager of a mutual fund that delivered a 35% rate of return in 2013, 3 percentage points above the 32% return on the S&P 500 in that year. Should you have congratulated the fund manager for her stock-picking prowess? It depends on the fund's beta. Suppose the fund specialized in high-beta stocks with an average beta of 1.5. Then you should *not* have been impressed. An index fund constructed to have a beta of 1.5 would have earned 32% × 1.5 = 48% in 2013, a great year for the stock market. So the mutual fund manager's fund actually *under*performed by about 48 − 35 = 13 percentage points.[3] The mutual fund's share-holders would have been better off in a high-beta index fund.

Of course, you cannot judge a mutual fund manager's skill based on only 1 year's performance. We simply point out that "beating the S&P" is child's play for a high-beta portfolio in a bull market like 2013.

The Portfolio Beta Determines the Risk of a Diversified Portfolio

You can also use beta to predict the *total risk* (standard deviation) of a diversified port-folio. Look back to Figure 11.9, which shows how the volatility of a portfolio return falls as more stocks are added and the portfolio becomes better diversified. The gain from diversification is rapid at first but slows down as specific risks are diversified away. With full diversification, only market risk remains.

Okay, but how much market risk remains? It depends on the beta of the portfolio. Suppose you construct a diversified portfolio of stocks with betas of about .5, like Coca-Cola and McDonald's. The portfolio beta will also be .5. Most of the individual stocks' specific risk would be diversified away. The market risk would remain, and the portfolio would end up half as variable as the market. If the standard deviation of the market is 20%, a fully diversified portfolio of stocks with betas of .5 has a standard deviation of .5 × 20 = 10%. We show this outcome in Figure 12.4. Suppose, on the other hand, you construct a fully diversified portfolio of stocks with betas clustered around 1.3, like Disney, Ford, and GE. In that case the portfolio standard deviation would be 1.3 × 20 = 26%.[4]

Of course, the average beta across all stocks must be 1.0. A fully diversified portfolio, including all stocks, will match the market and so have a beta of 1.0 and the same standard deviation as the market.

FIGURE 12.4 The risk of a fully diversified portfolio depends on the portfolio beta. In this example, the portfolio beta is .5 and the standard deviation of the portfolio "bottoms out" at 10%, half the market standard deviation of 20%.

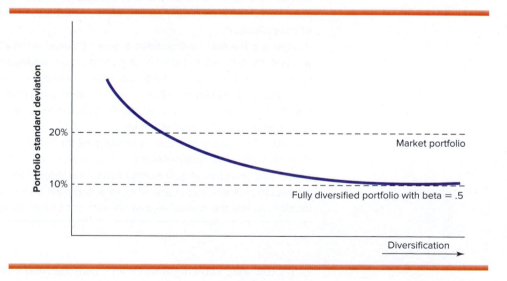

---

[3] The predicted rate of return of 1.5 × 32 = 48% is not quite right. We should have multiplied the beta of 1.5 by the *risk premium* earned on the market in 2013. The risk-free rate averaged about .5%, so the risk premium was 32 − .5 = 31.5%. The predicted risk premium was, therefore, 1.5 × 31.5 = 47.25%. The predicted return equals the interest rate plus the predicted risk premium, or .5 + 47.25 = 47.75%. Thus, the underperformance was 47.75 × 35 = 12.75%. Our initial calculation was only .25% too high, but the error would be larger with a higher interest rate.

[4] It can be difficult to achieve full diversification when constructing portfolios using stocks with very high or low betas. For example, a portfolio constructed from stocks with very high betas, such as U.S. Steel and Ford, could be concentrated in cyclical industries, and thus exposed to some undiversified industry risk in addition to market risk.

A wise and diversified investor does not judge the risk of individual stocks by their stand-alone volatility, but by their contributions to *portfolio* risk. By now you can see that the contributions depend on the stocks' betas. In the next sections, we will see how that observation leads to a model of risk and return and a way to estimate the opportunity cost of capital.

> ## 12.3   Self-Test
>
> Suppose you construct a portfolio from only 10 stocks with an average beta of 1.2. The market standard deviation is 20%. What can you say about the portfolio's standard deviation? Is it 24%? Less? More? Why?

12.3   Risk and Return

In Chapter 11, we looked at past returns on selected investments. The least risky investment was U.S. Treasury bills. Because the return on Treasury bills is fixed, it is unaffected by what happens to the market. Thus, the beta of Treasury bills is zero. The *riskiest* investment that we considered was the market portfolio of common stocks. This has average market risk: Its beta is 1.0.

Wise investors don't run risks just for fun. They are playing with real money and, therefore, require a higher average return from the market portfolio than from Treasury bills. The difference between the return on the market and the interest rate on bills is termed the **market risk premium.** Over the past century, the average market risk premium has been 7.6% a year. Of course, there is plenty of scope for argument as to whether the past century constitutes a typical period, but we will just assume here that the normal risk premium is a nice round 7%; that is, 7% is the additional return that an investor could reasonably expect on average from investing in the stock market rather than in Treasury bills.

In Figure 12.5*a*, we have plotted the risk and expected return from Treasury bills and the market portfolio. You can see that Treasury bills have a beta of zero and a risk-free return; we'll assume that return is 3%. The market portfolio has a beta of 1.0, an expected risk premium of 7%, and an expected return of $3 + 7 = 10\%$.

Now, given these two benchmarks, what expected rate of return should an investor require from a portfolio that is equally divided between Treasury bills and the market? Halfway between, of course. Thus in Figure 12.5*b*, we have drawn a straight line through the Treasury bill return and the expected market return. The portfolio (marked with an *X*) would have a beta of .5 and an expected return of 6.5%. This includes a risk premium of 3.5% above the Treasury bill return of 3%.

You can calculate this return as follows: Start with the difference between the expected market return r_m and the Treasury bill rate r_f. This is the expected market risk premium:

$$\text{Market risk premium} = r_m - r_f = 10\% - 3\% = 7\%$$

Beta measures risk relative to the market. Therefore, the portfolio's expected risk premium equals its beta times the market risk premium:

$$\text{Risk premium} = r - r_f = \beta(r_m - r_f)$$

For example, with a beta of .5 and a market risk premium of 7%,

$$\text{Risk premium} = \beta(r_m - r_f) = .5 \times 7\% = 3.5\%$$

market risk premium
Risk premium of market portfolio. Difference between market return and return on risk-free Treasury bills.

FIGURE 12.5 (a) Here we begin the plot of expected rate of return against beta. The first benchmarks are Treasury bills (beta = 0) and the market portfolio (beta = 1.0). We assume a Treasury bill rate of 3% and a market return of 10%. The market risk premium is 10 − 3 = 7%. (b) A portfolio split evenly between Treasury bills and the market will have beta = .5 and an expected return of 6.5% (point X). A portfolio invested 20% in the market and 80% in Treasury bills has beta = .2 and an expected rate of return of 4.4% (point Y). Note that the expected rate of return on any portfolio mixing Treasury bills and the market lies on a straight line. The risk premium is proportional to the portfolio beta.

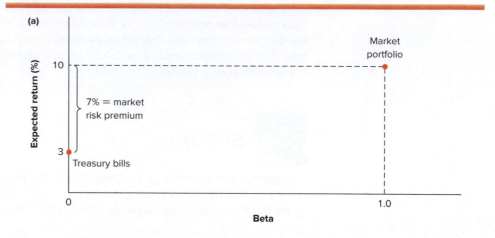

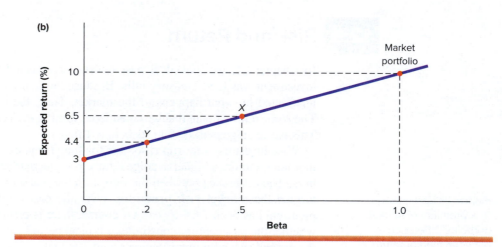

The total expected rate of return is the sum of the risk-free rate and the risk premium:

$$\text{Expected return} = \text{risk-free rate} + \text{expected risk premium} \qquad (12.2)$$

$$r = r_f + \beta(r_m - r_f)$$

$$= 3\% + 3.5\% = 6.5\%$$

You could have calculated the expected rate of return in one step from this formula:

$$\text{Expected return} = r = r_f + \beta(r_m - r_f)$$

$$= 3\% + (.5 \times 7\%) = 6.5\%$$

capital asset pricing model (CAPM)

Theory of the relationship between risk and return which states that the expected risk premium on any security equals its beta times the market risk premium.

This basic relationship should hold not only for our portfolios of Treasury bills and the market, but for *any* asset. This conclusion is known as the **capital asset pricing model, or CAPM.** The CAPM has a simple interpretation: **The expected rates of return demanded by investors depend on two things: (1) compensation for the time value of money (the risk-free rate, r_f) and (2) a risk premium, which depends on beta and the market risk premium.**

Note that the expected rate of return on an asset with $\beta = 1.0$ is just the market return. With a risk-free rate of 3% and market risk premium of 7%,

$$r = r_f + \beta(r_m - r_f)$$

$$= 3\% + (1 \times 7\%) = 10\%$$

12.4 Self-Test

What are the risk premium and expected rate of return on a stock with β = 1.5? Assume a Treasury bill rate of 6% and a market risk premium of 7%.

Why the CAPM Makes Sense

The CAPM assumes that the stock market is composed of well-diversified investors—investors operating at the bottom of the portfolio risk curves illustrated in Figures 11.9 and 12.4. The risks borne by such investors depend on their portfolio betas. This is realistic in a market dominated by large institutions, where even small fry can diversify at very low cost. The following example shows why this view of risk leads to the CAPM.

Example 12.3 ▶   How Would You Invest $1 Million?

Have you ever daydreamed about receiving a $1 million check, no strings attached, from an unknown benefactor? Let's daydream about how you would invest it.

We have two good candidates: Treasury bills, which offer an absolutely safe return, and the market portfolio (possibly via an index fund). The market has generated higher returns on average, but those returns have fluctuated a lot. (Look back to Figure 11.4.) So, your investment policy is going to depend on your tolerance for risk.

If you're a wimp, you may invest only a small part of your money in the market portfolio and lend the remainder to the government by buying Treasury bills. Suppose that you invest 20% of your money in the market portfolio and put the other 80% in U.S. Treasury bills. Then the beta of your portfolio will be a mixture of the beta of the market ($\beta_{market} = 1.0$) and the beta of the T-bills ($\beta_{T\text{-bills}} = 0$):

$$\text{Beta of portfolio} = \begin{pmatrix}\text{proportion} \\ \text{in market}\end{pmatrix} \times \begin{pmatrix}\text{beta of} \\ \text{market}\end{pmatrix} + \begin{pmatrix}\text{proportion} \\ \text{in T-bills}\end{pmatrix} \times \begin{pmatrix}\text{beta of} \\ \text{T-bills}\end{pmatrix}$$

$$\beta = (.2 \times \beta_{market}) \qquad\qquad + (.8 \times \beta_{T\text{-bills}})$$

$$= (.2 \times 1.0) \qquad\qquad + (.8 \times 0)$$

$$= .20$$

The fraction of funds that you invest in the market also affects your expected return. If you invest your entire million in the market portfolio, you earn the full market risk premium. But if you invest only 20% of your money in the market, your portfolio beta is .20 and you earn only 20% of the market risk premium.

$$\begin{matrix}\text{Expected risk} \\ \text{premium on portfolio}\end{matrix} = \begin{pmatrix}\text{proportion} \\ \text{in market}\end{pmatrix} \times \begin{pmatrix}\text{market risk} \\ \text{premium}\end{pmatrix} + \begin{pmatrix}\text{proportion} \\ \text{in T-bills}\end{pmatrix} \times \begin{pmatrix}\text{risk premium} \\ \text{on T-bills}\end{pmatrix}$$

$$= (.2 \times \text{expected market risk premium}) + (.8 \times 0)$$

$$= .2 \times \text{expected market risk premium}$$

$$= .2 \times 7 = 1.4\%$$

Notice that the portfolio risk premium equals the product of beta times the market risk premium.

The expected return on your portfolio is equal to the risk-free interest rate plus the expected risk premium:

$$\text{Expected portfolio return} = r_{portfolio} = 3 + 1.4 = 4.4\%$$

The expected return on this passive portfolio, therefore, gives a benchmark for the fair expected return on any other investment or asset with the same risk (beta). In Figure 12.5, panel *b*, we show the beta and expected return on this portfolio by the letter *Y*. ∎

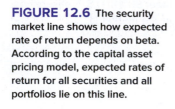

12.5   Self-Test

How would you construct a portfolio with a beta of .25? What is the expected return to this strategy? Assume Treasury bills yield 6% and the market risk premium is 7%.

The Security Market Line

security market line
Relationship between
expected return and beta.

Example 12.3 illustrates a general point: By investing some proportion of your money in the market portfolio and lending (or borrowing)[5] the balance, you can obtain any combination of risk and expected return along the sloping line in Figure 12.6. This line is known as the **security market line.**

The security market line describes the expected returns and risks from splitting your overall portfolio between risk-free securities and the market. It also sets a standard for other investments. Investors will be willing to hold other securities only if they offer equally good prospects. Thus, the required risk premium for any investment is given by the security market line:

Risk premium on investment = beta × expected market risk premium

Look back to Figure 12.5, panel *b*, which suggests that an individual common stock with $\beta = .5$ must offer a 6.5% expected rate of return when Treasury bills yield 3% and the market risk premium is 7%. You can now see why this has to be so. If that

FIGURE 12.6 The security market line shows how expected rate of return depends on beta. According to the capital asset pricing model, expected rates of return for all securities and all portfolios lie on this line.

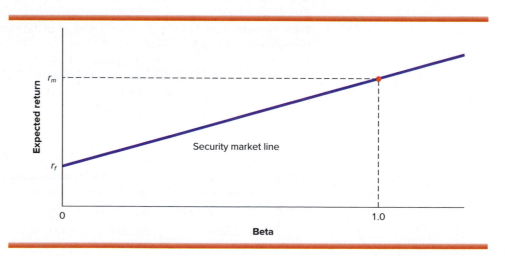

---

[5] Notice that the security market line extends above the market return at $\beta = 1.0$. How would you generate a portfolio with, say, $\beta = 2.0$? It's easy, but it's risky. Suppose you borrow $1 million and invest the loan plus $1 million in the market portfolio. That gives you $2 million invested and a $1 million liability. Your portfolio now has a beta of 2.0:

Beta of portfolio = (proportion in market × beta of market) + (proportion in loan × beta of loan)

$$\beta = (2 \times \beta_{market}) + (-1 \times \beta_{loan})$$
$$= (2 \times 1.0) + (-1 \times 0) = 2$$

Notice that the proportion in the loan is negative because you are borrowing, not lending money. By the way, borrowing from a bank or stockbroker would not be difficult or unduly expensive as long as you put up your $2 million stock portfolio as security for the loan. Can you calculate the risk premium and the expected rate of return on this borrow-and-invest strategy?

stock offered a lower rate of return, nobody would buy even a little of it—they could get 6.5% just by investing 50–50 in Treasury bills and the market. And if nobody wants to hold the stock, its price has to drop. A lower price means a better buy for investors—that is, a higher expected rate of return. The price will fall until the stock's expected rate of return is pushed up to 6.5%. At that price and expected return the CAPM holds.

If, on the other hand, our stock offered more than 6.5%, diversified investors would want to buy more of it. That would push the price up and the expected return down to the levels predicted by the CAPM.

This reasoning holds for stocks with any beta. Investors will demand that each security provide an expected rate of return that matches the expected rate of return they can obtain on equal-beta portfolios constructed from the market index and Treasury bills. That's why the CAPM makes sense and why the expected risk premium that investors demand from an investment should be proportional to its beta.

12.6 Self-Test

Suppose you invest $400,000 in Treasury bills and $600,000 in the market portfolio. What is the return on your portfolio if bills yield 6% and the expected return on the market is 13%? What does the return on this portfolio imply for the expected return on individual stocks with betas of .6?

Using the CAPM to Estimate Expected Returns

We can use the CAPM to calculate expected rates of return that investors demand on individual stocks or other securities. We need three numbers: the risk-free interest rate, the expected market risk premium, and beta. Suppose the interest rate on Treasury bills is 3% and the expected market risk premium is 7%. We take betas from Table 12.1. Table 12.2 puts these numbers together in the CAPM to get expected rates of return. Take Coca-Cola as an example:

$$\frac{\text{Expected}}{\text{return on Coca-Cola}} = \frac{\text{risk-free}}{\text{interest rate}} + \text{beta} \times \frac{\text{market}}{\text{risk premium}}$$

$$r = r_f + \beta \times (r_m - r_f) = 3\% + .49 \times 7\% = 6.4\%$$

U.S. Steel had the highest beta in our sample of companies and the highest required return of about 16%. At the other extreme, PG&E, a regulated public utility, had a very low beta and a low CAPM expected rate of return.

The calculations in Table 12.2 are easy, but don't assume that using the CAPM is a purely mechanical exercise. First, betas are estimates, not exact measurements. Coca-Cola's beta of .49 is a best statistical estimate, but its true beta could very well be .4 or .6. If you want to round Coca-Cola's beta to .50, that's fine with us. Second, very high or very low betas tend not to repeat in the future. For example, Ford's beta was above 2 as auto companies struggled in the recession of 2007–2009, but it has come down now that the company has regained financial health and profitability. Third, it's difficult to pin down the expected future market risk premium. Fourth, while the CAPM is widely used in practice, it is not the last word in risk and return in the stock market, as we will now see.

How Well Does the CAPM Work?

The basic idea behind the capital asset pricing model is that investors expect a reward for both waiting and worrying. The greater the worry, the greater the expected return. If you invest in a risk-free Treasury bill, you just receive the rate of interest. That's the

TABLE 12.2 Expected rates of return demanded by investors for selected companies

	Beta	Expected Return (%)
U.S. Steel	1.85	16.0
Disney	1.42	12.9
Ford	1.31	12.2
General Electric	1.20	11.4
Monsanto	1.19	11.3
Boeing	1.01	10.1
Union Pacific	1.00	10.0
Alphabet	0.96	9.8
ExxonMobil	0.94	9.6
Amazon	0.93	9.5
Intel	0.91	9.4
Pfizer	0.90	9.3
Starbucks	0.79	8.5
IBM	0.59	7.1
McDonald's	0.51	6.6
Coca-Cola	0.49	6.4
Campbell Soup	0.47	6.3
Walmart	0.26	4.8
Newmont Mining	0.24	4.7
PG&E	0.23	4.6

reward for waiting. When you invest in risky stocks, you demand an extra return or risk premium for worrying. When risk is higher, investors will not be willing to pay as much for the shares of the stock, and the price will fall until the rate of return they can expect to earn provides a "fair" expected risk premium. The capital asset pricing model states that this risk premium is equal to the stock's beta times the market risk premium.

How well does the CAPM work in practice? For example, is the expected return on stocks with betas of .5 halfway between the return on the market portfolio and the interest rate on Treasury bills? Unfortunately, the evidence is conflicting. Let's look back to the *actual* returns earned by investors in low-beta stocks and in high-beta stocks.

Imagine that 10 investors gathered together in a Wall Street bar in 1931 and agreed to establish investment trust funds for their children. Each investor decided to follow a different strategy. Investor 1 opted to buy the 10% of the New York Stock Exchange stocks with the lowest estimated betas; investor 2 chose the 10% with the next-lowest betas; and so on, up to investor 10, who proposed to buy the stocks with the highest betas. They also planned that at the end of each year they would reestimate the betas of all NYSE stocks and reconstitute their portfolios. And so they parted with much cordiality and good wishes.

In time, the 10 investors all passed away, but their children agreed to meet in early 2015 in the same bar to compare the performance of their portfolios. Figure 12.7 shows how they fared. Investor 1's portfolio turned out to be much less risky than the market; its beta was only .48. However, investor 1 also realized the lowest return, 8.2% above the risk-free rate of interest. At the other extreme, the beta of investor 10's portfolio was 1.54, about three times that of investor 1's portfolio. But investor 10 was rewarded with the highest return, averaging 15.6% a year above the interest rate. So, over this 84-year period, returns did indeed increase with beta.

As you can see from Figure 12.7, the market portfolio over the same 84-year period provided an average return of 12.2% above the interest rate[6] and (of course) had a beta

---

[6] In Figure 12.7, the stocks in the "market portfolio" are weighted equally. Because the stocks of small firms have provided higher average returns than those of large firms, the risk premium on an equally weighted index is higher than that on a value-weighted index. This is one reason for the difference between the 12.2% market risk premium in Figure 12.7 and the 7.6% premium reported in Table 11.1.

FIGURE 12.7 The capital asset pricing model states that the expected risk premium from any investment should lie on the security market line. The dots show the actual average risk premium from portfolios with different betas. The high-beta portfolios generated higher returns, just as predicted by the CAPM. But the high-beta portfolios plotted below the market line and the low-beta portfolios plotted above. A line fitted to the 10 portfolio returns would be "flatter" than the security market line.

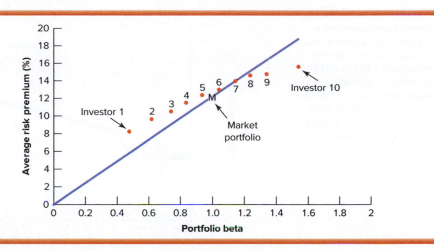

Source: This is an update of calculations that originally appeared in F. Black, "Beta and Return," *Journal of Portfolio Management* 20 (Fall 1993), pp. 8–18. We are grateful to Adam Kolasinski for recalculating and extending the plots.

of 1.0. The CAPM predicts that the risk premium should increase in proportion to beta, so the returns of each portfolio should lie on the upward-sloping security market line in Figure 12.7. Because the market provided a risk premium of 12.2%, investor 1's portfolio, with a beta of .48, should have provided a risk premium of 5.9% and investor 10's portfolio, with a beta of 1.54, should have given a premium of 18.8%. You can see that, while high-beta stocks performed better than low-beta stocks, the difference was not as great as the CAPM predicts.

Figure 12.7 provides broad support for the CAPM, though it suggests that the line relating return to beta has been too flat. But recent years have been less kind to the CAPM. For example, if the 10 friends had invested their cash in 1966 rather than 1931, there would have been very little relation between their portfolio returns and beta.[7] Does this imply that there has been a fundamental change in the relation between risk and return in the last 48 years, or did high-beta stocks just happen to perform worse during these years than investors expected? It is hard to be sure.

There is little doubt that the CAPM is too simple to capture everything that is going on in the market. For example, look at Figure 12.8. The orange line shows the cumulative difference between the returns on small-firm stocks and large-firm stocks. If you had bought the shares with the smallest market capitalizations and sold those with the largest capitalizations, this is how your wealth would have changed. You can see that small-cap stocks did not always do well, but over the long haul, their owners have made substantially higher returns. Since the end of 1926, the average annual difference between the returns on the two groups of stocks has been 3.3%. Now look at the blue line in Figure 12.8, which shows the cumulative difference between the returns on value stocks and growth stocks. *Value stocks* here are defined as those with high ratios of book value to market value. *Growth stocks* are those with low ratios of book to market. Notice that value stocks have provided a higher long-run return than growth stocks. Since 1926, the average annual difference between returns on value and growth stocks has been 4.8%.

The superior performance of small-firm stocks and value stocks does not fit well with the CAPM, which predicts that beta is the *only* reason that expected returns differ. If investors *expected* the returns to depend on firm size or book-to-market ratios, then the simple version of the capital asset pricing model cannot be the whole truth.

What's going on here? It is hard to say. Defenders of the capital asset pricing model emphasize that it is concerned with *expected* returns, whereas we can observe only

_____

[7] During this later period, the returns to the first seven investors increased in line with beta. However, the highest-beta portfolios performed poorly.

FIGURE 12.8 The orange
line shows the cumulative
difference between the returns
on small-firm and large-firm
stocks from 1926 to 2015.
The blue line shows the
cumulative difference between
the returns on high-book-to-
market-value stocks and low-
book-to-market-value stocks.

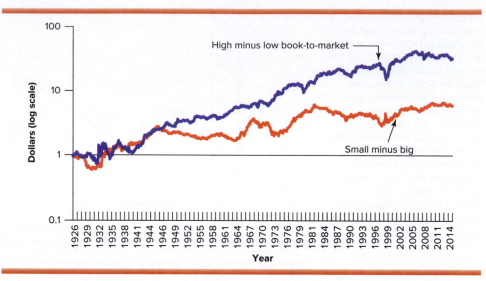

FIGURE 12.8 The orange line shows the cumulative difference between the returns on small-firm and large-firm stocks from 1926 to 2015. The blue line shows the cumulative difference between the returns on high-book-to-market-value stocks and low-book-to-market-value stocks.

Source: mba.tuck.dartmouth.edu/pages/faculty/ken.french/data_library.html. Used by permission of Kenneth R. French.

actual returns. Actual returns reflect expectations, but they also embody lots of "noise"—the steady flow of surprises that conceal whether on average investors have received the returns that they expected. Thus, when we observe that in the past small-firm stocks and value stocks have provided superior performance, we can't be sure whether this was simply a coincidence or whether investors have required a higher expected return to hold these stocks.

Such debates have prompted headlines like "Is Beta Dead?" in the business press. It is not the first time that beta has been declared dead, but the CAPM remains the leading model for estimating required returns. Only strong theories can have more than one funeral.

The CAPM is not the only model of risk and return. It has several brothers and sisters as well as second cousins. However, the CAPM captures in a simple way two fundamental ideas. First, almost everyone agrees that investors require some extra return for taking on risk. Second, investors appear to be concerned principally with the market risk that they cannot eliminate by diversification. That is why nearly three-quarters of financial managers use the capital asset pricing model to estimate the cost of capital.[8]

12.4   The CAPM and the Opportunity Cost of Capital

project cost of capital
Minimum acceptable
expected rate of return on
a project given its risk.

The discount rate for valuing a proposed capital investment project should be the *opportunity cost of capital,* defined as the expected rate of return that the company's shareholders could achieve by investing on their own. But the CAPM tells us (confirming common sense) that expected rates of return depend on risk, that is, on beta. Therefore, the opportunity cost of capital for a proposed project should depend on the project's beta. The **project cost of capital** is, therefore, its minimum acceptable expected rate of return, given its risk.

---

[8] See J. R. Graham and C. R. Harvey, "The Theory and Practice of Corporate Finance: Evidence from the Field," *Journal of Financial Economics* 61 (2001), pp. 187–243. A number of managers surveyed reported using more than one method to estimate the cost of capital. Seventy-three percent used the CAPM, while 39% stated they used the average historical stock return, and 34% used the CAPM with additional risk factors.

Example	12.4 ▶	Estimating the Opportunity Cost of Capital for a Project

Suppose that Coca-Cola is contemplating an investment of $10 million to expand a warehouse. It has forecast cash flows and calculated an internal rate of return (IRR) of 6%. We assume, as in Table 12.2, that the risk-free rate is 3% and the market risk premium is 7%. Should Coke invest?

To answer this question, you need to know the opportunity cost of capital r, defined as the expected rate of return that Coke's shareholders could achieve if the $10 million were paid out to them to invest on their own. The CAPM says that the expected rate of return demanded by investors depends on the project beta.

Suppose that the project's cash flows are an absolutely sure thing. Then, beta = 0 and the project cost of capital is

$$r = r_f + \beta \times (r_m - r_f) = 3\% + 0 \times 7\% = 3\%$$

If the project offers a 6% return when the opportunity cost of capital for the project is 3%, Coke should obviously go ahead.[9]

What about the 6.4% rate of return for Coke in Table 12.2? It's irrelevant if we are confident that the *project* is risk-free. Coke's stock offers more than the risk-free rate because it is risky, with a beta of .49. Coke's stockholders would all vote for Coke to invest on their behalf in a risk-free project earning 6% because the stockholders could get only 3% investing risk-free on their own. They can expect 6.4% by buying additional Coke shares, but that is a separate (and risky) decision.

Surefire projects rarely occur outside finance textbooks. So let's think about the opportunity cost of capital if the project has the same risk as the market portfolio. In this case, beta is 1.0 and the cost of capital is the expected rate of return on the market.

$$r = r_f + \beta \times (r_m - r_f) = 3\% + 1.0 \times 7\% = 10\%$$

Now that the project beta is 1.0, the project is no longer worth doing. The stockholders would vote against the project at a 6% expected return because they could earn a higher return, 10%, at the same level of risk (same beta) by investing on their own in the market portfolio.

When its beta is 1.0, the project is no longer attractive because, as Figure 12.9 shows, its expected rate of return now lies below the security market line. The project offers a lower rate of return than investors can expect on equally risky investments. Therefore, it is negative-NPV. ■

FIGURE 12.9 The expected return of this project is less than the expected return one could earn on stock market investments with the same market risk (beta). Therefore, the project's expected return lies below the security market line and the project should be rejected.

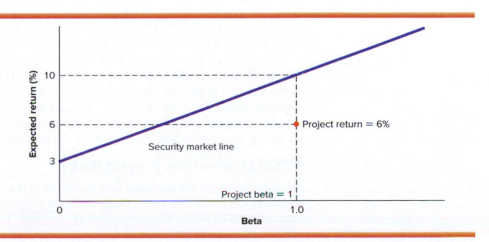

_____

[9] In Chapter 8, we described some special cases where you should prefer projects that offer a *lower* internal rate of return than the cost of capital. We assume here that your project is a "normal" one and that you prefer high IRRs to low ones.

If the CAPM holds, the security market line defines the opportunity cost of capital. If a project's expected rate of return plots above the security market line, then it offers a higher expected rate of return than investors could get on their own at the same beta.

12.7   Self-Test

Walmart is planning an Internet subsidiary to compete head-to-head with Amazon. It argues that it can compete aggressively in Internet retailing because it has a low beta and its shareholders will be content with an expected rate of return of only 4.8%. Is the argument correct?

The Company Cost of Capital

company cost of capital
Opportunity cost of capital for investment in the firm as a whole. The company cost of capital is the appropriate discount rate for an average-risk investment project undertaken by the firm.

The cost of capital depends on the use to which the capital is put. It depends on the risk (beta) of the project—not on the risk of the company investing in the project. If a company has a low-risk project, it should discount project cash flows at a correspondingly low rate. If it has a high-risk project, it should discount at a correspondingly high rate.

That is the principle. But you can imagine the chaos in practice if a large company had to set a different discount rate for every one of thousands of investment projects. Therefore, most companies estimate a **company cost of capital,** which depends on the average risk of its investments. Many companies use the company cost of capital for all capital-investment projects, which is fine provided that all projects are close enough to average risk. Others set the company cost of capital as a benchmark and adjust the discount rate up or down for riskier or safer projects.

Some companies set two or more discount rates for different types of projects. For example, several electric utilities have both regulated and "merchant" businesses. The regulated businesses are low-risk because they are not allowed to earn much more than a set rate of return. Their profit upside is limited, but so is the downside because they can pass most costs through to their customers and can petition to increase prices if their profits sag. (PG&E, which has the lowest beta in Table 12.2, is mostly a regulated business.) Merchant electricity production, on the other hand, is unregulated and must sell power at fluctuating market prices. Merchant producers can make or lose a lot of money, depending on uncertain demand and costs of production. Companies with both regulated and merchant businesses typically set *two* costs of capital, one for regulated investments and one for merchant investments.

Many U.S. corporations use the CAPM to compute their company costs of capital. Expected rates of return like those computed for Table 12.2 are only the first step, however. This is because they are *costs of equity,* that is, expected rates of return on common stock. But most companies use debt as well as equity financing. They calculate the company cost of capital as a weighted average of the cost of debt and the cost of equity. We explain how this is done in the next chapter.

What Determines Project Risk?

We have seen that the company cost of capital is the correct discount rate for projects that have the same risk as the company's existing business but *not* for those projects that are safer or riskier than the company's average. How do we know whether a project is unusually risky? Estimating project risk is never going to be an exact science, but here are two things to bear in mind.

First, we saw in Chapter 10 that operating leverage increases the risk of a project. When a large fraction of your costs is fixed, any change in revenues can have a dramatic effect on earnings. Therefore, projects that involve high fixed costs tend to have higher betas.

Second, many people intuitively associate risk with the variability of earnings. But much of this variability reflects diversifiable risk. Lone prospectors in search of gold look forward to extremely uncertain future earnings, but whether they strike it rich is not likely to depend on the performance of the rest of the economy. These investments (like Newmont Mining) have a high standard deviation but a low beta.

What matters is the strength of the relationship between the firm's earnings and the aggregate earnings of all firms. Cyclical businesses, whose revenues and earnings are strongly dependent on the state of the economy, tend to have high betas and a high cost of capital. By contrast, businesses that produce essentials, such as food, beer, and cosmetics, are less affected by the state of the economy. They tend to have low betas and a low cost of capital.

Don't Add Fudge Factors to Discount Rates

Risk to an investor arises because an investment adds to the spread of possible portfolio returns. To a diversified investor, risk is predominantly market risk. But in everyday usage *risk* simply means "bad outcome." People think of the "risks" of a project as the things that can go wrong. For example,

- A geologist looking for oil worries about the risk of a dry hole.
- A pharmaceutical manufacturer worries about the risk that a new drug that reverses balding may not be approved by the Food and Drug Administration.
- The owner of a hotel in a politically unstable part of the world worries about the political risk of expropriation.

Managers sometimes add fudge factors to discount rates to account for worries such as these.

This sort of adjustment makes us nervous. First, the bad outcomes we cited appear to reflect diversifiable risks that would not affect the expected rate of return demanded by investors. Second, the need for an adjustment in the discount rate usually arises because managers fail to give bad outcomes their due weight in cash-flow forecasts. They then try to offset that mistake by adding a fudge factor to the discount rate. For example, if a manager is worried about the possibility of a bad outcome such as a dry hole in oil exploration, he or she may reduce the value of the project by using a higher discount rate. That's not the way to do it. Instead, the possibility of the dry hole should be included in the calculation of the expected cash flows to be derived from the well. Suppose that there is a 50% chance of a dry hole and a 50% chance that the well will produce oil worth $20 million. Then the *expected* cash flow is not $20 million but $(.5 \times 0) + (.5 \times 20) = \$10$ million. You should discount the $10 million expected cash flow at the opportunity cost of capital; it does not make sense to discount the $20 million using a fudged discount rate.

Expected cash-flow forecasts should already reflect the probabilities of all possible outcomes, good and bad. If the cash-flow forecasts are prepared properly, the discount rate should reflect only the market risk of the project. It should not be fudged to offset errors or biases in the cash-flow forecast.

SUMMARY

How can you measure and interpret the market risk, or beta, of a security?
(LO12-1)

The contribution of a security to the risk of a diversified portfolio depends on its market risk. But not all securities are equally affected by fluctuations in the market. The sensitivity of a stock to market movements is known as **beta.** Stocks with a beta greater than 1.0 are particularly sensitive to market fluctuations. Those with a beta of less than 1.0 are not so sensitive to such movements. The average beta of all stocks is 1.0.

What is the relationship between the market risk of a security and the rate of return that investors demand of that security? (*LO12-2*)

The extra return that investors require for taking risk is known as the risk premium. The **market risk premium**—that is, the risk premium on the **market portfolio**—averaged 7.6% between 1900 and 2015. The **capital asset pricing model** states that the expected risk premium of an investment should be proportional to both its beta and the market risk premium. The expected **rate of return** from any investment is equal to the risk-free interest rate plus the risk premium, so the **CAPM** boils down to

$$r = r_f + \beta(r_m - r_f)$$

The **security market line** is the graphical representation of the CAPM equation. The security market line shows how the return that investors demand is related to the security's beta.

What determines the opportunity cost of capital for a project? (*LO12-3*)

The opportunity cost of capital is the return that investors give up by investing in the project rather than in securities of equivalent risk. The CAPM implies that the opportunity cost of capital depends on the project's beta. The **company cost of capital** is the expected rate of return demanded by investors in a company. It depends on the *average* risk of the company's assets and operations.

The opportunity cost of capital is determined by the use to which the capital is put. Therefore, required rates of return depend on the risk of the project, not on the risk of the firm's existing business. The **project cost of capital** is the minimum acceptable expected rate of return on a project given its risk.

Your cash-flow forecasts should already factor in the chances of pleasant and unpleasant surprises. Potential bad outcomes should be reflected in the discount rate only to the extent that they affect beta.

LISTING OF EQUATIONS

12.1 Beta of portfolio = (fraction of portfolio in stock 1 × beta of stock 1)

+ (fraction of portfolio in stock 2 × beta of stock 2)

12.2 Expected return = risk-free rate + expected risk premium

$$r = r_f + \beta(r_m - r_f)$$

QUESTIONS AND PROBLEMS

1. **Diversifiable Risk.** In light of what you've learned about market versus diversifiable (specific) risks, explain why an insurance company has no problem in selling life insurance to individuals but is reluctant to issue policies insuring against flood damage to residents of coastal areas. Why don't the insurance companies simply charge coastal residents a premium that reflects the actuarial probability of damage from hurricanes and other storms? (*LO12-1*)

2. **Specific versus Market Risk.** Figure 12.10 plots monthly rates of return from 2010 to 2015 for the Snake Oil mutual fund. Was this fund fully diversified? (*LO12-1*)

3. **Using Beta.** A stock with a beta of .8 has an expected rate of return of 12%. If the market return this year turns out to be 5 percentage points below expectations, what is your best guess as to the rate of return on the stock? (*LO12-1*)

4. **Specific versus Market Risk.** Figure 12.11 shows plots of monthly rates of return on three stocks versus the stock market index. (The plots are similar to those in Figure 12.2.) The beta and standard deviation of each stock is given beside its plot. (*LO12-1*)
   a. Which stock is safest for a diversified investor?
   b. Which stock is safest for an undiversified investor who puts all her funds in one of these stocks?
   c. Consider a portfolio with equal investments in each stock. What would this portfolio's beta have been?

d. Consider a well-diversified portfolio made up of stocks with the same beta as Ford. What are the beta and standard deviation of this portfolio's return? The standard deviation of the market portfolio's return is 20%.

e. What is the expected rate of return on each stock? Use the capital asset pricing model with a market risk premium of 8%. The risk-free rate of interest is 4%.

FIGURE 12.10 Monthly rates of return for the Snake Oil mutual fund and the Standard & Poor's Composite Index

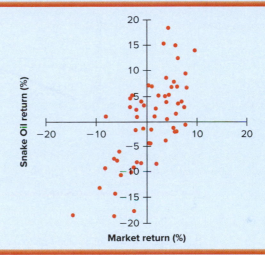

FIGURE 12.11 Monthly rates of return for (a) Ford, (b) Pfizer, and (c) Walmart, plus the market portfolio for the five years ending December 2015

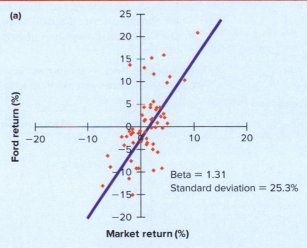

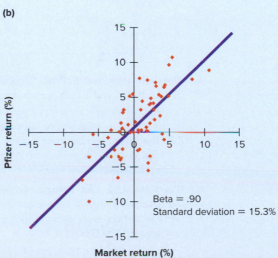

FIGURE 12.11 (*continued*)

(c)

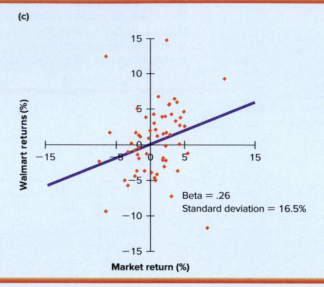

Beta = .26
Standard deviation = 16.5%

Market return (%)

5. **Beta.** Go to Connect and link to the material for Chapter 12, where you will find a spreadsheet containing 5 years of monthly prices for Hershey (HSY), U.S. Steel (X), and the S&P 500. Calculate the monthly price changes. (*LO12-1*)

   a. Calculate the beta of each firm. Use Excel's SLOPE function, which fits a regression line through a scatter diagram of two series of numbers.

   b. Does the relative magnitude of each beta make sense in terms of the business risk of the two firms? Explain.

6. **Calculating Beta.** Following are several months' rates of return for Tumblehome Canoe Company. Prepare a plot like Figure 12.1. What is Tumblehome's beta? (*LO12-1*)

Month	Market Return (%)	Tumblehome Return (%)
1	0	+1
2	0	−1
3	−1	−2.5
4	−1	−0.5
5	+1	+2
6	+1	+1
7	+2	+4
8	+2	+2
9	−2	−2
10	−2	−4

7. **Portfolio Risk and Return.** Suppose that the S&P 500, with a beta of 1.0, has an expected return of 10% and T-bills provide a risk-free return of 4%. (*LO12-1*)

   a. How would you construct a portfolio from these two assets with an expected return of 8%? Specifically, what will be the weights in the S&P 500 versus T-bills?

   b. How would you construct a portfolio from these two assets with a beta of .4?

   c. Find the risk premiums of the portfolios in parts (a) and (b), and show that they are proportional to their betas.

8. **Portfolio Risk and Return.** According to the CAPM, would the expected rate of return on a security with a beta less than zero be more or less than the risk-free interest rate? Why would investors invest in such a security? (*Hint:* Look back to the auto and gold example in Chapter 11.) (*LO12-1*)

9. **Risk and Return.** Suppose that the risk premium on stocks and other securities did, in fact, rise with total risk (i.e., the variability of returns) rather than just market risk. Explain how investors could exploit the situation to create portfolios with high expected rates of return but low levels of risk. (*LO12-2*)

10. **CAPM and Valuation.** You are considering acquiring a firm that you believe can generate expected cash flows of $10,000 a year forever. However, you recognize that those cash flows are uncertain. (*LO12-2*)

    a. Suppose you believe that the beta of the firm is .4. How much is the firm worth if the risk-free rate is 4% and the expected rate of return on the market portfolio is 11%?

    b. By how much will you overvalue the firm if its beta is actually .6?

11. **CAPM and Expected Return.** If the risk-free rate is 6% and the expected rate of return on the market portfolio is 13%, is a security with a beta of 1.25 and an expected rate of return of 16% overpriced or underpriced? (*LO12-2*)

12. **Portfolio Beta.** Look back at Table 12.1. (*LO12-2*)

    a. What is the beta of a portfolio that has 40% invested in Alphabet and 60% in McDonald's?

    b. Would you invest in this portfolio if you had no superior information about the prospects for either stock? Devise an alternative portfolio with the same expected return but less risk.

    c. Now repeat parts (a) and (b) with a portfolio that has 40% in Alphabet and 60% in Ford.

13. **CAPM and Expected Return.** Suppose that the Treasury bill rate is 6% and the expected return on the market is 10%. Use the betas in Table 12.1 to answer the following questions. (*LO12-2*)

    a. Calculate the expected return from Pfizer.

    b. What is the highest expected return offered by one of these stocks?

    c. What is the lowest expected return offered by one of these stocks?

    d. Would Ford offer a higher or lower expected return if the interest rate is 6% rather than 3%?

    e. Would Walmart offer a higher or lower expected return if the interest rate is 6% rather than 3%?

14. **Expected Returns.** Consider the following two scenarios for the economy and the expected returns in each scenario for the market portfolio, an aggressive stock A, and a defensive stock D. (*LO12-2*)

	Rate of Return		
Scenario	Market	Aggressive Stock A	Defensive Stock D
Bust	−8%	−10%	−6%
Boom	32	38	24

    a. Find the beta of each stock. In what way is stock D defensive?

    b. If each scenario is equally likely, find the expected rate of return on the market portfolio and on each stock.

    c. If the T-bill rate is 4%, what does the CAPM say about the fair expected rate of return on the two stocks?

    d. Which stock seems to be a better buy on the basis of your answers to parts (a), (b), and (c)?

15. **CAPM and Valuation.** A share of stock with a beta of .75 now sells for $50. Investors expect the stock to pay a year-end dividend of $2. The T-bill rate is 4%, and the market risk premium is 7%. If the stock is perceived to be fairly priced today, what must be investors' expectation of the price of the stock at the end of the year? (*LO12-2*)

16. **CAPM and Expected Return.** A share of stock with a beta of .75 now sells for $50. Investors expect the stock to pay a year-end dividend of $2. The T-bill rate is 4%, and the market risk premium is 7%. (*LO12-2*)

    a. Suppose investors believe the stock will sell for $52 at year-end. Is the stock a good or bad buy? What will investors do?

    b. At what price will the stock reach an "equilibrium" at which it is perceived as fairly priced today?

17. **CAPM and Expected Return.** The following table shows betas for several companies. Calculate each stock's expected rate of return using the CAPM. Assume the risk-free rate of interest is 4%. Use a 7% risk premium for the market portfolio. (*LO12-2*)

Company	Beta
Caterpillar	1.63
Cisco	1.24
Harley-Davidson	0.82
Hershey	0.24

18. **Portfolio Risk and Return.** Suppose that the S&P 500, with a beta of 1.0, has an expected return of 13% and T-bills provide a risk-free return of 4%. (*LO12-2*)
    a. What would be the expected return and beta of portfolios constructed from these two assets with weights in the S&P 500 of (i) 0; (ii) .25; (iii) .5; (iv) .75; (v) 1.0?
    b. On the basis of your answer to part (a), what is the trade-off between risk and return—that is, how does expected return vary with beta?
    c. What does your answer to part (b) have to do with the security market line relationship?

19. **Risk and Return.** True or false? Explain or qualify as necessary. (*LO12-2*)
    a. Investors demand higher expected rates of return on stocks with more variable rates of return.
    b. The capital asset pricing model predicts that a security with a beta of zero will provide an expected return of zero.
    c. An investor who puts $10,000 in Treasury bills and $20,000 in the market portfolio will have a portfolio beta of 2.0.
    d. Investors demand higher expected rates of return from stocks with returns that are highly exposed to macroeconomic changes.
    e. Investors demand higher expected rates of return from stocks with returns that are very sensitive to fluctuations in the stock market.
    f. The CAPM implies that if you could find an investment with a negative beta, its expected return would be less than the interest rate.
    g. If a stock lies below the security market line, it is undervalued.

20. **CAPM and Expected Return.** Stock A has a beta of .5, and investors expect it to return 5%. Stock B has a beta of 1.5, and investors expect it to return 13%. Use the CAPM to find the market risk premium and the expected rate of return on the market. (*LO12-2*)

21. **Leverage and Portfolio Risk.** Footnote 5 in the chapter asks you to consider a borrow-and-invest strategy in which you use $1 million of your own money and borrow another $1 million to invest $2 million in a market index fund. If the risk-free interest rate is 4% and the expected rate of return on the market index fund is 12%, what are the risk premium and expected rate of return on the borrow-and-invest strategy? Why is the risk of this strategy twice that of simply investing your $1 million in the market index fund? (*LO12-2*)

22. **CAPM and Expected Return.** If the expected rate of return on the market portfolio is 13% and T-bills yield 6%, what must be the beta of a stock that investors expect to return 10%? (*LO12-2*)

23. **Risk and Return.** True or false? Explain or qualify as necessary. (*LO12-2*)
    a. The expected rate of return on an investment with a beta of 2.0 is twice as high as the expected rate of return of the market portfolio.
    b. The contribution of a stock to the risk of a diversified portfolio depends on the market risk of the stock.
    c. If a stock's expected rate of return plots below the security market line, it is underpriced.
    d. A fully diversified portfolio with a beta of 2.0 is twice as volatile as the market portfolio.
    e. An undiversified portfolio with a beta of 2.0 is less than twice as volatile as the market portfolio.

24. **CAPM and Expected Return.** A mutual fund manager expects her portfolio to earn a rate of return of 11% this year. The beta of her portfolio is .8. (*LO12-2*)
    a. If the rate of return available on risk-free assets is 4% and you expect the rate of return on the market portfolio to be 14%, what expected rate of return would you demand before you would be willing to invest in this mutual fund?
    b. Is this fund attractive?

25. **Required Rate of Return.** Reconsider the mutual fund manager in Problem 24. How could you mix a stock index mutual fund with a risk-free position in Treasury bills (or a money market mutual fund) to create a portfolio with the same risk as the manager's but with a higher expected rate of return? What is the rate of return on that portfolio? (*LO12-2*)

26. **Required Rate of Return.** In view of your answer to Problem 25, explain why a mutual fund must be able to provide an expected rate of return in excess of that predicted by the security market line for investors to consider the fund an attractive investment opportunity. (*LO12-2*)

27. **CAPM.** The Treasury bill rate is 4%, and the expected return on the market portfolio is 12%. According to the capital asset pricing model: (*LO12-2*)
    a. What is the risk premium on the market?
    b. What is the required return on an investment with a beta of 1.5?
    c. If an investment with a beta of .8 offers an expected return of 9.8%, does it have a positive NPV?
    d. If the market expects a return of 11.2% from stock X, what is its beta?

28. **CAPM.** We Do Bankruptcies is a law firm that specializes in providing advice to firms in financial distress. It prospers in recessions, when other firms are struggling. Consequently, its beta is negative, −.2. (*LO12-2*)
    a. If the interest rate on Treasury bills is 5% and the expected return on the market portfolio is 15%, what is the expected return on the shares of the law firm according to the CAPM?
    b. Suppose you invested 90% of your wealth in the market portfolio and the remainder of your wealth in the shares in the law firm. What would be the beta of your portfolio?

29. **CAPM and Hurdle Rates.** A project under consideration has an internal rate of return of 14% and a beta of .6. The risk-free rate is 4%, and the expected rate of return on the market portfolio is 14%. (*LO12-3*)
    a. What is the required rate of return on the project?
    b. Should the project be accepted?
    c. What is the required rate of return on the project if its beta is 1.6?
    d. Should the project be accepted in this case?

30. **CAPM and Cost of Capital.** Suppose the Treasury bill rate is 4% and the market risk premium is 7%. (*LO12-3*)
    a. What are the project costs of capital for new ventures with betas of .75 and 1.75?
    b. Which of the following capital investments have positive NPVs?

Project	Beta	Internal Rate of Return (%)
P	1.0	14
Q	0	6
R	2.0	18
S	0.4	7
T	1.6	20

31. **CAPM and Valuation.** You are a consultant to a firm evaluating an expansion of its current business. The cash-flow forecasts (in millions of dollars) for the project are as follows:

Years	Cash Flow
0	−100
1–10	+15

On the basis of the behavior of the firm's stock, you believe that the beta of the firm is 1.4. Assuming that the rate of return available on risk-free investments is 4% and that the expected rate of return on the market portfolio is 12%, what is the net present value of the project? (*LO12-3*)

32. **CAPM and Cost of Capital.** Reconsider the project in Problem 31. (*LO12-3*)
    a. What is the project IRR?
    b. What is the cost of capital for the project?
    c. Does the accept-reject decision using IRR agree with the decision using NPV?

33. **CAPM and Valuation.** You are considering the purchase of real estate that will provide perpetual income that should average $50,000 per year. How much will you pay for the property if you believe its market risk is the same as the market portfolio's? The T-bill rate is 5%, and the expected market return is 12.5%. (*LO12-3*)

34. **Project Cost of Capital.** Suppose Cisco is considering a new investment in the common stock of a chocolate company. What is the required rate of return for this venture? Explain why the expected return on Cisco stock is not the appropriate required return. Use the data in Problem 17. (*LO12-3*)

WEB EXERCISES

1. You can find estimates of stock betas by logging on to **finance.yahoo.com** and looking at a company's profile. Try comparing the stock betas of Alphabet (GOOG), The Home Depot (HD), Procter & Gamble (PG), Altria Group (MO), and Caterpillar (CAT). Once you have read Section 12.3, use the capital asset pricing model to estimate the expected return for each of these stocks. You will need a figure for the current Treasury bill rate. You can find this also on **finance.yahoo.com** by clicking on *Bonds—Rates*. Assume for your estimates a market risk premium of 7%.

2. Log on to **www.fidelity.com** and look at the list of mutual funds that are managed by Fidelity. Some of these funds, such as the Growth Strategies Fund, appear from their names to be high risk. Others, such as the Balanced Fund, appear to be low risk. Pick several apparent high- and low-risk funds and then check whether their betas really do match the fund's name.

SOLUTIONS TO SELF-TEST QUESTIONS

12.1   See Figure 12.12. Anchovy Queen's beta is 1.0.

12.2   Beta = .79. This is a weighted average of the betas in Table 12.1, with 20% weights on Ford, Starbucks, Union Pacific, and IBM, and 10% weights on Newmont Mining and Walmart.

FIGURE 12.12 Each point shows the performance of Anchovy Queen stock when the market is up or down by 1%. On average, Anchovy Queen stock follows the market; it has a beta of 1.0.

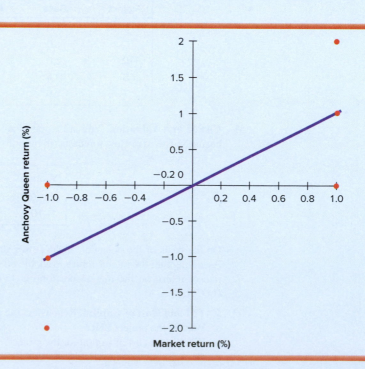

12.3 More than 24%. Diversification across only 10 stocks is not enough to eliminate all specific risk.

12.4 Risk premium = $\beta(r_m - r_f) = 1.5 \times 7 = 10.5\%$.

Expected return = $r = r_f + \beta(r_m - r_f) = 6 + (1.5 \times 7) = 16.5\%$

12.5 Put 25% of your money in the market portfolio and the rest in Treasury bills. The portfolio's beta is .25 and its expected return is

$$r_{\text{portfolio}} = (.75 \times 6) + (.25 \times 13) = 7.75\%$$

The expected return also may be computed as

$$r_f + \beta(r_m - r_f) = 6 + .25 \times 7 = 7.75\%$$

12.6 $r_{\text{portfolio}} = (.4 \times 6) + (.6 \times 13) = 10.2\%$. This portfolio's beta is .6, since \$600,000, which is 60% of the investment, is in the market portfolio. Investors in a stock with a beta of .6 would not buy it unless it also offered a rate of return of 10.2% and would rush to buy if it offered more. The stock price would adjust until the stock's expected rate of return was 10.2%.

12.7 The argument is wrong. The beta of the Internet marketing project would be similar to Amazon's beta, not Walmart's. Use of Walmart's low opportunity cost of capital would overvalue the project.

SOLUTIONS TO SPREADSHEET QUESTIONS

12.1 We would expect beta to fall from the value obtained in the spreadsheet. GE's return in August (when the market fell) is not as bad as originally assumed, and its return in October (when the market rose) is not as good as originally assumed. In both cases, GE's returns are less responsive to the market. In fact, beta falls from 1.11 to .64.

12.2 GE's beta is precisely the same as the original value. Increasing the assumed return in each month by a constant does not change the typical *responsiveness* of GE to variation in the return of the market index.

12.3 If, in the additional month of data, GE is down 8.6% while the market is up 4%, we would expect beta to fall. In this month, GE's stock moved in opposition to the market index. Adding this observation, therefore, reduces our estimate of GE's typical response to market movements. In fact, beta falls to .70. For similar reasons, the correlation coefficient falls from .82 to .44.

13

The Weighted-Average Cost of Capital and Company Valuation

LEARNING OBJECTIVES

After studying this chapter, you should be able to:

13-1 Calculate the weighted-average cost of capital.

13-2 Understand when the weighted-average cost of capital is—or isn't—the appropriate discount rate for a new project.

13-3 Measure a company's capital structure.

13-4 Estimate the expected returns on a firm's securities.

13-5 Use the weighted-average cost of capital to value a business given forecasts of its future cash flows.

RELATED WEBSITES FOR THIS CHAPTER CAN BE FOUND IN CONNECT.

Geothermal Corporation was founded to produce electricity from geothermal energy trapped under the earth. How should Geothermal determine its cost of capital? *Jennifer Boyer via Anosmia/Flickr/CC BY 2.0*

In the previous chapter, you learned how to use the capital asset pricing model to estimate the expected return on a company's common stock. If the firm is financed wholly by common stock, then the stockholders own all the firm's assets and are entitled to all the cash flows. In this case, the return required by investors in the common stock equals the company cost of capital.

Most companies, however, are financed by a mixture of securities, including common stock, bonds, and preferred stock. In this case, the company cost of capital is no longer the same as the expected return on the common stock. It depends on the expected return from *all* the securities that the company has issued.

The cost of capital also depends on taxes because interest payments made by a corporation are tax-deductible expenses. Therefore, the company cost of capital is usually calculated as a weighted average of the *after-tax* cost of debt interest and the "cost of equity"—that is, the expected rate of return on the firm's common stock. The weights are the fractions of debt and equity in the firm's capital structure. Managers refer to the firm's *weighted-average* cost of capital, or *WACC* (rhymes with "quack").

Managers use the firm's weighted-average cost of capital to evaluate average-risk investment projects. "Average risk" means that the project's risk matches the risk of the firm's existing assets and operations. This chapter explains how the weighted-average cost of capital is calculated in practice.

Managers calculating WACC can get bogged down in formulas. We want you to understand *why* WACC works, not just how to calculate it. Let's start with "Why?" We'll listen in as a young financial manager struggles to recall the rationale for project discount rates.

13.1   Geothermal's Cost of Capital

Jo Ann Cox, a recent graduate of a prestigious eastern business school, poured a third cup of black coffee and tried again to remember what she once knew about project hurdle rates. Why hadn't she paid more attention in Finance 101? Why had she sold her finance text the day after passing the finance final?

Costas Thermopolis, her boss and CEO of Geothermal Corporation, had told her to prepare a financial evaluation of a proposed expansion of Geothermal's production. She was to report at 9:00 Monday morning. Thermopolis, whose background was geophysics, not finance, not only expected a numerical analysis, but also expected her to explain it to him.

Thermopolis had founded Geothermal in 1996 to produce electricity from geothermal energy trapped deep under Nevada. The company had pioneered this business and had obtained perpetual production rights for a large tract on favorable terms from the U.S. government. When the oil shock in 2007–2008 drove up energy prices worldwide, Geothermal became an exceptionally profitable company. It was currently reporting a rate of return on book assets of 25% per year.

Now, in 2016, energy prices were no longer high and production rights were no longer cheap. The proposed expansion would cost $30 million and should generate a perpetual after-tax cash flow of $4.5 million annually. The projected rate of return was 4.5/30 = .15, or 15%, much less than the profitability of Geothermal's existing assets. However, once the new project was up and running, it would be no riskier than Geothermal's present business.

Jo Ann realized that 15% was not necessarily a bad return—though of course 25% would have been better. Fifteen percent might still exceed Geothermal's cost of capital—that is, exceed the expected rate of return that outside investors would demand to invest money in the project. If the cost of capital was less than the 15% expected return, expansion would be a good deal and would generate net value for Geothermal and its stockholders.

Jo Ann remembered how to calculate the cost of capital for companies that used only common stock financing. Briefly, she sketched the argument.

"I need the expected rate of return investors would require from Geothermal's real assets—the wells, pumps, generators, etc.[1] That rate of return depends on the assets' risk. However, the assets aren't traded in the stock market, so I can't observe how risky they have been. I can only observe the risk of Geothermal's common stock.

"But if Geothermal issues only stock—no debt—then owning the stock means owning the assets, and the expected return demanded by investors in the stock must also be the cost of capital for the assets." She jotted down the following identities:

$$\text{Value of business} = \text{value of stock}$$
$$\text{Risk of business} = \text{risk of stock}$$
$$\text{Rate of return on business} = \text{rate of return on stock}$$
$$\text{Investors' required return from business} = \text{investors' required return from stock}$$

If there were no company debt, this would be the right discount rate for Geothermal's expansion plan.

Unfortunately, Geothermal had borrowed a substantial amount of money; its stockholders did *not* have unencumbered ownership of Geothermal's assets. The expansion project would also justify some extra debt finance. Jo Ann realized that she would have to look at Geothermal's **capital structure**—its mix of debt and equity financing—and consider the expected rates of return required by debt as well as equity investors.

capital structure
The mix of long-term debt and equity financing.

---

[1] Investors will invest in the firm's securities only if they offer the same expected return as other equally risky securities. When securities are properly priced, the return that investors can expect from their investments is therefore also the return that they *require*.

Geothermal had issued 22.65 million shares, now trading at $20 each. Thus, shareholders valued Geothermal's equity at $20 × 22.65 million = $453 million. In addition, the company had issued bonds with a current market value of $194 million. The total market value of the company's debt and equity was therefore $194 + $453 = $647 million. Debt was 194/647 = .3, or 30% of the total.

"Geothermal's worth more to investors than either its debt or its equity," Jo Ann mused. "But I ought to be able to find the overall value of Geothermal's business by adding up the debt and equity." She sketched a rough balance sheet:

Assets		Liabilities and Shareholders' Equity		
Market value of assets = value of Geothermal's existing business	$647	Market value of debt	$194	(30%)
		Market value of equity	453	(70%)
Total value	$647	Total value	$647	(100%)

"Holy Toledo, I've got it!" Jo Ann exclaimed. "If I bought *all* the securities issued by Geothermal, debt as well as equity, I'd own the entire business. That means . . ." She jotted again:

$$\text{Value of business} = \frac{\text{value of portfolio of all the firm's}}{\text{debt and equity securities}}$$

$$\text{Risk of business} = \text{risk of portfolio}$$

$$\text{Rate of return on business} = \text{rate of return on portfolio}$$

$$\frac{\text{Investor's required return on business}}{\text{(company cost of capital)}} = \frac{\text{investors' required return on}}{\text{portfolio}}$$

"All I have to do is calculate the expected rate of return on a portfolio of all the firm's securities. That's easy. The debt's yielding 8%, and Fred, that nerdy banker, says that equity investors want 14%. Suppose he's right. The portfolio would contain 30% debt and 70% equity, so . . ."

$$\text{Portfolio return} = (.3 \times 8\%) + (.7 \times 14\%) = 12.2\%$$

It was all coming back to her now. The company cost of capital is just a weighted average of returns on debt and equity, with weights depending on relative market values of the two securities.

"But there's one more thing. Interest is tax-deductible. If Geothermal pays $1 of interest, taxable income is reduced by $1, and the firm's tax bill drops by 35 cents (assuming a 35% tax rate). The net cost is only 65 cents. So the after-tax cost of debt is not 8%, but .65 × 8 = 5.2%.

"Now I can finally calculate the weighted-average cost of capital:

$$\text{WACC} = (.3 \times 5.2\%) + (.7 \times 14\%) = 11.4\%$$

"Looks like the expansion's a good deal. Fifteen's better than 11.4. But I sure need a break."

13.2 The Weighted-Average Cost of Capital

company cost of capital
Opportunity cost of capital for investment in the firm as a whole. The company cost of capital is the appropriate discount rate for an average-risk investment project undertaken by the firm.

Jo Ann's conclusions were important. It should be obvious by now that the choice of the discount rate can be crucial, especially when the project involves large capital expenditures or is long-lived.

Think again what the **company cost of capital** is, and what it is used for. We *define* it as the opportunity cost of capital for the firm's existing assets; we *use* it to value new assets that have the same risk as the old ones. The company cost of capital is the minimum acceptable rate of return when the firm expands by investing in average-risk projects.

We first introduced the opportunity cost of capital in Chapter 1. "Opportunity cost" is a shorthand reminder that when the firm invests rather than returning cash to shareholders, the shareholders lose the opportunity to invest in financial markets. If the corporation acts in the shareholders' interests, it will invest their money only if it can find projects that offer higher rates of return than investors could achieve on their own. Therefore, the expected rates of return on investments in financial markets determine the cost of capital for corporate investments.

The company cost of capital is the opportunity cost of capital for the company as a whole. We discussed the company cost of capital in Chapter 12 but did not explain how to measure it when the firm has raised different types of debt and equity financing or how to adjust it for the tax-deductibility of interest payments. The weighted-average cost of capital formula handles these complications.

Calculating Company Cost of Capital as a Weighted Average

When only common stock is outstanding, calculating the company cost of capital is straightforward, though not always easy. For example, a financial manager could estimate beta and calculate shareholders' required rate of return using the capital asset pricing model (CAPM). This would be the expected rate of return investors require on the company's existing assets and operations and also the expected return they will require on new investments that do not change the company's market risk.

But most companies issue debt as well as equity. **The company cost of capital is a *weighted average* of the returns demanded by debt and equity investors. The weighted average is the expected rate of return investors would demand on a portfolio of all the firm's outstanding securities.**

Let's review Jo Ann Cox's calculations for Geothermal. To avoid complications, we'll ignore taxes for the next two or three pages. The total market value of Geothermal, which we denote as V, is the sum of the values of the outstanding debt D and the equity E. Thus, firm value is $V = D + E = \$194$ million $+ \$453$ million $= \$647$ million. Debt accounts for 30% of the value and equity accounts for the remaining 70%. If you held all the shares and all the debt, your investment in Geothermal would be $V = \$647$ million. Between them, the debtholders and equityholders own *all* the firm's assets. So V is also the value of these assets—the value of Geothermal's existing business.

Suppose that Geothermal's equity investors require a 14% rate of return on their investment in the stock. What rate of return must a new project provide in order that all investors—both debtholders and stockholders—earn a fair rate of return? The debtholders require a rate of return of $r_{debt} = 8\%$. So, each year the firm will need to pay interest of $r_{debt} \times D = .08 \times \$194$ million $= \$15.52$ million. The shareholders, who have invested in a riskier security, require an expected return of $r_{equity} = 14\%$ on their investment of $453 million. Thus in order to keep shareholders happy, the company needs additional income of $r_{equity} \times E = .14 \times \$453$ million $= \$63.42$ million. To satisfy both the debtholders and the shareholders, Geothermal needs to earn $15.52 million $+ \$63.42$ million $= \$78.94$ million. This is equivalent to earning a return of $r_{assets} = 78.94/647 = .122$, or 12.2%.

Figure 13.1 illustrates the reasoning behind our calculations. The figure shows the amount of income needed to satisfy the debt and equity investors. Notice that debtholders account for 30% of Geothermal's capital structure but receive less than 30% of its expected income. On the other hand, they bear less than a 30% share of risk because they have first cut at the company's income and also first claim on its assets if the company gets in trouble. Shareholders expect a return of more than 70% of Geothermal's income because they bear correspondingly more risk.

FIGURE 13.1 Geothermal's debtholders account for 30% of the company's capital structure, but they get a smaller share of expected income because their 8% return is guaranteed by the company. Geothermal's stockholders bear more risk and, to compensate, they receive, on average, greater return. Of course, if you buy all the debt and all the equity, you get all the income.

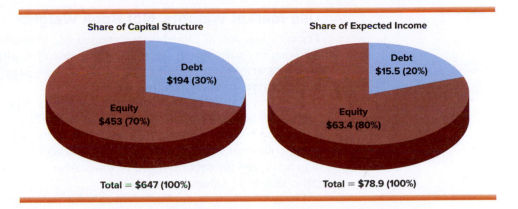

However, if you buy *all* Geothermal's debt and equity, you own its assets lock, stock, and barrel. You receive all the income and bear all the risks. The expected rate of return you'd require on this portfolio of securities is the same return you'd require from unencumbered ownership of the business. This rate of return—12.2%, ignoring taxes—is, therefore, the company cost of capital and the required rate of return from an expansion of the business.

The bottom line (still ignoring taxes) is

Company cost of capital = weighted average of debt and equity returns

The underlying algebra is simple. Debtholders need income of $(r_{debt} \times D)$, and the equity investors need expected income of $(r_{equity} \times E)$. The *total* income that is needed is $(r_{debt} \times D) + (r_{equity} \times E)$. The amount of their combined existing investment in the company is V. So to calculate the return that is needed on the assets, we simply divide the income by the investment:

$$r_{assets} = \frac{\text{total income}}{\text{value of investment}}$$

$$= \frac{(D \times r_{debt}) + (E \times r_{equity})}{V} = \left(\frac{D}{V} \times r_{debt}\right) + \left(\frac{E}{V} \times r_{equity}\right)$$

For Geothermal,

$$r_{assets} = (.30 \times 8\%) + (.70 \times 14\%) = 12.2\%$$

This figure is the expected return demanded by investors in the firm's assets.

13.1   Self-Test

Hot Rocks Corp., one of Geothermal's competitors, has issued long-term bonds with a market value of $50 million and an expected return of 9%. It has 4 million shares outstanding trading for $10 each. At this price, the shares offer an expected return of 17%. What is the weighted-average cost of capital for Hot Rocks' assets and operations? Assume Hot Rocks pays no taxes.

Use Market Weights, Not Book Weights

The company cost of capital is the expected rate of return that investors demand from the company's assets and operations. **The cost of capital must be based on what investors are actually willing to pay for the company's outstanding securities— that is, based on the securities' *market* values.**

Market values usually differ from the values recorded by accountants in the company's books. The book value of Geothermal's equity reflects money raised in the past from shareholders or reinvested by the firm on their behalf. If investors recognize Geothermal's excellent prospects, the market value of equity may be much higher than book, and the debt ratio will be lower when measured in terms of market values rather than book values.

Financial managers use book debt-to-value ratios for various purposes, and sometimes they unthinkingly look to the book ratios when calculating weights for the company cost of capital. That's a mistake because the company cost of capital measures what *investors* want from the company and so depends on how they value the company's securities. That value depends on future profits and cash flows, not on accounting history. Book values, while useful for many other purposes, measure only cumulative historical financing; they don't generally measure market values accurately.

13.2   Self-Test

Here is a book balance sheet for Duane S. Burg Associates. Figures are in millions.

Assets		Liabilities and Shareholders' Equity	
Assets (book value)	$75	Debt	$25
		Equity	50
	$75		$75

Unfortunately, the company has fallen on hard times. The 6 million shares are trading for only $4 apiece, and the market value of its debt securities is 20% below the face (book) value. Because of the company's large cumulative losses, it will pay no taxes on future income.

Suppose shareholders now demand a 20% expected rate of return. The bonds are now yielding 14%. What is the weighted-average cost of capital?

Taxes and the Weighted-Average Cost of Capital

So far, our examples have ignored taxes. When you calculate a project's NPV, you need to discount the cash flows *after* tax assuming that the project is wholly equity-financed. That is exactly the approach that we used in Chapter 9, when we valued Blooper's investment in the magnoosium mine. Sometimes, you may encounter companies that forecast cash flows *before* tax and then try to compensate for this by using a higher discount rate. It doesn't work; there is no simple adjustment to the discount rate that will allow you to discount pretax cash flows.

Taxes are also important because most companies are financed by both equity and debt. The interest payments on this debt are deducted from income before tax is calculated. Therefore, the cost to the company is reduced by the amount of this tax saving.

The interest rate on Geothermal's debt is $r_{debt} = 8\%$. However, with a corporate tax rate of $T_c = .35$, the government bears 35% of the cost of the interest payments. The government doesn't send the firm a check for this amount, but the income tax that the firm pays is reduced by 35% of its interest expense. Therefore, Geothermal's after-tax cost of debt is only $100 - 35 = 65\%$ of the 8% pretax cost:

$$\text{After-tax cost of debt} = (1 - \text{tax rate}) \times \text{pretax cost}$$
$$= (1 - T_c) \times r_{debt}$$
$$= (1 - .35) \times 8\% = 5.2\%$$

weighted-average cost of capital (WACC)
Expected rate of return on a portfolio of all the firm's securities, adjusted for tax savings due to interest payments.

We can now adjust our calculation of Geothermal's cost of capital to recognize the tax savings associated with interest payments:

$$\text{Company cost of capital, after-tax} = (.3 \times 5.2\%) + (.7 \times 14\%) = 11.4\%$$

Now we're back to the **weighted-average cost of capital,** or **WACC.** The general formula is

$$\text{WACC} = \left[\frac{D}{V} \times (1 - T_c)r_{debt}\right] + \left(\frac{E}{V} \times r_{equity}\right) \qquad (13.1)$$

13.3 Self-Test

Criss-Cross Industries has earnings before interest and taxes (EBIT) of $10 million. Interest payments are $2 million, and the corporate tax rate is 35%. Construct a simple income statement to show that the debt interest reduces the taxes the firm owes to the government. How much more tax would Criss-Cross pay if it were financed solely by equity?

Example 13.1 ▶ Weighted-Average Cost of Capital for Monsanto

In Chapter 12, we used the capital asset pricing model to estimate the expected return on Monsanto common stock. We will now use this estimate to figure out the company's weighted-average cost of capital.

Step 1. *Calculate capital structure using market value weights.* The total market value of Monsanto's securities is $V = D + E = \$8,429 + \$43,378 = \$51,807$ million. Debt as a proportion of the total value is $D/V = \$8,429/\$51,807 = .16$, and equity as a proportion of the total is $\$43,378/\$51,807 = .84$.

Step 2. *Determine the required rate of return on each security.* In Chapter 12, we estimated that Monsanto's shareholders required a return of 11.3%. The average yield on Monsanto's debt was about 5.3%.

Step 3. *Calculate a weighted average of the after-tax return on the debt and the return on the equity.[2]* The weighted-average cost of capital is

$$\text{WACC} = \left[\frac{D}{V} \times (1 - T_c)r_{debt}\right] + \left(\frac{E}{V} \times r_{equity}\right)$$
$$= [.16 \times (1 - .35)5.3\%] + (.84 \times 11.3\%) = 10.04\% \quad \blacksquare$$

13.4 Self-Test

Calculate WACC for Hot Rocks (Self-Test 13.1) and Burg Associates (Self-Test 13.2), assuming the companies face a 35% corporate income tax rate.

---

[2] Financial managers often use "equity" to refer to common stock, even though a firm's equity strictly includes both common and preferred stock. We continue to use r_{equity} to refer specifically to the expected return on the common stock.

What If There Are Three (or More) Sources of Financing?

We have simplified our discussion of the cost of capital by assuming the firm has only two classes of securities: debt and equity. Even if the firm has issued other classes of securities, our general approach to calculating WACC remains unchanged. We simply calculate the weighted-average after-tax return of each security type.

For example, suppose the firm also has outstanding preferred stock. Preferred stock has some of the characteristics of both common stock and fixed-income securities. Like bonds, preferred stock promises to pay a given, usually level, stream of dividends. Unlike bonds, however, there is no maturity date for the preferred stock. The promised dividends constitute a perpetuity as long as the firm stays in business. Moreover, a failure to come up with the cash to pay the dividends does not push the firm into bankruptcy. Instead, any unpaid dividends simply cumulate; the common stockholders do not receive dividends until the accumulated preferred dividends have been paid. Finally, unlike interest payments, preferred stock dividends are not considered tax-deductible expenses.

How would we calculate WACC for a firm with preferred stock as well as common stock and bonds outstanding? Using P to denote the value of preferred stock, we simply generalize Equation 13.1 for WACC as follows:

$$\text{WACC} = \left[\frac{D}{V} \times (1 - T_c)r_{\text{debt}}\right] + \left(\frac{P}{V} \times r_{\text{preferred}}\right) + \left(\frac{E}{V} \times r_{\text{equity}}\right) \qquad \text{(13.1a)}$$

The NPV of Geothermal's Expansion

We now return to Jo Ann Cox and Geothermal's proposed expansion. We want to make sure that both she and you know how to *use* the weighted-average cost of capital.

Remember that the proposed expansion costs $30 million and should generate a perpetual cash flow of $4.5 million per year. A simple cash-flow worksheet might look like this:[3]

Revenue	$10.00 million
− Operating expenses	−3.08
= Pretax operating cash flow	6.92
− Tax at 35%	−2.42
After-tax cash flow	$ 4.50 million

Note that these cash flows do not include the tax benefits of using debt. Geothermal's managers and engineers forecast revenues, costs, and taxes as if the project were to be all-equity-financed. The interest tax shields generated by the project's actual debt financing are not forgotten, however. They are accounted for by using the *after-tax* cost of debt in the weighted-average cost of capital.

Project net present value is calculated by discounting expected cash flow (which is a perpetuity) at Geothermal's 11.4% weighted-average cost of capital:

$$\text{NPV} = -30 + \frac{4.5}{.114} = +\$9.5 \text{ million}$$

Expansion will thus add $9.5 million to the net wealth of Geothermal's owners.

---

[3] For this example we ignore depreciation, a noncash but tax-deductible expense. (If the project were really perpetual, why depreciate?)

Checking Our Logic

Any project offering a rate of return more than 11.4% will have a positive NPV, assuming that the project has the same risk and financing as Geothermal's business. A project offering exactly 11.4% would just break even; it would generate just enough cash to satisfy both debtholders and stockholders.

Let's check that out. Suppose the revenues of the proposed expansion were only just sufficient to generate an NPV of zero. This would require revenues of only $8.34 million, resulting in pretax operating cash flow of $5.26 million and after-tax cash flow of $3.42 million:

Revenue	$8.34 million
− Operating expenses	−3.08
= Pretax operating cash flow	5.26
− Tax at 35%	−1.84
After-tax cash flow	$3.42 million

With an investment of $30 million, the internal rate of return on this perpetuity is exactly 11.4%:

$$\text{Rate of return} = \frac{3.42}{30} = .114, \text{ or } 11.4\%$$

and NPV is exactly zero:

$$\text{NPV} = -30 + \frac{3.42}{.114} = 0$$

When we calculated Geothermal's weighted-average cost of capital, we recognized that the company's debt ratio was 30%. When Geothermal's analysts use the weighted-average cost of capital to evaluate the new project, they are *assuming* that the $30 million additional investment would support the issue of additional debt equal to 30% of the investment, or $9 million. The remaining $21 million is provided by the shareholders either in the form of reinvested earnings or through the issue of additional shares.

The following table shows how the cash flows would be shared between the debtholders and shareholders assuming still that the project has zero NPV. We start with the pretax operating cash flow of $5.26 million:

Cash flow before tax and interest	$5.26 million
− Interest payment (.08 × $9 million)	−0.72
= Pretax cash flow	4.54
− Tax at 35%	−1.59
After-tax cash flow	$2.95 million

Project cash flows before tax and interest are forecast to be $5.26 million. Out of this figure, Geothermal needs to pay interest of 8% of $9 million, which comes to $.72 million. This leaves a pretax cash flow of $4.54 million, on which the company must pay tax. Taxes equal .35 × 4.54 = $1.59 million. Shareholders are left with $2.95 million, just enough to give them the 14% return that they need on their $21 million investment. (Note that 2.95/21 = .14, or 14%.) Therefore, everything checks out.

If a project has zero NPV when the expected cash flows are discounted at the weighted-average cost of capital, then the project's cash flows are just sufficient to give debtholders and shareholders the returns they require.

13.3   Interpreting the Weighted-Average Cost of Capital

When You Can and Can't Use WACC

Geothermal's weighted-average cost of capital is the rate of return that the firm must expect to earn on its average-risk investments in order to provide an adequate expected return to all its security holders. Strictly speaking, the weighted-average cost of capital is an appropriate discount rate only for a project that is a carbon copy of the firm's existing business. But, often, it is used as a companywide benchmark discount rate; the benchmark may be adjusted upward for unusually risky projects and downward for unusually safe ones.

There is a good musical analogy here. Most of us, lacking perfect pitch, need a well-defined reference point, like middle C, before we can sing on key. But anyone who can carry a tune gets *relative* pitches right. Businesspeople have good intuition about *relative* risks, at least in industries they are used to, but not about absolute risk or required rates of return. Therefore, they set a company- or industry-wide cost of capital as a benchmark. This is not the right hurdle rate for everything the company does, but judgmental adjustments can be made for riskier or less risky ventures.

Some Common Mistakes

One danger with the weighted-average formula is that it tempts people to make logical errors. Think back to Jo Ann Cox's estimate of Geothermal's cost of capital:

$$\text{WACC} = \left[\frac{D}{V} \times (1 - T_c)r_{\text{debt}}\right] + \left(\frac{E}{V} \times r_{\text{equity}}\right)$$

$$= [.3 \times (1 - .35) \times 8\%] + (.7 \times 14\%) = 11.4\%$$

Now suppose that, having read Jo Ann's report, Costas Thermopolis replies, "Aha! I have an idea. Geothermal has a good credit rating. It could easily push up its debt ratio to 50%. If the interest rate is 8% and the required return on equity is 14%, the weighted-average cost of capital would be only:

$$\text{WACC} = [.50 \times (1 - .35)8\%] + (.50 \times 14\%) = 9.6\%$$

At a discount rate of 9.6%, we can justify a lot more investment."

That reasoning will get the company into trouble. First, if Geothermal increased its borrowing, the lenders would almost certainly demand a higher rate of interest on the debt. Second, as the borrowing increased, the risk of the common stock would also increase and therefore the stockholders would demand a higher return.

There are actually two costs of debt finance. The explicit cost of debt is the rate of interest that bondholders demand. But there is also an implicit cost, because borrowing increases the required return to equity. When you jumped to the conclusion that Geothermal could lower its weighted-average cost of capital to 9.6% by borrowing more, you were recognizing only the explicit cost of debt and not the implicit cost.

13.5   Self-Test

Costas Thermopolis now points out that Geothermal proposes to finance its expansion entirely by borrowing at an interest rate of 8%. He argues that this is, therefore, the appropriate discount rate for the project's cash flows. Is he right?

How Changing Capital Structure Affects Expected Returns

We will illustrate how changes in capital structure affect expected returns by focusing on the simplest possible case, where the corporate tax rate T_c is zero.

Think about what would happen if Geothermal borrows an additional $100 million and uses the cash to buy back and retire $100 million of its common stock. If there are no corporate taxes, the change in capital structure does not affect the total cash that Geothermal pays out to its security holders, and it does not affect the risk of those cash flows. Therefore, if investors require a return of 12.2% on the total package of debt and equity before the financing, they must require the same 12.2% return on the package afterward. The weighted-average cost of capital is therefore unaffected by the change in the capital structure.

Is that surprising? After all, the required return on debt is lower than the required return on equity, so you might expect the additional borrowing to *reduce* the weighted average cost of capital. The reason that it does not do so is that the return on the individual securities changes. Because the company has more debt than before, the debt is riskier, and debtholders are likely to demand a higher return. Increasing the amount of debt also makes the equity riskier and increases the return that shareholders require. We will return to this point in Chapter 16.

What Happens When the Corporate Tax Rate Is Not Zero

We have shown that when there are no corporate taxes, the weighted-average cost of capital is unaffected by a change in capital structure. Unfortunately, taxes can complicate the picture.[4] For the moment, just remember:

- The weighted-average cost of capital is the right discount rate for average risk capital investments.
- The weighted-average cost of capital is the return the company needs to earn after tax in order to satisfy all its security holders.
- If the firm increases its debt ratio, both the debt and the equity will become riskier. The debtholders and equityholders require a higher return to compensate for increased risk.

13.4 Practical Problems: Measuring Capital Structure

We have explained the formula for calculating the weighted-average cost of capital. We will now look at some of the practical problems in applying that formula. We will give Jo Ann Cox a break, and suppose that you have been asked to estimate Big Oil's weighted-average cost of capital. Your first step is to work out Big Oil's capital structure. But where do you get the data?

Financial managers usually start with the company's accounts, which show the book value of debt and equity, whereas the weighted-average cost of capital formula calls for their *market* values. A little work and a dash of judgment are needed to go from one to the other.

Table 13.1 shows the debt and equity issued by Big Oil. The firm has borrowed $200 million from banks and has issued a further $200 million of long-term bonds. These bonds have a coupon rate of 8% and mature at the end of 12 years. Finally, there are 100 million shares of common stock outstanding, each with a par value of $1.

---

[4] There's nothing wrong with our formulas and examples, *provided* that the tax deductibility of interest payments doesn't change the aggregate risk of the debt and equity investors. However, if the tax savings from deducting interest are treated as safe cash flows, the formulas get more complicated. If you really want to dive into the tax-adjusted formulas showing how WACC changes with capital structure, we suggest Chapter 19 in R. A. Brealey, S. C. Myers, and F. Allen, *Principles of Corporate Finance*, 12th ed. (New York: McGraw-Hill Education, 2017).

TABLE 13.1 Big Oil's book (accounting) balance sheet (dollar values in millions)

Assets		Long-Term Liabilities and Equity		
Net working capital (= current assets − current liabilities)	$120	Bank debt	$200	25.0%
Property, plant, and equipment (PP&E)	620	Long-term bonds (12-year maturity, 8% coupon)	200	25.0
Other long-term assets	60	Common stock (100 million shares, par value = $1)	100	12.5
		Retained earnings	300	37.5
	$800		$800	100.0%

But the accounts also recognize that Big Oil has in past years plowed back into the firm $300 million of retained earnings. The total book value of the equity shown in the accounts is $100 million + $300 million = $400 million.

Notice that the right side of Table 13.1 contains long-term financing. Current liabilities have been subtracted on the left as an offset to current assets. Thus, *net* working capital equals current assets minus current liabilities. We set up the balance sheet in this way in order to compute the weighted-average cost of capital, which is normally defined as the combined cost of *long-term* debt financing and equity.[5] Thus, the balance sheet shows only sources of long-term financing on the right.

The figures shown in Table 13.1 are taken from Big Oil's annual accounts and are, therefore, book values. Sometimes the differences between book values and market values are negligible. For example, consider the $200 million that Big Oil owes the bank. The interest rate on bank loans is usually linked to the general level of interest rates. Thus, if interest rates rise, the rate charged on Big Oil's loan also rises to maintain the loan's value. As long as Big Oil is reasonably sure to repay the loan, it is worth close to $200 million. Most financial managers most of the time are willing to accept the book value of bank debt as a fair approximation of its market value.

What about Big Oil's long-term bonds? Since the bonds were originally issued, long-term interest rates have risen to 9%.[6] We can calculate the value today of each bond as follows:[7] There are 12 coupon payments of .08 × 200 = $16 million and then repayment of face value 12 years out. Thus, the final cash payment to the bondholders is $216 million. All the bond's cash flows are discounted back at the *current* interest rate of 9%:

$$PV = \frac{16}{1.09} + \frac{16}{(1.09)^2} + \frac{16}{(1.09)^3} + \cdots + \frac{216}{(1.09)^{12}} = \$185.7$$

Therefore, the bonds are worth only $185.7 million, 93% of their face value.

If you used the book value of Big Oil's long-term debt rather than its market value, you would be a little bit off in your calculation of the weighted-average cost of capital, but probably not seriously so.

The really big errors are likely to arise if you use the book value of equity rather than its market value. The $400 million book value of Big Oil's equity measures the total amount of cash that the firm has raised from shareholders in the past or has retained and invested on their behalf. But perhaps Big Oil has been able to find projects that were worth more than they originally cost, or perhaps the value of the

---

[5] Sometimes, companies finance long-term investment with short-term debt, rolling over the short-term debt as it matures. In this case, the permanent component of short-term debt could remain on the right side of the balance sheet, and the cost of short-term debt could be included in WACC. We assume that Big Oil's bank debt is part of its long-term financing.

[6] If Big Oil's bonds are traded, you can simply look up their price. (You can find prices for bond trades on **www.finra.org/marketdata**.) But many bonds are not regularly traded, and in such cases, you need to infer their price by calculating the bond's value using the rate of interest offered by similar bonds.

[7] We assume that coupon payments are annual. Most bonds in the United States actually pay interest twice a year.

TABLE 13.2 Big Oil's market-value balance sheet (dollar values in millions)

Assets		Liabilities and Equity		
Net working capital (= current assets − current liabilities)	$ 120.0	Bank debt	$ 200.0	12.6%
Value of PP&E and other long-term assets (including intangible assets)	1,465.7	Long-term bonds (market value = 93% par value)	185.7	11.7
		Total debt	385.7	24.3
		Common stock (100 million shares, par value = $1)	1,200.0	75.7
Value	$1,585.7	Value	$1,585.7	100.0%

assets has increased with inflation. Perhaps investors see great future investment opportunities for the company. All these considerations determine what investors are willing to pay for Big Oil's common stock.

Big Oil's stock price is $12 a share. Thus the total *market value* of the stock is

$$\text{Number of shares} \times \text{share price} = 100 \text{ million} \times \$12 = \$1,200 \text{ million}$$

In Table 13.2, we show a *market-value* balance sheet for Big Oil. You can see that debt accounts for 24.3% of company value ($D/V = .243$) and equity accounts for 75.7% ($E/V = .757$). These are the proportions to use when calculating the weighted-average cost of capital. Notice that if you looked only at the book values shown in Table 13.1, you would mistakenly conclude that debt and equity each accounted for 50% of value.

13.6 Self-Test

Here is the capital structure shown in Executive Fruit's *book* balance sheet:

Debt	$4.1 million	45.0%
Preferred stock	2.2	24.2
Common stock	2.8	30.8
Total	$9.1 million	100.0%

Explain why the percentage weights given here should *not* be used in calculating Executive Fruit's WACC.

13.5 More Practical Problems: Estimating Expected Returns

To calculate Big Oil's weighted-average cost of capital, you also need the rate of return that investors require from each security.

The Expected Return on Bonds

We know that Big Oil's bonds offer a yield to maturity of 9%. As long as the company does not go belly-up, that is the rate of return investors can expect to earn from holding Big Oil's bonds. If there is any chance that the firm may be unable to repay the debt, however, the yield to maturity of 9% represents the most favorable outcome and the *expected* return is lower than 9%.

For most large and healthy firms, the probability of bankruptcy is sufficiently low that financial managers are content to take the promised yield to maturity on the bonds as a measure of the expected return. But beware of assuming that the yield offered on the bonds of Fly-by-Night Corporation is the return that investors could *expect* to receive.

The Expected Return on Common Stock

Estimates Based on the Capital Asset Pricing Model   In the previous chapter, we showed you how to use the capital asset pricing model to estimate the expected rate of return on common stock. The capital asset pricing model tells us that investors demand a higher rate of return from stocks with high betas. The formula is

$$\begin{array}{c} \text{Expected return} \\ \text{on stock} \end{array} = \begin{array}{c} \text{risk-free} \\ \text{interest rate} \end{array} + \left(\begin{array}{c} \text{stock's} \\ \text{beta} \end{array} \times \begin{array}{c} \text{expected market} \\ \text{risk premium} \end{array} \right)$$

Financial managers and economists measure the risk-free rate of interest by the yield on Treasury debt securities. To measure the expected market risk premium, they usually look back at capital market history, which suggests that investors have received about an extra 7% a year from investing in common stocks rather than Treasury bills.[8] Yet, wise financial managers use this evidence with considerable humility, for who is to say whether investors in the past received more or less than they expected or whether investors today require a higher or lower reward for risk than their parents did?

Let's suppose Big Oil's common stock beta is estimated at .85, the risk-free interest rate (r_f) is 6%, and the expected market risk premium ($r_m - r_f$) is 7%. Then the CAPM would put Big Oil's cost of equity at

$$\text{Cost of equity} = r_{\text{equity}} = r_f + \beta(r_m - r_f)$$

$$= 6\% + .85(7\%) = 12\%$$

Estimates Based on the Dividend Discount Model   Whenever you are given an estimate of the expected return on a common stock, always look for ways to check whether it is reasonable. One check on the estimates provided by the CAPM can be obtained from the dividend discount model (DDM). In Chapter 7, we showed you how to use the constant-growth DDM formula to estimate the return that investors expect from different common stocks. Remember the formula: If dividends are expected to grow indefinitely at a constant rate g, then the price of the stock is equal to

$$P_0 = \frac{\text{DIV}_1}{r_{\text{equity}} - g}$$

where P_0 is the current stock price, DIV_1 is the forecast dividend at the end of the year, and r_{equity} is the expected return from the stock. We can rearrange this formula to provide an estimate of r_{equity}:

$$r_{\text{equity}} = \frac{\text{DIV}_1}{P_0} + g \tag{13.2}$$

In other words, the expected return on equity is equal to the dividend yield (DIV_1/P_0) plus the expected perpetual growth rate in dividends (g).

---

[8] The Treasury bill rate is the customary measure of the risk-free rate of interest. There is a mismatch, however, in using a short-term bill rate to calculate the cost of equity in a WACC. The WACC is used to discount cash flows that may arrive many years in the future. Discounting a distant future cash flow at a short-term rate doesn't make sense, especially when monetary policy forces the short-term rate down close to zero. Therefore, financial managers calculating WACC usually estimate the cost of equity using a long-term Treasury bond rate. In this case, the market risk premium must be defined as the expected difference between the returns on the stock market and on long-term Treasury bonds. Notice in Table 11.1 that the average return on Treasury bonds has been 1.3 percentage points above the average return on bills. Suppose a financial manager uses a long-term bond yield to estimate the cost of equity. If the manager relies on history, he or she would use a market risk premium that is 1.3 percentage points lower than the premium versus bills.

This constant-growth dividend discount model is widely used in estimating expected rates of return on common stocks of public utilities. Utility stocks have a fairly stable growth pattern and are therefore tailor-made for the constant-growth formula.

Remember that the constant-growth formula will get you into trouble if you apply it to firms with very high current rates of growth. Such growth cannot be sustained indefinitely. Using the formula in these circumstances will lead to an overestimate of the expected return.

Beware of False Precision   Do not expect estimates of the cost of equity to be precise. In practice, you can't know whether the capital asset pricing model fully explains expected returns or whether the assumptions of the dividend discount model hold exactly. Even if your formulas were right, the required inputs would be noisy and subject to error. Thus, a financial analyst who can confidently locate the cost of equity in a band of 2 or 3 percentage points is doing pretty well. In this endeavor, it is perfectly okay to conclude that the cost of equity is, say, "about 15%" or "somewhere in a range from 14% to 16%."[9]

Sometimes, accuracy can be improved by estimating the cost of equity or WACC for an industry or a group of comparable companies. This cuts down the "noise" that plagues single-company estimates. Suppose, for example, that you are able to identify three companies with investments and operations similar to Big Oil's. The average WACC for these three companies would be a valuable check on your estimate of WACC for Big Oil alone.

Or suppose that Big Oil is contemplating investment in oil refining. For this venture, Big Oil's existing WACC is probably not right; it needs a discount rate reflecting the risks of the refining business. It could therefore try to estimate WACC for a sample of oil refining companies. If too few "pure-play" refining companies were available—most oil companies invest in production and marketing as well as refining—an industry WACC for a sample of large oil companies could be a useful check or benchmark.

13.7   Self-Test

You have identified a group of oil companies with similar businesses and capital structures to Big Oil. The average estimated beta of their common stocks is 1.1. Use this "industry beta" to re-estimate the expected rate of return on Big Oil's common stock, assuming of course that the CAPM is true. Recalculate Big Oil's weighted-average cost of capital.

The Expected Return on Preferred Stock

Preferred stock that pays a fixed annual dividend can be valued from the perpetuity formula:

$$\text{Price of preferred} = \frac{\text{dividend}}{r_{\text{preferred}}}$$

where $r_{\text{preferred}}$ is the appropriate discount rate for the preferred stock. Therefore, we can infer the required rate of return on preferred stock by rearranging the valuation formula to

$$r_{\text{preferred}} = \frac{\text{dividend}}{\text{price of preferred}} \qquad \text{(13.3)}$$

---

[9] The calculations in this chapter have been done to one or two decimal places just to avoid confusion from rounding.

For example, if a share of preferred stock sells for $20 and pays a dividend of $2 per share, the expected return on preferred stock is $r_{\text{preferred}} = \$2/\$20 = 10\%$, which is simply the dividend yield.

Adding It All Up

Once you have worked out Big Oil's capital structure and estimated the expected return on its securities, you require only simple arithmetic to calculate the weighted-average cost of capital. Table 13.3 summarizes the necessary data. Now all you need to do is plug the data in Table 13.3 into the weighted-average cost of capital formula:

$$\text{WACC} = \left[\frac{D}{V} \times (1 - T_c)r_{\text{debt}}\right] + \left(\frac{E}{V} \times r_{\text{equity}}\right)$$

$$= [.243 \times (1 - .35)9\%] + (.757 \times 12\%) = 10.5\%$$

Suppose that Big Oil needs to evaluate a project with the same risk as its existing business. If the project would also support a 24.3% debt ratio, the 10.5% weighted-average cost of capital is the appropriate discount rate for the cash flows.

Real-Company WACCs

Big Oil is entirely hypothetical. Therefore, you might be interested in looking at Table 13.4, which gives some estimates of the weighted-average cost of capital for a sample of real companies.[10] As you do so, remember that any estimate of the cost of capital for a single company can be way off the true cost.[11] You should always try to check your estimate by looking at the cost of capital for a group of similar companies.

13.6 Valuing Entire Businesses

BEYOND THE PAGE

Valuing the deconstruction business

mhhe.com/brealey9e

Companies frequently buy and sell entire businesses. Do the methods that we have used in this chapter to value new projects also work for entire businesses?

Sure! As long as the company's debt ratio is expected to remain fairly constant, you can treat the company as one big project and discount its cash flows by the weighted-average cost of capital.[12] The result is the combined value of the company's debt and equity. If you want to know just the value of the equity, you must remember to subtract the value of the debt from the company's total value.

Suppose that you are interested in buying Establishment Industry's deconstruction division. The problem is to figure out what it is worth. Table 13.5 sets out your

TABLE 13.3 Data needed to calculate Big Oil's weighted-average cost of capital (dollar values in millions)

Security Type	Capital Structure		Required Rate of Return
Debt	$D = \$\ 385.7$	$D/V = 0.243$	$r_{\text{debt}} = 0.09$, or 9%
Common stock	$E = \$1,200.0$	$E/V = 0.757$	$r_{\text{equity}} = 0.12$, or 12%
Total	$V = \$1,585.7$		

Note: Corporate tax rate $= T_c = .35$. We assume that the interest rate on Big Oil's bank debt is the same as on its bonds.

---

[10] Notice that Ford's WACC is about average despite its very high cost of equity. This results from the company's very high debt ratio. Should Ford use a WACC of 9.5% when valuing a proposal to expand its operations? The answer is yes if a 79% debt ratio really is a sensible target capital structure. But if you believe that this debt ratio does not constitute a desirable long-term capital structure for Ford, then you would need to recalculate WACC with a lower ratio.

[11] For example, Ford's WACC would be underestimated if the company cannot sensibly continue to support such a high debt ratio.

[12] In Chapter 7, we showed how to value a business that is financed entirely by equity. In this section, we extend that discussion, and show how to deal with a business that is partly financed by debt.

TABLE 13.4 Calculating the weighted-average cost of capital for selected companies

	Expected Return on Equity (%)	Interest Rate on Debt (%)	Proportion of Equity (E/V)	Proportion of Debt (D/V)	WACC (%)
U.S. Steel	16.0	12.2	0.31	0.69	10.5
Disney	12.9	3.0	0.94	0.06	12.3
Ford	12.2	3.8	0.30	0.70	5.4
Monsanto	11.3	3.8	0.84	0.16	9.9
General Electric	11.4	4.3	0.63	0.37	8.2
Boeing	10.1	3.2	0.92	0.08	9.4
Union Pacific	10.0	3.1	0.85	0.15	8.8
Alphabet (Google)	9.8	2.9	1.00	0.00	9.8
ExxonMobil	9.6	2.8	0.93	0.07	9.0
Amazon	9.5	3.4	0.97	0.03	9.3
Intel	9.4	3.3	0.88	0.12	8.6
Pfizer	9.3	3.1	0.86	0.14	8.3
Starbucks	8.5	2.9	0.97	0.03	8.3
IBM	7.1	3.2	0.80	0.20	6.1
McDonald's	6.6	3.2	0.85	0.15	5.9
Coca-Cola	6.4	2.8	0.87	0.13	5.8
Campbell Soup	6.3	3.4	0.85	0.15	5.7
Walmart	4.8	2.7	0.81	0.19	4.2
Newmont Mining	4.7	5.6	0.60	0.40	4.3
Pacific Gas & Electric	4.6	3.3	0.60	0.40	3.6

Notes:
1. Expected return on equity is taken from Table 12.2.
2. Interest rate on debt is taken from recent trades on TRACE.
3. D is the book value of the firm's debt, and E is the market value of equity.
4. WACC $= (D/V) \times (1 - .35) \times r_{debt} + (E/V) \times r_{equity}$

TABLE 13.5 Forecasts of operating cash flow and investment for the deconstruction division (thousands of dollars). Rapid expansion means that free cash flow is negative in the early years, because investment outstrips the cash flow from operations. Free cash flow turns positive when growth slows down.

	Year					
	1	2	3	4	5	6
1. Sales	$1,200.0	$1,440.0	$1,728.0	$1,987.2	$2,285.3	$2,513.8
2. Costs	1,020.0	1,224.0	1,468.8	1,689.1	1,942.5	2,136.7
3. EBITDA* = 1 − 2	180.0	216.0	259.2	298.1	342.8	377.1
4. Depreciation	86.4	103.7	124.4	143.1	137.1	120.7
5. Profit before tax = 3 − 4	93.6	112.3	134.8	155.0	205.7	256.4
6. Tax at 35%	32.8	39.3	47.2	54.3	72.0	89.7
7. Profit after tax = 5 − 6	60.8	73.0	87.6	100.8	133.7	166.7
8. Operating cash flow = 4 + 7	147.2	176.7	212.0	243.8	270.8	287.3
9. Investment in fixed assets and net working capital	180.0	247.7	297.2	298.6	87.4	−16.5
10. Free cash flow = 8 − 9	−32.8	−71.0	−85.2	−54.8	183.4	303.8

* EBITDA = earnings before interest, taxes, depreciation, and amortization.

forecasts for the next 6 years. Row 8 shows the expected cash flow from operations. This is equal to the expected profit after tax plus depreciation. Remember, depreciation is not a cash outflow, and therefore you need to add it back when calculating the operating cash flow. Row 9 in the table shows the forecast investment in fixed assets and net working capital.

free cash flow (FCF)
Cash flow available for distribution to investors after firm pays for new investments or additions to working capital.

The operating cash flow *less* investment expenditures is the amount of cash that the business can pay out to investors after paying for all investments necessary for growth. This is the deconstruction division's **free cash flow (FCF)** (row 10 in the table). Notice that the free cash flow is negative in the early years. The firm is running a cash deficit not because it is unprofitable but because it is growing so fast and investing so much in the business.

The forecast cash flows in Table 13.5 do not include a deduction for debt interest. But we will not forget that acquisition of the deconstruction business will support additional debt. We will recognize this by discounting the free cash flows by the weighted-average cost of capital, which reflects both the firm's capital structure and the tax deductibility of its interest payments.

Suppose that a sensible capital structure for the deconstruction operation is 60% equity and 40% debt.[13] You estimate that the required rate of return on the equity is 12% and that the business could borrow at an interest rate of 5%. The weighted-average cost of capital is therefore

$$\text{WACC} = \left[\frac{D}{V} \times (1 - T_c)r_{\text{debt}}\right] + \left(\frac{E}{V} \times r_{\text{equity}}\right)$$

$$= [.4 \times (1 - .35)5\%] + (.6 \times 12\%) = 8.5\%$$

Calculating the Value of the Deconstruction Business

The value of the deconstruction operation is equal to the discounted value of the free cash flows (FCFs) out to a horizon year plus the forecast value of the business at the horizon, also discounted back to the present. That is,

$$\text{PV} = \underbrace{\frac{\text{FCF}_1}{1 + \text{WACC}} + \frac{\text{FCF}_2}{(1 + \text{WACC})^2} + \cdots + \frac{\text{FCF}_H}{(1 + \text{WACC})^H}}_{\text{PV (free cash flows)}} + \underbrace{\frac{\text{PV}_H}{(1 + \text{WACC})^H}}_{\text{PV (horizon value)}}$$

PV_H stands in for the value of free cash flows in periods $H + 1$, $H + 2$, and so on. We assume that beginning in year 6 the business is expected to settle down to steady growth of 5% a year, and so we have picked year 5 as the horizon year.

We saw in Chapter 7 that there are several common formulas or rules of thumb for estimating horizon value. Here we will just use the constant-growth formula that we introduced in that chapter:

$$\text{Horizon value} = \frac{\text{free cash flow in year 6}}{r - g} = \frac{303.8}{.085 - .05} = \$8,680 \text{ thousand}$$

We now have all we need to calculate the value of the deconstruction business today. We add up the present values of the free cash flows in the first 5 years and that of the horizon value:

PV (business) = PV (free cash flows years 1–5) + PV (horizon value)

$$= \frac{-32.8}{1.085} + \frac{-71.0}{(1.085)^2} + \frac{-85.2}{(1.085)^3} + \frac{-54.8}{(1.085)^4} + \frac{183.4}{(1.085)^5} + \frac{8,680}{(1.085)^5}$$

$$= \$5,697.5 \text{ thousand}$$

---

[13] By this we mean that it makes sense to finance 40% of the *present value* of the business by debt. Remember that we use market-value weights to compute WACC. Debt as a proportion of *book value* may be more or less than 40%.

Notice that when we use the weighted-average cost of capital to value a company, we are asking, "What is the combined value of the company's debt and equity?" If you need to value the equity, you must subtract the value of any outstanding debt. Suppose that the deconstruction business has been partly financed with $2,279,000 of debt, 40% of the overall value of about $5,697,500. Then the equity in the business is worth only $5,697,500 − $2,279,000 = $3,418,500.

13.8   Self-Test

Managers often use rules of thumb to check their estimates of horizon value. Suppose you observe that the value of the debt plus equity of a typical mature deconstruction business is 15 times its EBITDA. (EBITDA is defined at line 3 of Table 13.5.) If your operation sold in year 5 at a similar multiple of EBITDA, how would your estimate of the *present* value of the operation change?

SUMMARY

How do firms compute weighted-average costs of capital? (*LO13-1*)

Here's the WACC formula one more time:

$$\text{WACC} = \left[\frac{D}{V} \times (1 - T_c)r_{\text{debt}}\right] + \left(\frac{E}{V} \times r_{\text{equity}}\right)$$

The WACC is the expected rate of return on the portfolio of debt and equity securities issued by the firm. The required rate of return on each security is weighted by its proportion of the firm's total market value (not book value). Because interest payments reduce the firm's income tax bill, the required rate of return on debt is measured after tax, as $r_{\text{debt}} \times (1 - T_c)$.

Why do firms compute weighted-average costs of capital? (*LO13-2*)

Firms need a standard discount rate for average-risk projects. An "average-risk" project is one that has the same risk as the firm's existing operations and that supports the same relative amount of debt.

What about projects that are not average? (*LO13-2*)

The **weighted-average cost of capital** can still be used as a benchmark. The benchmark may be adjusted up for unusually risky projects and down for unusually safe ones.

What happens when capital structure changes? (*LO13-2*)

The rates of return on debt and equity will change. For example, increasing the debt ratio will increase the risk borne by both debt and equity investors and cause them to demand higher returns. However, this does *not* necessarily mean that the overall WACC will increase, because more weight is put on the cost of debt, which is less than the cost of equity. In fact, if we ignore taxes, the overall **cost of capital** will stay constant as the fractions of debt and equity change. This is discussed further in Chapter 16.

How do firms measure capital structure? (*LO13-3*)

Capital structure is the proportion of each source of financing in total market value. The WACC formula is usually written assuming the firm's capital structure includes just two classes of securities, debt and equity. If there is another class, say preferred stock, the formula expands to include it. In other words, we would estimate $r_{\text{preferred}}$, the rate of return demanded by preferred stockholders, determine P/V, the fraction of market value accounted for by preferred, and add $r_{\text{preferred}} \times P/V$ to the equation. Of course, the weights in the WACC formula always add up to 1. In this case $D/V + P/V + E/V = 1$.

How are the costs of debt and equity calculated?
(LO13-4)

The cost of debt (r_{debt}) is the market interest rate demanded by debtholders. In other words, it is the rate that the company would pay on *new* debt issued to finance its investment projects. The cost of preferred ($r_{preferred}$) is just the preferred dividend divided by the market price of a preferred share.

The tricky part is estimating the cost of equity (r_{equity}), the expected rate of return on the firm's shares. Financial managers commonly use the capital asset pricing model to estimate expected return. But for mature, steady-growth companies, it can also make sense to use the constant-growth dividend discount model. Remember, estimates of expected return are less reliable for a single firm's stock than for a sample of comparable-risk firms. Therefore, managers also consider WACCs calculated for industries.

Can WACC be used to value an entire business?
(LO13-5)

Just think of the business as a very large project. Forecast the business's operating cash flows (after-tax profits plus depreciation), and subtract the future investments in plant and equipment and in net working capital. The resulting **free cash flows** can then be discounted back to the present at the weighted-average cost of capital. Of course, the cash flows from a company may stretch far into the future. Financial managers therefore typically produce detailed cash flows only up to some horizon date and then estimate the remaining value of the business at the horizon.

LISTING OF EQUATIONS

13.1 $\text{WACC} = \left[\dfrac{D}{V} \times (1 - T_c)r_{debt}\right] + \left(\dfrac{E}{V} \times r_{equity}\right)$

13.1a $\text{WACC} = \left[\dfrac{D}{V} \times (1 - T_c)r_{debt}\right] + \left(\dfrac{P}{V} \times r_{preferred}\right) + \left(\dfrac{E}{V} \times r_{equity}\right)$

13.2 $r_{equity} = \dfrac{DIV_1}{P_0} + g$

13.3 $r_{preferred} = \dfrac{\text{dividend}}{\text{price of preferred}}$

QUESTIONS AND PROBLEMS

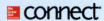

1. **Changes in Capital Structure.** Look at our calculation of Big Oil's WACC in Section 13.5. *(LO13-1)*
    a. Suppose Big Oil is excused from paying taxes. What would be its WACC?
    b. Now suppose that, after the tax rate has fallen to zero, Big Oil makes a large stock issue and uses the proceeds to pay off all its debt. What would be the cost of equity after the issue?
2. **WACC.** Here is some information about Stokenchurch Inc.:

    Beta of common stock = 1.2

    Treasury bill rate = 4%

    Market risk premium = 7.5%

    Yield to maturity on long-term debt = 6%

    Book value of equity = $440 million

    Market value of equity = $880 million

    Long-term debt outstanding = $880 million

    Corporate tax rate = 35%

    What is the company's WACC? *(LO13-1)*

3. **WACC.** Reactive Power Generation has the following capital structure. Its corporate tax rate is 35%. What is its WACC? (*LO13-1*)

Security	Market Value	Required Rate of Return
Debt	$20 million	6%
Preferred stock	10 million	8
Common stock	50 million	12

4. **WACC.** The common stock of Buildwell Conservation & Construction Inc. (BCCI) has a beta of .9. The Treasury bill rate is 4%, and the market risk premium is estimated at 8%. BCCI's capital structure is 30% debt, paying a 5% interest rate, and 70% equity. Buildwell pays tax at 40%. (*LO13-1*)

a. What is BCCI's cost of equity capital?
b. What is its WACC?
c. If BCCI is presented with a normal project with an internal rate of return of 12%, should it accept the project?

5. **Calculating WACC.** The total book value of WTC's equity is $10 million, and book value per share is $20. The stock has a market-to-book ratio of 1.5, and the cost of equity is 15%. The firm's bonds have a face value of $5 million and sell at a price of 110% of face value. The yield to maturity on the bonds is 9%, and the firm's tax rate is 40%. Find the company's WACC. (*LO13-1*)

6. **WACC.** Nodebt Inc. is a firm with all-equity financing. Its equity beta is .80. The Treasury bill rate is 4%, and the market risk premium is expected to be 10%. (*LO13-1*)

a. What is Nodebt's asset beta?
b. What is Nodebt's WACC?

7. **WACC.** Look at the following book-value balance sheet for University Products Inc. The preferred stock currently sells for $15 per share and pays a dividend of $2 a share. The common stock sells for $20 per share and has a beta of .8. There are 1 million common shares outstanding. The market risk premium is 10%, the risk-free rate is 6%, and the firm's tax rate is 40%. (*LO13-1*)

BOOK-VALUE BALANCE SHEET (Figures in $ millions)			
Assets		**Liabilities and Net Worth**	
Cash and short-term securities	$ 1	Bonds, coupon = 8%, paid annually (maturity = 10 years, current yield to maturity = 9%)	$10
Accounts receivable	3	Preferred stock (par value $20 per share)	2
Inventories	7	Common stock (par value $.10)	0.1
Plant and equipment	21	Additional paid-in stockholders' equity	9.9
		Retained earnings	10
Total	$32		$32

a. What is the market debt-to-value ratio of the firm?
b. What is University's WACC?

8. **Changes in Capital Structure.** Look back at Section 13.5. Suppose Big Oil is excused from paying taxes. It starts from the financing mix in Table 13.3, and then borrows an additional $200 million from the bank. It uses this cash to pay out a special $200 million dividend, leaving its assets and operations unchanged. (*LO13-1*)

a. What happens to Big Oil's WACC, still assuming it pays no taxes?
b. What happens to its cost of equity?

9. **WACC.** True or false? (*LO13-2*)

a. If a company uses its company cost of capital to value all projects, it will overestimate the value of high-risk projects.
b. It is okay to use the company cost of capital to value every project as long as the high risks of some projects are offset by the low risks of others.
c. A company can reduce the discount rate for a project by financing it with debt.

10. **Company versus Project Discount Rates.** Geothermal's WACC is 11.4%. Executive Fruit's WACC is 12.3%. Now Executive Fruit is considering an investment in geothermal power production. (*LO13-2*)

   a. Should it discount project cash flows at 12.3%?

   b. What would be a better discount rate for this investment?

11. **Project Discount Rate.** The total market value of the equity of Okefenokee Condos is $6 million, and the total value of its debt is $4 million. The treasurer estimates that the beta of the stock currently is 1.2 and that the expected risk premium on the market is 10%. The Treasury bill rate is 4%, and investors believe that Okefenokee's debt is essentially free of default risk. (*LO13-2*)

   a. What is the required rate of return on Okefenokee stock?

   b. Estimate the WACC assuming a tax rate of 40%.

   c. Estimate the discount rate for an expansion of the company's present business.

   d. Suppose the company wants to diversify into the manufacture of rose-colored glasses. The beta of optical manufacturers with no debt outstanding is 1.4. What is the required rate of return on Okefenokee's new venture? (You should assume that the risky project will not enable the firm to issue any additional debt.)

12. **Interpreting WACC.** An analyst at Dawn Chemical notes that its cost of debt is far below that of equity. He concludes that it is important for the firm to maintain the ability to increase its borrowing because if it cannot borrow, it will be forced to use more expensive equity to finance some projects. This might lead it to reject some projects that would have seemed attractive if evaluated at the lower cost of debt. Comment on this reasoning. (*LO13-2*)

13. **WACC and Taxes.** "The after-tax cost of debt is lower when the firm's tax rate is higher; therefore, the WACC falls when the tax rate rises. Thus, with a lower discount rate, the firm must be worth more if its tax rate is higher." Explain why this argument is wrong. (*LO13-2*)

14. **Project Discount Rate.** Universal Foods has a debt-to-value ratio of 40%, its debt is currently selling on a yield of 6%, and its cost of equity is 12%. The corporate tax rate is 40%. The company is now evaluating a new venture into home computer systems. The internal rate of return on this venture is estimated at 13.4%. WACCs of firms in the personal computer industry tend to average around 14%. (*LO13-2*)

   a. What is Universal's WACC?

   b. Will Universal make the correct decision if it discounts cash flows on the proposed venture at the firm's WACC?

   c. Should the new project be pursued?

15. **Capital Structure.** In 2015, Caterpillar Inc. had about 582 million shares outstanding. Their book value was $27.30 per share, and the market price was $71.50 per share. The company's balance sheet shows that the company had $25.2 billion of long-term debt, which was currently selling near par value. (*LO13-3*)

   a. What was Caterpillar's book debt-to-value ratio?

   b. What was its market debt-to-value ratio?

   c. Which of these two measures should you use to calculate the company's cost of capital?

16. **Capital Structure.** Here is a simplified balance sheet for Epicure Pizza (figures in $ millions):

Assets		Liabilities and Shareholders' Equity	
Current assets	$ 80	Current liabilities	$ 60
Fixed assets	125	Long-term debt	65
		Equity	80
Total	$205	Total	$205

Note: There are 16 million shares outstanding.

Epicure shares are currently priced at $12 each. (*LO13-3*)

a. You wish to calculate Epicure's WACC. What is the relevant figure for the company's debt ratio?

b. You now realize that since Epicure issued its debt, interest rates have fallen substantially. Do you need to revise your measure of the debt ratio upward or downward?

17. **Capital Structure.** Binomial Tree Farm's financing includes $5 million of bank loans and $6 million book value of 10-year bonds, which are selling at 95% of par value. Its common equity is shown in Binomial's Annual Report at $6.67. It has 500,000 shares of common stock outstanding which trade on the Wichita Stock Exchange at $18 per share. What debt ratio should Binomial use to calculate its WACC? (*LO13-3*)

18. **Cost of Debt.** Olympic Sports has two issues of debt outstanding. One is a 9% coupon bond with a face value of $20 million, a maturity of 10 years, and a yield to maturity of 10%. The coupons are paid annually. The other bond issue has a maturity of 15 years, with coupons also paid annually, and a coupon rate of 10%. The face value of the issue is $25 million, and the issue sells for 94% of par value. The firm's tax rate is 35%. (*LO13-4*)

a. What is the before-tax cost of debt for Olympic?

b. What is Olympic's after-tax cost of debt?

19. **Cost of Equity.** Bunkhouse Electronics is a recently incorporated firm that makes electronic entertainment systems. Its earnings and dividends have been growing at a rate of 30%, and the current dividend yield is 2%. Its beta is 1.2, the market risk premium is 8%, and the risk-free rate is 4%. (*LO13-4*)

a. Use the CAPM to estimate the firm's cost of equity.

b. Now use the constant growth model to estimate the cost of equity.

c. Which of the two estimates is more reasonable?

20. **Cost of Debt.** Micro Spinoffs Inc. issued 20-year debt a year ago at par value with a coupon rate of 8%, paid annually. Today, the debt is selling at $1,050. If the firm's tax bracket is 35%, what is its percentage cost of debt? (*LO13-4*)

21. **Cost of Preferred Stock.** Pangbourne Whitchurch has preferred stock outstanding. The stock pays a dividend of $4 per share, and sells for $40. The corporate tax rate is 35%. What is the percentage cost of the preferred stock? (*LO13-4*)

22. **Cost of Equity.** Reliable Electric is a regulated public utility, and it is expected to provide steady dividend growth of 5% per year for the indefinite future. Its last dividend was $5 per share; the stock sold for $60 per share just after the dividend was paid. What is the company's percentage cost of equity? (*LO13-4*)

23. **Company Cost of Capital.** The following table presents information for Golden Fleece Financial. Calculate the company cost of capital. Ignore taxes. (*LO13-4*)

Long-term debt outstanding	$300,000
Current yield to maturity on debt	8%
Number of shares of common stock	10,000
Price per share	$50
Book value per share	$25
Expected rate of return on stock	15%

24. **Company Valuation.** Icarus Airlines is proposing to go public, and you have been given the task of estimating the value of its equity. Management plans to maintain debt at 30% of the company's present value, and you believe that at this capital structure the company's debtholders will demand a return of 6% and stockholders will require 11%. The company is forecasting that next year's operating cash flow (depreciation plus profit after tax at 40%) will be $68 million and that investment in plant and net working capital will be $30 million. Thereafter, operating cash flows and investment expenditures are forecast to grow in perpetuity by 4% a year. (*LO13-5*)

a. What is the total value of Icarus?

b. What is the value of the company's equity?

25. **Company Valuation.** You need to estimate the value of Laputa Aviation. You have the following forecasts (in millions of dollars) of its profits and of its future investments in new plant and working capital:

	Year			
	1	**2**	**3**	**4**
Earnings before interest, taxes, depreciation, and amortization (EBITDA)	$80	$100	$115	$120
Depreciation	20	30	35	40
Pretax profit	60	70	80	80
Tax at 40%	24	28	32	32
Investment	12	15	18	20

From year 5 onward, EBITDA, depreciation, and investment are expected to remain unchanged at year-4 levels. Laputa is financed 50% by equity and 50% by debt. Its cost of equity is 15%, its debt yields 7%, and it pays corporate tax at 40%. (*LO13-5*)

a. Estimate the company's total value.
b. What is the value of Laputa's equity?

WEB EXERCISE

1. Estimate the weighted-average cost of capital for Home Depot (HD), Altria (MO), Caterpillar (CAT), Intel (INTC), and Monsanto (MON). You can estimate the expected stock returns for these companies by using the betas shown on finance.yahoo.com. You can also use Yahoo! Finance to find the relative proportions of equity and debt for each company. Remember, though, to use the market value of the equity, not its book value. Finding the yield on the debt is a little trickier. One possibility it to log on to www.bondsonline.com to find the current level of Treasury yields and the yield spreads (i.e., the extra yield for bonds with different ratings). An alternative is to look at the yields shown in the bonds section of Yahoo! Finance. Note: As we write this, Moody's ratings for the five companies vary from Baa for Altria, to A for Home Depot, Caterpillar, Intel, and Monsanto.

SOLUTIONS TO SELF-TEST QUESTIONS

13.1 Hot Rocks' 4 million common shares are worth $40 million. Its market-value balance sheet is:

Assets		**Liabilities and Shareholders' Equity**		
Assets	$90	Debt	$50	(56%)
	___	Equity	40	(44%)
Value	$90	Value	$90	

$$\text{WACC} = (.56 \times 9\%) + (.44 \times 17\%) = 12.5\%$$

We use Hot Rocks' pretax return on debt because the company pays no taxes.

13.2 Burg's 6 million shares are now worth only 6 million × $4 = $24 million. The debt is selling for 80% of book, or $20 million. The market-value balance sheet is:

Assets		**Liabilities and Shareholders' Equity**		
Assets	$44	Debt	$20	(45%)
	___	Equity	24	(55%)
Value	$44	Value	$44	

$$\text{WACC} = (.45 \times 14\%) + (.55 \times 20\%) = 17.3\%$$

Note that this question ignores taxes.

13.3   Compare the two income statements, one for Criss-Cross Industries and the other for a firm with identical EBIT but no debt in its capital structure. (All figures in millions.)

	Criss-Cross	Firm with No Debt
EBIT	$10.0	$10.0
Interest expense	2.0	0.0
Taxable income	8.0	10.0
Taxes owed	2.8	3.5
Net income	5.2	6.5
Total income accruing to debt- and equityholders	7.2	6.5

Notice that Criss-Cross pays $.7 million less in taxes than its debt-free counterpart. Accordingly, the total income available to debt-plus equityholders is $.7 million higher.

13.4   For Hot Rocks,

$$\text{WACC} = [.56 \times 9 \times (1 - .35)] + (.44 \times 17) = 10.8\%$$

For Burg Associates,

$$\text{WACC} = [.45 \times 14 \times (1 - .35)] + (.55 \times 20) = 15.1\%$$

13.5   Costas is wrong. The project is an expansion of the firm's existing line of business and presumably has some risk. Therefore, the appropriate discount rate is the company's weighted-average cost of capital, not just the rate at which it can borrow. Costas is ignoring the implicit cost of debt: that if the firm borrows to finance its expansion, leverage will be higher, the equity will be riskier, and equityholders will demand a higher expected rate of return.

13.6   WACC measures the expected rate of return demanded by debt and equity investors in the firm (plus a tax adjustment capturing the tax-deductibility of interest payments). Thus, the calculation must be based on what investors are actually paying for the firm's debt and equity securities. In other words, it must be based on market values.

13.7   From the CAPM:

$$r_{\text{equity}} = r_f + \beta_{\text{equity}}(r_m - r_f)$$
$$= 6\% + 1.10(7.0) = 13.7\%$$
$$\text{WACC} = .3(1 - .35)8\% + .7(13.7\%) = 11.15\%$$

13.8   Estimated horizon value for the deconstruction business is $15 \times$ year-5 EBITDA $= 15 \times 342.8 = \$5,142$ thousand. PV (horizon value) is $\$5,142/(1.085)^5 = \$3,149.7$ thousand. Adding in the PV of free cash flows for years 1 to 5 gives a present value for the business of $3,344.9 thousand.

MINICASE

Bernice Mountaindog was glad to be back at Sea Shore Salt. Employees were treated well. When she had asked a year ago for a leave of absence to complete her degree in finance, top management promptly agreed. When she returned with an honors degree, she was promoted from administrative assistant (she had been secretary to Joe-Bob Brinepool, the president) to treasury analyst.

Bernice thought the company's prospects were good. Sure, table salt was a mature business, but Sea Shore Salt had grown steadily at the expense of its less well known competitors. The company's brand name was an important advantage, despite the difficulty most customers had in pronouncing it rapidly.

Bernice started work on January 2, 2016. The first 2 weeks went smoothly. Then Mr. Brinepool's cost of capital memo (see Figure 13.2) assigned her to explain Sea Shore Salt's weighted-average

cost of capital to other managers. The memo came as a surprise to Bernice, so she stayed late to prepare for the questions that would surely come the next day.

Bernice first examined Sea Shore Salt's most recent balance sheet, summarized in Table 13.6. Then she jotted down the following additional points:

- The company's bank charged interest at current market rates, and the long-term debt had just been issued. Book and market values could not differ by much.
- But the preferred stock had been issued 35 years ago, when interest rates were much lower. The preferred stock, originally issued at a book value of $100 per share, was now trading for only $70 per share.

FIGURE 13.2 Mr. Brinepool's cost of capital memo

Sea Shore Salt Company
Spring Vacation Beach, Florida

CONFIDENTIAL MEMORANDUM

DATE: January 15, 2016
TO: S.S.S. Management
FROM: Joe-Bob Brinepool, President
SUBJECT: Cost of Capital

This memo states and clarifies our company's long-standing policy regarding hurdle rates for capital investment decisions. There have been many recent questions, and some evident confusion, on this matter.

Sea Shore Salt evaluates replacement and expansion investments by discounted cash flow. The discount or hurdle rate is the company's after-tax weighted-average cost of capital.

The weighted-average cost of capital is simply a blend of the rates of return expected by investors in our company. These investors include banks, bondholders, and preferred stock investors in addition to common stockholders. Of course many of you are, or soon will be, stockholders of our company.

The following table summarizes the composition of Sea Shore Salt's financing.

	Amount (in millions)	Percent of Total	Rate of Return
Bank loan	$120	20.0%	8%
Bond issue	80	13.3	7.75
Preferred stock	100	16.7	6
Common stock	300	50.0	16
	$600	100.0%	

The rates of return on the bank loan and bond issue are of course just the interest rates we pay. However, interest is tax-deductible, so the after-tax interest rates are lower than shown above. For example, the after-tax cost of our bank financing, given our 35% tax rate, is $8(1 - .35) = 5.2\%$.

The rate of return on preferred stock is 6%. Sea Shore Salt pays a $6 dividend on each $100 preferred share.

Our target rate of return on equity has been 16% for many years. I know that some newcomers think this target is too high for the safe and mature salt business. But we must all aspire to superior profitability.

Once this background is absorbed, the calculation of Sea Shore Salt's weighted-average cost of capital (WACC) is elementary:

$$\text{WACC} = 8(1 - .35)(.20) + 7.75(1 - .35)(.133) + 6(.167) + 16(.50) = 10.7\%$$

The official corporate hurdle rate is therefore 10.7%.

If you have further questions about these calculations, please direct them to our new Treasury Analyst, Ms. Bernice Mountaindog. It is a pleasure to have Bernice back at Sea Shore Salt after a year's leave of absence to complete her degree in finance.

TABLE 13.6 Sea Shore Salt's balance sheet, taken from the company's 2015 balance sheet (figures in $millions)

Assets		Liabilities and Net Worth	
Working capital	$200	Bank loan	$120
Plant and equipment	360	Long-term debt	80
Other assets	40	Preferred stock	100
		Common stock, including retained earnings	300
Total	$600	Total	$600

Notes:
1. At year-end 2015, Sea Shore Salt had 10 million common shares outstanding.
2. The company had also issued 1 million preferred shares with book value of $100 per share. Each share receives an annual dividend of $6.

- The common stock traded for $40 per share. Next year's earnings per share would be about $4 and dividends per share probably $2. (Ten million shares of common stock are outstanding.) Sea Shore Salt had traditionally paid out 50% of earnings as dividends and plowed back the rest.
- Earnings and dividends had grown steadily at 6% to 7% per year, in line with the company's sustainable growth rate:

$$\frac{\text{Sustainable}}{\text{growth rate}} = \frac{\text{return}}{\text{on equity}} \times \frac{\text{plowback}}{\text{ratio}}$$

$$= 4/30 \times .5$$

$$= .067, \text{ or } 6.7\%$$

Sea Shore Salt's beta had averaged about .5, which made sense, Bernice thought, for a stable, steady-growth business. She made a quick cost of equity calculation by using the capital asset pricing model (CAPM). With current interest rates of about 7%, and a market risk premium of 7%,

$$\text{CAPM cost of equity} = r_E = r_f + \beta(r_m - r_f)$$

$$= 7\% + .5(7\%) = 10.5\%$$

This cost of equity was significantly less than the 16% decreed in Mr. Brinepool's memo. Bernice scanned her notes apprehensively. What if Mr. Brinepool's cost of equity was wrong? Was there some other way to estimate the cost of equity as a check on the CAPM calculation? Could there be other errors in his calculations?

Bernice resolved to complete her analysis that night. If necessary, she would try to speak with Mr. Brinepool when he arrived at his office the next morning. Her job was not just finding the right number. She also had to figure out how to explain it all to Mr. Brinepool.

14

Introduction to Corporate Financing

LEARNING OBJECTIVES

After studying this chapter, you should be able to:

14-1 Explain why managers should assume that the securities they issue are fairly priced.

14-2 Summarize the changing ways that U.S. firms have financed their growth.

14-3 Interpret shareholder equity accounts in the firm's financial statements.

14-4 Describe voting procedures for the election of a firm's board of directors and other matters.

14-5 Describe the major classes of securities sold by the firm.

RELATED WEBSITES FOR THIS CHAPTER CAN BE FOUND IN CONNECT.

This is not the place where corporations go to raise the funds that they need. It is time to start learning about the different sources of finance. © Roberto Herrett/Alamy

Up to this point, we have concentrated almost exclusively on the firm's capital expenditure decisions. Now we move to the other side of the balance sheet to look at how the firm can finance those capital expenditures. To put it crudely, you have learned how to spend money; now you must learn how to raise it. In the next few chapters, therefore, we assume that the firm has already decided on which investment projects to accept, and we focus on the best way to finance these projects.

You will find that, in some ways, financing decisions are more complicated than investment decisions. You'll need to learn about the wide variety of securities that companies can issue. But there are also ways in which financing decisions are easier than investment decisions. For example, financing decisions do not have the same degree of finality as investment decisions. When Ford Motor Company decides to issue a bond, it knows that it can buy it back later if second thoughts arise.

It would be far more difficult for Ford to dismantle or sell an auto factory that is no longer needed.

In later chapters, we will look at some of the classic finance problems, such as how much firms should borrow and what dividends they should pay their shareholders. In this chapter, we set the scene with a brief overview of the types of long-term finance.

We begin our discussion of financing with a basic conceptual point. It is easier to make shareholders wealthier by your investment decisions than by your financing decisions. As we explain, competition between investors makes it difficult to find (or to issue) misvalued securities.

We then introduce you to the principal sources of finance, and we show how they are used by corporations. It is customary to classify these sources of finance as debt or equity. However, we will see that a simple division of sources of finance into debt and equity would miss the enormous variety of financing instruments that companies use today.

14.1 Creating Value with Financing Decisions

Smart investment decisions make shareholders wealthier. So do smart financing decisions. For example, if your company can borrow at 3% when the going rate is 4%, you have done your shareholders a good turn.

Unfortunately, this is more easily said than done. The problem is that competition in financial markets is more intense than in most product markets. In product markets, companies regularly find competitive advantages that allow positive-NPV investments. For example, a company may have only a few competitors that specialize in the same line of business in the same geographic area. Or it may be able to capitalize on patents or technology or on customer recognition and loyalty. All this opens up the opportunity to make superior profits and find projects with positive NPVs.

But there are few protected niches in *financial* markets. You can't patent the design of a new security. Moreover, in these markets you always face fast-moving competition, including all the other corporations seeking funds, to say nothing of the state, local, and federal governments, financial institutions, individuals, and foreign firms and governments that also come to New York, London, or Tokyo for financing. The investors who supply financing are numerous, and they are smart. Most likely, these investors can assess the values of securities at least as well as you can.

Of course, when you borrow, you would like to pay less than the going rate of interest. But if the loan is a good deal for your shareholders, it must be a bad deal for the lenders. So what are the chances that your firm could consistently trick investors into overpaying for its securities? Pretty slim. In general, firms should assume that financing will be raised on fair terms—in other words, that the securities they issue sell for their true values.

But what do we mean by *true value*? It is a potentially slippery phrase. True value does not mean ultimate future value—we do not expect investors to be fortune-tellers. It means a price that incorporates all the information *currently* available to investors. We came across this idea in Chapter 7, when we introduced the concept of *efficient capital markets* and showed how difficult it is for investors to obtain consistently superior performance. In an efficient capital market, all securities are fairly priced given the information available to investors. In that case, the sale of securities at their market price can never be a positive-NPV transaction.

All this means that it's harder to make or lose money by smart or stupid financing strategies. It is difficult to make money—that is, to find cheap financing—because the investors who supply the financing demand fair terms. At the same time, it's harder to lose money because competition among investors prevents any one of them from demanding more than fair terms.

Just remember as you read the following chapters: There are few free lunches on Wall Street . . . and few easy answers for the financial manager who must make corporate financing decisions.

14.2 Patterns of Corporate Financing

Firms have three broad sources of cash: They can plow back part of their profits, or they can raise money externally by an issue of either shares or debt. Look, for example, at Figure 14.1, which shows how FedEx and Dow Chemical (now part of DowDuPont) generated cash between 1990 and 2014. In each panel, the orange line shows the percentage yearly addition to the firm's capital provided by the sale of shares. The green line shows the addition that came from new issues of long- or short-term debt, and the blue line shows the contribution from **internally generated funds** (defined as depreciation plus earnings that are not paid out as dividends[1]).

internally generated funds
Cash reinvested in the firm; depreciation plus earnings not paid out as dividends.

---

[1] Remember that depreciation is a *noncash* expense. This means that it is treated as an expense even though it does not represent a use of cash. Therefore, we add it back to earnings to find the cash flow generated by the firm.

FIGURE 14.1 Sources of funds for FedEx and Dow Chemical

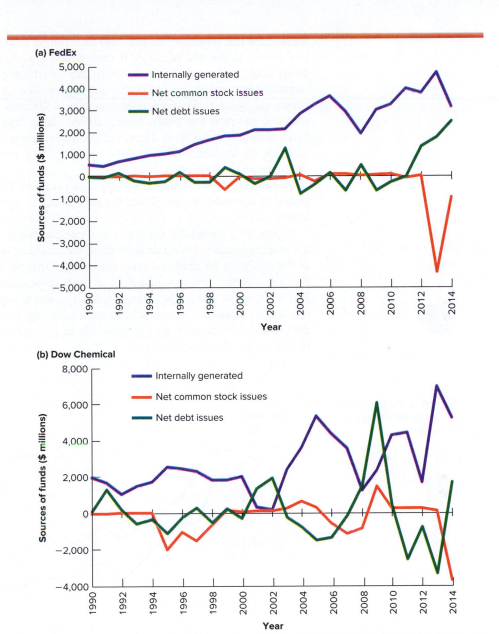

(a) FedEx

(b) Dow Chemical

There are both some similarities and some differences in our two examples. Let's start with the similarities. By far, the largest source of cash for both companies came from plowing back profits. The gap between this internally generated cash and the cash that the company needs is called the **financial deficit.** To make up the deficit, the company must either sell new equity or borrow. Neither FedEx nor Dow raised significant amounts of cash by selling new shares. In fact, as often as not they *used* cash to buy back shares that had been issued in earlier years. In Figure 14.1, these repurchases show up as negative issues of common stock. Toward the end of this period, both firms engaged in large stock repurchases, FedEx in 2013 and Dow in 2014. In total, over the 25-year period, both firms repurchased far more shares than they issued. (Dow made an issue of preferred stock in 2009. This is not shown in Figure 14.1.)

Instead of issuing equity, both companies occasionally raised considerable funds through large new issues of debt, but they did so for somewhat different reasons. For example, FedEx bought Kinko's in early 2004 for $2.4 billion in cash. To help

financial deficit
Difference between the cash companies need and the amount generated internally.

prepare for this purchase, FedEx sold $1.9 billion of short-term debt, called *commercial paper*, at the end of 2003. It then issued a package of 1-, 3-, and 5-year unsecured notes and used the proceeds to pay off the commercial paper. Much of this increased borrowing was also subsequently repaid over the next 4 years. Figure 14.1*a* shows the spike in FedEx's debt issuance in 2003 as well as the negative net debt issues in the next few years. FedEx's even larger debt issues in 2012 through 2014 had a different motivation. Here, the company seems to have deliberately decided to increase its leverage, issuing debt to raise the funds required for its large stock repurchases in those years.

In contrast, Dow Chemical's large debt issues in 2002 and 2009 coincided with a period of operating losses. Thus, the debt issues in those years largely substituted for internal funds.

Figure 14.2 shows the net effect of these financing decisions on the debt ratios of the two companies. Debt ratios here are measured in two ways: using the book value of the equity or its market value. For most of this period FedEx's steady accumulation of internal funds resulted in a fairly continuous decline in the debt ratio. But starting in 2012, the company's large stock repurchases and issues of debt resulted in dramatic increases in its debt ratio. By contrast, Dow's issues of debt in 2002 and 2009 to make up for shortfalls in profitability resulted in sharp increases in its debt ratio in those years.

FIGURE 14.2 Ratio of debt to debt plus equity for FedEx and Dow Chemical

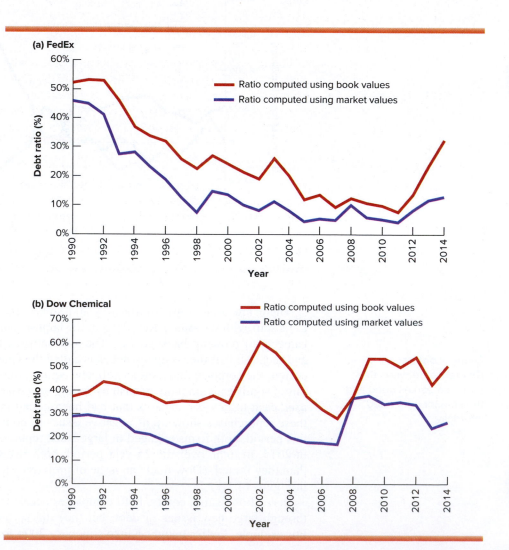

FIGURE 14.3 Sources of funds for U.S. nonfinancial corporations, 1991–2014

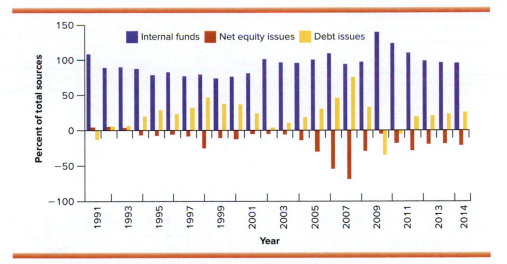

Source: Board of Governors of the Federal Reserve System, Division of Research and Statistics, "Financial Accounts of the United States," Table F.103, at **www.federalreserve.gov/releases/z1/current/data.htm**.

There is nothing particularly remarkable about the financial structure of either FedEx or Dow. However, some companies, such as Google, rely almost entirely on internal funds and have no debt. Others, such as Marriott, are at the opposite extreme. Marriott has $3.5 billion of long-term debt, and the book value of its equity is negative at −$2.2 billion.[2]

Figure 14.3 shows how corporate America as a whole has financed its investments. Notice again the importance of internal funds. Over the 24-year period, internally generated cash covered 95% of corporate capital requirements. The gap was more than made up by borrowing.[3] Equity issues in each year since 1994 have been negative; firms used some of their new cash to buy back stock.

Are Firms Issuing Too Much Debt?

We have seen that rather than sell additional common stock, firms have, on average, issued debt and used part of the proceeds to buy back some of their stock. Has this policy resulted in an increase in the proportion of debt that companies use?

Figure 14.4 provides some long-term perspective on the question. If all U.S. manufacturing corporations were merged into a single gigantic firm, this would be its ratio of debt to total capital. Debt ratios are lower when computed from market rather than book values. This is because the market value of equity is substantially greater than book value for most firms. Debt ratios using either measure increased until about 1990, but since then they have generally declined.[4]

Should we be worried when book debt ratios increase? It is true that high debt ratios mean that more companies are likely to fall into financial distress when a serious recession hits the economy. Undoubtedly GM, Chrysler, American Airlines, and the many other companies that faced insolvency in the recent recession would all have been in a stronger position if they had carried less debt. But it does not always follow that less risk is better. Finding the optimal debt ratio is like finding the optimal speed

---

[2] In other words, Marriott's accumulated losses exceed the total cumulative amount that it has raised from shareholders.

[3] The *type* of debt that firms use varies from year to year. For example, in 2009 the financial crisis led firms to repay bank debt and to issue instead huge amounts of corporate bonds. These variations do not show up in Figure 14.3.

[4] The rise in debt ratios in the first part of the period was not due to stock repurchases, since these were relatively uncommon until the mid-1980s.

FIGURE 14.4 The ratio of debt to debt plus equity for the nonfinancial corporate sector

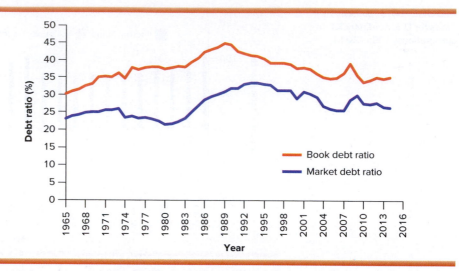

Source: Board of Governors of the Federal Reserve System, Division of Research and Statistics, "Financial Accounts of the United States," Table B.102, at **www.federalreserve.gov/releases/z1/current/data.htm**.

limit; we can agree that accidents at 30 miles per hour are less dangerous, other things being equal, than accidents at 60 miles per hour, but we do not, therefore, set the national speed limit at 30. Speed has benefits as well as risks. So does debt, as we will see in Chapter 16.

14.1   Self-Test

a. Which of the following sources of financing is most important for U.S. corporations as a whole: internal funds, net new borrowing, or stock issues?

b. Figure 14.3 indicates that net equity issues are negative for U.S. corporations as a whole. How is that possible? Don't U.S. corporations ever issue common stock?

14.3   Common Stock

We will now look more closely at the different sources of finance, starting with common stock. We will stick with our example of FedEx.

Most major corporations are far too large to be owned by one investor. For example, you would need to lay your hands on nearly $41 billion if you wanted to own the whole of FedEx. Therefore, the equity in large firms like FedEx is typically held by hundreds of thousands of different investors, each of whom holds a number of shares of common stock. These investors are therefore known as *shareholders,* or *stockholders.* At the end of 2014, FedEx had outstanding 276 million shares of common stock. Thus, if you were to buy one FedEx share, you would own 1/276,000,000, or about .00000036%, of the company. Of course, a large pension fund might hold many thousands of FedEx shares.

While 276 million shares are currently held by investors, FedEx has actually issued a total of 318 million shares. The difference in these values reflects 42 million shares that FedEx has bought back from investors. These repurchased shares are held in the company's treasury and are, therefore, known as **treasury stock.** The shares held by investors are said to be **issued** and **outstanding shares.** By contrast, treasury shares are said to be *issued but not outstanding.*

treasury stock
Stock that has been repurchased by the company and is held in its treasury.

issued shares
Shares that have been issued by the company.

outstanding shares
Shares that have been issued by the company and are held by investors.

If FedEx wishes to raise more money, it can sell more shares. However, there is a limit to the number that it can issue without the approval of the current shareholders. The maximum number of shares that can be issued is known as the **authorized share capital**—for FedEx, this is 800 million shares. FedEx has already issued 318 million shares, so it can issue nearly 500 million more without shareholders' approval.

Table 14.1 shows how the investment by FedEx's common stockholders is recorded in the company's books. The price at which each share is recorded is known as its **par value.** In FedEx's case each share has a par value of $.10. Thus, the total par value of the issued shares is 318 million shares × $.10 per share = $31.8 million. Par value has little economic significance.[5]

The price at which new shares are sold to investors almost always exceeds par value. The difference is entered into the company's accounts as **additional paid-in capital,** or *capital surplus.* For example, if FedEx sold an additional 1 million shares at $150 a share, the par value of the common stock would increase by 1 million × $.10 = $.1 million and additional paid-in capital would increase by 1 million × ($150 − $.10) = $149.9 million. You can see from this example that the funds raised from the stock issue are divided between par value and additional paid-in capital. Because the choice of par value in the first place was immaterial, so is the allocation between par value and additional paid-in capital.

Besides buying new stock, shareholders also indirectly contribute new capital to the firm whenever profits that could be paid out as dividends are instead plowed back into the company. Table 14.1 shows that **retained earnings,** the cumulative value of such reinvested profits, are $16,900 million.

Any money that FedEx spent to buy Treasury stock would also be shown on the balance sheet. Such money has been returned to stockholders and is, therefore, deducted from the stockholders' equity.

The sum of the par value, additional paid-in capital, and retained earnings, less repurchased stock and some miscellaneous other adjustments, is known as the *net common equity* of the firm. It equals the total amount contributed directly by shareholders when the firm issued new stock and indirectly when it plowed back part of its earnings. The book value of FedEx's net common equity is $14,993 million. With 276 million shares outstanding, this is equivalent to 14,993/276 = $54.32 a share. But the market price of FedEx's stock is about $150 per share, much higher than its book value. Evidently investors believe that FedEx's assets are worth much more than they originally cost.

authorized share capital
Maximum number of shares that the company is permitted to issue without shareholder approval.

par value
Value of security shown in the company's accounts.

additional paid-in capital
Difference between issue price and par value of stock. Also called *capital surplus.*

retained earnings
Earnings not paid out as dividends.

TABLE 14.1 Book value of common stockholders' equity of FedEx, May 31, 2014 (figures in $ millions)

Common shares ($.10 par value per share)	$ 32
Additional paid-in capital	2,786
Retained earnings	16,900
Treasury shares at cost	(4,897)
Other	172
Net common equity	$14,993
Note:	
Authorized shares (millions)	800
Issued shares, of which	318
Outstanding shares	276
Treasury shares	42

[5] Some companies issue shares with no par value, in which case the stock is listed in the accounts at an arbitrarily determined figure.

Ownership of the Corporation

A corporation is owned by its common stockholders. Some of this common stock is held directly by individual investors, but the greater proportion belongs to financial institutions such as mutual funds, pension funds, and insurance companies. For example, look at Figure 14.5. You can see that in the United States, almost 50% of common stock is held by U.S. financial institutions, with mutual funds holding about 26% and pension funds a further 14%.

What do we mean when we say that the stockholders *own* the corporation? First, the stockholders are entitled to whatever profits are left over after the lenders have received their due. Usually the company pays out part of these profits as dividends and plows back the remainder into new investments. Shareholders hope that these investments will enable the company to earn higher profits and pay higher dividends in the future.

Second, shareholders have the ultimate control over how the company is run. This does not mean that shareholders can do whatever they like. For example, the bank that lends to the company may place restrictions on how much extra borrowing the company can undertake. However, the contract with the bank can never restrict *all* the actions that the company might wish to undertake. The shareholders retain the residual rights of control over these decisions.

FIGURE 14.5 Holdings of corporate equities, September 30, 2015

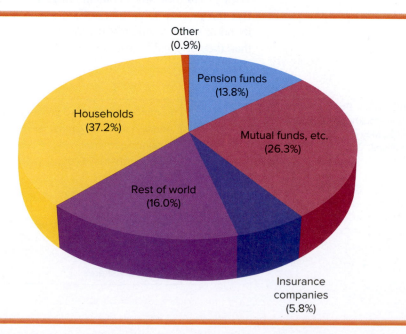

Source: Board of Governors of the Federal Reserve System, Division of Research and Statistics, "Financial Accounts of the United States," Table L.213, at **www.federalreserve.gov/releases/z1/current/data.htm**.

Occasionally, the company must get shareholder approval before it can take certain actions. For example, it needs shareholder agreement to increase the authorized capital or to merge with another company. On most other matters, shareholder control boils down to the right to vote on appointments to the board of directors.

The board of directors is supposed to represent the shareholders' interests. The board appoints and oversees management and must vote to approve important financial decisions, including major capital investments, payment of dividends, share repurchase programs, and new stock issues.

For public companies, the board usually includes the CEO, perhaps one or two other members of top management, and outside directors, who are not employees. The New York and NASDAQ stock exchanges require that a majority of the board consist of *independent* outside directors. Independent directors have "no material relationship" with the company aside from their service as directors and their ownership of the company's shares.

The CEO has traditionally also served as the *chair* of the board. The chair has extra influence, because he or she can set the agenda, which guides the board's deliberations. Some companies appoint a nonexecutive chair, thus separating the roles of chair and CEO and reducing the CEO's influence. In some other countries, such as Canada and the United Kingdom, the roles of chair and CEO are almost always separated.

The board compensation committee, which approves compensation for managers, must be entirely composed of independent directors. The compensation package is described in an annual Compensation Discussion and Analysis (CD&A), which is sent to shareholders along with director nominations and the company's annual report. Shareholders must be offered a nonbinding yes-or-no vote on the CD&A at least once every 3 years. The occasional "no" vote on management compensation is a disagreeable wake-up call for managers and directors. For example, when the shareholders of Charles River Laboratories voted "no" in 2013, the company made a number of changes to the compensation package before seeking (and obtaining) shareholder approval in 2014.

Voting Procedures

For many U.S. companies, the entire board of directors comes up for reelection every year. However, approximately 10% of large companies have *classified boards*, in which only one-third of the directors come up for reelection each year. Shareholder activists complain that such staggered elections make it more difficult for a dissident group of shareholders to replace the board and, therefore, help to entrench management. Staggered elections appear to protect management, deter proxy contests, and reduce the degree to which CEO compensation is linked to firm performance. In recent years, many companies have been successfully pressured by their shareholders to declassify their boards; declassification has generally resulted in an increase in stock price.

majority voting
Voting system in which each director is voted on separately.

In most companies, stockholders elect directors by a system of **majority voting.** In this case, each director is voted on separately, and stockholders can cast one vote for each share they own. In some companies, directors are elected by **cumulative voting.** The directors are then voted on jointly, and the stockholders can, if they choose, cast all their votes for just one candidate. For example, suppose that there are five directors to be elected and you own 100 shares. You, therefore, have a total of $5 \times 100 = 500$ votes. Under majority voting, you can cast a maximum of 100 votes for any one candidate. With a cumulative voting system, you can cast all 500 votes for your favorite candidate. Cumulative voting makes it easier for a minority group of the stockholders to elect a director to represent their interests. That is why minority groups devote so much effort to campaigning for cumulative voting.

cumulative voting
Voting system in which all the votes a shareholder is allowed to cast can be cast for one candidate for the board of directors.

On many issues, a simple majority of the votes cast is enough to carry the day, but there are some decisions that require a "supermajority" of, say, 75% of those eligible to vote. For example, a supermajority vote is sometimes needed to approve a merger. This makes it difficult for the firm to be taken over and, therefore, helps to protect the incumbent management.

Shareholders can either vote in person or appoint a proxy to vote. The issues on which they are asked to vote are rarely contested, particularly in the case of large publicly traded firms. Occasionally, however, there are **proxy contests** in which outsiders compete with the firm's existing management and directors for control of the corporation. But the odds are stacked against the outsiders, for the insiders can get the firm to pay all the costs of presenting their case and obtaining votes.

Classes of Stock

BEYOND THE PAGE

Alibaba and dual-class shares

mhhe.com/brealey9e

Usually companies have one class of common stock and each share has one vote. Occasionally, however, a firm may have two classes of stock outstanding, which differ in their right to vote. For example, when Google made its first issue of common stock, the founders were reluctant to give up control of the company. Therefore, the company created two classes of shares. The A shares, which were sold to the public, had 1 vote each, while the B shares, which were owned by the founders, had 10 votes each. Both classes of shares had the same cash-flow rights, but they had different control rights.

BEYOND THE PAGE

Google's stock split

mhhe.com/brealey9e

In some countries it is fairly common for firms to issue two classes of stock with different voting rights. That may be a good thing if the controlling shareholders then use their influence to improve profitability. However, you can see the dangers here. If an idle or incompetent management has a large block of votes, it may use these votes to stay in control. Or if another corporation has a controlling stake, it may exercise its influence to gain a business advantage.

14.4 Preferred Stock

BEYOND THE PAGE

Voting rights and private benefits

mhhe.com/brealey9e

Usually when investors talk about equity or stock, they are referring to common stock. But some companies also issue **preferred stock,** and this too is part of the company's equity. The sum of a company's common equity and preferred stock is known as its **net worth.**

For most companies, preferred stock is much less important than common stock. However, it can be a useful method of financing in mergers and certain other special situations.

Like debt, preferred stock promises a series of fixed payments to the investor, and with relatively few exceptions, preferred dividends are paid in full and on time. Nevertheless, preferred stock is legally an equity security. This is because payment of a preferred dividend is within the discretion of the directors. The only obligation is that no dividends can be paid on the common stock until the preferred dividend has been paid.[6] If the company goes out of business, the preferred stockholders get in the queue after the debtholders but before the common stockholders.

Preferred stock rarely confers full voting privileges. This is an advantage to firms that want to raise new money without sharing control of the firm with the new share-holders. However, if there is any matter that affects their place in the queue, preferred stockholders usually get to vote on it. Most issues also provide the holder with some voting power if the preferred dividend is skipped.

Companies cannot deduct preferred dividends when they calculate taxable income. Like common stock dividends, preferred dividends are paid from after-tax income. For most industrial firms, this is a serious deterrent to issuing preferred. However, regulated public utilities can take tax payments into account when they negotiate with regulators the rates they charge customers. So they can effectively pass the tax disadvantage of preferred on to the consumer. Preferred stock also has a particular attraction for banks because regulators allow banks to lump preferred in with common stock when calculating whether they have sufficient equity capital.

---

[6] These days this obligation is usually cumulative. In other words, before the common stockholders get a cent, the firm must pay any preferred dividends that have been missed in the past.

Preferred stock does have one tax advantage. If one corporation buys another's stock, only 30% of the dividends it receives is taxed. This rule applies to dividends on both common and preferred stock, but it is most important for preferred, for which returns are dominated by dividends rather than capital gains.

Suppose that your firm has surplus cash to invest. If it buys a bond, the interest will be taxed at the company's tax rate of 35%. If it buys a preferred share, it owns an asset like a bond (the preferred dividends can be viewed as "interest"), but the effective tax rate is only 30% of 35%, $.30 \times .35 = .105$, or 10.5%. It is no surprise that most preferred shares are held by corporations.

If you invest your firm's spare cash in a preferred stock, you will want to make sure that when it is time to sell the stock, it won't have plummeted in value. One problem with garden-variety preferred stock that pays a fixed dividend is that the preferred's market prices go up and down as interest rates change (because present values fall when rates rise). So one ingenious banker thought up a wrinkle: Why not link the dividend on the preferred stock to interest rates so that it goes up when interest rates rise and vice versa? The result is known as **floating-rate preferred.** If you own floating-rate preferred, you know that any change in interest rates will be counterbalanced by a change in the dividend payment, so the value of your investment is protected.

floating-rate preferred
Preferred stock for which the dividend rate is linked to current market interest rates.

14.3 Self-Test

A company in a 35% tax bracket can buy a bond yielding 10% or a preferred stock of the same firm that is priced to yield 8%. Which will provide the higher after-tax yield?

14.5 Corporate Debt

When they borrow money, companies promise to make regular interest payments and to repay the principal (i.e., the original amount borrowed). **However, corporations have limited liability. By this we mean that the promise to repay the debt is not always kept. If the company gets into deep water, the company has the right to default on the debt and to hand over its assets to the lenders.**

Clearly it will choose bankruptcy only if the value of the assets is less than the amount of the debt. In practice, when companies go bankrupt, this handover of assets is far from straightforward. For example, when Lehman Brothers filed for bankruptcy, the bankruptcy court was faced with 65,000 claims from creditors. The cost of shepherding Lehman through bankruptcy surpassed $2 billion.

Because lenders are not regarded as owners of the firm, they don't normally have any voting power. Also, the company's payments of interest are regarded as a cost and are therefore deducted from taxable income. Thus interest is paid out of *before-tax* income, whereas dividends on common and preferred stock are paid out of *after-tax* income. This means that the government provides a tax subsidy on the use of debt, which it does not provide on stock. We cover debt and taxes in Chapter 16.

Debt Comes in Many Forms

Some orderly scheme of classification is essential to cope with the almost endless variety of debt issues. We will walk you through the major distinguishing characteristics.

Interest Rate   The interest payment, or *coupon,* on most long-term loans is fixed at the time of issue. If a $1,000 bond is issued with a coupon of 10%, the firm continues to pay $100 a year regardless of how interest rates change. You may also encounter zero-coupon bonds. In this case, the firm does not make a regular interest payment. It just makes a single payment at maturity. Obviously, investors pay less for zero-coupon bonds.

Most loans from a bank and some long-term loans carry a *floating interest rate.* For example, your firm may be offered a loan at "1 percent over prime." The **prime rate** is the benchmark interest rate charged by banks to large customers with good to excellent credit. (But the largest and most creditworthy corporations can, and do, borrow at *less* than prime.) The prime rate is adjusted up and down with the general level of interest rates. When the prime rate changes, the interest on your floating-rate loan also changes.

Floating-rate loans are not always tied to the prime rate. Often they are tied to the rate at which international banks lend to one another. This is known as the *London Interbank Offered Rate,* or *LIBOR.*

prime rate
Benchmark interest rate charged by banks.

14.4 Self-Test

Would you expect the price of a 10-year floating-rate bond to be more or less sensitive to changes in interest rates than the price of a 10-year maturity fixed-rate bond?

---

funded debt
Debt with more than 1 year remaining to maturity.

Maturity   **Funded debt** is any debt repayable more than 1 year from the date of issue. Debt due in less than a year is termed *unfunded* and is carried on the balance sheet as a current liability. Unfunded debt is often described as short-term debt, and funded debt is described as long-term, although it is clearly artificial to call a 364-day debt short-term and a 366-day debt long-term (except in leap years).

There are corporate bonds of nearly every conceivable maturity. For example, in 2014, the French utility company EDF issued bonds that do not mature for 100 years. Some British banks have issued perpetuities—that is, bonds that may survive forever. At the other extreme, we find firms borrowing literally overnight.

sinking fund
Fund established to retire debt before maturity.

Repayment Provisions   Long-term loans are commonly repaid in a steady, regular way, perhaps after an initial grace period. For bonds that are publicly traded, this is done by means of a **sinking fund.** Each year, the firm puts aside a sum of cash into a sinking fund that is then used to buy back the bonds. When there is a sinking fund, investors are prepared to lend at a lower rate of interest. They know that they are more likely to be repaid if the company sets aside some cash each year than if the entire loan has to be repaid on one specified day.

Suppose that a company issues a 6%, 30-year bond at a price of $1,000. Five years later, interest rates have fallen to 4%, and the price of the bond has risen dramatically. If you were the company's treasurer, wouldn't you like to be able to retire the bonds and issue some new bonds at the lower interest rate? Well, with some bonds, known as **callable bonds,** the company does have the option to buy them back for the *call price.*[7] Of course, holders of these callable bonds know that the company will wish to buy the issue back if interest rates fall, and therefore, the price of the bond will not rise above the call price.

Figure 14.6 shows the risk of a call to the bondholder. The blue line is the value of a 30-year, 6% "straight," that is, noncallable, bond; the orange line is the value of a bond with the same coupon rate and maturity but callable at $1,060 (i.e., 106% of face value). At very high interest rates, the risk that the company will call the bonds is

callable bond
Bond that may be repurchased by the issuing firm before maturity at a specified call price.

---

[7] Sometimes callable bonds specify a period during which the firm is not allowed to call the bond if the purpose is simply to issue another bond at a lower interest rate.

FIGURE 14.6 Prices of callable versus straight debt. When interest rates fall, bond prices rise. But the price of the callable bond (orange line) is limited by the call price.

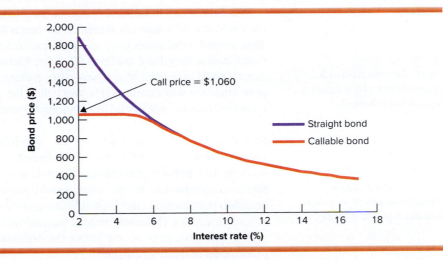

negligible, and the values of the two bonds are nearly identical. As rates fall, the straight bond continues to increase steadily in value, but because the capital appreciation of the callable bond is limited by the call price, its capital appreciation will lag behind that of the straight bond.

14.5   Self-Test

Suppose FedEx is considering two issues of 20-year maturity coupon bonds; one issue will be callable, the other not. For a given coupon rate, will the callable or noncallable bond sell at the higher price? If the bonds are both to be sold to the public at face value, which bond must have the higher coupon rate?

Country and Currency   These days, capital markets know few national boundaries and many large firms in the United States borrow abroad. For example, an American company may choose to finance a new plant in Switzerland by borrowing Swiss francs from a Swiss bank, or it may expand its Dutch operation by issuing a bond in Holland. Also many foreign companies come to the United States to borrow dollars, which are then used to finance their operations throughout the world.

In addition to these national capital markets, there is an international capital market centered mainly in London. Banks from all over the world have branches in London. They include such giants as Citicorp, UBS, Deutsche Bank, Bank of China, Mitsubishi UFJ, HSBC, and BNP Paribas. One reason they are there is to collect deposits in the major currencies. For example, suppose an Arab sheikh has just received payment in dollars for a large sale of oil. Rather than depositing the check in the United States, he may choose to open a dollar account with a bank in London. Dollars held in a bank outside the United States came to be known as **eurodollars.** Similarly, yen held outside Japan were termed euroyen, and so on.

eurodollars
Dollars held on deposit in a bank outside the United States.

The London bank branch that is holding the sheikh's dollar deposit may temporarily lend those dollars to a company, in the same way that a bank in the United States may relend dollars that have been deposited with it. Thus, a company can either borrow dollars from a bank in the United States or borrow dollars from a bank in London.[8]

[8] Because the Federal Reserve requires banks in the United States to keep interest-free reserves, there is in effect a tax on dollar deposits in the United States. Overseas dollar deposits are free of this tax, and therefore banks can afford to charge the borrower slightly lower interest rates.

If a firm wants to make an issue of long-term bonds, it can choose to do so in the United States. Alternatively, it can sell the bonds to investors in several countries. Because these international issues have usually been marketed by the London branches of international banks, they have traditionally been known as **eurobonds.** A eurobond may be denominated in dollars, yen, or any other currency. Unfortunately, when the single European currency was established it was called the *euro*. It is easy, therefore, to confuse a *eurobond* (a bond that is sold internationally) with a bond that is denominated in *euros*.

eurobond
Bond denominated in a currency not of the country in which it is issued.

Public versus Private Placements   Publicly issued bonds are sold to anyone who wishes to buy, and once they have been issued, they can be freely traded in the securities markets. In a **private placement,** the issue is sold directly to a small number of banks, insurance companies, or other investment institutions. Privately placed bonds cannot be resold to individuals in the United States and can be resold only to other qualified institutional investors. However, there is increasingly active trading *among* these investors.

private placement
Sale of securities to a limited number of investors without a public offering.

We will have more to say about the difference between public issues and private placements in the next chapter.

A Debt by Any Other Name   The word *debt* sounds straightforward, but companies enter into a number of financial arrangements that look suspiciously like debt, yet are treated differently in the accounts. Some of these obligations are easily identifiable. For example, accounts payable are simply obligations to pay for goods that have already been delivered and are, therefore, like a short-term debt.

Other arrangements are not so easy to spot. For example, instead of borrowing money to buy equipment, many companies **lease** or rent it on a long-term basis. In this case, the firm promises to make a series of payments to the lessor (the owner of the equipment). This is just like the obligation to make payments on an outstanding loan. What if the firm can't make the payments? The lessor can then take back the equipment, which is precisely what would happen if the firm had *borrowed* money from the lessor, using the equipment as collateral for the loan.

lease
Long-term rental agreement.

Postretirement health benefits and pension promises can also be huge liabilities for firms. For example, at the start of 2015, Ford faced an estimated $9 billion deficit on its pension plan. That is a debt the company will eventually need to pay.

There is nothing underhanded about such obligations. They are clearly shown on the company's balance sheet as a liability. Sometimes, however, companies go to considerable lengths to ensure that investors do *not* know how much they have borrowed. For example, Enron was able to borrow $658 million by setting up *special-purpose entities (SPEs)*, which raised cash by a mixture of equity and debt and then used that debt to help fund the parent company. None of this debt showed up on Enron's balance sheet.

Example   14.1 ▶   The Terms of Apple's Bond Issue

In February 2015, Apple made a huge $6.5 billion issue of debt. Part of this issue was in the form of 30-year bonds. Now that you are familiar with some of the jargon, you might like to look at Table 14.2, which summarizes the terms of Apple's bond issue. We have added some explanatory notes. ■

Innovation in the Debt Market

BEYOND THE PAGE

Innovations in bond design

mhhe.com/brealey9e

We have discussed domestic bonds and eurobonds, fixed-rate and floating-rate loans, secured and unsecured loans, and much more. You might think that this gives you all the choice you need. Yet issuers are always trying to devise new types of bonds that they hope will appeal to a particular clientele of investors. Just to give you a flavor of the inventiveness of financial managers, here are two examples of innovative bonds.

TABLE 14.2 Apple's debt issue

Comment	Description of Bond
1. Interest of 3.45% will be payable on February 9 and August 9 of each year. Thus every 6 months each note will pay interest of (.0345/2) × $1,000 = $17.25.	ISSUE: Apple Inc. 3.45% Notes
2. Investors will be repaid the $1,000 face value in 2045.	DUE: February 9, 2045
3. Moody's bond rating is Aa, the second-highest-quality rating.	RATING: Aa
4. A trustee is appointed to look after investors' interest.	TRUSTEE: Issued under an indenture between Apple and The Bank of New York Mellon Trust Company
5. The bonds are registered. The registrar keeps a record of who owns the bonds.	REGISTERED: Issued in registered, book-entry form
6. The company is not obliged to repay any of the bonds on a regular basis before maturity.	SINKING FUND: None
7. The company has the option to buy back the notes. The redemption price is the greater of $1,000 or a price that is determined by the value of an equivalent Treasury bond.	CALLABLE: In whole or in part at any time
8. The notes are senior debt, ranking equally with all Apple's other unsecured senior debt.	SENIORITY
9. The notes are not secured; that is, no assets have been set aside to protect the noteholders in the event of default. However, if Apple sets aside assets to protect any other bondholders, the notes will also be secured by these assets. This is termed a *negative pledge clause*.	SECURITY: The notes are unsecured. However, "if Apple shall incur, assume or guarantee any Debt, . . . it will secure . . . the debt securities then outstanding equally and ratably with . . . such Debt."
10. The principal amount of the issue was $2 billion. The notes were sold at 99.11% of their principal value.	OFFERED: $2,000,000,000 at 99.11%
11. The book runners are the managing underwriters to the issue and maintain the book of securities sold.	JOINT BOOK-RUNNING MANAGERS: Goldman, Sachs; Deutsche Bank Securities

Asset-Backed Bonds   Instead of borrowing money directly, companies sometimes bundle a group of loans and then sell the cash flows from these loans. This issue is known as an *asset-backed bond*. For example, automobile loans, student loans, and credit card receivables have all been bundled together and remarketed as asset-backed bonds. However, by far the most common application has been in the field of mortgage lending.

Suppose a mortgage lending company has made a large number of loans to buyers of homes or commercial real estate. However, the company doesn't want to wait until the loans are paid off; it can get its hands on the money now by selling *mortgage pass-through certificates* backed by the mortgage loans. The holders of these certificates are buying a share of the payments made by the underlying pool of mortgages. For example, if interest rates fall and the mortgages are repaid early, holders of the pass-through certificates are also repaid early. That is not generally popular with these holders because they get their money back just when they don't want it—when interest rates are low.

Sometimes, instead of issuing one class of pass-through certificates, companies have issued several different classes of security, known as *collateralized debt obligations* (or *CDOs*). For example, any mortgage payments might be used first to pay off the *senior* class of investors and only then will other, *junior* classes start to be repaid.

By 2007, more than half of the new issues of CDOs involved exposure to subprime mortgages. Because the mortgages were packaged together, senior investors in these CDOs were protected against the risk of default on any particular mortgage. However, even the senior tranches were exposed to the risk of an economywide slump in the housing market that would lead to widespread defaults

Economic catastrophe struck in the summer of 2007, when the investment bank Bear Stearns revealed that two of its hedge funds had invested heavily in CDOs that had become nearly worthless when mortgage default rates rose. Bear Stearns was rescued with help from the Federal Reserve, but the incident signaled the start of the credit crunch and the collapse of the CDO market. In 2008, new issues of CDOs fell by nearly 90%.

Mortality Bonds   Managers of life insurance companies agonize about the possibility of a pandemic or other disaster that results in a sharp increase in the death rate. In 2015, the French insurance company Axa sought to protect itself against this danger by issuing €285 million of *mortality bonds*. Axa's unusual bonds offer a tempting yield, but if mortality rates in the United States, France, and Japan exceed a predetermined threshold, the investors' funds are used to help pay Axa's life insurance obligations. So the investors are in a way betting that people will die on schedule.

There is a great variety of potential security designs. As long as you can convince investors of its attractions, you can issue a callable, subordinated, floating-rate bond denominated in euros. Rather than combining features of existing securities, you may be able to create an entirely new one. We can imagine a copper mining company issuing preferred shares on which the dividend fluctuates with the world copper price. We know of no such security, but it is perfectly legal to issue it and—who knows?—it might generate considerable interest among investors.

Variety is intrinsically good. People have different tastes, levels of wealth, rates of tax, and so on. Why not offer them a choice? Of course, the problem is the expense of designing and marketing new securities. But if you can think of a new security that will appeal to investors, you may be able to issue it on especially favorable terms and thus increase the value of your company.

14.6   Convertible Securities

warrant
Right to buy shares from a company at a stipulated price before a set date.

We have seen that companies sometimes have the option to repay an issue of bonds before maturity. There are also cases in which *investors* have an option. The most dramatic case is provided by a **warrant,** which is *nothing but* an option. Companies often issue warrants and bonds in a package.

Example 14.2 ▶   Warrants

Macaw Bill wishes to make a bond issue, which could include some warrants as a "sweetener." Each warrant might allow you to purchase one share of Macaw stock at a price of $50 any time during the next 5 years. If Macaw's stock performs well, that option could turn out to be very valuable. For instance, if the stock price at the end of the 5 years is $80, then you pay the company $50 and receive in exchange a share worth $80. Of course, an investment in warrants also has its perils. If the price of Macaw stock fails to rise above $50, then the warrants expire worthless. ■

convertible bond
Bond that the holder may exchange for a specified amount of another security.

A **convertible bond** gives its owner the option to exchange the bond for a predetermined number of common shares. The convertible bondholder hopes that the company's share price will zoom up so that the bond can be converted at a big profit. But if the shares zoom down, there is no obligation to convert; the bondholder remains just that. Not surprisingly, investors value this option to keep the bond or exchange it for shares, and therefore, a convertible bond sells at a higher price than a comparable bond that is not convertible.

The convertible is like a package of a bond and a warrant. But there is an important difference: When the owners of a convertible wish to exercise their options to buy shares, they do not pay cash—they just exchange the bond for shares of the stock.

BEYOND THE PAGE

   Tesla Motors convertible bond

mhhe.com/brealey9e

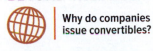
Companies may also issue convertible preferred stock. In this case the investor receives preferred stock with fixed dividend payments but has the option to exchange this preferred stock for the company's common stock.

We will have more to say about these and other options encountered by the financial manager in Chapter 23.

SUMMARY

Why should firms assume that the securities they issue are fairly priced? (*LO14-1*)

Managers want to raise money at the lowest possible cost, but their ability to find cheap financing is limited by the intense competition between investors. As a result of this competition, securities are likely to be fairly priced given the information available to investors. Such a market is said to be *efficient*.

What are recent trends in firms' use of different sources of finance? (*LO14-2*)

Internally generated cash is the principal source of company funds. In recent years, net equity issues have often been negative; that is, companies have repurchased more equity than they have issued. At the same time companies have issued large quantities of debt. However, large levels of **internally generated funds** have allowed book equity to increase despite the share repurchases, so the ratio of long-term debt to book value of equity has been fairly stable.

What information is contained in the shareholders' equity account in the firm's financial statements? (*LO14-3*)

The stockholders' equity account breaks down the book value of equity into **par value, additional paid-in capital, retained earnings,** and **treasury stock.** For most purposes, the allocation among the first three categories is not important. These accounts also show the total number of shares issued as well as shares repurchased by the company.

Who are the members of the company's board of directors and how are they elected? (*LO14-4*)

The CEO is almost always a director, often joined by a few other top managers. But for U.S. public companies, a majority of the board must be independent outside directors. Members of the compensation committee, which sets executive compensation, must all be independent directors.

Most companies use a **majority voting** system in which each director is voted on separately and stockholders cast one vote for each share they own. Less commonly, firms employ **cumulative voting,** which means that all directors are voted on jointly and stockholders may cast all their votes for just one candidate. Many companies have *classified* boards, in which case only a third of directors come up for reelection each year. However, companies have increasingly moved to declassify their boards so that all directors are voted on each year.

What are the major classes of securities issued by firms to raise capital? (*LO14-5*)

A company can issue a variety of securities such as common stock, preferred stock, and bonds. The **common stockholders** own the company. By this we mean that they are entitled to whatever profits are left over after other investors have been paid and that they have the ultimate control over how the company is run. Because shareholdings in the United States are usually widely dispersed, managers get to make most of the decisions, though their actions are monitored by the board of directors.

Preferred stock offers a fixed dividend but the company has the discretion not to pay it. It can't, however, then pay a dividend on the common stock. Despite its name, preferred stock is not a popular source of finance, but it is useful in special situations.

When companies issue **bonds,** they promise to make a series of interest payments and to repay the principal. However, this liability is limited. Stockholders have the right to default on their obligation and to hand over the assets to the debtholders. Unlike dividends on common stock and preferred stock, the interest payments on debt are regarded as a cost and therefore they are paid out of before-tax income. Here are some of the different forms of debt:

- *Fixed-rate* and *floating-rate* debt.
- *Funded (long-term)* and *unfunded (short-term)* debt.
- *Callable* and *sinking-fund* debt.
- *Domestic bonds* and *eurobonds.*
- *Publicly traded* debt and *private placements.*

The fourth source of finance consists of options and option-like securities. The simplest option is a **warrant,** which gives its holder the right to buy a share from the firm at a set price by a set date. Warrants are often sold in combination with other securities. **Convertible bonds** give their holder the right to convert the bond to shares. They therefore resemble a package of straight debt and a warrant.

QUESTIONS AND PROBLEMS

1. **Financing Decisions.** True or false? (*LO14-1*)
   a. Smart financial managers know that good financing decisions create as much value for the firm as good investment decisions.
   b. Competition between investors means that companies can generally sell their securities for more than they are worth.

2. **Sources of Finance.** True or false? (*LO14-2*)
   a. Net stock issues by U.S. nonfinancial corporations are, in most years, small but positive.
   b. Most capital investment by U.S. corporations is funded by retained earnings and reinvested depreciation.
   c. Debt ratios in the United States have generally increased over the past 20 years.

3. **Sources of Finance.** Fill in the blanks in the following passage by choosing the most appropriate term from the following list: *debt issues, higher, internally generated cash, lower, risen, financial deficit, fallen, negative, stayed roughly constant.* (*Note:* A term may be used more than once.) (*LO14-2*)

   By far the largest source of cash for most companies comes from ___(a)___. The gap between this cash and the cash that companies need is called the ___(b)___. On average, equity issues have been ___(c)___; in other words, companies have used the cash from ___(d)___ and retained earnings to buy back their stock. Debt ratios can be measured using either market values or book values. Generally, book debt ratios are ___(e)___ than market-value ratios. In the 30 or so years before 1990 both debt ratios have on average ___(f)___, but since then they have ___(g)___.

4. **Equity Accounts.** Match each of the following terms with the correct definition: (*LO14-3*)

   a. additional paid-in capital
   b. issued and outstanding
   c. retained earnings
   d. treasury stock
   e. authorized share capital
   f. par value

   A. The price at which each share is recorded in the company's books
   B. Held by investors
   C. Cumulative amount of profits that have been plowed back
   D. The difference between the amount of cash raised by an equity issue and the par value of the issue
   E. The maximum number of shares that can be issued without shareholder approval
   F. The amount that the company has spent buying back stock that it has not subsequently resold

5. **Equity Accounts.** The authorized share capital of the Alfred Cake Company is 100,000 shares. The equity is currently shown in the company's books as follows: (*LO14-3*)

Common stock ($1 par value)	$ 60,000
Additional paid-in capital	10,000
Retained earnings	30,000
Common equity	$100,000
Treasury stock (2,000 shares)	5,000
Net common equity	$ 95,000

  a. How many shares are issued?

  b. How many shares are outstanding?

  c. How many more shares can be issued without the approval of shareholders?

6. **Equity Accounts.** Common Products has just made its first issue of stock. It raised $2 million by selling 200,000 shares of stock to the public. These are the only shares outstanding. The par value of each share was $2. Fill in the following table: (*LO14-3*)

Common shares (par value)	_____(a)_____
Additional paid-in capital	_____(b)_____
Retained earnings	_____(c)_____
Net common equity	$2,500,000

7. **Equity Accounts.** (*LO14-3*)

  a. Rework Table 14.1, supposing that FedEx now issues 2 million shares at $150 a share. Which of the figures would change?

  b. What would happen to Table 14.1 if instead FedEx bought back 2 million shares at $150 per share?

8. **Voting for Directors.** If there are 10 directors to be elected and a shareholder owns 100 shares, indicate the maximum number of votes that he or she can cast for a favorite candidate under: (*LO14-4*)

  a. Majority voting.

  b. Cumulative voting.

9. **Voting for Directors.** The shareholders of the Pickwick Paper Company need to elect five directors. There are 400,000 shares outstanding. How many shares do you need to own to ensure that you can elect at least one director if the company has: (*LO14-4*)

  a. Majority voting?

  b. Cumulative voting?

  (*Hint:* How many votes in total will be cast? How many votes are required to ensure that at least one-fifth of votes are cast for your choice?)

10. **Preferred Stock.** True or false? (*LO14-5*)

  a. A company's equity includes both common and preferred stock.

  b. The sum of common equity and preferred stock is known as net worth.

  c. As its name implies, preferred stock is a more important source of financing than common equity.

  d. A corporation pays tax on only 30% of the common or preferred dividends it receives from other corporations.

  e. Because of the tax advantage, a large fraction of preferred shares is held by corporations.

11. **Preferred Stock.** Preferred stock of financially strong firms sometimes sells at lower yields than the bonds of those firms. For weaker firms, the preferred stock has a higher yield. What might explain this pattern? (*LO14-5*)

12. **Corporate Debt.** Haricot Corp. and Pinto Corp. both have profits of $100 million. Haricot is financed solely by equity, while Pinto has issued $150 million of 8% debt. If the corporate tax rate is 35%: (*LO14-5*)

  a. How much tax does each company pay?

  b. What is the total payout to investors (debtholders plus shareholders) of each company?

13. **Corporate Bonds.** Look at the terms of the Apple bond issue in Section 14.5. (*LO14-5*)

   a. Does the company have a call option?

   b. How much interest is paid on each Apple bond in a year?

   c. Can Apple issue secured debt that would come ahead of this issue?

   d. Does Apple's bond receive Moody's highest credit rating?

   e. Are the bonds repaid in one lump or by installments?

   f. Are Apple's bonds funded or unfunded debt?

14. **Corporate Bonds.** Other things equal, will the following provisions increase or decrease the yield to maturity at which a firm can issue a bond? (*LO14-5*)

   a. The borrower has the option to repay the loan before maturity.

   b. The bond is convertible into shares.

   c. The bond is a private placement.

15. **Callable Bonds.** (*LO14-5*)

   a. If interest rates fall, will callable or noncallable bonds rise more in price?

   b. Suppose that a company simultaneously issues a zero-coupon bond and a coupon bond with identical maturities. Both are callable at any time at their face value. Which bond is more likely to be called before maturity?

   c. Other things equal, which of the two bonds in part (a) is likely to offer the higher yield to maturity?

16. **Convertible Bonds.** Van Gogh Furniture has issued a zero-coupon 10-year bond that can be converted into 10 Van Gogh shares. Comparable nonconvertible bonds are yielding 8%. Van Gogh stock is priced at $50 a share. If you had to make a now-or-never decision on whether to convert or stay with the bond, which would you do? (*LO14-5*)

17. **Corporate Bonds.** Fill in the blanks by choosing the appropriate term from the following list: *lease, funded, floating-rate, eurobond, convertible, junior, call, sinking fund, prime rate, private placement, public issue, senior, unfunded, eurodollar rate, warrant, debentures, term loan.* (*LO14-5*)

   a. Debt maturing in more than 1 year is often called _____ debt.

   b. An issue of bonds that is sold simultaneously in several countries is traditionally called a(n) _____.

   c. If a lender ranks behind the firm's general creditors in the event of default, the loan is said to be _____.

   d. In many cases, a firm is obliged to make regular contributions to a(n) _____, which is then used to repurchase bonds.

   e. Some bonds give the firm the right to repurchase or _____ the bonds at specified prices.

   f. The benchmark interest rate that banks charge to their customers with good credit is generally termed the _____.

   g. The interest rate on bank loans is often tied to short-term interest rates. These loans are usually called _____ loans.

   h. Where there is a(n) _____, securities are sold directly to a small group of institutional investors. These securities cannot be resold to individual investors.

   i. In the case of a(n) _____, debt can be freely bought and sold by individual investors.

   j. A long-term rental agreement is called a(n) _____.

   k. A(n) _____ bond can be exchanged for shares of the issuing corporation.

   l. A(n) _____ gives its owner the right to buy shares in the issuing company at a predetermined price.

WEB EXERCISE

1. Pick two companies [Caterpillar (CAT) and Union Pacific (UNP) could be good candidates] and compare their sources of funds and financial structures. You can find summary cash-flow statements and balance sheets on finance.yahoo.com, but you may also find it useful to go to the companies' websites. What factors might explain the difference in the companies' financing patterns?

2. In Figure 14.3, we summarized the sources and uses of funds for U.S. nonfinancial corporations. The data for this figure can be found on www.federalreserve.gov/releases/z1/current/data.htm. Look at Table F.103 for the latest year. Find "total internal funds" (which appeared in

row 9 at the time we last looked), equity issues (line 47), debt issues (line 39), and loans (line 43). What proportion of the funds that companies raised in the latest year was generated internally, and how much had to be raised on the financial markets? Is this the usual pattern? Were companies on average issuing new equity or buying their shares back?

3. Construct a table similar to Table 14.1 for a company of your choice by looking up its annual report on the web. What is the difference between the company's outstanding and issued shares? Explain. Has the company in the past raised more money by issuing new shares or by plowing back earnings? Is that typical of U.S. public companies (see Section 14.2)?

SOLUTIONS TO SELF-TEST QUESTIONS

14.1 a. Internal funds are most important, followed by net new borrowing. Net equity issues are in last place.
  b. Stock repurchases have exceeded issues.

14.2 Par value of common shares must be $1 × 100,000 shares = $100,000. Additional paid-in capital is ($15 − $1) × 100,000 = $1,400,000. Because book value is $4,500,000, retained earnings must be $3,000,000. Therefore, the accounts look like this:

Common shares ($1 par value per share)	$ 100,000
Additional paid-in capital	1,400,000
Retained earnings	3,000,000
Net common equity	$4,500,000

14.3 The corporation's after-tax yield on the bonds is 10% − (.35 × 10%) = 6.5%. The after-tax yield on the preferred is 8% − [.35 × (.30 × 8%)] = 7.16%. The preferred stock provides the higher after-tax rate despite its lower before-tax rate.

14.4 Because the coupon on floating-rate debt adjusts periodically to current market conditions, the bondholder is less vulnerable to changes in market yields. The coupon rate paid by the bond is not locked in for as long a period of time. Therefore, prices of floaters should be less sensitive to changes in market interest rates.

14.5 The callable bond will sell at a lower price. Investors will not pay as much for the callable bond since they know that the firm may call it away from them if interest rates fall. Thus they know that their capital gains potential is limited, which makes the bond less valuable. If both bonds are to sell at face value, the callable bond must pay a higher coupon rate as compensation to the investor for the firm's right to call the bond.

15

How Corporations Raise Venture Capital and Issue Securities

LEARNING OBJECTIVES

After studying this chapter, you should be able to:

15-1 Understand how venture capital works.

15-2 Explain how firms make initial public offerings and the costs of such offerings.

15-3 Understand how established firms make subsequent public issues of securities.

15-4 Describe how companies may make private placements of securities.

RELATED WEBSITES FOR THIS CHAPTER CAN BE FOUND IN CONNECT.

Trading opens on NASDAQ for shares in Facebook. *© Zef Nikolla/Facebook/Bloomberg/Getty Images*

In 1976, two college dropouts, Steve Jobs and Steve Wozniak, sold their most valuable possessions, a van and a couple of calculators, and used the cash to start manufacturing computers in a garage. In 1980, when Apple Computer went public, the shares were offered to investors at $22 and jumped to $36. At that point, the shares owned by the company's two founders were worth $414 million.

In 1996, two Stanford computer science students, Larry Page and Sergey Brin, decided to collaborate to develop a web search engine. To help turn their idea into a commercial product, the two friends succeeded in raising almost $1 million from several wealthy investors. They also raised cash from two *venture capital* firms that specialized in helping young start-up businesses. Google went public in 2004 at a price of $85 a share, putting a value on the enterprise of $23 billion.

In 2004, Mark Zuckerberg, a Harvard sophomore, launched the Facebook website. It was initially restricted to Harvard students, but 2 years later was opened to everyone. In 2012, when Facebook went public, the stock was valued at a record $104 billion, and by the end of 2015, the company was worth nearly $300 billion.

Such stories illustrate that the most important asset of a new firm may be a good idea. But that is not all you need. To take an idea from the drawing board to a prototype and through to large-scale operations requires ever greater amounts of capital.

This chapter proceeds as follows: First we describe how venture capital firms provide equity capital and advice to help young companies over their awkward adolescent period, before they are large and successful enough to "go public" in an *initial public offering* or *IPO*. Then we describe how IPOs are accomplished.

A company's initial public offering is seldom its last. We saw in Chapter 14 that internally generated cash is not usually sufficient for capital investment and other cash requirements. Established companies make up the deficit by issuing more debt or equity. The remainder of this chapter looks at these debt and equity issues. You will learn about the costs and pros and cons of general cash offers, rights issues, and private placements.

15.1 Venture Capital

You have taken the big step. With a couple of friends, you have formed a corporation to open a chain of fast-food outlets, offering innovative combinations of national dishes such as sushi with sauerkraut, curry Bolognese, and chow mein with Yorkshire pudding. Breaking into the fast-food business costs money, but, after pooling your savings and borrowing to the hilt from the bank, you have raised $100,000 and purchased 1 million shares in the new company. At this *zero-stage* investment, your company's assets are $100,000 plus the *idea* for your new product.

That $100,000 is enough to get the business off the ground, but if the idea takes off, you will need more capital to pay for new restaurants. Many start-ups continue to grow with funds provided directly by managers or by their friends and families. Some thrive using bank loans and reinvested earnings. But you will probably need to find an investor who is prepared to back an untried company in return for part of the profits. Equity capital in young businesses is known as **venture capital,** which is provided by specialist venture capital firms, wealthy individuals, investment institutions such as pension funds, and sometimes mature corporations on the hunt for new technology or new products. Specialist venture capital (or "VC") firms are the most likely source if your start-up is high risk and high tech.

Most entrepreneurs are able to spin a plausible yarn about their company. But it is as hard to convince a venture capitalist to invest in your business as it is to get a first novel published. Your first step is to prepare a *business plan.* This describes your product, the potential market, the production method, and the resources—time, money, employees, plant, and equipment—needed for success. It helps if you can point to the fact that you are prepared to put your money where your mouth is. By staking all your savings in the company, you *signal* your faith in the business.

The venture capital company knows that the success of a new business depends on the effort its managers put in. Therefore, it will try to structure any deal so that you have a strong incentive to work hard. For example, if you agree to accept a modest salary (and look forward instead to increasing the value of your investment in the company's stock), the venture capital company knows you will be committed to working hard. However, if you insist on a watertight employment contract and a fat salary, you won't find it easy to raise venture capital.

You are unlikely to persuade a venture capitalist to give you several years of financing all at once. You will get only enough to reach the next key milestone or checkpoint. That gives the venture capitalist the opportunity to evaluate progress and decide whether investing in the next stage is worthwhile.

Suppose the first milestone for your restaurant chain is demonstrated profitability at the first two outlets. You budget an additional $500,000 investment to get to this milestone. Then you convince your friendly VC to buy 1 million new shares for $.50 each. This will give the VC one-half ownership of the firm: It owns 1 million shares, and you and your friends also own 1 million shares. Because the venture capitalist is paying $500,000 for a claim to half your firm, it is placing a $1 million value on the business. After this *first-stage* financing, your company's balance sheet looks like this:

venture capital
Money invested to finance a new firm.

FIRST-STAGE MARKET-VALUE BALANCE SHEET			
(Figures in $ millions)			
Assets		**Liabilities and Shareholders' Equity**	
Cash from new equity	$0.5	New equity from venture capital	$0.5
Other assets	0.5	Your original equity	0.5
Value	$1.0	Value	$1.0

15.1   Self-Test

> Why might the venture capital company prefer to put up only part of the funds up front? Would this affect the amount of effort put in by you, the entrepreneur? Is your willingness to accept only part of the venture capital that will eventually be needed a good signal of the likely success of the venture?

Suppose that 2 years later, your business has grown to the point at which it needs a further injection of equity. This *second-stage* financing might involve the issue of a further 1 million shares at $1 each. Some of these shares might be bought by the original VC firm and some by other venture capital firms. The balance sheet after the new financing would then be as follows:

SECOND-STAGE MARKET-VALUE BALANCE SHEET (Figures in $ millions)			
Assets		**Liabilities and Shareholders' Equity**	
Cash from new equity	$1	New equity from second-stage financing	$1
Other assets	2	Equity from first stage	1
		Your original equity	1
Value	$3	Value	$3

Notice that the value of the initial 1 million shares owned by you and your friends has now been marked up to $1 million. Does this begin to sound like a money machine? It was so only because you have made a success of the business and new investors are prepared to pay $1 to buy a share in the business. When you started out, it wasn't clear that sushi and sauerkraut would catch on. If it hadn't caught on, the venture capital firm could have refused to put up more funds.

You are not yet in a position to cash in on your investment, but your gain is real. The second-stage investors have paid $1 million for a one-third share in the company. (There are now 3 million shares outstanding, and the second-stage investors hold 1 million shares.) At least these impartial observers—who are willing to back up their opinions with a large investment—must have decided that the company was worth at least $3 million. Your one-third share is therefore also worth $1 million.

Venture Capital Companies

Some young companies grow with the aid of venture capital provided by wealthy individuals known as *angel investors.* Many others raise capital from specialist venture capital firms, which pool funds from a variety of investors, seek out fledgling companies to invest in, and then work with these companies as they try to grow. In addition, some large technology firms act as *corporate venturers* by providing capital to new and innovative companies. For example, over the past 20 years Intel has invested in more than 1,300 firms in 56 countries. In a recent development, young companies have also used the web to raise money from small investors. This development, known as *crowdfunding,* is described in the nearby box.

Most venture capital funds are organized as limited private partnerships with a fixed life of about 10 years. Pension funds and other investors are the limited partners. The management company, which is the general partner, is responsible for making and overseeing the investments and, in return, receives a fixed fee as well as a share of the profits. You will find that these venture capital partnerships are often lumped together with similar partnerships that provide funds for companies in distress or that buy out whole companies and then take them private. The general term for these activities is *private equity investing.*

BEYOND THE PAGE

U.S. venture capital

mhhe.com/brealey9e

A new way for entrepreneurs to finance start-ups has emerged. It is known as *crowdfunding*, which uses the Internet to raise money directly from a crowd of individuals.

HUDWAY was established in 2004 by two cousins to launch a number of IT products. By 2015, the company needed additional capital to develop a universal vehicle accessory that would turn a smartphone into a Head-Up Display (HUD). It had manufactured a test batch of 100 samples and was confident that it could go on to mass production. It set out its plans for HUD on Kickstarter, a crowdfunding platform, and invited offers of support. The concept proved enormously popular, and individuals pledged more than $500,000 of new capital. Many of these pledges were for just $1 but others were for $350.

Crowdfunding may be used by entrepreneurs seeking to raise millions of dollars for a new enterprise, but more often it is a method for individuals to raise a few thousand dollars. In contrast to traditional venture capital projects, a relatively small proportion of projects are high tech, and many are for artistic activities or movie production. The payoff for investors may be in cash but many crowdfunded projects, such as HUDWAY's, simply offer samples of their product.

Venture capital firms are not passive investors. They are usually represented on each company's board of directors, they help to recruit senior managers for the company, and they provide ongoing advice. This advice can be especially valuable to businesses in their early years and helps them to bring their products more quickly to market.

For every 10 first-stage venture capital investments, only 2 or 3 may survive as successful, self-sufficient businesses, and only 1 may pay off big. From these statistics come two rules of success in venture capital investment. First, don't shy away from uncertainty; accept a low probability of success. But don't buy into a business unless you can see the *chance* of a big, public company in a profitable market. There's no sense taking a big risk unless the reward is big if you win. Second, cut your losses; identify losers early, and if you can't fix the problem—by replacing management, for example—don't throw good money after bad. There's an old saying in the venture capital business: "The secret of success in VC is not picking winners, but shutting down the losers before you spend too much money on them."

Very few new businesses are big winners, but those that do win can be very profitable. So venture capitalists keep sane by reminding themselves of the success stories—those who got in on the ground floor of firms like Google, Microsoft, and FedEx.[1]

15.2 The Initial Public Offering

For many successful start-ups, there comes a time when they need more capital than can comfortably be provided by a small number of individuals or venture capitalists. At this point, one solution is to sell the business to a larger firm. But many entrepreneurs do not fit easily into a corporate bureaucracy and would prefer instead to remain the boss. In this case, the company may choose to raise money by selling shares to the public. **A firm *goes public* when it sells its first issue of shares in a general offering to investors. This first sale of stock is called an initial public offering,** or **IPO.**

initial public offering (IPO)
First offering of stock to the general public.

An IPO is termed a *primary* offering when new shares are sold to raise additional cash for the company. It is a *secondary* offering when the company's founders and the venture capitalist cash in on some of their gains by selling shares. A secondary offer, therefore, is no more than a sale of shares from the early investors in the firm to new investors, and the cash raised in a secondary offer does not flow to the company. Of course, IPOs can be and commonly are both primary and secondary: The firm raises new cash at the same time that some of the already existing shares in the firm are sold to the public. For example, in 2014 Alibaba's IPO raised $25 billion. About a third of the shares were sold by the company, but the remainder were sold by existing shareholders.

---

[1] Fortunately, the successes seem to have outweighed the failures. Cambridge Associates estimated that the average annual return on venture capital funds was about 18% for the 30 years ending in September 2015.

Some of the biggest secondary offerings have involved governments selling off stock in nationalized enterprises. For example, the U.S. Treasury raised $20 billion by selling its holdings in General Motors common and preferred stock. But this huge issue was dwarfed by the $70 billion that was raised in the same year by the sale of the Brazilian state-owned oil company Petrobras.

We have seen that companies may make an IPO to raise new capital or to enable the existing shareholders to cash out, but there can be other benefits. For example, the company's stock price provides a readily available yardstick of performance and allows the firm to reward the management team with stock options.

While there are advantages to having a market for your shares, we should not give the impression that firms everywhere aim to go public. In many countries, it is common for businesses to remain privately owned. Even in the United States, many firms choose to remain as private, unlisted companies. They include some very large operations, such as Koch Industries, Bechtel, Cargill, and Levi Strauss. Also, you should not think of the issue process in the United States as a one-way street; public firms often go into reverse and return to being privately owned. For a somewhat extreme example, consider the food service company Aramark. It began life in 1936 as a private company and went public in 1960. In 1984, the management bought out the company and took it private, and it remained private until 2001, when it had its second public offering. But the experiment did not last long, for 5 years later Aramark was the object of yet another buyout that took the company private once again. In December 2013, Aramark went public for a third time.

Managers often chafe at the red tape involved in running a public company and at the unrelenting pressure from shareholders to report increasing earnings. These complaints have become more vocal since the passage of the Sarbanes-Oxley Act. This act has sought to prevent a repeat of the corporate scandals that brought about the collapse of Enron and WorldCom, but a consequence has been an increased reporting burden on small public companies and a rise in the number of companies reverting to private ownership.

BEYOND THE PAGE

Largest U.S. private companies

mhhe.com/brealey9e

Arranging a Public Issue

underwriter
Firm that buys an issue of securities from a company and resells it to the public.

Once a firm decides to go public, the first task is to select the underwriters. **Underwriters are investment banking firms that act as financial midwives to a new issue. Usually they play a triple role—first providing the company with procedural and financial advice, then buying the stock, and finally reselling it to the public.** A small IPO may have only one underwriter, but larger issues usually require a syndicate of underwriters that buy the issue and resell it.

In the typical underwriting arrangement, called a *firm commitment*, the underwriters buy the securities from the firm and then resell them to the public. The underwriters receive payment in the form of a **spread**—that is, they are allowed by the company to sell the shares at a slightly higher price than they paid for them. But the underwriters also accept the risk that they won't be able to sell the stock at the agreed offering price. If that happens, they will be stuck with unsold shares and must get the best price they can for them. In the riskier cases, the underwriter may not be willing to enter into a firm commitment and, therefore, handles the issue on a *best efforts* basis. In this case the underwriter agrees to sell as much of the issue as possible but does not guarantee the sale of the entire issue.

spread
Difference between public offer price and price paid by underwriter.

Before any stock can be sold to the public, the company must register the issue with the Securities and Exchange Commission (SEC). This involves preparation of a detailed and sometimes cumbersome registration statement, which contains information about the proposed financing and the firm's history, existing business, and plans for the future. The SEC does not evaluate the wisdom of an investment in the firm, but it does check the registration statement for accuracy and completeness. The firm must

prospectus
Formal summary that
provides information on an
issue of securities.

underpricing
Issuing securities at an
offering price set below
their true value.

also comply with the "blue-sky" laws of each state, so named because they seek to protect the public against firms that fraudulently promise the blue sky to investors.[2]

The first part of the registration statement is distributed to the public in the form of a preliminary **prospectus.** One function of the prospectus is to warn investors about the risks involved in any investment in the firm. Some investors have joked that if they read prospectuses carefully, they would never dare buy any new issue. The appendix to this chapter provides a streamlined version of a possible prospectus for your restaurant business.

The company and its underwriters also need to set the issue price. To gauge how much the stock is worth, they may undertake discounted cash-flow calculations like those described in Chapter 7. They also look at the price-earnings ratios of the shares of the firm's principal competitors.

Before settling on the issue price, the underwriters generally arrange a "roadshow," which gives the underwriters and the company's management an opportunity to talk to potential investors. These investors may then offer their reaction to the issue, suggest what they think is a fair price, and indicate how much stock they would be prepared to buy. This allows the underwriters to build up a book of likely orders. Although investors are not bound by their indications, they know that if they want to maintain a good relationship with the underwriters, they must be careful not to renege on their expressions of interest.

The managers of the firm are eager to secure the highest possible price for their stock, but the underwriters are likely to be cautious because they will be left with any unsold stock if they overestimate investor demand. As a result, underwriters typically try to underprice the initial public offering. **Underpricing,** they argue, is needed to tempt investors to buy stock and to reduce the cost of marketing the issue to customers. **However, underpricing represents a cost to the existing owners because the new investors are allowed to buy shares in the firm at a favorable price.**

Sometimes new issues are dramatically underpriced. For example, when the prospectus for the IPO of eBay was first published, the underwriters indicated that the company would sell 3.5 million shares at a price between $14 and $16 each. However, the enthusiasm for eBay's web-based auction system was such that the underwriters increased the issue price to $18. The next morning dealers were flooded with orders to buy eBay; more than 4.5 million shares traded, and the stock closed the day at a price of $47.375.

The experience of eBay is not typical, but it is common to see the stock price increase significantly from the issue price in the days following the sale. For example, one study of 8,300 new issues between 1960 and 2015 found an average first-day price rise of 16.9%.[3] Such immediate price jumps suggest that investors would have been prepared to pay much more than they did for the shares.

Example 15.1 ▶   Underpricing of IPOs

Suppose an IPO is a secondary issue and the firm's founders sell part of their holding to investors. Clearly, if the shares are sold for less than their true worth, the founders will suffer an opportunity loss.

But what if the IPO is a primary issue that raises new cash for the company? Do the founders care whether the shares are sold for less than their market value? The following example illustrates that they should care.

[2] Sometimes states go beyond blue-sky laws in their efforts to protect their residents. When Apple Computer Inc. made its first public issue, the Massachusetts state government decided the offering was too risky for its residents and, therefore, banned the sale of the shares to investors in the state. The state relented later, after the issue was out and the price had risen. Massachusetts investors obviously did not appreciate this "protection."

[3] These figures are provided on Jay Ritter's home page, **bear.cba.ufl.edu/ritter**.

Suppose Cosmos.com has 2 million shares outstanding and now offers a further 1 million shares to investors at $50. On the first day of trading the share price jumps to $80, so the shares that the company sold for $50 million are now worth $80 million. The total market capitalization of the company is 3 million × $80 = $240 million.

The value of the founders' shares is equal to the total value of the company less the value of the shares that have been sold to the public—in other words, $240 million − $80 million = $160 million. The founders might justifiably rejoice at their good fortune. However, if the company had issued shares at a higher price, it would have needed to sell fewer shares to raise the $50 million that it needs and the founders would have retained a larger share of the company. For example, suppose that the outside investors, who put up $50 million, received shares that were *worth* only $50 million. In that case the value of the founders' shares would be $240 million − $50 million = $190 million.

The effect of selling shares below their true value is to transfer $30 million of value from the founders to the investors who buy the new shares. ■

Unfortunately, underpricing does not mean that anyone can become wealthy by buying stock in IPOs. If an issue is underpriced, everybody will want to buy it and the underwriters will not have enough stock to go around. You are, therefore, likely to get only a small share of these hot issues. If it is overpriced, other investors are unlikely to want it, and the underwriter will be only too delighted to sell it to you. This phenomenon is known as the *winner's curse.*[4] It implies that, unless you can spot which issues are underpriced, you are likely to receive a small proportion of the cheap issues and a large proportion of the expensive ones. Because the dice are loaded against uninformed investors, they will play the game only if there is substantial underpricing on average.

Example 15.2 ▶   Underpricing and the Winner's Curse

Suppose that an investor will earn an immediate 10% return on underpriced IPOs and lose 5% on overpriced IPOs. But because of high demand, you may get only half the shares you bid for when the issue is underpriced. Suppose you bid for $1,000 of shares in two issues, one overpriced and the other underpriced. You are awarded the full $1,000 of the overpriced issue but only $500 worth of shares in the underpriced issue. The net gain on your two investments is (.10 × $500) − (.05 × $1,000) = 0. Your net profit is zero, despite the fact that, on average, the IPOs are underpriced (10% underpricing versus 5% overpricing). You have suffered the winner's curse: You "win" a larger allotment of shares when they are overpriced. ■

15.2 Self-Test

What is the percentage profit earned by an investor who can identify the underpriced issues in Example 15.2? Who are such investors likely to be?

---

[4] The highest bidder in an auction is the participant who places the highest value on the auctioned object. Therefore, it is likely that the winning bidder has an overly optimistic assessment of true value. Winning the auction suggests that you have overpaid for the object–this is the winner's curse. In the case of IPOs, your ability to "win" an allotment of shares may signal that the stock is overpriced.

FIGURE 15.1 Total direct costs as a percentage of gross proceeds, 2004–2008. The total direct costs for initial public offerings (IPOs), seasoned equity offerings (SEOs), convertible bonds, and straight bonds are composed of underwriter spreads and other direct expenses.

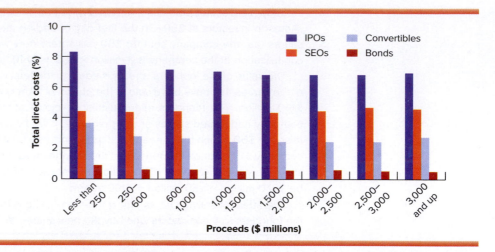

Source: We are grateful to Nickolay Gantchev for undertaking these calculations, which update tables in Immoo Lee, Scott Lochhead, Jay Ritter, and Quanshui Zhao, "The Costs of Raising Capital," *Journal of Financial Research* 19 (Spring 1996), pp. 59–74. Used with permission. Updates courtesy of Nickolay Gantchev.

flotation costs
The costs incurred when a firm issues new securities to the public.

BEYOND THE PAGE

The JOBS Act

mhhe.com/brealey9e

The costs of a new issue are termed **flotation costs.** Underpricing is not the only flotation cost. In fact, when people talk about the cost of a new issue, they often think only of the *direct costs* of the issue. For example, preparation of the registration statement and prospectus involves management, legal counsel, and accountants, as well as underwriters and their advisers. There is also the underwriting spread. (Remember, underwriters make their profit by selling the issue at a higher price than they paid for it.) For most issues of $20 million to $80 million, the spread is 7%.

Look at the dark blue bars (corresponding to IPOs) in Figure 15.1. These show the direct costs of going public. For all but the smallest IPOs, the underwriting spread and administrative costs are likely to absorb 7% to 8% of the proceeds from the issue. For the very largest IPOs, these direct costs may amount to only 5% of the proceeds.

Example 15.3 ▶ Costs of an IPO

The largest U.S. IPO was the $19.7 billion sale of stock by the credit card company Visa in 2008. A syndicate of 45 underwriters acquired a total of 446.6 million Visa shares for $42.768 each and then resold them to the public at an offering price of $44. The underwriters' spread was, therefore, $44 − $42.768 = $1.232. The firm also paid a total of $45.5 million in legal fees and other costs.[5] Therefore, the direct costs of the Visa issue were as follows:

Direct Expenses	
Underwriting spread	(446.6 million × $1.232) = $550.2 million
Other expenses	45.5
Total direct expenses	$595.7 million

The total amount of money raised by the issue was 446.6 million × $44 = $19,650 million. Of this sum, 3% was absorbed by direct expenses (that is, 595.7/19,650 = .030).

---

[5] These figures do not capture all administrative costs. For example, they do not include management time spent on the issue.

In addition to these direct costs, there was the cost of underpricing. By the end of the first day's trading, Visa's stock price had risen to $56.50, so investors valued Visa shares at 446.6 × $56.50 = $25,233 million. In other words, Visa sold stock for $25,233 − $19,650 = $5,583 million less than its market value. This was the cost of underpricing.

Managers commonly focus only on the direct costs of an issue. But, when we add in the cost of underpricing, the *total* cost of the Visa issue as a proportion of the market value of the shares was ($595.7 + $5,583)/$25,233 = .24, or 24%. ■

15.3   Self-Test

Suppose that the underwriters acquired Visa shares for **$45** and sold them to the public at an offering price of **$47**. If all other features of the offer were unchanged (and investors still valued the stock at **$56.50** a share), what would have been the direct costs of the issue and the costs of underpricing? What would have been the total costs (direct costs plus underpricing) as a proportion of the market value of the shares?

Other New-Issue Procedures

Almost all IPOs in the United States use the *bookbuilding* method. In other words, the underwriters build up a book of likely orders, buy the issue from the company at a discount, and then resell it to investors. This method is in some ways like an auction because potential buyers indicate how many shares they are prepared to buy at given prices. However, the indications are not binding and are used only as a guide to fix the price of the issue. The advantage of the bookbuilding method is that it allows underwriters to give preference to those investors whose bids are most helpful in setting the issue price and to offer them a reward in the shape of underpricing. But critics of the method point to the dangers of allowing the underwriters to decide who is allotted stock.

Stock can also be issued in an open auction. In this case, investors are invited to submit their bids, stating both an offering price and how many shares they wish to buy. The securities are then sold to the highest bidders. Most governments, including the U.S. Treasury, sell their bonds by auction. In the United States, auctions of common stock are fairly rare. However, in 2004 Google simultaneously raised eyebrows and $1.7 billion in the world's largest IPO to be sold by auction.

The Underwriters

We have described underwriters as playing a triple role—providing advice, buying a new issue from the company, and reselling it to investors. Underwriters don't just help the company to make its initial public offering; they are called in whenever a company wishes to raise cash by selling securities to the public.

Successful underwriting requires considerable experience and financial muscle. If a large issue fails to sell, the underwriters may be left with a loss of several hundred million dollars and some very red faces. Underwriting in the United States is, therefore, dominated by the major investment banking firms, which specialize in underwriting new issues, dealing in securities, and arranging mergers. They include such giants as JPMorgan Chase, Morgan Stanley, Goldman Sachs, Citi, and Bank of America Merrill Lynch. Large foreign banks, such as Deutsche Bank, Credit Suisse,

HSBC, and Barclays, are also heavily involved in underwriting securities that are sold internationally.

Underwriting is not always fun. In April 2008, the British bank HBOS offered its shareholders two new shares at a price of £2.75 for each five shares that they currently held.[6] The underwriters to the issue guaranteed that at the end of 8 weeks they would buy any new shares that the stockholders did not want. At the time of the offer, HBOS shares were priced at about £5, so the underwriters felt confident that they would not have to honor their pledge. Unfortunately, they reckoned without the turbulent market in bank shares that year. The bank's shareholders worried that the money they were asked to provide would largely go to bailing out the bondholders and depositors. By the end of the 8 weeks, the price of HBOS stock had slumped below the issue price, and the underwriters were left with 932 million unwanted shares worth £3.6 billion and a lot of egg on their faces.

Companies get to make only one IPO, but underwriters are in the business all the time. Wise underwriters, therefore, realize that their reputation is on the line and will not handle an issue unless they believe the facts have been presented fairly to investors. If a new issue goes wrong and the stock price crashes, the underwriters can find themselves very unpopular with their clients. For example, in 1999 the software company VA Linux went public at $30 a share. The next day trading opened at $299 a share, but then the price began to sag. Within 2 years, it had fallen below $2. Disgruntled VA Linux investors sued the underwriters for overhyping the issue. VA Linux investors were not the only ones to feel aggrieved. Investment banks soon found themselves embroiled in a major scandal as evidence emerged that they had deliberately oversold many of the issues that they underwrote during the dot-com boom years. There was further embarrassment when it emerged that several well-known underwriters had engaged in "spinning"—that is, allocating stock in popular new issues to managers of their important corporate clients. The underwriter's seal of approval for a new issue no longer seemed as valuable as it once had.

15.3   General Cash Offers by Public Companies

seasoned offering
Sale of additional securities by a firm that is already publicly traded.

After the initial public offering, a successful firm will continue to grow, and from time to time it will need to raise more money by issuing stock or bonds. An issue of additional stock by a company whose stock already is publicly traded is called a **seasoned offering.** Any issue of securities needs to be formally approved by the firm's board of directors. If a stock issue requires an increase in the company's authorized capital, it also needs the consent of the stockholders.

rights issue
Issue of securities offered only to current stockholders.

Public companies can issue securities either by making a general cash offer to investors at large or by making a **rights issue,** which is limited to existing shareholders. In the latter case, the company offers the shareholders the opportunity, or *right*, to buy more shares at an "attractive" price. For example, if the current stock price is $100, the company might offer investors an additional share at $50 for each share they hold.

Because the "attractive" offer is shared by and limited to all existing shareholders, it has no effect on their wealth. Suppose that before the issue, an investor has one share worth $100 and $50 in the bank. If the investor takes up the offer of a new share, that $50 of cash is transferred from the investor's bank account to the company's. The investor now has two shares that are a claim on the original assets worth $100 and on the $50 cash that the company has raised. So the two shares are worth a total of $150, or $75 each. The investor's wealth is unchanged.

---

[6] This arrangement is known as a *rights issue*. We describe rights issues shortly.

Example	15.4 ▶	Rights Issues

BEYOND THE PAGE

Rights issue
terminology

mhhe.com/brealey9e

We have already come across one example of a rights issue—the offer by the British bank HBOS, which ended up in the hands of its underwriters. Let us look more closely at another issue.

In September 2013, the British bank Barclays needed to raise £5.8 billion. It did so by offering its existing shareholders the right to buy one new share for every four that they currently held. The new shares were priced at £1.85 each, almost 40% below the preannouncement price.

Before the issue, Barclays had 12.68 billion shares outstanding, which were priced at £2.85 each. So investors valued the company at $12.68 \times £2.85 = £36.14$ billion. The new issue increased the total number of shares by $(1/4) \times 12.68 = 3.17$ billion and, therefore, raised 3.17 billion $\times £1.85 = £5.86$ billion. Thus, the issue increased the total value of the company to $36.14 + 5.86 = £42.00$ billion and reduced the value of each share to $42.00/15.85 = £2.65$.

Suppose that, just before the issue, you held four shares of Barclays plus £1.85 in cash. Your total wealth would be £13.25. If you decide to take up the rights issue, you would have to lay out all your cash to buy the one new share to which you are entitled, and you would end up with five shares worth $5 \times £2.65 = £13.25$. You would have gotten what you paid for. ∎

In some countries, the rights issue is the most common or only method for issuing stock, but in the United States rights issues are now very rare and most issues are in the form of a general cash offer.

General Cash Offers and Shelf Registration

general cash offer
Sale of securities open to all investors by an already-public company.

When a public company makes a **general cash offer** of debt or equity, it essentially follows the same procedure used when it first went public. This means that it must first register the issue with the SEC and draw up a prospectus.[7] Before settling on the issue price, the underwriters will usually contact potential investors and build up a book of likely orders. The company will then sell the issue to the underwriters, and they in turn will offer the securities to the public.

Companies do not need to prepare a separate registration statement every time they issue new securities. Instead, they are allowed to file a single registration statement covering financing plans for up to 2 years into the future. The actual issues can then be sold to the public with scant additional paperwork, whenever the firm needs cash or thinks it can issue securities at an attractive price. This is called **shelf registration**—the registration is put "on the shelf," to be taken down, dusted off, and used as needed.

shelf registration
A procedure that allows firms to file one registration statement for several issues of the same security.

Think of how you might use shelf registration when you are a financial manager. Suppose that your company is likely to need up to $200 million of new long-term debt over the next year or so. It can file a registration statement for that amount. It now has approval to issue up to $200 million of debt, but it isn't obliged to issue any. Nor is it required to work through any *particular* underwriters—the registration statement may name the underwriters the firm thinks it may work with, but others can be substituted later.

Now you can sit back and issue debt as needed, in bits and pieces if you like. Suppose JPMorgan comes across an insurance company with $10 million ready to invest in corporate bonds, priced to yield, say, 7.3%. If you think that's a good deal, you say OK and the deal is done, subject to only a little additional paperwork. JPMorgan then resells the bonds to the insurance company, hoping for a higher price than it paid for them.

---

[7] The procedure is similar when a company makes an international issue of bonds or equity, but as long as these issues are not sold publicly in the United States, they do not need to be registered with the SEC.

Here is another possible deal. Suppose you think you see a window of opportunity in which interest rates are "temporarily low." You invite bids for $100 million of bonds. Some bids may come from large investment bankers acting alone, others from ad hoc syndicates. But that's not your problem; if the price is right, you just take the best deal offered.

Thus, shelf registration offers several advantages:

1. Securities can be issued in dribs and drabs without incurring excessive costs.
2. Securities can be issued on short notice.
3. Security issues can be timed to take advantage of "market conditions" (although any financial manager who can reliably identify favorable market conditions might make a lot more money by quitting and becoming a bond or stock trader instead).
4. The issuing firm can make sure that underwriters compete for its business.

Not all companies eligible for shelf registration actually use it for all their public issues. Sometimes, they believe they can get a better deal by making one large issue through traditional channels, especially when the security to be issued has some unusual feature or when the firm believes it needs the investment banker's counsel or stamp of approval on the issue. Thus, shelf registration is less often used for issues of common stock than for garden-variety corporate bonds.

Costs of the General Cash Offer

Whenever a firm makes a cash offer, it incurs substantial administrative costs. Also, the firm needs to compensate the underwriters by selling them securities below the price that they expect to receive from investors. Look back at Figure 15.1, which shows the average underwriting spread and administrative costs for several types of security issues in the United States.

You can see that issue costs are higher for equity than for debt securities. This partly reflects the extra administrative costs of an equity issue. In addition, the underwriters demand extra compensation for the greater risk they take in buying and reselling equity.

Market Reaction to Stock Issues

Because stock issues usually throw a sizable number of new shares onto the market, it is widely believed that they must temporarily depress the stock price. If the proposed issue is very large, this price pressure may, it is thought, be so severe as to make it almost impossible to raise money.

This belief in price pressure implies that a new issue depresses the stock price temporarily below its true value. However, that view doesn't appear to fit very well with the notion of market efficiency. If the stock price falls solely because of increased supply, then that stock would offer a higher return than comparable stocks, and investors would be attracted to it as ants to a picnic.

Economists who have studied new issues of common stock have generally found that the announcement of the issue does result in a decline in the stock price. For industrial issues in the United States this decline amounts to about 3%.[8] While this may not sound overwhelming, such a price drop can be a large fraction of the money raised. Suppose that a company with a market value of equity of $5 billion announces its intention to issue $500 million of additional equity and thereby causes the stock price to drop by 3%. The loss in value is .03 × $5 billion, or $150 million. That's 30% of the amount of money raised (.30 × $500 million = $150 million).

---

[8] See, for example, P. Asquith and D. W. Mullins, "Equity Issues and Offering Dilution," *Journal of Financial Economics* 15 (January–February 1986), pp. 61–90; R. W. Masulis and A. N. Korwar, "Seasoned Equity Offerings: An Empirical Investigation," *Journal of Financial Economics* 15 (January–February 1986), pp. 91–118; and W. H. Mikkelson and M. M. Partch, "Valuation Effects of Security Offerings and the Issuance Process," *Journal of Financial Economics* 15 (January–February 1986), pp. 31–60.

What's going on here? Is the price of the stock simply depressed by the prospect of the additional supply? Possibly, but here is an alternative explanation.

Suppose managers (who have better information about the firm than outside investors) know that their stock is undervalued. If the company sells new stock at this low price, it will give the new shareholders a good deal at the expense of the old shareholders. In these circumstances managers might be prepared to forgo the new investment rather than sell shares at too low a price.

If managers know that the stock is *overvalued*, the position is reversed. If the company sells new shares at the high price, it will help its existing shareholders at the expense of the new ones. Managers might be prepared to issue stock even if the new cash were just put in the bank.

Of course investors are not stupid. They can predict that managers are more likely to issue stock when they think it is overvalued, and therefore they mark the price of the stock down accordingly. **The tendency for stock prices to decline at the time of an issue may have nothing to do with increased supply. Instead, the stock issue may simply be a** *signal* **that well-informed managers believe the market has overpriced the stock.**[9]

15.4 The Private Placement

private placement
Sale of securities to a limited number of investors without a public offering.

Whenever a company makes a public offering, it must register the issue with the SEC. It could avoid this costly process by selling the issue privately. There are no hard-and-fast definitions of a **private placement,** but the SEC has insisted that the security should be restricted largely to knowledgeable investors.

One disadvantage of a private placement is that the investor cannot easily resell the security. This is less important to institutions such as life insurance companies, which invest huge sums of money in corporate debt for the long haul. In 1990, the SEC relaxed its restrictions on who could buy unregistered issues. The new Rule 144a permitted large financial institutions to trade unregistered securities among themselves.

As you would expect, it costs less to arrange a private placement than to make a public issue. That might not be so important for the very large issues where costs are less significant, but it is a particular advantage for companies making smaller issues.

Another advantage of the private placement is that the debt contract can be custom-tailored for firms with special problems or opportunities. Also, if the firm wishes later to change the terms of the debt, it is much simpler to do this with a private placement where only a few investors are involved.

Therefore, it is not surprising that private placements occupy a particular niche in the corporate debt market, namely, loans to small and medium-size firms. These are the firms that face the highest costs in public issues, that require the most detailed investigation, and that may require specialized, flexible loan arrangements.

We do not mean that large, conventional firms should rule out private placements. Enormous amounts of capital are sometimes raised by this method. For example, in 2014 Medtronics, the medical technology company, borrowed $17 billion in a private placement. Nevertheless, the advantages of private placement—avoiding registration costs and establishing a direct relationship with the lender—are generally more important to smaller firms.

Of course, these advantages are not free. Lenders in private placements have to be compensated for the risks they face and for the costs of research and negotiation. They also have to be compensated for holding an asset that is not easily resold. All these factors are rolled into the interest rate paid by the firm. It is difficult to generalize about the differences in interest rates between private placements and public issues, but a typical yield differential is on the order of half a percentage point.

---

[9] This explanation was developed in S. C. Myers and N. S. Majluf, "Corporate Financing and Investment Decisions When Firms Have Information That Investors Do Not Have," *Journal of Financial Economics* 13 (1984), pp. 187–222.

SUMMARY

How do venture capital firms design successful deals? (*LO15-1*)

Infant companies raise **venture capital** to carry them through to the point at which they can make their first public issue of stock. Venture capital firms try to structure the financing to avoid conflicts of interest. If both the entrepreneur and the venture capital investors have an important equity stake in the company, they are likely to pull in the same direction. The entrepreneur's willingness to invest his or her own cash also *signals* management's confidence in the company's future. In addition, most venture capital is provided in stages that keep the firm on a short leash and force it to prove at each stage that it deserves the additional funds.

How do firms make initial public offerings, and what are the costs of such offerings? (*LO15-2*)

The **initial public offering** or **IPO** is the first sale of shares in a general offering to investors. The sale of the securities is usually managed by an underwriting firm that buys the shares from the company and resells them to the public. The **underwriter** helps to prepare a **prospectus,** which describes the company and its prospects. Underwriting firms have expertise in such sales because they are in the business all the time, whereas the company raises capital only occasionally. The costs of an IPO include direct costs, such as legal and administrative fees, as well as the underwriting spread—the difference between the price the underwriter pays to acquire the shares from the firm and the price the public pays the underwriter for those shares. Another major implicit cost is the **underpricing** of the issue—that is, shares are typically sold to the public somewhat below the true value of the security. This discount is reflected in abnormally high average returns to new issues on the first day of trading.

What are some of the significant issues that arise when established firms make a general cash offer of securities? (*LO15-3*)

There are always economies of scale in issuing securities. It is cheaper to go to the market once for $100 million than to make two trips for $50 million each. Consequently, firms "bunch" security issues. This may mean relying on short-term financing until a large issue is justified. Or it may mean issuing more than is needed at the moment to avoid another issue later.

A **seasoned offering** may depress the stock price. The extent of this price decline varies, but for issues of common stocks by industrial firms the fall in the value of the existing stock may amount to a significant proportion of the money raised. The likely explanation for this pressure is the information the market reads into the company's decision to issue stock.

Shelf registration often makes sense for debt issues by blue-chip firms. Shelf registration reduces the time taken to arrange a new issue, it increases flexibility, and it may cut underwriting costs. It seems best suited for debt issues by large firms that are happy to switch between investment banks. It seems least suited for issues of unusually risky securities or for issues by small companies that most need a close relationship with an investment bank.

How do companies make private placements? (*LO15-4*)

In **private placements,** the firm places the newly issued securities with a small number of large institutions. These arrangements avoid registration expenses, may be tailored to the special needs of the issuer, and, in the case of debt, allow for a more direct relationship with the lender. However, buyers need to be compensated for the fact that such issues are not easily resold. Private placements are well suited for small, risky, or unusual firms, but the advantages are not worth as much to blue-chip borrowers.

QUESTIONS AND PROBLEMS

1. **Venture Capital.** Look back at your restaurant chain venture. Suppose that when you first approach your friendly VC, he decides that your shares are worth only $.40 each. (*LO15-1*)

    a. How many shares will you need to sell to raise the additional $500,000?

    b. What fraction of the firm will you own after the VC investment?

2. **Venture Capital.** Ethelbert.com is a young software company owned by two entrepreneurs. It currently needs to raise $400,000 to support its expansion plans. A venture capitalist is prepared to provide the cash in return for a 40% holding in the company. Under the plans for the investment, the VC will hold 10,000 shares in the company and the two entrepreneurs will have combined holdings of 15,000 shares. (*LO15-1*)

    a. What is the total after-the-money valuation of the firm?
    b. What value is the venture capitalist placing on each share?

3. **Venture Capital.** True or false? (*LO15-1*)

    a. Venture capital companies know that managers are more likely to work hard if they can be assured of a good steady salary.
    b. Venture capital companies generally advance the money in stages.
    c. Venture capital companies are generally passive investors and are happy to let the companies in which they are invested get on with the job.
    d. Some young companies grow with the aid of equity investment provided by wealthy individuals known as angel investors.

4. **Venture Capital.** Complete the passage using the following terms: *limited partners, venture capital, private, underwriters, general partners, private equity, corporate venturers, partnerships, private, angel investors.* (*Note:* Not all terms will be used.) (*LO15-1*)

    Equity capital in young businesses is known as ___(a)___, and it is provided by specialist firms; wealthy individuals, known as ___(b)___; and large technology companies that act as ___(c)___. Venture capital funds are organized as ___(d)___. The management companies are the ___(e)___, and pension funds and other investors are the ___(f)___. Venture capital partnerships are often lumped together with similar partnerships that buy whole companies and take them ___(g)___. The general term for these firms is ___(h)___ companies.

5. **Venture Capital.** (*LO15-1*)

    a. "A signal is credible only if it is potentially costly." Explain why an entrepreneur's willingness to invest in her company's equity is a credible signal. Is a willingness to accept only part of the venture capital that will eventually be needed also a credible signal?
    b. "When managers take their reward in the form of increased leisure or executive jets, the cost is borne by the shareholders." Explain how venture capital financing tackles this problem.

6. **Venture Capital.** Here is a difficult question: Pickwick Electronics is a new high-tech company financed entirely by 1 million ordinary shares, all of which are owned by George Pickwick. The firm needs to raise $1 million now for stage 1 and, assuming all goes well, a further $1 million at the end of 5 years for stage 2. First Cookham Venture Partners is considering two possible financing schemes:

    • Buying 2 million shares now at their current valuation of $1.
    • Buying 1 million shares at the current valuation and investing a further $1 million at the end of 5 years at whatever the shares are worth.

    The outlook for Pickwick is uncertain, but as long as the company can secure the additional finance for stage 2, it will be worth either $2 million or $12 million after completing stage 2. (The company will be valueless if it cannot raise the funds for stage 2.) Show the possible payoffs for Mr. Pickwick and First Cookham, and explain why one scheme might be preferred. Assume an interest rate of zero. (*LO15-1*)

7. **Stock Issues.** True or false? (*LO15-1, LO15-2, and LO15-3*)

    a. Venture capitalists typically provide first-stage financing sufficient to cover all development expenses. Second-stage financing is provided by stock issued in an IPO.
    b. Underpricing in an IPO is a problem only when the original investors are selling part of their holdings.
    c. Stock price generally falls when the company announces a new issue of shares. This is attributable to the information released by the decision to issue.

8. **IPO Costs.** Moonscape has just completed an initial public offering. The firm sold 3 million shares at an offer price of $8 per share. The underwriting spread was $.50 a share. The firm incurred $100,000 in legal, administrative, and other costs. (*LO15-2*)

    a. What were flotation costs as a fraction of funds raised?
    b. Were flotation costs for Moonscape higher or lower than is typical for IPOs of this size (see Figure 15.1)?

9. **IPO Costs.** When Microsoft went public, the company sold 2 million new shares (the primary issue). In addition, existing shareholders sold .8 million shares (the secondary issue) and kept 21.1 million shares. The new shares were offered to the public at $21, and the underwriters received a spread of $1.31 a share. At the end of the first day's trading, the market price was $35 a share. (*LO15-2*)

   a. How much money did the company receive before paying its portion of the direct costs?

   b. How much did the existing shareholders receive from the sale of their shares before paying their portion of the direct costs?

   c. If the issue had been sold to the underwriters for $30 a share, how many shares would the company have needed to sell to raise the same amount of cash?

   d. How much better off would the existing shareholders have been?

10. **IPO Costs.** Having heard about IPO underpricing, I put in an order to my broker for 1,000 shares of every IPO he can get for me. After 3 months, my investment record is as follows: (*LO15-2*)

IPO	Shares Allocated to Me	Price per Share	Initial Return
A	500	$10	7%
B	200	20	12
C	1,000	8	−2
D	0	12	23

   a. What is the average underpricing in dollars of this sample of IPOs?

   b. What is the average initial return on my "portfolio" of shares purchased from the four IPOs that I bid on? When calculating this average initial return, remember to weight by the amount of money invested in each issue.

   c. "You have just encountered the problem of the winners' curse." True or false?

11. **IPO Costs.** Look at the illustrative new-issue prospectus in the appendix. (*LO15-2*)

   a. Is this issue a primary offering, a secondary offering, or both?

   b. What are the direct costs of the issue as a percentage of the total proceeds?

   c. Are these direct costs more than the average for an issue of this size?

   d. Suppose that on the first day of trading the price of Hotch Pot stock is $15 a share. What is the cost in dollars of the underpricing?

   e. After paying her share of the expenses, how much will the firm's president, Emma Lucullus, receive from the sale?

   f. What will be the value of the shares that Emma Lucullus retains in the company?

12. **IPO Costs.** Match Group went public in November 2015. The company sold 33,333,333 shares at $12 per share. The underwriting spread was $0.66 a share, and the direct expenses were $0.21 a share. (*LO15-2*)

   a. What was the percentage underwriting spread?

   b. How much did the company raise after all expenses?

   c. On its first day of trading the stock closed at $14.74. Calculate the dollar cost of underpricing.

13. **Underpricing.** In some U.K. IPOs, any investor may apply to buy shares. Mr. Bean has observed that, on average, these stocks are underpriced by about 9%, and for some years, he has followed a policy of applying for a constant proportion of each issue. Thus, he is disappointed and puzzled to find that this policy has not resulted in a profit. Explain to him why this is so. (*LO15-2*)

14. **Underpricing.** Fishwick Enterprises has 200,000 shares outstanding, half of which are owned by Jennifer Fishwick and half by her cousin. The two cousins have decided to sell 100,000 shares in an IPO. Half of these shares would be issued by the company to raise new cash, and half would be shares that are currently held by Jennifer Fishwick. Suppose that the shares are sold at an issue price of $50 but rise to $80 by the end of the first day's trading. Suppose also that investors would have been prepared to buy the issue at $80. (*LO15-2*)

   a. What percentage of the company will Jennifer own *after* the issue?

   b. What will her holding be worth at the end of the first day's trading?

   c. Suppose the issue had been priced at $80. How many shares would the company have needed to sell to raise the same gross proceeds from the IPO?

    d. What in this case would be Jennifer's wealth (cash plus the value of her remaining holding)?

    e. What is the cost of underpricing to Jennifer in dollars?

15. **Seasoned Issues.** Gravenstein Chemicals wishes to raise $5 million by an issue of stock. It expects direct expenses to absorb 1% of the money raised and the underwriters to charge a spread of 4%. If the announcement of the issue is likely to cause the price of Gravenstein stock to fall to $80 from its current level of $82, what is the minimum number of shares that the company must sell to ensure that it raises the required $5 million? (*LO15-3*)

16. **Rights Issues.** Associated Breweries is planning to market unleaded beer. To finance the venture, it proposes to make a rights issue with a subscription price of $10. One new share can be purchased for each two shares held. The company currently has outstanding 100,000 shares priced at $40 a share. Assuming that the new money is invested to earn a fair return, give values for the following: (*LO15-3*)

    a. Number of new shares.

    b. Amount of new investment.

    c. Total value of company after the issue.

    d. Total number of shares after the issue.

    e. Share price after the issue.

17. **Issue Methods.** Each of the terms listed below on the left is associated with one of the events on the right. Match each of the terms with the correct definition: (*LO15-3*)

    a. private placement

    b. firm commitment

    c. rights issue

    A. The underwriter agrees to buy the issue from the company at a fixed price.

    B. The company offers to sell stock only to existing stockholders.

    C. Sales of securities to a limited number of investors without a public offering.

18. **Issue Methods.** For each of the following pairs of issues, state which issue is likely to involve the lower proportionate underwriting and administrative costs. (*LO15-3*)

    a. A large issue or a small issue

    b. A bond issue or a common stock issue

    c. A small private placement of bonds or a small general cash offer of bonds

19 **Rights Issues.** Pandora Box Company Inc. makes a rights issue at a subscription price of $5 a share. One new share can be purchased for every five shares held. Before the issue there were 10 million shares outstanding and the share price was $6. (*LO15-3*)

    a. What is the total amount of new money raised?

    b. What is the expected stock price after the rights are issued?

    c. By what percentage would the total value of the company need to fall before shareholders would be unwilling to take up their rights?

    d. Suppose that you initially own 100 shares plus $100 in the bank. If you take up your rights issue, what will be your total wealth after the issue is completed?

    e. Suppose that the company now decides to issue the new stock at $4 instead of $5 a share. How many new shares would it have needed to raise the same sum of money?

    f. What is the expected stock price under this new arrangement after the rights are issued?

    g. If you take up your rights issue under this new arrangement, what will be your total wealth after the issue is completed?

    h. Which arrangement makes you better off: the first, the second, or neither?

20 **Issue Methods.** Match each of the following terms with the correct definition: (*LO15-3*)

    a. shelf registration

    b. seasoned issue

    c. primary issue

    d. secondary issue

    e. best efforts

    f. underwriters' spread

    g. blue-sky laws

    h. registration statement

    A. Sale of stock by a company to raise new cash

    B. The difference between the issue price and the price paid by the underwriters

    C. State rules governing the issue of securities

    D. Underwriter's agreement to sell as much of an issue as possible

    E. Sale of securities by existing investors

    F. Sale of additional stock by a public company

    G. Several issues of the same security may be sold under the same registration

    H. Document filed with SEC providing details of a new issue

21. **Issue Methods.** Young Corporation stock currently sells for $30 per share. There are 1 million shares currently outstanding. The company announces plans to raise $3 million by offering shares to the public at a price of $30 per share. (*LO15-3*)
    a. If the underwriting spread is 6%, how many shares will the company need to issue in order to be left with net proceeds (before other administrative costs) of $3 million?
    b. If other administrative costs are $60,000, what is the dollar value of the total direct costs of the issue?
    c. If the share price falls by 3% at the announcement of the plans to proceed with a seasoned offering, what is the dollar cost of the announcement effect?

22. **Issue Methods.** The market value of the research firm Fax Facts is $600 million. The firm issues an additional $100 million of stock, but as a result the stock price falls by 2%. What is the cost of the price drop to existing shareholders as a fraction of the funds raised? (*LO15-3*)

23. **Issue Methods.** Frank Enstein is the CEO of a private medical equipment company that is proposing to sell 100,000 shares of its stock in an open auction. Suppose the company receives the bids in the following table. What is the maximum price at which the company can sell its stock? (*LO15-3*)

Shares	Price
20,000	$80
10,000	78
15,000	73
25,000	70
10,000	69
8,000	67
14,000	66
15,000	65
30,000	61

24. **Underwriting.** Each of the terms listed below on the left is associated with one of the events on the right. Match each of the terms with the correct definition: (*LO15-3*)
    a. best efforts
    b. bookbuilding
    c. shelf registration

    A. Investors indicate to the underwriter how many shares they would like to buy in a new issue, and these indications are used to help set the price.
    B. The underwriter accepts responsibility only to try to sell the issue.
    C. Several tranches of the same security may be sold under the same registration. (A "tranche" is a batch, a fraction of a larger issue.)

25. **Issue Methods.** After each of the following issue methods, we have listed two types of issue. Choose the one more likely to employ that method. (*LO15-4*)
    a. Rights issue (*initial public offer / further sale of an already publicly traded stock*)
    b. Private placement (*issue of existing stock / bond issue by an industrial company*)
    c. Shelf registration (*initial public offer / bond issue by a large industrial company*)

26. **Issue Methods.** (*LO15-4*)
    a. Is a private placement more likely to be used for issues of seasoned stock or seasoned bonds by an industrial company?
    b. Is a rights issue more likely to be used for an initial public offering or for subsequent issues of stock?
    c. Is shelf registration more likely to be used for issues of unseasoned stocks or bonds by a large industrial company?

27. **Private Placements.** You need to choose between making a public offering and arranging a private placement. In each case, the issue involves $10 million face value of 10-year debt. You have the following data for each: (*LO15-4*)
    • *A public issue:* The interest rate on the debt would be 8.5%, and the debt would be issued at face value. The underwriting spread would be 1.5%, and other expenses would be $80,000.
    • *A private placement:* The interest rate on the private placement would be 9%, but the total issuing expenses would be only $30,000.
    a. What is the difference in the proceeds to the company net of expenses?
    b. Other things being equal, which is the better deal?

WEB EXERCISES

BEYOND THE PAGE

Twitter's IPO
prospectus

mhhe.com/brealey9e

1. In the appendix to this chapter, we provide a flavor of an IPO prospectus, and to see an actual prospectus, take a look at the nearby Beyond the Page feature. Try finding a prospectus for a recent IPO. We suggest that you first log on to finance.yahoo.com and click on the *Investing* tab to find a recent IPO by a U.S. company. Now log on to the SEC's huge database at www.sec.gov/edgar/searchedgar/webusers.htm. Edgar can be a bit complicated, but the final IPO prospectus should be shown as Form 424B4. On the basis of this prospectus, do you think the stock looks like an attractive investment? Which parts of the statement appear most useful? Which seem the least useful? What were the direct expenses of the issue?

2. We describe underpricing as part of the costs of a new issue. Jay Ritter's home page (site.warrington.ufl.edu/ritter/ipo-data/) is a mine of information on IPO underpricing. Look up his table of underpricing by year. Is underpricing less of a problem now than in the boom IPO years of 1998–2000? Now look at Jay Ritter's table of "money-left-on-the-table." Which company provided the greatest 1-day dollar gains to investors?

SOLUTIONS TO SELF-TEST QUESTIONS

15.1 Unless the firm can secure second-stage financing, it is unlikely to succeed. If the entrepreneur is going to reap any reward on his own investment, he needs to put in enough effort to get further financing. By accepting only part of the necessary venture capital, management increases its own risk and reduces that of the venture capitalist. This decision would be costly and foolish if management lacked confidence that the project would be successful enough to get past the first stage. A credible signal by management is one that only managers who are truly confident can afford to provide. (Words are cheap. So just saying that you are confident is not a credible signal.)

15.2 If an investor can distinguish between overpriced and underpriced issues, she will bid only on the underpriced ones. In this case she will purchase only issues that provide a 10% gain. However, the ability to distinguish these issues requires considerable insight and research. The return to the informed IPO participant may be viewed as a return on the resources expended to become informed.

15.3

Underwriting spread = 446.6 million × $2	$ 893.2 million
Other expenses	45.5
Total direct expenses	$ 938.7 million
Underpricing = 446.6 million × ($56.50 − $47)	4,242.7
Total expenses	$ 5,181.4 million
Market value of issue = 446.6 × $56.50	$25,232.9 million

Expenses as a proportion of market value = $5,181.4/25,232.9 = .205, or 20.5%.

MINICASE

Mutt.Com was founded in 2013 by two graduates of the University of Wisconsin with help from Georgina Sloberg, who had built up an enviable reputation for backing new start-up businesses. Mutt.Com's user-friendly system was designed to find buyers for unwanted pets. Within 3 years, the company was generating revenues of $3.4 million a year and, despite racking up sizable losses, was regarded by investors as one of the hottest new e-commerce businesses. Therefore, the news that the company was preparing to go public generated considerable excitement.

The company's entire equity capital of 1.5 million shares was owned by the two founders and Ms. Sloberg. The initial public offering involved the sale of 500,000 shares by the three existing shareholders, together with the sale of a further 750,000 shares by the company in order to provide funds for expansion.

The company estimated that the issue would involve legal fees, auditing, printing, and other expenses of $1.3 million, which would be shared proportionately between the selling shareholders and the company. In addition, the company agreed to pay the underwriters a spread of $1.25 per share (this cost also would be shared).

The roadshow had confirmed the high level of interest in the issue, and indications from investors suggested that the entire issue could be sold at a price of $24 a share. The underwriters, however, cautioned about being too greedy on price. They pointed out that indications from investors were not the same as firm orders. Also, they argued, it was much more important to have a successful issue than to have a group of disgruntled shareholders. They therefore suggested an issue price of $18 a share.

That evening, Mutt.Com's financial manager decided to run through some calculations. First, she worked out the net receipts to the company and the existing shareholders assuming that the stock was sold for $18 a share. Next, she looked at the various costs of the IPO and tried to judge how they stacked up against the typical costs for similar IPOs. That brought her up against the question of underpricing. When she had raised the matter with the underwriters that morning, they had dismissed the notion that the initial day's return on an IPO should be considered part of the issue costs. One of the members of the underwriting team had asked: "The underwriters want to see a high return and a high stock price. Would Mutt.Com prefer a low stock price? Would that make the issue less costly?" Mutt.Com's financial manager was not convinced but felt that she should have a good answer. She wondered whether underpricing was only a problem because the existing shareholders were selling part of their holdings. Perhaps the issue price would not matter if they had not planned to sell.

Is the initial day's return on the IPO a real cost to the firm? How much would that cost be if the stock is offered at $18 but actually could be sold for $24? How would you respond to the underwriter's questions, "Would Mutt.Com prefer a low stock price? Would that make the issue less costly?"

APPENDIX

Hotch Pot's New-Issue Prospectus[10]

Prospectus

800,000 Shares
Hotch Pot Inc.
Common Stock ($.01 par value)

Of the 800,000 shares of Common Stock offered hereby, 500,000 shares are being sold by the Company and 300,000 shares are being sold by the Selling Stockholders. See "Principal and Selling Stockholders." The Company will not receive any of the proceeds from the sale of shares by the Selling Stockholders.

Before this offering there has been no public market for the Common Stock. **These securities involve a high degree of risk. See "Certain Factors."**

THESE SECURITIES HAVE NOT BEEN APPROVED OR DISAPPROVED BY THE SECURITIES AND EXCHANGE COMMISSION NOR HAS THE COMMISSION PASSED ON THE ACCURACY OR ADEQUACY OF THIS PROSPECTUS. ANY REPRESENTATION TO THE CONTRARY IS A CRIMINAL OFFENSE.

	Price to Public	Underwriting Discount	Proceeds to Company*	Proceeds to Selling Shareholders†
Per share	$12.00	$1.30	$10.70	$10.70
Total†	$9,600,000	$1,040,000	$5,350,000	$3,210,000

* Before deducting expenses payable by the Company estimated at $400,000, of which $250,000 will be paid by the Company and $150,000 by the Selling Stockholders.
† The Company and the Selling Shareholders have granted to the Underwriters options to purchase up to 120,000 additional shares at the initial public offering price less the underwriting discount, solely to cover overallotment.

The Common Stock is offered, subject to prior sale, when, as, and if delivered to and accepted by the Underwriters and subject to approval of certain legal matters by their counsel and by counsel for the Company and the Selling Shareholders. The Underwriters reserve the right to withdraw, cancel, or modify such offer and reject orders in whole or in part.

Silverman Pinch Inc.   April 1, 2017

No person has been authorized to give any information or to make any representations, other than as contained therein, in connection with the offer contained in this Prospectus, and, if given or made, such information or representations must not be relied upon. This Prospectus does not constitute an offer of any securities other than the registered securities to which it relates or an offer to any person in any jurisdiction where such an offer would be unlawful. The delivery of this Prospectus at any time does not imply that information herein is correct as of any time subsequent to its date.

IN CONNECTION WITH THIS OFFERING, THE UNDERWRITER MAY OVERALLOT OR EFFECT TRANSACTIONS WHICH STABILIZE OR MAINTAIN THE MARKET PRICE OF THE COMMON STOCK OF THE COMPANY AT A LEVEL ABOVE THAT WHICH MIGHT OTHERWISE PREVAIL IN THE OPEN MARKET. SUCH STABILIZING, IF COMMENCED, MAY BE DISCONTINUED AT ANY TIME.

Prospectus Summary

The following summary information is qualified in its entirety by the detailed information and financial statements appearing elsewhere in this Prospectus.

The Company: Hotch Pot Inc. operates a chain of 140 fast-food outlets in the United States offering unusual combinations of dishes.

---

[10] Real prospectuses would be much longer than our simple example.

The Offering: Common Stock offered by the Company 500,000 shares; Common Stock offered by the Selling Stockholders 300,000 shares; Common Stock to be outstanding after this offering 3,500,000 shares.

Use of Proceeds: For the construction of new restaurants and to provide working capital.

The Company

Hotch Pot Inc. operates a chain of 140 fast-food outlets in Illinois, Pennsylvania, and Ohio. These restaurants specialize in offering an unusual combination of foreign dishes.

The Company was organized in Delaware in 2007.

Use of Proceeds

The Company intends to use the net proceeds from the sale of 500,000 shares of Common Stock offered hereby, estimated at approximately $5 million, to open new outlets in midwest states and to provide additional working capital. It has no immediate plans to use any of the net proceeds of the offering for any other specific investment.

Dividend Policy

The Company has not paid cash dividends on its Common Stock and does not anticipate that dividends will be paid on the Common Stock in the foreseeable future.

Certain Factors

Investment in the Common Stock involves a high degree of risk. The following factors should be carefully considered in evaluating the Company:

SUBSTANTIAL CAPITAL NEEDS   The Company will require additional financing to continue its expansion policy. The Company believes that its relations with its lenders are good, but there can be no assurance that additional financing will be available in the future.

COMPETITION   The Company is in competition with a number of restaurant chains supplying fast food. Many of these companies are substantially larger and better capitalized than the Company.

Capitalization

The following table sets forth the capitalization of the Company as of December 31, 2016, and as adjusted to reflect the sale of 500,000 shares of Common Stock by the Company.

	Actual	As Adjusted
		(in thousands)
Long-term debt	$ —	$ —
Stockholders' equity	30	35
Common stock—$.01 par value, 3,000,000 shares outstanding, 3,500,000 shares outstanding, as adjusted		
Paid-in capital	1,970	7,315
Retained earnings	3,200	3,200
Total stockholders' equity	$5,200	$10,550
Total capitalization	$5,200	$10,550

Selected Financial Data

[*The Prospectus typically includes a summary income statement and balance sheet.*]

Management's Analysis of Results of Operations and Financial Condition

Revenue growth for the year ended December 31, 2016, resulted from the opening of ten new restaurants in the Company's existing geographic area and from sales of a new range of desserts, notably crepe suzette with custard. Sales per customer increased by 20% and this contributed to the improvement in margins.

During the year the Company borrowed $600,000 from its banks at an interest rate of 2% above the prime rate.

Business

Hotch Pot Inc. operates a chain of 140 fast-food outlets in Illinois, Pennsylvania, and Ohio. These restaurants specialize in offering an unusual combination of foreign dishes. 50% of company's revenues derived from sales of two dishes, sushi and sauerkraut and curry bolognese. All dishes are prepared in three regional centers and then frozen and distributed to the individual restaurants.

Management

The following table sets forth information regarding the Company's directors, executive officers, and key employees:

Name	Age	Position
Emma Lucullus	28	President, Chief Executive Officer, and Director
Ed Lucullus	33	Treasurer and Director

Emma Lucullus Emma Lucullus established the Company in 2007 and has been its Chief Executive Officer since that date.

Ed Lucullus Ed Lucullus has been employed by the Company since 2007.

Executive Compensation

The following table sets forth the cash compensation paid for services rendered for the year 2016 by the executive officers:

Name	Capacity	Cash Compensation
Emma Lucullus	President and Chief Executive Officer	$130,000
Ed Lucullus	Treasurer	$95,000

Certain Transactions

At various times between 2007 and 2016, First Cookham Venture Partners invested a total of $1.5 million in the Company. In connection with this investment, First Cookham Venture Partners was granted certain rights to registration under the Securities Act of 1933, including the right to have their shares of Common Stock registered at the Company's expense with the Securities and Exchange Commission.

Principal and Selling Stockholders

The following table sets forth certain information regarding the beneficial ownership of the Company's voting Common Stock as of the date of this prospectus by (1) each person known by the Company to be the beneficial owner of more than 5% of its voting Common Stock, and (2) each director of the Company who beneficially owns voting Common Stock. Unless otherwise indicated, each owner has sole voting and dispositive power over his shares.

Name of Beneficial Owner	Shares Beneficially Owned prior to Offering		Shares to Be Sold	Shares Beneficially Owned after Offering	
	Number	Percent		Number	Percent
Emma Lucullus	400,000	13.3	25,000	375,000	12.9
Ed Lucullus	400,000	13.3	25,000	375,000	12.9
First Cookham Venture Partners	1,700,000	66.7	250,000	1,450,000	50.0
Hermione Kraft	200,000	6.7	—	200,000	6.9

Lock-Up Agreements

The holders of the Common Stock have agreed with the Underwriter not to sell, pledge, or otherwise dispose of their shares, other than as specified in this Prospectus, for a period of 180 days after the date of the Prospectus without the prior consent of Silverman Pinch.

Description of Capital Stock

The Company's authorized capital stock consists of 10,000,000 shares of voting Common Stock.

As of the date of this Prospectus, there are four holders of record of the Common Stock.

Under the terms of one of the Company's loan agreements, the Company may not pay cash dividends on Common Stock except from net profits without the written consent of the lender.

Underwriting

Subject to the terms and conditions set forth in the Underwriting Agreement, the Underwriter, Silverman Pinch Inc., has agreed to purchase from the Company and the Selling Stockholders 800,000 shares of Common Stock.

There is no public market for the Common Stock. The price to the public for the Common Stock was determined by negotiation between the Company and the Underwriter and was based on, among other things, the Company's financial and operating history and condition, its prospects, and the prospects for its industry in general, the management of the Company, and the market prices of securities for companies in businesses similar to that of the Company.

Legal Matters

The validity of the shares of Common Stock offered by the Prospectus is being passed on for the Company by Atticus and Finch and for the Underwriter by Stratton Oakmont.

Legal Proceedings

Hotch Pot was served in January 2017 with a summons and complaint in an action commenced by a customer who alleges that consumption of the Company's products caused severe nausea and loss of feeling in both feet. The Company believes that the complaint is without foundation.

Experts

The consolidated financial statements of the Company have been so included in reliance on the reports of Hooper Firebrand, independent accountants, given on the authority of that firm as experts in auditing and accounting.

Financial Statements

[Text and tables omitted.]

16

Debt Policy

LEARNING OBJECTIVES

After studying this chapter, you should be able to:

16-1 Show why capital structure does not affect firm value in perfect capital markets.

16-2 Calculate interest tax shields and explain why the U.S. tax system encourages debt finance.

16-3 Describe the costs of financial distress and explain the trade-off theory of capital structure.

16-4 Explain the benefits (and sometimes costs) of financial slack.

16-5 Specify characteristics that should affect a company's choice of capital structure.

RELATED WEBSITES FOR THIS CHAPTER CAN BE
FOUND IN CONNECT.

River Cruises is reviewing its capital structure. More debt would increase the expected return on its shares, but would it add value? *cliff1066™/Flickr/CC BY 2.0*

A firm's basic financial resource is the stream of cash flows produced by its assets and operations. When the firm is financed entirely by common stock, all those cash flows belong to the stockholders. When it issues both debt and equity, the firm splits the cash flows into two streams, a relatively safe stream that goes to the debtholders and a riskier one that goes to the stockholders.

The firm's mix of securities is known as its *capital structure*. Look at Table 16.1. You can see that in some industries, companies borrow much more heavily than in others. Biotech, software, and Internet companies rely almost wholly on equity finance. At the other extreme, corporations in the chemical, aerospace, and hotel industries rely much more on debt finance.

Capital structure is not immutable. Firms can change their capital structure, sometimes almost overnight. Shareholders want management to choose the mix of securities that maximizes firm value. But is there an optimal capital structure? We must consider the possibility that no combination has any greater appeal than any other. Perhaps the really important decisions concern the company's assets, and decisions about capital structure are mere details—matters to be attended to but not worried about.

In the first part of the chapter, we look at examples in which capital structure *doesn't* matter, and we point out some tempting financial fallacies that you should be prepared to resist. After that, we put back some of the things that do make a difference, such as taxes, bankruptcy, and the signals that your financing decisions may send to investors. We then draw up a checklist for financial managers who need to decide on the firm's capital structure.

The appendix to the chapter contains a brief discussion of what happens when firms cannot pay their debts and enter bankruptcy proceedings.

TABLE 16.1 Median ratios of long-term debt to total capital, 2015

Industry	Debt Ratio
Biotech	0.00
Software	0.00
Internet information providers	0.02
Semiconductors	0.09
Integrated oil and gas	0.34
Airlines	0.36
Gas utilities	0.43
Railroads	0.44
Chemicals	0.52
Aerospace	0.58
Hotels	0.64

Note: Debt to total capital ratio = $D/(D + E)$, where D and E are the book values of long-term debt and equity.
Source: Compustat.

BEYOND THE PAGE

Industry debt ratios in 2015

mhhe.com/brealey9e

16.1 How Borrowing Affects Value in a Tax-Free Economy

> It is after the ball game and the pizza man is delivering a pizza to Yogi Berra. "Should I cut it into four slices as usual, Yogi?" asks the pizza man. "No," replies Yogi, "Cut it into eight; I'm hungry tonight."

If you understand why more slices won't sate Yogi's appetite, you will have no difficulty understanding when a company's choice of **capital structure** does not increase the underlying value of the firm.

capital structure
The mix of long-term debt and equity financing.

Consider a simple balance sheet, with all entries expressed as current market values:

Assets	Liabilities and Stockholders' Equity
Value of cash flows from the firm's real assets and operations	Market value of debt
	Market value of equity
Value of firm	Value of firm

The right- and left-hand sides of a balance sheet are always equal. (Balance sheets have to balance!) Therefore, if you add up the market values of all the firm's debt and equity securities, you can calculate the value of all the future cash flows from the firm's real assets and operations.

In fact, the value of those cash flows *determines* the value of the firm and, therefore, determines the aggregate value of all the firm's outstanding debt and equity securities. If the firm changes its capital structure—say, by using more debt and less equity financing—overall value should not change.

Think of the left-hand side of the balance sheet as the size of the pizza; the right-hand side determines how it is sliced. A company can slice its cash flow into as many parts as it likes, but the value of those parts will always sum back to the value of the unsliced cash flow. (Of course, we have to make sure that none of the cash-flow stream is lost in the slicing. We cannot say "The value of a pizza is independent of how it is sliced" if the slicer is also a nibbler.)

The basic idea here (the value of a pizza does not depend on how it is sliced) has various applications. Yogi Berra got friendly chuckles for his misapplication. Franco Modigliani and Merton Miller received Nobel Prizes for applying it to corporate financing. Modigliani and Miller, always referred to as "MM," showed in 1958 that the value of a firm does not depend on how its cash flows are "sliced." More precisely, they demonstrated the following proposition: **When there are no taxes and capital markets function well, the market value of a company does not depend on its capital structure. In other words, financial managers cannot increase value by changing the mix of securities used to finance the company.**

Of course, this MM proposition rests on some important simplifying assumptions. For example, capital markets have to be "well functioning." This means that investors can trade securities without restrictions and can borrow or lend on the same terms as the firm. It also means that capital markets are efficient, so securities are fairly priced given the information available to investors. (We discussed market efficiency in Chapter 7.) MM's proposition also assumes that there are no distorting taxes, and it ignores the costs encountered if a firm borrows too much and lands in financial distress.

The firm's capital structure decision does matter if these assumptions are not true or if other practical complications are encountered. But the best way to *start* thinking about capital structure is to work through MM's argument. *To keep things as simple as possible, we will ignore taxes until further notice.*

MM's Argument—A Simple Example

Cleo, the president of River Cruises, is reviewing that firm's capital structure with Antony, the financial manager. Table 16.2 shows the current position. The company has no debt, and all its operating income is paid as dividends to the shareholders. The *expected* earnings and dividends per share are $1.25, but this figure is by no means certain—it could turn out to be more or less than $1.25. For example, earnings could fall to $.75 in a slump or they could jump to $1.75 in a boom.

The price of each share is $10. The firm expects to produce a level stream of earnings and dividends in perpetuity. No growth is forecast, so stockholders' expected return is equal to the dividend yield—that is, the expected dividend per share divided by the price, $1.25/$10.00 = .125, or 12.5%.

Cleo has come to the conclusion that shareholders would be better off if the company had equal proportions of debt and equity. Therefore, she proposes to issue $500,000 of debt at an interest rate of 10% and to use the proceeds to repurchase 50,000 shares. This is called a **restructuring.** Notice that the $500,000 raised by the new borrowing does not stay in the firm. It goes right out the door to shareholders in order to repurchase and retire 50,000 shares. Therefore, the assets and investment policy of the firm are not affected. Only the financing mix changes.

What would MM say about this new capital structure? Suppose the change is made. Operating income is the same, so the value of the "pie" is fixed at $1 million. With $500,000 in new debt outstanding, the remaining common shares must be worth $500,000, that is, 50,000 shares at $10 per share. The total value of the debt and equity is still $1 million.

restructuring
Process of changing the firm's capital structure without changing its real assets.

TABLE 16.2 River Cruises is entirely equity-financed. Although it expects to have an income of $125,000 in perpetuity, this income is not certain. This table shows the return to the stockholder under different assumptions about operating income. We assume no taxes.

Data			
Number of shares	100,000		
Price per share	$10		
Market value of shares	$1 million		

	State of the Economy		
	Slump	**Normal**	**Boom**
Operating income	$75,000	$125,000	$175,000
Earnings per share	$0.75	$1.25	$1.75
Return on shares	7.5%	12.5%	17.5%
		Expected outcome	

Because the value of the firm is the same, common shareholders are no better or worse off than before. River Cruises shares still trade at $10 each. The overall value of River Cruises' equity falls from $1 million to $500,000, but shareholders have also received $500,000 in cash.

Antony points all this out: "The restructuring doesn't make our stockholders any richer or poorer, Cleo. Why bother? Capital structure doesn't matter."

16.1   Self-Test

Suppose River Cruises issues $350,000 of new debt (rather than $500,000) and uses the proceeds to repurchase and retire common stock. How does this affect price per share? How many shares will be left outstanding?

How Borrowing Affects Earnings per Share

Cleo is unconvinced. She prepares Table 16.3 and Figure 16.1 to show how borrowing $500,000 could increase earnings per share. Comparison of Tables 16.2 and 16.3 shows that "normal" earnings per share increase to $1.50 (versus $1.25) after the restructuring. Table 16.3 also shows more "upside" (earnings per share of $2.50 versus $1.75) and more "downside" ($.50 versus $.75).

The orange line in Figure 16.1 shows how earnings per share would vary with operating income under the firm's current all-equity financing. It is, therefore, simply a plot of the data in Table 16.2. The blue line shows how earnings per share would vary if the company moves to equal proportions of debt and equity. Thus, it is a plot of the data in Table 16.3.

Cleo reasons as follows: "It is clear that debt could either increase or reduce the return to the equityholder. In a slump, the return to the equityholder is reduced by the use of debt, but otherwise it is *increased*. We could be heading for a recession but it doesn't look likely. Maybe we could help our shareholders by going ahead with the debt issue."

As financial manager, Antony replies as follows: "I agree that borrowing will increase earnings per share as long as there's no slump. But we're not really doing anything for shareholders that they can't do on their own. Suppose River Cruises does *not* borrow. In that case, an investor could go to the bank, borrow $10, and then invest

---

TABLE 16.3 River Cruises is wondering whether to issue $500,000 of debt at an interest rate of 10% and repurchase 50,000 shares. This table shows the return to the shareholder under different assumptions about operating income. Returns to shareholders are higher than they were in Table 16.2 in normal and boom times but lower in slumps.

Data			
Number of shares	50,000		
Price per share	$10		
Market value of shares	$500,000		
Market value of debt	$500,000		

Outcomes			
	State of the Economy		
	Slump	Normal	Boom
Operating income	$75,000	$125,000	$175,000
Interest	$50,000	$ 50,000	$ 50,000
Equity earnings	$25,000	$ 75,000	$125,000
Earnings per share	$0.50	$1.50	$2.50
Return on shares	5%	15%	25%
		Expected outcome	

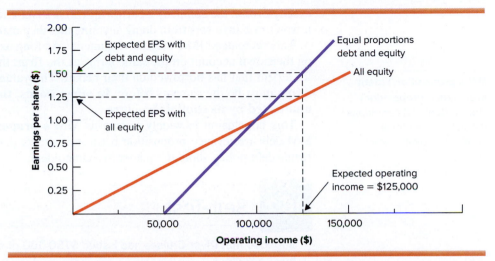

FIGURE 16.1 Borrowing increases River Cruises' earnings per share (EPS) when operating income is greater than $100,000 but reduces it when operating income is less than $100,000. Expected EPS rises from $1.25 to $1.50.

$20 in two shares. Such an investor would put up only $10 of her own money. Table 16.4 shows how the payoffs on this $10 investment vary with River Cruises' operating income. You can see that these payoffs are exactly the same as the investor would get by buying one share in the company after the restructuring. (Compare the last two lines of Tables 16.3 and 16.4.) It makes no difference whether shareholders borrow directly or whether River Cruises borrows on their behalf. Therefore, if River Cruises goes ahead and borrows, it will not allow investors to do anything that they could not do already, and so it cannot increase the value of the firm.

"We can run the same argument in reverse and show that investors also won't be any *worse* off after the restructuring. Imagine an investor who owns two shares in the company before the restructuring. If River Cruises borrows money, there is some chance that the return on the shares will be lower than before. If that possibility is not to our investor's taste, he can buy one share in the restructured company and also invest $10 in the firm's debt. Table 16.5 shows how the payoff on this investment varies with River Cruises' operating income. You can see that these payoffs are exactly the same as the investor got before the restructuring. (Compare the last lines of Tables 16.2 and 16.5.) By lending half of his capital (by investing in River Cruises' debt), the investor

TABLE 16.4 Individual investors can replicate River Cruises' borrowing by borrowing on their own. In this example, we assume that River Cruises has not restructured. However, the investor can put up $10 of her own money, borrow $10 more, and buy two shares at $10 apiece. This generates the same rates of return as in Table 16.3.

	State of the Economy		
	Slump	**Normal**	**Boom**
Earnings on two shares	$1.50	$2.50	$3.50
Less interest at 10%	$1.00	$1.00	$1.00
Net earnings on investment	$0.50	$1.50	$2.50
Return on $10 investment	5%	15%	25%
		Expected outcome	

TABLE 16.5 Individual investors can also undo the effects of River Cruises' borrowing. Here the investor buys one share for $10 and lends out $10 more. Compare these rates of return to the original returns of River Cruises in Table 16.2.

	State of the Economy		
	Slump	**Normal**	**Boom**
Earnings on one share	$0.50	$1.50	$2.50
Plus interest at 10%	$1.00	$1.00	$1.00
Net earnings on investment	$1.50	$2.50	$3.50
Return on $20 investment	7.5%	12.5%	17.5%
		Expected outcome	

exactly offsets the company's borrowing. So if River Cruises goes ahead and borrows, it won't *stop* investors from doing anything that they could previously do."

This recreates MM's original argument.[1] As long as investors can borrow or lend on their own account on the same terms as the firm, they are not going to pay more for a firm that has borrowed on their behalf. The value of the firm after the restructuring must be the same as before. **In other words, the value of the firm must be unaffected by its capital structure.**

This conclusion is widely known as **MM's proposition I.** It is also called the MM debt-irrelevance proposition because it shows that, under ideal conditions, the firm's debt policy shouldn't matter to shareholders.

MM's proposition I (debt-irrelevance proposition)
Under idealized conditions the value of a firm is unaffected by its capital structure.

16.2 Self-Test

Suppose that River Cruises had issued $750,000 of debt, using the proceeds to buy back stock.

a. What would be the impact of a $50,000 change in operating income on earnings per share?

b. Show how a conservative investor could "undo" the change in River Cruises' capital structure by varying the investment strategy shown in Table 16.5. *Hint:* The investor will have to lend $3 for every dollar invested in River Cruises' stock.

How Borrowing Affects Risk and Return

Figure 16.2 summarizes the implications of MM's debt irrelevance proposition for River Cruises. The upper pies represent firm value; the lower pies, expected, or "normal," operating income. Restructuring does not affect the size of the pies because the amount and risk of operating income are unchanged. Thus, if the firm raises $500,000 in debt and uses the proceeds to repurchase and retire shares, the remaining shares *must* be worth $500,000, and the total value of debt and equity *must* stay at $1 million.

The two bottom pies in Figure 16.2 are also the same size. But notice that the bottom right pie shows that shareholders can expect to earn more than half of River Cruises' normal operating income. They get more than half of the expected income "pie." Does that mean shareholders are better off? MM say no. Why? Because shareholders bear more risk.

FIGURE 16.2 "Slicing the pie" for River Cruises. The pies on the left assume the company has no debt. The pies on the right reflect the proposed restructuring. The restructuring splits firm value (top pies) 50–50. Shareholders get more than 50% of expected, or "normal," operating income (bottom pies), but only because they bear financial risk. Note that restructuring does not affect total firm value or operating income.

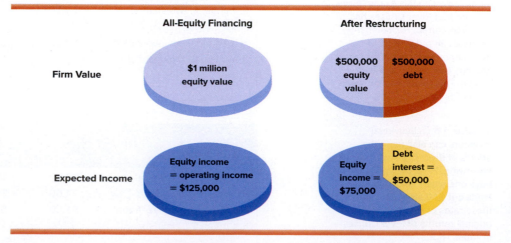

---

[1] There are many more general–and technical–proofs of the MM proposition. We will not pursue them here.

operating risk
Risk in firm's operating income. Also called *business risk.*

Look again at Tables 16.2 and 16.3. Restructuring does not affect operating income, regardless of the state of the economy. Therefore, debt financing does not affect the **operating risk** or, equivalently, the **business risk** of the firm. But with less equity outstanding, a change in operating income has a greater impact on earnings per share. Suppose operating income drops from $125,000 to $75,000. Under all-equity financing, there are 100,000 shares; so earnings per share fall by $.50. With 50% debt, there are only 50,000 shares outstanding; so the same drop in operating income reduces earnings per share by $1.

financial leverage
Debt financing to amplify the effects of changes in operating income on the returns to stockholders.

You can see now why the use of debt finance is known as **financial leverage** and a firm that has issued debt is described as a *levered firm.* The debt increases the uncertainty about percentage stock returns. If the firm is financed entirely by equity, a decline of $50,000 in operating income reduces the return on the shares by 5 percentage points. If the firm issues debt, then the same decline of $50,000 in operating income reduces the return on the shares by 10 percentage points. (Compare Tables 16.2 and 16.3.) In other words, the effect of leverage is to double the magnitude of the upside and downside in the return on River Cruises' shares. If borrowing doubles the upside and downside returns for River Cruises' stock, what happens to beta? It also doubles. For example, if beta is .33 (1/3) with 100% equity, it is .67 (2/3) with 50% debt and 50% equity.

financial risk
Risk to shareholders resulting from the use of debt.

Debt finance does not affect operating risk but it does add financial risk. With only half the equity to absorb the same amount of operating risk, risk per share must double.[2]

Consider now the implications of MM's proposition I for the expected return on River Cruises' stock. Before the proposed debt issue, the expected stream of earnings and dividends per share is $1.25. Because investment in the shares is risky, the shareholders require a return of 12.5%, or 2.5% above the interest rate. So the share price (which for a perpetuity is equal to the expected dividend divided by the required return) is $1.25/.125 = $10. The good news is that after the debt issue, expected earnings and dividends rise to $1.50. The bad news is that the risk of the shares has now doubled. So instead of being content with a return of 2.5% above the interest rate, shareholders now demand a return of 5% more than the interest rate—that is, a required return of 10 + 5 = 15%. The benefit from the rise in dividends is exactly canceled out by the rise in the required return. The share price after the debt issue is $1.50/.15 = $10, exactly the same as before.

	Current Structure: All Equity	Proposed Structure: Equal Debt and Equity
Expected earnings per share	$1.25	$1.50
Share price	$10	$10
Expected return on share	12.5%	15.0%

Thus, leverage increases the expected return to shareholders, but it also increases the risk. The two effects cancel, leaving shareholder value unchanged.

16.2 Debt and the Cost of Equity

What is River Cruises' cost of capital? With all-equity financing, the answer is easy. Stockholders pay $10 per share and expect earnings per share of $1.25. If the earnings per share are paid out in a perpetual stream, the expected return is $1.25/10 = .125, or 12.5%. This is the cost of equity capital, r_{equity}, and also r_{assets}, the expected return and cost of capital for the firm's assets.

---

[2] Think back to Section 10.4, where we showed that fixed costs increase the variability in a firm's profits. These fixed costs create *operating leverage*. It is exactly the same with debt. Debt interest is a fixed cost, and therefore, debt magnifies the variability of profits after interest. These fixed interest charges create financial leverage.

Because the restructuring does not change operating earnings or firm value, it should not change the cost of capital either. Suppose the restructuring takes place. Also, by a grand stroke of luck you simultaneously become a billionaire and buy *all* the outstanding debt and equity of River Cruises. What rate of return should you expect on this investment? Your answer should be 12.5% because, once you own all the debt and equity, you will effectively own all the assets and receive all the operating income.

You will indeed get 12.5%. Table 16.3 shows expected earnings per share of $1.50 and a share price that is unchanged at $10. Therefore, the expected return on equity is $1.50/\$10 = .15$, or 15% ($r_{\text{equity}} = .15$). The return on debt is 10% ($r_{\text{debt}} = .10$). Your overall return is

$$(.5 \times .10) + (.5 \times .15) = .125 = r_{\text{assets}}$$

There is obviously a general principle here: The appropriate weighted average of r_{debt} and r_{equity} takes you to r_{assets}, the opportunity cost of capital for the company's assets. The formula is

$$r_{\text{assets}} = (r_{\text{debt}} \times D/V) + (r_{\text{equity}} \times E/V)$$

where D and E are the amounts of outstanding debt and equity and V equals overall firm value, the sum of D and E. Remember that D, E, and V are market values, not book values.

This formula does not quite match the weighted-average cost of capital (WACC) formula presented in Chapter 13 because at this point we are still ignoring taxes.[3] Don't worry, we'll get to WACC in a moment. First let's look at the implications of MM's debt-irrelevance proposition for the cost of equity.

MM's proposition I states that the firm's choice of capital structure does not affect the firm's operating income or the value of its assets. So r_{assets}, the expected return on the package of debt and equity, is unaffected.

However, we have just seen that leverage does increase the risk of the equity and the return that shareholders demand. To see how the expected return on equity varies with leverage, we simply rearrange the formula for the company cost of capital as follows:

$$r_{\text{equity}} = r_{\text{assets}} + \frac{D}{E}(r_{\text{assets}} - r_{\text{debt}}) \tag{16.1}$$

which in words says that

$$\begin{array}{ccc}
\text{Expected} & \text{expected} & \left[\begin{array}{c} \text{debt-} \\ \text{equity} \times \left(\begin{array}{cc} \text{expected} & \text{expected} \\ \text{return on} - \text{return on} \\ \text{ratio} & \text{assets} & \text{debt} \end{array} \right) \end{array} \right] \\
\text{return} = \text{return} + \\
\text{on equity} & \text{on assets}
\end{array}$$

MM's proposition II
The required rate of return on equity increases as the firm's debt-equity ratio increases.

This is **MM's proposition II**. It states that the expected rate of return on the common stock of a levered firm increases in proportion to the debt-equity ratio (D/E), expressed in market values. Note that $r_{\text{equity}} = r_{\text{assets}}$ if the firm has no debt.

Example | 16.1 ▶ | River Cruises' Cost of Equity

We can check out MM's proposition II for River Cruises. Before the decision to borrow,

$$r_{\text{equity}} = r_{\text{assets}} = \frac{\text{expected operating income}}{\text{market value of all securities}}$$

$$= \frac{125,000}{1,000,000} = .125, \text{ or } 12.5\%$$

---

[3] See Sections 13.1 and 13.2.

If the firm goes ahead with its plan to borrow, the expected return on assets, r_{assets}, is still 12.5%. So the expected return on equity is

$$r_{equity} = r_{assets} + \frac{D}{E}(r_{assets} - r_{debt})$$

$$= .125 + \frac{500{,}000}{500{,}000}(.125 - .10)$$

$$= .15, \text{ or } 15\% \blacksquare$$

We pointed out in Chapter 13 that you can think of a debt issue as having an explicit cost and an implicit cost. The explicit cost is the rate of interest charged on the firm's debt. **But debt also increases financial risk and causes shareholders to demand a higher return on their investment. Once you recognize this implicit cost, debt is no cheaper than equity—the return that investors require on their assets is unaffected by the firm's borrowing decision.** Be sure to remember this point whenever you hear some layperson say "Debt is cheaper than equity."

16.3 Self-Test

When the firm issues debt, why does r_{assets}, the company cost of capital, remain fixed while the expected return on equity, r_{equity}, changes? Why is it not the other way around?

The implications of MM's proposition II are shown in Figure 16.3. No matter how much the firm borrows, the expected return on the package of debt and equity, r_{assets}, is unchanged, but the expected rate of return on the separate parts of the package does change. How is this possible? Because the proportions of debt and equity in the package are also changing. More debt means that the cost of equity increases, but at the same time the *amount* of equity is less.

In Figure 16.3, we have drawn the rate of interest on the debt as constant no matter how much the firm borrows. That is not wholly realistic. It is true that most large, conservative companies could borrow a little more or less without noticeably affecting the interest rate that they pay. But at higher debt levels, lenders become concerned that they may not get their money back and they demand higher rates of interest.

FIGURE 16.3 MM's proposition II with a fixed interest rate on debt. The expected return on River Cruises' equity rises in line with the debt-equity ratio. The weighted average of the expected returns on debt and equity is constant, equal to the expected return on assets.

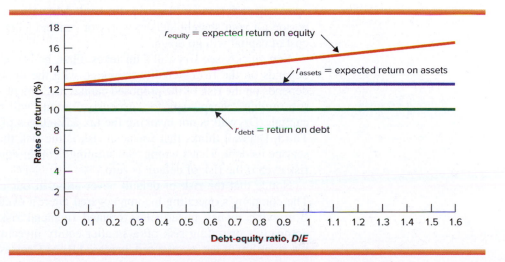

FIGURE 16.4 MM's proposition II when debt is not risk free. As the debt-equity ratio increases, debtholders demand a higher expected rate of return to compensate for the risk of default. The expected return on equity increases more slowly when debt is risky because the debtholders take on part of the risk. The expected return on the package of debt and equity, r_{assets}, remains constant.

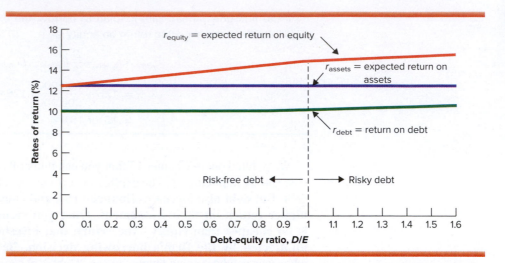

Figure 16.4 modifies Figure 16.3 to take account of this. You can see that as the firm borrows more, the risk of default increases and the firm has to pay higher rates of interest. Proposition II continues to predict that the expected return on the package of debt and equity does not change. However, the slope of the r_{equity} line now tapers off as D/E increases. Why? Essentially because holders of risky debt begin to bear part of the firm's operating risk. As the firm borrows more, more of that risk is transferred from stockholders to bondholders.

No Magic in Financial Leverage

MM's propositions boil down to a simple warning: *There is no magic in financial leverage.* Financial managers who ignore this warning can be sucked into serious practical mistakes. Here are two examples of tempting fallacies.

Debt Is Not Cheap Financing   Your surfactants business is under pressure from overseas producers. Claxon Drywall, a consultant, argues that you should double your planned capital investment in order to modernize plant and equipment and cut production costs. You point out that the expanded investment offers only a 9% return and is negative-NPV when forecast cash flows are discounted at your company's normal 11% cost of capital.

Drywall responds condescendingly: "Look, banks will be happy to lend you the money at 5%, and NPV at 5% is strongly positive. And there's no financial risk—your operating cash flows will service the bank debt with a large safety cushion. There's no reason for your shareholders to worry or demand a higher rate of return. Your overall cost of capital will go down."

You quickly see Drywall's mistakes. First, he is confusing the cost of debt, which depends on the firm's creditworthiness, with the opportunity cost of capital, which depends on the risk of the proposed capital investment. Second, he naively thinks that substituting "cheap" debt for "expensive" equity will bring down the overall cost of capital. (Drywall is not invoking the tax advantages of debt, which we cover below.) Third, Drywall thinks that financial risk is the risk that the firm will not be able to service its debt. That's wrong: Substituting debt for equity financing creates financial risk even if the risk of default is zero.

Notice that the risk of default never arose in our calculations for River Cruises. The company's operating income covered interest even when the economy slumped. Borrowing money nevertheless created financial risk because it concentrated the company's operating risk on a smaller equity investment. For example, it doubled the volatility of net income and increased River Cruises' beta from .33 to .67.

Beware of Hidden Debt   A law firm (*not* Dewey, Cheatem, and Howe) is expanding rapidly and must move to new office space. Business is good, and the firm is encouraged to purchase an entire building for $10 million. The building offers first-class office space, convenient to the firm's most important corporate clients, and provides space for future expansion.

Claxon Drywall appears again and encourages the firm not to buy the building but to sign a long-term lease for the building instead. "With lease financing, you'll save $10 million. You won't have to put up any equity investment," Drywall explains.

The senior law partner asks about the terms of the lease. "I've taken the liberty to check," Drywall says. "The lease will provide 100% financing. It will commit you to 20 fixed annual payments of $950,000, with the first payment due immediately."

"The initial payment of $950,000 sounds like a down payment to me," the senior partner observes sourly.

"Good point," Drywall says amiably, "but you'll still save $9,050,000 up front. You can earn a handsome rate of return on that money. For example, I understand you are considering branch offices in London and Brussels. The $9 million would pay the costs of setting up the new offices, and the cash flows from the new offices should more than cover the lease payments."

You can immediately see the dangers here. Committing to the lease amounts to taking on de facto debt of $9,050,000 after the first lease payment. (The lease payments are fixed obligations, just like debt service.) Is that prudent borrowing? Could the law firm make the lease payments if its business declined and a group of partners left?

It turns out that the 20 fixed payments of $950,000 would give the lessor an 8% rate of return.[4] That's the effective cost of debt embedded in the lease.[5] When Drywall says that the firm could cover the lease payments by opening branch offices, he is effectively arguing that investments in the branch offices are worthwhile if they offer a rate of return higher than 8%.

Drywall is again confusing the cost of debt, in this case 8%, with the opportunity cost of capital, which depends on the risk of investing in the branch offices.

What would MM say to the senior partner? First, they would ask whether the proposed branch offices have positive NPVs when forecast cash flows are discounted at the opportunity cost of capital. They would not object to borrowing $9,050,000 by way of the lease if the firm can use the money, if it can cover the lease payments with a reasonable safety cushion, and if 8% is a fair market rate for that amount of de facto borrowing. But they would caution that the extra borrowing will *not* reduce the overall company cost of capital. And they would insist that 8% is *not* the correct discount rate for cash flows from the new offices. Discounting at 8% implicitly assumes that there is magic in financial leverage. There is none.

MM would also suggest that we move on and think about debt and taxes.

16.3 Debt, Taxes, and the Weighted-Average Cost of Capital

The MM propositions suggest that debt policy should not matter. Yet financial managers do worry about debt policy, and for good reasons. Now we are ready to see why.

If debt policy were *completely* irrelevant, actual debt ratios would vary randomly from firm to firm and from industry to industry. Yet almost all airlines, utilities, and real estate development companies rely heavily on debt. And so do many firms in

---

[4] The present value of a 20-year annuity due of $950,000 is $10,073,000 at 8%. Or you can say that the present value at 8% of the 19 year-end payments is $9,123,000. With the initial payment of $950,000, the present value of all lease payments, again, is $10,073,000. Either way, the lessor earns slightly more than 8% on his or her money.

[5] We caution that leases are more complicated than implied here. For example, the lease would transfer ownership of the building and the law firm would lose depreciation tax shields.

capital-intensive industries like steel, aluminum, chemicals, and mining. On the other hand, it is rare to find a biotech or software company that is not predominantly equity financed. Glamorous growth companies seldom use much debt, despite rapid expansion and often heavy requirements for capital.

The explanation of these patterns lies partly in the things that we have so far left out of our discussion. Now we will put all these things back in, starting with taxes.

Debt and Taxes at River Cruises

Debt financing has one important advantage: The interest that the company pays is a tax-deductible expense, but equity income is subject to corporate tax.

To see the tax advantage of debt, let's look again at River Cruises. The left column of Table 16.6 assumes that the company has no debt. We now assume expected pretax income is $192,308, so expected income *after tax* at 35% remains $125,000. The right column shows what happens if the company borrows $500,000 at 10%.

Notice that the combined income of the debtholders and equityholders is higher by $17,500 when the firm is levered. This is because the interest payments are tax-deductible. Thus, every dollar of interest reduces taxes by $.35. The total amount of tax savings is simply .35 × interest payments. In the case of River Cruises, the **interest tax shield** is .35 × $50,000 = $17,500 each year. In other words, the "pie" of after-tax income that is shared by debt and equity investors increases by $17,500 relative to the zero-debt case. Because the debtholders receive no more than the going rate of interest, all the benefit of this interest tax shield is captured by the shareholders.

The interest tax shield is a valuable asset. Let's see how much it could be worth. Suppose that River Cruises plans to replace its bonds when they mature and to keep "rolling over" the debt indefinitely. It therefore looks forward to a permanent stream of tax savings of $17,500 per year.

If the debt is really fixed and permanent, and if River Cruises is confident that it will earn enough taxable income to cover the interest deductions, then the interest tax shields are a safe perpetuity. Suppose that the risk of the tax shields is the same as the interest payments generating them. Then we can discount at the 10% interest rate demanded by debt investors. The present value is

$$\text{PV interest tax shield} = \frac{\$17,500}{.10} = \$175,000$$

This simple calculation is a common rule of thumb. The rule takes the projected interest tax shield and divides by the cost of debt, as if the interest tax shield were perpetual and just as safe as the debt.[6]

Unfortunately, the rule almost always *overstates* the value of interest tax shields. First, the firm may not borrow permanently. Second, it may run into future losses and

interest tax shield
Tax savings resulting from deductibility of interest payments.

TABLE 16.6 River Cruises expects to earn $125,000 (now after tax at 35%) if there is no debt. But the total amount earned by debt and equity investors increases to $142,500 if there is $500,000 of debt. The increase of $17,500 occurs because interest is a tax-deductible expense. The interest tax shield reduces taxes by $17,500.

	Zero Debt	$500,000 Debt
Expected operating income	$192,308	$192,308
Debt interest at 10%	0	50,000
Before-tax income	192,308	142,308
Tax at 35%	67,308	49,808
After-tax income	125,000	92,500
Combined debt and equity income = after-tax income + interest	125,000	142,500

---

[6] Notice that the PV in this case equals the tax rate times the amount of debt outstanding. If the tax rate is T_C, the annual interest tax shield is $T_C \times r_{debt} \times D$. The tax shield is a perpetuity, so the PV calculation divides $T_C \times r_{debt} \times D$ by r_{debt}, and PV tax shield $= T_C \times D$.

not pay income taxes. If that happens, there are no taxes for interest to shield. Third, the formula assumes that the amount of debt is fixed regardless of how well the firm performs. It's more reasonable to assume that the firm will *rebalance* its capital structure over time to keep its debt *ratio* more or less constant. If the firm thrives and its value increases, it can borrow more. If the firm hits hard times and its value decreases, it can gradually pay down debt to a more comfortable level. Rebalancing means future debt and interest tax shields are no longer fixed amounts; they vary with the firm's performance and, therefore, should be discounted at a rate higher than the cost of debt.

Suppose that River Cruises will rebalance its debt in each and every future period, always keeping its debt ratio constant. In this case, the debt levels and interest tax shields fluctuate along with River Cruises' market value and are about as risky. This suggests a more conservative rule of thumb: Because the tax shields have the same risk as the rest of the firm, discount them at the same rate investors would use for operating income, which is 12.5% in our example.[7]

$$\text{PV interest tax shield} = \frac{\$17,500}{.125} = \$140,000$$

Even this more conservative PV calculation demonstrates that interest tax shields can add significant value for the firm and its shareholders.

16.4   Self-Test

Suppose River Cruises borrows only $300,000. Use the rules of thumb for valuing PV interest tax shield to answer the following questions:

a. What is the PV of interest tax shields if this borrowing is fixed and permanent?
b. What is this PV if River Cruises borrows permanently but rebalances its debt every future period to maintain a constant debt-to-value ratio?
c. The latter calculation is probably still too high. Why?

How Interest Tax Shields Contribute to the Value of Stockholders' Equity

MM's proposition I amounts to saying that "the value of the pizza does not depend on how it is sliced." The pizza is the firm's assets, and the slices are the debt and equity claims. If we hold the pizza constant, then a dollar more of debt means a dollar less of equity value.

But there is really a third slice—the government's. MM would still say that the value of the pizza—in this case, the company value *before* taxes—is not changed by slicing. But anything the firm can do to reduce the size of the government's slice obviously leaves more for the others. One way to do this is to borrow money. This reduces the firm's tax bill and increases the cash payments to the investors. The value of their investment goes up by the present value of the tax savings.

In a no-tax world, MM's proposition I states that the value of the firm is unaffected by capital structure. But MM also modified proposition I to recognize corporate taxes:

Value of levered firm = value if all-equity-financed + present value of tax shield

This formula is illustrated in Figure 16.5. It implies that borrowing increases firm value and shareholders' wealth.

---

[7] The annual interest tax shield is $T_C \times r_{debt} \times D$, as in footnote 6. But this PV calculation divides $T_C \times r_{debt} \times D$ by r_{assets}, so PV interest tax shield = $T_C \times D \times (r_{debt}/r_{assets})$.

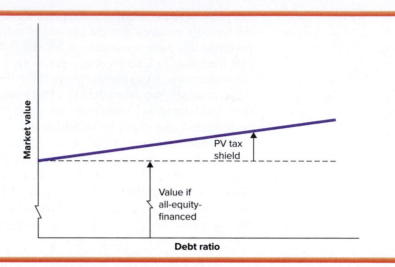

Corporate Taxes and the Weighted-Average Cost of Capital

We have shown that when there are corporate taxes, debt provides the company with a valuable tax shield. Few companies explicitly calculate the present value of interest tax shields associated with a particular borrowing policy. The tax shields are not forgotten, however, because they show up in the discount rate used to evaluate capital investments.

Because debt interest is tax deductible, the government in effect pays 35% of the interest cost. So to keep its investors happy, the firm has to earn the *after-tax* rate of interest on its debt plus the return required by shareholders. As we saw in Chapter 13, once we recognize the tax benefit of debt, the weighted-average cost of capital formula becomes

$$\text{WACC} = (1 - T_c)r_{\text{debt}}\left(\frac{D}{D+E}\right) + r_{\text{equity}}\left(\frac{E}{D+E}\right)$$

Notice that when we allow for the tax advantage of debt, the weighted-average cost of capital depends on the *after-tax* rate of interest $(1 - T_c) \times r_{\text{debt}}$.

| Example | 16.2 ▶ | WACC and Debt Policy |

BEYOND THE PAGE

 How the cost of capital changes with leverage

mhhe.com/brealey9e

We can use the weighted-average cost of capital formula to see how leverage affects River Cruises' cost of capital if the company pays corporate tax. When a company has no debt, the weighted-average cost of capital and the return required by shareholders are identical. For River Cruises, the WACC with all-equity financing is 12.5%, and the value of the all-equity firm is $1 million, just as in the no-tax examples earlier in this chapter.

Now we calculate River Cruises' WACC with $D = \$500,000$ of debt. If we use the more conservative rule of thumb[8] for the PV of the interest tax shields (see footnote 7), then company value $V = D + E$ increases by $.35 \times \$500,000 \times (.10/.125) = \$140,000$ to $\$1,140,000$. The equity value E is $\$1,140,000 - \$500,000 = \$640,000$.

---

[8] Recall that the more conservative rule of thumb assumes that the firm rebalances future debt levels to keep its debt *ratio* constant. This rule of thumb is the right match for a WACC calculation because use of WACC as a discount rate for long-lived assets also assumes constant debt ratios. For a more detailed analysis of the assumptions implicit in formulas for WACC and the cost of equity, see Chapter 19 in R. A. Brealey, S. C. Myers, and F. Allen, *Principles of Corporate Finance*, 12th ed. (New York: McGraw-Hill Education), 2017.

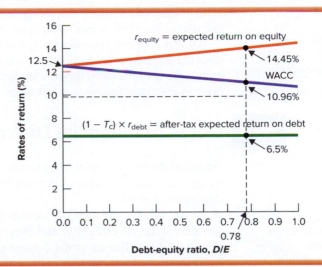

The right column in Table 16.6 shows equity income of $92,500 after interest and taxes, so the expected rate of return to shareholders is $92,500/640,000 = 14.45\%$ ($r_{equity} = .1445$). The interest rate is 10% ($r_{debt} = .10$), and the corporate tax rate is 35% ($T_C = .35$). This is all the information we need to see how taxes affect River Cruises' WACC:

$$\text{WACC} = \frac{D}{V} \times (1 - T_c)r_{debt} + \frac{E}{V} \times r_{equity} \tag{16.2}$$

$$= \left(\frac{500,000}{1,140,000}\right) \times (1 - .35).10 + \left(\frac{640,000}{1,140,000}\right) \times .1445 = .1096, \text{ or about } 11\%$$

Thus, interest tax shields increase the total value of River Cruises ($V = D + E$) by $140,000 and reduce its WACC from 12.5% to about 11%.

Figure 16.6 repeats Figure 16.3, except that it now recognizes the impact of interest tax shields. As the firm borrows more, the cost of equity rises, just as in Figure 16.3, although in this case to 14.45% instead of 15%.[9] But the after-tax cost of debt is only 6.5%. At borrowing of $500,000, the equity is worth $640,000, and the debt-equity ratio is $D/E = 500,000/640,000 = .78$. Figure 16.6 shows that WACC at this level of debt is 10.96%, the same as we calculated earlier. ■

The Implications of Corporate Taxes for Capital Structure

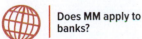
If borrowing provides an interest tax shield, the implied optimal debt policy appears to be embarrassingly extreme: All firms should borrow to the hilt. This maximizes firm value and minimizes the weighted-average cost of capital.

MM were not that fanatical about it. No one would expect the gains to apply at extreme debt ratios. For example, if a firm borrows heavily, all its operating income may go to pay interest. At this point, there are no corporate taxes to be paid and, therefore, no tax shields on additional debt. There is no point in such firms borrowing any more.

There may also be some tax *disadvantages* to borrowing, for bondholders have to pay personal income tax on any interest they receive. The top rate of tax on bond interest is about 40%. On the other hand, the maximum tax rate on both dividends and capital

---

[9] The reason that r_{equity} falls to 14.45% from its value of 15% in the no-tax case is that interest tax shields increase firm value and reduce D/E from $500,000/500,000 = 1.0$ in the no-tax case to $500,000/640,000 = .78$. By the way, MM's proposition II continues to work fine for the cost of equity as long as current and future debt-to-equity ratios are held constant. In this example,

$$r_{equity} = r_{assets} + (D/E) \times (r_{assets} - r_{debt}) = .125 + .78 \times (.125 - .10) = .1445, \text{ or } 14.45\%$$

gains is currently 23.8%.[10] Capital gains have the additional advantage that they are not taxed until the stock is sold. (The delay reduces the present value of the tax payment.)

All this suggests that there may come a point at which the tax savings from debt level off and may even decline. But it doesn't explain why highly profitable companies with large tax bills often thrive with little or no debt. There are clearly factors besides taxes to consider. One such factor is the likelihood of financial distress.

16.4 Costs of Financial Distress

Financial distress occurs when promises to creditors are broken or honored with difficulty. Sometimes, financial distress leads to bankruptcy. Sometimes, it means only skating on thin ice.

As we will see, financial distress is costly. Investors know that levered firms may run into financial difficulty, and they worry about the **costs of financial distress.** That worry is reflected in the current market value of the levered firm's securities. Even the most blue-chip firms are concerned about how their debt is perceived by investors. They want to maintain ready access to debt markets and to avoid the higher costs of debt that lenders are apt to demand at the first signs of financial weakness. Therefore, they want to maintain a good credit rating. Thus, you may hear a CFO say, "We want to maintain a single-A debt rating" or "We want to be a strong triple-B." But even high-rated firms sometimes fall into financial distress. For example, Eastman Kodak, which had a triple-A rating in the 1980s, fell into financial distress in the twenty-first century and filed for bankruptcy in 2012.

Even if the firm is not now in financial distress, investors factor the potential for future distress into their assessment of current value. This means that the overall value of the firm is

$$\begin{matrix} \text{Overall market} \\ \text{value} \end{matrix} = \begin{matrix} \text{value if all-equity-} \\ \text{financed} \end{matrix} + \begin{matrix} \text{PV tax} \\ \text{shield} \end{matrix} - \begin{matrix} \text{PV costs of} \\ \text{financial distress} \end{matrix}$$

The present value of the costs of financial distress depends both on the probability of distress and on the magnitude of the costs encountered if distress occurs.

Figure 16.7 shows how the trade-off between the tax benefits of debt and the costs of distress determines optimal capital structure. Think of a firm like River Cruises, which starts with no debt but considers moving to higher and higher debt levels, holding its assets and operations constant. **At moderate debt levels the probability of financial distress is trivial, and therefore, the tax advantages of debt dominate. But at some point, additional borrowing causes the probability of financial distress to increase rapidly, and the potential costs of distress begin to take a substantial bite out of firm value. The theoretical optimum is reached when the present value of tax savings from further borrowing is just offset by increases in the present value of costs of distress.**

This is called the **trade-off theory** of optimal capital structure. The theory says that managers will try to increase debt levels to the point where the value of additional interest tax shields is exactly offset by the additional costs of financial distress.

Now let's take a closer look at financial distress.

Bankruptcy Costs

In principle, bankruptcy is merely a legal mechanism for allowing creditors (i.e., lenders) to take over the firm when the decline in the value of its assets triggers a default on outstanding debt. If the company cannot pay its debts, the company is turned over

costs of financial distress Costs arising from bankruptcy or distorted business decisions before bankruptcy.

trade-off theory Debt levels are chosen to balance interest tax shields against the costs of financial distress.

---

[10] The tax rate on investment income generally rises with the investor's total income. The maximum rate is nominally 20%, but high-income investors (who hold a disproportionate share of stocks) also pay an additional 3.8% "surtax" on their investment earnings.

FIGURE 16.7 The trade-off theory of capital structure. The curved blue line shows how the market value of the firm at first increases as the firm borrows but finally decreases as the costs of financial distress become more and more important. The optimal capital structure balances the costs of financial distress against the value of the interest tax shields generated by borrowing.

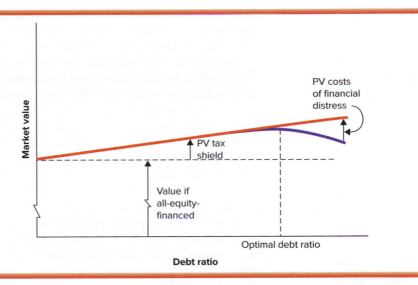

to the creditors, who become the new owners; the old stockholders are left with nothing. In this case, bankruptcy is not the *cause* of the decline in the value of the firm. It is the result.

In practice, of course, anything involving courts and lawyers cannot be free. The fees involved in a bankruptcy proceeding are paid out of the remaining value of the firm's assets. Creditors end up with what is left after paying the lawyers and other court expenses. If there is a possibility of bankruptcy, the current market value of the firm is reduced by the present value of these potential costs.

It is easy to see how increased leverage affects the costs of financial distress. The more the firm owes, the higher the chance of default and, therefore, the greater the expected value of the associated costs. This reduces the current market value of the firm.

Creditors foresee the costs and realize that if default occurs, the bankruptcy costs will come out of the value of the firm. For this, they demand compensation in advance in the form of a higher promised interest rate. This reduces the possible payoffs to stockholders and reduces the current market value of their shares by the present value of the expected future default costs.

> ### 16.5   Self-Test
>
> Suppose investors foresee $2 million of legal costs if the firm defaults on its bonds. How does this affect the value of the firm's bonds if bankruptcy occurs? How does the possibility of default affect the interest rate demanded by bondholders *today?* How does this possibility affect today's value of the firm's common stock?

We summarize bankruptcy procedures in the appendix to this chapter. Here we will focus only on *Chapter 11* of the bankruptcy code, which is the route usually taken by large firms that need help to climb out of financial distress. The purpose of Chapter 11 is to nurse the firm back to health and enable it to face the world again. This requires approval of a reorganization plan for who gets what; under the plan each class of creditors needs to give up its claim in exchange for new securities or a mixture of new securities and cash. The challenge is to design a new capital structure that will satisfy the creditors and allow the firm to solve the business problems that got it into trouble in the first place. Sometimes, it proves possible to satisfy both demands and the patient emerges fit and healthy. Often, however, the proceedings involve costly delays and legal tangles, and the business continues to deteriorate.

Bankruptcy costs can add up fast. The failed energy giant Enron paid nearly $800 million in legal, accounting, and other professional fees during the time that it spent in bankruptcy. As we write this, the costs of sorting out the 65,000 claims on the assets of Lehman Brothers have reached $2.2 billion.

Of course, these are exceptional cases, for only the largest firms can lay their hands on a billion dollars when bankrupt. But daunting as such numbers may seem, bankruptcy costs average only about 3% of the value of a firm in the year before bankruptcy.[11] The proportion is typically higher for small firms than for large ones; it seems that there are significant economies of scale in going bankrupt.

Thus far, we have discussed only the *direct* (i.e., legal and administrative) costs of bankruptcy. The *indirect* costs reflect the difficulties of running a company while it is going through bankruptcy. When Eastern Airlines entered bankruptcy in 1989, it was in severe financial trouble, but it still had some valuable, profit-making routes and some readily salable assets such as planes and terminal facilities. These assets were more than sufficient to repay in full its liabilities of $3.7 billion. However, the bankruptcy judge was determined to keep Eastern flying. Unfortunately, Eastern's losses continued to pile up. After the airline spent nearly 2 years under the "protection" of the bankruptcy court, the judge called it a day, the assets were sold off, and the creditors received less than $900 million. The unsuccessful attempt at resuscitation had cost Eastern's creditors $2.8 billion.

We don't know how much these indirect costs add to the expenses of bankruptcy. We suspect it is a significant number, particularly when bankruptcy proceedings are prolonged. Perhaps the best evidence is the reluctance of creditors to force a firm into bankruptcy. In principle, they would be better off to end the agony and seize the assets as soon as possible. But, instead, creditors often overlook defaults in the hope of nursing the firm over a difficult period. They do this in part to avoid the costs of bankruptcy. There is an old financial saying, "Borrow $1,000 and you've got a banker. Borrow $10,000,000 and you've got a partner."

Costs of Bankruptcy Vary with Type of Asset

Suppose your firm's only asset is a large downtown hotel, mortgaged to the hilt. A recession hits, occupancy rates fall, and the mortgage payments cannot be met. The lender takes over and sells the hotel to a new owner and operator. The stock is worthless and you use the firm's stock certificates for wallpaper.

What is the cost of bankruptcy? For Heartbreak Hotel, probably very little. The value of the hotel is, of course, much less than you hoped, but that is due to the lack of guests, not to bankruptcy. Bankruptcy does not damage the hotel itself. The direct bankruptcy costs are restricted to items such as legal and court fees, real estate commissions, and the time the lender spends sorting things out.

Suppose we repeat the story of Heartbreak Hotel for Fledgling Electronics. Everything is the same, except for the underlying assets. Fledgling is a high-tech going concern, and much of its value reflects investors' belief that its research team will come up with profitable ideas. Fledgling is a "people business"; its most important assets go down in the elevator and into the parking lot every night.

If Fledgling gets into trouble, the stockholders may be reluctant to put up money to cash in on those profitable ideas—why should they put up cash that will simply go to pay off the banks? Failure to invest is likely to be much more serious for Fledgling than for a company like Heartbreak Hotel.

---

[11] See, for example, L. A. Weiss, "Bankruptcy Resolution: Direct Costs and Violation of Priority of Claims," *Journal of Financial Economics* 27 (October 1990), pp. 285–314.

If Fledgling finally defaults on its debt, the lender would find it much more difficult to cash in by selling the assets. In fact, if trouble comes, many of those assets may drive into the sunset and never come back.

Some assets, like good commercial real estate, can pass through bankruptcy and reorganization largely unscathed; the values of other assets are likely to be considerably diminished. The losses are greatest for intangible assets that are linked to the continuing prosperity of the firm. That may be why debt ratios are low in the biotech industry, where company values depend on continued success in research and development. It may also explain the low debt ratios in many service companies, whose main asset is their skilled labor. The moral of these examples is this: **Do not think only about whether borrowing is likely to bring trouble. Think also of the value that may be lost if trouble comes.**

16.6 Self-Test

For which of the following companies would the costs of financial distress be most serious? Why?

- A 3-year-old biotech company. So far the company has no products approved for sale, but its scientists are hard at work developing a breakthrough drug.
- An oil production company with 50 producing wells and 20 million barrels of proven oil reserves.

Financial Distress without Bankruptcy

Not every firm that gets into trouble goes bankrupt. As long as the firm can scrape up enough cash to pay the interest on its debt, it may be able to postpone bankruptcy for many years. Eventually, the firm may recover, pay off its debt, and escape bankruptcy altogether.

A narrow escape from bankruptcy does *not* mean that costs of financial distress are avoided. When a firm is in trouble, suppliers worry that they may not be paid, potential customers fear that the firm will not be able to honor its warranties,[12] and employees start slipping out for job interviews. The firm's bondholders and stockholders both want it to recover, but in other respects, their interests may be in conflict. In times of financial distress, the security holders are like many political parties—united on generalities but threatened by squabbling on any specific issue. **Financial distress is costly when these conflicts get in the way of running the business. Stockholders are tempted to forsake the usual objective of maximizing the overall market value of the firm and to pursue narrower self-interest instead. They are tempted to play games at the expense of their creditors. These games add to the costs of financial distress.**

Think of a company—call it Double-R Nutting—that is teetering on the brink of bankruptcy. It has large debts and large losses. Double-R's assets have little value, and if its debts were due today, Double-R would default, leaving the firm bankrupt. The debtholders would perhaps receive a few cents on the dollar, and the shareholders would be left with nothing.

But suppose the debts are not due yet. That grace period explains why Double-R's shares still have value. There could be a stroke of luck that will rescue the firm and allow it to pay off its debts with something left over. That's a long shot—unless firm value increases sharply, the stock will be valueless. But the owners have a secret weapon: They control investment and operating strategy.

---

[12] In an attempt to stave off Chrysler's bankruptcy, the U.S. government sought to reassure the firm's customers by backing the warranties on its vehicles.

The First Game: Bet the Bank's Money   Suppose Double-R has the opportunity to take a wild gamble. If it does not come off, the shareholders will be no worse off; the company will probably go under anyway. But if the gamble does succeed, there will be more than enough assets to pay off the debt and the surplus will go into the shareholders' pockets. You can see why management might want to take the chance. In taking the gamble, they are essentially betting the debtholders' money, but if Double-R does hit the jackpot, the equityholders get most of the loot.

This was essentially the situation facing Federal Express while it was still struggling in 1974. It had only $5,000 left in its checking account but needed $24,000 for its weekly jet fuel payment. Fred Smith took the incentive to gamble literally. He took the firm's remaining $5,000 and boarded a plane for Las Vegas, where he won $27,000. When asked how he had mustered the nerve to do this, he replied, "What difference did it make? Without the funds for the fuel companies, we couldn't have flown anyway."[13] The effects of such distorted incentives to take on risk are usually not this blatant, but the results can be the same.

These kinds of **risk-shifting** strategies are costly for the bondholders and for the firm as a whole. Why are they associated with financial distress? Because the temptation to follow such strategies is strongest when the odds of default are high. A healthy firm would never invest in Double-R's lousy gamble because it would be gambling with its own money, not the bondholders'. A healthy firm's creditors would not be vulnerable to this type of game.

risk shifting
Firms threatened with default are tempted to shift to riskier investments.

The Second Game: Don't Bet Your Own Money   We have just seen how shareholders, acting in their narrow self-interest, may take on risky, unprofitable projects. These are errors of commission. We will now illustrate how conflicts of interest may also lead to errors of omission.

Suppose Double-R uncovers a relatively safe project with a positive NPV. Unfortunately, the project requires a substantial investment. Double-R will need to raise this extra cash from its shareholders. Although the project has a positive NPV, the profits may not be sufficient to rescue the company from bankruptcy. If that is so, all the profits from the new project will be used to help pay off the company's debt, and the shareholders will get no return on the cash they put up. Although it is in the firm's interest to go ahead with the project, it is not in the *owners'* interest, and the project will be passed up. A recent example of this problem occurred during the financial crisis when many banks, threatened with failure, discovered that their shareholders were reluctant to come to the rescue. The shareholders faced a **debt overhang** problem: Any cash that they contributed would simply be used to get existing debtholders and the government off the hook.

debt overhang
Firms threatened with default may pass up positive-NPV projects because bondholders capture part of the value added.

Our examples illustrate a general point. The value of any investment opportunity to the firm's *stockholders* is reduced because project benefits must be shared with the bondholders. Thus it may not be in the stockholders' self-interest to contribute fresh equity capital even if that means forgoing positive-NPV opportunities.

These two games illustrate potential conflicts of interest between stockholders and debtholders. The conflicts, which theoretically affect all levered firms, become much more serious when firms are staring bankruptcy in the face. **If the probability of default is high, managers and stockholders will be tempted to take on excessively risky projects. At the same time, stockholders may refuse to contribute more equity capital even if the firm has safe, positive-NPV opportunities. Stockholders would rather take money out of the firm than put new money in.**

[13] Roger Frock, *Changing How the World Does Business, FedEx's Incredible Journey to Success: The Inside Story* (San Francisco: Berrett-Koehler Publishers, 2006).

loan covenant
Agreement between firm and lender requiring the firm to fulfill certain conditions to safeguard the loan.

The company knows that lenders will demand a higher rate of interest if they are worried that games will be played at their expense. So to reassure lenders that its intentions are honorable, the firm will commonly agree to **loan covenants.** For example, it may promise to limit future borrowing and not to pay excessive dividends. Of course, no amount of fine print can cover every possible game that the company might play. For instance, no contract can ensure that companies will accept all positive-NPV investments and reject negative ones.

We do not mean to leave the impression that managers and stockholders always succumb to temptation unless restrained. Usually, they refrain voluntarily not only because of a sense of fair play, but also on pragmatic grounds: A firm or individual that makes a killing today at the expense of a creditor will be coldly received when the time comes to borrow again. Aggressive game playing is done only by firms in extreme financial distress (and sometimes by out-and-out crooks). Firms limit borrowing precisely because they don't wish to land in distress and be exposed to the temptation to play.

16.7   Self-Test

Suppose lenders foresee possible *future* risk-shifting and debt-overhang problems.

a. How do the lenders respond today?
b. How should the company respond today if the lenders' concerns are valid? Is there an argument for moving to a lower debt ratio?

We have now completed our review of the building blocks of the trade-off theory of optimal capital structure. In the next section, we will sum up that theory and briefly cover a competing "pecking order" theory.

16.5   Explaining Financing Choices

The Trade-Off Theory

Financial managers often think of the firm's debt-equity decision as a trade-off between interest tax shields and the costs of financial distress. Of course, there is controversy about how valuable interest tax shields are and what kinds of financial trouble are most threatening, but these disagreements are only variations on a theme. Thus, Figure 16.7 illustrates the debt-equity trade-off.

This trade-off theory predicts that target debt ratios will vary from firm to firm. Companies with safe, tangible assets and plenty of taxable income to shield ought to have high target ratios. Unprofitable companies with risky, intangible assets ought to rely primarily on equity financing.

All in all, this trade-off theory of capital structure tells a comforting story. It avoids extreme predictions and rationalizes moderate debt ratios. But what are the facts? Can the trade-off theory of capital structure explain how companies actually behave?

The answer is yes and no. On the yes side, the trade-off theory successfully explains many of the industry differences in capital structure that we encountered in Table 16.1. For example, high-tech growth companies, whose assets are risky and mostly

BEYOND THE PAGE

Do firms have a target debt ratio?

mhhe.com/brealey9e

intangible, normally use relatively little debt. Utilities or hotels can and do borrow heavily because their assets are tangible and relatively safe.

On the no side, there are other things the trade-off theory cannot explain. It cannot explain why some of the most successful companies thrive with little debt. Microsoft is a good example. The company has some debt outstanding, but it is a tiny fraction of the value of its common stock. Moreover, its holdings of cash and short-term investments are several times its outstanding debt. For example, in September 2015, Microsoft's outstanding long-term debt was about $28 billion, its holdings of cash and marketable securities were about $99 billion, and the market value of its common stock about $422 billion.

Granted, Microsoft's most valuable assets are intangible, and intangible assets and conservative capital structures should go together. But it pays large amounts in corporate tax. It could borrow enough to save millions of tax dollars without raising a whisker of concern about possible financial distress.

Microsoft illustrates an odd fact about real-life capital structures: The most profitable companies generally borrow the least. Here the trade-off theory fails, for it predicts exactly the reverse. Under the trade-off theory, high profits should mean more debt-servicing capacity and more taxable income to shield and therefore should result in a *higher* debt ratio.

BEYOND THE PAGE

Apple's debt issue

mhhe.com/brealey9e

16.8   Self-Test

Rank these industries in order of predicted debt ratios under the trade-off theory of capital structure: (a) Internet software; (b) auto manufacturing; (c) regulated electric utilities.

A Pecking Order Theory

There is an alternative theory that could explain why profitable companies borrow less. It is based on *asymmetric information*—managers know more than outside investors about the profitability and prospects of the firm. Thus, investors may not be able to assess the true value of a new issue of securities by the firm. They may be especially reluctant to buy newly issued common stock because they worry that the new shares will turn out to be overpriced.

Such worries can explain why the announcement of a stock issue can drive down the stock price.[14] If managers know more than outside investors, they will be tempted to time stock issues when their companies' stock is *overpriced*—in other words, when the managers are relatively pessimistic. On the other hand, optimistic managers will see their companies' shares as *underpriced* and decide *not* to issue. You can see why investors would learn to interpret the announcement of a stock issue as a "pessimistic manager" signal and mark down the stock price accordingly. You can also see why optimistic financial managers—and most managers *are* optimistic!—would view a common stock issue as a relatively expensive source of financing.

All these problems are avoided if the company can finance with internal funds, that is, with earnings that are retained and reinvested. But when external financing is required, the path of least resistance is debt, not equity. Issuing debt seems to have a trifling effect on stock prices. There is less scope for debt to be misvalued, and therefore, a debt issue is a less worrisome signal to investors.

---

[14] We described this "announcement effect" in Chapter 15.

pecking order theory
Firms prefer to issue debt rather than equity if internal finance is insufficient.

These observations suggest a **pecking order theory** of capital structure. It goes like this:

1. Firms prefer internal finance. Reinvesting retained earnings does not send adverse signals which could lower the stock price.
2. If external finance is required, firms issue debt first and issue equity only as a last resort. This pecking order arises because an issue of debt is less likely than an equity issue to be interpreted by investors as a bad omen.

In this story, there is no clear target debt-equity mix, because there are two kinds of equity, internal and external. The first is at the top of the pecking order, and the second is at the bottom. The pecking order explains why the most profitable firms generally borrow less; it is not because they have low target debt ratios but because they don't need outside money. Less profitable firms issue debt because they do not have sufficient internal funds for their capital investment program and because debt is first in the pecking order for *external* finance.

The pecking order theory does not deny that taxes and financial distress can be important factors in the choice of capital structure. However, the theory says that these factors are less important than managers' preference for internal over external funds and for debt financing over new issues of common stock.

For most U.S. corporations, internal funds finance the majority of new investment, and most external financing comes from debt. These aggregate financing patterns are consistent with the pecking order theory. Yet the pecking order seems to work best for mature firms. Fast-growing high-tech firms often resort to a series of common stock issues to finance their investments. Of course, you wouldn't expect the pecking order to apply to firms with extremely valuable growth opportunities. Such firms have good reasons to issue stock; they are credible issuers. Stock issues by growth firms do not send the same pessimistic signal as issues by mature firms.

The Two Faces of Financial Slack

Other things equal, it's better to be at the top of the pecking order than at the bottom. Firms that have worked down the pecking order and need external equity may end up living with excessive debt or bypassing good investments because shares can't be sold at what managers consider a fair price.

When asked about what factors are uppermost in their minds when they think about debt policy, financial managers commonly mention the tax advantage of debt and the importance of maintaining the firm's credit rating. But they place even greater emphasis on the need to retain flexibility so that the company has access to funds for pursuing new projects when they come along.[15] In other words, they place a high value on **financial slack.** Having financial slack means having cash, marketable securities, and ready access to the debt markets or to bank financing. Ready access basically requires conservative financing so that potential lenders see the company's debt as a safe investment.

In the long run, a company's value rests more on its capital investment and operating decisions than on financing. Therefore, you want to make sure your firm has sufficient financial slack so that financing is quickly available for good investments. Financial slack is most valuable to firms with plenty of positive-NPV growth opportunities. That is another reason growth companies usually aspire to conservative capital structures.

However, there is also a dark side to financial slack. Too much of it may encourage managers to take it easy, expand their perks, or empire-build with cash that should be paid back to stockholders. Michael Jensen has stressed this **free-cash-flow problem**: the tendency of managers with ample free cash flow (or unnecessary

BEYOND THE PAGE

Sealed Air Corporation

mhhe.com/brealey9e

financial slack
Ready access to cash or debt financing.

free-cash-flow problem
Companies with ample cash flow are tempted to overinvest and to operate inefficiently. Companies facing this problem may benefit from the discipline imposed by more debt and higher debt-service requirements.

---

[15] J. R. Graham and C. R. Harvey, "The Theory and Practice of Corporate Finance: Evidence from the Field," *Journal of Financial Economics* 61 (2001), pp. 187–243.

financial slack) to plow too much cash into mature businesses or ill-advised acquisitions. "The problem," Jensen says, "is how to motivate managers to disgorge the cash rather than investing it below the cost of capital or wasting it in organizational inefficiencies."[16]

If that's the problem, then maybe debt is an answer. Scheduled interest and principal payments are contractual obligations of the firm. Debt forces the firm to pay out cash. Perhaps the best debt level would leave just enough cash in the bank, after debt service, to finance all positive-NPV projects, with not a penny left over.

We do not recommend this degree of fine-tuning, but the idea is valid and important. For some firms, the threat of financial distress may have a good effect on managers' incentives. After all, skating on thin ice can be useful if it makes the skater concentrate. Likewise, managers of highly levered firms are more likely to work harder, run a leaner operation, and think more carefully before they spend money.

Is There a Theory of Optimal Capital Structure?

No. That is, there is no one theory that can capture everything that drives thousands of corporations' choices of capital structure. Instead, there are several theories, each more or less helpful, depending on the particular corporation's assets, operations, and circumstances.

In other words, relax: Don't waste time searching for a magic formula for the optimal debt ratio. Remember too that most value comes from the left side of the balance sheet, that is, from the firm's operations, assets, and growth opportunities. Financing is less important. Of course, financing can subtract value rapidly if you screw it up, but you won't do that.

In practice, financing choices depend on the relative importance of the factors discussed in this chapter. In some cases, reducing taxes will be the primary objective. Thus, high debt ratios are often found in developed commercial real estate, such as downtown office buildings. These can be safe, cash-cow assets if the office space is rented to creditworthy tenants. Bankruptcy costs are small, so it makes sense to lever up and save taxes.

For smaller growth companies, interest tax shields are less important than preserving financial slack. Profitable growth opportunities are valuable only if the company can be sure of finding the cash when it comes time to invest. Costs of financial distress are high for such companies, so it's no surprise that growth companies try to use mostly equity financing.

There's another reason that growth companies borrow less. Their growth opportunities are real options, that is, options to invest in real assets. Take an early stage biotech company. Its main asset is its research program and some promising compounds. But, if the research lives up to its early promise, the company will need to invest much more money to develop and market any resulting drugs. The fact that the company is putting down only part of the money up front creates leverage. It makes sense for it to offset the financial risk of its growth options by reducing the amount of debt on its balance sheet.

Growth options are less important for mature corporations. Such companies can and usually do borrow more. They often end up following the pecking order. These firms prefer to finance investment with retained earnings. They issue more debt when investments outrun retained earnings and pay down debt when earnings outpace investment.

Sooner or later, a corporation's operations age to the point where growth opportunities evaporate. In that case, the firm may issue large amounts of debt and retire equity to constrain investment and force payout of cash to investors.

These examples are not exhaustive, but they give some flavor of how a thoughtful CEO can set financing strategy.

---

[16] M.C. Jensen, "Agency Costs of Free Cash Flow, Corporate Finance and Takeovers," *American Economic Review* 26 (May 1986), p. 323.

SUMMARY

What is the goal of the capital structure decision? What is the financial manager trying to do? When would capital structure *not* matter? (*LO16-1*)

The goal is to maximize the overall market value of all the securities issued by the firm. Think of the financial manager as taking all the firm's real assets and selling them to investors as a package of securities. Some financial managers choose the simplest package possible: all-equity financing. Others end up issuing dozens of types of debt and equity securities. The financial manager must try to find the particular combination that maximizes the market value of the firm. If firm value increases, common stockholders will benefit.

But capital structure does not necessarily affect firm value. Modigliani and Miller's (MM's) famous **debt-irrelevance proposition** states that firm value can't be increased by changing **capital structure.** Therefore, the proportions of debt and equity financing don't matter. **Financial leverage** does increase the expected rate of return to shareholders, but the risk of their shares increases proportionally. MM show that the extra return and extra risk balance out, leaving shareholders no better or worse off.

Of course, MM's argument rests on simplifying assumptions. For example, it assumes efficient, well-functioning capital markets and ignores taxes and costs of financial distress. But even if these assumptions are incorrect in practice, MM's proposition is important. It exposes logical traps that financial managers sometimes fall into, particularly the idea that debt is "cheap financing" because the explicit cost of debt (the interest rate) is less than the cost of equity. Debt has an implicit cost, too, because increased borrowing increases **financial risk** and the cost of equity. When both costs are considered, debt is not cheaper than equity. MM show that if there are no corporate income taxes, the firm's weighted-average cost of capital does not depend on the amount of debt financing.

How do corporate income taxes modify MM's leverage-irrelevance proposition? (*LO16-2*)

Debt interest is a tax-deductible expense. Thus borrowing creates an **interest tax shield.** The present value of future interest tax shields can be very large, a substantial fraction of the value of outstanding debt. Of course, interest tax shields are valuable only for companies that are making profits and paying taxes.

If interest tax shields are valuable, why don't all taxpaying firms borrow as much as possible? (*LO16-3*)

The more firms borrow, the higher the odds of financial distress. The **costs of financial distress** can be broken down as follows:

- Direct bankruptcy costs, primarily legal and administrative costs.
- Indirect bankruptcy costs, reflecting the difficulty of managing a company when it is in bankruptcy proceedings.
- Financial decisions that are distorted by the threat of default and bankruptcy, including poor investment decisions caused by the conflicts of interest between debtholders and stockholders. These conflicts create potential **risk-shifting** and **debt-overhang** problems.

Combining interest tax shields and costs of financial distress leads to a **trade-off theory** of optimal capital structure. The trade-off theory says that financial managers should increase debt to the point where the value of additional interest tax shields is just offset by additional costs of possible financial distress.

The trade-off theory says that firms with safe, tangible assets and plenty of taxable income should operate at high debt levels. Less profitable firms, or firms with risky, intangible assets, ought to borrow less.

What's the pecking order theory? (*LO16-4*)

The **pecking order theory** says that firms prefer internal financing (i.e., earnings retained and reinvested) over external financing. If external financing is needed, they prefer to issue debt rather than issue new shares. The pecking order theory says that the amount of debt a firm issues will depend on its need for external financing. The theory also suggests that financial managers should try to maintain at least some **financial slack,** that is, a reserve of ready cash or unused borrowing capacity.

On the other hand, too much financial slack may lead to slack managers. High debt levels (and the threat of financial distress) can create strong incentives for managers to work harder, conserve cash, and avoid negative-NPV investments.

Is there a rule for finding optimal capital structure? (*LO16-5*)

Sorry, there are no simple answers for capital structure decisions. Debt may be better than equity in some cases, worse in others. But there are at least four dimensions for the financial manager to think about.

- *Taxes.* How valuable are interest tax shields? Is the firm likely to continue paying taxes over the full life of a debt issue? Safe, consistently profitable firms are most likely to stay in a taxpaying position.
- *Risk.* Financial distress is costly even if the firm survives it. Other things equal, financial distress is more likely for firms with high business risk. That is why risky firms typically issue less debt.
- *Asset type.* If distress does occur, the costs are generally greatest for firms whose value depends on intangible assets. Such firms generally borrow less than firms with safe, tangible assets.
- *Financial slack.* How much is enough? More slack makes it easy to finance future investments, but it may weaken incentives for managers. More debt, and therefore less slack, increases the odds that the firm may have to issue stock to finance future investments.

LISTING OF EQUATIONS

16.1 $r_{\text{equity}} = r_{\text{assets}} + \dfrac{D}{E}\,(r_{\text{assets}} - r_{\text{debt}})$

16.2 $\text{WACC} = \dfrac{D}{V} \times (1 - T_c)r_{\text{debt}} + \dfrac{E}{V} \times r_{\text{equity}}$

QUESTIONS AND PROBLEMS

1. **Debt Irrelevance.** True or false? MM's leverage-irrelevance proposition says: (*LO16-1*)
    a. The value of the firm does not depend on the fraction of debt versus equity financing.
    b. As financial leverage increases, the value of the firm increases by just enough to offset the additional financial risk absorbed by equity.
    c. The cost of equity increases with financial leverage only when the risk of financial distress is high.
    d. If the firm pays no taxes, the weighted-average cost of capital does not depend on the debt ratio.

2. **Debt Irrelevance.** River Cruises (see Section 16.1) is all-equity-financed with 100,000 shares. It now proposes to issue $250,000 of bonds and use the proceeds to repurchase 25,000 shares. Suppose an investor currently holds 1,000 shares in the company but is unhappy with its decision to borrow $250,000. Which of the following modifications to her own investment portfolio would offset the effects of the firm's additional borrowing? (*LO16-1*)
    a. Borrow $250 on her own account and use the cash to buy additional River Cruises' shares.
    b. Raise $250 by selling River Cruises' shares and use the cash to buy the company's debt.
    c. Keep her current holding of River Cruises' shares and borrow $250 to invest in the company's bond issue.

3. **Leverage and Earnings.** River Cruises (see Section 16.1) is all-equity-financed. Suppose it now issues $250,000 of debt at an interest rate of 10% and uses the proceeds to repurchase 25,000 shares. Assume that the firm pays no taxes and that debt finance has no impact on firm value. Rework Table 16.3 by selecting values for (a) to (j) below to show how earnings per share and share return vary with operating income after the financing. (*LO16-1*)

Current Data	
Number of shares	100,000
Price per share	$10
Market value of shares	$1 million

Outcomes			
	State of the Economy		
	Slump	**Normal**	**Boom**
Profits before interest	$75,000	$125,000	$175,000
Interest	(a)	(a)	(a)
Equity earnings	(b)	(c)	(d)
Earnings per share	(e)	(f)	(g)
Return on shares	(h)	(i)	(j)
		↑	
		Expected outcome	

4. **Leverage and P/E Ratios.** River Cruises (see Section 16.1) is all-equity-financed with 100,000 shares. It now proposes to issue $250,000 of debt at an interest rate of 10% and use the proceeds to repurchase 25,000 shares. Profits before interest are expected to be $125,000. (*LO16-1*)

   a. What is the ratio of price to expected earnings for River Cruises before it borrows the $250,000?
   b. What is the ratio after it borrows?

5. **Debt Irrelevance.** Companies A and B differ only in their capital structure. A is financed 30% debt and 70% equity; B is financed 10% debt and 90% equity. The debt of both companies is risk-free. (*LO16-1*)

   a. Rosencrantz owns 1% of the common stock of A. What other investment package would produce identical cash flows for Rosencrantz?
   b. Guildenstern owns 2% of the common stock of B. What other investment package would produce identical cash flows for Guildenstern?

6. **Debt Irrelevance.** What is wrong with the following arguments? (*LO16-1*)

   a. As the firm borrows more and debt becomes risky, both stock- and bondholders demand higher rates of return. Thus, by reducing the debt ratio, we can reduce both the cost of debt and the cost of equity, making everybody better off.
   b. Moderate borrowing doesn't significantly affect the probability of financial distress or bankruptcy. Consequently, moderate borrowing won't increase the expected rate of return demanded by stockholders.
   c. A capital investment opportunity offering a 10% internal rate of return is an attractive project if it can be 100% debt-financed at an 8% interest rate.
   d. The more debt the firm issues, the higher the interest rate it must pay. That is one important reason that firms should operate at conservative debt levels.

7. **Debt Irrelevance.** Digital Fruit is financed solely by common stock and has outstanding 25 million shares with a market price of $10 a share. It now announces that it intends to issue $160 million of debt and to use the proceeds to buy back common stock. There are no taxes. (*LO16-1*)

   a. What is the expected market price of the common stock after the announcement?
   b. How many shares can the company buy back with the $160 million of new debt that it will issue?
   c. What is the market value of the firm (equity plus debt) after the change in capital structure?
   d. What is the debt ratio after the change in capital structure?

8. **Leverage and Earnings.** Reliable Gearing currently is all-equity-financed. It has 10,000 shares of equity outstanding, selling at $100 a share. The firm is considering a capital restructuring. The low-debt plan calls for a debt issue of $200,000 with the proceeds used to buy back stock. The high-debt plan would exchange $400,000 of debt for equity. The debt will pay an interest rate of 10%. The firm pays no taxes. (*LO16-1*)

   a. What will be the debt-to-equity ratio if it borrows $200,000?
   b. If earnings before interest and tax (EBIT) are $110,000, what will be earnings per share (EPS) if Reliable borrows $200,000?
   c. What will EPS be if it borrows $400,000?

9. **Leverage and the Cost of Capital.** The common stock and debt of Northern Sludge are valued at $70 million and $30 million, respectively. Investors currently require a 16% return on the common stock and an 8% return on the debt. If Northern Sludge issues an additional $10 million of common stock and uses this money to retire debt, what happens to the expected return on the stock? Assume that the change in capital structure does not affect the interest rate on Northern's debt and that there are no taxes. (*LO16-1*)

10. **Leverage and the Cost of Capital.** "Increasing financial leverage increases both the cost of debt (r_{debt}) and the cost of equity (r_{equity}). So the overall cost of capital cannot stay constant." This problem is designed to show that the speaker is confused. Buggins Inc. is financed equally by debt and equity, each with a market value of $1 million. The cost of debt is 5%, and the cost of equity is 10%. The company now makes a further $250,000 issue of debt and uses the proceeds to repurchase equity. This causes the cost of debt to rise to 6% and the cost of equity to rise to 12%. Assume the firm pays no taxes. (*LO16-1*)

    a. How much debt does the company now have?
    b. How much equity does it now have?
    c. What is the overall cost of capital?

11. **Leverage and the Cost of Capital.** Astromet is financed entirely by common stock and has a beta of 1.0. The firm pays no taxes. The stock has a price-earnings multiple of 10 and is priced to offer a 10% expected return. The company decides to repurchase half the common stock and substitute an equal value of debt. Assume that the debt yields a risk-free 5%. Calculate the following: (*LO16-1*)

    a. The beta of the common stock after the refinancing
    b. The required return and risk premium on the common stock before the refinancing
    c. The required return and risk premium on the common stock after the refinancing
    d. The required return on the debt
    e. The required return on the company (i.e., stock and debt combined) after the refinancing

    If EBIT remains constant:

    f. What is the percentage increase in earnings per share after the refinancing?
    g. What is the new price-earnings multiple? (*Hint:* Has anything happened to the stock price?)

12. **Leverage and the Cost of Capital.** Hubbard's Pet Foods is financed 80% by common stock and 20% by bonds. The expected return on the common stock is 12%, and the rate of interest on the bonds is 6%. Assume that the bonds are default free and that there are no taxes. Now assume that Hubbard's issues more debt and uses the proceeds to retire equity. The new financing mix is 60% equity and 40% debt. If the debt is still default free, what happens to the following? (*LO16-1*)

    a. The expected rate of return on equity
    b. The expected return on the package of common stock and bonds

13. **Leverage and the Cost of Capital.** "MM totally ignore the fact that as you borrow more, you have to pay higher rates of interest." Explain carefully whether this is a valid objection. (*LO16-1*)

14. **Leverage and the Cost of Capital.** A firm currently has a debt-equity ratio of 1/2. The debt, which is virtually riskless, pays an interest rate of 6%. The expected rate of return on the equity is 12%. What would be the expected rate of return on equity if the firm reduced its debt-equity ratio to 1/3? Assume the firm pays no taxes. (*LO16-1*)

15. **Leverage and the Cost of Capital.** Archimedes Levers is financed by a mixture of debt and equity. There are no taxes. You have the following information about its cost of capital:

$$r_E = \text{(a)} \quad r_D = 12\% \quad r_A = \text{(b)}$$
$$\beta_E = 1.5 \quad \beta_D = \text{(c)} \quad \beta_A = \text{(d)}$$
$$r_f = 10\% \quad r_m = 18\% \quad D/V = 0.5$$

Can you fill in the blanks (a) to (d)? (*LO16-1*)

16. **Tax Shields.** River Cruises (see Section 16.1) is all-equity-financed with 100,000 shares. It now proposes to issue $250,000 of debt at an interest rate of 10% and to use the proceeds to repurchase 25,000 shares. Suppose that the corporate tax rate is 35%. Calculate the *dollar*

increase in the combined after-tax income of its debtholders and equityholders if profits before interest are: (*LO16-2*)

   a. $75,000.
   b. $100,000.
   c. $175,000.

17. **Tax Shields.** Establishment Industries borrows $800 million at an interest rate of 7.6%. Establishment will pay tax at an effective rate of 35%. What is the present value of interest tax shields if: (*LO16-2*)

   a. It expects to maintain this debt level into the far future?
   b. It expects to repay the debt at the end of 5 years?
   c. It expects to maintain a constant debt ratio once it borrows the $800 million and $r_{assets} = 10\%$?

18. **Tax Shields.** What is an interest tax shield? How does it increase the size of the "pie" for after-tax income stockholders? Explain. (*Hint:* Construct a simple numerical example showing how financial leverage affects the total cash flow available to debt and equity investors. Be sure to hold earnings before interest constant.) (*LO16-2*)

19. **Leverage and the Cost of Capital.** Dusit is financed 30% by debt yielding 8%. Investors require a return of 15% on Dusit's equity. (*LO16-2*)

   a. What is the company's weighted-average cost of capital if the corporate tax rate is 35%?
   b. What would be the company's cost of capital if it were exempted from corporate tax?

20. **Taxes and the Cost of Capital.** Here is Icknield's market-value balance sheet (figures in $ millions):

Net working capital	$ 550	Debt	$ 800
Long-term assets	2,150	Equity	1,900
Value of firm	$2,700		$2,700

The debt is yielding 7%, and the cost of equity is 14%. The tax rate is 35%. Investors expect this level of debt to be permanent. (*LO16-2*)

   a. What is Icknield's WACC?
   b. How would the market-value balance sheet change if Icknield retired all its debt?

21. **Taxes and the Cost of Capital.** Here are book- and market-value balance sheets of the United Frypan Company (figures in $ millions):

BOOK-VALUE BALANCE SHEET			
Net working capital	$ 20	Debt	$ 40
Long-term assets	80	Equity	60
	$100		$100

MARKET-VALUE BALANCE SHEET			
Net working capital	$ 20	Debt	$ 40
Long-term assets	140	Equity	120
	$160		$160

Assume that MM's theory holds except for taxes. There is no growth, and the $40 of debt is expected to be permanent. Assume a 35% corporate tax rate. (*LO16-2*)

   a. How much of the firm's value is accounted for by the debt-generated tax shield?
   b. What is United Frypan's after-tax WACC if $r_{debt} = 8\%$ and $r_{equity} = 15\%$?
   c. Now suppose that Congress passes a law that eliminates the deductibility of interest for tax purposes. What will be the new value of the firm, other things equal? Assume an 8% borrowing rate.

22. **Taxes.** MM's proposition I suggests that, in the absence of taxes, it makes no difference whether the firm borrows on behalf of its shareholders or whether they borrow directly. However, if there are corporate taxes, this is no longer the case. Construct a simple example to show that, with taxes, it is better for the firm to borrow than for the shareholders to do so. (*LO16-2*)

23. **Taxes.** MM's proposition I, when modified to recognize corporate taxes, suggests that there is a tax advantage to firm borrowing. If there is a tax advantage to firm borrowing, there is also a tax disadvantage to retaining and lending large amounts of cash. Explain why. (*LO16-2*)

24. **Tax Shields and WACC.** River Cruises' management now understands that the trade-off theory of optimal capital structure implies managers will increase debt as long as the value of additional interest tax shields exceeds the additional costs of potential financial distress. This trade-off gives rise to the hump-shaped curve in Figure 16.7, where the value of the firm is maximized at the optimal debt level. What will the curve of WACC as a function of debt level look like? (*LO16-2*)

    a. Start with a no-tax economy. Continue to assume that River Cruises' required return on assets is 12.5% and return on debt is 10%. In a spreadsheet, calculate r_{equity}, WACC, and r_{debt} for debt-equity ratios ranging from 0 to 2.5 in increments of .1. Does WACC vary with the *D/E* ratio? Compare your plot to Figure 16.3.

    b. Now assume the corporate tax rate is 35%. Repeat part (a). What happens to WACC as *D/E* increases?

    c. What seems to be the optimal capital structure?

    d. What considerations are missing that would affect the optimal capital structure seemingly implied by part (b)?

25. **Financial Distress.** True or false? (*LO16-3*)

    a. If the probability of default is high, managers and stockholders will be tempted to take on excessively risky projects.

    b. If the probability of default is high, stockholders may refuse to contribute equity even if the firm has safe, positive-NPV opportunities.

    c. When a company borrows, the expected costs of bankruptcy come out of the lenders' pockets and do not affect the market value of the shares.

26. **Costs of Financial Distress.** What are the drawbacks of operating a firm that is close to bankruptcy? Give some examples. (*LO16-3*)

27. **Costs of Financial Distress.** The Salad Oil Storage Company (SOS) has financed a large part of its facilities with long-term debt. There is a significant risk of default, but the company is not on the ropes yet. (*LO16-3*)

    a. Explain why SOS stockholders could lose by investing in a positive-NPV project financed by an equity issue.

    b. Explain why SOS stockholders could gain by investing in a highly risky, negative-NPV project.

28. **Costs of Financial Distress.** For which of the following firms would you expect the costs of financial distress to be highest? Explain briefly. (*LO16-3*)

    a. A computer software company that depends on skilled programmers to produce new products

    b. A shipping company that operates a fleet of modern oil tankers

29. **Costs of Financial Distress.** Let's go back to the Double-R Nutting Company. Suppose that Double-R's bonds have a face value of $50. Its current market-value balance sheet is:

Assets		Liabilities and Equity	
Net working capital	$20	Bonds outstanding	$25
Fixed assets	10	Common stock	5
Total assets	$30	Total liabilities and shareholders' equity	$30

Who would gain or lose from the following maneuvers? (*LO16-3*)

a. Double-R pays a $10 cash dividend.

b. Double-R halts operations, sells its fixed assets for $6, and converts net working capital into $20 cash. It invests its $26 in Treasury bills.

c. Double-R encounters an investment opportunity requiring a $10 initial investment with NPV = $0. It borrows $10 to finance the project by issuing more bonds with the same security, seniority, and so on, as the existing bonds.

d. Double-R finances the investment opportunity in part (c) by issuing more common stock.

30. **Trade-Off Theory.** Smoke and Mirrors currently has EBIT of $25,000 and is all-equity-financed. EBIT is expected to stay at this level indefinitely. The firm pays corporate taxes equal to 35% of taxable income. The discount rate for the firm's projects is 10%. (*LO16-3*)

a. What is the market value of the firm?

b. Now assume the firm issues $50,000 of debt paying interest of 6% per year, using the proceeds to retire equity. The debt is expected to be permanent. What will happen to the total value of the firm (debt plus equity)?

c. Recompute your answer to part (b) under the following assumptions: The debt issue raises the probability of bankruptcy. The firm has a 30% chance of going bankrupt after 3 years. If it does go bankrupt, it will incur bankruptcy costs of $200,000. The discount rate is 10%.

d. Should the firm issue the debt under these new assumptions?

31. **Pecking Order Theory.** What is the pecking order theory of optimal capital structure? If the theory is correct, what types of firms would you expect to operate at high debt levels? (*LO16-4*)

32. **Pecking Order Theory.** Alpha Corp. and Beta Corp. both produce turbo encabulators. Both companies' assets and operations are growing at the same rate, and their annual capital expenditures are about the same. However, Alpha Corp. is the more efficient producer and is consistently more profitable. According to the pecking order theory, which company should have the higher debt ratio? (*LO16-4*)

33. **Pecking Order Theory.** Construct a simple example to show that a firm's existing stockholders gain if it can sell overpriced stock to new investors and invest the cash in a zero-NPV project. (*LO16-4*)

a. Who loses from these actions?

b. If investors are aware that managers are likely to issue stock when it is overpriced, what will happen to the stock price when the issue is announced?

34. **Pecking Order Theory.** When companies announce an issue of common stock, the share price typically falls. When they announce an issue of debt, there is typically only a negligible change in the stock price. Can you explain why? (*LO16-4*)

35. **Financial Slack.** True or false? (*LO16-4*)

a. Financial slack means having cash in the bank or ready access to the debt markets.

b. Financial slack is most valuable to firms with few investment opportunities.

c. Managers with excessive financial slack may be tempted to spend it on poor investments.

36. **Theories of Capital Structure.** Fill in the missing entries by choosing from the following terms: *safe tangible assets, less, pecking order theory, capital, taxable income to shield, interest tax shields, financial distress, trade-off theory, more, risky assets.* (*Note:* Not all terms will be used.) (*LO16-5*)

Managers will try to increase debt levels to the point where the value of ___(a)___ is exactly offset by the additional costs of ___(b)___. This is known as the ___(c)___ of capital structure. The theory predicts that companies with ___(d)___ and plenty of ___(e)___ ought to borrow ___(f)___.

BEYOND THE PAGE

Sealed Air
Corporation

mhhe.com/brealey9e

37. **Optimal Capital Structure.** Access the Beyond the Page feature to read about Sealed Air's restructuring. (*LO16-5*)

a. What was the value of financial slack to Sealed Air before its restructuring?

b. What does the success of the restructuring say about optimal capital structure?

c. Would you recommend that all firms restructure as Sealed Air did?

WEB EXERCISES

1. Log on to finance.yahoo.com and click the *Key Statistics* link for Pfizer (PFE) and Coca-Cola (KO). Construct the debt ratio, debt/(debt + equity), for both firms. Now calculate their debt ratios by using the market value of equity but assuming that book value of debt approximates its market value. How does debt as a proportion of firm value change as you switch from book to market values?

2. On finance.yahoo.com find the profiles for PepsiCo (PEP) and IBM (IBM), and then look at each firm's annual balance sheet and income statement under *Financials*. Calculate the present value of the interest tax shield contributed by each company's long-term debt. Now suppose that each issues $3 billion more of long-term debt and uses the proceeds to repurchase equity. How would the interest tax shield change? In each case, assume that the debt is fixed and permanent.

SOLUTIONS TO SELF-TEST QUESTIONS

16.1 Price per share will stay at $10, so with $350,000, River Cruises can repurchase 35,000 shares, leaving 65,000 outstanding. The remaining value of equity will be $650,000. Overall firm value stays at $1 million. Shareholders' wealth is unchanged: They start with shares worth $1 million, receive $350,000, and retain shares worth $650,000.

16.2a.

Data		
Number of shares	25,000	
Price per share	$10	
Market value of shares	$250,000	
Market value of debt	$750,000	

	State of the Economy		
	Slump	Normal	Boom
Operating income ($)	75,000	125,000	175,000
Interest ($)	75,000	75,000	75,000
Equity earnings ($)	0	50,000	100,000
Earnings per share ($)	0	2.00	4.00
Return on shares	0%	20%	40%

Every change of $50,000 in operating income leads to a change in the return to equityholders of 20%. This is double the swing in equity returns when debt was only $500,000.

b. The stockholder should lend out $3 for every $1 invested in River Cruises' stock. For example, he could buy one share for $10 and then lend $30. The payoffs are:

	State of the Economy		
	Slump	Normal	Boom
Earnings on one share ($)	0	2.00	4.00
Plus interest at 10% ($)	3.00	3.00	3.00
Net earnings ($)	3.00	5.00	7.00
Return on $40 investment	7.5%	12.5%	17.5%

16.3 Business risk is unaffected by capital structure. As the financing mix changes, whatever equity is outstanding must absorb the fixed business risk of the firm. The less equity, the more risk absorbed per share. Therefore, as capital structure changes, r_{assets} is held fixed while r_{equity} adjusts.

16.4 Interest tax shields are $.35 \times .10 \times 300{,}000 = \$10{,}500$ per year.

   a. Discount the perpetuity at the cost of debt. $PV = 10{,}500/.10 = \$105{,}000$.

   b. In this case, the tax shields are about as risky as operating earnings. Discount at 12.5%. $PV = 10{,}500/.125 = \$84{,}000$.

   c. The company can't be sure that it will have enough taxable income to exploit interest tax shields in all future years.

16.5 In bankruptcy, bondholders will receive $2 million less. This lowers the expected cash flow from the bond and reduces its present value. Therefore, the bonds will be priced lower and must offer a higher interest rate. This higher rate is paid by the firm today. It comes out of stockholders' income. Thus common stock value falls.

16.6 The biotech company. Its assets are all intangible. If bankruptcy threatens and the best scientists accept job offers from other firms, there may not be much value remaining for the biotech company's debt and equity investors. On the other hand, bankruptcy would have little or no effect on the value of 50 producing oil wells and of the oil reserves still in the ground.

16.7 a. Lenders will demand a higher interest rate and possibly additional covenants or other restrictions on borrowing.

   b. The possibility of distorted future investment and operating decisions reduces the value of the firm today. The reduction in value is a cost of financial distress and a reason for a more conservative debt policy.

16.8 The electric utility has the most stable cash flow. It also has the highest reliance on tangible assets that would not be impaired by a bankruptcy. It should have the highest debt ratio. The software firm has the least dependence on tangible assets and the most on assets that have value only if the firm continues as an ongoing concern. It probably also has the most unpredictable cash flows. It should have the lowest debt ratio.

MINICASE

In March 2018, the management team of Londonderry Air (LA) met to discuss a proposal to purchase five shorthaul aircraft at a total cost of $25 million. There was general enthusiasm for the investment, and the new aircraft were expected to generate an annual cash flow of $4 million for 20 years.

The focus of the meeting was on how to finance the purchase. LA had $20 million in cash and marketable securities (see table), but Ed Johnson, the chief financial officer, pointed out that the company needed at least $10 million in cash to meet normal outflow and as a contingency reserve. This meant that there would be a cash deficiency of $15 million, which the firm would need to cover either by the sale of common stock or by additional borrowing. While admitting that the arguments were finely balanced, Mr. Johnson recommended an issue of stock. He pointed out that the airline industry was subject to wide swings in profits and the firm should be careful to avoid the risk of excessive borrowing. He estimated that in market value terms, the long-term debt ratio was about 59% and that a further debt issue would raise the ratio to 62%.

Mr. Johnson's only doubt about making a stock issue was that investors might jump to the conclusion that management believed the stock was overpriced, in which case the announcement might prompt an unjustified selloff by investors. He stressed, therefore, that the company needed to explain carefully the reasons for the issue. Also, he suggested that demand for the issue would be enhanced if at the same time LA increased its dividend payment. This would provide a tangible indication of management's confidence in the future.

These arguments cut little ice with LA's chief executive. "Ed," she said, "I know that you're the expert on all this, but everything you say flies in the face of common sense. Why should we want to sell more equity when our stock has fallen over the past year by nearly a fifth? Our stock is currently offering a dividend yield of 6.5%, which makes equity an expensive source of capital. Increasing the dividend would simply make it more expensive. What's more, I don't see the point of paying out more money to the stockholders at the same time that we are asking *them* for cash. If we hike the dividend, we will need to increase the amount of the stock issue; so we will just be paying the higher dividend out of the shareholders' own pockets. You're also ignoring the question of dilution. Our equity currently has a book value of $12 a share; it's not playing fair by our existing shareholders if we now issue stock for around $10 a share.

"Look at the alternative. We can borrow today at 6%. We get a tax break on the interest, so the after-tax cost of borrowing is $.65 \times 6 = 3.9\%$. That's about half the cost of equity. We expect to earn a return of 15% on these new aircraft. If we can raise money at 3.9% and invest it at 15%, that's a good deal in my book.

"You finance guys are always talking about risk, but as long as we don't go bankrupt, borrowing doesn't add any risk at all.

"Ed, I don't want to push my views on this—after all, you're the expert. We don't need to make a firm recommendation to the board until next month. In the meantime, why don't you get one of your new business graduates to look at the whole issue of how we should finance the deal and what return we need to earn on these planes?"

Use the most recently available financial data from 2017 to help evaluate Mr. Johnson's arguments about the stock issue and dividend payment as well as the reply of LA's chief executive. Who is correct? What is the required rate of return on the new planes?

**Summary financial statements for Londonderry Air, 2017
(Figures are book values, in millions of dollars)**

BALANCE SHEET			
Bank debt	$ 50	Cash	$ 20
Other current liabilities	20	Other current assets	20
10% bond, due 2032*	100	Fixed assets	250
Stockholders' equity†	120		
Total liabilities	$290	Total assets	$290

INCOME STATEMENT	
Gross profit	$57.5
Depreciation	20.0
Interest	7.5
Pretax profit	30.0
Tax	10.5
Net profit	19.5
Dividend	6.5

* The yield to maturity on LA debt currently is 6%.
† LA has 10 million shares outstanding, with a market price of $10 a share. LA's equity beta is estimated at 1.25, the market risk premium is 8%, and the Treasury bill rate is 3%.

APPENDIX

Bankruptcy Procedures

workout
Agreement between a company and its creditors establishing the steps the company must take to avoid bankruptcy.

bankruptcy
The reorganization or liquidation of a firm that cannot pay its debts.

liquidation
Sale of bankrupt firm's assets.

BEYOND THE PAGE

   U.S. bankruptcy filings

mhhe.com/brealey9e

reorganization
Restructuring of financial claims on failing firm to allow it to keep operating.

Firms that issue debt always bear a risk that when the debt comes due, they will not be able to pay their creditors. At that point, the firm may be forced into bankruptcy. We conclude this chapter with a brief overview of the bankruptcy process.

A corporation that cannot pay its debts will often try to come to an informal agreement with its creditors. This is known as a **workout.** A workout may take several forms. For example, the firm may negotiate an *extension,* that is, an agreement with its creditors to delay payments. Or the firm may negotiate a *composition*, in which the firm makes partial payments to its creditors in exchange for relief of its debts.

The advantage of a negotiated agreement is that the costs and delays of formal bankruptcy are avoided. However, the larger the firm and the more complicated its capital structure, the less likely it is that a negotiated settlement can be reached.

If the firm cannot get an agreement, then it may have no alternative but to file for **bankruptcy.**[17] Under the federal bankruptcy system, the firm has a choice of procedures. In about two-thirds of the cases, a firm will file for, or be forced into, bankruptcy under Chapter 7 of the 1978 Bankruptcy Reform Act. Then the firm's assets are **liquidated**—that is, sold—and the proceeds are used to pay creditors.

Secured creditors have first priority to the collateral pledged for their loans. Then come unsecured creditors in the following rank order: First come claims for expenses that arise after bankruptcy is filed, such as attorneys' fees or employee compensation earned after the filing. If such postfiling claims did not receive priority, no firm in bankruptcy proceedings could continue to operate. Next come claims for wages and employee benefits earned in the period immediately prior to the filing. Taxes are next in line, together with debts to some government agencies such as the Small Business Administration or the Pension Benefit Guarantee Corporation. Finally come general unsecured claims such as unsecured trade debt.

The alternative to a liquidation is a **reorganization,** which keeps the firm as a going concern and usually compensates creditors with new securities in the reorganized firm. Such reorganizations are generally in the shareholders' interests—they have little to lose if things deteriorate further and everything to gain if the firm recovers. Almost all large firms opt for a reorganization rather than a liquidation.

Firms attempting reorganization seek refuge under Chapter 11 of the Bankruptcy Reform Act. Chapter 11 is designed to keep the firm alive and operating and to protect the value of its assets while a plan of reorganization is worked out. During this period, other proceedings against the firm are halted, and the company is operated by existing management or by a court-appointed trustee.

The responsibility for developing a plan of reorganization may fall on the debtor firm. If no trustee is appointed, the firm has 120 days to present a plan to creditors. If this deadline is *not* met, or if a trustee is appointed, anyone can submit a plan—the trustee, for example, or a committee of creditors.

The reorganization plan is basically a statement of who gets what; each class of creditors gives up its claim in exchange for new securities. (Sometimes, creditors receive cash as well.) The problem is to design a new capital structure for the firm that will (1) satisfy the creditors and (2) allow the firm to solve the *business* problems that got the firm into trouble in the first place. Sometimes, only a plan of baroque complexity can satisfy these two requirements.

The reorganization plan goes into effect if it is accepted by creditors and confirmed by the court. Acceptance requires approval by a majority of each class of creditor. Once a plan is accepted, the court normally approves it, provided that *each* class of creditors has approved it and that the creditors will be better off under the plan than if the firm's assets were liquidated and distributed. The court may, under certain conditions, confirm a plan even if one or more classes of creditors vote against it. This is known as a *cram-down.*

The interests of the different classes of creditors do not always coincide. For example, junior creditors may threaten to slow the process as a way of extracting concessions from senior creditors.

---

[17] Occasionally, creditors will allow the firm to petition for bankruptcy after it has reached an agreement with the creditors. This is known as a *prepackaged bankruptcy*. The court simply approves the agreed workout plan.

BEYOND THE PAGE

Chapter 55

mhhe.com/brealey9e

The senior creditors may take less than 100 cents on the dollar and give something to junior creditors in order to expedite the process and reach an agreement.

Chapter 11 proceedings are often successful, and the patient emerges fit and healthy. But in other cases, cure proves impossible and the assets are liquidated. Sometimes, the firm may emerge from Chapter 11 for a brief period before it is once again submerged by disaster and back in bankruptcy. For example, TWA came out of bankruptcy at the end of 1993 and was back again less than 2 years later and then for a third time in 2001, prompting jokes about "Chapter 33." TWA has plenty of company in this regard. In recent years, about 80% of large firms have emerged from bankruptcy proceedings with a second life, but nearly one-third of those reorganized firms met with failure within 5 years.[18] Among other notable "serial failures" are Planet Hollywood, Grand Union, Memorex, Continental Airlines, and Harvard Industries.

The Choice between Liquidation and Reorganization

Here is an idealized view of the bankruptcy decision. Whenever a payment is due to creditors, management checks the value of the firm. If the firm is worth more than the promised payment, the firm pays up (if necessary, raising the cash by an issue of shares). If not, the equity is worthless, and the firm defaults on its debt and petitions for bankruptcy. If, in the court's judgment, the assets of the bankrupt firm can be put to better use elsewhere, the firm is liquidated and the proceeds are used to pay off the creditors. Otherwise, the creditors simply become the new owners and the firm continues to operate.

In practice, matters are rarely so simple. For example, we observe that firms often petition for bankruptcy even when the equity has a positive value. Moreover, the bankruptcy court may decide to keep the firm on life support even when the assets could be used more efficiently elsewhere. There are several reasons for this.

First, although the reorganized firm is legally a new entity, it is entitled to any tax-loss carry-forwards belonging to the old firm. If the firm is liquidated rather than reorganized, any tax-loss carry-forwards disappear. Thus, there is an incentive to continue in operation even if assets are better used by another firm.

Second, if the firm's assets are sold off, it is easy to determine what is available to pay the creditors. However, when the company is reorganized, it needs to conserve cash as far as possible. Therefore, claimants are generally paid in a mixture of cash and securities. This makes it less easy to judge whether they have received their entitlement. For example, each bondholder may be offered $300 in cash and $700 in a new bond that pays no interest for the first 2 years and a low rate of interest thereafter. A bond of this kind in a company that is struggling to survive may not be worth much, but the bankruptcy court usually looks at the face value of the new bonds and may, therefore, regard the bondholders as paid in full.

Senior creditors who know they are likely to get a raw deal in a reorganization are likely to press for a liquidation. Shareholders and junior creditors prefer a reorganization. They hope that the court will not interpret the pecking order too strictly and that they will receive some crumbs.

Third, although shareholders and junior creditors are at the bottom of the pecking order, they have a secret weapon: They can play for time. Bankruptcies of large companies often take several years before a plan is presented to the court and agreed to by each class of creditor. When they use delaying tactics, the junior claimants are betting on a turn of fortune that will rescue their investment. On the other hand, the senior creditors know that time is working against them, so they may be prepared to accept a smaller payoff as part of the price for getting a plan accepted. Also, prolonged bankruptcy cases are costly. (While their cases are extreme, we've seen that the Enron and Lehman bankruptcies have generated $800 million and more than $2 billion, respectively, in legal and administrative costs.) Senior claimants may see their money seeping into lawyers' pockets and, therefore, decide to settle quickly.

Fourth, while a reorganization plan is being drawn up, the company is allowed to buy goods on credit and borrow money. Postpetition creditors (those who extend credit to a firm already in bankruptcy proceedings) have priority over the old creditors, and their debt may even be secured by assets that are already mortgaged to existing debtholders. This also gives the prepetition creditors an incentive to settle quickly, before their claim on assets is diluted by the new debt.

Finally, profitable companies may file for Chapter 11 bankruptcy to protect themselves against "burdensome" suits. For example, in 1982 Manville Corporation was threatened by 16,000 damage

---

[18] "The Firms That Can't Stop Failing," *The Economist*, September 7, 2002.

suits alleging injury from asbestos. Manville filed for bankruptcy under Chapter 11, and the bankruptcy judge agreed to put the damage suits on hold until the company was reorganized. This took 6 years. Of course, legislators worry that these actions are contrary to the original intent of the bankruptcy acts.

The U.S. bankruptcy system is often described as debtor friendly. In some other countries, the bankruptcy regime is designed to recover as much cash as possible for the lenders. While critics of Chapter 11 complain about the costs of saving businesses that are not worth saving, commentators elsewhere bemoan the fact that their bankruptcy laws are causing the breakup of potentially healthy businesses.

Appendix Questions

1. **Bankruptcy.** True or false?
   a. When a company becomes bankrupt, it is usually in the interests of the equityholders to seek a liquidation rather than a reorganization.
   b. A reorganization plan must be presented for approval by each class of creditor.
   c. The Internal Revenue Service has first claim on the company's assets in the event of bankruptcy.
   d. In a reorganization, creditors may be paid off with a mixture of cash and securities.
   e. When a company is liquidated, one of the most valuable assets to be sold is often the tax-loss carry-forward.

2. **Bankruptcy.** Explain why equity can sometimes have a positive value even when companies petition for bankruptcy.

17

Payout Policy

LEARNING OBJECTIVES

After studying this chapter, you should be able to:

17-1 Describe how dividends are paid and shares are repurchased.

17-2 Explain why dividend increases and repurchases are good news for investors and why dividend cuts are bad news.

17-3 Explain why payout policy would not affect shareholder value in perfect and efficient financial markets.

17-4 Show how market imperfections, especially the different tax treatment of dividends and capital gains, can affect payout policy.

17-5 Understand how payout policy varies over the life cycle of the firm.

RELATED WEBSITES FOR THIS CHAPTER CAN BE FOUND IN CONNECT.

In 2015 Apple paid out $11.6 billion in dividends and used a further $34.7 billion to repurchase stock. How do companies such as Apple decide on the payout to shareholders? *Lydia Fizz/Flickr/CC BY 2.0*

Shareholders invest in the corporation when they buy newly issued shares and when the corporation reinvests earnings on the shareholders' behalf. The shareholders do not usually demand a prompt cash return on this investment. Some long-established companies have never paid a cash dividend. Sooner or later, however, most corporations do pay out cash to their shareholders. They pay dividends, or they use cash to buy back previously issued shares.

How much should a corporation pay out in a given year? Should the payout come as dividends or share repurchases? The answers to these two questions are the corporation's *payout policy*.

We start the chapter with a discussion of how dividends are paid and how firms repurchase their stock. We explain why dividend increases usually convey good news to investors and why dividend cuts convey bad news. Then we explain why payout policy should not affect shareholder wealth in an ideal world with perfect and efficient financial markets.

That leads us to the real-world complications that could favor one payout policy over another. Taxes, which favor repurchases, are probably at the head of the list.

We close with a discussion of total cash payout and how it is likely to change over the life cycle of the firm. Young, growing firms pay out little or nothing—they are raising cash from investors, not returning it. Mature firms pay out more and more as they age and investment opportunities shrink. A generous payout by aging firms is welcomed by investors, who worry that managers will otherwise waste free cash flow on empire-building and negative-NPV projects.

17.1 How Corporations Pay Out Cash to Shareholders

Corporations pay out cash to their shareholders in two ways. They can pay a cash dividend or repurchase some outstanding shares. Figure 17.1 shows annual repurchases and dividends in the United States since 1980. You can see that stock repurchases were rare before the mid-1980s but have since become far more common. In 2015, some of the most active stock repurchasers included Apple ($42 billion), Microsoft ($13 billion), Wells Fargo, and Intel ($10 billion each). The repurchase champion, however, is ExxonMobil, which has bought back more than 40% of its shares since 2000.

Most mature, profitable companies pay cash dividends. By contrast, growth companies typically pay small or no dividends. The no-dividend group includes household names such as Amazon, Facebook, eBay, and Alphabet (the parent company of Google). The no-dividend group also includes companies that used to pay dividends but have fallen on hard times and been forced to cut back dividends to conserve cash. An example is Ford Motor Company, which paid regular dividends for decades but then cut its dividend to zero in 2006 before resuming again in 2012.

Here is a table of payout practices for U.S. firms from 2003 to 2014:

		Pay Dividend?	
		Yes	No
Repurchase?	**Yes**	15%	11%
	No	18%	56%

You can see that firms are not obliged to choose between dividends and repurchase. On average, in any year, 15% of the firms both paid a dividend and also repurchased shares. The fraction that paid dividends but did not repurchase was 18%. The corresponding fraction for repurchases but no dividends was 11%. But 56% of firms neither paid dividends nor repurchased shares.

FIGURE 17.1 Dividends and stock repurchases in the United States, 1980–2014 (figures in $ billions)

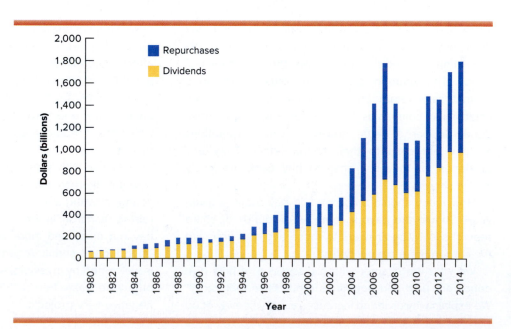

Source: Compustat, www.compustat.com.

FIGURE 17.2 The key dates for Coca-Cola's quarterly dividend

October 15, 2015	November 27, 2015	December 1, 2015	December 15, 2015
Coca-Cola declares regular quarterly dividend of $.33 per share.	Shares start to trade ex-dividend.	Dividend will be paid to share-holders registered on this date.	Dividend checks are mailed to shareholders.
Declaration date	Ex-dividend date	Record date	Payment date

How Firms Pay Dividends

cash dividend
Payment of cash by the firm to its shareholders.

In October 2015, Coca-Cola's board of directors met and decided to authorize a quarterly **cash dividend** of $.33 per share. Some of Coke's shareholders may have welcomed the cash, but others preferred to reinvest the dividend in the company. To help these investors, Coca-Cola offered an automatic dividend reinvestment plan, or DRIP. If a shareholder belonged to this plan, his or her dividends were automatically used to buy additional shares.[1]

Who receives the Coca-Cola dividend? That may seem an obvious question, but shares trade constantly, and the firm's records of who owns its shares are never fully up to date. So corporations have to specify a particular day's roster of shareholders who qualify to receive each dividend. Coca-Cola announced that it would send a dividend check on December 15 (the *payment date*) to all shareholders recorded in its books on December 1 (the *record date*).

ex-dividend
Without the dividend. Buyer of a stock after the ex-dividend date does not receive the most recently declared dividend.

On November 27, two business days before the record date, Coca-Cola stock began to trade **ex-dividend.** Investors who bought shares on or after that date did not have their purchases registered by the record date and were not entitled to the dividend. Other things equal, a stock is worth less if you miss out on the dividend. So when a stock "goes ex-dividend," its price falls by about the amount of the dividend.

Figure 17.2 illustrates the sequence of the key dividend dates. This sequence is the same whenever companies pay a dividend (though of course the actual dates will differ).

17.1 Self-Test

Mick Milekin buys 100 shares of Junk Bombs Inc. on Tuesday, June 2. The company has declared a dividend of $1 per share payable on June 30 to share-holders of record as of Wednesday, June 3. If the ex-dividend date is June 1, is Mick entitled to the dividend? When will the checks go out in the mail?

Limitations on Dividends

Suppose that an unscrupulous board decided to sell all the firm's assets and distrib-ute the money as dividends. That would not leave anything in the kitty to pay the firm's debts.

State law helps to protect the firm's creditors against excessive dividend payments. For example, most states prohibit a company from paying dividends if doing so would make the company insolvent.[2] Also, companies are not allowed to pay a dividend if it

---

[1] Often the new shares in an automatic dividend investment plan are issued at a small discount of around 5% from the market price; the firm offers this sweetener because it saves the underwriting costs of a regular share issue. Sometimes 10% or more of total dividends are reinvested under such plans.

[2] The statutes define insolvency in different ways. In some cases, it just means an inability to meet immediate obligations; in other cases, it means a deficiency of assets compared with all outstanding fixed liabilities.

cuts into legal capital. *Legal capital* is generally defined as the par value of the outstanding shares.[3]

Banks and other lenders may also demand dividend restrictions, particularly if they are worried about the borrower's creditworthiness. We mentioned that Ford eliminated its dividend in 2006. Ford had lost billions and had been forced to borrow heavily to finance its recovery plan. Its loan agreements prohibited dividends. Thus, Ford was only able to start paying dividends again in 2012 when its health had improved.

Stock Dividends and Stock Splits

stock dividends and splits
Distributions of additional shares to a firm's stockholders.

stock split
Distributions of additional shares to a firm's stockholders.

Coca-Cola's dividend was in cash, but companies sometimes declare **stock dividends.** For example, the firm could declare a stock dividend of 10%. In this case, it would send each shareholder 1 additional share for each 10 that the shareholder owns.

A stock dividend is very much like a **stock split.** In both cases, the shareholder is given a fixed number of new shares for each one held. For example, in a two-for-one stock split, each investor would receive one additional share for each share already held. The investor ends up with two shares rather than one. A two-for-one stock split is, therefore, like a 100% stock dividend. Both result in a doubling of the number of outstanding shares, but they do not affect the company's assets, profits, or total value.[4]

More often than not, however, the announcement of a stock split does result in a rise in the market price of the stock, even though investors are aware that the company's business is not affected. Perhaps low-priced shares are particularly favored by investors, or maybe investors take the decision as a signal of management's confidence in the future.[5]

Example **17.1 ▶**   Stock Dividends and Splits

Amoeba Products has issued 2 million shares currently selling at $15 each. Thus, investors place a total market value on Amoeba of $30 million. The company now declares a 50% stock dividend. This means that each shareholder will receive one new share for every two shares that are currently held. So the total number of Amoeba shares will increase from 2 million to 3 million. The company's assets are not changed by this paper transaction and are still worth $30 million. The value of each share after the stock dividend is, therefore, $30/3 = $10.

If Amoeba split its stock three for two, the effect would be the same.[6] In this case, two shares would split into three. (Amoeba's motto is "Divide and conquer.") So each shareholder has 50% more shares with the same total value. Other things equal, share price must decline by a third. ■

---

[3] Where there is no par value, legal capital consists of part or all of the receipts from past share issues.

[4] Unusually high stock prices can make trading difficult for some individual investors who are accustomed to buying shares in round lots of 100 shares each. So a corporation with stock that is selling for, say, $240 per share could use a six-for-one split to pull the price down into a more convenient "trading range" of around $40. It seems that sometimes individual investors may favor stocks with low prices and that companies respond to this change in demand by splitting their stock. See M. Baker, R. Greenwood, and J. Wurgler, "Catering through Nominal Share Prices," *Journal of Finance* 64 (December 2009), pp. 2559–2590.

[5] See E. F. Fama, L. Fisher, M. Jensen, and R. Roll, "The Adjustment of Stock Prices to New Information," *International Economic Review* 10 (February 1969), pp. 1–21. For evidence that companies which split their stock have above-average earnings prospects, see P. Asquith, P. Healy, and K. Palepu, "Earnings and Stock Splits," *Accounting Review* 64 (July 1989), pp. 387–403.

[6] The distinction between stock dividends and stock splits is a technical one. A stock dividend is shown on the balance sheet as a transfer from retained earnings to par value and additional paid-in capital. A split is shown as a proportional reduction in the par value of each share. Neither affects the total book value of stockholders' equity.

Sometimes, companies with very low stock prices use *reverse splits* to increase price per share. Citigroup, for example, announced a 1-for-10 reverse split in 2011. Citi had survived the financial crisis of 2007–2009, but its stock had fallen from pre-crisis levels of around $50 per share to a little above $4. The reverse split gave each shareholder 1 new share for every 10 old shares. Suddenly Citi stock was trading above $40. Of course, shareholders who purchased the stock pre-crisis remembered that the 10 shares they gave up in the split used to be worth $500.

Stock Repurchases

Another way for the firm to hand back cash to its stockholders is for it to repurchase some of its shares. For example, shortly after announcing its third-quarter dividend in 2015, Coca-Cola disclosed that it had spent $1.3 billion so far that year on repurchases. The company can keep these reacquired shares in its treasury and resell them if it needs money later. The shares can also be issued to managers who exercise stock options.

There are four main ways to implement a **stock repurchase:**

1. *Open-market repurchase.* The firm announces that it plans to buy stock in the secondary market, just like any other investor. This is by far the most common method. There are limits on how many of its own shares a firm is allowed to purchase on a given day, so repurchases are spread out over several months or years.
2. *Tender offer.* The firm offers to buy back a stated number of shares at a fixed price. If enough shareholders accept the offer, the deal is done.
3. *Auction.* The firm states a range of prices at which it is prepared to repurchase. Shareholders submit offers declaring how many shares they are prepared to sell at each price, and the firm calculates the lowest price at which it can buy the desired number of shares.
4. *Direct negotiation.* The firm may negotiate repurchase of a block of shares from a major shareholder. The most notorious examples are *greenmail transactions,* in which the target of an attempted takeover buys out the hostile bidder. "Greenmail" means that the shares are repurchased at a generous price that makes the bidder happy to leave the target alone.

17.2

The Information Content of Dividends and Repurchases

In 2004, a survey asked senior executives about their firms' dividend policies. Figure 17.3 summarizes the executives' responses. Three features stand out:

1. Managers are reluctant to make dividend changes that may have to be reversed, and they are willing to raise new financing if necessary to maintain payout.
2. Managers "smooth" dividends and hate to cut them back. Dividends tend to follow the growth in long-run, sustainable earnings. Transitory fluctuations in earnings rarely affect dividend payouts.
3. Managers focus more on dividend *changes* than on absolute levels. Thus, paying a $2 dividend is an important financial decision if last year's dividend was $1, but it's no big deal if last year's dividend was $2.

From these replies, you can see why an announcement of a dividend increase is good news for investors. Investors know that managers are reluctant to cut dividends and, therefore, will not increase them unless they are confident that the payment can be maintained. Therefore, the declaration of a dividend increase has **information content;** it signals managers' confidence in the future.

It is no surprise, therefore, to find that the announcement of a dividend increase prompts a small rise in the stock price and that a dividend cut results in a fall. For example, Healy and Palepu found that announcement of a company's first

---

stock repurchase
Firm distributes cash to stockholders by repurchasing shares.

BEYOND THE PAGE

The Lintner model of payout

mhhe.com/brealey9e

---

information content of dividends
Dividend increases convey managers' confidence about future cash flow and earnings. Dividend cuts convey lack of confidence and therefore are bad news.

FIGURE 17.3 A survey of financial executives suggested that their firms were reluctant to cut the dividend and tried to maintain a smooth series of payments.

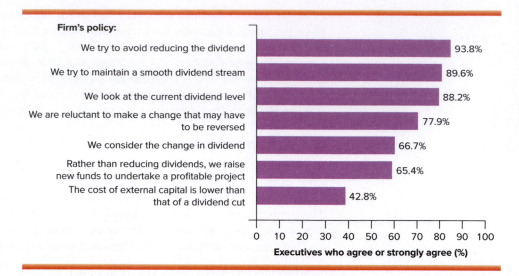

Source: A. Brav, J. R. Graham, C. R. Harvey, and R. Michaely, "Payout Policy in the 21st Century," *Journal of Financial Economics* 77 (September 2005), pp. 483–527.

dividend caused an immediate price increase of 4% on average.[7] Amihud and Li found that during the 1990s, the announcement of a dividend increase (by companies already paying a regular dividend) caused, on average, an immediate price rise of about .5%. A dividend cut resulted in a fall in price of about 2%.[8] Notice that investors do not get excited about the *level* of a company's dividend; they worry about the *change,* which they view as an indicator of management's confidence in the future.

Seasoned financial managers understand the information content of dividends and take care not to change dividends in a way that sends false signals to investors. But some dividend changes do not have any information content. For example, not all dividend cuts are bad news; if investors are convinced that there is a good reason for the cut, the stock price may emerge unscathed. The nearby box explains how investors went along with a dividend cut by JPMorgan Chase in 2009. Also, dividend cuts don't convey bad news when the information is already out and investors realize that the dividend cut is coming, as the following example illustrates.

Example **17.2** ▶   BP's Dividend Suspension

BP announced on June 16, 2010, that it planned to suspend dividends at least through the end of the year. The suspension freed up roughly $7.8 billion in cash, which could be used for the compensation fund that BP agreed to set up in the wake of the Gulf oil spill. Yet the announcement of the dividend cut barely moved BP's stock price. This cut was widely anticipated, so it wasn't new information. It was a response to a bad event that had *already* happened and knocked down BP's stock price. It was not interpreted as a signal of *fresh* bad news about BP. ■

BEYOND THE PAGE

   Repurchase motives

mhhe.com/brealey9e

There is also information content in stock repurchases. Repurchases can be signals of managers' optimism and may indicate their view that the company's shares are underpriced by investors. Investors may also applaud repurchases if they worry that the cash would otherwise be frittered away on unprofitable investments. (Of course, investors would be less thrilled if their favorite growth company suddenly announced

---

[7] P. Healy and K. Palepu, "Earnings Information Conveyed by Dividend Initiations and Omissions," *Journal of Financial Economics* 21 (1988), pp. 149–175.

[8] Y. Amihud and K. Li, "The Declining Information Content of Dividend Announcements and the Effect of Institutional Holdings," *Journal of Financial and Quantitative Analysis* 41 (2006), pp. 637–660. Amihud and Li also found that the information content of dividend announcements was much larger during the 1960s and 1970s.

a repurchase program because its managers could not think of anything better to do with the cash.) But announcement of a share repurchase program is not a commitment to continue repurchases in later years. So news about a planned repurchase is less strongly positive than the announcement of a dividend increase.

Many large, mature corporations such as Coca-Cola pay regular cash dividends and repurchase shares year in and year out. For them, repurchases are routine, one part of an overall payout strategy, and periodic announcements of repurchase programs convey less information.

17.3 Dividends or Repurchases? The Payout Controversy

It seems clear that a change in payout may provide information about management's confidence in the firm and so may affect the stock price. But this change in stock price would happen anyway as the information eventually seeped out through other channels. Can payout policy *change* the underlying value of the firm's common stock, or is it just a signal about that value?

This can be a difficult question to tackle because payout decisions are often intertwined with other financing or investment decisions. Some firms pay low dividends because management is optimistic about the firm's future and wishes to retain earnings for expansion. In this case, the payout decision is a by-product of the firm's capital budgeting decision. Another firm might finance capital expenditures largely by borrowing. This frees up cash that can be paid out to shareholders. In this case, the payout decision is a by-product of the borrowing decision.

We wish to isolate payout policy from other problems of financial management. The precise question we should ask is: What is the effect of a change in dividend payout *given* the firm's capital budgeting and borrowing decisions?

One nice feature of economics is that it can accommodate not just two, but three opposing points of view. And so it is with payout policy. On one side, there is a group that believes high dividends increase value. On the other side, there is a group that believes that high dividends bring high taxes and therefore reduce firm value. And in the center, there is a middle-of-the-road party that believes payout policy makes no difference. Let's start with the middle-of-the-roaders.

Franco Modigliani and Merton Miller (MM), who proved that debt policy doesn't matter in perfect financial markets, founded the middle-of-the-road party when they proved that dividend decisions also don't matter in perfect financial markets.[9] MM would admit that payout policy may matter in practice not just because of the

---

[9] M. H. Miller and F. Modigliani, "Dividend Policy, Growth and the Valuation of Shares," *Journal of Business* 34 (October 1961), pp. 411–433.

information content of dividends and repurchases, but also because of taxes and market imperfections. But understanding when and why payout policy does *not* matter will help us to understand when it may matter.

We start with a simple example illustrating MM's argument.

Dividends or Repurchases? An Example

Suppose you are CFO of Hewlard Pocket, a profitable and mature company. Growth is slowing down, and you plan to distribute free cash flow to stockholders. Does it matter whether you initiate dividends or a repurchase program? Does the choice affect the market value of your firm in any fundamental way?

Panel A of Table 17.1 shows the market value of Hewlard Pocket's assets and equity. The firm is worth $1.1 million. With 100,000 shares outstanding, price per share is $11. This is the price just before the ex-dividend date.

Panel B shows what happens after Pocket pays out a dividend of $1 per share, $100,000 in total. The cash account falls to $50,000, and the market value of the firm falls from $1.1 million to $1 million. Because there are 100,000 shares, price per share falls from $11 to $10.

The shareholders neither gain nor lose as a result of the dividend because the cash dividend exactly compensates them for the fall in share price. Suppose that you own 1,000 shares worth $11,000 before the dividend. After the dividend, you still have $11,000: $10,000 in stock plus $1,000 in cash.

Panel C shows what happens if Pocket pays no dividend but, instead, pays out $100,000 by repurchasing shares. It repurchases 9,091 shares at $11, leaving 100,000 − 9,091 = 90,909 shares outstanding. (Notice that the price stays at $11. Firm value is $1 million and price per share = $1,000,000/90,909 = $11.)

Suppose again that you own 1,000 shares worth $11,000 before the repurchase. If you sell the shares back to Pocket, you get $11,000 in cash. If you don't sell, your shares are still worth $11,000. It doesn't matter whether you sell or not—your wealth is the same. You are also exactly as well off with the repurchase as with the cash dividend.

Our example, therefore, confirms MM's argument by demonstrating that the choice between cash dividends and repurchases doesn't matter for shareholder wealth. (Some tax and other complications are still to come, of course.)

You may hear a claim that repurchases increase stock price. That's not quite right, as our example illustrates. A repurchase avoids the *fall* in stock price that would

TABLE 17.1 Hewlard Pocket's market value balance sheets illustrate the effects of dividends versus repurchases.

Assets		Liabilities and Shareholders' Equity	
A. Original Balance Sheet			
Cash	$ 150,000	Debt	$ 0
Other assets	950,000	Equity	1,100,000
Value of firm	$1,100,000	Value of firm	$1,100,000
Shares outstanding = 100,000			
Price per share = $1,100,000/100,000 = $11			
B. After Cash Dividend of $1 per Share			
Cash	$ 50,000	Debt	$ 0
Other assets	950,000	Equity	1,000,000
Value of firm	$1,000,000	Value of firm	$1,000,000
Shares outstanding = 100,000			
Price per share = $1,000,000/100,000 = $10			
C. After $100,000 Stock Repurchase Program			
Cash	$ 50,000	Debt	$ 0
Other assets	950,000	Equity	1,000,000
Value of firm	$1,000,000	Value of firm	$1,000,000
Shares outstanding = 90,909			
Price per share = $1,000,000/90,909 = $11			

otherwise occur on the ex-dividend date if the company used the cash to pay dividends rather than to repurchase stock. (Compare panels B and C in Table 17.1. Notice that with the repurchase the price per share stays at $11 instead of dropping to $10 ex-dividend.) Repurchases also reduce the number of outstanding shares, so future earnings per share increase, though *total* earnings are unaffected.

17.2   Self-Test

What would Table 17.1 look like if the dividend changes to $1.50 per share and the share repurchase to $150,000?

Repurchases and the Dividend Discount Model

Now here is a problem that often causes confusion: We stated in Chapter 7 that the value of a share of stock equals the discounted value of future dividends. Does this dividend discount model still work if the firm distributes cash by repurchases instead of dividends? The answer is yes, but you have to be careful to forecast dividends *per share*.

Let's start again with Table 17.1, panel B. Hewlard Pocket has just paid a dividend of $1 a share, and its 100,000 shares are now selling for $10 each. We add two assumptions. First, assume that the firm is expected to generate earnings of $100,000 per year, with no growth or decline ($g = 0$), and to pay out all earnings to stockholders. The stock price in panel B is ex-dividend, so the next payout of $100,000 ($1 per share) will come next period. Second, assume that the cost of equity is $r = .10$ (10%). We can apply the constant-growth dividend discount model from Chapter 7:

$$P_0 = \frac{DIV_1}{r - g} = \frac{\$1}{.10 - 0} = \$10$$

Now suppose that Pocket announces that henceforth it will pay out exactly 50% of earnings as cash dividends and 50% as repurchases. This means that next year's expected dividend is only $DIV_1 = \$.50$. On the other hand, the repurchases will reduce the number of shares outstanding, increasing earnings and dividends per share in year 2 and later years. It turns out that the $.50 reduction in the dividend will be exactly offset by the 5% growth in earnings and dividends per share.

Let's see how this works. Pocket will use $50,000 (50% of earnings) to repurchase shares in year 1. With that $50,000 and an ex-dividend stock price of $10.50 ($11 minus the $.50 dividend), it can repurchase $50,000/$10.50 = 4,762 shares. The number of shares outstanding, therefore, will fall from 100,000 to 95,238. Thus, the expected earnings per share in year 2 increase from $1 to $100,000/95,238 = $1.05 per share. The growth rate is 5%. Dividends per share in year 2 will also grow by 5% to $.525. And if you carry this example forward to year 3 and beyond, you will find that using 50% of earnings to repurchase shares continues to generate a growth rate in earnings and dividends per share of 5% per year.

You can probably see where this leads. The effect of the reduction in cash dividends is exactly offset by the growth in earnings and dividends per share that results from the stock repurchase. Again, we use the dividend discount model, this time with the lower dividend of $.50 and 5% growth:

$$P_0 = \frac{DIV_1}{r - g} = \frac{\$.50}{.10 - .05} = \$10$$

This result illustrates a general point: The dividend discount model is not upset by repurchases as long as you are careful to forecast earnings and dividends *per share*. But such forecasts may be difficult in practice because share repurchase programs are often volatile and erratic. If you are valuing a company that is likely to make frequent repurchases, it can be fiddly to keep track of the changing number of shares and the dividends per share. In such cases, you should consider using an alternative approach. This involves two steps:

Step 1. Calculate equity market capitalization (the value of all outstanding shares) by forecasting and discounting the free cash flow. Free cash flow is the amount that will be paid out to *all* current and future shareholders either as dividends or by stock repurchases (net of any issues of stock).

Step 2. Calculate price per share by dividing market capitalization by the number of shares currently outstanding. That way you don't have to worry about how payout is split between dividends and repurchases.

In our example, you would forecast total payout of $100,000 per year and market capitalization of $100,000/.10 = $1 million after dividends and repurchases in the current period. Price per share would be $1,000,000/100,000 = $10. (If we had started this example in panel C of Table 17.1, the number of shares would be 90,909 and price per share would be $1,000,000/90,909 = $11. The total market capitalization of the firm would still be $1,000,000.)

Dividends and Share Issues

Our Hewlard Pocket example showed that shareholders are no better or worse off if the company pays less in dividends and uses the cash that is saved to repurchase stock. But maybe companies can increase value by paying out *more* to shareholders either as dividends or through stock repurchases. Let's check.

Suppose that Pocket's cash holding is *not* surplus. Instead, the company has set aside $100,000 to buy a new fan pump. However, Pocket's president has read that the value of a stock is equal to the discounted stream of dividends. So he reasons that the company could increase the value of its stock by paying out that $100,000 as an extra dividend. The president's heart is in the right place. Unfortunately, his head isn't. To understand why, think about the effect of this proposed change in dividend policy *given the firm's capital budgeting and borrowing decisions.*

If Pocket buys its much-needed fan pump, the extra cash that is paid out needs to be replaced. If borrowing is fixed, the money must come from the sale of $100,000 in new shares. After Pocket pays the additional $100,000 dividend and replaces the cash by selling new shares, the company value is unchanged. But because the new stockholders are putting up $100,000, they will demand to receive shares worth $100,000. Because the total value of the company is the same, the value of the old stockholders' stake in the company falls by this $100,000. The old shareholders now have an extra $100,000 of cash in their pockets, but they have given up a $100,000 stake in the firm to those investors who buy the newly issued shares. Thus, the extra dividend that the old stockholders receive just offsets the loss in the value of the shares that they hold. In other words, Pocket is simply recycling cash: It pays out extra cash to its current investors (the dividend) but simultaneously takes back the same amount (through the share issue). To suggest that this makes investors better off is like advising the cook to cool the kitchen by leaving the refrigerator door open.

Does it make any difference to the old stockholders that they receive an extra dividend payment plus an offsetting capital loss? It might if that were the only way they could get their hands on the cash. But as long as there are efficient capital markets, they can raise cash by selling shares. Thus, Pocket's old shareholders can "cash in" either by persuading the management to pay a higher dividend or by selling some of their shares. In either case, there will be the same transfer of ownership and value from the old to the new stockholders. Because investors do not need dividends to convert their shares to cash, they will not pay higher prices for firms with higher dividend payouts. In other words, payout policy will have no impact on the value of the firm.

We have seen that MM's irrelevance argument holds both for increases in dividends and for reductions (always remembering that capital investment and borrowing are held constant). As our examples illustrate, payout policy is a trade-off between cash dividends and the issue or repurchase of common stock. In a perfect capital market, payout policy would have no impact on firm value. Of course, our examples of dividend irrelevance have ignored taxes, issue costs, and a variety of other real-world complications. We will turn to these intricacies shortly, but before we do, we note that the crucial assumption in our proof is that the sale or purchase of shares occurs at a fair price. The shares that Pocket buys back for $100,000 must be worth $100,000; those that it sells to raise $100,000 must also be worth that figure. In other words, dividend irrelevance assumes efficient capital markets.

17.4 Why Dividends May Increase Value

MM's conclusions follow from their assumptions of perfect and efficient capital markets. However, nobody claims their model is an exact description of the real world. Thus, the impact of payout policy finally boils down to arguments about imperfections and inefficiencies.

Those who believe that dividends are good argue that some investors have a natural preference for high-payout stocks. For example, some financial institutions are legally restricted from holding stocks lacking established dividend records. Trusts and endowment funds may prefer high-dividend stocks because dividends are regarded as spendable "income," whereas capital gains are only "additions to principal."

In addition, there is a natural clientele of investors, including the elderly, who look to their stock portfolios for a steady source of cash to live on. In principle, this cash can be generated from stocks paying no dividends at all; the investors can just sell off a small fraction of their holdings from time to time. But that can be inconvenient and lead to transaction costs.

Behavioral psychology may also help to explain why some investors prefer to receive regular dividends rather than sell small amounts of stock. We are all liable to succumb to temptation. Some of us may hanker after fattening foods, while others may be dying for a drink. We could seek to control these cravings by willpower, but that can be a painful struggle. Instead, it may be easier to set simple rules for ourselves ("cut out chocolate," or "wine only with meals"). In just the same way, we may welcome the self-discipline that comes from limiting our spending to dividend income.

All this may well be true, but it does not follow that you can increase the value of *your* firm by increasing dividend payout. Smart managers already have recognized that there is a clientele of investors who would be prepared to pay a premium for high-payout stocks. **There are natural clienteles for high-payout stocks, but it does not follow that any particular firm can benefit by increasing its dividends. The high-dividend clienteles already have plenty of high-dividend stocks to choose from.**

Suppose that the CEO of a software company announces at a press conference a plan to enter the market for mint toothpaste. When you ask why, the CEO points out that millions of people buy mint toothpaste. You would doubt the CEO's business sanity. Does the world need another mint toothpaste manufacturer? So why should you believe that because there is a clientele of investors who like high payouts, your company can increase value by manufacturing a high payout? That clientele was probably satisfied long ago.

Perhaps the most persuasive argument in favor of a high-payout policy is that it mitigates free-cash-flow problems. Suppose a company has plenty of cash but few profitable investment opportunities. Shareholders may fear that the money will be plowed back into building a larger empire rather than a more profitable one. In such cases, generous dividends or share repurchases deprive the managers of excess cash and encourage a more careful, value-oriented investment policy. Dividends provide more discipline than repurchases because financial managers rarely cut dividends except under great duress.

The accompanying figure shows how Apple's holdings of cash and marketable securities have grown over the past decade. By the start of 2012, Apple Inc. had accumulated cash and long-term securities of about $100 billion. Steve Jobs, the architect of Apple's explosive growth, had preferred to keep the war chest of cash for investment or possible acquisitions. Jobs's fiscal conservatism may seem quaint when Apple's forecasted income for 2012 was more than $40 billion. But Jobs could remember tough times for Apple; the company was near bankruptcy when Jobs took over in 1997. Apple had paid cash dividends in the early 1990s but was forced to stop in 1995 as its cash reserves dwindled.

After Jobs died in October 2011, the pressure from investors for payout steadily increased. "They have a ridiculous amount of cash," said Douglas Skinner, a professor of accounting at the Chicago Booth School of Business. "There is no feasible acquisition that Apple could do that would need that much cash."

On March 19, 2012, Apple announced that it would pay a quarterly dividend of $2.65 per share and spend $10 billion for share buybacks. It forecasted $45 billion in payout over the following 3 years. Apple's stock price jumped by $15.53 to $601 by the close of trading on the announcement day. Apple's dividend yield went from zero to $(2.65 \times 4)/601 = 1.8\%$.

Was Apple's payout sufficiently generous? Analysts' opinions varied. "A pretty vanilla return-of-cash program" (A. M. Sacconaghi, Bernstein Research). "It's not too piddling, and on the other hand not so large to signal that growth prospects are not what they thought" (David A. Rolfe, Wedgewood Partners). Bill Choi (Janney Montgomery Scott) pointed out that income-oriented mutual funds would now be more comfortable holding Apple stock.

Postscript: Apple more than kept its payout promise. In the 3 years to 2015, it distributed more than $65 billion through dividends and repurchases. Nevertheless, by the end of the period, its cash mountain was even higher than at the time of the 2012 announcement.

Source: N. Wingfield, "Flush with Cash, Apple Declares a Dividend and Buyback," *The New York Times*, March 20, 2012, pp. B1, B9.

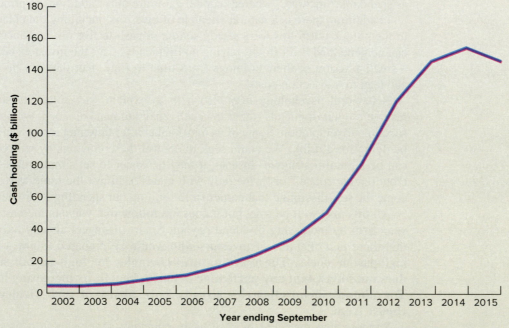

The growth in Apple's holdings of cash and marketable securities, 2002–2015

The nearby box describes how Apple decided to initiate dividends and repurchases in order to reduce its "cash mountain."

17.3   Self-Test

The Altria Group pays a generous cash dividend. Suppose an investor in Altria does not need a regular income. What could she do? If there were no trading costs, would she have any reason to care about Altria's payout policy? What if there is a brokerage fee on the purchase of new shares? What if Altria has a dividend reinvestment plan that allows the investor to buy shares at a 5% discount?

17.5 Why Dividends May Reduce Value

The low-dividend creed is simple. Companies can convert dividends into capital gains by shifting their payout policy. If dividends are taxed more heavily than capital gains, such financial alchemy should be welcomed by any taxpaying investor. Firms should pay the lowest cash dividend they can get away with. Surplus cash should be used to repurchase shares.

Table 17.2 illustrates this. It assumes that dividends are taxed at a rate of 40% but that capital gains are taxed at only 20%. The stocks of firms A and B are equally risky, and investors demand an expected *after-tax* rate of return of 10% on each. Investors expect A to be worth $112.50 per share next year. The share price of B is expected to be only $102.50, but a $10 dividend is also forecast, so the total pretax payoff is the same, $112.50.

Both stocks offer the same pretax dollar payoff. But to provide the same after-tax rate of return, B must sell for less than A, $97.78 rather than $100. The reason is obvious: Investors are willing to pay more for stock A because its return comes in the form of low-taxed capital gains. After tax, both stocks offer the same 10% expected return despite the fact that B's *pretax* return is higher.

Suppose the management of firm B eliminates the $10 dividend and uses the cash to repurchase stock instead. We saw earlier that a stock repurchase is equivalent to a cash dividend, but now we need to recognize that it is treated differently by the tax authorities. Stockholders who sell shares back to their firm pay tax only on any capital gains realized in the sale. By substituting a repurchase for a dividend, B's new policy would reduce the taxes paid by stockholders, and its stock price should rise.[10]

17.4 Self-Test

Look again at Table 17.2. What would happen to the price and pretax rate of return on stock B if the tax on capital gains were eliminated?

TABLE 17.2 Effects of a shift in dividend policy when dividends are taxed more heavily than capital gains. The high-payout stock (firm B) must sell at a lower price in order to provide the same after-tax return.

	Firm A	Firm B
Next year's price	$112.50	$102.50
Dividend	$0	$10.00
Total *pretax* payoff	$112.50	$112.50
Today's stock price	$100	$97.78
Capital gain	$12.50	$4.72
Before-tax rate of return (%)	$\frac{12.5}{100} = .125 = 12.5\%$	$\frac{14.72}{97.78} = .1505 = 15.05\%$
Tax on dividend at 40%	$0	$.40 \times \$10 = \$4.00$
Tax on capital gain at 20%	$.20 \times \$12.50 = \$2.50$	$.20 \times \$4.72 = \$.94$
Total after-tax income (dividends plus capital gains less taxes)	$(0 + 12.50) - 2.50 = \$10.00$	$(10 + 4.72) - (4.00 + .94) = \$9.78$
After-tax rate of return (%)	$\frac{10}{100} = .10 = 10\%$	$\frac{9.78}{97.78} = .10 = 10\%$

---

[10] The tax authorities have rules intended to prevent tax avoidance by substitution of repurchases for dividends. These rules are not applied to public corporations. But a private corporation that eliminates dividends and repurchases shares on a regular basis may find the repurchases reclassified as dividends for tax purposes.

Taxation of Dividends and Capital Gains under Current Tax Law

If dividends are taxed more heavily than capital gains, why should any firm ever pay a cash dividend? If cash is to be distributed to stockholders, isn't share repurchase the best channel for doing so?

In the United States, the case for low dividends was strongest before 1986. The top rate of tax on dividends was then 50%, while realized capital gains were taxed at 20%. However, the top tax rate is currently 23.8% on both dividends and capital gains.[11]

There is, however, one way that tax law still favors capital gains. Taxes on dividends have to be paid immediately, but taxes on capital gains can be deferred until shares are sold and the capital gains are realized. Stockholders can choose when to sell their shares and thus when to pay the capital gains tax.[12] The longer they wait, the less the present value of the capital gains tax liability.[13] Thus the *effective* capital gains tax rate can be less than the statutory rate.

The distinction between dividends and capital gains is less important for pension funds, endowments, and some other financial institutions that operate free of all taxes and, therefore, have no reason to prefer capital gains to dividends or vice versa. Only corporations have a tax reason to *prefer* dividends. They pay corporate income tax on only 30% of any dividends received.[14] Thus, the effective tax rate on dividends received by large corporations is 30% of 35% (the marginal rate of corporate income tax), or 10.5%. But they have to pay a 35% tax on the full amount of any capital gain.

The implications of these tax rules for payout policy are pretty simple. Capital gains have advantages to many investors, but they are far less advantageous than they were 30 or 40 years ago. Consequently, it is less easy today to make convincing arguments in favor of one kind of payout rather than another.

Taxes and Payout—A Summary

Taxes are important, but they cannot be the whole story of payout. Many companies paid generous dividends in the 1960s and 1970s, when U.S. tax rates on dividends were much higher than today. The shift from dividends to repurchases accelerated in the 2000s when tax rates on both dividends and capital gains were much lower than historical levels. Nevertheless, it seems safe to say that the tax advantages of repurchases are one reason that they have grown so much.

But financial markets clearly have room for a diversity of payout policies. Smaller growth companies reinvest all earnings and pay out nothing at all. Some pay out entirely through repurchases, some occasionally, some regularly. Some pay both dividends and repurchase. Very few companies pay out exclusively through cash dividends.

BEYOND THE PAGE

U.S. tax rates, 1960–2016

mhhe.com/brealey9e

17.6 Payout Policy and the Life Cycle of the Firm

MM said that payout policy does not affect shareholder value. Shareholder value is driven by investment policy, including exploitation of growth opportunities, and to

---

[11] The top tax rate on investment income is nominally given as 20%, but high-income investors (income above $250,000 for married couples) face an additional 3.8% surtax on their net investment income.

[12] If the stock is willed to your heirs, capital gains escape taxation altogether.

[13] Suppose the discount rate is 6%, and an investor in a 15% capital gains tax bracket has a $100 capital gain. If the stock is sold today, the capital gains tax will be $15. If sale is deferred 1 year, the tax due on that $100 gain still will be $15, but by virtue of delaying the sale for a year, the present value of the tax falls to $15/1.06 = $14.15. The effective tax rate falls to 14.15%. The longer the sale is deferred, the lower the effective tax rate.

[14] The percentage of dividend income on which tax is paid depends on the firm's ownership share in the company paying the dividend. If the share is less than 20%, taxes are paid on 30% of dividends received.

some extent, by debt policy (as we saw in the previous chapter). In MM's analysis, payout is a residual, a by-product of other financial decisions. The firm should make investment and financing decisions and then distribute whatever cash is left over. If payout is a residual, then payout decisions should evolve over the life cycle of the firm.

Young growth firms have plenty of profitable investment opportunities. During this time, it is efficient to retain and reinvest all operating cash flow. Why pay out cash to investors if the firm then has to replace the cash by borrowing or issuing more shares? Retaining cash avoids the costs of issuing securities and minimizes shareholders' taxes. Investors are not worried about wasteful overinvestment because investment opportunities are good, and managers' compensation is tied to stock price.

As the firm matures, positive-NPV projects become scarcer relative to cash flow. The firm begins to accumulate cash. Now investors begin to worry about free-cash-flow problems—for example, overinvestment or excessive perks. The investors pressure management to start paying out cash. Sooner or later, the managers comply—otherwise, stock price stagnates. The payout may come as share repurchases, but initiating a regular cash dividend sends a stronger and more reassuring signal of financial discipline. The commitment to financial discipline can outweigh the tax costs of dividends. (The middle-of-the-road party argues that the tax costs of paying cash dividends may not be that large, particularly in recent years, when U.S. personal tax rates on dividends and capital gains have been low.)

As the firm ages, more and more payout is called for. The payout may come as higher dividends or larger repurchases. Sometimes, the payout comes as the result of a takeover. Shareholders are bought out, and the firm's new owners generate cash by selling assets and restructuring operations. We discuss takeovers in Chapter 21.

The life cycle of the firm is not always predictable. It's not always obvious when the firm is "mature" and ready to start paying cash back to shareholders. The following three questions can help the financial manager decide:

1. Is the company generating positive free cash flow after making all investments with positive NPVs, and is the positive free cash flow likely to continue?
2. Is the firm's debt ratio prudent?
3. Are the company's holdings of cash a sufficient cushion for unexpected setbacks and a sufficient war chest for unexpected opportunities?

If the answer to all three questions is yes, then the free cash flow is surplus and payout is called for.

In March 2012, Apple answered yes to all three questions. Yes, it was continuing to accumulate cash at a rate of $30 billion per year. Yes, it had no debt to speak of. Yes because no conceivable investment or acquisition could soak up its excess cash flow.

Note that Apple did not just initiate a cash dividend. It announced a combination of dividends and repurchases. This two-part payout strategy is now standard for large, mature corporations. Note also that Apple did not initiate repurchases because its stock was undervalued but because it had surplus cash. So it's no surprise that repurchases increase when profits are high and more surplus cash is available.

SUMMARY

How are dividends paid, and how do companies decide how much to pay? (*LO17-1*)

Dividends come in many forms. The most common is the regular **cash dividend,** but sometimes companies pay a **stock dividend.** A firm is not free to pay dividends at will. For example, it may have accepted restrictions on dividends as a condition for borrowing money.

Dividends do not go up and down with every change in the firm's earnings. Instead, managers aim for smooth dividends and increase dividends gradually as earnings grow.

How are repurchases used to distribute cash to shareholders? (*LO17-1*)

Corporations also distribute cash by repurchasing shares. **Stock repurchases** have grown rapidly in recent years, but they do not always replace dividends. Mature firms that pay dividends also repurchase shares. On the other hand, thousands of U.S. corporations pay no dividends at all. When they pay out cash, they do so exclusively through repurchases.

Why are dividend increases and repurchases usually good news for investors? Why are dividend cuts bad news? (*LO17-2*)

Managers do not increase dividends unless they are confident that the firm will generate enough earnings to cover the payout. Therefore, announcement of a dividend conveys the managers' confidence to investors. Dividend cuts convey lack of confidence. Managers generally avoid them unless their firms are in trouble. This **information content of dividends** is the main reason that stock prices respond to dividend changes.

Repurchases are usually also good news. For example, announcement of a repurchase program can reveal managers' view that their company's stock is a "good buy" at the current price.

Cash payouts by dividends and repurchases can also reassure investors who worry that managers might otherwise spend the money on empire-building and negative-NPV projects.

Why would payout policy not affect firm value in an ideal world? (*LO17-3*)

If we hold the company's investment policy and capital structure constant, then payout policy is a trade-off between cash dividends and the issue or repurchase of common stock. In an ideally simple and perfect world, the choice would have no effect on market value. An increased cash dividend would require more shares issued or fewer shares repurchased. The increased cash in shareholders' wallets would be exactly offset by a lower share price. This is **MM's dividend-irrelevance proposition.**

How might differences in the tax treatment of dividends and capital gains affect payout policy? (*LO17-4*)

In the United States, individual investors currently pay tax on dividend income at a top rate of 23.8%. The top capital gains rate is also 23.8%, but the investor pays no tax on capital gains until his or her shares are actually sold. The longer the wait before the sale, the lower the present value of the tax. Thus, capital gains have a tax advantage for investors. The advantage was much greater in the 1970s and early 1980s, when the top tax rate on dividends was 50% and the top rate on capital gains only 20%.

If dividend income is taxed more heavily than capital gains, investors should shun high-dividend stocks. Instead of paying high dividends, corporations should shift to repurchases.

How does payout policy normally evolve over the life cycle of the firm? (*LO17-5*)

Young, rapidly growing firms are usually raising cash from investors, not distributing it. Such firms rarely pay dividends, although they may repurchase from time to time. Mature firms that generate positive free cash flow make regular payouts, often by repurchases as well as dividends. Commitment to a regular dividend can reassure investors who worry about free-cash-flow problems, that is, about overinvestment and inefficient operations.

QUESTIONS AND PROBLEMS

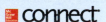

1. **How Corporations Pay Dividends.** Cash Cow International paid a regular quarterly dividend of $.075 a share. (*LO17-1*)

   a. Match each of the following dates to the correct term:

i.	May 7	A.	Record date
ii.	June 6	B.	Payment date
iii.	June 7	C.	Ex-dividend date
iv.	June 11	D.	Last with-dividend date
v.	July 2	E.	Declaration date

   b. On one of these dates the stock price is likely to fall by about the amount of the dividend. Which date?

   c. The stock price in early January was $27. What was the prospective dividend yield?

   d. The annual earnings per share were forecast at around $1.90. What was the percentage payout ratio?

2. **How Corporations Pay Dividends.** True or false? (*LO17-1*)
   a. A corporation cannot pay a dividend if its legal capital is impaired or if it is insolvent.
   b. The effective tax rate on capital gains can be less than the stated rate.
   c. Managers and investors are more concerned with dividend changes than dividend levels.
   d. Future stock price will be higher when a corporation distributes cash by repurchases rather than cash dividends.
   e. Stock dividends increase the number of shares that investors own and therefore increase shareholder wealth.
   f. By increasing the number of shares, stock dividends dilute each shareholder's interest in the company and therefore reduce wealth.

3. **How Corporations Pay Dividends.** Suppose that you own 1,000 shares of Nocash Corp. and the company is about to pay a 25% stock dividend. The stock currently sells at $100 per share. (*LO17-1*)
   a. What will be the number of shares that you hold after the stock dividend is paid?
   b. What will be the total value of your equity position after the stock dividend is paid?
   c. What will be the number of shares that you hold if the firm splits five-for-four instead of paying the stock dividend?

4. **Stock Repurchases.** True or false? (*LO17-1*)
   a. A company can keep repurchased stock in its treasury and reissue it later.
   b. The most common method for repurchasing stock is by auction.
   c. A greenmail transaction is one in which the target of a possible takeover buys back stock from the potential bidder.
   d. Most companies that distribute cash to investors do so either by paying dividends or by repurchase. It is very rare to find a company paying out cash by both methods.

5. **How Corporations Pay Dividends.** The stock of Payout Corp. will go ex-dividend tomorrow. The dividend will be $.50 per share, and there are 20,000 shares of stock outstanding. The market-value balance sheet for Payout is shown in the following table. (*LO17-1*)

Assets		Liabilities and Equity	
Cash	$100,000	Equity	$1,000,000
Fixed assets	900,000		

   a. What price is Payout stock selling for today?
   b. What price will it sell for tomorrow? Ignore taxes.
   c. Suppose that instead of paying a dividend, Payout Corp. announces that it will repurchase stock with a market value of $10,000. What happens to the stock price when the repurchase proposal is announced?
   d. Suppose that the stock is repurchased immediately after the announcement. What would be the stock price after the repurchase?

6. **Stock Repurchases.** Payout Corp. has regularly paid a quarterly dividend of $.50 per share on its 20,000 outstanding shares. Now suppose that Payout announces that instead of paying this dividend, it plans to repurchase $10,000 worth of stock instead. (*LO17-1*)
   a. What effect will the repurchase have on an investor who currently holds 100 shares and sells 1 of those shares back to the company in the repurchase?
   b. Compare the effects of the repurchase to the effects of the cash dividend that you worked out in Problem 5.

7. **How Corporations Pay Dividends.** Here are several "facts" about typical corporate dividend policies. Which are true and which are false? (*LO17-1*)
   a. The vast majority of companies pay out cash each year in the form of a dividend or a stock repurchase.
   b. Companies decide each year's dividend by looking at their capital expenditure requirements and then distributing whatever cash is left over.
   c. The share price generally falls on the dividend payment date.
   d. Managers often increase dividends temporarily when earnings are unexpectedly high for a year or two.

e. Companies undertaking substantial share repurchases usually finance them with an offsetting cut in cash dividends.

f. A company that declares a 10% stock dividend gives each shareholder 1 additional share for each 10 shares that he or she currently owns.

8. **Information Content.** Which of the following newspaper headlines would have the greatest positive impact on stock price? (*LO17-2*)

a. "Growler Corporation announces a $1 increase in its regular dividend."

b. "Growler Corporation announces a $1 special one-off dividend."

c. "Growler Corporation unexpectedly wins a lawsuit and collects cash amounting to $1 per Growler share. Growler plans to use the cash in a stock buyback program."

9. **Information Content of Dividends.** Why are dividend increases typically good news for investors and dividend cuts bad news? Explain briefly. (*LO17-2*)

10. **Payout Policy.** Mr. Milquetoast is enthusiastic about the prospects for Facebook. He wants to invest $100,000 in the stock but hesitates because Facebook has never paid a dividend. He needs to generate $5,000 per year in cash for living expenses. What should Mr. Milquetoast do? (*LO17-3*)

11. **Payout Policy.** Surf & Turf Hotels is a mature business, although it pays no cash dividends. Next year's earnings are forecast at $56 million. There are 10 million outstanding shares. The company has traditionally used 50% of earnings to repurchase shares of stock and has reinvested the remaining earnings. With reinvestment, the company has generated steady growth averaging 5% per year. Assume the cost of equity is 12%. (*LO17-3*)

a. Calculate Surf & Turf's current stock price, using the constant-growth DCF model from Chapter 7. (*Hint:* Take the easy route and start by calculating the total value of outstanding equity.)

b. Now Surf & Turf's CFO announces a switch from repurchases to a regular cash dividend. Next year's dividend will be $2.80 per share. The CFO reassures investors that the company will continue to pay out 50% of earnings and reinvest 50%. All future payouts will come as dividends, however. What would you expect to happen to Surf & Turf's stock price? Ignore taxes.

12. **Payout Policy.** Consolidated Pasta is currently expected to pay annual dividends of $10 a share in perpetuity on the 1 million shares that are outstanding. Shareholders require a 10% rate of return from Consolidated stock. (*LO17-3*)

a. What is the price of Consolidated stock?

b. What is the total market value of its equity?

Consolidated now decides to increase next year's dividend to $20 a share, without changing its investment or borrowing plans. Thereafter the company will revert to its policy of distributing $10 million a year.

c. How much new equity capital will the company need to raise to finance the extra dividend payment?

d. What will be the total present value of dividends paid each year on the new shares that the company will need to issue?

e. What will be the transfer of value from the old shareholders to the new shareholders?

f. Is this figure more than, less than, or the same as the extra dividend that the old shareholders will receive?

13. **Payout Policy.** Respond to the following two statements: (*LO17-3*)

a. "MM say that investors are equally happy with a dollar of dividends and a dollar of capital gains. That's crazy. Everyone knows that dividends are stable and capital gains risky. I'll take the dividend any day."

b. "Safer companies tend to pay more generous dividends. Therefore, a company can reduce the risk of its shares by increasing dividend payout."

14. **Payout Policy.** You own 2,000 shares of Patriot Corporation, which is about to double its dividend from $.75 to $1.50 per share. You do not need the extra dividend income, but you don't want to sell out. What would you do to offset the dividend increase? (*LO17-3*)

15. **Payout Policy.** Go back to the first Hewlard Pocket balance sheet. Pocket needs to hold on to $50,000 of cash for a future investment. Nevertheless, it decides to pay a cash dividend of

$2 per share and to replace the cash with a new issue of shares. After the dividend is paid and the new stock is issued: (*LO17-3*)

a. What will be the price per share?
b. What will be the total value of the company?
c. What will be the total value of the stock held by new investors?
d. What will be the wealth of the existing investors including the dividend payment?

16. **Payout Policy.** Go back again to the first Hewlard Pocket balance sheet. Now assume that Pocket wins a lawsuit and is paid $100,000 in cash. The market value of the equity rises by that amount, and Pocket decides to make a one-off payout of $2 per share instead of $1 per share. (*LO17-3*)

a. What will be Pocket's stock price if the payout comes as a cash dividend?
b. What will be Pocket's stock price if the payout comes as a share repurchase?

17. **Payout Policy.** House of Haddock has 5,000 shares outstanding and the stock price is $100. The company is expected to pay a dividend of $20 per share next year, and thereafter, the dividend is expected to grow indefinitely by 5% a year. The president, George Mullet, now makes a surprise announcement: He says that the company will henceforth distribute half the cash in the form of dividends and the remainder will be used to repurchase stock. (*LO17-3*)

a. What is the total value of the company before the announcement?
b. What is the total value after the announcement?
c. What is the value of one share before the announcement?
d. What is the new growth rate in the dividend stream? (Check your estimate of share value by discounting this stream of dividends per share.)

18. **Payout Policy.** We stated in Section 17.3 that MM's proof of dividend irrelevance assumes that any new shares are sold at a fair price. Consider the case in Problem 16 in which Hewlard Pocket pays the higher dividend of $2 a share and replaces the cash by issuing new stock. Suppose that the new shares are sold in a public issue at $8 a share, which is below the market price after the $2 dividend is paid. What is the loss suffered by the existing shareholders? Is dividend policy still irrelevant? Why or why not? (*LO17-3*)

19. **Payout Policy.** "Many companies use stock repurchases to increase earnings per share. For example, suppose that a company is in the following position:

Net profit	$10 million
Number of shares before repurchase	1 million
Earnings per share	$10
Price-earnings ratio	20
Share price	$200

"The company now repurchases 200,000 shares at $200 a share. The number of shares declines to 800,000 shares, and earnings per share increase to $12.50. Assuming the price-earnings ratio stays at 20, the share price must rise to $250." Discuss. (*LO17-3*)

20. **Payout Policy.** Little Oil has outstanding 1 million shares with a total market value of $20 million. The firm is expected to pay $1 million of dividends next year, and thereafter, the amount paid out is expected to grow by 5% a year in perpetuity. Thus, the expected dividend is $1.05 million in year 2, $1.1025 million in year 3, and so on. However, the company has heard that the value of a share depends on the flow of dividends, and therefore, it announces that next year's dividend will be increased to $2 million and that the extra cash will be raised immediately afterward by an issue of shares. After that, the total amount paid out each year will be as previously forecasted, that is, $1.05 million in year 2 and increasing by 5% in each subsequent year. (*LO17-3*)

a. At what price will the new shares be issued in year 1?
b. How many shares will the firm need to issue?
c. What will be the expected dividend payments on these new shares, and what, therefore, will be paid out to the old shareholders after year 1?
d. Recalculate the present value of the cash flows to current shareholders.

21. **Payout Policy.** Hors d'Age Cheeseworks has been paying a regular cash dividend of $4 per share each year for more than a decade. The company is paying out all its earnings as dividends

and is not expected to grow. There are 100,000 shares outstanding selling for $80 per share. The company has sufficient cash on hand to pay the next annual dividend.

Suppose that, starting in year 1, Hors d'Age decides to cut its cash dividend to zero and announces that it will repurchase shares instead. (*LO17-3*)

a. What is the immediate stock price reaction? Ignore taxes, and assume that the repurchase program conveys no information about operating profitability or business risk.

b. How many shares will Hors d'Age purchase?

c. Project future stock prices for both the old and new policies for years 1, 2, and 3.

22. **Payout Policy.** Big Industries has the following market-value balance sheet. The stock currently sells for $20 a share, and there are 1,000 shares outstanding. The firm will either pay a $1 per share dividend or repurchase $1,000 worth of stock. Ignore taxes. (*LO17-3*)

Assets		Liabilities and Equity	
Cash	$ 2,000	Debt	$10,000
Fixed assets	28,000	Equity	20,000

a. What will be the subsequent price per share if the firm pays a dividend?

b. What will be the subsequent price per share if the firm repurchases stock?

c. If total earnings of the firm are $2,000 a year, find earnings per share if the firm pays a dividend.

d. Now find earnings per share if the firm repurchases stock.

e. Find the price-earnings ratio if the firm pays a dividend.

f. Find the price-earnings ratio if the firm repurchases stock.

g. Adherents of the "dividends-are-good" school sometimes point to the fact that stocks with high dividend payout ratios tend to sell at above-average price-earnings multiples. Is Big Industries' P/E ratio higher if it pays a dividend?

h. Looking back at your answers to parts (a) to (f), do you think that the difference in P/E supports the "dividends-are-good" case?

23. **Payout Policy and Taxes.** What is the tax reason for not paying generous cash dividends? (*LO17-4*)

24. **Payout Policy and Taxes.** The expected pretax return on three stocks is divided between dividends and capital gains in the following way: (*LO17-4*)

Stock	Expected Dividend	Expected Capital Gain
A	$ 0	$10
B	5	5
C	10	0

a. If each stock is priced at $100, what are the expected net returns on each stock to (i) a pension fund that does not pay taxes, (ii) a corporation paying tax at 35%, and (iii) an individual with an effective tax rate of 15% on dividends and 10% on capital gains?

b. Suppose that investors pay 50% tax on dividends and 20% tax on capital gains. If stocks are priced to yield an 8% return after tax, what would A, B, and C each sell for? Assume the expected dividend is a level perpetuity.

25. **Payout Policy and Taxes.** For each of the following U.S. investors, state whether the investor has a tax reason to (i) prefer the company's payout to be in the form of dividends, (ii) prefer payout to be in the form of repurchases, or (iii) have no preference: (*LO17-4*)

a. A pension fund.

b. An individual investor in the top income tax bracket.

c. A corporation.

d. An endowment for a charity or university.

26. **Payout Policy and Taxes.** Good Values Inc. is all-equity-financed. The total market value of the firm currently is $100,000, and there are 2,000 shares outstanding. Ignore taxes. (*LO17-4*)

a. The firm has declared a $5 per share dividend. The stock will go ex-dividend tomorrow. At what price will the stock sell today?

b. At what price will the stock sell tomorrow?

c. Now assume that the tax rate on all dividend income is 30% and the tax rate on capital gains is zero. At what price will the stock sell, taking account of the taxation of dividends?

Now suppose that instead of paying a dividend, Good Values plans to repurchase $10,000 worth of stock.

d. What will be the stock price before the repurchase?

e. What will it be after the repurchase?

f. Does the existence of taxes tend to favor dividends or repurchases?

27. **Payout Policy and Taxes.** Investors require an after-tax rate of return of 10% on their stock investments. Assume that the tax rate on dividends is 30% while capital gains escape taxation. A firm will pay a $2 per share dividend 1 year from now, after which it is expected to sell at a price of $20. (*LO17-4*)

a. Find the current price of the stock.

b. Find the expected before-tax rate of return for a 1-year holding period.

c. Now suppose that the dividend will be $3 per share. If the expected after-tax rate of return is still 10% and investors still expect the stock to sell at $20 in 1 year, at what price must the stock now sell?

d. What is the before-tax rate of return?

e. Is this smaller or larger than your answer to part (b)?

28. **Payout Policy and Taxes.** Prowler Corporation wants to increase its debt ratio without changing its operations or capital investment outlays. Obviously, Prowler will have to increase borrowing, but how should it reduce equity? What would you recommend? (*LO17-4*)

29. **Life Cycle and Payout Policy.** MM show that in an idealized setting, firm value is not affected by payout policy. Yet we observe that more mature firms regularly pay higher dividends than do younger ones. Is this purely happenstance, or is there a real-world violation of the MM assumptions that may explain this pattern? (*LO17-5*)

30. **Life Cycle and Payout Policy.** In Section 17.2, we report results of a survey about corporate dividend policy. How might the tendencies documented in that survey result in more mature firms exhibiting systematically higher dividend payout ratios? (*LO17-5*)

31. **Life Cycle and Payout Policy.** Would you predict that mature or younger firms make greater use of repurchases relative to dividends? Why might one of these payout tools be better suited to younger firms? (*LO17-5*)

WEB EXERCISES

1. Go to the Industry Center on Yahoo! Finance at biz.yahoo.com/ic. Find the dividend yield of the typical firm in the biotech industry and the electric utilities industry. Which is higher? Can you come up with a good explanation for the difference?

2. Log on to the market data center of *The Wall Street Journal* online, online.wsj.com (find *Market Data* under the *Markets Tab*). Then click *U.S. Stocks* and *Dividends* to find a list of dividend declarations. What is the meaning of each event? What is the typical interval between each event?

SOLUTIONS TO SELF-TEST QUESTIONS

17.1 The ex-dividend date is June 1. Therefore, Mick buys the stock ex-dividend and will not receive the dividend. The checks will be mailed on June 30.

17.2

Assets			Liabilities and Equity		
After cash dividend					
Cash	$	0	Debt	$	0
Other assets		950,000	Equity		950,000
Value of firm		$950,000	Value of firm		$950,000
Shares outstanding = 100,000					
Price per share = $950,000/100,000 = $9.50					
After stock repurchase					
Cash	$	0	Debt	$	0
Other assets		950,000	Equity		950,000
Value of firm		$950,000	Value of firm		$950,000
Shares outstanding = 86,364					
Price per share = $950,000/86,364 = $11					

If a dividend is paid, the stock price falls by the amount of the dividend. If the company instead uses the cash for a share repurchase, the stock price remains unchanged at $11 but, with fewer shares left outstanding, the market value of the firm falls by the same amount as it would have if the dividend had been paid.

17.3 An investor who prefers a zero-dividend policy can reinvest any dividends received. This will cause the value of the shares held to be unaffected by payouts. The price drop on the ex-dividend date is offset by the reinvestment of the dividends. However, if the investor had to pay brokerage fees on the newly purchased shares, she would be harmed by a high-payout policy because part of the proceeds of the dividends would go toward paying the broker. On the other hand, if the firm offers a dividend reinvestment plan (DRIP) with a 5% discount, she is better off with a high-dividend policy. The DRIP is like a "negative trading cost." She can increase the value of her stock by 5% of the dividend just by participating in the DRIP. Of course, her gain is at the expense of shareholders that do not participate in the DRIP.

17.4 The price of the stock will equal the after-tax cash flows discounted by the required (after-tax) rate of return:

$$P = \frac{102.50 + 10 \times (1 - .4)}{1.10} = 98.64$$

Notice that the after-tax proceeds from the stock would increase by the amount that previously went to pay capital gains taxes, $.20 \times \$4.72 = \$.944$. The present value of this tax saving is $\$.944/1.10 = \$.86$. Therefore, the price increases to $\$97.78 + \$.86 = \$98.64$. The pretax rate of return falls to $(102.50 - 98.64 + 10)/98.64 = .1405$, or 14.05%, but the after-tax rate of return remains at 10%.

MINICASE

George Liu, the CEO of Penn Schumann, was a creature of habit. Every month, he and Jennifer Rodriguez, the company's chief financial officer, met for lunch and an informal chat at Pierre's. Nothing was ever discussed until George had finished his favorite *escalope de foie gras chaude*. At their last meeting in March, he had then toyed thoughtfully with his glass of Chateau Haut-Brion Blanc before suddenly asking, "What do you think we should be doing about our payout policy?"

Penn Schumann was a large and successful pharmaceutical company. It had an enviable list of highly profitable drugs, many of which had 5 or more further years of patent protection. Earnings in the latest 4 years had increased rapidly, but it was difficult to see that such rates of growth could continue. The company had traditionally paid out about 40% of earnings as dividends, though the

figure in 2017 was only 35%. Penn was spending more than $4 billion a year on R&D, but the strong operating cash flow and conservative dividend policy had resulted in a buildup of cash. Penn's recent income statements, balance sheets, and cash-flow statements are summarized in Tables 17.3, 17.4, and 17.5.

The problem, as Mr. Liu explained, was that Penn's dividend policy was more conservative than that of its main competitors. "Share prices depend on dividends," he said. "If we raise our dividend, we'll raise our share price, and that's the name of the game." Ms. Rodriguez suggested that the real issue was how much cash the company wanted to hold. The current cash holding was more than adequate for the company's immediate needs. On the other hand, the research staff had been analyzing a number of new compounds with promising applications in the treatment of liver diseases.

If this research were to lead to a marketable product, Penn would need to make a large investment. In addition, the company might require cash for possible acquisitions in the biotech field. "What worries me," Ms. Rodriguez said, "is that investors don't give us credit for this and think that we are going to fritter away the cash on negative-NPV investments or easy living. I don't think we should commit to paying out high dividends, but perhaps we could use some of our cash to repurchase stock."

"I don't know where anyone gets the idea that we fritter away cash on easy living," replied Mr. Liu, as he took another sip of wine, "but I like the idea of buying back our stock. We can tell shareholders that we are so confident about the future that we believe buying our own stock is the best investment we can make." He scribbled briefly on his napkin. "Suppose we bought back 50 million shares at $105. That would reduce the shares outstanding to 488 million. Net income last year was nearly $4.8 billion, so earnings per share would increase to $9.84. If the price-earnings multiple stays at 11.8, the stock price should rise to $116. That's

an increase of over 10%." A smile came over Mr. Liu's face. "Wonderful, he exclaimed, "here comes my *homard à nage*. Let's come back to this idea over dessert."

Evaluate the arguments of Jennifer Rodriguez and George Liu. Do you think the company is holding too much cash? If you do, how do you think it could be best paid out?

TABLE 17.3 Penn Schumann Inc. balance sheet
(figures in millions of dollars)

	2017	2016
Cash and short-term investments	$ 7,061	$ 5,551
Receivables	2,590	2,214
Inventory	1,942	2,435
Total current assets	$11,593	$10,200
Property, plant, and equipment	$21,088	$19,025
Less accumulated depreciation	5,780	4,852
Net fixed assets	$15,308	$14,173
Total assets	$26,901	$24,373
Payables	$ 6,827	$ 6,215
Short-term debt	1,557	2,620
Total current liabilities	$ 8,384	$ 8,835
Long-term debt	3,349	3,484
Shareholders' equity	15,168	12,054
Total liabilities and equity	$26,901	$24,373
Note:		
Shares outstanding (millions)	538	516
Market price per share ($)	105	88

TABLE 17.4 Penn Schumann Inc. income statement
(figures in millions)

	2017	2016
Revenue	$16,378	$13,378
Costs	8,402	7,800
Depreciation	928	850
EBIT	$ 7,048	$ 4,728
Interest	323	353
Tax	1,933	1,160
Net income	$ 4,792	$ 3,215
Dividends	1,678	1,350
Earnings per share ($)	8.91	6.23
Dividends per share ($)	3.12	2.62

TABLE 17.5 Penn Schumann Inc. statement of cash flows
(figures in millions)

	2017
Net income	$ 4,792
Depreciation	928
Decrease (increase) in receivables	(376)
Decrease (increase) in inventories	493
Increase (decrease) in payables	612
Total cash from operations	$ 6,449
Capital expenditures	(2,063)
Increase (decrease) in short-term debt	(1,063)
Increase (decrease) in long-term debt	(135)
Dividends paid	(1,678)
Cash provided by financing activities	$(2,876)
Net increase in cash	$ 1,510

18

Long-Term Financial Planning

LEARNING OBJECTIVES

After studying this chapter, you should be able to:

18-1   Describe the contents and uses of a financial plan.

18-2   Construct a simple financial planning model.

18-3   Estimate the effect of growth on the need for external financing.

RELATED WEBSITES FOR THIS CHAPTER CAN BE FOUND IN CONNECT.

Financial planners don't guess the future; they prepare for it. © nikkytok/Shutterstock RF

It's been said that a camel looks like a horse designed by a committee. If a firm made every decision piecemeal, it would end up with a financial camel. That is why smart financial managers consider the overall effect of future investment and financing decisions.

Think back to Chapter 1, where we discussed the job of the financial manager. The manager must consider what investments the firm should undertake and how the firm should raise the cash to pay for those investments. By now you know a fair amount about how to make investment decisions that increase shareholder value and about the different securities that the firm can issue. But because new investments need to be paid for, those decisions cannot be made independently. They must add up to a sensible whole. That's why financial planning is needed. The financial plan allows managers to think about the implications of alternative financial strategies and to tease out any inconsistencies in the firm's goals.

Financial planning also helps managers to avoid some surprises and consider how they should react to those surprises that *cannot* be avoided. In Chapter 10, we stressed that good financial managers insist on understanding what makes projects work and what could go wrong with them. The same approach should be taken when investment and financing decisions are considered as a whole.

Finally, financial planning helps establish goals to motivate managers and provide standards for measuring performance.

We start the chapter by summarizing what financial planning involves, and we describe the contents of a typical financial plan. We then discuss the use of financial models in the planning process. Finally, we examine the relationship between a firm's growth and its need for new financing.

18.1   What Is Financial Planning?

Firms must plan for both the short term and the long term. Short-term planning rarely looks further ahead than the next 12 months. It seeks to ensure that the firm has enough cash to pay its bills and that short-term borrowing and lending are arranged to the best advantage. We discuss short-term planning in the next chapter.

Here we are concerned with long-term planning, where a typical **planning horizon** is 5 years, although some firms look out 10 years or more. For example, it can take at least 10 years for an electric utility to design, obtain approval for, build, and test a major generating plant.

Long-term planning focuses on the big picture. For example, it looks at future investment plans by each line of business and avoids getting bogged down in details. Of course, some individual projects may be large enough to have significant individual impact. When the telecom giant Verizon chose to spend billions of dollars to deploy fiber-optic-based broadband technology to its residential customers, you can bet that this project was explicitly analyzed as part of its long-range plans. Normally, however, planners do not work on a project-by-project basis. Instead, they are content with rules of thumb that relate average levels of fixed and short-term assets to annual sales.

The long-term financial plan considers the investment that will be needed to meet the firm's goals and the finance that must be raised. But you can't think about these things without also tackling other important issues. For example, you need to consider possible dividend policies. You can't turn dividends on and off like a faucet, but the more that is paid out to shareholders, the more external financing that will be needed. You also need to think about what is an appropriate debt ratio for the firm. A conservative capital structure may mean greater reliance on new share issues. The financial plan helps you to think about these choices. Finally, by establishing a set of coherent goals, the plan makes it easier to look back at how well the firm has achieved its goals.

Why Build Financial Plans?

Firms spend considerable energy, time, and resources building elaborate financial plans. What do they get for this investment?

Contingency Planning   Planning is not just forecasting. Forecasting concentrates on the most likely outcomes, but planners need to worry about unlikely events as well as likely ones. If you think ahead about what could go wrong, then you are less likely to ignore the danger signals, and you can respond faster to trouble.

Companies have developed a number of ways of asking "what-if" questions about both individual projects and the overall firm. For example, as we saw in Chapter 10, managers often work through the consequences of their decisions under different scenarios. One scenario might envisage high interest rates contributing to a slowdown in world economic growth and lower commodity prices. A second scenario might involve a buoyant domestic economy, high inflation, and a weak currency.

The idea is to formulate responses to possible surprises. What will you do, for example, if sales in the first year turn out to be 10% below forecast? A good financial plan should help you adapt as events unfold.

Considering Options   Planners need to think whether there are opportunities for the company to exploit its existing strengths by moving into a wholly new area. Often they may recommend entering a market for "strategic" reasons—that is, not because the immediate investment has a positive net present value but because it establishes the firm in a new market and creates options for possibly valuable follow-on investments.

For example, Verizon's costly fiber-optic initiative would never be profitable strictly in terms of its most common current uses. But the new technology gives Verizon *options* to offer services that may be highly valuable in the future, such as the rapid delivery of an array of home entertainment services. The justification for the huge investment lies in these potential growth options.

Forcing Consistency   Financial plans draw out the connections between the firm's plans for growth and the financing requirements. For example, a forecast of 25% growth might require the firm to issue securities to pay for necessary capital expenditures, while a 5% growth rate might enable the firm to finance capital expenditures by using only reinvested profits.

Financial plans should help to ensure that the firm's goals are mutually consistent. For example, the chief executive might say that she is shooting for a profit margin of 10% and sales growth of 20%, but financial planners need to think whether the higher sales growth may require price cuts that will reduce profit margin.

Moreover, a goal that is stated in terms of accounting ratios is not operational unless it is translated back into what that means for business decisions. For example, a higher profit margin can result from higher prices, lower costs, or a move into new, high-margin products. Why then do managers define objectives in this way? In part, such goals may be a code to communicate real concerns. For example, a target profit margin may be a way of saying that in pursuing sales growth, the firm has allowed costs to get out of control.

The danger is that everyone may forget the code and the accounting targets may be seen as goals in themselves. No one should be surprised when lower-level managers focus on the goals for which they are rewarded. For example, when Volkswagen management set a goal of 6.5% profit margin, some VW groups responded by developing and promoting expensive, high-margin cars. Less attention was paid to marketing cheaper models, which had lower profit margins but higher sales volume. As soon as this became apparent, Volkswagen announced that it would de-emphasize its profit margin goal and would instead focus on return on investment. It hoped that this would encourage managers to get the most profit out of every dollar of invested capital.

18.2 Financial Planning Models

Financial planners often use financial planning *models* to help them explore the consequences of alternative strategies. These range from simple models, such as the one presented later in this chapter, to models that incorporate hundreds of equations.

Financial planning models support the financial planning process by making it easier and cheaper to construct forecast financial statements. The models automate an important part of planning that would otherwise be time-consuming, and labor-intensive.

Components of a Financial Planning Model

A completed financial plan for a large company is a substantial document. A smaller corporation's plan would have the same elements but less detail. For the smallest businesses, financial plans may be entirely in the financial managers' heads. The basic elements of the plans will be similar, however, for firms of any size.

Financial plans include three components: inputs, the planning model, and outputs. The relationship among these components is represented in Figure 18.1. Let's look at them in turn.

FIGURE 18.1 The components of a financial plan

Inputs   The inputs to the financial plan consist of the firm's current financial statements and its forecasts about the future. Usually, the principal forecast is the likely growth in sales because many of the other variables such as labor requirements and inventory levels are tied to sales. These forecasts are only in part the responsibility of the financial manager. Obviously, the marketing department will play a key role in forecasting sales. In addition, because sales will depend on the state of the overall economy, large firms will seek forecasting help from firms that specialize in preparing macroeconomic and industry forecasts.

The Planning Model   The financial planning model calculates the implications of the manager's forecasts for profits, new investment, and financing. The model consists of equations relating output variables to forecasts. For example, the equations can show how a change in sales is likely to affect costs, working capital, fixed assets, and financing requirements. The financial model could specify that the total cost of goods produced may increase by 80 cents for every $1 increase in total sales, that accounts receivable will be a fixed proportion of sales, and that the firm will need to increase fixed assets by 8% for every 10% increase in sales.

Outputs   The output of the financial model consists of projected financial statements such as income statements, balance sheets, and statements describing sources and uses of cash. These statements are called **pro formas,** which means that they are forecasts based on the inputs and the assumptions built into the plan. Usually, the output of financial models also includes many of the financial ratios we discussed in Chapter 4. These ratios indicate whether the firm will be financially fit and healthy at the end of the planning period.

pro formas
Projected or forecast financial statements.

18.3   A Long-Term Financial Planning Model for Dynamic Mattress

To see how one might construct a planning model, we will drop in on the financial manager of Dynamic Mattress and look at how she uses a simple spreadsheet program to draw up the firm's long-term plan. The starting point is Dynamic's latest financial statements. Table 18.1 shows its 2016 income statement and year-end balance sheet. (Note that we have collapsed individual current assets and liabilities into a single figure for net working capital.)

Now that we know where the company has been, we begin to focus on where it might be heading. Suppose that Dynamic's analysis leads it to forecast a 20% annual growth in the company's sales over the next several years. As the company grows, it will require additional investments in both working and physical capital. Can the company realistically expect to finance this growth using reinvested earnings, or must it plan to raise additional capital by issuing debt or equity? Spreadsheet programs are tailor-made for such questions. Let's investigate.

Dynamic's financial manager begins by forecasting a growth rate for sales. She then considers how other key variables such as assets or cost of goods sold will increase as sales increase. She estimates that these variables will be directly proportional to sales. Forecasting models like this, which assume a stable relation between sales and other key variables, are known as **percentage of sales models.**

percentage of sales model
Planning model in which sales forecasts are the driving variables and most other variables are proportional to sales.

The basic *sources and uses relationship* tells us that Dynamic's sources of funds must be adequate to cover its uses of funds. If the company's operations do not provide enough funds to pay for uses, then it will need to raise additional capital from external sources, for example, by issuing debt or equity. Dynamic's *required exter-*

TABLE 18.1 Financial statements for Dynamic Mattress Company (figures in $ millions). Figures subject to rounding error.

Income Statement	2016
1. Revenue	$2,200.0
2. Cost of goods sold	2,024.0
3. Depreciation	23.5
4. EBIT (1 − 2 − 3)	$ 152.5
5. Interest expense	6.0
6. Earnings before taxes (4 − 5)	$ 146.5
7. Taxes (50% of 6)	73.3
8. Net income (6 − 7)	$ 73.3
9. Dividends	46.7
10. Reinvested earnings (8 − 9)	$ 26.6
11. Operating cash flow (3 + 8)	$ 96.8

Balance Sheet (year-end)	2015	2016
Assets		
12. Net working capital	$192.0	$ 242.0
13. Fixed assets	268.5	275.0
14. Total net assets (12 + 13)	$460.5	$ 517.0
Liabilities and Shareholders' Equity		
15. Long-term debt	$ 60.0	$ 90.0
16. Shareholders' equity	400.5	427.0
17. Total liabilities and shareholders' equity (15 + 16)	$460.5	$ 517.0

nal capital equals the difference between the funds that the firm will require for its investments and dividend payments and the funds that it will raise from its business operations:

$$\text{Required external capital} = \text{investment in net working capital} + \text{investment in fixed assets} + \text{dividends} - \text{cash flow from operations}$$

Thus, there are three steps to finding how much extra capital Dynamic will need to raise and the implications for its debt ratio.

Step 1   Project the cash flow generated by the firm's operations. These projections are based on the forecasted 20% increase in revenues. The first column of the income statement in Table 18.2 shows this figure for Dynamic in the latest year, 2016, and is taken from Table 18.1. The next column shows the forecasted values for 2017. The column on the right provides comments on where these values come from. You can see that most of these values are in fact simply fixed proportions of the firm's sales projection. The forecast relations among these variables are summarized below the table. These relations apply to forecasts for years 2017 and beyond (but not necessarily to 2016 or earlier years).

We see that if sales increase by 20%, the firm is projected to earn net income of $88.7 million. Its operating cash flow will be the sum of this net income plus the $24.8 million depreciation allowance, which is treated as an expense on the income statement, but is not a cash outflow. (Recall that we first encountered this relation in Chapter 9, Equation 9.3, where we found that one way to compute operating cash flow is as after-tax net income plus depreciation.) Dynamic's forecasted operating cash flow for 2017 is 88.7 + 24.8 = $113.5 million.

TABLE 18.2 Pro forma financial statements for Dynamic Mattress, assuming that external capital is in the form of debt (figures in $ millions, subject to rounding error)

Income Statement	2016	2017	Comment
1. Revenue	$2,200.0	$2,640.0	20% forecast growth rate
2. Cost of goods sold	2,024.0	2,428.8	92% of sales
3. Depreciation	23.5	24.8	9% of net fixed assets at end of previous year
4. EBIT	$ 152.5	$ 186.5	(1) − (2) − (3)
5. Interest expense	6.0	9.0	10% of debt at end of previous year
6. Earnings before taxes	$ 146.5	$ 177.5	(4) − (5)
7. Taxes at 50%	73.3	88.7	50% of (6)
8. Net income	$ 73.3	$ 88.7	(6) − (7)
9. Dividends	46.7	53.2	60% of (8)
10. Reinvested earnings	$ 26.6	$ 35.5	40% of (8)

Balance Sheet (year-end)	2016	2017	
Assets			
11. Net working capital	$ 242.0	$ 290.4	11% of (1)
12. Net fixed assets	275.0	330.0	12.5% of (1)
13. Total net assets	$ 517.0	$ 620.4	(12) + (13)
Liabilities and Equity			
14. Long-term debt[a]	$ 90.0	$ 157.9	Increases by external financing
15. Shareholders' equity[b]	427.0	462.5	Increases by reinvested earnings
16. Total liabilities and shareholders' equity	$ 517.0	$ 620.4	(15) + (16)
Sources and Uses of Funds			
17. Operating cash flow	$ 96.8	$ 113.5	(3) + (8)
18. Increase in working capital	50.0	48.4	change in (11)
19. Investments in fixed assets	30.0	79.8	(3) + change in (12)
20. Dividends	46.7	53.2	(9)
21. Total uses of cash	126.7	181.4	(18) + (19) + (20)
22. Required external capital	30.0	67.9	(21) − (17)
Financial Ratios			
23. Debt ratio	0.17	0.25	(14)/(16)
24. Interest coverage	25.4	20.7	(4)/(5)

[a] Long-term debt, the balancing item, increases by required external capital.
[b] Shareholders' equity equals its value in the previous year plus retained earnings.
Note: Parameter values in Table 18.2:
Growth rate of sales = 0.20, Corporate tax rate = 0.50, Interest rate paid on debt outstanding at start of year (end of previous year) = 0.10, Net working capital/sales = 0.11, Fixed assets/sales = 0.125, Cost of goods sold/sales = 0.92, Payout ratio = 0.60, Depreciation/net fixed assets at start of year (end of previous year) = 0.09.

Step 2 Project the funds that the company will require to support both its investments in net working capital and fixed assets as well as the funds it intends to pay out as dividends. The sum of these expenditures gives you the total uses of capital. If the total uses of capital exceed the cash flow generated by operations, Dynamic will need to raise additional long-term capital.

The second column of Table 18.2 shows that Dynamic will need to increase its working capital by $48.4 million in 2017 to support its higher level of sales. It will also need to increase *net fixed assets*—that is, fixed assets net of accumulated depreciation—by $55 million. However, because depreciation in 2017 would otherwise reduce the book value of fixed assets by $24.8 million, an increase of $55 million in net fixed assets will actually require total investment of $55 + $24.8 = $79.8 million. In general, total investment = increase in gross fixed assets = increase in net fixed assets + depreciation. Finally, at its 60% payout ratio, the firm expects to pay out $53.2 million in dividends in 2017.

$$\text{Total uses of cash} = \text{investment in fixed assets}$$
$$+ \text{ investment in net working capital (NWC)} + \text{dividends}$$
$$= (\text{increase in net fixed assets} + \text{depreciation})$$
$$+ \text{ increase in NWC} + \text{dividends}$$
$$= (55 + 24.8) + 48.4 + 53.2 = \$181.4 \text{ million}$$

Thus, we can project Dynamic's required external capital in 2017 as the difference between its uses and sources of funds: $181.4 − 113.5 = $67.9 million. The sources and uses panel toward the bottom of Table 18.2 summarizes these calculations.

Step 3   Finally, construct a forecast, or *pro forma*, balance sheet that incorporates the additional assets and the new levels of debt and equity. This step requires the firm to take a stand on how it will raise the $67.9 million. Will it issue debt? Equity? Some combination of the two? The CFO has asked to see how Dynamic's debt ratio would change if it raises all external funds by issuing new debt. So, in Table 18.2, debt serves as the **balancing item,** or *plug*. The balancing item is the variable that adjusts to ensure that the firm's total sources of funds (including external finance) are equal to its uses. Notice that long-term debt increases by $67.9 million from the end of 2016 to the end of 2017, exactly the amount of required external capital. In contrast, shareholders' equity increases by only $35.5 million, the amount of earnings reinvested in the firm in 2016. Therefore, the ratio of debt to total net assets increases, from .17 to .25.

Is this the best policy? The model is silent on this issue. Financial planning models can only ensure that the assumptions about growth, financing, and financial position are mutually *consistent*—they cannot tell you which plan is best. Dynamic's financial manager may feel uncomfortable with the implied increase in leverage and with the long-term implications of relying on debt to finance Dynamic's growth. She will certainly want to raise this concern with the CFO.

Spreadsheet 18.1 extends these projections over a longer time frame, assuming Dynamic continues to use debt as the balancing item and that it can sustain a 20% growth rate. As the firm grows, it will require ever-larger investments in fixed assets and working capital. If the company continues to rely on debt finance, its leverage will increase rapidly. By 2020, its debt ratio will have risen from 17% to 43% and the interest coverage ratio will have declined from 25.4 to 9.5. The interest payments would still be comfortably covered by earnings, and most financial managers could live with this amount of debt. However, the company cannot continue to borrow at this rate for much longer, and the debt ratio might already be close to the limit set by the company's banks and bondholders.

An obvious alternative is for Dynamic to issue a mix of debt and equity, but there are other possibilities that the financial manager may want to explore. One option may be to hold back dividends during this period of rapid growth. Another option might be to investigate whether the company could cut back on net working capital. For example, it may be able to economize on inventories or speed up the collection of receivables. The model makes it easy to examine these alternatives.

Our financial plan solved for the amount of debt that it will need to issue, given its growth plans and an unwillingness to issue equity. Debt issues were, therefore, the balancing item. But the firm might wish to consider alternative balancing items. For example, it might choose to keep a fixed debt-equity *ratio*. In this case, the balancing item would be the total amount of external capital (debt plus equity) required, which would be split between debt and equity.

balancing item
Variable that adjusts to maintain the consistency of a financial plan. Also called *plug*.

BEYOND THE PAGE

Dynamic Mattress's spreadsheet

mhhe.com/brealey9e

SPREADSHEET 18.1 A long-term planning model for Dynamic Mattress

	A	B	C	D	E	F	G	H	I	J	K
1											
2	**Model inputs for years 2017 and beyond**			**Income Statement**	**2015**	**2016**	**2017**	**2018**	**2019**	**2020**	**Formula for column G**
3	Growth rate (%)	20%		Revenue		2200.0	2,640.0	3,168.0	3,801.6	4,561.9	F3*(1+$B3)
4	Tax rate (%)	50%		Cost of goods sold		2024.0	2,428.8	2,914.6	3,497.5	4,197.0	G3*B8
5	Interest rate on debt (%)	10%		Depreciation		23.5	24.8	29.7	35.6	42.8	F17*B10
6	NWC/sales	0.110		EBIT		152.5	186.5	223.7	268.5	322.2	G3-G4-G5
7	Fixed assets/sales	0.125		Interest expense		6.0	9.0	15.8	24.0	34.0	B5*F21
8	COGS/sales	0.920		Earnings before taxes		146.5	177.5	207.9	244.4	288.1	G6-G7
9	Payout ratio	0.600		Taxes at 50%		73.3	88.7	104.0	122.2	144.1	B4*G8
10	Depreciation/fixed assets	0.090		Net income		73.3	88.7	104.0	122.2	144.1	G8-G9
11				Dividends		46.7	53.2	62.4	73.3	86.4	G10*B9
12				Reinvested earnings		26.6	35.5	41.6	48.9	57.6	G10-G11
13											
14				**Balance Sheet (year-end)**	**2015**	**2016**	**2017**	**2018**	**2019**	**2020**	**Formula for column G**
15				**Assets**							
16				Net working capital	192.0	242.0	290.4	348.5	418.2	501.8	B6*G3
17				Net fixed assets	268.5	275.0	330.0	396.0	475.2	570.2	B7*G3
18				Total net assets	460.5	517.0	620.4	744.5	893.4	1072.1	G16+G17
19											
20				**Liabilities and Equity**							
21				Long-term debt[a]	60.0	90.0	157.9	240.4	340.4	461.5	F21+G32
22				Shareholders' equity[b]	400.5	427.0	462.5	504.1	553.0	610.6	F22+G12
23				Total liabilities and shareholders' equity	460.5	517.0	620.4	744.5	893.4	1072.1	G21+G22
24											
25				**Sources and Uses of Funds**							
26				Operating cash flow (3 + 8)		96.8	113.5	133.7	157.9	186.8	G5+G10
27				Increase in working capital		50.0	48.4	58.1	69.7	83.6	G16-F16
28				Investments in fixed assets		30.0	79.8	95.7	114.8	137.8	G17-F17+G5
29				Dividends		46.7	53.2	62.4	73.3	86.4	G11
30				Total uses of cash		126.7	181.4	216.2	257.9	307.9	SUM(G27:G29)
31											
32				Required external financing		30.0	67.9	82.5	100.0	121.0	G30-G26
33											
34				**Financial Ratios**							
35				Debt ratio		0.17	0.25	0.32	0.38	0.43	G21/G23
36				Interest coverage		25.4	20.7	14.2	11.2	9.5	G6/G7

[a] Long-term debt, the balancing item, increases by required external financing.
[b] Shareholders' equity equals its value in the previous year plus retained earnings.

TABLE 18.3 Required external financing in 2017 for Dynamic Mattress. Higher growth rates require more external capital.

Growth Rate (%)	Required External Financing ($ millions)
0	−28.5
5.9	0
10	19.7
20	67.9
30	116.1

Example 18.1 ▶ What Happens If the Growth Rate Changes?

We can use Spreadsheet 18.1 to explore the effect of sales growth on the need for external capital. We can alter the assumed growth rate in the spreadsheet and see the effect on required external financing. For example, we saw in Table 18.2 that when the growth rate was 20%, required external capital in 2017 was $67.9 million. In our model, net assets are proportional to sales, so when we assume a higher growth rate of sales, assets also increase at a faster rate. The additional capital necessary to pay for those additional assets implies a greater need for external financing.

   Table 18.3 shows how required external financing responds to a change in the growth rate. Notice that at a 5.9% growth rate, required external financing is zero. At higher growth rates, the firm requires external financing. At lower growth rates, reinvested earnings exceed the addition to assets and there is a surplus of funds from internal sources; this shows up as negative required external financing. Later in the chapter, we will explore the limits to internal growth more systematically. ■

18.1 Self-Test

Suppose that Dynamic Mattress is committed to a 20% growth rate and to paying out 60% of its net income as dividends. However, it now wishes to maintain its debt-equity ratio at .211, its value in 2016. How much equity and how much debt must be issued in 2017?

Pitfalls in Model Design

The model that we have developed for Dynamic Mattress is too simple for practical application. You probably have already thought of several ways to improve it—by keeping track of the outstanding shares, for example, and reporting earnings and dividends per share. Or you might want to distinguish between short-term lending and borrowing opportunities, now buried in net working capital.

   The percentage of sales model assumes almost all the forecasts for the company are proportional to the forecasted level of sales. However, in reality, many variables will not be proportional to sales. For example, important components of working capital such as inventory and cash balances will generally rise less rapidly than sales. In addition, fixed assets such as plant and equipment are not usually added in small increments as sales increase. The Dynamic Mattress plant may well be operating at less than full capacity so that the company can initially increase output without any additions to capacity. Eventually, however, if sales continue to increase, the firm may need to make a large new investment in plant and equipment.

Example 18.2 ▶ Required External Funds and Excess Capacity

Suppose that Carter Tools has $50 million invested in fixed assets and generates sales of $60 million. The company is currently working at 80% of capacity. Suppose that a 50% increase in sales is forecast. How much investment in fixed assets would be required?

Sales can increase without the need for new investments in fixed assets until the company is at 100% of capacity. Therefore, sales can increase to $60 million × 100/80 = $75 million before the firm reaches full capacity given its current level of fixed assets. At full capacity, therefore, the ratio of assets to sales would be $50 million/$75 million = ⅔.

The 50% increase in forecast sales would imply a sales level of $60 million × 1.5 = $90 million. To support this level of sales, the company needs at least $90 million × ⅔ = $60 million of fixed assets. This calls for a $10 million investment in additional fixed assets. ■

You may want to modify your model to allow for the fact that investment in new plant occurs in large increments. But beware of adding too much complexity: There is always the temptation to make a model bigger and more detailed. You may end up with an exhaustive model that is too cumbersome for routine use. The fascination of detail, if you give in to it, distracts attention from crucial decisions like stock issues and payout policy.

18.2   Self-Test

Suppose that at its current level of assets and sales, Carter Tools in Example 18.2 is working at 75% of capacity.

a. How much can sales expand without any further investment in fixed assets?
b. How much investment in fixed assets would be required to support a 50% expansion in sales?

Choosing a Plan

We've pointed out that financial planning models help the manager to develop *consistent* forecasts of crucial financial variables. For example, if you wish to value Dynamic Mattress, you need forecasts of future free cash flows. These are easily derived from our financial planning model.[1] However, a planning model does not tell you whether the plan is optimal. It does not even tell you which alternatives are worth examining. For example, we saw that Dynamic Mattress is planning for a rapid growth in sales and earnings per share. But is that good news for the shareholders? Well, not necessarily; it depends on the opportunity cost of the capital that Dynamic Mattress needs to invest. If the new investment earns more than the cost of capital, it will have a positive NPV and add to shareholder wealth. If the investment earns less than the cost of capital, shareholders will be worse off, even though the company expects steady growth in earnings.

The capital that Dynamic Mattress needs to raise depends on its decision to pay out 60% of its earnings as a dividend. But the financial planning model does not tell us whether this dividend payment makes sense or what mixture of equity or debt the company should issue. In the end the management has to decide. We would like to tell you exactly how to make the choice, but we can't. There is no model that encompasses all the complexities encountered in financial planning and decision making.

We commented earlier that financial planning is not just about exploring how to cope with the most likely outcomes. It also needs to ensure that the firm is prepared for unlikely or unexpected ones. For example, Dynamic's manager would certainly wish to consider how the company's capital requirement would change if profit margins come under pressure and the company generated less cash from its operations. Planning models make it easy to explore the consequences of such events.

---

[1] Look back at Table 13.5, where we set out the free cash flows for the deconstruction division. A financial planning model would be a natural tool for deriving these figures.

18.3   Self-Test

Which of the following questions will a financial plan help to answer?

a. Is the firm's assumption for asset growth consistent with its plans for debt and equity issues and dividend policy?

b. Will accounts receivable increase in direct proportion to sales?

c. Will the contemplated debt-equity mix maximize the value of the firm?

18.4   External Financing and Growth

Financial models such as the one that we have developed for Dynamic Mattress can help managers trace through the financial consequences of their growth plans. But there is a danger that the complexities of a full-blown financial model can obscure basic issues. Therefore, managers also use some simple rules of thumb to draw out the relationship between a firm's growth objectives and its requirement for external financing.

Recall that in 2016 Dynamic Mattress had sales of $2,200 million and ended the year with total net assets (net fixed assets plus net working capital) of $517 million. In other words, each dollar of sales required $.235 of net assets. The company forecasts that sales in 2017 will increase by $440 million. So, if the ratio of net assets to sales remains constant, net assets in 2017 will need increase by

$$\text{Increase in net assets} = \frac{\text{net assets}}{\text{sales}} \times \text{increase in sales}$$

$$= .235 \times 440 = \$103.4 \text{ million}$$

Part of this increase can be financed by reinvested earnings, which in 2017 are $35.5 million. Thus the amount of external financing needed is:[2]

$$\text{Required external capital} = \text{increase in net assets} - \text{reinvested earnings}$$

$$= \frac{\text{net assets}}{\text{sales}} \times \text{increase in sales} - \text{reinvested earnings}$$

$$= .235 \times 440 - 35.5 = \$67.9 \text{ million}$$

Sometimes, it is useful to write this calculation in terms of growth rates. If net assets are proportional to sales, then the higher sales volume will also require a 20% addition to net assets. Thus,

$$\text{Increase in net assets} = \text{growth rate} \times \text{initial net assets} = .20 \times 517.0 = \$103.4 \text{ million}$$

and therefore,

$$\text{Required external financing} = (\text{growth rate} \times \text{initial net assets}) \quad\quad \textbf{(18.1)}$$
$$- \text{reinvested earnings}$$
$$= .20 \times 517.0 - 35.5 = \$67.9 \text{ million}$$

---

[2] This formula for required external capital appears to differ from the approach we took earlier. But they are fully consistent. We previously stated that required external finance is the difference between total investments in fixed and working capital and cash flow from operations.

Required external capital = Δ net working capital + investment in fixed assets + dividends − cash flow from operations = Δ NWC + (increase in net fixed assets + depreciation) + dividends − (net income + depreciation)

Notice that the two terms involving depreciation cancel out and that the change in net working capital plus the change in net fixed assets equals the change in total net assets. Therefore,

Required external capital = increase in total net assets + dividends − net income

= increase in total net assets − reinvested earnings

This simple equation highlights that the amount of external financing depends on the firm's projected growth. If Dynamic's net assets remain a constant percentage of sales, then the company needs to raise $67.9 million to support a 20% addition to sales. The faster the firm grows, the more it needs to invest and, therefore, the more new capital it needs to raise.

The sloping line in Figure 18.2 illustrates how required external capital increases with the growth rate. At low growth rates, the firm generates more funds than necessary for expansion. In this sense, its requirement for further external funds is negative. It may choose to use its surplus earnings to pay off some of its debt or buy back its stock. In fact, the vertical intercept in Figure 18.2, at zero growth, is the negative of the addition to retained earnings. When growth is zero, no funds are needed for expansion, so all that addition is surplus.

Table 18.3 showed that with very low projected growth rates, reinvested earnings are more than sufficient to pay for the necessary investments. Required external capital is, therefore, negative. But as growth rates increase, more funds are needed to pay for the necessary additions to fixed assets and working capital. The maximum growth rate that the firm can achieve without raising external funds is called the **internal growth rate.** The growth rate is "internal" because it can be maintained without resorting to external sources of capital.

internal growth rate
Maximum rate of growth without external financing.

Notice that if we set required external financing to zero, we can solve Equation 18.1 for the internal growth rate as

$$\text{Internal growth rate} = \text{reinvested earnings}/\text{net assets}$$

Thus, the firm's rate of growth without additional external sources of capital will equal the ratio of reinvested earnings to net assets. A firm with a high volume of reinvested earnings relative to its assets can generate a higher growth rate without needing to raise more capital.

We can gain more insight into what determines the internal growth rate by multiplying the top and bottom of the expression for internal growth by *net income* and *equity* as follows:

$$\text{Internal growth rate} = \frac{\text{reinvested earnings}}{\text{net income}} \times \frac{\text{net income}}{\text{equity}} \times \frac{\text{equity}}{\text{net assets}} \quad \textbf{(18.2)}$$

$$= \text{plowback ratio} \times \text{return on equity} \times \frac{\text{equity}}{\text{net assets}}$$

A firm can achieve a higher growth rate without raising external capital if (1) it plows back a high proportion of its earnings, (2) it has a high return on equity (ROE), and (3) it has a low debt-to-asset ratio.

FIGURE 18.2 External financing and growth

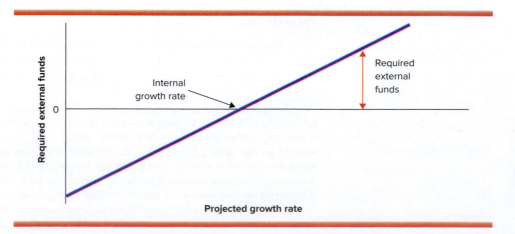

Example	18.3 ▶	Internal Growth for Dynamic Mattress

Dynamic Mattress has chosen a plowback ratio of 40%. Equity outstanding at the start of 2017 is $427 million, and outstanding net assets are $517 million. Dynamic's return on equity[3] is ROE = 17.9%, and its ratio of equity to net assets is 427/517 = .826. If it is unwilling to raise new capital, its maximum growth rate is

$$\text{Internal growth rate} = \text{plowback ratio} \times \text{ROE} \times \frac{\text{equity}}{\text{net assets}}$$

$$= .4 \times .179 \times .826 = .059, \text{ or } 5.9\%$$

Look back at Table 18.3 and you will see that at this growth rate, external financing is, in fact, zero. This growth rate is much lower than the 20% growth that Dynamic forecasts, which explains the company's need for external financing. ■

Instead of focusing on the maximum growth rate that can be supported without raising *any* external capital, firms may also be interested in the growth rate that can be sustained without additional *equity* issues. Of course, if the firm is able to issue enough debt, virtually any growth rate can be financed. It makes more sense to assume that the firm has settled on an optimal capital structure that it will maintain even as equity is augmented by reinvested earnings. The firm issues only enough debt to keep its debt-equity ratio constant. The **sustainable growth rate** is the highest growth rate the firm can maintain without increasing its financial leverage. It turns out that the sustainable growth rate depends only on the plowback ratio and return on equity:[4]

sustainable growth rate
The firm's growth rate if it plows back a constant fraction of earnings, maintains a constant return on equity, and keeps its debt ratio constant.

$$\text{Sustainable growth rate} = \text{plowback ratio} \times \text{return on equity} \qquad (18.3)$$

---

[3] Actually, calculating ROE to find the internal growth rate can be a bit tricky. Dynamic is forecasting a growth rate of 20% and an ROE of 88.7/427 = 20.8%, but if it grows more slowly, sales, net income and ROE will all be lower. In other words, ROE may depend on the growth rate. We saw in Table 18.3 that a growth rate of 5.9% implies external financing of zero in 2017; we will choose the ROE corresponding to the internal growth rate of 5.9%. If you input 5.9% as the growth rate in the Dynamic Mattress spreadsheet, you will find that net income in 2017 is $76.3 million while equity outstanding at the beginning of 2017 (end of 2016) is $427, which implies an ROE of 76.3/427 = .179. Notice that although it is common to calculate ROE by dividing income by either end-of-year or year-average shareholders' equity, neither of those conventions will work in this application. To find the internal growth rate, we need to view ROE as analogous to the rate of return on a stock, that is, as money earned during the year per dollar of shareholders' equity at the start of the year.

[4] Here is a proof:

$$\text{Required equity issues} = \text{growth rate} \times \text{net assets} + \text{reinvested earnings} - \text{new debt issues}$$

We find the sustainable growth rate by setting required new equity issues to zero and solving for growth:

$$\text{Sustainable growth rate} = \frac{(\text{reinvested earnings} + \text{new debt issues})}{\text{net assets}}$$

$$= \frac{(\text{reinvested earnings} + \text{new debt issues})}{(\text{debt} + \text{equity})}$$

However, because both debt and equity are growing at the same rate, new debt issues must equal reinvested earnings multiplied by the ratio of debt to equity, D/E. Therefore, we can write the sustainable growth rate as

$$\text{Sustainable growth rate} = \frac{\text{reinvested earnings} \times (1 + D/E)}{(\text{debt} + \text{equity})}$$

$$= \frac{\text{reinvested earnings} \times (1 + D/E)}{\text{equity} \times (1 + D/E)} = \frac{\text{reinvested earnings}}{\text{equity}}$$

$$= \frac{\text{reinvested earnings}}{\text{net income}} \times \frac{\text{net income}}{\text{equity}} = \text{plowback} \times \text{ROE}$$

You may remember this formula from Chapter 7, where we first used the dividend discount model to value the firm.

Example   18.4 ▶   Sustainable Growth Rate

Dynamic Pillows Inc. currently has an equity-to-net-asset ratio of .8. Its ROE is 18%. The firm currently reinvests one-third of its earnings back into the firm. Moreover, it plans to keep leverage unchanged, so it will issue an additional 20 cents of debt for every 80 cents of reinvested earnings. Given this policy, its maximum growth rate is

$$\text{Sustainable growth rate} = \text{plowback ratio} \times \text{ROE}$$
$$= 1/3 \times .18 = .06, \text{ or } 6\%$$

If the firm is willing to plow back a higher proportion of its earnings, it can issue more debt without increasing its leverage. Both the greater reinvested profits and the additional debt issues would allow it to grow more rapidly. You can confirm in Self-Test 18.4 [see part (b)] that if the firm increases its plowback ratio, its sustainable growth rate will be higher. ■

18.4   Self-Test

Suppose Dynamic Pillows reduces the dividend payout ratio to 25%. Calculate its growth rate assuming (a) that no new debt or equity will be issued or, alternatively, (b) that the firm maintains its debt-to-equity ratio at .25.

SUMMARY

What are the contents and uses of a financial plan?
(*LO18-1*)

Most firms take financial planning seriously and devote considerable resources to it. The tangible product of the planning process is a financial plan describing the firm's financial strategy and projecting its future consequences by means of **pro forma** balance sheets, income statements, and statements of sources and uses of funds. The plan establishes financial goals and is a benchmark for evaluating subsequent performance. Usually, it also describes why that strategy was chosen and how the plan's financial goals are to be achieved.

Planning, if it is done right, forces the financial manager to think about events that could upset the firm's progress and to devise strategies to be held in reserve for counterattack when unfortunate surprises occur. Planning is more than forecasting because forecasting deals with the most likely outcome. Planners also have to think about events that *may* occur even though they are unlikely.

In long-range, or strategic, planning, the **planning horizon** is usually 5 years or more. This kind of planning deals with aggregate decisions; for example, the planner would worry about whether the division should commit to heavy capital investment and rapid growth, but not whether the division should choose machine tool A versus tool B. In fact, planners must be constantly on guard against the fascination of detail because giving in to it means slighting crucial issues like investment strategy, debt policy, and the choice of a target dividend payout ratio.

The plan is the end result. The process that produces the plan is valuable in its own right. Planning forces the financial manager to consider the combined effects of all the firm's investment and financing decisions. This is important because these decisions interact and should not be made independently.

How are financial planning models constructed? (*LO18-2*)	There is no theory or model that leads straight to *the* optimal financial strategy. Consequently, financial planning proceeds by trial and error. Many different strategies may be projected under a range of assumptions about the future before one strategy is finally chosen. The dozens of separate projections that may be made during this trial-and-error process generate a heavy load of arithmetic and paperwork. Firms have responded by developing corporate planning models to forecast the financial consequences of specified strategies and assumptions about the future. One very simple starting point may be a **percentage of sales model,** in which many key variables are assumed to be directly proportional to sales. Planning models are efficient and widely used. But remember that there is not much finance in them. Their primary purpose is to produce accounting statements. The models do not search for the best financial strategy but only trace out the consequences of a strategy specified by the model user.
What is the effect of growth on the need for external financing? (*LO18-3*)	Higher growth rates will lead to greater need for investments in fixed assets and working capital. The **internal growth rate** is the maximum rate at which the firm can grow if it relies entirely on reinvested profits to finance its growth, that is, the maximum rate of growth without requiring external financing. The **sustainable growth rate** is the rate at which the firm can grow without changing its leverage ratio or issuing new equity.

LISTING OF EQUATIONS

18.1 Required external financing = growth rate × initial net assets − reinvested earnings

18.2 Internal growth rate = plowback ratio × return on equity × $\dfrac{\text{equity}}{\text{net assets}}$

18.3 Sustainable growth rate = plowback ratio × return on equity

QUESTIONS AND PROBLEMS

1. **Financial Planning.** True or false? (*LO18-1*)
   a. Financial planning should attempt to minimize risk.
   b. The primary aim of financial planning is to obtain better forecasts of future cash flows and earnings.
   c. Financial planning is necessary because financing and investment decisions interact and should not be made independently.
   d. Firms' planning horizons rarely exceed 3 years.
   e. Individual capital investment projects are not considered in a financial plan unless they are very large.
   f. Financial planning requires accurate and consistent forecasting.
   g. Financial planning models should include as much detail as possible.

2. **Financial Models.** What are the dangers and disadvantages of using a financial model? Discuss. (*LO18-1*)

3. **Using Financial Plans.** Corporate financial plans are often used as a basis for judging subsequent performance. What can be learned from such comparisons? What problems might arise, and how might you cope with such problems? (*LO18-1*)

4. **Financial Targets.** Managers sometimes state a target growth rate for sales or earnings per share. Do you think that either of these makes sense as a corporate goal? If not, why do you think that managers focus on them? (*LO18-1*)

5. **Percentage of Sales Models.** Percentage of sales models usually assume that costs, fixed assets, and working capital all increase at the same rate as sales. When do you think that these assumptions do not make sense? Would you feel happier using a percentage of sales model for short-term or long-term planning? (*LO18-2*)

6. **Relationships among Variables.** Comebaq Computers is aiming to increase its market share by slashing the price of its new range of personal computers. Are costs and assets likely to increase or decrease as a proportion of sales? Explain. (*LO18-2*)

7. **Balancing Items.** What are the possible choices of balancing items when using a financial planning model? Discuss whether some are generally preferable to others. (*LO18-2*)

8. **Financial Planning Models.** The following tables summarize the 2017 income statement and end-year balance sheet of Drake's Bowling Alleys. Drake's financial manager forecasts a 10% increase in sales and costs in 2018. The ratio of sales to average assets is expected to remain at .40. Interest is forecasted at 5% of debt at the start of the year. (*LO18-2*)
   a. What is the implied level of assets at the end of 2018?
   b. If the company pays out 50% of net income as dividends, how much cash will Drake's need to raise in the capital markets in 2018?
   c. If Drake's is unwilling to make an equity issue, what will be the debt ratio at the end of 2018?

INCOME STATEMENT, 2017		
(Figures in $ thousands)		
Sales	$1,000	(40% of average assets)[a]
Costs	750	(75% of sales)
Interest	25	(5% of debt at start of year)[b]
Pretax profit	$ 225	
Tax	90	(40% of pretax profit)
Net income	$ 135	

BALANCE SHEET, YEAR-END			
(Figures in $ thousands)			
Assets	$2,600	Debt	$ 500
		Equity	2,100
Total	$2,600	Total	$2,600

[a] Assets at the end of 2016 were $2,400,000.
[b] Debt at the end of 2016 was $500,000.

BEYOND THE PAGE

Dynamic
Mattress's
spreadsheet

mhhe.com/brealey9e

9. **Financial Planning Models.** The Beyond the Page features for this chapter include the spreadsheets for Dynamic Mattress's long-term plan. How would its financial plan change if the dividend payout ratio were cut to 40%? Use the revised model to generate a new financial plan for 2019. Show how the financial statements given in Spreadsheet 18.1 would change. What would be required external financing? (*LO18-2*)

10. **Percentage of Sales Models.** Here are the abbreviated financial statements for Planner's Peanuts: (*LO18-2*)

INCOME STATEMENT, 2017	
Sales	$2,000
Cost	1,500
Net income	$ 500

BALANCE SHEET, YEAR-END					
	2016	2017		2016	2017
Assets	$2,500	$3,000	Debt	$ 833	$1,000
			Equity	1,667	2,000
Total	$2,500	$3,000	Total	$2,500	$3,000

   a. If sales increase by 20% in 2018 and the company uses a strict percentage of sales planning model (meaning that all items on the income and balance sheet also increase by 20%), what must be the balancing item?
   b. What will be the value of this balancing item?

11. **Financial Planning Models.** The following tables contain financial statements for Dynastatics Corporation. Although the company has not been growing, it now plans to expand and will increase net fixed assets (i.e., assets net of depreciation) by $200,000 per year for the next 3 years, and it forecasts that the ratio of revenues to total assets will remain at 1.50. Annual depreciation is 10% of net fixed assets at the beginning of the year. Fixed costs are expected to remain at $56,000 and variable costs at 80% of revenue. The company's policy is to pay out two-thirds of net income as dividends and to maintain a book debt ratio of 25% of total capital. (*LO18-2*)

INCOME STATEMENT, 2017	
(Figures in $ thousands)	
Revenue	$1,800
Fixed costs	56
Variable costs (80% of revenue)	1,440
Depreciation	80
Interest (8% of beginning-of-year debt)	24
Taxable income	200
Taxes (at 40%)	80
Net income	$ 120
Dividends	$80
Addition to retained earnings	$40

BALANCE SHEET, YEAR-END	
(Figures in $ thousands)	
	2017
Assets	
Net working capital	$400
Fixed assets	800
Total assets	$1,200
Liabilities and shareholders' equity	
Debt	$300
Equity	900
Total liabilities and shareholders' equity	$1,200

a. Produce income statements and balance sheets for 2018 through 2020. Assume that net working capital will equal 50% of fixed assets.

b. Now assume that the balancing item is debt and that no equity is to be issued. Prepare pro forma balance sheets for 2018 through 2020.

c. What is the projected debt ratio for 2020?

12. **Using Percentage of Sales.** Eagle Sports Supply has the following financial statements. Assume that Eagle's assets are proportional to its sales. (*LO18-2*)

INCOME STATEMENT, 2017	
Sales	$950
Costs	250
Interest	50
Taxes	150
Net income	$500

BALANCE SHEET, YEAR-END					
	2016	**2017**		**2016**	**2017**
Assets	$2,700	$3,000	Debt	$ 900	$1,000
			Equity	1,800	2,000
Total	$2,700	$3,000	Total	$2,700	$3,000

a. Find Eagle's required external funds if it maintains a dividend payout ratio of 70% and plans a growth rate of 15% in 2018.

b. If Eagle chooses not to issue new shares of stock, what variable must be the balancing item?

c. What will be the value of this balancing item?

d. Now suppose that the firm plans instead to increase long-term debt only to $1,100 and does not wish to issue any new shares of stock. What is now the balancing item?

e. What will be the value of this new balancing item?

13. **Using Percentage of Sales.** The 2017 financial statements for Growth Industries are presented below. Sales and costs are projected to grow at 20% a year for at least the next 4 years. Both current assets and accounts payable are projected to rise in proportion to sales. The firm is currently operating at full capacity, so it plans to increase fixed assets in proportion to sales. Interest expense will equal 10% of long-term debt outstanding at the start of the year. The firm will maintain a dividend payout ratio of .40. Construct a spreadsheet model for Growth Industries similar to the one in Spreadsheet 18.1. (*LO18-2*)

a. How much external capital will the company require in 2021?

b. What will be the company's debt ratio at the end of 2021?

INCOME STATEMENT, 2017	
Sales	$200,000
Costs	150,000
EBIT	$ 50,000
Interest expense	10,000
Taxable income	$ 40,000
Taxes (at 35%)	14,000
Net income	$ 26,000
Dividends	$10,400
Addition to retained earnings	$15,600

BALANCE SHEET, YEAR-END, 2017				
Assets			**Liabilities**	
Current assets			Current liabilities	
Cash	$ 3,000		Accounts payable	$ 10,000
Accounts receivable	8,000		Total current liabilities	$ 10,000
Inventories	29,000		Long-term debt	100,000
Total current assets	$ 40,000		Stockholders' equity	
			Common stock plus additional	
Net plant and equipment	160,000		paid-in capital	15,000
			Retained earnings	75,000
			Total liabilities plus	
Total assets	$200,000		stockholders' equity	$200,000

14. **Capacity Use and External Financing.** Now suppose that the fixed assets of Growth Industries (from the previous problem) are operating at only 75% of capacity. What is the required external financing over the next year? (*LO18-2*)

15. **Capacity Use and External Financing.** If Growth Industries from Problem 13 is operating at only 75% of capacity, how much can sales grow before the firm will need to raise any external funds? Assume that once fixed assets are operating at capacity, they will need to grow thereafter in direct proportion to sales. (*LO18-2*)

16. **Feasible Growth Rates.** (*LO18-3*)

a. What is the internal growth rate of Eagle Sports (see Problem 12) if the dividend payout ratio is fixed at 70% and the equity-to-asset ratio is fixed at ⅔?

b. What is the sustainable growth rate?

17. **Growth Rates.** Loreto Inc. has the following financial ratios: asset turnover = 1.40; profit margin = 5%; payout ratio = 25%; equity/assets = .60. (*LO18-3*)
    a. What is Loreto's sustainable growth rate?
    b. What is its internal growth rate?

18. **Required External Financing.** If Planner's Peanuts dividend payout ratio in Problem 10 is fixed at 50%, calculate the required total external financing for growth rates in 2018 of (a) 15%, (b) 20%, and (c) 25%. (*LO18-3*)

19. **Feasible Growth Rates.** What is the maximum possible growth rate for Planner's Peanuts (see Problem 10) if the payout ratio remains at 50% and: (*LO18-3*)
    a. No external debt or equity is to be issued?
    b. Alternatively, the firm maintains a fixed debt ratio but issues no equity?

20. **Sustainable Growth.** Plank's Plants had net income of $2,000 on sales of $50,000 last year. The firm paid a dividend of $500. Total assets were $100,000, of which $40,000 was financed by debt. (*LO18-3*)
    a. What is the firm's sustainable growth rate?
    b. If the firm grows at its sustainable growth rate, how much debt will be issued next year?
    c. What would be the maximum possible growth rate if the firm did not issue any debt next year?

21. **Sustainable Growth.** A firm has decided that its optimal capital structure is 100% equity-financed. It perceives its optimal dividend policy to be a 40% payout ratio. Asset turnover is sales/assets = .8, the profit margin is 10%, and the firm has a target growth rate of 5%. (*LO18-3*)
    a. Is the firm's target growth rate consistent with its other goals?
    b. If not, what would asset turnover need to be to achieve its goals?
    c. How high would the profit margin need to be instead?

22. **Internal Growth.** Go-Go Industries is growing at 30% per year. It is all-equity-financed and has total assets of $1 million. Its return on equity is 25%. Its plowback ratio is 40%. (*LO18-3*)
    a. What is the internal growth rate?
    b. What is the firm's need for external financing this year?
    c. By how much would the firm increase its internal growth rate if it reduced its payout ratio to zero?
    d. By how much would such a move reduce the need for external financing?

23. **Sustainable Growth.** A firm's profit margin is 10%, and its asset turnover ratio is .6. It has no debt, has net income of $10 per share, and pays dividends of $4 per share. What is the sustainable growth rate? (*LO18-3*)

24. **Internal Growth.** An all-equity-financed firm plans to grow at an annual rate of at least 10%. Its return on equity is 18%. What is the maximum possible dividend payout rate the firm can maintain without resorting to additional equity issues? (*LO18-3*)

25. **Internal Growth.** Suppose the firm in the previous question has a debt-equity ratio of ⅓. What is the maximum dividend payout ratio it can maintain without resorting to any external financing? (*LO18-3*)

26. **Internal Growth.** A firm has an asset turnover ratio of 2.0. Its plowback ratio is 50%, and it is all-equity-financed. What must its profit margin be if it wishes to finance 10% growth using only internally generated funds? (*LO18-3*)

27. **Internal Growth.** If the profit margin of the firm in the previous problem is 6%, what is the maximum payout ratio that will allow it to grow at 8% without resorting to external financing? (*LO18-3*)

28. **Internal Growth.** If the profit margin of the firm in Problem 26 is 6%, what is the maximum possible growth rate that can be sustained without external financing? (*LO18-3*)

29. **Internal Growth.** For many firms, cash and inventory needs may grow less than proportionally with sales. When we recognize this fact, will the firm's internal growth rate be higher or lower than the level predicted by the following formula? (*LO18-3*)

$$\text{Internal growth rate} = \frac{\text{reinvested earnings}}{\text{net assets}}$$

WEB EXERCISES

1. Log on to finance.yahoo.com, and compare Wendy's International (WEN) and McDonald's (MCD) internal growth rates and sustainable growth rates by using recent annual data. (Note that the internal growth rate is calculated by using the earnings reinvested in the firm in the current year, not total retained earnings from the balance sheet.) Yahoo! also shows the earnings growth that analysts are forecasting for each firm. Are the forecasts supported by the past performance of each firm?

2. Go to finance.yahoo.com. Find the (annual) balance sheet and income statement for American Electric Power (AEP). Suppose the company plans on 4% revenue growth over the next year. Under a percentage of sales approach, where assets and costs (except for depreciation) are proportional to sales, find AEP's required external funding over the next year. Assume that it will maintain the same dividend payout ratio as in the current year and that its average tax rate will be the same next year as it was in the most recent year.

3. Log on to Yahoo's Industry center at biz.yahoo.com/ic/. The industry browser provides some financial ratios for different sectors. What is the sustainable rate of growth for a sample of different industries if the component firms maintain their plowback ratios and returns on equity? (*Note:* Although Yahoo does not report the plowback ratio, you can calculate it by multiplying the dividing yield by the P/E ratio.) Do you think that those industries with a high return on equity can continue to earn such a high return on new investment?

SOLUTIONS TO SELF-TEST QUESTIONS

18.1 The *total amount* of external financing is unchanged because the dividend payout is unchanged. The $67.9 million increase in total assets in 2017 will now be financed by a mixture of debt and equity. If the debt-equity ratio is to remain unchanged, the ratio of equity to total assets also must be unchanged at 427/517 = .826. The firm will need to increase equity by .826 × $67.9 = $56.1 million and debt by .174 × $67.9 = $11.8 million. Because reinvested earnings already increase shareholders' equity by $35.5 million, the firm would issue an additional $20.6 million of new equity and $11.8 million of debt.

18.2 a. The company currently runs at 75% of capacity given the current level of fixed assets. Sales can increase until the company is at 100% of capacity; therefore, sales can increase to $60 million × (100/75) = $80 million.

   b. If sales were to increase by 50% to $90 million, new fixed assets would need to be added. The ratio of assets to sales when the company is operating at 100% of capacity [from part (a)] is $50 million/$80 million = ⅝. Therefore, to support sales of $90 million, the company needs at least $90 million × ⅝ = $56.25 million of fixed assets. This calls for a $6.25 million investment in additional fixed assets.

18.3 a. This question is answered by the planning model. Given assumptions for asset growth, the model will show the need for external financing, and this value can be compared to the firm's plans for such financing.

   b. Such a relationship may be assumed and built into the model. However, the model does not help to determine whether it is a reasonable assumption.

   c. Financial models do not shed light on the best capital structure. They can tell us only whether contemplated financing decisions are consistent with asset growth.

18.4 a. The equity-to-asset ratio is .8. If the payout ratio were reduced to 25%, the maximum growth rate assuming no external financing would be .75 × 18% × .8 = 10.8%.

   b. A debt-equity ratio of .25 implies the equity-to-asset ratio is maintained at .8. For example, if debt is 1 and equity is 4, then equity/assets = 4/(1 + 4) = .80. If the firm can issue enough debt to maintain its equity-to-asset ratio unchanged, the sustainable growth rate will be plowback ratio × return on equity = .75 × 18% = 13.5%.

MINICASE

Garnett Jackson, the founder and CEO of Tech Tune-Ups, stared out the window as he finished his customary peanut butter and jelly sandwich, contemplating the dilemma currently facing his firm. Tech Tune-Ups is a start-up firm, offering a wide range of computer services to its clients, including online technical assistance, remote maintenance and backup of client computers through the Internet, and virus prevention and recovery. The firm has been highly successful in the 2 years since it was founded; its reputation for fair pricing and good service is spreading, and Mr. Jackson believes the firm is in a good position to expand its customer base rapidly. But he is not sure that the firm has the financing in place to support that rapid growth.

Tech Tune-Ups' main capital investments are its own powerful computers, and its major operating expense is salary for its consultants. To a reasonably good approximation, both of these factors grow in proportion to the number of clients the firm serves.

Currently, the firm is a privately held corporation. Mr. Jackson and his partners, two classmates from his undergraduate days, have contributed $250,000 in equity capital, largely raised from their parents and other family members. The firm has a line of credit with a bank that allows it to borrow up to $400,000 at an interest rate of 8%. So far, the firm has used $200,000 of its credit line. If and when the firm reaches its borrowing limit, it will need to raise equity capital and will probably seek funding from a venture capital firm. The firm is growing rapidly, requiring continual investment in additional computers, and Mr. Jackson is concerned that it is approaching its borrowing limit faster than anticipated.

Mr. Jackson thumbs through past financial statements and estimates that each of the firm's computers, costing $10,000, can support revenues of $80,000 per year but that the salary and benefits paid to each consultant using one of the computers is $70,000. Sales revenue in 2016 was $1.2 million, and sales are expected to grow at a 20% annual rate in the next few years. The firm pays taxes at a rate of 35%. Its customers pay their bills with an average delay of 3 months, so accounts receivable at any time are usually around 25% of that year's sales.

Mr. Jackson and his co-owners receive minimal formal salary from the firm, instead taking 70% of profits as a "dividend," which accounts for a substantial portion of their personal incomes. The remainder of the profits are reinvested in the firm. If reinvested profits are not sufficient to support new purchases of computers, the firm borrows the required additional funds using its line of credit with the bank.

Mr. Jackson doesn't think Tech Tune-Ups can raise venture funding until after 2018. He decides to develop a financial plan to determine whether the firm can sustain its growth plans using its line of credit and reinvested earnings until then. If not, he and his partners will have to consider scaling back their hoped-for rate of growth, negotiate with their bankers to increase the line of credit, or consider taking a smaller share of profits out of the firm until further financing can be arranged.

Mr. Jackson wiped the last piece of jelly from the keyboard and settled down to work.

Can you help Mr. Jackson develop a financial plan? Do you think his growth plan is feasible?

19

Short-Term Financial Planning

LEARNING OBJECTIVES

After studying this chapter, you should be able to:

19-1 Show how long-term financing policy affects short-term financing requirements.

19-2 Trace a firm's sources and uses of cash and evaluate its need for short-term borrowing.

19-3 Develop a short-term financing plan that meets the firm's need for cash.

RELATED WEBSITES FOR THIS CHAPTER CAN BE FOUND IN CONNECT.

Short-term financial planning ensures that you have enough cash on hand to pay the bills. © Studio 52/Shutterstock RF

Much of this book is devoted to long-term financial decisions, such as the investment decision or the choice of capital structure. These decisions are called long term for two reasons. First, they usually involve long-lived assets or liabilities. Second, they are not easily reversed and so may commit the firm to a particular course of action for many years.

Short-term financial plans generally involve short-lived assets and liabilities, and usually the decisions are easily reversed. Compare, for example, a 60-day bank loan for $50 million with a $50 million issue of a 20-year bond. The bank loan is clearly a short-term decision. The firm can repay it 2 months later and be right back where it started. A firm might conceivably issue a 20-year bond in January and repay it in March, but it would be extremely inconvenient and expensive to do so. In practice, such a bond is a long-term decision not just because of its 20-year maturity, but also because the decision cannot easily be reversed.

A financial manager responsible for short-term financial decisions does not have to look too far into the future. The decision to take a 60-day bank loan could properly be based on cash-flow forecasts for the next few months only. In contrast, the decision to issue a bond will normally reflect forecast cash requirements 5, 10, or more years into the future.

Short-term financial decisions do not involve many of the difficult conceptual issues encountered elsewhere in this book. In a sense, short-term decisions are easier than long-term decisions—but they are not less important. A firm can identify extremely valuable capital investment opportunities, find the precise optimal debt ratio, follow the perfect dividend policy, and yet founder because no one bothers to raise the cash to pay this year's bills—hence the need for short-term planning.

We start the chapter by showing how long-term financing decisions affect the short-term financial planning problem. We then demonstrate how financial managers forecast month-by-month cash requirements or surpluses and how they use these forecasts to develop short-term financing strategies.

19.1 Links between Long-Term and Short-Term Financing

All businesses require capital—that is, money invested in plant, machinery, inventories, accounts receivable, and all the other assets that it takes to run a business. The total cost of these assets is the firm's *cumulative capital requirement.* For most firms, the cumulative capital requirement grows irregularly, like the wavy line in Figure 19.1. This line shows a clear upward trend as the firm's business grows. But the figure also shows seasonal variation around the trend, with the capital requirement peaking late in each year. In addition, there would be unpredictable week-to-week and month-to-month fluctuations, but we have not attempted to show these in Figure 19.1.

The firm's cumulative capital requirement (red line) is the cumulative investment in all the assets needed for the business. The figure presents three possible strategies for the actual amount of long-term financing raised over time (lines A, B, and C). The requirement for short-term financing is the difference between long-term financing and the cumulative capital requirement. When long-term financing does not cover the cumulative capital requirement, the firm must raise short-term capital to make up the difference. When long-term financing more than covers the cumulative capital requirement, the firm has surplus cash available that can be lent out. Thus, the amount of long-term financing raised, given the capital requirement, determines whether the firm is a short-term borrower or lender.

Line A envisions the greatest amount of long-term financing and implies that the firm has a permanent cash surplus. The firm never needs short-term financing and, in fact, always has extra cash to invest. In contrast, if long-term financing follows line C, then long-term capital is always less than cumulative requirements and the firm always needs short-term financing. Finally, if long-term financing follows line B, which is probably the most common strategy, the firm is a short-term lender during part of the year and a borrower during the rest. When the red line is above line B, the firm needs to raise short-term finance. When it is below, the firm has excess cash that can be invested to earn interest.

What is the *best* level of long-term financing relative to the cumulative capital requirement? It is hard to say. There is no convincing theoretical analysis of this question. We can make some practical observations, however:

1. *Matching maturities.* When financial managers are asked the most important reason for choosing between short- and long-term debt, they generally say that they try to

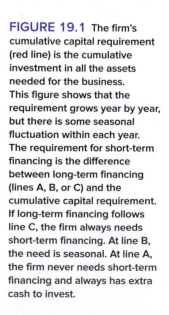

FIGURE 19.1 The firm's cumulative capital requirement (red line) is the cumulative investment in all the assets needed for the business. This figure shows that the requirement grows year by year, but there is some seasonal fluctuation within each year. The requirement for short-term financing is the difference between long-term financing (lines A, B, or C) and the cumulative capital requirement. If long-term financing follows line C, the firm always needs short-term financing. At line B, the need is seasonal. At line A, the firm never needs short-term financing and always has extra cash to invest.

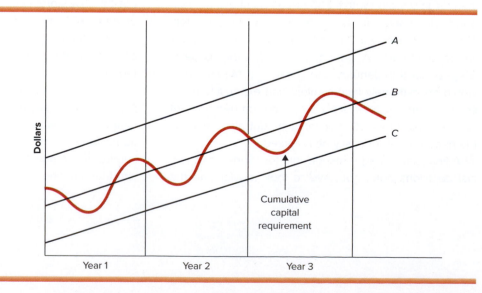

"match" the maturities of their assets and liabilities.[1] That is, they largely finance long-lived assets such as plant and machinery with long-term borrowing and equity. Short-term assets such as inventory and accounts receivable are financed by short-term debt.

2. *Permanent working capital requirement.* Most firms make a permanent investment in net working capital (current assets less current liabilities). This investment is financed from long-term sources.

3. *Maintaining liquidity.* Current assets can be converted into cash more easily than long-term assets. So firms with large holdings of current assets enjoy greater liquidity. Of course, some current assets are more readily converted into cash than others. Inventories are converted into cash only when the goods are produced, sold, and paid for. Receivables are more liquid; they become cash as customers pay their bills. Short-term securities can generally be sold if the firm needs cash on short notice and are therefore more liquid still.

Some firms choose to maintain more liquidity than others. For example, many high-tech companies, such as Intel and Cisco, hold huge amounts of marketable securities. On the other hand, firms in old-line manufacturing industries—such as chemicals, paper, or steel—manage with a far smaller reserve of liquidity. Why is this? One reason is that companies with rapidly growing profits may generate cash faster than they can redeploy it in new positive-NPV investments. This produces a surplus of cash that can be invested in short-term securities. Of course, companies faced with a growing mountain of cash may eventually respond by adjusting their payout policies. In Chapter 17, we saw how Apple proposed to reduce its cash mountain by paying a special dividend and repurchasing its stock.

Many companies with large cash reserves, including Apple, have businesses located in countries with low rates of corporate tax. Because profits are not taxed in the United States until the companies repatriate them, there is a powerful incentive to let the cash build up abroad.

There are some advantages to holding a reservoir of cash, particularly for smaller firms that face relatively high costs of raising funds on short notice. For example, biotech firms require large amounts of cash to develop new drugs. These firms generally have substantial cash holdings to fund their R&D programs and to exploit any successful drug developments.

Financial managers of firms with a surplus of long-term financing and with cash in the bank don't have to worry about finding the money to pay next month's bills. The cash can help to protect the firm against a rainy day and give it breathing space to make changes to operations. However, there are also drawbacks to surplus cash. Holdings of marketable securities are at best a zero-NPV investment for a taxpaying firm.

Pinkowitz and Williamson looked at the value that investors place on a firm's cash and found that, on average, shareholders valued a dollar of cash at $1.20.[2] Investors placed a particularly high value on liquidity for firms with plenty of growth opportunities. At the other extreme, Pinkowitz and Williamson found that when a firm was likely to face financial distress, a dollar of cash within the firm was often worth less than a dollar to the shareholders. Presumably shareholders worried that the cash would just be used to pay off the bondholders.

---

[1] A survey by Graham and Harvey found that managers considered that the desire to match the maturity of the debt with that of the assets was the single most important factor in their choice between long-term and short-term debt. See J. R. Graham and C. R. Harvey, "The Theory and Practice of Corporate Finance: Evidence from the Field," *Journal of Financial Economics* 61 (May 2001), pp. 187–243.

[2] L. Pinkowitz and R. Williamson, "The Market Value of Cash," *Journal of Applied Corporate Finance* 19 (2007), pp. 74–81.

19.2 Tracing Changes in Cash

BEYOND THE PAGE

Dynamic Mattress's short-term plan

mhhe.com/brealey9e

In the last chapter, we looked over the shoulder of the CFO of Dynamic Mattress while she prepared the company's long-term financial plan. Our task now is to see how Dynamic develops a short-term financial plan. We begin with Tables 19.1 and 19.2, which summarize the company's latest income statement and year-end balance sheets.[3]

Table 19.2 shows that in 2016, Dynamic's cash balance increased from $20 million to $30.4 million. What caused this increase? Did the extra cash come from Dynamic's issue of long-term debt, from reinvested earnings, from cash released by reducing inventory, or from extra credit extended by Dynamic's suppliers? (Note the increase in accounts payable.)

The correct answer? All of the above. There is rarely any point in linking a particular source of funds with a particular use. Instead, as we saw in Chapter 3, financial analysts trace the sources and uses of cash in the statement of cash flows like the one shown in Table 19.3. The positive entries in that table correspond to activities that generated cash and the negative entries refer to activities that absorbed cash. So, we see that Dynamic generated cash through the following means:

1. It earned $73.3 million of net income (operating activity).
2. It set aside $23.5 million as depreciation. Remember that depreciation is not a cash outlay. Thus, it must be added back to obtain Dynamic's cash flow (operating activity).

TABLE 19.1 2016 income statement for Dynamic Mattress Company (figures in $ millions, subject to rounding error)

Sales	$2,200.0
Operating costs	2,024.0
Depreciation	23.5
EBIT	$ 152.5
Interest	6.0
Pretax income	$ 146.5
Tax at 50%	73.3
Net income	$ 73.3

Note: Dividend = $46.8 million; reinvested earnings = $26.5 million.

TABLE 19.2 Year-end balance sheets for Dynamic Mattress Company (figures in $ millions, subject to rounding error)

Assets	2015	2016	Liabilities and Shareholders' Equity	2015	2016
Current assets			Current liabilities		
Cash	$ 20.0	$ 30.4	Debt due within a year (bank loans)	$ 25.0	$ 0
Marketable securities	0.0	25.0	Accounts payable	110.0	135.0
Accounts receivable	124.0	150.0	Total current liabilities	$135.0	$135.0
Inventory	183.0	171.6	Long-term debt	60.0	90.0
Total current assets	$327.0	$377.0	Net worth (equity and retained earnings)	400.5	427.0
Fixed assets			Total liabilities and owners' equity	$595.5	$652.0
Gross investment	$345.0	$375.0			
Less depreciation	76.5	100.0			
Net fixed assets	$268.5	$275.0			
Total assets	$595.5	$652.0			

[3] Notice that when Dynamic developed its long-term plan, it collapsed all current assets and liabilities into a single figure for net working capital. That broad-brush treatment is not appropriate for short-term planning, and therefore Table 19.2 spells out the individual components of net working capital. Notice also that because we report current assets and current liabilities separately in Table 19.2 (rather than reporting only *net* working capital), total assets are $652 million rather than $517 million, the value of the net assets, reported in Table 18.1. The difference in these figures is $135 million, the value of Dynamic's current liabilities.

TABLE 19.3 2016 statement of cash flows for Dynamic Mattress Company (figures in $ millions, subject to rounding error)

Cash Provided by Operations:	
Net income	$ 73.3
Depreciation	23.5
Changes in working capital items:	
Decrease (increase) in accounts receivable	− 26.0
Increase (decrease) in inventories	11.4
Increase (decrease) in accounts payable	25.0
Total decrease (increase) in working capital	$ 10.4
Cash flow provided by operations	−$107.2
Cash Flows from Investments:	
Investments in fixed assets	−$ 30.0
Cash Provided by (Used for) Financing Activities:	
Increase (decrease) in bank loans	−$ 25.0
Increase (decrease) in long-term debt	30.0
Dividends	− 46.8
Sale (purchase) of marketable securities	− 25.0
Issue (repurchase) of common stock	0.0
Cash provided by (used for) financing activities	−$ 66.8
Net Increase (Decrease) in Cash	**$ 10.4**

3. It reduced inventory, releasing $11.4 million (operating activity).
4. It increased its accounts payable, in effect borrowing an additional $25 million from its suppliers (operating activity).
5. It issued $30 million of long-term debt (financing activity).

Dynamic used cash for the following purposes:

1. It allowed accounts receivable to expand by $26 million (operating activity). In effect, it lent this additional amount to its customers.
2. It invested $30 million (investing activity). This shows up as the increase in gross fixed assets in Table 19.2.
3. It paid a $46.8 million dividend (financing activity). (*Note:* The $26.5 million increase in Dynamic's equity in Table 19.2 is due to reinvested earnings: $73.3 million of equity income, less the $46.8 million dividend.)
4. It purchased $25 million of marketable securities (financing activity).
5. It repaid $25 million of short-term bank debt (financing activity).

19.1 Self-Test

How will the following affect *cash* and *net working capital* (*current assets − current liabilities*)?

a. The firm takes out a short-term bank loan and uses the funds to pay off some of its accounts payable.
b. The firm uses cash on hand to buy raw materials.
c. The firm repurchases outstanding shares of stock.
d. The firm sells long-term bonds and puts the proceeds in its bank account.

19.3 Cash Budgeting

Table 19.3 showed why Dynamic's cash balance rose in 2016. But the financial manager needs to forecast the company's cash needs in 2017 and ensure that the company will be able to pay its upcoming bills. To discover how much cash the company may need requires the manager to prepare a cash budget based on the expected *future* sources and uses of cash.

There are three steps to preparing this cash budget:

Step 1. Forecast the sources of cash. The largest inflow of cash usually comes from payments by the firm's customers.

Step 2. Forecast the uses of cash.

Step 3. Calculate whether the firm is facing a cash shortage or surplus.

The company then uses these forecasts to draw up a plan for investing cash surpluses or financing any deficit.

Preparing the Cash Budget

Step 1: Forecast Sources of Cash   We will illustrate the preparation of the cash budget by continuing the example of Dynamic Mattress.

Most of Dynamic's cash inflow comes from the sale of mattresses. Therefore, we start with a sales forecast by quarter for 2017:[4]

Quarter:	First	Second	Third	Fourth
Sales ($ millions)	560	502	742	836

But unless customers pay cash on delivery, these sales will become accounts receivable before they become cash. Cash flow comes from *collections* on accounts receivable.

Most firms keep track of the average time it takes customers to pay their bills. From this, they can forecast what proportion of a quarter's sales is likely to be converted into cash in that quarter and what proportion is likely to be carried over to the next quarter as accounts receivable.

Suppose that 70% of sales are collected in the immediate quarter and the remaining 30% in the next. Table 19.4 shows forecast collections under this assumption. For example, you can see that in the first quarter collections from current sales are 70% of $560, or $392 million. But the firm also collects 30% of the previous quarter's sales, or .3 × $396.7 = $119.0 million. Therefore, total collections are $392 + $119.0 = $511.0 million.

Dynamic started the first quarter with $150.0 million of accounts receivable. The quarter's sales of $560 million were *added* to accounts receivable, but $511.0 million

TABLE 19.4 To forecast Dynamic Mattress's collections on accounts receivable in 2017, you need to forecast sales and collection rates (figures in $ millions, subject to rounding error)

	First Quarter	Second Quarter	Third Quarter	Fourth Quarter
1. Receivables at start of period	$150.0	$199.0	$181.6	$253.6
2. Sales	560.0	502.0	742.0	836.0
Collections:				
70% of sales in current period	392.0	351.4	519.4	585.2
30% of sales in last period	119.0[a]	168.0	150.6	222.6
3. Total collections	511.0	519.4	670.0	807.8
4. Receivables at end of period (1) + (2) − (3)	199.0	181.6	253.6	281.8

[a] We assume sales in the last quarter of the previous year were $396.7 million.

---

[4] For simplicity, we present a quarterly forecast. However, most firms would forecast by month instead of by quarter. Sometimes weekly or even daily forecasts are made.

TABLE 19.5 Dynamic Mattress's cash budget for 2017 (figures in $ millions, subject to rounding error)

	First Quarter	Second Quarter	Third Quarter	Fourth Quarter
Sources of Cash:				
Collections on accounts receivable	$511.0	$519.4	$670.0	$807.8
Other	0	0	77.0	0
Total sources	$511.0	$519.4	$747.0	$807.8
Uses of Cash:				
Payments of accounts payable	$250.0	$250.0	$267.0	$261.0
Increase in inventory	150.0	150.0	170.0	180.0
Labor and other expenses	136.0	136.0	136.0	136.0
Capital expenditures	70.0	10.0	8.0	14.5
Taxes, interest, and dividends	46.0	46.0	46.0	46.0
Total uses	$652.0	$592.0	$627.0	$637.5
Sources minus uses	**−$141.0**	**−$ 72.6**	**$120.0**	**$170.3**
Calculation of Short-Term Borrowing Requirement:				
Cash at start of period	$ 30.4	−$110.6	−$ 183.2	−$ 63.2
Change in cash balance	− 141.0	− 72.6	120.0	170.3
Cash at end of period[a]	−$ 110.6	−$183.2	−$ 63.2	$ 107.1
Minimum operating balance	25.0	25.0	25.0	25.0
Cumulative financing required[b]	135.6	208.2	88.2	− 82.1

[a] Firms cannot literally hold a negative amount of cash. This line shows the amount of cash the firm will have to raise to pay its bills.
[b] A negative sign indicates that no short-term financing is required. Instead, the firm has a cash surplus.

of collections were *subtracted*. Therefore, as Table 19.4 shows, Dynamic ended the quarter with accounts receivable of 150 + 560 − 511 = $199 million. The general formula is

Ending accounts receivable = beginning accounts receivable + sales − collections

The first three rows of Table 19.5 show forecasted sources of cash for Dynamic Mattress. Collection of receivables is the main source, but it is not the only one. Perhaps the firm plans to dispose of some land or expects a tax refund or payment of an insurance claim. All such items are included as "other" sources. It is also possible that the firm may raise additional capital by borrowing or selling stock, but we don't want to prejudge that question. Therefore, for the moment we just assume that Dynamic will not raise further long-term finance.

Step 2: Forecast Uses of Cash   So much for the incoming cash. Now for the outgoing. There always seem to be many more uses for cash than there are sources. The second section of Table 19.5 shows how Dynamic expects to use cash. For simplicity, we have condensed the uses into five categories:

1. *Payments of accounts payable.* Dynamic has to pay its bills for raw materials, parts, electricity, and so on. The cash-flow forecast assumes all these bills are paid on time, although Dynamic could probably delay payment to some extent. Delayed payment is sometimes called *stretching your payables*. Stretching is one source of short-term financing, but for most firms, it is an expensive source because, by stretching, they lose discounts given to firms that pay promptly. (This is discussed in more detail in Chapter 20.)

2. *Increase in inventories.* The expected increase in sales in 2017 requires additional investment in inventories.

3. *Labor, administrative, and other expenses.* This category includes all other regular business expenses.
4. *Capital expenditures.* Note that Dynamic Mattress plans a major outlay of cash in the first quarter to pay for a long-lived asset.
5. *Taxes, interest, and dividend payments.* This includes interest on currently outstanding long-term debt and dividend payments to stockholders.

Step 3: Calculate the Cash Balance   The forecast net inflow of cash (sources minus uses) is shown by the bold line in Table 19.5. Note the large negative figure for the first quarter: a $141.0 million forecast *outflow.* There is a smaller forecast outflow in the second quarter and then substantial cash inflows in the second half of the year.

The bottom part of Table 19.5 calculates how much financing Dynamic will have to raise if its cash-flow forecasts are right. It starts the year with $30.4 million in cash. There is a $141.0 million cash outflow in the first quarter, and so Dynamic will have to obtain at least $141.0 − 30.4 = $110.6 million of additional financing. This would leave the firm with a forecasted cash balance of exactly zero at the start of the second quarter.

Most financial managers regard a planned cash balance of zero as driving too close to the edge of the cliff. They establish a minimum operating cash balance to absorb unexpected cash inflows and outflows. We assume that Dynamic's minimum operating cash balance is $25 million.

This means it will have to raise $110.6 + $25 = $135.6 million in the first quarter and $72.6 million more in the second quarter. Thus, its *cumulative* financing requirement is $208.2 million by the second quarter. Fortunately, this is the peak: The cumulative requirement declines in the third quarter by $120 million to $88.2 million. In the final quarter, Dynamic is out of the woods: Its cash balance is $107.1 million, well above its minimum operating balance.

Our next step is to develop a short-term financing plan that covers the forecasted requirements in the most economical way. We move on to that topic after two general observations:

1. The large cash outflows in the first two quarters do not necessarily spell trouble for Dynamic Mattress. In part, they reflect the capital investment made in the first quarter: Dynamic is spending $70 million, but it should be acquiring an asset worth that much or more. The cash outflows also reflect low sales in the first half of the year; sales recover in the second half.[5] If this is a predictable seasonal pattern, the firm should have no trouble borrowing to help it get through the slow months.
2. Table 19.5 is only a best guess about future cash flows. It is a good idea to think about the *uncertainty* in your estimates. For example, you could undertake a sensitivity analysis, in which you inspect how Dynamic's cash requirements would be affected by a shortfall in sales or by a delay in collections.

19.2 Self-Test

Calculate Dynamic Mattress's quarterly cash receipts, net cash flow, and cumulative short-term financing required if customers pay for only 60% of purchases in the current quarter and pay the remaining 40% in the following quarter.

---

[5] Maybe people buy more mattresses late in the year when the nights are longer.

19.4 Dynamic's Short-Term Financial Plan

Dynamic's cash budget defines its problem. Its financial manager must find short-term financing to cover the firm's forecast cash requirements. There are dozens of sources of short-term financing, but, for simplicity, we will assume that Dynamic has just two options:

1. *Bank loan.* Dynamic has an existing arrangement with its bank, allowing it to borrow up to $100 million at an interest rate of 10% per year, or 2.5% per quarter. It can borrow and repay the loan whenever it chooses, but the company may not exceed its credit limit.
2. *Stretching payables.* Dynamic can also raise capital by putting off payment of its bills. The financial manager believes that Dynamic can defer up to $100 million in each quarter. Thus, $100 million can be saved in the first quarter by not paying bills in that quarter. (Note that the cash-flow forecasts in Table 19.5 assumed that these bills will be paid in the first quarter.) If deferred, these payments must be made in the second quarter, but up to $100 million of the second quarter bills can be deferred to the third quarter, and so on.

Stretching payables is often costly, even if no ill will is incurred.[6] The reason is that suppliers may offer discounts for prompt payment. Dynamic loses this discount if it pays late. In this example, we assume the lost discount is 5% of the amount deferred. In other words, if a $100 payment is delayed, the firm must pay $105 in the next quarter. This is like borrowing at a quarterly interest rate of 5%, or equivalently at an annualized rate over 20% (more precisely, $1.05^4 - 1 = .216$, or 21.6%).

Dynamic Mattress's Financing Plan

With these two options, the short-term financing strategy is obvious. Use the bank loan first, if necessary up to the $100 million limit. If there is still a shortage of cash, stretch payables. Table 19.6 shows the resulting plan. In the first quarter of 2017, the plan calls for borrowing the full amount from the bank ($100 million) and stretching $10.6 million of payables (see lines 1 and 2 of panel B). In addition, the company sells the $25 million of marketable securities it held at the end of 2016. Thus, it raises $100 + $10.6 + $25 = $135.6 million of cash in the first quarter (see the last line of panel B).

In the second quarter, Dynamic needs to raise an additional $72.6 million to support its operations. It also owes interest of $2.5 million on its bank loan. It must retire the payables that it stretched last quarter. With the 5% interest on that implicit loan from its suppliers, this adds $10.6 + $.5 million to the funds it must raise in the second quarter. Finally, if it wants to raise cash to compensate for the interest it had been earning on the securities it sold in the first quarter, it will require another $.50 million.[7] In total, therefore, it must come up with $86.7 million in the second quarter.

In the third quarter, the firm generates a $120 million cash-flow surplus from operations. Part of that surplus, $86.7 million, is used to pay off the stretched payables from the second quarter, as it is required to do. A small portion is used to

---

[6] In fact, ill will is likely to be incurred. Firms that stretch payments risk being labeled as credit risks. Since stretching is so expensive, suppliers reason that customers will resort to it only when they cannot obtain credit at reasonable rates elsewhere. Suppliers naturally are reluctant to act as the lender of last resort.

[7] This last term is a little tricky. Strictly speaking, the interest the firm no longer earns on the securities it sold is more of an opportunity cost than an absolute requirement for new funds. However, some firms such as Apple or Google have enormous quantities of cash, and they may view the earnings on those funds as a non-trivial portion of the company's target cash flow. We assume here that Dynamic chooses to replace its lost interest earnings, and builds that replacement into its financing plan.

TABLE 19.6 Dynamic
Mattress's financing plan, 2017
(figures in $ millions, subject to
rounding error)

	Quarter:	First	Second	Third	Fourth
A. Cash Requirements					
Cash required for operations[a]		$135.6	$ 72.6	−$120.0	−$170.3
Interest on bank loan[b]		0.0	2.5	2.5	1.9
Interest on stretched payables[c]		0.0	0.5	4.3	0.0
Repayments of last quarter's stretched payables		0.0	10.6	86.7	0.0
Lost interest on sold securities[d]		0.0	0.5	0.5	0.5
Total cash required		$135.6	$ 86.7	−$ 25.9	−$167.9
B. Cash Raised in Quarter					
Bank loan		$100.0	$ 0.0	$ 0.0	$ 0.0
Stretched payables		10.6	86.7	0.0	0.0
Securities sold		25.0	0.0	0.0	0.0
Total cash raised		$135.6	$ 86.7	$ 0.0	$ 0.0
C. Repayments					
Of bank loan		$ 0.0	$ 0.0	$ 25.9	$ 74.1
D. Addition to Cash Balances and Security Holdings					
		$ 0.0	$ 0.0	$ 0.0	$ 93.9
E. Bank Loan					
Beginning of quarter		$ 0.0	$100.0	$100.0	$ 74.1
End of quarter		100.0	100.0	74.1	0.0

[a] Cash required for operations in each quarter equals the change in cumulative financing required from the last line of Table 19.5. A negative cash requirement implies a positive cash flow from operations.
[b] The interest rate on the bank loan is 2.5% per quarter, applied to the bank loan outstanding at the start of the quarter. Thus, the interest due in the second quarter is .025 × $100 million = $2.5 million.
[c] The "interest" cost of the stretched payables is 5% of the payment deferred. For example, in the second quarter, 5% of the $10.5 million of deferred payments is about $0.53 million.
[d] The interest loss on securities sold is 2% per quarter. Thus, in the second quarter, Dynamic needs to find an additional .02 × $25 million = $.5 million.

pay interest on its outstanding loans. It uses the remaining cash-flow surplus, $25.9 million (last line of panel A), to pay down its bank loan. In the fourth quarter, the firm has a surplus funds from operations of $170.3 million. It pays off the interest and remaining principal on the bank loan and is able to put $93.9 million in cash and marketable securities.

19.3   Self-Test

a. Revise Dynamic Mattress's short-term financial plan, assuming that it can borrow only $80 million from the bank.
b. In the end, the bank loan is repaid, whether it is $100 million as in Table 19.6, or $80 million as it is here. Why, then, does the company end up with less addition to cash balances in the fourth quarter in this revised plan?

Evaluating the Plan

Does the plan shown in Table 19.6 solve Dynamic's short-term financing problem? No—the plan is feasible, but Dynamic can probably do better. The most glaring weakness is its reliance on stretching payables, an extremely expensive financing device. Remember that it costs Dynamic 5% per quarter to delay paying bills—an effective interest rate of greater than 20% per year.

The first plan would merely stimulate the financial manager to search for cheaper sources of short-term borrowing. The financial manager would ask several other questions as well. For example:

1. Does Dynamic need a larger reserve of cash or marketable securities to guard against, say, its customers stretching *their* payables (thus slowing down collections on accounts receivable)?
2. Does the plan yield satisfactory current and quick ratios?[8] Its bankers may be worried if these ratios deteriorate.
3. Are there intangible costs to stretching payables? Will suppliers begin to doubt Dynamic's creditworthiness?
4. Does the plan for 2017 leave Dynamic in good financial shape for 2018? (Here the answer is yes because Dynamic will have paid off all short-term borrowing by the end of the year.)
5. Should Dynamic try to arrange long-term financing for the major capital expenditure in the first quarter? This seems sensible, following the rule of thumb that long-term assets deserve long-term financing. It would also dramatically reduce the need for short-term borrowing. A counterargument is that Dynamic is financing the capital investment *only temporarily* by short-term borrowing. By year-end, the investment is paid for by cash from operations. Thus Dynamic's initial decision not to seek immediate long-term financing may reflect a preference for ultimately financing the investment with retained earnings.
6. Perhaps the firm's operating and investment plans can be adjusted to make the short-term financing problem easier. Is there any easy way of deferring the first quarter's large cash outflow? For example, suppose that the large capital investment in the first quarter is for new mattress-stuffing machines to be delivered and installed in the first half of the year. The new machines are not scheduled to be ready for full-scale use until August. Perhaps the machine manufacturer could be persuaded to accept 60% of the purchase price on delivery and 40% when the machines are installed and operating satisfactorily.
7. Should Dynamic release cash by reducing the level of other current assets? For example, it could reduce receivables by getting tough with customers who are late paying their bills. (The cost is that, in the future, these customers may take their business elsewhere.) Or it may be able to get by with lower inventories of mattresses. (The cost here is that it may lose business if there is a rush of orders that it cannot supply.)

Short-term financing plans must be developed by trial and error. You lay out one plan, think about it, and then try again with different assumptions on financing and investment alternatives. You continue until you can think of no further improvements.

Trial and error is important because it helps you understand the real nature of the problem the firm faces. Here we can draw a useful analogy between the process of planning and Chapter 10's discussion of project analysis. In Chapter 10, we described sensitivity analysis and other tools used by firms to find out what makes capital investment projects tick and what can go wrong with them. Dynamic's financial manager faces the same kind of task here: not just to choose a plan but to understand what can go wrong and what will be done if conditions change unexpectedly.

A Note on Short-Term Financial Planning Models

Working out a consistent short-term plan requires burdensome calculations. Fortunately, much of the arithmetic can be delegated to a computer. Many large firms have built short-term financial planning models to do this. Smaller companies do not face so much detail and complexity and often find it easier to work with a spreadsheet

---

[8] These ratios are discussed in Chapter 4.

program on a personal computer. In either case, the financial manager specifies forecasted cash requirements or surpluses, interest rates, credit limits, and so on, and the model grinds out a plan like the one shown in Table 19.6.

The computer also produces balance sheets, income statements, and whatever special reports the financial manager may require. Smaller firms that do not want custom-built models can rent general-purpose models offered by banks, accounting firms, management consultants, or specialized computer software firms.

Spreadsheet 19.1 shows Dynamic's cash budget. The spreadsheet is the source of the cash-flow forecasts that appeared in Tables 19.4 and 19.5. Look at column E of the spreadsheet. It shows which entries are simply numerical assumptions (e.g., the sales assumptions in row 5) and which are computations based on other variables (e.g., the collections on sales in the last and current periods in rows 7 and 8). The formulas quickly show you how the various items in the cash budget are linked.

SPREADSHEET 19.1 Dynamic Mattress's cash budget, 2017 (figures in $ millions)

	A	B	C	D	E	F
1	Quarter:	First	Second	Third	Fourth	Formula in Col C
2						
3	**A. Accounts Receivable**					
4	Receivables (beginning of period)	150.0	199.0	181.6	253.6	B10
5	Sales	560.0	502.0	742.0	836.0	502
6	Collections					
7	On sales in current period (70%)	392.0	351.4	519.4	585.2	0.7*C5
8	On sales in previous period (30%)[a]	119.0	168.0	150.6	222.6	0.3*B5
9	Total collections	511.0	519.4	670.0	807.8	C7+C8
10	Receivables (end of period)	199.0	181.6	253.6	281.8	C4+C5−C9
11						
12	**B. Cash Budget**					
13	Sources of cash					
14	Collections of accounts receivable	511.0	519.4	670.0	807.8	C9
15	Other	0.0	0.0	77.0	0.0	0
16	Total sources	511.0	519.4	747.0	807.8	C14+C15
17	Uses of cash					
18	Payments of accounts payable	250.0	250.0	267.0	261.0	250
19	Increase in inventory	150.0	150.0	170.0	180.0	150
20	Labor and other expenses	136.0	136.0	136.0	136.0	136
21	Capital expenses	70.0	10.0	8.0	14.5	10
22	Taxes, interest, and dividends	46.0	46.0	46.0	46.0	46
23	Total uses	652.0	592.0	627.0	637.5	SUM(C18:C22)
24						
25	**Net cash inflow = sources − uses**	−141.0	−72.6	120.0	170.3	C16−C23
26						
27	**C. Short-Term Financing Requirements**					
28	Cash at start of period	30.4	−110.6	−183.2	−63.2	B30
29	+ Net cash inflow	−141.0	−72.6	120.0	170.3	C25
30	= Cash at end of period[b]	−110.6	−183.2	−63.2	107.1	C28+C29
31	Minimum operating balance	25.0	25.0	25.0	25.0	B31
32	Cumulative financing required[c]	135.6	208.2	88.2	−82.1	C31−C30

[a] Sales in the fourth quarter of the previous year were $396.7 million.
[b] Firms cannot literally hold negative cash. This line shows the amount of cash the firm will have to raise to pay its bills.
[c] A negative sign indicates that no short-term financing is required. Instead the firm has a cash surplus.

SUMMARY

How does long-term financing policy affect short-term financing requirements? (*LO19-1*)

The nature of the firm's short-term financial planning problem is determined by the amount of long-term capital it raises. A firm that issues large amounts of long-term debt or common stock, or that retains a large part of its earnings, may find that it has permanent excess cash. Other firms raise relatively little long-term capital and end up as permanent short-term debtors. Most firms attempt to find a golden mean by financing all fixed assets and part of current assets with equity and long-term debt. Such firms may invest cash surpluses during part of the year and borrow during the rest of the year.

How does the firm's sources and uses of cash relate to its need for short-term borrowing? (*LO19-2*)

The starting point for short-term financial planning is an understanding of sources and uses of cash. Firms forecast their net cash requirement by forecasting collections on accounts receivable, adding other cash inflows, and subtracting all forecast cash outlays. If the forecast cash balance is insufficient to cover day-to-day operations and to provide a buffer against contingencies, the firm will need to find additional finance.

How do firms develop a short-term financing plan that meets their need for cash? (*LO19-3*)

The search for the best short-term financial plan inevitably proceeds by trial and error. The financial manager must explore the consequences of different assumptions about cash requirements, interest rates, limits on financing from particular sources, and so on. Firms commonly use computerized financial models to help in this process.

QUESTIONS AND PROBLEMS

1. **Working Capital Management.** How would each of the following six different transactions affect Dynamic Mattress's (i) cash and (ii) net working capital? (*LO19-1*)
    a. Paying out an extra $2 million cash dividend
    b. A customer paying a $2,500 bill resulting from a previous sale
    c. Paying $5,000 previously owed to one of its suppliers
    d. Borrowing $1 million long-term and investing the proceeds in inventory
    e. Borrowing $1 million short-term and investing the proceeds in inventory
    f. Selling $5 million of marketable securities for cash

2. **Sources and Uses of Cash.** Create the statement of cash flows from the following entries: (*LO19-2*)

Net income	$1,500
Dividends	900
Additions to inventory	120
Additions to receivables	150
Depreciation	90
Reduction in payables	550
Net issuance of long-term debt	300
Sale of fixed assets	600

3. **Short-Term Financial Plans.** Fill in the blanks in the following statements. (*LO19-2*)
    a. A firm has a cash surplus when its ____(i)____ exceeds its ____(ii)____. The surplus is normally invested in ____(iii)____.
    b. In developing the short-term financial plan, the financial manager starts with a(n) ____(iv)____ budget for the next year. This budget shows the ____(v)____ generated or absorbed by the firm's operations and also the minimum ____(vi)____ needed to support these operations. The manager may also wish to invest in ____(vii)____ as a reserve for unexpected cash requirements.

4. **Sources and Uses of Cash.** How would each of the following events affect the firm's balance sheet? State whether each change is a source or use of cash. (*LO19-2*)

   a. An automobile manufacturer increases production in response to a forecast increase in demand. Unfortunately, the demand does not increase.
   b. Competition forces the firm to give customers more time to pay for their purchases.
   c. The firm sells a parcel of land for $100,000. The land was purchased 5 years earlier for $200,000.
   d. The firm repurchases its own common stock.
   e. The firm pays its quarterly dividend.
   f. The firm issues $1 million of long-term debt and uses the proceeds to repay a short-term bank loan.

5. **Sources and Uses of Cash.** What will be the effect of each of the following transactions on cash, net working capital, and the current ratio? Assume that the current ratio is above 1.0. (*LO19-2*)

   a. The firm borrows $1,000 in a short-term loan from its bank and pays $500 in accounts payable.
   b. The firm issues $1,000 in long-term bonds and uses the proceeds to pay $800 in payables and purchase $200 in marketable securities.

6. **Sources and Uses of Cash.** Table 19.7 shows Dynamic Mattress's year-end 2014 balance sheet, and Table 19.8 shows its income statement for 2015. Use these tables (and Table 19.2) to work out the statement of cash flows for 2015. Group these items into sources of cash and uses of cash. (*LO19-2*)

7. **Short-Term Planning.** Paymore Products places orders for goods equal to 75% of its sales forecast in the next quarter. What will orders be in each quarter of the year if the sales forecasts for the next five quarters are as shown in the following table? (*LO19-2*)

	Quarter in Coming Year				Following Year
	First	**Second**	**Third**	**Fourth**	**First Quarter**
Sales forecast	$372	$360	$336	$384	$384

TABLE 19.7 Year-end balance sheet for Dynamic Mattress for 2014 (figures in $ million)

Assets		Liabilities and Shareholders' Equity	
Current assets		Current liabilities	
Cash	$ 20	Bank loans	$ 20
Marketable securities	10	Accounts payable	75
Accounts receivable	110		
Inventory	150		
Total current assets	$290	Total current liabilities	$ 95
Fixed assets			
Gross investment	250	Long-term debt	25
Less depreciation	70	Net worth (equity and retained earnings)	350
Net fixed assets	$180		
Total assets	$470	Total liabilities and net worth	$470

Note: Dividend = $30 million and reinvested earnings = $10 million.

TABLE 19.8 Income statement for Dynamic Mattress for 2015 (figures in $ millions)

Sales	$1,500.0
Operating costs	1,408.5
	$ 91.5
Depreciation	6.5
EBIT	$ 85.0
Interest	5.0
Pretax income	$ 80.0
Tax at 50%	40.0
Net income	$ 40.0

Note: Dividend = $30 million and reinvested earnings = $10 million.

8. **Forecasting Payments.** Calculate Paymore's cash payments (from Problem 7) to its suppliers under the assumption that the firm pays for its goods with a 1-month delay. Therefore, on average, two-thirds of purchases are paid for in the quarter that they are purchased, and one-third are paid in the following quarter. (*LO19-2*)

9. **Forecasting Collections.** Now suppose that Paymore's customers (from Problem 7) pay their bills with a 2-month delay. What is the forecast for Paymore's cash receipts in each quarter of the coming year? Assume that sales in the last quarter of the previous year were $336. (*LO19-2*)

10. **Forecasting Net Cash Flow.** Assuming that Paymore's labor and administrative expenses (from Problem 7) are $65 per quarter and that interest on long-term debt is $40 per quarter, work out the net cash inflow for Paymore for the coming year using a table like Table 19.5. (*LO19-2*)

11. **Short-Term Financing Requirements.** Suppose that Paymore's cash balance (from Problem 7) at the start of the first quarter is $40 and its minimum acceptable cash balance is $30. Work out the short-term financing requirements for the firm in the coming year using a table like Table 19.5. The firm pays no dividends. (*LO19-3*)

12. **Short-Term Financing Plan.** Now assume that Paymore (from Problem 7) can borrow up to $100 from a line of credit at an interest rate of 2% per quarter. Prepare a short-term financing plan. Use Table 19.6 to guide your answer. (*LO19-3*)

13. **Dynamic's Short-Term Plan.** Each of the following events affects one or more of the tables in Sections 19.2 and 19.3. Show the effects of each event by adjusting the tables listed in parentheses. Treat each event independently. (*LO19-2, LO19-3*)

    a. Dynamic repays only $10 million of short-term debt in 2016. (Tables 19.2 and 19.3)

    b. Dynamic issues an additional $40 million of long-term debt in 2016 and invests $25 million in a new warehouse. (Tables 19.2 and 19.3)

    c. In 2016, Dynamic reduces the quantity of stuffing in each mattress. Customers don't notice, but operating costs fall by 10%. The firm's dividend payout ratio remains unchanged. (Tables 19.1,19.2, and 19.3)

    d. Starting in the third quarter of 2017, Dynamic employs new staff members who prove very effective in persuading customers to pay more promptly. As a result, 90% of sales are paid for immediately and 10% are paid in the following quarter. (Tables 19.4 and 19.5)

    e. Starting in the first quarter of 2017, Dynamic cuts wages by $20 million a quarter. (Table 19.5)

    f. In the second quarter of 2017, a disused warehouse catches fire mysteriously. Dynamic receives a $50 million check from the insurance company. (Table 19.5)

    g. Dynamic's treasurer decides he can scrape by on a $10 million operating cash balance. (Table 19.5)

14. **Forecasting Collections.** Here is a forecast of sales by National Bromide for the first 4 months of 2017 (figures in thousands of dollars):

Month:	1	2	3	4
Cash sales	15	24	18	14
Sales on credit	100	120	90	70

On average, 50% of credit sales are paid for in the current month, 30% in the next month, and the remainder in the month after that. What are the expected cash collections in months 3 and 4? (*LO19-3*)

15. **Forecasting Payments.** (*LO19-3*)

    a. If a firm pays its bills with a 30-day delay, what fraction of its purchases will be paid for in the current quarter?

    b. What fraction will be paid in the following quarter?

    c. What if its payment delay is 60 days?

16. **Impact of Long-Term Financing.** Suppose that Dynamic Mattress issued $5 million of additional long-term debt and used the proceeds to add to its cash balances. Recalculate its short-term financing plan (Table 19.6) now that it has raised $5 million of additional long-term financing. (*LO19-3*)

17. **Short-Term Plan.** Recalculate Dynamic Mattress's 2017 financing plan (Table 19.6), assuming that the firm wishes to maintain a minimum cash balance of $30 million instead of $25 million. Assume the firm can convince the bank to extend its line of credit to $105 million. (*LO19-3*)

18. **Cash Budget.** The following data are from the budget of Ritewell Publishers. Half the company's sales are transacted on a cash basis. The other half are paid for with a 1-month delay. The company pays all of its credit purchases with a 1-month delay. Credit purchases in January were $30, and total sales in January were $180. (*LO19-3*)

	February	March	April
Total sales	$200	$220	$180
Cash purchases	70	80	60
Credit purchases	40	30	40
Labor and administrative purchases	30	30	30
Taxes, interest, and dividends	10	10	10
Capital expenditures	100	0	0

Complete the following cash budget:

	February	March	April
Sources of cash			
Collections on current sales			
Collections on amounts receivable			
Total sources of cash			
Uses of cash			
Payments of accounts payable			
Cash purchases			
Labor and administrative expenses			
Capital expenditures			
Taxes, interest, and dividends			
Total uses of cash			
Net cash inflow			
Cash at start of period	100		
+ Net cash inflow			
= Cash at end of period			
+ Minimum operating cash balance	100	100	100
= Cumulative short-term financing required			

19. **Forecasts of Payables.** Dynamic Futon forecasts the following purchases from suppliers: (*LO19-3*)

  a. Forty percent of goods are supplied cash-on-delivery. The remainder are paid with an average delay of 1 month. If Dynamic Futon starts the year with payables of $22 million, what is the forecasted level of payables for each month?

  b. Suppose that, from the start of the year, the company stretches payables by paying 40% after 1 month and 20% after 2 months. (The remainder continue to be paid cash-on-delivery.) Recalculate payables for each month assuming that there are no cash penalties for late payment.

	Jan.	Feb.	Mar.	Apr.	May	June
Value of goods ($ millions)	32	28	25	22	20	20

20. **Dynamic's Short-Term Plan.** Work out a short-term financing plan for Dynamic Mattress Company, assuming the limit on the line of credit is raised from $100 to $120 million. Otherwise, keep to the assumptions used in developing Table 19.6. (*LO19-3*)

21. **Dynamic's Short-Term Plan.** Dynamic Mattress decides to lease its new mattress-stuffing machines rather than buy them. As a result, capital expenditure in the first quarter is reduced by $50 million, but the company must make lease payments of $2.5 million for each of the four quarters. Assume that the lease has no effect on tax payments until after the fourth quarter. Construct two tables like Tables 19.5 and 19.6 showing Dynamic's cumulative financing requirement and a new financing plan. Check your answer using Dynamic's spreadsheet. (*LO19-3*)

WEB EXERCISE

1. Download the annual report of Abercrombie & Fitch (ANF) and Kellogg (K). How do these firms differ in terms of short term financing strategies? For example, which firm relies more on lines of credit? Look at their quarterly financial statements on finance.yahoo.com. Which firm has greater seasonality in sales? Does this seem related to their use of bank loans?

SOLUTIONS TO SELF-TEST QUESTIONS

19.1 a. This transaction merely substitutes one current liability (short-term debt) for another (accounts payable). Neither cash nor net working capital is affected.
      b. This transaction will increase inventory at the expense of cash. Cash falls but net working capital is unaffected.
      c. The firm will use cash to buy back the stock. Both cash and net working capital will fall.
      d. The proceeds from the sale will increase both cash and net working capital.

19.2

Quarter:	First	Second	Third	Fourth
A. Accounts Receivable				
Receivables (beginning of period)	150.1	215.3	192.1	288.1
Sales	560.0	502.0	742.0	836.0
Collections				
On sales in current period (60%)	336.0	301.2	445.2	501.6
On sales in previous period (40%)	158.7	224.0	200.8	296.8
Total collections	494.7	525.2	646.0	798.4
Receivables (end of period)	215.3	192.1	288.1	325.7
B. Cash Budget				
Sources of cash				
Collections of accounts receivable	494.7	525.2	646.0	798.4
Other	0.0	0.0	77.0	0.0
Total sources	494.7	525.2	723.0	798.4
Uses of cash				
Payments of accounts payable	250.0	250.0	267.0	261.0
Increase in inventory	150.0	150.0	170.0	180.0
Labor and other expenses	136.0	136.0	136.0	136.0
Capital expenses	70.0	10.0	8.0	14.5
Taxes, interest, and dividends	46.0	46.0	46.0	46.0
Total uses	652.0	592.0	627.0	637.5
Net cash inflow = sources − uses	−157.3	−66.8	96.0	160.9
C. Short-Term Financing				
Requirements				
Cash at start of period	30.4	−126.9	−193.7	−97.7
+ Net cash inflow	−157.3	− 66.8	96.0	160.9
= Cash at end of period	−126.9	−193.7	−97.7	63.2
Minimum operating balance	25.0	25.0	25.0	25.0
Cumulative financing required	151.9	218.7	122.7	−38.2

19.3   a.

Quarter:	First	Second	Third	Fourth
A. Cash Requirements				
Cash required for operations	135.6	72.6	−120.0	−170.3
Interest on bank loan	0.0	2.5	2.5	2.4
Interest on stretched payables	0.0	1.5	5.4	0.0
Repayments of last quarter's stretched payables	0.0	30.6	107.7	0.0
Lost interest on sold securities	0.0	0.5	0.5	0.5
Total cash required	135.6	107.7	−3.9	−167.4
B. Cash Raised in Quarter				
Bank loan	80.0	0.0	0.0	0.0
Stretched payables	30.6	107.7	0.0	0.0
Securities sold	25.0	0.0	0.0	0.0
Total cash raised	135.6	107.7	0.0	0.0
C. Repayments				
Of bank loan	0.00	0.00	3.9	96.1
D. Addition to Cash Balances or Security Holdings	0.00	0.00	0.00	71.3
E. Bank Loan				
Beginning of quarter	0.0	100.0	100.0	96.1
End of quarter	100.0	100.0	96.1	0.0

b.   The implicit interest rate on stretching payables is higher than the rate on the bank loan. In the first quarter, if the company can borrow only $80 million, it must stretch payables by $30.6 million rather than $10.6 million (as in Table 19.6). Borrowing at the higher interest rate means that Dynamic incurs higher total interest payments and faces a greater need to raise cash in the second quarter. This, in turn, slows the rate at which it can pay off the bank loan. Therefore, the interest due on the bank loan in the fourth quarter is higher, and that higher interest payment absorbs some of the funds that would have been available to invest in cash or securities. The model allows us to trace the chain of implications over the course of the year.

MINICASE

Capstan Autos operated an East Coast dealership for a major Japanese car manufacturer. Capstan's owner, Sidney Capstan, attributed much of the business's success to its no-frills policy of competitive pricing and immediate cash payment. The business was basically a simple one—the firm imported cars at the beginning of each quarter and paid the manufacturer at the end of the quarter. The revenues from the sale of these cars covered the payment to the manufacturer and the expenses of running the business, as well as providing Sidney Capstan with a good return on his equity investment.

By the fourth quarter of 2021, sales were running at 250 cars a quarter. Because the average sale price of each car was about $20,000, this translated into quarterly revenues of 250 × $20,000 = $5 million. The average cost to Capstan of each imported car was $18,000. After paying wages, rent, and other recurring costs of $200,000 per quarter and deducting depreciation of $80,000, the company was left with earnings before interest and taxes (EBIT) of $220,000 a quarter and net profits of $140,000.

The year 2022 was not a happy year for car importers in the United States. Recession led to a general decline in auto sales, while the fall in the value of the dollar shaved profit margins for many dealers in imported cars. Capstan, more than most firms, foresaw the difficulties ahead and reacted at once by offering 6 months' free credit while holding the sale price of its cars constant. Wages and other costs were pared by 25% to $150,000 a quarter, and the company effectively eliminated all capital expenditures. The policy appeared successful. Unit sales fell by 20% to 200 units a quarter, but the company continued to operate at a satisfactory profit (see table).

The slump in sales lasted for 6 months, but as consumer confidence began to return, auto sales began to recover. The company's new policy of 6 months' free credit was proving sufficiently popular that Sidney Capstan decided to maintain the policy. In the third quarter of 2022, sales had recovered to 225 units; by the fourth quarter, they were 250 units; and by the first quarter of the next year, they had reached 275 units. It looked as if, by the second quarter of 2023, the company could expect to sell 300 cars. Earnings before interest and taxes were already in excess of their previous high, and Sidney Capstan was able to congratulate himself on weathering what looked to be a tricky period. Over the

18-month period, the firm had earned net profits of more than half a million dollars, and the equity had grown from just over $1.5 million to about $2 million.

Sidney Capstan was, first and foremost, a superb salesman and always left the financial aspects of the business to his financial manager. However, there was one feature of the financial statements that disturbed Sidney Capstan—the mounting level of debt that, by the end of the first quarter of 2023, had reached $9.7 million. This unease turned to alarm when the financial manager phoned to say that the bank was reluctant to extend further credit and was even questioning its current level of exposure to the company.

Mr. Capstan found it impossible to understand how such a successful year could have landed the company in financial difficulties. The company had always had good relationships with its bank, and the interest rate on its bank loans was a reasonable 8% a year (or about 2% a quarter). Surely, Mr. Capstan reasoned, when the bank saw the projected sales growth for the rest of 2023, it would realize that there were plenty of profits to enable the company to start repaying its loans.

Mr. Capstan kept coming back to three questions: Was his company really in trouble? Could the bank be right in its decision to withhold further credit? And why was the company's indebtedness increasing when its profits were higher than ever?

SUMMARY INCOME STATEMENT
(All figures except unit sales in $ thousands)

	Year: 2021	2022				2023
Quarter:	4	1	2	3	4	1
1. Number of cars sold	250	200	200	225	250	275
2. Unit price	20	20	20	20	20	20
3. Unit cost	18	18	18	18	18	18
4. Revenues (1) × (2)	5,000	4,000	4,000	4,500	5,000	5,500
5. Cost of goods sold (1) × (3)	4,500	3,600	3,600	4,050	4,500	4,950
6. Wages and other costs	200	150	150	150	150	150
7. Depreciation	80	80	80	80	80	80
8. EBIT (4) − (5) − (6) − (7)	220	170	170	220	270	320
9. Net interest	4	0	76	153	161	178
10. Pretax profit (8) − (9)	216	170	94	67	109	142
11. Tax [.35 × (10)]	76	60	33	23	38	50
12. Net profit (10) − (11)	140	110	61	44	71	92

SUMMARY BALANCE SHEETS
(Figures in $ thousands)

	End of 3rd Quarter 2021	End of 1st Quarter 2023
Cash	$ 10	$ 10
Receivables	0	10,500
Inventory	4,500	5,400
Total current assets	$4,510	$15,910
Fixed assets (net)	1,760	1,280
Total assets	$6,270	$17,190
Bank loan	230	9,731
Payables	4,500	5,400
Total current liabilities	$4,730	$15,131
Shareholders' equity	1,540	2,059
Total liabilities plus equity	$6,270	$17,190

20

Working Capital Management

LEARNING OBJECTIVES

After reading this chapter, you should be able to:

20-1 Understand why firms need to invest in net working capital.

20-2 Describe the usual steps in a firm's credit management policy.

20-3 Measure the implicit interest rate on credit sales.

20-4 Describe how firms assess the probability a customer will pay its bills.

20-5 Understand when it makes sense to grant credit to customers.

20-6 Cite the costs and benefits of holding inventories.

20-7 Compare the different techniques that firms use to make and receive payments.

20-8 Compare alternatives for investing idle cash and interpret interest rates in the money market.

20-9 Understand the principal sources of short-term loans.

RELATED WEBSITES FOR THIS CHAPTER CAN BE FOUND IN CONNECT.

Most of this book is devoted to long-term financial decisions such as capital budgeting and the choice of capital structure. In the previous chapter, we started our analysis of short-term planning decisions by looking at how firms ensure that they have enough cash to pay their bills. It is now time to look more closely at the management of short-term assets and liabilities, known collectively as *working capital.*

There are four principal types of current assets. All need to be managed. We begin with accounts receivable. Companies frequently sell goods on credit, so it may be weeks or even months before they receive payment. The unpaid bills show up in the balance sheet as accounts receivable. We will explain how the company's credit manager sets the terms of payment, decides which customers should be offered credit, and ensures that they pay promptly.

The second major short-term asset is inventory. To do business, firms need reserves of raw materials, work in progress, and finished goods. But these inventories can be expensive to store, and they tie up capital. Inventory management involves a trade-off between these costs and benefits. In manufacturing companies, the production manager is most likely to make this judgment without direct input from the financial manager. Therefore, we spend less time on this topic than on the management of the other components of working capital.

Our next task is to discuss the firm's cash balances. The first problem is to decide how much cash the firm should retain and, therefore, how much can be invested in interest-bearing securities. The second is to ensure that cash payments are handled efficiently. You want to collect payments as quickly as possible and put them to work earning interest. We will describe some of the techniques that firms use to move money around efficiently.

Managing the firm's cash is an important part of working capital management. Stowing it away in a large safe is not the answer. © *Ingram Publishing RF*

We describe some of the firm's choices for how to invest excess funds in a variety of short-term securities, which are the fourth major component of working capital.

Finally, we take a brief look at the sources of short-term borrowing, which constitutes an important short-term liability for many firms.

20.1 Working Capital

Short-term, or *current,* assets and liabilities are collectively known as *working capital.* Table 20.1 gives a breakdown of current assets and liabilities for all manufacturing corporations in the United States.

Components of Working Capital

Current Assets   One important current asset is *accounts receivable.* These consist of sales to other companies or to individuals that have not yet been paid for.

The second important current asset consists of *inventories* of raw materials, work in process, and finished goods. Table 20.1 shows that firms in the United States have roughly the same amount invested in inventories as in accounts receivable.

The remaining current assets consist largely of cash and marketable securities. The cash includes dollar bills, but most of the cash is in the form of bank deposits. Companies invest excess cash in a variety of short-term securities such as Treasury bills issued by the U.S. government.

Now take a look at Figure 20.1, which shows the relative importance of current assets in different industries. For example, current assets constitute almost half of total assets of aerospace companies while they account for less than 20% of the assets of drink and tobacco companies. For some companies, "current assets" means principally inventory; for others, it means accounts receivable or cash and securities. For example, you can see that inventory accounts for the majority of the current assets of retail firms, receivables are more important for aerospace companies, and cash and securities make up the bulk of the current assets of computer and electronics companies.

Current Liabilities   We have seen that a principal current asset for most companies consists of bills that have not yet been paid. Somebody's credit must be somebody else's debt. Therefore, it is not surprising that one of the main current liabilities is *accounts payable*—that is, outstanding payments that are due to other companies. The other major current liability consists of short-term borrowing.

Working Capital and the Cash Cycle

net working capital
Current assets minus current liabilities. Often called *working capital.*

The difference between current assets and current liabilities is known as **net working capital,** but financial managers often refer to the difference simply (but imprecisely) as *working capital.* Usually, current assets exceed current liabilities—that is, firms have positive net working capital. For U.S. manufacturing companies, current assets are, on average, about a third higher than current liabilities.

The working capital that a company needs depends on its business process. Consider a company, let's call it Digital Souvenirs, that makes small novelty items for gift shops. It buys raw materials, processes them into finished goods, and then sells these goods on credit. Figure 20.2 summarizes the whole cycle of its operations.

TABLE 20.1 Current assets and liabilities of U.S. manufacturing corporations, first quarter 2016 (figures in $ billions)

Current Assets		Current Liabilities	
Cash	$ 338	Short-term loans	$ 241
Marketable securities	170	Accounts payable	554
Accounts receivable	700	Accrued income tax	27
Inventories	791	Payments due on long-term debt	167
Other current assets	409	Other current liabilities	838
Total	$2,408	Total	$1,827

Source: U.S Department of Commerce, *Quarterly Financial Report for Manufacturing, Mining, Trade, and Selected Service Industries,* **https://www.census.gov/econ/qfr/mmws/current/qfr_pub.pdf.**

FIGURE 20.1 Current assets as a percentage of total assets in different industries

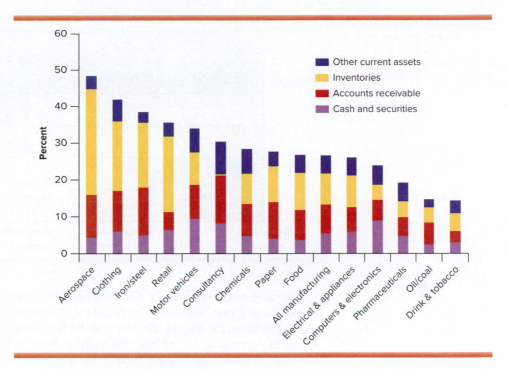

Source: U.S Department of Commerce, Quarterly Financial Report for Manufacturing, Mining, Trade, and Selected Service Industries, **https://www.census.gov/econ/qfr/mmws/current/qfr_pub.pdf.**

FIGURE 20.2 Simple cycle of the company's operations

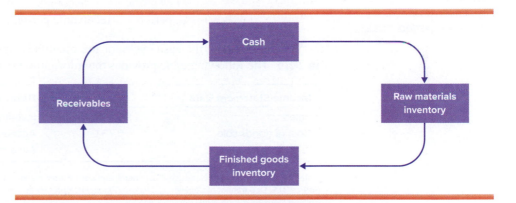

If you prepare Digital's balance sheet at the beginning of the process, you see cash (a current asset). If you delay a little, you find less cash: It has been spent on inventories of raw materials, which then give way to inventories of finished goods (also current assets). When the goods are sold, the inventories in turn give way to accounts receivable (another current asset), and finally, when the customers pay their bills, the firm takes out its profit and replenishes its cash balance.

At each stage in this process, Digital maintains an investment in working capital, even though the particular component of working capital may be changing. Figure 20.3 depicts four key dates in the production cycle that affect the amount of this investment. The delay between the initial investment in inventories and the final sales date is called the *inventory period* (or average days in inventory, a measure that should be familiar to you from Chapter 4). The delay between the time that the goods are sold and when the customers finally pay their bills is the *accounts receivable period* (or average collection period, another measure that should be familiar). The total length of time from the purchase of raw materials until the final payment by the customer is termed the *operating cycle:*

Operating cycle = inventory period + accounts receivable period

FIGURE 20.3 Digital's operating and cash cycle

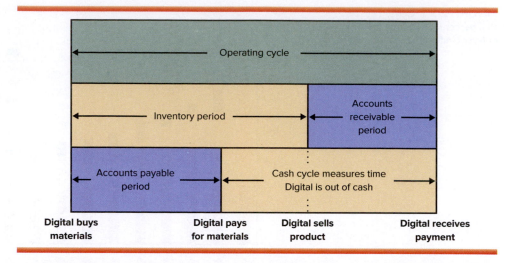

Digital is not out of cash for the entire operating cycle. Although the company starts by purchasing raw materials, it does not pay for them immediately. The longer that it defers payment, the shorter the time that the firm is out of cash. The interval between the firm's payment for its raw materials and the collection of payment from the customer is known as the **cash cycle** or **cash conversion period:**

cash cycle
Period between a firm's payment for materials and cash receipts from sales. Also called *cash conversion period.*

$$\text{Cash cycle} = \text{operating cycle} - \text{accounts payable period}$$

$$= \left(\begin{array}{c} \text{inventory} \\ \text{period} \end{array} + \begin{array}{c} \text{accounts} \\ \text{receivable period} \end{array} \right) - \begin{array}{c} \text{accounts payable} \\ \text{period} \end{array}$$

We can compute the cash cycle for the manufacturing sector in the United States in 2015. The following table provides the information that you need:

Income Statement Data		Balance Sheet Data	
Sales	$6,435	Inventory	$787
Cost of goods sold	5,731	Accounts receivable	705
		Accounts payable	566

Note: Cost of goods sold includes selling, general, and administrative expenses.
Source: U.S. Department of Commerce, *Quarterly Financial Report for Manufacturing, Mining, Trade, and Selected Service Industries,* June 2016, Tables 1.0 and 1.1.

There are three elements to the cash cycle:

$$\text{Inventory period} = \frac{\text{inventory}}{\text{annual cost of goods sold}/365} = \frac{787}{5,731/365} = 50.1 \text{ days}$$

$$\text{Accounts receivable period} = \frac{\text{accounts receivable}}{\text{annual sales}/365} = \frac{705}{6,435/365} = 40.0 \text{ days}$$

$$\text{Accounts payable period} = \frac{\text{accounts payable}}{\text{annual cost of goods sold}/365} = \frac{566}{5,731/365} = 36.0 \text{ days}$$

The cash cycle is

$$\begin{array}{c} \text{Inventory} \\ \text{period} \end{array} + \begin{array}{c} \text{accounts receivable} \\ \text{period} \end{array} - \begin{array}{c} \text{accounts payable} \\ \text{period} \end{array} = 50.1 + 40.0 - 36.0 = 54.1 \text{ days}$$

Therefore, it is taking U.S. corporations an average of nearly 8 weeks from the time that they lay out money on inventories to the time that they collect payment from their customers.

Of course, the cash cycle is much longer in some businesses than in others. For example, aerospace companies typically hold large inventories and offer long payment periods. Their cash cycle is nearly 6 months, and they need to make a substantial investment in net working capital. By contrast, many retail companies with their low investment in receivables have a cash cycle of just a few weeks. These companies often have negative net working capital.

BEYOND THE PAGE

The cash cycle

mhhe.com/brealey9e

20.1   Self-Test

a. Would you expect Tiffany, which sells fine jewelry, or Target, which sells a wide range of household goods at competitive prices, to have the longer cash cycle?

b. Use the following data to calculate the cash cycle of each firm (all values are in millions of dollars). What factor has the greatest impact on the difference in their cash cycles?

	Tiffany	Target
Sales	$4,248	$72,618
Cost of goods sold	1,713	51,278
Inventories	2,344	8,534
Accounts receivable	294	1,114
Accounts payable	366	11,244

We stated that the cash cycle depends on the firm's business, but this does not mean that it is cast in stone. Working capital can be *managed*. Therefore, it is now time to look more closely at the main items of working capital. We start with accounts receivable and move on to inventories, cash, and marketable securities. We conclude with a look at a major current liability, short-term debt.

20.2   Accounts Receivable and Credit Policy

We start our tour of current assets with the firm's accounts receivable. When one company sells goods to another, it does not usually expect to be paid immediately. The unpaid bills, or **trade credit,** compose the bulk of accounts receivable. The remainder is made up of **consumer credit,** bills awaiting payment by the final customer.

Credit management involves the following five steps:

trade credit
Bills awaiting payment from one company to another.

consumer credit
Bills awaiting payment from the final customer to a company.

1. You must establish the terms of sale on which you propose to sell your goods. For example, how long will you give customers to pay their bills? Will you offer a discount for immediate payment?
2. You must decide what evidence you require that the customer owes you money. For example, is a signed receipt enough, or do you insist on a formal IOU?
3. You need to work out which customers are likely to pay their bills. This is called *credit analysis.*
4. You must decide on credit policy. How much credit will you extend to each customer? How much risk are you prepared to take on marginally creditworthy prospects?
5. Finally, you have to collect the money when it becomes due. What do you do about reluctant payers or deadbeats?

We discuss these topics in turn.

Terms of Sale

Whenever you sell goods, you need to set the **terms of sale.** For example, if you are supplying goods to a wide variety of irregular customers, you may require cash on delivery (COD). And if you are producing goods to the customer's specification or incurring heavy delivery costs, then it may be sensible to ask for cash before delivery (CBD).

In many other cases, payment is not made until after delivery, so the buyer receives *credit.* Each industry seems to have its own typical credit arrangements. These have a rough logic. For example, the seller will naturally demand earlier payment if its customers are financially less secure, if their accounts are small, or if the goods are perishable or quickly resold.

When you buy goods on credit, the supplier will state a final payment date. To encourage you to pay *before* the final date, the seller will often offer a cash discount for prompt settlement. For example, a manufacturer may require payment within 30 days but give a 5% discount to customers who pay within 10 days. These terms would be referred to as 5/10, net 30:

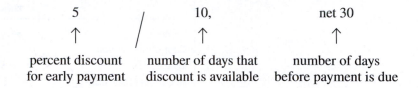

Similarly, if a firm sells goods on terms of 2/30, net 60, customers receive a 2% discount for payment within 30 days or else must pay in full within 60 days. If the terms are simply net 30, then customers must pay within 30 days of the invoice date and no discounts are offered for early payment.

20.2   Self-Test

Suppose that a firm sells goods on terms of 2/10, net 20. On May 1, you buy goods from the company with an invoice value of $20,000. How much would you need to pay if you took the cash discount? What is the latest date on which the cash discount is available? By what date should you pay for your purchase if you decide not to take the cash discount?

For many items that are bought regularly, it is inconvenient to require separate payment for each delivery. A common solution is to pretend that all sales during the month in fact occur at the end of the month (EOM). Thus, goods may be sold on terms of net 10 EOM. In this case, the customer needs to pay within 10 days of the end of the month.

A firm that buys on credit is, in effect, borrowing from its supplier. It saves cash today but will have to pay later. This is an implicit loan from the supplier. Of course, if it is free, a loan is always worth having. But if you pass up a cash discount, then the loan may prove to be very expensive. For example, a customer who buys on terms of 3/10, net 30, may decide to forgo the cash discount and pay on the 30th day. The customer obtains an extra 20 days' credit by deferring payment from 10 to 30 days after the sale but pays about 3% more for the goods. This is equivalent to borrowing money at a rate of 74.3% a year. To see why, consider an order of $100. If the firm pays within 10 days, it gets a 3% discount and pays only $97. If it waits the full 30 days, it pays $100. The extra 20 days of credit increase the payment by the fraction 3/97 = .0309, or 3.09%. Therefore, the implicit interest charged to extend the trade credit is 3.09% *per 20 days*. There are 365/20 = 18.25 twenty-day periods in a year, so the effective annual rate of interest on the loan is $(1.0309)^{18.25} - 1 = .743$, or 74.3%.

The general formula for calculating the implicit annual interest rate for customers who do not take the cash discount is

$$\text{Effective annual rate} = \left(1 + \frac{\text{discount}}{\text{discounted price}}\right)^{365/\text{extra days credit}} - 1 \qquad \textbf{(20.1)}$$

The discount divided by the discounted price is the percentage increase in price paid by a customer who forgoes the discount. In our example, with terms of 3/10, net 30, the percentage increase in price is 3/97 = .0309, or 3.09%. This is the implicit rate of interest *per period*. The period of the loan is the number of extra days of credit that you can obtain by forgoing the discount. In our example, this is 20 days. To annualize this rate, we compound the per-period rate by the number of periods in a year.

Of course, any firm that delays payment beyond day 30 gains a cheaper loan but damages its reputation for creditworthiness.

Example **20.1** ▶   Trade Credit Rates

What is the implied interest rate on trade credit if the discount for early payment is 5/10, net 60?

The cash discount in this case is 5% and customers who choose not to take the discount receive an extra 60 − 10 = 50 days credit. So the effective annual interest is

$$\text{Effective annual rate} = \left(1 + \frac{\text{discount}}{\text{discounted price}}\right)^{365/\text{extra days credit}} - 1$$

$$= \left(1 + \frac{5}{95}\right)^{365/50} - 1 = .454, \text{or } 45.4\%$$

In this case, the customer who does not take the discount is effectively borrowing money at an annual interest rate of 45.4%. ■

You might wonder why the effective interest rate on trade credit is typically so high. At such steep effective rates, most purchasers will choose to pay early and receive the discount. Those who don't are probably strapped for cash. It makes sense to charge these firms a high rate of interest.

20.3 **Self-Test**

What would be the effective annual interest rate in Example 20.1 if the terms of sale were 5/10, net 50? Why is the rate higher?

Credit Agreements

open account
Agreement whereby sales on credit are made with no formal debt contract.

The terms of sale define the amount of any credit but not the nature of the contract. Repetitive sales are almost always made on **open account** and involve only an implicit contract. There is simply a record in the seller's books and a receipt signed by the buyer.

Sometimes, you might want a clear commitment from the buyer before you deliver the goods. In this case, the common procedure is to arrange a *commercial draft.* This is simply jargon for an order to pay.[1] It works as follows: The seller prepares a draft ordering payment by the customer and sends this draft to the customer's bank. If immediate payment is required, the draft is termed a *sight draft;* otherwise, it is known as a *time draft.* Depending on whether it is a sight or a time draft, the customer either tells the bank to pay up or acknowledges the debt by adding the word "accepted" and a signature. Once accepted, a time draft is like a postdated check and is called a *trade acceptance.* This trade acceptance is then forwarded to the seller, who holds it until the payment becomes due.

If your customer's credit is shaky, you may ask the customer to arrange for a bank to accept the time draft. In this case, the bank guarantees the customer's debt, and the draft is called a *banker's acceptance.* Banker's acceptances are often used in overseas trade. They are actively bought and sold in the money market, the market for short-term high-quality debt.

Credit Analysis

credit analysis
Procedure to determine the likelihood a customer will pay its bills.

Credit analysis seeks to judge whether customers are likely to pay their debts. The most obvious indication is whether they have paid promptly in the past. Prompt payment is usually a good omen, but beware of the customer who establishes a high credit limit on the basis of small payments and then disappears, leaving you with a large unpaid bill.

If you are dealing with a new customer, you will probably check with a credit agency. Dun & Bradstreet, which is by far the largest of these agencies, provides credit ratings on a huge number of domestic and foreign firms. In addition to its rating service, Dun & Bradstreet provides on request a full credit report on a potential customer.

Credit agencies usually report the experience that other firms have had with your customer, but you can also get this information by contacting these firms directly or through a credit bureau.

Your bank can also make a credit check. It will contact the customer's bank and ask for information on the customer's average bank balance, access to bank credit, and general reputation.

In addition to checking with your customer's bank, it might make sense to discover what everybody else in the financial community thinks about your customer's credit standing. Does that sound expensive? Not if your customer is a public company. You just look at the Moody's or Standard & Poor's rating for the customer's bonds.[2] You can also compare prices of these bonds with the prices of other firms' bonds. (Of course, the comparisons should be between bonds of similar maturity, coupon, and so on.)

If you don't wish to rely on the judgment of others, you can do your own homework. Ideally, this would involve a detailed analysis of the company's business prospects and financing, but this is usually too expensive. Therefore, credit analysts concentrate on the company's financial statements, using rough rules of thumb to judge whether the firm is a good credit risk. The rules of thumb are based on *financial ratios.* Chapter 4 described how these ratios are calculated and interpreted.

Numerical Credit Scoring   Analyzing credit risk is like detective work. You have a lot of clues—some important, some fitting into a neat pattern, others contradictory. You must weigh these clues to come up with an overall judgment.

---

[1] For example, a check is an example of a draft. Whenever you write a check, you are ordering the bank to make a payment.

[2] We described bond ratings in Chapter 6, Section 6.6.

When the firm has a small, regular clientele, the credit manager can easily handle the process informally and make a judgment about what are often termed the *five Cs of credit:*

1. The customer's *character.*
2. The customer's *capacity* to pay.
3. The customer's *capital.*
4. The *collateral* provided by the customer.[3]
5. The *condition* of the customer's business.

When the company is dealing directly with consumers or with a large number of small trade accounts, some streamlining is essential. In these cases, it may make sense to use a scoring system to prescreen credit applications.

If you apply for a credit card or a bank loan, you will probably be asked to complete a questionnaire that provides details about your job, home, and financial health. This information is then used to calculate an overall credit score.[4] If you do not make the grade on the score, you are likely to be refused credit or subjected to a more detailed analysis. In a similar way, banks and the credit departments of industrial firms also use mechanical credit-scoring systems to assess the financial health of potential commercial customers.

Suppose that you are given the task of developing a credit-scoring system that will help to decide when it makes sense to extend credit to the firm's customers. You start by comparing the financial statements of companies that went bankrupt over a 40-year period with those of surviving firms. Figure 20.4 shows what you find. Panel *a* illustrates that, as early as 4 years before they went bankrupt, failing firms were earning a much lower return on assets (ROA) than survivors. Panel *b* shows that on average they also had a high ratio of liabilities to assets, and panel *c* shows that EBITDA (earnings before interest, taxes, depreciation, and amortization) was low relative to the firms' total liabilities. Thus, bankrupt firms were less profitable (low ROA), were more highly leveraged (high ratio of liabilities to assets), and generated relatively little cash (low ratio of EBITDA to liabilities). In each case, these indicators of the firms' financial health steadily deteriorated as bankruptcy approached.

Rather than focusing on individual ratios, it makes more sense to combine the ratios into a single score. Banks and consultancies have employed a variety of statistical techniques to develop a combined credit score. For example, an early and still widely used approach, the Z-score model developed by Edward Altman, uses multiple discriminant analysis to separate the creditworthy sheep from the impecunious goats.[5]

The Credit Decision

credit policy
Standards set to determine the amount and nature of credit to extend to customers.

You have taken the first three steps toward an effective credit operation. In other words, you have fixed your terms of sale, you have decided whether to sell on open account or to ask your customers to sign an IOU, and you have established a procedure for estimating the probability that each customer will pay up. Your next step is to decide on **credit policy.**

---

[3] For example, the customer can offer bonds as collateral. These bonds can then be seized by the seller if the customer fails to pay.

[4] The most commonly used consumer credit score is the FICO score developed by Fair Isaac Corp., which uses data provided by any one of three credit bureaus—Experian, TransUnion, or Equifax.

[5] See E. I. Altman, "Financial Ratios and the Prediction of Corporate Bankruptcy," *Journal of Finance* 23 (September 1968), pp. 589–609.

FIGURE 20.4 Financial ratios of failing and nonfailing firms

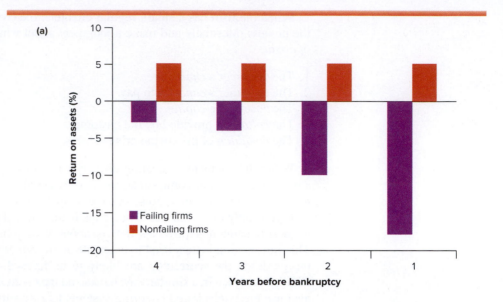

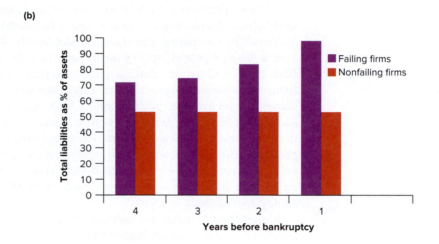

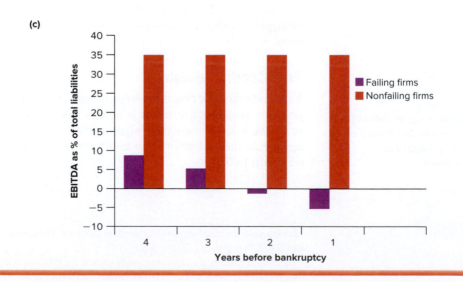

Source: W. H. Beaver, M. F. McNichols, and J.-W. Rhie, "Have Financial Statements Become Less Informative? Evidence from the Ability of Financial Ratios to Predict Bankruptcy," *Review of Accounting Studies* 10 (2005), pp. 93–122.

FIGURE 20.5 If you refuse credit, you make neither profit nor loss. If you offer credit, there is a probability p that the customer will pay and you will make REV − COST and there is a probability $(1 − p)$ that the customer will default and you will lose COST.

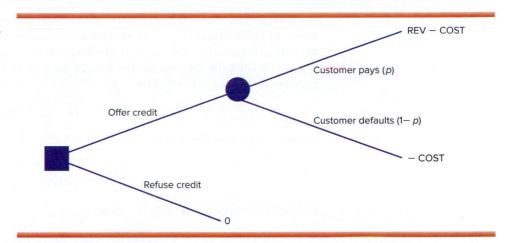

If there is no possibility of repeat orders, the credit decision is relatively simple. Figure 20.5 summarizes your choice. On the one hand, you can refuse credit and pass up the sale. In this case, you make neither profit nor loss. The alternative is to offer credit. If you offer credit and the customer pays, you benefit by the profit margin on the sale. If the customer defaults, you lose the cost of the goods delivered. **The decision to offer credit depends on the probability of payment. You should grant credit if the expected profit from doing so is greater than the profit from refusing.**

Suppose that the probability that the customer will pay up is p. If the customer does pay, you receive additional revenues (REV) and you deliver goods that you incurred costs to produce; your net gain is the present value of REV − COST. Unfortunately, you can't be certain that the customer will pay; there is a probability $(1 − p)$ of default. Default means you receive nothing but still incur the additional costs of the delivered goods. The *expected profit*[6] from the two sources of action is therefore as follows:

Action	Expected Profit
Refuse credit:	0
Grant credit:	$p \times \text{PV(REV} - \text{COST)} - (1 - p) \times \text{PV(COST)}$

You should grant credit if the expected profit from doing so is positive.

Example 20.2 ▶   **The Credit Decision**

Consider the case of the Cast Iron Company. On each nondelinquent sale, Cast Iron receives revenues with a present value of $1,200 and incurs costs with a present value of $1,000. Therefore, the company's expected profit if it offers credit is

$$p \times \text{PV(REV} - \text{COST)} - (1 - p) \times \text{PV(COST)} = p \times 200 - (1 - p) \times 1{,}000$$

If the probability of collection is 5/6, Cast Iron can expect to break even:

$$\text{Expected profit} = 5/6 \times 200 - (1 - 5/6) \times 1{,}000 = 0$$

Thus, Cast Iron's policy should be to grant credit whenever the chances of collection are better than 5 out of 6. ■

---

[6] Notice that we use the present values of costs and revenues. This is because there sometimes are significant lags between costs incurred and revenues generated. Also, while we follow convention in referring to the "expected profit" of the decision, it should be clear that our equation for expected profit is in fact the net present value of the decision to grant credit. As we emphasized in Chapter 1, the manager's task is to add value, not to maximize accounting profits.

In this last example, the net present value of granting credit is positive if the probability of collection exceeds 5/6. In general, this break-even probability can be found by setting the net present value of granting credit equal to zero and solving for p. It turns out that the formula for the break-even probability is simply the ratio of the present value of costs to revenues:

$$p \times PV(REV - COST) - (1 - p) \times PV(COST) = 0$$

Break-even probability of collection, then, is

$$p = \frac{PV(COST)}{PV(REV)}$$

and the break-even probability of *default* is

$$(1 - p) = 1 - PV(COST)/PV(REV) = PV(PROFIT)/PV(REV)$$

In other words, the break-even probability of default is simply the profit margin on each sale. If the default probability is larger than the profit margin, you should not extend credit.

Think what this implies. Companies that operate on low profit margins should be cautious about granting credit to high-risk customers. Firms with high margins can afford to deal with more doubtful ones.

20.4   Self-Test

What is the break-even probability of collection if the present value of the revenues from the sale is $1,100 rather than $1,200? Why does the break-even probability increase? Use your answer to decide whether firms that sell high-profit-margin or low-margin goods should be more willing to issue credit.

So far, we have ignored the possibility of repeat orders. But one of the reasons for offering credit today is that you may get yourself a good, regular customer.

Suppose Cast Iron has been asked to extend credit to a new customer. You can find little information on the firm, and you believe that the probability of payment is no better than .8. If you grant credit, the expected profit on this order is negative:

$$\text{Expected profit on initial order} = p \times PV(REV - COST) - (1 - p) \times PV(COST)$$
$$= (.8 \times 200) - (.2 \times 1,000) = -\$40$$

You decide to refuse credit. This is the correct decision *if* there is no chance of a repeat order. But now consider future periods. If the customer does pay up, there will be a reorder next year. Having paid once, the customer will seem less of a risk. For this reason, any repeat order may be very profitable.

Think back to Chapter 10, and you will recognize that the credit decision bears many similarities to our earlier discussion of real options. By granting credit now, the firm retains the option to grant credit on an entire sequence of potentially profitable repeat sales. This option can be very valuable and can tilt the decision toward granting credit. Even a dubious prospect may warrant some initial credit if there is a chance that the company will develop into a profitable steady customer.

Example	20.3 ▶	Credit Decisions with Repeat Orders

To illustrate, let's look at an extreme case. Suppose that if a customer pays up on the first sale, you can be *sure* you will have a regular and completely reliable customer. In this case, the value of such a customer is not the profit on one order but an entire stream of profits from repeat purchases.

For example, suppose that the customer will make one purchase each year from Cast Iron. If the discount rate is 10% and the profit on each order is $200 a year, then the present value of a perpetual stream of business from a good customer is not $200 but $200/.10 = $2,000. There is a probability p that Cast Iron will secure a good customer with a value of $2,000. There is a probability of $(1 - p)$ that the customer will default, resulting in a loss of $1,000. So, once we recognize the benefits of securing a good and permanent customer, the expected profit from granting credit is

$$\text{Expected profit} = (p \times 2,000) - (1 - p) \times 1,000$$

This is positive for any probability of collection above .33. Thus the break-even probability falls from 5/6 to 1/3. **If one sale may lead to profitable repeat sales, the firm should be more inclined to grant credit on the initial purchase.** ∎

20.5 Self-Test

How will the break-even probability vary with the discount rate? Try a rate of 20% in Example 20.3. What is the intuition behind your answer?

Of course, real-life situations are generally far more complex than our simple examples. Customers are not all good or all bad. Many pay late consistently; you get your money, but it costs more to collect and you lose a few months' interest. And estimating the probability that a customer will pay up is far from an exact science. Then there is uncertainty about repeat sales. There may be a good chance that the customer will give you further business, but you can't be sure of that and you can't know for how long she or he will continue to buy from you.

Like almost all financial decisions, credit allocation involves a strong dose of judgment. Our examples are intended as reminders of the issues involved rather than as cookbook formulas. Here are the basic things to remember:

1. *Maximize profit.* As credit manager, your job is not to minimize the number of bad accounts; it is to maximize profits. You are faced with a trade-off. The best that can happen is that the customer pays promptly; the worst is default. In the one case, the firm receives the full additional revenues from the sale less the additional costs; in the other, it receives nothing and loses the costs. You must weigh the chances of these alternative outcomes. If the margin of profit is high, you are justified in a liberal credit policy; if it is low, you cannot afford many bad debts.

2. *Concentrate on the dangerous accounts.* You should not expend the same effort on analyzing all credit decisions. If an application is small or clear-cut, your decision should be largely routine; if it is large or doubtful, you may do better to move straight to a detailed credit appraisal. Most credit managers don't make credit decisions on an order-by-order basis. Instead, they set a credit limit for each customer. The sales representative is required to refer the order for approval only if the customer exceeds this limit.

3. *Look beyond the immediate order.* Sometimes it may be worth accepting a relatively poor risk as long as there is a likelihood that the customer will grow into a regular and reliable buyer. (This is why credit card companies are eager to sign up college students even though few students can point to an established credit history.) New businesses must be prepared to incur more bad debts than established businesses because they have not yet formed relationships with low-risk customers. This is part of the cost of building up a good customer list.

Collection Policy

It would be nice if all customers paid their bills by the due date. But they don't, and since you may also "stretch" your payables from time to time, you can't altogether blame them.

Slow payers impose two costs on the firm. First, they require the firm to spend more resources in collecting payments. They also force the firm to invest more in working capital. Recall from Chapter 4 that accounts receivable are proportional to the average collection period (also known as days' sales in receivables):

$$\text{Accounts receivable} = \text{daily sales} \times \text{average collection period}$$

collection policy
Procedures to collect and
monitor receivables.

When your customers stretch payables, you end up with a longer collection period and a greater investment in accounts receivable. That's why you need a **collection policy.**

The credit manager keeps a record of payment experiences with each customer. In addition, the manager monitors overdue payments by drawing up a schedule of the aging of receivables. The **aging schedule** classifies accounts receivable by the length of time they are outstanding. This may look roughly like Table 20.2. The table shows that customer A, for example, is fully current: There are no bills outstanding for more than a month. Customer Z, however, might present problems, as there are $15,000 in bills that have been outstanding for more than 3 months.

aging schedule
Classification of accounts
receivable by time
outstanding.

20.6   Self-Test

Suppose a customer who buys goods on terms 1/10, net 45, always forgoes the cash discount and pays on the 45th day after sale. If the firm typically buys $10,000 of goods a month, spread evenly over the month, what will the aging schedule look like?

TABLE 20.2 An aging schedule of receivables

Customer's Name	Less than 1 Month	1–2 Months	2–3 Months	More than 3 Months	Total Owed
A	$ 10,000	$ 0	$ 0	$ 0	$ 10,000
B	8,000	3,000	0	0	11,000
.	.	.	.	.	.
.	.	.	.	.	.
.	.	.	.	.	.
Z	5,000	4,000	6,000	15,000	30,000
Total	$200,000	$40,000	$15,000	$43,000	$298,000

When a customer is in arrears, the usual procedure is to send a *statement of account* and to follow this at intervals with increasingly insistent emails, letters, or telephone calls. If none of these has any effect, most companies turn the debt over to a collection agency or an attorney.

Large firms can reap economies of scale in record keeping, billing, and so on, but the small firm may not be able to support a fully fledged credit operation. However, it can obtain some scale economies by farming out part of the job to a *factor*. The factor and its client's firm agree on credit limits for each customer, and the client notifies each customer that the factor has purchased the debt (i.e., the trade credit). The factor then takes on the responsibility (and risk) of collecting the bills and pays the invoice value to the client minus a fee of 1% or 2%. Factoring not only saves companies the chore of collecting their debts; by providing funds up-front, it can also offer a valuable source of short-term capital.

Factoring is fairly prevalent in Europe but accounts for only a small proportion of debt collection in the United States. It is most common in industries such as clothing and toys. These are characterized by many small producers and retailers that do not have long-term relationships with each other. Because a factor may be employed by a number of manufacturers, it sees a larger proportion of the transactions than any single firm and, therefore, is better placed to judge the creditworthiness of each customer.[7]

There is always a potential conflict of interest between the collection department and the sales department. Sales representatives commonly complain that they no sooner win new customers than the collection department frightens them off with threatening letters. The collection manager, on the other hand, bemoans the fact that the sales force is concerned only with winning orders and does not care whether the goods are subsequently paid for. This conflict is another example of the agency problem introduced in Chapter 1. **Good collection policy balances conflicting goals. The company wants cordial relations with its customers. It also wants them to pay their bills on time.**

There are instances of cooperation between sales managers and the financial managers who worry about collections. For example, the specialty chemicals division of a major pharmaceutical company actually made a business loan to an important customer that had been suddenly cut off by its bank. The pharmaceutical company bet that it knew its customer better than the customer's bank did—and the pharmaceutical company was right. The customer arranged alternative bank financing, paid back the pharmaceutical company, and became an even more loyal customer. It was a nice example of financial management supporting sales.

It is not common for suppliers to make business loans in this way, but they lend money *indirectly* whenever they allow a delay in payment. Trade credit can be an important source of funds for indigent customers that cannot obtain a bank loan. But that raises an important question: If the bank is unwilling to lend, does it make sense for you, the supplier, to continue to extend trade credit? Here are two possible reasons that it may make sense: First, as in the case of our pharmaceutical company, you may have more information than the bank about the customer's business. Second, you need to look beyond the immediate transaction and recognize that your firm may stand to lose some profitable future sales if the customer goes out of business.[8]

---

[7] This point is made in S. L. Mian and C. W. Smith, Jr., "Accounts Receivable Management Policy: Theory and Evidence," *Journal of Finance* 47 (March 1992), pp. 169–200.

[8] Of course, banks also need to recognize the possibility of continuing business from the firm. The question, therefore, is whether suppliers have a *greater* stake in the firm's continuing prosperity. For some evidence on the determinants of the supply and demand for trade credit, see M. A. Petersen and R. G. Rajan, "Trade Credit: Theories and Evidence," *Review of Financial Studies* 10 (Fall 1997), pp. 661–692.

20.3 Inventory Management

The second important current asset is *inventory*. Inventories may consist of raw materials, work in process, or finished goods awaiting sale and shipment. Firms are not obliged to carry these inventories. For example, they could buy materials day by day, as needed. But then they would pay higher prices for ordering in small lots, and they would risk production delays if the materials were not delivered on time. They can avoid that risk by ordering more than the firm's immediate needs. Similarly, firms could do away with inventories of finished goods by producing only what they expect to sell tomorrow. But this also could be a dangerous strategy. A producer with only a small inventory of finished goods is more likely to be caught short and unable to fill orders if demand is unexpectedly high. Moreover, a large inventory of finished goods may allow longer, more economical production runs.

But there are also costs to holding inventories that must be set against these benefits. These are called *carrying costs*. For example, money tied up in inventories does not earn interest; storage and insurance must be paid for; and there may be a risk of spillage or obsolescence. Therefore, production managers need to strike a sensible balance between the benefits of holding inventory and the costs.

Example 20.4 ▶   Inventory Management

BEYOND THE PAGE

How Akron's inventory costs change with order size

mhhe.com/brealey9e

Here is a simple inventory problem. Akron Wire Products uses 255,000 tons a year of wire rod. Suppose that it orders Q tons at a time from the manufacturer. Just before delivery, its inventories of wire have run down to zero. Just *after* delivery, it has an inventory of Q tons. Thus, Akron's inventory of wire rod roughly follows the sawtooth pattern in Figure 20.6.

There are two costs to holding this inventory. First, there are carrying costs, such as the cost of storage, and the opportunity cost of the capital that is tied up in inventory. Suppose these costs work out to an annual figure of about $55 per ton. The second type of cost is the order cost. Each order that Akron places with the manufacturer involves a fixed handling and delivery charge of $450.

Here, then, is the kernel of the inventory problem: As Akron increases its order size, the number of orders falls but average inventory rises. Figure 20.7 shows that cost related to the number of orders declines, though at a decreasing rate, while carrying cost related to inventory size rises. It is worth increasing order size as long as the decline in order cost outweighs the rise in carrying cost. The optimal inventory policy is one in

---

FIGURE 20.6 A simple inventory rule. The company waits until inventories of materials are exhausted and then reorders a constant quantity.

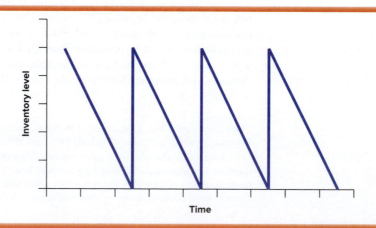

FIGURE 20.7 As the inventory order size increases, order costs fall and inventory carrying costs rise. Total costs are minimized when the saving in order costs equals the increase in carrying costs.

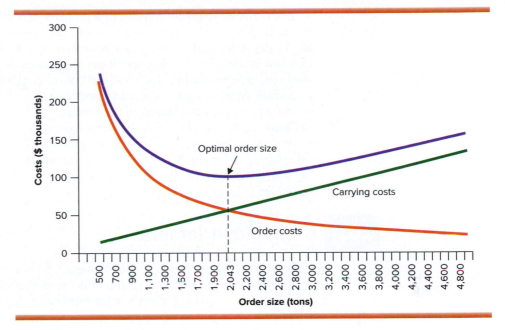

which these two effects exactly offset each other. In our example, this occurs when the firm places about 250 orders a year (roughly one order every working day) and the size of each order is $Q = 2,043$ tons. The optimal order size (2,043 tons in our example) is known as the *economic order quantity*, or *EOQ*.[9] ∎

In calculating the economic order quantity for Akron Wire, we made several unrealistic assumptions. For instance, most firms do not use up their inventory of raw material at a constant rate, and they would not wait until stocks had completely run out before replenishing them. But this simple model does capture some essential features of inventory management:

- Optimal inventory levels involve a trade-off between carrying costs and order costs.
- Carrying costs include the cost of storing goods as well as the cost of capital tied up in inventory.
- A firm can manage its inventories by waiting until they reach some minimum level and then replenishing them by ordering a predetermined quantity.
- When carrying costs are high and order costs are low, it makes sense to place more frequent orders and maintain lower levels of inventory. If order costs are high, you will want to make larger and therefore less frequent orders.
- Inventory levels do not rise in direct proportion to sales. As sales increase, the optimal inventory level rises, but less than proportionately.

just-in-time approach
System of inventory management that requires minimum inventories of materials and very frequent deliveries by suppliers.

Corporations today get by with lower levels of inventory than they used to. Thirty years ago, inventories held by U.S. companies accounted for 12% of firm assets. Today, the figure is a little over 8%. One way that companies have reduced inventory levels is by moving to a **just-in-time approach.** Just-in-time was pioneered by Toyota

---

[9] When the firm uses up materials at a constant rate, as in our example, there is a simple formula for calculating the economic order quantity (EOQ). It is

$$\text{Optimal order size} = Q = \sqrt{\frac{2 \times \text{sales} \times \text{cost per order}}{\text{carrying cost}}}$$

In our example, $Q = \sqrt{\dfrac{2 \times 255,000 \times 450}{55}} = 2,043$ tons.

in Japan. Toyota keeps inventories of auto parts to a minimum by ordering supplies only as they are needed. Thus, deliveries of components to its plants are made throughout the day at intervals as short as 1 hour. Toyota is able to operate successfully with such low inventories only because it has a set of plans to ensure that strikes, traffic snarl-ups, or other hazards don't halt the flow of components and bring production to a standstill. Many companies in the United States have learned from Toyota's example and have pared their investment in inventories.

Firms are also finding that they can reduce their inventories of finished goods by producing their goods to order. For example, Dell Computer discovered that it did not need to keep a large stock of finished machines. Its customers are able to use the Internet to specify what features they want on their PC. The computer is then assembled to order and shipped to the customer.[10]

20.4 Cash Management

Short-term securities pay interest; cash doesn't. So why do corporations and individuals hold billions of dollars in cash and demand deposits? Why, for example, don't you take all *your* cash and invest it in interest-bearing securities? The answer of course is that cash gives you more *liquidity* than do securities. You can use it to buy things. It is hard enough to get New York cab drivers to give you change for a $20 bill, but try asking them to split a Treasury bill.

When you have only a small proportion of your wealth in cash, a little extra can be extremely useful; when you have a substantial holding, any additional liquidity is not worth much. Therefore, as financial manager, you want to hold cash balances up to the point where the marginal value of the liquidity is equal to the value of the interest forgone.

In choosing between cash and short-term securities, the financial manager faces a task like that of the production manager. After all, cash is just another raw material that you need to do business, and there are costs and benefits to holding large "inventories" of cash. If the cash were invested in securities, it would earn interest. On the other hand, you can't use those securities to pay the firm's bills. If you had to sell them every time you needed to pay a bill, you could incur heavy transaction costs. The financial manager must trade off the cost of keeping an inventory of cash (the lost interest) against the benefits (the saving on transaction costs).

For very large firms, the transaction costs of buying and selling securities are trivial compared with the opportunity cost of holding idle cash balances. Suppose that the interest rate is 3% per year, or roughly $3/365 = .0082\%$ per day. Then the daily interest earned on $1 million is $.000082 \times \$1,000,000 = \$82$. Even at a cost of $50 per transaction, which is generous, it pays to buy Treasury bills today and sell them tomorrow rather than to leave $1 million idle overnight.

A corporation such as Walmart, with nearly $500 billion of annual sales, has an average daily cash flow of $\$500,000,000,000/365 = \$1,370$ million. Firms of this size end up buying or selling securities once a day, every day, unless by chance they have only a small positive cash balance at the end of the day.

Banks have developed a variety of ways to help such firms invest idle cash. For example, they may provide *sweep programs,* in which the bank automatically "sweeps" surplus funds into a higher-interest account. Why then do these large firms hold any significant amounts of cash in non-interest-bearing accounts? For two reasons: First, cash may be left in accounts to compensate banks for the

---

[10] These examples of just-in-time and build-to-order production are taken from T. Murphy, "JIT When ASAP Isn't Good Enough," *Ward's Auto World,* May 1999, pp. 67–73; R. Schreffler, "Alive and Well," *Ward's Auto World,* May 1999, pp. 73–77; "A Long March: Mass Customization," *The Economist,* July 14, 2001, pp. 63–65.

services they provide. Second, large corporations may have literally hundreds of accounts with dozens of different banks. It is often less expensive to leave idle cash in some of these accounts than to monitor each account daily and make daily transfers between them.

One major reason for the proliferation of bank accounts is decentralized management. If you give a subsidiary operating freedom to manage its own affairs, you must also give it the right to spend and receive cash. Good cash management nevertheless implies some degree of centralization. You cannot maintain your desired inventory of cash if all the subsidiaries in the group are responsible for their own private pools of cash. And you certainly want to avoid situations in which one subsidiary is investing its spare cash at 3% while another is borrowing at 5%. It is not surprising, therefore, that even in highly decentralized companies there is generally central control over cash balances and bank relations.

Check Handling and Float

Traditionally, most large bills in the United States have been paid with checks. But check handling is a cumbersome and labor-intensive task, and it can take several days for a check to clear. Suppose, for example, that you renew your auto insurance by writing a check for $600, which you mail to your insurance company. A day or so later, the insurance company receives your check and deposits it in its bank account. But this money isn't available to the company immediately. The company's bank won't actually have the money in hand until it sends the check to your bank and receives payment. Because the bank has to wait, it makes the insurance company wait, too— usually 1 or 2 business days. Until the check has been presented and cleared, that $600 will continue to sit in your bank account.

Checks that have been mailed but not yet cleared are known as *float*. In our example, float provided you with an extra $600 in your bank account while your check went first to the insurance company, then to the company's bank, and finally to your own bank. This may make float seem like a marvelous invention, but unfortunately, it can also work in reverse. Every time someone writes *you* a check, you have to wait several days after depositing it before you may spend the money.

Changes in federal law in the last several years have helped to speed up collections. The Check Clearing for the 21st Century Act, usually known as "Check 21," allows banks to send digital images of checks to one another rather than sending the checks themselves. So cargo planes and trucks no longer need to crisscross the country to take bundles of checks from one bank to another. The cost of processing checks is also being reduced by a technological innovation known as *check conversion*. In this case, when you write a check, the details of your bank account and the amount of the payment are automatically captured at the point of sale, your check is handed back to you, and your bank account is immediately debited.

concentration account
Customers make payments to a regional collection center, which then transfers funds to an account at a principal bank.

Firms that receive a large volume of paper checks have devised a number of ways to ensure that the cash becomes available as quickly as possible. For example, a retail chain may arrange for each branch to deposit receipts in a collection account at a local bank. Surplus funds are then periodically transferred electronically to a **concentration account** at one of the company's principal banks. There are two reasons that concentration banking allows the company to gain quicker use of its funds. First, because the store is nearer to the bank, transfer times are reduced. Second, because the customer's check is likely to be drawn on a local bank, the time taken to clear the check is also reduced.

lock-box system
System whereby customers send payments to a post-office box and a local bank collects and processes checks.

Concentration banking is often combined with a **lock-box system.** In this case, the firm's customers are instructed to send their payments to a regional post-office box. The local bank then takes on the administrative chore of emptying the box and depositing the checks in the company's local deposit account.

Example 20.5 ▶   Lock-Box Systems

Suppose that you are thinking of opening a lock box. The local bank shows you a map of mail delivery times. From that and knowledge of your customers' locations, you come up with the following data:

Average number of daily payments to lock box = 150
Average size of payment   = $1,200
Rate of interest *per day*   = .02%
Saving in mailing time   = 1.2 days
Saving in processing time   = .8 day

On this basis, the lock box would reduce float by

150 items per day × $1,200 per item × (1.2 + .8) days saved = $360,000

Invested at .02% per day, that gives a daily return of

$$.0002 \times \$360,000 = \$72$$

The bank's charge for operating the lock-box system depends on the number of checks processed. Suppose that the bank charges $.26 per check. That works out to 150 × $.26 = $39 per day. You are ahead by $72 − $39 = $33 per day, plus whatever your firm saves from not having to process the checks itself. ■

20.7   Self-Test

How will the following conditions affect the price that a firm should be willing to pay for a lock-box service?

a. The average size of its payments increases.
b. The number of payments per day increases (with no change in average size of payments).
c. The interest rate increases.
d. The average mail time saved by the lock-box system increases.
e. The processing time saved by the lock-box system increases.

Other Payment Systems

Checks are not the only way to pay for larger purchases or send payments to another location. Some of the more important payment methods are set out in Table 20.3.

Figure 20.8 compares use of these payment systems around the world. Payment patterns vary widely across countries. For example, look at the bottom (orange) portion of the bars in the figure. Checks are virtually unheard of in Sweden and Switzerland. Most payments there are made by debit cards or credit transfer. By contrast, the French and Americans love to write checks. Each year, U.S. individuals and firms write about 14 billion checks. But even in the United States, check writing is steadily giving way to electronic payments. The number of checks written in the United States fell by 40% between 2010 and 2014.

In fact, the use of checks continues to decline around the world as the market share of credit and debit cards continues to grow. In addition, mobile phone technology and the Internet are encouraging the development of new infant payment systems.

TABLE 20.3 Small face-to-face purchases are commonly paid for in cash, but here are some of the other ways that you can pay your bills

Check When you write a check, you are instructing your bank to pay a specified sum on demand to the particular firm or person named on the check.

Credit card A credit card, such as a Visa or MasterCard, gives you a line of credit that allows you to make purchases up to a stated limit. At the end of each month, either you pay the credit card company for these purchases or you will be charged interest on any outstanding balance.

Charge card (or travel and entertainment card) A charge card may look like a credit card and you can spend money with it like a credit card. But with a charge card, the day of reckoning comes at the end of each month, when you must pay for all purchases that you have made. In other words, you must pay off your entire balance every month.

Debit card A debit card allows you to have your purchases from a store charged directly to your bank account. The deduction is usually made electronically and is immediate. Often, debit cards may also be used to make withdrawals from a cash machine (ATM).

Credit transfer With a credit transfer, you ask your bank to set up a standing order to make a regular set payment to a supplier. For example, standing orders are often used to make regular fixed mortgage payments.

Direct payment A direct payment (also called direct debit) is an instruction to your bank to allow a company to collect varying amounts from your account, as long as you have been given advance notice of the collection amounts and dates. For example, an electric utility company may ask you to set up a direct debit that allows it to receive automatic payment of your electricity bills from your bank account.

FIGURE 20.8 Payment methods by country, 2014 (percentage of total non-cash transactions)

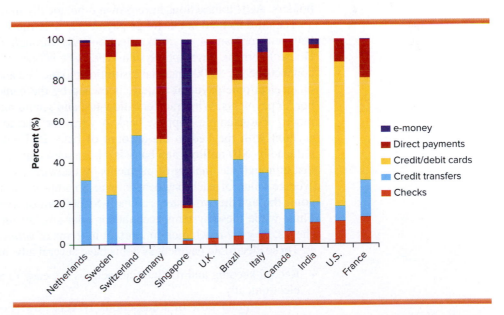

Source: Bank for International Settlements, "Statistics on Payment and Settlement Systems in the CPMI Countries," www.bis.org/publ, December 2015.

Electronic Funds Transfer

As we've just noted, payments are increasingly being made electronically throughout the world. The most familiar forms of electronic payment are the credit card and debit card, but there are three other important ways that money can travel electronically. It can do so by direct payment, direct deposit, or wire transfer.

TABLE 20.4 Use of payment systems in the United States, 2014

	Number of Payments (millions)	Value of Payments ($ trillions)
Checks	9,702	14
ACH	18,298	40
Fedwire	135	885
CHIPS	109	391

Source: Bank for International Settlements, "Statistics on payment, clearing and settlement systems in the CPMI countries," December 2015.

Direct payment systems (also known as *direct debit* systems) are used for recurring expenditures, such as utility bills, insurance premiums, and mortgage or loan payments. For example, if you have taken out a student loan, you may have authorized the lender to take the payment directly from your bank account each month. The student loan company simply needs to provide its bank with a file showing details of each student, the amount to be debited, and the date. The payment then travels electronically through the **Automated Clearing House (ACH)** system. You are saved from the chore of writing regular checks, and the firm knows exactly when the cash is coming in and avoids the labor-intensive process of handling thousands of checks.

Automated Clearing House (ACH)

An electronic network for cash transfers in the United States.

The Automated Clearing House system also allows money to flow in the reverse direction. Thus, while a *direct payment* transaction provides an automatic debit, a *direct deposit* constitutes an automatic credit. Direct deposits are used to make bulk payments such as wages or dividends. Again, the company provides its bank with a file of instructions. The bank then debits the company's account and transfers the cash via the Automated Clearing House to the bank accounts of the firm's employees or shareholders. ACH transactions have grown dramatically in recent years.

The third method of electronic payment is wire transfer. Most large-value payments between companies are made electronically through Fedwire or CHIPS (Clearing House Interbank Payments System). Fedwire is operated by the Federal Reserve and connects nearly 8,000 financial institutions to the Fed and so to each other. CHIPS, the other electronic payment system, is owned by the banks and used mainly for cross-border payments. Wire transfers allow fast and secure movement of very large sums of money. For example, suppose bank A wires the Fed to transfer $10 million from its account with the Fed to the account of bank B. Bank A's account is immediately reduced by $10 million, and bank B's is increased at the same time. Table 20.4 shows that although the *number* of payments by Fedwire and CHIPS is relatively small, the average value of each payment is over $5 million, and the total value of payments going through the two systems is nearly $1,300 trillion a year ($1,300,000,000,000,000). Thus, while these systems account for a far smaller *number* of transactions than do checks, they are much more important in terms of *value*.

These electronic payment systems have several advantages:

- Record keeping and routine transactions are easy to automate when money moves electronically.
- The marginal cost of transactions is very low. For example, a transfer using Fedwire typically costs about $20, while it costs only a few cents to make each ACH payment.
- Float is reduced and the company can ensure that its payments arrive exactly on time.

International Cash Management

Cash management in domestic firms is child's play compared with that in large multinational corporations operating in dozens of different countries, each with its own currency, banking system, and legal structure.

A single centralized cash management system is an unattainable ideal for these companies, although they are edging toward it. For example, suppose that you are treasurer of a large multinational company with operations throughout Europe. You could allow the separate businesses to manage their own cash, but that would be costly and would almost certainly result in each one accumulating little hoards of cash. The solution is to set up a regional system. In this case, the company establishes a local concentration account with a bank in each country. Any surplus cash is swept daily into central multicurrency accounts in London or another European banking center. This cash is then invested in marketable securities or used to finance any subsidiaries that have a cash shortage.

Payments can also be made out of the regional center. For example, to pay wages in each European country, the company just needs to send its principal bank a computer file with details of the payments to be made. The bank then finds the least costly way to transfer the cash from the company's central accounts and arranges for the funds to be credited on the correct day to the employees in each country.

Most large multinationals have several banks in each country, but the more banks they use, the less control they have over their cash balances. So development of regional cash management systems favors banks that can offer a worldwide branch network. These banks can also afford the high costs of setting up computer systems for handling cash payments and receipts in different countries.

20.5 Investing Idle Cash: The Money Market

In September 2015, Apple was sitting on a $206.4 billion mountain of cash and fixed income investments, amounting to two-thirds of the company's total assets. Of this sum, $11.4 billion was kept as cash and the remainder was invested as follows:

Fixed Income Investments	Value at Cost ($ millions)
Money market mutual funds	$ 3,570
U.S. Treasury and agency securities	40,766
Non-U.S. government securities	6,356
Certificates of deposit and time deposits	4,347
Commercial paper	6,016
Corporate securities	116,908
Municipal securities	947
Mortgage- and asset-backed securities	16,121
Total	$195,031

money market
Market for short-term financial assets.

Most companies do not have the luxury of such huge cash surpluses, but, like Apple, they park any cash that is not immediately needed in short-term investments. The market for these investments is known as the **money market.** The money market has no physical marketplace. It consists of a loose collection of banks and dealers linked together by telephones or through the web. But a huge volume of securities is regularly traded on the money market, and competition is vigorous.

Large corporations manage their own money market investments, but small companies sometimes find it more convenient to hire a professional investment management firm or to put their cash into a money market fund. This is a mutual fund that invests only in low-risk, short-term securities. Despite its large cash surplus, Apple invested a small proportion of its money in money market funds.

Money Market Investments

Only fixed-income securities with maturities less than 1 year are considered to be part of the money market. However, most instruments in the money market actually have considerably shorter maturity. Limiting maturity has two advantages for the cash manager. Recall from Chapter 6 that risk due to interest rate fluctuations increases with maturity. Very short-term securities, therefore, have almost no interest rate risk. Second, it is far easier to gauge the risk of default over short horizons. One need not worry as much about deterioration in financial strength over a 90-day horizon as over the 30-year life of a bond. These considerations imply that high-quality money market securities are a safe "parking spot" to keep idle balances until they are converted back to cash.

Most money market securities are also highly marketable or *liquid,* meaning that it is easy and cheap to sell the asset for cash. This property, too, is an attractive feature of securities used as temporary investments until cash is needed.

Some of the important instruments of the money market are:

Treasury bills.   Treasury bills are issued weekly by the U.S. government and mature in 4 weeks, 3 months, 6 months, and 12 months. They are the safest and most liquid money market instrument.

Commercial paper.   This is short-term, usually unsecured, debt issued by large and well-known companies. While maturities can range up to 270 days before registration with the SEC is required, most commercial paper is issued with maturities of less than 2 months. Because there is no active trading in commercial paper, it has low marketability. Therefore, it would not be an appropriate investment for a firm that could not hold it until maturity. Moody's, Standard & Poor's, and Fitch rate commercial paper in terms of the default risk of the issuer. We will have more to say about commercial paper in the next section.

Certificates of deposit.   CDs are time deposits at banks, usually in denominations greater than $100,000. Unlike demand deposits (checking accounts), time deposits cannot be withdrawn from the bank on demand: The bank pays interest and principal only at the maturity of the deposit. However, short-term CDs (with maturities less than 3 months) are actively traded, so a firm can easily sell the security if it needs cash.

Repurchase agreements.   Also known as *repos,* repurchase agreements are, in effect, collateralized loans. A government bond dealer sells Treasury securities to an investor, with an agreement to repurchase them at a later date at a higher price. The increase in price serves as implicit interest, so the investor in effect is lending money to the dealer, first giving money to the dealer and later getting it back with interest. The bills serve as collateral for the loan: If the dealer fails, and cannot buy back the bill, the investor can keep it. Repurchase agreements are usually very short-term, with maturities of only a few days.

Calculating the Yield on Money Market Investments

BEYOND THE PAGE

Calculating the yield on Treasury bills

mhhe.com/brealey9e

Many money market investments are pure discount securities. This means that they don't pay interest. The return consists of the difference between the amount you pay and the amount you receive at maturity. The discount from face value is your implicit interest payment, and the interest rate on a money market investment is commonly quoted on a discount basis. For example, suppose that 3-month bills are issued at an discount from face value of 6% annualized. This is a rather complicated way of saying that the price of a 3-month bill is $100 - (3/12) \times 6 = 98.5$. Therefore, for every $98.5 that you invest today, you receive $100 at the end of 3 months. The return over 3 months is $1.5/98.5 = .0152$, or 1.52%. This is equivalent to an annual rate of return of 6.23%. Note that the return is always higher than the discount because you pay less than face value when you buy the bond. When you read that an investment is selling at a discount of 6%, it is very easy to slip into the mistake of thinking that this is its return.

| Example | 20.6 ▶ | Money Market Rates |

A Treasury bill with face value of $100,000 and maturity of 6 months is sold for $98,000. The rate on this bill on a discount basis would be quoted as 4%. The actual discount from face value over 6 months is, therefore, 2%. The *effective* annual yield on this half-year investment can be found by solving

$$98{,}000 \times (1 + r)^{1/2} = 100{,}000$$

which implies that $r = .0412$, or 4.12%. ■

Yields on Money Market Investments

When we value long-term debt, it is important to take account of default risk. Almost anything may happen in 30 years, and even today's most respectable company may get into trouble eventually. Therefore, corporate bonds offer higher yields than Treasury bonds.

Short-term debt is not risk free either. During the financial crisis, seven companies stopped payments on their commercial paper. They included Lehman Brothers, which defaulted on a record $3 billion of paper. Fortunately, such examples are exceptions; in general, the danger of default is less for money market securities issued by corporations than for corporate bonds. There are two reasons for this. First, as we pointed out earlier, the range of possible outcomes is smaller for short-term investments. Even though the distant future may be clouded, you can usually be confident that a particular company will survive for at least the next month. Second, for the most part, only well-established companies can borrow in the money market. If you are going to lend money for just a few days, you can't afford to spend too much time in evaluating the loan. Thus, you will consider only blue-chip borrowers.

Despite the high quality of money market investments, there are often significant differences in yield between corporate and U.S. government securities. Why is this? One answer is the risk of default. Another is that the investments have different degrees of liquidity, or "moneyness." Investors like Treasury bills because they are easily turned into cash on short notice. Securities that cannot be converted quickly and cheaply into cash need to offer relatively high yields.

During times of market turmoil, investors may place a higher value on having ready access to cash. On these occasions the yield on illiquid securities can increase dramatically. This happened in 2007, when banks across the world revealed huge losses in the U.S. subprime mortgage market. Fearful that some banks would be forced into sales of their positions, investors shrank from illiquid securities, and there was a "flight to quality." The spread between the yields on commercial paper and Treasury bills increased to over 100 basis points (1.00%), four times its level at the beginning of the year.

The International Money Market

In addition to the domestic money market, there is also an international market for short-term dollar investments, which is known as the *eurodollar* market. Eurodollars have nothing to do with the euro, the currency of the European Monetary Union (EMU). They are simply dollars deposited in a bank in Europe. For example, suppose that an American auto producer buys 1,000 ounces of palladium from Anglo Platinum (Amplats), the South African mining giant. It pays for the purchase with a check for $1.5 million drawn on JPMorgan Chase. Amplats then deposits the check with its account at Barclays Bank in London. As a result, Barclays has an asset in the form of a $1.5 million credit in its account with JPMorgan Chase. It also has an offsetting liability in the form of a dollar deposit. Because that dollar deposit is placed in Europe, it is called a eurodollar deposit.[11]

Just as there is both a domestic U.S. money market and a eurodollar market, so there is both a domestic Japanese money market and a market in London for euroyen. So if a U.S. corporation wishes to make a short-term investment in yen, it can deposit the yen with a bank in Tokyo or it can make a euroyen deposit in London. Similarly, there is both a domestic money market in the euro area as well as a money market for euros in London. And so on.

Major international banks in London lend dollars to one another at the dollar *London Interbank Offered Rate* (LIBOR). Similarly, they lend yen to each other at the yen LIBOR interest rate, and they lend euros at the euro interbank offered rate, or Euribor. These interest rates are used as a benchmark for pricing many types of short-term loans in the United States and in other countries. For example, a corporation in the United States may issue a floating-rate note with interest payments tied to dollar LIBOR.

20.6 Managing Current Liabilities: Short-Term Debt

Our focus so far in this chapter has been on the management of the principal current assets. But financial managers also need to worry about the company's current liabilities. We will look at just one important current liability, short-term debt.

Bank Loans

The simplest and most common source of short-term finance is a loan from a bank. Companies sometimes wait until they need the money before they apply for a bank loan, but in the majority of cases the firm will arrange a **revolving line of credit** that permits it to borrow from the bank up to an agreed limit. The company can borrow and repay whenever it wants until the agreement expires. In return, the company will agree to pay the bank a commitment fee of up to .5% on any unused amount.

Many bank loans have durations of only a few months. For example, a firm may need a loan to cover a seasonal increase in inventories, and the loan is then repaid as the goods are sold. Such a loan is described as *self-liquidating;* in other words, the sale of goods provides the cash to repay the loan. However, banks also make term loans, which last for several years.

Some bank loans are too large for a single lender. In these cases, the borrower may pay an arrangement fee to a lead bank, which then parcels out the loan or credit line among a syndicate of banks. For example, in 2015 the brewing giant Anheuser-Busch InBev announced a record $70 billion syndicated loan to help pay for the acquisition of its rival, SABMiller. The loan was raised in multiple currencies and with several different maturities.

Most short-term bank loans are made at a fixed rate of interest, which is often quoted as a discount. For example, if the interest rate on a 1-year loan is stated as a discount of 5%, the borrower receives $100 − $5 = $95 and undertakes to pay $100 at the end of the year. The return on such a loan is not 5% but 5/95 = .0526, or 5.26%.

revolving line of credit
Agreement by a bank that a company may borrow at any time up to an established limit.

20.8 Self-Test

First National Bank of Baboquivari has offered to lend your firm $1 million for 3 months at an 8% discount. What is the effective interest rate on this loan? (*Hint:* You may find it helpful to look back at Example 20.6.)

---

[11] Amplats could equally well deposit the check with the London branch of a U.S. bank or a Japanese bank. It would still have made a eurodollar deposit.

BEYOND THE PAGE

 The LIBOR scandal

mhhe.com/brealey9e

For longer-term bank loans, the interest rate is usually linked to the general level of interest rates. A common benchmark is LIBOR, the interest rate at which the major international banks borrow dollars from one another.[12] Thus, if the rate is set at "1% over LIBOR," the borrower may pay 5% in the first 3 months when LIBOR is 4%, 6% in the next 3 months when LIBOR is 5%, and so on.

Secured Loans

If a bank is concerned about a firm's credit risk, the firm will need to provide security or *collateral* for the loan. Sometimes, this security will include both current and fixed assets. However, if the bank is lending on a short-term basis, the collateral is generally restricted to liquid assets such as receivables, inventories, or securities. For example, a firm may decide to borrow short-term money secured by its accounts receivable. When its customers pay their bills, it can use the cash collected to repay the loan.

Banks will not usually lend the full value of the assets that are used as security. So a firm that puts up $100,000 of receivables as security may find that the bank is prepared to lend only $75,000. The safety margin (or haircut, as it is called) is likely to be even larger in the case of loans that are secured by inventory.

Accounts Receivable Financing

When a loan is secured by receivables, the firm assigns the receivables to the bank. If the firm fails to repay the loan, the bank can collect the receivables from the firm's customers and use the cash to pay off the debt. However, the firm is still responsible for the loan even if the receivables ultimately cannot be collected. The risk of default on the receivables is therefore borne by the firm.

Inventory Financing

Banks may also be willing to accept inventory as collateral, but they are choosy about the inventory they will accept. They want to make sure that they can identify and sell it if you default. Automobiles and other standardized nonperishable commodities are good security for a loan; work in progress and ripe strawberries are poor collateral.

To ensure that the borrower doesn't sell the inventory and run off with the money, lenders often insist on *field warehousing*. In this case, an independent warehouse company hired by the bank supervises the inventory pledged as collateral for the loan. As the firm sells its product and uses the revenue to pay back the loan, the bank directs the warehouse company to release the inventory back to the firm. If the firm defaults on the loan, the bank keeps the inventory and sells it to recover the debt.

Sometimes, however, the collateral that the company provides is illusory and the borrower does run off with the money. Consider, for example, the story of the great salad oil swindle. Fifty-one banks and companies made loans of nearly $200 million to the Allied Crude Vegetable Oil Refining Corporation in the belief that these loans were secured by valuable salad oil. Unfortunately, they did not notice that Allied's tanks contained false compartments that were mainly filled with seawater. When the fraud was discovered, the president of Allied went to jail, and the 51 lenders stayed out in the cold looking for their $200 million. The nearby box presents a similar story that illustrates the potential pitfalls of secured lending. Here, too, the loans were not as "secured" as they appeared: The supposed collateral did not exist.

Commercial Paper

When banks lend money, they provide two services. They match up would-be borrowers and lenders, and they check that the borrower is likely to repay the loan. Banks recover the costs of providing these services by charging borrowers on average a higher interest rate than they pay to lenders. These services are less necessary for large, well-known companies that regularly need to raise large amounts of cash. Such

---

[12] Occasionally, the interest rate is linked to the bank's prime rate or to the federal funds rate, which is the interest rate at which banks in the United States lend excess reserves to each other.

The National Safety Council of Australia's Victoria Division had been a sleepy outfit until John Friedrich took over. Under its new management, NSC members trained like commandos and were prepared to go anywhere and do anything. They saved people from drowning, fought fires, found lost bushwalkers, and went down mines. Their lavish equipment included 22 helicopters, eight aircraft, and a mini-submarine. Soon, the NSC began selling its services internationally.

Unfortunately, the NSC's paramilitary outfit cost millions of dollars to run—far more than it earned in revenue. Friedrich bridged the gap by borrowing $A236 million of debt. The banks were happy to lend because the NSC's debt appeared well secured. At one point, the company showed $A107 million of receivables (i.e., money owed by its customers), which it pledged as security for bank loans. Later checks revealed that many of these customers did not owe the NSC a cent. In other cases, banks took comfort in the fact that their loans were secured by containers of valuable rescue gear. There were more than 100 containers stacked around the NSC's main base. Only a handful contained any equipment, but these were the ones that the bankers saw when they came to check that their loans were safe. Sometimes, a suspicious banker would ask to inspect a particular container. Friedrich would then explain that it was away on exercise, fly the banker across the country in a light plane, and point to a container well out in the bush. The container would, of course, be empty, but the banker had no way to know that.

Six years after Friedrich was appointed CEO, his massive fraud was uncovered. But a few days before a warrant could be issued, Friedrich disappeared. Although he was eventually caught and arrested, he shot himself before he could come to trial. Investigations revealed that Friedrich was operating under an assumed name, having fled from his native Germany, where he was wanted by the police. Many rumors continued to circulate about Friedrich. He was variously alleged to have been a plant of the CIA and the KGB, and the NSC was said to have been behind an attempted counter-coup in Fiji. For the banks there was only one hard truth: Their loans to the NSC, which had appeared so well secured, would never be repaid.

Source: Adapted from T. Sykes, *The Bold Riders* (St. Leonards, Australia: Allen & Unwin, 1994), chap. 7.

commercial paper
Short-term unsecured notes issued by firms.

companies have found it profitable to bypass the bank and to sell short-term debt, known as **commercial paper,** directly to large investors.

In the United States commercial paper has a maximum maturity of 270 days because longer maturities would require registration with the Securities and Exchange Commission. Most paper matures in 60 days or less. Commercial paper is not secured, but companies generally back their issue of paper by arranging a special backup line of credit with a bank. This guarantees that they can find the money to repay the paper, and the risk of default is therefore small.

Recent years have not been kind to the commercial paper market. When Lehman Brothers went bankrupt in 2008, it defaulted on its outstanding commercial paper. The commercial paper market seized up; many companies either found it impossible to issue commercial paper or were obliged to pay very high rates of interest. The resulting interruption of credit to the corporate sector was a major cause of the recession that followed the financial crisis. Even before the crisis, however, all was not well. In 2001, two large California utilities—Pacific Gas & Electric and Southern California Edison—became the first companies for 10 years to default on their nonfinancial commercial paper.

SUMMARY

Why do firms need to invest in net working capital?
(*LO20-1*)

The most important current assets are cash, marketable securities, accounts receivable, and inventories. The most important current liabilities are bank loans and accounts payable.

Net working capital results from the lags between the time that the firm obtains the raw materials for its product and the time that its customers pay for their purchases. The **cash cycle** is the length of time from the *payment* for these raw materials to the date that the customers pay their bills.

What are the usual steps in credit management? (*LO20-2*)

The first step in credit management is to set normal **terms of sale.** This means that you must decide the length of the payment period and the size of any cash discounts. In most industries, these conditions are fairly standardized.

Your second step is to decide the form of the contract with your customer. Most domestic sales are made on **open account.** In this case, the only evidence that the customer owes you money is the entry in your ledger and a receipt signed by the customer. Sometimes, you may require a more formal commitment before you deliver the goods. For example, the supplier may arrange for the customer to provide a trade acceptance.

The third task is to assess each customer's creditworthiness. When you have made an assessment of the customer's credit standing, the fourth step is to establish sensible credit policy. Finally, once the credit policy is set, you need to establish a collection policy to identify and pursue slow payers.

How do we measure the implicit interest rate on credit? (*LO20-3*)

The effective interest rate for customers who buy goods on credit rather than taking the discount for quicker payment is

$$\left(1 + \frac{discount}{discounted\ price}\right)^{365/extra\ days\ credit} - 1$$

How do firms assess the probability that a customer will pay? (*LO20-4*)

Credit analysis is the process of deciding which customers are likely to pay their bills. There are various sources of information: your own experience with the customer, the experience of other creditors, the assessment of a credit agency, a check with the customer's bank, the market value of the customer's securities, and an analysis of the customer's financial statements. Firms that handle a large volume of credit information often use a formal system for combining the various sources into an overall credit score.

How do firms decide whether it makes sense to grant credit to a customer? (*LO20-5*)

Credit policy refers to the decision to extend credit to a customer. The job of the credit manager is not to minimize the number of bad debts; it is to maximize profits. This means that you need to weigh the odds that the customer will pay, providing you with a profit, against the odds that the customer will default, resulting in a loss. Remember not to be too shortsighted when reckoning the expected profit. It is often worth accepting the marginal applicant if there is a chance that the applicant may become a regular and reliable customer.

If credit is granted, the next problem is to set a **collection policy.** This requires tact and judgment. You want to be firm with the truly delinquent customer, but you don't want to offend the good one by writing demanding letters just because a check has been delayed in the mail. You will find it easier to spot troublesome accounts if you keep a careful **aging schedule** of outstanding accounts.

What are the costs and benefits of holding either inventories or cash? (*LO20-6*)

The benefit of higher inventory levels is the reduction in order costs associated with restocking and the reduced chances of running out of material. The costs are the carrying costs, which include the cost of space, insurance, spoilage, and the opportunity cost of the capital tied up in inventory. Cash provides liquidity, but it doesn't pay interest. Securities pay interest, but you can't use them to buy things. As financial manager you want to hold cash up to the point where the incremental or marginal benefit of liquidity is equal to the cost of holding cash, that is, the interest that you could earn on securities.

What are some of the ways that companies receive and make payments? (*LO20-7*)

When you mail a check, it may take several days before it is presented and cleared. During this time, the money will continue to sit in your bank account. Checks that have been mailed but not yet cleared are known as *float.* Unfortunately, float also works in reverse. Every time someone writes *you* a check, there is a delay before the money ends up in your bank account. Companies that receive a large volume of checks employ techniques such as **lock-box banking** and **concentration accounts** to speed up the process of depositing and clearing checks.

Check usage is on the decline. Instead, money increasingly travels electronically. For example, your mortgage payment will probably be taken directly *from* your bank account each month, and your salary will probably be paid directly *into* your account. Large-value payments between companies are made electronically by means of the Fedwire and CHIPS systems. The number of payments going through these two systems is quite small, but their value is huge.

Where do firms invest excess funds until they are needed to pay bills? (*LO20-8*)

Firms can invest idle cash in the **money market,** the market for short-term financial assets. These assets tend to be short-term, low-risk, and highly liquid, making them ideal instruments in which to invest funds for short periods of time before cash is needed. The most important money market instruments are Treasury bills, commercial paper, certificates of deposit, and repurchase agreements.

What are the principal sources of short-term borrowing? (*LO20-9*)

A major source of short-term financing is bank loans. Often, firms pay a regular fee for a **line of credit** that allows them to borrow from the bank up to an agreed limit. Bank loans may be secured on the firm's receivables or inventory. Large well-known firms may also issue their own short-term debt to investors. This is known as **commercial paper.**

LISTING OF EQUATION

20.1   Effective annual rate $= \left(1 + \dfrac{\text{discount}}{\text{discounted price}}\right)^{365/\text{extra days credit}} - 1$

QUESTIONS AND PROBLEMS

1. **Working Capital.** A junior analyst at Camberwell Corp. has jumbled the items on its balance sheet. Can you help him calculate the value of (a) Camberwell's current assets, (b) its current liabilities, and (c) its net working capital? (*LO20-1*)

Bank debt	$ 9.1 million
Other current liabilities	12.2
Plant and equipment	34.8
Long-term debt	12.1
Accounts receivable	8.7
Marketable investments	6.4
Inventories	7.9
Goodwill	3.8
Other current assets	13.0
Accounts payable	8.4
Cash	3.7

2. **Cash Cycle.** Will each of the following events increase or decrease the cash cycle? (*LO20-1*)
   a. Higher financing rates induce the firm to reduce its level of inventory.
   b. The firm obtains a new line of credit that enables it to avoid stretching payables to its suppliers.
   c. The firm factors its accounts receivable.
   d. A recession occurs, and the firm's customers increasingly stretch their payables.

3. **Managing Working Capital.** A new computer system allows your firm to monitor inventory more accurately and anticipate future inventory shortfalls. As a result, the firm feels more able to pare down its inventory levels. Will the new system increase or decrease (a) working capital and (b) the cash cycle? (*LO20-1*)

4. **Cash Cycle.** The following table shows income statement and balance sheet data for five U.S. industries in 2015. Calculate the cash cycle for each industry. (*LO20-1*)

INCOME STATEMENT AND BALANCE SHEET DATA (Figures in $ millions)					
	Food	Pharmaceuticals	Oil and Coal	Computers and Peripherals	Food Stores
Income Statement Data:					
Sales	$676.7	$396.8	$1,049.2	$206.1	$463.7
Cost of goods sold	614.2	328.9	990.6	166.3	439.8
Balance Sheet Data:					
Inventory	$ 64.1	$ 52.4	$ 49.5	$ 8.8	$ 25.1
Accounts receivable	51.4	60.6	73.2	20.2	5.7
Accounts payable	41.8	39.2	76.3	28.3	21.6

Note: Cost of goods sold includes selling, general, and administrative expenses.
Source: U.S. Department of Commerce, *Quarterly Financial Report for Manufacturing, Mining, Trade Corporations, and Selected Service Industries,* September 2015.

5. **Cash Cycle.** Calculate (a) the accounts receivable period, (b) accounts payable period, (c) inventory period, and (d) cash cycle for the following firm: (*LO20-1*)

Income Statement Data:	
Sales	$5,000
Cost of goods sold	4,200
Balance Sheet Data:	
Inventory	550
Accounts receivable	110
Accounts payable	270

6. **Cash Cycle.** Will the following increase or decrease the cash cycle? (*LO20-1*)
   a. Customers are given a larger discount for cash transactions.
   b. The inventory turnover ratio falls from 8 to 6.
   c. New technology streamlines the production process.
   d. The firm adopts a policy of reducing outstanding accounts payable.
   e. The firm starts producing more goods in response to customers' advance orders instead of producing for inventory.
   f. A temporary glut in the commodity market induces the firm to stock up on raw materials while prices are low.

7. **Cash Cycle.** A firm is considering several policy changes to increase sales. It will increase the variety of goods it keeps in inventory, but this will increase inventory by $10,000. It will offer more liberal sales terms, but this will result in average receivables increasing by $65,000. These actions are expected to increase sales by $800,000 per year, and cost of goods will remain at 80% of sales. Because of the firm's increased purchases for its own production needs, average payables will increase by $35,000. What effect will these changes have on the firm's cash cycle? (*LO20-1*)

8. **Terms of Sale.** Complete the passage below by selecting the appropriate terms from the following list (some terms may be used more than once): *acceptance, open, commercial, trade, the United States, his or her own, draft, account, bank, banker's, the customer's.* (*LO20-2*)

   Most goods are sold on ____(a) ____. In this case, the only evidence of the debt is a record in the seller's books and a signed receipt. An alternative is for the seller to arrange a(n) ____(b) ____ ordering payment by the customer. In order to obtain the goods, the customer must acknowledge this order and sign the document. This signed acknowledgment is known as a(n) ____(c) ____. Sometimes, the seller may also ask ____(d) ____ bank to sign the document. In this case, it is known as a(n) ____ (e)____.

9. **Payment Lag.** The lag between the purchase date and the date on which payment is due is known as the *terms lag*. The lag between the due date and the date on which the buyer actually pays is termed the *due lag,* and the lag between the purchase and actual payment dates is the *pay lag.* Thus, pay lag = terms lag + due lag. Would the following events likely increase or decrease each of these lags? (*LO20-2*)

   a. The company imposes a service charge on late payers.
   b. A recession causes customers to be short of cash.
   c. The company changes its terms from net 10 to net 20.

10. **Terms of Sale.** For each of the following pairs, is firm A or firm B more likely to grant the longer credit period? (*LO20-2*)

   a. Firm A sells hardware; firm B sells bread.
   b. Firm A's customers have an inventory turnover ratio of 10; firm B's customers have a turnover of 15.
   c. Firm A sells mainly to electric utilities; firm B sells to fashion boutiques.

11. **Trade Credit Rates.** Company X sells on a 1/20, net 60, basis. Company Y buys goods with an invoice of $1,000. (*LO20-3*)

   a. How much can company Y deduct from the bill if it pays on day 20?
   b. How many extra days of credit can company Y receive if it passes up the cash discount?
   c. What is the effective annual rate of interest if Y pays on the due date rather than day 20?

12. **Trade Credit Rates.** A firm currently offers terms of sale of 3/20, net 40. What effect will the following actions have on the implicit interest rate charged to customers that pass up the cash discount? Will the implicit interest rate increase or decrease? (*LO20-3*)

   a. The terms are changed to 4/20, net 40.
   b. The terms are changed to 3/30, net 40.
   c. The terms are changed to 3/20, net 30.

13. **Trade Credit and Receivables.** A firm offers terms of 3/15, net 30. Currently, two-thirds of all customers take advantage of the trade discount; the remainder pay bills at the due date. (*LO20-3*)

   a. What will be the firm's typical value for its accounts receivable period?
   b. What is the average investment in accounts receivable if annual sales are $20 million?
   c. What would likely happen to the firm's accounts receivable period if it changed its terms to 4/15, net 30?

14. **Terms of Sale.** Microbiotics currently sells all of its frozen dinners cash-on-delivery but believes it can increase sales by offering supermarkets 1 month of free credit. The price per carton is $50, and the cost per carton is $40. (*LO20-3*)

   a. If unit sales will increase from 1,000 cartons to 1,060 per month, what is the expected profit from offering the credit? The interest rate is 1% per month, and all customers will pay their bills.
   b. What if the interest rate is 1.5% per month?
   c. What if the interest rate is 1.5% per month but the firm can offer the credit only as a special deal to new customers, while old customers will continue to pay cash on delivery?

15. **Credit Analysis.** Financial ratios were described in Chapter 4. If you were the credit manager, to which financial ratios would you pay most attention? (*LO20-4*)

16. **Credit Analysis.** Use the data in Example 20.2. But now suppose that 10% of Cast Iron's customers are slow payers and that slow payers have a probability of 30% of defaulting on their bills. If it costs $5 to determine whether a customer has been a prompt or slow payer in the past, should Cast Iron undertake such a check? (What are the expected savings and expected profit from the credit check? The answers will depend on both the probability of uncovering a slow payer and the savings from denying slow payers credit.) (*LO20-4*)

17. **Credit Analysis.** Look back at Problem 16, but now suppose that if a customer defaults on a payment, you can eventually collect about half the amount owed to you. Will you be more or less tempted to pay for a credit check once you account for the possibility of partial recovery of debts? (*LO20-4*)

18. **Credit Analysis.** Galenic Inc. is a wholesaler for a range of pharmaceutical products. Before deducting any losses from bad debts, Galenic operates on a profit margin of 5%. For a long time

the firm has employed a numerical credit-scoring system based on a small number of key ratios. This has resulted in a bad debt ratio of 1%.

Galenic has recently commissioned a detailed statistical study of the payment record of its customers over the past 8 years and, after considerable experimentation, has identified five variables that could form the basis of a new credit-scoring system. On the evidence of the past 8 years, Galenic calculates that for every 10,000 accounts it would have experienced the following default rates:

Credit Score under Proposed System	Number of Accounts		
	Defaulting	Paying	Total
Better than 80	60	9,100	9,160
Worse than 80	40	800	840
Total	100	9,900	10,000

By refusing credit to firms with a poor credit score (worse than 80), Galenic calculates that it would reduce its bad debt ratio to 60/9,160, or just under .7%. While this may not seem like a big deal, Galenic's credit manager reasons that this is equivalent to a decrease of one-third in the bad debt ratio and would result in a significant improvement in the profit margin. (*LO20-4*)

a. What is Galenic's current profit margin, allowing for bad debts?
b. Assuming that the firm's estimates of default rates are right, by how much would the new credit-scoring system affect profits?
c. Why might you suspect that Galenic's estimates of default rates will not be realized in practice?
d. Suppose that one of the variables in the proposed new scoring system is whether the customer has an existing account with Galenic (new customers are more likely to default). Would you be more or less likely to accept the proposal? (*Hint:* Think about repeat sales.)

19. **Credit Decision/Repeat Sales.** Locust Software sells computer training packages to its business customers at a price of $101. The cost of production (in present value terms) is $96. Locust sells its packages on terms of net 30 and estimates that about 7% of all orders will be uncollectible. An order comes in for 20 units. The interest rate is 1% per month. (*LO20-5*)

a. What is the expected profit of extending credit if this is a one-time order? The sale will not be made unless credit is extended.
b. What is the break-even probability of collection?
c. Now suppose that if a customer pays this month's bill, it will place an identical order in each month indefinitely and can be safely assumed to pose no risk of default. Should credit be extended?
d. What is the break-even probability of collection in the repeat-sales case?

20. **Credit Decision.** Look back at Example 20.2. Cast Iron's costs have increased from $1,000 to $1,050. Assuming that there is no possibility of repeat orders and that the probability of successful collection from the customer is $p = .95$, answer the following: (*LO20-5*)

a. What is the expected profit of granting credit? Should Cast Iron grant or refuse credit?
b. What is the break-even probability of collection?

21. **Credit Decision.** The Branding Iron Company sells its irons for $60 apiece wholesale. Production cost is $50 per iron. There is a 25% chance that a prospective customer will go bankrupt within the next half-year. The customer orders 1,000 irons and asks for 6 months' credit. What is the expected profit of accepting the order? Should Branding Iron accept the order? Assume the discount rate is 8% per year, there is no chance of a repeat order, and the customer will either pay in full or not pay at all. (*LO20-5*)

22. **Credit Policy.** As treasurer of the Universal Bed Corporation, Aristotle Procrustes is worried about his bad debt ratio, which is currently running at 6%. He believes that imposing a more stringent credit policy might reduce sales by 5% and reduce the bad debt ratio to 4%. If the cost of goods sold is 80% of the selling price, what is the impact of changing credit policy on expected profit? Should Mr. Procrustes adopt the more stringent policy? (*LO20-5*)

23. **Credit Decision/Repeat Sales.** Surf City sells its network browsing software for $15 per copy to computer software distributors and allows its customers 1 month to pay their bills. The cost

of the software is $10 per copy. The industry is very new and unsettled, however, and the probability that a new customer granted credit will go bankrupt within the next month is 25%. The firm is considering switching to a cash-on-delivery credit policy to reduce its exposure to defaults on trade credit. The discount rate is 1% per month. (*LO20-5*)

a. What is the impact on the firm's expected profits of switching to a cash-on-delivery policy? If it switches, sales will fall by 40%.

b. How would your answer change if a customer that is granted credit and pays its bills can be expected to generate repeat orders with negligible likelihood of default for each of the next 6 months? Similarly, customers that pay cash also will generate on average 6 months of repeat sales.

24. **Credit Policy.** A firm currently makes only cash sales. It estimates that allowing trade credit on terms of net 30 would increase sales from 100 to 110 units per month. The price per unit is $101, and the cost (in present value terms) is $80. The interest rate is 1% per month. (*LO20-5*)

a. What would be the NPV of a change in the firm's credit policy?

b. How would your answer to part (a) change if 5% of all customers will fail to pay their bills under the new credit policy?

c. What if 5% of only the *new* customers fail to pay their bills? The current customers take advantage of the 30 days of free credit but remain safe credit risks.

25. **Credit Policy.** Jim Khana, the credit manager of Velcro Saddles, is reappraising the company's credit policy. Velcro sells on terms of net 30. Cost of goods sold is 85% of sales. Velcro classifies customers on a scale of 1 to 4. During the past 5 years, the collection experience for the four groups of customers was as follows:

Classification	Defaults as Percentage of Sales	Average Collection Period in Days for Nondefaulting Accounts
1	0	45
2	2	42
3	10	50
4	20	85

The average interest rate was 15%. What is the expected profit for each group in Velcro's credit policy? Should the firm deny credit to any of its customers? Which groups? What other factors should be taken into account before changing this policy? (*LO20-5*)

26. **Inventory Management.** True or false? (*LO20-6*)

a. Inventory levels tend to rise proportionately more than sales.

b. Carrying costs include the cost of the capital tied up in inventory.

c. Optimal inventory levels involve a trade-off between carrying costs and ordering costs.

d. As order size increases, carrying costs and optimal inventory levels decline.

27. **Inventory Management.** Which of the following should increase the optimal level of inventories? (*LO20-6*)

a. Freight rates decline.

b. Interest rates rise.

c. The cost of insuring the warehouse and contents rises.

d. Changing consumer taste causes an increased rate of obsolescence in the firm's products.

28. **Inventory Management.** Redraw Figure 20.7 assuming that carrying costs are $60 a ton and that each order involves a fixed charge of $400. (*LO20-6*)

a. What is the optimal order quantity?

b. Using your plot from part (a), about how many orders should the firm place a year?

c. What is the average size of the firm's inventory?

29. **Inventory Management.** In 2017, Cumnor Towers had sales of $618 million and cost of goods sold of $522 million. Its average inventory was $50 million. (*LO20-6*)

a. What was Cumnor's average inventory period?

b. How much would the value of the company increase if Cumnor could permanently reduce its average inventory period by 10 days? Assume that there are no offsetting costs to this change.

30. **Cash Management.** Suppose that the rate of interest increases from 4% to 8% per year. Would firms' cash balances go up or down relative to sales? Explain. (*LO20-7*)

31. **Float.** On January 25, Coot Company has $250,000 deposited with a local bank. On January 27, the company writes and mails checks of $20,000 and $60,000 to suppliers. At the end of the month, Coot's financial manager deposits a $45,000 check received from a customer in the morning mail and picks up the end-of-month account summary from the bank. The manager notes that only the $20,000 payment of the 27th has cleared the bank. What is the company's available balance with its bank? (*LO20-7*)

32. **Float.** Most banks now allow you to pay your bills online. You log on to your account to tell the bank which payments it should send out on your behalf. Whereas most banks charge you for writing paper checks, they do not charge for this Internet bill-paying service and, in fact, do not even charge you for their cost of postage. Why are the banks willing to provide this service to you for no fee? (*LO20-7*)

33. **Float.** General Products writes checks that average $20,000 daily. These checks take an average of 6 days to clear. It receives payments that average $22,000 daily. It takes 3 days before these checks are available to the firm. What would be the annual savings if General Products could obtain access to the payments it receives within 2 days? The interest rate is 6% per year. (*LO20-7*)

34. **Lock Boxes.** Anne Teak, the financial manager of a furniture manufacturer, is considering operating a lock-box system. She forecasts that 400 payments a day will be made to lock boxes with an average payment size of $2,000. The bank's charge for operating the lock boxes is $.40 a check. The interest rate is .015% per day. (*LO20-7*)

    a. If the lock box makes the cash available 2 days earlier, what is the net daily advantage of the system?
    b. Is it worthwhile to adopt the system?
    c. What minimum reduction in the time required to collect and process each check is needed to justify use of the lock-box system?

35. **Cash Management.** Complete the passage below by choosing the appropriate terms from the following list: *lock-box banking, Fedwire, concentration banking.* (*LO20-7*)

    Firms can increase their cash resources by speeding up collections. One way to do this is to arrange for payments to be made to regional offices that pay the checks into local banks. This is known as ____(a)____. Surplus funds are then transferred from the local banks to one of the company's main banks. Transfers can be made electronically through the ____(b)____ system. Another technique is to arrange for a local bank to collect the checks directly from a post office. This is known as ____(c)____.

36. **Lock Boxes.** Sherman's Sherbet currently takes about 6 days to collect and deposit checks from customers. A lock-box system could reduce this time to 4 days. Collections average $15,000 daily. The interest rate is .02% per day. (*LO20-7*)

    a. By how much will the lock-box system reduce float?
    b. What is the daily interest savings of the system?
    c. Suppose the lock-box service is offered for a fixed monthly fee instead of payment per check. What is the maximum monthly fee that Sherman's should be willing to pay for this service? (Assume a 30-day month.)

37. **Lock Boxes.** The financial manager of JAC Cosmetics is considering opening a lock box in Pittsburgh. Checks cleared through the lock box will amount to $300,000 per month. The lock box will make cash available to the company 3 days earlier. Suppose that the bank offers to run the lock box for a fee of $.10 per check cleared. What must the average check size be for the fee alternative to be less costly? Assume an interest rate of 6% per year. (*LO20-7*)

38. **Collection Policy.** Major Manufacturing currently has one bank account located in New York to handle all of its collections. The firm keeps an additional cash balance with the bank of $300,000 to pay for these services. It is considering opening a bank account with West Coast National Bank to speed up collections from its many California-based customers. Major estimates that the West Coast account would reduce collection time by 1 day on the $1 million a day of business that it does with its California-based customers. If it opens the account, it can reduce the balance with its New York bank to $200,000 because it will do less business in New York. However, West Coast will require an additional cash balance of $200,000. What would be the profitability of the new account? (*LO20-7*)

39. **Money Markets.** What happens to the spread between commercial paper rates and Treasury bill rates when there is a "flight to quality"? Why is commercial paper considered less liquid than Treasury bills? (*LO20-7*)

40. **Money Markets.** A Treasury bill with face value of $100,000 and maturity of 3 months sells for $99,000. (*LO20-8*)
    a. What would be the rate quoted on this bill on a discount basis?
    b. What would be its effective annual interest rate?

41. **Factoring and Discount Interest.** A firm sells its $1,000,000 receivables to a factor that specializes in collecting receivables for $960,000. The average collection period is 1 month. What is the effective annual rate on this arrangement? (*LO20-8*)

42. **Factoring and Discount Interest.** A firm sells its accounts receivables to a factor at a 1.5% discount. The average collection period is 1 month. What is the effective annual interest rate on this arrangement? What is the implicit effective annual interest rate if the average collection period is 1.5 months? (*LO20-8*)

43. **Money Markets.** Name the instrument that best fits each of the following descriptions: (*LO20-9*)
    a. Short-term unsecured loan issued directly by the company.
    b. An agreement by a government bond dealer to buy back a bond that it has sold.
    c. A short-term security issued at a discount by the government.
    d. Evidence that a company owns a bank time deposit.

44. **Lines of Credit.** The chapter notes that firms commonly pay commitment fees to banks when obtaining a line of credit. Yet when the line is first taken out, it commonly is not drawn down (i.e., the firm does not initiate any borrowing from its line). Why do these firms pay for something that seems to be not currently needed? (*LO20-9*)

45. **Short-Term Debt.** Pick the term from the following list that best fits each description: *haircut; commercial paper; collateral; revolving line of credit; self-liquidating loan; LIBOR; syndicated loan.* (*LO20-9*)
    a. Interest rate at which major international banks borrow from each other.
    b. An additional margin of collateral for a loan.
    c. A large loan provided by a group of banks.
    d. Arrangement that allows the company to borrow, repay, and re-borrow up to an agreed limit.
    e. Sale of the current assets provides the cash to repay the loan.
    f. Unsecured debt maturing in 270 days or less.
    g. Security for a loan.

WEB EXERCISES

For Exercises 1 through 4, obtain financial statements for the firms either from the company websites or from a service such as finance.google.com *or* finance.yahoo.com.

1. Look at the financial statements of Ascena Retail Group (ASNA) and The Buckle Inc. (BKE), two fashion-clothing retailers. Compare the inventory level and turnover of each. What might explain the differences you uncover?

2. Check out the recent performance of a nice coffee shop with attached free reading rooms: Barnes & Noble Inc. (BKS). BKS is sometimes characterized as an "inventory business." In what way is this the case?

3. Compare and contrast the accounts receivable turnover and days' sales outstanding for Yum! Brands (YUM) and the casino and gaming firm Wynn Resorts (WYNN). Read the business description for information that may explain the level of each company's investment in accounts receivable.

4. Log on to finance.yahoo.com and find the condensed balance sheets and income statements for Merck (MRK) and Consolidated Edison (ED). Calculate their net working capital and the cash cycle. By how much would the investment in net working capital fall if each firm could reduce its cash cycle by one day?

5. When credit managers need a credit check on a small business, they often look up the Dun & Bradstreet report on the company. You can see a sample Comprehensive Report by logging on to **www.dnb.com**. On the basis of this report, would you be prepared to extend credit to this company? Why or why not?

6. Credit scoring is widely used to rate applicants for personal loans. Several websites provide a free calculator that you can use to estimate your FICO score. Try varying some of the inputs and see how your credit rating changes. How much would the rating change if you missed a loan payment?

7. Log on to the web page of a major bank such as Wells Fargo (**www.wellsfargo.com**) or Bank of America (**www.bankofamerica.com**). How do these banks help corporations to manage their cash? For example, check out each bank's Treasury management services. Among their offerings, you will find lock-box services as well as electronic check processing.

SOLUTIONS TO SELF-TEST QUESTIONS

20.1 One would expect Tiffany to have the longer cash cycle. It holds an inventory of expensive jewelry that can take a long time to sell. Target's goods are priced to sell quickly. In fact, the following calculations show that the difference in the cash cycle of the two firms is driven primarily by their very different inventory periods.

	Tiffany	Target
Sales ($ millions)	$4,248	$72,618
COGS ($ millions)	$1,713	$51,278
Inventories ($ millions)	$2,344	$ 8,534
Accounts receivable ($ millions)	$ 294	$ 1,114
Accounts payable ($ millions)	$ 366	$11,244
Inventory period (days)	499	61
Accounts receivable period (days)	25	6
Payables period (days)	78	80
Cash cycle (days)	446	−13

20.2 To get the cash discount, you have to pay the bill within 10 days, that is, by May 11. With the 2% discount, the amount that needs to be paid by May 11 is $20,000 × .98 = $19,600. If you forgo the cash discount, you do not have to pay your bill until May 21, but on that date the amount due is $20,000.

20.3 The cash discount in this case is 5%, and customers who choose not to take the discount receive an extra 50 − 10 = 40 days credit. So the effective annual interest is

$$\text{Effective annual rate} = \left(1 + \frac{\text{discount}}{\text{discounted price}}\right)^{365/\text{extra days credit}} - 1$$

$$= \left(1 + \frac{5}{95}\right)^{365/40} - 1 = .597, \text{or } 59.7\%$$

In this case, the customer who does not take the discount is effectively borrowing money at an annual interest rate of 59.7%. This is higher than the rate in Example 20.1 because fewer days of credit are obtained by forfeiting the discount.

20.4 The present value of costs is still $1,000. Present value of revenues is now $1,100. The break-even probability is defined by

$$p \times 100 - (1 - p) \times 1,000 = 0$$

which implies that $p = .909$. The break-even probability is higher because the profit margin is now lower. The firm cannot afford as high a bad debt ratio as before because it is not making as much on its successful sales. We conclude that high-margin goods will be offered with more liberal credit terms.

20.5 The higher the discount rate, the less important are future sales. Because the present value of repeat sales is lower, the break-even probability on the initial sale is higher. For instance, we saw that the break-even probability was 1/3 when the discount rate was 10%. When the discount rate is 20%, the present value of a perpetual flow of repeat sales falls to $200/.20 = $1,000, and the break-even probability increases to 1/2:

$$1/2 \times \$1,000 - 1/2 \times \$1,000 = 0$$

20.6 The customer pays bills 45 days after the invoice date. Because goods are purchased daily, at any time there will be bills outstanding with "ages" ranging from 1 to 45 days. At any time, the customer will have 30 days' worth of purchases, or $10,000, outstanding for a period of up to 1 month and have 15 days' worth of purchases, or $5,000, outstanding for between 1 month and 45 days. The aging schedule will appear as follows:

Age of Account	Amount
<1 month	$10,000
1–2 months	5,000

20.7 The benefit of the lock-box system, and the price the firm should be willing to pay for the system, is higher when:

a. Payment size is higher (because interest is earned on more funds).
b. Payments per day are higher (because interest is earned on more funds).
c. The interest rate is higher (because the cost of float is higher).
d. Mail time saved is higher (because more float is saved).
e. Processing time saved is higher (because more float is saved).

20.8 The discount for 3 months is 8/4 = 2%. For every $100 that you undertake to repay in month 6, you receive up-front $100 − $2 = $98. The 3-month interest rate is 100/98 − 1 = .02041. The effective annual rate on the loan is, therefore, $1.02041^4 - 1 = .0842$, or 8.42%.

MINICASE

George Stamper, a credit analyst with Micro-Encapsulators Corp. (MEC), needed to respond to an urgent e-mail request from the southeast sales office. The local sales manager reported that she had an opportunity to clinch an order from Miami Spice (MS) for 50 encapsulators at $10,000 each. She added that she was particularly keen to secure this order because MS was likely to have a continuing need for 50 encapsulators a year and could, therefore, prove a very valuable customer. However, orders of this size to a new customer generally required head office agreement, so it was George's responsibility to make a rapid assessment of MS's creditworthiness and to approve or disapprove the sale.

George knew that MS was a medium-size company with a patchy earnings record. After growing rapidly in the 1980s, MS had encountered strong competition in its principal markets, and earnings had fallen sharply. George was not sure exactly to what extent this was a bad omen. New management had been brought in to cut costs, and there were some indications that the worst was over for the company. Investors appeared to agree with this assessment, because the stock price had risen to $5.80 from its low of $4.25 the previous year. George had in front of him MS's latest financial statements, which are summarized in Table 20.5. He rapidly calculated a few key financial ratios.

George also made a number of other checks on MS. The company had a small issue of bonds outstanding, which were rated B by Moody's. Inquiries through MEC's bank indicated that MS had unused lines of credit totaling $5 million but had entered into discussions with its bank for a renewal of a $15 million bank loan that was due to be repaid at the end of the year. Telephone calls to MS's other suppliers suggested that the company had recently been 30 days late in paying its bills.

George also needed to take into account the profit that the company could make on MS's order. Encapsulators were sold on standard terms of 2/30, net 60. So if MS paid promptly, MEC would receive additional revenues of 50 × $9,800 = $490,000. However, given MS's cash position, it was more than likely that it would forgo the cash discount and would not pay until sometime after the 60 days. Because interest rates were about 8%, any such delays in payment could reduce the present value to MEC of the revenues. George also recognized that there were production and transportation costs in filling MS's order. These worked out at $475,000, or $9,500 a unit. Corporate profits were taxed at 35%.

What can you say about Miami Spice's creditworthiness? What is the break-even probability of default? How is it affected by the delay before MS pays its bills? How should George Stamper's decision be affected by the possibility of repeat orders?

TABLE 20.5 Miami Spice: Summary financial statements (figures in $ millions)

Balance Sheet	2017	2016
Assets		
Current assets		
Cash and marketable securities	$ 5.0	$ 12.2
Accounts receivable	16.2	15.7
Inventories	27.5	32.5
Total current assets	$ 48.7	$ 60.4
Fixed assets		
Property, plant, and equipment	$228.5	$228.1
Less accumulated depreciation	129.5	127.6
Net fixed assets	$ 99.0	$100.5
Total assets	$147.7	$160.9
Liabilities and Shareholders' Equity		
Current liabilities		
Debt due for repayment	$ 22.8	$ 28.0
Accounts payable	19.0	16.2
Total current liabilities	$ 41.8	$ 44.2
Long-term debt	$ 40.8	$ 42.3
Shareholders' equity		
Common stock*	10.0	10.0
Retained earnings	55.1	64.4
Total shareholders' equity	65.1	74.4
Total liabilities and shareholders' equity	$147.7	$160.9

Income Statement	2017	2016
Revenue	$149.8	$134.4
Cost of goods sold	131.0	124.2
Other expenses	1.7	8.7
Depreciation	8.1	8.6
Earnings before interest and taxes	9.0	− 7.1
Interest expense	5.1	5.6
Income taxes	1.4	− 4.4
Net income	$ 2.5	−$ 8.3
Allocation of net income		
Addition to retained earnings	1.5	− 9.3
Dividends	1.0	1.0

* 10 million shares, $1 par value.

21

Mergers, Acquisitions, and Corporate Control

LEARNING OBJECTIVES

After studying this chapter, you should be able to:

21-1 Explain why it may make sense for companies to merge.

21-2 Estimate the gains and costs of mergers to the acquiring firm.

21-3 Describe ways that companies change their ownership or management.

21-4 Describe takeover defenses.

21-5 Explain some of the motivations for leveraged and management buyouts.

21-6 Summarize the evidence on whether mergers increase efficiency and on how any gains from mergers are distributed between shareholders of the acquired and acquiring firms.

RELATED WEBSITES FOR THIS CHAPTER CAN BE FOUND IN CONNECT.

Most mergers are arranged amicably, but when a firm underperforms, it is likely to be gobbled up by a stronger rival.
© Ingram Publishing/SuperStock RF

The scale and pace of merger activity have often been remarkable. For example, Table 21.1 lists just a few recent mergers. Notice that many of the largest mergers have involved firms in different countries. Look also at Figure 21.1, which shows the value of global mergers for each year from 1995 to 2015. The year 2015 was a record one for mergers with 35,000 deals worth $4.6 trillion. During such periods of intense merger activity, financial managers spend considerable time either searching for firms to acquire or worrying whether some other firm is about to take over their company.

When one company buys another, it is making an investment, and the basic principles of capital investment decisions apply. You should go ahead with the purchase if it makes a net contribution to shareholders' wealth. But mergers are often awkward transactions to evaluate, and you have to be careful to define benefits and costs properly.

Many marriages between companies are amicable, but sometimes one party is dragged kicking and screaming to the altar. We review these hostile takeovers and the principal methods of attack and defense.

When a firm is taken over, its management is usually replaced. That is why we describe takeovers as part of a broader market for corporate control. Activity in this market goes far beyond ordinary acquisitions. Ownership or management also changes if there is a proxy contest, a leveraged buyout, or a divestiture. We therefore look at these ways to change control of the firm.

We close the chapter with a discussion of who gains and loses from mergers, and we discuss whether mergers are beneficial on balance.

TABLE 21.1 Some important recent merger announcements (Note: Some of these mergers had not been completed by September 2016)

Industry	Acquiring Company	Selling Company	Payment ($ billions)
Telecom	Charter Communications	Time Warner Cable	79
Pharmaceuticals	Actavis (Ireland)*	Allergan	71
Brewing	Anheuser-Busch InBev	SABMiller	68
Pay TV	AT&T	DirectTV	67
Computing	Dell	EMC	67
Chemicals	Bayer (Germany)	Monsanto	66
Chemicals	Dow Chemical	DuPont	55
Health insurance	Anthem	Cigna	54
Cement	Holcim (Switzerland)	Lafarge (France)	47
Food	H.J. Heinz	Kraft Foods	46
Semiconductors	Avago Technologies (Singapore/U.S.)	Broadcom	37
Pharmaceuticals	Shire (U.K.)	Baxalta	32
Pharmaceuticals	Abbott Laboratories	St. Jude Medical	31
Software	Microsoft	LinkedIn	28
Tobacco	Reynolds American	Lorillard	27
Pharmaceuticals	Actavis (Ireland)	Forest Laboratories	25
Telecom	Altice (Netherlands)	SFR (France)	24

* After completing this acquisition, Actavis changed its name to Allergan.

FIGURE 21.1 The number of mergers in the United States, 1995–2015

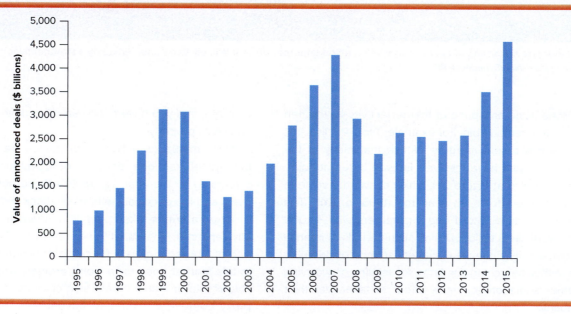

Source: dealogic.

21.1   Sensible Motives for Mergers

Mergers are often categorized as *horizontal, vertical,* or *conglomerate.* A horizontal merger is one that takes place between two firms in the same line of business; the merged firms are former competitors. Most recent mergers have been of this type. For example, the financial crisis led to a number of mammoth bank mergers, such as those between Bank of America and Merrill Lynch and between Wells Fargo and Wachovia. Other headline-grabbing horizontal mergers have involved telecom and cable companies, such as Liberty Global's acquisition of Virgin Media, Charter Communications' merger with Time Warner Cable, and Altice's merger with Cablevision.

A *vertical merger* involves companies at different stages of production. The buyer expands back toward the source of raw materials or forward in the direction of the ultimate consumer. Thus, a soft-drink manufacturer might buy a sugar producer (expanding backward) or a fast-food chain as an outlet for its product (expanding forward). The acquisition of the Nokia Handset and Services Business by Microsoft for around $7.9 billion was an example of a vertical merger. Microsoft intended to install its Windows phone operating system on Nokia mobile phones. (In the end, however, the venture failed, and Microsoft eventually had to write off nearly its entire investment in Nokia.)

A *conglomerate merger* involves companies in unrelated lines of business. For example, the Indian company Tata Group is a huge, widely diversified company. Its acquisitions have been as diverse as Eight O'Clock Coffee, Corus Steel, Jaguar Land Rover, British Salt, and the Ritz Carlton, Boston. No U.S. company is as diversified as Tata, but in the 1960s and 1970s, it was common in the United States for unrelated businesses to merge. The number of U.S. conglomerate mergers declined in the 1980s. In fact, much of the action in the 1980s came from breaking up the conglomerates that had been formed 10 to 20 years earlier.

21.1 Self-Test

Are the following hypothetical mergers horizontal, vertical, or conglomerate?

a. The computer manufacturer Lenovo acquires Dell.
b. Dell acquires Safeway (a supermarket chain).
c. Safeway acquires Campbell Soup.
d. Campbell Soup acquires Lenovo.

Many mergers and acquisitions are motivated by possible gains in efficiency from combining operations. These mergers create *synergies.* By this, we mean that the two firms are worth more together than apart.

With these distinctions in mind, we are about to consider why firms may sometimes be worth more together than apart. We proceed with some trepidation. Though mergers often lead to real benefits, the apparent gains are frequently mirages that tempt unwary or overconfident managers into takeover disasters. This was the case for AOL, which spent a record-breaking $156 billion in 2000 to acquire Time Warner. The aim was to create a company that could offer consumers a comprehensive package of media and information products. It didn't work, and in less than 10 years, the two companies threw in the towel and split up. By that point, more than $200 billion of value had evaporated.

Many mergers that appear to make sense fail because managers cannot handle the complex task of integrating two firms with different production processes, pay structures, and accounting methods. Moreover, the value of most businesses depends on *human* assets—managers, skilled workers, scientists, and engineers. If these people are not happy in their new roles in the merged firm, the best of them will leave. Beware of paying too much for assets that go down in the elevator and out to the parking lot at the close of each business day.

Consider the $38 billion merger between Daimler-Benz and Chrysler. Although it was hailed as a model for consolidation in the auto industry, the early years were bedeviled by conflicts between two very different cultures:

> German management-board members had executive assistants who prepared detailed position papers on any number of issues. The Americans didn't have assigned aides and formulated their decisions by talking directly to engineers or other specialists. A German decision worked

its way through the bureaucracy for final approval at the top. Then it was set in stone. The Americans allowed midlevel employees to proceed on their own initiative, sometimes without waiting for executive-level approval.

. . . Cultural integration also was proving to be a slippery commodity. The yawning gap in pay scales fueled an undercurrent of tension. The Americans earned two, three, and, in some cases, four times as much as their German counterparts. But the expenses of U.S. workers were tightly controlled compared with the German system. Daimler-side employees thought nothing of flying to Paris or New York for a half-day meeting, then capping the visit with a fancy dinner and a night in an expensive hotel. The Americans blanched at the extravagance.[1]

Nine years after acquiring Chrysler, Daimler announced that it was offloading an 80% stake in Chrysler to a leveraged-buyout firm, Cerberus Capital Management. Daimler actually paid Cerberus $677 million to take Chrysler off its hands. Cerberus in return assumed about $18 billion in pension and employee health care liabilities and agreed to invest $6 billion in Chrysler and its finance subsidiary.

These observations illustrate the difficulties in realizing the benefits of merger. There are also occasions when the merger does achieve the intended synergies, but the buyer nevertheless loses because it pays too much. The buyer may overestimate the value of stale inventory or underestimate the costs of renovating old plant and equipment, or it may overlook the warranties on a defective product. For example, when Bank of America took over Countrywide Financial in 2007, it was blindsided by the extent of Countrywide's mortgage-related losses as well as the legal liabilities it inherited from Countrywide's lending practices. Bank of America's losses on the merger are now estimated at more than $50 billion.

With these caveats in mind, we will now consider some possible sources of synergy.

Economies of Scale

Just as most of us believe that we would be happier if only we were a little richer, so managers always seem to believe their firm would be more competitive if only it were just a little bigger. They hope for *economies of scale,* that is, the opportunity to spread fixed costs across a larger volume of output. For example, when Heinz and Kraft Foods announced plans to merge in 2015, they forecast annual cost savings of $1.5 billion by the end of 2017. These savings would mostly come from economies of scale in the North American market, where there would be opportunities to shut down less efficient manufacturing facilities and reduce labor costs. Also, the larger combined sales would help the company to drive better bargains with retailers and restaurants.[2] Beware of overly optimistic predictions of cost savings, however. The nearby box tells the story of one bank merger that resulted in a spectacular debacle rather than the predicted synergies.

These economies of scale are the natural goal of horizontal mergers. But they have been claimed in conglomerate mergers, too. The architects of these mergers have pointed to the economies that come from sharing central services such as accounting, financial control, and top-level management.

Economies of Vertical Integration

Large companies commonly like to gain as much control and coordination as possible over the production process by expanding back toward the output of the raw material and forward to the ultimate consumer. One way to achieve this is to merge with a supplier or a customer.

Vertical integration facilitates coordination and administration. We illustrate with an extreme example: Think of an airline that does not own any planes. If it sells tickets

---

[1] From Bill Vlasic and Bradley A. Stertz, *Taken for a Ride: How Daimler-Benz Drove Off with Chrysler,* pp. 302, 319 © 2000 HarperCollins Publishers.

[2] See "Analysis of the Kraft-Heinz Merger," *Forbes,* March 30, 2015.

When three of Japan's largest banks combined to form Mizuho Bank, it brought together assets of $1.5 trillion, more than twice those of the world leader Deutsche Bank. The name "Mizuho" means "rich rice harvest," and the bank's management forecast that the merger would create a rich harvest of synergies. In a message to shareholders, the bank president claimed that the merger would create "a comprehensive financial services group that will surge forward in the 21st century." He predicted that the bank would "lead the new era through cutting-edge comprehensive financial services . . . by exploiting to the fullest extent the Group's enormous strengths, which are backed by a powerful customer base and state-of-the-art financial and information technologies." The cost of putting the banks together was forecast at ¥130 billion, but management predicted future benefits of ¥466 billion a year.

Within a few months of the announcement, reports began to emerge of squabbles among the three partners. One problem area was IT. Each of the three merging banks had a different supplier for its computer system. At first, it was proposed to use just one of these three systems, but then the banks decided to connect the three different systems together by using "relay" computers.

Three years after the initial announcement, the new company opened for business on April 1, 2002. Five days later, computer glitches resulted in a spectacular foul-up. Some 7,000 of the bank's cash machines did not work; 60,000 accounts were debited twice for the same transaction; and millions of bills went unpaid. *The Economist* reported that 2 weeks later, Tokyo Gas, the biggest gas company, was still missing ¥2.2 billion in payments and the top telephone company, NTT, which was looking for ¥12.7 billion, was forced to send its customers receipts marked with asterisks in place of figures because it did not know which of about 760,000 bills had been paid.

One of the objects behind the formation of Mizuho was to exploit economies in its IT systems. The launch fiasco illustrated dramatically that it is easier to predict such merger synergies than to realize them.

Source: The creation of Mizuho Bank and its launch problems are described in "Undispensable: A Fine Merger Yields One Fine Mess," *The Economist,* April 25, 2002 © The Economist Newspaper Limited, London (April 25, 2002).

for a flight from Boston to San Francisco, it then rents a plane from a separate company. Perhaps this arrangement might work on a small scale, but it would be an administrative nightmare for a major carrier that would have to coordinate hundreds of rental agreements each day. It is not surprising that all major airlines have integrated backward by buying and flying their own airplanes rather than patronizing rent-a-plane companies.

As this example suggests, vertical mergers often make sense when two businesses are inextricably linked. For example, a smelter may need to be located next to a mine to reduce the costs of transporting the ore. While it may be possible in such cases to organize the activities as separate firms operating under a long-term contract, such a contract can never allow for every conceivable change in circumstance. Therefore, when two parts of an operation are highly dependent on each other, it can make sense to combine them within the same firm, which then decides how the assets are best used.

Vertical integration has fallen out of fashion recently. Many companies are finding it more efficient to *outsource* many of their activities. For example, back in the 1950s and 1960s, General Motors was thought to have a cost advantage over its competitors because it produced a greater fraction of its components in-house. By the 1990s, Ford and Chrysler had the advantage. They could buy the parts more cheaply from outside suppliers. This was partly because the outside suppliers tended to use nonunion labor. But it also appears that manufacturers have more bargaining power when they are dealing with independent suppliers rather than with another part of the corporate family. In 1998, GM decided to spin off Delphi, its automotive parts division, as a separate company. After the spin-off, GM continued to buy parts from Delphi in large volumes, but it negotiated the purchases at arm's length.

Combining Complementary Resources

Many small firms are acquired by large firms that can provide the missing ingredients necessary for the firm's success. The small firm may have a unique product but lack the engineering and sales organization necessary to produce and market it on a large scale. The firm could develop engineering and sales talent from scratch, but it may be quicker and cheaper to merge with a firm that already has ample talent. The two firms have *complementary resources*—each has what the other needs—so it may make sense for them to merge. Also the merger may open up opportunities that neither firm would pursue otherwise.

In recent years, many of the major pharmaceutical firms have faced the loss of patent protection on their more profitable products and have not had an offsetting pipeline of promising new compounds. This has prompted an increasing number of acquisitions of biotech firms. For example, in 2015, Shire spent $5.9 billion to acquire Dyax, a biotech company with a breakthrough rare disease treatment. Shire calculated that its bigger global reach would help to get the full potential from this product.

Mergers as a Use for Surplus Funds

Suppose that your firm is in a mature industry. It is generating a substantial amount of cash, but it has few profitable investment opportunities. Ideally, such a firm should distribute the surplus cash to shareholders by increasing its dividend payment or by repurchasing its shares. Unfortunately, energetic managers are often reluctant to shrink their firm in this way.

If the firm is not willing to purchase its own shares, it can instead purchase someone else's. Thus, firms with a surplus of cash and a shortage of good investment opportunities often turn to mergers *financed by cash* as a way of deploying their capital.

Firms that have excess cash and do not pay it out or redeploy it by acquisition often find themselves targets for takeover by other firms that propose to redeploy the cash for them. During the oil price slump of the early 1980s, many cash-rich oil companies found themselves threatened by takeover. This was not because their cash was a unique asset. The acquirers wanted to capture the companies' cash flow to make sure it was not frittered away on negative-NPV oil exploration projects. We return to this *free-cash-flow* motive for takeovers later in the chapter.

Eliminating Inefficiencies

Cash is not the only asset that may be wasted by poor management. There are always firms with unexploited opportunities to cut costs and increase sales and earnings. Such firms are natural candidates for acquisition by other firms with better management. In some instances "better management" may simply mean the determination to force painful cuts or realign the company's operations. Notice that the motive for such acquisitions has nothing to do with benefits from combining two firms. Acquisition is simply the mechanism by which a new management team replaces the old one.

A merger may not be the only way to improve management, but sometimes, there is no simple and practical alternative. Managers are naturally reluctant to fire or demote themselves, and stockholders of large public firms do not usually have much *direct* influence on how the firm is run or who runs it.

If this motive for merger is important, one would expect to observe that acquisitions often precede a change in the management of the target firm. This seems to be the case. For example, Martin and McConnell found that the chief executive is four times more likely to be replaced in the year after a takeover than during earlier years.[3] The firms that they studied had generally been poor performers. Apparently, many of these firms fell on bad times and were rescued by merger.

Industry Consolidation

The biggest opportunities to improve efficiency seem to come in industries with too many firms and too much capacity. These conditions often trigger a wave of mergers and acquisitions, which then force companies to cut capacity and employment and

---

[3] K. J. Martin and J. J. McConnell, "Corporate Performance, Corporate Takeovers, and Management Turnover," *Journal of Finance* 46 (June 1991), pp. 671–687.

release capital for reinvestment elsewhere in the economy. For example, when U.S. defense budgets fell after the end of the Cold War, a round of consolidating takeovers followed in the defense industry.

The banking industry is another example. The United States entered the 1980s with far too many banks, largely as a result of restrictions on interstate banking. When those restrictions were loosened and technology improved, hundreds of small banks were swept up into regional or "super-regional" banks. Europe also experienced a wave of bank mergers as companies sought to gain the financial muscle to compete in a Europe-wide banking market. These included the mergers of UBS and Swiss Bank Corp. (1997), BNP and Banque Paribas (1998), Banco Santander and Banco Central Hispanico (1999), and Commerzbank and Dresdner Bank (2009).

21.2   Dubious Reasons for Mergers

The benefits that we have described so far all make economic sense. Other arguments sometimes given for mergers are more dubious. Here are two.

Diversification

We have suggested that the managers of a cash-rich company may prefer to see that cash used for acquisitions. That is why we often see cash-rich firms in stagnant industries merging their way into fresh woods and pastures new. But what about diversification as an end in itself? It is obvious that diversification reduces risk. Isn't that a gain from merging?

The trouble with this argument is that diversification is easier and cheaper for the stockholder than for the corporation. Why should firm A buy firm B to diversify when the shareholders of firm A can buy shares in firm B to diversify their own portfolios? It is far easier and cheaper for individual investors to diversify than it is for firms to combine operations. There is little evidence that investors pay a premium for diversified firms; in fact, discounts are more common.

The Bootstrap Game

During the 1960s, some conglomerate companies made acquisitions that offered no evident economic gains. Nevertheless, the conglomerates' aggressive strategy produced several years of rising earnings per share. To see how this can happen, let us look at the acquisition of Muck and Slurry by the well-known conglomerate World Enterprises.

Example 21.1 ▶   The Bootstrap Game

The position before the merger is set out in the first two columns of Table 21.2. Notice that because Muck and Slurry has relatively poor growth prospects, its stock sells at a lower price-earnings ratio than World Enterprises (line 3). The merger, we assume, produces no economic benefits, so the firms should be worth exactly the same together as apart. The value of World Enterprises after the merger is therefore equal to the sum of the separate values of the two firms (line 6).

Because World Enterprises stock is selling for double the price of Muck and Slurry stock (line 2), World Enterprises can acquire the 100,000 Muck and Slurry shares for 50,000 of its own shares. Thus, World will have 150,000 shares outstanding after the merger.

World's total earnings double as a result of the acquisition (line 5), but the number of shares increases by only 50%. Its earnings *per share* rise from $2.00 to $2.67. We call this a *bootstrap effect* because there is no real gain created by the merger and no increase in the two firms' combined value. Since World's stock price is unchanged by the acquisition of Muck and Slurry, the price-earnings ratio falls (line 3).

TABLE 21.2 Impact of merger on market value and earnings per share of World Enterprises

	World Enterprises (before merger)	Muck and Slurry	World Enterprises (after acquiring Muck and Slurry)
1. Earnings per share	$2	$2	$2.67
2. Price per share	$40	$20	$40
3. Price-earnings ratio	20	10	15
4. Number of shares	100,000	100,000	150,000
5. Total earnings	$200,000	$200,000	$400,000
6. Total market value	$4,000,000	$2,000,000	$6,000,000
7. Current earnings per dollar invested in stock (line 1 divided by line 2)	$0.05	$0.10	$0.067

Note: When World Enterprises purchases Muck and Slurry, there are no gains. Therefore, total earnings and total market value should be unaffected by the merger. But earnings *per share* increase. World Enterprises issues only 50,000 of its shares (priced at $40) to acquire the 100,000 Muck and Slurry shares (priced at $20).

Before the merger, $1 invested in World Enterprises bought 5 cents of current earnings and rapid growth prospects. On the other hand, $1 invested in Muck and Slurry bought 10 cents of current earnings but slower growth prospects. If the *total* market value is not altered by the merger, then $1 invested in the merged firm gives World shareholders 6.7 cents of immediate earnings but slower growth than before the merger. Muck and Slurry shareholders get lower immediate earnings but faster growth. Neither side gains or loses *provided* that everybody understands the deal.

Financial manipulators sometimes try to ensure that the market does *not* understand the deal. Suppose that investors are fooled by the exuberance of the president of World Enterprises and mistake the 33% postmerger increase in earnings per share for *sustainable* growth. If they do, the price of World Enterprises stock rises and the shareholders of both companies receive something for nothing. ■

You should now see how to play the bootstrap game. Suppose that you manage a company enjoying a high price-earnings ratio. The reason it is high is that investors anticipate rapid growth in future earnings. You achieve this growth not by capital investment, product improvement, or increased operating efficiency, but by purchasing slow-growing firms with low price-earnings ratios. The long-run result will be slower growth and a depressed price-earnings ratio, but in the short run, earnings per share can increase dramatically. If this fools investors, you may be able to achieve the higher earnings per share without suffering a decline in your price-earnings ratio. But in order to *keep* fooling investors, you must continue to expand by merger *at the same compound rate.* Obviously, you cannot do this forever; one day, expansion must slow down or stop. Then earnings growth will cease, and your house of cards will fall. **Buying a firm with a lower P/E ratio can increase earnings per share. But the increase should not result in a higher share price. The short-term increase in earnings should be offset by lower future earnings growth.**

21.2 Self-Test

Suppose that Muck and Slurry has even worse growth prospects than in our example and its share price is only $10. Recalculate the effects of the merger in this case. You should find that earnings per share increase by a greater amount because World Enterprises can now buy the same *current* earnings for fewer shares.

21.3   The Mechanics of a Merger

Buying a company is a much more complicated affair than buying a piece of machinery. We are not going to get into the tax or accounting complexities here, but we will describe the different forms that an acquisition can take and the way that an acquisition can be stymied by an antitrust ruling.

The Form of Acquisition

There are three ways for one firm to acquire another. One possibility is to *merge* the two companies into one, in which case the acquiring company assumes *all* the assets and *all* the liabilities of the other. The acquired firm ceases to exist, and its former shareholders receive cash and/or securities in the acquiring firm. A **merger** must have the approval of at least 50% of the shareholders of each firm.[4]

merger
Combination of two firms into one, with the acquirer assuming assets and liabilities of the target firm.

An alternative procedure is for the acquiring firm to buy the target firm's stock in exchange for cash, shares, or other securities. The acquired firm may continue to exist as a separate entity, but it is now owned by the acquirer. The approval and cooperation of the target firm's managers are generally sought, but even if they resist, the acquirer can attempt to purchase a majority of the outstanding shares. By offering to buy shares directly from shareholders, the acquiring firm can bypass the target firm's management altogether. The offer to purchase stock is called a **tender offer.** If the tender offer is successful, the buyer obtains control and can, if it chooses, toss out incumbent management.

tender offer
Takeover attempt in which outsiders directly offer to buy the stock of the firm's shareholders.

The third approach is to buy the target firm's assets. In this case, ownership of the assets needs to be transferred, and payment is made to the selling firm rather than directly to its stockholders.

The terminology of mergers and acquisitions (M&A) can be confusing. These phrases are used loosely to refer to any kind of corporate combination or takeover. But strictly speaking, *merger* means the combination of all the assets and liabilities of two firms. The purchase of the stock or assets of another firm is an **acquisition.**

acquisition
Takeover of a firm by purchase of that firm's common stock or assets.

Mergers, Antitrust Law, and Popular Opposition

Mergers may be blocked by the federal government if they are thought to be anticompetitive or to create too much market power. Even the threat of government opposition may be enough to scupper the companies' plans. For example, in 2015, the $70 billion takeover of Time Warner Cable by Comcast was abandoned after regulators raised concerns that the deal would give Comcast an unfair advantage in the cable TV market.

Companies that do business outside the United States also have to worry about foreign antitrust laws. For example, when Deutsche Börse and the New York Stock Exchange announced plans to merge, the European Commission ruled that the move would create an unduly dominant position in the market for European derivatives.

Mergers may also be stymied by political pressures and popular resentment even when no formal antitrust issues arise. In recent years, national governments in Europe have become involved in almost all high-profile cross-border mergers and are likely to intervene actively in any hostile bid. For example, the news in 2005 that PepsiCo might bid for Danone aroused considerable hostility in France. The prime minister added his support to opponents of the merger and announced that the French government was drawing up a list of strategic industries that should be protected from foreign ownership. It was unclear whether yogurt production would be one of these strategic industries.

---

[4] Corporate charters and state laws sometimes specify a higher percentage.

Economic nationalism is not confined to Europe. For example, in the wake of concern over cyber espionage, a U.S. House of Representatives committee recommended in 2012 that the federal government should block mergers of U.S. firms with Chinese telecommunications companies.

Cross-Border Mergers and Tax Inversion

In 2013, the U.S pharmaceutical company Actavis took over Warner-Chilcott of Ireland. As part of the deal, the company announced that it would reincorporate in Ireland, where the corporate tax rate is 12.5%, much lower than the combined U.S. federal and state corporate tax rate. In the following year, Actavis acquired both Forest Labs and Allergan and, as a result, they both changed their headquarters to Ireland.

These deals are examples of *tax inversion*. The United States taxes a company's profits even if the profits are earned overseas. Other countries tax only those profits that are earned domestically. When a U.S. corporation moves abroad because of a merger, it must still pay U.S. tax on its U.S. profits, but it no longer pays U.S. tax on profits earned elsewhere. Because the corporate tax rate in the United States is much higher than in most other developed countries, there has been a strong incentive for companies to move their domicile abroad. Tax inversion deals have prompted concerns about the loss of tax revenue and accusations of unpatriotic corporate behavior. In response, the U.S. government has enacted several regulations that somewhat reduce the opportunities for tax inversion.

21.4   Evaluating Mergers

If you are given the responsibility for evaluating a proposed merger, you must think hard about the following two questions:

1. Is there an overall economic gain to the merger? In other words, is the merger value-enhancing? Are the two firms worth more together than apart?
2. Do the terms of the merger make my company and its shareholders better off? There is no point in merging if the cost is too high and all the economic gain goes to the other company.

Answering these deceptively simple questions is rarely easy. Some economic gains can be nearly impossible to quantify, and complex merger financing can obscure the true terms of the deal. But the basic principles for evaluating mergers are not too difficult.

Mergers Financed by Cash

We will concentrate on a simple numerical example. Your company, Cislunar Foods, is considering acquisition of a smaller food company, Targetco. Cislunar is proposing to finance the deal by purchasing all of Targetco's outstanding stock for $19 per share. Some financial information on the two companies is given in Table 21.3.

BEYOND THE PAGE

 Merger calculator

mhhe.com/brealey9e

Question 1   Why would Cislunar and Targetco be worth more together than apart? Suppose that operating costs can be reduced by combining the companies' marketing, distribution, and administration. Revenues can also be increased in Targetco's region. The rightmost column of Table 21.3 contains projected revenues, costs, and earnings for the two firms operating together: annual operating costs postmerger will be $2 million less than the sum of the separate companies' costs, and revenues will be $2 million more. Therefore, projected earnings increase by $4 million.[5] We will assume that the increased earnings are the only synergy to be generated by the merger.

---

[5] To keep things simple, the example ignores taxes and assumes that both companies are all-equity-financed. We also ignore the interest income that could have been earned by investing the cash used to finance the merger.

TABLE 21.3 Cislunar Foods is considering an acquisition of Targetco. The merger would increase the companies' combined earnings by $4 million.

	Cislunar Foods	Targetco	Combined Companies	
Revenues	$150	$20	$172	(+2)
Operating costs	$118	$16	$132	(−2)
Earnings	$ 32	$ 4	$ 40	(+4)
Cash	$ 55	$ 2.5		
Other assets' book value	$185	$17.0		
Total assets	$240	$19.5		
Price per share	$ 48	$16		
Number of shares	10.0	2.5		
Market value	$480	$40		

Note: Figures in millions except price per share.

The economic gain to the merger is the present value of the extra earnings. If the earnings increase is permanent (a level perpetuity) and the cost of capital is 20%,

$$\text{Economic gain} = \text{PV(increased earnings)} = \frac{4}{.20} = \$20 \text{ million}$$

This additional value is the basic motivation for the merger.

Question 2   What are the terms of the merger? What is the cost to Cislunar and its shareholders?

Targetco's management and shareholders will not consent to the merger unless they receive at least the stand-alone value of their shares. They can be paid in cash or by new shares issued by Cislunar. In this case, we are considering a cash offer of $19 per Targetco share, $3 per share over the prior share price. Targetco has 2.5 million shares outstanding, so Cislunar will have to pay out $47.5 million, a premium of $7.5 million over Targetco's prior market value. On these terms, Targetco stockholders will capture $7.5 million out of the $20 million gain from the merger. That ought to leave $12.5 million for Cislunar.

This is shown in the Cash Purchase column of Table 21.4. The total value of the merged firm, $492.5 million, is the sum of the original values of the two firms *plus* the economic gain from the merger *minus* the cash paid by Cislunar to Targetco's shareholders. That cash leaves the merged firm. Shares outstanding of Cislunar remain at 10 million, so price per share rises by $1.25 to $49.25, giving Cislunar shareholders a gain of $1.25 per share × 10 million shares = $12.5 million.

Therefore, the merger makes sense for Cislunar for two reasons. First, it adds $20 million of overall value. Second, the terms of the merger give only $7.5 million of that $20 million overall gain to Targetco's stockholders, leaving $12.5 million for Cislunar. You could say that the *cost* of acquiring Targetco is $7.5 million—the difference between the cash payment and the value of Targetco as a separate company:

$$\text{Cost} = \text{cash paid out} - \text{Targetco value} = \$47.5 - 40 = \$7.5 \text{ million}$$

Of course, the Targetco stockholders are ahead by $7.5 million. *Their gain is your cost.* As we've already seen, Cislunar stockholders come out $12.5 million ahead. This is the merger's NPV for Cislunar:

$$\text{NPV} = \text{economic gain} - \text{cost} = \$20 - 7.5 = \$12.5 \text{ million}$$

Writing down the economic gain and cost of a merger in this way separates the motive for the merger (the economic gain, or value added) from the terms of the merger (the *division* of the gain between the two merging companies).

TABLE 21.4 Financial forecasts after the Cislunar–Targetco merger. The middle column assumes a cash purchase at $19 per Targetco share. The right column assumes Targetco stockholders receive one new Cislunar share for every three Targetco shares.

	Cash Purchase	Exchange of Shares
A. Value of Firms		
Original value of Cislunar	$480	$480
+ Original value of Targetco	40	40
+ Economic gain from merger	20	20
− Cash paid to Targetco shareholders	47.5	0
= Value of Cislunar after merger	$492.5	$540
Cislunar shares outstanding postmerger	10	10.833
Cislunar price per share postmerger	$49.25	$ 49.85
B. Gains from Merger		
Value of original Cislunar shareholders: postmerger	$492.5	$498.5 (= 10 × $49.85)
− Value of Cislunar shares: premerger	480	480
= Cislunar shareholders' gain from merger	$ 12.5	$ 18.5
Value received by Targetco shareholders	$ 47.5 (cash payment)	$ 41.5 (= .833 × $49.85) (value of shares in merged firm)
− Value of Targetco shares premerger	40	40
= Targetco shareholders' gain from merger	$7.5	$ 1.5
Sum of gains to Cislunar and Targetco shareholders	12.5 + 7.5 = $20	18.5 + 1.5 = $20

Note: Figures in millions except price per share.

21.3 Self-Test

The Great White Shark Company makes a surprise cash offer of $22 a share for Goldfish Industries. Before the offer, Goldfish was selling for $18 a share. Goldfish has 1 million shares outstanding. What must Great White believe about the present value of the improvement it can bring to Goldfish's operations?

Mergers Financed by Stock

What if Cislunar wants to conserve its cash for other investments and, therefore, decides to pay for the Targetco acquisition with new Cislunar shares? The deal calls for Targetco shareholders to receive one Cislunar share in exchange for every three Targetco shares.

It's the same merger, but the financing is different. The right column of Table 21.4 works out the consequences. The value of the merged firm is $540 million in this case because no cash is paid out to the original Targetco shareholders. Instead, they are given shares in the merged firm, specifically one share of Cislunar for every three of their 2.5 million original shares in Targetco, a total of .833 million shares. This means that there will be 10.833 million shares in the merged firm, resulting in a share price of $540/10.833 = $49.85.

The value of the shares given to Targetco's original shareholders is .833 million × $49.85 = $41.5 million, representing an increase of $1.5 million over the value of their original holdings. Following the merger, Cislunar's original shareholders hold stock with total market value of 10 million × $49.85 = $498.5 million, an increase of $18.5 million over their original value.

In both cases, the total gains to Cislunar's original shareholders and Targetco's shareholders sum to $20 million, the economic gain of the merger. But given the terms of this share exchange, less of the gain is captured by Targetco's shareholders.

They get 833,333 shares at $49.85, or $41.5 million, a premium of only $1.5 million over Targetco's prior market value:

$$\text{Cost} = \text{value of shares issued} - \text{Targetco value}$$
$$= \$41.5 - 40 = \$1.5 \text{ million}$$

The merger's NPV to Cislunar's original shareholders is

$$\text{NPV} = \text{economic gain} - \text{cost} = 20 - 1.5 = \$18.5 \text{ million}$$

Note that Cislunar stock rises by $1.85 from its prior value. The total increase in value for Cislunar's original shareholders, who retain 10 million shares, is $18.5 million.

Evaluating the terms of a merger can be tricky when there is an exchange of shares. The target company's shareholders will retain a stake in the merged firms, so you have to figure out what the firm's shares will be worth *after* the merger is announced and its benefits appreciated by investors. Notice that we started with the total market value of Cislunar and Targetco postmerger, took account of the merger terms (833,333 new shares issued), and worked back to the postmerger share price. Only then could we work out the division of the merger gains between the two companies.

There is a key distinction between cash and stock for financing mergers. If cash is offered, the cost of the merger is not affected by the size of the merger gains. If stock is offered, the cost depends on the gains because the gains show up in the postmerger share price, and these shares are used to pay for the acquired firm.

Stock financing also mitigates the effects of over- or undervaluation of either firm. Suppose, for example, that A overestimates B's value as a separate entity, perhaps because it has overlooked some hidden liability. Thus, A makes too generous an offer. Other things equal, A's stockholders are better off if it is a stock rather than a cash offer. With a stock offer, the inevitable bad news about B's value will fall partly on B's former stockholders.

21.4 Self-Test

Suppose Targetco shareholders demand 1 Cislunar share for every 2.5 Targetco shares. Otherwise, they will not accept the merger. Under these revised terms, is the merger still a good deal for Cislunar?

A Warning

The cost of a merger is the premium the acquirer pays for the target firm over its value as a separate company. If the target is a public company, you can measure its separate value by multiplying its stock price by the number of outstanding shares. Watch out, though: If investors expect the target to be acquired, its stock price may overstate the company's separate value. The target company's stock price may already have risen in anticipation of a premium to be paid by an acquiring firm.

Another Warning

Some companies begin their merger analyses with a forecast of the target firm's future cash flows. The forecasts include any revenue increases or cost reductions attributable to the merger. The cash flows are then discounted back to the present and compared with the purchase price:

$$\text{Estimated net gain} = \text{DCF valuation of target including merger benefits}$$
$$- \text{cash required for acquisition}$$

This is a dangerous procedure. Even the brightest and best-trained analyst can make large errors in valuing a business. The estimated net gain may come up positive not because the merger makes sense, but simply because the analyst's cash-flow forecasts are too optimistic. On the other hand, a good merger may not be pursued if the analyst fails to recognize the target's potential as a stand-alone business.

A better procedure *starts* with the target's current and stand-alone market value and concentrates instead on the *changes* in cash flow that would result from the merger. **Always ask why the two firms should be worth more together than apart. Remember,** *you add value only if you can generate additional economic benefits*—**some competitive edge that other firms can't match and that the target firm's managers can't achieve on their own.**

It makes sense to keep an eye on the value that investors place on the gains from merging. If A's stock price falls when the deal is announced, investors are sending a message that the merger benefits are doubtful *or* that A is paying too much for these benefits.

21.5   The Market for Corporate Control

The shareholders are the owners of the firm. But most shareholders do not feel like the boss, and with good reason. Try buying a share of IBM stock and marching into the boardroom for a chat with your employee, the chief executive officer.[6]

The *ownership* and *management* of large corporations are almost always separated. Shareholders do not directly appoint or supervise the firm's managers. They elect the board of directors, who act as their agents in choosing and monitoring the managers of the firm. Shareholders have a direct say in very few matters. Control of the firm is in the hands of the managers, subject to the general oversight of the board of directors.

This system of governance creates potential *agency costs.* Agency costs occur when managers or directors take actions adverse to shareholders' interests.

The temptation to take such actions may be ever-present, but there are many forces and constraints working to keep managers' and shareholders' interests in line. As we pointed out in Chapter 1, managers' paychecks in large corporations are almost always tied to the profitability of the firm and the performance of its shares. Boards of directors take their responsibilities seriously—they may face lawsuits if they don't—and, therefore, are reluctant to rubber-stamp obviously bad financial decisions.

But what ensures that the board has engaged the most talented managers? What happens if managers are inadequate? What if the board of directors is derelict in monitoring the performance of managers? Or what if the firm's managers are fine but resources of the firm could be used more efficiently by merging with another firm? Can we count on managers to pursue arrangements that would put them out of jobs?

These are all questions about *the market for corporate control,* the mechanisms by which firms are matched up with management teams and owners who can make the most of the firm's resources. You should not take a firm's current ownership and management for granted. If it is possible for the value of the firm to be enhanced by changing management or by reorganizing under new owners, there will be incentives for someone to make a change.

There are four ways to change the management of a firm: (1) a successful proxy contest in which a group of stockholders votes in a new group of directors, who then pick a new management team; (2) the purchase of one firm by another in a merger or acquisition; (3) a leveraged buyout of the firm by a private group of investors; and (4) a divestiture, in which a firm either sells part of its operations to another company or spins it off as an independent firm.

We will review briefly each of these methods.

---

[6] Try buying a million shares and you may get a better welcome.

21.6   Method 1: Proxy Contests

Shareholders elect the board of directors to keep watch on management and replace unsatisfactory managers. If the board is lax, shareholders are free to elect a different board. In theory, this ensures that the corporation is run in the best interests of shareholders.

In practice, things are not so clear-cut. Ownership in large corporations is widely dispersed. Usually, even the largest single shareholder holds only a small fraction of the shares. Most shareholders have little notion who is on the board or what the members stand for. Management, on the other hand, deals directly with the board and has a personal relationship with its members. In many corporations, management sits on the committee that nominates candidates for the board. It is not surprising that some boards seem less than aggressive in forcing managers to run a lean, efficient operation and to act primarily in the interests of shareholders.

proxy contest
Takeover attempt in which outsiders compete with management for shareholders' votes. Also called *proxy fight.*

When a group of investors believe that the board and its management team should be replaced, they can launch a **proxy contest.** A *proxy* is the right to vote another shareholder's shares. In a proxy contest, the dissident shareholders attempt to obtain enough proxies to elect their own slate to the board of directors. Once the new board is in control, management can be replaced and company policy changed. A proxy fight is, therefore, a direct contest for control of the corporation.

The problem with proxy fights is that they can cost millions of dollars. Dissidents who engage in them must use their own money, but management can draw on the corporation's funds and lines of communication with shareholders to defend itself. To level the playing field somewhat, the SEC has proposed new rules to make it easier to mount a proxy fight.

Institutional shareholders, such as large hedge funds, have become more aggressive in pressing for managerial accountability and have been able to gain concessions by threatening proxy fights. For example, in 2008 shareholder activist Carl Icahn indicated his intention to put himself forward for nomination to the board of Motorola. Icahn controlled less than 7% of the votes and failed to prevent the reelection of the existing board. Nevertheless, the pressure from Icahn had an effect: Motorola agreed to nominate two new board members and to consult with Icahn about a possible spin-off of the company's handset division.

21.7   Method 2: Takeovers

If the management of one firm believes that another company's management is not acting in the best interests of investors, it can go over the heads of that firm's management and make a *tender offer* directly to its stockholders. The management of the target firm may advise its shareholders to accept the offer and sell their shares, or it may fight the bid in the hope that the acquirer will either raise its offer or walk away from the deal. If the tender offer is successful, the new owner can then install its own management team. Thus, corporate takeovers are the arenas where contests for corporate control are often fought.

In the United States, the rules for tender offers are set largely by the Williams Act of 1968 and by state laws. The courts act as a referee to see that the contests are conducted fairly. The problem in setting these rules is that it is unclear who requires protection. Should the management of the target firm be given more weapons to defend itself against unwelcome predators? Or should it simply be encouraged to sit the game out? Or should it be obliged to conduct an auction to obtain the highest price for its shareholders? And what about would-be acquirers? Should they be forced to reveal their intentions at an early stage, or would that allow other firms to piggyback on their good ideas by entering bids of their own? Keep these questions in mind as you read Example 21.2.

| Example | 21.2 ▶ | Allergan Fights Off an Unwelcome Predator |

Allergan is a U.S. specialty pharmaceutical company, best known as the maker of Botox. In 2014, its independence was threatened by the Canadian firm, Valeant, which, in an unusual move, teamed up with the hedge fund, Pershing Square, to acquire Allergan. Between February and April 2014, Bill Ackman, the manager of Pershing, built up a holding of 9.7% of Allergan's shares. Then on April 21, Valeant announced its offer for Allergan of $47 billion in a mixture of stock and cash, a premium of about 17% over Allergan's previous day's market value.

Allergan's management rejected the offer as undervaluing the company. It accused Valeant of following a strategy of gobbling up acquisitions and starving them of funds. In turn, Valeant accused Allergan's management of spending too freely on research and development and on sales and marketing. It promised that it would cut the combined company's R&D spending by 69%.

As soon as Allergan became aware of Valeant's offer, the board sought to protect itself by putting in place a poison pill. If any single shareholder acquired a holding of more than 10% of Allergan stock, the poison pill would allow Allergan to offer its other shareholders additional shares at a substantial discount. The immediate effect of Allergan's pill was to stop Pershing from increasing its holding.

In May, Valeant moved to anticipate any antitrust objections to the merger by selling off the rights to some of its skin care products that competed with Allergan's. It then raised its offer to $49.4 billion, and 3 days later, raised it again to $53 billion. Subsequently in October, Valeant wrote to Allergan that it was prepared to raise its offer to at least $59 billion, though it stopped short of actually doing so.

As Allergan's board continued to reject Valeant's offers, Pershing proposed to call a special meeting of Allergan's shareholders to replace the board with new members who would be more receptive to Valeant's bid. Such a meeting would require the support of 25% of Allergan's shareholders. Because the poison pill effectively grouped together any shareholders who acted jointly, Pershing needed to be sure that any demand for a special meeting would not trigger the poison pill. Pershing got its way: Allergan settled the pending litigation by agreeing to hold the special shareholder meeting in December, giving Pershing the chance to attempt its threatened replacement of Allergan's board.

But not everything was going well for Pershing and Valeant. In November 2014, a federal court federal district court ruled that there were serious questions as to whether Pershing's collaboration with Valeant involved insider trading and enjoined Pershing Square from voting its shares at Allergan's special meeting unless it disclosed the facts underlying its exposure to liability for insider trading.

Although the poison pill could not prevent Pershing from calling the special meeting to unseat Allergan's directors, it did give Allergan breathing space. So, while the parties were fighting their battles in the courts, Allergan started looking around for a more congenial partner. At first, it thought it had found one in Salix Pharmaceuticals. A combined company of Allergan and Salix would have been too large a fish for Valeant to swallow. Reports of the negotiations with Salix led Pershing to threaten that, if Allergan went ahead with a bid for Salix, Pershing would immediately bring litigation against Allergan's board for breach of fiduciary duty. But by then Allergan had become disenchanted with the possible Salix merger. Shortly afterward, it found a more attractive partner in Actavis. In November 2014, Allergan agreed to a $66 billion offer from Actavis, and the long, acrimonious battle for Allergan was finally over.

Postscript: Allergan still continued to make the headlines. As we saw earlier in the chapter, after the merger, Actavis sold off much of its existing business and changed its name to Allergan. In 2015, Allergan again found itself involved in a merger negotiation as the pharmaceutical giant Pfizer launched a friendly $160 billion bid for the company. But that deal fell through in 2016 when the U.S. government announced new rules limiting the tax benefits of mergers with foreign companies. Much of what made the merger attractive to Pfizer had been Allergan's tax domicile in Ireland, which has lower corporate tax rates than the United States. Valeant also continued to make the news, but it was not news that its shareholders wanted to hear. Its shares plummeted more than 90% after the company uncovered accounting irregularities, warned of a potential default on its $30 billion of debt, and revealed it was under investigation by the SEC. ■

What are the lessons? First, the example illustrates some of the strategems of merger warfare. Firms like Allergan that are worried about being taken over usually prepare their defenses in advance. Like Allergan, they may deter potential bidders by devising poison pills, which make the company unappetizing. For example, the poison pill may give existing shareholders the right to buy the company's shares at half-price as soon as a bidder acquires more than 10% of the shares. The bidder is not entitled to the discount. Thus, the bidder resembles the mythological Tantalus—as soon as it has acquired 10% of the shares, control is lifted away from its reach.

Often, firms that are vulnerable to attack will persuade shareholders to agree to **shark-repellent** changes to the corporate charter. For example, the charter may be amended to require that any merger must be approved by a *supermajority* of 80% of the shares rather than the normal 50%.

These takeover defenses rarely make a company impregnable. In Valeant's case, its offensive gained ground, but with great expense and at a very slow pace. This gave Allergan the opportunity to find a white knight in the form of Actavis that would come to its rescue.

BEYOND THE PAGE

Oracle's bid for
PeopleSoft

mhhe.com/brealey9e

shark repellent
Amendment to a company charter made to forestall takeover attempts.

21.8   Method 3: Leveraged Buyouts

leveraged buyout (LBO)
Acquisition of a firm by a private group using substantial borrowed funds.

management buyout (MBO)
Acquisition of the firm by its own management in a leveraged buyout.

Leveraged buyouts, or **LBOs,** differ from ordinary acquisitions in two ways. First, a large fraction of the purchase price is debt-financed. Some, perhaps all, of this debt is junk, that is, below investment grade. Second, the shares of the LBO no longer trade on the open market. The remaining equity in the LBO is privately held by a small group of (usually institutional) investors and is known as *private equity*. When this group is led by the company's management, the acquisition is called a **management buyout (MBO).** Many LBOs are, in fact, MBOs.

In the 1970s and 1980s, many management buyouts were arranged for unwanted divisions of large, diversified companies. Smaller divisions outside the companies' main lines of business often lacked top management's interest and commitment, and divisional management chafed under corporate bureaucracy. Many such divisions flowered when spun off as MBOs. Their managers, pushed by the need to generate cash for debt service and encouraged by a substantial personal stake in the business, found ways to cut costs and compete more effectively.

During the 1980s, private-equity activity shifted to buyouts of entire businesses, including large, mature public corporations. The largest, most dramatic, and best-documented LBO of them all was the $25 billion takeover of RJR Nabisco in 1988 by Kohlberg Kravis Roberts (KKR). The players, tactics, and controversies of LBOs are writ large in this case.

Example **21.3 ▶**   RJR Nabisco[7]

On October 28, 1988, the board of directors of RJR Nabisco revealed that Ross Johnson, the company's chief executive officer, had formed a group of investors prepared to buy all the firm's stock for $75 per share in cash and take the company private. Johnson's group was backed up and advised by Shearson Lehman Hutton, the investment bank subsidiary of American Express.

---

[7] The story of the RJR Nabisco buyout is reconstructed by B. Burrough and J. Helyar in *Barbarians at the Gate: The Fall of RJR Nabisco* (New York: Harper & Row, 1990) and is the subject of a movie with the same title.

RJR's share price immediately moved to about $75, handing shareholders a 36% gain over the previous day's price of $56. At the same time, RJR's bonds fell because it was clear that existing bondholders would soon have a lot more company.

Johnson's offer lifted RJR onto the auction block. Once the company was in play, its board of directors was obliged to consider other offers, which were not long coming. Four days later, a group of investors led by LBO specialist Kohlberg Kravis Roberts bid $90 per share, $79 in cash plus preferred stock valued at $11.

The bidding finally closed on November 30, some 32 days after the initial offer was revealed. In the end, it was Johnson's group against KKR. KKR offered $109 per share, after adding $1 per share (roughly $230 million) at the last hour. The KKR bid was $81 in cash, convertible subordinated debentures valued at about $10, and preferred shares valued at about $18. Johnson's group bid $112 in cash and securities.

But the RJR board chose KKR. True, Johnson's group had offered $3 per share more, but its security valuations were viewed as "softer" and perhaps overstated. Also, KKR's planned asset sales were less drastic; perhaps its plans for managing the business inspired more confidence. Finally, the Johnson group's proposal contained a management compensation package that seemed extremely generous and had generated an avalanche of bad press.

But where did the merger benefits come from? What could justify offering $109 per share, about $25 billion in all, for a company that only 33 days previously had been selling for $56 per share?

KKR and other bidders were betting on two things. First, they expected to generate billions of additional dollars from interest tax shields, reduced capital expenditures, and sales of assets not strictly necessary to RJR's core businesses. Asset sales alone were projected to generate $5 billion. Second, they expected to make those core businesses significantly more profitable, mainly by cutting back on expenses and bureaucracy. Apparently there was plenty to cut, including the RJR "Air Force," which, at one point, operated 10 corporate jets.

But while KKR's new management team was cutting costs and selling assets, prices in the junk bond market were rapidly declining, implying much higher future interest charges for RJR and stricter terms on any refinancing. In mid-1990, KKR made an additional equity investment, and later that year, the company announced an offer of cash and new shares in exchange for $753 million of junk bonds. By 1993, the burden of debt had been reduced from $26 billion to $14 billion. For RJR, the world's largest LBO, it seemed that high debt was a temporary, not permanent, virtue. ∎

Barbarians at the Gate?

The buyout of RJR crystallized views on LBOs, the junk bond market, and the takeover business. For many, it exemplified all that was wrong with finance in the 1980s, especially the willingness of "raiders" to carve up established companies, leaving them with enormous debt burdens, basically in order to get rich quick.

There was plenty of confusion, stupidity, and greed in the LBO business. Not all the people involved were nice. On the other hand, LBOs generated enormous increases in market value, and most of the gains went to selling stockholders, not raiders. For example, the biggest winners in the RJR Nabisco LBO were the company's stockholders.

The most important sources of added value in the buyout of RJR came from making the firm leaner and meaner. The company's new management was obliged to pay out massive amounts of cash to service the LBO debt. It also had an equity stake in the business and therefore strong incentives to sell off nonessential assets, cut costs, and improve operating profits.

LBOs are usually *diet deals*. But there may be other motives. Here are some of them.

The Junk Bond Markets   LBOs and debt-financed takeovers may have been driven by artificially cheap funding from the junk bond markets. With hindsight, it seems that investors in junk bonds underestimated the risks of default. Default rates climbed painfully between 1989 and 1991, yields rose dramatically, and new issues dried up. For a while, junk-financed LBOs disappeared from the scene.

Leverage and Taxes   As we explained in Chapter 16, borrowing money saves taxes. But taxes were not the main driving force behind LBOs. The value of interest tax shields was just not big enough to explain the observed gains in market value.

Of course, if interest tax shields were the main motive for LBOs' high debt, then LBO managers would not be so concerned to pay off debt. We saw that this was one of the first tasks facing RJR Nabisco's new management.

Other Stakeholders   It is possible that the gain to the selling stockholders is just someone else's loss and that no value is generated overall. Therefore, we should look at the total gain to *all* investors in an LBO, not just the selling stockholders.

Bondholders are the obvious losers. The debt they thought was well-secured may turn into junk when a debt-financed LBO dramatically increases leverage. We noted how market prices of RJR Nabisco debt fell sharply when Ross Johnson's first LBO offer was announced. But again, the value losses suffered by bondholders in LBOs are not nearly large enough to explain stockholder gains.

Leverage and Incentives   Managers and employees of LBOs work harder and often smarter. They have to generate cash to service the extra debt. Moreover, managers' personal fortunes are riding on the LBO's success. They become owners rather than organization men or women.

It is hard to measure the payoff from better incentives, but there is some evidence of improved operating efficiency in LBOs. Kaplan, who studied 48 management buyouts between 1980 and 1986, found average increases in operating income of 24% over the following 3 years. Ratios of operating income and net cash flow to assets and sales increased dramatically. He observed cutbacks in capital expenditures but not in employment. Kaplan suggests that these operating changes "are due to improved incentives rather than layoffs or managerial exploitation of shareholders through inside information."[8]

Free Cash Flow   The free-cash-flow theory of takeovers is basically that mature firms with a surplus of cash will tend to waste it. This contrasts with standard finance theory, which says that firms with more cash than positive-NPV investment opportunities *should* give the cash back to investors through higher dividends or share repurchases. But we see firms like RJR Nabisco spending on corporate luxuries and questionable capital investments. One benefit of LBOs is to put such companies on a diet and force them to pay out cash to service debt.

The free-cash-flow theory predicts that mature, "cash cow" companies will be the most likely targets of LBOs. We can find many examples that fit the theory, including RJR Nabisco. The theory says that the gains in market value generated by LBOs are just the present values of the future cash flows that would otherwise have been frittered away.[9]

We have reviewed several motives for LBOs. We do not say that all LBOs are good. On the contrary, there have been many mistakes, and even soundly motivated LBOs are risky, as the bankruptcies of a number of highly leveraged transactions have demonstrated. Yet we do take issue with those who portray LBOs *solely* as undertaken by Wall Street barbarians breaking up the traditional strength of corporate America.

[8] S. Kaplan, "The Effects of Management Buyouts on Operating Performance and Value," *Journal of Financial Economics* 24 (October 1989), pp. 217–254.

[9] The free-cash-flow theory's chief proponent is Michael Jensen. See M. C. Jensen, "The Eclipse of the Public Corporation," *Harvard Business Review* 67 (September–October 1989), pp. 61–74; and "The Agency Costs of Free Cash Flow, Corporate Finance and Takeovers," *American Economic Review* 76 (May 1986), pp. 323–329.

21.9   Method 4: Divestitures, Spin-Offs, and Carve-Outs

In the market for corporate control, fusion—mergers and acquisitions—gets the most publicity. But fission—the divestiture of assets or entire businesses—can be just as important. Often, one firm may sell part of its business to another firm. For example, we saw in Section 21.7 how the generic drug company Actavis merged with Allergan, a specialty pharmaceutical company. After the merger, Actavis changed its name to Allergan and sold off its generic drug business to Teva Pharmaceutical Industries.

Instead of selling part of their operations, companies sometimes *spin off* a business by separating it from the parent firm and distributing to their shareholders the stock in the newly independent company. For example, after Carl Icahn pressured Motorola to spin off its mobile devices division, the division was launched as an independent company, Motorola Mobility. Motorola's shareholders received shares in the spun-off firm and, thus, could trade their Motorola Mobility shares as well as those of the slimmed-down original company, now renamed Motorola Solutions.[10]

Motorola is by no means alone in wanting to split up. Recent spinner-offers include DuPont, Conagra, eBay, Emerson, and Procter & Gamble.

Carve-outs are similar to spin-offs except that shares in the new company are not given to existing stockholders but, instead, are sold in a public offering. Sometimes, companies carve out a small proportion of the company to establish a market in the subsidiary and subsequently spin off the remainder of the shares. The nearby box describes how the computer company Palm was first carved and then spun.

The most frequent motive for spin-offs is improved efficiency. Companies sometimes refer to a business as being a "poor fit." By spinning off a poor fit, the management of the parent company can concentrate on its main activity. If each business must stand on its own feet, there is no risk that funds will be siphoned off from one in order to support unprofitable investments in the other. Moreover, if the two parts of the business are independent, it is easy to see the value of each and to reward managers accordingly.

21.10   The Benefits and Costs of Mergers

Merger Waves

Look back at Figure 21.1, which shows the number of mergers in the United States for each year since 1962. Notice that mergers come in waves. There was an upsurge in merger activity from 1967 to 1969 and then again in the late 1990s. Another merger boom began in 2003; this petered out with the onset of the financial crisis but then revived in 2014–2015.

We don't really understand why merger activity is so volatile and why it seems to be associated with the level of stock prices. None of the motives that we review in this chapter are related to the general level of stock prices. Neither do they wax and wane with the booms and busts in merger activity.

Some mergers may result from mistakes in valuation on the part of the stock market. In other words, the buyer may believe that investors have underestimated the value of the seller or may hope that they will overestimate the value of the combined firm. But we see (with hindsight) that mistakes are made in bear markets as well as bull markets. Why don't we see just as many firms hunting for bargain acquisitions when the stock market is low? It is possible that "suckers are born every minute," but why do they seem more prone to be harvested in bull markets?

---

[10] Seven months after the spin-off, Google acquired Motorola Mobility for $12.5 billion but less than 2 years later sold it to Lenovo for just below $3 billion. The investment may have been disappointing for Google, but not as disappointing as the final sales price suggests, since Google retained the majority of Motorola's patent portfolio, which was probably the key motivation behind its original purchase.

When 3Com acquired U.S. Robotics in 1997, it also became the owner of Palm, a small start-up business developing handheld computers. It was a lucky purchase because over the next 3 years, the PalmPilot came to dominate the market for handheld computers. But as Palm began to take up an increasing amount of management time, 3Com concluded that it needed to return to its knitting and focus on its basic business of selling computer network systems. It, therefore, announced that it would carve out 5% of its holding of Palm through an initial public offering. At the same time, it published plans to spin off the remaining 95% of Palm shares later in 2000 by giving 3Com shareholders about 1.5 Palm shares for each 3Com share that they owned.

The Palm carve-out occurred at close to the peak of the high-tech boom and got off to a dazzling start. The shares were issued in the IPO at $38 each. On the first day of trading, the stock price touched $165 before closing at $95. Therefore, anyone owning a share of 3Com stock could look forward later in the year to receiving about 1.5 shares of Palm worth 1.5 × 95 = $142.50. But apparently 3Com's shareholders were not fully convinced that their newfound wealth was for real, for on the same day, 3Com's stock price closed at $82, or more than $60 a share *less* than the market value of the shares in Palm that they were due to receive.*

Three years after 3Com spun off its holding in Palm, Palm itself entered the spin-off business by giving shareholders stock in PalmSource, a subsidiary that was responsible for developing and licensing the Palm operating system. The remaining business, renamed palmOne, would focus on making mobile gadgets. The company gave three reasons for its decision to split into two. First, like 3Com's management, Palm's management believed that the company would benefit from clarity of focus and mission. Second, it argued that shareholder value could "be enhanced if investors could evaluate and choose between both businesses separately, thereby attracting new and different investors." Finally, it seemed that Palm's rivals were reluctant to buy software from a company that competed with them in making handheld hardware.

* This difference would seem to present an arbitrage opportunity. An investor who bought 1 share of 3Com and sold short 1.5 shares of Palm would receive an immediate cash flow of $60 *and* own 3Com's other assets for free. The difficulty in executing this arbitrage is explored in O. A. Lamont and R. H. Thaler, "Can the Market Add and Subtract? Mispricing in Tech Stock Carve-Outs," *Journal of Political Economy* 111 (April 2003), pp. 227–268.

There are undoubtedly good acquisitions and bad acquisitions, but economists find it hard to agree on whether acquisitions are beneficial *on balance*. In general, shareholders of the target firm make a healthy gain. For example, one study found that following the announcement of the bid, the stock price of the target company jumped by 16% on average.[11] On the other hand, it appears that investors expected the acquiring companies to just about break even, for the price of their shares fell by .7%. The value of the total package—buyer plus seller—increased by 1.8%. Of course, these are averages; selling shareholders, for example, have sometimes obtained much higher returns. When Hewlett-Packard won its takeover battle to buy data-storage company 3Par, it paid a premium of 230%, or about $1.5 billion, for 3Par's stock.

Because buyers roughly break even and sellers make substantial gains, it seems that there are positive overall benefits from mergers. But not everybody is convinced. Some believe that investors analyzing mergers pay too much attention to short-term earnings gains and don't notice that these gains are at the expense of long-term prospects.

We can't observe how companies would have fared in the absence of a merger, so it is difficult to measure the effects on profitability. However, several studies of merger activity suggest that mergers *do* seem to improve real productivity. For example, Healy, Palepu, and Ruback examined 50 large mergers and found an average increase in the companies' pretax returns of 2.4 percentage points.[12] They argue that this gain came from generating a higher level of sales from the same assets. There was no evidence that the companies were mortgaging their long-term futures by cutting back on long-term investments; expenditures on capital equipment and research and development tracked the industry average.

[11] See G. Andrade, M. Mitchell, and E. Stafford, "New Evidence and Perspectives on Mergers," *Journal of Economic Perspectives* 15 (Spring 2001), pp. 103–120.

[12] See P. Healy, K. Palepu, and R. Ruback, "Does Corporate Performance Improve after Mergers?" *Journal of Financial Economics* 31 (April 1992), pp. 135–175. The study examined the pretax returns of the merged companies relative to industry averages.

If you are concerned with public policy toward mergers, you do not want to look only at their impact on the shareholders of the companies concerned. For instance, we have already seen that, in the case of RJR Nabisco, some part of the shareholders' gain was at the expense of the bondholders and the Internal Revenue Service (through the enlarged interest tax shield). The acquirer's shareholders may also gain at the expense of the target firm's employees, who, in some cases, are laid off or are forced to take pay cuts after takeovers.

Perhaps the most important effect of acquisition is felt by the managers of companies that are not taken over. For example, one effect of LBOs was that the managers of even the largest corporations could not feel safe from challenge. Perhaps the threat of takeover spurs the whole of corporate America to try harder. Unfortunately, we don't know whether on balance the threat makes for more active days or more sleepless nights.

The threat of takeover may be a spur to inefficient management, but it is also costly. The companies need to pay for the services provided by the investment bankers, lawyers, and accountants. In addition, mergers can soak up large amounts of management time and effort. When a company is planning a takeover, it can be difficult to give as much attention as one should to the firm's existing business.

Even if the gains to the community exceed these costs, one wonders whether the same benefits could not be achieved more cheaply another way. For example, are leveraged buyouts necessary to make managers work harder? Perhaps the problem lies in the way that many corporations reward and penalize their managers. Perhaps many of the gains from takeover could be captured by linking management compensation more closely to performance.

SUMMARY

Why may it make sense for companies to merge? (*LO21-1*)

A merger may be undertaken in order to replace an inefficient management. But sometimes, two businesses may be more valuable together than apart. Gains may stem from economies of scale, economies of vertical integration, the combination of complementary resources, or redeployment of surplus funds. We don't know how frequently these benefits occur, but they do make economic sense. Sometimes, mergers are undertaken to diversify risks or artificially increase growth of earnings per share. These motives are dubious.

How should the gains and costs of mergers to the acquiring firm be measured? (*LO21-2*)

A merger generates an economic gain if the two firms are worth more together than apart. The *gain* is the difference between the value of the merged firm and the value of the two firms run independently. The *cost* is the premium that the buyer pays for the selling firm over its value as a separate entity. When payment is in the form of shares, the value of this payment naturally depends on what those shares are worth after the merger is complete. You should go ahead with the merger if the gain exceeds the cost.

In what ways do companies change the composition of their ownership or management? (*LO21-3*)

If the board of directors fails to replace an inefficient management, there are four ways to effect a change: (1) Shareholders may engage in a **proxy contest** to replace the board; (2) the firm may be taken over by another; (3) the firm may be purchased by a private group of investors in a leveraged buyout; or (4) it may sell off part of its operations to another company.

What are some takeover defenses? (*LO21-4*)

Mergers are often amicably negotiated between the management and directors of the two companies; but if the seller is reluctant, the would-be buyer can decide to make a tender offer for the stock. We sketched some of the offensive and defensive tactics used in takeover battles. These defenses include **shark repellents** (changes in the company charter meant to make a takeover more difficult to achieve) and **poison pills** (measures that make takeover of the firm more costly).

What are some of the motivations for leveraged and management buyouts of the firm? (*LO21-5*)

In a **leveraged buyout (LBO)** or **management buyout (MBO),** all public shares are repurchased and the company "goes private." LBOs tend to involve mature businesses with ample cash flow and modest growth opportunities. LBOs and other debt-financed takeovers are driven by a mixture of motives, including (1) the value of interest tax shields; (2) transfers of value from bondholders, who may see the value of their bonds fall as the firm piles up more debt; and (3) the opportunity to create better incentives for managers and employees, who have a personal stake in the company. In addition, many LBOs have been designed to force firms with surplus cash to distribute it to shareholders rather than plowing it back. Investors feared such companies would otherwise channel free cash flow into negative-NPV investments.

Do mergers increase efficiency, and how are the gains from mergers distributed between shareholders of the acquired and acquiring firms? (*LO21-6*)

We observed that when the target firm is acquired, its shareholders typically win: Target firms' shareholders earn abnormally large returns. The bidding firm's shareholders roughly break even. This suggests that the typical merger generates positive net benefits, but competition among bidders and active defense by management of the target firm pushes most of the gains toward selling shareholders.

QUESTIONS AND PROBLEMS

1. **Merger Types.** Are the following hypothetical mergers horizontal, vertical, or conglomerate? (*LO21-1*)
    a. General Motors acquires Ford.
    b. Ford acquires Walmart.
    c. Walmart acquires Kraft Heinz.
    d. Kraft Heinz acquires General Motors.

2. **Merger Motives.** Do each of the following motives for mergers make economic sense? Answer yes or no. (*LO21-1*)
    a. Merging to achieve economies of scale
    b. Merging to reduce risk by diversification
    c. Merging to redeploy cash generated by a firm with ample profits but limited growth opportunities
    d. Merging to increase earnings per share

3. **Merger Motives.** Explain why it might or might not make good sense for Northeast Heating and Northeast Air Conditioning to merge into one company. (*LO21-1*)

4. **The Bootstrap Game.** The Muck and Slurry merger has fallen through (see Section 21.1). But World Enterprises is determined to report earnings per share of $2.67. It therefore acquires the Wheelrim and Axle Company. You are given the following data:

	World Enterprises	Wheelrim and Axle	Merged Firm
Earnings per share	$2.00	$2.50	$2.67
Price per share	$40	$25	_____
Price-earnings ratio	20	10	_____
Number of shares	100,000	200,000	_____
Total earnings	$200,000	$500,000	_____
Total market value	$4,000,000	$5,000,000	_____

Once again, there are no gains from merging. In exchange for Wheelrim and Axle shares, World Enterprises issues just enough of its own shares to ensure its $2.67 earnings per share objective. (*LO21-1*)

a. Complete the preceding table for the merged firm.
b. How many shares of World Enterprises are exchanged for each share of Wheelrim and Axle?
c. What is the cost of the merger to World Enterprises?
d. What is the change in the total value of the World Enterprises shares that were outstanding before the merger?

5. **Mergers and P/E Ratios.** Castles in the Sand currently sells at a price-earnings multiple of 10. The firm has 2 million shares outstanding and sells at a price per share of $40. Firm Foundation has a P/E multiple of 8, has 1 million shares outstanding, and sells at a price per share of $20. (*LO21-1*)

a. If Castles acquires the other firm by exchanging one of its shares for every two of Firm Foundation, what will be the earnings per share of the merged firm?
b. What will happen to Castles' price per share?
c. Show that shareholders of neither Castles nor Firm Foundation realize any change in wealth.
d. What should be the P/E of the new firm if the merger has no economic gains?
e. What will happen to Castles' price per share if the market does not realize that the P/E ratio of the merged firm ought to differ from Castles' premerger ratio?
f. How are the gains from the merger split between shareholders of the two firms if the market is fooled as in part (e)?

6. **Stock versus Cash Offers.** Sweet Cola Corp. (SCC) is bidding to take over Salty Dog Pretzels (SDP). SCC has 3,000 shares outstanding, selling at $50 per share. SDP has 2,000 shares outstanding, selling at $17.50 a share. SCC estimates the economic gain from the merger to be $15,000. (*LO21-2*)

a. If SDP can be acquired for $20 a share, what is the NPV of the merger to SCC?
b. What will SCC sell for when the market learns that it plans to acquire SDP for $20 a share?
c. What will SDP sell for?
d. What are the percentage gains to the shareholders of each firm?
e. Now suppose that the merger takes place through an exchange of stock. On the basis of the premerger prices of the firms, SCC sells for $50, so instead of paying $20 cash, SCC issues .40 of its shares for every SDP share acquired. What will be the price of the merged firm?
f. What is the NPV of the merger to SCC when it uses an exchange of stock? Why does your answer differ from part (a)?

7. **Merger Gains.** Acquiring Corp. is considering a takeover of Takeover Target Inc. Acquiring has 10 million shares outstanding, which sell for $40 each. Takeover Target has 5 million shares outstanding, which sell for $20 each. If the merger gains are estimated at $25 million, what is the highest price per share that Acquiring should be willing to pay to Takeover Target shareholders? (*LO21-2*)

8. **Mergers Gains.** If Acquiring Corp. from Problem 7 has a price-earnings ratio of 12 and Takeover Target has a P/E ratio of 8, what should be the P/E ratio of the merged firm? Assume in this case that the merger is financed by an issue of new Acquiring Corp. shares. Takeover Target will get one Acquiring share for every two Takeover Target shares held. (*LO21-2*)

9. **Merger Gains and Costs.** Velcro Saddles is contemplating the acquisition of Skiers' Airbags Inc. The values of the two companies as separate entities are $20 million and $10 million, respectively. Velcro Saddles estimates that by combining the two companies, it will reduce marketing and administrative costs by $500,000 per year in perpetuity. Velcro Saddles is willing to pay $14 million cash for Skiers'. The opportunity cost of capital is 8%. (*LO21-2*)

a. What is the gain from the merger?
b. What is the cost of the cash offer?
c. What is the NPV of the acquisition under the cash offer?

10. **Stock versus Cash Offers.** Suppose that instead of making a cash offer as in Problem 9, Velcro Saddles considers offering Skiers' shareholders a 50% holding in Velcro Saddles. (*LO21-2*)

a. What is the value of the stock in the merged company held by the original Skiers' shareholders?
b. What is the cost of the stock alternative?
c. What is the merger's NPV under the stock offer?

11. **Stock versus Cash Offers.** As financial manager of Britwell Inc., you are investigating a possible acquisition of Salome. You have the basic data given in the following table. You estimate that investors expect a steady growth of about 6% in Salome's earnings and dividends. Under new management, this growth rate would be increased to 8% per year without the need for additional capital. (*LO21-2*)

	Britwell	Salome
Forecast earnings per share	$5.00	$1.50
Forecast dividend per share	$3.00	$0.80
Number of shares	1,000,000	600,000
Stock price	$90	$20

a. What is the gain from the acquisition?
b. What is the cost of the acquisition if Britwell pays $25 in cash for each share of Salome?
c. What is the cost of the acquisition if Britwell offers one share of Britwell for every three shares of Salome?
d. How would the cost of the cash offer change if the expected growth rate of Salome was not changed by the merger?
e. How would the cost of the share offer change if the expected growth rate was not changed by the merger?

12. **Merger Gains.** Immense Appetite Inc. believes that it can acquire Sleepy Industries and improve efficiency to the extent that the market value of Sleepy will increase by $5 million. Sleepy currently sells for $20 a share, and there are 1 million shares outstanding. (*LO21-2*)

a. Sleepy's management is willing to accept a cash offer of $25 a share. Can the merger be accomplished on a friendly basis?
b. What will happen if Sleepy's management holds out for an offer of $28 a share?

13. **Market for Corporate Control.** Why are both tender offers and proxy contests threatening to the current management of a firm? What are less contentious mechanisms that may lead to a change in management? (*LO21-3*)

14. **Merger Tactics.** Connect each term to its correct definition or description. (*LO21-4*)

a. LBO
b. poison pill
c. tender offer
d. shark repellent
e. proxy contest

A. Attempt to gain control of a firm by winning the votes of its stockholders
B. Changes in the corporate charter that are designed to deter an unwelcome takeover
C. Measure in which shareholders are issued rights to buy shares if the bidder acquires a large stake in the firm
D. Offer to buy shares directly from stockholders
E. Buyout of a company or business by private investors, largely debt-financed

15. **Merger Tactics.** In Section 21.7, we described how Valeant and its ally, Pershing Square, lost the battle to acquire Allergan. Sometimes, the losers in a takeover battle can also win if they own a toe-hold stake in the target's stock. Between April and June 2014, Pershing acquired a 9.7% stake in Allergan at an estimated average price of $128 a share. In November, Actavis offered $219 per share for each of Allergan's 299 million shares. What was Pershing's profit on its holding? (*LO21-4*)

16. **LBO Facts.** True or false? (*LO21-5*)

a. One of the first tasks of an LBO's financial manager is to pay down debt.
b. Leveraged buyouts reduce the free cash flow available to the firm.
c. Targets for LBOs in the 1980s tended to be profitable companies in mature industries with limited investment opportunities.

17. **Merger Facts.** True or false? (*LO21-6*)

a. Sellers usually gain in mergers.
b. Buyers usually gain in mergers.
c. Firms that do unusually well tend to be acquisition targets.
d. Merger activity in the United States varies dramatically from year to year.
e. On average, mergers produce substantial economic gains.
f. Tender offers require the approval of the selling firm's management.
g. The cost of a merger is always independent of the economic gain produced by the merger.

WEB EXERCISE

1. Look at a recent example of a merger announcement, and log on to the website of the acquiring company. What reasons does the acquirer give for buying the target? How does it intend to pay for the target—with cash, shares, or a mixture of the two? Can you work out how much the target's shareholders will gain from the offer? Is it more or less than would be the case for an average merger? Now log on to **finance.yahoo.com** and find out what happened to the stock price of the acquiring company when the merger was announced. Were shareholders pleased with the announcement?

SOLUTIONS TO SELF-TEST QUESTIONS

21.1 a. Horizontal merger. Lenovo is in the same industry as Dell.
      b. Conglomerate merger. Dell and Safeway are in different industries.
      c. Vertical merger. Safeway is expanding backward to acquire one of its suppliers, Campbell Soup.
      d. Conglomerate merger. Campbell Soup and Lenovo are in different industries.

21.2 Given current earnings of $2 a share and a share price of $10, Muck and Slurry would have a market value of $1,000,000 and a price-earnings ratio of only 5. It can now be acquired for only 25,000 of World Enterprises shares. Therefore, the merged firm will have 125,000 shares outstanding and earnings of $400,000, resulting in earnings per share of $3.20, higher than the $2.67 value in the third column of Table 21.2.

21.3 The cost of the merger is $4 million: the $4 per share premium offered to Goldfish shareholders times 1 million shares. If the merger has positive NPV to Great White Shark, the gain must be greater than $4 million.

21.4 Yes. Look again at Table 21.4. Total market value is still $540 million, but Cislunar will have to issue 1 million shares to complete the merger. Total shares in the merged firm will be 11 million. The postmerger share price is $49.09, so Cislunar and its shareholders still come out ahead.

MINICASE

McPhee Food Halls operated a chain of supermarkets in the west of Scotland. The company had had a lackluster record, and since the death of its founder in late 2007, it had been regarded as a prime target for a takeover bid. In anticipation of a bid, McPhee's share price moved up from £4.90 in March 2012 to a 12-month high of £5.80 on June 10, despite the fact that the London stock market index as a whole was largely unchanged.

Almost nobody anticipated a bid coming from Fenton, a diversified retail business with a chain of clothing and department stores. Though Fenton operated food halls in several of its department stores, it had relatively little experience in food retailing. Fenton's management had, however, been contemplating a merger with McPhee for some time. The managers not only felt that they could make use of McPhee's food retailing skills within their department stores, but they also believed that better management and inventory control in McPhee's business could result in cost savings worth £10 million.

Fenton's offer of 8 Fenton shares for every 10 McPhee shares was announced after the market close on June 10. Because McPhee had 5 million shares outstanding, the acquisition would add an additional $5 \times (8/10) = 4$ million shares to the 10 million Fenton shares that were already outstanding. While Fenton's management believed that it would be difficult for McPhee to mount a successful takeover defense, the company and its investment bankers privately agreed that the company could afford to raise the offer if it proved necessary.

Investors were not persuaded of the benefits of combining a supermarket with a department store company, and on June 11 Fenton's shares opened lower and drifted down £.10 to close the day at £7.90. McPhee's shares, however, jumped to £6.32 a share.

Fenton's financial manager was due to attend a meeting with the company's investment bankers that evening, but before doing so, he decided to run the numbers once again. First, he reestimated the gain and cost of the merger. Then, he analyzed that day's fall in Fenton's stock price to see whether investors believed there were any gains to be had from merging. Finally, he decided to revisit the issue of whether Fenton could afford to raise its bid at a later stage. If the effect was simply a further fall in the price of Fenton stock, the move could be self-defeating.

Does the market believe that the merger will create net gains? What are the costs and benefits of the proposed merger for Fenton's shareholders? Would Fenton be wise to raise its bid?

International Financial Management

LEARNING OBJECTIVES

After studying this chapter, you should be able to:

22-1 Understand the difference between spot and forward exchange rates.

22-2 Understand the basic relationships among spot exchange rates, forward exchange rates, interest rates, and inflation rates.

22-3 Formulate simple strategies to protect the firm against exchange rate risk.

22-4 Perform an NPV analysis for projects with cash flows in foreign currencies.

RELATED WEBSITES FOR THIS CHAPTER CAN BE FOUND IN CONNECT.

Coca-Cola does business around the world. What new issues does international business raise for the financial manager?
© Barry Lewis/Alamy

Thus far, we have talked mostly about doing business at home. But many companies have substantial overseas interests. Of course, the objectives of international financial management are still the same. You want to buy assets that are worth *more* than they cost, and you want to pay for them by issuing liabilities that are, if possible, worth *less* than the money raised. But when you try to apply these criteria to an international business, you come up against some new wrinkles.

You must, for example, know how to deal with more than one currency. Therefore, we open this chapter with a look at foreign exchange markets.

The financial manager must also remember that interest rates differ from country to country. For example, in

December 2015, the 10-year interest rate was about 8.2% in Greece, 6.9% in Brazil, 2.2% in the United States, and actually negative, −.2%, in Switzerland. We will discuss the reasons for these differences in interest rates, along with some of the implications for financing overseas operations.

Exchange rate fluctuations can knock companies off course and transform black ink into red. We will, therefore, discuss how firms can protect themselves against exchange risks.

We will also discuss how international companies decide on capital investments. How do they choose the discount rate? You'll find that the basic principles of capital budgeting are the same as those for domestic projects, but there are a few pitfalls to watch for.

22.1 Foreign Exchange Markets

An American company that imports goods from France will probably need to exchange its dollars for euros in order to pay for its purchases. Another company exporting to France may receive euros, which it then sells in exchange for dollars. Both firms must make use of the foreign exchange market, where currencies are traded.

The foreign exchange market has no central marketplace. All business is conducted via computer terminals and telephone. The principal dealers are the large commercial banks, and a corporation that wants to buy or sell currency usually does so through a commercial bank.

Turnover in the foreign exchange markets is huge. In London alone, nearly $1.9 trillion of currency changes hands each day. That is equivalent to an annual turnover of around $500 trillion ($500,000,000,000,000). New York accounts for a further $800 billion of turnover per day. Compare this with the trading volume of the New York Stock Exchange, where about $40 billion of stock typically changes hands on any given day.

Spot Exchange Rates

Suppose you ask someone the price of bread. He may tell you that you can buy two loaves for a dollar, or he may say that one loaf costs 50 cents. If you ask a foreign exchange dealer to quote you a price for Ruritanian rurs, she may tell you that you can buy 100 rurs for a dollar or that 1 rur costs $.01. The first quote (the number of rurs that you can buy for a dollar) is known as an *indirect quote* of the **exchange rate.** The second quote (the number of dollars that it costs to buy 1 rur) is known as a *direct quote.* Of course, both quotes provide the same information. If you can buy 100 rurs for a dollar, then you can easily calculate that the cost of buying 1 rur is 1/100 = $.01.

(Ruritania is a fictional country, which for arithmetic convenience has a currency that trades for exactly 100 rurs per U.S. dollar. We will use Ruritania in several examples.)[1]

Table 22.1 shows the exchange rate for several actual countries on December 17, 2015. The second column of the table shows the name of the currency and its common

exchange rate
Amount of one currency needed to purchase one unit of another.

TABLE 22.1 Exchange rates in December 2015

Country	Currency	Exchange Rate
Europe		
Eurozone countries	Euro (EUR or €)	1.084*
Sweden	Krona (SEK)	8.569
Switzerland	Franc (CHF)	0.995
United Kingdom	Pound (GBP or £)	1.491*
Americas		
Brazil	Real (BRL)	3.941
Canada	Dollar (CAD)	1.389
Mexico	New peso (MXN)	17.013
Asia/Africa		
Australia	Dollar (AUD)	1.390
China	Yuan (CNY)	6.483
China (Hong Kong)	Dollar (HKD)	7.753
India	Rupee (INR)	66.225
Japan	Yen (JPY or ¥)	121.359
South Africa	Rand (ZAR)	15.090
South Korea	Won (KRW)	1,176.471

* Direct quotes (number of U.S. dollars per unit of foreign currency). Other quotes are indirect (units of foreign currency per U.S. dollar).
Source: Financial Times, December 18, 2015, available at **www.ft.com**.

---

[1] Ruritania was conceived by Anthony Hope as the setting for his 1984 novel, *The Prisoner of Zenda.* The Ruritanian rur was first proposed by Ludwig von Mises in his 1912 book, *The Theory of Money and Credit.*

abbreviation. For example, the Mexican peso is usually abbreviated as MXN and the U.S. dollar as USD. By custom, the prices of most currencies are expressed as indirect quotes. Thus, the third column of Table 22.1 shows that you could buy 17.013 Mexican pesos for 1 dollar. This is sometimes written as MXN17.013 = USD1.

To complicate matters, there are two currencies whose prices are generally expressed as direct quotes. These are the euro and the British pound. For example, you can see that it cost $1.084 to buy 1 euro. We, therefore, write the euro exchange rate as USD1.084 = EUR1.

22.1   Self-Test

Use the exchange rates in Table 22.1. How many euros can you buy for 1 dollar (an indirect quote)? How many dollars can you buy for 1 yen (a direct quote)?

Example 22.1 ▶   A Yen for Trade

How many yen will it cost a Japanese importer to purchase $10,000 worth of oranges from a California farmer? How many dollars will that farmer need in order to buy and import a Japanese tractor priced in Japan at 4.5 million yen?

The exchange rate is JPY121.359 = USD1. The $10,000 of oranges will require the Japanese importer to come up with 10,000 × 121.359 = 1,213.59 yen. The tractor will require the American importer to come up with 4,500,000/121.359 = $37,080. ∎

---

spot rate of exchange
Exchange rate for an immediate transaction.

The exchange rates in the last column of Table 22.1 are the prices of currency for immediate delivery. These are known as **spot rates of exchange.** For example, the spot rate of exchange for Brazilian reals is BRL3.941 = USD1. In other words, it costs 3.941 Brazilian reals to buy 1 dollar for immediate delivery.

Exchange rates are generally quoted against the dollar. For example, Table 22.1 shows that $1 can buy either 121.359 Japanese yen or 1,176.471 Korean won. This implies that 121.359 yen are equivalent to 1,176.471 won and, therefore, that 1 yen is equivalent to 1,176.471/121.359 = 9.694 won. An exchange rate between two currencies other than the U.S. dollar is known as a *cross-rate*. In our example, the cross-rate of exchange between the Japanese yen and the South Korean won is KRW9.694 = JPY1.

Cross-rates between any two currencies are locked down by the exchange rate for each currency versus the U.S. dollar. Otherwise, investors could make an easy, risk-free arbitrage profit. For example, suppose that a (really stupid) bank quotes a rate of KRW8 = JPY1. Here's what you do: You take $1 and exchange it for 1,176.471 Korean won, which you then use to buy 1,176.471/8 = 147.059 Japanese yen. These, in turn, can be exchanged back to U.S. dollars for 147.059/121.359 = $1.211 You have just taken advantage of a misalignment of prices to make a surefire 21.1% profit.[2] Of course, in real life you and other investors would transact with millions of dollars, not with one dollar at a time. The bank would be forced to revise its quote in short order.

22.2   Self-Test

Use the exchange rates in Table 22.1. What is the cross-rate between the Mexican peso and the Hong Kong dollar? How could you make money if a bank quoted you a rate of 2.5 pesos per Hong Kong dollar?

---

[2] In practice, foreign exchange dealers quote a spread between the prices at which they are prepared to buy and sell foreign currency, and this spread would reduce your profit. The spread is very small on large trades, but it is a major cost for small transactions by individuals.

Most countries allow their currencies to *float,* so the exchange rate fluctuates from minute to minute and day to day. When the currency increases in value, which means that you need less of the foreign currency to buy 1 dollar, the currency is said to *appreciate.* When you need more of the currency to buy 1 dollar, the currency is said to *depreciate.*

22.3 Self-Test

Table 22.1 shows that the exchange rate for the Australian dollar in December 2015 was AUD1.390 = USD1. A year earlier, the spot rate of exchange for the Australian dollar was AUD1.224 = USD1. Thus, in 2015 you could buy more Australian dollars for a U.S. dollar than a year earlier. Did the Australian dollar appreciate or depreciate?

Some countries try to avoid fluctuations in the value of their currency and seek instead to maintain a fixed exchange rate. But fixed rates seldom last forever. If everybody tries to sell the currency, eventually the country will be forced to allow the currency to depreciate. When this happens, exchange rates can change dramatically. For example, as a major oil producer, Azerbaijan has had a policy of pegging its currency, the manat, to the dollar. But with the fall in oil prices, this peg became unsustainable, and in December 2015, the Azerbaijani central bank announced that it would allow its currency to float. Overnight the manat depreciated by 32%.

Forward Exchange Rates

Fluctuations in exchange rates can get companies into hot water. For example, suppose you have agreed to buy a consignment of machinery from Ruritania. The machinery will be delivered at the end of 12 months at a cost of 100 million Ruritanian rurs (RURs). Currently, 1 dollar buys 100 rurs (RUR100 = USD1). So, if the exchange rate does not change, the machinery will cost you $1 million. But what if the rur appreciates? For example, suppose that when you come to buy the rurs at the end of the year, one dollar buys only 80 rurs (RUR80 = USD1). Then the *dollar* cost of your machinery has risen to $1.25 million (100 million/80 = $1.25 million).

You can avoid this exchange rate risk and fix your dollar cost by *buying forward,* that is, by arranging *now* to buy rurs at a prespecified price on a future date. This arrangement is called a foreign exchange *forward contract.* Suppose you enter into a forward contract with a bank to buy 100 million rurs 12 months from now at a price of RUR105 = USD1. You don't pay anything now; you simply fix today the price that you will pay in the future. After 12 months, the bank pays you 100 million rurs and you hand over in exchange $.952 million (100/105 = $.952 million).[3]

The spot exchange rate is the rate that you pay to obtain foreign currency today. The exchange rates in Table 22.1 are all spot exchange rates. The price of currency for delivery at a future date is called the **forward exchange rate.** The forward exchange rate is not usually the same as the spot rate. In our example, 1 dollar bought 100 Ruritanian rurs in the spot market but 105 rurs in the forward market. In this case, the rur is said to trade at a forward *discount* relative to the dollar. It's a discount because rurs are cheaper—each dollar can buy more rurs—if purchased forward rather than spot. If each dollar bought *fewer* rurs in the forward market, the rur would trade at a forward *premium* relative to the dollar.

A forward purchase or sale is a made-to-order transaction between you and the bank. It can be for any currency, any amount, and any delivery day. You could buy,

forward exchange rate
Exchange rate agreed upon today for a future transaction.

---
[3] If the forward exchange rate is RUR105 = USD1, then 1 rur will cost you 1/105 = $.00952, and 100 million rurs will cost 100 million × $.00952 = $.952 million.

say, 99,999 Vietnamese dong or 101,000 Haitian gourdes for a year and a day forward as long as you can find a bank ready to deal. There is also an organized market for currency for future delivery known as the currency *futures* market. Futures contracts are highly standardized versions of forward contracts—they exist only for the main currencies, they are for specified amounts, and the choice of delivery dates is limited. But trading is easy on futures exchanges—you don't have to negotiate a one-off contract with a bank. Almost everything we will say about the pricing of forward contracts applies also to futures. We will describe futures markets in greater detail in Chapter 24.

22.4　Self-Test

A skiing vacation at Whistler in Canada costs 1,300 Canadian dollars.

a. How many U.S. dollars does that represent? Use the exchange rates in Table 22.1.

b. Suppose that the Canadian dollar appreciates by 10% relative to the U.S. dollar, so each U.S. dollar buys 10% fewer Canadian dollars than before. What is the new indirect exchange rate?

c. If the Canadian vacation continues to cost the same number of Canadian dollars, what will happen to the cost in U.S. dollars?

22.2　Some Basic Relationships

The financial manager of an international business must cope with fluctuations in exchange rates and must be aware of the distinction between spot and forward exchange rates. She must also recognize that two countries may have different interest rates. To develop a consistent international financial policy, the financial manager needs to understand how exchange rates are determined and why one country may have a lower interest rate than another.

To keep life as simple as possible, we will stick with our fictitious company doing business in Ruritania. Here are four basic questions that its financial manager needs to consider:

1. Why is the interest rate in Ruritania not the same as the rate in the United States?
2. What is the relationship between the spot exchange rate for the rur today and the expected exchange rate at some future date?
3. How do different rates of inflation in Ruritania and the United States affect each country's interest rate and the exchange rate?
4. What explains the difference between the forward exchange rate for the rur and the spot rate?

These are complex issues, but as a first cut, we suggest that you think of spot and forward exchange rates, interest rates, and inflation rates as being linked as shown in Figure 22.1.

Exchange Rates and Inflation

Consider first the relationship between changes in the exchange rate and inflation rates (the two boxes on the right of Figure 22.1). The idea here is simple: If one country suffers a higher rate of inflation than another, then the value of that country's currency will decline.

But let's slow down and consider *why* changes in inflation and spot interest rates are linked. Suppose you notice that gold can be bought in New York for $1,200 an ounce and sold in Ruritania for 130,000 rurs an ounce. If there are no restrictions on the

FIGURE 22.1 Some simple theories linking spot and forward exchange rates, interest rates, and inflation rates

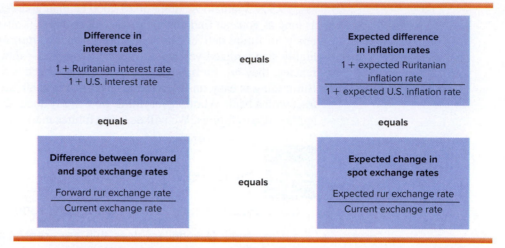

transport of gold, you could be onto a good thing. You buy gold for $1,200 and take it on the first plane to Ruritania, where you sell it for 130,000 rurs. The current exchange rate for the Ruritanian rur is RUR100 = USD1. So you can exchange your 130,000 rurs for 130,000/100 = $1,300. You have made a gross profit of $100 an ounce. Of course, you have to pay transportation and insurance costs, but there should still be something left over for you.

You returned from your trip with a surefire profit. But surefire profits rarely exist, and when they do exist, they don't last long. As others notice the disparity between the price of gold in Ruritania and the price in New York, the price will be forced down in Ruritania (or up in New York) until the profit opportunity disappears. This ensures that the dollar price of gold is the same in the two countries.

Our conclusion that gold is worth the same regardless of currency is an example of the **law of one price.** Just as the price of goods in Walmart must be roughly the same as the price of goods in Target, so the prices of goods in Ruritania when converted into dollars should be roughly the same as the prices in the United States:

$$\text{Dollar price of goods in U.S.} = \frac{\text{Rur price of goods in Ruritania}}{\text{Number of rurs per dollar}}$$

Gold is a standard and easily transportable commodity, but the same forces push the domestic and foreign prices of other goods toward equality. Those goods that can be bought more cheaply abroad will be imported, which will force down the price of the domestic product. Those goods that can be produced more cheaply at home will be exported, and that will force down the price of the foreign product.

No one who has compared prices in foreign stores with prices at home really believes that the law of one price holds exactly. Look at Table 22.2, which shows the local price of a Big Mac in different countries converted into dollars. You can see that the price varies considerably across countries. For example, in Switzerland Big Macs cost 31% more than in the United States, but in Russia the price of a Big Mac is about 69% less than in the United States.[4]

This suggests a possible way to make a quick buck. Why don't you buy a hamburger-to-go in Russia for $1.53 and take it for resale in Switzerland, where the price in dollars is $6.44? The answer, of course, is that the gain would not cover the costs. The law of one price works very well for commodities like gold, where transportation costs are small. It works far less well for Big Macs and worse still for haircuts and appendectomies, which cannot be transported at all.

law of one price
Theory that prices of goods in all countries should be equal when translated to a common currency, or, more generally, that two assets providing the same cash flows cannot sell for different prices.

---

[4] Of course, it could also be that Big Macs come with a bigger smile in Switzerland. If the quality of the hamburgers or the service differs, we are not comparing like with like.

TABLE 22.2 Price of Big Mac hamburgers in different countries

Country	Local Price Converted to U.S. Dollars	Country	Local Price Converted to U.S. Dollars
Australia	$3.74	Norway	$5.21
Brazil	3.35	Russia	1.53
China	2.68	South Africa	1.77
Euro area	4.00	Switzerland	6.44
Japan	3.12	United Kingdom	4.22
Indonesia	2.19	United States	4.93

Source: "The Big Mac Index: After the Dips," *The Economist,* January 2016.

purchasing power parity (PPP)

Theory that the cost of living in different countries is equal and exchange rates adjust to offset inflation differentials across countries.

We need a weaker version of the law of one price, a diluted law that captures the main idea but allows for exceptions. The weaker version is **purchasing power parity, or PPP.** PPP states that although some goods, such as Big Macs and haircuts, may cost different amounts in different countries, the overall cost of living should be similar. PPP implies that the relative costs of living in two countries will not be affected by differences in their inflation rates. Instead, different inflation rates in local currencies will be offset by changes in exchange rates.

If purchasing power parity holds, then your forecast of the difference in inflation rates is also your best forecast of the change in the spot rate of exchange. For example, suppose you need a forecast of the exchange rate for the Ruritanian rur. Purchasing power parity says that you should focus on the difference between the inflation rates in Ruritania and the United States.

The current exchange rate for the rur is RUR100 = USD1. If the cost of living is the same in Ruritania and the United States, then 100 rurs buys the same bundle of goods and services as $1. Suppose that economists are forecasting an inflation rate of 6% in Ruritania and 1% in the United States. Then, at the end of 1 year, 106 rurs will buy the same quantity of goods as $1.01, and $1 will have the same purchasing power as RUR100 × (1.06/1.01) = RUR105. Purchasing power parity implies that the expected exchange rate at the end of the year is RUR105 = USD1. Because inflation is expected to be higher in Ruritania, the rur is forecast to depreciate.

Look back at the two right-hand boxes in Figure 22.1. We can now fill in those boxes for the Ruritanian rur:[5]

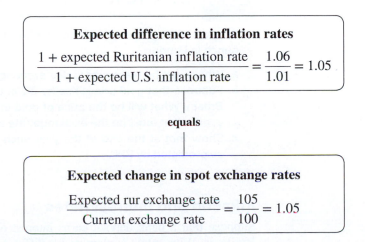

Expected difference in inflation rates

$$\frac{1 + \text{expected Ruritanian inflation rate}}{1 + \text{expected U.S. inflation rate}} = \frac{1.06}{1.01} = 1.05$$

equals

Expected change in spot exchange rates

$$\frac{\text{Expected rur exchange rate}}{\text{Current exchange rate}} = \frac{105}{100} = 1.05$$

---

[5] A warning: Notice that the relationships in Figure 22.1 all apply to *indirect* exchange rates, i.e., foreign currency per dollar. Remember that the pound/U.S. dollar and euro/U.S. dollar exchange rates are conventionally expressed as direct rates. To use our formulas for euros and pounds, you must first convert the quoted rates to indirect rates.

Now we have some helpful advice for the U.S. company doing business in Ruritania. If the financial manager needs to forecast the future spot exchange rate for Ruritanian rurs, he or she should start by looking at the difference in expected inflation rates in Ruritania versus in the United States.

Real and Nominal Exchange Rates

Financial managers distinguish nominal exchange rates from real exchange rates. *Nominal exchange rates* tell you how many euros or yen or pounds you can buy for your dollar. *Real exchange rates* measure the quantity of goods you can buy for that dollar in Europe or Japan or the United Kingdom. For example, if the value of the Ruritanian rur declines, you will be able to purchase more rurs for your dollar, but if Ruritania experiences higher inflation, those rurs may buy you only the same amount of goods. In this case the *nominal* exchange rate has declined but the *real* exchange rate is unchanged. Purchasing power parity theory implies that any change in the nominal exchange rate will be offset by a change in the relative price of goods in the two countries, leaving the real exchange rate unaffected.

Figure 22.2 plots the nominal and real exchange rates since 1900 in three countries. For example, the first plot shows that in 2015 one pound (£1) bought only 31% of the dollars that it did a century earlier. But this decline in the nominal value of the pound was offset by the higher inflation rate in the United Kingdom. The plot shows that, over more than a century, the inflation-adjusted, or real, exchange rate was little changed. The plots for France and Italy tell a similar story.

Of course, purchasing power parity theory is not the whole truth, and in the short term, real exchange rates do change, sometimes quite sharply. For example, the real value of the euro fell by about 20% in the 14 months ending November 2015. European goods became much cheaper in the United States than they had been. Such changes in real exchange rates can be a major headache for anyone making short-term currency forecasts. But if you are a financial manager called on to make a long-term forecast of an exchange rate, you probably can't do much better than to assume that changes in the nominal value of the currency will offset the difference in inflation rates. That is the message of purchasing power parity theory.

22.5 | Self-Test

Suppose that gold currently costs $1,000 an ounce in New York and £600 an ounce in London.

a. What must be the pound/dollar exchange rate?
b. Suppose that gold prices rise by 2% in the United States and by 5% in Great Britain. What will be the price of gold in the two currencies at the end of the year? What must be the exchange rate at the end of the year?
c. Show that at the end of the year each dollar buys about 3% more pounds, as predicted by PPP.

Inflation and Interest Rates

Suppose that a bank deposit earns interest of 3% in the United States and 8.1% in Ruritania. What might explain such a difference?

We can start by looking back to Chapter 5, where we distinguished nominal and real rates of interest. Bank deposits promise you a fixed nominal rate of interest, but they don't promise what that money will buy. If you invest $100 for a year at an interest rate of 3%, you will have 3% more dollars at the end of the year than you did at the start. But you may not be 3% better off. Some of the gain would be needed to compensate for inflation.

FIGURE 22.2 Nominal versus real exchange rates in (*a*) the United Kingdom, (*b*) France, and (*c*) Italy; December 1899 = 100 (Values are shown on log scale.)

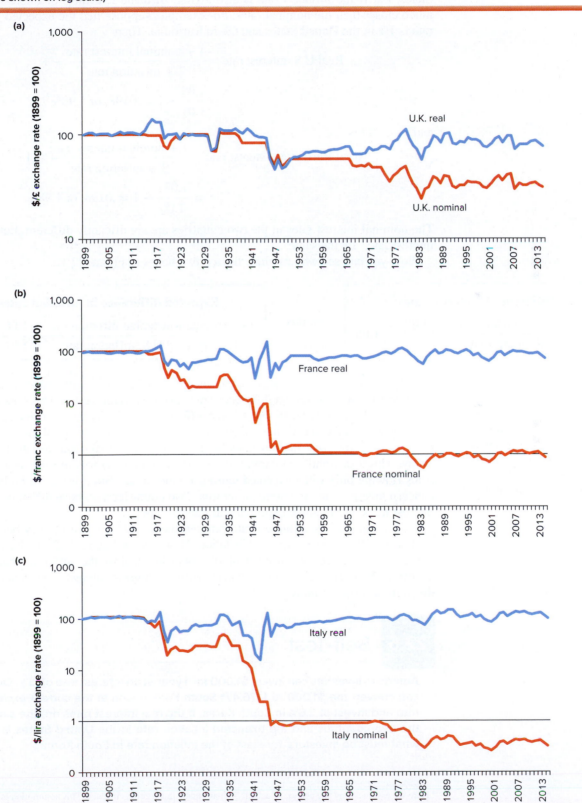

Note: Since 1999, both the lira and the French franc have been replaced by the euro.
Source: E. Dimson, P. R. Marsh, and M. Staunton, *Triumph of the Optimists: 101 Years of Global Investment Returns* (Princeton, NJ: Princeton University Press, 2002). Updates courtesy of *Triumph*'s authors.

In our example, the nominal rate of interest is higher in Ruritania than in the United States, but if the inflation rate is also higher, then the real rates of interest may be much closer than the nominal rates. For example, suppose that the expected inflation rate is 1% in the United States and 6% in Ruritania. Then

$$\text{Real U.S. interest rate} = \frac{1 + \text{nominal interest rate}}{1 + \text{inflation rate}} - 1$$

$$= \frac{1.03}{1.01} - 1 = .0198, \text{ or } 1.98\%$$

and

$$\text{Real Ruritanian interest rate} = \frac{1 + \text{nominal interest rate}}{1 + \text{inflation rate}} - 1$$

$$= \frac{1.081}{1.06} - 1 = .0198, \text{ or } 1.98\%$$

The nominal interest rates in the two countries are significantly different, but the real interest rates are the same.

Now you can see why we drew the top two boxes in Figure 22.1:

Difference in interest rates		**Expected difference in inflation rates**
$\dfrac{1 + \text{Ruritanian interest rate}}{1 + \text{U.S. interest rate}} = \dfrac{1.081}{1.03} = 1.05$	**equals**	$\dfrac{1 + \text{expected Ruritanian inflation rate}}{1 + \text{expected U.S. inflation rate}} = \dfrac{1.06}{1.01} = 1.05$

international Fisher effect
Theory that real interest rates in all countries should be equal, with differences in nominal rates reflecting differences in expected inflation.

If expected real interest rates are the same everywhere, then differences in the nominal interest rate must reflect differences in expected inflation rates. This conclusion is often called the **international Fisher effect,** after the economist Irving Fisher. As long as capital can flow unimpeded across national borders, capital market equilibrium requires that *real* interest rates be the same in any two countries. Just as water always flows downhill, so capital always flows where returns are greatest. Capital stops flowing only when expected returns are the same.[6] But it is the *real* returns that concern investors, not the nominal returns. Two countries may have different nominal interest rates but the same expected real interest rate.

How similar are real interest rates around the world? It is hard to say because we cannot directly observe *expected* inflation. However, in Figure 22.3, we have plotted the average interest rate in each of 67 countries against the inflation that in fact occurred. You can see that the countries with the highest interest rates generally had the highest inflation rates.

22.6 | Self-Test

American investors can invest $1,000 for 1 year at an interest rate of .3%. Or they can convert the $1,000 to 1,176,471 South Korean won at the current exchange rate and invest at 2.6% in South Korea. If the real interest rates are the same in the two countries and the expected inflation rate in the United States is 1.7%, what must be investors' forecast of the inflation rate in South Korea?

---

[6] Here we assume away any chance of default on loans made in a foreign currency. This assumption is fine for the most important currencies, including the U.S. dollar, pound, euro, Swiss franc, and yen. The assumption is not acceptable for some developing countries where local politics are unstable. We have assumed that loans in Ruritanian rurs are default-risk-free. But if investors worry about default or expropriation by the Ruritanian government, they may demand a higher real interest rate on rur loans.

FIGURE 22.3 Countries with the highest interest rates generally have the highest inflation. In this diagram, each of the 67 points represents the experience of a different country.

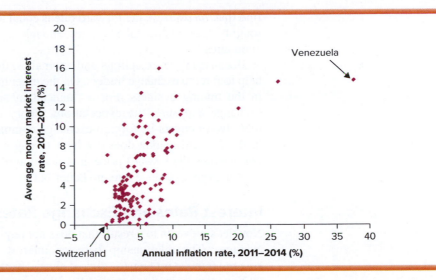

The Forward Exchange Rate and the Expected Spot Rate

If you buy Ruritanian rurs forward, you get more rurs for your U.S. dollar than if you buy them spot. So the rur is selling at a forward discount. Now let us think how this discount may be related to expected changes in spot rates of exchange.

The spot rate for the rur is RUR100 = USD1, and the 1-year forward rate is RUR105 = USD1. Would you sell rurs forward if you were confident that they would rise in value? Probably not. You would be tempted to wait until the end of the year and get a better price for your rurs in the spot market. If other traders felt the same way, nobody would sell rurs forward. On the other hand, if traders expected the rur to fall sharply in value, they might be reluctant to *buy* forward and, in order to attract buyers, the number of rurs that you could buy for a U.S. dollar in the forward market would need to rise.[7] Trading would stabilize when the forward rate adjusts to equal the expected future spot rate.

expectations theory of exchange rates

Theory that the expected spot exchange rate equals the forward rate.

This is the reasoning behind the **expectations theory of exchange rates,** which predicts that the forward rate equals the expected future spot exchange rate. Put another way, we can say that the *percentage* difference between the forward rate and today's spot rate is equal to the expected *percentage* change in the spot rate:

This is the third leg of our quadrilateral in Figure 22.1.

Difference between forward and spot exchange rates	equals	**Expected change in spot exchange rate**
$\dfrac{\text{Forward rur exchange rate}}{\text{Current exchange rate}} = \dfrac{105}{100} = 1.05$		$\dfrac{\text{Expected rur exchange rate}}{\text{Current exchange rate}} = \dfrac{105}{100} = 1.05$

The expectations theory of forward rates does not imply that managers are perfect forecasters. Sometimes, the actual future spot rate will turn out to be above the previous forward rate. Sometimes, it will fall below. But if the theory is correct, we should

---

[7] This reasoning ignores risk. If a forward purchase reduces your risk sufficiently, you *might* be prepared to buy forward even if you expected to pay more as a result. Similarly, if a forward sale reduces risk, you *might* be prepared to sell forward even if you expected to receive less as a result.

find that, *on average,* the forward rate is equal to the future spot rate. This prediction is roughly true, if we take a long enough average,[8] but there are exceptions and anomalies.[9]

Because of the exceptions and anomalies, the expectations hypothesis is not much help to foreign exchange traders. On the other hand, financial managers are not usually in the trading business. For a financial manager who consistently hedges foreign exchange exposure, the expectations theory offers some reassurance. A company that always covers its foreign exchange commitments by buying or selling currency in the forward market does not have to pay a premium to avoid exchange rate risk: *On average,* the forward price at which it agrees to exchange currency will equal the eventual spot exchange rate, no better but no worse.

Interest Rates and Exchange Rates

Now let's move on to a result that does not require qualification or appeals to long-run averages: The relationship between interest rates and exchange rates, known as *covered interest rate parity,* almost always works, even in the short run.

You are an investor with $1 million to invest for 1 year. The interest rate in Ruritania is 8.1%, and in the United States it is 3%. Is it better to invest your money in Ruritania or in the United States?

The answer seems obvious: Isn't it better to earn an interest rate of 8.1% than 3%? But appearances may be deceptive. If you lend in Ruritania, you first need to convert your $1 million into rurs. When the loan is repaid at the end of the year, you need to convert your rurs back into U.S. dollars. Of course, you don't know what the exchange rate will be at the end of the year, but you can fix the future value of your rurs by selling them forward. If the forward rate of exchange is sufficiently low, you may do just as well keeping your money in the United States.

Let's check which loan is the better deal:

- *U.S. dollar loan.* The rate of interest on a U.S. dollar loan is 3%. Therefore, at the end of the year, you get $1 million × 1.03 = $1.03 million.
- *Ruritanian rur loan.* The current (spot) rate of exchange is RUR100 = USD1. Therefore, you can convert your million dollars into RUR100 million. The interest rate on a rur loan is 8.1%, so at the end of the year you will have RUR100 million × 1.081 = RUR108.1 million. You don't know what the exchange rate will be at the end of the year, but that doesn't matter. You can nail down the rate at which you convert your rurs back into U.S. dollars. The 1-year forward exchange rate is RUR105 = USD1. Therefore, by selling the rurs forward, you make sure that you will get RUR108.1/105 = $1.03 million.

Thus, the two investments offer exactly the same rate of return. They have to, because they are both risk-free. If the domestic interest rate were different from the "covered" foreign rate, you would have a money machine: You could borrow in the market with the lower rate and lend in the market with the higher rate.

---

[8] It seems that companies are sometimes prepared to give up return in order to *buy* forward currency and other times they are prepared to give up return in order to *sell* forward currency. The forward rate *overstates* the likely future spot rate about half the time, and about half the time it *understates* the likely spot rate. The over- and underpredictions average out in the long run.

[9] Scholars who have studied exchange rates have found that forward rates typically exaggerate the likely change in the spot rate. When the forward rate appears to predict a sharp rise in the spot rate, the forward rate tends to overestimate the rise in the spot rate. When the forward rate appears to predict a fall, it tends to overestimate this fall. There is even evidence that when the forward rate predicts a rise, the spot rate is more likely to fall than rise. For a readable discussion of this puzzling finding, see K. A. Froot and R. H. Thaler, "Anomalies: Foreign Exchange," *Journal of Political Economy* 4 (1990), pp. 179–192.

We now have the final leg of our quadrilateral in Figure 22.1:

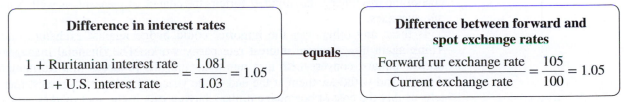

Difference in interest rates		Difference between forward and spot exchange rates
$$\frac{1 + \text{Ruritanian interest rate}}{1 + \text{U.S. interest rate}} = \frac{1.081}{1.03} = 1.05$$	equals	$$\frac{\text{Forward rur exchange rate}}{\text{Current exchange rate}} = \frac{105}{100} = 1.05$$

interest rate parity
Theory that forward premium equals the interest rate differential.

This link between the forward exchange rate and the difference in interest rates is called **interest rate parity.** Whereas the other relationships shown in Figure 22.1 tend to hold approximately, interest rate parity almost always holds with precision. This should not be surprising because there would be easy opportunities for riskless arbitrage whenever parity is violated. In fact, foreign currency dealers set the forward exchange rate by looking at the difference between the interest rates on deposits in different currencies.

Interest rate parity also holds an important lesson for managers. International capital markets and currency markets function well and offer no free lunches. You can't assume that it is cheaper to borrow in a currency with a low nominal rate of interest. If you hedge or "cover" your exchange rate exposure, interest rate parity implies that the all-in cost of borrowing will be the same in any currency.[10] If you don't cover, exchange rate movements can easily erase the apparent advantage of a low interest rate.

Interest rate parity means that covered interest rates are the same in all major currencies. A financial manager who attempts to borrow in currencies with low interest rates can profit only by taking a bet on future exchange rates.

22.7   Self-Test

By 2020, Ruritanian exchange rates had moved to RUR120 = USD1 (spot) and RUR126.92 = USD1 (1-year forward). One-year interest rates were 4% in the United States and 10% in Ruritania. Confirm covered interest rate parity.

22.3   Hedging Currency Risk

Transaction Risk

Firms with international operations are subject to currency risk. As exchange rates fluctuate, the dollar value of their revenues or expenses also fluctuates. It is useful to distinguish two types of exchange rate risk: *transaction risk* and *economic risk.*

Transaction risk arises when the firm agrees to pay or receive a known amount of foreign currency. For example, our importer of machinery was committed to pay RUR100 million at the end of 12 months. If the value of the rur appreciates rapidly over this period, that machinery will cost more dollars than the importer expected.

Transaction risk is easily identified and hedged. For every rur our importer is committed to pay, she can buy 1 rur forward. If she buys RUR100 million forward, the importer fixes the entire dollar cost of the machinery and avoids the risk of an appreciation of the rur.

Of course, it is possible that the rur will *depreciate* sharply over the year,[11] in which case the importer would regret that she did not wait to buy the rurs more cheaply in the

---

[10] A covered foreign interest rate means that you borrow or lend in a foreign currency and hedge the exchange rate risk by entering a forward currency contract. In our example, you could lend RUR100 million, which grows with 8.1% interest to RUR108.1 million. You therefore would sell RUR108.1 million forward to lock in the dollar value of your year-end proceeds.

[11] By this we mean that the rur falls by more than predicted by the forward rate.

spot market. Unfortunately, you cannot have your cake and eat it. By fixing the dollar cost of the machinery, the importer forfeits the chance of pleasant, as well as unpleasant, surprises.

Is there any other way the importer could hedge against exchange rate loss? Think again how covered interest rate parity works. The financial manager could borrow dollars, convert them into rurs today, put the proceeds in a Ruritanian bank deposit, and withdraw them at the end of the year to pay her bill. Interest rate parity tells us that the cost of borrowing dollars, buying rurs in the spot market, and leaving them on deposit is exactly the same as the cost of buying rurs forward.

What is the cost of protection against currency risk? You sometimes hear managers say that it is equal to the difference between the forward rate and *today's* spot rate. This is wrong. If our importer did not hedge, she would pay the spot price for rurs when the payment is due at the end of the year. Therefore, the cost of hedging is the difference between the forward rate and the expected spot rate when payment is due.

Should companies hedge, or should they just sit back and absorb currency fluctuations? We generally vote for hedging. First, it makes life simpler for the firm and allows it to concentrate on its own business. Second, it does not cost much. (In fact, the cost is zero if the forward rate equals the expected spot rate, as our simple theories imply.) Third, the foreign exchange market seems reasonably efficient, at least for the major currencies. Speculation should be a zero-sum game, barring the unlikely case where the financial manager knows more than the pros who make the foreign exchange market.

Economic Risk

Even if a firm neither owes nor is owed foreign currency, it still may be affected by currency fluctuations. For example, in 2011 the Swiss National Bank announced that it would not allow the value of the Swiss franc to rise above 1.2 francs to the euro, and there it pretty much stayed until January 2015 when the bank suddenly announced that it was removing the peg. The next day, the franc climbed by more than 20% against the euro. Many Swiss exporters faced a difficult choice: maintain the euro price of their product, thus accepting a reduced price in their home currency, or raise the euro price, becoming less competitive against other European producers. Swiss exporters had *economic exposure* to the exchange rate because the exchange rate change affected their competitive position.

One solution is for the company to undertake *operational hedging* by balancing production closely with sales. For example, 35% of Nestlé's sales are in the euro area, but so are 35% of its production costs. It gains protection from currency risks because its costs and revenues in different currencies are balanced.

Swiss luxury goods manufacturers have less operational hedging. A substantial proportion of the costs for Swiss companies Swatch and Richemont arise in Switzerland, and they export the bulk of their output.[12] For these companies, appreciation of the Swiss franc is a potential concern. Therefore, they mitigate this currency risk by using financial hedges. For example, much of Richemont's borrowing is in dollars rather than Swiss francs. So, if the franc appreciates against the dollar, the pressure on Richemont's profits is offset in part by a reduction in the number of francs needed to service its dollar debt. In addition, the company uses currency forwards to fix the price at which it can buy or sell foreign currency.

22.8   Self-Test

A Ford dealer in the United States never needs to buy or sell foreign currency. Does that mean it has no currency risk? Explain.

---

[12] Swatch produces high-quality watches. Richemont is the world's second largest luxury goods producer with a variety of brand names such as Cartier, Dunhill, and Piaget.

22.4 International Capital Budgeting

Net Present Values for Foreign Investments

Exports by the soft-drink manufacturer Ecsy-Cola Corporation have risen to the point that it is considering establishing a small manufacturing and sales operation overseas in Ruritania. Ecsy-Cola's decision to invest overseas should be based on the same criteria as a decision to invest in the United States. The company needs to forecast the incremental cash flows from the project, discount the cash flows at the opportunity cost of capital, and accept those projects with a positive NPV.

Suppose Ecsy-Cola's Ruritanian facility is expected to generate the following cash flows *in Ruritanian rurs:*

	0	1	2	3	4	5
Cash flow (millions of rurs)	−380	100	125	150	175	200

The interest rate in the United States is 3%. Ecsy's financial manager estimates that the company requires an additional expected return of 10% to compensate for the risk of the project, so the opportunity cost of capital for the project is $3 + 10 = 13\%$.

Notice that Ecsy's opportunity cost of capital is stated in terms of the return on a dollar-denominated investment, but the cash flows are given in rurs. A project that offers a 13% expected return in rurs could fall far short of offering the required return in dollars if the value of the rur is expected to decline. Conversely, a project that offers an expected return of less than 13% in rurs may be worthwhile if the rur is likely to appreciate.

You cannot compare the project's return measured in one currency with the return that you require from investing in another currency. If the opportunity cost of capital is measured as a dollar-denominated return, cash flows should also be forecast in dollars.

To translate the rur cash flows into dollars, Ecsy needs a forward exchange rate. Where does this come from? Forward exchange rates for longer than a year are not usually quoted in the financial press, but they can be estimated using interest rate parity. For example, suppose that the financial manager looks in the newspaper and finds that the current exchange rate is RUR100 = USD1 and that the interest rate is 3% in the United States and 8.1% in Ruritania. Thus, the manager sees right away that the rur is likely to sell at a forward discount of 5% a year. For example, the 1-year forward rate is

$$\text{Forward rate for year 1} = \text{spot rate in year 0} \times \frac{1 + \text{rur interest rate}}{1 + \text{dollar interest rate}}$$

$$= \text{RUR100/USD1} \times \frac{1.081}{1.03} = \text{RUR104.95/USD1}$$

The implied forward exchange rates for each year of the project are calculated similarly, as follows:[13]

Year	Forward Exchange Rate (RUR per USD)
1	$100 \times (1.081/1.03) = \text{RUR104.95/USD1}$
2	$100 \times (1.081/1.03)^2 = \text{RUR110.15/USD1}$
3	$100 \times (1.081/1.03)^3 = \text{RUR115.60/USD1}$
4	$100 \times (1.081/1.03)^4 = \text{RUR121.33/USD1}$
5	$100 \times (1.081/1.03)^5 = \text{RUR127.33/USD1}$

---

[13] We assume that the 3% and 8.1% interest rates are the same for longer maturities.

The financial manager can use these forward exchange rates to convert the rur cash flows into dollars:

Year:	0	1	2	3	4	5
Cash flow (millions of rurs)	−380	100	125	150	175	200
Forward exchange rate (rurs to the dollar)	100	104.95	110.15	115.60	121.33	127.33
Cash flow (millions of dollars)	− 3.8	0.9528	1.1348	1.2976	1.4424	1.5707

Now the manager discounts these dollar cash flows at the 13% dollar cost of capital:

$$\text{NPV} = -3.8 + \frac{.9528}{1.13} + \frac{1.1348}{1.13^2} + \frac{1.2976}{1.13^3} + \frac{1.4424}{1.13^4} + \frac{1.5707}{1.13^5}$$

$$= \$.568 \text{ million, or } \$568{,}000$$

Notice that the manager discounted cash flows at 13%, not at the U.S. risk-free interest rate of 3%. The cash flows are risky, so a risk-adjusted interest rate is appropriate. The positive NPV tells the manager that the project is worth undertaking; it increases shareholder wealth by $568,000.

Notice also that the firm does *not* have to forecast the future rur/dollar exchange rate to translate its rur cash flows into dollar equivalents. It instead uses the forward exchange rates implied by the interest rate differential in the two countries. No currency forecast is needed because the company can hedge its foreign exchange exposure.

If it does hedge, for example, by selling rurs forward, then its rur cash flows will be brought back into dollars at the forward exchange rates implied by the interest rate differential. In other words, the firm can, if it chooses, nail down the dollar cash flows that we have just calculated. The decision to accept or reject the project, therefore, is separate from the firm's particular view about the future exchange rate.

What if the management actually expects the rur to appreciate rather than depreciate? Should it use its own forecasts of the future exchange rate instead of the forward exchange rates implied by interest rate parity? No! For a project to be attractive, it must be able to stand on its own, based on *hedged* cash flows. It would be foolish for a firm to accept a poor project just because it forecasts exchange rate appreciation. If management is confident in its predictions of future exchange rates, it would be better to speculate on the currency directly rather than use a negative-NPV project to gain exposure to the currency. (Of course, before it speculates, management ought to think very carefully about why it believes its exchange rate forecast is superior to the market's. After all, Ecsy's comparative advantage is presumably in manufacturing fizzy drinks, not in exchange rate speculation.)

22.9   Self-Test

Suppose that the nominal interest rate in Ruritania is 6% rather than 8.1%. The spot exchange rate is still RUR100 = USD1, and the expected rur cash flows on Ecsy's project are also the same as before.

a. What do you deduce about the likely difference in the inflation rates in Ruritania and the United States?
b. Would you now be able to buy more or fewer rurs in the forward market than when the rur interest rate was 8.1%?
c. Do you think that the NPV of Ecsy's project will now be higher or lower than the figure we calculated above? Check your answer by calculating NPV under this new assumption.

Political Risk

So far, we have focused on the management of exchange rate risk, but managers also worry about *political risk*. They worry that a government will change the rules of the game, breaking a promise or an understanding, after the investment is made. Of course, political risks are not confined to overseas investments. Businesses in every country are exposed to the risk of unanticipated actions by governments, and when political risk increases, share prices become more volatile. The danger for foreign companies is that they may be a particular target for government actions.

Consultancy services offer analyses of political and economic risks and draw up country rankings.[14] For example, Table 22.3 is an extract from the 2014 political risk rankings provided by the PRS Group. Each country is scored on 12 dimensions and a total score is calculated. Norway comes top of the class overall, while Somalia languishes at the bottom.

Some managers dismiss political risk as an act of God, like a hurricane or earthquake. But the most successful multinational companies structure their business to reduce political risk. Foreign governments are not likely to expropriate a local business if it cannot operate without the support of its parent. For example, the foreign subsidiaries of American computer software or pharmaceutical companies would have relatively little value if they were cut off from the know-how of their parents. Such operations are much less likely to be expropriated than, say, a mining operation that can be operated as a stand-alone venture.

We are not recommending that you turn your silver mine into a pharmaceutical company, but you may be able to plan your overseas manufacturing operations to improve your bargaining position with foreign governments. For example, Ford has integrated its overseas operations so that the manufacture of components, subassemblies, and complete automobiles is spread across plants in a number of countries. None of these plants would have much value on its own, and Ford can switch production between plants if the political climate in one country deteriorates.

TABLE 22.3 Political risk scores for a sample of countries, 2014

Country	Total
Maximum score	**100.0**
Norway	90.8
Switzerland	89.5
Germany	85.3
Canada	82.3
Korea, Republic	81.8
Japan	81.0
Australia	78.0
United Kingdom	76.5
United States	75.5
China, People's Rep.	73.3
France	70.5
Russia	70.0
Brazil	68.8
India	65.8
Venezuela	54.8
Somalia	37.5

Source: PRS Group, *International Country Risk Guide,* a publication of The PRS Group, Inc., **www.prsgroup.com**, 2014.

[14] For a discussion of these services, see C. Erb, C. R. Harvey, and T. Viskanta, "Political Risk, Financial Risk, and Economic Risk," *Financial Analysts Journal* 52 (1996), pp. 28–46. Campbell Harvey's web page (www.duke.edu/charvey) is also a useful source of information on political risk.

Multinational corporations have also devised financing arrangements to help keep foreign governments honest. For example, suppose your firm is contemplating an investment of $500 million to reopen the San Tomé silver mine in Costaguana with modern machinery, smelting equipment, and shipping facilities.[15] The Costaguanan government agrees to invest in roads and other infrastructure and to take 20% of the silver produced by the mine in lieu of taxes. The agreement is to run for 25 years.

The project's NPV on these assumptions is quite attractive. But what happens if a new government comes into power 5 years from now and imposes a 50% tax on "any precious metals exported from the Republic of Costaguana"? Or changes the government's share of output from 20% to 50%? Or simply takes over the mine "with fair compensation to be determined in due course by the Minister of Natural Resources of the Republic of Costaguana"?

No contract can absolutely restrain sovereign power. But you can arrange project financing to make these acts as painful as possible for the foreign government. For example, you might set up the mine as a subsidiary corporation, which then borrows a large fraction of the required investment from a consortium of major international banks. If your firm guarantees the loan, make sure the guarantee stands only if the Costaguanan government honors its contract. The government will be reluctant to break the contract if doing so causes a default on the loans and undercuts the country's credit standing with the international banking system.

The Cost of Capital for Foreign Investment

We did not say how Ecsy-Cola arrived at a 13% dollar discount rate for its Ruritanian project. That depends on the risk of overseas investment and the reward that investors require for taking this risk. Unfortunately, there is no tidy theory of risk and return in an international context.[16]

Remember that the risk of an investment cannot be considered in isolation; it depends on the securities that the investor holds in his or her portfolio. For example, suppose Ecsy-Cola's shareholders invest mainly in companies that do business in the United States. They could view the Ruritanian market, though volatile, as driven by different forces and therefore a diversifiable risk. If the correlation between the Ruritanian and U.S. markets is relatively low, an investment in the Ruritanian soft-drink business would appear to be a relatively low-risk project to Ecsy-Cola's shareholders. That would not necessarily be true of all investors, for example, those who are already heavily exposed to the fortunes of the Ruritanian market.[17]

Avoiding Fudge Factors

We don't pretend that we can put an absolutely precise figure on the cost of capital for foreign investment. But we disagree with the practice of *automatically* increasing the domestic cost of capital when foreign investment is considered.

Some financial managers automatically mark up the required return for foreign investment because it is more costly to manage an operation in a foreign country and because they worry about the risks of expropriation, foreign exchange restrictions, or unfavorable tax changes. In other words, they add a fudge factor to the discount rate to offset these costs and risks.

---

[15] The early history of the San Tomé mine is described in Joseph Conrad's *Nostromo*.

[16] Why is there no tidy theory? One fundamental reason is that economists have never been able to agree on what makes one country different from another. Is it just that they have different currencies? Or is it that their citizens have different tastes and consume different things? Or is it that they are subject to different regulations and taxes? The answers to these questions affect the relationship among security prices in different countries.

[17] One can imagine an integrated world in which all investors diversify worldwide, regardless of their domiciles. In this ideal case, U.S. and Ruritanian investors would view the risks of Ecsy-Cola's investment identically. But in reality investors' portfolios are strongly weighted toward their home countries. This weighting is called a "home bias." We do not yet have an integrated world capital market.

Those managers should leave the discount rate alone and reduce expected cash flows instead. For example, let's go back to Ecsy-Cola's cash-flow forecast of 100 million Ruritanian rurs in year 1. Now the company gets word of a proposed 100 million rur "incorporation fee" to be imposed in "the first year of operations for all new foreign investments." The odds that the fee will be imposed are judged at 5%.

Now the *expected* cash flow for year 1 is not 100 million rurs but .95 × 100 million = 95 million rurs. Ecsy should recalculate NPV using this forecast. It should make similar cash-flow adjustments for possible political risks in later years.

Adjusting cash flows brings management's assumptions about political risks out in the open for scrutiny and sensitivity analysis. There may be some discount rate fudge factor that gives the correct NPV, but financial managers have no practical way of knowing what the fudge factor is until the cash flows are adjusted and NPV is recalculated. Once the adjusted NPV is in hand, the fudge factor is not needed.

SUMMARY

What is the difference between spot and forward exchange rates? (*LO22-1*)

The **exchange rate** is the amount of one currency needed to purchase one unit of another currency. The **spot rate of exchange** is the exchange rate for an immediate transaction. The **forward rate** is an exchange rate agreed upon today for a transaction at a specified future date.

What are the basic relationships among spot exchange rates, forward exchange rates, interest rates, and inflation rates? (*LO22-2*)

To produce order out of chaos, the international financial manager needs some model of the relationships between exchange rates, interest rates, and inflation rates. Four very simple theories prove useful:

- In its strict form, **purchasing power parity** states that $1 must have the same purchasing power in every country. You only need to take a vacation abroad to know that this doesn't square well with all the facts. Nevertheless, *on average,* changes in exchange rates tend to match differences in inflation rates and, if you need a long-term forecast of the exchange rate, it is difficult to do much better than to assume that the exchange rate will offset the effect of any differences in the inflation rates.
- In an open world, capital market *real* rates of interest would have to be the same. Thus, differences in *nominal* interest rates would result from differences in expected inflation rates. This **international Fisher effect** suggests that firms should not simply borrow where interest rates are lowest. Those countries are also likely to have the lowest inflation rates and the strongest currencies.
- The **expectations theory of exchange rates** tells us that the forward rate equals the expected spot rate (though it is very far from being a perfect forecaster of the spot rate).
- **Interest rate parity** theory states that the interest differential between two countries must be equal to the difference between the forward and spot exchange rates. In the international markets, arbitrage ensures that parity almost always holds.

What are some simple strategies to protect the firm against exchange rate risk? (*LO22-3*)

Our simple theories about forward rates have two practical implications for the problem of hedging overseas operations. First, the expectations theory suggests that hedging exchange risk is on average costless. Second, there are two ways to hedge against exchange risk: One is to buy or sell currency forward; the other is to lend or borrow abroad. Interest rate parity tells us that the cost of the two methods should be the same.

How do we perform an NPV analysis for projects with cash flows in foreign currencies? (*LO22-4*)

Overseas investment decisions are no different in principle from domestic decisions. You need to forecast the project's cash flows and then discount them at the opportunity cost of capital. But it is important to remember that if the opportunity cost of capital is stated in dollars, the cash flows must also be converted to dollars. This requires a forecast of foreign exchange rates. We suggest that you rely on the simple parity relationships and use the interest rate differential to produce these forecasts.

QUESTIONS AND PROBLEMS

connect

1. **Exchange Rates.** Use Table 22.1 to answer the following questions: (*LO22-1*)
    a. How many euros can you buy for $100? How many dollars can you buy for 100 euros?
    b. How many Swiss francs can you buy for $100? How many dollars can you buy for 100 Swiss francs?
    c. If the British pound depreciates with respect to the dollar, will the exchange rate quoted in Table 22.1 increase or decrease?
    d. Someone offers you the choice between a U.S. and a Canadian dollar. Which do you choose?

2. **Exchange Rates.** Look at Table 22.1. How many Mexican pesos can you buy for $1? How many yen can you buy? How many yen would it cost to buy 1 Mexican peso? (*LO22-1*)

3. **Exchange Rates.** Suppose that 2-year interest rates are 5.2% in the United States and 1.0% in Japan. The spot exchange rate is JPY98.63 = USD1. Suppose that 1 year later, interest rates are 3% in both countries, while the value of the yen has appreciated to JPY96.00 = USD1. (*LO22-1*)

    a. Benjamin Pinkerton from New York invested in a U.S. 2-year zero-coupon bond at the start of the period and sold it after 1 year. What was his return?
    b. Madame Butterfly from Osaka bought some dollars. She invested them in a one-year dollar bond and sold it after 1 year. What was her return in yen?
    c. Suppose that Madame Butterfly had correctly forecast the price at which she sold her bond and that she hedged her investment against currency risk. What would have been her return in yen?

4. **Exchange Rates.** Look at Table 22.2 which shows the dollar price of Big Macs in different countries. Use the exchange rates in Table 22.1 to calculate the price of a Big Mac in the local currency in each of the following countries: (a) Australia, (b) Brazil, (c) China, (d) the euro area, (e) Japan, (f) Switzerland, and (g) the U.K. (*LO22-1*)

5. **Exchange Rate Relationships.** Look at Table 22.1. (*LO22-2*)
    a. How many Brazilian reals do you get for your dollar?
    b. If the 1-year forward rate on the real is BRL4.012 = USD1, is the real at a forward discount or premium?
    c. If the 1-year interest rate on dollars is 1%, what do you think is the interest rate on the real?
    d. According to the expectations theory, what is the expected spot rate for the real in 1 year's time?
    e. According to purchasing power parity, what is the difference in the expected rate of price inflation in the United States and the rate in Brazil?

6. **Exchange Rate Relationships.** The spot and 1-year forward rates on the New Zealand dollar are currently NZD1.485 = USD1 and NZD1.455 = USD1, respectively. If the expectations theory of forward rates is correct, would you expect the New Zealand dollar to appreciate or depreciate over the coming year? (*LO22-2*)

7. **Exchange Rate Relationships** Choose the correct phrase to complete this sentence:
    The difference in interest rates between Ruritania and the United States equals: (*LO22-2*)
    a. The forward rur rate divided by the current spot rate.
    b. The forward rur rate divided by the expected spot rate.
    c. The current rur rate divided by the Ruritanian inflation rate.

8. **Exchange Rate Relationships.** Assume that the simple exchange rate relationships described in Section 22.2 hold exactly. (*LO22-2*)
    a. Dollar interest rate = 5%; Laputian interest rate = 10%; 1-year forward exchange rate = LAP100 = USD1. What is the current spot exchange rate?
    b. Current Lilliputian exchange rate = LIL40 = USD1; expected exchange rate at end of year = LIL45 = USD1; Lilliputian 1-year interest rate = 15%. What is the U.S. dollar interest rate?
    c. The U.S. inflation rate is 6%; the inflation rate in Blefuscu is twice that of the United States; the 1-year forward exchange rate = BLE25 = USD1. What is the current exchange rate between Blefuscu and the United States?

9. **Exchange Rate Relationships.** The following table shows the local prices of a Grande Latte coffee in Starbucks in 2015: (*LO22-2*)

	Price of Coffee	Exchange Rate
India	INR200.00	INR66.225 = USD1
Malaysia	MYR12.20	MYR4.287 = USD1
Mexico	MXN43.00	MXN17.013 = USD1
Philippines	PHP150.00	PHP47.28 = USD1
South Korea	KRW5100.00	KRW1176.471 = USD1
United States	USD3.55	

Source: www.humuch.com.

a. Calculate the dollar price of a latte in each country.
b. Does purchasing power parity hold?
c. What would the local price of a latte need to be in each country to ensure that the cost was the same as in the United States? In each case state whether the currency would need to appreciate or depreciate to equalize the prices.

10. **Exchange Rate Relationships.** Look at Table 22.1. If the 1-year forward exchange rate for the Brazilian real is USD1 = BRL4.480 and the 1-year interest rate on dollars is .5%, what do you think is the 1-year interest rate in Brazil? (*LO22-2*)

11. **Exchange Rate Relationships.** The following table shows interest rates and exchange rates for the U.S. dollar and the Narnian leo. The spot exchange rate is 15 leos = $1. Complete the missing entries. (*Hint:* Remember to convert the interest rate to a 1- or 3-month rate when appropriate.) (*LO22-2*)

	1 Month	3 Months	1 Year
Dollar interest rate (annually compounded)	4.0	4.5	(a)
Narnian interest rate (annually compounded)	9.2	(b)	9.8
Forward leos per dollar	(c)	14.822	15.600

12. **Exchange Rate Relationships.** In 2010, many investors borrowed money in countries such as the United States, where interest rates were low, and invested the money in countries such as Australia, where rates were high. This is called a "carry trade." The risk of such a trade is that the Australian dollar may depreciate sharply. Could you eliminate this risk by entering into a forward exchange contract and still make money? (*LO22-2*)

13. **Exchange Rate Relationships.** Suppose the interest rate on 1-year loans in the United States is 3% while in Mexico the interest rate is 8%. The spot exchange rate is MXN18 = USD1 and the 1-year forward rate is MXN24 = USD1. (*LO22-2*)

a. In what country would you choose to borrow?
b. In which would you choose to lend?

14. **Exchange Rate Relationships.** Suppose that the inflation rate in the United States is 4% and in Canada it is 5%. Would you expect the Canadian dollar to appreciate or depreciate against the U.S. dollar? (*LO22-2*)

15. **Exchange Rate Risk.** Dick Johnson, the treasurer of Sonora Mining, has noticed that the interest rate in Japan is below the rates in most other countries. He is, therefore, suggesting that the company should make an issue of Japanese yen bonds. What considerations ought he first to take into account? (*LO22-3*)

16. **Exchange Rate Risk.** An importer in the United States is due to take delivery of silk scarves from Europe in 6 months. The price is fixed in euros. Which of the following transactions could eliminate the importer's exchange risk? (*LO22-3*)

a. Buy euros forward.
b. Sell euros forward.
c. Borrow euros; buy dollars at the spot exchange rate.
d. Sell euros at the spot exchange rate; lend dollars.

17. **Exchange Rate Risk.** An American investor buys 100 shares of London Enterprises at a price of £50 when the exchange rate is USD2 = GBP1. A year later, the shares are selling at £52. No dividends have been paid. (*LO22-3*)

    a. What is the rate of return to an American investor if the exchange rate is still USD2 = GBP1?
    b. What if the exchange rate is USD2.20 = GBP1?
    c. What if the exchange rate is USD1.80 = GBP1?

18. **Exchange Rate Risk.** Sanyo produces audio and video consumer goods and exports a large fraction of its output to the United States under its own name and the Fisher brand name. It prices its products in yen, meaning that it seeks to maintain a fixed price in terms of yen. Suppose the yen moves from JPY101.359 = USD1 to JPY108.50 = USD1. What currency risk does Sanyo face? How can it reduce its exposure? (*LO22-3*)

19. **Exchange Rate Risk.** A firm in the United States is due to receive payment of €1 million in 8 years' time. It would like to protect itself against a decline in the value of the euro but finds it difficult to find a forward contract for such a long period. Is there any other way in which it can protect itself? (*LO22-3*)

20. **Exchange Rate Risk.** General Gadget Corp. (GGC) is a U.S.-based multinational firm that makes electrical coconut scrapers. These gadgets are made only in the United States using local inputs. The scrapers are sold mainly to Asian and West Indian countries where coconuts are grown. (*LO22-3*)

    a. If GGC sells scrapers in Trinidad, what is the currency risk faced by the firm?
    b. In what currency should GGC borrow funds to pay for its investment in order to mitigate its foreign exchange exposure?
    c. Suppose that GGC begins manufacturing its products in Trinidad using local (Trinidadian) inputs and labor. How does this affect its exchange rate risk?

21. **Exchange Rate Risk.** Alpha and Omega are U.S. corporations. Alpha has a plant in Hamburg, Germany, that imports components from the United States, assembles them, and then sells the finished product in Germany. Omega is at the opposite extreme: It also has a plant in Hamburg, but it buys its raw material in Germany and exports its output back to the United States. How is each firm likely to be affected by a fall in the value of the euro? How could each firm hedge itself against exchange risk? (*LO22-3*)

22. **Exchange Rate Risk.** You have bid for a possible export order that would provide a cash inflow of €1 million in 6 months. The spot exchange rate is USD1.30 = EUR1, and the 1-year forward rate is USD1.28 = EUR1. There are two sources of uncertainty: (i) The euro could appreciate or depreciate, and (ii) you may or may not receive the export order. Fill in the following table to illustrate in each case the profits or losses that you would make if you sell €1 million forward. Assume that the exchange rate in 1 year will be either USD1.20 = EUR1 or USD1.40 = EUR1. (*LO22-3*)

	Total Profit/Loss	
Spot Rate	**Receive Order**	**Lose Order**
USD1.20 = EUR1	(a)	(c)
USD1.40 = EUR1	(b)	(d)

23. **Exchange Rate Risk.** The current exchange rate is USD2 = GBP1. ClickEasy is a large British firm that exports computer games to the United States. If the dollar depreciates relative to the pound, ClickEasy will increase the dollar price it charges its U.S. customers. But it cannot raise its U.S. price enough to fully offset any dollar depreciation because if it does so, it will lose customers to its U.S. competitors. Its rule of thumb is that for every 10-cent increase in the exchange rate (e.g., from USD2 = GBP1 to USD2.10 = GBP1), it will increase prices by $5 (e.g., from $200 to $205 per game). Given this rule, it will lose only some of its U.S. sales.

    Suppose its forecast of annual sales in the United States as a function of the dollar price is

    $$\text{Quantity sold} = 1,000,000 - 100 \times \text{price in dollars}$$

    Answer the following questions: (*LO22-3*)

a. Plot the British pound value of ClickEasy's revenue from its U.S. sales as a function of the exchange rate for exchange rates ranging from USD1.50 = GBP1 to USD3.00 = GBP1. What is its exchange rate exposure?

b. Suppose each exchange rate scenario in part (a) is equally likely. What would ClickEasy's expected dollar revenue be? What would be its pound revenue in each scenario if it sold forward that number of U.S. dollars at a forward exchange rate of USD2 = GBP1? Does this seem like an effective hedge?

24. **International Investment Decisions.** It is the year 2020 and Pork Barrels Inc. is considering construction of a new barrel plant in Spain. The forecast cash flows in millions of euros are as follows:

C_0	C_1	C_2	C_3	C_4	C_5
−80	+10	+20	+23	+27	+25

The spot exchange rate is USD1.2 = EUR1. The interest rate in the United States is 8%, and the euro interest rate is 6%. You can assume that pork barrel production is effectively risk-free. (*LO22-4*)

a. Calculate the NPV of the euro cash flows from the project. What is the NPV in dollars?

b. What are the dollar cash flows from the project if the company hedges against exchange rate changes?

c. Suppose that the company expects the euro to depreciate by 5% a year. Does this make the project less attractive?

d. Suppose that Pork Barrels decides to go ahead with the project despite its concerns about the euro. Would the company do better to finance it by borrowing the present value of the project in euros or in dollars?

25. **International Investment Decisions.** It is 2020 and Carpet Baggers Inc. is proposing to construct a new bagging plant in a country in Europe. The two prime candidates are Germany and Switzerland. The forecast cash flows from the proposed plants are as follows:

	C_0	C_1	C_2	C_3	C_4	C_5	C_6	IRR (%)
Germany (millions of euros)	− 60	+10	+15	+15	+20	+20	+20	18.8
Switzerland (millions of Swiss francs)	−120	+20	+30	+30	+35	+35	+35	12.8

The spot exchange rate for euros is USD1.3 = EUR1, while the rate for Swiss francs is CHF1.5 = USD1. The interest rate is 5% in the United States, 4% in Switzerland, and 6% in the euro countries. The financial manager has suggested that if the cash flows were stated in dollars, a return in excess of 10% would be acceptable. (*LO22-4*)

a. What is the dollar NPV of the German project?

b. What is the dollar NPV of the Swiss project?

c. Should the company go ahead with the German project, the Swiss project, or neither?

26. **International Investment Decisions.** Suppose that you (foolishly) use your own views about exchange rates when valuing an overseas investment proposal. Specifically, suppose that you believe that the rur will depreciate by 2% per year. Recalculate the NPV of Ecsy-Cola's project from Section 22.4. (*LO22-4*)

27. **International Investment Decisions.** An American firm is evaluating an investment in Mexico. The project costs 500 million pesos, and it is expected to produce an income of 250 million pesos a year in real terms for each of the next 3 years. The expected inflation rate in Mexico is 4% a year, and the firm estimates that an appropriate discount rate for the project would be about 8% above the risk-free rate of interest. Calculate the net present value of the project in U.S. dollars. Exchange rates are given in Table 22.1. The interest rate is about 4.3% in Mexico and 1.5% in the United States. (*LO22-4*)

WEB EXERCISES

1. There are plenty of good sites that show current and past spot rates of exchange. Forward rates are less easy to come by, but the Bank of England website gives spot and forward rates for the pound (we suggest that you download the forward rate itself rather than the forward premium). Can you deduce from these whether the interest rate is higher in the United States than in the United Kingdom? *Warning:* Look out for the difference between direct and indirect quotes.

2. Log on to www.prsgroup.com, and get a free sample of the *International Country Risk Guide*. For which characteristics does the United States score well? For which does it score badly? Is Norway still close to top of the class?

SOLUTIONS TO SELF-TEST QUESTIONS

22.1 Direct quote: USD1.084 = EUR1
Indirect quote: 1/1.084, or EUR.9225 = USD1
Indirect quote: JPY121.359 = USD1
Direct quote: 1/121.359, or USD.0082 = JPY1

22.2 One Hong Kong dollar is worth 17.013/7.753 = 2.194 Mexican pesos (and one peso is worth 7.753/17.013 = .456 Hong Kong dollar). If a bank quotes 2.5 pesos per Hong Kong dollar, you could take one U.S. dollar, buy 7.753 Hong Kong dollars, and then exchange the Hong Kong dollars for $7.753 \times 2.5 = 19.383$ pesos. Then you could change the pesos back into 19.383/17.013 = 1.139 U.S. dollars. The profit is $.139.

22.3 The U.S. dollar buys more Australian dollars, so the Australian dollar has depreciated with respect to the U.S. dollar.

22.4 a. 1,300/1.389 = $935.93.
 b. Indirect exchange rate: USD1 = $.9 \times 1.389 = $CAD1.250.
 c. 1,300/1.250 = $1,040.00. The U.S. dollar price increases.

22.5 a. Because the gold price must be the same in the two countries, GBP600 = USD1,000. Therefore, GBP.6 = USD1. The direct quote would be 1/.6 = USD1.667 = GBP1.0.
 b. In the United States, price = $1,000 \times 1.02 = $1,020. In Great Britain, price = £600 \times 1.05 = £630. The new exchange rate is, therefore, USD1,020 = GBP630, or USD1.619 = GBP1.
 c. Initially $1 buys 1/1.667 = £.6. At the end of the year, $1 buys 1/1.619 = £.6177, which is 3% higher than the original value of £.6.

22.6 The real interest rate in the United States is $1.003/1.017 - 1 = -.0138$, or -1.38%. If the real rate is the same in South Korea, then expected inflation must be (1 + nominal rate)/(1 + real rate) − 1 = 1.026/.9862 − 1 = .0403, or 4.03%.

22.7 Suppose you want Ruritanian rurs next year. You can put $1 aside, earn interest at 4%, and buy rurs at the forward price of 126.92. You end up with $1 \times 1.04 \times 126.92 = 132$ rurs. As the alternative, you can buy 120 rurs at spot and earn 10% in Ruritania. You end up in exactly the same place, with $120 \times 1.1 = 132$ rurs.

22.8 If the euro or the yen depreciates against the dollar, then foreign cars are likely to become cheaper. The Ford dealer therefore has economic risk even though it never needs to buy or sell foreign currency.

22.9 a. If real interest rates are the same in the two countries, the difference in the inflation rates is now $1.06/1.03 - 1 = .0291$, or 2.91%.
 b. Less. For example, the 1-year forward rate should now be (1.06/1.03) × 100, or RUR102.91 = USD1. A dollar now buys fewer rurs in the forward market than before (or, equivalently, each rur is now worth more dollars in the forward market).
 c. The rur cash inflows from Ecsy's project can now be exchanged for more dollars. So net present value increases:

Year:	0	1	2	3	4	5
Cash flow (millions of rurs)	−380	100	125	150	175	200
Forward exchange rate (rurs to the dollar)	100	102.91	105.91	108.99	112.17	115.44
Cash flow (millions of dollars)	−3.8	0.9717	1.1802	1.3762	1.5601	1.7326
PV at 13%	−3.8	0.8599	0.9243	0.9538	0.9569	0.9404

NPV = $.835 million

MINICASE

"Jumping jackasses! Not another one!" groaned George Luger. It was a memo from the CEO of DVR Importers dated December 31, 2016. It was the third memo from the CEO that he had received that day. It read as follows:

> From: CEO's Office
>
> To: Company Treasurer
>
> George,
>
> I have been looking at some of our foreign exchange deals and they don't seem to make sense.
>
> First, we have been buying yen forward to cover the cost of our imports. You have explained that this insures us against the risk that the dollar may depreciate over the next year, but it is incredibly expensive insurance. Each dollar buys only 108.173 yen when we buy forward, compared with the current spot rate of 111.715 yen to the dollar. We could save a fortune by buying yen as and when we need them rather than buying them forward.
>
> Another possibility has occurred to me. If we are worried that the dollar may depreciate (or do I mean "appreciate"?), why don't we buy yen at the low spot rate of ¥111.715 to the dollar and then put them on deposit until we have to pay for the DVRs? That way we can make sure that we get a good rate for our yen.
>
> I am also worried that we are missing out on some cheap financing. We are paying about 6% to borrow dollars for one year, but Ben Hur was telling me at lunch that we could get a one-year yen loan for about 2%. I find that a bit surprising, but if that's the case, why don't we repay our dollar loans and borrow yen instead?
>
> Perhaps we could discuss these ideas at next Wednesday's meeting. I would be interested in your views on the matter.
>
> Jill Edison

How should George respond to Jill's memo? For example:

1. Is the forward purchase of the yen "incredibly expensive insurance"?

2. Would the company be better if it purchased yen and "then put them on deposit"?

3. Should the company "repay [its] dollar loans and borrow yen instead"?

23

Options

LEARNING OBJECTIVES

After studying this chapter, you should be able to:

23-1 Calculate the payoff to buyers and sellers of call and put options.

23-2 Understand the determinants of option values.

23-3 Recognize options in capital investment proposals.

23-4 Identify options that are provided in financial securities.

RELATED WEBSITES FOR THIS CHAPTER CAN BE FOUND IN CONNECT.

Just another day on the options exchange. But why does the financial manager of an industrial company need to understand options?
© Scott Olson/Getty Images

When the Chicago Board Options Exchange (CBOE) was established in 1973, few observers guessed what a success it would be. Today, the CBOE trades options to buy or sell about 50 billion shares of stock a year. In addition to trading options on individual stocks, you can now trade options on stock indexes, bonds, commodities, and foreign exchange.

You will see that options can be valuable tools for managing the risk characteristics of an investment portfolio. But why should the financial manager of an industrial company read further? There are several reasons. First, most capital budgeting projects have options embedded in them that allow the company to expand at a future date or to bail out. These options enable the company to profit if things go well but give downside protection when they don't.

Second, many of the securities that firms issue include an option. For example, companies often issue convertible bonds. The holder has the option to exchange the bond for common stock. Some corporate bonds also contain a call provision, meaning that the issuer has the option to buy back the bond from the investor.

Finally, managers routinely use currency, commodity, and interest rate options to protect the firm against a variety of risks.

In one chapter, we can provide you with only a brief introduction to options. Our first goal is to explain how options work and how option value is determined. Then we will tell you how to recognize some of the options that crop up in capital investment proposals and in company financing.

For simplicity, we will use the example of traded options on shares of Alphabet (the parent company of Google) to illustrate the nature of options and how they are valued, but we hope that our brief survey will convince you that the interest of financial managers in options goes far beyond these traded options.

23.1 Calls and Puts

call option

Right to buy an asset at a specified exercise price on or before the expiration date.

A **call option** gives its holder the *right* to buy stock for a fixed *exercise price* (also called the *strike price*) on or before a specified expiration date.[1] For example, if you buy a call option on Alphabet stock with an expiration date in June and an exercise price of $750, you have the right to buy the stock at a price of $750 anytime until June.

You need not exercise a call option; you will choose to exercise only if the share price exceeds the exercise price. If it does not do so, the option will be left unexercised and will be valueless. But suppose that when the option expires, Alphabet shares are selling above the exercise price, say, at $820. In this case, you will choose to exercise your option to pay $750 for shares worth $820. Your payoff will equal the difference between the $820 for which you can sell the shares and the $750 that you must pay when you exercise the option. More generally, when the stock price is greater than the exercise price, the payoff from your call option is equal to the difference between the stock price and the exercise price.

In summary, the value of the call option at expiration is as follows:

Stock Price at Expiration	Value of Call at Expiration
Greater than exercise price	Stock price − exercise price
Less than exercise price	Zero

Of course, that payoff is not all profit: You have to pay for the option. The price of the call is known as the option *premium*. Option buyers pay the premium for the right to exercise later. Your *profit* equals the ultimate payoff to the call option (which may be zero) minus the initial premium.

Example 23.1 ▶   Call Options on Alphabet

In December 2015, a call option on Alphabet stock with a June 2016 expiration and an exercise price of $750 sold for $58.00. If you bought this call, you gained the right to purchase Alphabet shares for $750 at any time until the option expired the following June. The price of Alphabet stock in December was about $750. So, if the stock price did not rise by June, the call would not be worth exercising and you would lose your investment of $58.00. On the other hand, even a relatively modest rise in the stock price could give you a rich profit on your option. For example, if Alphabet sold for $850 in June, the proceeds from exercising the call would be

$$\text{Proceeds} = \text{stock price} - \text{exercise price} = \$850 - \$750 = \$100$$

and the net profit on the call would be

$$\text{Profit} = \text{proceeds} - \text{original investment} = \$100 - \$58.00 = \$42.00$$

In 6 months, you would have earned a return of $42.00/$58.00 = .72, or 72%. ■

put option

Right to sell an asset at a specified exercise price on or before the option's expiration date.

Whereas a call option gives you the right to buy a share of stock, a **put option** gives you the right to *sell* it for the exercise price. If you own a put on a share of stock and the stock price turns out to be greater than the exercise price, you will not want to exercise your option to sell the shares for the exercise price. The put will be left unexercised and will expire valueless. But if the stock price turns out to be less than the exercise price, it will pay to buy the share in the market at the low price and then exercise your option to sell it for the exercise price. The put would then be worth the difference between the exercise price and the stock price.

---

[1] In some cases, the option can be exercised only on its expiration date, and it is then conventionally known as a *European call;* in other cases, it can be exercised on or before that date, and it is known as an *American call.*

In general, the value of the put option at expiration is as follows:

Stock Price at Expiration	Value of Put at Expiration
Greater than exercise price	Zero
Less than exercise price	Exercise price − stock price

Example 23.2 ▶   Put Options on Alphabet

In December 2015, it cost $60.30 to buy a put option on Alphabet stock with a June 2016 expiration and an exercise price of $750. Suppose that Alphabet is selling for $650 when the put option expires. Then, if you hold the put, you can buy a share of stock in the market for $650 and exercise your right to sell it for $750. The put will be worth $750 − $650 = $100. Because you paid $60.30 for the put originally, your net profit is $100 − $60.30 = $39.70. As a put buyer, your worry is that the stock price will rise above the $750 exercise price. If that happens, you will let the put option expire worthless, and you will lose the $60.30 that you originally paid for it. ■

Table 23.1 shows how the values of Alphabet calls and puts are affected by the level of the stock price on the expiration date. You can see that once the stock price is above the exercise price, the call value on the expiration date rises dollar for dollar with the stock price, and once the stock price is below the exercise price, the put value rises a dollar for each dollar *decrease* in the stock price. Figure 23.1 plots the values of each option on the expiration date.

Table 23.2 shows the prices of nine options on Alphabet stock in December 2015. Notice that for any particular expiration date, call options are worth more when the exercise price is lower, while puts are worth more when the exercise price is higher. This makes sense: You would rather have the right to buy at a low price and the right to sell at a high price. Notice also that for any particular exercise price the longer-dated options are the most valuable. This also makes sense. An option that expires in January 2017 gives you everything that a shorter-dated option offers and more. Naturally, you would be prepared to pay for the chance to keep your options open for as long as possible.

TABLE 23.1 How the value of an Alphabet option on its expiration date varies with the price of the stock on that date (exercise price = $750)

Stock Price:	$650	$700	$750	$800	$850
Call value	0	0	0	$50	$100
Put value	$100	$50	0	0	0

FIGURE 23.1 Values of call options and put options on Alphabet stock on option expiration date (exercise price = $750)

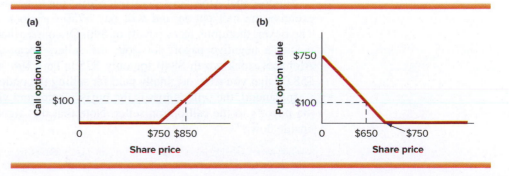

TABLE 23.2 Examples of options on Alphabet shares in December 2015 when Alphabet stock was selling for $750

Expiration Date	Exercise Price	Call Price	Put Price
March 2016	$700	$ 64.73	$ 25.00
	750	42.00	47.67
	800	21.50	84.00
June 2016	700	86.00	41.60
	750	58.00	60.30
	800	35.60	90.90
January 2017	700	105.11	63.54
	750	81.80	76.50
	800	61.10	106.00

23.1 Self-Test

a. What will be the proceeds and net profits (i.e., net of the option premium) to an investor who purchases the January 2017 expiration Alphabet call option with exercise price of $800 if the stock price at expiration is $710? What if the stock price at expiration is $880? Use the data in Table 23.2.

b. Now answer part (a) for an investor who purchases a March 2016 expiration Alphabet put option with exercise price $800.

Selling Calls and Puts

The traded options that you see quoted in the financial pages are not sold by the companies themselves but by other investors. If one investor buys an option on Alphabet stock, some other investor must be on the other side of the bargain. We will look now at the position of the investor who sells an option.[2]

We have already seen that the Alphabet calls that expire in June 2016 with an exercise price of $750 are trading at $58.00. Thus if you *sell* the June call option on Alphabet stock, the buyer pays you $58.00. However, in return you promise to sell Alphabet shares at a price of $750 to the call buyer if he decides to exercise his option. The option seller's obligation to *sell* Alphabet is just the other side of the coin to the option holder's right to *buy* the stock. The buyer pays the option premium for the right to exercise; the seller *receives* the premium but may be required at a later date to deliver the stock for an exercise price that is less than the market price of the stock. If the share price is below the exercise price of $750 when the option expires in June, holders of the call will not exercise their option and you, the seller, will have no further liability. However, if the price of Alphabet is greater than $750, it will pay the buyer to exercise and you must give up your shares for $750 each. You lose the difference between the share price and the $750 that you receive from the buyer.

Suppose that Alphabet's stock price turns out to be $840. In this case, the buyer will exercise the call option and will pay $750 for stock that can be resold for $840. The buyer, therefore, has a payoff of $90. Of course, that positive payoff for the buyer means a negative payoff for you, the seller, because you are obliged to deliver Alphabet stock worth $840 for only $750. This $90 loss more than wipes out the $58.00 that you were originally paid for selling the option.

In general, the seller's loss is the buyer's gain, and vice versa. Figure 23.2a shows the payoffs to the call option seller. Note that this figure is just Figure 23.1a drawn upside down.

---

[2] The option seller is known as the *writer*.

FIGURE 23.2 Payoffs to sellers of call and put options on Alphabet stock (exercise price = $750)

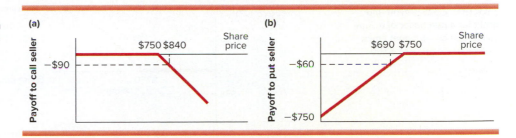

The position of an investor who sells the Alphabet put option can be shown in just the same way by standing Figure 23.1*b* on its head. The put *buyer* has the right to sell a share for $750; so the *seller* of the put has agreed to pay $750 for the share if the put buyer should demand it. Clearly, the seller will be safe as long as the share price remains above $750, but his payoff will be negative if the share price falls below this figure. The worst thing that can happen to the put seller is for the stock to be worthless. The seller would then be obliged to pay $750 for a worthless stock. The payoff to the seller would be −$750. Note that the advantage always lies with the option buyer, and the obligation lies with the seller. Therefore, the buyer must pay the seller to acquire the option.

Table 23.3 summarizes the rights and obligation of buyers and sellers of calls and puts.

23.2   Self-Test

a. What will be the proceeds and net profits to an investor who sells the March expiration Alphabet call option with exercise price of $800 if the stock price at expiration is $740? What if the stock price at expiration is $890? Use the data in Table 23.2.

b. Now answer part (a) for an investor who sells a March expiration Alphabet put option with exercise price $800.

Payoff Diagrams Are Not Profit Diagrams

Figures 23.1 and 23.2 show only the possible *payoffs* when the option expires; they do not account for the initial cost of buying the option or the initial proceeds from selling it.

This is a common point of confusion. For example, the payoff diagram in Figure 23.1*a* makes purchase of a call look like a sure thing—the payoff is at worst zero, with plenty of upside if Alphabet's stock price goes above $750 by the expiration date. But compare this with the *profit diagram* in Figure 23.3, which subtracts the $58.00 cost of the call in December 2015 from the payoff at expiration. The call buyer loses money unless the share price in June exceeds $750 + $58.00 = $808.00.

Take another example: The payoff diagram in Figure 23.2*b* makes selling a put look like a sure loser—the *best* payoff is zero. But the profit diagram in Figure 23.4, which recognizes the $60.30 received by the seller, shows that the seller gains at all prices above $750 − $60.30 = $689.70.

Profit diagrams like those in Figures 23.3 and 23.4 may be helpful to the options beginner, but options experts rarely draw them. Now that you've graduated from the

---

TABLE 23.3 Rights and obligations of various option positions

	Buyer	Seller
Call option	Right to buy asset	Obligation to sell asset
Put option	Right to sell asset	Obligation to buy asset

FIGURE 23.3 Payoff and profit for a purchaser of a June call option on Alphabet stock with exercise price of $750

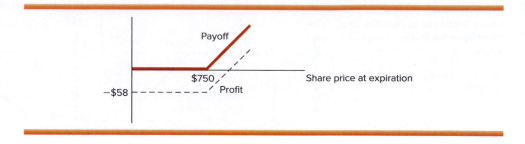

FIGURE 23.4 Payoff and profit for a seller of a put option on Alphabet with exercise price of $750

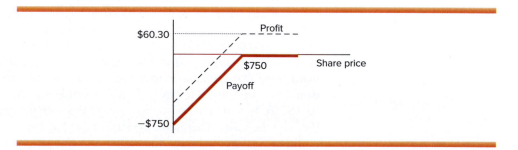

first options class, we won't draw them either. We will stick to payoff diagrams because you have to focus on payoffs at expiration to understand options and to value them properly.

Financial Alchemy with Options

Options can be used to modify the risk characteristics of a stock. Suppose, for example, that you are generally optimistic about Alphabet's prospects but you perceive enough risk that a large investment in the stock would cause you sleepless nights. Here is a strategy that might appeal to you: Buy the stock, but also buy a put option on the stock with exercise price $750. If the stock price rises from its current level of $750, your put turns out to be worthless, but you win on your investment in the stock. If the stock price falls, your losses are limited because the put gives you the right to sell your stock for the $750 exercise price. Thus, the value of your stock-plus-put position cannot be less than $750.

Here is another way to view your overall position. You hold the stock and the put option. The ultimate value of each component of the portfolio is as follows:

	Stock Price < $750	Stock Price ≥ $750
Value of stock	Stock price	Stock price
Value of put option	$750 − stock price	0
Total value	$750	Stock price

No matter how far the stock price falls, the total value of your portfolio cannot fall below the $750 exercise price.

The value of your position when the option expires is graphed in Figure 23.5. You have downside protection at $750 but still share in any increase in the stock price. This strategy is called a *protective put* because the put option gives protection against losses. Of course, such protection is not free. Look again at Table 23.2 and you will find the cost of such protection. "Stock price insurance" at a level of $750 between December and June cost $60.30 per share; this was the December price of a put option with exercise price $750 and June expiration.

FIGURE 23.5 Payoff to protective put strategy. If the ultimate stock price exceeds $750, the put is valueless but you own the stock. If it is less than $750, you can sell the stock for the exercise price.

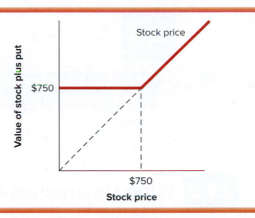

Some More Option Magic

Look again at Figure 23.5, which shows the possible payoffs at expiration from holding both a share of Alphabet stock and a put option to sell it for $750. Does this picture look somewhat familiar? It should. Turn back to panel *a* of Figure 23.1, which shows the payoffs from holding a call option on Alphabet stock with an exercise price of $750. The only difference between the two sets of payoffs is that the combination of the stock and put option always provides exactly $750 more than the call option. In other words, regardless of the final stock price, holding the stock plus a put option gives the same payoff as an alternative strategy of buying a call option plus investing the present value of $750 in a bank deposit.

Think what happens if you follow this second strategy. If the stock price is below $750 when the option expires, your call option will be valueless but you will still have $750 in the bank. On the other hand, if the stock price rises above $750, you will take your money out of the bank, use it to exercise the call, and own the stock. The following table confirms that this second investment package gives you exactly the same payoffs as you get from holding the stock and a put option:

	Payoffs at Expiration	
	Stock price ≤ $750	Stock price > $750
Call option	0	Stock price − $750
Bank deposit paying $750	$750	$750
Total value	$750	Stock price

BEYOND THE PAGE

   Option payoffs

mhhe.com/brealey9e

If you plan to hold each of these packages until the options expire, the packages must sell for the same price today. This gives us a fundamental relationship between the price of a call and the price of a put:[3]

Price of stock + price of put = price of call + present value of exercise price

This basic relationship between share price, call and put prices, and the present value of the exercise price is called *put-call parity*.

---

[3] This relationship assumes that the two options have the same exercise price and expiration date. Alphabet stock does not pay a dividend. If it did pay a dividend before expiration, the formula should be expanded to:

Stock price − PV(dividends before expiration) + put price = call price + PV(exercise price)

Notice that several of the prices in Table 23.2 are inconsistent with this formula. There are two reasons for this. First, we rounded Alphabet's stock price. Second, there were very few trades that day in some of these options and the prices are not all recorded at the same time.

23.3 **Self-Test**

A 1-year *call* option on Witterman stock with an exercise price of **$60** costs **$8.05**. The stock price is **$55**, and the interest rate on a bank deposit is **4%**. What is the value of a 1-year *put* option on Witterman with an exercise price of **$60**?

23.2 # What Determines Option Values?

In Table 23.2, we set out the prices of different Alphabet options. But we said nothing about how the market values of options are determined. It is time to do so.

Upper and Lower Limits on Option Values

We know what an option is worth when it expires. Consider, for example, the option to buy Alphabet stock at $750. If the stock price is below $750 at the expiration date, the call will be worthless; if the stock price is above $750, the call will be worth the value of the stock minus the $750 exercise price. The relationship is depicted by the heavy orange line in Figure 23.6.

Even before expiration, the price of the option can never remain *below* the heavy orange line in Figure 23.6. For example, if our option were priced at $20 and the stock at $800, it would pay any investor to buy the option, exercise it for an additional $750, and then sell the stock for $800. That would give a "money machine" with a profit of $800 − ($20 + $750) = $30. Money machines can't last. The demand for options from investors using this strategy would quickly force the option price up at least to the heavy orange line in the figure. The heavy orange line is therefore a lower limit on the market price of the option. Thus

$$\text{Lower limit on value of call option} = \text{the greater of zero or (stock price − exercise price)}$$

FIGURE 23.6 Value of a call before its expiration date (dashed line). The value depends on the stock price. The call is always worth more than its value if exercised now (heavy orange line). It is never worth more than the stock price itself (blue line).

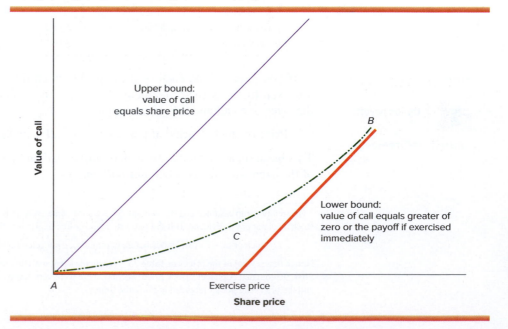

The diagonal blue line in Figure 23.6, which is the plot of the stock price, is the *upper* limit to the option price. Why? Because the stock itself gives a higher final payoff whatever happens. If when the option expires the stock price ends up above the exercise price, the option is worth the stock price *less* the exercise price. If the stock price ends up below the exercise price, the option is worthless but the stock's owner still has a valuable security. Thus, the extra payoff to holding the stock rather than the option is as follows:

Stock Price at Expiration	Stock Payoff	Option Payoff	Extra Payoff from Holding Stock Rather than Option
Greater than $750	Stock price	Stock price − $750	$750
Less than or equal to $750	Stock price	$0	Stock price

The Determinants of Option Value

The option price must lie between the upper and lower limits in Figure 23.6. In fact, the price will lie on a curved, upward-sloping line like the dashed curve shown in the figure. This line begins its travels where the upper and lower bounds meet (at zero). Then it rises, gradually becoming parallel to the lower bound. This line tells us an important fact about option values: Given the exercise price, *the value of a call option increases as the stock price increases.*

That should be no surprise. Owners of call options are clearly happy when the stock price is much higher than the exercise price and are willing to pay more for options that are deeper "in the money." If you look back at the prices of the Alphabet options, you will see that the price of the call is higher when the stock price is above the exercise price. But let us look more carefully at the shape and location of the dashed line. Three points, *A*, *B*, and *C*, are marked on the dashed line. As we explain each point, you will see why the option price has to behave as the dashed line predicts.

Point *A* *When the stock is worthless, the option is worthless.* A stock price of zero means that there is no possibility the stock will ever have any future value.[4] If so, the option is sure to expire unexercised and worthless, and it is worthless today.

Point *B* *When the stock price becomes very high, the option price approaches the stock price less the present value of the exercise price.* Notice that the dashed line representing the option price in Figure 23.6 eventually becomes parallel to the ascending heavy orange line representing the lower bound on the option price. The reason is as follows: The higher the stock price, the greater the odds that the option will eventually be exercised. If the stock price is high enough, exercise becomes a virtual certainty; the probability that the stock price will fall below the exercise price before the option expires becomes trivial.

If you own an option that you know will be exchanged for a share of stock, you effectively own the stock now. The only difference is that you don't have to pay for the stock (by handing over the exercise price) until later, when formal exercise occurs. In these circumstances, buying the call is equivalent to buying the stock now with deferred payment and delivery. The value of the call is, therefore, equal to the stock price less the present value of the exercise price.[5]

This brings us to another important point about options. Investors who acquire stock by way of a call option are buying on "installment credit." They pay the purchase

<hr>

[4] If a stock can be worth something in the future, then investors will pay *something* for it today, although possibly a very small amount.

[5] We assume here that the stock pays no dividends until after the option expires. If dividends were paid, you *would* care about when you get to own the stock because the option holder misses out on any dividends.

price of the option today, but they do not pay the exercise price until they actually exercise the option. The delay in payment is particularly valuable if interest rates are high and the option has a long maturity. Thus, *the value of a call option increases with both the rate of interest and the time to expiration.*

23.4   Self-Test

How would the value of a put option be affected by an increase in the exercise price? Explain.

Point C   *The option price always exceeds its minimum value* (except at expiration or when the stock price is zero). We have seen that the dashed and heavy lines in Figure 23.6 coincide when stock price is zero (point A), but elsewhere the lines diverge; that is, the option price must exceed the minimum value given by the heavy orange line. You can see why by examining point C.

At point C, the stock price exactly equals the exercise price. The option therefore would be worthless if it expired today. However, suppose that the option will not expire until 3 months hence. Of course, we do not know what the stock price will be at the expiration date. It could be higher than the exercise price, or it could be be lower. The possible payoffs to the option are therefore:

Outcome	Payoff
Stock price rises	Stock price – exercise price (option is exercised)
Stock price falls	Zero (option expires worthless)

If there is some chance of a positive payoff, and if the worst payoff is zero, then the option must be valuable. That means the option price at point C exceeds its lower bound, which at point C is zero. In general, the option price will exceed the lower bound as long as there is time left before expiration.

One of the most important determinants of the *height* of the dashed curve (i.e., of the difference between actual and lower-bound value) is the likelihood of substantial movements in the stock price. An option on a stock whose price is unlikely to change by more than 1% or 2% is not worth much; an option on a stock whose price may halve or double is very valuable.

For example, suppose that a call option has an exercise price of $750 and the stock price will be either $650 or $850 when the option expires. The possible payoffs to the option are as follows:

Stock price at expiration	$650	$850
Call value at expiration	0	$100

Now suppose that the value of the stock when the option expires can be $600 or $900. The *average* of the possible stock prices is the same as before, but the volatility is greater. In this case, the payoffs to the call are:

Stock price at expiration	$600	$900
Call value at expiration	0	$150

A comparison of the two cases highlights the valuable asymmetry that options offer. If the stock price turns out to be below the exercise price when the option expires, the option is valueless regardless of whether the shortfall is a cent or a dollar.

However, the option holder reaps all the benefits of stock price advances. Thus, in our example, the option is worth only $100 if the stock price reaches $850, but it is worth $150 if the stock price rises to $900. Therefore, volatility helps the option holder.

The probability of large stock price changes during the remaining life of an option depends on two things: (1) the variability of the stock price *per unit of time* and (2) the length of time until the option expires. Other things equal, you would like to hold an option on a volatile stock. Given volatility, you would like to hold an option with a long life ahead of it because that longer life means that there is more opportunity for the stock price to change. The value of an option increases with both the variability of the share price and the time to expiration.

It's a rare person who can keep all these properties straight at first reading. Therefore, we have summed them up in Table 23.4.

23.5 Self-Test

Rework our numerical example for a put option with an exercise price of $750. Show that put options also are more valuable when the stock price is more volatile.

Option-Valuation Models

BEYOND THE PAGE

A simple option-valuation model

mhhe.com/brealey9e

If you want to value an option, you need to go beyond the qualitative statements of Table 23.4; you need an exact option-valuation model—a formula that you can plug numbers into and come up with a figure for option value.

Valuing complex options is a high-tech business and well beyond the scope of this book. Our aim here is not to make you into instant option whizzes, but we can illustrate the basics of option valuation by walking you through an example. The trick to option valuation is to find a combination of borrowing and an investment in the stock that exactly replicates the option. The nearby box illustrates a simple version of one of these option-valuation models.

This model achieves simplicity by assuming that the share price can take on only two values at the expiration date of the option. This assumption is clearly unrealistic, but it turns out that the same approach can be generalized to allow for a large number of possible future share prices rather than just the two values in our example.

In 1973 Fischer Black, Myron Scholes, and Robert Merton came up with a formula showing that even when share prices are changing continuously, an option can still be replicated by a series of levered investments in the stock. The Black-Scholes formula is regularly used by option traders, investment bankers, and financial managers to value a wide variety of options. Scholes and Merton shared the 1997 Nobel Prize in economics for their work on the development of this formula.[6] The nearby Spreadsheet Solutions box shows you how to set up a Black-Scholes calculator in Excel.

TABLE 23.4 What the price of a call option depends on

If the following variables increase, . . .	. . . the value of a call option will
Stock price	Increase
Exercise price	Decrease
Interest rate	Increase
Time to expiration	Increase
Volatility of stock price	Increase

[6] Fischer Black passed away in 1995.

It is December 2015, and you are contemplating the purchase of a call option on Alphabet stock. The call has a June 2016 expiration date and an exercise price of $750. Alphabet's stock price is also currently $750, so the option will be valueless unless the stock price appreciates over the next 6 months. The outlook for Alphabet stock is uncertain, and all you know is that at the end of the 6 months, the price will either rise by 17.5% to 1.175 × $750 = $881.25 or fall by the same proportion to $750/1.175 = $638.30. Finally, the rate of interest on a bank loan at this time is about 1% for 6 months.

The following chart depicts the outlook for three alternative investments:

Alphabet Stock		Call Option		Bank Loan	
December	June	December	June	December	June
$750 → $881.25 / 638.30		? → $131.25 / $0		$100 → $101 / $101	

The first investment is Alphabet stock. Its current price is $750, but the price could rise to $881.25 or fall to $638.30. The second investment is the call option. When the call expires in June, the option will be valueless if the stock price falls, and it will be worth $881.25 − $750 = $131.25 if the stock price rises to $881.25. We don't know (yet) what the call is worth today, so for the time being, we put a question mark against the December value. Our third investment is a $100 bank loan at an interest rate of 1% for 6 months. The payoff on the $100 bank loan is $101 no matter what happens to the price of Alphabet stock.

Now consider two investment strategies. The first (strategy A) is to buy 100 call options. The second (strategy B) is to buy 54.02 Alphabet shares and borrow the present value of $34,481. Table 23.5 shows the possible payoffs from the two strategies. Notice that when you borrow from the bank you receive a *positive* cash flow now but have a negative cash flow when the loan is repaid in June.

You can see that, regardless of whether the stock price falls to $638.30 or rises to $881.25, the payoffs from the two strategies are identical. To put it another way, you can exactly replicate an investment in call options by a combination of a bank loan and an investment in the stock.[*] If two investments give the same payoffs in all circumstances, then their value must be the same today. In other words, the cost of buying 100 call options must be exactly the same as borrowing PV($34,481) from the bank and buying 54.02 Alphabet shares:

$$\text{Price of 100 calls} = \$40,515 - \$34,140 = \$6,375$$
$$\text{Price of 1 call} = \$6,375/100 = \$63.75$$

Presto! You have just valued a call option.

[*] The only tricky part in valuing the Alphabet option was to work out the number of shares that were needed to replicate the call option. Fortunately, there is a simple formula which says that the number of shares is equal to:

$$\frac{\text{Spread of possible option prices}}{\text{Spread of possible stock prices}} = \frac{\$131.25 - 0}{\$881.25 - 638.30} = .5402$$

To replicate 1 call option, you need to buy .5402 of a share. To replicate 100 calls, you need to buy 54.02 shares of stock.

TABLE 23.5 It is possible to replicate the payoffs from Alphabet call options by borrowing to invest in Alphabet stock

		Payoff in June If Stock Price Equals	
	Cash Flow in June 2016	$638.30	$881.25
Strategy A			
Buy 100 calls	?	$ 0	+$13,125
Strategy B			
Buy 54.02 shares	−$40,515	+$34,481	+$47,606
Borrow PV($34,481)	+ 34,140	− 34,481	− 34,481
	−$ 6,375	$ 0	+$13,125

Note: PV($34,481) paid 6 months from now is $34,481/1.01 = $34,140.

Today, there are many ever-more-sophisticated variants on the Black-Scholes formula that can better capture some aspect of real-life markets. As computer power continues to increase, these models can be made more complex and increasingly accurate.

Rather than using an estimate of volatility to calculate the value of an option, investors sometimes use option prices to back out an estimate of future volatility. The nearby box describes how these estimates of volatility are used to create a "fear index."

You may like to try your hand at using the Black-Scholes option-pricing formula to value the Alphabet option. You can use the spreadsheet provided in Connect, but it takes only a few moments to construct your own Excel program to calculate Black-Scholes values. The following spreadsheet shows how you do it. First, type in the formulas shown on the right side of the spreadsheet in cells E2 to E8. Now enter the data for the Alphabet June 2016 call in cells B2 to B6. Notice that

the values for the standard deviation and interest rate are entered as decimals.[*] On past evidence, the standard deviation of Alphabet's annual returns has been about 25%, so we enter the standard deviation in cell B2 as .25. The last two lines of the output column show that the Black-Scholes formula gives a value of $56.36 for the Alphabet call option, pretty close to its market price in December 2015. (Don't worry about the other lines of output.)

Spreadsheet Questions

1. Use the option-pricing spreadsheet to calculate the value of the Alphabet call option at stock prices ranging from $250 to $1,250 at intervals of $50. (Use an annual interest rate of 2.01%, equivalent to 1% per 6 months.)
2. Plot the values as a function of the stock price. How does your graph compare to the plot in Figure 23.6?

BEYOND THE PAGE

The Black-Scholes model

mhhe.com/brealey9e

	A	B	C	D	E	F	G	H	I	J
1	**Inputs**			**Outputs**			**Formula for Output in Column E**			
2	Standard deviation (annual)	0.25		PV(Ex. Price)	742.5743		B6/(1+B4)^B3			
3	Maturity (in years)	0.5		d1	0.1447		(LN(B5/E2)(B2*B3^0.5)+B2*B3^0.5/2)			
4	Risk-free rate (effective annual rate)	0.0201		d2	−0.0321		E3-B2*B3^.5			
5	Stock price	750		N(d1)	0.5575		NORMSDIST(E3)			
6	Exercise price	750		N(d2)	0.4872		NORMSDIST(E4)			
7				B/S call value	56.3584		B5*E5 − E2*E6			
8				B/S put value	48.9326		E7+E2 − B5			

* Chapter 11 described how to calculate standard deviations. Notice also that in cell E2, we compute the present value of the exercise price by treating the interest rate as an effective annual yield. You should be aware, however, that many Black-Scholes calculators require that the interest rate be expressed as a continuously compounded rate. See Chapter 5, Table 5.7, if you need a review of continuous compounding.

23.6 Self-Test

Use the simple option-valuation model in the Finance in Practice box as a model to help you answer this question: Suppose that the price of Fly-by-Night stock is $30 and could either double to $60 or halve to $15 over the next 3 months. Show that the following two strategies have exactly the same payoffs regardless of whether the stock price rises or falls:

Strategy A. Buy three call options with an exercise price of $30.
Strategy B. Buy two shares and borrow the present value of $30.

What is your cash outflow today if you follow strategy B? What does this tell you about the value of three call options? Assume that the interest rate is 1% per 3 months.

The Market Volatility Index, or VIX, measures the volatility implied by near-term options on the Standard & Poor's 500 Index and is, therefore, an estimate of expected future market volatility over the next 30 calendar days. Implied market volatilities have been calculated by the Chicago Board Options Exchange (CBOE) since January 1986, though in its current form the VIX dates back only to 2003.

Investors regularly trade volatility. They do so by buying or selling VIX futures and options contracts. Since these were introduced by the CBOE, they have become two of the most successful innovations ever introduced by the exchange.

Because VIX measures investor uncertainty, it has been dubbed the "fear index." The market for index options tends to be dominated by equity investors who buy put options on the index when they are concerned about a potential drop in the stock market. Any subsequent decline in the value of their portfolio is then offset by the increase in the value of the put option. The more that investors value such insurance, the higher the price of index put options. Thus, VIX is an indicator that reflects the price of portfolio insurance.

Between January 1986 and December 2015, the VIX has averaged 21.0%, almost identical to the long-term level of market volatility that we cited in Chapter 11. The high point for the index was on October 19, 1987, when the VIX closed at 151%. Fortunately, market volatility returned fairly rapidly to less heady levels.

Although the VIX is the most widely quoted measure of volatility, volatility measures are also available for several other U.S. and overseas stock market indexes.

BEYOND THE PAGE

 **Implied volatilities**

mhhe.com/brealey9e

23.3 Spotting the Option

In our discussion so far, we may have given you the impression that financial managers are concerned only with traded options to buy or sell shares. But once you have learned to recognize the different kinds of options, you will find that they are everywhere. Unfortunately, they rarely come with a large label attached. Often, the trickiest part of the problem is to identify the option.

We will start by looking briefly at options on real assets and then turn to options on financial assets. You should find that you have already encountered many of these options in earlier chapters.

Options on Real Assets

In Chapter 10, we pointed out that the capital investment projects that you accept today may affect the opportunities you have tomorrow. Today's capital budgeting decisions need to recognize these future opportunities.

Other things equal, a capital investment project that generates new opportunities is more valuable than one that doesn't. A flexible project—one that doesn't commit management to a fixed operating strategy—is more valuable than an inflexible one. When a project is flexible or generates new opportunities for the firm, it is said to contain **real options.**

If you look out for real options, you'll find them almost everywhere. The nearby Finance in Practice box provides an illustration of a firm that took real options into account in an important capital budgeting decision. In Chapter 10, we looked at several ways that companies may build future flexibility into a project. Here is a brief reminder of two types of real options that we introduced in that chapter.

real options
Options to invest in, modify, postpone, or dispose of a capital investment project.

The Option to Expand   Many capital investment proposals include an option to expand in the future. For instance, some of the world's largest oil reserves are found in the tar sands of Alberta, Canada. Unfortunately, in many cases, the cost of extracting oil is higher than the current market price. Yet oil companies have been prepared to pay considerable sums for these tracts of barren land. The reason? Ownership of the tar sands gives the companies an option. If prices remain below the cost of extraction, much of the Alberta sands will remain undeveloped. But if prices rise above the cost of extraction, those land purchases could prove very valuable. Thus, ownership gives the companies a real option—a call option to extract the oil.

When Allegheny Corporation acquired open gas-fired power plants in Mississippi and Tennessee, these plants were expected to sit idle most of the year and, when operating, to produce electricity at a cost at least 50% higher than the most efficient state-of-the-art facilities. Allegheny's decision to acquire these power plants resulted from a sophisticated application of real options analysis.

The firm observed that electricity prices in an increasingly free energy market can be wildly volatile. For example, during some power shortages in the Midwest during the hot summer months, the cost of 1 megawatt-hour of electricity has increased briefly from a typical level of $40 to several thousand dollars. The option to obtain additional energy in these situations obviously would be quite valuable.

Allegheny concluded that it would pay to acquire some cheap power plants, even if they were relatively high-cost electricity producers. Most of the time, the plants will sit idle, with market prices for electricity below the marginal cost of production. But every so often, when electricity prices spike, the plants can be fired up to produce electricity—at a great profit. Even if they operate only a few weeks a year, they can be positive-NPV investments.

These plants are in effect call options on electrical power. The options are currently out of the money, but the possibility that power prices will increase makes these calls worth more than their price. The decision to build them therefore makes the firm more valuable.

The Option to Abandon   Suppose that you need a new plant ready to produce turboencabulators in 3 years. You have a choice of designs. If design A is chosen, construction must start immediately. Design B is more expensive, but you can wait a year before breaking ground.

If you know with certainty that the plant will be needed, you should opt for design A. But suppose that there is some possibility that demand for turboencabulators will fall off and that, in a year's time, you will decide the plant is not required. Then design B may be preferable because it gives you the option to bail out at low cost any time during the next 12 months.

You can think of the option to abandon as a put option. The exercise price of the put is the amount that you could recover if you abandon the project. The abandonment option makes design B more attractive by limiting the downside exposure. The more uncertain is the need for the new plant, the more valuable is the downside protection offered by the option to abandon.

23.7 Self-Test

A real estate developer buys 70 acres of land in a rural area, planning to build a subdivision on the land if and when the population from the city begins to expand into the area. If population growth is less than anticipated, the developer believes that the land can be sold to a country club that would build a golf course on the property.

a. In what way does the possibility of sale to the country club provide a put option to the developer?

b. What is the exercise price of the option? The asset value?

c. How does the golf course option increase the NPV of the land project to the developer?

Options on Financial Assets

The Alphabet options that we considered earlier were sold by one group of investors to another. They had no effect on the company's cash flows. However, firms may also issue options to their managers or investors, and these do have a potential impact on the companies' cash flows. Here are a few examples.

Executive Stock Options   In fiscal 2014, Larry Ellison, the chairman of Oracle, was paid a salary of just $1, but before you send him a food parcel, note that he also received options worth $64 million. The amount of Larry Ellison's compensation is unusual, but these days, the senior managers of most major U.S. corporations are compensated largely with stock options.

These stock options are valuable and, therefore, are an expense just like salaries and wages. The Financial Accounting Standards Board (FASB) now requires companies to use an option-valuation model, such as the Black-Scholes model, to estimate the fair value of option grants and to recognize this value when calculating expenses. For example, in fiscal 2015, Oracle granted options to its directors, management, and employees to buy 34 million shares of the company's stock. The company's accounts showed that, according to the Black-Scholes model, the average value of each of these options was $9.62.

Stock options, such as those provided by Oracle, are an important part of managers' compensation. There is nothing wrong with that if the options encourage managers to work hard to increase the value of their companies' stock. However, in recent years, some companies illegally boosted the value of the stock options that they had given to managers by backdating the grant of their executive stock options.

warrant
Right to buy shares from a company at a stipulated price before a set date.

Warrants   A **warrant** is a long-term call option on the company's stock. For example, in return for helping to bail out the Bank of America in 2008, the U.S. Treasury received 150 million Bank of America warrants. Each warrant entitled the Treasury to buy one share in the bank for $13.30 at any time before January 2019.

In March 2010, the Treasury sold the warrants to investors for $8.35 each. At that time, the price of Bank of America stock was $16.40 a share. So, investors who bought the warrants would realize a profit if the stock price rose above $13.30 + $8.35 = $21.65.

Warrants are sometimes issued when a firm becomes bankrupt; the bankruptcy court offers the firm's bondholders warrants in the reorganized company as part of the settlement. At other times, warrants are given to underwriters as part of their compensation for managing an issue of securities. When a company issues a bond, it will occasionally add some warrants as a "sweetener." Because these warrants are valuable to investors, they are prepared to pay a higher price for a package of bonds and warrants than for the bond on its own. Managers sometimes look with delight at this higher price, forgetting that, in return, the company has incurred a liability to sell its shares to the warrant holders at what, with hindsight, may turn out to be a low price.

convertible bond
Bond that the holder may exchange for a specified amount of another security.

Convertible Bonds   The **convertible bond** is a close relative of the bond-warrant package. It allows the bondholder to exchange the bond for a given number of shares of common stock. Therefore, it is a package of a straight bond and a call option. The exercise price of the call option is the value of the "straight bond" (i.e., a bond that is not convertible). It will be profitable to convert if the value of the stock to which the investor is entitled exceeds the value of the straight bond.

The owner of a convertible bond owns a bond and a call option on the firm's stock. So does the owner of a package of a bond and a warrant. However, there are differences, the most important being that a convertible bond's owner must give up the bond to exercise the option. The owner of a package of bonds and warrants exercises the warrants for cash and keeps the bond.

| **Example** | **23.3** ▶ | Convertible Bonds |

In September 2014, Twitter issued $.9 billion of 1% coupon convertible notes maturing in 2021. Each of these bonds can be converted before maturity into 12.8793 shares of common stock. In other words, the owner of the convertible has the option to return the bond to the company and receive 12.8793 shares in exchange. The number of shares that are received for each bond is called the bond's *conversion ratio*. The conversion ratio of the Twitter bond is 12.8793.

In order to receive 12.8793 shares of Twitter stock, you must surrender bonds with a face value of $1,000. Therefore, to receive *one* share, you have to surrender a face amount of $1,000/12.8793 = $77.64. This figure is called the *conversion price*. Anybody who originally bought the bond at $1,000 in order to convert it into 12.8793 shares paid the equivalent of $77.64 a share.

When the convertible was issued, Twitter's stock price was $52.57. So, if investors were obliged to convert their bond immediately, their investment would have been worth 12.8793 × $52.57 = $677. This was the bond's *conversion value*. Of course, investors did not need to convert in 2014. They obviously hoped that Twitter's stock price would zoom up, making conversion profitable. But they had the comfort of knowing that if the stock price did not zoom, they could choose not to convert and simply hold on to the bond. The value of the bond if it could not be converted is known as its *bond value*. ■

Because the owner of the convertible always has the option *not* to convert, bond value establishes a lower bound, or floor, to the price of a convertible. Of course, this floor is not completely flat. If the firm falls on hard times, the bond may not be worth much. In the extreme case where the firm becomes worthless, the bond is also worthless.

When the firm does well, conversion value exceeds bond value. In this case, the investor would choose to convert if forced to make an immediate choice. Bond value exceeds conversion value when the firm does poorly. In these circumstances, the investor would hold on to the bonds if forced to choose. Convertible holders do not have to make a now-or-never choice for or against conversion. They can wait and then, with the benefit of hindsight, take whatever course turns out to give them the highest payoff. Thus, a convertible is always worth more than both its bond value and its conversion value (except when time runs out at the bond's maturity).

We stated earlier that it is useful to think of a convertible bond as a package of a straight bond and an option to buy the common stock in exchange for the straight bond. The value of this call option is equal to the difference between the convertible's market price and its bond value.

23.8 Self-Test

a. As we write this in April 2016, the price of Twitter stock is $16.90. What is the April 2016 conversion value of the Twitter convertible bond in Example 23.3? What has happened to its conversion price?

b. When it made the convertible bond issue, Twitter estimated that a straight, nonconvertible issue of 1% 7-year bonds would need to yield 5.75%. In this case, what was the bond value of of each $1,000 convertible note? (Assume annual coupon payments.) If the convertible was issued at face value, what value were investors placing on the conversion option?

Callable Bonds   Unlike warrants and convertibles, which give the *investor* an option, a **callable bond** gives an option to the *issuer*. A company that issues a callable bond has an option to buy the bond back at the stated exercise or "call" price. Therefore, you can think of a callable bond as a *package* of a straight bond (a bond that is not callable) and a call option held by the issuer.

The option to call the bond is obviously attractive to the issuer. If interest rates decline and bond prices rise, the company has the opportunity to repurchase the bond at a fixed call price. Therefore, the option to call the bond puts a ceiling on the bond price.

callable bond
Bond that may be repurchased by the issuing firm before maturity at a specified call price.

Of course, when the company issues a callable bond, investors are aware of this ceiling on the bond price and will pay less for a callable bond than for a straight bond. The difference between the value of a straight bond and a callable bond with the same coupon rate and maturity is the value of the call option that investors have given to the company:

Value of callable bond = value of straight bond − value of the issuer's call option

---

23.9 Self-Test

A few companies have in the past issued "puttable bonds," which allow the investor to redeem the bond at face value or let the bond remain outstanding until maturity. Suppose a 20-year puttable bond is issued with the investor allowed after 5 years to redeem the bond at face value.

a. On what asset is the option written? (What asset do the option holders have the right to sell?)
b. What is the exercise price of the option?
c. In what circumstances will the option be exercised?
d. Does the put option make the bond more or less valuable?

SUMMARY

What is the payoff to buyers and sellers of call and put options? (*LO23-1*)

There are two basic types of options. A **call option** is the right to buy an asset at a specific exercise price on or before the exercise date. A **put** is the right to sell an asset at a specific exercise price on or before the exercise date. The payoff to a call is the value of the asset minus the exercise price if the difference is positive, and zero otherwise. The payoff to a put is the exercise price minus the value of the asset if the difference is positive, and zero otherwise. The payoff to the seller of an option is the negative of the payoff to the option buyer.

What are the determinants of option values? (*LO23-2*)

The value of a call option depends on the following considerations:

- To exercise the call option, you must pay the exercise price. Other things equal, the less you are obliged to pay, the better. Therefore, the value of the option is higher when the exercise price is low relative to the stock price.
- Investors who buy the stock by way of a call option are buying on installment credit. They pay the purchase price of the option today, but they do not pay the exercise price until they exercise the option. The higher the rate of interest and the longer the time to expiration, the more this "free credit" is worth.
- No matter how far the stock price falls, the owner of the call cannot lose more than the price of the call. On the other hand, the more the stock price rises above the exercise price, the greater the profit on the call. Therefore, the option holder does not lose from increased variability if things go wrong, but gains if they go right. The value of the option increases with the variability of stock returns. Of course, the longer the time to the final exercise date, the more opportunity there is for the stock price to vary.

What options may be present in capital investment proposals? (*LO23-3*)

The importance of building flexibility into investment projects (discussed in Chapter 10) can be reformulated in the language of options. For example, many capital investments provide the flexibility to expand capacity in the future if demand turns out to be buoyant.

They are, in effect, providing the firm with a call option on the extra capacity. Firms also think about alternative uses for their assets if things go wrong. The option to abandon a project is a put option; the put's exercise price is the value of the project's assets if shifted to an alternative use. The ability to expand or to abandon are both examples of **real options.**

What options may be provided in financial securities? (*LO23-4*)

Many of the securities that firms issue contain an option. For example, a **warrant** is nothing but a long-term call option issued by the firm. **Convertible bonds** give the investor the option to buy the firm's stock in exchange for the value of the underlying bond. Unlike warrants and convertibles, which give an option to the investor, **callable bonds** give the option to the issuing firm. If interest rates decline and the value of the underlying bond rises, the firm can buy the bonds back at a specified exercise price.

QUESTIONS AND PROBLEMS

🔲 connect

1. **Option Payoffs.** Fill in the blanks by choosing the appropriate terms from the following list: *call, exercise, put.* (*LO23-1*)
   A(n) ____ (a) ____ option gives its owner the opportunity to buy a stock at a specific price, which is generally called the ____ (b) ____ price. A(n) ____ (c) ____ option gives its owner the opportunity to sell stock at a specified ____ (d) ____ price.

2. **Option Payoffs.** Turn back to Table 23.2, which lists prices of various Alphabet options. Use the data in the table to calculate the payoff and the profits for investments in each of the following June maturity options, assuming that the stock price on the expiration date is $750. (*LO23-1*)
   a. Call option with exercise price of $700
   b. Put option with exercise price of $700
   c. Call option with exercise price of $750
   d. Put option with exercise price of $750
   e. Call option with exercise price of $800
   f. Put option with exercise price of $800

3. **Option Payoffs.** In the film *Casino Royale,* the villain, Le Chiffre, plans to destroy an airliner being developed by Skyfleet. To profit from this, he first buys options on Skyfleet stock. Fortunately, James Bond foils the plot and Le Chiffre is bankrupted. Was Le Chiffre buying calls or puts? (*LO23-1*)

4. **Option Payoffs.** (*LO23-1*)
   a. Turn back again to Table 23.2, which lists prices of various Alphabet options. Use the data in the table to calculate the payoff and the profits for investments in each of the following January 2017 maturity options, assuming that the stock price on the expiration date is $780.
      i. Call option with exercise price of $700
      ii. Put option with exercise price of $700
      iii. Call option with exercise price of $750
      iv. Put option with exercise price of $750
      v. Call option with exercise price of $800
      vi. Put option with exercise price of $800
   b. Now repeat part (a), assuming that the stock price on the expiration date is $690.
   c. Are the prices of the January 2017 options more or less than those of the corresponding June 2016 options that you looked at in Problem 2?

5. **Option Payoffs.** (*LO23-1*)
   a. Note Figure 23.7a. Match the graph with one of the following positions:
      i. Call buyer
      ii. Call seller
      iii. Put buyer
      iv. Put seller
   b. Now do the same with Figure 23.7b.

FIGURE 23.7 See Problem 5.

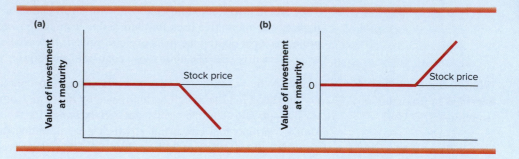

6. **Option Payoffs.** "The buyer of a call and the seller of a put both hope that the stock price will rise. Therefore, the two positions are identical." Is the speaker correct? (*LO23-1*)

7. **Option Payoffs.** Suppose that you hold a share of stock and a put option on that share with an exercise price of $100. What is the value of your portfolio when the option expires if: (*LO23-1*)

    a. The stock price is below $100?
    b. The stock price is above $100?

8. **Option Payoffs.** Mixing options and securities can often create interesting payoffs. For each of the following combinations, show what the payoff would be when the option expires if (i) the stock price is below the exercise price and (ii) the stock price is above the exercise price. Assume that each option has the same exercise price and expiration date. (*LO23-1*)

    a. Buy a call and invest the present value of the exercise price in a bank deposit.
    b. Buy a share and a put option on the share.
    c. Buy a share, buy a put option on the share, and sell a call option on the share.
    d. Buy a call option and a put option on the share.

9. **Option Payoffs.** Look at Figure 23.8, which shows the possible future payoffs in June 2016 from a particular package of investments in Alphabet options. Incidentally, this package of investments is called a "straddle" by option buffs. (*LO23-1*)

    a. What package of investments would provide you with this set of payoffs?
    b. How much would the package have cost you in December 2015? (See Table 23.2.)
    c. Would it have made sense to hold this package if you thought that the price of Alphabet stock was unlikely to change much?

FIGURE 23.8 This strategy provides a payoff of $0 if the Alphabet stock price remains at $750 and a payoff of $750 if Alphabet's stock price either falls to zero or rises to $1,500. See Problem 9.

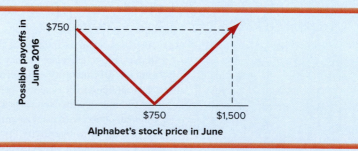

10. **Option Payoffs.** Look at Figure 23.9, which shows the possible future payoffs in June 2016 from a particular package of investments in Alphabet options. This package of investments is called a "butterfly" by option buffs. (*LO23-1*)

    a. What package of investments would provide you with this set of payoffs?
    b. How much would the package have cost you in December 2015? (See Table 23.2.)
    c. Would it have made sense to hold this package if you thought that the price of Alphabet stock was unlikely to change much?

FIGURE 23.9 This strategy provides a total payoff of $50 if the stock price is $750 and a payoff of zero if Alphabet's stock price in June is either (*a*) $700 or less or (*b*) $800 or more. See Problem 10.

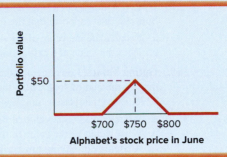

11. **Option Values.** Look at the data in Table 23.2. (*LO23-2*)
    a. What is the price of a call option with an exercise price of $750 and expiration in March 2016? What if expiration is in January 2017?
    b. Why do you think the January 2017 calls cost more than the March 2016 calls?
    c. Is the same true of put options? Why?

12. **Option Values.** Answer the following questions by choosing from the following options: *stock price; stock price − exercise price; the greater of zero or stock price − exercise price; the lesser of zero or stock price − exercise price; exercise price* (*LO23-2*)
    a. Which is the lower bound to the price of a call option?
    b. Which is the upper bound?

13. **Option Values.** What is a call option worth if: (*LO23-2*)
    a. The stock price is zero?
    b. The stock price is extremely high relative to the exercise price?

14. **Option Values.** Table 23.2 shows call options on Alphabet stock with the same exercise date in June 2016 and with exercise prices $700, $750, and $800. Notice that the price of the middle call option (with exercise price $750) is less than halfway between the prices of the other two calls (with exercise prices $700 and $800). Suppose that this were not the case. For example, suppose that the price of the middle call were the average of the prices of the other two calls. Show that if you sell two of the middle calls and use the proceeds to buy one each of the other calls, your proceeds in June may be positive but cannot be negative, despite the fact that your net outlay today would be zero. What can you deduce from this example about option pricing? (*LO23-2*)

15. **Option Values.** How does the price of a put option respond to the following changes, other things equal? Does the put price go up or down? (*LO23-2*)
    a. Stock price increases.
    b. Exercise price is increased.
    c. Risk-free interest rate increases.
    d. Expiration date of the option is extended.
    e. Volatility of the stock price falls.
    f. Time passes, so the option's expiration date comes closer.

16. **Option Values.** (*LO23-2*)
    a. Circular File stock is selling for $25 a share. You see that call options on the stock with exercise price $20 are selling at $3. What should you do? What will happen to the option price as investors identify this opportunity?
    b. Now you observe that put options on Circular File with exercise price $30 are selling for $4. What should you do?

17. **Option Values.** As manager of United Bedstead, you own substantial executive stock options. These options entitle you to buy the firm's shares during the next 5 years at a price of $100 a share. The plant manager has just outlined two alternative proposals to reequip the plant. Both proposals have the same net present value, but project A is substantially riskier than B. At first you are undecided which to choose, but then you selfishly remember your stock options. Which project is better for your wealth? (*LO23-2*)

18. **Option Values.** Look once more at the Alphabet call option that we valued in Section 23.2. Suppose (just suppose) that the interest rate on bank loans is 20%. (*LO23-2*)

    a. Recalculate the value of the Alphabet call option.

    b. Does the value of a call option increase or decrease if interest rates rise?

19. **Option Values.** Look again at the Alphabet call option that we valued in Section 23.2. Suppose that by the end of June 2016, the price of Alphabet stock could double to $1,500 or halve to $375. Everything else is unchanged from our example. (*LO23-2*)

    a. What would be the value of the Alphabet call in June 2016 if the stock price is $1,500?

    b. What would be the value of the call if the stock price in June is $375?

    c. A strategy of buying three calls provides exactly the same payoffs as borrowing the present value of $X from the bank and buying two shares. What is X in this example?

    d. What is the net cash flow in December 2015 from the policy of borrowing PV($X) and buying two shares?

    e. What is the value of the call option?

    f. We have now assumed greater stock volatility than in our example in Section 23.2. Has this increased or decreased the value of the option?

20. **Option Values.** (*LO23-2*)

    a. Use the Black-Scholes formula to find the value of a call option on the following stock. (You can find the spreadsheet in this chapter as well as in Connect.)

i. Time to expiration	1 year
ii. Standard deviation	40% per year
iii. Exercise price	$50
iv. Stock price	$50
v. Interest rate	4% (effective annual yield)

    b. Now recalculate the value of this call option, but use the following parameter values. Each change should be considered independently. Confirm that the value of the option changes in agreement with the prediction of Table 23.4.

i. Time to expiration	2 years
ii. Standard deviation	50% per year
iii. Exercise price	$60
v. Stock price	$60
vi. Interest rate	6%

    c. In which case did increasing the value of the input *not* increase your calculation of option value?

21. **Option Values.** Option prices are determined in part by volatility, and traders sometimes use the volatility estimates built into option prices to assess market conditions. The volatility estimate built into S&P 500 options may be found at Yahoo! Finance (get quotes for ticker symbol VIX). If you look at the historical plot of the VIX, you'll see that it spikes during periods of turbulence (e.g., the subprime crisis in 2008 or the lead-up to the Brexit vote in June 2016), and for this reason it is often called a "fear gauge." Let's see how traders back out these estimates of volatility from option prices. To do so, consider the option in the previous problem. Assume that option traders see the option selling at a price of $9.50 and wonder what volatility level this price implies. (*LO23-2*)

    a. Go to the Black-Scholes spreadsheet in this chapter (available in Connect) and go to the sheet *Implied Volatility*. In the box on the right, enter the value of $9.50. Press *Find Std Dev* and you will see the option's *implied volatility*—that is, the volatility level implied by its market price. This sort of inference is the basis for the VIX.

    b. What happens to implied volatility if you enter a lower call value? Why has it decreased?

22. **Option Risk.** Look back at Table 23.2. Suppose that by January 2017, the price of Alphabet could either rise from its December 2015 level to $750 × 1.22 = $915.00 or fall to $750/1.22 = $614.75. (*LO23-2*)

    a. What would be your percentage return on a January expiration call option with an exercise price of $750 if the stock price rose?

    b. What would be your percentage return if the stock price fell?

    c. Which is riskier: the stock or the option?

23. **Real and Financial Options.** Fill in the blanks. (*LO23-3*)

    a. An oil company acquires mining rights to a silver deposit. It is not obliged to mine the silver, however. The company has effectively acquired a(n) ____(a)____ option, where the exercise price is the cost of opening the mine and extracting the silver.

    b. Some preferred shareholders have the right to redeem their shares at par value after a specified date. (If they hand over their shares, the firm sends them a check equal to the shares' par value.) These shareholders have a(n) ____(b)____ option.

    c. A firm buys a standard machine with a ready secondhand market. The secondhand market gives the firm a(n) ____(c)____ option.

24. **Real Options.** Describe each of the following situations in the language of options. State in each case whether the situation involves a call or a put and the option's exercise price. (*LO23-3*)

    a. A company has drilling rights to undeveloped heavy crude oil in southern California. Development and production of the oil now is a negative-NPV endeavor. The break-even price is $120 per barrel, versus a spot price of $80. However, the decision to develop can be put off for up to 5 years.

    b. A restaurant produces net cash flows, after all out-of-pocket expenses, of $700,000 per year. There is no upward or downward trend in the cash flows, but they fluctuate. The real estate occupied by the restaurant is owned, and it could be sold for $5 million.

25. **Real Options.** Price support systems for various agricultural products have allowed farmers to sell their crops to the government for a specified "support price" of, say, $5 a bushel. (*LO23-3*)

    a. Has the government given the farmers a call or a put option?

    b. What is the exercise price of this option?

26. **Real Options.** After dramatic increases in oil prices in the 1970s, the U.S. government funded several projects to create synthetic oil or natural gas from abundant U.S. supplies of coal and oil shale. Although the cost of producing such synthetic fuels at the time was greater than the price of oil, it was argued that the projects still could be justified for their insurance value because the cost of synthetic fuel would be essentially fixed while the price of oil was risky. Evaluate the synthetic fuel program as an option on fuel sources. (*LO23-3*)

    a. Is it a call or a put option?

    b. What is the exercise price?

    c. How would uncertainty in the future price of oil affect the amount the United States should have been willing to spend on such projects?

27. **Financial Options.** A 10-year maturity convertible bond with a 6% coupon on a company with a bond rating of Aaa is selling for $1,050. Each bond can be exchanged for 20 shares, and the stock price currently is $50 per share. Other Aaa-rated bonds with the same maturity would sell at a yield to maturity of 8%. (*LO23-4*)

    a. What is the value of the bondholders' call option?

    b. What is the difference between the value of the convertible and the value of the shares it can be converted into?

28. **Financial Options.** Some investment management contracts give the portfolio manager a bonus proportional to the amount by which a portfolio return exceeds a specified threshold. (*LO23-4*)

    a. In what way is this an implicit call option on the portfolio?

    b. Can you think of a way in which such contracts can lead to incentive problems? For example, what happens to the value of the prospective bonus if the manager invests in very volatile stocks?

29. **Financial Options.** The Rank and File Company is considering a stock issue to raise $50 million. An underwriter offers to guarantee the success of the issue by buying any unwanted stock at the $25 issue price. The underwriter's fee is $2 million. (*LO23-4*)

    a. What kind of option does Rank and File acquire if it accepts the underwriter's offer?

    b. What determines the value of the option?

30. **Financial Options.** (*LO23-4*)

   a. Some banks have offered their customers an unusual type of time deposit. The deposit does not pay any interest if the market falls, but instead, the depositor receives a proportion of any rise in the Standard & Poor's Index. What implicit option do the investors hold? How should the bank invest the money in order to protect itself against the risk of offering this deposit?

   b. You can also make a deposit with a bank that does not pay interest if the market index rises but makes an increasingly large payment as the market index falls. How should the bank protect itself against the risk of offering this deposit?

31. **Financial Options.** The FDIC insures bank deposits. If a bank's assets are insufficient to pay off all depositors, the FDIC will contribute enough money to ensure that all depositors can be paid off in full. (We ignore the $250,000 maximum coverage on each account.) In what way is this guarantee of deposits the provision of a put option by the FDIC? (*Hint:* Write out the funds the FDIC will have to contribute when bank assets are less than deposits owed to depositors.) What is the exercise price of the put option? (*LO23-4*)

WEB EXERCISES

1. You can find option prices on finance.yahoo.com. Enter the company symbol and then click on *Options*. Try looking up option prices for Intel (INTC) and Pfizer (PFE). Does the price of calls increase or decrease with (a) the exercise price and (b) time to expiration? Would your answer be the same for puts? Why or why not?

2. Try using the Black-Scholes model to value a call option on Facebook or Amazon. The inputs are the same as those in our simple valuation example, except that instead of putting in the spread of possible stock prices, you must put in the standard deviation of stock returns. Assume a standard deviation of 45% for Facebook and 27% for Amazon. (At the time of writing, neither firm pays a dividend.) How different are the values you obtain from the prices shown on finance.yahoo.com? What happens to the option value if you change the standard deviation? Can you explain?

3. Find IBM's most recent income statement. What was the value that IBM assigned to the stock options it granted its employees in the most recent year? How did IBM estimate the value?

SOLUTIONS TO SELF-TEST QUESTIONS

23.1 a. The January call with exercise price $800 costs $61.10. If the stock price at the expiration date is $710, the call expires valueless and the investor loses the entire $61.10. If the stock price is $880, the value of the call at expiration is $880 − $800 = $80 and the investor's profit is $80 − $61.10 = $18.90.

   b. The March put with exercise price $800 costs $84.00. If the stock price at the expiration date is $710, the value of the put is $800 − $710 = $90 and the investor's profit is $90 − $84.00 = $6.00. If the stock price is $880, the put expires valueless and the investor loses the entire $84.00.

23.2 a. The call seller receives $21.50 for writing the call. If the stock price at expiration is $740, the call expires valueless and the investor keeps the entire $21.50 as a profit. If the stock price is $890, the value of the call at expiration is $890 − $800 = $90. In other words, the call seller must deliver a stock worth $890 for an exercise price of only $800. The investor's net profit is negative at $21.50 − $90 = −$68.50. The call seller makes a loss whenever the value of the call at expiration is more than the initial premium received for writing the option. In other words, he loses if the stock price is above $800 + $21.50 = $821.50.

   b. The put seller receives $84.00 for writing the put. If the stock price at expiration is $740, the final value of the put is $800 − $740 = $60. In other words, the put seller must pay an exercise price of $800 for a stock worth only $740. The investor's net profit is $84.00 − $60 = $24.00. If the stock price is $890, the put expires valueless and the put seller keeps the entire $84.00 as a profit. The put seller makes a loss when the value of the put at expiration is greater than the initial premium received for writing the option. In other words, he loses if the stock price is below $800 − $84 = $716.

23.3 Put-call parity states that price of stock + price of put = price of call + present value of exercise price. Therefore, in the case of Witterman,

$$\$55 + \text{price of put} = \$8.05 + \frac{\$60}{1.04}$$

and price of put = $8.05 + $57.69 − $55 = $10.74.

23.4 The value of a put option is higher when the exercise price is higher. You would be willing to pay more for the right to sell a stock at a high price than the right to sell it at a low price.

23.5 First, consider the payoff to the put holder in the lower-volatility scenario:

Stock price	$650	$850
Put value	$100	0

In the higher-volatility scenario, the value of the stock can be $600 or $900. Now the payoff to the put is:

Stock price	$600	$900
Put value	$150	0

The expected value of the payoff of the put is higher in the high-volatility scenario.

23.6 The payoffs are as follows:

		Payoff in 3 Months If Stock Price Equals:	
	Cash Flow Today	$15	$60
Strategy A			
Buy three calls	?	$ 0	+$ 90
Strategy B			
Buy two shares	−$60.00	+$30	+$120
Borrow PV($30)	+ 29.70	− 30	− 30
	−$30.30	$ 0	+ $90

Note: PV($30) at an interest rate of 1% for 3 months is 30/1.01 = $29.70.

The initial net cash outflow from strategy B is $30.30. Because the three calls offer the same payoffs in the future, they must also cost $30.30. One call is worth 30.30/3 = $10.10.

23.7 a. The developer has the option to sell the potential housing development to the country club. This abandonment option is like a put that guarantees a minimum payoff from the investment.
   b. The exercise price of the option is the price at which it can be sold to the country club. The asset value is the present value of the project if maintained as a housing development. If this value is less than the value as a golf course, the project will be sold.
   c. The abandonment option increases NPV by placing a lower bound on the possible payoffs from the project.

23.8 a. Conversion value = 12.8793 × $16.90 = $217.66.
        Conversion price = $1,000/12.8793 = $77.64 (unchanged).
   b. Bond value = $10/1.0575 + . . . + 10/1.0575^6 + 1,010/1.0575^7 = $732.46. The value that investors placed on the conversion option at the time of issue was, therefore, 1,000 − 732.46 = $267.54.

23.9 a. In 5 years, the bond will be a 15-year maturity bond. The bondholder can sell the bond back to the firm at face value. The bondholder therefore has a put option to sell a 15-year bond for face value even if interest rates have risen and the bond would otherwise sell below face value.
   b. The exercise price is the face value of the bond.
   c. The bondholder will sell the bond back to the company if interest rates increase or the company's credit deteriorates.
   d. More valuable. The bondholder now has the right, but not the obligation, to sell the bond at face value in 5 years.

SOLUTIONS TO SPREADSHEET QUESTIONS

1.

Stock	Call
350	0.0002
400	0.0056
450	0.0693
500	0.4715
550	2.0690
600	6.5216
650	15.5839
700	32.3137
750	56.3584
800	87.7736
850	125.3553
900	167.5610
950	212.9332
1,000	260.3160

2.

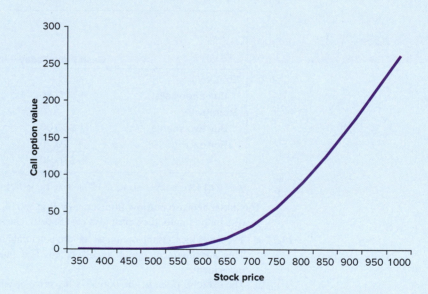

For stock prices below about $400, the option value is close to zero. As the stock price increases, the slope of the plot approaches 1.

24

Risk Management

LEARNING OBJECTIVES

After studying this chapter, you should be able to:

24-1 Understand why companies hedge to reduce risk.

24-2 Use options, futures, and forward contracts to devise simple hedging strategies.

24-3 Explain how companies can use swaps to manage the risk of securities that they have issued.

RELATED WEBSITES FOR THIS CHAPTER CAN BE FOUND IN CONNECT.

We often assume that risk is beyond our control. A business is exposed to unpredictable changes in raw material costs, tax rates, technology, and a long list of other variables. There's nothing the manager can do about it.

This is not wholly true. To some extent, a manager can *select* which risks to accept. For example, in the previous chapter, we saw that companies can lessen the risk of an investment by building in flexibility. A company that uses standardized equipment that can be easily resold is taking less risk than a similar firm that uses specialized equipment with no alternative uses. In this case, the option to resell the equipment serves as an insurance policy.

Sometimes, rather than building flexibility into the project, companies accept the risk but then use financial instruments to offset it. This practice of taking offsetting risks is known as *hedging*. In this chapter, we will explain how hedging works and we will describe some of the specialized financial instruments that have been devised to help manage risk. These instruments include options, futures, forwards, and swaps. Each of these instruments provides a payoff that depends on the price of some underlying commodity or financial asset. Because their payoffs derive from the prices of other assets, they are often known collectively as *derivative instruments* (or *derivatives* for short).[1]

This is just about the shortest chapter in the book, little more than a chef's taster. It provides only a quick overview of a huge topic. For example, it doesn't explain how to value derivatives or how to set up a hedge. But most companies employ derivatives extensively to

Risk management does not mean avoiding risk. It means deciding what risks to take. © Don Mason/age fotostock RF

adjust their risk, and it is important that you have some basic understanding of what they are and how they can be used (and misused).

PART SEVEN

Special Topics

---

[1] Derivatives often conjure up an image of wicked speculators. Derivative instruments attract their share of speculators, some of whom may be wicked, but they are also used by sober and prudent businesspeople who simply want to reduce risk.

693

24.1 Why Hedge?

In this chapter, we will explain *how* companies hedge the risks of their business. But first, we should give some of the reasons *why* they do it.

Surely, the answer to this question is obvious. Isn't less risk always better than more? Well, not necessarily. Even if hedging is costless, transactions undertaken *solely* to reduce risk are unlikely to add value. There are two basic reasons for this:

- *Reason 1: Hedging is a zero-sum game.* A company that hedges a risk does not eliminate it. It simply passes the risk on to someone else. For example, suppose that a heating-oil distributor agrees with a refiner to buy all of next winter's heating-oil deliveries at a fixed price. This contract is a zero-sum game because the refiner loses what the distributor gains and vice versa. If next winter's price of heating oil turns out to be unusually high, the distributor wins from having locked in a below-market price, but the refiner is forced to sell below market. Conversely, if the price of heating oil is unusually *low*, the refiner wins because the distributor is forced to buy at the high fixed price. Of course, neither party knows next winter's price at the time that the deal is struck, but they consider the range of possible prices and negotiate terms that are fair (zero NPV) on both sides of the bargain.

- *Reason 2: Investors' do-it-yourself alternative.* Companies cannot increase the value of their shares by undertaking transactions that investors can easily do on their own. We came across this idea when we discussed whether leverage increases company value, and we met it again when we came to dividend policy. It also applies to hedging. For example, when the shareholders in our heating-oil distributor invested in the company, they were presumably aware of the risks of the business. If they did not want to be exposed to the ups and downs of energy prices, they could have protected themselves in several ways. Perhaps they own shares in both the distributor and the refiner and do not care whether one wins at the other's expense.

Of course, shareholders can adjust their exposure only when companies keep investors fully informed of the transactions that they have made. For example, when a group of European central banks announced in 1999 that they would limit their sales of gold, the gold price immediately shot up. Investors in gold-mining shares rubbed their hands at the prospect of rising profits. But when they discovered that some mining companies had protected themselves against price fluctuations and would *not* benefit from the price rise, the hand-rubbing turned to hand-wringing.

Some stockholders of these gold-mining companies wanted to make a bet on rising gold prices; others didn't. But all of them gave the same message to management. The first group said, "Don't hedge! I'm happy to bear the risk of fluctuating gold prices, because I think gold prices will increase." The second group said, "Don't hedge! I'd rather do it myself."

We have seen that although hedging reduces risk, this doesn't in itself increase firm value. So when does it make sense to hedge? Sometimes, hedging is worthwhile because it makes financial planning easier and reduces the odds of an embarrassing cash shortfall. A shortfall might mean only an unexpected trip to the bank, but on other occasions the firm might have to forgo worthwhile investments, and in extreme cases the shortfall could trigger bankruptcy. Why not reduce the odds of these awkward outcomes with a hedge?

We saw in our discussion of debt policy in Chapter 16 that financial distress can result in indirect as well as direct costs to a firm. Costs of financial distress arise from disruption to normal business operations as well as from the effect that financial distress has on the firm's investment decisions. The better the risk management policies, the less chance that the firm will incur these costs of distress. As a side benefit, better risk management increases the firm's debt capacity.

In some cases, hedging also makes it easier to decide whether an operating manager deserves a stern lecture or a pat on the back. Suppose that your export division shows a 50% decline in profits when the dollar unexpectedly strengthens against other currencies. How much of that decrease is due to the exchange rate shift and how much to poor management? If the company had protected itself against the effect of exchange rate changes, it's probably bad management. If it wasn't protected, you have to make a judgment with hindsight, probably by asking, "What would profits have been *if* the firm had hedged against exchange rate movements?"

Finally, hedging extraneous events can help focus the operating manager's attention. We know we shouldn't worry about events outside our control, but most of us do anyway. It's naive to expect the manager of the export division not to worry about exchange rate movements if his bottom line and bonus depend on them. The time spent worrying could be better spent if the company hedged itself against such movements.

A sensible risk strategy needs answers to the following questions:

- *What are the major risks that the company faces, and what are the possible consequences?* Some risks are scarcely worth a thought, but there are others that might bankrupt the company.
- *Is the company being paid for taking these risks?* Managers are not paid to avoid all risks, but if they can reduce their exposure to risks for which there are no compensating rewards, they can afford to place larger bets when the odds are stacked in their favor.
- *Can the company take any measures to reduce the probability of a bad outcome or to limit its impact?* For example, most businesses install alarm and sprinkler systems to prevent damage from fire and invest in backup facilities in case damage does occur.
- *Can the company purchase fairly priced insurance to offset any losses?* Insurance companies have some advantages in bearing risk. In particular, they may be able to spread the risk across a portfolio of different insurers.
- *Can the company use derivatives, such as options or futures, to hedge the risk?* In the remainder of this chapter, we explain when and how derivatives may be used.

The Evidence on Risk Management

There are three principal ways to manage risk. First, the firm can reduce risk by building flexibility into its operations. For example, a petrochemical plant that is designed to use either oil or natural gas as a feedstock reduces the chance of an unfavorable shift in the price of raw materials. Or think of a company that reduces the risk of a disaster by test marketing a new product before launching it nationally. Both firms are using *real options* to limit their risk.

A second way to reduce risk is to buy an insurance policy against such hazards as fire, accidents, and theft. Insurance may make sense when the insurance company can diversify away the risk.

derivatives
Contracts such as options and futures, whose payoffs are determined by the values of other financial variables.

Finally, the firm may enter into specialized financial contracts that fix its costs or prices. These contracts are known collectively as **derivatives,** and they include options, futures, and swaps. Derivatives are most often used to protect against economywide risks.

A survey of the world's 500 largest companies found that almost all the companies use derivatives in some way to manage their risk.[2] Ninety-four percent employ them to manage currency risk. Eighty-eight percent use them to control interest rate risk and 51% to manage the risk of fluctuations in commodity prices.

Risk policies differ. For example, some natural resource companies work hard to hedge their exposure to price fluctuations; others shrug their corporate shoulders and let prices wander as they may. Explaining why some hedge and others don't is not easy. One study of oil and gas companies found that the firms hedged most if they had high debt ratios, no debt ratings, and low dividend payouts.[3] It seems that for these firms, hedging programs were designed to reduce the likelihood of financial distress and to improve the firms' access to debt finance.

---

[2] International Swap Dealers Association (ISDA), "2009 Derivatives Usage Survey," www.isda.org.

[3] G. D. Haushalter, "Financing Policy, Basis Risk and Corporate Hedging," *Journal of Finance* 55 (February 2000), pp. 107–152.

24.2 Reducing Risk with Options

In the previous chapter, we introduced you to put and call options. Managers regularly buy options on currencies, interest rates, and commodities to limit their downside risk. Many of these options are traded on options exchanges, but often they are simply private deals between the corporation and a bank.

Consider, for example, the problem faced by the Mexican government. Thirty percent of its revenue comes from Pemex, the state-owned oil company. So, if oil prices fall, the government may be compelled to reduce its planned spending.

The government's solution has been to arrange an annual hedge against a possible fall in the oil price. For example, in late 2014, the Mexican government bought put options that gave it the right to sell 228 million barrels of oil over the coming year at an exercise price of $76.40 per barrel. If oil prices rose above this figure, Mexico would reap the benefit. But if oil prices fell *below* $76.40 a barrel, the payoff to the put options would exactly offset the revenue shortfall. In effect, the options put a floor of $76.40 a barrel on the value of its oil. Of course, the hedge did not come free. The Mexican government is reported to have spent $773 million to buy the contracts.

Figure 24.1 illustrates the nature of Mexico's insurance strategy. Panel *a* shows the revenue derived from selling 228 million barrels of oil. As the price of oil rises or falls, so do the government's revenues. Panel *b* shows the payoffs to the government's options to sell 228 million barrels at $76.40 a barrel. The payoff on these options rises as oil prices fall below $76.40 a barrel. This payoff exactly offsets any decline in oil revenues. Panel *c* shows the government's *total* revenues after buying the put options. For prices below $76.40 per barrel, revenues are fixed at 228 × $76.40 = $17,419 million. But for every dollar that oil prices rise *above* $76.40, revenues increase by $228 million. The profile in panel *c* should be familiar to you. It represents the payoffs to the protective put strategy that we first encountered in Section 23.1.[4]

24.3 Futures Contracts

futures contract
Exchange-traded promise to buy or sell an asset in the future at a prespecified price.

Suppose you are a wheat farmer. You are optimistic about next year's wheat crop, but still you can't sleep. You are worried that when the time comes to sell the wheat, prices may have fallen through the floor. The cure for insomnia is to sell wheat *futures*. In this case, you agree to deliver so many bushels of wheat in (say) September at a price that is set today. Do not confuse this **futures contract** with an option, where the holder has a *choice* whether to make delivery; your futures contract is a firm promise to deliver wheat at a fixed selling price.

A miller is in the opposite position. She needs to *buy* wheat after the harvest. If she would like to fix the price of this wheat ahead of time, she can do so by *buying* wheat futures. In other words, she agrees to take delivery of wheat in the future at a price that is fixed today. The miller also does not have an option; if she still holds the futures contract when it matures, she is obliged to take delivery.

Let's suppose the farmer and the miller strike a deal. They enter a futures contract. What happens? First, no money changes hands when the contract is initiated.[5] The miller agrees to buy wheat at the futures price on a stated *future* date (the contract maturity date). The farmer agrees to sell at the same price and date. Second, the futures

---

[4] The Mexican government option position was slightly more complicated than our description. On some of the production, it agreed to take a hit if prices fell below $60 a barrel. On this portion of production, government revenues were protected only against prices between $60 and $80.

[5] Actually, each party will be required to set up a margin account to guarantee performance on the contract. Despite this, the futures contract still may be considered as essentially requiring no money down. First, the amount of margin is small. Second, it may be posted in interest-bearing securities, so that the parties to the trade need not suffer an opportunity cost from placing assets in the margin account.

FIGURE 24.1 How options protected Mexico against a sharp fall in oil prices

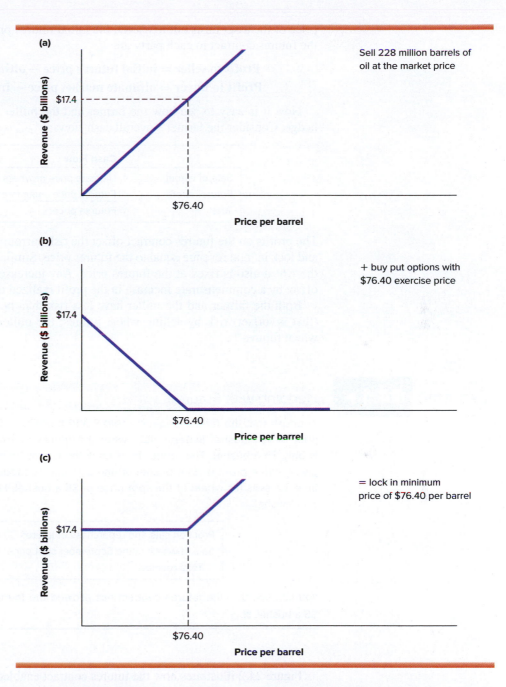

(a)

Sell 228 million barrels of oil at the market price

Revenue ($ billions)

$17.4

$76.40

Price per barrel

(b)

+ buy put options with $76.40 exercise price

Revenue ($ billions)

$17.4

$76.40

Price per barrel

(c)

= lock in minimum price of $76.40 per barrel

Revenue ($ billions)

$17.4

$76.40

Price per barrel

contract is a binding obligation, not an option. Options give the right to buy or sell *if* buying or selling turns out to be profitable. The futures contract *requires* the farmer to sell and the miller to buy regardless of who profits and who loses. **Just remember, no money changes hands when a futures contract is entered into. The contract is a binding obligation to buy or sell at a fixed price at contract maturity.**

The profit on the futures contract is the difference between the initial futures price and the ultimate price of the asset when the contract matures. For example, if the futures price is originally $5 and the market price of wheat turns out to be $5.50, the farmer delivers and the miller receives the wheat for a price $.50 below market value. The farmer loses $.50 per bushel and the miller gains $.50 per bushel as a result of the futures transaction. In general, the seller of the contract benefits if the price initially locked in turns out to exceed the price that could have been obtained at contract maturity. Conversely, the buyer of the contract benefits if the ultimate market price of the asset turns out to exceed the initial futures price. Therefore, the profits on the futures contract to each party are

Profit to seller = initial futures price − ultimate market price

Profit to buyer = ultimate market price − initial futures price

Now it is easy to see how the farmer and the miller can both use the contract to hedge. Consider the farmer's overall cash flows:

	Cash Flow
Sale of wheat	Ultimate price of wheat
Futures profit	Futures price − ultimate price of wheat
Total	Futures price

The profits on the futures contract offset the risk surrounding the sales price of wheat and lock in total revenue equal to the futures price. Similarly, the miller's all-in cost for the wheat also is fixed at the futures price. Any increase in the cost of wheat will be offset by a commensurate increase in the profit realized on the futures contract.

Both the farmer and the miller have less risk than before. The farmer has hedged (that is, offset) risk by selling wheat futures; the miller has hedged risk by buying wheat futures.[6]

Example 24.1 ▶   Hedging with Futures

Suppose that the farmer originally sold 5,000 bushels of September wheat futures at a price of $6 a bushel. In September, when the futures contract matures, the price of wheat is only $5 a bushel. The farmer buys back the wheat futures at $5 just before maturity, giving him a profit of $1 a bushel on the sale and subsequent repurchase. At the same time, he sells his wheat at the spot price of $5 a bushel. His total receipts are therefore $6 a bushel:

Profit on sale and repurchase of futures	$1
Sale of wheat at the September spot price	5
Total receipts	$6

You can see that the futures contract has allowed the farmer to lock in total proceeds of $6 a bushel. ■

Figure 24.2 illustrates how the futures contract enabled the farmer in Example 24.1 to hedge his position. Panel *a* shows how the value of 5,000 bushels of wheat varies with the spot price of wheat. The value rises by $5,000 for every dollar increase in wheat prices. Panel *b* is the profit on a futures contract to deliver 5,000 bushels of wheat at a futures price of $6 per bushel. The profit will be zero if the ultimate price of wheat equals the original futures price, $6. The profit on the contract to deliver at $6 rises by $5,000 for every dollar the price of wheat *falls* below $6. The exposures to the price of wheat depicted in panels *a* and *b* obviously cancel out. Panel *c* shows that the total value of the 5,000 bushels plus the futures position is unaffected by the ultimate price of wheat, and equals $6 × 5,000 = $30,000. In other words, the farmer has locked in proceeds of $6 per bushel, equal to the original futures price.

---

[6] Neither has eliminated all risk. For example, the farmer still has quantity risk. He does not know for sure how many bushels of wheat he will produce.

FIGURE 24.2 The farmer can use wheat futures to hedge the value of the crop. See Example 24.1.

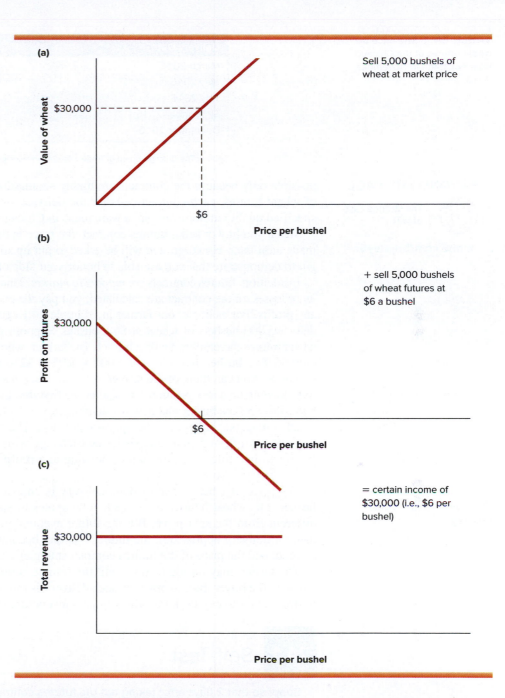

(a)

Sell 5,000 bushels of wheat at market price

(b)

+ sell 5,000 bushels of wheat futures at $6 a bushel

(c)

= certain income of $30,000 (i.e., $6 per bushel)

The Mechanics of Futures Trading

In practice, the farmer and miller would not sign the futures contract face-to-face. Instead, each would go to an organized futures exchange such as the Chicago Board of Trade.[7]

Table 24.1 shows the price of wheat futures at the Chicago Board of Trade in November 2015, when the price for immediate delivery was about $4.87 a bushel. Notice that there is a choice of possible delivery dates. If, for example, you were to sell wheat for delivery in May 2016, you would get a lower price than by selling December 2016 futures.

The miller would not be prepared to buy futures contracts if the farmer were free to deliver half-rotten wheat to a leaky barn at the end of a cart track. Futures trading is

---

[7] The Chicago Board of Trade is part of the CME Group.

TABLE 24.1 The price of wheat futures at the Chicago Board of Trade in November 2015

Delivery Date	Price per Bushel
March 2016	$4.88
May 2016	4.91
July 2016	5.01
September 2016	5.17
December 2016	5.28

Source: The Chicago Board of Trade website, **www.cmegroup.com**.

BEYOND THE PAGE

The strange case of WTI

mhhe.com/brealey9e

possible only because the contracts are highly standardized. For example, in the case of wheat futures, each contract calls for the delivery of 5,000 bushels of wheat of a specified quality at, for example, a warehouse in Chicago or Burns Harbor.

When you buy or sell a futures contract, the price is fixed today, but payment is not made until later. However, you will be asked to put up some cash or securities as *margin* to demonstrate that you are able to honor your side of the bargain.

In addition, futures contracts are *marked to market.* This means that each day any profits or losses on the contract are calculated; you pay the exchange any losses and receive any profits. For example, our farmer in Example 24.1 entered into a futures contract to deliver 5,000 bushels of wheat at $6 a bushel. Suppose that the next day, the price of wheat futures increases to $6.05 a bushel. The farmer, who has agreed to deliver wheat at only $6.00 a bushel, has a loss of 5,000 × $.05 = $250 and must pay this sum to the exchange. You can think of the farmer as buying back his futures position each day and then opening up a new position. Thus, after the first day, the farmer has realized a loss on his trade of $.05 a bushel and now has an obligation to deliver wheat for $6.05 a bushel.

Of course, our miller is in the opposite position. The rise in the futures price leaves her with a *profit* of 5 cents a bushel. The exchange will, therefore, pay her this profit. In effect, the miller sells her futures position at a profit and opens a new contract to take delivery at $6.05 a bushel.

spot price
Price paid for immediate delivery.

The price of wheat for immediate delivery is known as the **spot price.** When the farmer sells wheat futures, the price that he agrees to take for his wheat may be very different from the spot price. But the future eventually becomes the present. As the date for delivery approaches, the futures contract becomes more and more like a spot contract and the price of the futures contract snuggles up to the spot price.

The farmer may decide to wait until the futures contract matures and then deliver wheat to the buyer. But, in practice, such delivery is rare because it is more convenient for the farmer to buy back the wheat futures just before maturity.[8]

24.1   Self-Test

Suppose that 2 days after taking out the futures contract, the price of September wheat increases from $6.05 to $6.20 a bushel. What additional payments will be made by or to the farmer and the miller? What will be their remaining obligation at the end of this second day?

Commodity and Financial Futures

We have shown how the farmer and the miller can both use wheat futures to hedge their risk. It is also possible to trade futures in a wide variety of other commodities, such as sugar, soybean oil, pork bellies, orange juice, crude oil, and copper.

---

[8] In the case of some of the financial futures described later, you cannot deliver the asset. At maturity, the buyer simply receives (or pays) the difference between the spot price and the price at which he or she has agreed to purchase the asset.

TABLE 24.2 Some financial futures contracts

Contract	Principal Exchange
U.S. Treasury notes and bonds	CBT
Eurodollar deposits	CME
Standard & Poor's Index	CME
Euro	CME
Yen	CME
German government bonds (Bunds)	Eurex

Key to abbreviations:
CBT   Chicago Board of Trade
CME   Chicago Mercantile Exchange

Commodity prices can bounce up and down like a bungee jumper. For example, at the start of 2009, copper prices were about $3,000 a ton. Just 2 years later, they were over $10,000. For a large user of copper, such as General Cable, these price fluctuations could knock the company badly off course. General Cable, therefore, reduces its exposure to movements in the price of copper and other metals by hedging with commodity futures. A number of copper producers have also found that hedging increases their debt capacity. For example, in 2014, when a group of banks agreed to lend $165 million for a copper mine in Indonesia, they insisted that the company hedge its exposure to copper prices.

For many firms, the wide fluctuations in interest rates and exchange rates have become at least as important a source of risk as changes in commodity prices. You can use *financial futures* to hedge against these risks.

Financial futures are similar to commodity futures, but instead of placing an order to buy or sell a commodity at a future date, you place an order to buy or sell a financial asset at a future date. You can use financial futures to protect yourself against fluctuations in short- and long-term interest rates, exchange rates, and the level of share prices.

Table 24.2 lists some of the more popular financial futures contracts.

24.2 Self-Test

You plan to issue long-term bonds in 9 months but are worried that interest rates may have increased in the meantime. How could you use financial futures to protect yourself against a general rise in interest rates?

24.4 Forward Contracts

Each day, billions of dollars of futures contracts are bought and sold. We have seen that this liquidity is possible only because futures contracts are standardized. Futures contracts mature on a limited number of dates each year (take another look at the wheat contract in Table 24.1), and the contract size is standardized. For example, a contract may call for delivery of 5,000 bushels of wheat, 100 ounces of gold, or 62,500 British pounds. If the terms of a futures contract do not suit your particular needs, you may be able to buy or sell a **forward contract.**

Forward contracts are custom-tailored futures contracts.[9] **You can write a forward contract with any maturity date for delivery of any quantity of goods.**

forward contract
Agreement to buy or sell an asset in the future at an agreed price.

---

[9] One difference between forward and futures contracts is that forward contracts are not marked to market. Thus, with a forward contract, you settle up any profits or losses when the contract matures.

For example, suppose that you know that you will need to pay out yen in 3 months' time. You can fix today the price that you will pay for the yen by arranging with your bank to buy yen forward. At the end of the 3 months, you pay the agreed sum and take delivery of the yen.

Example 24.2 ▶   Forward Contracts

Computer Parts Inc. has ordered memory chips from its supplier in Japan. The bill for ¥53 million must be paid on July 27. The company can arrange with its bank today to buy this number of yen forward for delivery on July 27 at a forward price of ¥110 per dollar. Therefore, on July 27, Computer Parts pays the bank $53 million/110 = $481,818 and receives ¥53 million, which it can use to pay its Japanese supplier. By committing forward to exchange $481,818 for ¥53 million, its dollar costs are locked in. Notice that if the firm had not used the forward contract to hedge and the dollar had depreciated over this period, the firm would have had to pay a greater amount of dollars. For example, if the dollar had depreciated to ¥100 = $1, the firm would have had to exchange $530,000 for the ¥53 million necessary to pay its bill. The firm could have used a futures contract to hedge its foreign exchange exposure, but standardization of futures would not allow for delivery of precisely ¥53 million on precisely July 27. ∎

The most active trading in forwards is in foreign currencies, but companies also enter into forward rate agreements (FRAs) that allow them to fix in advance the interest rate at which they borrow or lend.

24.5 Swaps

Interest Rate Swaps

Suppose Computer Parts from Example 24.2 decides to produce memory chips instead of purchasing them from outside suppliers. It has issued $100 million in floating-rate bonds to help finance the construction of a new plant. (Recall from Chapter 14 that floating-rate loans make interest payments that go up and down with the general level of interest rates. The coupon payments on the bonds are tied to a specific short-term interest rate.) But the financial manager is concerned that interest rates are becoming more volatile, and she would like to lock in the firm's interest expenses. One approach would be to buy back the floating-rate bonds and replace them with a new issue of fixed-rate debt. But it is costly to issue new debt to the public; in addition, buying back the outstanding bonds in the market will result in considerable trading costs.

> **swap**
> Arrangement by two counterparties to exchange one stream of cash flows for another.

A better approach to hedge out its interest rate exposure is for the firm to enter into an interest rate **swap.** The firm will pay or "swap" a fixed payment for another payment that is tied to the level of interest rates. Thus, if rates do rise, increasing the firm's interest expense on its floating-rate debt, its cash flow from the swap agreement will rise as well, offsetting its exposure.

Suppose the firm pays the LIBOR rate on its floating-rate bonds. (Recall that LIBOR, or London Interbank Offer Rate, is the interest rate at which banks borrow from each other in the eurodollar market. It is the most frequently used short-term interest rate in the swap market.) The firm's interest expense each year, therefore, equals the LIBOR rate times $100 million. It would like to transform this obligation into one that will not fluctuate with interest rates.

Suppose that current rates in the swaps market are "LIBOR for 5% fixed." This means that Computer Parts can enter into a swap agreement to *pay* 5% on "notional

FIGURE 24.3 Interest rate swap. Computer Parts currently pays the LIBOR rate on its outstanding bonds (the arrow on the left). If the firm enters a swap to pay a fixed rate of 5% and receive a floating rate of LIBOR, its exposure to LIBOR will cancel out and its net cash outflow will be a fixed rate of 5%.

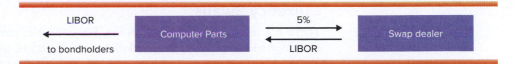

principal" of $100 million to a swap dealer and *receive* payment of the LIBOR rate on the same amount of notional principal. The dealer and the firm are called *counterparties* in the swap. The firm pays the dealer .05 × $100 million and receives LIBOR × $100 million in return. The firm's *net* cash payment to the dealer is therefore (.05 − LIBOR) × $100 million. (If LIBOR exceeds 5%, the firm receives money from the dealer; if it is less than 5%, the firm pays money to the dealer.) Figure 24.3 illustrates the cash flows paid by Computer Parts and the swap dealer.

Table 24.3 shows Computer Parts's net payments for three possible interest rates. The total payment on the bond-with-swap agreement equals $5 million regardless of the interest rate. The swap has transformed the floating-rate bond into synthetic fixed-rate debt with an effective coupon rate of 5%. The firm has thus hedged away its interest rate exposure without actually having to replace its floating-rate bonds with fixed-rate bonds. Swaps offer a much cheaper way to "rearrange the balance sheet."[10]

There are many other applications of interest rate swaps. For example, suppose a portfolio manager is holding a portfolio of long-term bonds but is worried that interest rates may increase and bond prices fall. She can enter into a swap to pay a fixed rate and receive a floating rate, thereby converting the holdings into a synthetic floating-rate portfolio (see Self-Test 24.3).

24.3   Self-Test

Consider the portfolio manager who is holding $100 million in long-term 5% coupon bonds and wishes to reduce price risk by transforming the holding into a synthetic floating-rate bond. Assume that the bonds currently pay a 5% fixed rate and that swap dealers currently offer terms of 5% fixed for LIBOR. What swap would the manager establish? Show the total income on the fund in a table like Table 24.3, and illustrate the cash flows in a diagram like Figure 24.3.

TABLE 24.3 An interest rate swap can transform floating-rate bonds into synthetic fixed-rate bonds

	LIBOR Rate		
	4.5%	**5.0%**	**5.5%**
Interest paid on floating-rate bonds (= LIBOR × $100 million)	$4,500,000	$5,000,000	$5,500,000
+ Cash payment on swap [= (.05 − LIBOR) × notional principal of $100 million]	500,000	0	−500,000
Total payment	$5,000,000	$5,000,000	$5,000,000

---

[10] You might wonder what's in this arrangement for the swap dealer. The dealer will profit by charging a bid-ask spread. Because the dealer pays LIBOR in return for 5% in this swap, it might search for another trader who wishes to receive a fixed rate and pay LIBOR. The dealer will pay a 4.9% rate to that trader in return for the LIBOR rate. So, the dealer pays a fixed rate and receives floating with one trader but pays floating and receives fixed with the other. Its net cash flow is thus fixed and equal to .1% of notional principal.

Currency Swaps

There are many other types of swaps. For example, currency swaps allow firms to exchange a series of payments in dollars (which may be tied to a fixed or floating rate) for a series of payments in another currency (which also may be tied to a fixed or floating rate). These swaps can, therefore, be used to manage exposure to exchange rate fluctuations.

Example 24.3 ▶   Currency Swaps

Suppose that the Possum Company wishes to borrow Swiss francs (CHF) to help finance its European operations. Because Possum is better known in the United States, the financial manager believes that the company can obtain more attractive terms on a dollar loan than on a Swiss franc loan. Therefore, the company borrows $10 million for 5 years at 5% in the United States. At the same time, Possum arranges with a swap dealer to trade its future dollar liability for Swiss francs. Under this arrangement, the dealer agrees to pay Possum sufficient dollars to service its dollar loan, and in exchange, Possum agrees to make a series of annual payments in Swiss francs to the dealer.

Possum's cash flows are set out in Table 24.4. Line 1 shows that when Possum takes out its dollar loan, it promises to pay annual interest of $.5 million and to repay the $10 million that it has borrowed. Lines 2a and 2b show the cash flows from the swap, assuming that the spot exchange rate for Swiss francs is $1 = CHF2. Possum hands over to the dealer the $10 million that it borrowed and receives in exchange 2 × $10 million = CHF20 million. In each of the next 4 years, the dealer pays Possum $.5 million, which it uses to pay the annual interest on its loan. In year 5, the dealer pays Possum $10.5 million to cover both the final year's interest and the repayment of the loan. In return for these future dollar receipts, Possum agrees to pay the dealer CHF1.2 million in each of the next 4 years and CHF21.2 million in year 5.

Notice that Possum's payments equal those it would have made if it had borrowed CHF20 million at an interest rate of 6%. Therefore, the combined effect of Possum's two steps (line 3) is the conversion of its 5% dollar loan into a 6% Swiss franc loan. The device that makes this possible is the currency swap. ■

24.4   Self-Test

Suppose that the spot exchange rate had been $1 = CHF3 and that Swiss interest rates were 8%. Recalculate the Swiss franc cash flows that the dealer would agree to (line 2b of Table 24.4) and Possum's net cash flows (line 3).

And Some Other Swaps

While interest rate and currency swaps are the most popular type of contract, there is a wide variety of other possible swaps or related contracts.

TABLE 24.4 Cash flows from Possum's dollar loan and currency swap (figures in millions)

	Year 0		Years 1–4		Year 5	
	$	CHF	$	CHF	$	CHF
1. Issue dollar loan	+10		−0.5		−10.5	
2. Arrange currency swap						
a. Possum receives $	−10		+0.5		+10.5	
b. Possum pays CHF		+20		−1.2		−21.2
3. Net cash flow	0	+20	0	−1.2	0	−21.2

Inflation swaps allow a company to protect against inflation risk. One party in the swap receives a fixed payment, while the other receives a payment that is linked to the rate of inflation. In effect, the swap creates a made-to-measure inflation-linked bond, which can be of any maturity.

You can also enter into a total return swap where one party (party A) makes a series of agreed payments, and the other (party B) pays the total return on a particular asset. This asset might be a common stock, a loan, a commodity, or a market index. For example, suppose that B owns $10 million of IBM stock. It now enters into a 2-year swap agreement to pay A each quarter the total return on this stock. In exchange, A agrees to pay B interest of LIBOR + 1%. Although ownership of the IBM stock does not change hands, the effect of this total return swap is the same as if B had sold the asset to A and bought it back at an agreed future date.

24.6   Innovation in the Derivatives Market

Almost every day, some new derivative contract seems to be invented. At first, there may be just a few private deals between a bank and its customers, but if the contract proves popular, one of the futures exchanges may try to muscle in on the business.

Derivatives dealers try to identify the major risks that face businesses and then design a contract that will allow them to lay off these risks. For example, a major hazard for many financial institutions is the possibility that a large customer will get into difficulties and default on its debts. Credit default swaps offer a way for the lender to insure against such a default. The provider of the insurance promises to pay out if the borrower defaults on its debts and in return charges a premium for taking on the risk.

Iron ore prices are volatile. With fluctuating demand from China, iron ore prices nearly tripled between early 2009 and 2011 before slumping by 75% over the next 5 years. The futures exchanges reasoned that both producers and users might welcome a contract that allowed them to hedge these price movements. Therefore, in July 2010, the New York Mercantile Exchange (part of the CME Group) introduced a futures contract based on the price of iron ore landed in China.

Real estate businesses and builders worry about fluctuations in house prices. So wouldn't it be nice if they could stop worrying and hedge themselves against these fluctuations? Well, now they can do so by dealing in real estate futures or options on the Chicago Mercantile Exchange. Real estate futures were launched in 2006 and enable participants to protect themselves against changes in house prices in 10 U.S. cities.

It seems to be very difficult to predict which new contracts will succeed and which will bomb. By the time you read this, iron ore contracts may have been forgotten, and everyone will be talking about the new growth market in _____ derivatives. Perhaps you can help fill in the missing word.

24.7   Is "Derivative" a Four-Letter Word?

BEYOND THE PAGE

Major derivatives losses

mhhe.com/brealey9e

Our earlier examples of the farmer and the miller showed how derivatives—futures, options, or swaps, for example—can be used to reduce business risk. However, if you were to copy the farmer and sell wheat futures without an offsetting holding of wheat, you would not be *reducing* risk; you would be *speculating*.

A successful futures market needs speculators who are prepared to take on risk and provide the farmer and the miller with the protection they need. For example, if an excess of farmers wished to sell wheat futures, the price of futures would be forced down until enough speculators were tempted to buy in the hope of a profit. If there is a

In October 2010, Jérôme Kerviel became the world's poorest man when a French court sentenced him to 5 years in prison and fined him €4.9 billion. Until his arrest 2 years earlier, he had been a trader in the French bank Société Générale. But then it was discovered that he had engaged in unauthorized trading, resulting in record losses for the bank of €4.9 billion, or $7.2 billion.

Kerviel joined the back office of SocGen in 2000. Five years later, he realized his dream when he was promoted to be a trader on the Delta One desk, which mainly trades equities, futures, and exchange-traded funds. In most banks, the Delta One desk focuses on arbitrage opportunities, and Kerviel's job was to exploit small price differences between equity futures contracts, rather than to bet on the market's direction.

Soon after taking up his new position, Kerviel took an unauthorized bet on a downturn in the market. The trade proved successful and resulted in a profit of €500,000. Although it was not hedged and exceeded Kerviel's credit limit, the bank took no action. Spurred on by this success, Kerviel continued to take unhedged bets on his outlook for the market. To hide the fact that his trades were unhedged, he created a series of fictitious offsetting trades.

For a while, fortune smiled on Kerviel, and by 2007, he had made a profit of €1.4 billion. But in January 2008, everything started to unravel. As stock prices collapsed, Kerviel took larger and larger bets that the markets would recover. Every time he lost, Kerviel doubled up on his bets. By mid-January, he had about €50 billion—more than the bank's total market capitalization—riding on a market turnaround. By late January, the bank had learned the full extent of Kerviel's positions and frantically moved to close them out. The resulting loss of €4.9 billion amounted to more than 10% of the value of the bank's equity.

Société Générale's failure to spot the unauthorized trading was the subject of much criticism. Some commented that a trader who had worked in the back office would be particularly well informed about ways to hide his activities. Banks took comfort in the fact that such a breakdown in controls could never happen again—that is, until 2011, when the Swiss Bank UBS revealed that a trader who had been promoted from the back office to the Delta One desk had lost more than $2 billion in unauthorized trading.

Postcript: In September of 2016, Kerviel enjoyed a remarkable reversal of fortune when an appeals court in France reduced his fine from €4.9 billion to only €1 million. A windfall gain of nearly €4.9 billion in one day beats winning the lottery.

surplus of millers wishing to buy wheat futures, the reverse will happen. The price will be forced up until speculators are drawn in to sell.

Speculation may be necessary to a thriving derivatives market, but it can get companies into serious trouble. In 1995, Baring Brothers, a blue-chip British merchant bank with a 200-year history, became insolvent. The reason: Nick Leeson, a trader in its Singapore office, had lost $1.4 billion speculating in futures on the Japanese stock market index. Barings has plenty of company. For example, the nearby Finance in Practice box describes how the French bank Société Générale took a $7.2 billion bath from unauthorized trading by one of its staff, and in 2011, the Swiss bank UBS joined the billion-dollar club when a rogue trader notched up losses of $2.3 billion.

Do these horror stories mean that firms should ban the use of derivatives? Of course not. But they do illustrate that derivatives need to be used with care. **Speculation is foolish unless you have reason to believe that the odds are stacked in your favor. If you are not better informed than the highly paid professionals in banks and other institutions, you should use derivatives for hedging, not for speculation.**

BEYOND THE PAGE

Metallgesellschaft

mhhe.com/brealey9e

BEYOND THE PAGE

Long-term capital management (LTCM)

mhhe.com/brealey9e

SUMMARY

Why do companies hedge to reduce risk? (*LO24-1*)

Fluctuations in commodity prices, interest rates, or exchange rates make planning difficult and can throw companies badly off course. Financial managers, therefore, look for opportunities to manage these risks, and a number of specialized instruments have been invented to help them. These are collectively known as *derivative instruments*. They include options, futures, forwards, and swaps.

How can futures and forward contracts be used to devise simple hedging strategies? (*LO24-2*)

Futures contracts are agreements made today to buy or sell an asset in the future. The price is fixed today, but the final payment does not occur until the delivery date. Futures contracts are highly standardized and are traded on organized exchanges. Commodity futures allow firms to fix the future price that they pay for a wide range of agricultural commodities, metals, and oil. Financial futures help firms to protect themselves against unforeseen movements in interest rates, exchange rates, and stock prices.

Forward contracts are equivalent to tailor-made futures contracts. For example, firms often enter into forward agreements with a bank to buy or sell foreign exchange or to fix the interest rate on a loan to be made in the future.

How can companies use swaps to change the risk of securities that they have issued? (*LO24-3*)

Swaps allow firms to exchange one series of future payments for another. For example, the firm might agree to make a series of regular payments in one currency in return for receiving a series of payments in another currency.

QUESTIONS AND PROBLEMS

1. **Risk Management.** True or false? (*LO24-1*)
   a. Hedging is a zero-sum game.
   b. Reducing risk always increases company value.
   c. Hedging can reduce the likelihood of financial distress.
   d. Investors may prefer to hedge themselves.
   e. Risk may be reduced by real options.
   f. Derivatives include futures, forwards, preferred stock, and swaps.

2. **Risk Management.** Large businesses spend millions of dollars annually on insurance. Why? Should they insure against all risks, or does insurance make more sense for some risks than others? (*LO24-1*)

3. **Commodity Futures.** Match each of the following terms with one of the definitions below: *spot price, futures price, forward contract, marked to market, expected spot price* (*LO24-2*)
   a. Price for immediate delivery
   b. A tailor-made futures contract
   c. The expected price in the future
   d. System in which profits and losses are settled with the futures exchange on a daily basis
   e. The price fixed today for delivery in the future

4. **Commodity Futures.** True or false? (*LO24-2*)
   a. Buyers of futures contracts generally wait until the contract matures and then take delivery of the commodity.
   b. The great advantage of a futures contract is that the buyer is not obliged to deliver the contract at maturity. He will do so only if the price at maturity is above the contract price.
   c. Because the buyer of the futures can sell his contract before maturity rather than take delivery, the futures contract is equivalent to a call option.
   d. In contrast to a futures contract, a forward contract requires payment up front.

5. **Commodity Futures.** What do you think are the advantages of holding futures rather than the underlying commodity? What do you think are the disadvantages? (*LO24-2*)

6. **Hedging Strategies.** "The farmer does not avoid risk by selling wheat futures. If wheat prices rise above $6.40 a bushel, then he will suffer losses if he has sold wheat futures at $6.40. Is this fair comment? (*LO24-2*)

7. **Hedging Strategies.** (*LO24-2*)
   a. An investor currently holding $1 million in long-term Treasury bonds becomes concerned about increasing volatility in interest rates. She decides to hedge her risk by using Treasury bond futures contracts. Should she buy or sell such contracts?
   b. The treasurer of a corporation that will be issuing bonds in 3 months also is concerned about interest rate volatility and wants to lock in the price at which he can sell 8% coupon bonds. Should he buy or sell Treasury bond futures contracts to hedge his firm's position?

8. **Hedging.** When the euro strengthened, German luxury-car manufacturers found it increasingly difficult to compete in the U.S. market. How could they have hedged themselves against this risk? Would a company that was hedged have been in a better position to compete? Explain why or why not. (*LO24-2*)

9. **Hedging.** Assume that the 1-year interest rate is 4% and the 2-year interest rate is 5%. You approach a bank and ask at what rate the bank will promise to make a 1-year loan in 12 months' time. The bank offers to make a forward commitment to lend to you at 10%. (*LO24-2*)

   a. Would you accept the offer?
   b. Can you think of a simple, cheaper alternative?

10. **Hedging.** Phoenix Motors wants to lock in the cost of 10,000 ounces of platinum to be used in next quarter's production of catalytic converters. It buys 3-month futures contracts for 10,000 ounces at a price of $1,650 per ounce. (*LO24-2*)

    a. Suppose the spot price of platinum falls to $1,500 in 3 months' time. Does Phoenix have a profit or loss on the futures contract?
    b. Has it locked in the cost of purchasing the platinum it needs?
    c. How does your answer to part (a) change if the spot price of platinum increases to $1,800 after 3 months?
    d. How does your answer to part (b) change?

11. **Hedging.** A gold-mining firm is concerned about short-term volatility in its revenues. Gold currently sells for $1,600 an ounce, but the price is extremely volatile and could fall as low as $1,520 or rise as high as $1,680 in the next month. The company will bring 1,000 ounces of gold to the market next month. (*LO24-2*)

    a. What will be the total revenues if the firm remains unhedged for gold prices of (i) $1,520, (ii) $1,600, and (iii) $1,680 an ounce?
    b. The futures price of gold for delivery 1 month ahead is $1,620. What will be the firm's total revenues if the firm enters into a 1-month futures contract to deliver 1,000 ounces of gold?
    c. What will be the total revenues if the firm buys a 1-month put option to sell gold for $1,000 an ounce? The put option costs $110 per ounce.

12. **Hedging.** Your firm has just tendered for a contract in Japan. You won't know for 3 months whether you get the contract, but if you do, you will receive a payment of ¥10 million 1 year from now. You are worried that if the yen declines in value, the dollar value of this payment will be less than you expect, and the project could even show a loss. Discuss the possible ways that you could protect the firm against a decline in the value of the yen. Illustrate the possible outcomes if you do get the contract and if you don't. (*LO24-2*)

13. **Commodity Futures.** Listed here are some commodity futures contracts, and some possible users of these contracts. State (i) which contract each user would be most likely to use to hedge its risk and (ii) whether it would be likely to buy or sell the contract. (*LO24-2*)

a. oil futures	A. An airline
b. wheat futures	B. A Kansas wheat farmer
c. lumber futures	C. A Texas cattle ranch
d. copper futures	D. A meatpacker
e. live cattle futures	E. A home builder
	F. An oil producer
	G. A milling company
	H. A mining company
	I. A timber company
	J. A cable manufacturer

14. **Commodity Futures.** Log on to the online *Wall Street Journal,* www.wsj.com, and find the prices of gold futures (look for *Market Data Center* under the *Markets* tab). (*LO24-2*)

    a. What is the date of the most distant contract?
    b. Is the futures price higher or lower than the current spot price?
    c. Suppose that you buy 100 ounces of gold futures for this date. When do you receive the gold?
    d. When do you pay for it?

15. **Marking to Market.** Yesterday you sold 6-month futures on Standard & Poor's Index at a price of 2,100. Today the S&P closed at 2,080, and S&P futures closed at 2,120. You get a call from your broker, who reminds you that your futures position is marked to market every-day. Is she asking you to pay money, or is she about to offer to pay you? (*LO24-3*)

16. **Marking to Market.** Suppose that in the 5 days following a farmer's sale of September wheat futures at a futures price of $5.83, the futures price is:

Day	1	2	3	4	5
Price	$5.83	$5.89	$5.70	$5.50	$5.60

At the end of day 5, the farmer decides to quit wheat farming and buys back his futures contract. What payments are made between the farmer and the exchange on:

a. Day 1?

b. Day 2?

c. Day 3?

d. Day 4?

e. Day 5?

What is the total payment over the 5 days? Would the total payment be any different if the contract was not marked to market? (*LO24-3*)

17. **Swaps.** Look back at our example of the interest rate swap in Section 24.5. Since Computer Parts entered into the swap, interest rates have risen. Is the company showing a profit or a loss on the contract? (*LO24-3*)

WEB EXERCISES

1. Log on to www.cmegroup.com and find the recent quotes for soybean futures. What is the longest maturity for this contract? Is there more trading in the nearer or more distant contracts? Does it cost more to buy soybeans for delivery in the next few months or for later delivery?

2. Every 3 years, the Bank for International Settlements undertakes a survey of derivatives trading that is available on its website, www.bis.org. Which are the most important types of derivative contract? Which have been growing most rapidly? Why? Who do you think would find them useful?

SOLUTIONS TO SELF-TEST QUESTIONS

24.1 The farmer has a further loss of 15 cents a bushel ($6.20 − $6.05) and will be required to pay this amount to the exchange. The miller has a further profit of 15 cents per bushel and will receive this from the exchange. The farmer is now committed to delivering wheat in September for $6.20 per bushel, and the miller is committed to paying $6.20 per bushel.

24.2 You sell long-term bond futures with a delivery date of 9 months. Suppose, for example, that you agree to deliver long-term bonds in 9 months at a price of $100. If interest rates rise, the price of the bond futures will fall to (say) $95. (Remember that when interest rates rise, bond prices fall.) In this case, the profit that you make on your bond futures offsets the lower price that the firm is likely to receive on the sale of its own bonds. Conversely, if interest rates fall, the company will make a loss on its futures position but will receive a higher price for its own bonds.

24.3 The manager wants to convert the fixed-rate bond, whose value will fall if interest rates rise, into a "synthetic" floating-rate bond. Floating-rate bonds always pay close to current-market interest rates, and therefore, their prices have little exposure to interest rate fluctuations.

The manager should enter a swap to pay a 5% fixed rate and receive LIBOR on notional principal of $100 million. The cash flows will then rise in tandem with the LIBOR rate:

	LIBOR Rate		
	4.5%	**5.0%**	**5.5%**
Interest received on fixed-rate bonds (= .05 × $100 million)	$5,000,000	$5,000,000	$5,000,000
+ Cash flow on swap [= (LIBOR − .05) × notional principal of $100 million]	−500,000	0	+500,000
Total income	$4,500,000	$5,000,000	$5,500,000

The total income equals LIBOR × $100 million, so this position is, in effect, a synthetic floating-rate bond tied to LIBOR. The diagram describing the cash flows of each party to the swap is as follows:

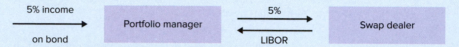

24.4   The following table shows revised cash flows from Possum's dollar loan and currency swap (figures in millions). The Swiss franc cash flows correspond to the payments on a CHF30 million bond with a coupon rate of 8%.

	Year 0		Years 1–4		Year 5	
	$	**CHF**	**$**	**CHF**	**$**	**CHF**
1. Issue dollar loan	+10		−0.5		−10.5	
2. Arrange currency swap						
a. Possum receives $	−10		+0.5		+10.5	
b. Possum pays CHF		+30		−2.4		−32.4
3. Net cash flow	0	+30	0	−2.4	0	−32.4

Notice that in exchange for $10 million today, the dealer is now prepared to pay CHF30 million. Because the Swiss interest rate is now 8%, the dealer will expect to earn .08 × 30 = CHF2.4 million interest on its Swiss franc outlay.

What We Do and Do Not Know about Finance

It is time to sum up. We begin this chapter with a very brief recap of the six most important ideas in finance. By now, these should be second nature to you.

Of course, there are still many puzzles that remain to be worked out. We will give you our list of the nine most important unsolved problems in finance.

We have tried to provide you with the essentials of finance, but it would be a dull subject if you could learn all that there is to know in one book. Therefore, we provide a short road map of the important topics that you may encounter in more advanced finance classes.

Too bad Einstein didn't tackle the unsolved problems of finance. © *Keystone-France/Gamma-Keystone/Getty Images*

25.1   What We Do Know: The Six Most Important Ideas in Finance

What would you say if you were asked to name the six most important ideas in finance? Here is our list.

Net Present Value (Chapter 5)

When you wish to know the value of a used car, you look at prices in the secondhand car market. Similarly, when you wish to know the value of a future cash flow, you look at prices quoted in the capital markets, where claims to future cash flows are traded (remember, those highly paid investment bankers are just secondhand cash-flow dealers). If you can buy cash flows for your shareholders at a cheaper price than they would have to pay in the capital market, you have increased the value of their investment.

This is the simple idea behind *net present value (NPV)*. When we calculate a project's NPV, we are asking whether the project is worth more than it costs. We are estimating its value by calculating what its cash flows would be worth if a claim on them were offered separately to investors and traded in the capital markets.

This is why we calculate NPV by discounting future cash flows at the opportunity cost of capital—that is, at the expected rate of return offered by securities having the same degree of risk as the project. In well-functioning capital markets, all equivalent-risk assets are priced to offer the same expected return. When we discount at the opportunity cost of capital, we are calculating the price that would provide investors with that rate of return.

Like most good ideas, the net present value rule is obvious when you think about it. But notice what an important idea it is. The NPV rule allows thousands of shareholders, who may have vastly different levels of wealth and attitudes toward risk, to participate in the same enterprise and to delegate its operation to a professional manager. They give the manager one simple instruction: "Maximize net present value."

Risk and Return (Chapters 11 and 12)

Some people say that modern finance is all about the capital asset pricing model. That's nonsense. If the capital asset pricing model had never been invented, our advice to financial managers would be essentially the same. The attraction of the model is that it gives us a manageable way of thinking about the required return on a risky investment.

Again, it is an attractively simple idea. There are two kinds of risks—those that you can diversify away and those that you can't. The only risks people care about are the ones that they can't get rid of—the nondiversifiable ones.

You can measure the *nondiversifiable,* or *market, risk* of an investment by the extent to which the value of the investment is affected by a change in the *aggregate* value of all the assets in the economy. This is called the *beta* of the investment. The required return on an asset increases in line with its beta.

Many people are worried by some of the rather strong assumptions behind the capital asset pricing model, or they are concerned about the difficulties of estimating a project's beta. They are right to be worried about these things. One day, we will have much better theories than we do now,[1] but we are prepared to bet that these more sophisticated theories will retain the two crucial ideas behind the capital asset pricing model:

- Investors don't like risk and require a higher return to compensate.
- The risk that matters is the risk that investors cannot get rid of.

---

[1] We confess we have been making this prediction for 35 years. One day we will be right.

Efficient Capital Markets (Chapter 7)

The third fundamental idea is that security prices accurately reflect available information and respond rapidly to new information as soon as it becomes *available*. This *efficient-market theory* comes in three flavors, corresponding to different definitions of "available information." The weak form (or random-walk theory) says that prices reflect all the information in past prices; the semistrong form says that prices reflect all publicly available information; and the strong form holds that prices reflect all acquirable information.

Don't misunderstand the efficient-market idea. It doesn't say that there are no taxes or costs; it doesn't say that there aren't some clever people and some stupid ones; it doesn't say that investors don't make mistakes. It merely implies that competition in capital markets is very tough—there are no money machines, and security prices reflect the true underlying values of assets on the basis of the best information available to investors.

The efficient-market hypothesis has been extensively tested, and the tests have revealed several pricing "anomalies," or seeming profit opportunities with simple investment strategies. We showed you just a few examples of these anomalies in Chapter 7. But the academic journals are now filled with dozens and dozens more of these puzzles. Does this mean that investors are leaving easy money on the table?

Unfortunately for all of us, this body of evidence has *not* translated into easy money. Superior returns are elusive, and only a very few mutual fund managers have been able to generate such returns with any consistency. Implementing the anomalies in real markets is apparently far more difficult than finding them on databases of past returns.

MM's Irrelevance Propositions (Chapters 16 and 17)

The irrelevance propositions of Modigliani and Miller (MM) imply that you can't increase value through financing policies unless these policies also increase the total cash flow available to investors. Financing decisions that simply repackage the same cash flows don't add value.

Financial managers often ask how much their company should borrow. MM's response is that as long as borrowing does not alter the *total* cash flow generated by the firm's assets, it does not affect firm value.

Miller and Modigliani used a similar argument to show that payout policy does not affect value unless it affects the total cash flow available to present and future shareholders. If investment and borrowing are fixed, the only way that the company can pay an increased dividend is by cutting back on share repurchases or by issuing more shares. In either case the firm is simply putting cash in one of your pockets and taking it out of another.

The same ideas can be run in reverse. Just as splitting up the cash flows doesn't add value, neither does combining different cash-flow streams. This implies that you can't increase value by putting two whole companies together unless you thereby increase total cash flow. Thus there are no benefits to mergers solely for diversification.

You can think of these irrelevance propositions as a form of "conservation of value." You can't increase value simply by putting two companies together, nor can you create value by splitting up total cash flow into several pieces, for example, into debt and equity claims. The whole is just the sum of the parts.

Option Theory (Chapter 23)

In everyday conversation, we often use the word "option" as synonymous with "choice" or "alternative"; thus, we speak of someone as *having a number of options*. In finance, an *option* refers specifically to the opportunity to trade in the future on terms that are fixed today. Smart managers know that it is often worth paying today for the option to buy or sell an asset tomorrow.

We saw in Chapters 10 and 23 that companies are willing to pay extra for capital projects that give them future flexibility. Also, many securities provide the company or the investor with options. For example, a convertible bond gives the owner an option to exchange the bond for shares.

Managers spend much more time thinking about options than they used to. This is partly because they increasingly use options to help limit risk. Also, managers and economists are more aware that many assets contain disguised real options. For example, the opportunity to abandon a project and recover its salvage value is a put option.

If options are so prevalent, it is important to know how to value them. One of the great finance developments of recent years was the discovery by Black, Scholes, and Merton of a formula to value options. We reviewed briefly the determinants of option value in Chapter 23.

Agency Theory

A modern corporation is a team effort involving many players, including management, employees, shareholders, and bondholders. The members of this corporate team are bound together by a series of formal and informal contracts to ensure that they pull together.

For a long time, economists assumed that all players acted instinctively for the common good. But in the last 20 years, we have learned a lot about the possible conflicts of interest and how companies try to overcome such conflicts. These ideas are collectively known as *agency theory*.

Consider, for example, the relationship between the firm's shareholders and managers. The shareholders (the *principals*) want managers (their *agents*) to maximize firm value. To encourage managers to do so, firms seek to tie the managers' compensation to the value they have added. Moreover, managers who persistently neglect shareholders' interests face the threat that their firm will be taken over and they will be turfed out.

Although we didn't allocate a separate chapter to agency theory, the theory has helped us to think about such questions as these:

- How can an entrepreneur persuade venture capital investors to join in his or her enterprise? (Chapter 15)
- What are the reasons for all the fine print in bond agreements? (Chapter 16)
- Are mergers, acquisitions, and LBOs simply attempts to "rip off" other players, or do they change management's incentives to maximize company value? (Chapter 21)

Are these six ideas exciting theories or plain common sense? Call them what you will, they are basic to the financial manager's job. If, after reading this book, you really understand these ideas and know how to apply them, you have learned a great deal.

25.2 What We Do Not Know: Nine Unsolved Problems in Finance

Because the unknown is never exhausted, the list of what we do not know about finance could go on forever. Here are nine unsolved problems that seem ripe for productive research.

What Determines Project Risk and Present Value?

A good capital investment is one that has a positive NPV. We have talked at some length about how to calculate NPV, but we have given you very little guidance about how to find positive-NPV projects, other than to say in Chapter 10 that projects have positive NPVs when the firm has some competitive advantage. But why do some companies earn superior returns while others in the same industry do not?

When are superior returns merely windfall gains, and when can they be anticipated, created, and planned for? What is their source, and how long do they persist before competition wears them away? Very little is known about any of these important questions.

Here is a related question: Why are some real assets risky and others relatively safe? In Chapter 12 we suggested a few reasons for differences in project betas—differences in operating leverage, for example, or in the extent to which a project's cash flows respond to the performance of the national economy. These are useful clues, but we have, as yet, no general procedure for estimating project betas. Assessing project risk is, therefore, still largely a seat-of-the-pants matter.

Risk and Return—Have We Missed Something?

In 1848, John Stuart Mill wrote, "Happily there is nothing in the laws of value which remains for the present or any future writer to clear up; the theory is complete." Economists today are not so sure about that. For example, the capital asset pricing model is an enormous step toward understanding the effect of risk on the value of an asset, but there are many puzzles left, some statistical and some theoretical.

The statistical problems arise because the capital asset pricing model is hard to prove or disprove conclusively. It appears that average returns from low-beta stocks are too high (i.e., higher than the capital asset pricing model predicts), and those from high-beta stocks are too low. But this could be a problem with the way the tests are conducted and not with the model itself.

We also described the puzzling discovery that expected returns appear to be related to firm size and to the ratio of the book value of the stock to its market value. Of course, these findings could be just a coincidence—an accidental result that is unlikely to be repeated. But if they are not a coincidence, the capital asset pricing model cannot be the whole truth. Perhaps firm size and the book-to-market ratio are related to some other variable x that, along with beta, truly determines the expected returns demanded by investors. But we cannot yet identify variable x and prove that it matters.

Meanwhile, work is proceeding on the theoretical front to relax the simple assumptions underlying the capital asset pricing model. Here is one example: Suppose that you love fine wine. It may make sense for you to buy shares in a grand cru chateau, even if that soaks up a large fraction of your personal wealth and leaves you with a relatively undiversified portfolio. However, you are *hedged* against a rise in the price of fine wine: Your hobby will cost you more in a bull market for wine, but your stake in the chateau will make you correspondingly richer. Thus, you are holding a relatively undiversified portfolio for a good reason. We would not expect you to demand a premium for bearing that portfolio's undiversifiable risk.

In general, if two people have different tastes, it may make sense for them to hold different portfolios. You may hedge your consumption needs with an investment in wine making, whereas somebody else may do better to invest in Baskin-Robbins. The capital asset pricing model isn't rich enough to deal with such a world. It assumes that all investors have similar tastes; the "hedging motive" does not enter, and therefore, they hold the same portfolio of risky assets.

Merton has extended the capital asset pricing model to accommodate the hedging motive.[2] If enough investors are attempting to hedge against the same thing, this model implies a more complicated risk–return relationship. However, it is not yet clear who is hedging against what, so the model remains difficult to test. Given the rich possibilities for these extra hedging motives, there are many plausible alternative risk measures beyond beta and many potential competitors to the simple capital asset pricing model.

In the meantime, we must recognize the CAPM for what it is: an incomplete but extremely useful way of linking risk and return. Recognize too that its most basic message, that diversifiable risk doesn't matter, is accepted by nearly everyone.

---

[2] See R. Merton, "An Intertemporal Capital Asset Pricing Model," *Econometrica* 41 (1973), pp. 867–887.

Are There Important Exceptions to the Efficient-Market Theory?

The efficient-market theory is persuasive, but no theory is perfect—there must be exceptions.

Some of the apparent exceptions could simply be coincidences, for the more that researchers study stock performance, the more strange coincidences they are likely to find. For example, there is evidence that daily returns around new moons have been roughly double those around full moons.[3] It seems difficult to believe that this is anything other than a chance relationship—fun to read about but not a concern for serious investors or financial managers. But not all exceptions can be dismissed so easily. We saw that in the years following their initial public offerings, the stocks of these firms perform relatively poorly. Some scholars believe that this may mean that the stock market is inefficient and investors have consistently been slow to react to the initial offering. Of course, we can't expect investors never to make mistakes. If they have been slow to react in the past, it will be interesting to see whether they learn from their mistake and price the stocks more efficiently in the future.

Some researchers believe that the efficient-market theory ignores important aspects of human behavior. For example, psychologists find that people place too much emphasis on recent events when they are predicting the future. We don't yet know how far such behavioral observations can help us to understand apparent anomalies.

During the dot-com boom of the late 1990s, stock prices rose to astronomical levels. The NASDAQ Composite Index rose 580% from the beginning of 1995 to its peak in March 2000 and then fell by nearly 80%. Maybe such extreme price movements can be explained by standard valuation techniques. However, others argue that stock prices are liable to speculative bubbles, where investors are caught up in a whirl of irrational exuberance. Now it may well be true that some of us are liable to become overexcited, but why don't professional investors bail out of the overpriced stocks? Perhaps they would do so if it were their own money at stake, but maybe there is something in the way that their performance is measured and rewarded that encourages them to run with the herd.

These are important questions. Much more research is needed before we have a full understanding of why asset prices sometimes seem to get so out of line with what appears to be their discounted future payoffs.

Is Management an Off-Balance-Sheet Liability?

In Chapter 7, we argued that the market value of the firm should equal intrinsic value, the value of the firm as a going concern. But sometimes it appears that price does not equal intrinsic value. For example, closed-end funds are firms whose only asset is a portfolio of common stocks; intrinsic value should be easy to observe here, yet the stock of closed-end funds often sells for less than the value of the fund's portfolio. Other examples abound. For instance, real estate stocks often appear to sell for less than the market value of the firm's net assets. In the early 1980s, the market values of many large oil companies were less than the market values of their oil reserves. Analysts joked that you could buy oil cheaper on Wall Street than in west Texas.

These are cases where it is relatively easy to compare the market value of the firm with the value of its underlying assets. It is possible that these examples may be the tip of the iceberg and similar discrepancies may be widespread in other firms where value is harder to measure. If so, the tip of the iceberg could turn out to be a hot potato.

---

[3] K. Yuan, L. Zheng, and Q. Zhu, "Are Investors Moonstruck? Lunar Phases and Stock Returns," *Journal of Empirical Finance* 13 (2006), pp. 1–23.

We don't understand why firms may sell for less than the market value of their assets. One possibility is that gaps between market value and asset value reflect the value of management. Of course, if market value is less than the value of assets, then the market seems to view managers' value added as negative. That is why we suggest that management may be an off-balance-sheet liability. Perhaps investors are worried that managers extract too much of the firm's cash flow for their own interests or pet projects. Of course, managers commit their human capital to the firm and rightfully expect a reasonable return on their personal investment. In most firms, managers and employees coinvest with stockholders and creditors—human capital from the insiders and financial capital from outside investors. So far, we know very little about how this coinvestment works.

How Can We Explain Capital Structure?

Modigliani and Miller's article about capital structure emphasized that the value of a firm depends on real variables—the goods it produces, the prices it charges, and the costs that it incurs. Financing decisions merely affect the way that the cash flows are packaged for distribution to investors. What goes into the package is more important than the package itself.

Does it really not matter how much your firm borrows? We have come across several reasons why it *may* matter. Tax is one possibility. Debt provides a corporate tax shield, and this tax shield may more than compensate for any extra personal tax that the investor has to pay on debt interest. Perhaps managers are concerned with potential bankruptcy costs. Perhaps differences in capital structure reflect differences in the relative importance of growth opportunities. So far, none of these possibilities has been either proved relevant or definitely excluded.

The upshot of the matter is that we still don't have an accepted, coherent theory of capital structure. It is not for want of argument on the subject. Perhaps we are asking too much. There may be no *one* theory that can capture everything that drives the debt and equity choices of thousands of corporations.

How Can We Resolve the Payout Controversy?

We spent all of Chapter 17 on payout policy without being able to resolve the dividend controversy. Many people believe dividends are good; others believe they are bad and repurchases are good; and still others believe that as long as the firm's investment decisions are unaffected, the payout decision is largely irrelevant. If pressed, we largely take the middle view, but we can't be dogmatic about it.

Perhaps the problem is that we are asking the wrong question. Instead of inquiring whether dividends are good or bad, perhaps we should be asking *when* it makes sense to pay out high or low dividends. Investors in mature firms with few investment opportunities may welcome the financial discipline imposed by a high dividend payout, while for younger firms or firms with a large cash surplus, the tax advantage of stock repurchase may be more influential.

The way that companies distribute cash has changed over the last few decades. An increasing number of companies do not pay any dividends, while the volume of stock repurchase has mushroomed. This may partly reflect an increase in the proportion of small high-growth firms with lots of investment opportunities, but this does not appear to be the complete explanation. Understanding these shifts in payout policy may help us to understand how that policy affects firm value.

How Can We Explain Merger Waves?

There are many plausible reasons why two firms might wish to merge. If you single out a *particular* merger, it is usually possible to think up a reason why that merger could make sense. But that leaves us with a special hypothesis for each merger. What we need is a *general* hypothesis to explain merger waves. For example, nobody seemed to be merging in 2002, yet only 4 years later, mergers were back in fashion. Why?

We can think of other instances of financial fashions. For example, from time to time there are hot new-issue periods when there seems to be an endless supply of speculative new issues and an insatiable demand for them. In recent years, economists have been developing new theories of speculative bubbles. Perhaps such theories will help to explain these mystifying financial fashions.

What Is the Value of Liquidity?

Unlike Treasury bills, cash pays no interest. On the other hand, cash provides more liquidity than Treasury bills. The value of this liquidity declines as you hold increasing amounts of cash. When you have only a small proportion of your assets in cash, a little extra can be extremely useful; when you have a substantial holding, any additional liquidity is not worth much. Unfortunately, we don't really understand how to value the liquidity service of cash, and therefore, we can't say how much cash is enough or how readily the firm should be able to raise it. In our chapters on working capital management, we largely finessed these questions by speaking vaguely of the need to ensure an "adequate" liquidity reserve.

A better knowledge of liquidity would also help us to understand how corporate bonds are priced. We already know part of the reason that corporate bonds sell for lower prices than Treasury bonds—corporate bonds are risky. However, the differences between the prices of corporate bonds and Treasury bonds are too large to be explained just by the possibility that the company will default. It seems likely that the price difference is partly due to the fact that corporate bonds are less liquid than Treasury bonds. But until we know how to price differences in liquidity, we can't really say much more than this.

Investors seem to value liquidity much more highly at some times than at others. When liquidity suddenly dries up, firms can find it very difficult to borrow. This happened in the financial crisis of 2007–2009 when investors became concerned about the rising default levels in the subprime mortgage market. Many banks that had sold these mortgages had subsequently repackaged them and traded the packages to financial institutions both in the United States and abroad. As the music began to stop, no one was quite sure who would be left holding the parcel. Dealers became increasingly reluctant to quote a price for buying or selling bonds, and banks became wary about lending to each other. Those banks that earlier in the year had been able to borrow at .1% above the Federal Reserve's target interest rate found that they now needed to pay a spread of over 4%—if they could borrow at all.

Why Are Financial Systems Prone to Crisis?

Financial markets work well most of the time, but we don't understand why they sometimes shut down or clog up, and we can offer relatively little advice to managers as to how to respond.

The crisis that started in 2007 was an unwelcome reminder of the fragility of financial systems. One moment everything seems to be going fine; the next moment markets crash and banks fail, and before long, the economy is in recession. We know that major banking crises are often preceded by credit booms and asset price bubbles. When the bubbles burst, housing prices and stock prices fall, often precipitously, and deep recession follows.

Our understanding of these financial crises is limited. We need to know what causes them, how they can be prevented, and how they can be managed when they do occur. Crisis prevention will have to incorporate good governance systems, well-constructed compensation schemes, and efficient risk management. Understanding financial crises will occupy economists and financial regulators for many years to come. Let's hope that they figure out the last one before the next one knocks on the door.

That concludes our list of unsolved problems. We have given you the nine uppermost in our minds. If there are others that you find more interesting and challenging, by all means construct your own list and start thinking about it.

25.3 A Final Word

We titled this chapter "What We Do and Do Not Know about Finance." We should perhaps have added, somewhat immodestly, a third section, "What We Know about Finance but Haven't Told You." After all, this book is an introduction to finance and there are plenty of topics that we have only skimmed over. Here are just three examples:

- Investment decisions always have side effects on financing—every dollar has to be raised somehow. Sometimes, these side effects may be important. For instance, if the project allows the company to issue more debt, it may bring with it valuable tax shields. How can companies allow for these financing side effects when evaluating new investment projects? We touched on this issue in Chapter 13 when we showed you how to calculate the weighted-average cost of capital, but there is a huge body of knowledge about how best to allow for financing side effects in project valuation.
- We stressed in Chapter 14 the wide variety of claims that companies can sell to raise money. We described the principal ones, but there are others that we largely ignored. Leasing is an example. Companies lease assets rather than buy them because it is convenient and because, in some circumstances, there can be tax advantages. A lot is now known about how to value leases.
- Treasurers of large corporations worry about fluctuations in exchange rates, interest rates, and commodity prices. Various tools—including options, futures, forwards, and swaps—have been invented to help managers hedge against these risks. Many of the best brains in finance have been applied to devising and valuing these new instruments. We only touched on the problem of option valuation and said nothing at all about valuing futures. It's an exciting area, and there is no shortage of books and articles to help you learn more.

We hope that you will be tempted by this introduction to dive more deeply into the inviting waters of finance.

QUESTIONS AND PROBLEMS

If you have reached this far, you deserve a break. So we haven't provided any heavyweight problems at the end of this chapter. Instead, we have included a quiz of the "Trivial Pursuit" variety. You don't need to know the answers to be a financial wizard, and for the most part they are not to be found in earlier chapters. However, they may help you to impress your friends at smart dinner parties.[4]

1. What do these countries' currencies have in common?
   - Australia
   - Canada
   - Hong Kong
   - New Zealand
   - Singapore
   - Taiwan
   - United States

   [Score 10]

---

[4] The answers are given in the Answers to Quiz.

2. What do the following countries' currencies have in common?

- Estonia
- Finland
- Ireland
- Greece
- Portugal

[Score 10]

3. Government bonds are known by a variety of names. In which countries are the following government bonds issued?

- Bunds
- JGBs
- Gilts
- OATs
- Tesobonos

[Score 2 for each correct answer]

4. Each of these indexes measures stock market performance in a different country. What are the countries?

- CAC Index
- DAX Index
- FTSE Index
- Hang Seng Index
- Nikkei Index

[Score 2 for each correct answer]

5. In which city is each of these futures markets located?

- CME
- SHFE
- LME
- NYMEX
- TFX

[Score 2 for each correct answer]

6. Name the company:

a. Among the world's largest insurance companies, this firm required emergency loans of more than $80 billion from the U.S. government to cover its losses on credit default swaps.

b. In 2007, depositors in this U.K. bank formed long queues as they rushed to withdraw their money.

c. This former investment banking giant filed for bankruptcy in September 2008—at the time, the largest-ever U.S. bankruptcy.

d. This bank failed after a 10-day bank run in September 2008—the largest bank failure in U.S. history.

[Score 2.5 for each correct answer]

7. Match the two merging firms.

Acquiring Firms	Acquired Firms
Heinz	Lafarge
Microsoft	Skype
United Technologies	Goodrich
Holcim	Xstrata
Glencore	Kraft

[Score 2 for each correct answer]

8. To which country does each of the following banks belong?
   - ICICI
   - BBVA
   - Sberbank
   - Bank of Communications (BoCom)
   - Mizuho Bank

   [Score 2 for each correct answer]

9. In which state are the major U.S. corporations commonly incorporated?
   - Alabama
   - California
   - Delaware
   - Illinois
   - Maryland

   [Score 10]

10. Spot the "odd one out."
    - Butterfly
    - Odd lot
    - Straddle
    - Vertical spread

    [Score 10]

11. What do the following abbreviations stand for?
    - CFTC
    - FDIC
    - PCAOB
    - FSOC
    - SEC

    [Score 2 for each correct answer]

12. Spot the "odd one out."
    - Delta Air Lines
    - United Airlines
    - Southwest Airlines
    - American Airlines
    - US Airways

    [Score 10]

13. Match up the following events and dates:
    - 1963   The first financial futures contract was traded in Chicago.
    - 1972   The first swap was arranged (between the World Bank and IBM).
    - 1973   The first eurobond was issued (by the Italian company Autostrade).
    - 1981   The first traded options market was formed in the United States.
    - 1997   The U.S. Treasury first issued indexed bonds.

    [Score 2 for each correct answer]

14. Match each of the following Asian countries with its currency:
    - China   Baht
    - South Korea   Dong
    - Myanmar (Burma)   Kyat
    - Thailand   Won
    - Vietnam   Yuan

    [Score 2 for each correct answer]

15. In which year did the U.S. stock market decline by 43%?

   - 1931
   - 1939
   - 1987

   [Score 10]

16. Stocks are often referred to by their ticker symbols. To which companies do the following symbols refer?

   - LUV
   - RIG
   - HOG
   - BID
   - ZEUS

   [Score 2 for each correct answer]

17. Each of the following organizations made large losses from trading. Match each firm with a major cause of the loss.

   - Barings   Copper futures
   - Metallgesellschaft Nikkei Index futures
   - Allied Irish Bank   Oil futures
   - Procter & Gamble   Currencies
   - Sumitomo Corporation Swaps

   [Score 2 for each correct answer]

18. What do the following professors of finance have in common?

   - Harry Markowitz
   - Merton Miller
   - William Sharpe
   - Eugene Fama
   - Robert Shiller
   - Robert Merton
   - Myron Scholes

   [Score 10]

19. Match each of the following individuals with one of the quotations.

   - Gordon Gekko   a. "When the music stops . . . things will be complicated. But as
   - Charles Prince   long as the music is playing, you've got to get up and dance.
   - John Maynard Keynes   We're still dancing."
   - John D. Rockefeller b. "Where are the customers' yachts?"
   - Fred Schwed   c. "Believing that fundamental conditions of the country are
                            sound . . . my son and I have for some days been purchasing
                            sound common stocks."
                         d. The stock market "is, so to speak, a game of Snap, of Old Maid,
                            of Musical Chairs—a pastime in which he is a victor who says
                            Snap neither too soon nor too late, who passes the Old Maid to
                            his neighbor before the game is over, who secures a chair for
                            himself when the music stops."
                         e. "Greed is good."

   [Score 2 for each correct answer]

20. International bond issues are often known by nicknames. For example, an international bond issued in Southeast Asia is known as a "dragon bond." What is the common term for a bond issued by a foreign company in the bond market of each of the following countries?

   - Japan
   - Netherlands
   - Spain
   - United Kingdom
   - United States

   [Score 2 for each correct answer]

ANSWERS TO QUIZ

1. Each of their currencies is called the dollar.

2. They are all members of the European Monetary Union (EMU) and, therefore, all use the euro.

3. Bunds = Germany
   JGBs (Japanese Government Bonds) = Japan
   Gilts = United Kingdom
   OATs (Obligations Assimilables du Trésor) = France
   Tesobonos = Mexico

4. CAC Index = France
   DAX Index = Germany
   FTSE Index = United Kingdom
   Hang Seng Index = Hong Kong
   Nikkei Index = Japan

5. CME (Chicago Mercantile Exchange) = Chicago
   SHFE (Shanghai Futures Exchange) = Shanghai
   LME (London Metal Exchange) = London
   NYMEX (New York Mercantile Exchange) = New York
   TFX (Tokyo Financial Exchange) = Tokyo

6. a. AIG
   b. Northern Rock
   c. Lehman Brothers
   d. Washington Mutual

7.

Acquiring Firms	Acquired Firms
Heinz	Kraft
Microsoft	Skype
Holcim	Lafarge
United Technologies	Goodrich
Glencore	Xstrata

8. ICICI = India
   BBVA = Spain
   Sberbank = Russia
   Bank of Communications = China
   Mizuho Bank = Japan

9. Delaware

10. "Odd lot" refers to an order to buy or sell fewer than 100 shares. The other terms all refer to combinations of options.

11. CFTC = Commodity Futures Trading Commission
    FDIC = Federal Deposit Insurance Corporation
    PCAOB = Public Company Accounting Oversight Board
    FSOC = Financial Stability Oversight Council
    SEC = Securities and Exchange Commission

12. Southwest is the only one of these airlines that has not been through Chapter 11 bankruptcy proceedings.

13. 1963   The first eurobond was issued (by the Italian company Autostrade).
    1972   The first financial futures contract was traded in Chicago.
    1973   The first traded options market was formed in the United States.
    1981   The first swap was arranged (between the World Bank and IBM).
    1997   The U.S. Treasury first issued indexed bonds.

14. China = Yuan

    South Korea = Won

    Myanmar = Kyat

    Thailand = Baht

    Vietnam = Dong

15. 1931

16. LUV = Southwest Airlines

    RIG = Transocean

    HOG = Harley-Davidson

    BID = Sotheby's

    ZEUS = Olympic Steel

17. Barings   Nikkei Index futures

    Metallgesellschaft   Oil futures

    Allied Irish Bank   Currencies

    Procter & Gamble   Swaps

    Sumitomo Corporation   Copper futures

18. Each received the Nobel Prize for his contribution to financial economics.

19. Gordon Gekko (in the movie *Wall Street*) = e

    Charles Prince (CEO of Citigroup commenting in 2007 on why the bank's leveraged lending was expanding so rapidly) = a

    John Maynard Keynes (writing in *The General Theory of Employment, Interest and Money, 1936*) = d

    John D. Rockefeller (at the start of the 1929 Great Crash) = c

    Fred Schwed (in a 1940 book of that title) = b

20. Japan = Samurai bond

    Netherlands = Rembrandt bond

    Spain = Matador bond

    United Kingdom = Bulldog bond

    United States = Yankee bond

If you scored:

0–50	You weren't trying.
51–80	Not bad.
81–120	You are probably going to be an investment banker.
121–160	You are probably an investment banker *already*.
161–200	You probably cheated.

APPENDIX A
Present Value and Future Value Tables

TABLE A.1 Future value of $1 after t years $= (1 + r)^t$

	Interest Rate per Year														
Number of Years	1%	2%	3%	4%	5%	6%	7%	8%	9%	10%	11%	12%	13%	14%	15%
1	1.0100	1.0200	1.0300	1.0400	1.0500	1.0600	1.0700	1.0800	1.0900	1.1000	1.1100	1.1200	1.1300	1.1400	1.1500
2	1.0201	1.0404	1.0609	1.0816	1.1025	1.1236	1.1449	1.1664	1.1881	1.2100	1.2321	1.2544	1.2769	1.2996	1.3225
3	1.0303	1.0612	1.0927	1.1249	1.1576	1.1910	1.2250	1.2597	1.2950	1.3310	1.3676	1.4049	1.4429	1.4815	1.5209
4	1.0406	1.0824	1.1255	1.1699	1.2155	1.2625	1.3108	1.3605	1.4116	1.4641	1.5181	1.5735	1.6305	1.6890	1.7490
5	1.0510	1.1041	1.1593	1.2167	1.2763	1.3382	1.4026	1.4693	1.5386	1.6105	1.6851	1.7623	1.8424	1.9254	2.0114
6	1.0615	1.1262	1.1941	1.2653	1.3401	1.4185	1.5007	1.5869	1.6771	1.7716	1.8704	1.9738	2.0820	2.1950	2.3131
7	1.0721	1.1487	1.2299	1.3159	1.4071	1.5036	1.6058	1.7138	1.8280	1.9487	2.0762	2.2107	2.3526	2.5023	2.6600
8	1.0829	1.1717	1.2668	1.3686	1.4775	1.5938	1.7182	1.8509	1.9926	2.1436	2.3045	2.4760	2.6584	2.8526	3.0590
9	1.0937	1.1951	1.3048	1.4233	1.5513	1.6895	1.8385	1.9990	2.1719	2.3579	2.5580	2.7731	3.0040	3.2519	3.5179
10	1.1046	1.2190	1.3439	1.4802	1.6289	1.7908	1.9672	2.1589	2.3674	2.5937	2.8394	3.1058	3.3946	3.7072	4.0456
11	1.1157	1.2434	1.3842	1.5395	1.7103	1.8983	2.1049	2.3316	2.5804	2.8531	3.1518	3.4785	3.8359	4.2262	4.6524
12	1.1268	1.2682	1.4258	1.6010	1.7959	2.0122	2.2522	2.5182	2.8127	3.1384	3.4985	3.8960	4.3345	4.8179	5.3503
13	1.1381	1.2936	1.4685	1.6651	1.8856	2.1329	2.4098	2.7196	3.0658	3.4523	3.8833	4.3635	4.8980	5.4924	6.1528
14	1.1495	1.3195	1.5126	1.7317	1.9799	2.2609	2.5785	2.9372	3.3417	3.7975	4.3104	4.8871	5.5348	6.2613	7.0757
15	1.1610	1.3459	1.5580	1.8009	2.0789	2.3966	2.7590	3.1722	3.6425	4.1772	4.7846	5.4736	6.2543	7.1379	8.1371
16	1.1726	1.3728	1.6047	1.8730	2.1829	2.5404	2.9522	3.4259	3.9703	4.5950	5.3109	6.1304	7.0673	8.1372	9.3576
17	1.1843	1.4002	1.6528	1.9479	2.2920	2.6928	3.1588	3.7000	4.3276	5.0545	5.8951	6.8660	7.9861	9.2765	10.7613
18	1.1961	1.4282	1.7024	2.0258	2.4066	2.8543	3.3799	3.9960	4.7171	5.5599	6.5436	7.6900	9.0243	10.5752	12.3755
19	1.2081	1.4568	1.7535	2.1068	2.5270	3.0256	3.6165	4.3157	5.1417	6.1159	7.2633	8.6128	10.1974	12.0557	14.2318
20	1.2202	1.4859	1.8061	2.1911	2.6533	3.2071	3.8697	4.6610	5.6044	6.7275	8.0623	9.6463	11.5231	13.7435	16.3665

	Interest Rate per Year														
Number of Years	16%	17%	18%	19%	20%	21%	22%	23%	24%	25%	26%	27%	28%	29%	30%
1	1.1600	1.1700	1.1800	1.1900	1.2000	1.2100	1.2200	1.2300	1.2400	1.2500	1.2600	1.2700	1.2800	1.2900	1.3000
2	1.3456	1.3689	1.3924	1.4161	1.4400	1.4641	1.4884	1.5129	1.5376	1.5625	1.5876	1.6129	1.6384	1.6641	1.6900
3	1.5609	1.6016	1.6430	1.6852	1.7280	1.7716	1.8158	1.8609	1.9066	1.9531	2.0004	2.0484	2.0972	2.1467	2.1970
4	1.8106	1.8739	1.9388	2.0053	2.0736	2.1436	2.2153	2.2889	2.3642	2.4414	2.5205	2.6014	2.6844	2.7692	2.8561
5	2.1003	2.1924	2.2878	2.3864	2.4883	2.5937	2.7027	2.8153	2.9316	3.0518	3.1758	3.3038	3.4360	3.5723	3.7129
6	2.4364	2.5652	2.6996	2.8398	2.9860	3.1384	3.2973	3.4628	3.6352	3.8147	4.0015	4.1959	4.3980	4.6083	4.8268
7	2.8262	3.0012	3.1855	3.3793	3.5832	3.7975	4.0227	4.2593	4.5077	4.7684	5.0419	5.3288	5.6295	5.9447	6.2749
8	3.2784	3.5115	3.7589	4.0214	4.2998	4.5950	4.9077	5.2389	5.5895	5.9605	6.3528	6.7675	7.2058	7.6686	8.1573
9	3.8030	4.1084	4.4355	4.7854	5.1598	5.5599	5.9874	6.4439	6.9310	7.4506	8.0045	8.5948	9.2234	9.8925	10.6045
10	4.4114	4.8068	5.2338	5.6947	6.1917	6.7275	7.3046	7.9259	8.5944	9.3132	10.0857	10.9153	11.8059	12.7614	13.7858
11	5.1173	5.6240	6.1759	6.7767	7.4301	8.1403	8.9117	9.7489	10.6571	11.6415	12.7080	13.8625	15.1116	16.4622	17.9216
12	5.9360	6.5801	7.2876	8.0642	8.9161	9.8497	10.8722	11.9912	13.2148	14.5519	16.0120	17.6053	19.3428	21.2362	23.2981
13	6.8858	7.6987	8.5994	9.5964	10.6993	11.9182	13.2641	14.7491	16.3863	18.1899	20.1752	22.3588	24.7588	27.3947	30.2875
14	7.9875	9.0075	10.1472	11.4198	12.8392	14.4210	16.1822	18.1414	20.3191	22.7374	25.4207	28.3957	31.6913	35.3391	39.3738
15	9.2655	10.5387	11.9737	13.5895	15.4070	17.4494	19.7423	22.3140	25.1956	28.4217	32.0301	36.0625	40.5648	45.5875	51.1859
16	10.7480	12.3303	14.1290	16.1715	18.4884	21.1138	24.0856	27.4462	31.2426	5.5271	40.3579	45.7994	51.9230	58.8079	66.5417
17	12.4677	14.4265	16.6722	19.2441	22.1861	25.5477	29.3844	33.7588	38.7408	44.4089	50.8510	58.1652	66.4614	75.8621	86.5042
18	14.4625	16.8790	19.6733	22.9005	26.6233	30.9127	35.8490	41.5233	48.0386	55.5112	64.0722	73.8698	85.0706	97.8622	112.4554
19	16.7765	19.7484	23.2144	27.2516	31.9480	37.4043	43.7358	51.0737	59.5679	69.3889	80.7310	93.8147	108.8904	126.2422	146.1920
20	19.4608	23.1056	27.3930	32.4294	38.3376	45.2593	53.3576	62.8206	73.8641	86.7362	101.7211	119.1446	139.3797	162.8524	190.0496

TABLE A.2 Discount factors: Present value of \$1 to be received after t years $= 1/(1 + r)^t$

						Interest Rate per Year									
Number of Years	1%	2%	3%	4%	5%	6%	7%	8%	9%	10%	11%	12%	13%	14%	15%
1	0.9901	0.9804	0.9709	0.9615	0.9524	0.9434	0.9346	0.9259	0.9174	0.9091	0.9009	0.8929	0.8850	0.8772	0.8696
2	0.9803	0.9612	0.9426	0.9246	0.9070	0.8900	0.8734	0.8573	0.8417	0.8264	0.8116	0.7972	0.7831	0.7695	0.7561
3	0.9706	0.9423	0.9151	0.8890	0.8638	0.8396	0.8163	0.7938	0.7722	0.7513	0.7312	0.7118	0.6931	0.6750	0.6575
4	0.9610	0.9238	0.8885	0.8548	0.8227	0.7921	0.7629	0.7350	0.7084	0.6830	0.6587	0.6355	0.6133	0.5921	0.5718
5	0.9515	0.9057	0.8626	0.8219	0.7835	0.7473	0.7130	0.6806	0.6499	0.6209	0.5935	0.5674	0.5428	0.5194	0.4972
6	0.9420	0.8880	0.8375	0.7903	0.7462	0.7050	0.6663	0.6302	0.5963	0.5645	0.5346	0.5066	0.4803	0.4556	0.4323
7	0.9327	0.8706	0.8131	0.7599	0.7107	0.6651	0.6227	0.5835	0.5470	0.5132	0.4817	0.4523	0.4251	0.3996	0.3759
8	0.9235	0.8535	0.7894	0.7307	0.6768	0.6274	0.5820	0.5403	0.5019	0.4665	0.4339	0.4039	0.3762	0.3506	0.3269
9	0.9143	0.8368	0.7664	0.7026	0.6446	0.5919	0.5439	0.5002	0.4604	0.4241	0.3909	0.3606	0.3329	0.3075	0.2843
10	0.9053	0.8203	0.7441	0.6756	0.6139	0.5584	0.5083	0.4632	0.4224	0.3855	0.3522	0.3220	0.2946	0.2697	0.2472
11	0.8963	0.8043	0.7224	0.6496	0.5847	0.5268	0.4751	0.4289	0.3875	0.3505	0.3173	0.2875	0.2607	0.2366	0.2149
12	0.8874	0.7885	0.7014	0.6246	0.5568	0.4970	0.4440	0.3971	0.3555	0.3186	0.2858	0.2567	0.2307	0.2076	0.1869
13	0.8787	0.7730	0.6810	0.6006	0.5303	0.4688	0.4150	0.3677	0.3262	0.2897	0.2575	0.2292	0.2042	0.1821	0.1625
14	0.8700	0.7579	0.6611	0.5775	0.5051	0.4423	0.3878	0.3405	0.2992	0.2633	0.2320	0.2046	0.1807	0.1597	0.1413
15	0.8613	0.7430	0.6419	0.5553	0.4810	0.4173	0.3624	0.3152	0.2745	0.2394	0.2090	0.1827	0.1599	0.1401	0.1229
16	0.8528	0.7284	0.6232	0.5339	0.4581	0.3936	0.3387	0.2919	0.2519	0.2176	0.1883	0.1631	0.1415	0.1229	0.1069
17	0.8444	0.7142	0.6050	0.5134	0.4363	0.3714	0.3166	0.2703	0.2311	0.1978	0.1696	0.1456	0.1252	0.1078	0.0929
18	0.8360	0.7002	0.5874	0.4936	0.4155	0.3503	0.2959	0.2502	0.2120	0.1799	0.1528	0.1300	0.1108	0.0946	0.0808
19	0.8277	0.6864	0.5703	0.4746	0.3957	0.3305	0.2765	0.2317	0.1945	0.1635	0.1377	0.1161	0.0981	0.0829	0.0703
20	0.8195	0.6730	0.5537	0.4564	0.3769	0.3118	0.2584	0.2145	0.1784	0.1486	0.1240	0.1037	0.0868	0.0728	0.0611

						Interest Rate per Year									
Number of Years	16%	17%	18%	19%	20%	21%	22%	23%	24%	25%	26%	27%	28%	29%	30%
1	0.8621	0.8547	0.8475	0.8403	0.8333	0.8264	0.8197	0.8130	0.8065	0.8000	0.7937	0.7874	0.7813	0.7752	0.7692
2	0.7432	0.7305	0.7182	0.7062	0.6944	0.6830	0.6719	0.6610	0.6504	0.6400	0.6299	0.6200	0.6104	0.6009	0.5917
3	0.6407	0.6244	0.6086	0.5934	0.5787	0.5645	0.5507	0.5374	0.5245	0.5120	0.4999	0.4882	0.4768	0.4658	0.4552
4	0.5523	0.5337	0.5158	0.4987	0.4823	0.4665	0.4514	0.4369	0.4230	0.4096	0.3968	0.3844	0.3725	0.3611	0.3501
5	0.4761	0.4561	0.4371	0.4190	0.4019	0.3855	0.3700	0.3552	0.3411	0.3277	0.3149	0.3027	0.2910	0.2799	0.2693
6	0.4104	0.3898	0.3704	0.3521	0.3349	0.3186	0.3033	0.2888	0.2751	0.2621	0.2499	0.2383	0.2274	0.2170	0.2072
7	0.3538	0.3332	0.3139	0.2959	0.2791	0.2633	0.2486	0.2348	0.2218	0.2097	0.1983	0.1877	0.1776	0.1682	0.1594
8	0.3050	0.2848	0.2660	0.2487	0.2326	0.2176	0.2038	0.1909	0.1789	0.1678	0.1574	0.1478	0.1388	0.1304	0.1226
9	0.2630	0.2434	0.2255	0.2090	0.1938	0.1799	0.1670	0.1552	0.1443	0.1342	0.1249	0.1164	0.1084	0.1011	0.0943
10	0.2267	0.2080	0.1911	0.1756	0.1615	0.1486	0.1369	0.1262	0.1164	0.1074	0.0992	0.0916	0.0847	0.0784	0.0725
11	0.1954	0.1778	0.1619	0.1476	0.1346	0.1228	0.1122	0.1026	0.0938	0.0859	0.0787	0.0721	0.0662	0.0607	0.0558
12	0.1685	0.1520	0.1372	0.1240	0.1122	0.1015	0.0920	0.0834	0.0757	0.0687	0.0625	0.0568	0.0517	0.0471	0.0429
13	0.1452	0.1299	0.1163	0.1042	0.0935	0.0839	0.0754	0.0678	0.0610	0.0550	0.0496	0.0447	0.0404	0.0365	0.0330
14	0.1252	0.1110	0.0985	0.0876	0.0779	0.0693	0.0618	0.0551	0.0492	0.0440	0.0393	0.0352	0.0316	0.0283	0.0254
15	0.1079	0.0949	0.0835	0.0736	0.0649	0.0573	0.0507	0.0448	0.0397	0.0352	0.0312	0.0277	0.0247	0.0219	0.0195
16	0.0930	0.0811	0.0708	0.0618	0.0541	0.0474	0.0415	0.0364	0.0320	0.0281	0.0248	0.0218	0.0193	0.0170	0.0150
17	0.0802	0.0693	0.0600	0.0520	0.0451	0.0391	0.0340	0.0296	0.0258	0.0225	0.0197	0.0172	0.0150	0.0132	0.0116
18	0.0691	0.0592	0.0508	0.0437	0.0376	0.0323	0.0279	0.0241	0.0208	0.0180	0.0156	0.0135	0.0118	0.0102	0.0089
19	0.0596	0.0506	0.0431	0.0367	0.0313	0.0267	0.0229	0.0196	0.0168	0.0144	0.0124	0.0107	0.0092	0.0079	0.0068
20	0.0514	0.0433	0.0365	0.0308	0.0261	0.0221	0.0187	0.0159	0.0135	0.0115	0.0098	0.0084	0.0072	0.0061	0.0053

TABLE A.3 Annuity table: Present value of $1 per year for each of t years $= 1/r - 1/[r(1 + r)^t]$

	Interest Rate per Year														
Number of Years	1%	2%	3%	4%	5%	6%	7%	8%	9%	10%	11%	12%	13%	14%	15%
1	0.9901	0.9804	0.9709	0.9615	0.9524	0.9434	0.9346	0.9259	0.9174	0.9091	0.9009	0.8929	0.8850	0.8772	0.8696
2	1.9704	1.9416	1.9135	1.8861	1.8594	1.8334	1.8080	1.7833	1.7591	1.7355	1.7125	1.6901	1.6681	1.6467	1.6257
3	2.9410	2.8839	2.8286	2.7751	2.7232	2.6730	2.6243	2.5771	2.5313	2.4869	2.4437	2.4018	2.3612	2.3216	2.2832
4	3.9020	3.8077	3.7171	3.6299	3.5460	3.4651	3.3872	3.3121	3.2397	3.1699	3.1024	3.0373	2.9745	2.9137	2.8550
5	4.8534	4.7135	4.5797	4.4518	4.3295	4.2124	4.1002	3.9927	3.8897	3.7908	3.6959	3.6048	3.5172	3.4331	3.3522
6	5.7955	5.6014	5.4172	5.2421	5.0757	4.9173	4.7665	4.6229	4.4859	4.3553	4.2305	4.1114	3.9975	3.8887	3.7845
7	6.7282	6.4720	6.2303	6.0021	5.7864	5.5824	5.3893	5.2064	5.0330	4.8684	4.7122	4.5638	4.4226	4.2883	4.1604
8	7.6517	7.3255	7.0197	6.7327	6.4632	6.2098	5.9713	5.7466	5.5348	5.3349	5.1461	4.9676	4.7988	4.6389	4.4873
9	8.5660	8.1622	7.7861	7.4353	7.1078	6.8017	6.5152	6.2469	5.9952	5.7590	5.5370	5.3282	5.1317	4.9464	4.7716
10	9.4713	8.9826	8.5302	8.1109	7.7217	7.3601	7.0236	6.7101	6.4177	6.1446	5.8892	5.6502	5.4262	5.2161	5.0188
11	10.3676	9.7868	9.2526	8.7605	8.3064	7.8869	7.4987	7.1390	6.8052	6.4951	6.2065	5.9377	5.6869	5.4527	5.2337
12	11.2551	10.5753	9.9540	9.3851	8.8633	8.3838	7.9427	7.5361	7.1607	6.8137	6.4924	6.1944	5.9176	5.6603	5.4206
13	12.1337	11.3484	10.6350	9.9856	9.3936	8.8527	8.3577	7.9038	7.4869	7.1034	6.7499	6.4235	6.1218	5.8424	5.5831
14	13.0037	12.1062	11.2961	10.5631	9.8986	9.2950	8.7455	8.2442	7.7862	7.3667	6.9819	6.6282	6.3025	6.0021	5.7245
15	13.8651	12.8493	11.9379	11.1184	10.3797	9.7122	9.1079	8.5595	8.0607	7.6061	7.1909	6.8109	6.4624	6.1422	5.8474
16	14.7179	13.5777	12.5611	11.6523	10.8378	10.1059	9.4466	8.8514	8.3126	7.8237	7.3792	6.9740	6.6039	6.2651	5.9542
17	15.5623	14.2919	13.1661	12.1657	11.2741	10.4773	9.7632	9.1216	8.5436	8.0216	7.5488	7.1196	6.7291	6.3729	6.0472
18	16.3983	14.9920	13.7535	12.6593	11.6896	10.8276	10.0591	9.3719	8.7556	8.2014	7.7016	7.2497	6.8399	6.4674	6.1280
19	17.2260	15.6785	14.3238	13.1339	12.0853	11.1581	10.3356	9.6036	8.9501	8.3649	7.8393	7.3658	6.9380	6.5504	6.1982
20	18.0456	16.3514	14.8775	13.5903	12.4622	11.4699	10.5940	9.8181	9.1285	8.5136	7.9633	7.4694	7.0248	6.6231	6.2593

	Interest Rate per Year														
Number of Years	16%	17%	18%	19%	20%	21%	22%	23%	24%	25%	26%	27%	28%	29%	30%
1	0.8621	0.8547	0.8475	0.8403	0.8333	0.8264	0.8197	0.8130	0.8065	0.8000	0.7937	0.7874	0.7813	0.7752	0.7692
2	1.6052	1.5852	1.5656	1.5465	1.5278	1.5095	1.4915	1.4740	1.4568	1.4400	1.4235	1.4074	1.3916	1.3761	1.3609
3	2.2459	2.2096	2.1743	2.1399	2.1065	2.0739	2.0422	2.0114	1.9813	1.9520	1.9234	1.8956	1.8684	1.8420	1.8161
4	2.7982	2.7432	2.6901	2.6386	2.5887	2.5404	2.4936	2.4483	2.4043	2.3616	2.3202	2.2800	2.2410	2.2031	2.1662
5	3.2743	3.1993	3.1272	3.0576	2.9906	2.9260	2.8636	2.8035	2.7454	2.6893	2.6351	2.5827	2.5320	2.4830	2.4356
6	3.6847	3.5892	3.4976	3.4098	3.3255	3.2446	3.1669	3.0923	3.0205	2.9514	2.8850	2.8210	2.7594	2.7000	2.6427
7	4.0386	3.9224	3.8115	3.7057	3.6046	3.5079	3.4155	3.3270	3.2423	3.1611	3.0833	3.0087	2.9370	2.8682	2.8021
8	4.3436	4.2072	4.0776	3.9544	3.8372	3.7256	3.6193	3.5179	3.4212	3.3289	3.2407	3.1564	3.0758	2.9986	2.9247
9	4.6065	4.4506	4.3030	4.1633	4.0310	3.9054	3.7863	3.6731	3.5655	3.4631	3.3657	3.2728	3.1842	3.0997	3.0190
10	4.8332	4.6586	4.4941	4.3389	4.1925	4.0541	3.9232	3.7993	3.6819	3.5705	3.4648	3.3644	3.2689	3.1781	3.0915
11	5.0286	4.8364	4.6560	4.4865	4.3271	4.1769	4.0354	3.9018	3.7757	3.6564	3.5435	3.4365	3.3351	3.2388	3.1473
12	5.1971	4.9884	4.7932	4.6105	4.4392	4.2784	4.1274	3.9852	3.8514	3.7251	3.6059	3.4933	3.3868	3.2859	3.1903
13	5.3423	5.1183	4.9095	4.7147	4.5327	4.3624	4.2028	4.0530	3.9124	3.7801	3.6555	3.5381	3.4272	3.3224	3.2233
14	5.4675	5.2293	5.0081	4.8023	4.6106	4.4317	4.2646	4.1082	3.9616	3.8241	3.6949	3.5733	3.4587	3.3507	3.2487
15	5.5755	5.3242	5.0916	4.8759	4.6755	4.4890	4.3152	4.1530	4.0013	3.8593	3.7261	3.6010	3.4834	3.3726	3.2682
16	5.6685	5.4053	5.1624	4.9377	4.7296	4.5364	4.3567	4.1894	4.0333	3.8874	3.7509	3.6228	3.5026	3.3896	3.2832
17	5.7487	5.4746	5.2223	4.9897	4.7746	4.5755	4.3908	4.2190	4.0591	3.9099	3.7705	3.6400	3.5177	3.4028	3.2948
18	5.8178	5.5339	5.2732	5.0333	4.8122	4.6079	4.4187	4.2431	4.0799	3.9279	3.7861	3.6536	3.5294	3.4130	3.3037
19	5.8775	5.5845	5.3162	5.0700	4.8435	4.6346	4.4415	4.2627	4.0967	3.9424	3.7985	3.6642	3.5386	3.4210	3.3105
20	5.9288	5.6278	5.3527	5.1009	4.8696	4.6567	4.4603	4.2786	4.1103	3.9539	3.8083	3.6726	3.5458	3.4271	3.3158

TABLE A.4 Annuity table: Future value of $1 per year for each of t years $= [(1 + r)^t - 1]/r$

	Interest Rate per Year														
Number of Years	1%	2%	3%	4%	5%	6%	7%	8%	9%	10%	11%	12%	13%	14%	15%
1	1.0000	1.0000	1.0000	1.0000	1.0000	1.0000	1.0000	1.0000	1.0000	1.0000	1.0000	1.0000	1.0000	1.0000	1.0000
2	2.0100	2.0200	2.0300	2.0400	2.0500	2.0600	2.0700	2.0800	2.0900	2.1000	2.1100	2.1200	2.1300	2.1400	2.1500
3	3.0301	3.0604	3.0909	3.1216	3.1525	3.1836	3.2149	3.2464	3.2781	3.3100	3.3421	3.3744	3.4069	3.4396	3.4725
4	4.0604	4.1216	4.1836	4.2465	4.3101	4.3746	4.4399	4.5061	4.5731	4.6410	4.7097	4.7793	4.8498	4.9211	4.9934
5	5.1010	5.2040	5.3091	5.4163	5.5256	5.6371	5.7507	5.8666	5.9847	6.1051	6.2278	6.3528	6.4803	6.6101	6.7424
6	6.1520	6.3081	6.4684	6.6330	6.8019	6.9753	7.1533	7.3359	7.5233	7.7156	7.9129	8.1152	8.3227	8.5355	8.7537
7	7.2135	7.4343	7.6625	7.8983	8.1420	8.3938	8.6540	8.9228	9.2004	9.4872	9.7833	10.0890	10.4047	10.7305	11.0668
8	8.2857	8.5830	8.8923	9.2142	9.5491	9.8975	10.2598	10.6366	11.0285	11.4359	11.8594	12.2997	12.7573	13.2328	13.7268
9	9.3685	9.7546	10.1591	10.5828	11.0266	11.4913	11.9780	12.4876	13.0210	13.5795	14.1640	14.7757	15.4157	16.0853	16.7858
10	10.4622	10.9497	11.4639	12.0061	12.5779	13.1808	13.8164	14.4866	15.1929	15.9374	16.7220	17.5487	18.4197	19.3373	20.3037
11	11.5668	12.1687	12.8078	13.4864	14.2068	14.9716	15.7836	16.6455	17.5603	18.5312	19.5614	20.6546	21.8143	23.0445	24.3493
12	12.6825	13.4121	14.1920	15.0258	15.9171	16.8699	17.8885	18.9771	20.1407	21.3843	22.7132	24.1331	25.6502	27.2707	29.0017
13	13.8093	14.6803	15.6178	16.6268	17.7130	18.8821	20.1406	21.4953	22.9534	24.5227	26.2116	28.0291	29.9847	32.0887	34.3519
14	14.9474	15.9739	17.0863	18.2919	19.5986	21.0151	22.5505	24.2149	26.0192	27.9750	30.0949	32.3926	34.8827	37.5811	40.5047
15	16.0969	17.2934	18.5989	20.0236	21.5786	23.2760	25.1290	27.1521	29.3609	31.7725	34.4054	37.2797	40.4175	43.8424	47.5804
16	17.2579	18.6393	20.1569	21.8245	23.6575	25.6725	27.8881	30.3243	33.0034	35.9497	39.1899	42.7533	46.6717	50.9804	55.7175
17	18.4304	20.0121	21.7616	23.6975	25.8404	28.2129	30.8402	33.7502	36.9737	40.5447	44.5008	48.8837	53.7391	59.1176	65.0751
18	19.6147	21.4123	23.4144	25.6454	28.1324	30.9057	33.9990	37.4502	41.3013	45.5992	50.3959	55.7497	61.7251	68.3941	75.8364
19	20.8109	22.8406	25.1169	27.6712	30.5390	33.7600	37.3790	41.4463	46.0185	51.1591	56.9395	63.4397	70.7494	78.9692	88.2118
20	22.0190	24.2974	26.8704	29.7781	33.0660	36.7856	40.9955	45.7620	51.1601	57.2750	64.2028	72.0524	80.9468	91.0249	102.4436

	Interest Rate per Year														
Number of Years	16%	17%	18%	19%	20%	21%	22%	23%	24%	25%	26%	27%	28%	29%	30%
1	1.0000	1.0000	1.0000	1.0000	1.0000	1.0000	1.0000	1.0000	1.0000	1.0000	1.0000	1.0000	1.0000	1.0000	1.0000
2	2.1600	2.1700	2.1800	2.1900	2.2000	2.2100	2.2200	2.2300	2.2400	2.2500	2.2600	2.2700	2.2800	2.2900	2.3000
3	3.5056	3.5389	3.5724	3.6061	3.6400	3.6741	3.7084	3.7429	3.7776	3.8125	3.8476	3.8829	3.9184	3.9541	3.9900
4	5.0665	5.1405	5.2154	5.2913	5.3680	5.4457	5.5242	5.6038	5.6842	5.7656	5.8480	5.9313	6.0156	6.1008	6.1870
5	6.8771	7.0144	7.1542	7.2966	7.4416	7.5892	7.7396	7.8926	8.0484	8.2070	8.3684	8.5327	8.6999	8.8700	9.0431
6	8.9775	9.2068	9.4420	9.6830	9.9299	10.1830	10.4423	10.7079	10.9801	11.2588	11.5442	11.8366	12.1359	12.4423	12.7560
7	11.4139	11.7720	12.1415	12.5227	12.9159	13.3214	13.7396	14.1708	14.6153	15.0735	15.5458	16.0324	16.5339	17.0506	17.5828
8	14.2401	14.7733	15.3270	15.9020	16.4991	17.1189	17.7623	18.4300	19.1229	19.8419	20.5876	21.3612	22.1634	22.9953	23.8577
9	17.5185	18.2847	19.0859	19.9234	20.7989	21.7139	22.6700	23.6690	24.7125	25.8023	26.9404	28.1287	29.3692	30.6639	32.0150
10	21.3215	22.3931	23.5213	24.7089	25.9587	27.2738	28.6574	30.1128	31.6434	33.2529	34.9449	36.7235	38.5926	40.5564	42.6195
11	25.7329	27.1999	28.7551	30.4035	32.1504	34.0013	35.9620	38.0388	40.2379	42.5661	45.0306	47.6388	50.3985	53.3178	56.4053
12	30.8502	32.8239	34.9311	37.1802	39.5805	42.1416	44.8737	47.7877	50.8950	54.2077	57.7386	61.5013	65.5100	69.7800	74.3270
13	36.7862	39.4040	42.2187	45.2445	48.4966	51.9913	55.7459	59.7788	64.1097	68.7596	73.7506	79.1066	84.8529	91.0161	97.6250
14	43.6720	47.1027	50.8180	54.8409	59.1959	63.9095	69.0100	74.5280	80.4961	86.9495	93.9258	101.4654	109.6117	118.4108	127.9125
15	51.6595	56.1101	60.9653	66.2607	72.0351	78.3305	85.1922	92.6694	100.8151	109.6868	119.3465	129.8611	141.3029	153.7500	167.2863
16	60.9250	66.6488	72.9390	79.8502	87.4421	95.7799	104.9345	114.9834	126.0108	138.1085	151.3766	165.9236	181.8677	199.3374	218.4722
17	71.6730	78.9792	87.0680	96.0218	105.9306	116.8937	129.0201	142.4295	157.2534	173.6357	191.7345	211.7230	233.7907	258.1453	285.0139
18	84.1407	93.4056	103.7403	115.2659	128.1167	142.4413	158.4045	176.1883	195.9942	218.0446	242.5855	269.8882	300.2521	334.0074	371.5180
19	98.6032	110.2846	123.4135	138.1664	154.7400	173.3540	194.2535	217.7116	244.0328	273.5558	306.6577	343.7580	385.3227	431.8696	483.9734
20	115.3797	130.0329	146.6280	165.4180	186.6880	210.7584	237.9893	268.7853	303.6006	342.9447	387.3887	437.5726	494.2131	558.1118	630.1655

Glossary

A

acquisition   Takeover of a firm by purchase of that firm's common stock or assets.

additional paid-in capital   Difference between issue price and par value of stock. Also called *capital surplus.*

agency cost   Value lost from agency problems or from the cost of mitigating agency problems.

agency problem   Managers are agents for stockholders and are tempted to act in their own interests rather than maximizing value.

aging schedule   Classification of accounts receivable by time outstanding.

annual percentage rate (APR)   Interest rate that is annualized in the United States using simple interest.

annuity   Level stream of cash flows at regular intervals with a finite maturity.

annuity due   Level stream of cash flows starting immediately.

annuity factor   Present value of an annuity of $1 per period.

authorized share capital   Maximum number of shares that the company is permitted to issue without shareholder approval.

Automated Clearing House (ACH)   An electronic network for cash transfers in the United States.

average tax rate   Total taxes owed divided by total income.

B

balance sheet   Financial statement that shows the firm's assets and liabilities at a particular time.

balancing item   Variable that adjusts to maintain the consistency of a financial plan. Also called *plug.*

bankruptcy   The reorganization or liquidation of a firm that cannot pay its debts.

beta   Sensitivity of a stock's return to the return on the market portfolio.

bond   Security that obligates the issuer to make specified payments to the bondholder.

book value   Net worth of the firm according to the balance sheet.

break-even analysis   Analysis of the level of sales at which the project breaks even.

business risk   See *operating risk.*

C

call option   Right to buy an asset at a specified exercise price on or before the expiration date.

callable bond   Bond that may be repurchased by the issuing firm before maturity at a specified call price.

capital asset pricing model (CAPM)   Theory of the relationship between risk and return which states that the expected risk

premium on any security equals its beta times the market risk premium.

capital budget   List of planned investment projects.

capital budgeting decision   Decision to invest in tangible or intangible assets. Also called *capital expenditure (CAPEX) decision.*

capital budgeting or capital expenditure (CAPEX) decision   See *capital budgeting decision.*

capital markets   Markets for long-term financing.

capital rationing   Limit set on the amount of funds available for investment.

capital structure   The mix of long-term debt and equity financing.

CAPM   See *capital asset pricing model.*

cash conversion period   See *cash cycle.*

cash cycle   Period between a firm's payment for materials and cash receipts from sales. Also called *cash conversion period.*

cash dividend   Payment of cash by the firm to its shareholders.

chief financial officer (CFO)   Supervises all financial functions and sets overall financial strategy.

collection policy   Procedures to collect and monitor receivables.

commercial paper   Short-term unsecured notes issued by firms.

common stock   Ownership shares in a publicly held corporation.

common-size balance sheet   All items in the balance sheet are expressed as a percentage of total assets.

common-size income statement   All items on the income statement are expressed as a percentage of revenues.

company cost of capital   Opportunity cost of capital for investment in the firm as a whole. The company cost of capital is the appropriate discount rate for an average-risk investment project undertaken by the firm.

compound interest   Interest earned on interest.

concentration account   System whereby customers make payments to a regional collection center which transfers funds to a principal bank.

constant-growth dividend discount model   Version of the dividend discount model in which expected dividends grow at a constant rate.

consumer credit   Bills awaiting payment from the final customer to a company.

controller   Responsible for budgeting, accounting, and taxes.

convertible bond   Bond that the holder may exchange for a specified amount of another security.

corporate governance   The laws, regulations, institutions, and corporate practices that protect shareholders and other investors.

corporation   A business organized as a separate legal entity owned by stockholders.

cost of capital   Minimum acceptable rate of return on capital investment.

costs of financial distress   Costs arising from bankruptcy or distorted business decisions before bankruptcy.

coupon   The interest payments paid to the bondholder.

coupon rate   Annual interest payment as a percentage of face value.

credit analysis   Procedure to determine the likelihood a customer will pay its debts.

credit policy   Standards set to determine the amount and nature of credit to extend to customers.

credit risk   See *default risk*.

cumulative voting   Voting system in which all the votes a shareholder is allowed to cast can be cast for one candidate for the board of directors.

current yield   Annual coupon payment divided by bond price.

D

debt overhang   Firms threatened with default may pass up positive-NPV projects because bondholders capture part of the value added.

decision tree   Diagram of sequential decisions and possible outcomes.

default premium   The additional yield on a bond that investors require for bearing credit risk.

default risk   The risk that a bond issuer may default on its bonds. Also called *credit risk*.

degree of operating leverage (DOL)   Percentage change in profits given a 1% change in sales.

depreciation tax shield   Reduction in taxes attributable to depreciation.

derivatives   Contracts such as options and futures, whose payoffs are determined by the values of other financial variables.

discount factor   Present value of a $1 future payment.

discount rate   Interest rate used to compute present values of future cash flows.

discounted cash flow (DCF)   Method of calculating present value by discounting future cash flows.

diversification   Strategy designed to reduce risk by spreading the portfolio across many investments.

dividend discount model   Discounted cash-flow model that states that today's stock price equals the present value of all expected future dividends.

Dow Jones Industrial Average   Index of the investment performance of a portfolio of 30 "blue-chip" stocks.

Du Pont formula   ROA equals the product of asset turnover and operating profit margin.

E

economic value added (EVA)   Net income minus a charge for the cost of capital employed. Also called *residual income*.

effective annual interest rate   Interest rate that is annualized using compound interest.

efficient market   Market in which prices reflect all available information.

equivalent annual annuity   The cash flow per period with the same present value as the cost of buying and operating a machine.

eurobond   Bond denominated in a currency not of the country in which it is issued.

eurodollars   Dollars held on deposit in a bank outside the United States.

ex-dividend   Without the dividend. Buyer of a stock after the ex-dividend date does not receive the most recently declared dividend.

exchange rate   Amount of one currency needed to purchase one unit of another.

expectations theory of exchange rates   Theory that the expected spot exchange rate equals the forward rate.

F

face value   Payment at the maturity of the bond. Also called *principal* or *par value*.

financial assets   Financial claims to the income generated by the firm's real assets.

financial deficit   Difference between the cash companies need and the amount generated internally.

financial institution   A bank, insurance company, or similar financial intermediary.

financial intermediary   An organization that raises money from investors and provides financing for individuals, corporations, or other organizations.

financial leverage   Debt financing. Leverage amplifies the effects of changes in operating income on the returns to stockholders.

financial market   Market where securities are issued and traded.

financial risk   Risk to shareholders resulting from the use of debt.

financial slack   Ready access to cash or debt financing.

financing decision   Decision on the sources and amounts of financing.

fixed costs   Costs that do not depend on the level of output.

fixed-income market   Market for debt securities.

floating-rate preferred   Preferred stock for which the dividend rate is linked to current market interest rates

flotation costs   The costs incurred when a firm issues new securities to the public.

forward contract   Agreement to buy or sell an asset in the future at an agreed price.

forward exchange rate   Exchange rate agreed today for a future transaction.

free cash flow (FCF)   Cash flow available for distribution to investors after firm pays for new investments or additions to working capital.

free-cash-flow problem   Companies with ample cash flow are tempted to overinvest and to operate inefficiently. Companies facing this problem may benefit from the discipline imposed by more debt and higher debt-service requirements.

funded debt Debt with more than 1 year remaining to maturity.

future value (FV) Amount to which an investment will grow after earning interest.

futures contract Exchange-traded promise to buy or sell an asset in the future at a prespecified price.

G

GAAP See *generally accepted accounting principles.*

general cash offer Sale of securities open to all investors by an already-public company.

generally accepted accounting principles (GAAP) U.S. procedures for preparing financial statements.

H

hedge fund Private investment fund that pursues complex, high-risk investment strategies.

I

income statement Financial statement that shows the revenues, expenses, and net income of a firm over a period of time.

inflation Rate at which prices as a whole are increasing.

information content of dividends Dividend increases convey managers' confidence about future cash flow and earnings. Dividend cuts convey lack of confidence and therefore are bad news.

initial public offering (IPO) First offering of stock to the general public.

interest rate parity Theory that forward premium equals the interest rate differential.

interest rate risk The risk in bond prices due to fluctuations in interest rates.

interest tax shield Tax savings resulting from deductibility of interest payments.

internal growth rate Maximum rate of growth without external financing.

internal rate of return (IRR) Discount rate at which project NPV = 0.

internally generated funds Cash reinvested in the firm; depreciation plus earnings not paid out as dividends.

international Fisher effect Theory that real interest rates in all countries should be equal, with differences in nominal rates reflecting differences in expected inflation.

intrinsic value Present value of future cash payoffs from a stock or other security.

investment grade Bonds rated Baa or above by Moody's or BBB or above by Standard & Poor's or Fitch.

investment opportunity frontier Plot of the combinations of expected return versus standard deviation for various portfolio weights.

IPO See *initial public offering.*

IRR See *internal rate of return.*

issued shares Shares that have been issued by the company.

J

junk bond Bond with a rating below Baa or BBB.

just-in-time approach System of inventory management that requires minimum inventories of materials and very frequent deliveries by suppliers.

L

law of one price Theory that prices of goods in all countries should be equal when translated to a common currency, or, more generally, that two assets providing the same cash flows cannot sell for different prices.

lease Long-term rental agreement.

leveraged buyout (LBO) Acquisition of a firm by a private group using substantial borrowed funds.

limited liability The owners of a corporation are not personally liable for its obligations.

liquidation Sale of bankrupt firm's assets.

liquidation value Net proceeds that could be realized by selling the firm's assets and paying off its creditors.

liquidity The ability to sell an asset on short notice at close to the market value.

loan covenant Agreement between firm and lender requiring the firm to fulfill certain conditions to safeguard the loan.

lock-box system System whereby customers send payments to a post-office box and a local bank collects and processes checks.

M

majority voting Voting system in which each director is voted on separately.

management buyout (MBO) Acquisition of the firm by its own management in a leveraged buyout.

marginal tax rate Additional taxes owed per dollar of additional income.

market capitalization Total market value of equity, equal to share price times number of shares outstanding.

market index Measure of the investment performance of the overall market.

market portfolio Portfolio of all assets in the economy. In practice a broad stock market index is used to represent the market.

market risk Economywide (macroeconomic) sources of risk that affect the overall stock market. Also called *systematic risk.*

market risk premium Risk premium of market portfolio. Difference between market return and return on risk-free Treasury bills.

market value The current price of an asset or liability.

market value added   Market capitalization minus book value of equity.

market-to-book ratio   Ratio of market value of equity to book value of equity.

market-value balance sheet   Balance sheet showing market rather than book values of assets, liabilities, and stockholders' equity.

maturity premium   Extra annual return from investing in long- versus short-term Treasury securities.

merger   Combination of two firms into one, with the acquirer assuming assets and liabilities of the target firm.

MM's dividend-irrelevance proposition   Under idealized conditions, the value of the firm is unaffected by dividend policy.

MM's proposition I (debt-irrelevance proposition)   Under idealized conditions the value of a firm is unaffected by its capital structure.

MM's proposition II   The required rate of return on equity increases as the firm's debt-equity ratio increases.

modified accelerated cost recovery system (MACRS) Depreciation method that allows higher tax deductions in early years and lower deductions later.

money market   Market for short-term financing (less than 1 year).

mutual fund   An investment company that pools the savings of many investors and invests in a portfolio of securities.

mutually exclusive projects   Two or more projects that cannot be pursued simultaneously.

N

net present value (NPV)   Present value of cash flows minus investment.

net working capital   Current assets minus current liabilities. Often called *working capital.*

net worth   Book value of common stockholders' equity plus preferred stock.

nominal interest rate   Rate at which money invested grows.

NPV break-even point   Minimum level of sales needed to cover all costs including the cost of capital.

O

open account   Agreement whereby sales on credit are made with no formal debt contract.

operating leverage   Degree to which costs are fixed.

operating profit margin   After-tax operating income as a percentage of sales.

operating risk   Risk in firm's operating income. Also called *business risk.*

opportunity cost   Benefit or cash flow forgone as a result of an action.

opportunity cost of capital   The minimum acceptable rate of return on capital investment is set by the investment opportunities available to shareholders in financial markets.

outstanding shares   Shares that have been issued by the company and are held by investors.

P

P/E ratio   Ratio of stock price to earnings per share.

par value   Value of security shown in the company's accounts.

payback period   Time until cash flows recover the initial investment in the project.

payout ratio   Fraction of earnings paid out as dividends.

pecking order theory   Firms prefer to issue debt rather than equity if internal finance is insufficient.

pension fund   Fund set up by an employer to provide for employees' retirement.

percentage of sales model   Planning model in which sales forecasts are the driving variables and most other variables are proportional to sales.

perpetuity   Stream of level cash payments that never ends.

planning horizon   Time horizon for a financial plan.

plowback ratio   Fraction of earnings retained by the firm.

poison pill   Measure taken by a target firm to avoid acquisition; for example, by granting existing shareholders the right to buy additional shares at an attractive price if a bidder acquires a large holding.

preferred stock   Stock that takes priority over common stock in regard to dividends.

present value (PV)   Value today of a future cash flow.

present value of growth opportunities (PVGO)   Net present value of a firm's future investments.

price-earnings multiple (P/E ratio)   Ratio of stock price to earnings per share.

primary market   Market for the sale of new securities by corporations.

primary offering   The corporation sells shares in the firm.

prime rate   Benchmark interest rate charged by banks.

private placement   Sale of securities to a limited number of investors without a public offering.

pro formas   Projected or forecast financial statements.

profitability index   Ratio of net present value to initial investment.

project cost of capital   Minimum acceptable expected rate of return on a project given its risk.

prospectus   Formal summary that provides information on an issue of securities.

protective covenants   Conditions imposed on borrowers to protect lenders from unreasonable risks.

proxy contest   Takeover attempt in which outsiders compete with management for shareholders' votes. Also called *proxy fight.*

purchasing power parity (PPP)   Theory that the cost of living in different countries is equal and exchange rates adjust to offset inflation differentials across countries.

put option   Right to sell an asset at a specified exercise price on or before the expiration date.

R

rate of return   Total income per period per dollar invested.

real assets   Assets used to produce goods and services.

real interest rate   Rate at which the purchasing power of an investment increases.

real options   Options to invest in, modify, postpone, or dispose of a capital investment project.

reorganization   Restructuring of financial claims on failing firm to allow it to keep operating.

restructuring   Process of changing the firm's capital structure without changing its real assets.

retained earnings   Earnings not paid out as dividends.

return on assets (ROA)   Net income plus after-tax interest as a percentage of total assets.

return on capital (ROC)   Net income plus after-tax interest as a percentage of long-term capital.

return on equity (ROE)   Net income as a percentage of shareholders' equity.

revolving line of credit   Agreement by a bank that a company may borrow at any time up to an established limit.

rights issue   Issue of securities offered only to current stockholders.

risk premium   Expected return in excess of risk-free return as compensation for risk.

risk shifting   Firms threatened with default are tempted to shift to riskier investments.

S

scenario analysis   Project analysis given different combinations of assumptions.

seasoned offering   Sale of additional securities by a firm that is already publicly traded.

secondary market   Market in which previously issued securities are traded among investors.

secured debt   Debt that, in the event of a default, has first claim on specified assets.

security market line   Relationship between expected return and beta.

sensitivity analysis   Analysis of the effects on project profitability of changes in sales, costs, and so on.

shark repellent   Amendment to a company charter made to forestall takeover attempts.

shelf registration   A procedure that allows firms to file one registration statement for several issues of the same security.

simple interest   Interest earned only on the original investment; no interest is earned on interest.

sinking fund   Fund established to retire debt before maturity.

specific risk   Risk factors affecting only that firm. Also called *diversifiable risk.*

spot price   Price paid for immediate delivery.

spot rate of exchange   Exchange rate for an immediate transaction.

spread   Difference between public offer price and price paid by underwriter.

stakeholder   Anyone with a financial interest in the corporation.

Standard & Poor's Composite Index   Index of the investment performance of a portfolio of 500 large stocks. Also called the *S&P 500.*

standard deviation   Square root of variance. A measure of volatility.

statement of cash flows   Financial statement that shows the firm's cash receipts and cash payments over a period of time.

stock dividends and splits   Distributions of additional shares to a firm's stockholders.

stock repurchase   Firm distributes cash to stockholders by repurchasing shares.

stock split   Distributions of additional shares to a firm's stockholders.

straight-line depreciation   Constant depreciation for each year of the asset's accounting life.

sustainable growth rate   The firm's growth rate if it plows back a constant fraction of earnings, maintains a constant return on equity, and keeps its debt ratio constant.

swap   Arrangement by two counterparties to exchange one stream of cash flows for another.

T

tender offer   Takeover attempt in which outsiders directly offer to buy the stock of the firm's shareholders.

terms of sale   Credit, discount, and payment terms offered on a sale.

trade credit   Bills awaiting payment from one company to another.

trade-off theory   Debt levels are chosen to balance interest tax shields against the costs of financial distress.

treasurer   Responsible for financing, cash management, and relationships with banks and other financial institutions.

treasury stock   Stock that has been repurchased by the company and is held in its treasury.

U

underpricing   Issuing securities at an offering price set below the true value of the security.

underwriter   Firm that buys an issue of securities from a company and resells it to the public.

V

variable costs   Costs that change as the level of output changes.

variance   Average value of squared deviations from mean. A measure of volatility.

venture capital   Money invested to finance a new firm.

W

WACC See *weighted-average cost of capital.*

warrant Right to buy shares from a company at a stipulated price before a set date.

weighted-average cost of capital (WACC) Expected rate of return on a portfolio of all the firm's securities, adjusted for tax savings due to interest payments. WACC is the correct discount rate for projects that have similar risks to the company's existing business.

workout Agreement between a financially distressed company and its creditors establishing the steps the company must take to avoid bankruptcy.

Y

yield curve Plot of relationship between bond yields to maturity and time to maturity.

yield to maturity Discount rate at which the present value of the bond's payments equals the price.

Global Index

A

Actavis, 612, 620, 626, 630
Airbus, 14
Altice, 512, 613
Anglo Platinum, 595
Antitrust laws, 619–620
Argentina, default on bonds, 183
Aristotle, 24
Australia
  bank loans, 98
  corporate governance, 18
  exchange rate Dec. 2015, 640
  financial reporting
    standards, 72
  Gorgon natural gas project, 6,
    24, 239
  Macquarrie Bank, 42, 43
  National Safety Council, 598
  political risk score, 655
  risk premium, 338
Autonomy, 6, 71
Avago Technologies, 512
Axa, 434
Azerbaijani central bank, 642

B

Banco Central Hispanico, 617
Banco Santander, 617
Bank loans, Australia, 598
Bank mergers
  Europe, 617
  Japan, 614
Bank of China, 430
Bankruptcy, Parmalat, 25
Banque Paribas, 617
Barclays Bank, 17, 595
  rights issue, 451
  as underwriter, 450
Barings Brothers Bank collapse,
  25, 706
Barrick, 17
Belgium, risk premium, 338
Big Mac index, 644
Black, Conrad, 16, 17
BNP, 617
BNP Paribas, 430
Board of directors, 17
  France, 18
  Germany, 18
Bonds, in Italy, 126n
Brazil
  10-year interest rate, 639
  exchange rate Dec. 2015, 640
  financial reporting
    standards, 72
  payment systems, 591
  political risk score, 655
British Salt, 613
Buying forward, 642

C

Canada
  CEOs and chairpersons, 427
  corporate governance, 18
  exchange rate Dec. 2015, 640
  financial reporting standards, 72
  Hudson's Bay Company, 9
  payment systems, 591
  risk premium, 338
  Valeant, 626–627
Capital budgeting; see
    International capital
    budgeting
Capital investment, 639
Capital market equilibrium, 648
Capital markets, 38
  few national boundaries,
    431–432
Carrefour, 17
Cartier, 652n
Cash flows
  adjusting, 657
  expected, 657
  hedged, 654
  in international capital
    budgeting, 653–654
Caue Itabriitos iron-ore project, 5
Channel Tunnel, 24
China
  exchange rate Dec. 2015, 640
  financial reporting
    standards, 72
  and iron ore prices, 705
  political risk score, 655
  rare earth metals, 320
China Telecom, 37
Citicorp, 430
Coca-Cola Company, overseas
    business, 639
Code of Hammurabi, 24
Columbia Pipeline Group, 5
Commerzbank, 617
Compound growth, 24
Conrad, Joseph, 656n
Consols, 135–136
Corporate governance
  Australia, 18
  Canada, 18
  Europe, 18
  Germany, 18
  Japan, 18
  United Kingdom, 18
Corporate scandal, Australia, 598
Corus Steel, 613
Cost of capital
  automatic increases in, 656
  in international capital
    budgeting, 656
Covered foreign interest rate, 651n
Covered interest rate parity, 650, 652

Covidien, 512
Credit Suisse, as underwriter, 449
Cross-rates, 641n
Currency appreciation, 642
Currency depreciation, 642
Currency risk, 651

D

Daimler-Benz, failed merger,
  613–614
Danone, 619
Dasault Falcon jets, 5
Default
  Argentine bonds, 183
  by Greece, 25
  on loans, 648
  on microloans, 36
Denmark, risk premium, 338
Deutsche Bank, 37, 45, 430
  as underwriter, 449
Deutsche Börse, 37, 619
Dimsom, Elroy, 647n
Direct quote, 640
Discount rate
  fudge factors, 657
  national 10-year differences,
    639
Diversifiable risk, 656
Dojima Rice Market, 24
Dresdner Bank, 617
Dunhill, 652n

E

East India Company, 2
Economic risk, 651, 652
EDF, 430
Erb, C., 655n
Euribor, 586
Euro, 25, 432, 595–596
  decline in 2015, 646
  and Swiss franc, 652
Euro interbank offered rate, 586
Eurobonds, 432
Eurodollar market, 24, 596
Eurodollars, 431, 595–596
Euronext, 198
Europe
  antitrust laws, 619–620
  bank mergers, 617
  corporate governance, 18
  coupon payments, 171
  euro currency, 432
  exchange rates Dec. 2015, 640
  factoring in, 585
  in financial crisis of 2007–2009,
    50–51
European Central Bank, 51
European Commission, 619

European Monetary Union, 25, 595
European Union
  central banks and gold sales,
    694
  financial reporting standards, 73
  principles-based accounting, 73
Euroyen, 431, 586
Exchange rate fluctuations
  coping with, 643
  effect on companies, 639
Exchange rate risk; see also
    Currency risk
  avoiding, 642
Exchange rates
  Big Mac index, 644–645
  cross-rates, 641
  definition, 640
  expectations theory of, 649–650
  expected spot rate, 649–650
  fixed, 642
  floating, 642
  forecasting, 646, 654
  forward rate, 642–643, 649–650
  futures market, 643
  indirect, 645n
  inflation and interest rates,
    646–649
  and interest rates, 650–651
  international Fisher effect, 648
  and law of one price, 644
  nominal rate, 646
  purchasing power parity, 645
  quotations for Dec. 2015, 640
  real rate, 646
  spot rate, 640–642
  yen and dollar, 641
Expectations theory of exchange
    rates, 649–650
Expected inflation, 648
Expected return, 655
Expropriation risk, 655, 656

F

Factoring, 585
FedEx, international expansion,
  4–5
Ferrari, 37
Fidelity Investments, 40
Financial hedge, 652
Financial managers
  coping with exchange rate
    fluctuations, 643
  and exchange rates, 639
  hedging currency risk,
    651–652
  hedging exchange rate risk, 560
  marking up required returns,
    656
  and nominal vs. real interest
    rate, 646

Financial markets
    capital markets, 38
    fixed-income markets, 38
    microfinance, 36
    money markets, 38
Financial Times Company, 333
Financial Times Stock Exchange,
    333
Finland, risk premium, 338
Fisher, Irving, 648
Fixed exchange rates, 642
Fixed-income markets, 38
Floating exchange rates, 642
Ford Motor Company, overseas
    operations, 655
Forecasting
    change in spot rate, 645
    exchange rates, 654
    inflation rate, 645
Foreign exchange markets, 38
    buying forward, 642–643
    case, 663
    conducted via computers or
        telephones, 640
    cross-rates, 641
    currency appreciation, 642
    currency depreciation, 642
    daily turnover, 640
    direct quote, 640
    exchange rate fluctuations, 649
    exchange rates quoted against
        dollar, 641
    expectations theory of exchange
        rates, 649–650
    expected spot rate, 649–650
    fixed exchange rates, 642
    floating exchange rates, 642
    forward contract, 642
    forward premium, 642
    forward rate, 642–643, 649–650
    forward rate vs. spot rate, 650n
    futures market, 643
    hedging in
        economic risk, 651, 652
        factors favoring, 652
        financial hedge, 652
        forward hedge, 652
        interest rate parity, 652
        operational hedge, 652
        transactions risk, 651–652
    indirect quote, 640
    interest rate parity, 651
    and interest rates, 650–651
    international Fisher effect, 648
    liquidity in, 46
    quotations for Dec. 2015, 640
    setting forward rate, 651
    spot exchange rate, 640–642
    spread, 641n
Foreign investment
    capital cost of, 656
    and net present value, 653
    political risk, 655–656
    required return, 656
Forward contract, 642
Forward discount, 642

Forward exchange rate
    definition, 642
    expectations theory, 649–650
    and expected spot rate, 649–650
    financial manager understanding
        of, 643
    forward premium, 642
    in hedging, 652
    interest rate parity, 651
    and interest rates, 650–651
    in international capital
        budgeting, 653–654
    simple theories, 644
    spot rate understated by, 650n
Forward premium, 642
France
    Axa, 434
    boards of directors, 18
    EDF, 430
    identification of corporations,
        8n
    Lafarge, 512
    nominal vs. real exchange rate,
        647
    payment systems, 590, 591
    political risk score, 655
    risk premium, 338
    SFR, 512
    Société Générale losses, 706
Frankfurt stock exchange, 198
Friedrich, John, 598
Froot, K. A., 650n
Fudge factors, 656–657
Futures contracts, 643
Futures market, 24, 643

G

Germany
    boards of directors, 18
    corporate governance, 18
    identification of corporations,
        8n
    payment systems, 591
    political risk score, 655
    risk premium, 338
    Volkswagen, 19
Gold price, 644
Gold sales, by European central
    banks, 694
Gorgon natural gas project, 6, 24,
    239
Greece
    10-year interest rate, 639
    debt default, 25
    in financial crisis of 2007–2009,
        50–51
Gresham's law, 2

H

Harvey, Campbell R., 655n
HBOS
    rights issue, 451
    share issue, 450

Heathrow Airport, 5
Hedged cash flows, 654
Hedging
    currency risk
        economic risk, 652
        factors favoring, 652
        financial hedge, 652
        by financial managers, 650
        operational hedge, 652
        transaction risk, 651–652
    in international capital
        budgeting, 654
Holcim, 512
Holland, 430
Hollinger International, 16, 17
Hong Kong, 22
    exchange rate Dec. 2015, 640
Hope, Anthony, 640n
HSBC, 24, 430
    as underwriter, 450
Hudson's Bay Company, 9
Hujdur, Vahid, 36
Hungary, inflation in, 25

I

India
    exchange rate Dec. 2015, 640
    financial reporting
        standards, 72
    payment systems, 591
    political risk score, 655
Indirect exchange rate, 645n
Indirect quote, 640
Indonesia, copper mine, 701
Inflation
    Big Mac index, 644–645
    and exchange rates, 643–646
    expected, 648
    in Hungary, 25
    and interest rates, 646–649
    international Fisher effect, 648
    law of one price, 644
    purchasing power parity, 645
    in Venezuela, 25
    in Yugoslavia, 25
Inflation rate
    Switzerland 2011–2014, 649
    Venezuela 2011–2014, 649
Inflation-indexed debt, 25
Intercontinental Exchange, 38
Interest rate parity, 651, 652
Interest rates, 430
    euro interbank offered rate, 586
    and exchange rates, 650–651
    and inflation, 646–649
    international Fisher effect, 648
    London Interbank Offered Rate,
        586, 597, 702–703
    microloans, 36
    national 10-year differences,
        639
    national differences, 639
    nominal vs. real, 646
    risk-adjusted, 654

International Accounting Standard
    Board, 72
International banking, 24, 586
International capital budgeting,
    639
    avoiding fudge factors, 656–657
    cash flows, 653–654
    cost of capital, 655
    and forward exchange rate,
        653–654
    net present value analysis,
        653–654
    political risk, 655–656
International capital markets
    currency risk, 651
    economic risk, 51, 652
    transaction risk, 651–652
International cash management,
    592–593
International financial management
    basic relationships
        exchange rates and inflation,
            643–646
        expectations theory, 649–650
        expected spot rate, 640–650
        forward rate, 649–650
        inflation and interest rates,
            646–649
        interest rate parity, 651
        interest rates and exchange
            rates, 650–651
        international Fisher effect,
            648
        law of one price, 644
        purchasing power parity,
            644–645
        questions for financial
            managers, 639
        real vs. nominal exchange
            rates, 646–647
    capital budgeting, 653–657
    case, 663
    foreign exchange markets,
        640–643
    hedging currency risk, 651–652
International Financial Reporting
    Standards, 72, 73
International Fisher effect, 648
International Monetary Fund,
    25, 51
International money market,
    595–596
Investment decisions
    Channel Tunnel, 24
    Gorgon natural gas project, 24
    for selected companies, 5
    Toyota, 275
    Virgin Atlantic Airlines, 14
Investors, worldwide, 36
Ireland
    Actavis, 612, 620, 626, 630
    Covidien, 512
    in financial crisis of 2007–2009,
        51
    risk premium, 338
    Warner-Chilcott, 620

Iron ore prices, and China, 705
Israel
    inflation-indexed debt, 25
    Pebbles, 5
Italy
    government borrowing, 126,
        127–128
    Medici empire, 24
    nominal *vs.* real exchange rate,
        647
    Parmalat bankruptcy, 72
    payment systems, 591
    risk premium, 338

J

Jaguar Land Rover, 613
Japan
    bank mergers, 615
    corporate governance, 18
    Dojima Rice Market, 24
    exchange rate Dec. 2015, 640
    money market, 596
    Nikkei index, 226
    political risk score, 655
    real estate bubble, 222–227
    risk premium, 338
    stock market bubble, 226
    Tokugawa era, 24
Joint stock companies, 24
JPMorgan Chase, 595
Just-in-time systems, 587–588

K

Kerviel, Jérôme, 706
Korean Air, 319

L

Lafarge, 512
Latin Monetary Union, 25
Law of one price, 644
Leeson, Nick, 25, 706
Loans, default on, 648
London, 22
    banks in, 430
    foreign exchange markets, 640
    Heathrow Airport, 5
    international banks, 586
London Interbank Offered Rate,
    430, 586, 597, 702–703
London stock exchange, 198
Luxota, 5
LVMH, 5

M

Macquarrie Bank, 42, 43
Maldives, 198
Manchester United, 37
Marsh, Paul R., 647n
Medici empire, 24

Mergers, global value of, 611
Mexico
    exchange rate Dec. 2015, 640
    oil prices, 696, 697
Micro loans, 36
Mises, Ludwig von, 640n
Mitsubishi UFJ, 430
Mizuho Bank, 615
Money
    in 17th century, 24
    Gresham's law, 24
Money market interest, 649
Money markets, 38
    international, 595–596
    Japan, 586
Mongolia, tugrik, 119n
Morgan Stanley Capital
    International, 333
Multinational companies, political
    risk for, 656

N

National Safety Council, Australia,
    598
Nestlé, 652
Net present value in international
    capital budgeting, 653–654
Netherlands
    Altice, 512
    payment systems, 591
    risk premium, 338
New Zealand, risk premium, 338
Nikkei index, 226, 333
Nokia, 613
Nominal exchange rate
    definition, 646
    in France, 647
    in Italy, 647
    in United Kingdom, 647
Nominal interest rate, 646
Nomura, 43
Norway
    political risk score, 655
    risk premium, 338
Novartis, 37

O

Oil prices
    decline, 642
    and Pemex, 696, 697
Operational hedging, 652
Opportunity cost of capital, 653
Options, 24

P

Parmalat bankruptcy, 25, 72
Payment systems, for selected
    countries, 591
Pebbles, 5
Pemex, 696, 697
Perpetuities, 135–136, 430

Petrobas, 37
Piaget, 652n
Poison pill, 626, 627
Political risk
    expropriation risk, 655, 656
    heavy taxes, 656
    in international capital
        budgeting, 655–656
    management's assumptions, 657
    scores for selected countries,
        655
    unanticipated government
        actions, 655
Portugal
    in financial crisis of 2007–2009,
        51
    risk premium, 337, 338
Principles-based accounting, 73
PRS Group, 655
Purchasing power parity
    Big Mac index, 644–645
    definition, 645
    real *vs.* nominal exchange rate,
        646

R

Rare earth metals, 320
Real estate bubble, Japan, 226–227
Real exchange rate
    definition, 646
    in France, 647
    in Italy, 647
    in United Kingdom, 647
Real interest rate, 646
Required return on foreign
    investments, 656
Research in Motion, 17
Rice futures, 24
Richemont, 652
Rio Tinto, 17
Risk premium, for selected
    countries, 337–338
Risk-adjusted interest rates, 654
Risk, diversifiable, 656
Rolls-Royce, 315
Russia, political risk score, 655

S

Samsung Electronics, 278
Secured loans, hazardous, 598
SFR, 512
Shire, 512
Siemens, 17
Singapore, 22
    Avago Technologies, 512
    payment systems, 591
Smith, Adam, 18
Société Générale losses, 706
Somalia, political risk score, 655
Sony Corporation, 37
South Africa
    exchange rate Dec. 2015, 640
    risk premium, 338

South Korea
    exchange rate Dec. 2015, 640
    political risk score, 655
South Sea Bubble, 24
Sovereign debt default, 25
Soviet Union, 24
Spain
    in financial crisis of 2007–2009,
        51
    risk premium, 338
Speculation
    on currency, 654
    at Société Générale, 706
    zero-sum game, 652
Spot rate of exchange
    and cross-rates, 641
    for December 2015, 640
    definition, 641
    expectations theory, 649–650
    financial manager understanding
        of, 643
    forecasting, 646
    versus forward rate, 642–643,
        649–650
    in hedging, 652
    and interest rate differences,
        650–651
    interest rate parity, 651
    overstated by forward rate, 650n
    simple theories, 644
Spread, in foreign exchange
    markets, 641n
Staunton, Mike, 647n
Stock market bubble, Japan, 226
Subsidiary corporation, 656
Swatch, 652
Sweden
    exchange rate Dec. 2015, 640
    payment systems, 590, 591
    risk premium, 338
Swiss Bank Corp., 613
Swiss francs, 430
Swiss National Bank, ending franc–
    euro exchange rate, 652
Switzerland
    10-year interest rate, 639
    exchange rate Dec. 2015, 640
    Holcim, 512
    inflation rate 2011-2014, 649
    payment systems, 590, 591
    political risk score, 655
    risk premium, 337, 338
Sykes, T., 598n

T

Tata Group, 613
Taxation, as political risk, 656
Thaler, R. H., 650n
Thales, 24
Tokyo, 22
Tokyo Gas, 615
Toyota Motor Corporation, 275,
    587–588
Trans Canada, 5

Transaction risk, 651–652
Tristar engine, 315
Tugrik, 119n

U

UBS, 430, 617
Uhlfelder, Eric, 36
Underwriters
    Barclays, 450
    Credit Suisse, 449
    Deutsche Bank, 449
    HSBC, 450
Unilever, 37
United Kingdom
    Autonomy sale to Hewlett-
        Packard, 6

banks in London, 431
Barings Brothers Bank collapse,
    25, 706
CEOs and chairpersons, 427
consols, 135–136
corporate governance, 18
exchange rate Dec. 2015, 640
HBOS, 450, 451
Heathrow Airport, 5
identification of
    corporations, 8n
inflation-indexed debt, 25
nominal *vs.* real exchange rate,
    647
payment systems, 591
perpetuities, 430
political risk score, 655

risk premium, 338
shareholders' rights, 16
Shire, 512

V

Vale, 5
Valeant, 626–627
Venezuela
    inflation in, 25
    inflation rate 2011–2014, 649
    political risk score, 655
Virgin Atlantic Airlines, 6, 38
    investment decisions, 14
    investment/financing
        decisions, 5

Virgin Media, 613
Viskanta, T., 655n
Vivendi, 72
Volkswagen, software scandal, 19

W

Wagner, Deidre, 36
Warner-Chilcott, 620
Wealth of Nations (Smith), 18n

Y

Yen, 641
Yugoslavia, inflation in, 25

Subject Index

A

Abbott Laboratories, 612
Accelerated depreciation, 20
Accounting
  calculating profits, 65
  cash *versus* accrual, 65–66
  practice and malpractice
    constant scrutiny of
      companies, 70
    convergence of standards, 72
    cookie jar reserves, 71
    Enron scandal, 71–72
    and Financial Accounting
      Standards Board, 70
    and investors, 71
    off-balance sheet assets and
      liabilities, 71
    principles-based, 72–73
    and Public Company
      Accounting Oversight
      Board, 72
    revenue recognition, 71
    rules-based, 72–73
    and Sarbanes-Oxley Act, 72
    scandals, 72
    transparency, 72
  profits adjusted, 284
Accounting break-even point,
  311–312
Accounting income *vs.* economic
  value added, 92
Accounting information, 57
Accounting profits *vs.* cash flows,
  277
Accounting rate of return
  and economic value added, 93
  problems with, 95
  return on assets, 94
  return on capital, 93–94
  return on equity, 95
Accounting standards, 18, 72
Accounting targets, 531
Accounts, dangerous, 583
Accounts payable
  on balance sheet, 59
  as current liability, 572
  as debt, 432
  payments, 57
  stretching, 557, 559
Accounts receivable
  on balance sheet, 58
  in cash budgeting, 556–557
  and credit policy, 575–585
  as current asset, 571, 572
Accounts receivable
  financing, 597
Accounts receivable period, 573
Accrual accounting, 65–66
Acid-test ratio, 104
Acin, I. F., 337n

Ackman, Bill, 628
Acquisitions; *see also* Mergers
  beneficial on balance, 631
  bootstrap game, 616–617
  to create synergy, 613
  definition, 619
  form of, 619
  as investment, 611
  and investors, 631
  management buyouts, 627
  and managers of companies not
    taken over, 632
  preceding management change,
    616
Activist shareholders, 17–18, 427
Additional paid-in capital, 425
Administrative costs, 558
After-tax cost of debt, 397
After-tax cost of debt and
  interest, 391
After-tax income, 429
After-tax interest, 92n
After-tax rate of interest, 480
After-tax rate of return, 517
Agency costs, 15, 624
Agency problems
  and activist investors, 17–18
  control of, 16
  in crisis of 2007–2009, 51
  definition, 15
  losses from, 15
  scandals, 15
  and stakeholders, 16
Agency theory, questions arising
  from, 716
Aggressive stock, 362
Aging schedule, 584
AIG, 49, 176
Airlines, macro risks, 353
Alaska Air Group, 47–48
Alcoa
  cost of capital, 93
  economic value added, 93
  long-term capital, 93
  market-to-book ratio, 90
  market value added, 90
  return on capital, 93
Alibaba, 444
Allegheny Corporation, 679
Allen, F., 401n, 480n
Allergan, 612, 628–629, 630
Allied Crude Vegetable Oil
  Refining Corporation, 597
Alphabet, 203, 506, 665, 668–669
  beta, 367
  call options, 666
  call price, 668
  exercise price, 668
  and option valuation models,
    676–677
  put options, 667

  standard deviation for common
    stock, 343
  stock prices, 666–667
  weighted average cost of
    capital, 407
Altman, Edward I., 579
Altria Group, 516
Amazon, 506
  beta, 367
  as growth company, 202–204
  market-to-book value, 204
  market *vs.* book value, 201
  price-earnings ratio, 204
  standard deviation for common
    stock, 343
  stock price, 201, 202–203
  weighted average cost of
    capital, 407
AMD, 184
American Airlines, 423
American call, 666n
American Electric Power
  market-to-book value, 204
  market *vs.* book value, 201
  price-earnings ratio, 204
  stock price, 201
American Express, 627
Amihud, Y., 510
Amortizing loan, 149
Andrade, G., 631n
Angel investors, 443
Anheuser-Busch, 612
  and SABMiller, 596
Annually compounded rate, 147
Annual percentage rate, 146–147
Annuities
  vs. annuity due future value,
    143–144
  definition, 135
  financial calculators for, 145
  future value, 140–141
  lottery winnings, 138–139
  present value, 141
  spreadsheet solutions, 145–146
  valuing, 136–139
Annuity due
  versus annuity future value, 143
  definition, 143
  future value, 143–144
  present value, 143
Annuity factor, 137
Annuity formula for coupon
  payments, 170
Annuity table, 138
Anthem, 612
Antitakeover tactics
  poison pill, 626
  shark repellent, 627
Antitrust law, and mergers, 619–620
AOL–Time Warner merger failure,
  613

Apple Inc., 20, 506, 519, 553
  bond issue, 38
  cash holdings, 516
  cash holdings 2015, 593
  cost of capital, 93
  debt issue, 432–433
  dividends in 2015, 505
  economic value added, 92–93
  financing decisions 1996–2016,
    34–35
  initial public offering, 37, 441
  investments, 593
  long-term capital, 93
  market capitalization, 34
  market-to-book ratio, 90
  market value added, 90
  retained earnings, 35
  return on capital, 93
  revenues, 36
Apple iPhone 7, 278
Approximation rule, 151
Aramark, 445
Arbitrage opportunity, 631
ARM loans, 49n
Arthur Andersen, 25
Articles of incorporation, 15
Asked price, 168, 169
Asked yield to maturity, 168, 169
Ask price, 199
Asquith, P., 452n, 508n
Asset-backed bonds, 433–434
Asset bubbles, 720
Asset risk *vs.* portfolio risk,
  343–350
Assets
  aggregate value of all, 714
  on balance sheet, 58
  and bankruptcy costs, 484–485
  book *vs.* market value, 61–63
  collateral, 185
  equivalent-risk, 714
  financial *vs.* real, 6–7
  intangible, 3, 6, 102, 119, 202,
    239
  leased, 101n, 721
  versus liabilities, 60
  liquid, 58, 103
  needed by corporations, 3
  risky *vs.* safe, 717
  tangible, 3, 6, 58, 119
  of target firm, 619
  total return swaps, 705
  underlying, 718
Asset turnover ratio, 96, 98
Asset turnover *vs.* profit margin,
  89–99
Asymmetric information, 488
AT&T, 612
Auction
  for initial public offerings, 449
  for stock repurchase, 509

Auditing oversight, 72
Authorized share capital, 425
Automated Clearing House, 592
Automatic dividend reinvestment plan, 507
Average collection period, 97
Average-risk investment projects, 391
Average tax rate, 75

B

Backup line of credit, 598
Baker, M., 508n
Balance sheet
  accounts payable, 59
  accounts receivable, 57
  asset classes, 60
  book *vs.* market value, 61–63
  common-size, 60–61
  consolidated, 58
  current assets, 58
  current liabilities, 59
  definition, 58
  depreciation, 56
  effect of transactions, 66–67
  FedEx, 201
  first-stage financing, 442
  fixed assets, 56
  goodwill on, 59
  Hewlett-Packard, 512
  intangible assets, 59
  liabilities, 58–60
  liquid assets, 58
  long-term liabilities, 59
  main items on, 60
  market value of assets omitted, 95
  net current assets, 59
  net working capital, 58
  other current assets, 58
  second-stage financing, 443
  shareholders' equity, 60
  tangible assets, 68
  and value of the firm, 468
Balancing item, 535
Bank accounts
  effective interest rate, 147
  proliferation of, 589
Banker's acceptance, 578
Bank loans, 6–7
  accounts receivable financing, 597
  collateral for, 597
  interest rates, 596
  inventory financing, 597
  long-term loans, 597
  revolving line of credit, 596
  secured loans, 597
  self-liquidating, 596
  for short-term financing, 551, 559, 596
  term loans, 596
Bank of America, 36, 37, 40, 43, 46, 49, 50, 612, 680

cost of capital, 93
  economic value added, 92–93
  long-term capital, 93
  losses from Countrywide Financial, 614
  market-to-book ratio, 90
  market value added, 90
  return on capital, 93
Bank of America Merrill Lynch, 449
Bank runs, 46n
Bankruptcy, 429
  Arthur Andersen, 25
  and credit scoring, 579, 580
  definition, 482–483
  Eastern Airlines, 484
  Eastman Kodak, 482
  Energy Future Holdings, 7
  Enron Corporation, 25, 484
  financial distress without, 485–487
  of large companies, 502
  LBOs ending in, 629
  Lehman Brothers, 484
  low probability of, 403–404
  Manville Corporation, 502–503
  and trade-off theory, 482
  TWA, 502
  and warrants, 680
  WorldCom, 25
Bankruptcy costs, 482–485
  direct, 484
  indirect, 484
  varying with type of asset, 484–485
Bankruptcy procedures
  Chapter 11, 483–484, 501–502
  Chapter 7, 501
  creditors, 501–502
  liquidation, 501
  liquidation *vs.* reorganization, 502–503
  negotiated agreement, 501
  reorganization, 501, 502–503
  workout, 501
Bankruptcy Reform Act of 1978, 501
Banks and banking
  check handling and float, 589
  commercial banks, 42
  concentration accounts, 589
  credit checks, 578
  dividend restrictions, 507–508
  electronic funds transfer, 591–592
  functions, 21
  industry consolidation, 617
  investment banks, 42–43
  liquidity, 46n
  lock-box system, 589–590
  proliferation of accounts, 589
  savings and loan associations, 42n
  savings banks, 42n
  subprime mortgages, 49
  sweep programs, 588–589

Barber, Brad, 220–221
Barnes and Noble, 17
Baskin-Robbins, 717
BATS Exchange, 199
Bear Stearns, 49, 51, 433–434
Beaver, W. H., 580
Bechtel, 445
Before-tax income, 429
Behavioral finance
  attitudes toward risk, 227
  beliefs about probabilities, 227–228
  sentiment, 228
Behavioral psychology, 515
Benefit-cost ratio, 253
Berkshire Hathaway, 19n
Berra, Yogi, 468
Best-efforts basis, 445
Beta(s), 714
  accessing estimates of, 365
  aggressive stocks, 362
  Coca-Cola Company, 375
  common stock, 363–365
  defensive stock, 362
  definition, 362
  estimating project cost of capital, 379
  example, 362–363
  "is beta dead" question, 378
  learning from, 367–370
  measuring, 362–365
  Pacific Gas and Electric, 365, 375
  portfolio, 367–371
  to predict total risk, 370–371
  for real companies, 365
  for selected companies, 367
  spreadsheet solutions, 364
  Treasury bills, 371
  Union Pacific, 368–369
  U.S. Steel, 365, 375
  Vanguard Growth and Income Fund, 368–369
  Vanguard 500 Index Fund, 369
Bexalta, 612
Bid-ask spread, 199
Bid price, 168, 169, 199
Bill and Melinda Gates Foundation, 139
Black, Fischer, 675, 716
Black-Scholes option valuation model, 675–677, 680, 716
Blockholders, 17
Bloomingdale's strategy, 98
Blue-sky laws, 446
Board of directors, 9, 427
  classified, 427
  in corporate governance, 17
  election of, 17
  responsibilities, 624
  staggered elections, 427
Boeing 737, 318
Boeing 787, 239
Boeing Company, 4, 21, 46, 319
  beta, 367
  standard deviation for common stock, 343

weighted average cost of capital, 407
Bond dealers, 169
Bondholders
  convertible bonds, 681
  and default risk, 185
  losers in LBOs, 629
  risk of calls for, 430–431
  and risk-shifting strategies, 486
  RJR Nabisco, 632
  tax on interest, 481–482
  and warrants, 680
Bond market
  bond dealers, 169
  junk bonds, 628–629
  size of, 168
  trading in, 169
Bond prices
  calculating, 170–171
  at discount, 175
  in financial press, 168, 169
  fluctuations less than stocks, 336
  as function of interest rate, 174
  and interest rates, 169–174
  long- *vs.* short-term bonds, 180
  at premium, 175
  and semiannual coupon payments, 171
  of strips, 179–180
  varying with interest rates, 172–174
Bond rating services, 183
Bonds; *see also* Corporate bonds; Treasury bonds
  callable, 430–431
  called, 38
  characteristics, 168–169
  compared to stock, 38
  convertible, 187, 434, 665
  coupon payments, 702
  differences among, 168
  differing maturities, 168
  engraved certificate, 167
  expected return, 403–404
  floating interest payments, 38
  floating-rate, 187, 702
  histograms, 340
  inflation-indexed, 181
  inflation-linked, 705
  information on Internet, 186
  interest rate risk, 174
  and interest rates, 335–336
  investment grade, 47
  junk bonds, 47
  liquid, 184
  long-term, 180
  municipal, 183
  plain vanilla, 187
  and preferred stock, 398
  rate of return, 176–179
  total direct costs, 448
  types of issuers, 167
  yield curve, 179–182
  yield to maturity, 174–176
  zero-coupon, 187

Bond valuation, 169–170
    spreadsheet solutions, 178–179
Bond-with-swap agreements, 703
Bookbuilding method, 449
Book debt ratios, 101
Book value
    company cost of capital not
        based on, 396
    and debt ratio, 101
    definition, 61, 201
    versus market value, 61–63,
        201–203
    net common equity, 425
    and salvage value, 291
    for selected companies, 201
Book-value balance sheet, 62–63
Bootstrap game, 617–618
Borrowing
    and capital structure, 719
    and change in dividend policy,
        514
    effect on value, 468
        debt and cost of equity,
            473–477
        earnings per share, 470–472
        MM proposition I, 468–470
        and restructuring, 469–470
        risk and return, 472–473
        taxation, 478–479
    during financial crises, 720
    and financial risk, 476
    by growth companies, 490
    loan covenants, 487
    MM proposition I, 468
    MM proposition II, 475–476
    MM propositions, 715
    tax disadvantages, 481–482
BP, dividend suspension, 510
Brav, A., 510
Break-even analysis, 310–313
    accounting break-even point,
        311–312
    to answer what-if questions, 303
    defined in terms of NPV, 311
    definition, 311
    and economic value added, 312n
    example, 314–315
    at Lockheed, 315
    NPV, 312–315
    operating leverage, 315–317
    sales volume, 311
Brealey, R. A., 401n, 480n
Bridge loans, 42n
Brin, Sergey, 441
Bristol-Myers Squibb, 184
    channel stuffing, 71
Broadcom, 612
Brokerage firms, 198
Buffett, Warren, 19n
Build-to-order production, 588n
Bureau of Labor Statistics, 148n
Burroughs, B., 627n
Business organizations
    constant scrutiny of, 70–71
    corporations, 8–9
    countercyclical firms, 344

cyclical, 381
debt-equity mix, 394
dividend discount model for
    valuing, 218–220
life cycle of the firm, 518–519
limited liability partnerships, 10
limited partnerships, 10
macro risks, 353
no-dividend group, 506
partnerships, 10
private unlisted companies, 444
professional corporations, 10
sole proprietorships, 10
valuing entire economies,
    406–409
Business plan, 442
Business risk, 473
Busse, J. A., 222n

C

Cablevision, 613
California State Teachers'
    Retirement System, 20
Callable bonds, 430–431, 681–682
Callaway Golf, 47–48
Called bonds, 38
Call options
    Alphabet, 666
    and convertible bonds, 680
    definition, 666
    exercise price, 666
    factors affecting price, 675
    and interest rate, 674
    option to expand, 678
    payoff diagram, 669–670
    price and protective put, 671
    profit diagram, 669–670
    versus put options, 666–667
    selling, 668–669
    and stock prices, 671
    and stock price value, 673–675
    on straight bonds, 680
    value at expiration, 674
    value before expiration date, 672
    values and stock prices,
        673–675
    values at expiration, 666
    and warrants, 680
Call price, 681
Cambridge Associates, 444n
Cambridge Bancorp, 42
Campbell Soup
    beta, 367
    market-to-book value, 204
    market *vs.* book value, 201
    price-earnings ratio, 204
    standard deviation for common
        stock, 343
    stock price, 201
    weighted average cost of capital,
        407
Capital; *see also* Opportunity cost
    of capital
    long-term financing, 6

tied up in inventory, 586
total requirement, 552–553
Capital asset pricing model, 394
    assumptions, 373
    assumptions about, 717
    assumptions behind, 714
    attraction of, 714
    basis of, 375–376
    to calculate company cost of
        capital, 397
    to estimated expected return,
        375
    estimating common stock
        returns, 404
    example, 373
    expected *vs.* actual returns,
        377–378
    growth stocks, 377
    hedging motive, 717
    "is beta dead" question, 378
    making sense of, 373
    operation of, 375–378
    and opportunity cost of capital
        company cost of capital, 379
        determining project risk,
            379–380
        fudge factors, 381
    portfolio beta, 377
    and risk premium, 377
    security market line, 374–375
    and small-firm stocks, 377
    statistical problems, 717
    value stocks, 377
Capital budget
    cash-flow estimates, 303
    and competitive advantage, 304
    definition, 304
    post-approval planning, 304
    and senior management, 304
Capital budgeting; *see also*
        Discounted cash-flow
        analysis
    beware of allocated overhead
        costs, 280
    and change in dividend policy,
        514
    consistent forecasts, 305
    forget sunk costs, 278–279
    include all indirect effects, 278
    include opportunity costs, 279
    recognize investment in working
        capital, 279–280
    remember terminal cash flow,
        280
    what-if questions crucial to,
        306–307
Capital budgeting decisions, 6, 239
    decision rules, 261
    and financial managers, 11
    and real options, 317–318
    and value of the firm, 197
Capital budgeting technique, 262
Capital expenditure decisions, 6
Capital expenditures, 558
Capital gains, 205
    advantages, 482

dividends converted to, 517
taxation of, 518
Capital gains tax, 75
Capital investment, 283
    in cash-flow analysis, 286–287
    cash flow from, 283
    company cost of capital,
        380–381
    long life of, 278
Capital investment projects
    case, 270
    criteria, 239
    decision rules
        assets with different lives,
            259
        comparisons, 261
        internal rate of return rule,
            246
        net present value rule, 241
        payback rule, 255
        profitability index, 253
    definition, 239
    internal rate of return rule,
        245–253
        choosing between mutually
            exclusive projects, 271
        financial calculators for, 240
        long-lived projects, 246–248
        with multiple internal rates of
            return, 271
        versus NPV rule, 246
        opportunity cost of capital,
            246
        pitfalls, 239–240, 248–253
        project rate of return, 246
        spreadsheet solutions, 249
    investment in intangible assets,
        239
    long-term consequences, 239
    mutually exclusive projects
        investment timing, 257–258
        long- *vs.* short-lived projects,
            258–260
        replacement problem,
            260–261
    net present value rule, 239
        financial calculators for, 240
        mutually exclusive projects,
            244
        spreadsheet solutions, 245
        valuing long-lived projects,
            242–244
    opportunity cost of capital, 241
    options embedded in, 665
    option to expand, 678
    payback rule, 240
        discounted payback, 256
        payback period, 255
        primary users, 256
        problems with, 255
        simplicity of, 256
    profitability index, 240
    profitability rule
        capital rationing, 254
        pitfalls, 254
        purpose, 253–254

Capital investment projects *Cont.*
  and risk, 240, 241
  and shareholders, 239
  timing of decision, 241
Capital market history
  estimating cost of capital from, 336–337
  historical record, 333–336
  market indexes, 333
Capital markets
  definition, 38
  efficient, 420
  few national boundaries, 431–432
  tough competition in, 715
  well-functioning, 714
Capital rationing
  definition, 254
  hard *vs.* soft, 254
  and NPV rule, 262
Capital structure
  after bankruptcy, 483–484
  changes in, 467
  and costs of financial distress, 482–487
  debt and cost of equity, 469–470, 476–477
  decision, 6
  definition, 392, 467, 468
  effect of changes on returns, 401
  effect of debt on earnings per share, 470–472
  effect of debt on risk and return, 472–473
  and financial leverage
    debt not cheap, 476
    hidden debt, 477
  financing choice
    financial slack, 489–490
    pecking order theory, 488–489
    trade-off theory, 487–488
  industry differences, 468
  measuring, 401–403
  MM proposition I, 468–469
  MM proposition II, 474–476
  optimal, 467, 490
  restrictions, 469–470
  and taxation, 477–482
    implications, 481–482
    interest tax shield, 478–480
    weighted average cost of capital, 480–481
  trade-off theory, 482, 487–488
  and value of the firm, 468–473
  value of the firm unaffected by, 472
Capital surplus, 425
Careers in finance, 21–22
Cargill, 444
Carrying costs, 586, 587
Carve-outs, 630, 631
Cash
  advantages of holding, 553
  calculating, 65
  current assets, 104, 572

current assets converted into, 553
  forecasting sources of, 556–557
  forecasting uses of, 557–558
  held by Apple, 516
  versus installment plan, 130
  investment of idle, 593–596
  liquidity of, 588
  during market turmoil, 595
  mergers financed by, 620–622
  reasons for holding, 588
  reduction in, 285
  reinvested, 35–36
  requirements for, 67
  versus short-term securities, 588
  sources and uses of, 11
  sources of, 420–421
  total uses of, 535
  tracing changes in, 554
  transported over time, 45
Cash accounting, 65–66
Cash balances, 558
  as current asset, 571
  versus free cash flow, 70
  versus retained earnings, 60n
Cash budgeting
  calculating cash balance, 558
  financial manager forecasts, 556
  forecasting sources of cash, 556–557
  forecasting uses of cash, 557–558
  preparation steps, 556
  spreadsheet, 562
Cash conversion cycle
  accounts payable period, 574
  accounts receivable period, 574
  computing, 574
  definition, 574
  example, 574
  inventory period, 574
  length of, 575
  operations cycle, 573–574
Cash coverage ratio, 101–102
Cash cycle, 574
Cash dividends
  definition, 507
  reduction offset by savings, 513
  versus repurchase, 506
Cash-flow analysis
  capital investment, 286–287
  changes in working capital, 288
  operating cash flow, 287–288
  total project cash flow, 288
Cash flow from financing, 68
Cash flow from investing, 67–68
Cash flow from operations, 67, 69
Cash flow projection, 533–534
Cash flows; *see also* Free cash flow; Operating cash flows
  versus accounting profits, 277
  basic financial resource, 467
  on bonds, 171
  calculating
    capital investment, 283

changes in working capital, 284–285
    operational cash flow, 284
  calculations
    capital investment, 283
    changes in working capital, 285–286
    operating cash flow, 283
  from capital investment, 283
  from changes in working capital, 285–286
  in corporations, 11
  daily at Walmart, 588
  discounted to common date, 127
  discounting, 404n
  discounting future, 714
  estimated in nominal terms, 281
  forecasts, 303
  identifying
    discount cash flows, not profit, 276–277
    discount incremental cash flows, 278
    discount nominal cash flows, 281–282
    separate investment from financing decisions, 282–283
  versus income
    cash *vs.* accrual accounting, 65–66
    depreciation, 64–65
  incremental, 271
  and inflation, 281–282
  later than sales, 277
  long-lived projects, 242
  in merger analysis, 621–622
  midyear convention, 289n
  modified sequence, 272
  multiple, 128–131
  versus net income, 67
  nominal, 281
  present value of, 245
  present value of future, 125–126
  versus profit, 66–67
  project, 282–283, 305–306, 399
  real *vs.* nominal, 148–149
  split by debt and equity, 467
  splitting, 715
  terminal, 28
  from Treasury bonds, 169
  and value of the firm, 468
Cash inflow, 11, 66
Cash management
  Automated Clearing House, 592
  cash *vs.* short-term securities, 588
  check handling and float, 589–590
  concentration account, 589
  decentralized, 589
  degree of centralization, 589
  electronic funds transfer, 591–592
  lock-box system, 589–590
  money market investments, 594

payment systems, 590–591
  reasons for holding cash, 588
  sweep programs, 588–589
  transaction costs, 588
Cash outflow, 66
Cash payments, valuing
  from annuities, 136
  from lottery winnings, 138, 144
  from perpetuities, 135–136
Cash ratio, 104
Caterpillar Inc., 8n
CEOs, 10, 427
  and Sarbanes-Oxley Act, 17
Cerberus Capital Management, 613–614
Certificates of deposit, 594
Channel stuffing, 71
Chapter 11 bankruptcy, 502–503
Chapter 7 bankruptcy, 501
Charge card, 591
Charter Communications, 612, 613
Check conversion, 589
Check Handling for the 21st Century Act, 589
Checking handling, 589
Checks, 591
Check 21, 589
Chesapeake Energy, 198
Chicago Board of Trade, 699, 700
Chicago Board Options Exchange, 665, 678
Chicago Mercantile Exchange, 24, 38, 705
Chief financial officers, 10
  and Sarbanes-Oxley Act, 17
  survey of, 337n
Choi, Bill, 516
Chrysler Corporation, 423, 624
  merger failure, 613–614
Cigna, 612
Cisco Systems, 553
Citi, 449
Citigroup, 17, 43, 50n, 509
Classified board of directors, 427
Clearing House Interbank Payments System, 592
Closed-end funds, 40n, 718
  and ETFs, 45n
Closely held corporations, 9, 35–36
CME Group, 699n, 705
CNBC, 222
Coca-Cola Company, 91, 370, 379, 507, 508, 509
  beta, 367, 375
  cost of capital, 93
  dividend policy, 511
  long-term capital, 93
  market-to-book ratio, 90
  market value added, 90
  return on capital, 93
  standard deviation for common stock, 343
  weighted average cost of capital, 407

Collateral, 185
  inventory financing, 597
  secured loans, 597
Collateralized debt obligations, 433–434
Collateralized loans, 594
Collection policy
  aging schedule, 583
  conflicting goals, 585
  costs imposed by slow payers, 584
  definition, 583
  and factoring, 585
  versus sales department, 585
  statement of account, 584
  trade credit, 585
Comcast, 619
Commercial banks, 42
  compared to investment banks, 43n
  major, 43
  number of, in U.S., 42
Commercial draft, 578
Commercial paper, 38, 422
  backup line of credit, 598
  defaults, 598
  definition, 598
  maturities, 598
  in money market, 594
Commodity futures, 700–701
Commodity options, 665
Commodity price risk, 695
Commodity prices, 47
Common-size balance sheet
  definition, 60
  Home Depot, 61
Common-size income statement
  definition, 64
  Home Depot, 64
Common stock
  additional paid-in capital, 425
  authorized share capital, 425
  book value of FedEx, 425
  capital surplus, 425
  and company cost of capital, 394
  definition, 198
  dividend discount model, 206–209
    with constant growth, 209–214, 214–217
    with no growth, 209
    valuation, 206–218
  dividends on, 398
  expected rate of return, 205, 380, 394
    avoiding false precision, 405
    based on capital asset pricing model, 404
    based on dividend discount model, 404–405
    and cost of capital, 391
    and volatility, 344
  histograms, 339, 340
  initial public offerings, 444–450
  intrinsic value, 204–205

issued shares, 424
listings on exchanges, 198
measuring risk of
  betas, 362–365
    portfolio betas, 367–371
    total risk, 365–367
net common equity, 425
number of FedEx shares, 424
outstanding shares, 424
and ownership of corporations, 426–427
par value, 425
payout policy and value of, 511
price and intrinsic value, 204–205
rates of return 1900–2015, 335
and retained earnings, 425
returns on, 363
riskiest securities, 331–336
standard deviation for selected companies, 343
treasury stock, 424
valuation by comparables, 203–204, 217
voting procedures, 427–428
Company cost of capital
  based on market value, 396
  calculating as weighted average, 394–395
  and common stock, 394
  definition, 380, 393, 394
  and expected return on common stock, 391
  as opportunity cost of capital, 380, 394
Company values, 47–48
Compensation committee, 427
Competition
  in capital markets, 715
  in financial markets, 420
  Home Depot *vs.* Lowe's, 107
Competitive advantage
  in product markets, 420
  in project analysis, 304
Competitiveness, 6
Complementary resources, combined by merger, 615–616
Compound growth, 123
Compounding
  continuous, 147
  power of, 123
Compound interest
  definition, 120
  effective annual interest rate, 146–147
  and future value, 120–123
  present value calculation using, 125–126
  and purchase price of Manhattan, 122–123
Conagra, 630
Concentration system, 589
Conflicts of interest
  eliminating, 305
  sales *vs.* collection department, 585

shareholders *vs.* debt holders, 486–487
Conforming loans, 50n
Conglomerate mergers
  bootstrap game, 617–618
  definition, 612–613
Consistency in financial planning, 531
Consistent forecasts, 305
Consolidated balance sheet, 58
Consolidated Edison, stock price, 202–203
Constant dollar, 149
Constant-growth dividend discount model
  caveat on, 212
  definition, 210
  estimating growth rate, 211
  example, 210–211, 212–213
  and forecasting, 209–210
  formula, 210
  present value of perpetuities, 210
Consumer credit, 575
Consumer Price Index
  gasoline prices, 149
  for selected years, 148
Continental Airlines, 502
Contingency planning, 530
Continuous compounding, 147
Controller, 10, 11
Conversion price, 680–681
Conversion value, 580
Convertible bonds, 187, 434, 665
  options on, 680–681
  total direct costs, 448
Convertible preferred stock, 435
Convertible securities
  bonds, 434
  preferred stock, 435
  warrants, 434
Cookie jar reserves, 71
Coolidge, Calvin, 336
Corning, 184
Corporate bonds
  Apple Inc., 432–433
  asset-backed, 433–434
  callable, 430–431, 681–682
  convertible, 187, 665, 680–681
  coupon payments, 702
  default premium, 183
  default risk, 167, 182–185
  FedEx, 186
  floating-rate, 702
  interest rate, 167
  investment grade, 183
  junk bonds, 183
  liquid, 184
  long-term, 402
  mortality bonds, 434
  number of defaults, 183–184
  private placement, 432
  protecting against default risk, 185
  public placement, 432
  rating services, 183

RJR Nabisco, 187
  value of straight *vs.* callable, 682
  with warrants, 680
  yield, 183
  zero-coupon, 187
Corporate debt
  Apple Inc., 432–433
  compared to preferred stock, 428
  forms of
    accounts payable, 432
    callable bonds, 430–431
    country and currency, 431–432
    funded debt, 430
    interest rates, 429–430
    leases, 432
    maturities, 430
    public or private placement, 432
    repayment provisions, 430–431
    sinking fund, 430
    unfunded debt, 430
  interest rates, 429–430
  limited liability, 430
Corporate finance
  basic objective, 87
  complicated decisions, 419
  creating value with decisions, 240
  versus investment decisions, 419
  patterns of
    cash sources, 420, 423
    commercial paper, 422
    debt issues, 421–422
    debt ratios, 422, 423–424
    financial deficits, 421
    internally generated funds, 420–421, 423
Corporate financing
  common stock, 424–428
  convertible securities, 434–435
  and corporate debt, 429–434
  preferred stock, 428–429
  too much debt, 423–424
Corporate governance
  activist shareholders, 17–18
  and agency costs, 624
  board of directors, 17
  definition, 17
  information for investors, 18
  interest of managers and shareholders, 3
  legal requirements, 17
  and takeovers, 18
Corporate performance measures
  economic value added, 91–95
  financial leverage, 10–102
  financial ratios, 88–89
  form efficiency, 96
  interpreting financial ratios, 101–107
  liquidity, 103–104
  market value, 89–91
  market value added measures, 89–91
  return on assets, 97–99
  role of financial ratios, 108–109

Corporate raiders, 20
Corporate scandals, 15, 72, 597
Corporate tax
    and dividend policy, 518
    expense deduction, 73
    implications for capital
        structure, 481–482
    interest deduction, 73–74
    interest rate shield, 479
    loss carryback, 74
    state taxes, 73n
    tax rates, 73
    and weighted average cost of
        capital, 480–481
Corporate tax rate, with weighted
    average cost of capital, 401
Corporate venturers, 443
Corporations
    acceptable risks, 693
    agency problems, 15–16
    and agency theory, 716
    assets needed by, 3
    bank as source of loans to, 42
    boards of directors, 9, 427
    capital budgeting process, 11
    capital surplus, 425
    cash flows, 11
    CEOs, 427
    closely held, 9
    common stock, 424–426
    compensation committee, 427
    current assets, 572
    current liabilities, 572
    debt vs. equity financing, 38,
        197
    definition, 8
    disadvantages, 9
    executive compensation, 16–17
    financial environment, 33
    financial manager roles, 10–11
    financing assets, 3
    financing choices, 36
    flow of savings to, 35–43
    goals
        market value maximization,
            12–15
        profit maximization, 13
        value maximization, 3, 12
    initial public offerings, 37
    investment banks, 10
    limited liability, 8, 429
    ownership of, 426–428
    preferred stock, 424–429
    principal financial decisions, 21
    public companies, 9
    reinvested cash, 35–36
    reliance on dividend discount
        model, 220
    reliance on valuation by
        comparables, 220
    retained earnings, 425
    separation of ownership and
        control, 9, 12
    stakeholders, 16
    tax avoidance, 20
    tax drawback, 9

    as team effort, 57
    two sets of books, 291
    voting procedures, 427–428
Correlations across industries,
    347–348
Cost(s)
    of debt, 475
    disadvantage for corporations, 9
    of financial distress
        bankruptcy costs, 482–485
        liquidation vs. reorganization,
            502–503
        without bankruptcy, 406–407
    fixed, 307, 315
    of general cash offers, 452
    of initial public offerings, 448
    of liquidation, 501
    new products, 6
    of proxy contests, 625
    of shutting down, 280
    sunk costs, 278–279
    variable, 307, 315–316
Cost-benefit analysis of mergers,
    631–632
Cost-cutting projects, 284
Cost of capital; see also
        Company cost of capital;
        Opportunity cost of capital
    definition, 48
    and economic value added,
        91, 93
    historical evidence to estimate,
        336–337
    measuring, 336
    nominal, 281
    project, 378–379
    and rate of return, 331
    and taxes, 391
Cost of equity, 380, 391
    and debt, 473–477
    lacking precision, 405
    MM proposition I, 474
Cost of goods sold, 65
Costs(s)
    of financial distress
Costs of financial distress
    bankruptcy costs, 482–484
    bankruptcy procedures, 501–502
    definition, 482
    investor assessment, 481
    liquidation vs. reorganization,
        502–503
    and trade-off theory, 481
    varying by type of asset,
        484–485
    without bankruptcy, 485–487
Countercyclical firms, 344
Counterparties, 703
Countrywide Financial, 614
Coupon, 168, 169
Coupon bonds, debentures, 168
Coupon payments, 179, 702
    semiannual, 171–172
    valuing, 170
Coupon rate, 173
Cowgill, B., 39

Cox, Jo Ann, 392–394, 398–400,
    401
Credit
    backup line of, 598
    five Cs of, 579
    free, 126–127
    shaky, 578
Credit agencies, 578
Credit agreements
    banker's acceptance, 578
    commercial draft, 578
    open accounts, 577
    sight draft, 578
    time draft, 578
    trade acceptance, 578
Credit analysis
    agencies for, 578
    based on financial ratios, 578
    definition, 578
    and five Cs of credit, 579
    numerical credit scoring,
        578–579
    Z score model, 579
Credit booms, 720
Credit bureaus, 579n
Credit card, 591
Credit checks, 578
Credit decision
    credit policy, 579–581
    dangerous accounts, 583
    and default, 581
    looking beyond immediate
        order, 584
    maximizing profit, 583
    and probability of payment, 581
    with repeat orders, 582–583
    without repeat orders, 581–582
Credit default swaps, 705
Credit manager responsibilities, 583
Creditors, 501
    and bankruptcy costs, 482–483
    and bankruptcy procedures,
        501–502
    junior, 502
    liquidation vs. reorganization,
        502–503
    postpetition, 502
    prepetition, 502
    secured, 501
    senior, 501, 502
Credit policy
    aging schedule, 584
    collection policy, 584–595
    consumer credit, 575
    credit agreements, 577–579
    credit analysis, 578–579
    credit decision, 579–4584
    definition, 579
    open account, 577
    steps, 575
    terms of sale, 575–577
    trade credit, 575
Credit ratings, 47–48, 578
Credit risk, 183
Credit sales, 92n
Credit scoring, 578–579

Credit transfer, 591
Crowdfunding, 443, 444
Cruz, Ted, 39
Cumulative capital requirement
    best level of
        maintaining liquidity, 553
        matching maturities, 552–553
        permanent working capital, 553
    long- vs. short-term financing,
        552–553
    seasonal variations, 552
Cumulative financing requirement,
    558
Cumulative voting, 427
Currency options, 665
Currency risk, 695
Currency swaps, 704–705
Current assets, 60
    on balance sheet, 58
    and cash, 104
    converted into cash, 553
    as percentage of total assets, 573
    types of, 571
    in working capital, 572
Current dollar, 149
Current expenditures, 65
Current liabilities, 60
    on balance sheet, 59
    managing, 596–598
    in working capital, 572
Current yield, 125
Cutoff period, 255
Cyclical businesses, 381

D

Dangerous accounts, 583
Debentures, 168
Debit card, 591
Debt; see also Corporate debt
    best level of, 489
    as book value, 95
    commercial paper, 422
    compared to preferred stock,
        428
    and cost of equity, 473–477
    and expected return to
        shareholders, 472–473
    explicit costs, 475
    and financial risk, 475
    fixed rate, 703
    funded vs. funded, 430
    Geothermal Corp., 392–393
    hidden, 477
    implicit costs, 475
    inflation-indexed, 25
    long-term, 595
    MM Proposition I, 474
    MM Proposition II, 474
    secured, 185
    short-term, 595
    subordinated, 185
    and taxation, 478–479
    and uncertainty of stock returns,
        473

Debt burden, 102
Debt-equity mix, 535
Debt-equity mix target, 489
Debt-equity ratio, 100, 535
Debt financing
　business risk, 473
　versus equity financing, 197
　and financial leverage, 473
　financial risk, 473
　MM proposition I, 473
　operating risk, 473
Debt holders
　rate of return for, 394–395
　versus shareholders, 486–487
Debt investors, 6
Debt issues, 421–422
　too much, 423–424
Debt market innovations
　asset-backed bonds, 433–434
　collateralized debt obligations,
　　433–434
　mortality bonds, 434
　mortgage pass-through
　　certificates, 433
Debt overhang problem, 486
Debt policy
　and capital structure choices
　　financial slack, 489–490
　　optimal capital structure, 490
　　pecking order theory,
　　　488–489
　　trade-off theory, 487–488
　case, 499–500
　and cost of equity, 473–477
　costs of financial distress
　　bankruptcy procedures,
　　　501–502
　　liquidation *vs.* reorganization,
　　　502–503
　effect on value of the firm
　　capital structure, 468–469
　　earnings per share, 470–472
　　and restructuring, 469
　　risk and return, 472–473
　and financial distress
　　bankruptcy costs, 482–485
　　without bankruptcy, 485–487
　and financial leverage
　　debt not cheap, 476
　　hidden debt, 477
　loan covenants, 487
　MM proposition II, 474–475
　not irrelevant, 477–478
　and risk management, 694
　and taxation
　　and capital structure, 481–482
　　interest rate shield, 478–479
　　value of shareholders' equity,
　　　479
　　weighted average cost of
　　　capital, 480–481
Debt ratio, 100–101, 406, 422,
　423–424
　and book value, 101
　higher, 488
　RJR Nabisco, 187

Debt securities
　complexity of, 38
　over-the-counter trading, 38
Debt-to-book ratio, 396
Decision rules
　for assets with different lives,
　　259
　case, 270
　comparison of, 261
　internal rate of return, 246, 248,
　　261
　investment timing, 258
　net present value, 241, 246, 261
　payback rule, 255, 261
　presumably inferior, 262
　profitability index, 253, 261
Decision tree, 318
Default
　break-even probability, 582
　on mortgages, 103
　by WorldCom, 184
Default premium, 183
Default rate, junk bonds, 628–629
Default risk
　bank loans, 597
　commercial paper, 598
　corporate bonds, 182–185
　for corporate bonds, 167
　and credit decision, 581
　definition, 183
　low on Treasury bonds, 167
　municipal bonds, 183n
　protecting against
　　protective covenants, 185
　　security, 185
　　seniority, 185
　and risky projects, 486–487
Defensive stock, 362
Defined-benefit plans, 41n
Defined contribution plans, 41
Deflation, 149
Degree of operating leverage, 316
Dell Inc., 588, 612
Delphi division of General Motors,
　615
Delta Airlines, 343
　economic value added, 93
　market-to-book ratio, 90
　market value added, 90
Depreciation, 69
　accelerated, 20
　on balance sheet, 58
　deducting, 101–102
　on income statement, 64–65
　of intangible assets, 102
　modified accelerated cost
　　recovery system,
　　290–291
　and project cash flows, 284
　purpose of, 61
　and salvage value, 291
　on statement of cash flows,
　　67–68
　straight-line, 291
　and taxes, 73
Depreciation tax shield, 284, 290

Derivatives, 38
　copper futures, 701
　credit default swaps, 705
　definition, 693
　forward contracts, 701–702
　futures contracts, 696–701
　identifying risks, 705
　innovations in market, 705
　iron ore futures, 705
　options, 696
　percentage of companies using,
　　695
　speculation *vs.* risk reduction,
　　705–706
　survey on uses of, 695
　swaps, 702–705
　types of, 695
Diet deals, 628
Dimon, James, 511
Dimson, Elroy, 333–334, 335,
　　339, 341
Direct costs
　of bankruptcy, 484
　of initial public offering, 448
Direct debit, 591
Direct debit system, 592
Direct deposit, 592
Direct negotiation for stock
　　repurchase, 509
Direct payment, 591
Direct payment systems, 592
DirecTV, 612
Discount bonds, 175
Discounted cash-flow analysis
　calculating cash flow, 283–286
　case, 301
　definition, 275
　dominant tool for managers, 262
　example
　　calculating NPV, 28–289
　　cash-flow analysis, 286–288
　　depreciation, 290
　　forecasting working capital,
　　　289
　　project analysis, 291–293
　　salvage value, 291
　　spreadsheet solutions, 292
　identifying cash flows, 276–282
　long-lived capital investments,
　　278
　and real options, 317
　separating investment from
　　financing decisions,
　　282–283
　spreadsheet solutions, 292–293
　for valuing businesses,
　　218–220
Discounted cash-flow calculations,
　124
Discounted cash-flow methods,
　248
Discounted cash-flow rate of
　　return, 247
Discounted cash flows, 714
Discounted-payback period, 256
Discount factor, 125

Discounting
　cash flow, not profit, 276–277
　cash flows, 404n
　in incremental cash flows,
　　278–279
　nominal cash flow, 281–282
　real cash flow, 281
Discount rate, 209
　for differing project, 380
　and internal rate of return rule,
　　247
　nominal, 281
　weighted average cost of capital,
　　400
　for yield to maturity, 176
Diversifiable risks, 351–353
Diversification, 362
　definition, 343
　to eliminate specific risk, 351, 361
　and investment opportunity
　　frontier, 346–347
　by investors, 45, 331
　mutual funds, 368–370
　and portfolio betas, 370–371
　as reason for merger, 617
　slowing down of, 370
Divestitures, 630
Dividend discount model
　Blue Skies example, 207–208
　for common stock valuation,
　　206–210
　with constant growth, 208–214
　corporate reliance on, 220
　definition, 206
　estimating common stock
　　returns, 404–405
　forecasting dividends, 206–207
　with no growth, 209
　with nonconstant growth,
　　214–217
　and stock repurchases, 219–220,
　　513–514
　valuation formula, 206–207
Dividend policy, 715
　Apple Inc., 505, 516
　capital budgeting and changes
　　in, 514
　case, 526–527
　and corporate tax, 518
　decrease in value of the firm,
　　517–518
　and financial planning, 530
　high-payout, 515
　increase in value of the firm,
　　515
　JPMorgan Chase, 511
　and legal capital, 508
　low-payout policy, 517
　managerial views, 509–510
　MM proposition I, 514–515
　news of increase, 509–510
　payout controversy
　　capital budgeting decisions,
　　　514
　　dividend discount model,
　　　513–514

Dividend policy   *Cont.*
  dividends and repurchases,
    512–513
  dividends and share values,
    514–515
  investment and financing
    decisions, 511
  MM proposition I, 511–512
  resolving controversy about, 719
  restrictions, 507–508
  state laws, 507–508
  stock dividends, 508–509
  stock splits, 508–509
  tax effects, 517–518
Dividend reinvestment plan, 507
Dividends, 13–14, 204
  Alphabet in 2015, 505
  in cash forecasts, 558
  Coca-Cola Company, 507
  converted into capital
    gains, 517
  and financial managers, 510
  forecasting, 206
  information content, 509–510
  limitations, 507–508
  McDonald's, 215–216
  payment date, 507
  payout ratio, 211–212
  popular views of, 719
  on preferred stock, 398, 428
  record date, 507
  and share issues, 514–515
  and stock repurchase, 509
  versus stock repurchase,
    512–513
  and stock repurchases,
    219–220
  suspended by BP, 510
  taxation of, 75, 517–518
  in U.S. 1980–2014, 506
  value of, 215
Dividend yield, 200, 205
Dodd-Frank law, 16–17
Dot-com boom, 228
Dot-com bubble, 227, 718
Dow Chemical, 612
  cash source, 420–421
  debt issues, 422
  market-to-book value, 204
  market *vs.* book value, 201
  price-earnings ratio, 204
  stock price, 201
Dow Du Pont, cash source,
    420–421
Dow Jones Industrial Average, 333
  decline by 1932, 336
Dow Jones Wilshire 5000, 333
Dun & Bradstreet, 578
DuPont, 612, 630
Du Pont formula
  definition, 98
  profit margin, 97–99
  return on assets, 98–99
  return on equity, 102
  and return on equity, 102
Dyax, 616

E

Earning power
  extra, 202
  future, 202
Earnings, 60n
  plowback ratio, 211–212
  plowed back into investments,
    213–214
  volatility of, 381
Earnings before interest, taxes,
    depreciation, and
    amortization, 102n, 579
Earnings before interest and taxes,
    64, 73–74, 101
Earnings per share, 209
  effects of borrowing, 470–472
  FedEx, 200
  MM proposition I, 469–470
  and operating income, 473
  and return on equity, 211–212
Eastman Kodak, 482
Easy money policies, 49
eBay, 202
  underpricing initial public
    offering, 446
EBIT; *see* Earnings before interest
    and taxes
EBITDA; *see* Earnings
    before interest, taxes,
    depreciation, and
    amortization
Economic nationalism, 620
Economic order quantity, 586
Economic value added
  versus accounting income, 92
  and accounting rate of return, 93
  and break-even analysis, 312n
  calculating, 91–92
  and cost of capital, 91, 93
  definition, 91
  Home Depot, 92
  problems with, 95
  for selected companies, 93
Economies of scale, from merger,
    614
Economies of vertical integration,
    614–615
Edman, A., 18n
Effective annual interest rate
  annual percentage rate, 146–147
  in bank accounts, 147
  calculating, 147
  definition, 146
  quote variations, 146
Effective annual rate, 171n
Efficiencies, motive for spin-offs,
    630
Efficiency measures
  asset turnover ratio, 96
  inventory turnover, 96
  receivables turnover, 96–97
Efficient capital markets, 420
Efficient market, 221–224
Efficient market hypothesis
  exceptions to

behavioral aspects, 718
  coincidences, 718
  forms of, 715
  and market anomalies, 225–226
  relative merits of, 715
  semi-strong form, 225
  strong form, 225
  testing for anomalies, 715
  weak form, 225
Eight O'Clock Coffee, 613
Einstein, Albert, 713
Electric utilities, less than average
    macro risk, 353
Electronic communication
    networks, 198
Electronic funds transfer, 591–592
  advantages, 592
  Automated Clearing House, 592
  Clearing House Interbank
    Payments System, 592
  direct deposit, 592
  direct payment, 592
  wire transfer, 592
Ellison, Larry, 16, 17n, 680
EMC, 612
Emerson Electric, 630
Energy Future Holdings, 7
Enron Corporation, 25, 71, 72,
    445, 484
  special-purpose entities, 432
Entergy, 5, 7, 38, 47–48
Entrepreneurs
  business plan, 442
  crowdfunding, 443, 444
  venture capital, 441–444
Equifax, 579n
Equipment, long- *vs.* short-lived,
    257, 258–260
Equity
  as book value, 95
  common and preferred stock,
    397n
  cost of, 391
  internal and external, 489
Equity financing, 102
  versus debt financing, 197
  growth rate without additional,
    541
Equity investors, 6
Equity issues, 423
Equity markets, 37
Equivalent annual annuity,
    259–260
Equivalent-risk assets, 714
Ethics of value maximization,
    18–19
European call, 666n
EVA Dimensions, 90, 95
Excess capacity, 537–538
Exchange rate fluctuations, 704
Exchange rates
  and currency swaps, 704
Exchange-traded funds, 45r–46,
    221
Exchange-traded portfolio, 221
Ex-dividend, 507

Executive compensation, 16–17
  stock options, 680
Executive stock options, 680
Exercise price
  Alphabet, 666
  call options, 666
  call price, 668
  definition, 666
  put options, 666, 667, 679
  and sock prices, 673
  and stock prices, 671
Expected cash flow
  forecasts, 381
Expected rate of return, 241, 331
  bonds, 403–404
  common stock, 205, 380, 394,
    404–405
  effect of capital structure
    changes, 401
  equivalent-risk assets, 714
  and opportunity cost of capital,
    91
  preferred stock, 405–406
  on risky securities, 48
  using capital asset pricing model
    estimates, 375
  and volatility, 344
Expense deduction, 73
Expenses, noncash, 400n
Experian, 579n
Expiration date, 666, 667, 672–673
External financing
  and growth rate, 539–542
  required, 537–538
  required capital, 532–533
Extra earning power, 202
Extraneous events, 695
ExxonMobil, 5, 91, 94, 353–354,
    506
  beta, 367
  cost of capital, 93
  economic value added, 93
  long-term capital, 93
  market-to-book ratio, 90
  market value added, 90
  return on capital, 93
  standard deviation for common
    stock, 343
  weighted average cost of capital,
    407

F

Facebook, 5, 506
  initial public offering, 217, 441
  reinvesting earnings, 11
Face value, 168
Factoring, 585
Fair Isaac Corporation, 579n
Fama, Eugene F., 508n
Fannie Mae, 49, 50, 176
Fashion, changes in, 320
Fast-Track Wireless, 12
Fear index, 676, 678
Federal Reserve System

easy money policy, 49
Fedwire, 592
in financial crisis of 2007–2009, 49
interest-free reserves, 431n
target interest rate, 720
tight money policy, 172
FedEx, 3, 423, 486
    acquisition of Kinko's, 4, 421–422
    acquisitions, 4
    balance sheet, 201
    bond issues, 186
    book value, 201
    book value of shareholders' equity, 425
    cash source, 420–421
    dividend yield, 200
    financing decisions, 4–5
    founding of, 4
    initial public offering, 4, 198
    international expansion, 4–5
    investment decisions, 4–5
    limit order book, 199
    market cap, 199–200
    market-to-book value, 204
    market vs. book value, 201
    number of shares outstanding, 424
    price-earnings ratio, 204
    share price history, 200
    stock price, 199–200, 201
    and venture capitalists, 4–5
    website, 4
Fedwire, 592
Fernandez, P., 337n
FICO score, 579n
Fidelity Investments, 40
Field warehousing, 597
Finance
    careers in, 21–22
    at FedEx, 5
    history of, 24–25
    reputation in, 19
    unsolved problems
        capital structure, 719
        exceptions to efficient market theory, 718
        financial crises, 720–721
        merger waves, 719–720
        payout controversy, 719
        present value determinants, 716–717
        project risk determinants, 716–717
        risk and return, 717
        value of liquidity, 720
        value of the firm, 718–719
Finance lease, 100n
Financial Accounting Standards Board
    on accounting methods, 70
    on option valuation models, 680
Financial analysts, 21, 22, 333
Financial assets, 40
    definition, 6–7

options on, 679–682
    callable bonds, 681–682
    convertible bonds, 680–681
    executive stock options, 680
    warrants, 680
trading of, 7
types of, 6–7
Financial calculators
    for annuities, 145
    for bond prices, 170–171
    brands of, 250
    to find discount factor, 125
    to find future value, 131–132
    to find present value, 131–132
    to find yield, 177
    for future value, 122
    for internal rate of return, 250
    for net present value, 250
    for present value, 125
Financial crises, attempts to understand, 720–721
Financial crisis of 2007–2009, 24
    debt overhang problem, 486
    financial system meltdown, 49–51
    fragility of financial system, 720
    lack of liquidity, 720
    lessons from, 51
    mortgage-backed securities, 49–50
    origin of, 49
    share price decline, 336
    spread of, 50–51
    subprime mortgages, 49
    and Treasury bonds, 176–177
    Troubled Asset Relief Program, 511
Financial distress
    bankruptcy procedures, 501–502
    costs of, 694
        bankruptcy costs, 482–485
        liquidation vs. reorganization, 502–503
        without bankruptcy, 486–487
    impact on managers, 486–487
Financial environment, 33
Financial futures, 24
    definition, 701
    at maturity, 70n
    prices as of Dec. 1015, 700
    trading mechanics, 699–700
Financial Industry Regulatory Authority, 185, 186
Financial institutions; see also Financial markets
    commercial banks, 42
    definition, 42
    employment in, 21
    in financial crisis of 2007–2009, 49–51
    as financial intermediaries, 42
    flow of savings to corporations, 35–43
    functions
        diversification, 45–46
        payment mechanism, 45–46

providing liquidity, 45
    risk transfer, 45–46
    transporting cash over time, 45
importance for companies, 34–35
insurance companies, 43
investment banks, 42–43
as investors, 75
understanding, 33
Financial instruments for hedging, 693, 721
Financial intermediaries
    compared to manufacturing corporations, 40
    definition, 41
    financial institutions as, 42
    hedge funds, 41
    mutual funds, 41
    pension funds, 41
Financial investments
    payoff on, 693
    risk management, 693
Financial leverage
    cash coverage ratio, 101–102
    debt not cheap, 476
    debt ratio, 100–101
    definition, 100, 473
    excluding short-term debt, 101
    hidden debt, 477
    Home Depot, 101–102
    and return on equity, 102
    times interest earned ratio, 101
Financial managers
    capital budgeting decisions, 6
    and capital budgeting process, 11
    chief financial officer, 11
    conflicts of interest, 3
    consideration of investments, 529
    controller, 12
    day-to-day activities, 7–8
    on dividends, 510
    essential roles, 11
    forecasting cash needs, 556
    and life cycle of the firm, 519
    measuring capital structure, 401–403
    and MM propositions, 715
    and outside investors, 11–12
    and project viability, 529
    questions faced by, 3
    questions on project analysis, 303–304
    short-term decisions, 551
    and trade-off theory, 487–488
    treasurer, 12
    understanding financial institutions, 33
    value added by, 3, 87
    worries about takeovers, 611
Financial markets
    commodities markets, 38–39
    competition in, 420
    definition, 37

derivatives market, 38–39
few protected niches in, 421
in financial crisis of 2007–2009, 49–51
functions
    diversification, 45–46
    payment mechanism, 45–46
    providing liquidity, 45
    risk transfer, 45–46
    transporting cash across time, 45
importance for companies, 34–35
information provided by
    commodity prices, 47
    company values, 47
    cost of capital, 48
    stock prices, 48
options markets, 38–39
prediction market, 39
primary market, 37
secondary market, 37
shareholder access to, 12
Financial plan
    choosing, 538
    consistent goals, 531
    to establish goals, 529
    implications of alternative strategies, 529
    reasons for long-term, 551
Financial planning; see also Short-term financial planning
    and alternative strategies, 531
    to avoid surprises, 529
    benefits of
        considering options, 530–531
        contingency planning, 530
        forcing consistency, 531
    and dividend policy, 530
    focus on big picture, 530
    versus forecasting, 530
    for investment decisions, 529
    issues involved in, 530
    long-term by Verizon, 530–531
    planning horizon, 530
    short-term easier than long-term, 552–553
    short- vs. long-term, 530
    strategy reasons, 530
    what-if questions, 530
Financial planning models
    assumptions consistency, 535
    balancing item, 535
    case, 549
    cash-flow projections, 533
    components
        inputs, 531–532
        outputs, 531–532
        planning model, 531–532
    consistent assumptions, 535
    definition, 531
    example, 532–537
    external financing and growth rate, 539–542
    funding projections, 534–535
    and growth rate changes, 537

Financial planning models   *Cont.*
  net fixed assets increase,
    534–535
  percentage of sales model,
    532–537
  pitfalls in design, 537
  pro forma balance sheet, 535
  required external capital,
    530–533
  required funds and excess
    capacity, 537–538
  spreadsheet, 536
Financial ratios
  assets turnover ratio, 96
  average collection period, 97
  calculating, 88
  credit analysis based on, 578
  failing and nonfailing firms, 580
  interpreting, 104–107
  inventory turnover ratio, 96
  leverage ratios, 100–102
  liquidity ratios, 103–104
  major industry groups, 107
  median, for nonfinancial
    corporations, 108
  organizational chart, 88
  price-earnings ratio, 200
  profitability ratios, 93–97
  profit margin, 97–98
  purpose, 78
  receivables turnover, 96–97
  related to shareholder value,
    88–89
  role of, 108–109
  sales to assets, 96
  types of, 88
Financial reporting, 72
Financial risk, 473, 475, 476
Financial scandals, 19, 25
Financial slack
  and debt policy, 489–490
  definition, 489
  no-cash-flow problem, 489–490
Financial statements
  balance sheet, 58–61
  book values *vs.* market values,
    61–63
  generally accepted accounting
    principles, 61
  income statement, 63–67
  obtaining, 61
  pro forma, 532, 534
  and Sarbanes-Oxley Act, 72
  Securities and Exchange
    Commission
    requirements, 58
  statement of cash flows, 67–69
  statement of shareholders'
    equity, 58n
Financial system
  forms of financing, 35
  fragility of, 720
  prone to crises, 720–721
Financing
  capital structure choices
    financial slack, 489–490

pecking order theory, 488–489
theory of optimal capital
  structure, 490
trade-off theory, 487
debt-equity mix, 394
debt *vs.* equity, 38
first-stage, 442
forms of, 35
general cash offering, 450–453
initial public offerings, 444–450
internal *vs.* external, 488–489
of mergers
  by cash, 620–622
  by stock, 622–623
by a mixture of securities, 391
multiple sources of, 398
private placement, 453
second-stage, 443
side effects, 721
total, of U.S. corporations, 43–44
venture capitalists, 441–444
Financing decisions, 3
  Apple Inc. 1996–2016, 34–35
  and boards of directors, 17
  capital structure decision, 6
  compared to investment
    decisions, 6–7
  by corporations, 21
  effect on value, 715
  FedEx, 4–5
  financial asset issues, 6–7
  versus investment decisions, 419
  by investors, 6
  Microsoft Corporation, 6
  and payout policy, 511
  recent examples, 5
  separate from investment
    decisions, 282–283
  and shareholder value, 88
  and time value of money, 119
Fire insurance, 352
Firm commitment, 445
First-stage financing, 442
Fisher, L., 508n
Fixed assets, 60
  on balance sheet, 58
Fixed costs, 307
  break-even point, 315
  and operating leverage, 315n
Fixed-income market, 38
Fixed-income securities, 593
Fixed-rate debt, 703
Flexible production facilities, 320
Flight to quality, 595
Float, 589
Floatation costs, 447–448
Floating interest payments, 38
Floating interest rate, 430
Floating-rate bonds, 187, 702
Floating-rate loans, 430
Floating-rate preferred, 429
Food companies, less than average
  macro risk, 353
Ford, Harrison, 361
Ford Motor Company, 5, 370, 419,
  506, 508, 624

beta, 367
standard deviation for common
  stock, 343
weighted average cost of capital,
  407
Forecast bias
  and favorite projects, 306
  and hurdle rate, 306
  overoptimism, 306
  problem of allowing unbiased
    forecasts, 306
  reducing, 305–306
Forecasting
  calculating implications of, 532
  in cash budgeting, 556
    sources of cash, 556–557
    uses of cash, 557–558
  cash flows, 303, 381, 533–534
  consistent, 305
  and constant-growth dividend
    discount model, 209–210
  contrasted with financial
    planning, 530
  critical financial variables, 538
  dividends, 206
  dividends per share, 513–514
  growth in sales, 532
  incremental cash flows, 278
  in merger analysis, 621–622
  operating cash flows, 287–288,
    407–408
  plans for growth, 531
  profits, 303–304
  stock prices, 206
  working capital, 289
Forest Laboratories, 612
Forward contracts
  definition, 701
  example, 702
  and futures contracts, 701
  not marked to market, 701n
  for risk management, 693,
    701–702
Forward rate agreements, 702
Fraud, 19
Freddie Mac, 49, 50n, 72, 176
Free cash flow, 408–409
  versus cash balances, 70
  components, 69–70
  definition, 69–70, 218–219
  Home Depot, 69–70
Free-cash-flow problem, 489–490
  and high-payout policy, 515
Free-cash-flow theory of takeovers,
  616, 629
Free credit, 126–127
Freeport-McMoRan, 280
French, Kenneth R., 378
Friedman, Milton, 24
Frock, Roger, 486n
Fudge factors, 381
Funded debt, 430
Futures contracts, 38
  characteristics, 696–699
  commodity futures, 700–701
  copper prices, 701

daily turnover, 701
definition, 696
financial futures, 701
and forward contracts, 701–702
hedging with, 691, 700–701
iron ore, 705
margin account, 696n
maturity date, 696
mechanics of trading, 699–700
  margin requirement, 700
  marked to market, 700
  spot price, 700
versus options, 695–697
profit on, 697–698
real estate, 705
for risk management, 693,
  696–701
standardized, 701
wheat futures, 696–700
Future value
  of annuities, 140–141
  calculating, 120, 122
  case, 165
  compound interest, 120–123
  definition, 120
  financial calculators for,
    131–132
  multiple cash flows, 128–129
  and purchase price of
    Manhattan, 122–123
  simple interest, 120
  spreadsheet solutions, 132–135
Future value table, 122

G

Gambling *vs.* investing, 331
Gantchev, Nickolay, 448
Gasoline prices, 149
Gates, Bill, 139, 152, 153
General Cable, 701
General cash offers
  costs of, 452
  definition, 451
  market reaction to, 452–453
  rights issue, 450–451
  seasoned offering, 450
  shelf registration, 451–452
General Dynamics, 4
General Electric, 47–48, 348,
  364, 370
  beta, 367
  market-to-book value, 204
  market *vs.* book value, 201
  price-earnings ratio, 204
  standard deviation for common
    stock, 343
  stock price, 201
  weighted average cost of
    capital, 407
Generally accepted accounting
  principles, 70–71
  definition, 61
  shifts to international
    standards, 72

General Mills, 343
General Motors, 239, 423, 445, 511, 624
General partners, 10
Geothermal Corporation, 391, 397
  capital structure, 392
  company cost of capital, 394–395
  company cost of debt, 396
  cost of capital, 392
  debt-equity mix, 394
  NPV of expansion, 398–399
  weighted average cost of capital, 394–395, 400
Gere, Richard, 20
Global Crossing, 72
Goals
  in financial planning, 531
  financial planning to establish, 529
  investment needed to meet, 530
Going-concern value, 202
Goldman Sachs, 10, 21, 22n, 43, 449
Goodwill, on balance sheet, 59
Google Finance, 61
Google Inc., 39, 203, 217, 449, 506, 630n, 665
  initial public offering, 441
  weighted average cost of capital, 407
Gordon, Myron, 210
Government-sponsored entities, 50n
Gradley, Richard, 22
Graham, J. R., 70n, 337n, 378n, 510, 553n
Grand Union, 502
Green, T. C., 222n
Greenbacks, 24
Greenmail transactions, 509
Greenwood, R., 508n
Growth companies, 202–204
  less borrowing by, 490
  small or no dividends, 506
Growth rate, 531
  financial planning and changes in, 537
  internal, 540–541
  sustainable, 211, 212, 540–541
Growth stocks, 213, 214
Guiso, L., 18n
Gulf oil spill of 2010, 510

H

H. J. Heinz Company, 612, 614
Hard capital rationing, 254
Harvard Industries, 502
Harvey, C. R., 70n, 337n, 378n, 510, 553n
Haushalter, G. D., 695n
Healy, P., 508n, 509–510, 631
Hedge funds, 41
  investment strategies, 41

large fees, 41n
vulture funds, 41
Hedging
  and capital asset pricing model, 717
  extraneous events, 694–695
  and financial distress, 694
  financial instruments for, 693, 721
  with forward contracts, 701–702
  with futures contracts, 696–701
  innovation in derivatives market, 705
  no increase in firm value, 694
  and operations manager, 694
  with options, 696
  problems with derivatives, 705–706
  reasons for
    investor do-it-yourself alternatives, 694
    as zero-sum game, 694
  risk reduction *vs.* speculation, 705–706
  and sensible risk strategy, 695
  with swaps, 702–705
  types of derivatives, 695
Helyar, J., 627n
Hewlett-Packard, 17, 513, 514, 631
  acquisition of Autonomy, 6, 71
  market value balance sheet, 512
Hidden debt, 477
High-dividend stock, 515
Histograms, 339–341
Historical cost, 61, 201
Hobbit, The, 239
Home Depot, 16, 91
  after-tax operating income, 92
  assets turnover ratio, 96
  balance sheet, 58–60, 90
  book *vs.* market value, 60
  brand name, 95
  common-size balance sheet, 60–61
  common-size income statement, 64
  cost of capital, 92, 94
  credit sales, 92n
  earnings, 60n
  EBIT, 64
  economic value added, 90, 92
  equity components, 60
  financial leverage, 100–102
  financial measures, 106
  financial ratios over time, 106
  free cash flow, 68–70, 69–70
  income for investors, 92
  income statement, 89
  inventory turnover ratio, 96
  and Lowe's, 105–106
  market capitalization, 89, 92
  market-to-book ratio, 90
  market value added, 89
  net working capital, 103–104
  receivables turnover ratio, 96–97

return on assets, 94
return on capital, 93–94
return on equity, 95
shareholder value, 90–91
statement of cash flows, 67–69
summary of performance measures, 105
Horizontal merger
  definition, 612–613
  economies of scale from, 614
Horizon value, 408–409
Horizon value formulas, 219
Hostile takeovers, 611
Housing prices, 48
HUDWAY, 444
Hurdle rate, 14, 48
  offset bias by increasing, 306

I

IBM, 38, 353–354, 624, 705
  beta, 367
  standard deviation for common stock, 343
  weighted average cost of capital, 407
Icahn, Carl, 625, 630
Income
  after-tax, 429
  before-tax, 429
  versus cash flow
    cash *vs.* accrual accounting, 65–66
    depreciation, 65–66
  ordinary, 75
Income statement
  break-even sales volume, 311
  capital expenditures, 65
  cash *vs.* accrual accounting, 65–66
  common size, 66–67
  cost of capital omitted, 91
  definition, 63
  depreciation, 64–65
  earnings disposition, 66–67
  effect of transactions, 66–67
  Home Depot, 63–65
  income *vs.* cash flow, 64–67
  profit *vs.* cash flow, 66–67
  retained earnings, 66–67
  and statement of cash flows, 67
Income stocks, 213
Incremental cash flows, 271
  discounting, 276
  forecasting, 278
  and overhead costs, 280
Indexed bonds, 181
Index mutual funds, 45
Indirect costs of bankruptcy, 484
Indirect effects, 278
Industries
  current assets as percentage of total assets, 573
  financial ratios, 107
Industry consolidation

banks, 617
from mergers, 616–617
Inefficiencies eliminated by merger, 616
Inflation, 25
  and bond prices, 181
  and cash flows, 281–282
  and Consumer Price Index, 148, 149
  definition, 148
  effect on Bill Gates, 152
  and price of gasoline, 149
  and time value of money
    and interest rates, 149–150
    real *vs.* nominal cash flows, 148–149
    real *vs.* nominal NPV calculation, 153
    valuing real cash payments, 151
Inflation-indexed bonds, 181
Inflation-indexed debt, 25
Inflation-linked bonds, 705
Inflation rate
  and cash flows, 148–149
  impact on cash flows, 281
  in U.S. 1900–2015, 149
Inflation swaps, 705
Information
  asymmetric, 488
  value of, 309
Information content
  of dividends, 509–510
  in stock repurchases, 510–511
Initial public offering
  Alibaba, 444
  Apple Inc., 35, 441
  average return on, 225
  case, 459–460
  definition, 37, 198, 444
  Facebook, 217, 441
  FedEx, 4
  followed by poor performance, 718
  Google Inc., 441
  Internet 1990-2000, 37
  as primary offering, 444
  secondary offerings, 444
  total direct costs, 448
  underwriters, 449–450
  underwriting arrangements
    best-efforts basis, 445
    and blue-sky laws, 446
    bookbuilding method, 449
    firm commitment, 445
    floatation costs, 448–449
    issue pricing, 446
    and open auction, 449
    prospectus, 446
    road shows, 446
    Securities and Exchange Commission regulations, 4
    spread, 445
    underpricing, 446–447
    Visa, 448–449

Inputs, in financial planning, 531–532
Insider trading, 626
Insolvency, 507n
Installment credit, 675
Installment plan, 130
Institutional shareholders, 625
Insurance against risk, 695
Insurance companies/industry
  employment in, 21
  functions, 43
  locations, 22
  losses by, 45n
Intangible assets, 3
  on balance sheet, 59
  depreciation of, 102
  and going-concern value, 202
  heavy involvement in, 239
  investment in, 6, 119
Intel Corporation, 61, 123, 506, 553
  beta, 367
  as corporate venturer, 443
  standard deviation for common stock, 343
  weighted average cost of capital, 407
Interest
  in cash forecasts, 558
  deductible, 393
  floating payment, 38
  foregone by holding cash, 588
  tax deductible, 480
Interest coverage ratio, 101
Interest deduction, 73–74
Interest-free reserves, 431n
Interest payment, 100
Interest rate options, 665
Interest rate risk, 594, 695
  for bonds, 174
Interest rates
  after-tax, 480
  annual percentage rate, 146–147
  bank loans, 596
  and bond prices, 169–174
  comparing, 146
  on corporate debt, 428–430
  effective annual, 146–147
  floating, 430
  fluctuating, 167
  and inflation, 150–151
  information on, 47
  on interbank loans, 49n
  and internal rate of return, 251–252
  and investors, 180
  MM proposition II, 475–476
  nominal, 150–151
  in nominal terms, 281
  and present value calculation, 127–128
  prime rate, 430
  real, 150–151
  10-year Treasury bonds, 172
  trade credit, 577
  Treasury bonds, 167

and value of call option, 674
and value of long-term bonds, 335–336
Interest rate swaps, 702–703
Interest tax shield
  calculating, 478–479
  definition, 478
  and value of shareholders' equity, 479
Internal growth rate, 540–541
Internally generated funds, 420–421, 423
Internal rate of return, 239–240
  financial calculators for, 250
  incremental cash flows, 271
  and interest rates, 251–252
  modified, 253, 271–272
  versus opportunity cost of capital, 248
  spreadsheet solutions, 249
  summary of, 261
Internal rate of return rule
  agreement with NPV rule, 246, 248
  for long-lived projects, 246–248
  modified, 271–272
  multiple rates of return, 252–253
  mutually exclusive projects, 271
  versus NPV rule, 245–246
  pitfalls
    lending or borrowing, 251–252
    mutually exclusive projects, 249–251
    mutually exclusive projects involving different outlays, 261
Internal Revenue Service, 290, 632
  on depreciation, 73
  loss carryback, 74
Internet
  bond information from, 186
  initial public offerings, 37
Intrinsic value, 206
  of common stock, 204–205
  definition, 204
Inventories
  carrying costs, 586, 587
  for collateral, 597
  composition of, 586
  as current asset, 571, 572
  increase in, 557–558
  shortages, 587
Inventory financing, 597
Inventory management
  build-to-order goods, 588
  carrying costs, 586, 587
  costs of holding inventory, 586
  economic order quantity, 587
  essential features of, 587
  just-in-time systems, 96, 578–588
  optimal policy, 586–587
  order cost, 568–587
Inventory turnover ratio, 96

Investing *vs.* gambling, 331
Investment banks, 42–43
  advice on takeovers, 42
  bridge loans, 42n
  compared to commercial banks, 43n
  as corporations, 10
  functions, 21
  largest in U.S., 449
  in New York, 22
  as underwriters, 449–450
  underwriting, 42
  underwriting arrangements, 449–450
Investment criteria
  comparison of, 261
  comparisons of, 261
  internal rate of return, 245–253
  mutually exclusive projects, 255–261
  net present value, 239–245
  payback rule, 255–256
  profitability index, 253–255
Investment decisions, 3; *see also* Capital budgeting decisions; Financial investment criteria
  central to success, 239
  compared to financing decisions, 6–7
  by corporations, 21
  failure of, 6
  FedEx, 4–5
  financial planning for, 529
  versus financing decisions, 419
  and NPV, 318
  and payout policy, 511
  recent examples, 5
  separate from financing decisions, 282–283
  and shareholder value, 88, 518–519
  side effects of financing, 721
  small, 6
Investment grade bonds, 47, 183
Investment horizon, 206–209, 215
Investment management departments, 22
Investment opportunity frontier, 346–347
Investment risk, 15
  measuring, 339–343
  and speed of possible returns, 339–340
Investments
  acquisitions as, 611
  and cost of capital, 48
  earnings plowed back into, 213–214
  effect on market value, 13–14
  example, 373
  and going-concern value, 202
  growth 1899-2009, 334
  hurdle rate, 48
  in inventories, 65
  kinds of, 119

least risky and riskiest, 371–372
long-term consequences, 6
long-term with short-term debt, 402n
money market, 593–594
in net working capital, 279–280
opportunities for young firms, 519
positive-NPV, 421
rates of return, 14
reasons for, 119
and risk, 241
risky, 15
taxation of income from, 75
by venture capitalists, 4, 5
Investment strategies, 41
Investment timing
  decision, 257–258
  decision rule, 258
Investment trade-off, and value maximization, 13–14
Investors
  acquiring stock by way of call options, 674
  and acquisitions, 631
  advantages of mutual funds, 40
  angel, 443
  blockholders, 17
  bond information on interest rates, 186
  and convertible bonds, 680–681
  in debt *vs.* equity, 6
  dislike of risk, 714
  diversification by, 45–46, 331
  and financial managers, 11–12
  finding undervalued stock, 220
  flight to quality, 595
  and general cash offers, 453
  and hedging choice, 694
  and high-payout stock, 515
  and high stock prices, 508n
  information for, 18
  information provided to, 47–48
  and interest rates, 180
  investment horizon, 206–209
  irrational exuberance, 228
  junior, 433
  mistakes by, 48n
  news of dividend increase, 509
  number of securities to choose from, 333
  preference for liquid bonds, 184
  preference for regular dividends, 515
  pressure on Apple, 516
  pricing common stocks, 226
  required rate of return, 394
  risk averse, 12
  risk measurement, 339–341
  risk tolerant, 12
  sellers of options, 668
  senior, 433
  short selling, 20
  in 3Com, 631
  trading financial assets, 7
  and trading volatility, 678

valuing liquidity, 720
  and warrants, 680
  worldwide, 36
  in young companies, 206
Iowa Electronics Market, 39
Iron ore futures, 705
Irrational exuberance, 228
"Is beta dead" question, 378
Issued shares, 424
Issue pricing, 446

J

JCPenney, 17
Jegadeesh, N., 225n
Jensen, Michael, 489–490, 508n,
    629n
Jobs, Steve, 441, 516
John Deere, investment and
    financing decisions, 5
Johnson, Ross, 627–628, 629
Johnson & Johnson, 184, 203
  investments by, 218
  market-to-book value, 204
  market vs. book value, 201
  price-earnings ratio, 204
  sources of value, 202
  stock price, 201
JPMorgan Chase, 7, 42, 48, 449, 510
  dividend policy, 511
Jumbo mortgages, 50n
Junior creditors, 501, 502
Junior investors, 433
Junk bond market, 628–629
Junk bonds, 47, 183
  default rate, 628–629
Just-in-time systems, 96, 587–588

K

Kane, J., 50
Kaplan, S., 629
Kellogg, 343
Kickstarter, 444
Kinko's, 4, 421–422
Koch Industries, 445
Kohlberg Kravis Roberts, 627–628
Korwas, A. N., 452n
Kozlowski, Dennis, 15, 17
Kraft Foods, 612

L

Labor costs, 558
Lamont, A. A., 631n
Lazard, 42
LBO; see Leveraged buyouts
Leases, 432
  cost of debt embedded in, 477
Leasing, 721
Lee, Immoo, 448
Legal capital, 508
Lehman Brothers collapse, 8, 24, 25,
    49, 51, 176, 483, 595, 598

Level cash flows
  annuities due, 134–144
  annuity factor, 137
  future value of annuities,
      140–142
  lottery winnings, 138–139, 144
  mortgage payments, 139–140
  retirement savings, 142–143
  valuing annuities, 136–139
  valuing perpetuities, 135–136
Leverage
  effect on cost of financial
      distress, 483
  and incentives, 629
  and return on equity, 102
  and taxes, 629
Leveraged buyouts, 100
  and bondholders, 629
  cash cow targets, 629
  compared to other acquisitions,
      627
  definition, 627
  diet deals, 628
  for division of companies, 627
  ending in bankruptcy, 629
  free-cash-flow theory, 629
  and incentives, 629
  junk bond market, 628–629
  junk debt, 627
  management buyouts, 627
  private equity activity, 627
  RJR Nabisco, 627–628, 629
  and stakeholders, 629
  and taxes, 629
Leverage ratios
  cash coverage ratio, 101–102
  debt ratio, 100–101
  return on equity, 102
  times interest earned ratio, 101
Levered firm, 473
Levi Strauss, 444
Li, K., 510
Liabilities
  versus assets, 60
  on balance sheet, 58–60
  book vs. market value, 61
  long-term, 62
Liberty Global, 613
Life cycle of the firm, 518–519
Life insurance companies
  as lenders, 21
  mortality bonds, 434
Limited liability, 10, 429
  definition, 8
Limited liability companies, 10
Limited liability partnerships, 10
Limited partners, 10
Limit order book, 199
Line of credit
  backup, 598
  revolving, 596
LinkedIn, 612
Liquid assets, 58, 103
Liquidation
  definition, 501
  versus reorganization, 502–503

Liquidation value, 201–202
Liquid bonds, 184
Liquidity
  advantages of, 553
  and corporate bond pricing, 720
  definition, 46, 103
  disappearance of, 51
  drawback, 103
  from holding cash, 588
  lacking in financial crisis, 720
  maintaining, 553
  measuring, 103–104
  money market securities, 594
  pricing differences in, 720
  provided by financial
      institutions, 46
  valued by investors, 720
  value decline, 720
Liquidity ratios
  cash ratio, 104
  less desirable characteristics,
      103
  net working capital to total
      assets ratio, 103–104
  quick ratio, 104
Loan covenants, 487
Loans
  amortizing, 149
  ARM loans, 49n
  from banks, 6–7
  bridge loans, 42n
  collateralized, 594
  conforming, 50n
  to corporations, 42
  floating-rate, 430
  NINJA, 49
Lock-box system, 589–590
Lockhead, Scott, 448
Lockheed, 278–279, 315
Long-lived projects
  calculating rate of return for,
      246–248
  cash flows from, 242–244
  and net present value, 242–244
Long-term bonds, 402
Long-term debt, 38, 595
Long-term debt-equity ratio, 100
Long-term debt ratio, 100–101
Long-term financial planning; see
      also Financial planning
  links to short-term financing
  alternative approaches, 553
  cumulative capital
      requirement, 552–553
  maintaining liquidity, 553
  time horizon, 552
  permanent cash surplus, 552
Long-term financing, 43, 402n
Long-term financing decisions,
    552
Long-term liabilities, 60, 62
Long-term Treasury bonds, 184,
    334, 405
Lorillard, 612
Loss carryback, 74
Loss of degree of freedom, 342n

Lottery winnings, 138–139, 144
Low dividend payout policy, 517
Lowe's, 105
  financial measures, 106
  and Home Depot, 106–107
Low-quality earnings, 71

M

Machine replacement timing,
    260–261
Machine tool manufacturers, macro
    risks, 353
Macro risk, 352–353
Madoff, Bernard, 19
Magnoosium, 288n
Majluf, N. S., 453n
Majority voting, 427
Makkula, Mike, 34
Management
  and agency theory, 716
  changes in, 624
  means of changing
    carve-outs, 630
    divestitures, 630
    LBOs, 627–630
    proxy contests, 625
    spin-offs, 630
    takeovers, 625–627
  replacement of, 611
  separation of ownership and,
      624
Management buyouts
  definition, 627
  study of, 629
Managers
  acceptable risks, 693
  of companies not taken over,
      632
  conflicts of interest, 305
  constant scrutiny of, 70–71
  effect of bankruptcy threat,
      486–487
  interests aligned with
      shareholders, 624
  of LBOs, 629
  market share goal, 13
  profit maximization by, 13
  replaced after mergers, 611
  self-interest, 15
  and shareholders, 3
  use of discounted cash-flow
      analysis, 262
  use of weighted average cost of
      capital, 391
  views of dividend policies,
      509–510
Manhattan Island purchase price,
    122–123
Manville Corporation, 502–503
Margin account, 696n
Marginal tax rate, 74
Margin requirement, 700
Marked to market, 700, 701n
Market, reasons for entering, 530

Marketable securities
    Apple Inc., 516
    as current asset, 572
Market anomalies; *see* Stock
        market
Market capitalization
    Apple Inc., 34
    definition, 89
    FedEx, 199
    Home Depot, 89–91
    Microsoft, 7
    for selected companies, 90
Market for corporate control
    and agency costs, 624
    definition, 611, 624
    and separation of ownership and
        management, 624
    and shark repellent, 627
    ways to change management
        divestitures, spin-offs, and
            carve-outs, 630
        leveraged buyouts, 627–630
        proxy contests, 625
        takeovers, 625–627
Market indexes
    historical record, 333–336
    list of, 333
Marketing department, 532
Market order, 198–199
Market portfolio
    definition, 362
    rates of return, 336
Market price, 202, 240
Market risk, 45
    and beta of portfolio, 370
    definition, 351
    higher rate of return to
        compensate for, 361
    as macro risk, 352–353
    measuring, 714
        betas, 361–365
        portfolio beta, 367
        total risk, 365–367
    risk management, 353–354
    versus specific risk, 350–351,
        361
Market risk premium, 371–372
Market share, 13
Market-to-book ratio
    definition, 90–91
    for selected companies, 90
Market-to-book value, for selected
        companies, 204
Market turmoil, 595
Market value, 240
    versus asset value, 719
    versus book value, 61–63,
        201–203
    company cost of capital based
        on, 396
    definition, 62, 201
    drawbacks
        fluctuations, 91
        investor expectations, 91
        privately owned
            companies, 91

effect of investments, 13–14
    Geothermal Corporation, 394
    Hewlett-Packard, 512
    investment trade-off, 13–14
    lender interest in, 101
    maximization, 12–15
    and opportunity cost of capital,
        14–15
    for selected companies, 201
    stock price, 202
Market value added
    definition, 89
    Home Depot, 89–90
    for selected companies, 90
Market-value balance sheet, 62–63
Market Volatility Index, 678
Marriott, 423
Marsh, Paul R., 333–334, 335,
        339, 341
Martin, K. J., 616n
Massachusetts Bay Colony, 24
MasterCard, 591
Masulis, R. W., 452n, 490n
Matching maturities, 552–553
Maturities
    of bonds, 38
    corporate debt, 430
    differing, 168
    matching, 552–553
    money market investments, 594
    money market securities, 594
    short-term, 334
Maturity date, 38
    forward contracts, 701
    futures contracts, 696
    lacking for preferred stock, 398
Maturity premium, 334–335
McConnell, J. J., 616n
McDonald's, 362, 370
    beta, 367
    market-to-book value, 204
    market *vs.* book value, 201
    price-earnings ratio, 204
    standard deviation for common
        stock, 343
    stock price, 201
    stock valuation, 215–216
    weighted average cost of capital,
        407
McNichols, M. F., 580
Medtronic, 453, 612
Memorex, 502
Mergers
    benefits and costs of, 630–632
    case, 636–637
    conglomerate, 612–613
    cross-border, and tax inversion,
        620
    defining costs and benefits, 611
    definition, 612–613, 619
    difficulty of realizing benefits
        of, 613–614
    dubious reasons for
        bootstrap game, 617–618
        diversification, 617
    evaluation of

cash financing, 620–622
    stock financing, 622–623
    warnings, 623–624
explaining waves of, 630–632,
        719–720
failures of, 613–614
financed by cash, 616
global value of, 611
horizontal, 612–613
hostile takeovers, 611
and management replacement,
        611
market for corporate control
    agency costs, 624
    divestitures, spin-offs, and
        carve-outs, 630
    leveraged buyouts, 627–629
    management buyouts, 627
    management changes, 624
    proxy contests, 625
    takeovers, 625–627
mechanics of
    and antitrust laws, 619–620
    form of acquisition, 619
    and popular opposition,
        619–620
    tender offer, 619–620
number of, in 2015, 611
recent, 611, 612
sensible reasons for
    better management, 616
    combining complementary
        resources, 615–616
    to create synergies, 613
    economies of scale, 614
    economies of vertical
        integration, 614–615
    eliminating inefficiencies,
        616
    industry consolidation,
        616–617
    use for surplus funds, 616
success of
    eliminating inefficiencies,
        616
    industry consolidation,
        616–617
in United States 1995–2015, 612
vertical, 612–613
warfare strategies, 626–627
Merrill Lynch, 25, 43n, 49, 51, 612
Merton, Robert, 675, 716, 717
Mian, S. L., 585n
Michaely, R., 510
Microsoft Corporation, 94, 95,
        200, 488, 506, 612, 613
    cost of capital, 93
    economic value added, 92–93
    financing decisions, 6
    long-term capital, 93
    market-to-book ratio, 90
    market value added, 90
    return on capital, 93
Midyear convention, 289n
Mikkelson, W. H., 452n
Mill, John Stuart, 717

Miller, Merton H., 468, 511, 715,
        719
Minuit, Peter, 122, 123
Mitchell, M., 631n
MM proposition I, 715
    risk and return, 472–473
    and corporate tax, 479
    cost of equity, 469–470
    debt *vs.* earnings per share,
        470–472
    definition, 469, 472
    on dividends, 514–515
    interest rate shield, 479
    and payout policy, 511–512
    and restructuring, 469–470
    shareholder risk, 470–472
    simplifying assumptions, 469
    value of the firm, 468–469, 472
MM proposition II, 715
    debt-equity ratio, 474–475
    definition, 474
Modified accelerated cost recovery
        system, 290–291
Modified cash-flow sequence, 272
Modified internal rate of return,
        253, 271–272
Modigliani, Franco, 468, 511, 715,
        719
Momentum factor, 225
Money management, 21–22
Money managers, 221
Money market
    calculating yield, 594
    corporate *vs.* U.S. securities, 595
    default risk, 595
    definition, 38, 593
    during financial crisis, 595
    fixed-income securities, 594
    interest rate risk, 594
    interest rates, 595
    international, 595–596
    investments
        certificates of deposit, 594
        commercial paper, 594
        repurchase agreements, 594
        Treasury bills, 594
    liquidity in, 594
    during market turmoil, 595
    mutual fund, 593
    short maturities, 594
    yield on investments, 595
Monsanto
    beta, 367
    standard deviation for common
        stock, 343
    weighted average cost of capital,
        397, 407
Moody's Investors Services, 183,
        578
Moore, Gordon, 123
Morgan Stanley, 10, 21, 25, 42, 449
Mortality bonds, 434
Mortgage-backed securities, 49,
        50, 51
Mortgage pass-through certificates,
        433

Mortgage payments, 139–140, 141
Mortgages
    default rates, 103
    jumbo, 50n
    subprime, 49, 50
Moskowitz, T. J., 225n
Motorola, 625, 630
Motorola Mobility, 630
Mullins, D. W., 452n
Multiple cash flows
    future value, 128–129
    present value, 130–131
    spreadsheet solutions, 134–135
Multiple rates of return, 252–253
Municipal bonds, default risk, 183n
Murphy, T., 588n
Mutual funds, 21–22, 593
    advantages to investors, 40
    closed-end fund, 40n, 718
    definition, 41
    definition and functions, 41
    and exchange-traded funds, 45n
    index, 45
    as investment companies, 40
    management fees, 40
    number of, 40
    open-end fund, 40n
    risks, 368–370
Mutually exclusive projects,
        256–261
    choice between long- vs. short-
        lived equipment, 258–260
    choosing among, 244
    internal rate of return for
        choosing, 271
    and internal rate of return rule,
        249–251
    investment timing decision,
        257–258
    machine replacement problem,
        260–261
    trade-offs, 258
Myers, S. C., 401n, 453n, 480n

N

Nardelli, Robert, 16
NASDAQ, 37, 198, 427
    decline in 2002, 336
    and dot-com bubble, 227
NASDAQ Composite Index, 718
Negative-risk asset, 36
Net asset value, 40n
Net common equity, 425
Net current assets, 59
Net fixed assets, 534–535
Net income
    versus cash flows, 67
    and internal growth rate, 540
Net present value, 14n
    calculating, 241, 276–277, 396
    calculating cost of capital, 241
    definition, 241
    determining, 241
    financial calculators for, 250

of Geothermal expansion,
        398–399
    gold standard of investment
        criteria, 262
    granting credit, 582
    versus internal rate of return
        rule, 245–246
    and investment decisions, 318
    long-lived projects, 242–244
    to measure cost of projects, 275
    to measure worth of projects,
        288–289
    mutually exclusive projects, 244
    negative, 276
    of new machines, 260–261
    office block project, 240–241
    opportunity cost of capital, 241,
        242–243
    positive, 239, 303
    versus profitability index,
        253–254
    and profit calculation, 277
    in project analysis, 291–293
    and risk, 241
    in sensitivity analysis, 307
    spreadsheet solutions, 245
    steps in calculating, 244
    summary of, 261
    and sunk costs, 278
    and timing option, 319–320
Net working capital, 59; see also
        Working capital
    definition, 103, 572
    Home Depot, 103–104
    recognizing investment in, 279
    and total assets ratio, 103–104
Net worth, 428
New issue puzzle, 225–226
Newmont Mining, 381
    beta, 367
    market return, 366–367
    standard deviation, 349–350
    standard deviation for common
        stock, 343
    weighted average cost of capital,
        407
New product development, 441
New product launch, 278
New products, costs and risks, 6
New York, foreign exchange
        turnover, 640
New York Composite Index, 223
New York Mercantile Exchange,
        47, 705
New York Stock Exchange, 9, 33,
        37, 38, 427, 619
    daily trading volume, 198
    formation of, 24
    trading volume, 640
NINJA loans, 49
No-dividend companies, 506
No-growth dividend discount
        model, 209
Nominal cash flows, 148–149, 281
Nominal cost of capital, 281
Nominal discount rate, 281

Nominal dollar, 149
Nominal interest rate, 150, 181–
        182, 281
Nominal NPV calculation, 153
Noncash expenses, 400n
Nonconstant growth dividend
        discount model
    estimates of McDonald's value,
        215
    formula, 215
    investment horizon, 215
    terminal value, 216
    valuation errors, 216
    value of dividends, 215
Nondiversifiable risks, 714
NPV; see Net present value
NPV break-even point, 312–314
NPV profile, 247, 249
    of projects, 246
NPV rule
    agreement with internal rate of
        return rule, 248
    and capital rationing, 262
    choosing among projects, 244
    definition, 241
    merits of, 714
    steps, 275
NPV zero, 246–247
Numerical credit scoring, 578–579

O

Odean, Terrance, 220–221
Off-balance sheet assets and
        liabilities, 71
Oil companies, 616
One at a time variables, 307
Ooi, Y. H., 225n
Open account, 577
Open auction, stock sales, 449
Open-end fund, 40n
Open-market repurchase, 509
Operating cash flow, 278–288
    cost-cutting projects, 284
    dealing with depreciation, 284,
        288
    example, 285
    forecasting, 287–288
    forecasts, 407–408
    formula, 284
    new projects, 283
Operating cycle, 573–574
Operating income
    effect on earnings per share,
        472–473
    and restructuring, 473
Operating leverage
    definition, 315–316
    degree of, 316
    and project risk, 317, 380
Operating profit margin, 98
Operating risk, 473
Opportunity cost
    in cash-flow analysis, 279
    definition, 279

for funds invested, 170
Opportunity cost of capital, 33,
        48, 336
    and CAPM
        company cost of capital, 380
        determining project risk,
            380–381
        estimating, 379
        fudge factors, 381
        project cost of capital,
            378–379
    as company cost of capital, 394
    definition, 14, 241, 378
    discounting future cash flows
        as, 714
    and expected rate of return, 91
    formula, 474
    versus internal rate of return,
        248
    and internal rate of return rule,
        246
    investment risk, 15
    measuring, 15
    and net present value, 241,
        242–243
    and rate of return, 339
Optimal capital structure, 490
Option(s)
    as choices, 715
    in financial planning, 530–531
Option premium, 668
Option price, 673, 675
Options
    American call, 666n
    call options, 666–668
    determinants of value
        high stock price, 673–674
        stock price exceeds minimum
            value, 674
        worthless stock price, 673
    embedded in capital budgeting
        projects, 665
    European call, 666n
    on financial assets, 679–682
        callable bonds, 681–682
        convertible bonds, 680–681
        executive stock options, 680
    versus futures, 696–697
    increased use of, 716
    Market Volatility Index, 678
    modifying risk characteristics of
        stock, 670–671
    payoff diagram, 669–670
    versus payoff from holding
        stock, 671
    payoffs, 668, 669–670
    positions, right, and obligations,
        669
    profit diagram, 669–670
    protective put, 670
    put-call parity, 671
    put options, 666–668
    on real assets
        option to abandon, 679
        option to expand, 678
    real estate, 705

Options *Cont.*
    for risk management, 665, 693, 696
    selling, 668–669
    types traded, 665
    upper and lower limits on value, 672–673
    value at expiration date, 672–673
    yearly trading volume, 665
Option to abandon, 319, 679
Option to expand, 317–318, 678
Option valuation models
    Black-Scholes formula, 675–677, 716
    fear index, 676, 678
    Financial Accounting Standards Board standards, 680
    simple model, 676
Oracle Corporation, 16, 17, 680
Order costs, 586
Ordinary income, 75
Ordinary least squares regression, 365n
Ortiz, A., 337n
Other current assets, 58
Outputs in financial planning, 531–532
Outsourcing *vs.* vertical integration, 624
Outstanding shares, 424
Overconfidence, 27
Overhead costs, 280
Overpricing, 488
Over-the-counter trading, 38

P

Pacific Gas & Electric, 375, 380, 598
    beta, 365, 367, 375
    weighted average cost of capital, 407
Page, Larry, 441
Palepu, K., 508n, 510, 631
Palm, 630, 631
PalmOne, 631
Palm Pilot, 631
Paper money, 24
Partch, M. M., 452n
Partnerships
    definition, 10
    limited, 10
    tax advantage, 10
    unlimited liability, 10
Par value, 168
    common stock, 425
Paulson, John, 20
Payables; *see* Accounts payable
Payback period, 255
    summary of, 261
Payback rule, 240
    cutoff period, 255
    definition, 255
    discounted payback period, 256
    and net present value, 255

payback period, 255
    problems with, 255
    reasons for using, 255–256
    simplicity, 256
Payment mechanism, 46–47
Payment systems, 590–591
Payoff
    on financial investments, 693
    on options, 668, 669–670
    protective put strategy, 670
Payoff diagram, 669–670
Payout date, 507
Payout policy
    Apple Inc., 505
    and capital budgeting, 514
    case, 526–527
    controversy
        dividends and share issues, 514–515
        dividends *vs.* repurchase, 512–513
        MM proposition I, 511–512
        repurchase and dividend discount model, 513–514
    definition, 505
    high-dividend policy, 515
    information content
        dividends, 509–510
        stock repurchase, 510–511
    and life cycle of the firm, 518–519
    low-dividend policy, 517
    managerial views, 509
    means used
        cash dividends, 506–508
        stock dividends, 508
        stock repurchase, 506, 509
        stock splits, 508
    MM propositions, 715
    opposing points of view, 511
    real-world complications, 505
    reasons for dividend value decrease, 517–518
    reasons for dividend value increase, 515–516
    resolving dividend controversy, 719
    tax implications, 518
    and value of common stock, 511
Payout ratio, 211
Pecking order theory of capital structure
    asymmetric information, 488
    definition, 489
    internal and external funds, 488–489
Pedersen, L. H., 225n
Penkowitz, L., 553
Penn Central Railroad, 24
Pension benefit Guarantee Corporation, 501
Pension funds
    long-run investment, 41
    taxation of, 75
    total assets in 2015, 41
    types of, 41

Pensions, 432
PepsiCo, 619
    market-to-book value, 204
    market *vs.* book value, 201
    price-earnings ratio, 204
    stock price, 201
Percentage of sales models
    assumptions and complexities, 537
    balancing item, 535
    definition, 532
    steps in, 533–535
Perpetuities
    definition, 135
    preferred stock as, 398
    present value, 210
    valuing, 135–136
Pershing Square, 626
Personal tax
    average rate, 74
    on capital gains, 75
    on dividend income, 75
    double taxation, 75
    on investment earnings, 75
    marginal rate, 74
    on ordinary income, 75
    tax rate, 75
Petersen, M. A., 585n
Pfizer, 333
    beta, 367
    standard deviation for common stock, 343
    weighted average cost of capital, 407
Pharmaceutical firms, 616
Plain vanilla bonds, 187
Planet Hollywood, 502
Planning horizon, 530
Planning model, 531–532
Plowback ratio, 211
Plug, 535
Poison pill, 626, 627
Ponzi, Charles, 19n
Ponzi scheme, 19
Portfolio
    macro risks, 353
    measures of performance, 334–336
    types of, 333
    volatility, 344–350
Portfolio betas, 367–371
Portfolio deviation, 343–344
Portfolio return, 345
Portfolio risk, 331, 371
    versus asset risk, 343–350
    calculating, 347–350
    economic scenarios for, 344–346
    investment opportunity frontier, 346–347
    market *vs.* specific risk, 350–351
Positive NPV, 249, 303
Positive-NPV investments, 257, 421
Postpetition creditors, 502
Postretirement health benefits, 432

Powerball lottery, 138–139, 144
Power Computing Corporation, 34
Prediction markets, 39
Preferred stock
    characteristics, 398
    convertible, 435
    definition, 428
    dividends, 428
    expected return, 405–406
    floating-rate, 429
    lack of voting rights, 428
    and net worth, 428
    tax advantage, 429
Premium bonds, 275
Prepetition creditors, 502
Present value
    of annuities, 137, 141
    bonds, 170
    calculating, 124
    calculations, 288–289
    of cash payments, 152
    compound interest calculations, 125
    coupon payments, 171
    of coupon payments, 173
    definition, 124
    determinants, 716–717
    discounted cash-flow calculation, 124
    discount factor, 125
    discount rate, 124
    financial calculators for, 131–132
    finding interest rates, 127–128
    formula, 125
    of free credit, 126–127
    of future cash flows, 125
    multiple cash flows, 130–131
    of perpetuities, 210
    and project decisions, 240–241
    and risk, 241
    saving for future purchases, 124
    spreadsheet solutions, 132–135
    stock valuation, 204–205
Present value of its growth opportunities, 214, 217
Present value table, 126
Presidential election of 2016, 39
Pretax returns, 517
Pretty Woman, 20
Price-earnings multiple, 200
Price-earnings ratio, 200, 203
    and bootstrap game, 617
    high, 214
    infinite, 214
    for selected companies, 204
Pricing anomalies, 715
Primary issue, 37
Primary market, 198
    definition, 37
Primary offering, 198, 444
Prime rate, 430
Principal, 168
Principles-based accounting, 72–73
Private equity, 628

Private placements
advantages, 453
definition, 453
disadvantages, 453
and Rule 144a (SEC), 453
Private unlisted companies, 444
Probabilities, 227–228
Procter & Gamble, 5, 17, 630
stock buyback, 11
Production to order, 588
Product markets, 420
Professional corporations, 10
Profit
adjusted in accounting, 284
calculating, 65
versus cash flow, 66–67,
276–277
as earned, 277
Facebook, 217
forecasts to calculate, 303–304
on futures contracts, 697–698
negative at Amazon, 202
and net present value, 277
Profitability index, 240
capital rationing, 254
definition, 253
and investment of securities, 253
pitfalls, 254
positive NPV, 253
summary of, 261
Profitability ratios
asset turnover, 98
inventory turnover, 98
receivables turnover, 96–97
return on assets, 94
return on capital, 93–94
return on equity, 95
Profit diagram, 669–670
Profit margin
definition, 97
high or low, 98
operating, 98
versus turnover, 98–99
Profit maximization, 13
and credit decision, 583
Pro forma financial statements,
532, 534
Project analysis, 291–293
accounting, 311–312
break-even analysis, 312–315
case, 328–329
investment process
analysis of competitive
advantage, 304
capital budget, 304–305
consistent forecasts, 305
eliminating conflicts of
interest, 305
net present value, 312–315
operating leverage, 315–317
questions for financial
managers, 303–304
real options
flexible production facilities,
320
option to abandon, 319

option to expand, 317–319
timing option, 319–320
reducing forecast bias, 305
what-if questions, 303
crucial to capital budgeting,
306–307
scenario analysis, 310
sensitivity analysis,
307–310
Project cash flows, 282–283,
305–306, 399
Project cost of capital, 378–379
Project modification, 317
Project net present value, 398
Project rate of return, 246–247
Project risk, 317, 331
determinants, 716–717
determining, 380–381
and diversification, 343–351
asset *vs.* portfolio risk,
344–350
market risk *vs.* specific risk,
350–351
estimating cost of capital,
336–338
measuring
benchmarks, 338
standard deviation, 338–341
variance, 338–341
variations in stock returns,
341–343
operating leverage, 317
and opportunity cost of capital,
380–381
rates of return, 331, 343–344
thoughts on
dangerous but diversifiable
risks, 351–352
market risks as macro risk,
352–353
risks are measurable,
353–354
wildcat oil wells, 351–352
Projects; *see also* Capital
investment projects;
Mutually exclusive
projects
built-in flexibility, 303, 693
calculating NPV, 714
cost-cutting, 284
debt overhang problem, 486
determining value of, 278
in financial planning, 530
flexible, 678
long-lived, 242–244, 246–248
NPV profile, 246
possible variations in, 304
risk-free, 336
and stock valuation, 197
termination of, 319
understanding viability of, 529
value *vs.* cost
investment decisions,
240–241
measuring worth, 239–240
Property, plant, and equipment, 58

Prospectus
definition, 446
example, 461–464
general cash offering, 451
Protective covenants, 185
Protective put, 670
Proxy, 625
Proxy contests, 428, 625
Public companies, 9
becoming privately
owned, 445
under constant scrutiny, 70–71
Public Company Accounting
Oversight Board, 72
Purchasing power, 148
Put-call parity, 671
Put options
Alphabet, 657
definition, 666
option to abandon, 679
payoff diagram, 669–670
price and price of call, 671
profit diagram, 669–670
protective put, 670
and risk characteristics of
stocks, 670
selling, 668–669
and stock prices, 670–671

Q

Quick ratio, 104
Qwest Communications, 72

R

Rajan, R. G., 585n
Rajgopal, S., 70n
Random walk, 221–224
Random walk hypothesis, 715
Rate of return rule, 246
Rates of return, 15; *see also*
Expected rate of return
assumptions, 344
on bonds, 176–179
calculating, 246–248
common stock 1900–2015, 335
common stock fluctuations, 335
and cost of capital, 331
discount rate, 209
dividend yield, 200
expected by shareholders, 33
Geothermal Corporation, 394
hurdle rate, 14
least risky and riskiest
investments, 371–372
on market portfolio, 336
measuring variations in,
341–343
multiple, 252–253
nominal, 331–332
and opportunity cost of capital,
339
portfolio, 343–344
projected, 392

real, 331–332
and risk, 343–344
scenarios, 346
security market line, 374–375
Treasury bills, 335, 337
Treasury bonds, 177
on various portfolios, 333–336
versus yield to maturity,
176–177
Raw materials, depreciation on,
320
Raw materials inventories, 572
Real assets, 6–7, 678
definition, 678
option to abandon, 319, 679
option to expand, 317–318, 678
Real cash flows, 148–149, 281
Real cash payments, 151–152
Real dollars, 149
Real estate futures, 705
Real interest rate, 150, 181–182,
281
Real options
decision tree for, 318
definition, 317
flexible production facilities,
320
option to abandon, 319
option to expand, 317–318
timing option, 319–320
Real *vs.* nominal NPV, 153
Receivables, 58; *see also* Accounts
receivable
aging schedule, 584
definition, 96
loans secured by, 597
Receivables turnover ratio,
96–97
Record date, 507
Registration statement
general cash offers, 451
initial public offerings, 445
Regression line, 365n
Reinhardt, U. E., 315n
Reinvestment, 35
Related diversification, 613
Relational Investors, 20
Reorganization
definition, 501
versus liquidation, 502–503
Reorganization plan, 483–484, 501
Repayment process, 430–431
Replacement problem, 257,
260–261
Repurchase agreements
in money market, 594
Reputation, in finance, 19
Required external financing, 532–
533, 537–538
Required internal capital, 538–542,
539n
Required return, 714
Residual claimants, 60
Residual income, 91; *see also*
Economic value added
Restricted stock, 16

Restructuring
    and cost of capital, 474
    effect of capital structure,
        469–470, 472
    MM proposition I, 469–470,
        472
    and risk and return, 472
Retained earnings, 425
    Apple Inc., 35
    versus cash balances, 60n
    on income statement, 64
Retirement, saving for, 142
Return on assets
    definition, 93, 94
    Du Pont formula, 98–99
    Home Depot, 1–5, 93–94
    profit margin, 97–98
Return on capital
    calculating, 94
    definition, 93
    Home Depot, 93–94
    for selected companies, 93–94
Return on equity, 541n
    definition, 92, 95
    and earnings per share, 211–212
    and financial leverage, 100
    Home Depot, 93–94, 95
    and leverage, 102
Returns; see also Expected rate of
        return; Rates of return
    asset vs. market risk, 344–350
    on common stock, 363
    equally likely scenarios, 344
    factors affecting, 362
    historical record, 333–336
    measuring variations in,
        341–343
    standard deviation of, 341–342
    two forms of, 332
    U.S. Steel stock, 365
    weighted average, 345
Revenue recognition, 71
Revenues
    Apple Inc., 36
    Facebook, 217
    not constant, 312–313
Reverse splits, 509
Revolving line of credit, 596
Reynolds American, 612
Rhie, J.-W., 580
Rieker, M., 511
Rights issue
    definition, 450
    rare in U.S., 451
Risk(s)
    acceptable, 693
    asset, 343–350
    asset vs. portfolio, 344–350
    attitudes toward, 227
    business risk, 473
    common stock, 335–336
    credit, 183
    default, 185
    and depreciation, 343–344
    of different securities, 334–335
    diversifiable, 351–352

of diversified portfolio, 370
    financial, 475–476
    identifying, 705
    interest rate risk, 594
    investment, 15
    investors' dislike of, 714
    macro, 353
    market risk, 45, 351, 714
    market vs. specific risk,
        350–351
    measurable, 353–354
    in mutual funds, 368–370
    need to measure, 331
    in new products, 6
    nondiversifiable, 714
    and NPV rule, 714
    operating, 473
    portfolio, 331
    and present value, 241
    private placements, 453
    project, 317, 379–380
    reallocating, 45–46
    shareholder, 470–472
    spreadsheet solutions, 364
    in stock ownership, 198
    strategy for shifting, 486
    total, 370–371
Risk and return
    beta of investment, 714
    capital asset pricing model,
        714, 717
    effect of borrowing, 472–473
    historical record, 333–336
    market indexes, 333
    and market risk, 714
    market risk premium,
        371–372
    on portfolio, 346
    statistical problems, 717
Risk averse, 12, 15
Risk-free return, 371
Risk management, 353–354
    derivative instruments, 695
    derivatives market innovation,
        705
    evidence on, 695
    financial instruments for, 693,
        721
    with forward contracts, 701–702
    with futures contracts, 696–701
    identifying risks, 705
    with options, 696
    policy differences, 695
    problems with derivatives,
        705–706
    reasons for hedging, 694–695
    sensible strategy issues, 695
    with swaps, 702–705
    three ways of, 695
Risk measurement
    histograms, 339–340
    variance in standard deviation,
        338–341
    variation in stock returns, 341
Risk premium, 335, 370n
    average, 337

average expected, 337n
    future, 337
    for selected countries, 338
    for United States, 337, 338
Risk reduction
    versus speculation, 705–706
    transactions solely for, 694
Risk-shifting strategies, 486
Risk tolerant, 12
Risk transfer, 45–46
Ritter, Jay, 225n, 446n, 448
Ritz-Carlton, 613
RJR Nabisco, 24–25, 627–628,
        629, 632
    debt ratio, 187
Roadshows, 446
Rodriguez, Albert, 22
Rolfe, David A., 516
Roll, R., 508n
Ruback, R., 631
Rules-based accounting, 72–73

S

SABMiller, 596, 612
Sacconaghi, A. M., 516
Salad oil scandal, 597
Sales
    before cash flow, 277
    channel stuffing, 71
Sales department, 585
Sales-to-assets ratio, 96
Sales volume, break-even, 311
Salix Pharmaceuticals, 626
Salvage value, 283
    and book value, 291
Sapienza, P., 18n
Sarbanes-Oxley Act, 445
    and boards of directors, 17
    CEO and CFO requirements, 17
    reasons for, 25, 72
Savings
    flow to corporations, 35–42
    in hedge funds, 41
    in mutual funds, 40
    in pension funds, 41
    for retirement, 142
Savings and loan associations,
        42n, 50
Savings banks, 42n
Scenario analysis
    to answer what-if questions, 303
    definition, 310
Scenarios, equally likely, 344
Scholes, Myron, 675, 716
Schreffler, R., 588n
Schwartz, S. L., 226
Seasoned equity offerings, 448
Seasoned offering, 450
Secondary market, 198
    definition, 37
Secondary offerings, 444–446
Secondary transactions, 37
Second-stage financing, 443
Secured creditors, 501

Secured debt, 185
Secured loans, 597
Securities, 7
    commercial paper, 38
    convertible, 434–435
    derivatives, 38
    differing risks, 334–335
    in efficient capital markets, 420
    equally risky, 205
    financing by a mixture of, 391
    fixed-income, 593
    large number of, 333
    long-term debt, 38
    in money market, 594
    mortgage-backed, 49, 50, 51
    prices and available information,
        715
    short-term, 38
    transaction costs, 588
Securities and Exchange
        Commission, 18, 594,
        598, 625
    and accounting standards, 72
    and channel stuffing, 71
    financial statement filing, 58
    initial public offering
        regulations, 445–446
Security market line
    definition, 374
    expected return on betas,
        374–375
    rejecting, 379
Self-liquidating loans, 596
Self-regulatory organization, 186
Semiannual coupon payments, 171
Semi-strong form efficiency, 225,
        715
Senior creditors, 501
Senior investors, 433
Seniority, 185
Sensitivity analysis
    to answer what-if questions, 303
    definition, 307
    example, 307
    fixed costs, 307
    limitations, 309–310
    NPV calculations, 307
    one at a time variables, 307
    and project modification, 317
    unknown unknowns, 307
    value of information, 309
    variable costs, 307
Sentiment, 228
Separation of ownership and
        management, 9, 12, 624
Shareholders; see also Dividend
        policy; Payout policy
    access to financial markets, 12
    activists, 17–18, 427
    adjusting exposure, 694
    and agency theory, 716
    and NPV rule, 714
    blockholders, 17
    and capital investment
        decisions, 239
    versus debtholders, 486–487

definition, 8
delegation of decision making, 12
demand for information, 57
and ethics of value maximization, 18–19
institutional, 625
and integrity, 18
investment trade-off, 13–14
limited liability, 8
and managers, 3
managers' interests aligned with, 624
as partial owners, 197
profit maximization, 13
in proxy contests, 625
reasons for investing, 505
and reorganization, 502
residual claimants, 60
risk averse, 12
risk tolerant, 12
and risky projects, 486
taxation of, 9
in 3Com, 631
value maximization goal, 12–15
voting procedures
    cumulative voting, 427
    majority voting, 427
    proxy contests, 428
Walmart, 12
Shareholders' equity
on balance sheet, 60
book value, 201
book vs. market value, 62, 201–203
eBay, 202
FedEx, 425
and interest tax shield, 479, 489
statement of, 58n
Shareholder value, 87
driven by investment decisions, 518–519
financial ratios related to, 88–89
and financing decisions, 88
and investment decisions, 88
Shearson Lehman Hutton, 627
Shelf registration
advantages, 452
definition, 451
Shortage costs, 586
Short sellers, 41
Short selling, 20
Short-term debt, 101, 402n, 595
bank loans, 596–597
commercial paper, 597–598
Short-term financial decisions, 551
Short-term financial planning, 530
Short-term financing
case, 568–569
cash budgeting, 556–558
computer-generated, 561–562
links to long-term planning
    advantages of liquidity, 553
    alternative approaches, 553
    cumulative capital requirement, 552–553

time horizon, 552
nature of decisions, 551
note on planning models, 561–562
plan execution and evaluation, 559–561
plan to cover forecasted requirements, 558
sources
    bank loans, 596–597
    commercial paper, 597–598
sources of
    bank loans, 551, 559, 596–597
    commercial paper, 597–598
    stretching payables, 559
tracing changes in cash, 554–555
trial and error process, 561
Short-term maturity, 334
Short-term securities, 38
    versus cash, 588
    as current asset, 571
    in money market, 594
Shutdown costs, 283
Shutting down, 280
Sidel, R., 511
Sight draft, 578
Simple interest, 120
Simple option valuation model, 676
Single cash flow, 133–134
Sinking fund, 430
Skinner, Douglas, 516
Small Business Administration, 501
Smith, C. W., Jr., 585n
Soft capital rationing, 254
Sole proprietors, 10, 15
Solera, Sherry, 22
Sommer, Jeff, 221n
Southern California Edison, 598
Southwest Airlines, 14n
Specialists, 198
Special-purpose entities, 432
Specific risk
    definition, 351
    diversification to eliminate, 351
    versus market risk, 350–351, 361
    origin of, 351
Speculation vs. risk reduction, 705–706
Speculative bubbles, 718
Speculative grade bonds, 183
Spinning, 450
Spin-offs, 630
    Delphi from General Motors, 615
Spot price, 700
Spread
    bond prices, 168
    definition, 445
    underwriting, 448
Spreadsheets
    for annuities, 145–146

for bond prices, 170–171
bond valuation, 178–179
calculating risk and betas, 364
calculating volatility, 348
capital budgeting, 562
capital investment, 288–289
cash budget, 562
discounted cash-flow analysis, 292–293
to find future value, 132–135
to find present value, 132–135
internal rate of return, 249
for multiple cash flows, 134–135
net present value, 245
present value of cash flows, 245
for single cash flow, 133–134
to solve Manhattan price problem, 133
Sprint, 184
cost of capital, 93
economic value added, 93
long-term capital, 93
market-to-book ratio, 90
market value added, 90
retained capital, 93
St. Jude Medical, 612
Stafford, E., 631n
Stakeholders
    definition, 16
    and LBOs, 629
Standard & Poor's, 578
    bond ratings, 183
    and performance of money managers, 221
Standard & Poor's Composite (500) Index, 45, 226, 333, 348, 362, 678
    decline in 2002, 336
    standard deviation for common stock, 343
Standard & Poor's Depository Receipts, 45
Standard & Poor's Index Spiders, 46
Standard deviation, 339–341
    calculating, 340–341
    definition, 340
    formula, 340
    Newmont Mining, 350
    for selected companies, 343
    spreadsheet solutions, 348
    stock market returns, 341
    U.S. Steel, 349–350
Starbucks, 20, 36, 334
    beta, 367
    standard deviation for common stock, 343
    weighted average cost of capital, 407
Start-ups
    angel investors, 443
    business plan, 442
    and corporate venturers, 443
    crowdfunding, 443, 444
    initial public offerings, 444–450

private equity investing, 443
    success rate, 444
    and venture capital, 441–444
Statement of account, 585
Statement of cash flows
    capital expenditures, 68
    cash flow from financing, 68
    cash flow from investing, 67–68
    cash flow from operations, 67
    definition, 67
    depreciation allowance, 67
    free cash flow, 69–70
    Home Depot, 67–69
    and income statement, 67
Statement of shareholders' equity, 58n
State-owned enterprises, 254
States
    blue-sky laws, 446
    corporate taxes, 73n
    laws on dividend payout, 507–508
State Street Global Advisors, 46
Statistical problems, 716
Staunton, Mike, 334, 335, 339, 341
Stern Stewart & Company, 91
Stertz, Bradley A., 614n
Stock; see also Common stock; Initial public offering; Preferred stock
    aggressive, 362
    classes of, 428
    compared to bonds, 38
    correlations across industries, 347–348
    defensive, 362
    dividend yield, 200
    factors affecting returns, 362
    fairly valued, 222
    FedEx initial public offering, 4
    as financial asset, 6–7
    growth stock, 213
    high-dividend, 515
    income stock, 213
    incremental risk, 347–348
    initial public offerings, 198
    large number of, 333
    McDonald's, 215–216
    measuring variations in returns, 341–343
    mergers financed by, 621–633
    need to know valuation, 197
    overpriced, 488
    overvalued, 453
    ownership risk, 198
    primary issue, '37
    primary offerings, 198
    private placements, 453
    restricted, 16
    rights issue, 450–451
    risk characteristics, 670
    seasoned offerings, 450
    in secondary market, 198
    short selling, 20
    trading ex-dividend, 507
    trading range, 508n

Stock *Cont.*
  underpriced, 488
  undervalued, 220, 453
  valuation difficulty, 217
  vesting, 16n
Stockbroker firms, 22
Stock dividends, 508–509
Stock exchanges
  BATS Exchange, 199
  brokerage firms, 198
  daily trading volume, 198
  electronic communication
      networks, 198
  limit order book, 199
  market orders, 198–199
  NASDAQ, 198, 333, 427
  New York Stock Exchange, 198,
      333, 427
  sources of trading data, 199n
  specialists, 198
Stockholders, 8
  see also Shareholders
Stock market
  after crash of 1929, 336
  anomalies, 715
    momentum factor, 225
    new issue puzzle, 225–226
  crashes, 24
  decline in 2008, 15
  dot-com bubble, 718
  efficiency and bubbles, 226–227
  efficient, 221–224
  equity market, 37
  fluctuations, 362
  functions, 37
  primary market, 37, 198
  random walk, 221–224
  reaction to general cash offers,
      452–453
  secondary market, 37, 198
  and shareholder value, 87
  short selling, 20
  tests of efficiency, 226
  volatility, 342–343
Stock market bubbles, 226–227,
    228
Stock market indexes; *see* Market
    indexes
Stock market listings, 199–200
Stock options, 16, 680
Stock prices, 48
  after initial public offerings, 718
  Amazon, 202–203
  ask price, 199
  and behavioral finance, 227–228
  bid-ask spread, 199
  bid price, 199
  book values, 201–203
  and call options, 666, 670–671
  and competition, 222
  in competitive markets, 205
  Consolidated Edison, 202–203
  cycles, 224
  and exercise price, 673
  Facebook, 217
  FedEx, 199–200
  FedEx history, 200

  forecasting, 206
  high, 508n
  and intrinsic value, 204–205
  liquidation values, 201–203
  market fluctuations, 362
  market values, 201–203
  no-growth shares, 209
  and put options, 666, 670–671
  reaction to general cash offers,
      452–453
  reasons for knowing, 197
  and repurchase, 512–513
  for selected companies, 201
  and selling calls and puts,
      668–669
  speculative bubbles, 718
  3Com, 631
  Twitter, 681
  underpricing, 446–447
  and value of call options,
      673–675
  variability per unit of time, 674
Stock repurchase
  and dividend discount model,
      219–220, 513–514
  versus dividends, 512–513
  implementing
    auction, 509
    direct negotiation, 509
    open-market repurchase, 509
    tender offer, 509
  information content, 509–510
  most active companies, 506
  in U.S. 1980–2014, 506
Stock splits, 508–509
  reverse, 509
Stock trading, 37
Straight-line depreciation, 291
Strategy, and Du Pont formula, 98
Stretching payables, 557, 559
Strips, 187
Strong form efficiency, 225, 715
Structured investment
    vehicles, 103
Subordinated debt, 185
Subprime mortgages, 25, 49, 50,
    103, 433–434
Sunk costs, 278–279
Surplus funds, mergers as use for,
    616
Surprises
  avoiding, 529
  and contingency planning, 530
Sustainable growth rate, 211, 212,
    540–541
Swaps
  counterparties, 703
  credit default swaps, 705
  currency swaps, 704
  definition, 702
  for exchange rate fluctuations,
    704
  for hedging, 702
  inflation swaps, 705
  interest rate swaps, 702–703
  for risk management, 693,
    702–705

  total return swaps, 705
Sweep programs, 588–589
Synergies
  elusive, 614
  mergers to create, 613
  sources of
    combining complementary
      resources, 615–616
    economies of scale, 614
    economies of vertical
      integration, 614–615
Synthetic fixed-rate debt, 703

T

Takeovers, 18
  definition, 619
  fighting off, 628–629
  financial manager worries
    about, 611
  free-cash-flow theory, 616, 629
  and greenmail transactions, 509
  hostile, 611
  oil industry in 1980s, 616
  and poison pill, 626, 627
  by proxy contests, 625
  in 1980s, 24–25
  shark repellent, 627
  spun to unofficial management,
    632
  tender offer, 625
Tangible assets, 3
  on balance sheet, 58
  investment in, 6
  investments in, 119
Target interest rate, 720
Taxation
  capital gains, 518
  of capital gains, 75
  in cash forecasts, 558
  corporate tax, 73–74
  and cost of capital, 391
  and debt, 478–479
  of dividend, 517–518
  of dividends, 75
  double, 75
  interest rate shield, 478–479
  of investment income, 75
  and LBOs, 629
  and municipal bonds, 183n
  of mutual funds, 40n
  of partnerships, 10
  of pension funds, 75
  personal tax, 74–75
  preferred stock dividends, 398
  of preferred stock dividends,
    428–429
  of shareholders, 9
  and weighted average cost of
    capital, 396–397
Tax avoidance, 20
Tax inversion, 620
Tax rates
  average, 75
  corporate taxes, 73
  on dividends, 74–75

  investment income, 518n
  marginal, 74
Technologies, obsolete, 257
Tender offer
  rules for, 625
  for stock repurchase, 509
10 K forms, 58
10 Q forms, 58
Terminal cash flow, 280
Terminal price, 216
Term loans, 596
Terms of sale
  cash before delivery, 576
  cash discounts, 576
  cash on delivery, 576
  credit sale, 576
  definition, 576
  end-of-month sale, 576
  implicit rate of interest per
    period, 577
  interest rates, 577
  payment date, 576
  trade credit
    as implicit loan, 576
    interest rates, 577
Thaler, R., 631n
3Par, 631
Thermopolis, Costas, 392, 400
3Com, 631
3M Corporation, 333
Tight money policy, 172
Time deposits
  certificates of deposit, 594
  current assets, 553
Time draft, 578
Time horizon
  of investors, 202
  long-term financing, 530
  long *vs.* short-term financing,
    552–553
Times interest earned ratio, 101
Time value of money
  annuity due, 143–144
  calculation for annuity
    problems, 144–146
    using financial calculators,
      145
    using spreadsheets, 145–146
  calculations
    using financial calculators,
      131–132
    using spreadsheets, 132–135
  definition, 119
  effective annual interest rate,
    146–148
  and financing decisions, 119
  future value and compound
    interest, 120–123
  future value of annuity, 140–143
  and inflation
    interest rates, 149–151
    real or nominal NPV
      calculation, 153
    real *vs.* nominal cash,
      148–149
    valuing real cash payments,
      151–153

level cash flows, 135–143
multiple cash flows, 128–131
present value, 123–128
Time Warner, 613
cost of capital, 93
economic value added, 93
market-to-book ratio, 90
market value added, 90
retained capital, 93
total long-term capital, 93
Time Warner Cable, 612, 613, 619
Timing option, 319–320
Timken Company, 20
TIPS; see Treasury Inflation
Protected Securities
Total assets, 94–95
Total capitalization, 92, 94
Total capital requirement; see
Cumulative capital
requirement
Total project cash flow, 288
Total return swaps, 705
Total risk
and market risk, 356–367
predicted by betas, 370–371
Trade acceptance, 578
Trade credit
collection policy, 585
definition, 575
interest rates, 577
management of, 575
sources of funds, 585
supply and demand
determinants, 585n
Trade-off theory of capital
structure, 482, 487–488
Trading range, 508n
Transaction costs, buying and
selling securities, 588
Transparency, 71
Trans Union, 579n
Travel and entertainment card, 591
Treasurer, 10, 11
Treasury bills, 404n
average rate of return, 335
histograms, 340
least risk investment, 371
low risks, 334
in money market, 594
and opportunity cost of capital,
339
rates of return, 337
Treasury bonds
asked price, 168, 169
asked yield to maturity, 168, 169
bid price, 168, 169
coupon, 168
in crisis of 2007–2009, 176–177
face value, 168
interest payments, 168
interest rate fluctuations,
172–174
and interest rates, 169–174
long-term, 180, 334, 405
low default risk, 167
low interest rate, 167
mini bonds, 179

as notes, 168
number of, outstanding, 168
in open auction, 449
par value, 168
present value calculation, 170
sample of quotes 2015, 169
semiannual coupon payments,
171–172
size of public holdings, 168
spread, 168
strips, 179–180, 187
trading in, 169
yield curve, 179–182
yield spread 1953-2016, 184
Treasury Department
purchase of toxic assets, 49
sale of warrants, 680
sell-off of General Motors stock,
445
Treasury Inflation Protected
Securities, 25, 181
Treasury stock, 60, 428
Troubled Asset Relief Program, 511
True value, 421
Trump, Donald, 39
Truth-in-lending laws, 146n
Turnover vs. profit margin, 89–99
TWA, 502
Twitter, 217
convertible bonds, 680–681
Two-for-one stock split, 508
TXU, 7
Tyco, 15, 17

U

Uhlfelder, Eric, 36
Underlying assets, 718
Underpricing, 488
definition, 446
eBay, 446
example, 446–447
and winner's curse, 447
Underwriters
best-efforts basis, 445
blockbuilding, 449
case, 459–460
characteristics, 449–450
definition, 445
firm commitment, 445
floatation costs, 448–449
general cash offers, 451
issue pricing, 446
prospectus, 446
reputation, 340
road shows, 446
Securities and Exchange
Commission regulations,
445–446
spinning by, 450
state blue-sky laws, 446
underpricing by, 446–447
VA Linux scandal, 340
and winner's curse, 447
Underwriters spread, 448
Underwriting, 42

Unethical financial transactions, 3
Unfunded debt, 430
Union Pacific
beta, 367, 368–369
standard deviation for common
stock, 343
weighted average cost of
capital, 407
Union Power, 5
United States
current assets of corporations,
572
current liabilities of
corporations, 572
dividends 1980-2014, 506
dot-com bubble, 227
inflation rate 1900–2015, 149
largest investment banks, 449
mergers 1995–2015, 612
number of commercial banks, 42
payment systems, 590, 591, 592
risk premium, 337, 338
semiannual coupon payments,
171
stock repurchases 1980–2014, 506
and tax inversion, 620
10-year interest rate, 639
total financing of corporations,
43–44
United States Postal Service, 4
Unknown unknowns, 307
Unlimited liability, 10
Unrelated diversification, 613
U.S. Robotics, 631
U.S. Steel, 362
beta, 365, 367, 375
market return, 366
standard deviation, 349–350
standard deviation for common
stock, 343
weighted average cost of
capital, 407
U.S. dollar, nominal vs. real
value, 149

V

VA Linux, 450
Valuation
common stocks
by comparables, 203–204,
217, 220
dividend discount model,
206–208
price and intrinsic value,
204–206
corporate reliance on, 220
growth stocks, 213–214
long-lived projects, 242–244
option models, 716
Black-Scholes formula,
675–677
Financial Accounting
Standards Board standards,
680
simple model, 676

Valuation errors, 216
Valuation formula, 206–207
Valuation horizons, 219
Value
book vs. market, 61–63
of a business, 219
callable bonds, 682
of call options
determinants, 673–674
upper and lower limits,
672–673
valuation models, 675–678
distribution of, 13
effect of financing decisions,
715
of entire businesses, 406–409
and financing decisions, 6
of no-growth stocks, 209
and payout policy, 715
from sound financing, 87
true, 421
of underlying assets, 718
Value added
for additional economic
benefits, 622
by financial managers, 3
financial ratios to understand,
88–89
measures needed for, 87
Value maximization, 3
ethics of, 18–19
investment trade-off, 13–14
and managerial practices, 13
necessary for survival, 13
opportunity cost of capital, 14
shareholder goal, 12
Value of the firm, 219
asset value vs. market
value, 719
based on capital
investment, 489
and capital budgeting
decisions, 197
and capital structure, 719
and debt policy
capital structure, 468–469
earnings per share, 470–472
restructuring, 469
risk and return, 472–473
determined by cash flows, 468
and dividend policy, 515–518
interest rate shield, 479
intrinsic value vs. price, 718
and liquidation, 502–503
in liquidation, 502–503
liquidation value, 201–202
management's contribution, 719
market value, 201–202
not increased by hedging, 694
unaffected by capital structure,
472
underlying assets, 718–719
valuing entire businesses,
406–409
Value stocks, 377
Vanguard Explorer Fund, 40
Vanguard 500 Index Fund, 369

Vanguard Growth and Income
    Fund
    beta, 368–369
Vanguard 5000 Index Fund, 45
Variable costs
    break-even point, 311
    definition, 307
    increase in, 315–316
    operating leverage, 315–317
Variance, 339–341
    calculating, 340, 341
    definition, 340
    formula, 340
    loss of degree of freedom, 342n
Venture capital, 35
    from angel investors, 443
    and business plan, 442
    definition, 442
    first-stage financing, 442
    second-stage financing, 443
    for start-ups, 441
Venture capital firms, 441
    on board of directors, 444
    characteristics, 443–444
    limited private partnerships, 443
    for start-ups, 442–443
    success rate, 444
Venture capitalists, 4, 5
Verizon, 239, 530–531
Vertical integration
    economies of, 614–615
    versus outsourcing, 624
Vertical merger, 612–613
Vertical mergers, 615
Vesting, 16n
Visa, 591
    initial public offering, 448–449
Vlasic, Bill, 614n
Volatility
    of earnings, 381
    near-term options, 678
    of portfolio, 344–350
    spreadsheet solutions, 348
Volkswagen, 531
Voting procedures
    with common stock, 427–428
    lacking with preferred stock,
        428
Vulture funds, 41

W

Wachovia, 25, 612
Wall Street Journal, 168, 197,
        199–200, 216
Wall Street Walk, 18, 20
Walmart, 6, 184, 644
    beta, 367
    cost of capital, 93
    daily cash flow, 588

economic value added, 92–93
    investment and financing
        decisions, 5
    long-term capital, 93
    market-to-book ratio, 90
    market-to-book value, 204
    market value added, 90
    market *vs.* book value, 201
    number of shareholders, 12
    price-earnings ratio, 204
    return on capital, 93
    standard deviation for common
        stock, 343
    stock price, 201
    weighted average cost of capital,
        407
Walmart strategy, 98
Walt Disney Company, 370
    beta, 367
    standard deviation for common
        stock, 343
    weighted average cost of capital,
        407
Warrants, 434, 680
Weak-form efficiency, 225, 715
Webb, Susan, 22
Websites, for bond information,
        186
Weighted average cost of
        capital, 92n
    accounting cash flows, 404n
    calculating
        expected return on bonds,
            403–404
        expected return on common
            stock, 404–405
        expected return on preferred
            stock, 405–406
        real companies, 406
        summary on, 406
    case, 415–417
    company cost of capital
        calculation, 393–395
    and corporate tax, 480–481
    formula, 397, 406, 480
    interpreting
        corporate tax rate, 401
        effect of capital structure
            changes, 401
        former myths, 400
        when usable, 400
    managerial use of, 391
    measuring capital structure,
        401–403
    Monsanto, 397
    multiple sources of financing,
        398
    for selected companies, 407
    and taxes, 396–397
    value of deconstruction,
        408–409

valuing entire businesses,
        406–409
Weighted average of returns, 345
Weiss, L. A., 484n
Wells Fargo, 506, 612
What-if questions
    crucial to capital budgeting,
        306–307
    in financial planning, 530
    importance of, 306
    in project analysis, 293, 303
    scenario analysis, 310
    sensitivity analysis, 307–310
Wheat futures
    contracts, 696–700
Wildcat oil wells, 351–353
Williams Act of 1968, 625
Williamson, R., 553
Wilshire 5000 Market Index, 221
Wingfield, N., 516
Winner's curse, 447
Wire transfer, 592
Wolfers, J., 39
Working capital, 279
    and business process, 572–575
    cash conversion period,
        574–575
    in cash-flow analysis, 288
    changes in, 285–286, 288
    components
        changes with operations
            cycle, 572–575
        current assets, 572
        current liabilities, 572
    current assets, 571
    definition, 572
    forecasting, 289
    increase or decrease, 286
    sources of, 28
Working capital management
    accounts receivable and credit
        policy
        collection policy, 584–585
        credit agreements, 577–578
        credit analysis, 578–579
        credit decision, 579–584
        steps, 575
        terms of sale, 575–577
    case, 608–609
    cash management
        cash *vs.* short-term securities,
            588–589
        check handling and float,
            589–590
        electronic funds transfer,
            591–592
        international, 592–593
        payment systems, 590–591
    inventory management, 586–588
    money market investments,
        593–596

short-term debt
        bank loans, 596–597
        commercial paper, 597–598
Working capital requirement, 553
Workout, 501
WorldCom, 25, 72, 445
    bankruptcy, 184
Wozniak, Steve, 441
Writer, 668n
Wurgler, J., 508n

Y

Yahoo!, 17
Yahoo! Finance, 61, 199–200, 365
Yield
    corporate *vs.* Treasury bonds,
        183
    corporate *vs.* U.S. securities, 595
    financial calculators for, 177
    on long-term bonds, 180
    money market investments,
        594–595
    on 7-year nominal bonds, 182
    on 7-year TIPS, 182
Yield curve
    Treasury bonds
        definition, 180
        nominal *vs.* real interest rate,
            181–182
        upward-sloping, 180
Yield spread, corporate *vs.*
        Treasury bonds, 184
Yield to maturity, 174–176
    asked, 168, 169
    calculating, 176
    current yield, 175
    definition, 175
    measure of total return, 175–176
    promised *vs.* expected, 185
    versus rate of return, 176–177
    for selected companies, 184
Yuan, K., 718n
Yum! Brands, 47–48

Z

Zero-coupon bonds, 187
Zero NPV, 246–247
Zero-sum game, hedging as, 694
Zhao, Quanshui, 448
Zheng, L., 718n
Zhu, Q., 718n
Ziemba, W. T., 226
Zilzewitz, E., 39
Zingales, L., 18n
Z score model, 579
Zuckerberg, Mark, 441
Zuckerman, G., 22n

SOME USEFUL FACTS AND FORMULAS

Du Pont Formulas (4.5)

Return on assets = asset turnover × profit margin

Return on equity = $\dfrac{\text{assets}}{\text{equity}}$ × asset turnover

$\qquad\qquad$ × profit margin × debt burden

Time Value of Money

Future Value (5.1)

The value to which a $1 investment will grow after t years with compound interest at an annual interest rate of r percent is $FV = (1 + r)^t$

Present Value (5.2)

The value today of $1 to be received in t years is $PV = \dfrac{1}{(1+r)^t}$

Annuities (5.5)

The present value of a stream of income of $1 per year for t years is $PV = \dfrac{1}{r} - \dfrac{1}{r(1+r)^t}$

The future value of a stream of income of $1 per year for t years is $FV = \dfrac{(1+r)^t - 1}{r}$

Effective Annual Rate (5.7)

The annually compounded rate on a loan given a stated APR and m compounding periods per year is

Effective annual rate = $\left(1 + \dfrac{\text{APR}}{m}\right)^m - 1$

Real versus Nominal Quantities (5.8)

The purchasing power of a future cash flow in terms of today's dollars is

Real value of cash flow at time t = $\dfrac{\text{nominal cash flow}}{(1 + \text{inflation rate})^t}$

The growth of purchasing power from an investment is

Real interest rate = $\dfrac{1 + \text{nominal interest rate}}{1 + \text{inflation rate}} - 1$

$\qquad\qquad\quad \approx$ nominal rate − inflation rate

Stock Valuation

Dividend Discount Model (7.3)

The value of a share of stock equals the present value of dividends paid until the horizon date, H, plus the present value of the anticipated sales price of the stock, P_H.

$$P_0 = \dfrac{\text{DIV}_1}{1+r} + \dfrac{\text{DIV}_2}{(1+r)^2} + \ldots + \dfrac{\text{DIV}_H + P_H}{(1+r)^H}$$

Constant-Growth Dividend Discount Model (7.4)

If the initial dividend is DIV_1 (paid in 1 year), and if the dividend grows thereafter at a constant rate of g, the present value of the dividend stream is $P_0 = \dfrac{\text{DIV}_1}{r - g}$

Capital Budgeting

Break-Even Point (10.4)

The sales revenue necessary for the firm to break even (in terms of accounting profits) is

Break-even revenue = $\dfrac{\text{fixed costs including depreciation}}{\text{additional profit from each additional dollar of sales}}$

Operating Leverage (10.4)

The degree of operating leverage, DOL, is the sensitivity of profits to changes in sales:

$\text{DOL} = \dfrac{\text{percentage change in profits}}{\text{percentage change in sales}} = 1 + \dfrac{\text{fixed costs}}{\text{profits}}$

Risk and Return

Measures of Risk and Return (11.3, 12.1)

Mean or expected return = probability-weighted average of possible outcomes

Variance $= \sigma^2 =$ mean of squared deviations around the mean

Standard deviation $= \sigma = \sqrt{\text{variance}}$

Beta $= \beta =$ expected increase in stock return for an extra 1% increase in the return on the market index

Capital Asset Pricing Model (12.3)

The expected rate of return on a risky security equals the rate of return on risk-free assets plus a risk premium that depends on the security beta:

$r = r_f + \beta(r_m - r_f)$

Capital Structure

Weighted-Average Cost of Capital (13.2)

$$\text{WACC} = \left[\dfrac{D}{V} \times r_{\text{debt}}(1 - T_c)\right] + \dfrac{E}{V} \times r_{\text{equity}}$$

where T_c is the corporate tax rate, D is debt, E is equity, and $V = D + E$

Return on Assets (16.2)

Return on assets equals the weighted average of the returns of the firm's outstanding securities:

$$r_{assets} = r_{debt} \frac{D}{V} + r_{equity} \frac{E}{V}$$

(assuming no taxes)

Value of Interest Tax Shields (16.3)

If a firm maintains a fixed amount of debt in perpetuity, then the present value of the tax savings equals $T_c \times$ debt.

If the firm will indefinitely maintain a constant debt *ratio*, then the PV of the interest tax shield is $T_C \times$ current debt $\times (r_{debt}/r_{assets})$.

Financial Planning

Internal Growth Rate (18.4)

The steady rate at which a firm can grow without issuing new debt or equity is

Plowback ratio $\times$ return on equity $\times \dfrac{\text{equity}}{\text{assets}}$

Sustainable Growth Rate (18.4)

The steady rate at which a firm can grow without issuing new equity or changing leverage is

Plowback ratio $\times$ return on equity

Cash Cycle (20.1)

Inventory period + receivables period − accounts payable period

Working Capital Management

Effective Annual Rate on Trade Credit (20.2)

$$\text{Effective annual rate} = \left(1 + \frac{\text{discount}}{\text{discounted price}}\right)^{365/\text{extra days credit}} - 1$$

International Finance (22.2)

Interest rate parity : $\dfrac{1 + r_{foreign}}{1 + r_\$} = \dfrac{f_{foreign/\$}}{s_{foreign/\$}}$

where r is the interest rate, s is the spot exchange rate, and f is the forward exchange rate expressed as an indirect quote (foreign currency per \$)

International Fisher effect: $\dfrac{1 + r_{foreign}}{1 + r_\$} = \dfrac{1 + i_{foreign}}{1 + i_\$}$

where r is the interest rate and i is the inflation rate

Expectations theory: $\dfrac{f_{foreign/\$}}{s_{foreign/\$}} = \dfrac{E(s_{foreign/\$})}{s_{foreign/\$}}$

Purchasing power parity: $\dfrac{1 + i_{foreign}}{1 + i_\$} = \dfrac{E(s_{foreign/\$})}{s_{foreign/\$}}$